Uncertainty in Artificial Intelligence

Proceedings of the Seventh Conference (1991)

Uncertainty in Artificial Intelligence

Proceedings of the Seventh Conference (1991)

July 13–15, 1991

Seventh Conference on
Uncertainty in Artificial Intelligence

University of California at Los Angeles

Edited by

Bruce D. D'Ambrosio
Oregon State University
Corvallis, Oregon

Philippe Smets
IRIDIA, Université Libre de Bruxelles
Brussels, Belgium

Piero P. Bonissone
General Electric CRD
Schenectady, New York

Morgan Kaufmann Publishers
San Mateo, California

Sponsoring Editor **Michael B. Morgan**
Production Editor **Yonie Overton**
Cover Designer **Sandra Popovich**
Compositor **Technically Speaking Publications**

Morgan Kaufmann Publishers, Inc.
Editorial Office:
2929 Campus Drive, Suite 260
San Mateo, California 94403

95 94 93 92 91   5 4 3 2 1

Library of Congress Cataloging-in-Publication Data is available for this book.
Library of Congress Catalogue Card Number: 91-640658
ISBN 1-55860-203-8

Preface

This collection of papers, like its predecessors, reflects the cutting edge of research on the automation of reasoning with uncertainty. This volume contains the papers presented at the Seventh Conference on Uncertainty in Artificial Intelligence, held on July 13–15, 1991 at the University of California at Los Angeles (UCLA).

Our particular thanks go to the many referees who have been part of the review process for this conference. Every accepted paper has been reviewed by an average of three referees to guarantee the quality of the selected papers. We gratefully acknowledge the work of the following reviewers:

A. Agogino, F. Bacchus, J. Bigham, P. Bonissone, J. Breese, M. Clarke, G. Cooper, B. D'Ambrosio, M. Delgado, D. Dubois, L. Farinas del Cero, M. Fehling, J. Fox, R. Fung, D. Geiger, R. Goldman, P. Haddawy, J. Halpern, S. Hanks, D. Heckerman, M. Henrion, E. Horvitz, Y. Hsia, R. Kennes, J. Kohlas, V. Kreinovich, R. Kruse, H. Kyburg, J. Lang, K. Laskey, T. Levitt, R. Lopez de Mantaras, R. Loui, A. Mamdani, A. Mayer, S. Moral, H. Nguyen, G. Paass, R. Patil, G. Provan, E. Ruspini, A. Saffiotti, K. Schill, D. Schwartz, R. Shachter, P. Shenoy, P. Smets, T. Stratt, M. Wellman, N. Wilson, M. Wong, R. Yager, and J. Yen.

We also extend our gratitude to Mike Morgan and Yonie Overton for their efficient and knowledgeable support.

We want to thank the Computer Science Department of Oregon State University in Corvallis, Oregon, IRIDIA of the Université Libre de Bruxelles in Brussels, Belgium, and the General Electric Corporate Research and Development Center in Schenectady, New York for the financial and moral support given to the organizers.

Finally, we would like to emphasize that, for the first time in the history of this conference, about a third of the papers come from European researchers. This result is partially attributable to the existence of a large consortium of European researchers working in the domain of uncertainty in AI. The researchers in the ESPRIT Basic Research Action, entitled Defeasible Reasoning and Uncertainty Management Systems (DRUMS), have been a major source of European participation in this conference.

We hope that this kind of international contact will lead to future joint research and successful collaborations between the United States and Europe.

Bruce D. D'Ambrosio
Program Co-chair

Philippe Smets
Program Co-chair

Piero P. Bonissone
Conference Chair

Contents

ARCO1: An Application of Belief Networks to the Oil Market

Bruce Abramson
University of Southern California
Department of Computer Science
Los Angeles, CA 90089-0782

Abstract

Belief networks are a new, potentially important, class of knowledge-based models. ARCO1, currently under development at the Atlantic Richfield Company (ARCO) and the University of Southern California (USC), is the most advanced reported implementation of these models in a financial forecasting setting. ARCO1's underlying belief network models the variables believed to have an impact on the crude oil market. A pictorial market model—developed on a MAC II—facilitates consensus among the members of the forecasting team. The system forecasts crude oil prices via Monte Carlo analyses of the network. Several different models of the oil market have been developed; the system's ability to be updated quickly highlights its flexibility.

1 Introduction

Belief networks are a class of models that have recently become important to researchers at the intersection of artificial intelligence (AI) and decision analysis (DA). Despite their underlying sophistication, belief networks are conceptually simple. Any directed acyclic graph (DAG) in which (i) nodes represent individual variables, items, characteristics, or knowledge sources, (ii) arcs demonstrate influence among the nodes, and (iii) functions associated with the arcs indicate the nature of that influence, qualifies as a belief network (Abramson 1990). Belief networks were originally introduced as a middle ground between psychologically valid elicitation procedures and mathematically valid representations of uncertainty (Howard and Matheson 1984). As such, they begin with an understanding of the heuristics and biases that typically plague experts (Kahneman, Slovic, and Tversky 1982), the DA elicitation techniques that help overcome these biases (von Winterfeldt and Edwards 1986), and the axioms of Bayesian probability theory (Savage 1954, Edwards, Lindman, and Savage 1963). These basic principles have led to a variety of inference and decision algorithms (Pearl 1988, Shachter 1986, 1988).

Several powerful belief network-based systems have been discussed in the literature. The two most developed of these systems, MUNIN (Andreassen et. al. 1987) and Pathfinder (Heckerman, Horvitz, and Nathwani 1990), deal with medical diagnoses. ARCO1 marks the first reported forecasting application. This paper outlines the modeling effort that went into ARCO1, and reports its preliminary models of the 1990 oil market and its forecasts of 1990 prices. For a more detailed treatment of this material, see (Abramson and Finizza in press).

2 Domain Specifics

Models of the world oil market can be broadly classified into as either optimization models or target capacity utilization (TCU) models (Energy Modeling Forum 1982, Gately 1984, Powell 1990). Optimization models, which are generally based on economic theories of depletable resources and/or cartels, are used primarily for long term projections (Marshalla and Nesbitt, 1986). Since our aim was to develop a system for short term forecasts, we chose to develop ARCO1 as a TCU model.

The central determinant of prices in a TCU framework is the relationship of calculated production to exogenously determined capacity; the resulting measure of market tightness indicates price pressure. Our choice of this framework as the basis of ARCO1's model stresses the importance of subjective political variables. Since capacity is exogenously determined and short term crude oil demand is highly price inelastic and almost completely specified by seasonal patterns, short term price forecasts can be (more or less) reduced to forecasts of production. Production levels, in turn, are essentially set by the political decisions of the governments of oil producing countries;

OPEC's Persian Gulf members (Saudi Arabia, Iran, Iraq, Kuwait, UAE, and Qatar) are particularly important, because they tend to be the only producers with substantial slack capacity. Thus, the inclusion of political analyses and adjustments to *production* calculations appear to be much more appropriate than politically motivated judgemental adjustments to mechanically forecast *price* calculations.

ARCO1's base case was a model of the 1990 oil market designed in early 1990 using historical data through the fourth quarter of 1989 and subjective assessments provided between November 1989 and February 1990. This model, depicted in Figure 1, has already undergone revisions and will continue to be revised. It contains about 140 equations, many with time lags and some expressed as conditional probabilities. Section 3 enumerates these variables and relationships. It is important to stress, however, that the system is more than simply a model. ARCO1 was designed to facilitate scenario development and simulation exercises. One such exercise is discussed in Section 4; it concerns a scenario developed in late-August/early-September 1990 to reflect the altered political realities of the Persian Gulf.

3 Model Variables

This section explains ARCO1's variables, as shown in Figures 1 and 2. The variables can be broken into seven categories and eight time periods. The time periods range, by quarter, from the first quarter of 1989 through the fourth quarter of 1990. The categories, in turn, are historical, annual, tax, demand, supply, politics, and price.

Historical Variables represent events that have already occurred; their values were retrieved from the appropriate references.

Annual Variables are not expected to change over the course of the year.

- **NC Cap:** physical production capacity of non-core OPEC countries (i.e., OPEC countries outside the Persian Gulf).
- **NC Prod:** actual production of non-core OPEC countries.
- **World Growth:** world GDP growth is broken into four components: lesser developed countries (LDC), Western Europe (WE), US, and Japan. Coefficients relating the four components of the world economy to the single world growth variable were calculated by linear regression.

Tax Variables relate to US tax policy. Two types of potentially relevant legislation are envisioned: an oil import fee (OI Fee) and an increase in the federal gasoline tax (GT indicates whether or not the tax will be passed. GT Impact translates the tax from dollars-per-gallon to dollars-per-barrel). If an oil import fee is imposed, its presumed effect would be to place an $18 per barrel floor on imported oil prices. Increases in the federal gasoline tax could range from $.01 to $.50 per gallon.

Demand Variables are used to calculate total free world demand. Demand calculations, (at least in the developed world), are more straightforward than supply calculations because there are fewer phenomena that allow a small group of decision makers to affect the market. The only demand-side peculiarity identified, in fact, was fuel switching, a decision on the part of the managers of dual-fired utility plants to switch to oil use; its impact is restricted to times when prices are maintained below $15 per barrel, and may range as high as 2 MMBD (million barrels per day).

- **Level:** prevailing price at start of quarter.
- **Duration:** length of time over which the current price level has prevailed.
- **Fuel Switching:** amount of increased demand due to the adoption of oil by utility plants with dual-fired furnaces. Conditionally dependent on price level and duration.
- **Demand:** total world demand, by quarter. Functional specification was determined by an *ad hoc* combination of regression techniques and scenario analysis.

Supply Variables are used to calculate free world supply.

- **US Prod:** US production levels.
- **NO Prod:** other non-OPEC (non-US) production.
- **C Cap:** physical production capacity of core OPEC countries.
- **Delta I:** the change in inventory levels.
- **O Call:** effective demand for OPEC oil, or the call on OPEC. Defined as total world demand minus oil supplied by other sources.
- **Core Demand:** effective demand for oil from core OPEC countries, defined as the amount demanded from OPEC minus the amount supplied by non-core countries.
- **Core Production:** amount produced by the core OPEC countries, given as core demand plus a "political hedge factor."
- **Cap Ut:** defined as the percentage of core OPEC capacity being used for production.
- **Supply:** total world supply of crude.
- **DeltaY Core Prod:** one year change in production by core OPEC countries.

DeltaQ Core Prod: one quarter change in production by core OPEC countries.

DeltaY Sweet: the one year change in production of light, sweet crude, (all non-OPEC production).

Political Variables were introduced to capture subjective measures of core OPEC politics. Two different aspects of the political situation are considered: general intra-gulf relations (Intragulf) and the degree of conflict arising from unhappiness with market share (Market Share). These two variables are then combined and mapped into production to yield a "political hedge to production" factor (Politics).

Price Variables directly represent the price of various grades of crude, OPEC (Saudi basket) and WTI (West Texas Intermediate, the benchmark US crude).

OPEC: the price of OPEC oil, given as a regression-weighted function.

Time: introduced to measure the trend of a steadily increasing shortage of sweet crude.

SS Diff: difference in price between sweet and sour crude. It is measured by a complex formula.

WTI: price of WTI oil, subject to the possible imposition of an oil import fee.

4 Scenarios

The previous section defined the variables and influences captured by ARCO1's model of the 1990 oil market. Value ranges and precise dependence (algebraic, econometric, and probabilistic) were omitted from the discussion, as they are from Figure 1's picture of the network; they are neither central to the model of the domain nor of particular interest to most AI researchers. They are, however, crucial if the model is to produce any useful results. This distinction is characteristic of belief networks; network structure (i.e., nodes and arcs) describes the domain, while network parameters (i.e., historical data, prior probabilities, and numeric relationships) allow specific questions to be answered. Viewed another way, the model illustrated in Figure 1 captures one year of the oil market. A fixed set of parameters (such as those that we used in our studies) captures a time frame (the year 1990). Thus, recasting the model for 1991 should require nothing more than reviewing and updating the network's parameters. (It would, in fact, be this simple were the network structure completely satisfactory. Several potentially hazy areas—notably US tax policy, inventory behavior, and Gulf politics—have already been detected, and are currently under revision. Once a fully satisfactory network structure has been derived, however, updates should be restricted to parameter changes. Structural changes should be few and far between, and should correspond to fundamental changes in the market).

The discussion of variables and influence, then, was intended to convey a broad understanding of the oil market. Forecasts, on the other hand, require data. The basic model was used to create two sets of scenarios for 1990: a base case and a constrained capacity case. The base case was designed in early 1990, and covers all four quarters of the year. The constrained capacity case was designed in late August/early September 1990, when a fundamental market shift occurred; it assumes an effective boycott of Iraqi and Kuwaiti oil, and that all other producers produce at maximum capacity. A revised network, shown in Figure 2, was constructed. It accounted for historical data through the end of the second quarter, and produced forecasts for the third and fourth quarters of 1990. These cases were developed to demonstrate the system's flexibility, not its accuracy. Recall that the system's processing power is still restricted to Monte Carlo analyses; this entire phase of development must be viewed more as a proof-of-concept than as a demonstration of power.

4.1 Base Case

The base case for 1990 is described by the network of Figure 1. Specific values for historical and exogenous variables were retrieved from the appropriate sources. For further details and the actual values assigned to these variables, see (Abramson and Finizza in press). Many of the probabilistic assessments and regression weights are currently under review and have yet to be released. Qualitative analyses of US tax policy, fuel switching, and Gulf politics, however, certainly warrant further discussion.

US tax policy is one instance of an important set of judgemental variables that doesn't fit into data-driven models. Since the US is the world's largest consumer of oil, as well as its largest importer and one of its largest producers, US policies can affect the market in several ways. First, increased taxation could lead to slowly declining demand. Second, US taxes could have a direct impact on the price of imported oil, consequently an indirect impact on world prices and on domestically produced crude. Since crude oil spot prices are typically quoted for WTI, (as traded on NYMEX, the New York Mercantile Exchange), the price of domestic oil is of central importance. The analysis of US tax policy considered the possibility of two relevant taxes: an increase in the federal gasoline tax, and the imposition of an oil import fee (at an $18 floor). The general assessment was that the increased gasoline tax was the more likely of the two, and that if passed, would decrease the likelihood of an oil import fee. (Note that the federal gasoline tax was, in fact, increased for 1991 as part of the budget package eventually passed in October 1990).

Fuel switching, (a managerial decision at dual-fired utility plants to burn oil rather than natural gas), is another area that generally eludes data-driven models. This decision, unlike most others affecting the market, is an essentially macro-level demand decision; universal switching to oil could increase demand by as much as 2 MMBD. ARCO1's model included a fairly detailed analysis of fuel switching. Without getting into specifics, the thrust of the analysis is that oil warrants consideration at prices below $15 per barrel. If low prices are maintained for an extended period of time, many managers will opt for oil. The lower the prices and the longer they are maintained, the greater the demand.

Political analyses and projections are necessarily softer (i.e., more subjective) than their economic counterparts. As a result, they are invariably omitted from technical models, and relegated to the role of *a posteriori* judgemental adjustments. ARCO1's structure helped initiate a quantitative—albeit subjective—analysis of core OPEC (Persian Gulf) politics. The first step in the analysis lay in realizing that politics is really significant only as it affects production. Thus, rather than being an adjustment to price, politics is viewed as an adjustment to OPEC production. The second step used this observation to identify two relevant characteristics of Gulf politics: (i) general political amicability among the core OPEC members, and (ii) each country's satisfaction with its market share (and thus, implicitly, compliance with OPEC quotas). The third step placed these variables on a subjective five-point scales (harmony-to-war and strict compliance-to-rampant cheating, respectively). The fourth step specified conditional probabilities relating the two, and the fifth step mapped them into oil production above or below natural demand. This type of political analysis is inexact, and will certainly need to be refined, updated, and changed. (One such change is discussed in the next section). Its inclusion in the model, however, establishes a clear "political module" into which all updates can easily be inserted.

4.2 Constrained Capacity Case

The constrained capacity (or boycott) case was designed after Iraq's invasion of Kuwait on August 2, 1990. The behavior of the oil market following the Iraqi invasion and the subsequent world reaction indicated that a fundamental change had occurred, and that all existing short-term models were in need of (at least some) revision. The modularity of ARCO1's underlying network facilitated these changes; the constrained capacity network is shown in Figure 2.

The network that corresponds to this case incorporated several assumptions that actually made the analysis *easier* than it was in the base case. First, (and most obviously), it was designed seven months later and with two additional quarters of historical data. Thus, nodes corresponding to first and second quarter 1989 were dropped, and actual numbers for first and second quarters 1990 were included. Second, it began with the assumptions that the boycott of Iraq and Kuwait would be effective, and that everyone else in the world would raise their production levels to their maximum physical capacity. Since all non-OPEC producers were already assumed to be producing to capacity, and the production levels of non-core OPEC countries had been fixed at 90% of their capacity, few changes were needed outside OPEC's core. Core production, however, was pushed up to the combined capacities of Saudi Arabia, Iran, UAE, and Qatar. Capacity utilization, originally introduced as a measure of pressure on production and the key to the model, was fixed at 1.0. As a result, the entire political analysis module was dropped from the network; despite the obvious volatility of the political situation, the impact on production was assumed to be steady throughout the rest of the year. (The model assumed that no settlement negotiated before the end of the year would restore the situation *ante*). Fuel switching was dropped from the analysis because the possibility of sustained prices under $15 per barrel disappeared, and US tax policy was excluded (perhaps unreasonably) because it did not appear likely to have much of an impact before the end of 1990. Most of the other analyses remained as they had been in the base case.

One point worth noting is that this constrained capacity case is significantly outside the range of possibilities that were envisioned when the base case was designed. The initial political assessment, in fact, assumed that the pattern set during the Iran/Iraq war would continue: lack of cohesion among Gulf countries would lead to overproduction and low prices. The possibility of a consumers boycott was not even considered. Nevertheless, the model was flexible enough to be updated (quickly and painlessly) in the presence of new data.

5 Forecasts

The first phase of ARCO1's development stressed model construction. The system's ultimate objective, however, is to *use* these models to forecast the market. ARCO1's underlying belief networks captured information about direct interrelationships among the variables affecting the oil market. Implicit in these direct relationships lies information about the market's indirect relationships. The task of the forecasting/processing engine must be to explicate the indirect relationships between exogenous variables and future prices.

Although a wide range of statistical procedures are (theoretically) available to ARCO1, only one simple technique has been fully implemented to date: Monte Carlo analysis. The implementation of Monte Carlo on the network was fairly straightforward. Exogenous variables, (represented by rooted nodes, or nodes with no ingoing arcs), were specified as either constant values or as unconditional (prior) probability distributions. In either case, assigning a single value to an exogenous variable was straightforward. Once all rooted nodes were instantiated, nodes pointed to only by rooted nodes, (i.e., variables directly dependent only on exogenous variables), could similarly be instantiated. This procedure continued until the entire network (or, alternatively, the mid-network node selected as the forecast's target) was instantiated. This assignment of a single value to each variable constitutes a single fully-specified scenario (i.e., all variables are instantiated); the procedure is guaranteed to terminate because a belief network is a DAG (i.e., it contains no cycles). Multiple fully-specified scenarios lead to a distribution of values across the target variable, and thus a probabilistically reported forecast.

Results were generated by Monte Carlo analyses of the 1990 networks; they are not meant to be either complete or conclusive, but simply illustrative of the claim that the system works. The variables targeted by these forecasts were the network's sinks, namely WTI or WTIp (by quarter). The WTIp variables recognize the possibility of an oil import fee placing an $18 floor on domestic oil prices; they adopt the price calculated for WTI if no fee is imposed, but report a price of $18 if the fee is passed and the calculated price is less than or equal to $18. Three sets of simulations were run. The first set studied the full base case, simulating the network shown in Figure 1. The second set retained the base case assumptions, but updated the network with actual data for the first two quarters of 1990. The third set simulated the constrained capacity case, using the network of Figure 2. (As the data will show, however, this third set of simulations was not really necessary). In each of these simulations, 100 scenarios were generated for each target variable. (Simulations of 100 scenarios are not really adequate. The small size was necessitated by implementation inefficiencies. Many of them have already been corrected; our current implementation is running ten to twenty times as quickly). The results of these simulations are shown in Table 1.

The 1990 base case forecast indicated a relatively flat market. All four quarters generated average prices between $20 and $22, with an annual average of $21.14. The [$18,$21] range accounted for 246 of the 400 scenarios (61.5%), with just over half of them (50.5%) falling between $19 and $21. The distribution of the remaining 154 scenarios, however, was far from uniform. Only 34 scenarios (8.5%) projected prices at or below $17, and 23 of these actually hit the $17 level; the [$14,$16] range accounted for only 11 of 400 possible cases (2.75%). Thus, the probability of a significant downward trend under the base case conditions was highly unlikely. On the upside, however, there appeared to be more room for runaway prices. 67 scenarios (16.75%) generated prices in the [$22,$25] range, 43 in the [$26,$30] range (10.75%), and 10 in the [$31,$40] range (2.5%).

Recall that these results were based on assumptions available at the beginning of 1990. The actual average WTI price for the first quarter of 1990 was $21.70, within $1 (or about 1/3 of a standard deviation) from the forecast mean. In the second quarter, average WTI price was $17.76, about $3 (or one standard deviation) from the forecast mean. Thus, ARCO1's forecasts prior to the Iraqi invasion of Kuwait (and the ensuing fundamental shift in the market) were relatively accurate. The insertion of first and second quarter data, however, allowed us to re-run the simulations for the third and fourth quarter. These updates were produced using data available in July 1990. They are well within the range of projections made by most industry analysts at the time. Unfortunately, the market shifted sharply in August. When Iraq invaded Kuwait, the US successfully led the United Nations to establish an effective embargo of Iraqi and Kuwaiti oil, and all other producers decided to increase production, the global supply picture was altered drastically. Simulations of our constrained capacity case yielded the very tight forecasts shown in the final column of Table 1.

The conditions underlying the constrained capacity scenario are sufficiently restrictive to remove virtually all uncertainty from the system; detailed simulation and statistical analyses were unnecessary. Under its assumptions, supply is entirely fixed, and demand is assumed to vary more-or-less in line with world GDP growth. Thus, prices generated under this scenario (at least for the near term) are effectively fixed. Despite the volatility of spot prices throughout the third and fourth quarters of 1990, ARCO1's constrained capacity forecasts were remarkably accurate; the (true) average prices were $26.31 for the third quarter and $31.91 for the fourth. Technical volatility, however, does highlight a potential problem facing the system. The networks discussed in this paper all focus on market fundamentals. Volatility caused by war fears, unusually high risk factors, and other technical factors, tend to elude fundamental analyses. In a disequilibrated (or day-traded) market, forecasts produced by ARCO1 are unlikely to be useful. In a stable, fundamental-based setting, however, the information captured by ARCO1's network does appear to model our understanding of the crude oil market in a manner amenable to producing relatively accurate forecasts.

6 Conclusions

ARCO1 is a knowledge-based system designed to help the members of ARCO's corporate planning group who are involved with forecasting the price of crude oil. The system is based on a belief network, a type of graphical model that is rapidly gaining popularity in

1990 Base Case (original)			1990 Base Case (updated)		Constrained Capacity Case
Quarter	μ	σ	μ	σ	Prices
1Q 1990	20.87	2.9	NA	NA	NA
2Q 1990	20.62	3.3	NA	NA	NA
3Q 1990	21.23	4.1	19.18	2.5	25
4Q 1990	21.84	4.4	20.79	4.4	29-31

Table 1: Means and standard deviations of the forecasts generated by Monte Carlo analyses. All numbers in are approximate, and quoted in dollars per barrel.

both the AI and DA research communities. ARCO1's construction was involved and time-consuming. As the first reported forecasting system of its type, it suggested many interesting basic research issues, most of which have yet to be explored. The underlying software is evolutionary; it grows in response to need. Since the first crucial stage of the system's development was the construction of a belief network model of the domain, work to date has emphasized modeling rather than forecasting. As a result, the forecasting applications may appear somewhat trivial—albeit surprisingly accurate. This paper was intended more as a proof-of-concept than as a demonstration-of-power. A great deal of evaluation—of both the underlying models and their forecasts—still need to be done.

7 Acknowledgements

Domain expertise was provided by ARCO's Anthony Finizza, Mikkal Herberg, Peter Jaquette, and Paul Tossetti. The code underlying the system was written by Keung-Chi Ng.

8 References

Abramson, B., 1990. On Knowledge Representation in Belief Networks. *Proceedings of the 3rd International Conference on Information Processing and Management of Uncertainty in Knowledge-Based Systems.*

Abramson, B. and A. J. Finizza, In press. Using Belief Networks to Forecast Oil Prices. *International Journal of Forecasting.*

Andreassen, S., M. Woldbye, B. Falck, and S. Anderson, 1987. MUNIN - A Causal Probabilistic Network for the Interpretation of Electromyographic Findings. In *Proceedings of the 10th International Joint Conference on Artificial Intelligence*, pages 366–372.

Edwards, W., H. Lindman, and L. Savage, 1963. Bayesian Statistical Inference for Psychological Research. *Psychological Review*, 70(3):193–242.

Energy Modeling Forum, 1982. World Oil. Technical Report EMF 6, Stanford University, 1982.

Gately, D., 1984. A Ten-Year Retrospective: OPEC and the World Oil Market. *Journal of Economic Literature*, 22:1100–14.

Heckerman, D., E. Horvitz, and B. Nathwani, 1990. Toward Normative Expert Systems: The Pathfinder Project. Technical Report KSL-90-08, Stanford University.

Howard, R.A. and J. E. Matheson, 1984. Influence Diagrams. In R. A. Howard and J. E. Matheson, editors, *Readings on the Principles and Applications of Decision Analysis, vol. II*, pages 721–762. Strategic Decisions Group.

Kahneman, D., P. Slovic, and A. Tversky, editors, 1982. *Judgement Under Uncertainty: Heuristics and Biases.* Cambridge University Press.

Marshalla, R.A. and D. Nesbitt, 1986. Future World Oil Prices and Production Levels: An Economic Analysis. *The Energy Journal*, 7(1):1–22.

Pearl, J., 1988. *Probabilistic Reasoning in Intelligent Systems.* Morgan Kaufmann.

Powell, S., 1990. The Target Capacity-Utilization Model of OPEC and the Dynamics of the World Oil Market. *The Energy Journal*, 11(1):27–63.

Savage, L.J., 1954. *The Foundations of Statistics.* Wiley.

Shachter, R.D., 1986. Evaluating Influence Diagrams. *Operations Research*, 34(6):871–882.

Shachter, R.D., 1988. Probabilistic Inference and Influence Diagrams. *Operation Research*, 36:589–604, 1988.

von Winterfeldt, D. and W. Edwards, 1986. *Decision Analysis and Behavioral Research.* Cambridge University Press.

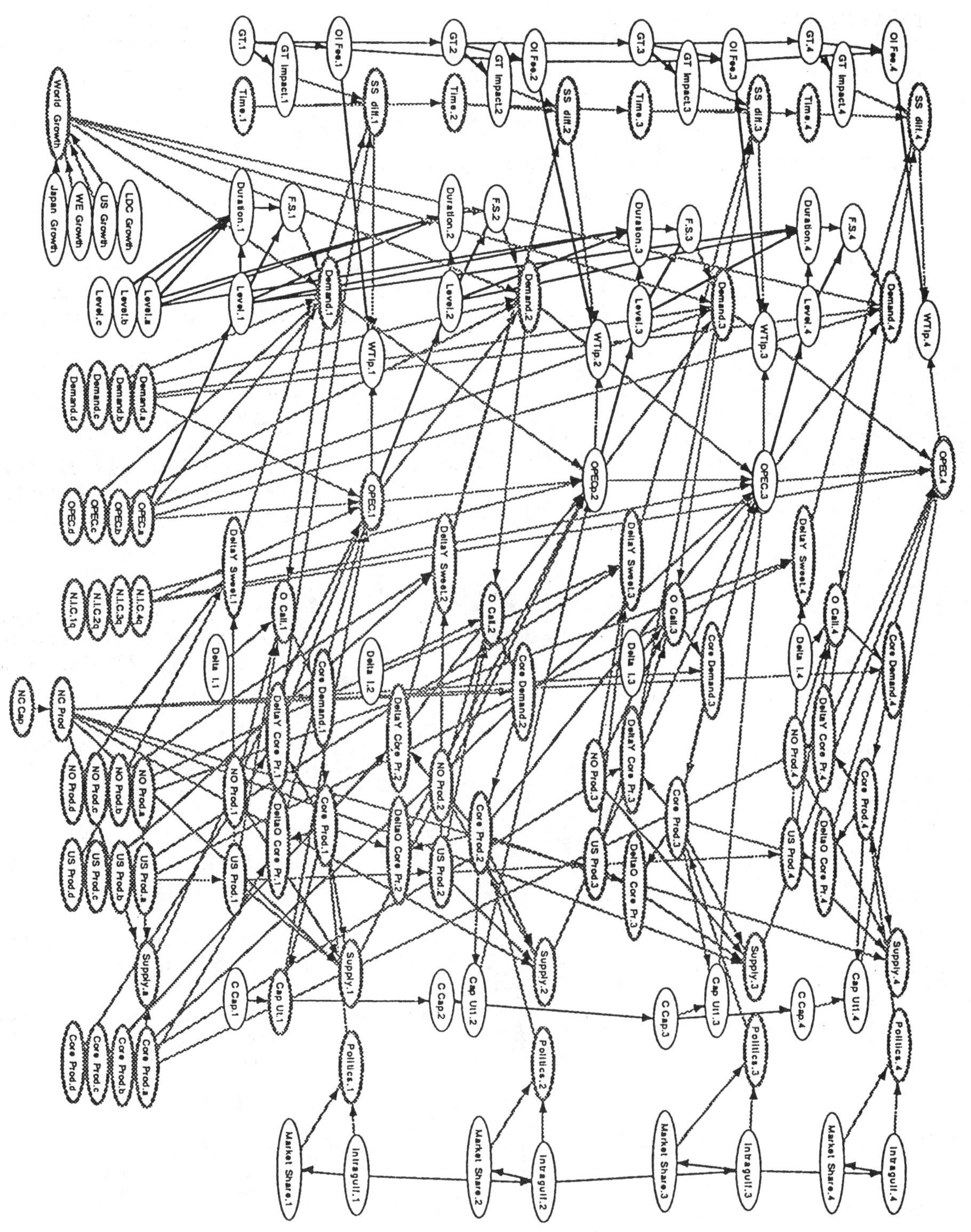

Figure 1: The network used to capture the 1990 base case. This model was designed in early 1990, using historical data through the fourth quarter of 1989 and subjective assessments provided by February 1990. Variables labelled ".1," ".2," ".3," and ".4" correspond to the first, second, third, and fourth quarters of 1990, respectively. Variables labelled ".d," ".c," ".b," and ".a" correspond to the first, second, third, and fourth quarters of 1989, respectively.

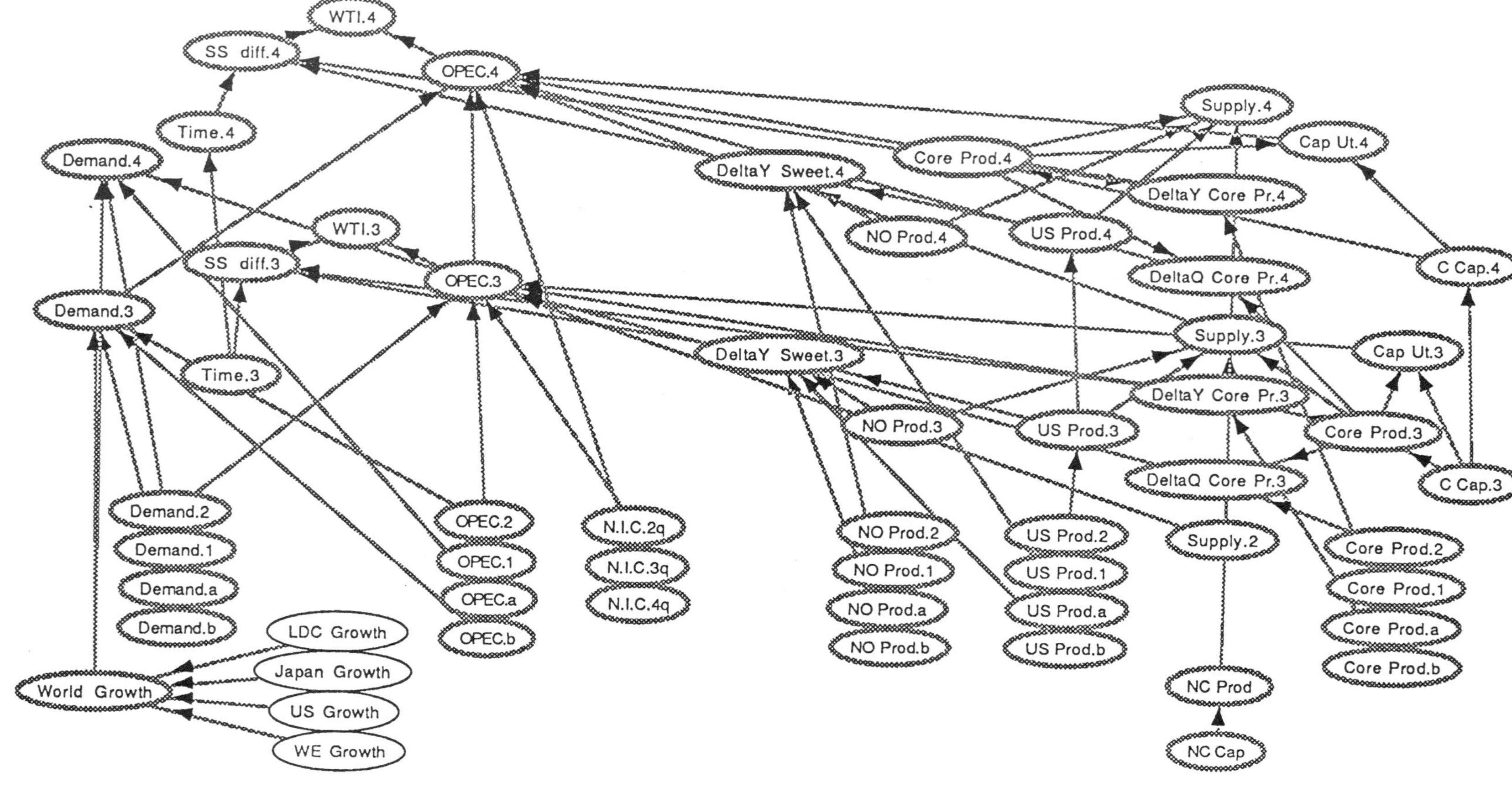

Figure 2: The network used to capture the constrained capacity case. This model was designed in September 1990, using historical data through the second quarter of 1989 and subjective assessments provided in August/September 1990. Variables labelled ".1," ".2," ".3," and ".4" correspond to the first, second, third, and fourth quarters of 1990, respectively. Variables labelled ".d," and ".c" correspond to the first, second, third, and fourth quarters of 1989, respectively.

"Conditional Inter-Causally Independent" node distributions, a property of "noisy-or" models

John Mark Agosta
Robotics Laboratory
Stanford University
Stanford, CA 94305
johnmark@flamingo.stanford.EDU

Abstract

This paper examines the interdependence generated between two parent nodes with a common instantiated child node, such as two hypotheses sharing common evidence. The relation so generated has been termed "inter-causal." It is shown by construction that inter-causal independence is possible for binary distributions at one state of evidence. For such "CICI" distributions, the two measures of inter-causal effect, "multiplicative synergy" and "additive synergy" are equal. The well known "noisy-or" model is an example of such a distribution. This introduces novel semantics for the noisy-or, as a model of the degree of conflict among competing hypotheses of a common observation.

In a general Bayesian network, the relation between a pair of nodes can be *predictive*, meaning we are interested in the effect of a node upon its successors, or, oppositely, *diagnostic*, where we infer the state of a node from knowledge of its successors. We can define yet a third relation between nodes that are neither successors of each other, but share a common successor. Such a relation has been termed *inter-causal.* [Henrion and Druzel 1990, p.10] For example, in the simplest diagram with this property, nodes A and B in Figure one are inter-causally related to each other by their common evidence at node e. This relation is a property of the clique formed by "marrying the parents" of e, not by the individual effects of the arcs into e. In this paper I derive the quantitative inter-causal properties due to evidence nodes constructed from the noisy-or" model.

The interest in inter-causal relations occurs in the process of *abduction*, that is, reasoning from evidence back to the hypotheses that explain the evidence. This arises in problems of interpretation, where more than one hypothesis may be suggested by a piece of evidence. [Goldman and Charniak 1990] Having multiple explanations denotes the ambiguity due to not having enough information to entirely resolve which hypothesis offers the true explanation. This paper shows how to construct an evidence node that expresses this ambiguity by the degree of conflict between hypotheses. We apply this elsewhere [Agosta 1991] as a component in building a "recognition network" where relevant hypotheses are created "on the fly" as possible interpretations of the evidence.

The implicit relation between A and B due to shared evidence has been extensively explored as the property of one hypothesis to "explain away" another. These are cases where, given evidence and the assertion of one hypothesis, the other hypothesis can be disqualified as a cause of the evidence. This paper explores how this dependency induced between hypotheses changes with the evidence. Interestingly, with binary variables, the induced dependency may vary, and as shown by the noisy-or, disappear for certain states of evidence.

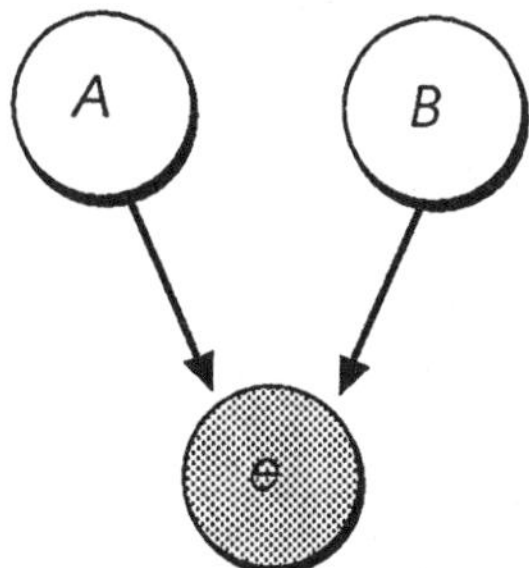

Figure 1: The relationship between hypotheses is determined by their common evidence

1 EVIDENCE NODES THAT ARE COMMON TO MULTIPLE PARENTS

This paper characterizes quantitatively the dependency between A and B that stems from the likelihood matrix at e. Capital letters such as A and B denote unobserved random variables and lower case letters denote variables when they have been observed: e^+ for $E = true$ and e^- for $E = false$.

Dependencies between two hypotheses' existence can occur in two senses: they *conflict*, so as the probability of one hypothesis' existence increases, the other decreases—we say one tends to *exclude* the other; or, as one increases the other increases also. The latter relation shall be called *collaboration.* First I discuss some of the basic independence properties of the network shown in figure one as it depends on the state of node e. Next I consider how the conditional distribution of node e leads to conditional dependence of its parents, using the "noisy-or" model as an example for node e. Finally I propose a quantitative parameterization of the dependence generated between the parent nodes.

1.1 INTER-CAUSAL INDEPENDENCE

The definition of d-separation [Pearl 1988, p.117] provides general conditions about the conditional independence of nodes that are parents of a common evidence node. In figure one, nodes A and B must be independent when their common successor is uninstantiated, or has any instantiated successors. The converse is not always true: it is possible to construct cases where A and B remain conditionally independent after e has been observed.[1] The d-separation theorem applies to the structure of the network: this conditional case extends it to the property of the distributions for a common successor node.

To construct such an independence conserving node, consider first the case where all variables are binary valued. The likelihood matrix for node e is:

$$\begin{bmatrix} r & s \\ t & u \end{bmatrix} \stackrel{\text{def}}{=} p\{e^- \mid A\,B\} \text{ such that}$$

$$r \stackrel{\text{def}}{=} p\{e^- \mid A = a^+\ B = b^+\},$$

$$s \stackrel{\text{def}}{=} p\{e^- \mid A = a^-\ B = b^+\} \text{ and so on.}$$

Taking expectation over B, the likelihood ratio seen by A, $p\{e^- | a^+\} \ / \ p\{e^- | a^-\}$, will be in the range between r/s and t/u. It is evident that, if the likelihood ratios in each row are the same, then the likelihood ratio seen by the other parent, A, will be constant for any value of B. Thus the expected likelihood ratio for A will be independent of the distribution of the other parent, node B. The same argument applies to the columns, and so to the relation of B upon A.

This property generalizes to random variables with more than two states where each row in the likelihood matrix differs only by a ratio, so that the row space is of rank one. Using a well known result from linear algebra, the row rank equals the column rank, so the same argument applies to the columns' likelihood ratios. This suggests a way to construct such a matrix:

Proposition 1: Independence is preserved between direct predecessors A and B of a common successor node E for one state of the evidence e^-, if the combined likelihood matrix is proportional to the "outer product" of the vectors for each individual likelihood:

$$p\{e^- \mid A\,B\} \propto p\{e^- \mid A\}p\{e^- \mid B\}.$$

This is shown by solving for $p\{A | B\,e^-\}$ for any $p\{A\}$, with Bayes' rule:

$$\begin{aligned} &p\{A | B\,e^-\} \\ &= \frac{p\{e^- \mid A\,B\}p\{A\}}{E_A[p\{e^- \mid A\,B\}p\{A\}]} \\ &\quad \text{Substituting in the likelihood, and simplifying:} \\ &= \frac{p\{e^- \mid A\}p\{e^- \mid B\}p\{A\}}{E_A[p\{e^- \mid A\}p\{e^- \mid B\}p\{A\}]} \\ &= \frac{p\{e^-\,A\}}{p\{e^-\}} = p\{A | e^-\}. \end{aligned}$$

I will call this independence condition between predecessor nodes conditional on one state of the common evidence "conditional inter-causal independence," or CICI. This condition on the likelihood distribution serves as a qualification on the conditions of d-separation for specified states of evidence at E.

Since the likelihood matrix appears in both numerator and denominator of Bayes' rule, scaling the likelihood by a constant affects neither l.h.s. nor r.h.s. Thus in the binary case, where the likelihoods are $a = p\{e^- | a^+\}$, $b = p\{e^- | b^+\}$, the outer product of the two likelihood vectors with a scaling factor, c, is general form for a CICI relation matrix:

$$\begin{bmatrix} r & s \\ t & u \end{bmatrix} = \begin{bmatrix} abc & (1-a)bc \\ a(1-b)c & (1-a)(1-b)c \end{bmatrix}.$$

I will call this the "singular matrix" model. The independence constraint removes one degree of freedom, leaving the matrix to be specified with three parameters. For binary variables, this constraint is equivalent to the relation matrix having a determinant equal to zero. This follows from the proposition:

Corollary 1: The determinant of a likelihood matrix of binary valued random variables, $p\{e | A\,B\}$, of rank one equals zero. Thus $\det p\{e | A\,B\} = 0$ implies that $p\{A | Be\} = p\{A | e\}$. Multiplying out the determinant gives $\det p\{e | A\,B\} = ru - st$, the quantity referred to as "multiplicative synergy" by Henrion. [Henrion, Druzdzel 1990]

[1] W. Buntine has pointed out that this is also a well known property of the logistic distribution, which may be thought of as a continous version of the noisy-or.

This independence relation $p\{A|BE\} = p\{A|E\}$ holds for CICI nodes at both certainty for one value of $e = E$ as well as for complete ignorance of E. The next questions are 1) whether this independence is implied for all distributions $p\{E\}$, and conversely 2) whether there are necessarily states of E for which CICI nodes do create conditional dependence. If 1) is true, CICI evidence nodes would be degenerate and serve no purpose.

To answer the first question we test if is it possible to have a relation matrix that is rank one at each state of the evidence. In that case the relation matrix would be factorable for every state of the evidence. In the binary case, this pair of constraints for both $E = e^+$ and $E = e^-$ can be shown, with some algebra, to imply that the likelihood ratios for one of the two parents must be constant and equal to one. This means that effectively there is no arc from that parent to the evidence. This independence is implied by a more general result of [Geiger and Heckerman 1990] about "transitive distributions" for which connectedness in graphical representations is equivalent to dependence among the distributions. Strictly positive binary distributions are one case of transitive distributions.

Now the converse, to show when the likelihood is factorable at one state of evidence it creates dependencies among parents at others. Let the evidence be a binary node, factorable at $E = e^-$. Then by Bayes rule, at the other state of the evidence:

$$\frac{p\{B|A e^+\}}{p\{B\}} = \frac{p\{e^+|AB\}}{p\{e^+|A\}} = \frac{(1 - p\{e^-|A\}p\{e^-|B\})}{1 - p\{e^-|A\}}$$

The right side cannot be factored into A and B factors, and is dependent upon A.

1.2 The noisy or

The noisy-or model is an example that illustrates the dependencies generated by CICI likelihoods:

Proposition 2: A "noisy-or" is a case of a CICI node. This can be shown by writing the noisy-or for evidence e^+ as

$$p\{e^+|AB\} = \begin{bmatrix} 1 - q_0q_1q_2 & 1 - q_0q_1 \\ 1 - q_0q_2 & 1 - q_0 \end{bmatrix},$$

where $q_i = 1 - p_i$, the reliability probabilities. It is evident that for evidence e^- , the likelihood matrix is a matrix of ones minus this. Calculating its determinant,

$$\det|1 - p\{e^+|AB\}| = \det p\{e^-|AB\} = 0.$$

With CICI nodes I will, by convention, label the evidence e^- at which independence occurs.

The other way to build a CICI node is from the "singular matrix model," mentioned in the previous section, where the singular matrix represents the likelihood $p\{e^-|AB\}$. What is the relation between these two models? They both have three degrees of freedom. Equating and solving obtains $c = q_0$, $q_2 = b/(1-b)$, $q_1 = a/(1-a)$. Since all terms must be probabilities in the range of $(0,1)$, the noisy-or can be identified with the singular matrix model only when the singular matrix parameters are restricted to $0 < a, b < 1/2$. This is because the noisy-or model enforces a size ordering among matrix entries, the largest entry being in the upper left hand corner. There are three other cases, $0 < a < 1/2 \leq b < 1$, $0 < b < 1/2 \leq a < 1$ and $1/2 \leq a, b < 1$. These are equivalent to the noisy-or matrix with the row terms switched, the column terms switched, or both switched. These four generalizations cover the range of binary CICI relation nodes.

1.3 THE DEGREE OF INTER-CAUSAL EFFECT

We have seen that inter-causal independence among a node's parents depends upon the common node's evidence. In the binary case, forcing inter-causal independence at one state of the evidence precludes it from the other state. We have also seen that, in the binary case, the rank one condition for independence is easily tested by looking for a zero determinant of the likelihood matrix. The next question is, what does the value of a non-zero determinant indicate about the effect of A upon B?

1.3.1 Qualitative effects

The value of this determinant varies from minus unity to plus unity as the relation between parents goes from extreme exclusion to extreme collaboration. At each extreme the parents A and B are deterministically dependent. Then either the parents are mutual exclusive, a condition already discussed, or they are forced to have identical distributions. To force identity between parents, the relation matrix becomes an identity matrix. For exclusion it is one minus this matrix—zeros on the diagonal and ones off-diagonal. Call these extremes "complete collaboration and "complete exclusion." Thus a relation matrix with complete collaboration for e^+ will have complete exclusion for e^-. These two matrices and their linear combinations are not CICI matrices, except for the trivial case of a constant matrix.

To be able to use the determinant measure—the multiplicative synergy—to characterize the relation between parents, I must first establish that the sign of this property of the likelihood matrix is invariant to Bayes' rule: The next theorem shows that the sign of the multiplicative synergy equals the sign of the CICI relation between parents not just for $p\{e|AB\}$, but for $p\{A|Be\}$, and all other permutations that may be generated by Bayes' rule.

Lemma: Multiplication of a likelihood matrix, $L(X,Y)_{ij}$ by any positive probability vector $v(X)_i$ does not change the sign of the likelihood's determinant.

To show this: Multiplication by a row vector variable is equivalent to a term-by-term multiplication of matrices where the vector is replicated to fill out the columns of its matrix. This, in turn, is equivalent to matrix multiplication where the vector values fill the diagonal of a matrix, with all other entries zero. Write this diagonal matrix derived from the vector as $d(v)_{ii}$. From linear algebra there is the result that the determinant of a product equals the product of each matrix's determinant, thus

$$\det d(v)_{ii} L(X,Y)_{ij} = \det d(v)_{ii} \det L(X,Y)_{ij}.$$

The determinant of the diagonal matrix is merely the product of terms along the diagonal, a number between zero and one. We can now show:

Proposition 3: Exclusion or collaboration (the sign of the multiplicative synergy) is given by the sign of the determinant of $p\{e|AB\}$ and is invariant to all permutations derivable by Bayes' rule of this likelihood matrix for a given conditioning.

Bayes' rule consists of multiplying the likelihood matrix by one probability vector, the prior, then dividing it by another, the pre-posterior. By the previous lemma, multiplication by the prior multiplies the likelihood's determinant by a positive number. Division by the pre-posterior likewise multiplies it by the reciprocal, another positive number. Both operations preserve the sign of the likelihood determinant. Note that since the conditioning of the likelihood must be preserved;$\det p\{e^+|AB\} > 0$ does not necessarily imply that $\det p\{a^+|EB\} > 0$.

1.3.2 Comparision to other measures of diagnostic and inter-causal relations

Inter-causality has been examined as a qualitative relation by Wellman. [Wellman 1988] In the tradition of non-numeric, automatic reasoning methods for planning, he has developed an abstraction of influence diagrams where each influence is described by its sign. These "qualitative probabilistic networks" can formulate decision tradeoffs by considering dominance relationships among alternatives. Such networks are constructed from two kinds of qualitative relations: the first, *qualitative influences*, describes the relation between two variables; the second is the relation between influences that he terms *qualitative synergy*, which corresponds to inter-causality. Here is his definition of synergy, in our notation: [p. 74]

Definition:(Qualitative synergy) Variables A and B are positively synergistic on E, written $Y^+(E|AB)$, or just $Y^+ E$, if and only if, for every x, a_1, a_2, b_1, b_2, e_0, $a_1 \geq a_2$, $b_1 \geq b_2$ implies

$$p\{e_0|a_1 b_1 x\} - p\{e_0|a_2 b_1 x\} \\ \leq p\{e_0|a_1 b_2 x\} - p\{e_0|a_2 b_2 x\}.$$

Similarly in the last relation, substitute "$\geq$" for negatively synergistic and "=" for zero synergy.

Henrion has called this quantity "additive synergy" to distinguish it from the multiplicative synergy measure defined previously. In comparison to Wellman, our definition of "quantitative additive synergy" takes the liberty of assigning a value to Y whose sign corresponds to the sign of the synergy:

$$Ye^+ \stackrel{\text{def}}{=} Y(E = e^+|AB) = r + u - s - t.$$

Wellman does recognize in his examples the implied inter-causal relation between A and B due to the synergistic properties of the likelihood. As a further distinction, Wellman takes pains to extend his definition over all states of conditioning variables x, which he calls the *context*. This would be useless for our quantitative definition; however it serves his purpose of determining dominance relations. Unlike his definition however, I define a $Y\,e$ for each conditioning of E in the likelihood matrix. Since qualitative synergy is derived from a stochastic dominance relation on continuous variables, to apply it to the case of binary variables he introduces a sign ordering convention such that $e^+ > e^-$. In my framework, his definition is equivalent to just the case where $E = e^+$. As such, the manner in which this relation depends upon the evidential support at E is not developed in his examples.

1.3.3 Relation between additive and multiplicative synergies

As seen, for purposes of characterizing the effects between inter-causal nodes, I have modified definitions of synergy to be conditional on the states of binary variables. The next part develops a constraint among determinants (multiplicative synergy measures) of the same relation matrix with different states of binary evidence.

Proposition 4: Additive synergy equals the sum of the determinant measures, $\det e$, for both states of evidence. Expressed as a formula,

$$Ye^+ = \det e^+ - \det e^-,$$

where $\det e^+$ is defined to equal determinant $|p\{E = e^+ | AB\}|$, and likewise $\det e^-$ to equal the determinant $|p\{E = e^- | AB\}|$. Further, Y changes sign when the state of evidence is negated. To demonstrate, since E is a binary variable,

$$\begin{aligned} Ye^- &= Y(E = e^- | A\,B) \\ &= 1 - r + 1 - u - (1 - s) - (1 - t) \\ &= s + t - r - u = -Ye^+. \end{aligned}$$

To see the relation between multiplicative and additive synergies, write out

$$\begin{aligned} \det e^- &= (1 - r)(1 - u) - (1 - s)(1 - t) \\ &= s + t - r - u + ru - st \\ &= Ye^- + \det e^+, \\ \text{or} \quad & Ye^+ = \det e^+ - \det e^- \end{aligned}$$

Proposition 5: Multiplicative and additive synergy are equal for CICI relation matrices. If one of the states of evidence forces independence (e.g., is CICI) then the determinant for that state disappears. Thus for CICI nodes the relation between additive and multiplicative synergy is: $\det e^+ = Ye^+$, that is, both measures are equivalent.

The additive-multiplicative synergy relation makes it easy to show the following:

Proposition 6: Noisy-or matrices are exclusionary nodes for $E = e^+$.

Since $\det e^- = 0$, one can use the previous result to show $Ye^+ < 0$. See [Agosta 1991].

A typical situation expressed by a noisy-or is the relation between seeing cat prints in someone's house and inferring which kind of cat they have as a pet. The exclusionary property of noisy-or nodes is the essence of their ability to "explain away" one hypothesized cause as another cause becomes more likely. Thus upon seeing paw prints, one cause—a pet blue Persian—tends to exclude their being also a short haired red tabby in the house.[2] If we comb the house and find no paw prints, the explanations remain independent: we are no wiser about relative probabilities of the household's domestic animals, even though we may justifiably tend to doubt they own a pet.

How would collaborative nodes, e.g. $Ye^+ > 0$ nodes, be constructed? Recall the result in Linear Algebra that switching a pair of rows or columns of a matrix switches the sign of a matrix's determinant. Thus they can be built from exclusionary nodes by switching the off-diagonal and on-diagonal elements.

[2]For the model to apply strictly, there should be no relation between lovers of different kinds of cats; that is, being a Persian owner should not, in itself, make the household more or less likely to own a short haired tabby. (This example is inspired by [M. Henrion, 1990].)

1.3.4 The range of inter-causal dependency

How can the dependency be described quantitatively? This inter-causal dependency is not just a consequence of the diagnostic dependencies between the parents, A and B, and the evidence; rather it may be thought of as the relation between these dependencies. At the extremes of complete inter-causal dependency, the individual (marginal) likelihoods $p\{E| A\}$ and $p\{E| B\}$ are completely determined by the marginals of the other predecessor: there is no additional freedom in the diagnostic relation between hypothesis and evidence. In comparison, when A and B are inter-causally conditionally independent, the diagnostic support between hypothesis and evidence for each can be specified independently.

As a consequence of proposition 3, there is a qualitative correspondence, where the sign of the determinant of likelihood matrix terms $p\{e| A\,B\}$ corresponds to the sign of the induced dependency of $p\{A| B\}$. Their quantitative relation is not as obvious. Note that unlike the determinant, $\det e^+$, $p\{A| B\}$ is homogeneous of zeroth order in the likelihood terms. That is, scaling the entries in the likelihood matrix does not change the dependence among parents, as can be seen from the following version of Bayes' rule:

$$p\{B| A\,e\} = \frac{p\{e| A\,B\}p\{B\}}{E_B[p\{e| A\,B\}]}$$

This means that multiplying all terms of $p\{e| A\,B\}$ by a constant changes the value of the determinant but leaves $p\{B| A\,e\}$ unchanged, destroying the one to one correspondence between the multiplicative synergy and any quantitative characterization of the inter-causal relation $p\{e| A\,B\}$.

To explore the quantitative relation, the next section shows the construction of the algebraic solution for one parent's belief as a function of the rest of the clique's nodes.

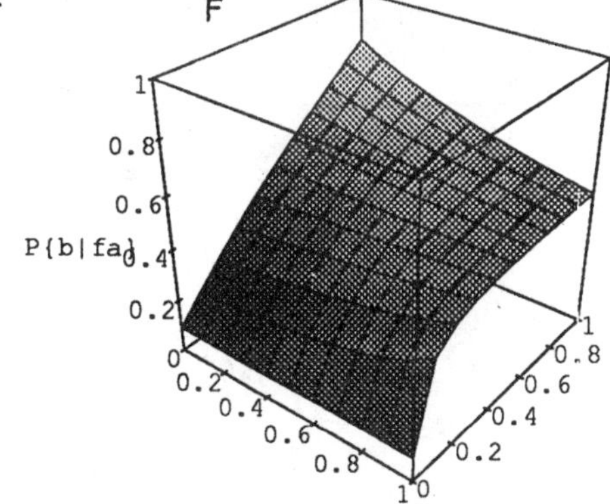

Figure 2: The noisy-or belief surface

2 CONSTRUCTIVE SOLUTION OF THE BINARY VARIABLE INTER-CAUSAL DEPENDENCY

By deriving the belief of one parent as a function of the probabilities of the other nodes in the clique, one may examine its quantitative behavior completely. This function is a three-dimensional surface, a marginal probability of one parent as a function of the support for their common evidence and the other parent. This "belief function surface" shows the combined effect on one parent of the diagnostic and inter-causal influences.

The solution technique used is similar to the clique potential methods. All the nodes are formed into one clique potential, Ψ, proportional to the joint for the state space of all nodes. The probability that we solve for is the posterior on B as a function of the probabilities of other nodes in the network. To make precise the sensitivity of one node's marginal on other nodes' probabilities, think of the "knobs" to control the other nodes as pi (π) and lambda (λ) messages to the nodes; π messages as the root nodes, and λ messages to leaf nodes. These messages can be specified independently of each other, whereas in general the marginal probabilities of nodes cannot, since they are not independent. In this case there is one λ message, to the evidence node, E, and two π messages, one for each parent, of which we are mainly interested in the π for the "other" parent, A.

The posterior on B is a function of both parent priors, $\pi(a)$ and $\pi(b)$, the evidence likelihood matrix, $p\{E|AB\}$, and the "evidential support," or the λ message that the evidence receives. To show the functional dependence, I write $p\{B|\pi(a)\,\pi(b)\,\lambda(e)\}$. It is important to distinguish this from $p\{B|AE\}$, which is a tabulation of probabilities at each combination of points in the state space, rather than a function of probabilities. The potential, Ψ, is a $2\times 2\times 2$ matrix, the product of all terms. To obtain the posterior on B, sum over all other variables, then normalize by the sum of all eight terms. These definitions are used for clarity:

$$a \stackrel{\text{def}}{=} \pi(A=a^+), b \stackrel{\text{def}}{=} \pi(B=b^+), f \stackrel{\text{def}}{=} \lambda(E=e^+),$$

so that,

$$\Psi(a,b,f) = \pi(A)\pi(B)\lambda(E)p\{E|AB\}.$$

Thus,

$$p\{B|\pi(a)\pi(b)\lambda(e)\} = \frac{\sum_{AE}\Psi(a,b,f)}{\sum_{ABE}\Psi(a,b,f)}$$

$$= \frac{\begin{array}{c} b[a(fr+(1-f)(1-r)) \\ +(1-a)(sf+(1-f)(1-s))], \\ (1-b)[a(ft+(1-f)(1-t)) \\ +(1-a)(uf+(1-f)(1-u))] \end{array}}{\sum_{ABE}\Psi(a,b,f)}$$

The numerator is a two-valued vector for b^+ and b^-. It is normalized by the denominator, which is precisely the sum of the two terms in the numerator. Figure two shows a graph of this "belief surface" as a function of f and a, for $\pi(b) = 1/2$. The values from this example are for a symmetric noisy-or likelihood matrix. The conditional independence of the parent node probabilities is evident by the constant value of the function for all values of a at both $f = 0$; that is, $e^- = E$ and $f = 1/2$, complete ignorance of E. The exclusionary property is evident along the edge $f = 1$, where B is inversely related to a. The graph may be thought of as a combination of the diagnostic relation, where decreasing f increases the belief in both parents, together with an inter-causal exclusionary relation when $e^+ = E$. The inter-causal relation is slight when $1/2 \leq f \leq 0$ since at both extremes of this interval the inter-causal dependence disappears.

The exclusive relation between the beliefs of A and B are described by the $f = \lambda(e) = 1$ edge of the belief function surface, shown here in figure three:

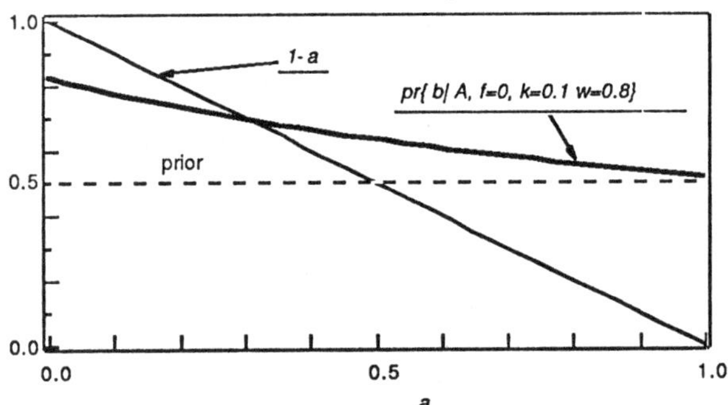

Figure 3: Partial exclusion of a CICI relation, bounded below by its prior. The other line shows the complete exclusion relation.

The two beliefs move in opposite directions, with $p\{B|\pi(a)\,\pi(b)\,\lambda(e)=1\}$ having a maximum approximately at w and a minimum no lower than $\pi(b)$. Previously I mentioned a relation matrix for complete exclusion, which forced $p\{B|e\}+p\{A|e\} = 1$. In comparison to this *partial exclusion* at $f = 1$, the complete exclusion probability, $p\{B|e\}$, descends to zero from unity. The outstanding difference between complete exclusion and that generated by a CICI node is this lower bound that prevents B's belief from ever being driven below its value without the CICI node. Thus "CICI partial exclusion" cannot defeat other support for a node's belief.

The degree of inter-causal exclusion is limited by the diagnostic effect when their combination operates in opposite directions. One way to think of this is that the positive effect of the diagnostic support dominates the negative effect of exclusion. In the "cat household" example, if we see a blue Persian after having seen paw prints, our belief in the presence of a short haired red tabby cannot be less than our prior belief about the tabby. To formalize this property of CICI nodes:

Proposition 7: For $p\{ e^+ | A\, B \}$ in the form of a noisy-or, $p\{ B | A\, e^+ \} > \pi(b)$ for all values of $\pi(a)$. In terms of the graph in figure two, this constrains the e^+ half of the belief function surface to lie above the prior value, and the e^- half to lie below. The surface intersects the $\pi(b)$ valued horizontal plane only along the $E = 1/2$ line.

To show

$$p\{ B | \pi(a) = 1 \pi(b) \lambda(e) = 1 \} > \pi(b),$$

write it out in functional form;

$$\frac{br}{br + (1-b)t} > b,$$

which reduces to $r > t$, an assumption of the noisy-or.

In a corresponding manner the size ordering relative to B of the other three vertices of the belief surface can be demonstrated. Each vertex value is an increasing function of the prior on B and the ratio of a pair of elements in the likelihood matrix. For both $p\{ B | e^- a^+ \}$ and $p\{ B | e^- a^- \}$, the "independent edge" vertices, the ratios are equal: $(1-r)/(1-t) = (1-s)/(1-u)$. This is just a restatement of the $\det e^- = 0$ condition.

The "independent edge" value $p\{ B | e^- \}$ and the "positive exclusion" value $p\{ B | a^- e^+ \}$, the two extreme values of the surface, describe the surface completely, and have physical significance in the model. I will use them to effectively factor the relation into a two parameter model of the likelihood, in the "factored" form of a symmetric noisy-or:

$$p\{ e^- | AB \} = \begin{bmatrix} k^2 w & kw \\ kw & w \end{bmatrix} \text{ for } 0 < k < 1, 0 < w < 1.$$

With the belief surface we can describe qualitatively both parameters' effects. As w increases, the "positive exclusion" vertex, $p\{ B | a^- e^+ \}$, increases also. As k decreases, the vertex probabilities become more extreme. At the same time, the "negative exclusion" vertex approaches $\pi(b)$. This is also true for non-symmetric noisy-or's, thus the degree of freedom that was lost to the symmetry assumption has only marginal effect on the surface shape. Further, when $\pi(b)$ approaches either zero or one it pulls the whole surface with it, for instance as $\pi(b) \to 1$ then $p\{ B | A\, E \} \to 1$.

To derive the vertex values in the limit of small k and large w, approximate the values by first order expansions in k and w . First this lemma, by which one may approximate rational functions whose numerator and denominator differ by a "small" amount:

Lemma: Since

$$\frac{1}{1-z} = 1 + z + \frac{z^2}{1-z}$$

this approximation holds:

$$\frac{1}{1-z} = 1 + z + O(z^2) \geq 1 + z, \text{ for } z \text{ small.}$$

With this formula the best linear approximation to a rational polynomial is obtained without the need to write out the derivative.

Proposition 8: The "independent edge" probability $p\{ B | e^- \}$ at $\pi(b) = 1/2$ is independent of w and equals $k/(1+k)$. This follows exactly since

$$p\{ B | e^- \} = \frac{bk}{1 + b(k-1)}.$$

Further, k sets an upper bound for this probability, since it follows that for all k and b,

$$p\{ B | e^- \} < k.$$

Proposition 9: The "negative exclusion" corner $p\{ B | a^- e^- \}$ approaches B from above, such that

$$p\{ B | a^- e^- \} \geq b[1 + kw(1-b)].$$

Since the inequality is bounded by $O(z^2)$, this probability approaches b, linearly in k, as k approaches 0. When k is small $p\{ B | a^- e^- \}$ is well approximated by b.

Proposition 10: The "positive exclusion" probability $p\{ B | a^- e^+ \}$ is bounded below to $O(z^2)$ such that

$$p\{ B | a^- e^+ \} > 1 - \frac{(1-b)(1-w)}{b(1-kw)}.$$

Further, when k is small and b is near 1/2, this limit is approximately equal to w.

To summarize, it is a good approximation that the belief surface, and hence any CICI distribution, can be specified by limits to the minimum and maximum values of the surface, which imply the conditional probabilities of the parent nodes at different states of evidence. These probabilities lead directly to estimates of the symmetric CICI likelihood parameters; k approaching the "independent edge" conditional probability, and w approaching the "positive exclusion" conditional probability. The remaining vertex, the "negative exclusion" conditional probability closely approximates the parent's prior. The error in the approximation is second order in k and $1 - w$, and the approximation becomes exact as $k \rightarrow 0$ and $w \rightarrow 1$.

3 DISCUSSION

A major finding of this paper is that the CICI effect of evidence is secondary to its diagnostic effects. Thus the relative effect between hypotheses—call it the observed exclusion—is also a consequence of the degree of direct support for the hypotheses as much as it is affected by the partial exclusion controled by the noisy-or parameter, w. The more that two related hypotheses have direct support, the less that secondary inter-causal effects appear. Thus the refutational effect of w on a hypothesis due to conflicting hypotheses decreases as other support for the hypothesis increases.

This paper has explored the properties of CICI evidence nodes. The properties are two: First, when it is certain that the evidence is absent, e.g. at e^-, the CICI node leaves dependencies among the hypothesis set unchanged. For hypotheses that are otherwise independent, this reduces the connectivity of the network, and thus simplifies the complexity of the probability updating algorithm. Secondly, at the other extreme when the evidence, e^+, is present, the CICI node generates partial exclusion (or collaboration) among the set, in the sense that the exclusion can not decrease other evidential support, only increase support in the lack of other evidence.

There are several consequences of building a network of nodes with these properties. First, the conditional independence property implies the exclusion property, so we either accept both, or neither. It is a general property of common evidence nodes, not only CICI nodes, that shared evidence generates dependencies among hypotheses; and we have seen that we cannot have independence among the existence of hypotheses for all states of evidence. As a consequence, it is probabilistically inconsistent to treat common evidence separately, inferring each hypothesis independently. This can be summed up in the phrase "ambiguity implies conflict," meaning that alternate, competing explanations must probabilistically exclude each other. Conversely, they could also be collaborating explanations that become coupled by common evidence. What is not possible is for two perfectly good explanations of a common effect to be probabilistically independent of each other for all states of the evidence.

Multiple parent nodes are the elements from which to build networks of multiply connected hypotheses. This technique is similar to other "constraint propagation networks" of hypotheses where typically inter-hypothesis constraints are expressed without intervening nodes. Constraint networks typically can propagate a small change through all nodes in a network, because of their similar properties to sets of simultaneous equations. In comparision, inter-causal constraints tend to have a quickly attentuated effect among chains of nodes, since the percent change diminishes from a node to its neighbor. Inter-causal constraints are best thought of as resulting in a secondary set of effects that tend to increase the discrimination of diagnostic inference among hypotheses.

Acknowledgements

My grateful acknowledgements to Tom Binford, Max Henrion, Harold Lehmann, Gregory Provan, Ross Shachter and Mike Wellman for their comments and suggestions. Also to Wally Mann and Margaret Miller for help with the figures.

References

Agosta, J. M., "The structure of Bayes networks for visual recognition," *Proc. 4th conf. on uncertainty in A.I.*, 1988, pp.1-8.

_____, *Probabilistic recognition networks, an application of influence diagrams to visual recognition*, PhD Thesis, submitted April 1991.

Geiger, D. and D. Heckerman, "Separable and Transitive Graphoids", *Proc. of the 6th conf. on uncertainty and A.I.*, 1990, pp. 538-545.

Goldman, R. P. and E. Charniak, "Dynamic construction of belief networks," *Proc. of the 6th Conf in Uncertainty and A.I.*, 1990, pp. 90-97.

Henrion, M. and M. Druzdzel, "Qualitative propagation and scenario-based approaches to explanation of probabilistic reasoning," *Proc. of the 6th Conf on uncertainty and A.I.*, 1990, pp. 10-20.

Pearl, J., *Probabilistic Reasoning in Intelligent Systems*, (San Mateo, CA: Morgan Kaufman:, 1988.)

Wellman, M. P., *Formulation of Tradeoffs in planning under uncertainty*,(Massachusetts: Cambridge, MIT Thesis MIT/LCS/TR-427, August 1988.)

Combining Multiple-valued Logics in Modular Expert Systems

Jaume Agustí-Cullell Francesc Esteva Pere García Lluís Godó Carles Sierra

Centre d'Estudis Avançats de Blanes, CSIC
C/ Sta. Barbara s/n
17300 BLANES Girona Spain.
Tel. 34-72-336101 Fax: 34-72-337806
e-mails: agusti,esteva,pere,godo,sierra@ceab.es

Abstract

The way experts manage uncertainty usually changes depending on the task they are performing. This fact has lead us to consider the problem of communicating modules (task implementations) in a large and structured knowledge based system when modules have different uncertainty calculi. In this paper, the analysis of the communication problem is made assuming that (i) each uncertainty calculus is an inference mechanism defining an entailment relation, and therefore the communication is considered to be inference-preserving, and (ii) we restrict ourselves to the case which the different uncertainty calculi are given by a class of truth-functional Multiple-valued Logics.

1 INTRODUCTION

Most expert system (ES) building tools with uncertainty management capabilities provide a unique and global method for representing and combining evidence. Nevertheless, human experts usually change the way they manage uncertainty depending on the task they are performing. To be able to model this behaviour, an ES building tool must allow to attach different uncertainty calculi to the structures implementing the different tasks (in modular ES shells the notion of task is usually implemented as goal-oriented modules). However, tasks or modules in a knowledge base are not independent one of each other, they need to cooperate and communicate, as human experts do when solving complex problems. This can be shown in the following example.

A physician diagnosing a pneumonia could ask to a radiologist about the results of a radiological analysis. The simplest and more frequent type of communication is to get an "atomic" answer like

> *"it is likely that the patient has a cavitation in his left lung."*

Then, to use this information in his own reasoning, the physician must only interpret in his language the linguistic expression *likely* used by the radiologist, and perhaps to identify it with another uncertainty term, say for example *acceptable*, used by himself. But the communication could have been richer than that "atomic" answer, and consist of a more complex piece of information. For instance, the radiologist could have answered:

> *"if from a clinical point of view you are very confident that the patient has a bacterial disease and he is also inmunodepressed, then its nearly sure he has a cavitation in his left lung."*

As in the previous case, to use the radiologist information the physician must again interpret it. However, this time the interpretation can not be only a matter of uncertainty terms (*very confident, nearly sure*) but also a matter of way of reasoning, if he wants to make use of this information in other situations (i.e., patients) which do not match exactly the one expressed above.

Therefore, if in a knowledge base we have different uncertainty calculi for different tasks (or modules), and these modules need to communicate, a correspondence between their uncertainty calculi must be established. To model the first type of communication shown in the example, in a modular ES shell only a way of translating the languages of different uncertainty calculi, attached to different modules, is required. However, to model the second type of communication the correspondence is also required to be made inference-preserving. The need to preserve sometimes inferences through the communication among tasks can be made clearer by means of another little example from an existing expert system, PNEUMON-IA[1] [Verdaguer, 1989], for the diagnosis of

[1] PNEUMON-IA is an application developped in the modular rule-based expert system shell MILORD [Sierra, 1989], that manages linguistically expressed uncertainty (see section 3 for more details)

pneumoniae. The module (task) *Bacteria* of this expert system comprises the following rule:

[If a patient has leukopenia and left-deviation then he has a bacterial disease, ***sure****]*

stating that the certainty about the bacterianicity of a disease depends on the certainty of the facts *leukopenia* and *left-deviation*, which are investigated in another module named *Laboratory*. Let's suppose that these two modules have different uncertainty calculi. Then we could have two types of communication between them. A first possibility is that *Bacteria* asks to *Laboratory* for the two facts, translates the answers and makes its "and" combination to conclude about bacterianicity. The second possibility is *Bacteria* asks the certainty value of the non-atomic sentence "*leucopenia and left-deviation*" and translates it. In this last case the "and" combination of the certainty values is performed in the *Laboratory* module, and the result is afterwards translated to the *Bacteria* uncertainty calculus and used to conclude about bacterianicity. It seems clear that in order to keep the coherence of the whole diagnosis task, the certainty degree of bacterianicity found out in each case should be the same. To make this sure, the correspondence between the uncertainty calculi of those modules should preserve the inferences made in the *Laboratory* module when moving to the *Bacteria* module.

The general problem of analyzing conditions under which a correspondence or communication between different tasks with different uncertainty calculi preserves inference is a very hard one. In order to deal with this problem, several approaches could be taken into account, from pure logical ones to more cognitive ones. In [Meseguer, 1989], in another but not very different setting, it is argued that "*if the approach taken lacks a logical basis to serve as a criterion of correctness the result may be quite ad hoc and unsatisfactory, and it will probably involve a good deal of costly engineering trial and error*". Following this argument, the approach we have chosen is a logical one, but without forgetting cognitive aspects. More concretely, our analysis will be carried out from two main points:

- first, we will consider uncertainty calculi as inference mechanisms defining logical entailment relationships. Therefore, correspondences (or communications) between different uncertainty calculi will be analyzed as mappings between different entailment systems.

- and second, we will use finite truth-functional multiple-valued logics (MV-logics, for short) as uncertainty calculi, as long as this is a simplified view of the uncertainty reasoning model that our laboratory has been working with in developing applications with the MILORD system [Sierra, 1989], mainly in the medical diagnosis field.

The paper is structured in the following way. After this introductory section, in section two there is a general overview on entailment systems and their inference-preserving mappings. In section three, we describe the class of finite truth-functional multiple-valued logics we will use as uncertainty calculi for different tasks. Section four is devoted to a detailed study of inference-preserving mappings for our uncertainty calculi, and finally, an interactive algorithm for defining such inference preserving correspondences is proposed. This algorithm has been thought as a mechanism to support human experts when developing applications.

2 ENTAILMENT SYSTEMS

Inference engines of many rule-based ES can be considered as implementations of proof calculi (from a set of axioms and a set of inference rules) of some underlying Logical Systems. As it is known, every logical system should have a syntactical and semantical formalizations. The theories of Institutions and Entailments Systems allow to formalize an intuitive notion of logical system from the model and proof theoretic approach point of view respectively ([Goguen and Burstall, 1983], [Meseguer, 1989], [Harper et al., 1989]). In this way the Institution approach takes the satisfaction relation between models and sentences as basic whereas the Entailment System approach takes the entailment relation.

The communication problem among tasks or modules has been introduced as the problem of defining inference preserving mappings. Therefore, in this paper we focus our attention in the entailment systems approach rather than in the Institutions one, and thus, we are mainly interested in correspondences between different entailment systems.

Although a categorical definition of Entailment Systems has been given [Meseguer, 1989], for our purposes an *Entailment System* will consist of a pair $(L, \vdash)$, where L is a *language* (a set of sentences, usually built from a set of connectives and a signature that provides a set of sorted symbols), and $\vdash$ is an *entailment relation* on $2^L xL$, i.e. a relation satisfying the following properties:

E1.- *reflexivity*: for any sentence E, $\{E\} \vdash E$
E2.- *monotonicity*: if $\Gamma \vdash E$ and $\Gamma \subseteq \Gamma'$ then $\Gamma' \vdash E$
E3.- *transitivity*: if $\Gamma \vdash E_i$, for $i \in I$ and
$\Gamma \cup \{E_i, i \in I\} \vdash E$ then $\Gamma \vdash E$,

where Γ and Γ' are sets of sentences, and E and E_i are sentences of L.

In [Meseguer, 1989] the following notion of a map of entailment systems has been proposed.

Definition 2.1. (map of entailment systems) *Given the entailment systems $(L, \vdash)$ and $(L', \vdash')$, a mapping $H: L \rightarrow L'$ is said to be a map of entailment systems if the following condition*

If $\Gamma \vdash E$ then $H(\Gamma) \vdash' H(E)$,

holds for all set of sentences Γ and for all sentence E of L. The map H is said to be conservative if $\Gamma \vdash E$ whenever $H(\Gamma) \vdash' H(E)$.

A map between entailment systems allows to preserve inference in a strict sense. In particular, when the map is conservative one entailment system is an extension of the other one. However these strong conditions sometimes can be weakened in the uncertainty reasoning framework. From the point of view of the correspondence problem between different tasks with different uncertainty calculi, when a task imports information from another task, it doesn't need always to deduce exactly the same conclusions as the previous one could deduce. Sometimes it only needs that its conclusions be coherent with the deduction system of the other task . In other words, it allows its reasoning to be less accurate when dealing with the other task information, but not incorrect in any case. To model this last situation a definition weaker than the conservative one is introduced below. We will call it *weak conservative*.

Definition 2.2. (weak conservative map). *Given entailment systems (L, |-) and (L', |-') a map H from L to L' is called weak conservative if the following condition holds:*

If H(Γ) |-' E' then there exists a sentence E of L such that Γ |- E and H(E) |-' E'

for all set of sentences Γ of L and all sentence E' of L '.
If H is also a map of entailment systems we call it weak conservative map .

3 A CLASS OF MULTIPLE-VALUED LOGICS FOR THE UNCERTAINTY MANAGEMENT IN RULE-BASED EXPERT SYSTEMS

Taking the uncertainty management of MILORD as a reference, in this section we consider a restricted type of MV-logics which are expressive enough to model the uncertainty reasoning used in many rule-based systems. The uncertainty management approach used in MILORD has the following characteristics [Godo et al., 1989]:
1) The expert defines a set of linguistic terms expressing uncertainty corresponding to the verbal scale he will use to weight facts and rules.
2) The set of linguistic terms is supposed to be ordered, at least partially, according to the amount of uncertainty they express, being always the booleans 'true' and 'false' their maximum and minimum elements respectively.
3) The combination and propagation of uncertainty is performed by operators defined over the set of linguistic terms, basically conjunction, disjunction, negation and detachment operators. A method for the elicitation of these operators from the expert has been proposed in (Lopez de Mantaras et al., 90). The main difference of this approach with respect to other ones is that no underlying numerical representation of the linguistic terms is required. Linguistic terms are treated as mere labels. The only a priori requirement is that these labels should represent an ordered set of expressions about uncertainty. For each logical connective, a set of desirable properties of the corresponding operator is listed. Many of these properties are a finite counterpart of those of the uncertainty calculi based on t-norms and t-conorms, which are in turn the basis of the usual [0,1]-valued systems underlying Fuzzy Sets Theory [Alsina et al., 1983]. The listed properties act as constraints on the set of possible solutions. In this way, all operators fulfilling them are generated. This approach has been implemented by formulating it as a constraint satisfaction problem [Godo and Meseguer, 1991]. Finally, the expert may select the one he thinks fits better his own way of uncertainty management in the current task.

These characteristics make clear that the logics associated to the different MILORD uncertainty calculi are a class of finite multiple-valued logics, taking the linguistic terms as truth-values and the operators as the interpretations of the logical connectives. In other words, each linguistic term set, together with its set of operators, defines a truth-values algebra and therefore a corresponding multiple-valued logic. In (Agustí-Cullell et al., 1990), MV-logics have been analyzed from the semantic point of view and formalized as families of Institutions.

Following that line, the main characteristics of our MV-logics for uncertainty management we are concerned with are given by:

- An **algebra of truth-values:** a finite algebra $A = \langle A_n, \mathbf{0}, \mathbf{1}, N, T, I \rangle$ such that:
  1) The set of truth-values A_n is a chain[2] represented by
  $$\mathbf{0} = a_0 < a_1 < ... < a_{n-1} = \mathbf{1},$$
  where **0** and **1** are the booleans *False* and *True* respectively.
  2) The negation operator N is an unary operation such that the following properties hold:
  N1: if $a < b$ then $N(a) > N(b)$
  N2: $N^2 = Id$.
  3) The "and" operation T is any binary operation such that the following properties hold:
  T1: $T(a,b) = T(b,a)$
  T2: $T(a,T(b,c)) = T(T(a,b),c)$
  T3: $T(0,a) = 0$
  T4: $T(1,a) = a$
  T5: if $a \leq b$ then $T(a,c) \not> T(b,c)$ for all c.
  Note that in the unit interval these properties define t-norms functions if we add the condition of continuity.
  4) The implication operator I is defined by residuation with respect to T,.
  $$I(a,b) = Max\{ c \in A_n \text{ such that } T(a,c) \leq b \}$$
  i.e., I is the finite counterpart of an R-implication generated by the "and" operator T [Trillas and Valverde, 1985].
- A set of **Connectives**: "not"(¬), "and"(&) and "implication"(-->)
- A set of **Sentences**: sentences are pairs of classical-like propositional sentences and intervals of truth-values. The classical like-propositional sentences are built from a set of atomic symbols and the above set of connectives. However the sentences we will consider through this case study are only of the following types:

(p_1, V),
$(p_1 \,\&\, p_2 \,\&\, ... \,\&\, p_n , V)$,
$(p_1 \,\&\, p_2 \,\&\, ... \,\&\, p_n \text{ --> } q, V)$,

where $p_1, ..., p_n$ are literals (atoms or negations of atoms), q is an atomic sentence and V is a subset of truth-values. For each truth-values algebra A, L_A will stand for

[2] Usually the set of truth-values A_n stands for a totally ordered set of linguistic terms that the expert uses to express uncertainty, but nothing changes if it is only partially ordered.

the set of sentences with intervals of truth-values belonging to A
- **Models:** are defined by valuations, i.e. mappings ρ from to the firsts components of sentences to A_n provided that:

$\rho(\neg p) = N(\rho(p))$
$\rho(p_1 \& p_2) = T(\rho(p_1), \rho(p_2))$
$\rho(p \dashrightarrow q) = I(\rho(p), \rho(q))$

- **Satisfaction Relation**: between models and sentences is defined by:

$M_\rho \models (p, V)$ if, and only if $\rho(p) \in V$,

where M_ρ stands for the model defined by a valuation ρ.
- **Entailment Relation**: the minimal one generated by
1) the following set of axioms:
(A-1) $((p_1\&p_2)\&p_3 \text{-->} p_1\&(p_2\&p_3)$, **1**)
(A-2) $(p_1\&(p_2\&p_3) \text{-->} (p_1\&p_2)\&p_3$, **1**)
(A-3) $(p_1\&p_2 \text{-->} p_2\&p_1$, **1**)
(A-4) $(\neg\neg p \text{-->} p$, **1**)
2) the following inference rules, which are sound with respect to the satisfaction relation (Agustí-Cullell et al., 1990):
(RI-1) WEAKENING: Γ, (p, V) |- (p, V'), where V ⊆ V' and Γ is a set of sentences,
(RI-2) NOT-introduction: (p, V) |- (¬p, N(V)),
(RI-3) AND-introduction:
$(p_1, V_1), (p_2, V_2) \vdash (p_1 \& p_2, T(V_1, V_2))$,
(RI-4) MODUS PONENS:
$(p, V_1), (p \text{-->} q, V_2) \vdash (q, MP(V_1, V_2))$, being

$$MP(a,b) = \begin{cases} \emptyset, & \text{if } a \text{ and } b \text{ are inconsistent} \\ [a,\mathbf{1}], & \text{if } b = \mathbf{1} \\ T(a,b), & \text{otherwise} \end{cases}$$

where *a* and *b* are said to be inconsistent if there exists no *c* such that I(a,c) = b.

Notice that these inference rules are the only ones that an inference engine would need when working on sets of sentences of the above specified types, very common in fact in rule-based ES. However, instead of the rule RI-4 and for the sake of simplicity, we will consider the following inference rule:

(RI-4') MODIFIED MODUS PONENS:
$(p, V_1), (p \text{-->} q, V_2) \vdash (q, T(V_1, V_2))$.

Although it is correct for instance in the usual case of upper intervals of truth-values, this inference rule is not logically sound in general with respect to the semantics (satisfaction relation) above defined. Nevertheless, it is a well known fact that, from the cognitive point of view, detachment operators share the same properties required to conjunction operators [Bonissone, 1987]. These arguments, together with self-evident simplicity reasons, have lead us to adopt the inference rule RI-4'. Therefore, from now on, given a truth-values algebra A we will denote by MVL_A the multiple-valued logic defined above, and by $(L_A, \vdash_A)$ its associated entailment system. The language of this entailment system is L_A and its entailment relation is the minimal one determined by axioms A-1, A-2, A-3 and A-4, and by inference rules RI-1, RI-2, RI-3 and RI-4'.

On the other hand, the disjunction operator needed for parallel combination can be obtained from the negation and conjunction operators using the De Morgan laws. For these reasons, and for deductive purposes, only the ordered set of truth-values (linguistic terms) and the conjunction and negation operators should be specified in the truth-values algebra definitions. Therefore, from now on, truth-values algebras will be represented by <A,T,N>, omitting the booleans **0** and **1**, as long as they belong to all algebras.

4 INFERENCE PRESERVING MAPS BETWEEN MV-LOGICS

The aim of this section is to analyze the problem of preserving inference in communicating modules, assuming that each one has its own finite MV-logic as uncertainty calculus. In section two, maps and weak conservative maps of entailment systems have been introduced in order to model inference preserving correspondences. In the first subsection of this section, it is shown that morphisms and quasi-morphisms of truth-values algebras generate maps and weak conservative maps respectively of the corresponding entailment systems. In the second and third subsection, morphisms and quasi-morphisms of truth-values algebras are studied. Finally, in the fourth subsection an interactive algorithm to define such mappings to assist human experts when developing applications, is proposed.

4.1 WEAK CONSERVATIVE MAPS

Now we consider the problem of finding inference preserving correspondences between two of these logics MVL_A and MVL_B, where $A = \langle A_n, T, N\rangle$ and $B = \langle B_m, T', N'\rangle$ are their corresponding truth-values algebras. As it has been noted in section 2, the mappings between their entailment systems $(L_A, \vdash_A)$ and $(L_B, \vdash_B)$ we are mainly interested in are the *weak conservative* ones. In order to give a sufficient condition for a mapping $f: A_n \longrightarrow B_m$ to generate a weak conservative mapping between the entailment systems of MVL_A and MVL_B, we need some new definitions and results:

Given a truth-values algebra $A = \langle A_n,T,N\rangle$, we consider the set of intervals of A_n, $I(A_n) = \{[a,b] \mid a,b \in A_n\}$ where $[a,b] = \{x \mid x \in A_n,\ a \le x \le b\}$. We can define the following order relation in $I(A_n)$:

$$I_1 \le^* I_2 \ \text{ if } a \le b \text{ for all } a \in I_1 \text{ and for all } b \in I_2.$$

Let's consider now the following operations on $I(A_n)$
1) $N^*([a,b]) = [N(b), N(a)]$
2) $T^*([a_1,b_1],[a_2,b_2]) = [T(a_1,a_2), T(b_1,b_2)]$

It is easy to check that N* is a negation mapping and T* fulfils T1÷T5. Moreover, identifying every element *a* of A_n with the interval *[a,a]* of $I(A_n)$, $\langle A_n, T, N\rangle$ is a subalgebra of $\langle I(A_n),T^*,N^*\rangle$, that is, we have the following proposition.

Proposition 4.1. *Any truth-value algebra $<A_n, T, N>$ can be extended to an algebra $<I(A_n), T^*, N^*>$ of the same type that has $<A_n, T, N>$ as a subalgebra.*

It is worth noticing that $(I(A_n), \leq^*)$ is only a partial ordered set with minimum $\mathbf{0} = [0,0]$ and maximum $\mathbf{1} = [1,1]$, and N* and T* are univocally defined by N and T. Next we give a small example of an algebra of intervals generated by a truth-values algebra of four elements

Example. Let A = {0 < a < b < 1} the chain of four elements. The set of intervals of A is I(A) = {[0,a], [0,b], [0,1], [a,b], [a,1], [b,1], [0,0], [a,a], [b,b], [1,1] }. Identifying every interval [x,x] with the element x of A, the order relation on A and I(A) can be represented by the graphs of figure 1.

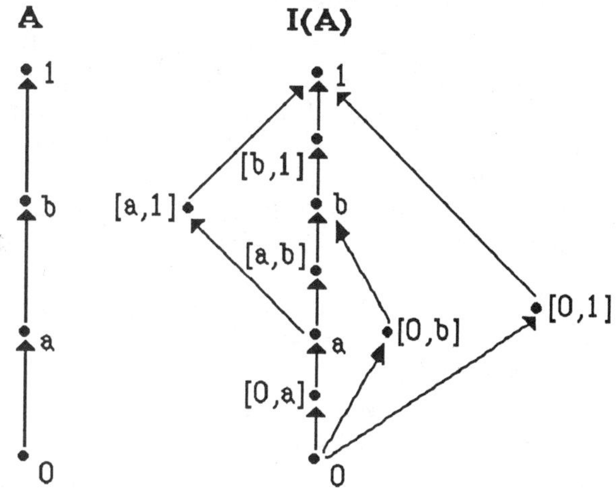

Figure 1: Graphs of the order relation of A and I(A).

Next we introduce what we call a **quasi-morphism** of algebras as a weakened notion of morphism, allowing to map values of an algebra into intervals of the other. This tries to capture the possibility of being imprecise when renaming truth-values from a MV-logic to another.

Definition 4.1. *Given two truth-values algebras $A = <A_n, T_1, N_1>$ and $B = <Bm, T_2, N_2>$, a mapping $f: A_n \longrightarrow I(B_m)$ is a quasi-morphism from A to B if the following conditions hold:*

1) f is non-decreasing, i.e. if $a \leq b$, then $f(a) \not> f(b)$,
2) $f(0) = 0$,
3) $f(N_1(x)) = N_2^*(f(x))$,
4) $f(T_1(x,y)) \subset T_2^*(f(x),f(y))$,

It is clear from this definition that :

(i) algebra morphisms are a particular case of algebra quasi-morphisms, identifying every element *b* of B with the interval [b,b]. Moreover, a quasi-morphism f is a morphism if, and only if, $f(A_m) \subset B_m$.

(ii) algebra morphisms from $<A_n, T_1, N_1>$ to $<I(B_m), T_1^*, N_2^*>$ are also quasi-morphisms.

Theorem 4.2. *Let MVL_A and MVL_B be the multiple-valued logics defined on the truth-values algebras $A = <A_n, T, N>$ and $B = <B_m, T', N'>$ respectively. Then every quasi-morphism of A to B generates a weak conservative mapping between the entailment systems of MVL_A and MVL_B.*

Proof. Let $f: A_n \longrightarrow I(B_m)$ be a quasi-morphism between A and B, and let $\Gamma = \{(p_1, V_1), ..., (p_n, V_n)\}$ a set of sentences of MVL_A. We will denote by H_f the translation function from MVL_A to MVL_B defined by $H_f((s,V)) = (s,f(V))$.Obviously H_f translates axioms of MVL_A into axioms of MVL_B. Suppose that in MVL_B a sentence E' = (q, V') can be derived from $H_f(\Gamma) = \{(p_1, f(V_1)), ..., (p_n, f(V_n))\}$ and axioms of MVL_B by applying a sequence of RI-1, RI-2, RI-3 and RI-4' inference rules and let's denote by *g'* the composition of their corresponding inference functions (only functions N' and T' will appear). Then it must be the case that $g'(f(V_1), ..., f(V_n)) \subset V'$. We have to show that there exists a sentence E of MVL_A such that it can be derived from $\Gamma \mid\!-_A E$ and that $H_f(E) \mid\!-_B E'$. Let E be the sentence $(q, g(V_1, ..., V_n))$, where *g* is the function obtained from g' replacing the occurrences of N' and T' by N and T. Then it is clear that $\Gamma \mid\!-_A E$ holds and, because f is a quasi-morphism, we have $f(g(V_1, ..., V_n)) \subset g'(f(V_1), ..., f(V_n)) \subset V'$, so $H_f(E) \mid\!-_B$ E' also holds and the theorem have been proved.◆

In the particular case of algebra morphisms, the following proposition shows that they also generate maps of entailment systems.

Proposition 4.3. *Let MVL_A and MVL_B be the multiple-valued logics defined on the truth-values algebras $A = <A_n, T, N>$ and $B = <B_m, T', N'>$ respectively. Then every order-preserving morphism of A to B generates a map between the entailment systems of MVL_A and MVL_B.*

4.2 MORPHISMS OF TRUTH-VALUES ALGEBRAS

In this subsection we turn our attention to the problem of relating truth-values algebras by means of order-preserving mappings which are algebra morphisms, and some necessary and/or sufficient conditions for their existence are given. Although there can exist algebra morphisms which are not order-preserving, for cognitive and logical reasons it seems reasonable to require this condition. Therefore, as long as we are only interested in order-preserving mappings, from now on, and for the sake of simplicity, we will use the term *morphisms* as an abbreviation of order-preserving morphism with f(0) = 0.

We begin with some well-known results on negation operators. For each chain A_n, there exists only one negation N and it is defined by

$$N(a_i) = a_{n-i-1}.$$

Then every chain A_n can be partitioned in three subsets:

- the set of negative elements $\mathcal{N}_n = \{x \mid x < N(x)\}$
- the set of fixed elements $\mathcal{F}_n = \{x \mid x = N(x)\}$
- the set of positive elements $\mathcal{P}_n = \{x \mid x > N(x)\}$

being these subsets $\mathcal{F}_n = \{ a_k \}$, $\mathcal{N}_n = \{ a_i \mid i<k \}$, $\mathcal{P}_n = \{ a_i \mid i>k \}$, if n =2k+1, and $\mathcal{F}_n = \emptyset$, $\mathcal{N}_n = \{ a_i \mid i<k \}$ and $\mathcal{P}_n = \{ a_i \mid i \geq k \}$, if n=2k.

The following equalities also hold: $N(\mathcal{N}_n) = \mathcal{P}_n$, $N(\mathcal{F}_n) = \mathcal{F}_n$ and $N(\mathcal{P}_n) = \mathcal{N}_n$.

Proposition 4.4. *Given two chains A_n and B_m, a mapping $f: A_n \longrightarrow B_m$ is a morphism with respect to the negation operator if, and only if, the following conditions hold:*

1. *$f_{|\mathcal{N}_n}$ is an order preserving mapping from $\mathcal{N}_n$ to $\mathcal{N}_m \cup \mathcal{F}_m$ such that $f(\mathbf{0}) = \mathbf{0}$*
2. *$f(\mathcal{F}_n) = \mathcal{F}_m$*
3. *If a_i belongs to $\mathcal{P}_n$, $f(a_i) = N'(f(a_{n-i-1}))$, where N' is the negation associated to B_m.*

From this proposition it is easy to show that:

- If *n* is odd then, in order to be f a *morphism*, *m* must be also odd, as long as $f(\mathcal{F}_n) = \mathcal{F}_m \neq \emptyset$.
- In the case of being *n* even or both *n* and *m* odd, every mapping $f_1: \mathcal{N}_n \longrightarrow \mathcal{N}_m \cup \mathcal{F}_m$ defines a negation morphism *f* in the following way:

$$f(a_i) = \begin{cases} f_1(a_i), & \text{if } a_i \in \mathcal{N}_n \\ b_r, & \text{if } a_r \in \mathcal{F}_n \text{ and } \mathcal{F}_m = \{b_r\} \\ N'(f_1(N(a_i))), & \text{if } a_i \in \mathcal{P}_n \end{cases}$$

and reciprocally, every negation morphism *f* is defined by the mapping $f_1 = f_{|\mathcal{N}_n}$.

We follow now with two propositions about how "and" operations can defined in order to have algebra morphisms.

Proposition 4.5. *Let $< A_n, N, T >$ be a truth-values algebra and let B_m a chain containing A_n such that the negation N' associated to B fulfils $N'_{|A_n} = N$, i.e. if $a_i = b_j$ then $N(a_i) = b_{m-j-1}$. Then there exists at least an "and" operation T' on B_m such that $<A_n, N, T>$ is a subalgebra of $< B_m, N', T' >$.*

Proof. It can be easily checked that the mapping T' defined as:

$$T'(p,q) = \begin{cases} T(p^-,q^-), & \text{if } p \neq 1 \text{ and } q \neq 1 \\ p, & \text{if } q = 1 \\ q, & \text{if } p = 1 \end{cases}$$

where $p^- = \max\{ x \in A_n \mid x \leq p \}$, is an "and" operation on B_m, and that it also verifies $T'_{|A_n \times A_n} = T$.◆

Proposition 4.6. *Let $<A_n, T, N>$ be a truth-values algebra and let $f: A_n \longrightarrow B_m$ be a negation morphism. Then there exists an "and" operation T' on B_m such that f is an algebra morphism if, and only if, f is compatible with T, that is, for all $a,b,c,d \in A_n$, $f(a) = f(b)$ and $f(c) = f(d)$ imply $f(T(a,c)) = f(T(b,d))$.*

Proof. Obviously, if f is an algebra morphism it is compatible with T. On the other hand, if f is compatible with T, the relation $\approx_f$ defined as

$$a \approx_f b \quad \text{if}_{DEF} \quad f(a) = f(b)$$

is a congruence relation on A_n. Let $< A_n/\approx_f, T_f, N_f>$ be the quotient algebra. Therefore, identifying $A_n/\approx_f$ with $f(A_n)$, f will be a morphism from $<A_n, T, N>$ to $< f(A_n), T_f, N_f>$. By proposition 4.5 there exists T' on B_m such that $< f(A_n), T_f, N_f>$ is a subalgebra of $<B_m, T', N'>$, where N' is the negation associated to B_m.◆

Now, taking into account the above results, it is interesting to point out some considerations about the problem of algebra morphism generation. In the following A will stand for a truth-values algebra $<A_n, T, N>$ and B_m for a chain of m elements.

1) If *n* is odd and *m* even, there is no possible morphism between A and B, being B any truth-values algebra defined on B_m. Then, this case will not be considered any more.

2) In order to define a morphism $f: A_n \longrightarrow B_m$ with respect to the negation operator we only need to take any mapping $f_1: \mathcal{N}_n \longrightarrow \mathcal{N}_m \cup \mathcal{F}_m$ with $f_1(0) = 0$ and to extend it in the way above indicated.

3) The generation of possible operations T' on B_m, together with renaming mappings f from A_n to B_m such that f: $<A_n, T, N> \longrightarrow <B_m, T', N'>$ are morphisms, is a process that can be automated without difficulties. The problem reduces to:

- first, to generate all mappings f from all order preserving mappings $f_1: \mathcal{N}_n \longrightarrow \mathcal{N}_m \cup \mathcal{F}_m$ with $f_1(0) = 0$,
- second, to check which ones are compatible with T,
- and third, to generate all algebras B_m containing $f(A_m)$ as subalgebra.

This method will provide us with a family of suitable algebras $<B_m, T', N'>$ for each mapping f_1.

4) Nevertheless, in general, it can be the case that the set of possible solutions would be empty. As an example, consider the algebra $<A_4,T,N>$, where $A_4 = \{0<a_1<a_2<1\}$, and the "and" operation T is the one given in figure 2.

T	0	a_1	a_2	1
0	0	0	0	0
a_1	0	0	0	a_1
a_2	0	0	a_1	a_2
1	0	a_1	a_2	1

Figure 2: “And” operation in a chain of four elements

It is easy to check that there exists no renaming mapping from A_4 to B_3 such that a morphism between $<A_4,T,N>$ and $<B_3, T', N'>$ can be defined for any "and" operation T'. Let $B_3 = \{0<b<1\}$, and thus $\mathcal{N}' = \{0\}$, $\mathcal{F}' = \{b\}$, and $\mathcal{P}' = \{1\}$. It is clear that if $f_1:\{0,a_1\} \longrightarrow \{0,b\}$ is order-preserving and $f_1(0) = 0$, then there are only two possibilities:

1) $f_1(a_1) = 0$, and then the mapping $f: A_4 \longrightarrow B_3$ is defined by $f(0) = f(a_1)$ and $f(a_2) = f(1) = 1$, but f is not compatible with T, because $f(a_2) = f(1)$ but $f(T(a_2,a_2)) = 0 \neq 1 = f(T(a_2,1))$;

2) $f_1(a) = b$, and then the mapping f: $A_4 \longrightarrow B_3$ is defined by $f(0) = 0$, $f(a_1) = f(a_2) = b$, and $f(1) = 1$, but again f is not compatible with T, because $f(a_1) = f(a_2)$ but $f(T(a_1,a_1)) = 0 \neq b = f(T(a_2,a_2))$.

4.3 QUASI-MORPHISMS OF TRUTH-VALUES ALGEBRAS

As we have seen in last section, given any truth-values algebras A and B, it is not always possible to find a morphism between them. However, this is not the case of quasi-morphisms because of the additional freedom of mapping (or renaming) a truth-value of A to an interval of B. This point is proved in the following proposition.

Proposition 4.7: *Let* $A = \langle A_n, T_1, N_1 \rangle$ *and* $B = \langle B_m, T_2, N_2 \rangle$ *be two truth-values algebras. Let* $C = \langle C_k, T', N' \rangle$ *be an algebra that can be imbedded in both A and B, and let* h_1 *and* h_2 *their corresponding monomorphisms. Then there exists at least one quasi-morphism f from A to B such that* $f(h_1(c)) = h_2(c)$, *for all* $c \in C_k$.

Proof. First of all, notice that given A and B there always exists the algebra C, because at least the algebra of booleans satisfies the required condition for any pair of truth-values algebras. So, let h_1 and h_2 be the corresponding monomorphisms from C to A and B respectively, and consider the mapping f: $A_n \dashrightarrow I(B_m)$ defined by:

$$f(x) = [\, h_2(c_x^-), h_2(c_x^+) \,]$$

where $c_x^- = \max\{ c \text{ of } C_k \mid h_1(c) \leq x \}$ and $c_x^+ = \min\{ c \text{ of } C_k \mid h_1(c) \geq x \}$. Straightforward computation shows that the required properties for *f* to be a quasi-morphism hold.◆

As an example, let's consider the algebras $A = \langle A_5, T, N \rangle$ and $B = \langle B_7, T', N' \rangle$, where the "and" operations T and T' are given in figure 3 respectively.

T	0	a_1	a_2	a_3	1
0	0	0	0	0	0
a_1	0	0	a_1	a_1	a_1
a_2	0	a_1	a_2	a_2	a_2
a_3	0	a_1	a_2	a_3	a_3
1	0	a_1	a_2	a_3	1

T'	0	b_1	b_2	b_3	b_4	b_5	1
0	0	0	0	0	0	0	0
b_1	0	b_1	b_1	b_1	b_1	b_1	b_1
b_2	0	b_1	b_2	b_2	b_2	b_2	b_2
b_3	0	b_1	b_2	b_3	b_3	b_3	b_3
b_4	0	b_1	b_2	b_3	b_4	b_4	b_4
b_5	0	b_1	b_2	b_3	b_4	b_5	b_5
1	0	b_1	b_2	b_3	b_4	b_5	1

Figure 3. "And" operations in chains of five and seven elements

It can be checked that there is no morphism from A to B. On the other hand $C = \langle C_3, T'', N'' \rangle$, being $C_3=\{0<b<1\}$ and $T''(x,y) = \min(x,y)$, is the maximal subalgebra that can be imbedded into A and B, and the monomorphisms h_1 and h_2 are defined by:

$h_1(0) = 0$ $\quad$ $h_2(0) = 0$
$h_1(b) = a_2$ $\quad$ $h_2(b) = b_3$
$h_1(1) = 1$ $\quad$ $h_2(1) = 1$

respectively. The above proposition 4.7 assures that the mapping f: $A_5 \to I(B_7)$ defined by:

$f(0) = 0$
$f(a_1) = [0,b_3]$
$f(a_2) = b_3$
$f(a_3) = [b_3,1]$
$f(1) = 1$

is a quasi-morphism from A to B.

4.4 PRAGMATICS OF INFERENCE PRESERVING MAPPINGS

In the previous sections we have seen that when two modules, that use different multiple-valued logical languages, need to communicate, an inference preserving mapping between their logics has to be defined. The process of defining these mappings could be supported by an interactive algorithm based on the notion of morphism and quasi-morphism between truth-values algebras. This process could be as follows:
Initially the expert determines a MV-logic for each module, giving the set of truth-values and the "and" truth-table, and proposes as many as needed renaming functions between different truth-values sets. Then, for each pair of modules having different MV-logics, the interactive algorithm will take their truth-values algebras and the renaming between them and check if the initial renaming is an algebra quasi-morphism. If not, the algorithm presents to the expert the set of possible modifications of the renaming function, each one being a morphism or a quasi-morphism. The expert may then select the one that fits better his aims. If no selection is made, possible modifications of the "and" truth-table are suggested, keeping the initial renaming function. Finally, if there has not been any solution, possible modifications of both renaming and truth-table are suggested.

Next, we give an scheme of the algorithm in a Pascal-like style. The notation used is the one of the previous sections.

```
Quasi-morphism_generator((An, T) (Bm, T'), f) =
                ; An and Bm are the truth-values sets,
                ; T and T' are the "and" connectives
                ; and f is a renaming from An to I(Bm)
;1: Renaming checking
        if quasi-morphism?(A, B, f)
                ; A = (An, T) and B = (Bm, T')
                ; This predicate is implicitly defined
```

```
                ; in the previous sections.
        Then Return (A, B, f)
                ; If the renaming given by the expert
                ; determines a quasi-morphism we return
                ; it.
;2: Renaming generation
        R = {f: An → I(Bm) | quasi-morphism?(A, B, f) }
                ; R is the set of all acceptable
                ; renaming functions
                ; The way they are computed is described
                ; below.
        print(R)
        if select(r)
                ; r ∈ R is selected by the expert
        then return (A, B, r)
;3: "And" truth-tables generation
        C = { T' / T' is an "and" operation on Bm and
        quasi-morphism?(A, (Bm, T'), f) }
        print(C)
        if select(c)
                ; c ∈ C is selected by the expert
        then return (A, (Bm, c), f)
;4: Renaming and "and" truth-table generation
        RC = { (f, T') / f: An → I(Bm) and
        quasi-morphism?(A, (Bm, T'), f) }
        print(RC)
        if select((x, y))
                ; (x,y) ∈ RC is selected by the expert
        then return (A, (Bm, y), x)
        else return nil
```

In the following a constructive description of predicates and functions used in the algorithm is given.

a) Renaming checking: It is only a checking predicate. It checks if a given function (renaming) is a quasi-morphism from A to B, where A and B are two given algebras.

b) Renaming generation: Let A and B be two truth-values algebras. *Renaming generation* is a predicate that returns all possible quasi-morphisms from the truth-values algebra A to the interval algebra I(B). The method to find these quasi-morphisms is the following:

1. Define the operations T'* and N'* on I(B).
2. Define mappings f_1: $\mathcal{N} \cup \mathcal{F}$ ----> $\mathcal{N}'^* \cup \mathcal{F}'^*$ such that $f_1(0) = 0$, $f_1(\mathcal{F}) = \mathcal{F}'^*$ and $x \le y$ implies $f_1(x) \not\geq f_1(y)$.
3. For every f_1, define the negation morphism f by,

$$f(x) = \begin{cases} f_1(x), & \text{if } x \in \mathcal{N} \cup \mathcal{F} \\ N'^*(f_1(N(x))), & \text{if } x \in \mathcal{P} \end{cases}$$

4 Check if f is a quasi-morphism.

Remarks: The solutions, if any, contain as a particular case all the possible morphisms from A to B. By proposition 4.7, for every pair of algebras A and B, the *renaming generation* set (A,B) is not empty.

c) "And" truth-table generation: Let A be a truth-value algebra, let B_m be a chain of m elements and let f be a renaming function from A_n to $I(B_m)$. *"And" truth-table generation* is a predicate that returns "and" operations on B_m such that f be a quasi-morphism. The method for finding "and" operations is the following:

1. If f is not a negation morphism, it returns the empty set.
2. Find all "and" operations T' on B_m.
3. Check if f is a quasi-morphism.

Remarks: A general algorithm for finding truth-values algebras over a partially ordered set of n elements is given in [Godo and Meseguer, 1991].

d) Renaming and truth-table generation: Let A be a truth-value algebra and let B_m be a chain of m elements. *Renaming and truth-table generation* is a function that, given A_n and B_m, returns pairs (T',f), where T' is an "and" operation on B_m and f is a quasi-morphism from A to $\langle I(B_m),T'^*,N'^*\rangle$. In this case, the method for finding pairs (T', f) is the following one:

1. Define N'* on $I(B_m)$.
2. Define all the possible functions f_1 as in the case of *renaming generation.*
3. For every f_1, define the negation morphisms as in the case of *renaming generation.*
4. Find all "and" operations T' on B_m.
5. Check if f is a quasi-morphism.

Final remarks:

1.- All these methods can be automated.

2.- Some of the functions can return the empty set. (see examples of subsections 4.2 and 4.3)

3.- An order of preference on the sets *R*, *C* and *RC* should be given. There are many possibilities to do this. For example, several distances with respect to the initial renaming and truth-table operation can be defined on the above sets to obtain preference orderings. It seems reasonable that in all cases algebra morphisms should be preferred to algebra quasi-morphisms.

4.- The complexity of the algorithm is exponential in the number of truth-values. However, two factors make acceptable the execution time of the algorithm: (i) the number of different uncertainty linguistic terms used by an expert is usually not greater then nine [Miller, 1967], and (ii) the strong conditions required to "and" operations (see section 3) restrict the combinatorial explosion in the generation of such operations..

5 CONCLUSIONS AND FUTURE WORK

In this paper, the problem of communicating tasks with different uncertainty calculi has been introduced in a very general framework. This problem arises when dealing with large knowledge-based systems in which a better modelling of reasoning for different tasks requires working together with different uncertainty reasoning systems In the framework of rule-based expert systems, this problem has been analyzed in detail in the particular case in which different MV-logics are used to model the management of uncertainty in different tasks. Necessary and/or sufficient conditions for the correspondence mappings between them to be inference preserving have been given. Also an interactive algorithm to define such mappings has been proposed to assist the human expert in relating tasks or modules by inference preserving correspondences. However the general problem of communicating different uncertainty reasoning systems is very complex, and further research is needed as much in the field of distributed knowledge based systems as in the case of considering more complex models of uncertainty reasoning systems.

Acknowledgements

This research has been partially supported by the CICYT id.880j382 project SPES, and by the ESPRIT-II Basic Research Action DRUMS.

References

Agustí-Cullell J., Esteva F., Garcia P., Godo L.(1990) *'Formalizing Multiple-valuated Logics as Institutions'*.Short version in Proceedings of Third International IPMU Conference, Paris, pp.355-357. Full version will appear in Lecture Notes on Computer Science in June 1991.

Alsina C., Trillas E., Valverde L.(1983)*' On some logical connectives for Fuzzy Set Theory'*. Journal of Mathematical Analysis and Applications, 93, pp. 15-26.

Bonissone P.P. (1987) *'Summarizing and propagating uncertain information by triangular norms'* International Journal of aproximate reasoning 1 (1). pp. 71-101.

Godo L., Lopez de Mantaras R., Sierra C., Verdaguer A. (1989) *'MILORD:The architecture and management of linguistically expressed uncertainty'*. Int. Journal of Intelligent System Vol. 4 nº 4, pp. 471-501.

Godo L., Meseguer P. (1991) *'A constraint-based approach to generate finite truth-values algebras'*. Research Report IIIA-CEAB 91/9.

Goguen J., Burstall R.M., (1983) *'Introducing Institutions'* . Proc. Workshop on Logics of Programs, Carnegie-Mellon University. Springer LNCS 164, pp. 221-256.

Harper R., Sannella D., Tarleckil A. (1989) *'Structure and Representation in LF'* Proc.4th. IEEE Symposium on Logic of Computer Science.

Lopez de Mantaras R. (1990) *'Approximate Reasoning Models '* Elllis Horwood Ltd.

Miller G.A. (1967) *'The Magical Number Seven Plus or Minus Two: Some Limits on our Capacity for Processing Information'* in The Psychology of Communication, Penguin Books Inc.

Meseguer J. (1989) *'General Logics '*. In H.D. Ebbinghaus el al. (eds) Proc. Logic Colloquium '87. North - Holland.

Sierra C. (1989) *' MILORD: Arquitectura multi-nivell per a sistemes experts en classificació"* Ph. D. Universitat Politècnica de Catalunya . Barcelona.

Trillas E., Valverde L. (1985) *'On mode and implication in approximate reasoning '* in Gupta et al. (Eds.) Approximate reasoning in expert systems. pp. 157-166. North-Holland.

Verdaguer, A. (1989) *'PNEUMON-IA; desenvolupament i validació d'un sistema expert d'ajuda al diagnòstic mèdic'* Ph. D. Thesis. Universitat Autònoma de Barcelona.

Constraint Propagation with Imprecise Conditional Probabilities

Stéphane AMARGER **Didier DUBOIS** **Henri PRADE**

Institut de Recherche en Informatique de Toulouse (I.R.I.T.) - Université Paul Sabatier
118 route de Narbonne
31062 TOULOUSE Cedex - FRANCE
email: [amarger, dubois, prade]@irit.fr

Abstract

An approach to reasoning with default rules where the proportion of exceptions, or more generally the probability of encountering an exception, can be at least roughly assessed is presented. It is based on local uncertainty propagation rules which provide the best bracketing of a conditional probability of interest from the knowledge of the bracketing of some other conditional probabilities. A procedure that uses two such propagation rules repeatedly is proposed in order to estimate any simple conditional probability of interest from the available knowledge. The iterative procedure, that does not require independence assumptions, looks promising with respect to the linear programming method. Improved bounds for conditional probabilities are given when independence assumptions hold.

1 INTRODUCTION

In commonsense reasoning it is very usual to manipulate rules with exceptions. One of the most important cases of such rules consists in default statements containing explicit or implicit numerical quantifiers. Even when they are explicit these quantifiers may be only vaguely stated as for instance in the proposition "most students are young" ; see (Zadeh, 1985). The numerical approach interprets the linguistic term "most" in this example as an ill-defined numerical quantifier expressing the proportion of young people among students, in a certain context (for simplicity we assume here that 'young' has a clear-cut meaning and is not viewed as a fuzzy predicate ; see (Dubois and Prade, 1988) for preliminary results on the handling of fuzzy predicates in this framework). More generally, we may have some imprecise statement about the value of the probability of not encountering an exception, i.e. in our example, the conditional probability P(young | student) is bounded from below by some number in [0,1]. This type of incomplete statistical information is considered by Kyburg (1974) as a large part of our commonsense knowledge. P(young | student) is often also regarded as a degree of certainty that a student taken at random is indeed young.

Different kinds of treatment can be imagined for rules of the kind "if A then B with probability $P(B \mid A)$." This can be illustrated considering the above rule and another which can be chained with it, namely, "if B then C with probability $P(C \mid B)$." Applying Bayes rule we have $P(C \mid A) \geq P(B \cap C \mid A) = P(C \mid A \cap B) \cdot P(B \mid A)$ (here we use the same symbol '$\cap$' for denoting the conjunction of propositions or the intersection of the classes of items which satisfy the propositions). Then assuming irrelevance of A with respect to C in the context B, namely assuming here that $P(C \mid A \cap B) = P(C \mid B)$, we obtain the lower bound $P(C \mid B) \cdot P(B \mid A)$ for $P(C \mid A)$. But without this kind of assumption, as soon as $P(C \mid B) \neq 1$, nothing can be said about the value of $P(C \mid A)$ which can take any value in the interval [0,1]. Indeed nothing forbids to have $A \cap C = \emptyset$ (leading to $P(C \mid A) = 0$) as well as $A \subseteq C$ (leading to $P(C \mid A) = 1$) for instance. Interestingly enough if we add some information about $P(A \mid B)$ we may obtain non-trivial bounds for $P(C \mid A)$ just from bounds on $P(B \mid A)$, $P(A \mid B)$ and $P(C \mid B)$. Then more generally we may choose either i) to exploit the available knowledge on conditional probabilities for computing the best possible upper and lower bounds for some other conditional probabilities of interest, or ii) to take advantage of independence assumptions (which are perhaps hard to check) and prior probabilities for computing probability estimates (Pearl, 1988). The first approach may give no informative result, but when results are informative, they are very strong. On the contrary, the Bayesian approach always gives informative results, but these results can always be questioned by the arrival of new pieces of information. In this paper we investigate the first approach in detail.

Formally, let X be a set of objects, A and B be two subsets of X, and Q_B^A be a subset of values (which may reduce to a single value) expressing what is known about the proportion of A's which are B's. Q_B^A is a subinterval of the unit interval [0,1], corresponding to the default rule "Q_B^A A's are B's." This knowledge is understood as a constraint acting on the cardinality of B relative to A, i.e.:

$$\frac{|A \cap B|}{|A|} \in Q_B^A \subseteq [0,1]$$

where $|A|$ is the cardinality of the subset A. More generally, it is equivalent to a piece of information of the form $P(B \mid A) \in [P_*(B \mid A), P^*(B \mid A)]$ where only the two bounds $P_*(B \mid A)$ and $P^*(B \mid A)$ are known. Indeed relative cardinality is a particular case of conditional probability, where the underlying distribution is uniformly distributed over X. Thus proportions and probabilities obey the same mathematical laws and we shall use them in an interchangeable way in the following.

We use a network representation, as for instance the one on Figure 1, where the two directed edges between two nodes A and B are weighted by Q_A^B and Q_B^A, i.e. what is known of the proportions of B's which are A's and of A's which are B's. Note that in terms of conditional probabilities we assume information on both $P(A \mid B)$ and $P(B \mid A)$, which contrasts with Bayesian networks (Pearl, 1988). Besides $P(A)$ will be interpreted as $P(A \mid X)$ where X stands for the set of all considered objects or in logical terms corresponds to the ever-true proposition. Hence all probabilities that we handle are (bounds of) conditional probabilities in a network where cycles are allowed, and no prior probability information is required in order to start the inference process in the approach described in this paper (contrary to Quinlan (1983)'s INFERNO system or Baldwin (1990)'s support logic programming).

Other works have been published, that handle probability bounds (see (Dubois et al., 1990) for a survey). However, these works always assume knowledge about unconditional probabilities (i.e. $P(A) = P(A \mid X)$ in our framework) and are often oriented towards the computation of unconditional probabilities $P(B)$. This is not true here. The reasoning systems of Bacchus (1990) aim at embedding the type of knowledge we deal with into a formal logical setting. Contrastedly our aim is to specify efficient inference algorithms.

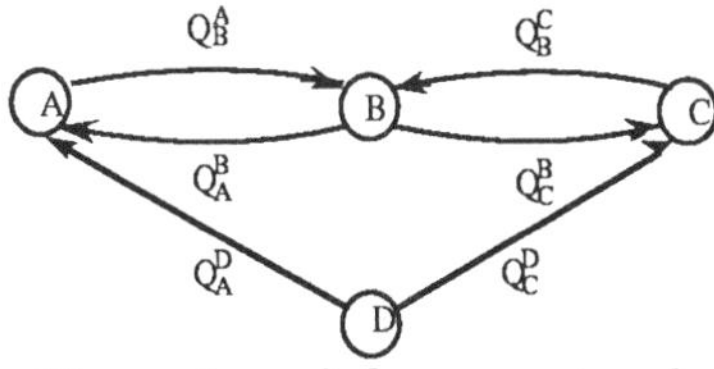

Figure 1 : an inference network

In the following sections, we are going to present computational methods that can handle imprecisely-known conditional probabilities. This work pursues an earlier investigation. In Dubois and Prade (1988), see also LéaSombé (1990), a first local pattern of reasoning, corresponding to the transitive chaining syllogism was studied. In (Dubois et al., 1990) two other local patterns enable us to estimate conditional probabilities involving conjunctions of events or contexts in their expression. A more complete set of propagation rules is presented in (Amarger et al. 1991).

After presenting the problem is section 2, section 3 recalls how our problem can be reduced to linear programming. Section 4 presents a generalized version of Bayes' theorem which can help improve the known bounds on an inference network in a single propagation step. Section 5 recalls the previously studied inference patterns involving conjunctions and disjunctions of two terms and discusses the handling of negation. Section 6 presents the general strategy that exploits two propagation rules in order to answer queries about conditional probabilities of interest. Section 7 illustrates the approach on an example. Section 8 discusses the handling of conjunction and disjunction in queries. Section 9 considers the introduction of independence assumptions in the chaining of conditional probabilities. In the conclusion, analogies with non-monotonic reasoning are pointed out.

2 STATEMENT OF THE PROBLEM

We suppose that we know some default rules containing numerical quantifiers or conditional probabilities such as "Q_B^A A's are B's" or "if A then B with probability $P(B \mid A)$."

The objective of our research is to answer queries like : "what proportion of A's are C's ?," "what proportion of A's and B's are C's ?," "what proportion of C's are A's and B's ?," "what proportion of A's or B's are C's ?," or "what proportion of C's are A's or B's ? ;" or similar queries stated in terms of conditional probabilities, from the available knowledge about the values of other proportions or conditional probabilities. This corresponds respectively to evaluate the probabilities $p = P(C \mid A)$, $P(C \mid A \cap B)$, $P(A \cap B \mid C)$, $P(C \mid A \cup B)$ or $P(A \cup B \mid C)$. The possible values of p usually form an interval $[p_*, p^*]$, and not just a single value, where p_* is the lowest value and p^* the highest value possibly taken by the conditional probability. Usually, a good local uncertainty propagation method will provide bounds that bracket $[p_*, p^*]$, i.e. the deduction method will be sound. If it supplies exact bounds, it is called complete. The inference patterns we shall use in the following sections are sound and are also complete when we consider just the elementary network corresponding to the statement of the pattern, i.e. they are said to be *locally complete.*

Our view of a knowledge base in this paper is thus a collection of general statements regarding a population X of objects ; these statements express in imprecise terms the proportions of objects in various subclasses of X, that belong to other subclasses. This knowledge base allows for answering queries about a given object, given a subclass to which it belongs (also called its "reference class" by Kyburg). To do so we just apply to this object the properties of this subclass, implicitly assuming that it is a typical element of this class. If more information become available for this object, we just change its reference class accordingly.

Computing bounds for $P(B \mid A)$ is a matter of constraint propagation, and is not based on updating a probability distribution, contrary to Bayesian reasoning. Namely, given that we know that an object of interest is in subclass A, we certainly do not interpret this fact as P(A) = 1. Indeed adding the constraint P(A) = 1 to the knowledge base may lead to modify the set of probability measures that obey the constraints induced by probability bounds (e.g. $P(C \mid A \cap B)$ must become equal to $P(C \mid B)$). This is because P(A) = 1 means that X – A is an empty set ; on the contrary, a "fact" "$x \in A$" in our system just indicates that we look for the properties of members of subset A. Although in Bayesian reasoning, computing P(B I A) is the same as assuming the posterior probability of A is 1 because the probability distribution on X is unique, these two operations no longer coincide with probability bounds : one is just focusing on a reference class (what can be said about B, for members of A?) while the other is knowledge updating (see Dubois and Prade, 1991b). Dubois and Prade (1991b) further discuss the difference between focusing and updating in the framework of belief functions. As for the difference between computing P(B I A) and P(B) when A is an accepted fact, this topic has been considered in the philosophical literature for a long time. See e.g. Suppes (1966).

3 A LINEAR PROGRAMMING METHOD

It has been shown in (Paass, 1988) that reasoning from numerically quantified general rules may be modelled as an optimization problem. Namely, if there are n atomic symbols in the network, there are 2^n possible worlds, and we can express all constraints on conditional probabilities as linear constraints where the variables x_i correspond to the unknown probabilities of possible worlds i. The calculation of bounds on an unknown conditional probability P(A I B) comes down to find the maximum and the minimum of a rational fraction whose numerator sums the probabilities x_i of the possible worlds where A and B are true, and whose denominator sums the probabilities x_i of the possible worlds where B is true, under the constraints induced by the already known probability bounds and to the requirement that the x_i's sum to one.

The same approach may be used to solve any query. As we can see we are faced with a fractional linear programming problem of the form (P),

$$(P)\left\{\text{Opti}\ \frac{c \cdot {}^t x}{d \cdot {}^t x},\ x \geq 0 \ \text{ under } \ \mathbb{1} \cdot {}^t x = 1,\ M \cdot x \leq 0\right\}$$

where $\mathbb{1}$ is the "unit vector," c, d, x are row vectors, M is a matrix, "Opti" is either "Max" or "Min," and t denotes the transposition, can be transformed into an equivalent linear program (P'). Indeed, as pointed out by (Charnes and Cooper, 1962), letting $y_i = x_i/(d \cdot {}^t x)$, we obtain :

$$(P')\ \{\text{Opti}\ c \cdot {}^t y,\ y \geq 0 \ \text{ under } \ M \cdot y \leq 0,\ d \cdot {}^t y = 1\}$$

So, as explained and exemplified in (Amarger et al., 1990), the calculation of bounds for P(B I A) requires that two linear programs be solved (one to compute the exact lower bound and one to compute the exact upper bound). But, even if with this method we are able to precisely compute the best bounds bracketing the conditional probability of interest, it is hard to try to provide an explanation for the obtained results in terms of the available knowledge we start with.

This reduction of a fractional linear programming problem induced by probability constraints to a linear programming problem has been also pointed out and used in (van der Gaag, 1990), where also local computation methods are proposed on the basis of the decomposition of the linear system into subsystems, and exploiting independence relationships when they are known. Methods based on local inference patterns may provide less precise results (although they are guaranteed to be sound), but are faster and their results easier to explain.

4 GENERALIZED BAYES' THEOREM

In the framework of numerical quantifiers, because we manipulate conditional probabilities, it would be interesting to use the Bayes' theorem :

$$\forall A, B,\ \ P(A|B) = P(B|A) \cdot P(A) / P(B)$$

But, in our approach we do not assume that P(A) and P(B) are known. A more general identity, where only conditional probabilities appear can be established :

Proposition 1 : Generalized Bayes' theorem

$$\forall A_1, \ldots, A_k,\ P(A_1|A_k) = P(A_k|A_1) \prod_{i=1}^{k-1} \frac{P(A_i|A_{i+1})}{P(A_{i+1}|A_i)}$$

when all involved quantities are positive.

This identity is easily proved replacing conditional probabilities P(A I B) by their expressions $P(A \cap B)/P(B)$. Note that this identity tells us that given a cycle $A_1, A_2, \ldots, A_k, A_{k+1} = A_1$ in a probabilistic network, the 2.k quantities $\{P(A_i \mid A_{i+1}), i \in]k]\} \cup \{P(A_{i+1} \mid A_i), i \in]k]\}$ (where $]k] \equiv]0, k] \cap \mathbb{N}$) are not independent when positive: any 2.k - 1 of these quantities determine the remaining one. Now, because we use upper and lower probabilities, we extend this theorem as follows:

Proposition 2 : Generalized Bayes' theorem - upper/lower probabilities case.

Given k sets $A_1, A_2, \ldots, A_k$, with $k > 2$, the following inequalities should hold :

• lower bound :

$$\forall A_1, \ldots, A_k,\ P_*(A_1|A_k) \geq P_*(A_k|A_1) \prod_{i=1}^{k-1} \underline{d}_{i,i+1}$$

with: $\forall i, j \in]k],\ \underline{d}_{i,j} = P_*(A_i|A_j) / P^*(A_j|A_i)$.

• upper bound :

$$\forall A_1, \ldots, A_k,\ P^*(A_1|A_k) \leq P^*(A_k|A_1) \prod_{i=1}^{k-1} \overline{d}_{i,i+1}$$

with: $\forall$ i, j $\in$]k], $\bar{d}_{i,j} = P^*(A_i|A_j)/P_*(A_j|A_i)$.

A simpler version of Proposition 2 is used by Fertig and Breese (1990) for arc reversal in influence diagrams where probabilities are incompletely known. Proposition 2 is the basis of a first inference rule for tightening probability bounds in a set of ill-known conditional probabilities.

Namely given a knowledge base $\mathcal{K} = \{(P_*(A_i \mid A_j), P^*(A_i \mid A_j)), i, j \in]n]\}$; we can associate to it a network G with n nodes $A_1, A_2,\ldots, A_n$ and whose arcs (A_i,A_j) are weighted by $\underline{d}_{i,i+1}$. Proposition 2 leads to update $P_*(A \mid B)$, and $P^*(A \mid B)$ in one step as follows

$$P_*(A \mid B) = P_*(B \mid A)\cdot \max_{\substack{\text{over all paths } A_1,\ldots,A_k \text{ in } G\\ \text{with } 2<k\le n,\ A_1=A,\ A_k=B}} \left\{\prod_{i=1}^{k-1} \underline{d}_{i,i+1}\right\} \quad (1)$$

$$P^*(A \mid B) = P^*(B \mid A)\cdot \min_{\substack{\text{over all paths } A_k,\ldots,A_1 \text{ in } G\\ \text{with } 2<k\le n,\ A_1=A,\ A_k=B}} \left\{\prod_{i=1}^{k-1} 1/\underline{d}_{i,i+1}\right\} \quad (2)$$

The second update is easily explained noticing that $\bar{d}_{i,i+1} = 1/\underline{d}_{i+1,i}$. Note that these changes in probability bounds do not correspond to a revision of the knowledge, but only to constraint propagation steps ; namely the set of probability measures such that $\forall$ i, j, $P_*(A_i \mid A_j) \le P(A_i \mid A_j) \le P^*(A_i \mid A_j)$ never changes.

As it can be guessed, the propagation of the constraint expressed by Proposition 1 is achieved by computing the longest (i.e. most weighted) elementary paths from A to B and from B to A in the network G where arcs (A,B) and (B,A) have been suppressed. Here the length of the path is the product of all weights of arcs in the path. For reason of computing accuracy, it is better to compute the length of the paths using a standard (max, +) path algebra, changing $\underline{d}_{i,i+1}$ into Log $\underline{d}_{i,i+1}$. Then any shortest path algorithm will do. Note that the length of a circuit $A_1,\ldots, A_k, A_{k+1} = A_1$ in G is such that $\underline{d}_{1,2} \cdot \underline{d}_{2,3}\ldots \underline{d}_{k-1,k} \cdot \underline{d}_{k,1} \le 1$; indeed, this inequality reads

$$\prod_{i=1}^{k-1} P_*(A_i \mid A_{i+1}) \Big/ \prod_{i=1}^{k-1} P^*(A_{i+1} \mid A_i) \le P^*(A_1 \mid A_k) / P_*(A_k \mid A_1)$$

and is a consequence of Proposition 1. Hence in the network with weights of the form Log $\underline{d}_{i,j}$, no circuit will be of positive length. Hence longest paths between nodes will always exist.

The constraint propagation steps (1) and (2) can be used as an inference rule that we shall denote BG (Bayes generalized) in the following.

5 LOCAL INFERENCE RULES

The first local inference pattern, already examined in (Dubois and Prade, 1988) and in (Dubois et al., 1990), corresponds to the evaluation of a missing arc in the inference network, and can be viewed as the counterpart of node removal in influence diagrams.

The problem solved by this pattern, also called "**quantified syllogism rule**" (QS) is the following: given bounds on P(A I B), P(B I A), P(C I B) and P(B I C), what are the bounds on P(C I A) (thus removing node B). The following bounds can be shown to be the tightest ones :

lower bound :

$$P_*(C \mid A) = P_*(B \mid A) \max\left(0, 1 - \frac{1 - P_*(C \mid B)}{P_*(A \mid B)}\right) \quad (3)$$

upper bound :

$$P^*(C|A) = \min\left(1, 1 - P_*(B|A) + \frac{P_*(B|A) . P^*(C|B)}{P_*(A|B)}, \frac{P^*(B|A)P^*(C|B)}{P_*(A|B)P_*(B|C)}, \frac{P^*(B|A)P^*(C|B)}{P_*(A|B)P_*(B|C)}[1 - P_*(B|C)] + P^*(B|A)\right) \quad (4)$$

The application of QS to the network with nodes A, B, C for the calculation of P(C I A) is denoted QS(C, B, A) = (C, A). For a proof that these bounds are optimal see (Dubois and Prade, 1988 ; Dubois et al., 1990).

This pattern can be extended to more than 3 nodes in sequence. It can be proved that optimality is preserved. Especially, given (A, B, C, D), it is equivalent to remove B first (computing P(C I A)), then C, or C first (computing P(D I B)), and then B, in order to get P(D I A), i.e. there is an associativity property.

Proposition 3 : QS(QS(D,C,B),A) = QS(D,QS(C,B, A))

Proof : First, consider the network {A, B, C} ; applying QS we get bounds for P(C I A) and P(A I C). Then we could think of applying QS again in order to improve bounds of P(C I B) for instance. Clearly this process will not lead to improve these bounds. Indeed if these bounds were improved using P(B I A), P(A I B), and the calculated bounds on P(C I A), P(A I C), it would indicate that quantities P(B I C) or P(C I B) are related to P(B I A) or P(A I B). But this is clearly not true. Similarly the knowledge about P(D I C) and P(C I D) has no influence on P(B I C) and P(C I B), hence has no influence on the optimal bounds of P(C I A) and P(A I C). The optimality of the QS rule then implies that the result of applying it on P(C I A), P(A I C), P(C I D), P(D I C) will also give optimal bounds on P(D I A) and P(A I D). The same reasoning applies if we compute P(D I B), P(B I D) first. In both cases we get optimal bounds on P(D I A) and P(A I D). Associativity then follows from optimality. Q.E.D.

This result could also be derived by the study of the linear program associated to the network, looking for decomposability properties of the constraint matrix.

Clearly, this property of QS is very nice and easily generalizes to a network with any number of nodes. Thus on a "linear chain" beginning with node A_1 and ending with node A_k, we can apply QS iteratively, from left to right, in order to evaluate $P(A_k \mid A_1)$ for instance, without resorting to linear programming.

In (Dubois et al., 1990) the expression of bounds on $P(A \cap B \mid C)$ and $P(C \mid A \cap B)$ in terms of more elementary conditional probabilities $P(A \mid C)$, $P(C \mid A)$, $P(C \mid B)$, $P(B \mid C)$, $P(A \mid B)$ and $P(B \mid A)$ have been established starting with a complete network with nodes A, B, C. The case of disjunction is solved in (Amarger et al., 1991) where probabilities of the form $P(A \cup B \mid C)$ and $P(C \mid A \cup B)$ are explicitly obtained under the same setting. Disjunction and conjunction are addressed in Section 8 using the two rules QS and BG.

The case of negation is especially interesting. Indeed, given $P(B \mid A)$ and $P(A \mid B)$, we obviously know $P(\neg B \mid A)$ and $P(\neg A \mid B)$ where $\neg$ denotes complementation. However it is easy to verify that $P(A \mid \neg B)$ and $P(B \mid \neg A)$ remain totally unknown. It is indeed easy to check that

$$P(A \mid \neg B) = P(A \mid B)\cdot\left(\left(1/P(B \mid A)\right) - 1\right)\cdot P(B)/P(\neg B) \quad (5)$$

In other words, answering queries of the form "How many not B's are A's" require the knowledge of unconditional probabilities. A possible other way of dealing with negation is to introduce the closed world assumption which can be stated as follows : if sets A, B and C_i, $i \in]n]$ appear in the network, then let us assume that the universe is reduced to $A \cup B \cup \bigcup_{i \in]n]} C_i$. In other words, we assume that the set $\neg A \cap \neg B \cap \bigcap_{i \in]n]} \neg C_i$ is empty, or at least that $P(\neg A \cap \neg B \cap \bigcap_{i \in]n]} \neg C_i) = 0$. In the trivial case where we consider the classes A and B only, it leads to $P(\neg A \cap \neg B) = 0$, and then $P(A \mid \neg B) = P(A \mid A \cap \neg B) = 1$. So, if we "open" the world by considering C also, then we assume $P(\neg A \cap \neg B \cap \neg C) = 0$. Since $\neg B = [\neg B \cap (A \cup C)] \cup [\neg B \cap \neg(A \cup C)] = \neg B \cap (A \cup C) \cup (\neg A \cap \neg B \cap \neg C)$, then $P(\neg B) = P(\neg B \cap (A \cup C))$. Thus we change the question "what is the value of $P(A \mid \neg B)$?" into "what is the value of $P(A \mid \neg B \cap (A \cup C))$?". A systematic way of dealing with these questions require a proper handling of Boolean expressions in conditional probabilities.

6 A CONSTRAINT PROPAGATION BASED ON INFERENCE RULES

In the previous sections, we have presented two local inference rules, and now, the problem is to use these rules in order to perform automated reasoning with the whole network. The aim of this section is to build a reasoning strategy in order to be able to answer any *simple* query (i.e. a query of the form "what is the proportion of A's which are C's?," where A and C are atoms in the language). The network is supposed to be made out of simple conditional probabilities of the form $P(A \mid B)$ where A and B are atomic symbols.

Graphically, to answer a query like "what proportion of X's are Y's ?" is equivalent to generate the new arc <X, Y> in a network like the one of Figure 1. Our approach is local in the sense that the patterns are designed to provide answers to particular queries using local inference rules. Consequently, one can observe the influence of each piece of knowledge on the result ; global methods do not offer such a possibility. Even though a particular pattern corresponds to an elementary network, the inference patterns can work on any network, whatever its structure, unlike the Bayesian approach which needs an acyclic network topology (e.g. directed cycles are prohibited) adapted to the propagation mechanism ; see (Lauritzen and Spiegelhalter, 1988 and Pearl, 1988).

Of course, in practice, in order to answer a particular query, it may exist several possibilities for applying the inference patterns to the network, corresponding to different paths. Since the inference rules are sound, one can easily combine the different results provided by all the applications of rules because their intersection still provides a sound result. Indeed, let us suppose that $Q_1 = [p_{*1}, p^*_1]$ and $Q_2 = [p_{*2}, p^*_2]$ are two intervals that contains the value p we want to estimate ; then we have : $p \in Q_1 \cap Q_2 = [\max(p_{*1}, p_{*2}), \min(p^*_1, p^*_2)]$. This generalizes to the intersection of any number of intervals ; and the emptiness of the intersection would be the proof that the data we start with are not consistent.

We will first use a saturation strategy in order to extract as much information as we can from the network, namely, try to get probability intervals as tight as possible for all conditional probabilities $P(A \mid B)$. The result is called the *saturated network.*

We are going to use two tools : rule QS (corresponding to the basic quantified syllogism) presented in Section 5., in order to add links to the network, and the generalized Bayes' theorem (rule BG) presented in Section 4.

Step 1 : recursively apply QS, to generate the missing arcs. This step is performed until the probability intervals can no more be improved.

Step 2 : recursively apply BG to improve the arcs generated by Step 1.

Then, the general algorithm is :

(a) perform Step 1

(b) perform Step 2

(c) if the probability intervals have been improved go to (a), otherwise stop

Note that the two steps are very complementary. Indeed, step 1 uses an optimal rule but a local one, while step 2 uses a suboptimal method but considers more than 3-tuples of nodes.

Another important problem encountered in inference system is the consistency of the knowledge base. Using the global method presented in Section 3., if one of the two linear programs we have to solve (or both) has no solution, we can say that there is an inconsistency in the constraints of the linear programs, i.e. an inconsistency in the knowledge base. Solving only one linear program is enough to find out an inconsistency (if any) among the constraints expressing the knowledge base. If there is some inconsistency, exhibiting the Simplex array, we will be able to determine where is the inconsistency, i.e. which arcs are inconsistent. So, our system is of the following general form :

(a) consistency checking by linear programming
 if an inconsistency is detected, exit
(b) saturation of the network
(c) answering user's queries.

The considered queries are of the form P(A | B) ?.

Using results in established in (Dubois et al., 1990; Amarger et al., 1991) we can also handle queries of the form P(A ∪ B | C) ?, P(A ∩ B | C) ?, P(C | A ∩ B) ?,...Of course, steps (a) and (b) may take a long time computation, but they only are performed once for all at the beginning of the session, in order to ensure that the user works with a consistent knowledge base, and to make all the information explicit.

7 AN EXAMPLE

In this section, our purpose is to point out the results given by both the quantified syllogism and generalized Bayes' theorem. The algorithm we use is written in "C" on a Sun 3/50 workstation without arithmetical co-processor and the Floyd algorithm is used to compute the longest paths (see (Gondran and Minoux, 1985) for instance). The example we use is already considered in (Dubois et al., 1990), and is pictured in Figure 2 and, in the following, we use the incidence matrix notation to let the saturated network be more readable.

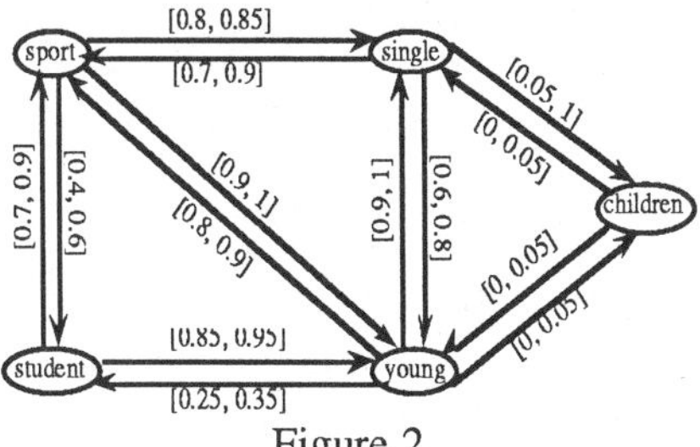

Figure 2

So, using the above algorithm (the details are given in (Amarger, Dubois, Prade 1991)), we get the "saturated" network (the improved bounds are underlined):

	student	sport	single	young	children
student	[1.00;1.00]	[0.90;0.90]	[0.61;1.00]	[0.85;0.85]	[0.00;0.27]
sport	[0.40;0.40]	[1.00;1.00]	[0.85;0.85]	[0.90;0.96]	[0.00;0.15]
single	[0.22;0.36]	[0.70;0.70]	[1.00;1.00]	[0.80;0.80]	[0.05;0.10]
young	[0.35;0.35]	[0.84;0.88]	[0.90;0.90]	[1.00;1.00]	[0.00;0.05]
children	[0.00;0.09]	[0.00;0.13]	[0.00;0.05]	[0.00;0.04]	[1.00;1.00]

The computation of the complete "saturated" matrix was made in 10 seconds (CPU and I/O time).

The optimal solution computed by the global method presented in Section 3., and in (Amarger et al., 1990) is exactly the same as the one computed by the "local method" based on QS and BG. Let us note that the "global method" is written in "C", on a Sun 3/50 workstation, without arithmetical co-processor; and the computation of each element of the "optimal" matrix is made in 12 seconds (CPU and I/O time). So, combining a locally optimal method (QS) with a global but suboptimal method (generalized Bayes' theorem), we get results as good as the ones given by a globally optimal method (Simplex based method of Section 3.), but with a much smaller computation time, in our example.

8 CONJUNCTION AND DISJUNCTION

The results involving conjunction and disjunction solved in previous papers are not general enough to be very useful in practice. Their merits are but tutorial. Especially, their extension to disjunctions and conjunctions of more than two terms look untractable in an analytic form. Even the case when only three symbols A, B and C are involved, and where bounds on the six conditional probability values involving these symbols are known, will lead to unwieldy expressions because the six values are related via the generalized Bayes' theorem.

A more realistic approach to the problem of handling disjunctions and conjunctions is to introduce new nodes in the network, that account for the concerned conjunctions and disjunctions, and apply the iterative algorithm (or linear programming) to answer the query. As an example, let us consider the query "what is the probability of C given A and B", where the background network includes nodes A, B, C only; (see Figure 3)

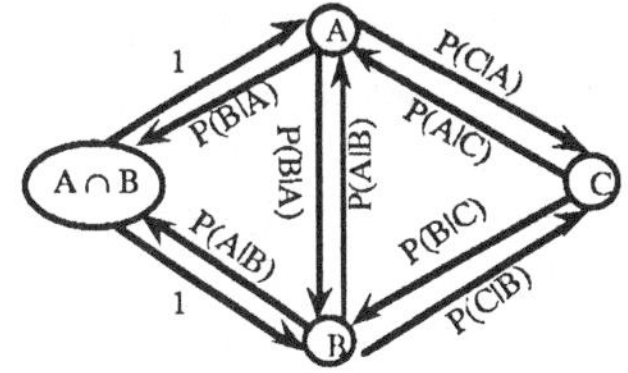

Figure 3 : Introducing a new node "A ∩ B"

To deal with this problem we create a node named A ∩ B. A description of the conjunction in terms of conditional probabilities leads to force $P_*(A \mid A \cap B) = 1$, $P_*(B \mid A \cap B) = 1$, $P(A \cap B \mid B) = P(A \mid B)$ and $P(A \cap B \mid A) = P(B \mid A)$, and to add these arcs to the network (see Figure 3). Then the calculation of $P(C \mid A \cap B)$ can be addressed by the repeated use of the Quantified Syllogism pattern and the generalized Bayes rule in this network.

In order to catch a feeling of what kinds of results can be produced by this method, let us deal with the case when the six values P(A I C), P(C I A), P(B I C), P(C I B), P(A I B), P(B I A) are precisely known in Figure 3. Of course they obey the generalized Bayes theorem, so that only five of them need to be known. The calculation of bounds for $P(C \mid A \cap B)$ can be performed by applying twice the syllogism rule, cancelling A between $A \cap B$ and C, and cancelling B between $A \cap B$ and C. Applying (1) and (3) with the following substitution : A becomes $A \cap B$, B becomes A, we get

$$\max\left(0,\ 1-\frac{1-P(C \mid A)}{P(B \mid A)}\right) \le P(C \mid A \cap B) \le \min\left(1,\ \frac{P(C \mid A)}{P(B \mid A)}\right)$$

Similarly, exchanging A and B in the above inequalities, we get :

$$\max\left(0,\ 1-\frac{1-P(C \mid B)}{P(A \mid B)}\right) \le P(C \mid A \cap B) \le \min\left(1,\ \frac{P(C \mid B)}{P(A \mid B)}\right)$$

Joining these results together, we obtain

$$\max\left(0, 1-\frac{1-P(C \mid A)}{P(B \mid A)}, 1-\frac{1-P(C \mid B)}{P(A \mid B)}\right) \le P(C \mid A \cap B) \quad (6)$$

$$P(C \mid A \cap B) \le \min\left(1, \frac{P(C \mid B)}{P(A \mid B)}, \frac{P(C \mid A)}{P(B \mid A)}\right) \quad (7)$$

It can be checked that this is exactly what has been obtained in (Dubois et al., 1990), i.e. when we have no knowledge about P(B I C) and P(A I C). To improve these bounds requires the use of the generalized Bayes theorem. As shown in (Dubois et al., 1990) only the lower bound of $P(C \mid A \cap B)$ can be improved knowing P(B I C) and P(A I C). However the following extra inequalities are not related to the generalized Bayes theorem nor to the quantified syllogisms

$$P(C \mid A \cap B) \ge \frac{P(C \mid A)}{P(B \mid A)} + \frac{P(C \mid B)}{P(A \mid B)} \cdot \left(1 - \frac{1}{P(B \mid C)}\right) \quad (8)$$

$$P(C \mid A \cap B) \ge \frac{P(C \mid B)}{P(A \mid B)} + \frac{P(C \mid A)}{P(B \mid A)} \cdot \left(1 - \frac{1}{P(A \mid C)}\right) \quad (9)$$

These inequalities are simple consequences of the additivity of probabilities applied to $A \cap B \cap C$ under the form

$$P(A \cap B \cap C) = P(A \cap C) + P(B \cap C) - P((A \cap C) \cup (B \cap C)) \ge P(A \cap C) + P(B \cap C) - P(C)$$

Hence additivity is not presupposed by the description of node $A \cap B$ in Figure 3. Proceeding similarly for $P(A \cap B \mid C)$, the syllogism rule leads to the following bounds

$$\max\left(0, P(A \mid C)\left(1+\frac{(P(B \mid A)-1)}{P(C \mid A)}\right), P(B \mid C)\left(1+\frac{(P(A \mid B)-1)}{P(C \mid B)}\right)\right)$$
$$\le P(A \cap B \mid C) \le$$
$$\min\left(P(A \mid C), P(B \mid C), \frac{P(A \mid C)P(B \mid A)}{P(C \mid A)}, \frac{P(B \mid C)P(A \mid B)}{P(C \mid B)}\right)$$

Note that in the above expression, the two last terms in the 'min' are equal due to the generalized Bayes' theorem. Using results in (Dubois et al., 1990), it can be checked that the upper bound is optimal while the lower bound is sound but not optimal. Indeed we do not recover the obvious bound, again related to additivity :

$$P(A \cap B \mid C) \ge \max(0, P(A \mid C) + P(B \mid C) - 1) \quad (10)$$

More specifically, given only P(A I C) = 1 and P(B I C) = 1, the repeated use of the syllogism rule and the generalized Bayes' rule are not capable of producing $P(A \cap B \mid C) = 1$ (a result produced by the above bound). Indeed, if we add the node AB to represent $A \cap B$, we have to saturate the following network

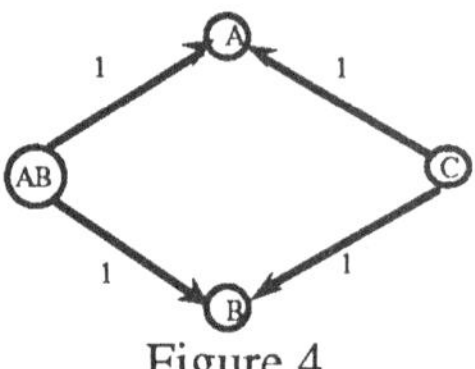

Figure 4

All that this network tells is that $AB \subseteq A \cap B$ and $C \subseteq A \cap B$, but clearly, $AB \cap C$ can be anything. Also, even assuming that $P(A \mid B) \ne 1$ and $P(B \mid A) \ne 1$ are known and letting P(AB I A) = P(B I A), P(AB I B) = P(A I B) cannot improve the lower bound of P(AB I C) using the syllogism rule, nor the generalized Bayes rule. This point indicates that some of the lower bounds already obtained in (Dubois et al., 1990), for the conjunction will be useful to implement, in order to improve the performance of the iterative procedure, i.e. the inequalities (8), (9) and (10).

Another point to notice is that the constraint P(AB I A) = P(B I A) is stronger than letting $P^*(AB \mid A) = P^*(B \mid A)$, $P_*(AB \mid A) = P_*(B \mid A)$, when only bounds on P(B I A) are known, indeed, the equality of the bounds can go along with the inequality $P(AB \mid A) \ne P(B \mid A)$. Let us consider the query about $P(C \mid A \cup B)$. To deal with this case, we create a node named $A \cup B$, and arcs joining this node to the network, so as to describe the disjunction in terms of conditional probabilities namely $P(A \cup B \mid A) = 1$ and $P(A \cup B \mid B) = 1$. The calculation of $P(A \mid A \cup B)$ and $P(B \mid A \cup B)$ is slightly less straightforward, namely

$$P(A \mid A \cup B) = \frac{P(A)}{P(A \cup B)} = \frac{P(A)}{P(A)+P(B)-P(A \cap B)} = \frac{P(A \mid B)}{P(A \mid B)+P(B \mid A)-P(A \mid B) \cdot P(B \mid A)}$$

since $P(B)/P(A) = P(B \mid A)/P(A \mid B)$. The complete study of this case is left to the reader. A lack of optimality similar to the one encountered with conjunction will be observed.

9 INDEPENDENCE ASSUMPTIONS

Although our approach does not require independence assumptions, it should be possible to use them if they hold, in order to improve bounds. This section gives preliminary results on that point, for the syllogism rule

QS. Let us consider conditional independence relations. There are three possible ones on {A, B, C}:

i) $P(B \cap C \mid A) = P(B \mid A) \cdot P(C \mid A)$
ii) $P(A \cap C \mid B) = P(A \mid B) \cdot P(C \mid B)$
iii) $P(A \cap B \mid C) = P(A \mid C) \cdot P(B \mid C)$

First, note that i) and iii) are symmetric with respect to each other, exchanging C and A. We shall thus just consider i) and ii). ii) has already been considered in the introduction and we shall check that we cannot do better: ii) is indeed equivalent to the irrelevance property $P(C \mid B) = P(C \mid A \cap B)$. Hence the independence property can be exploited by substituting $P(C \mid B) = P(C \mid A \cap B)$ in the bounds on $P(C \mid A \cap B)$ (equations (6), (7)). Only the bounds where $P(C \mid A)$ appear are useful. We get (for precise values)

$$1 - \left(1 - P(C \mid A)/P(B \mid A)\right) \le P(C \mid B) \le P(C \mid A)/P(B \mid A)$$

from which it follows :

$$P(C \mid B) \cdot P(B \mid A) \le P(C \mid A) \le 1 - P(B \mid A) + P(C \mid B) \cdot P(B \mid A) \quad (11)$$

the lower bound improves (3) and the upper bound improves the second term in the general upper bound (4). Particularly, when $P(B \mid A) = 1$ it can be checked that ii) entails $P(C \mid A) = P(C \mid B)$. For bounds on $P(A \mid C)$, just exchange A and C in the above inequalities, and get

$$P(A \mid B)P(B \mid C) \le P(A \mid C) \le 1 - P(B \mid C) + P(A \mid B)P(B \mid C) \quad (12)$$

The above inequalities can influence $P(C \mid A)$ using the generalized Bayes rule since

$$P(A \mid C) = P(C \mid A) \cdot P(A \mid B) \cdot P(B \mid C)/P(B \mid A) \cdot P(C \mid B)$$

can be substituted in (12) and enable to catch the inequality

$$P(C \mid A) \le \frac{P(B \mid A)P(C \mid B)}{P(A \mid B)P(B \mid C)}(1 - P(B \mid C) + P(A \mid B)P(B \mid C)) \quad (13)$$

that comes on top of (11) (the lower bound of (11) is obtained again this way). It improves the last term appearing in the upper bound in (4).

Let us turn to i). It yields a new expression for $P(C \mid A)$ under the from $P(B \cap C \mid A)/P(B \mid A)$. Let us write it by letting $P(A \mid B \cap C)$ appear;using the generalized Bayes rule:

$$P(C \mid A) = \frac{P(A \mid B \cap C) \cdot P(C \mid B)}{P(A \mid B)}$$

Now using optimal bounds (6) and (7) on $P(A \mid B \cap C)$, and given that $P(A \mid C)$ is unknown there comes

$$\max\left(0, 1 - \frac{1 - P(C \mid B)}{P(A \mid B)}\right) \le P(C \mid A) \le \min\left(1, \frac{P(C \mid B)}{P(A \mid B)}\right) \quad (14)$$

Again, if $P(C \mid B) = 1$, we conclude that $P(C \mid A) = 1$. Moreover if $P(A \mid B) = 1$, then $P(C \mid A) = P(C \mid B)$. The lower bound in (14) improves (3), and the upper bound may improve the third term in (4).
Independence assumption iii) leads to a similar bracketting of $P(A \mid C)$, just exchanging C and A in (14) :

$$\max\left(0, 1 - \frac{1 - P(A \mid B)}{P(C \mid B)}\right) \le P(A \mid C) \le \min\left(1, \frac{P(A \mid B)}{P(C \mid B)}\right) \quad (15)$$

(15) and the generalized Bayes rule enable special bounds for $P(C \mid A)$ to be found under assumption iii), namely :

$$\frac{P(B \mid A)}{P(B \mid C)}\left[1 - \frac{1 - P(C \mid B)}{P(A \mid B)}\right] \le P(C \mid A) \le \frac{P(B \mid A)}{P(B \mid C)} \quad (16)$$

Again the lower bound in (16) improves (3), and the upper bound may improve the third term in (4).

To summarize, when independence assumptions are declared, namely i), ii), iii), bounds on $P(C \mid A)$ given in (3) and (4) can be improved by means of (14), (11) and (13), and (16) respectively. Of course, these types of independence assumption can be more directly exploited in queries involving conjunctions or disjunctions.

10 CONCLUSION

The approach proposed in this paper to handle conditional probabilities in knowledge networks presupposes assumptions that contrast with the ones underlying Bayesian networks. In Bayesian networks, a single joint probability distribution is reconstructed from the acyclic network using conditional independence assumptions, and given some a priori probabilities on the roots of the acyclic network. Here, nothing is assumed about a priori (unconditional) probabilities, no independence assumption is taken for granted, and, the more cycles there are, the more informative the network is.

Results obtained so far indicate that the two inference rules that we use in turn, namely the syllogism rule (QS) and the generalized Bayes' theorem (BG), are powerful and can compete with a brute force linear programming approach, as regards the quality of the obtained probability bounds. Our inference technique seems to be more efficient than linear programming since each run of each step of the inference procedure is polynomial in the number of nodes in the network. However, more investigation is needed on complexity aspects, and to better grasp the distance to optimality of the inference procedure.

It has been indicated how to deal with conditional probabilities involving conjunctions and disjunctions of two terms, and negation of terms. However the obtained optimal bounds are rather heavy mathematical expressions for conjunctions and disjunctions, and it seems difficult to extrapolate them to more than two terms. It has been shown how to solve the problem of conjunction and disjunction by introducing auxiliary nodes in the original network. In the future, we plan to treat negation likewise and to generalize the node addition approach to the combination of more than two primitive terms.

In the long run, we plan to develop a computerized tool (parts of which are already implemented) that can handle a knowledge base in the form of a pair (W,Δ) where W is a set of facts and Δ a sets of conditional probabilities. A query Q can then be solved by computing $P(Q \mid W)$ where W is the conjunction of available facts, and $P(Q \mid W)$ is obtained under the form of bounds derived from the saturated network built with Δ. This mode of reasoning is similar to what happens in non-monotonic logic. More specifically some of the propagation rules proposed here bear some interesting analogies with some derived inference rules in a well-behaved non-monotonic logic. For instance the BG rule corresponds to

$$\frac{\alpha_1 \mid\!\sim \alpha_2, \alpha_2 \mid\!\sim \alpha_3, \ldots, \alpha_{n-1} \mid\!\sim \alpha_n, \alpha_n \mid\!\sim \alpha_1}{\alpha_1 \mid\!\sim \alpha_n} \text{ (loop)}$$

where $\mid\!\sim$ denotes the non-monotonic consequence relation discussed in (Kraus and al, 1990). The QS rule gives

$$\frac{\alpha_1 \mid\!\sim \alpha_2, \alpha_2 \mid\!\sim \alpha_1, \alpha_2 \mid\!\sim \alpha_3}{\alpha_1 \mid\!\sim \alpha_3} \text{ (equivalence)}$$

the basic lower bound for $P(A \cap B \mid C)$ (see (Amarger et al., 1990)) corresponds to

$$\frac{\gamma \mid\!\sim \alpha, \gamma \mid\!\sim \beta}{\gamma \mid\!\sim \alpha \wedge \beta} \text{ (right and)}$$

These analogies are no longer surprizing since such kinds of links between probabilistic reasoning and non-monotonic logic have been already laid bare by (Pearl, 1988) and the authors (Dubois and Prade, 1991). But the correspondence pointed out above suggests to consider a nonmonotonic logic where primitive inference rules are the above rules, i.e.rules which are usually considered as derived ones. This point is worth studying in the future.

Among topics of interest for future research, a more detailed comparison with the Bayesian approach would be quite interesting, of course. It would allow the loss of information due to the absence of a priori probabilities to be quantified. It has been demonstrated how to allow for independence assumptions in our approach. Clearly it generates non-linear constraints in the optimization problem associated to a query. But it seems that the inference procedure can cope with these assumptions in a nicer way, just by modifying the constraint propagation rules accordingly. Another topic is the extension of our method to fuzzy quantifiers, already considered in (Dubois and Prade, 1988) for the syllogism rule.

Acknowledgements

This work is partially supported by the DRUMS project (Defeasible Reasoning and Uncertainty Management Systems), funded by the Commission of the European Communities under the ESPRIT BRA n° 3085.

References

S. Amarger, R. Epenoy, and S. Grihon (1990) Reasoning with conditional probabilities. A linear programming based method. *Proc. of the DRUMS Esprit Project, RP2 Workshop*, Albi (France), April 1990, (published by IRIT, Toulouse (France)), pp. 154-167.

S. Amarger, D. Dubois, and H. Prade (1991) Handling imprecisely-known conditional probabilities. UNICOM *"Seminar AI and Computer Power – The Impact on Statistics"*, Brunel Conf. Center, West London, 13-14 March.

F. Bacchus (1990) *Representing and Reasoning with Probabilistic Knowledge*. Cambridge, Ma.: MIT Press.

J. Baldwin (1990) Computational models of uncertainty reasoning in expert systems. *Computers and Math. with Appl.* 19, 105-119

A. Charnes and W.W. Cooper (1962) Programming with linear fractional functions. *Naval Res. Logist. Quart.*, 9, 181-186.

D. Dubois and H. Prade (1988) On fuzzy syllogisms. *Comp. Intel.* (Canada), 4, 171-179.

D. Dubois and H. Prade (1991a) Conditional objects and non-monotonic reasoning. *Proc. of the 2d. Int. Conf. on Principles of Knowledge Representation and Reasoning (KR'91)*, Morgan Kaufmann, 175-185

D. Dubois and H. Prade (1991b) Evidence knowledge and belief functions. To appear in *Int. J. of Approx. Reas.*

D. Dubois, H. Prade, and J-M. Toucas (1990) Inference with imprecise numerical quantifiers. In : *Intelligent Systems: State of the Art and Future Directions* (Z. Ras, M. Zemankova, eds.), Chichester: Ellis Horwood, 52-72.

K.W. Fertig and J.S. Breese (1990) Interval influence diagrams. In : *Uncertainty in Artificial Intelligence 5* (M. Henrion et al., eds.), North-Holland,149-171.

M. Gondran and M. Minoux (1985) *Graphes and algorithmes*. Eyrolles, Paris.

S. Kraus, D. Lehmann, and M. Magidor (1990) Nonmonotonic reasoning, preferential models and cumulative logics. *Artificial Intel.*, 44, 167-207.

H. Kyburg (1974) *The Logical Foundation of Statistical Inference*. D. Reidel, Dordrecht.

S.L. Lauritzen and D.J. Spiegelhalter (1988) Local computation with probabilities on graphical structures and their application to expert systems. *J. of the Royal Statistical Society*, B 50(2), 157-224.

Léa Sombé (P. Besnard, M-O. Cordier, D. Dubois, L. Fariñas del Cerro, C. Froidevaux, Y. Moinard, H. Prade, C. Schwind, and P. Siegel) (1990) *Reasoning Under Incomplete Information in Artificial Intelligence : a Comparison of Formalisms Using a Single Example*. Wiley, New-York .

G. Paass (1988) Probabilistic Logic. In : *Non-Standard Logics for Automated Reasoning* (D. Dubois, P. Smets, A. Mamdani, H. Prade, eds.), Academic Press (London), Ch. 8, 213-251.

J. Pearl (1988) *Probabilistic Reasoning in Intelligent Systems : Networks of Plausible Inference*. San Mateo, Ca.: Morgan Kaufmann.

J.R. Quinlan (1983) INFERNO:a cautious approach to uncertain inference. *The Comp. Res.*, 12, 255-269.

P. Suppes (1966) Probabilistic inference and the concept of total evidence. In *Aspects of Inductive Logic* (J. Hintikka and P. Suppes, Eds.) North-Holland, Amsterdam, 49-65

L.C. van der Gaag (1990) Computing probability intervals under independency constraints. *Proc. of the 6th Conf. on Uncertainty in Artificial Intelligence*, Cambridge, Mass., July 27-29, 491-495

L.A. Zadeh (1985) Syllogistic reasoning in fuzzy logic and its application to usuality and reasoning with dispositions. *IEEE Trans. on Systems, Man and Cybernetics*, 15(6), 745-763.

BAYESIAN NETWORKS APPLIED TO THERAPY MONITORING

Carlo Berzuini[1], Riccardo Bellazzi
Dipartimento di Informatica e Sistemistica
Universita'di Pavia
27100 Pavia (Italy)

David Spiegelhalter
Medical Research Council
Biostatistics Unit
Cambridge CB2 2BW, U.K.

Abstract

We propose a general Bayesian network model for application in a wide class of problems of therapy monitoring. We discuss the use of stochastic simulation as a computational approach to inference on the proposed class of models. As an illustration we present an application to the monitoring of cytotoxic chemotherapy in breast cancer.

1. INTRODUCTION

Of interest here is the general problem of *monitoring* and *controlling* a biomedical process over time. The basic premise is that a *model* of the process of interest is available, which allows *learning* from past data and *predicting* the future evolution of the process. Such a model may provide an intelligent system with a basis for :

(a) activating alarms which indicate significant deviations from expected progress ;

(b) using the accumulating data about the process to "learn" about the model parameters, for a more sensitive monitoring and for more accurate patient-specific predictions;

In this paper we propose a model structure that appears to be generic to the monitoring problem, and therefore likely to be useful in a wide class of clinical monitoring problems. Typical applications may involve short-term drug delivery, or medium term treatment, or long-term monitoring of chronic disease. In drug delivery the process of interest is the temporal variation of the drug concentration in body compartments, and the goal is to suggest dosage adjustments that are necessary to achieve concentrations which lie between specific desired limits.

In the management of a chronic disease the monitored process is typically the patient's progression through stages of the disease, and the goal of the monitoring is to predict possible risks and benefits of changes in therapy. An application to medium-term treatment monitoring is used in this paper as an illustration.Clinical practice in medium- or long-term monitoring situations often involves simple rules in which an observed change in the process provokes a corresponding action. Usually these rules are grossly inappropriate for particular patients. Our approach should allow a progress with respect to such a scheme, in that the rules would be replaced by an adaptive model, or the model might be used to evaluate the reliability of the rules.

In the field of drug dosage individualization a Bayesian approach has previously been suggested (eg. D'Argenio 1988, Sheiner 1982). However a flexible framework for model development and for inference computations in this area has not previously been proposed.

In this paper we use a *Bayesian network* both as a representation of the model and as a computational framework for inference. Bayesian networks are able to crystallize in a graphical representation the rich mixture of causal knowledge and conditional independence assumptions that underlies a complex probabilistic model. At a high level, the network will display the way in which the basic sub-systems relate and interlock to form the complete mosaic that represents the process of interest. This is particularly useful in models that involve development over time. At a lower level, the network will display in detail the conditional independence relationships among individual variables in each portion of the global model.

The computation of inferences on the model can be conveniently performed using a stochastic simulation algorithm, called the Gibbs sampler [Geman & Geman, 1984] [Pearl, 1987] [Gelfand, 1988] [Henrion, 1990] [Shachter, 1990]. The essence of this algorithm consists of sampling the joint posterior distribution of unobserved

[1]*Mailing address*: Carlo Berzuini, Dipartimento di Informatica e Sistemistica, via Abbiategrasso 209. 27100 Pavia (Italy). FAX: (39) 382-422881

variables/parameters in the model. The result is an *approximation* of the desired posteriors.

In alternative, one might use algorithm for the exact calculation of posteriors (see, for example, Lauritzen and Spiegelhalter, 1988). However, algorithms for "exact" probability propagation may raise difficulties in certain situations. The first is when the graph is too tightly connected, which will particularly occur when population parameters are not precisely specified. The second is when continuous variables are involved: "exact" propagation currently requires that these variables are discretized, and a recent proposed "exact" method for propagating probabilities on networks with mixed qualitative and quantitative variables [Lauritzen, 1990] seems to assume heavy restrictions on the distributions involved. A compile-time discretization may be hampered by the difficulty of deciding the most appropriate binning and bounding; a run-time ("dynamic") discretization may led to a significant overhead, particularly if the involved distributions are complex.

Thanks to the availability of standard routines for sampling from continuous distributions [Ripley, 1987], stochastic simulation takes advantage of what we know to hamper the applicability of exact methods, namely the continuous nature of the variables, particularly non-Gaussian distributions.

abstraction, a node at a given level representing one or more nodes at lower levels. This greatly facilitates insight into the model.

In this section we consider a top-level view of our model, which is shown in Fig.1.

We suppose that a response relationship of interest has been observed on *N cases*, typically patients, that are somehow similar. The *N*-th patient, called the *target case*, is currently under observation. Node ***X*** represents future evolution of the target case, conditional on a plan for future therapeutic action.

Usually there will be a substantial patient *heterogeneity* in their response to the therapy, and part of this variation will be "explained" by a set z of covariates (eg. age, sex) that affect an individual's response characteristics. We let z_i denote the covariate vector for the *i*-th patient. To handle patient heterogeneity, we introduce *patient-specific* unknown *response parameter vectors*, $\theta_1,...,\theta_N$. We regard the generic θ_i as drawn from a density $p(\theta_i \mid z_i,\beta,\kappa)$, where the unknown parameters β represent effects associated with the individual covariates, and κ is a vector of distributional parameters. For notational economy we pool β and κ, which we call the *hyperparameters*, into a single parameter vector $\pi=(\beta,\kappa)$,

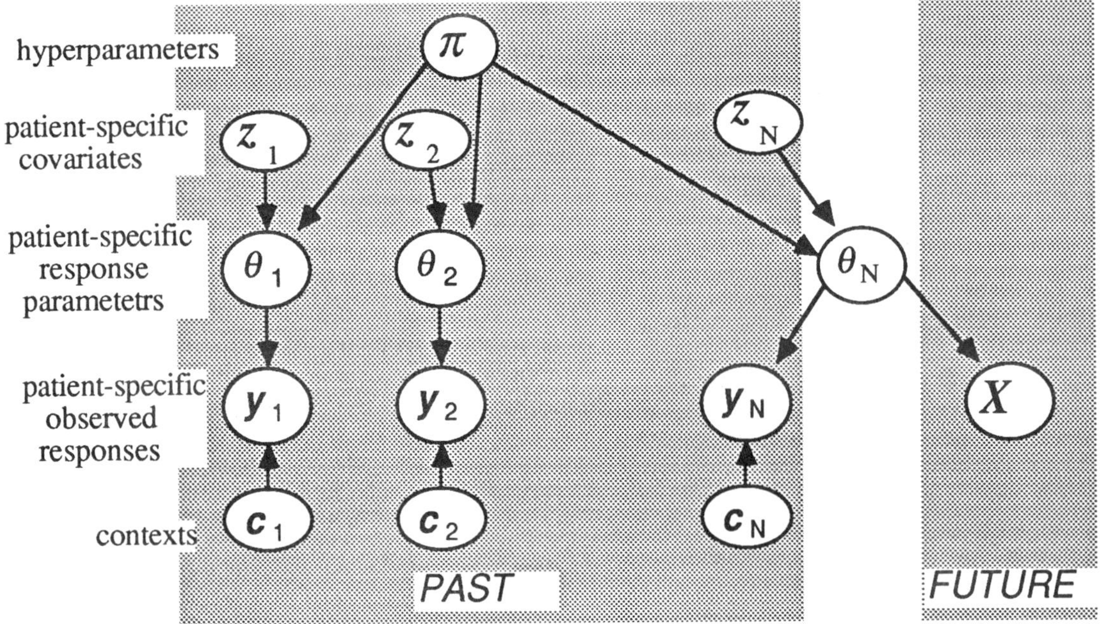

Figure 1. High-level view of the general Bayesian network model for therapeutic monitoring

2. HIGH-LEVEL VIEW OF THE MODEL

One of the advantages of Bayesian networks is that they can be developed at progressively higher levels of detail. One then obtains network models at different levels of

called the *hyperparameter vector*. We assume that the generic θ_i completely defines the response characteristics for the *i*-th patient.

Therefore, the vector of the actual observations on the response of the *i*-th patient, denoted as y_i, can be viewed as a random vector drawn from the density $p(y_i$

$|\theta_i, c_i)$,where the vector c_i summarizes the *known* values of a set of context variables, describing *contingent* conditions such as dose schedules, observation times, or contingent aspects of the patient such as, for example, values of physiological quantities at drug administration.

3. INFERENCE

The inference procedure starts with using "population" information :

$$D = \{y_1,...,y_{N-1}, c_1,...,c_{N-1}, z_1,... ,z_{N-1}, z_N\}$$

to shape a prior distribution for the unknown parameters θ_N for the target case. Then, case-specific response data $\{y_N, c_N\}$ are used to update such prior into a posterior distribution that reflects all the current information about the target case, while "borrowing strength" from the whole past experience D. A classical maximum-likelihood approach tends to yield a poor estimate of θ_N or of linear transformations of it if the record $\{y_N, c_N\}$ contains poor information. By contrast, in our approach the estimates of those components or transformations of θ_N which are poorly estimated from the patient's-specific data will be drawn towards the population average, so that more reasonable values should be obtained.

A further benefit of our approach is that the estimation of θ_N is done through a *sequential updating* procedure : as new data from the monitored patient (or from data-base patients) become available they are incorporated to yield a revised posterior distribution of θ_N, and thus a revised predictive distribution of X. Significant changes in the patient's behaviour, possibly pointing to important patho-physiological events, should be mirrored by concomitant patterns of change of the posterior of θ_N.

The inference involves four basic steps of probability propagation over the net of Fig.1. These steps are separately described in the following. Below the description of each single step, the relevant portion of the net of Fig. 1 is shown.

population updating: initially we pretend to be completely uninformed about the value of the hyperparameters π, and represent this "ignorance" by associating with node π a "vague" *hyperprior* distribution, denoted $p_0(\pi)$. Then information $D = \{y_1,...,y_{N-1}, z_1,...,z_{N-1}, c_1,...,c_{N-1}\}$ is used to update $p_0(\pi)$, using probability propagation over the network below, into an *a posteriori* distribution $p_1(\pi | D)$, called the *population distribution* of π ;

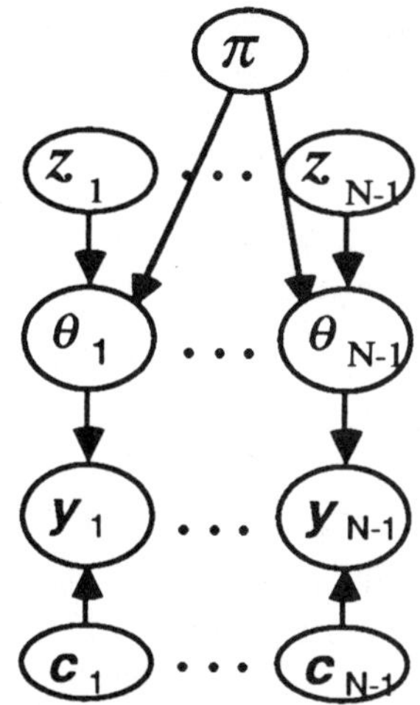

collapsing: prior to considering the specific data $\{y_N, c_N\}$, all we know about the target case is the corresponding covariate vector z_N and the fact that he/she/it is a member of the same population from which the remaining N-1 data base cases were drawn. This leads to regard the parameters θ_N for the target case as those of a generic population individual with covariables z_N, and to view θ_N as drawn from the distribution :

$$p_0(\theta_N | z_N, D) = \int_{\Omega} p_\theta(\theta_N | \pi, z_N) p_1(\pi | D) d\pi \qquad (1)$$

where Ω denotes relevant domain of π.

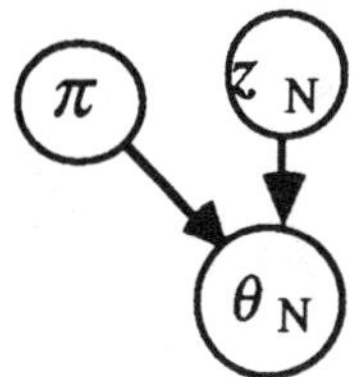

case-specific updating past data $\{y_N, c_N\}$ obtained from the target case are used to update the prior $p_0(\theta_N | z_N, D)$ into a posterior distribution $p_1(\theta_N | z_N, y_N, c_N, D)$ which, by Bayes' theorem, is given by :

$$p_1(\theta_N | z_N, y_N, c_N, D) \propto p_0(\theta_N | z_N, D) \times p(y_N | \theta_N, c_N) \qquad (2)$$

and that describes our uncertainty about the response parameters for the target case, *after considering all relevant (population- and patient-specific) available information.*

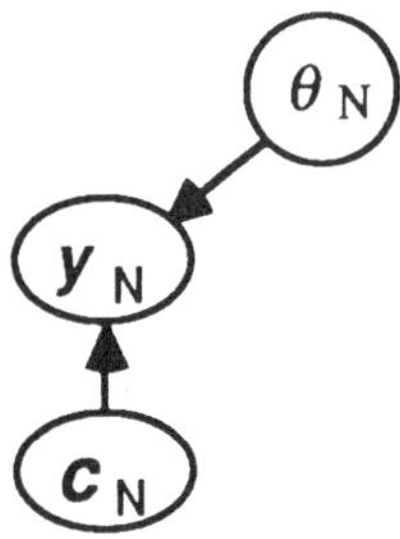

prediction: $p_1(\theta_N | z_N, y_N, c_N, D)$ is used to obtain a predictive distribution of X, denoted $p_P(X)$. Future patient's evolution is predicted under different hypothesized decision plans for a more rational decision. $p_P(X)$ is defined by :

$$p_P(X) = \int_{\Sigma} p(X | \theta_N) p_1(\theta_N | z_N, y_N, c_N, D)\, d\theta_N \quad (3)$$

where Σ denotes relevant domain of θ_N.

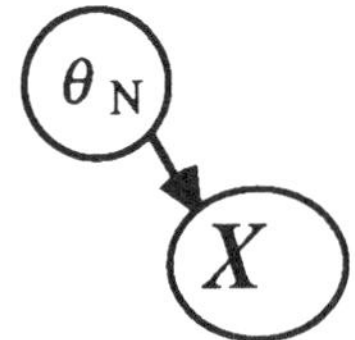

4. COMPUTING THE INFERENCES VIA STOCHASTIC SIMULATION

The computations required in the above described inference phases can be conveniently performed by *sampling* techniques. For example, collapsing requires the integration (1). This can be performed by first drawing a sample $\pi^{(0)}$ from $p_1(\pi | D)$, then a sample $\theta^{(0)}$ from $p_\theta(\theta_N | \pi^{(0)}, z_N)$, then a new sample $\pi^{(1)}$ from $p_1(\pi | D)$ and a new sample $\theta^{(1)}$ from $p_\theta(\theta_N | \pi^{(1)}, z_N)$, and so on. This resampling is repeated a high number of times, say L. At the end, one can straightforwardly use the set of generated samples $\{\theta^{(0)}, \theta^{(1)}, \ldots, \theta^{(L)}\}$ to calculate any marginal or summary of $p_0(\theta_N | z_N, D)$, eg. selected percentiles of the distribution of a given component of θ_N.

Note that the densities that appear in (1)-(2) are multivariate, which seems to imply that the sampling steps involved in collapsing and case-specific updating must be actually performed on multivariate densities. As a matter of fact, one may draw samples from a multivariate distribution by actually sampling univariate distributions. A first possibility is to exploit conditional independence. For example, if the components of π are conditionally independent given D, then one can draw samples from the multivariate density $p_1(\pi | D)$ by actually sampling individual densities $p_1(\pi_h | D)$.

Case-specific updating and prediction are conveniently carried out by an iterative stochastic simulation algorithm, called the *Gibbs sampler*, that uses a Bayesian network representation of the relationships among variables $(\theta_N, z_N, y_N, c_N)$ as the computational framework for the necessary calculations. Such a network will obviously depend on the specific application, since it describes in all details the structure of the conditional independencies among individual variables in the problem.

Perhaps the key reference to Gibbs sampling is Geman & Geman [Geman & Geman, 1984], who discuss its application to image analysis. A thorough review of the method is given by Gelfand & Smith [Gelfand, 1988]. Within the AI literature, the method has been explored, under the name of *Markov stochastic simulation*, by several authors, eg. Pearl [Pearl, 1987] and Henrion [Henrion, 1990].

To perform the Gibbs sampling, initial values are assigned to each unobserved variable in the network. Then, for each unobserved variable in turn, the current value is replaced by a value drawn from the full conditional distribution of that variable given the current values of its "neighbours" in the net (parents, children and parents of the children, observed and unobserved). This resampling is repeated many times. Under certain regularity conditions, Geman & Geman [Geman & Geman, 1984] show that the resampling process is an irreducible Markov chain that converges to an equilibrium distribution given by the full posterior distribution of the unknown variables. Thus, after the sampling, any posterior summaries or marginal components of such multivariate posterior can be straightforwardly calculated from the set of generated samples.

5. SPECIFIC MODEL FOR CYTOTOXIC CHEMOTHERAPY MONITORING IN BREAST CANCER

As an illustration example, we consider an application to the monitoring of patients affected by breast-cancer who are being given cycles of post-operative cytotoxic chemotherapy. From a clinical perspective, it is desirable that the patient receives an adequate dose, while guarding excessive toxicity which leaves the patient vulnerable to bouts of infection.

We need a low-level network model that describes the relationships among individual response parameters, context variables and response observations in this specific application. The idea is one of introducing suitable and reasonable conditional independence assumptions among the variables in order that the problem can be decomposed into manageable sub-problems, and that subsequent quantification of the model is straightforward.

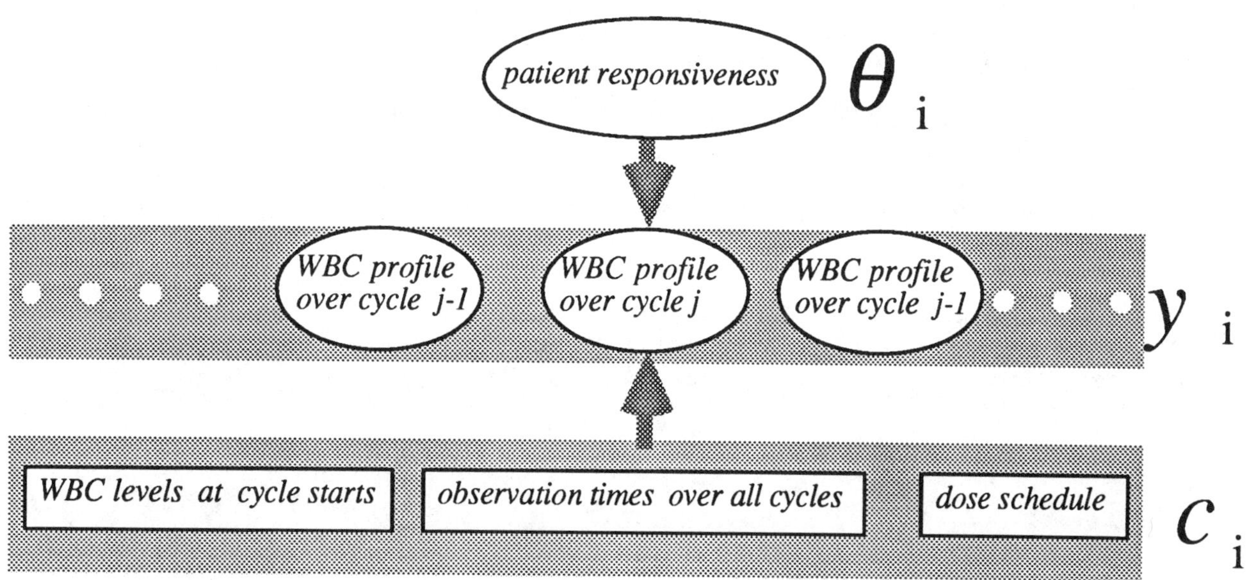

Figure 2. Intermediate-level view of a Bayesian network for the monitoring of cytotoxic chemotherapy in breast cancer. The figure shows only a portion of model for the generic i-th patient. A big shaded arrow pointing from a layer to another means that each node in the first layer sends an arrow to each node in the latter layer.

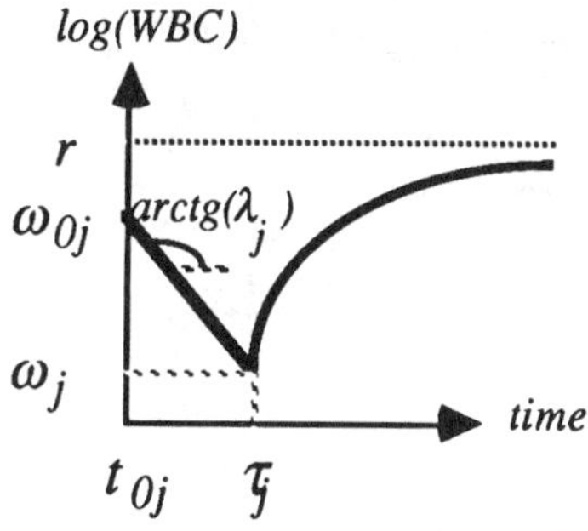

Figure 3. log-WBC-count profile over j-th cycle for a generic patient

Our proposed model, which has been described in more detail by Bellazzi *et al* (1991), is shown in Fig.2. This model represents the assumption that observations on individual cycles of treatment are conditionally independent given some patient-specific parameters, such as those representing the sensitivity and responsiveness of the patient.

We assume that the level of white blood cell (*WBC*) count is the most important aspect of bone-marrow toxicity. High toxicity is reflected by a low WBC count. Several features might be straightforwardly combined with the WBC count in our model, but nothing essential is lost if we restrict to a simple model. We let w_{kj} denote k-th log-*WBC*-count measurement within the j-th cycle of treatment, and let t_{kj} denote the time of this measurement, taken from the instant at which the drug is administered at the beginning of the cycle. The stylized profile shown in Fig. 3 is assumed to be a realistic model of the log-*WBC*-count profile over the generic treatment cycle.

The intercept w_{0j} represents the log-*WBC* count at drug administration. The downward slope is denoted as λ_j, the recovery rate as γ (assumed independent of the cycle) and the change point as τ_j. The minimum log-*WBC* level reached during the cycle j, denoted as ω_j, is a simple function of $\{w_{0j}, \lambda_j, \tau_j\}$.
By adding gaussian white noise errors e_{kj}, $k = 1,\ldots, 5$; $j=1,\ldots, NC$, we obtain the following longitudinal regression model for the log-*WBC* profile over treatment cycle j :

$$
\begin{aligned}
&\lambda_j = k \times dose_j \times \alpha \\
&\omega_j = w_{0j} - k \times dose_j \times \alpha \times \tau \qquad (4)\\
&w_{kj} = w_{0j} - \lambda_j \times (t_{kj} - t_{0j}) + e_{kj} \quad \text{if} \quad 0 < t_{kj} < \tau \\
&w_{kj} = \omega_j + (r - \omega_j)(1 - exp\{-\gamma \times (t_{kj} - \tau)\}) + e_{kj} \quad \text{if } \tau < t_{kj} \\
&e_{kj} \sim No(0, \sigma^2)
\end{aligned}
$$

with :

k	observation within cycle ($k = 1,\ldots,5$)
j	cycle number
e_{kj}	realisation of a gaussian random variable with mean 0 and variance σ^2;
$dose_j$	*standardized dose* = actual dose given to the patient at cycle j divided by square meters of body surface area ;

α — *patient's sensitivity* to the drug (α =1 : *normal patient*; α =1.5 : *sensitive patient*; α =2 : *very sensitive patient*);

k — expected fall in the log-*WBC* count count in unit time, for a normal patient given a unit dose of treatment ;

r — "normal" log-*WBC* count (the value at the start of the therapy).

$$\pi_{.1} + \pi_{.2} + \pi_{.3} = 1.$$

The parameters $\pi_{.m}$, m =1,..., 3 are hyperparameters. The parameter σ is more conveniently treated as continuous. A suitable class of prior distributions for σ is the inverse gamma :

$$1/\sigma \sim \Gamma(a , b) \quad (7)$$

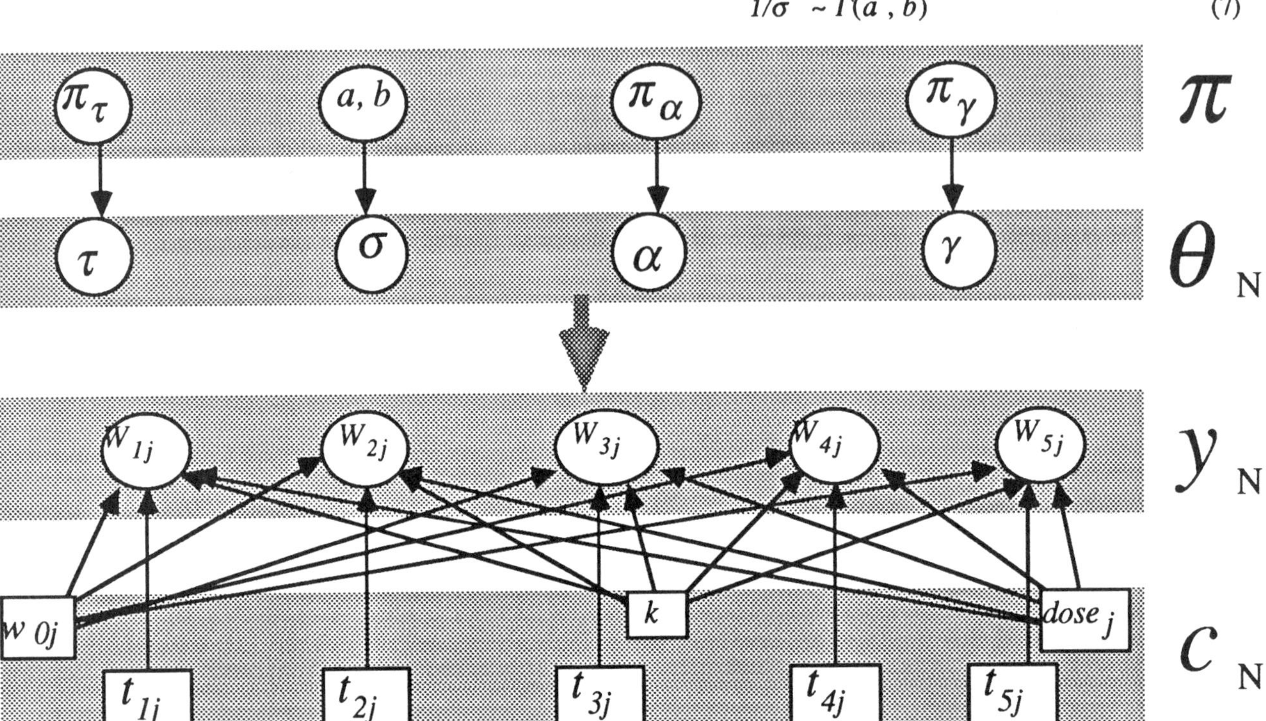

Figure 4 Bayesian Network representation of our patient-model for toxicity. Layers (from top to bottom) contain : hyperparameters, response parameters, response observations (WBC counts), context variables. A big shaded arrow pointing from a layer to another means that each node in the first layer sends an arrow to each node in the latter layer.

From (4) it follows that the conditional distribution attached to the generic observed log-WBC-count w_{kj} is gaussian, and specified by :

$$p(w_{kj} | \textit{all other variables}) =$$
$$= No(w_{0j} - k \; dose_j \; \alpha(t_{kj} - t_{0j}), \sigma^2) \quad \text{if } \tau_j < t_{kj} \quad (5)$$
$$= No(\omega_j + (r - \omega_j)(1 - exp\{-\gamma \times (t_{kj} - \tau)\}), \sigma^2) \quad \text{if } \tau_j \geq t_{kj}$$

A complete Bayesian formulation of the model requires us to specify conditional distributions of response parameters { $\alpha, \gamma, \tau, \sigma$ } given a suitable set of hyperparameters. We decided to take α, γ, τ as 3-level discrete random variables with respective prior probability mass functions:

$$p(\alpha = m) = \pi_{\alpha m}, \; p(\gamma = m) = \pi_{\gamma m}, \; p(\tau = m) = \pi_{\tau m} \quad (6)$$
$$m = 1, ..., 3$$

which preserves conjugacy with respect to (5). The quantities a , b are hyperparameters.

Finally we need to attach prior distributions to the hyperparameters. A suitable prior for each hyperparameter is the *uniform* distribution over a suitable interval. Such a "vague" hyperprior expresses our *a priori* total ignorance about such hyperparameters.

The qualitative relationships implicit in equations (4)-(7) are depicted in the Bayesian Network shown in Fig. 3. The meaning of a generic arrow *x* -->*y* may be interpreted to be "*x contributes to define the distribution from which y is generated*". The distributional specifications described above provide a complete quantification of the network, in that they specify the conditional distribution of each random variable given its parents in the network.

Note that the network contains a node for each single observation on WBC. Implicit in the network structure is the assumption that these observations are conditionally independent given the response parameters and the context variables. This is correct as long as one neglects correlation among errors e_{kj}.

One could acknowledge the fact that response parameters may vary from cycle to cycle by introducing cycle specific parameters α_j, σ_j and so on, and impose a structure (eg. a time series model) that expresses the temporal relatedness among these, but we shall not pursue this here.

5.3 Numerical results

A computer program, called GAMEES (Bellazzi, 1991), has been developed for general purpose Bayesian network modelling and inference using stochastic simulation. The network structure is entered into the computer through a graphical interface. The program requests the user to enter only essential aspects of the overall multi-level network structure. The program then internally generates all the implied repetitive structure. GAMEES incorporates a wide library of sampling routines and sampling control strategies for carrying out all the inference steps described in section 3 and processing the generated samples. The population-updating phase is carried out through a connection between the Bayesian network and a patient data-base.

By means of GAMEES, we applied the model of Fig.3 to the treatment records of 11 patients undergoing breast-cancer post-operative chemotherapy. These records contained data from 2 to 3 treatment cycles per patient, each cycle yielding at most 5 data points.

Population updating and *collapsing* yielded population priors for response parameters. In particular, for parameter α we obtained : $p_1(\alpha = 1) = 0.33$ and $p_1(\alpha = 1.5) = 0.36$ and $p_1(\alpha = 2) = 0.31$, indicating that patients with "normal" sensitivity are slightly more frequent than others.

The data from the chosen *target patient* spanned 5 treatment cycles. Fig.*5a* shows the data from the target patient superimposed to a "cloud of points" that represents a collection of profiles simulated using population distributions for the response parameters. The profiles appear to be very dispersed, reflecting high heterogeneity within the population. It is apparent that the target patient is much more sensitive than the population average, and that a prediction of the response for the target patient based on population distributions of the unknown model parameters would be inappropriate.

Patient-specific updating was first carried out on the basis of first cycle data from the target patient. 500 Gibbs sampling runs were employed. The convergence of the algorithm was monitored by plotting profiles of values generated sequentially during the Gibbs sampling, one plot for each of the four unknown response parameters. A reasonably stationary behaviour of the four profiles was achieved after 100 runs, although substantial cyclicity persisted. Subsequent samples were picked up at a rate of one out of every five to reduce autocorrelation. The obtained predictive distribution of subsequent WBC count evolution over cycles 2 to 5 is represented in Fig.*5b* by a cloud of points. Big points represent actual observations. One may note that the prediction fits the actually observed patient's data much better than the population-based prediction of Fig. *5a*. Moreover, the good fit between actual observations made in cycles 2 to 5 and the corresponding prediction indicates that the patient is "responding as expected". Any discrepancy may lead to a decision (e.g. to change therapy) and can also be used to update response parameters.

Fig.*5c* displays the prediction of the patient's response over cycles 4 and 5, based on data of cycles 1 to 3.

Fig.*5d* shows the evolution of the estimated posterior distribution for parameter α over the cycles of therapy. Note that the sequential updates gradually shift our belief towards the highest value for parameter α, thus strengthening our opinion that the patient is "very sensitive". Another useful summary would be a plot of percentile curves for posteriors of interest.

7. CONCLUSIONS

We have described an approach to therapy monitoring that we hope of potential usefulness in many areas of clinical monitoring, such as short-term drug delivery, medium-term therapy managing and long-term monitoring of chronic diseases. An important characteristic of this approach is the capability of learning at a population level and adapting to a specific patient.

In the future we intend to explore, in different application areas, the possibility of developing these models into even larger networks by extending them to include processes that develop on different temporal scales, such as when short-term drug delivery and medium-term clinical outcomes are taken into account jointly. A suitable conditional independence structure would make a large network model manageable, allowing its various portions to be studied individually, so that different areas of expertise might be cooperatively brought to bear.

An investigation of the possibilities to combine the modelling approach proposed in this paper with other approaches, such as compartmental modelling, provides much scope for further work. In particular, compartmental modeling of the underlying drug metabolism might provide an essential tool for achieving meaningful and parsimonious parametrisations of the response relationship to be modelled. This would allow patho-physiological knowledge to be brought to bear, and would be particularly useful when multiple response curves, generated by the same underlying metabolic dynamics are involved.

Acknowledgements

M.Leaning made essential contributions to the development of the application. R.Bianchi and S.Quaglini implemented (together with R.Bellazzi) the GAMEES program. This work was partly supported by an EEC grant (AIM Project 1005).

References

Bellazzi, R., Berzuini, C., Quaglini, S., Spiegelhalter, D., Leaning, M. (1991), Cytotoxic chemotherapy monitoring using stochastic simulation on graphical models. *to appear on the Proceedings of the AIME-91 Conference, Maastricht, Nederland, july 1991.*

D'Argenio, D.Z. and Maneval, D.C. (1988). Estimation approaches for modeling sparse data systems, *Proceedings of the IFAC Symposium on Modeling and Control in Biomedical Systems, 6-8 april, Venice, Italy* (C.Cobelli and L.Mariani, eds.). Pergamon Press, New York.

Gelfand, A. and Smith, A.F.M. (1988), Sampling based approaches to calculating marginal densities. *Technical Report*, University of Nottingham, U.K.

Geman, S. & Geman, D. (1984), Stochastic relaxation, Gibbs distributions, and the Bayesian restoration of images. *IEEE Transactions on Pattern Analysis and Machine Intelligence*, PAMI-6, pp. 721-741.

Henrion, M. (1990), An Introduction to Algorithms for Inference in Belief Nets, in: *Uncertainty in Artificial Intelligence 5* (M.Henrion, R.D.Shachter, L.N. Kanal and J.F.Lemmer eds.), Elsevier Science Publishers B.V. (North-Holland).

Lauritzen, S.L. & Spiegelhalter, D.J. (1988) Local computations with probabilities on graphical structures and their application to expert systems (with discussion). *J. Roy. Statist. Soc., B*, **50**, 157-224.

Lauritzen, S. (1990), Propagation of probabilities, Means and Variances in Mixed Graphical Association Models, *Technical Report R 90-18*, Institute for Electronic Systems, Department of Mathematics and Computer Science, University of Aalborg, Denmark, april 1990.

Pearl, J. (1987), Evidential reasoning using stochastic simulation of causal models. *Artificial Intelligence*, **32**, no.2, 245-252.

Ripley, B.D. (1987), *Stochastic Simulation*, Wiley, New York.

Shachter, R.D., Peot, M. (1990), Simulation Approaches to General Probabilistic Inference on Belief Networks, in: *Uncertainty in Artificial Intelligence 5* (M.Henrion, R.D.Shachter, L.N. Kanal and J.F.Lemmer eds.), Elsevier Science Publishers B.V. (North-Holland).

Sheiner, L.B., Beal, S.L., (1982), Bayesian individualisation of pharmakokinetics: simple implementation and comparison with non Bayesian methods. *J. Pharm. Sci.*, **71**, 1344-1348.

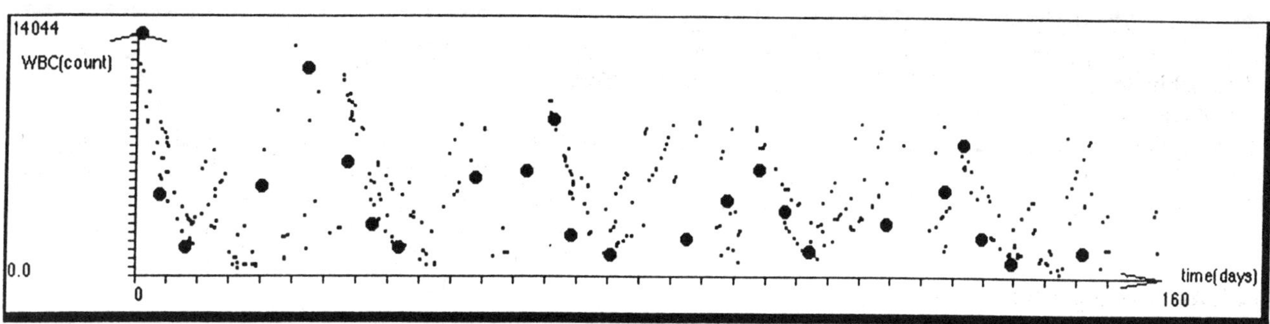
14044
WBC(count)
0.0
0
time(days)
160

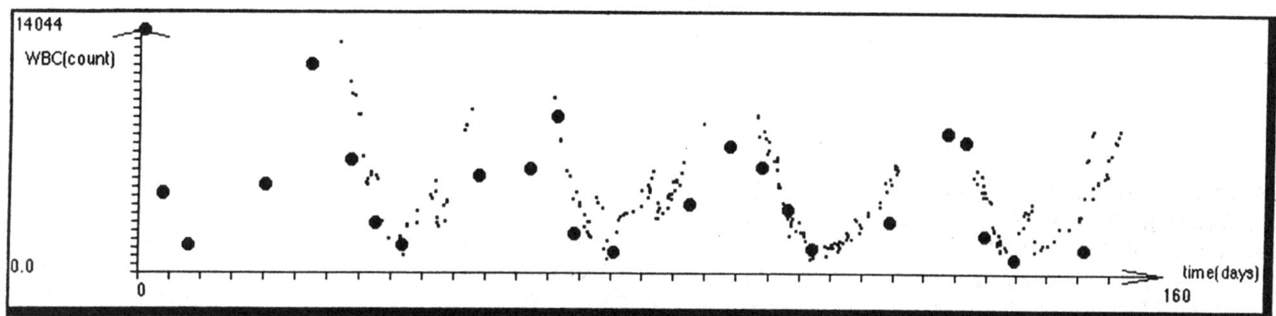
14044
WBC(count)
0.0
0
time(days)
160

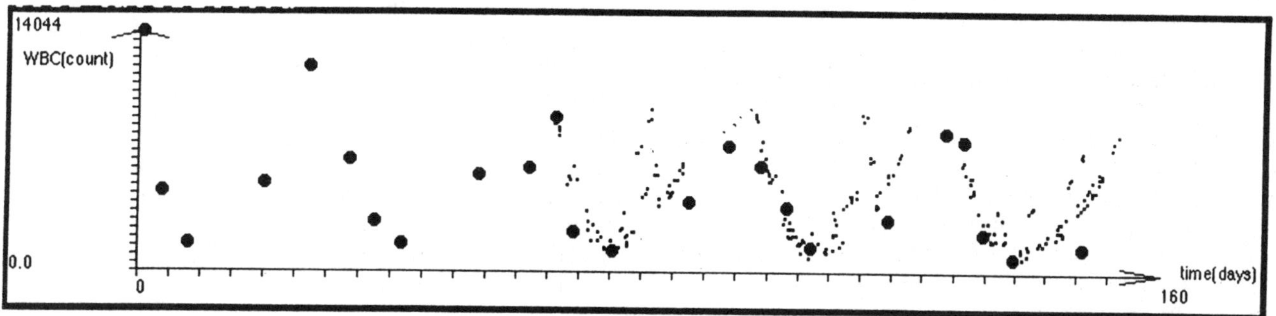
14044
WBC(count)
0.0
0
time(days)
160

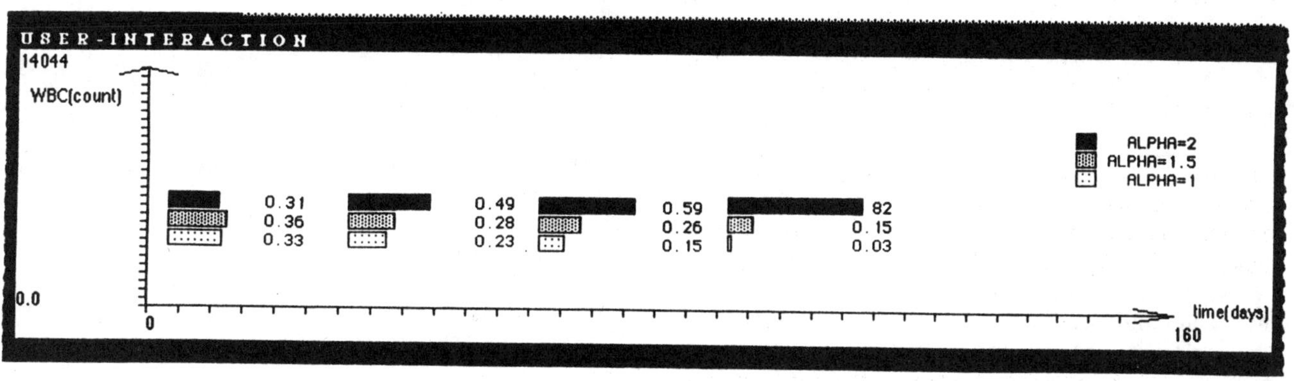
USER-INTERACTION
14044
WBC(count)
ALPHA=2
ALPHA=1.5
ALPHA=1
0.31
0.36
0.33
0.49
0.28
0.23
0.59
0.26
0.15
82
0.15
0.03
0.0
0
time(days)
160

Some Properties of Plausible Reasoning

Wray Buntine
RIACS*and AI Research Branch
NASA Ames Research Center, MS 244-17
Moffett Field, CA, 94025, USA
wray@ptolemy.arc.nasa.gov

Abstract

This paper presents a plausible reasoning system to illustrate some broad issues in knowledge representation: dualities between different reasoning forms, the difficulty of unifying complementary reasoning styles, and the approximate nature of plausible reasoning. These issues have a common underlying theme: there should be an underlying belief calculus of which the many different reasoning forms are special cases, sometimes approximate. The system presented allows reasoning about defaults, likelihood, necessity and possibility in a manner similar to the earlier work of Adams. The system is based on the belief calculus of subjective Bayesian probability which itself is based on a few simple assumptions about how belief should be manipulated. Approximations, semantics, consistency and consequence results are presented for the system. While this puts these often discussed plausible reasoning forms on a probabilistic footing, useful application to practical problems remains an issue.

1 INTRODUCTION

There are many styles of knowledge representation and inference involving some form of uncertainty or inconsistency: reasoning about likelihoods, independence and related notions such as causality, confirmation, defaults and statistical frequencies, and tasks such as analogy, abduction and belief revision. In knowledge representation there is now a recognised need for the unification and development of these multiple, complementary forms of reasoning (Brachman, 1990). To do this unification an underlying belief calculus is needed as a common base for the different reasoning forms. First, this paper presents a system unifying defaults, likelihood, necessity and possibility. Because the system uses Bayesian probability as the underlying belief calculus, independence, abduction, belief revision and many other facets of plausible reasoning could be integrated as well, although it is not done so here. Second this paper argues that plausible reasoning can be interpreted as a form of approximate reasoning. This has important implications to the implementation of plausible reasoning systems. For instance, error can accumulate in a long chain of plausible reasoning, so potential error should be tracked. So this paper also discusses approximate methods for tracking error. Also, we cannot expect plausible reasoning to be correct every time. Many of the so-called paradoxes in plausible reasoning arise because it is assumed that plausible reasoning will always lead to a correct conclusion.

The system presented here, like most Bayesian methods, is based on a few basic assumptions together with a few approximations. The assumptions are about how belief can be modelled and updated and have been presented in (Horvitz et al., 1986). The same Bayesian principles have led to the development of algorithms for learning (Buntine, 1991a), uncertain inference, and many more applications outside of artificial intelligence. Bayesian methods are claimed to be normative, which means they set a standard for plausible reasoning and implies they will not suffer from the standard paradoxes that are discussed in the non-monotonic literature (Hanks and McDermott, 1987; Poole, 1989; Pearl, 1988; Etherington et al., 1990). (Treatment of several paradoxes are given here and in (Buntine, 1991b).) The system presented here only implements one facet of the Bayesian approach and therefore is incomplete and may require extending with one of many complementary modes of normative reasoning, such as the making of default assumptions about independence (Goldszmidt and Pearl, 1990b).

The next section informally introduces the notation for a qualitative and a quantitative logic that each demonstrate a different level of approximation for reasoning about defaults and likelihoods. The default component of the qualitative logic corresponds to the var-

*Research Institute for Advanced Computer Science.

ious conditional logics developed for default reasoning (Delgrande, 1988; Pearl, 1988; Geffner, 1988) but most closely to Adams' improper conditional (Adams, 1966). The quantitative logic has its roots in remarks made by Adams. The qualitative system is presented here only for contrast with the quantitative system, because the quantitative system has many advantages with little extra overhead. The third section covers the theory of the two systems, semantics, consistency and consequence. Since the qualitative logic is an extension of Adams conditional logic (Adams, 1966; Adams, 1975), applied to default reasoning by Geffner and Pearl (Pearl, 1988; Geffner, 1988), this greatly extends and simplifies Adams' and Goldszmidt and Pearl's (Goldszmidt and Pearl, 1990a) consistency and consequence tests by incorporating necessity, possibility, and likelihood in a quantitative framework. The quantitative framework allows approximate default and likelihood reasoning and tracking of accumulated error at the same time. The fourth section illustrates the use of the logics on some standard problems from the literature. The fifth section uses the logics to illustrate some major properties of plausible reasoning.

It is beyond the scope of this paper to cover the basic notions of probability and decision theory underlying subsequent sections. Suitable introductions from an AI perspective can be found in (Langlotz and Shortliffe, 1989; Horvitz et al., 1988; Pearl, 1988).

2 NOTATION

DP is a propositional[1] logic annotated with probability bounds, and has a probabilistic rather than a possible world semantics. This allows inequality reasoning as an approximation to normative reasoning about point probabilities. QDP drops the numeric subscripts from DP and is designed to be a qualitative counterpart of DP. It is intended to be an approximation to DP for reasoning about "small" but not infinitesimal probabilities. The semantics of QDP complements DP and is based on order of magnitude reasoning, but also has an infinitesimal semantics similar to Adams' conditional logic.

DP is built on the language D_P that is constructed from the propositional language together with four modal operators: the unary connectives $\Box$ (necessity), $\diamond$ (possibility), and the binary connectives $\Rightarrow$ (default with error bound) and $\approx\!\succ$ (likelihood with lower bound). There is no nesting of these operators. The operators can be interpreted as follows. (Below A and B both represent arbitrary propositions.)

[1]Although propositional sentences are dealt with throughout, pseudo-first-order sentences will sometimes be used. They are effectively propositional if there are known to be a finite number of constants, no quantifiers are allowed, and a sentence with variables is intended to represent a sentence schema.

$\Box A$: A is necessarily true in any situation.

$\diamond A$: Some situation can possibly arise in which A is true.

$A \Rightarrow_\epsilon B$: Given that you know just A about the current situation, you can infer B by default (with error in belief at most ϵ).

$A \approx\!\succ_e B$: Given that you know just A about the current situation, B is at least likely (with belief no less than e).

These four operators are joined using the standard boolean connectives ($\neg$ (negation), $\rightarrow$ (conditional), $\wedge$ (conjunction), etc.) to form the language D_P. This language also has a qualitative version, QD_P, which has the numeric subscripts dropped. The semantics for the language implements this by making ϵ and e infinitesimal; not because we believe them to be infinitesimal but as a mathematical abstraction to obtain approximate behaviour of the operators for ϵ and e small. QD_P has successively weaker forms of the likelihood operator. $A \approx\!\succ B$ denotes "likely," whereas $A \approx\!\succ^2 B$ would denote "barely likely," etc. This is related to the iterated likelihood operator found in (Halpern and Rabin, 1987) and has a formal justification in Theorem 3 part 2.

$A \approx\!\succ^n B$: Given that you know just A about the current situation, B is at least likely to be ... to be likely (to order n).

The default and likelihood operators are "improper" according to Adams' terminology (Adams, 1966). This means $A \Rightarrow B$ and $A \approx\!\succ B$ will both hold true if A is necessarily $false$. The "proper" versions must have A being possible, so correspond to $\diamond A \wedge (A \Rightarrow B)$, and $\diamond A \wedge (A \approx\!\succ B)$ respectively.

The logics, being probabilistically based, are easily able to express sentences such as "an Australian is likely to drink Foster's": *Australian* $\approx\!\succ$ *Drinks-Foster's*; whereas *Australian* $\approx\!\succ^2$ *Drinks-another-Foster's* expresses the fact that, at least occasionly, an Australian will drink even more Foster's. Surprisingly enough, they also able to express sentences more in the spirit of autoepistemic (Moore, 1985) and default logics (Reiter, 1980). We can interpret the sentence "a professor has a Ph.D. unless known otherwise" two ways:

$$\diamond(Prof(x) \wedge Phd(x)) \longrightarrow (Prof(x) \Rightarrow Phd(x)) ,$$
$$\diamond(Prof(x) \wedge Phd(x)) \longrightarrow \Box(Prof(x) \rightarrow Phd(x)) .$$

Read as "if it is possible that a particular professor has a PhD, then the professor *most likely* has a Ph.D.," and "if it is possible that a particular professor has a PhD, then the professor *definitely* has a Ph.D." respectively. The default logic representation, from $Prof(x) \wedge M\ Phd(x)$ infer $Phd(x)$, corresponds to the second reading. So the possibility operator, "$\diamond$", behaves rather like the M operator of default logic.

3 THEORY

This section presents the semantics for the two logics and then discusses their intended use in plausible reasoning. Basic consistency and consequence theorems are given.

3.1 SEMANTICS

In DP, "$\models_{Pr} D$" denotes that $D \in D_P$ is true for the probability distribution Pr. Pr plays a role not unlike an interpretation in standard propositional logic.

Definition 1 *Given a probability distribution Pr on propositions, "$\models_{Pr}$" is defined on sentences from D_P as follows.*

1. *$\models_{Pr} \Box A$ if and only if $Pr(A) = 1$.*
2. *$\models_{Pr} A \Rightarrow_\epsilon B$ if and only if $Pr(B|A) \geq 1 - \epsilon$.*
3. *$\models_{Pr} \neg D$ if and only if not $\models_{Pr} D$.*
4. *$\models_{Pr} D \rightarrow E$ if and only if not $\models_{Pr} D$ or $\models_{Pr} E$.*

Possibility and likelihood are by definition dual operators for necessity and default respectively. "$\Diamond A$" is defined as "$\neg\Box\neg A$", so $\models_{Pr} \Diamond A$ if and only if $Pr(A) > 0$. "$A \rightsquigarrow_e B$" is defined as "$\neg(A \Rightarrow_e \neg B)$", so $A \rightsquigarrow_e B$ if and only if $Pr(B|A) > e$.

Definition 2 *A sentence $D \in D_P$ is a* theorem *of the probabilistic logic DP if $\models_{Pr} D$ for all possible probability distributions Pr.*

Consistency and consequence for sentences are defined in the usual manner based on the notion of a theorem.

To obtain qualitative rules about default and likelihood from the quantitative rules in DP, we can perform order of magnitude reasoning. We can consider a representative default error, ϵ, where ϵ might be less than 0.01, or whatever the decision context requires. Likewise, we can consider a representative default likelihood, e, where e might be greater than 0.05, say. In order to approximate the behaviour of our reasoning with these particular limits in mind, we can parameterise the system by ϵ and e and consider only approximate calculations to $O(\epsilon)$ and $O(e)$. QD_P is defined in a manner such that ϵ and e are arbitrarily small, but ϵ is also arbitrarily smaller than e.

Definition 3 *A sentence $D \in QD_P$ is a* theorem *of the qualitative probabilistic logic QPD if there exists a theorem $D' \in D_P$ corresponding to D (that is, identical except for any super or subscripts), in which all subscripts to "$\Rightarrow$" and "$\rightsquigarrow$" are parameterised by some variables ϵ and e and each subscript to "$\Rightarrow$" is of order ϵ as ϵ approaches 0 and e remains finite, and each subscript in D' corresponding to "$\rightsquigarrow^n$" in D is of order e^n as e and $\frac{\epsilon}{e}$ approach 0. This is denoted "$\models_{QDP} D$".*

Again, consistency and consequence are defined in the usual manner.

This definition can be reinterpreted to give an infinitesimal semantics close to that of Adams. Lemma 1 below (Buntine, 1991b) does this using a standard clausal form for defaults and another for likelihoods that collects all necessities and possibilities into the left-hand side of the clause.

Lemma 1

$$\models_{QDP} \Box U \wedge_{i \in I_V} \Diamond V_i \wedge_{i \in I_A} A_i \Rightarrow B_i \longrightarrow \vee_{i \in I_C} G_i \Rightarrow H_i ,$$

if and only if there exists a δ and η such that for all $\epsilon < \eta$

$$\models_{DP} \Box U \ \wedge_{i \in I_V} \Diamond V_i \ \wedge_{i \in I_A} A_i \Rightarrow_\epsilon B_i \longrightarrow \vee_{i \in I_C} G_i \Rightarrow_{\delta\epsilon} H_i .$$

Similarly,

$$\models_{QDP} \Box U \ \wedge_{i \in I_V} \Diamond V_i \ \wedge_{i \in I_A} A_i \rightsquigarrow^{n_i} B_i \longrightarrow \vee_{i \in I_C} G_i \rightsquigarrow^{m_i} H_i ,$$

if and only if there exists a δ and η such that for all $\epsilon < \eta$

$$\models_{DP} \Box U \ \wedge_{i \in I_V} \Diamond V_i \ \wedge_{i \in I_A} A_i \rightsquigarrow_{\epsilon^{n_i}} B_i \longrightarrow \vee_{i \in I_C} G_i \rightsquigarrow_{\delta\epsilon^{m_i}} H_i .$$

For the D_P sentences in the lemma, δ is an *error propagation factor*, and $\delta\epsilon$ and $\delta\epsilon^{m_i}$ are the *error propagation functions* respectively. For the default clause, the larger the value of δ, the faster error can propagate when the clause is applied in some chain of reasoning. Since a smaller likelihood represents more room for error, in the likelihood clause the smaller the value of δ, the faster error will propagate when the clause is applied in some chain of reasoning.

For instance, the sentence

$$(A \rightsquigarrow_e C) \wedge (B \rightsquigarrow_d C) \rightarrow A \vee B \rightsquigarrow_f C ,$$

is a theorem of DP with the error propagation function f given by

$$f \leq \frac{ed}{e + d - ed} \leq \min(e, d) .$$

Therefore we can drop the subscripts to get a QDP theorem as well.

3.2 THEOREMS

DP and QDP give a system for reasoning qualitatively and quantitatively about probability inequalities. However, normative reasoning according to Bayesian principles is based on point probabilities. Often in normative reasoning, we have a specific decision context in mind and we wish to determine if the probability of some proposition is less than or greater than some fixed probability (determined by the loss function). DP and QDP are then approximations for dealing with this special case. QDP is merely an abstraction of DP given here to show the connection of DP with existing conditional and probabilistically motivated logics. Because of the inability of QDP to keep track of error, it would be a potentially unsafe system to use in practice.

If the problem contains a good deal of uncertainty so the errors are large, or the loss function for the decisions to be made requires careful evaluation of comparative probabilities, it may be more appropriate to conduct a careful probabilistic analysis instead of using the approximate methods suggested here. If however, the errors are small, it is shown in this section we can do consistency and consequence tests in DP using qualitative reasoning about defaults and likelihood, and follow this with some simple error propagation calculations to calculate upper bounds on propagated errors. These approximate probability calculations may then be a sufficient basis for making decisions. Details of this approach are described in this section. This makes DP a safe alternative to QDP when approximate reasoning seems appropriate.

Notice though that whether a sentence from D_P is consistent or is a consequence of some other can be converted to a set of simplex problems in the variables, as done with Probabilistic Logic (Nilsson, 1986). We shall not pursue this approach, however, since we are concerned with approximate modelling of default and likelihood reasoning, for which "propagation errors" can be calculated rapidly using other more approximate means, as shown below.

Algorithms for consistency and consequence are given here for the numerically annotated logic DP. To obtain results for QDP, simply drop the subscripts, and in the case of likelihoods, be careful to check the orders of magnitude of the error propagation functions. Since each of the theorems below allows arbitrary possibilities to be included, the algorithms can be readily converted to the proper versions of the operators.

The algorithms rely on first computing the subset of the default (likelihood) operators that must have their antecedents necessarily false. For instance, in $(A \Rightarrow B) \wedge (A \Rightarrow \neg B) \wedge (C \Rightarrow D)$, A must be necessarily false since both B and $\neg B$ cannot be "typical" at the same time. So both the first two defaults must have their antecedents necessarily false. These computed subsets for defaults (likelihoods) are referred to as the maximum (minimum) inconsistent set. An algorithm for computing the maximum inconsistent set of a DP sentence with defaults is given in Figure 1. The algorithm for computing the minimum inconsistent set for a DP sentence containing no defaults is given in Figure 2. Logical tests for consistency and consequence are given in Theorem 2 for D_P clauses containing no likelihood operator. The role of the maximum inconsistent set can best be seen by looking at parts 1 and 4 of the theorem.

> **Input:** A D_P sentence $\Box U \bigwedge_{i\in I_V} \Diamond V_i \bigwedge_{i \in I_A} A_i \Rightarrow_{\epsilon_i} B_i$, where $\epsilon_i < \frac{1}{|I_A|}, \frac{1}{2}$ for $i \in I_A$.
> **Output:** The maximum inconsistent set, I_{max}.
> **Algorithm:** Let $I = I_A$. If there exists a $j \in I$ such that $U \wedge A_j \bigwedge_{i \in I} (A_i \rightarrow B_i)$ is satisfiable, then remove that j from I. Repeat this until no j found or $I = \emptyset$. I_{max} is then given by I.

Figure 1: The defaults-inconsistency algorithm

> **Input:** A D_P sentence $\Box U \bigwedge_{i\in I_V} \Diamond V_i \bigwedge_{i \in I_A} A_i \not\succ_{e_i} B_i$, where $e_i < \frac{1}{|I_A|}$ for $i \in I_A$.
> **Output:** The minimum inconsistent set, I_{min}.
> **Algorithm:** Let $I = \emptyset$. If there exists a $j \in I_A - I$ such that $U \bigwedge_{i \in I} \neg A_i \wedge A_j \wedge B_j$ is unsatisfiable, then add that j to I and repeat until no j found. I_{min} is now given by I.

Figure 2: The likelihood-inconsistency algorithm

Theorem 2 *Consider the D_P sentence D given by $\Box U \bigwedge_{i\in I_V} \Diamond V_i \bigwedge_{i \in I_A} A_i \Rightarrow_{\epsilon_i} B_i$, where $\epsilon_i < \frac{1}{|I_A|}, \frac{1}{2}$ for $i \in I_A$. Let I_{max} denote the (unique) maximum inconsistent set for the sentence.*

1. *The sentence D is inconsistent if and only if there exists some $j \in I_V$ such that $U \wedge V_j \bigwedge_{i \in I_{max}} \neg A_i$ is unsatisfiable.*
2. *The D_P sentence $C \Rightarrow_\delta B$ is a consequence of D for some $\delta < \frac{1}{2}$ if and only if $D \wedge (C \Rightarrow_\delta \neg B)$ is inconsistent. $\delta = \sum_{i \in I_A} \epsilon_i$ is a correct error propagation function.*
3. *The D_P sentence $\Diamond C$ is a consequence of D if and only if $D \wedge \Box\neg C$ is inconsistent.*
4. *The D_P sentence $\Box C$ is a consequence of D if and only if D itself is inconsistent or $\models U \bigwedge_{i \in I_{max}} \neg A_i \rightarrow C$.*

Notice by part 1, if the DP sentence contains proper default operators (so possibilities are included), then the sentence will necessarily be inconsistent if the maximum inconsistent set is non-empty. The corresponding property applies to likelihoods.

Tests for consistency and consequence using the likelihood operator are given in Theorem 3. Methods for computing tighter bounds for the error propagation function, linear in some cases, are given in (Buntine, 1991b).

Theorem 3 *Consider the D_P sentence D given by*

$\Box U \ \wedge_{i \in I_V} \diamond V_i \ \wedge_{i \in I_A} A_i \approx\!\succ_{e_i} B_i$, *where* $e_i < \frac{1}{|I_A|}$ *for* $i \in I_A$. *Let* I_{min} *denote the (unique) minimum inconsistent set.*

1. *The sentence D is inconsistent if and only if there exists some* $j \in I_V$ *such that* $U \wedge_{i \in I_{min}} \neg A_i \wedge V_j$ *is unsatisfiable.*

2. *The* D_P *sentence* $C \approx\!\succ_f B$ *is a consequence of D for some* $f < 1$ *if and only if D is inconsistent or the likelihood inconsistency algorithm in Figure 3 terminates yielding a consequence. If consequence holds, then a lower bound on f, the error propagation function, is given by* $f \geq \left(\frac{e}{1+e}\right)^{|I_A|}$, *where* $e = \min_{i \in I_A} e_i$, *although the error propagation function can be less, for instance, linear in the* e_i *in some cases.*

3. *The* D_P *sentence* $\diamond C$ *is a consequence of D if and only if* $D \wedge \Box \neg C$ *is inconsistent.*

4. *The* D_P *sentence* $\Box C$ *is a consequence of D if and only if D is inconsistent or* $\models U \ \wedge_{i \in I_{min}} \neg A_i \rightarrow C$.

Input: A consistent D_P sentence $\Box U \wedge_{i \in I_V} \diamond V_i \wedge_{i \in I_A} A_i \approx\!\succ_{e_i} B_i$, where $e_i < \frac{1}{|I_A|}$ for $i \in I_A$, its minimum inconsistent set I_{min}, and a likelihood $C \approx\!\succ_f D$.

Output: Whether the likelihood is a consequence of the sentence for some value of f.

Algorithm: If $U \wedge_{i \in I_{min}} \neg A_i \wedge C \wedge \neg B$ is unsatisfiable, return *is a consequence* for any f. Set $I = \emptyset$. If there exists some $j \in I_A - I_{min} - I$ such that

$$\models U \ \wedge_{i \in I_{min}} \neg A_i \ \wedge A_j \wedge B_j \ \wedge_{i \in I} (A_i \rightarrow B_i) \rightarrow C \wedge B \quad .$$

then add that j to I. Otherwise return *not a consequence*. Repeat this process until $U \wedge_{i \in I_{min}} \neg A_i \wedge C \wedge \neg B \wedge_{i \in I} A_i$ is unsatisfiable or $I = I_A - I_{min}$. If termination occurred because $I = I_A - I_{min}$, return *not a consequence*, else return *is a consequence* for some f.

Figure 3: The likelihood-consequence algorithm

Also, $(A \approx\!\succ B) \rightarrow \neg(A \Rightarrow \neg B)$ is a theorem of QDP. This property can be used, for instance, to convert a QDP formula containing a mixture of defaults and likelihoods into a stronger formula containing just defaults, and so prove consistency of the weaker formula.

4 EXAMPLES

The logics are illustrated here on some standard paradoxes from the knowledge representation literature. Others handled are the "Yale shooting problem" and "Can Joe read and write?" (Buntine, 1991b).

4.1 THE LOTTERY PARADOX

Suppose a lottery has 1,000,000 participants. The following two sentences are theorems of DP. The first follows from Theorem 2, and the second is its dual constructed by converting defaults to likelihoods and rearranging:

$$\bigwedge_{i=1}^{1,000,000} (true \Rightarrow_\epsilon \langle \text{person } i \text{ wont win lottery} \rangle) \longrightarrow$$
$$(true \Rightarrow_{1,000,000*\epsilon} \langle \text{no-one will win lottery} \rangle) \ ,$$

with its dual,

$$(true \approx\!\succ_\epsilon \langle \text{someone will win lottery} \rangle) \longrightarrow$$
$$\bigvee_{i=1}^{1,000,000} (true \approx\!\succ_{\frac{\epsilon}{1,000,000}} \langle \text{person } i \text{ will win lottery} \rangle) \ .$$

Moreover, replacing 1,000,000 by 999,999 yields sentences that are not theorems of QDP. Ignoring the error bounds as done in QDP, the first sentence would seem to read "if, by default, any particular person will not win the lottery, then, by default, no-one will win the lottery at all". Likewise, the second DP sentence would seem to read: "if it is likely that someone will win the lottery, then for some lottery entrant, it is likely they will win the lottery" (clearly not the case before the draw).

The two readings are versions of the lottery paradox that are the dual of each other. In the first DP sentence the natural value for ϵ is $\frac{1}{1,000,000}$; this leaves the sentence impotent because the error bound in the conclusion becomes 1. In DP there is no paradoxical reading. QDP unfortunately drops the subscripts (both are of order ϵ as ϵ approaches 0) and loses the error information. QDP suffers from the lottery paradox because it disregards the approximate nature of the default and likelihood operators. In the first sentence above, taking the conjunction of one million different approximate statements leads to an incorrect statement because the error in each accumulates.

Because of the cheap cost of maintaining approximate error calculations, as demonstrated in Theorem 3 for DP, there would seem little reason for using a purely qualitative system such as QDP.

4.2 THE "VANISHING" EMUS

The modelling of default reasoning based on infinitesimal probabilities has been criticised on the grounds that it makes "subclasses vanish" (Neufeld et al., 1990, p123). Etherington, Kraus and Perlis (Etherington et al., 1990) show a related problem applies to default logic and circumscription.

Consider the following rules:

$$Emu(x) \rightarrow Bird(x) \;,$$
$$Emu(x) \Rightarrow \neg Flies(x) \;,$$
$$Bird(x) \Rightarrow Flies(x) \;.$$

We can conclude (using Theorem 2) that "typically, birds aren't emus", $Bird(x) \Rightarrow \neg Emu(x)$, and "typically, things aren't emus", $true \Rightarrow \neg Emu(x)$.

If we take the infinitesimal semantics of the default operator literally then we could conclude that "no birds are emus", or "nothing is an emu". The real intent of the probabilistic semantics presented here, however, is about approximations so a more correct reading of the conclusion is that the emu is an uncommon or non-typical bird, which in reality is true of emus.

Circumscription, when presented with this same problem will deduce there are no emus to minimise the exceptions (Etherington et al., 1990). Etherington, Kraus and Perlis invent the notion of scope to overcome the same kind of difficulties in default logics and circumscription (Etherington et al., 1990):

> We contend that the intention of default reasoning is generally not to determine the properties of every individual in the domain, but rather those of some particular individuals of interest.

QDP resolves the same paradoxes using a related principle that falls out naturally from the Bayesian framework and can be stated as follows:

> The intention of default reasoning is generally to determine reasonable properties of an individual in the domain. While these may be reasonable individually, they are not necessarily correct so one cannot reasonably say they apply uniformly.

5 CONCLUSION

The systems presented here do not do full normative Bayesian reasoning but instead are approximations valid in certain situations (as explained at the beginning of Section 3.2). Approximations have two effects: they can make a system incomplete or incorrect. DP has retained correctness but become incomplete. In QDP correctness is also lost by doing order of magnitude reasoning. One result of incompleteness is that on many general problems these systems will need complementary reasoning forms in order to produce a result. A result of incorrectness is that errors in reasoning can creep in, especially when they are hidden in qualitative reasoning which has a logical form making it appear deceptively accurate. As shown with the examples, both these results are a source of material for paradoxes if the underlying approximations are not understood.

This section discusses the issues raised by this: unifying complementary reasoning forms, the nature of approximate reasoning, and the dualities between default and likelihood reasoning. These insights, together with Theorems 2 and 3 form the major contributions of this paper. This gives us a much deeper insight into the problems of knowledge representation and inference involving some form of uncertainty.

5.1 DUALITIES

One of the first things taught to students of logic is the duality between disjunction and conjunction ($\neg(A \wedge B) \leftrightarrow (\neg A \vee \neg B)$ and $\neg(A \vee B) \leftrightarrow (\neg A \wedge \neg B)$). In modal logic, duality also holds between necessity and possibility ($\Box A \;\leftrightarrow\; \neg \diamond \neg A$ and $\diamond A \;\leftrightarrow\; \neg\Box\neg A$). In DP the corresponding duality applies between default and likelihood. This means, for instance, that we can obtain dual forms for all DP theorems and to a limited degree some QDP theorems (the QDP definitions are only approximately dual) by converting defaults to likelihoods and vice versa. Versions of some QDP theorems and their (rearranged) duals are given in Table 1.

1	$(C \Rightarrow A) \;\wedge\; (C \Rightarrow \neg A) \;\rightarrow\; \Box\neg C$
2	$(C \Rightarrow A) \;\wedge\; (C \Rightarrow B) \;\rightarrow\; C \Rightarrow (A \wedge B)$
3	$(C \Rightarrow A) \;\rightarrow\; (C \wedge A \Rightarrow B) \;\rightarrow\; (C \Rightarrow B)$
4	$(A \vee B) \Rightarrow C \;\rightarrow\; (A \Rightarrow C) \;\vee\; (B \Rightarrow C)$

1	$\diamond C \;\rightarrow\; (C \approx\!\succ A) \;\vee\; (C \approx\!\succ \neg A)$
2	$C \approx\!\succ (A \vee B) \;\rightarrow\; (C \approx\!\succ A) \;\vee\; (C \approx\!\succ B)$
3	$(C \approx\!\succ B) \;\rightarrow\; (C \approx\!\succ A) \;\vee\; (C \wedge A \approx\!\succ B)$
4	$(A \approx\!\succ C) \;\wedge\; (B \approx\!\succ C) \;\rightarrow\; (A \vee B) \approx\!\succ C$

Table 1: Some theorem schemata (1st table) and their duals (2nd)

These duality properties come about because of the basic properties of negation and by the dual definitions for the operators. A more remarkable but not so exact duality can be seen in the consistency and consequence theorems for default and likelihood. Compare the algorithms for the maximum and minimum inconsistent sets, and compare each of the results in Theorems 2 and 3. These theorems are not duals according to the definition of default and likelihood. For instance, the dual results to Theorem 2 would show a disjunction of likelihoods can be a consequence of a single likelihood rather than show a single likelihood can be a consequence of a conjunction of likelihoods, the situation of Theorem 3. The theorems are proven using quite different methods (for instance the results for likelihood are considerably harder to prove than those for default). Yet the theorems and algorithms have a remarkably similar form. Their major difference is that error combines slowly (linearly) for defaults but rapidly (multiplicatively) for likelihoods, though linearly in some special cases (Buntine, 1991b). Because likelihood errors combine rapidly, people often keep track of the degree of likelihood. For instance, likelihoods are used to rank order hypotheses in model-based diagnosis and abduction. Another result of this difference is that while considerable research has focussed on default reasoning, none to date has considered variable strength defaults as for instance allowed using error propagation functions and Theorem 2. In contrast, likelihood reasoning systems suggested in the literature introduced qualitative variable strength likelihoods from the beginning (Halpern and Rabin, 1987).

5.2 UNIFYING COMPLEMENTARY REASONING FORMS

The treatment of the two paradoxes "Can joe read and write?" and the Yale shooting problem are an example of how independence becomes an important complementary reasoning form for conditional logics. Both these problems yield no paradox in QDP, NP (Delgrande, 1988) and related conditional logics because no default conclusions can be made at all. This holds because the antecedents of a conditional default or likelihood rule cannot be arbitrarily specialised with some additional knowledge. That is, the QD_P sentence $(B \Rightarrow C) \rightarrow (A \wedge B \Rightarrow C)$ is not a theorem of QDP. For instance, the often useful transitive relation $(A \Rightarrow B) \wedge (B \Rightarrow C) \rightarrow A \Rightarrow C$ is not a theorem of QDP. However, the QD_P sentence

$$((B \Rightarrow C) \rightarrow (A \wedge B \Rightarrow C)) \longrightarrow ((A \Rightarrow B) \wedge (B \Rightarrow C) \rightarrow A \Rightarrow C)$$

is a theorem of QDP. This means knowledge of the form $(B \Rightarrow C) \rightarrow (A \wedge B \Rightarrow C)$ will play a vital role in enabling default and likelihood conclusions like transitivity. If A is independent of C given B then we have this knowledge.

Given that we need complementary reasoning forms, how do we unify them? It would be nice if we could somehow keep the different reasoning styles in separate modules, as suggested in hybrid reasoning systems (Frisch and Cohn, 1991). However, experience gained in the exercise here indicates this may not usually be possible. The unifying of necessity and possibility reasoning with default reasoning and likelihood reasoning, as presented in Theorems 2 and 3, required careful integration of the several approaches. Another unification that needs to be made is to integrate symbolic reasoning about independence (Lauritzen et al., 1990; Pearl, 1988) into the algorithms presented in Theorems 2 and 3.

5.3 APPROXIMATE REASONING

Qualitative reasoning about default and likelihood is interpreted here as an approximate form of reasoning that is bound to sometimes produce incorrect results. By investigating the quantitative counterpart to these reasoning forms, we are able to see more closely how this error propagates and accumulates and how we might track it, and we are able to better understand the assumptions under which the system operates. A qualitative system, for instance, has an implicit assumption that all errors ϵ are identical. With the quantitative system, however, we are able to allow the errors to vary—a more realistic situation.

Of course, all these rough approximations could be circumvented if we would adhere to more complete, fully normative Bayesian reasoning in the first place. This raises the important question: When do approximate systems such as DP buy us improved performance in an application over more complete probabilistic approaches? Comparative studies here do not exist. Approximate systems such as DP could be appropriate for generating a comprehensible explanation of probabilistic results obtained, for instance, by other numeric methods. Also, approximate systems due to their more simplistic framework, may be more appropriate for rapid turn-around in system development and user training. They may therefore serve as a useful complement to a more complete probabilistic approach rather than as a replacement. Only application experience will tell.

References

Adams, E. (1966). Probability and the logic of conditionals. In Hintikka, J. and Suppes, P., editors, *Aspects of Inductive Logic*, pages 265–316. North-Holland, Amsterdam.

Adams, E. (1975). *The Logic of Conditionals.* Reidel, Boston.

Brachman, R. (1990). The future of knowledge representation. In *Eighth National Conference on Artificial Intelligence*, pages 1082–1092, Boston, Massachusetts.

Buntine, W. (1991a). Classifiers: A theoretical and empirical study. In *International Joint Conference on Artificial Intelligence*, Sydney. Morgan Kaufmann.

Buntine, W. (1991b). Modelling default and likelihood reasoning as probabilistic reasoning. *Annals of Mathematics and AI.* To appear.

Delgrande, J. (1988). An approach to default reasoning based on a first-order conditional logic: revised report. *Artificial Intelligence*, 36:63–90.

Etherington, D., Kraus, S., and Perlis, D. (1990). Nonmonotonicity and the scope of reasoning: Preliminary report. In *Eighth National Conference on*

Artificial Intelligence, pages 600–607, Boston, Massachusetts.

Frisch, A. and Cohn, A. (1991). Thoughts and afterthoughts on the 1988 workshop on principles of hybrid reasoning. *AI Magazine*, 11(5):77–83.

Geffner, H. (1988). On the logic of defaults. In *Seventh National Conference on Artificial Intelligence*, pages 449–454, Saint Paul, Minnesota.

Goldszmidt, M. and Pearl, J. (1990a). Deciding consistency of databases containing defeasible and strict information. In Henrion, M., Schachter, R., Kanal, L., and Lemmer, J., editors, *Uncertainty in Artificial Intelligence 5*. Elsevier Science Publishers, Amsterdam. An extended version appears as UCLA Cognitive Systems Laboratory, Technical Report CSD-890034 (R-122).

Goldszmidt, M. and Pearl, J. (1990b). A maximum entropy approach to nonmonotonic reasoning. In *Eighth National Conference on Artificial Intelligence*, pages 646–652, Boston, Massachusetts.

Halpern, J. and Rabin, M. (1987). A logic to reason about likelihood. *Artificial Intelligence*, 32:379–405.

Hanks, S. and McDermott, D. (1987). Nonmonotonic logic and temporal projection. *Artificial Intelligence*, 33:379–412.

Horvitz, E., Breeze, J., and Henrion, M. (1988). Decision theory in expert systems and artificial intelligence. *International Journal of Approximate Reasoning*, 2:247–302.

Horvitz, E., Heckerman, D., and Langlotz, C. (1986). A framework for comparing alternative formalisms for plausible reasoning. In *Fifth National Conference on Artificial Intelligence*, pages 210–214, Philadelphia.

Langlotz, C. and Shortliffe, E. (1989). Logical and decision theoretic methods for planning under uncertainty. *AI Magazine*, 10(1):39–48.

Lauritzen, S., Dawid, A., Larsen, B., and Leimer, H.-G. (1990). Independence properties of directed Markov fields. *Networks*, 20:491–505.

Moore, R. (1985). Semantical considerations on nonmonotonic logic. *Artificial Intelligence*, 25:75–94.

Neufeld, E., Poole, D., and Aleliunas, R. (1990). Probabilistic semantics and defaults. In Schachter, R., Levitt, T., Kanal, L., and Lemmer, J., editors, *Uncertainty in Artificial Intelligence 4*. North Holland.

Nilsson, N. (1986). Probabilistic logic. *Artificial Intelligence*, 28:71–87.

Pearl, J. (1988). *Probabilistic Reasoning in Intelligent Systems*. Morgan and Kauffman.

Poole, D. (1989). What the lottery paradox tells us about default reasoning. In *First International Conference on Principles of Knowledge Representation and Reasoning*, pages 333–340, Toronto.

Reiter, R. (1980). A logic for default reasoning. *Artificial Intelligence*, 13:81–132.

Theory Refinement on Bayesian Networks

Wray Buntine
RIACS and AI Research Branch
NASA Ames Research Center, Mail Stop 244-17
Moffet Field, CA 94035, USA
Phone: +1 (415) 604-3389
wray@ptolemy.arc.nasa.gov

Abstract

Theory refinement is the task of updating a domain theory in the light of new cases, to be done automatically or with some expert assistance. The problem of theory refinement under uncertainty is reviewed here in the context of Bayesian statistics, a theory of belief revision. The problem is reduced to an incremental learning task as follows: the learning system is initially primed with a partial theory supplied by a domain expert, and thereafter maintains its own internal representation of alternative theories which is able to be interrogated by the domain expert and able to be incrementally refined from data. Algorithms for refinement of Bayesian networks are presented to illustrate what is meant by "partial theory", "alternative theory representation", etc. The algorithms are an incremental variant of batch learning algorithms from the literature so can work well in batch and incremental mode.

1 Introduction

Theory refinement is the task of updating a domain theory in the light of new cases. The key idea is to use the expert's prior domain knowledge to prime a learning system during the knowledge acquisition process. Subsequent refinement of theory proceeds by having the learning system accept examples or ask key questions of the expert. Shapiro (Shapiro, 1983), for instance, developed a comprehensive theory and suite of algorithms for the task of refining Horn clause theories (logic programs). Ginsberg *et al.* applied a more heuristic approach to the refinement of a rule base in the context of medical diagnosis (Ginsberg et al., 1988). Recent research in this area (Ourston and Mooney, 1990; Towell et al., 1990) grew out the need to make the many inductive learning algorithms available more knowledge intensive, so they can mimic some of the perceived benefits of analytic learning methods such as explanation based learning. But this research faces the problems of "imperfect and uncertain domain theories" and "noisy training cases" not well handled by analytic methods.

A recent example of this hybrid learning approach is as follows (Towell et al., 1990): a rule-base of knowledge about the domain is transcribed into a neural network to initialize the network; the new training cases are then run in a back-propagation algorithm to refine the network. This approach addresses the following research question: how can we build a learning algorithm that covers the full spectrum from theory refinement, to standard batch learning (starting with a non-informative theory, and assuming learning occurs from just one batch of cases), to incremental learning (assuming new cases come in smaller batches and the theory is gradually refined)?

A second recent example of theory refinement is of Bayesian networks sometimes used in medical expert systems (Lauritzen and Spiegelhalter, 1988). While experts can set up an appropriate graphical structure and estimate the needed probabilities, new examples may arrive on a daily basis so the expert system needs to be refined. Spiegelhalter *et al.* argue that the expert's experience and confidence in setting up the initial model needs to be quantified (Spiegelhalter and Lauritzen, 1989) (for instance, how many examples was it based on) in order to do refinement carefully. It could be that the expert's initial model is based on many cases and is very reliable, and the 10 new noisy cases obtained happen to be unusual so they wrongly suggest the expert's initial model requires major refinement. Spiegelhalter *et al.*'s approach addresses a second research question: given some new and possibly anomalous cases, when do we start refining, how drastically do we refine, and when do we disregard the anomalous cases as noise? Spiegelhalter, however, did not address the issue of refining the structure of a Bayesian network, only the continuous parameters of the probability distributions.

This paper considers these two broad research questions together. The approach to theory refinement suggested is as follows: the learning system is primed with a partial theory supplied by a domain expert, and thereafter maintains its own alternative theory representation which is able to be interrogated by the domain expert and able to be incrementally refined from data. Furthermore, the partial theory is such that it can initially be null, and that it incorporates a quantification of the expert's experience so that the "right" amount of refinement is done given new cases. Another approach to learning networks that incorporates a partial theory is given by by (Srinivas et al., 1990).

The general approach developed here is based on Bayesian principles for belief updating that form the basis of several learning algorithms (Buntine, 1990b; Cooper and Herskovits, 1991). The principles specify precisely a "normative" approach to theory refinement, and the approach suggested here approximates this. The normative property is a claim that the principles set a standard which other theory refinement or learning algorithms must approximate; if they fail to do so they will return poorer refined/learned theories on average. Another popular learning framework in the computing area is uniform convergence, of which the PAC model is an instance (Haussler, 1991). This is an approach that approximates the normative Bayesian approach when sample sizes are large. Several researchers have reported (unsurprisingly) that the Bayesian approach is superior with smaller size training samples (Buntine, 1990b; Opper and Haussler, 1991) in a range of batch learning problems.

Some previous methods for learning Bayesian networks (Geiger et al., 1990; Spirtes and Glymour, 1990; Verma and Pearl, 1990; Srinivas et al., 1990) are closer to the large sample uniform convergence framework because they assume independence information can be unambiguously determined. Some of these algorithms also make the assumption (Geiger et al., 1990; Spirtes and Glymour, 1990; Verma and Pearl, 1990) that the unknown probability distribution is a DAG-isomorph (Pearl, 1988). This means all independencies in the problem must be perfectly captured by some Bayesian network, which may not be the case in a particular problem (for instance, all non-chordal Markov networks are not DAG-isomorphic). These algorithms can seemingly "discover causality from data", but existence of some "causality" is immediate from the assumption of DAG-isomorphism. How restrictive will this assumption be in practice and how sensitive are the algorithms to its failure? The approach here in contrast requires that some ordering (possibly causal) of the variables is supplied to the system. This assumes nothing about the underlying probability distribution because a Bayesian network can always be found for some ordering. The algorithms presented do, however, assume that every example in the training sample has variable values fully specified. (While this assumption can be relaxed, it can involve considerable computational cost if done properly.)

In the approach presented here, the initial partial theory obtained from the domain expert is interpreted as *a prior* information about the space of possible theories, and the alternative theory representation is interpreted as a subspace of alternative theories that are reasonable *a posterior*, represented in a compact form. Simple learning approaches approximate this space of alternative theories by taking a single high posterior structure (Cooper and Herskovits, 1991; Buntine, 1990a) however experiments show that averaging over a larger sized space yields considerable improvement (Buntine, 1990a)[1]. This improved performance corresponds to the improved accuracy gained in the *TOPN* system when the system approximates posteriors using a thousand alternative disease sets instead of a single disease set (Henrion, 1990).

A space of alternative theories is difficult to present to a domain expert but can be readily summarized in several ways for expert interrogation during theory refinement: two approaches are described here. The theory refinement algorithm of course applies Bayes theorem to this space of alternatives. To generate a space of reasonable alternatives, it does a search of the space of high posteriors in a similar style and with the same motivation as the *TOPN* system and the Bayesian averaging method for trees (Buntine, 1990a).

The theory refinement approach is developed here for Bayesian networks. These networks are first introduced and then the representation of partial theories and their transformation to a prior is described. The representation for alternative theories is described, and then the theory refinement and interrogation algorithms are presented. These major sections describe the approach but assume that conditional probability distributions for each node in a Bayesian network are represented with a full conditional joint distribution, and that all values of variables are supplied with each training case. Of course, in larger practical systems, these two assumptions rarely apply. The final section describes how noisy-or gates and other lower-dimensional conditional distributions can have their parameters learnt within the same theory refinement framework.

2 Bayesian Networks

Bayesian networks specify dependence properties between variables by using a directed acyclic graph. They describe probabilistic models useful for non-directed classification. That is, one can predict (and compute likelihoods for) one subset of variables from any other. In contrast, class probability trees (Quin-

[1]Similar results are reported in (Spirtes et al., 1990), although their justification is different.

lan, 1986; Buntine, 1990a) only allow directed classification because they only yield predictions about a special target variable usually referred to as the class.

Figure 1 shows a simple Bayesian network. The set

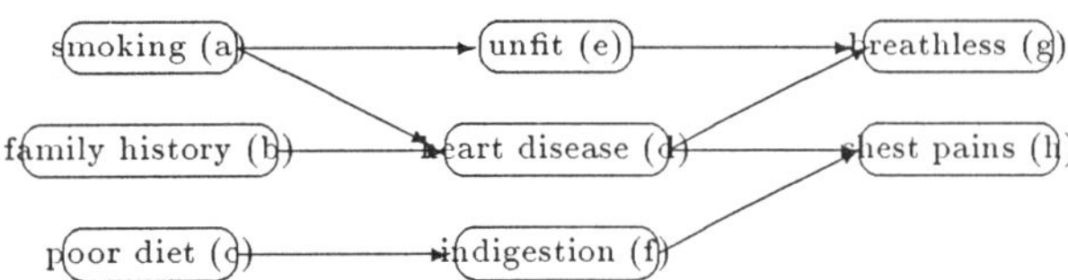

Figure 1: Bayesian network for a simple system

of variables that have outgoing arcs to a variable x are called the parents of the variable x. Each variable also has an associated conditional probability table which gives probabilities for different values of the variable conditioned on values of its parent variables. For instance for the graph in the figure, we need values for $Pr(e|a)$, $Pr(d|a,b)$, $Pr(g|e,d)$, etc., because a is the only parent of e, etc. Given the *parent structure* specifying the network and the *conditional probability tables*, methods exist for computing arbitrary conditional and marginal likelihoods between variables (Lauritzen and Spiegelhalter, 1988).

The following notation is used here. A Bayesian network consists of a set of discrete variables $\mathcal{X}$ where each variable $x \in \mathcal{X}$ has a set of parent variables Π_x. The full parent structure is denoted Π. For instance, for the graph in the figure, $\Pi_e = \{a\}$, $\Pi_d = \{a,b\}$, etc. The set of possible values for the variable x is $v(x)$ and for the cartesian product of variables in Π_x is $v(\Pi_x)$. For instance, if a, b and d are boolean, then $v(a) = \{true, false\}$, and $v(\Pi_d) = \{(true,true),(true,false),(false,true),(false,false)\}$. Also, m_x denotes the cardinality of $v(x)$.

Given an assignment I to the variables in $\mathcal{X}$, $\mathcal{X} = I$, denote corresponding assignments to $x \in \mathcal{X}$ by $I_{|x}$, and to $\Pi_x \subset \mathcal{X}$ by $I_{|\Pi_x}$. For instance, if $\mathcal{X} = \{u,v,w\}$ and $\Pi_u = \{v,w\}$ for u, v and w boolean, then if $I = (true, false, true)$, then $I_{|u} = true$ and $I_{|\Pi_u} = (false, true)$. Also, θ denotes the matrix of conditional probabilities for x given that the parent variables are Π_x and conditioned on their values. So $Pr(x = i \mid \Pi_x = j, \Pi_x, \theta) = \theta_{x=i|j}$. With these, we are able to determine the probability of the full set of variables $\mathcal{X}$ using the standard expansion

$$Pr(\mathcal{X} = I \mid \Pi, \theta) = \prod_{x \in \mathcal{X}} \theta_{x=I_{|x}|I_{|\Pi_x}} .$$

This gives the likelihood for a single example given Π and θ, and a product of these forms gives the likelihood for an independently and identically distributed training sample, used in calculating various posteriors.

3 Partial Bayesian networks

An initial partial theory given by the expert is to be transformed to a prior probability over the space of theories. Since a Bayesian network is fully specified by a parent structure Π together with conditional probabilities θ, an initial partial theory then somehow specifies a prior distribution $Pr(\Pi, \theta)$. This section describes the information obtained from the expert and how it is converted into a prior on Bayesian networks.

Experience shows that experts are often able to suggest roughly which variables influence which. This is because experts are usually better at expressing qualitative knowledge than quantitative, and because weak domain theories often indicate influence but not its exact equational form. If variables are ordered according to time of occurrence, for instance family history of heart disease pre-dates heart disease, then many of the potential influences (those following in time) are made impossible. The partial theory obtained from the expert is an ordering of variables and a Bayesian network specified pictorially in shades of grey. Black arcs indicate definite parents (with a prior of 1). Missing arcs indicate definite non-parents (with a prior of 0). Grey arcs indicate parents whose status we are uncertain about, with prior belief proportional to the grey level (or to allow greater range, with log prior mapped to the grey level). This tells the theory refinement algorithm how eager it should be to modify a potential parent's status in the light of new evidence.

We ask the expert to provide a total ordering, "$\prec$", on variables such that a variable's parents must be a subset of those variables less than it (i.e. $y \in \Pi_x$ only if $y \prec x$). We then ask the expert to indicate how strongly s/he believes each potential parent is a parent, measured in units of subjective probability. Denote this information by E. So for variables $x, y \in \mathcal{X}$ such that $y \prec x$, this is the prior probability that y is a parent of x, denoted $Pr(y \rightarrow x \mid \prec, E)$. Assuming independence, a full prior on any given parent structure conditioned on the total ordering of variables is now

$$Pr(\Pi \mid \prec, E) = \prod_{x \in \mathcal{X}} Pr(\Pi_x \mid \prec, E) ,$$

assuming Π is consistent with $\prec$, where

$$\Pr(\Pi_x \mid \prec, E) = \left(\prod_{y \in \Pi_x} Pr(y \rightarrow x \mid \prec, E) \right) \cdot \left(\prod_{y \notin \Pi_x} (1 - Pr(y \rightarrow x \mid \prec, E)) \right) .$$

To extend this simple model of a partial theory we could also introduce correlations between potential parents.

So a partial Bayesian network is specified by a total ordering of variables $\prec$ together with a prior probability for each potential parent E, which allows us to evaluate $Pr(y \to x \mid \prec, E)$. To complete the prior, we need to specify $Pr(\theta \mid \Pi, \prec, E)$.

We assume θ is independent of $\prec$ and E given Π so develop a prior for $Pr(\theta \mid \Pi)$. We choose a prior that is a conjugate prior (it yields a posterior in the same functional form, so makes the mathematics simple (Berger, 1985)) and assumes the least amount of information is known about the conditional probability tables. This is a product of standard non-informative priors on multinomial distributions (each conditional probability distribution is a multinomial), the symmetric Dirichlet prior (Buntine, 1990b; Berger, 1985), and assumes prior independence between cells in the conditional probability table:

$$Pr(\theta \mid \Pi) = \prod_{x \in \mathcal{X}} \prod_{j \in v(\Pi_x)} \frac{\prod_{i \in v(x)} \theta_{i|j}^{\alpha_x - 1}}{Beta_{m_x}(\alpha_x, \ldots, \alpha_x)},$$

where $Beta_{m_x}$ is the m_x dimensional Beta function given by

$$Beta_C(n_1, \ldots, n_C) = \frac{\prod_{i=1\ldots C} \Gamma(n_i)}{\Gamma(\sum_{i=1\ldots C} n_i)},$$

Γ is the Gamma function, e.g. $\Gamma(n+1) = n!$, and α_x is a parameter to the prior for each variable x. A particular Bayesian network is often equivalent to a set of other Bayesian networks with some arc directions changed (Verma and Pearl, 1990). With

$$\alpha_x = \frac{\alpha}{m_x |v(\Pi_x)|}, \qquad (1)$$

this prior gives equivalent networks equivalent priors, and means marginal priors for individual variables are non-informative. (The proof of this is more involved than we have space for.)

4 Representing alternative Bayesian networks

Given a total ordering on variables, the theory refinement algorithm given in the next section considers reasonable alternative parent sets for each variable determined according to some criteria of reasonableness. For the variable x alternative parent sets Π_x will be a collection of subsets of $\{y : y \prec x\}$. Combining these gives a space of alternative parent structures that can then be represented by taking the cartesian product across $\mathcal{X}$ of the sets of reasonable parent sets. For each possible parent structure Π, we also have to know its posterior probability and sufficient information to update this given new examples. This space of parent structures and the additional information can be thought of as similar to a version space (Mitchell, 1982). However, because of the inherent uncertainty of the theories considered here, the "version space" cannot be updated by considering consistency with the training sample, most specific generalizations, etc. Instead Bayes theorem indicates the normative way of updating the "version space" of alternative parent structures and our posterior belief in them.

Unfortunately, the full space of parent structures is super exponential, so we cannot store and update details about each one. To overcome this we can store those whose posterior is quite high in relative terms since these are the only structures that are significant. This section outlines how we can calculate the posterior for a given parent structure, and how a reasonable set of alternative parent structures can be stored. We refer to this representation of the set of reasonable parent structures, their conditional probability tables and associated statistics as a *combined Bayesian network*. "Reasonable" in this context is given a more precise meaning in the next section where it is shown how to maintain and update combined Bayesian networks.

Let P_x denote a set containing sets of reasonable parent variables for the variable x, so we have fair belief that the "true" $\Pi_x \in P_x$. Then the space of reasonable parent structures Π given the total ordering $\prec$ is given by the cartesian product $\bigotimes_{x \in X} P_x$. Let the number of different reasonable parents $\sum_{x \in \mathcal{X}} |P_x|$ be denoted by P (we note this now because it is useful in determining the operation count for later algorithms).

Each reasonable parent structure Π has an associated subjective posterior probability indicating how strongly we currently believe it is the "true" structure. Having seen the sample *Sample*, and obtained the information $\prec$ and E from the expert, this is $Pr(\Pi \mid Sample, \prec, E)$. According to standard rules of probability, this can be calculated as

$$\begin{aligned} & Pr(\Pi \mid Sample, \prec, E) \\ & \quad \propto Pr(\Pi \mid \prec, E) \cdot \int_\theta Pr(\theta \mid \Pi) Pr(Sample \mid \Pi, \theta) \\ & \quad = \prod_{x \in \mathcal{X}} Pr(\Pi_x \mid Sample, \prec, E) \qquad (2) \end{aligned}$$

where

$$\begin{aligned} & Pr(\Pi_x \mid Sample, \prec, E) \\ & \quad \propto Pr(\Pi_x \mid \prec, E) \\ & \qquad \prod_{j \in v(\Pi_x)} \frac{Beta_{m_x}(n_{x=1|j} + \alpha_x, \ldots, n_{x=m_x|j} + \alpha_x)}{Beta_{m_x}(\alpha_x, \ldots, \alpha_x)}, \end{aligned}$$

and $n_{x=i|j}$ is the number of examples in the training sample *Sample* with $x = i$ and $\Pi_x = j$, assuming every example in *Sample* has variable values fully specified. The solution to the integral follows by using standard properties of the Dirichlet integral (Buntine, 1990b). The counts $n_{x=i|j}$ are the only parameters in the posterior affected by the training sample and they are referred to as sufficient statistics (Berger, 1985); these need to be maintained during incremental learning.

Finally, each reasonable parent structure also has estimates for the parameters θ specifying the conditional probability tables. The estimated table for the variable x is given by $\mathbf{E}_{\theta|Sample,\Pi}\left(\theta_{x=i|j}\right)$. According to standard rules of probability, these can be calculated as

$$\begin{aligned} &\mathbf{E}_{\theta|Sample,\Pi}\left(\theta_{x=i|j}\right) \\ &\quad= \frac{\int_\theta \theta_{x=i|j} Pr(Sample \mid \Pi, \theta) Pr(\theta \mid \Pi)}{\int_\theta Pr(Sample \mid \Pi, \theta) Pr(\theta \mid \Pi)} \\ &\quad= \frac{n_{x=i|j} + \alpha_x}{n_{x=.|j} + m_x \alpha_x}, \qquad (3) \end{aligned}$$

where $n_{x=.|j} = \sum_{i=1\ldots m_x} n_{x=i|j}$. The integrations are done using standard properties of the Dirichlet integral and simplified using recursive properties of the Gamma function ($\Gamma(x+1) = x\Gamma(x)$).

With this basic information, we are now ready to describe the representation for a combined Bayesian network. In order to reconstruct the necessary conditional probability tables, compute the posteriors, etc. for each set of parent variables $\Pi_x \in P_x$, it is sufficient that the corresponding counts $n_{x=i|j}$ are kept. To save computation the posterior $Pr(\Pi_x \mid Sample, \prec, E)$ and the totals $n_{x=.|j}$ are also kept. To access all alternative parent sets $\Pi_x \in P_x$ efficiently they are stored in a lattice structure where subset and superset parent sets are linked together in a web, denoted the parent lattice for x. The full set of lattices is of size P which is $\geq |\mathcal{X}|$. Because this is potentially exponential in $|\mathcal{X}|$, only those parent sets with significant posterior probabilities are stored and linked. For instance, we might only store those parent sets with posterior within a factor of 1/1000 of the maximum posterior parent set found so far to, for instance, restrain P to be $O(|\mathcal{X}|)$. The structure updating algorithm does this. By increasing this factor close to 1, we are always guaranteed to make the full set of lattices manageable in size but at the expense of losing accuracy in theory refinement. But because posterior probabilities usually vary exponentially in learning, the set of reasonable parent sets should be manageable.

The root node of the parent lattice for x is the empty set and the *leaves* are the sets Π_x which have no supersets contained in P_x. We refer to this entire representation as a combined Bayesian network. Notice that we can easily fill in a lattice $P_x = \{\{a\}, \{a,b\}, \{a,c\}, \{a,d\}\}$ by adding $\{a,b,c\}$ and $\{a,c,d\}$ or $\{a,b,c,d\}$ to reduce the number of leaves, although some of these new leaves may have insignificant posterior probabilities.

To assist in the search and update of the lattice during theory refinement, nodes (i.e. parent sets and associated statistics) are labeled as alive, dead or asleep. Alive nodes represent the set of "reasonable" alternatives having high posteriors, and correspond to those parent sets in P_x. Dead nodes exist in the lattice as dead-end markers in the search space, they have been explored, have been forever determined as "unreasonable" alternatives and are not to be further expanded. Asleep nodes are similar but are only considered unreasonable for now and may be made alive later on. Furthermore, nodes can be either open or closed, depending on whether they require further expansion during search.

5 Theory Refinement

This section proposes several algorithms for the modification and interrogation of a combined Bayesian network. Most algorithms are linear-time in $|v(\Pi_x)|$, $|\mathcal{X}|$, P, which itself may be $O(|\mathcal{X}|)$, and other relevant variables. The structure update algorithm is an adjustable search algorithm so its time can vary from anything to fast greedy search to a slower beam search.

5.1 Parameter Updates

When the training sample *Sample* is extended, and we require a rapid incremental update of the combined Bayesian network, then a simple parameter update can be done without altering the structure of the parent lattices. This means, for each variable $x \in X$ and for each reasonable parent set $\Pi_x \in P_x$, we have to increment the corresponding cell counts, and update the posteriors. Normally, this process should effect only the alive nodes in the parent lattice. For instance, suppose *Sample* is extended to *Sample*$'$ with the new example having $x = i$ and $\Pi_x = j$, then we should increment $n_{x=i|j}$ and

$$\begin{aligned} &Pr(\Pi_x \mid Sample', \prec, E) \\ &\quad= Pr(\Pi_x \mid Sample, \prec, E) \\ &\qquad\quad \frac{(n_{x=i|j} + \alpha_x)(n_{x=.|j} - 1 + m_x\alpha_x)}{(n_{x=.|j} + m_x\alpha_x)(n_{x=i|j} - 1 + \alpha_x)}. \end{aligned}$$

This follows from recursive properties of the Gamma function. The full update process will therefore take $O(P)$ operations. If we increase *Sample* by adding N extra examples in a batch then we can repeat this process N times. This process can be further sped up by initially updating only the leaf nodes in the parent lattices because the change in example counts can then be filtered upwards without reference to the examples.

5.2 Structure Updates

Given additional time, an any-time search can be begun to extend and modify the reasonable parent structures P_x and the corresponding parent lattices to ensure high posterior parent sets are represented. This algorithm is first presented here as a one-time batch algorithm (starting from an empty lattice), and then differentiated to produce the incremental version. The algorithm presented is a simple beam search algorithm with three parameters such that $1 > C > D > E$. These are used to vary the search, as explained below. Alternatively, a branch and bound algorithm could be developed using upper bounds on posterior probabilities, or a corresponding decision theoretic search algorithm.

The batch beam search algorithm finds many parent sets with posteriors within a given factor C of the best found. The beams searched are those parents sets within a factor D of the best found. The algorithm is presented in pseudo-code in Figure 2. This search

> **Input:** A variable x and a prior on its parent sets $Pr(\Pi_x)$, and a training sample.
>
> **Output:** The parent lattice for x corresponding to this sample.
>
> **Algorithm:** Set *Best-posterior* to the posterior for $\Pi_x = \emptyset$. Set *Open-list* to $\{\emptyset\}$. This maintains a list of parent sets within a factor C of *Best-posterior*, those to be further expanded during search. Set *Alive-list* to $\{\emptyset\}$. This maintains a list of parent sets within a factor D of *Best-posterior*, that are considered alive in the parent lattice. Repeat the process below until *Open-list* becomes empty. Take the top parent set Π_x from *Open-list*. If its posterior is $< E \cdot$ *Best-Posterior*, mark this parent set dead. If its posterior is $< D \cdot$ *Best-Posterior* ignore this parent set and proceed. Otherwise, generate all its children and calculate their posterior probabilities conditioned on the training sample. If the greatest posterior is $>$ *Best-Posterior*, then update *Best-Posterior* and modify *Alive-list* to reflect the new maximum. Mark all children with posterior $< E \cdot$ *Best-Posterior* such that the sample size is $O(|\mathcal{X}||v(\Pi_x)|)$ as dead. Add all children with posterior $> D \cdot$ *Best-Posterior* to *Open-list*. Add all children with posterior $> C \cdot$*Best-Posterior* to *Alive-list* and mark them as alive. Mark all remaining unmarked children as asleep.

Figure 2: The batch learning algorithm

is made easier by the fact the posterior probabilities on alternative structures tend to vary exponentially as structures change, and high posterior structures tend to clump together. This makes the beam search more efficient. Also, parent sets are marked dead if at any time they have a posterior less than a factor E of the best and have fairly stable probability estimates. Many parent sets will be marked dead as posteriors for poor parent structures decrease exponentially with increasing sample size. Since dead nodes cannot be expanded, this further reduces the search. Finally, notice that if C and D are set close to 1, then the algorithm becomes a greedy search for a high posterior parent set.

A process reproducing the result of this algorithm can be run incrementally. This would be needed when an additional batch of examples is received. If asleep nodes have not been updated with previous additional samples because the parameter update process of the previous section was used, then these asleep nodes should first have their parameters updated and *Best-Posterior* recalculated. Processing after this is interruptible to achieve the any-time feature of the search. Adjust *Alive-list* and *Open-list* to reflect the new *Best-Posterior*. Finally expand nodes from *Open-list* and continue with the search. Some nodes may oscillate on and off *Alive-list* and *Open-list* because the posterior ordering of parent sets will oscillate as the training samples increases and the posteriors are modified. This is the problem of repeated restructuring reported by Crawford to occur in incremental learning algorithms (Crawford, 1989). This can be prevented by making a differential on C and D between placing a node on and taking a node off.

5.3 Structure posteriors

One useful form of feedback to the expert is to return information in exactly the same format initially obtained from the expert, a partial Bayesian network. This means calculating the posterior probability (conditioned on the training sample) that variable y will be a parent of x

$$\begin{aligned} & Pr(y \rightarrow x \mid Sample, \prec, E) \\ = & \sum_{\Pi_x \in P_x \,\wedge\, y \in \Pi_x} Pr(\Pi_x \mid Sample, \prec, E) \,. \end{aligned}$$

The full calculation for all variables will take $O(|\mathcal{X}| \cdot P)$ operations. This information could be pictorially represented as a graph with arcs done in shades of grey to indicate strength of belief. Standard asymptotic properties of Bayesian methods assure us that as the sample size gets arbitrarily large, these posterior probabilities will converge to either 0 or 1.

5.4 Alternative Bayesian networks

Another useful form of feedback for the expert is to return some "good" Bayesian networks stored in the combined Bayesian network. We can do this by selecting for each $x \in \mathcal{X}$, a set of parents Π_x and an associated conditional probability distribution. To ensure these are truly representative networks, we can return a collection of networks together in a compressed format corresponding to a single Bayesian network, denoted a *smoothed Bayesian network*. A similar operation has been presented for class probability trees (Buntine, 1990a).

For each variable x, we choose a leaf $L_x \in P_x$ from the parent lattice for x using a probabilistic method described later. This provides one potential parent set for x. However, there may be more high posterior parents sets in P_x that are subsets of L_x. We shall average each of their corresponding conditional probability tables together to obtain a single representative conditional probability table.

Denote by S_x the set of parent sets that are subsets of L_x,

$$S_x = \{\Pi_x : \Pi_x \in P_x \wedge \Pi_x \subseteq L_x\} \subseteq P_x .$$

Then we can merge all these parent sets and average their conditional probability tables together to obtain a single representation of them all. This is done with the following formulae: the posterior probability that the "true" set of parents for x is in S_x,

$$Pr(S_x \mid Sample, \prec, E) = \sum_{\Pi_x \in S_x} Pr(\Pi_x \mid Sample, \prec, E) ,$$

the posterior expected conditional probability table for x conditioned on L_x assuming that the "true" set of parents for x is in S_x,

$$\begin{aligned} & \mathrm{E}_{\Pi_x,\theta|S_x,Sample,\prec,E}\left(Pr(x=i \mid L_x=j,\Pi_x,\theta)\right) \\ &= \sum_{\Pi_x \in S_x} Pr(x=i \mid \Pi_x = j_{|\Pi_x}, \Pi_x, Sample) \\ &\quad \cdot \frac{Pr(\Pi_x \mid Sample, \prec, E)}{Pr(S_x \mid Sample, \prec, E)} , \end{aligned}$$

(note the 1st probability on the right-hand side of the equation is calculated using Equation (3)) and the posterior expected probability that y is a parent of x assuming that the "true" set of parents for x is in S_x,

$$\begin{aligned} & Pr(y \rightarrow x \mid S_x, Sample, \prec, E) \\ &= \frac{\sum_{\Pi_x \in S_x \wedge y \in \Pi_x} Pr(\Pi_x \mid Sample, \prec, E)}{Pr(S_x \mid Sample, \prec, E)} . \end{aligned}$$

We use these formulae as follows: for each x we choose a leaf L_x in P_x randomly in proportion with $Pr(S_x \mid Sample, \prec, E)$. For the full set of variables this takes $O(P)$ operations. Because this process relies on selection of leaves from the parent lattice, it may be advantageous to reduce the number of leaves, as discussed with the structure update algorithm. For a variable x, we can display its set of parents pictorially using grey scales as discussed previously, but using $Pr(y \rightarrow x \mid S_x, Sample, \prec, E)$ as the probability y is a parent of x. For the full set of variables this takes $O(|\mathcal{X}| \cdot P)$ operations. Finally, we can generate the conditional probability tables for x given the value of L_x by computing $\mathrm{E}_{\Pi_x,\theta|S_x,Sample,\prec,E}\left(Pr(x=i \mid L_x=j,\Pi_x,\theta)\right)$. This represents the average of the various conditional probability tables corresponding to parent sets in S_x. Empirically, this has the effect of smoothing the conditional probability tables for x given L_x computed using Equation (3). This takes $O(\sum_{x \in \mathcal{X}} m_x |v(L_x)||S_x|)$ operations.

Given only a small training sample, this technique is likely to produce many different smoothed Bayesian networks corresponding to the many different alive leaves in the parent lattices. Perusal of these will give the expert some idea of the current variability in choice of a "good" Bayesian network. As the training sample size increases, asymptotic properties of Bayesian methods assure us the sets of high posterior parents and their conditional probability tables will become roughly equivalent so the different smoothed Bayesian networks produced will differ much less and eventually converge.

6 Extensions

This section briefly considers relaxing one of the assumptions made in the previous section: full conditional joint distributions exist at each node. Further extensions would be the handling of "missing values", where some examples have variable values missing, and the handling of expert designated "hidden variables" in the structure. Both problems can be handled the EM algorithm (Dempster et al., 1977).

While full conditional joint distributions are more general than any other model, their specification requires an exponential number of parameters. When estimating parameter values from data, this can be a severe problem as it is when trying to elicit the same probabilities from an expert. One way around this is to introduce approximate distributions of lower dimension. We have two issues to consider here: (1) How do you learn parameters for a specific conditional distribution? (2) How do you then patch the distribution learnt into the broad framework given previously?

There are many ways of representing restricted conditional probability distributions: trees (Buntine, 1990a), logistic regression and other qualitative models popular in economic statistics (Amemiya, 1985), and the noisy-or gate popular in AI (Pearl, 1988).

The noisy-or gate is described as follows. Suppose boolean variable x is conditioned on boolean variables $x_1, \ldots, x_n$. The noisy-or has parameters $q_0, \ldots, q_n$,

$$\begin{aligned} & Pr(x \mid x_1, \ldots x_n, q) \\ &= q_0 \prod_{i=1,\ldots n} q_i^{1_{x_i}} && \text{when } x \text{ is false, and} \\ &= 1 - q_0 \prod_{i=1,\ldots n} q_i^{1_{x_i}} && \text{when } x \text{ is true,} \end{aligned}$$

where the indicator function 1_{x_i} is 1 when x_i is true and zero otherwise. A similar conditional probability distribution is the multivariate logistic regression function, which in a slightly modified form applies to boolean variable x conditioned on to boolean variables $x_1, \ldots, x_n$ and is

$$\begin{aligned} & Pr(x \mid x_1, \ldots x_n, r) \\ &= \frac{r_0 \prod_{i=1,\ldots n} r_i^{1_{x_i}}}{1 + r_0 \prod_{i=1,\ldots n} r_i^{1_{x_i}}} && \text{when } x \text{ is false, and} \end{aligned}$$

$$= \frac{1}{1 + r_0 \prod_{i=1,\ldots n} r_i^{1_{x_i}}} \qquad \text{when } x \text{ is true.}$$

(It is usually given with parameters $r_i = e^{r'_i}$.) The two forms approximate each other when the product is small. More generally, the logistic function is a symmetrized version of the noisy-or. Versions of the function exist when the variables are many-valued discrete variables, and to introduce higher-order correlations between variables. The logistic function has the same functional form as a simple (or "idiot") Bayes classifier, and can be obtained by taking the conditional distribution from a quadratic exponential distribution on discrete variables $x, x_1, \ldots x_n$.

To incorporate these methods into the framework just given, we need to be able to calculate the posterior expected parameter values, and the (relative) posterior probability that the noisy-or function or the logistic regression function is "true", independently of the parameter values. Since each conditional distribution is associated with a particular set of parent variables, the parameter values and the posterior can then be placed in a parent lattice of the combined Bayesian network. The posterior can be used, for instance, to search the space of logistic regressions over different parent sets using the algorithm of Figure 2, and also used when determining structure posteriors.

Posterior expected parameter values, and the (relative) posterior probability for both noisy-or and logistic regression models are readily estimated using standard maximum likelihood and Bayesian methods. It is simple to show that the sample likelihood functions for both the noisy-or and the logistic regression function is convex. So with a dominant likelihood term, the posterior on the parameters is unimodal and the maximum posterior parameters can be found using search methods such as scoring, Newton-Raphson, or conjugate gradient (Amemiya, 1985). A multivariate normal approximation for the posterior at this point (Berger, 1985, p224) can then be used to marginalize out the parameters and approximate the posterior probability that the noisy-or function of the logistic regression function is "true". Notice that because the numeric search algorithms are iterative, they are readily placed in an incremental framework. Given a few new training cases, start the iterative search at the previous maximum posterior point and convergence will be rapid to the new point (because the posterior is unimodal, there will be no catastrophic changes of the maximum posterior point).

7 Conclusion

This paper has presented a representation and some theory refinement algorithms for learning Bayesian networks. These have the following important properties:

- The representation can be initiated with a partial Bayesian network that quantifies the expert's experience and confidence. A similar approach was suggested in (Srinivas et al., 1990). Thereafter the representation maintains several reasonable hypotheses in a form of version space.
- The algorithms approximate the normative Bayesian solution to the corresponding batch learning problem. An analogous approximation for class probability trees significantly outperformed standard statistical and AI methods (Buntine, 1990a) on a large range of problems. A weaker approximation for batch learning (which finds a single high posterior network) has been reported to work well empirically (Cooper and Herskovits, 1991), and the parameter updating component of the algorithm corresponds to previous work (Spiegelhalter and Lauritzen, 1989).
- There is an incremental algorithm that allows any-time return for varied processing times between receipt of new examples. The development of the algorithm illustrates how a batch learning algorithm can be converted to an incremental learning algorithm.
- There are several algorithms that allow a user to interrogate the current hypotheses about Bayesian networks and to get some idea of their variability.
- The algorithms have parameters that allow fuller approximation of the normative solution. These parameters allow one to trade-off space/time complexity with (average-case) quality of learned theories (compare with (Buntine, 1990a; Henrion, 1990)).
- Extensions have been suggested to show how to handle different conditional probability models such as noisy-or gates and logistic functions.

Experience with a similar approach for learning trees suggests the algorithms, with some additional hacking, should work well.

Acknowledgements

Several of these ideas have been suggested independently by Bob Fung, and I have also benefited from discussion with him. The writing of this paper was motivated by some comments made by Pat Langley.

References

Amemiya, T. (1985). *Advanced Econometrics.* Harvard University Press, Cambridge, MA.

Berger, J. O. (1985). *Statistical Decision Theory and Bayesian Analysis.* Springer-Verlag, New York.

Buntine, W. (1990a). Learning classification trees. Technical Report FIA-90-12-19-01, RIACS and NASA Ames Research Center, Moffett Field, CA. Paper presented at Third International Workshop on Artificial Intelligence and Statistics.

Buntine, W. (1990b). *A Theory of Learning Classification Rules.* PhD thesis, University of Technology, Sydney. Forthcoming.

Cooper, G. and Herskovits, E. (1991). A Bayesian method for the induction of probabilistic networks from data. Technical Report KSL-91-02, Knowledge Systems Laboratory, Medical Computer Science, Stanford University.

Crawford, S. (1989). Extensions to the CART algorithm. *International Journal of Man-Machine Studies*, 31(2):197–217.

Dempster, A., Laird, N., and Rubin, D. (1977). Maximum likelihood from incomplete data via the EM algorithm. *J. Roy. Statist. Soc. B*, 39:1–38.

Geiger, D., Paz, A., and Pearl, J. (1990). Learning causal trees from dependence information. In *Eighth National Conference on Artificial Intelligence*, pages 770–771, Boston, Massachusetts.

Ginsberg, A., Weiss, S., and Politakis, P. (1988). Automatic knowledge base refinement for classification systems. *Artificial Intelligence*, 35(2):197–226.

Haussler, D. (1991). A decision theoretic generalization of the PAC learning model and its application to some feed-forward neural networks. *Information and Control.* To appear.

Henrion, M. (1990). Towards efficient inference in multiply connected belief networks. In Oliver, R. and Smith, J., editors, *Influence Diagrams, Belief Nets and Decision Analysis*, pages 385–407. Wiley.

Lauritzen, S. and Spiegelhalter, D. (1988). Local computations with probabilities on graphical structures and their application to expert systems. *J. Roy. Statist. Soc. B*, 50(2):240–265.

Mitchell, T. (1982). Generalization as search. *Artificial Intelligence*, 18(2):203–226.

Opper, M. and Haussler, D. (1991). Generalised performance of Bayes optimal classification algorithm for learning a perceptron. In *COLT'91: 1991 Workshop on Computational Learning Theory.* Morgan Kaufmann. Manuscript.

Ourston, D. and Mooney, R. (1990). Changing the rules: A comprehensive approach to theory refinement. In *Eighth National Conference on Artificial Intelligence*, pages 815–820, Boston, Massachusetts.

Pearl, J. (1988). *Probabilistic Reasoning in Intelligent Systems.* Morgan and Kauffman.

Quinlan, J. (1986). Induction of decision trees. *Machine Learning*, 1(1):81–106.

Shapiro, E. (1983). *Algorithmic Program Debugging.* MIT Press.

Spiegelhalter, D. and Lauritzen, S. (1989). Sequential updating of conditional probabilities on directed graphical structures. Research Report R-89-10, Institute of Electronic Systems, Aalborg University, Aalborg, Denmark.

Spirtes, P. and Glymour, C. (1990). An algorithm for fast recovery of sparse causal graphs. Report CMU-LCL-90-4, Laboratory for Computational Linguistics, Carnegie Mellon University.

Spirtes, P., Scheines, R., and Glymour, C. (1990). Simulation studies of the reliability of computer-aided model specification using TETRAD II. EQS and LISREL programs. *Sociological Methods and Research*, 19(1):3–66.

Srinivas, S., Russell, S., and Agogino, A. (1990). Automated construction of sparse Bayesian networks. In Henrion, M., Schachter, R., Kanal, L., and Lemmer, J., editors, *Uncertainty in Artificial Intelligence 5*, pages 295–308. Elsevier Science Publishers, Amsterdam.

Towell, G., Shavlik, J., and Noordewier, M. (1990). Refinement of approximate domain theories by knowledge-based neural networks. In *Eighth National Conference on Artificial Intelligence*, pages 861–866, Boston, Massachusetts.

Verma, T. and Pearl, J. (1990). Equivalence and synthesis of causal models. In *Sixth Workshop on Uncertainty in Artificial Intelligence*, Cambridge, MA.

COMBINATION OF UPPER AND LOWER PROBABILITIES

Jose E. Cano, **Serafín Moral,** **Juan F. Verdegay-López**

Departamento de Ciencias de la Computación e I.A. Universidad de Granada. 18071 Granada, Spain.

Abstract

In this paper, we consider several types of information and methods of combination associated with incomplete probabilistic systems. We discriminate between 'a priori' and evidential information. The former one is a description of the whole population, the latest is a restriction based on observations for a particular case. Then, we propposе different combination methods for each one of them. We also consider conditioning as the heterogeneous combination of 'a priori' and evidential information. The evidential information is represented as a convex set of likelihood functions. These will have an associated possibility distribution with behavior according to classical Possibility Theory.

1 INTRODUCTION

In Probability Theory the main method of incorporating new information is through conditioning. In general, there is no doubt about how to represent initial information and how to update it in the light of new observations. However, when we work with probabilistic intervals, there is a bit of a mess. Several formulas of combining and conditioning are available, the main problem being which formula or method to use in a particular case. The reason for this is the lack of a firm semantic basis.

In this paper we present a method of tackling incomplete probabilistic information, which tries to avoid this kind of ambiguity. The main feature is the clear distinction between evidential and 'a priori' information. Evidential information will be represented as a convex set of likelihood functions with an associated possibility distribution. The interpretation of these possibilities will have a probabilistic basis. However their behavior will be very similar to classical possibility distributions (Dubois, Prade 1988; Zadeh 1978).

We shall discriminate between the combination of evidential information and the combination of 'a priori' information. Conditioning will be a kind of heterogeneous combination: 'a priori' and evidential information. The result is called 'a posteriori' information. This 'a posteriori' information is different from that resulting from applying known formulas of calculating conditional information: Dempster conditioning (Dempster 1967) and upper and lower conditioning (Dempster 1967; Campos, Lamata, Moral 1990; Fagin, Halpern 1990).

The problem of applying Dempster-Shafer Theory of Evidence (Dempster 1967; Shafer 1976) to upper and lower probabilities is that there is only one way of combining information, the so called Dempster rule of combination. Furthermore, the most used conditioning is Dempster conditioning (Dempster 1967; Moral, Campos 1990) which is a particular case of Dempster rule. So all information is combined in an homogeneous way. This gives rise to cases in which Dempster rule seems reasonable and cases in which the results are not very intuitive. In general, Dempster conditioning produces very narrow intervals, if upper and lower probabilities interpretation is considered (Pearl 1989).

2 'A PRIORI' INFORMATION

Let X be a variable taking values on a finite set $U = \{u_1, ..., u_m\}$. An 'a priori' information about X is a convex set of probabilities,

$$\mathcal{H} = \left\{ \sum_{i=1}^{n} \alpha_i P_i \mid \sum_{i=1}^{n} \alpha_i = 1 \right\}$$

where $\{P_1, P_2, ... P_n\}$ is a finite set of probabilities on U. In general, this information is applicable under a determined set of conditions Co under which X takes its values. The meaning is that one element of $\mathcal{H}$ is the true probability distribution associated with X, under conditions Co. Given a set of possible probabilities $\mathcal{C} = \{P_1, P_2, ... P_n\}$, we may associate a convex set of probabilities with it, its convex hull

$$\overline{\mathcal{C}} = \left\{ \sum_{i=1}^{n} \alpha_i P_i \mid \sum_{i=1}^{n} \alpha_i = 1 \right\}$$

$\mathcal{C}$ and $\overline{\mathcal{C}}$ may be considered for the same experiment with different interpretations. For example, let us consider that we have two urns, U_1 and U_2. U_1 has 99 red balls and one black. U_2 has one red ball and 99 black ones. If we pick up a ball randomly from one of the two urns then, we have two possible probabilities, $\mathcal{C} = \{P_1, P_2\}$, for the color of the ball, one for each urn. However, if the experiment is to select an urn and then pick a ball, the frequencies of the colors will be given by one probability $\alpha P_1 + (1-\alpha)P_2$, where α is the probability of selecting U_1, and $(1-\alpha)$ the probability of selecting U_2. As α is unknown, we have a convex set of probabilities $\overline{\mathcal{C}}$. We will always consider the second interpretation. That is, that we have a previous experiment consisting in randomly selecting one of the possible probability distributions. Therefore a set of probability distributions will be equivalent to its convex hull.

Above assumption may have some problems. For example, assume that we have two variables, X_1 and X_2, which are known to be independent. For the first variable we have the convex set of possible probabilities $\mathcal{C}_1 = \overline{\{P_1, Q_1\}}$, and for the second variable, the convex set $\mathcal{C}_2 = \overline{\{P_2, Q_2\}}$. Given these conditions, the possible set of probabilities for the variable $X = (X_1, X_2)$ is

$$\mathcal{C} = \{p \mid p(a_1, a_2) = h_1(a_1)h_2(a_2), h_1 \in \mathcal{C}_1, h_2 \in \mathcal{C}_2\}$$

However, this set $\mathcal{C}$ is not neccesarily convex. We may have:

- $P_1.P_2, Q_1.Q_2 \in \mathcal{C}$
- Sometimes the convex combination

$$\alpha(P_1.P_2) + (1-\alpha)(Q_1.Q_2)$$

is not equal to a product such as

$$(\beta P_1 + (1-\beta)Q_1).(\gamma P_2 + (1-\gamma)Q_2),$$

that is, an element from $\mathcal{C}$.

This has been considered also by B. Tessem (1989), in a slightly different problem: The induced set of probabilities in X_2, from a convex set of 'a priori' distributions on X, and a convex set of conditionals. It is shown that this set is not necessarily convex.

We shall always represent uncertainty as a convex set of probabilities. Then, in situations like this, we shall do an approximation of the possible set of probabilities calculating its convex hull. From a practical point of view, this approximation is equivalent to assuming that the selection of probabilities for X_1 and X_2 may be done in a dependent way. That is, with probability α we may choose P_1 for X_1 and P_2 for X_2; and with probability $1-\alpha$ it is possible to choose Q_1 for X_1 and Q_2 for X_2. This does not imply that the variables X_1 and X_2 are dependent. In fact, the individual probabilities are combined by multiplication ($P_1.P_2$ and $Q_1.Q_2$). Only the probability distributions are selected on a dependent way. In a particular case, it may occurs that the selection of probabilities is independent. But then, we are adding some extra probabilities. From this point of view, we are losing some information, but we lose it for the sake of simplicity. Convex sets are more manageable than general sets.

The combination of 'a priori' convex sets of probability distributions has been considered in Campos, Lamata, Moral (1988). If we have two 'a priori' convex sets of probabilities $\mathcal{C}_1$ and $\mathcal{C}_2$ given for the same set of conditions, then the conjunction will be the intersection of the convex hulls, $\overline{\mathcal{C}}_1 \cap \overline{\mathcal{C}}_2$. The disjunction will be the convex hull of the union: $\overline{\mathcal{C}_1 \cup \mathcal{C}_2}$.

This kind of combination is the one applied in situations like the following: We know that if we pick up a ball from this urn the probability of being red is between 0.75 and 0.85, and from other source we obtain that this probability is between 0.8 and 0.9. Then we may apply this combination (conjunction in this case) and deduce that the probability is between 0.8 and 0.85.

If $\mathcal{C}_1$ and $\mathcal{C}_2$ are convex sets of probabilities, but relative to different contexts Co_1 and Co_2, then no 'a priori' information may be deduced in the context $Co_1 \cup Co_2$ (both conditions are verified), except if one of the probabilities is degenerated. The following situation is perfectly possible:

- $\mathcal{C}_1 = \{p_1\}$ in conditions Co_1, where

$$p_1(a_1) = 0.99,\ p_1(a_2) = 0.01$$

- $\mathcal{C}_2 = \{p_2\}$ in conditions Co_2, where

$$p_2(a_1) = 0.99,\ p_2(a_2) = 0.01$$

- $\mathcal{C}_3 = \{p_3\}$ in conditions $Co_1 \cup Co_2$, where

$$p_3(a_1) = 0,\ p_3(a_2) = 1$$

However, if we have the following information,

- I1: "Most of Computer Science students (CS) are single (S)"
- I2: "Most of young people (Y) are single (S)"

Where I1 and I2 may be translated in the probabilistic information,

- Under conditions $Co_1 = \{CS\}$

$$p_1(S) = 0.99 \quad p_1(\neg S) = 0.01$$

- Under conditions $Co_2 = \{Y\}$

$$p_2(S) = 0.99 \quad p_2(\neg S) = 0.01$$

and nothing is known about the probability of being single under conditions {CS,Y}, then common sense says that in this case it would not be wrong to assume that "Most young people studing Computer Science are single". It migth occur that young Computer Science students are a rare combination and most of them are married. But if nothing is said about this, then it may be considered that there are not strange interactions and that under conditions Co_1 and Co_2 we may use $\mathcal{C}_3 = \mathcal{C}_1 \cap \mathcal{C}_2 = \{p_1\} = \{p_2\}$.

In short, to do the combination of 'a priori' probabilitic convex sets is neccesary to determine whether they are given in the same context. In shuch a case, we calculate the conjunction by the intersection of convex sets and the disjunction by the convex hull of the union. If the sets of probabilities are given under two different contexts, then nothing can be said about the combination. However, when there is no more available information, then the former combination could be considered by default, but taking into account that this is an additional assumption we make about the problem.

Very often, 'a priori' information is given by means of probability intervals or probability envelopes. A probability envelope is a pair of applications

$$l, u : \mathcal{P}(U) \longrightarrow [0,1]$$

such that there exist a family $\mathcal{P}$ of probability measures verifying

$$l(A) = \inf_{P \in \mathcal{P}} P(A) \qquad u(A) = \sup_{P \in \mathcal{P}} P(A)$$

It is clear that given a set of probabilities, $\mathcal{C}_1$, we may associate with it a probability envelope. However a probability envelope (l, u) may be defined from different sets of probabilities. But, in every case, there is always a maximal family given by

$$\mathcal{P} = \{P | l(A) \leq P(A) \leq u(A), \forall A \subseteq \mathcal{U}\}$$

If $\mathcal{C}$ is a set of probabilities and we calculate the associated envelope (l, u), this envelope is equivalent to a maximal family $\mathcal{P}$. Always, we have $\mathcal{C} \subseteq \mathcal{P}$. Then, if we transform a set $\mathcal{C}$ on an envelope we may consider that some information is lost (there are more probabilities being possible).

3 EVIDENTIAL INFORMATION

3.1 LIKELIHOOD FUNCTIONS

Assume that we do not have an 'a priori' information about X, but we have observed O, and we have a family of conditional probabilities,

$$P(O|X = a_i),\ \ a_i \in U.$$

Taking into account that nothing is known about 'a priori' probabilities of a_i are not known then nothing can be said about 'a posteriori' probabilities of a_i after observing O, with the exception that if $P(O|a_i) = 0$ then we can conclude that a_i is impossible. Cosider the following example: We have $U = \{a_1, a_2\}$ and

$$P(O|a_1) = 1, P(O|a_2) = 0.001$$

Then after observing O, we may have $p(a_2|O) = 1$ $(p(a_2|O) = 0)$ if the unknown 'a priori' probability was $p(a_2) = 1$ $(p(a_2) = 0)$. However, it is clear that after observing O, a_2 should be considered less possible than a_1. In conclussion the information provided by O can not be represented by probabilities or interval probabilities. We shall do as in Clasical Non-Bayesian Statistics and say that O defines a likelihood function, l_o, on U, which is a mapping from U on the interval $[0,1]$, given by

$$l_o(a_i) = P(O|X = a_i),\ \ a_i \in U.$$

This likelihood may be interpreted as a possibility distribution, π_o, which is not neccesarily normalized (Smets 1982).

The possibility measure associated with π_o is defined (Zadeh 1978) as a mapping

$$\Pi_o : \mathcal{P}(U) \longrightarrow [0,1]$$

given by

$$\Pi_o(A) = \max_{a \in A} \pi_o(a)$$

The following proposition relates a possibility measure with probability bounds.

Proposition.- Given a possibility measure Π_o on U, then

$$\Pi_o(A) \geq P(O \cap A)$$

and these bounds are optimal under information O.

Proof.-

$$P(O \cap A) = \sum_{a_i \in A} P(O \cap \{a_i\}) =$$

$$\sum_{a_i \in A} P(O|a_i).p(a_i) = \sum_{a_i \in A} \pi_o(a_i).p(a_i)$$

Now, taking into account that,

$$\sum_{a_i \in A} p(a_i) = P(A) \leq 1,$$

we get the required inequality,

$$P(O \cap A) \leq \max_{a_i \in A} \pi_o(a_i) = \Pi_o(A).$$

The bounds are optimal in the sense that being

$$\Pi_o(A) = \max_{a_i \in A} \pi_o(a_i)$$

then, if

$$\max_{a_i \in A} \pi_o(a_i) = \pi_o(a_k), \quad a_k \in A$$

we may consider the 'a priori' probability

- $p(a_k) = 1$,
- $p(a_i) = 0$, *otherwise*

With this 'a priori' probability,

$$P(O \cap A) = p(a_k)P(O|a_k) = \Pi_o(A),$$

that is, equality is given. ■

These bounds are not associated with conditional probabilities, $P(.|O)$, but with probabilities of consistency with information O. To consider real conditional probabilities we have to divide by $P(O)$, but this probability is unknown, and we only have an upper bound $\Pi_o(U)$. The normalization by this value may be considered as an upper relative degree of consistency,

$$g_o{}^*(A) = \frac{\Pi_o(A)}{\Pi_o(U)}$$

From this upper value, we may define the lower limit as

$$g_{o*}(A) = 1 - g_o{}^*(\overline{A}).$$

3.2 CONVEX SETS OF LIKELIHOOD FUNCTIONS

On the other hand, it is possible that the exact values of conditional probabilities are not known. For example, we only have probability intervals

$$b_i \leq P(O|X = a_i) \leq c_i$$

In this case, observation O does not define only one likelihood function, but a convex set of likelihoods, those verifying $a_i \leq l(a_i) \leq c_i$. This convex set will be called the evidential information associated with O and denote it by E_o.

An evidential information also has an associated possibility distribution,

$$\pi_o(a_i) = \max_{l \in E_o} l(a_i)$$

This possibility distribution also verifies a similar proposition to the above, relative to probability bounds. In the same way, we may associate the pair of lower-upper measures $(g_{o*}, g_o{}^*)$.

With the same reasoning as in 'a priori' information, it will be considered that a set of likelihood functions, E, is equivalent to its convex hull, $\overline{E}$. A special likelihood function is the null likelihood, l_N , defined as

$$l_N(a_i) = 0, \quad \forall a_i \in U$$

This likelihood function comes from an observation, O, for which

$$P(O|a_i) = 0$$

are possible conditional probabilities (there may be another possible conditional probabilities defining other likelihood functions associated with observation O).

It is clear that after observing O, these conditional probabilities are impossible, because we have

$$P(O) = \sum_i P(O|a_i)p(a_i) = 0$$

Then l_N has to be considered as an impossible likelihood. It could be thought that when l_N appears it would be better to remove it. In fact, the removing of something impossible must not change our state of mind. But for the same reason the inclussion of l_N should not have any effect in our final results. This will happen in our model: never the final probability intervals will chage because of the inclussion or elimination of l_N.

Taking the above reasons into account we shall extend our original equivalence relation among sets of likelihood functions, considering that two sets, E_1 and E_2, are equivalent if and only if $\overline{E_1 \cup \{l_N\}} = \overline{E_2 \cup \{l_N\}}$. That is, if previously including the null linkelihood their convex hulls are equal. The effect of this equivalence relation will be that if we have a likelihood, l, we do not have to consider any likelihood $\alpha.l$ (where $\alpha \leq 1$). This is not strange. Having l, the likelihood $\alpha.l$ ($\alpha \leq 1$) defines the same relative possibilities, but with a lower normalization factor.

In the following, the convex set $\overline{E \cup \{l_N\}}$ will be denoted as $C(E)$.

The disjunction and conjunction of evidential information are defined in an analogous way to the disjunction and conjunction of 'a priori' information.

If E_1 and E_2 are two sets of evidential information, the disjunction, $E_1 \vee E_2$, is defined as $C(E_1 \cup E_2)$. The conjunction, $E_1 \wedge E_2$, is defined as the intersection of the convex hulls: $C(E_1) \cap C(E_2)$.

Here is important to distinguish between the conjunction of evidential information, $C(E_1) \cap C(E_2)$ and the evidential observation associated with the conjunction of two observations O_1 and O_2, $E_{O_1 \wedge O_2}$. The first is applied when we know that E_1 and E_2 are two convex sets of likelihood functions associated with the same observation and is performed calculating $C(E_1) \cap C(E_2)$. The last, when we have two sets of likelihoods corresponding to two observations, O_1 and O_2, and we want to calculate the evidential information associated with $O_1 \wedge O_2$. The same is applied for the disjunction.

For the calculus of evidential information $E_{O_1 \wedge O_2}$ from the evidential information E_{O_1} and E_{O_2}, we have to calculate the possible values for the probability $P(O_1 \wedge O_2|a_i)$ from the values of $P(O_1|a_i)$ and $P(O_2|a_i)$. The only thing we can say is that

$$\max\{0, P(O_1|a_i) + P(O_2|a_i) - 1\} \leq P(O_1 \wedge O_2|a_i) \leq$$

$$\leq \min\{P(O_1|a_i), P(O_2|a_i)\}$$

then we have to consider in $E_{O_1 \wedge O_2}$ all the likelihood functions, l, verifying

$$\max\{0, l_1(a_i) + l_2(a_i) - 1\} \leq l(a_i) \leq$$

$$\leq Min\{l_1(a_i), l_2(a_i)\}$$

where $l_1 \in E_{O_1}, l_2 \in E_{O_2}$.

For the associated possibility distribution, we get

$$\pi_{O_1 \wedge O_2}(a_i) = \min\{\pi_{O_1}(a_i), \pi_{O_2}(a_i)\}$$

that is, the same formula as in classical Possibility Theory (Dubois, Prade 1988), but without assuming any additional assumption of coherence or compatibility of observations.

If we assume that O_1 and O_2 are conditionally independent given the value of X then we get:

$$\pi_{O_1 \wedge O_2}(a_i) = \pi_{O_1}(a_i).\pi_{O_2}(a_i).$$

Another assumptions may be make to obtain different combination formulas for operations on observations.

4 COMBINATION OF 'A PRIORI' AND EVIDENTIAL INFORMATION

Here, it is considered the combination of a convex set of 'a priori' probabilities, $\mathcal{C}$, with an evidential information, E. The method is a generalization of Bayes Theorem and is based on the formula of conditioning in Moral, Campos (1990). The generalization given here is different from the one given by Smets (1978, 1981). The main difference comes from the fact that we assume that an observation defines a consonant evidence (a possibility) and Smets works with general evidential information. Also, in our approach, we distinguish between evidential and 'a priori' information using different methods according to the particular situation.

The combination of a probability measure p about the values of X and a possibility associated with observation O : $\pi_o(a_i) = p(O|X = a_i)$, is given by the function,

$$h(a_i) = p(a_i).\pi_o(a_i).$$

We shall denote this function h by $p \times \pi_o$. After normalization, h determines the values of conditional probability,

$$p(X = a_i|O) = \frac{h(a_i)}{\sum_j h(a_j)}$$

The normalization factor may be considered as the likelihood of the 'a priori' probability given O. A very small likelihood of h may make us suspect the initial values of probability and therefore, the resulting conditional probabilities. Furthermore, in this case these values will be very sensitive to the lack of accuracy of initial probabilities.

The above expression is precisely Bayes formula, developed in two stages: first combination and after normalization. In a similar way, we shall define the combination of an 'a priori' convex set of probability distributions and an evidential information E_o as the set,

$$H = C(\{p \times \pi | p \in \mathcal{C}, \pi \in E_o\}) = \mathcal{C} \otimes E_o$$

As before, and by analogous reasons we shall assume that two combination sets, H_1 and H_2, are equivalent if $C(H_1) = C(H_2)$.

To assign probability intervals (Moral, Campos 1990) to the set H we select the extreme points of H, $h_1, ..., h_n$. Each h_k different from the null function can define a probability value, normalizing it by its likelihood,

$$p_k(X = a_i|O) = \frac{h_k(a_i)}{\sum_j h_k(a_j)}$$

We could now calculate the upper and lower probability values by means of the expression,

$$t_o{}^*(A|O) = \max_k P_k(A|O),$$

$$t_{o*}(A|O) = \min_k P_k(A|O)$$

This is equivalent to upper-lower conditioning (Dempster 1967; Fagin, Halpern 1990). But in this method there is some missing information. In effect, given that h_k is the true combination, then in this case, the probability of observation O is $\sum_j h_k(a_j)$. According to our definition of possibility, this defines a possibility about the combination functions and the corresponding conditional probabilities, given by

$$\pi(p_k(.|O)) = \sum_j h_k(x_j)$$

That is, we do not only have a set of conditional probabilities, we also have a possibility about them. This possibility also defines upper and lower probabilities: If $D \subseteq \{p_1(.|O), ..., p_m(.|O)\}$, then

$$g_o{}^*(D) = \frac{\Pi(D)}{\max_k \pi(p_k(.|O))},$$

$$g_{o*}(D) = 1 - g_o{}^*(\overline{D}).$$

Now, we define the upper and lower conditional intervals in the following way. The upper and lower values of B given observation O, are calculated by means of Choquet integral (Choquet 1953) of conditional probabilities with respect to the measures g_o^* and g_{o*}, respectively:

$$P_o^*(B) = I(P_k(B|O)/g_o{}^*),$$

$$P_{o*}(B) = I(P_k(B|O)/g_{o*}),$$

these integrals being defined in the following way,

$$I(h/g) = \int_0^\infty g(H_\alpha)d\alpha$$

where

- h is a function $h : U \longrightarrow R_o^+$
- $H_\alpha = \{x \in U | h(x) \geq \alpha\}$
- g is a monotone fuzzy measure (non necessarily additive (Sugeno 1974)).

It is important to point out that the result of the combination is the set H, not the intervals. For example, we may have the same intervals coming from pure possibilistic information or a convex set of probability distributions. However, after combining each one of them with new information, the intervals may become very different. The following example illustrates these ideas.

Example.- Let us consider a set $U = \{1, 2, 3\}$ and an obsevation O_1 such that

$$p(O_1|1) = 1, \quad p(O_1|2) = 0.5, \quad p(O_1|3) = 0.2$$

The intervals defined by this observation are

$$\begin{array}{rr} \emptyset \longrightarrow [0,0] & \{1\} \longrightarrow [0.5,1] \\ \{2\} \longrightarrow [0,0.5] & \{3\} \longrightarrow [0,0.2] \\ \{1,2\} \longrightarrow [0.8,1] & \{1,3\} \longrightarrow [0.5,1] \\ \{2,3\} \longrightarrow [0,0.5] & \{1,2,3\} \longrightarrow [1,1] \end{array}$$

Now assume that we have a convex set of probability distributions, $\mathcal{C}$, with extreme points

	1	2	3
p_1	1	0	0
p_2	0.5	0.5	0
p_3	0.5	0.3	0.2
p_4	0.8	0	0.2

The intervals associated with it are the same as before. However the information is different and it is combined in a different way. Assume now that we have observation O_2 and

$$p(O_2|1) = 0.1, \quad p(O_2|2) = 0.6, \quad p(O_2|3) = 1$$

If we assume that O_1 and O_2 are conditionally independent given the value of X, then the conjunction of these two observations gives rise to the following possibility and intervals.

$$\pi_{o_1 \wedge o_2}(1) = 0.1 \quad \pi_{o_1 \wedge o_2}(2) = 0.3 \quad \pi_{o_1 \wedge o_2}(2) = 0.2$$

$$\begin{array}{ll} \emptyset \longrightarrow [0,0] & \{1\} \longrightarrow [0,0.33] \\ \{2\} \longrightarrow [0.33,1] & \{3\} \longrightarrow [0,0.67] \\ \{1,2\} \longrightarrow [0.33,1] & \{1,3\} \longrightarrow [0,0.67] \\ \{2,3\} \longrightarrow [0.67,1] & \{1,2,3\} \longrightarrow [1,1] \end{array}$$

If we combine observation O_2 with the convex set $\mathcal{C}$, we get the convex set H with extreme points

	1	2	3
h_1	0	0	0
h_2	0.1	0	0
h_3	0.05	0.3	0
h_4	0.05	0.18	0.2
h_5	0.08	0	0.2

The corresponding normalized probabilities and possibilities are

1	2	3	π
undefined	*undefined*	*undefined*	0
1	0	0	0.1
0.14	0.86	0	0.35
0.12	0.42	0.46	0.43
0.29	0	0.71	0.28

The intervals, calculated using Choquet integral are,

$$\begin{array}{ll} \emptyset \longrightarrow [0,0] & \{1\} \longrightarrow [0.12,0.40] \\ \{2\} \longrightarrow [0.15,0.78] & \{3\} \longrightarrow [0.09,0.63] \\ \{1,2\} \longrightarrow [0.37,0.91] & \{1,3\} \longrightarrow [0.22,0.85] \\ \{2,3\} \longrightarrow [0.60,0.88] & \{1,2,3\} \longrightarrow [1,1] \end{array}$$

which are really different to the corresponding to the combination of O_1 and O_2.

The most important thing to remark in this combination method is that it is a mixture of Classical Statistics based on likelihood functions and Bayesian Statistics. When we have a probabilistic 'a priori' information then Bayes Theorem is obtained. When we do not have 'a priori' information a likelihood function or its corresponding possibility is considered. When we have an 'a priori' information consisting on a convex set of probabilities, then Bayes Theorem is applied to each individual probability but, at the same time, it is defined a likelihood about the possible probabilities. Then we are using at the same time Bayes Theorem and likelihood functions, the first is applied to transform probabilities, the second to change our belief about what is the true probability. The following example illustrates these ideas.

Example.- Assume as above that we have two urns U_1 and U_2 with red and black balls:

$U1$	99 *red*	1 *black*
$U2$	1 *red*	99 *black*

Consider that we pick up two balls with replacement from the same urn and the events are denoted as follows:

- B1 The first ball is black
- R1 The first ball is red
- B2 The second ball is black
- R2 The second ball is red

For the color of the two balls we have an 'a priori' information with two extreme probabilities, one for each urn:

	$R1 \cap R2$	$R1 \cap B2$	$B1 \cap R2$	$B1 \cap B2$
p_1	0.9801	0.0099	0.0099	0.0001
p_2	0.0001	0.0099	0.0099	0.9801

Assume now that we observe the colour of the first ball: red. This defines the following likelihood

	$R1 \cap R2$	$R1 \cap B2$	$B1 \cap R2$	$B1 \cap B2$
l	1	1	0	0

The combination of 'a priori' information and the likelihood is

	$R1 \cap R2$	$R1 \cap B2$	$B1 \cap R2$	$B1 \cap B2$
h_1	0.9801	0.099	0	0
h_2	0.0001	0.099	0	0

If we normalize the probabilities calculating the corresponding possibilities we get

	$R2$	$B2$	π
$p_1(.\|R1)$	0.99	0.01	0.99
$p_2(.\|R1)$	0.01	0.99	0.01

Observe as we have transformed each probability distribution according to Bayes rule. But also, the combination defines a possibility about which is the true probability (or what is equivalent: which is the true urn). Note also that here the probabilities for the second ball are the same as before the first ball is observed. However, knowing that the first ball is red defines a likelihood about which is the true urn, that changes our belief about the colour of the second ball. The integration of conditional probabilities and possibilities by using Choquet integral produces the following intervals:

$$\begin{array}{ll} R2 & [0.9801, 0.9900] \\ B2 & [0.0100, 0.0199] \end{array}$$

These intervals incorporate not only the changes on conditonal probabilities but also our chages on belief about the urns, that is, the bayesian updating and the likelihood information.

Acknowledgments

We are indebted to L.M. de Campos, M. Delgado and M.T. Lamata for their help in completing this work. We are also very grateful to Ph. Smets by his valuable and useful comments.

This research has been supported by the Commission of European Communities under Project DRUMS (Esprit B.R.A. 3085).

References

Campos L.M. de, Lamata M.T., Moral S. (1988) Logical connectives for combining fuzzy measures. In: Methodologies for Intelligent Systems (Z.W. Ras, L. Saitta, eds.) Elsevier (New York) 11,18.

Campos L.M. de, Lamata M.T., Moral S.(1990) The concept of conditional fuzzy measure. International Journal of Intelligent Systems 5, 237-246.

Choquet G. (1953/54) Theorie of capacities. Ann. Inst. Fourier 5, 131-292.

Dempster A.P. (1967) Upper and lower probabilities induced by a multivalued mapping. Ann. Math. Statist. 38, 325-339.

Dubois D., Prade H. (1988). Possibility Theory. An Approach to Computerized Processing of Information. Plenum Press (New York).

Fagin R., Halpern J.Y. (1990) A new approach to updating beliefs. Research Report RJ 7222. IBM Almaden Research Center.

Moral S., Campos L.M. de (1990) Updating uncertain information. Proceedings 3rd. IPMU Conference, Paris 1990, 452-454.

Pearl J. (1989) Reasoning with belief functions: a critical assessment. Tech. Rep. R-136. University of California, Los Angeles.

Shafer G. (1976) A Mathematical Theory of Evidence. Princeton University Press (Princeton).

Smets Ph. (1982) Possibilistic Inference from Statistical Data. Proceedings of the Second World Conference on Mathematics at the Service of Man (A. Ballester, eds.) 611-613.

Smets Ph. (1978) Un Modele Mathematico-Statistique Simulant le Processus du Diagnostic Medical. Doctoral Disertation. Universite Libre de Bruxelles, Bruxelles.

Smets Ph. (1981) Medical Diagnosis: Fuzzy Sets and Degrees of Belief. Fuzzy Sets and Systems 5, 259-266.

Sugeno M. (1974) Theory of Fuzzy Integrals and its Applications. Ph. D. Thesis, Tokyo Institute of Technology.

Tessen B. (1989) Interval Representation of Uncertainty in Artificial Intelligence. Ph. D. Thesis, Departament of Informatics, University of Bergen, Norway.

Zadeh L.A. (1978) Fuzzy sets as a basis for a theory of possibility. Fuzzy Sets and Systems 1, 3-28.

A Probabilistic Analysis of Marker-Passing Techniques for Plan-Recognition

Glenn Carroll
Department of Computer Science
Brown University

Eugene Charniak
Department of Computer Science
Brown University

Abstract

Useless paths are a chronic problem for marker-passing techniques. We use a probabilistic analysis to justify a method for quickly identifying and rejecting useless paths. Using the same analysis, we identify key conditions and assumptions necessary for marker-passing to perform well.

1 Introduction

A recognition problem is one of inferring the presence of some entity from some input, typically from observing the presence of other entities and the relations between them. We will make the common assumption that high-level recognition is accomplished by selecting an appropriate *schema* from a schema library. A schema is a generalized internal description of a class of entities in terms of their parts, their properties, and the relations between them. In the schema selection paradigm, to recognize a "foo" in the input is to create a schema instance foo1 of type foo and assign a high degree of belief in the proposition that foo1 exists. (Henceforth we will assign the degree of belief in the existence of a schema instance to the proposition that the instance is of the appropriate type, e.g., that foo1 is of type foo.) In plan recognition, the generalized plans are schemas. While the system which we will discuss has been applied to plan recognition in the context of story understanding, we will continue to talk of schema, since we wish to emphasize that our system is applicable to high-level recognition in general.

A crucial problem faced by schema selection is that of searching the schema library for the right schema; typically a single piece of local evidence is multiply ambiguous as to the schema which it could indicate. For example, an act of getting a rope might fit into many schemas.

One of the few concrete suggestions here has been *marker passing* (Alterman [1985]; Charniak [1983]; Charniak [1986]; Collins & Quillian [1969]; Hendler [1988]; Norvig [1987a]). Marker-passing uses a breadth-first search to find paths between concepts in an associative network made up of concepts and their part-subpart relations. In our case, the concepts will be schemas, i.e. plans and/or actions. The idea is that a path between two schemas suggests which schema(s) to consider for recognition. For example, a knob instance and a hinge instance might suggest a door (instance); since there are links between the schemas door and knob and between door and hinge in the associative network (they are part-subpart relations), there is therefore a path from knob to door to hinge. Unfortunately, most marker-passer systems have found many more bad paths, suggesting incorrect schemas, than good ones (Charniak [1986]; Norvig [1987b]). We will show in this paper that the good/bad path ratio can be raised quite high by exploiting probability information; we realize this benefit by (cheaply) controlling the marker-passer's search, both extending it in promising directions and terminating it in unpromising ones.

In this paper we will give a probabilistic account of marker passing. This account will have two goals — first it should shed further light on when marker-passing is an appropriate technique, and second it should show how to improve the performance of marker-passing algorithms by increasing the likelihood that the paths generated will, in fact, suggest the correct schema. In section 2 we will consider schema evaluation within a probabilistic framework. That is, given we have a potential schema, how do we evaluate the probability that it is the correct explanation of the input. In particular, we will be adopting a Bayesian network (or belief network) formulation of the problem, so the probability distributions correspond to DAGs with probabilities associated with each node. Section 3 will then be concerned with schema selection, i.e., how our marker passing system works, and how the schema suggestions (paths) from the marker-passer map to Bayesian networks. In Section 4 we will show how to use probability information from the knowledge base to intelligently limit the marker-passing search. Specifically, we will describe how to calculate on the fly a measure which is an upper bound on the joint probability of the schemas which a candidate path suggests. Thanks to properties of the marker-passer paths and our probabilistic model, we can avoid constructing and evaluating a Bayesian network to evaluate each path, an NP-hard problem (Cooper [1987]), so our evaluation need not be expensive. This section has the bulk of the new work in the paper. We summarize and explain results in section 5.

The opening sections of this paper alternate somewhat irregularly between the marker-passer and the Bayesian network; while it might appear to be simpler to fully describe first one and then the other, this would leave much of what we have to say completely unmotivated and very likely obscure. Once we reach section 4, we treat the two systems together, showing how paths map to Bayesian networks, and how path calculations yield an upper bound on the joint probability of the nodes in the Bayesian network.

2 Probabilistic Schema Evaluation

We adopt a standard first-order theory of schema in which a schema is a set and asserting that an entity is an instance of that schema is asserting that it is an element of the set. We use the predicate inst for this purpose.

(inst *instance schema*).

Schemas are related in the usual isa-hierarchy (subset) as in

(isa *specific-schema general-schema*).

In this paper we assume that isa relations form a tree, not a lattice, and thus all the immediate isa subsets of a given parent are disjoint.

Slots or roles in schemas are represented using functions from a schema instance to the slot-filler schema instance. Equality is used to assert that a particular entity fills that role. For example, to assert that a particular store store-25 fills the store-of role in supermarket-shopping-3 we assert

(== (store-of supermarket-shopping-3) store-25)

Facts about the relations between the parts of a schema are then universally quantified facts about the corresponding functions. For example, to say that every store-of a supermarket-shopping must be filled with an instance of a supermarket (another schema) we would say

(inst ?x supermarket-shopping) → (inst (store-of ?x) supermarket)

To abbreviate this we will write: (role supermarket-shopping store-of supermarket). More generally,

(role $schema_1$ *slot* $schema_2$)

states that anything which fills *slot* in $schema_1$ must be an instance of $schema_2$. Note that role is not a predicate of our plan recognition language, but is rather an abbreviation for formulas of the above form.

In our probabilistic version we will determine the probability of a plan by embedding inst and == statements in a Bayesian network. We will not attempt to summarize Bayesian networks but rather will assume the reader has a working knowledge of them. (See (Pearl [1988]) for a good introduction.) Equality (==) statements will become random variables with possible values 1 and 0 (true and false). inst statements become random variables which can take any maximally specific schema type as their value[1]. Thus the probability of the statement (inst sms1 supermarket-shopping) would become the probability that the instance sms1 takes on the value supermarket-shopping. However, often we will talk as if the statement (inst sms1 supermarket-shopping) appears in the network (with values 1 and 0). Most of the time the two representations are interchangeable.

We intend our prior and conditional probabilities to come from a sample space of explanations for some large corpus of stories. For example, the prior probability of a supermarket-shopping plan would be the number of supermarket-shopping plans that appear in our set of explanatory plans, divided by the total number of explanatory plans. See (Goldman [1991]) for a detailed description of the probability model.

3 Probabilistic Schema Selection

3.1 Marker-Passing

Marker-passing searches for paths between schemas in a graph whose nodes are schemas and whose arcs are isa and role statements. Marker-passing works as follows: the marker-passer is given some schema, derived from a new inst statement, e.g., (inst supermarket1 supermarket). It places a mark on that schema, and then proceeds in breadth-first order to place marks on all the neighbors in the graph, their neighbors' neighbors, and so on. For example, our supermarket schema has two neighbors, supermarket-shopping, which is connected by the statement (role supermarket-shopping store-of supermarket) and store-, which is connected by the statement (isa supermarket store-). Both of these would be marked after supermarket, and then their neighbors would be marked. Each mark has a numeric value, which generally diminishes according to its distance from the original mark (c.f., "zorch" in (Charniak [1986])). This value is used to cut off marker-passing, since otherwise we would continue until the entire graph was covered. For our value, we

[1]Thus, the sum over all possible values is 1.0, which would not be true if they could take on non-maximally specific types.

use an upper bound on the schemas and relations suggested by the path; we will be precise in section 4. After marking a node, the marker-passer checks for marks from some other origin on the same node. If such a mark is found, both it and the new mark are back-traced to their respective origins, and the resulting lists of statements are glued together to form a path. For example, suppose we found a mark on supermarket-shopping which had originated at go. We would have as a path:

```
(inst supermarket2 supermarket)
(role supermarket-shopping store-of
supermarket)
(isa shopping supermarket-shopping)
(role shopping go-step go)
(inst go1 go)
```

We include the original inst statements, even though the marker-passer does not, strictly speaking, pass marks over these links. It will be convenient for us to refer to them as part of the path, and they serve to disambiguate this path from other paths which may have the same links but different origins.

The marker-passer returns a list of all the paths which it found once the marking has terminated. For more detail on how marker-passing works, see (Hendler [1988]).

3.2 Valid Paths and Interpretations

Intuitively, we wish to interpret a path as a claim about how its ends are related to each other. In order to do this, we need to translate the path through the semantic network (a list of inst, isa, and role statements) into a set of Bayesian network nodes (inst and equality statements) and arcs. Before we describe this mapping, we must confess that our marker-passing system is not precisely the very simple one described above. We employ a DFA at each node in our network to control the marker-passing, allowing us to restrict the form of paths which we generate and report. This allows us to skip paths which are malformed in the sense that either they cannot be translated into a consistent set of statements in our schema theory, or they embody demonstrably bad schema suggestions. A valid path is one which is not malformed in the above sense.

Notation. By isa- we mean isa with the order of arguments reversed. So,

(isa *specific-frame general-frame*) iff (isa- *general-frame specific-frame*)

Similarly for role and role-:

(role *filler-frame filled-frame slot*) iff (role- *filled-frame filler-frame slot*)

In future discussions we will often fail to distinguish between the predicates and their "-" versions.

Definition 3.1. *A* valid path *from* i_1 *to* i_2 *has the form*

(inst i_1 s_1) ($pred_1$ s_1 s_2) ... ($pred_n$ s_n s_{n+1}) (inst i_2 s_{n+1})

where

- $pred_i$ *may be one of* isa, isa-, role *and* role-,
- *at least one* role *appears among the* $pred_i$.
- *no sequence* (isa ...)(isa- ...) *appears among the* $pred_i$
- *if* $pred_i$ *is a* role-, *then no* $pred_k$ *where* $k > i$ *can be a* role

Our last two restrictions prohibit *isa-plateaus*, where an isa is followed by an isa-, and slot-filler valleys, where a role- is followed by a role, possibly with isa's between them. We have calculated, off-line, the joint probability of the statements associated with paths which violate the above restrictions; in all cases the joint probability falls below our threshold for being worth computing[2].

We will now define the statements associated with a path P, written $S(P)$.

Notation. By $P[n]$ we mean the nth statement of a path P.

The *relevant instance* at $P[n]$ (written $I(P[n])$) is defined as follows:

Definition 3.2.

1. *If (inst i s)* $= P[n]$, *then* $I(P[n]) = i$.
2. *If (isa* s_1 s_2*)* $= P[n]$ *and* $I(P[n-1]) = i$, *then* $I(P[n]) = i$. *Similarly for isa-.*
3. *If (role* s_1 *slot* s_2*)* $= P[n]$ *then* $I(P[n]) = i'$, *where* i' *is a new constant term.*

$S(P)$ is defined as follows:

Definition 3.3.

1. *If (inst i t)* $= P[n]$, *then (inst i t)* $\in S(P)$.
2. *If (isa* s_1 s_2*)* $= P[n]$ *and (inst i t)* $\in S(P)$, *then (inst i* s_2*)* $\in S(P)$. *Similarly for isa-.*
3. *If (role* s_1 *slot* s_2*)* $= P[n]$, *then* {*(inst* i_n s_2*) (==(slot* i_n*) i))*} $\subset S(P)$, *where* $i_n = I(P[n])$. *Similarly for role-.*

Intuitively we wish to interpret a path P as a claim about how its ends are related to each other. "Every $s \in S(P)$ is true" is intended to be the formalization of

[2] To summarize: for isa-plateaus, the left and right side of the Bayesian net in which we embed the statements are independent, so they cannot support one another. For the slot-filler valleys, there is no evidence to support the object which must appear in two schemas. See (Charniak & Carroll [1991]) for details.

```
(inst supermarket2 supermarket)
(role supermarket-shopping store-of
supermarket)
(isa- shopping supermarket-shopping)
(role go shopping go-step) \nopagebreak
(inst go1 go)
```

FIG. 3.1. An Example Marker-passer Path.

```
(inst supermarket2 supermarket)
(== (store-of shopping3) supermarket2)
(inst shopping3 supermarket-shopping)
(inst shopping3 shopping)
(== (go-step shopping3) go1)
(inst go1 go)
```

FIG. 3.2. $S(P)$ For Example Path.

this claim. For example, the path in Figure 3.1 would have as its $S(P)$ the statements shown in Figure 3.2. We actually need only a subset of $S(P)$, namely the *relevant statements* associated with P, (written $RS(P)$) which we will define below. First we give two more definitions necessary for defining $RS(P)$.

We define isa* as

DEFINITION 3.4. *$\forall t, t'$ (isa* t t') iff ((isa t t') or $\exists t''$[(isa t t'') and (isa* t'' t')]).*

We define the *relevant type* of an inst (written $RT(i)$) to be the most specific schema type of the node; more formally,

DEFINITION 3.5. *$RT(i) = t$ such that* (inst i t) $\in S(P)$ *and $\forall t'$((inst i t') $\in S(P) \rightarrow$ (isa* t t') or $t = t'$).*

We define the *relevant statements* associated with P as

DEFINITION 3.6.

1. *If (inst i t) $\in S(P)$ and $RT(i) = t$ then (inst i t) $\in RS(P)$.*
2. *If (== (slot i) j) $\in S(P)$, then (== (slot i) j) $\in RS(P)$.*

In effect, we remove superfluous instance statements from $S(P)$, whose statements are stll implied by those retained in $RS(P)$.

Our formal measure of a path P is defined by embedding the members of $RS(P)$ in a Bayesian network, and then evaluating the probability that each node is true, given the evidence. In general there may be several paths for the same entities, indicating alternative possible plans. In what follows we will be looking at Bayesian networks in which there is only one $RS(P)$. The idea is that we are interested in getting a preliminary guess as to how likely a particular interpretation–an $RS(P)$– is, and we can do this without detailed comparisons with its competitors.

3.3 Vertebrate Bayesian Networks

With each path P we will associate a Bayesian network with a particular structure which will prove important to our calculations. We call such networks *vertebrate* Bayesian networks, because they have *spines*.

DEFINITION 3.7. *A Bayesian network is a "vertebrate" Bayesian network iff it consists of two parts, to be defined below, called the* spine, *and the* interior.

Intuitively, a spine is the geometrical backbone of its Bayesian network.

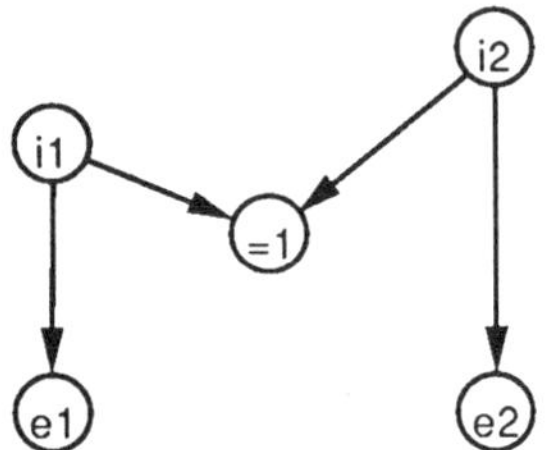

FIG. 3.3. The basic spine.

NOTATION. We use i_j to name inst nodes.

Recall that equality nodes represent slot-filler relationships for us.

NOTATION. We use $=_j$ to name equality nodes, indicating in this case that the parent node i_j is the slot filler.

There are other types of nodes which act as evidence for our equality and inst nodes. For example, the appearance of a word in text provides evidence for the existence of a particular inst. Although these nodes come in several flavors, we can treat them generically for our purposes, so we will name all of them simply "evidence" nodes.

NOTATION. We use e_j to name evidence nodes.

Our definition describes a structure topologically; thus, we imply that a node subscripted by j is not equal to any node subscripted by k, where $k \neq j$.

Legal spines are recursively defined as follows:

DEFINITION 3.8.

Base step: *Any Bayesian network whose node set is $\{i_1, i_2, =_1, e_1, e_2\}$ and whose edge set is $\{i_1 \rightarrow e_1, i_2 \rightarrow e_2, i_1 \rightarrow =_1, i_2 \rightarrow =_1\}$ is a spine. See Figure 3.3.*

Recursion: *If S is a spine with the nodes i_1 and e_1 and the edge $i_1 \rightarrow e_1$, then S' is a spine, where*

$$N(S') = N(S) \cup \{i', =_{i'}\} \quad (1)$$

and

$$
\begin{aligned}
E(S') &= \{E(S) - \{i_1 \rightarrow e_1\}\} \cup \\
&\quad \{i_1 \rightarrow i', i' \rightarrow e_1, \\
&\quad i_1 \rightarrow =_{i'}, i' \rightarrow =_{i'}\} \qquad (2)
\end{aligned}
$$

See Figure 3.4.

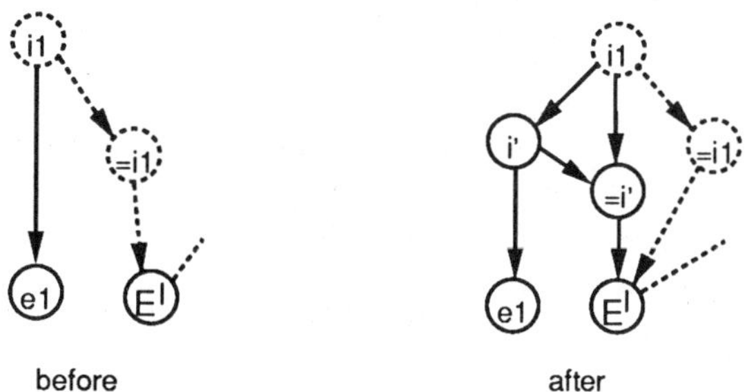

FIG. 3.4. Before and after nodes are added to a spine.

As for the "interior" of a vertebrate Bayesian network, intuitively it is the evidence supporting the equality nodes of the vertebrate Bayesian network. We may assume, without loss of generality that there is only once such evidence node E^I. More formally:

DEFINITION 3.9. *If V is a vertebrate Bayesian network with spine S, and S has the non-evidence nodes N and the evidence nodes E, then the interior of V is an evidence node E^I disjoint from E and a set of edges D from every equality node in N to E^I.*

The assumption that there will be supporting evidence, some E^I node, is the crucial one for marker-passing. When there is no evidence, the posterior probabilities of the abductive hypotheses generated from our paths turn out to be abysmally low; plainly put, they are bad guesses. In general, we believe that

CLAIM 3.1. *A domain is suitable for search by means of marker-passing only if there will usually be supporting evidence for paths returned by the marker-passer.*

We will support our claim by showing that, in our domain, which meets the evidence condition, we can increase the ratio of good to bad paths returned from the marker-passer to better than 90%. Our claim should not be interpreted as saying that the marker-passer has no responsibility for the quality of paths it returns; quite the opposite is true. Most of the remainder of this paper will focus on the calculations which allow us to determine whether or not a path is worthwhile, *assuming that there is evidence for it.* If we could not make these calculations, then doubtless many of the paths which would be returned would in fact *fail* to have associated evidence. We can safely throw them out because they are bad paths *regardless* of whether they have evidence.

3.4 Relating Paths to Networks

We will now show that each path corresponds to a unique vertebrate Bayesian network, and that the joint probability of $S(P)$ in the network can be calculated from each step of the path.

THEOREM 3.1. *If P is a valid path, then there exists a unique vertebrate Bayesian network V such that the statements in $RS(P)$ have formulas in one-to-one correspondence with the non-evidence nodes of V.*

Proof. The proof is by induction on the length of the path.

The basis follows from the definition of the simplest spine, and $RS(P)$ for the shortest valid path. The spine and $RS(P)$ have one == node (statement, respectively) and two inst nodes (statements, respectively). For the induction step, suppose we have proved there is a unique network for P. Let P' have the same structure as P, with an extra isa statement inserted in some location which does not violate our constraints for path validity. We first note that isa statements do not add statements to $RS(P)$, they only change the schemas named in statements already there. Hence, if we have a vertebrate Bayesian network for P, we can use the same structure (with different relevant types for some nodes) for P'.

If P' is P with an extra role statement (again, inserted in some location which respects path validity), this corresponds to applying clause 2, the recursion step, of the definition of a spine. The role statement adds an == statement and an inst statement to $RS(P)$, and applying clause 2 adds the corresponding nodes to the network. Since each step determines a unique transformation and each transformation results in a unique vertebrate Bayesian network, P corresponds to a unique vertebrate Bayesian network, which we call $V(P)$, or, where unambiguous, just V. □

From the above, it should be obvious that we can construct a vertebrate Bayesian network by sequentially processing a path from left to right, adding new nodes and arcs for each role statement we come across, and changing the relevant type of our last added node when we encounter an isa-. We will use this fact, together with some distribution properties of vertebrate Bayesian networks to calculate our measure of path utility without vertebrate Bayesian network corresponding to the path.

4 Path Calculations

4.1 The Spinal Contribution

Our calculations will not compute the exact joint probability of the network which we construct. Instead we will compute an upper bound on the joint probability,

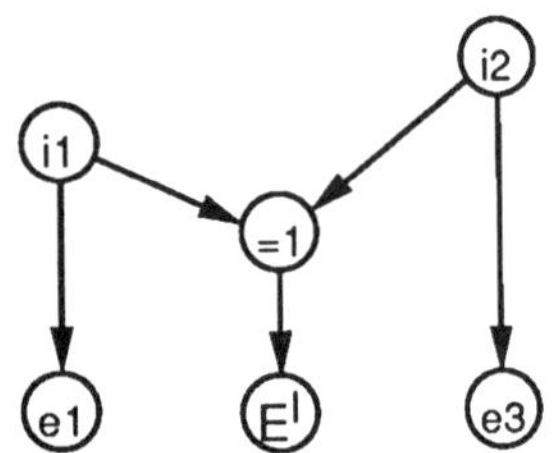

FIG. 4.1. The basic vertebrate Bayesian network.

under assumptions to be detailed below, which we call the ***spinal contribution.*** We will define the spinal contribution momentarily, in terms of the joint probability of the network. To begin with, the exact joint probability of the simplest vertebrate Bayesian network (the basic spine with an added interior evidence node, E^I, pictured in Figure 4.1) is

$$\frac{p(e_1|i_1)p(E^I| =_1)p(e_3|i_2)p(i_1)p(i_2)p(=_1 |i_1, i_2)}{p(e_1, E^I, e_3)} \quad (3)$$

We use conditional probability and independence to transform the denominator into

$$p(e_1)p(e_3)p(E^I|e_1, e_3) \quad (4)$$

For the numerator, we note that

$$p(e_1|i_1) = p(i_1|e_1)p(e_1)/p(i_1) \quad (5)$$

and similarly for $p(e_3|i_2)$.

The slot-filler term, $p(=_1 |i_1, i_2)$, requires some discussion. Recall that role statements specify a particular type for each slot that a schema has. The probability that i_1 fills this particular slot in i_2 is the probability that any two things of the specified type are equal. This, in turn, is equal to the prior probability of any two things being equal, divided by the prior probability of a thing being the specified type.

NOTATION. We write $p(==)$ for the prior probability of any two things being equal.

This allows us to rewrite the last term in our formula as follows:

$$p(=_1 |i_1, i_2) = p(==)/p(i_1) \quad (6)$$

Applying the substitutions in equations 4, 5, and 6 to 3, and then cancelling and regrouping yields

$$\left(\frac{p(i_1|e_1)p(i_2|e_3)}{p(i_1)}\right)\left(\frac{p(==)p(E^I| =_1)}{p(E^I|e_1, e_3)}\right) \quad (7)$$

The right-hand group of terms will appear in the exact calculations for every vertebrate Bayesian network, with the difference that E^I may be conditioned on more nodes, if they are present. By our earlier assumptions about the distributions for E^I, this group has an upper bound of 1.0.

The left-hand group of terms we call the *spinal contribution* of our joint probability; more generally, any terms not included in the bounded group, will be part of the spinal contribution, and calculating it will be the focus of the rest of this section. Since those terms not in the spinal contribution have an upper bound of 1.0, the spinal contribution is an upper bound on the joint probability of the network.

4.2 Calculations

THEOREM 4.1. *As a path P is traversed, our measure of the spinal contribution of the corresponding vertebrate Bayesian network fragment, $SC(V)$, can be computed recursively in the following manner:*

1. *The initial value, corresponding to the* (inst i_1 s_1) *node/statement* [3] *is $p(i_1|e_1)$, our current belief in the node.*
2. *As each subsequent statement is traversed, we compute the new value by multiplying the current value by the number given in table 4.1.*

TABLE 4.1. Spinal Contribution Multipliers

Link	*Multiplier*
(role s_1 slot s_2)	$p(s_1)/p(s_2)$
(role- s_1 slot s_2)	*1.0*
(isa s_1 s_2)	*1.0*
(isa- s_1 s_2)	$p(s_2)/p(s_1)$
(inst i_1 s_1)	$p(i_1|e_1)/p(s_1)$

Proof. Omitted due to space limitations. See (Charniak & Carroll [1991]) . □

4.3 Internal Calculations

Marker-passing produces whole paths as output; internally, however, it builds these from two half-paths which resulted from passing marks from two differing origins (at different times). We would like to use our measure of spinal contribution to cut off the depth of marker-passing, which requires that we compute it as the half-path is built, before the two halves are put together. We now show that this is possible, and that the calculations for an entire path, above, comprise the bulk of the work for computing half-paths. Our lemma concerns the spine, not the entire vertebrate Bayesian network, since the interior evidence node is not part of our spinal contribution.

DEFINITION 4.1. *By* cleaving *a vertebrate Bayesian network graph at some* inst *node n, we mean that*

- *the cleaved node n appears in both halves*

[3]This is a node in the Bayesian network, and a statement in the path. Since we will be discussing probabilities from now on, we will generally call them nodes.

- *the left half includes the evidence node* e_1*, all* inst *nodes* i_1 *through* i_n *and all arcs between them, and similarly for the right half*
- *equality nodes with both parents among* inst *nodes* i_1 *through* i_n *and all arcs incident to them are in the left half, and similarly for the right*

See Figure 4.2.

LEMMA 4.2. *A spine can be cleaved into two halves* H_1 *and* H_2 *at any* inst *node, such that the spinal contribution of the whole graph is given by*

$$SC(V) = SC(H_1) \times SC(H_2)/p(n) \qquad (8)$$

where n is the node at which the graph is cleaved.

Proof. Omitted due to space limitations. See (Charniak & Carroll [1991]) . □

Lemma 4.2 means that we can track the spinal contribution incrementally as we extend a half-path. When the measure drops below a threshold, T, we can cut safely cut off marker-passing; that is, we will miss no complete paths whose measure would be above T^2. Currently we have T set at 30. We have arrived at this value through experimentation with a set of paths generated from a set of stories which we use for debugging and tuning our system. Generally, there is a large gap, a factor of 10 or more, between the spinal contribution of those paths which have the right explanations and those which do not. While our system does rely on the prior probabilities for our schema, this gap suggests that we can get by with priors that are only approximately correct.

5 Results

We have employed our marker-passer in the Wimp3 story understanding system (Goldman [1991]) to find explanatory plans. The results quoted in table 5.1 are those obtained both on Wimp3's debugging corpus of 25 1-to-4 line "stories" and on its evaluation corpus[4] of 25 stories. We counted paths at four points in the flow of control. First, we counted paths which left the marker passer. As described above, we integrated the probability valuation of paths into the marker-passing mechanism itself, using it to control the spread of marks. This makes it impossible to estimate how many paths were eliminated due to low probability values. Likewise, we cannot say how many paths were eliminated by employing DFA's to prohibit generation of invalid paths. We can only give the total number of paths returned, with the invalid and low probability paths already weeded out. Second, we counted paths which were "asserted", i.e., used for forward-chaining and Bayesian network construction. These are paths which passed various secondary filters reported in (Carroll & Charniak [1989]). Third, we counted paths whose resulting statements were actually evaluated using our Bayesian network evaluation mechanism. Some paths could be eliminated without evaluation, as we will describe shortly. Finally, we counted those paths which we approved after evaluation; for a path to be approved the posterior probability of the suggested plans given the evidence had to be 1,000 times higher than the prior probability for the plans. The ratio of approved paths to asserted paths was 68% for the debugging corpus, and 59% for the test corpus, a significant improvement on the 10% good to bad path ratio reported earlier, (Charniak Neat 1986 Norvig 1987 Berkeley]) and strong support for our claim that the key to the viability of marker-passing is the supporting evidence, our E^I.

TABLE 5.1. Results Summary

corpus	paths reported	paths asserted	paths evaluated	paths approved
debug	985	115	83	78
test	747	109	68	64

Our analysis suggested one more improvement which could be made. As we commented earlier, the marker passer's probability calculations are an upper bound, based on the assumption that there is evidence in favor of the path (other than the nodes at either end). That is, after the marker passer produces an acceptable path P, Wimp3 constructs a Bayesian network which includes $RS(P)$. Among the paths which were not approved, we found that there was often no evidence supporting some of the statements in $RS(P)$. While we cannot determine whether evidence is missing before network construction, we can do so before network evaluation. While the former takes time linear in the size of the network (making reasonable assumptions about the process), the latter, in general, takes exponential time (and is NP-hard). Indeed, network evaluation accounts for approximately 90% of Wimp3's running time, and thus the only really bad paths are those which cannot be removed before network evaluation and are not approved afterwards. Weeding out paths with no evidence accounts for the difference between paths which were asserted–used for network construction–and paths which were evaluated. A combined total of 151 paths had to be evaluated by Wimp3, and, of these, all but 9 were good, for a percentage of about 94%. This leads us to extend our claim to say that: *A domain is suitable for search by means of marker-passing only if there will usually be supporting evidence for paths returned by the marker-passer, or paths without evidence can be cheaply identified.*

[4]The debugging corpus is used for testing and tuning of parameters. The evaluation corpus is for evaluation only, and is therefore a cleaner test, in some sense.

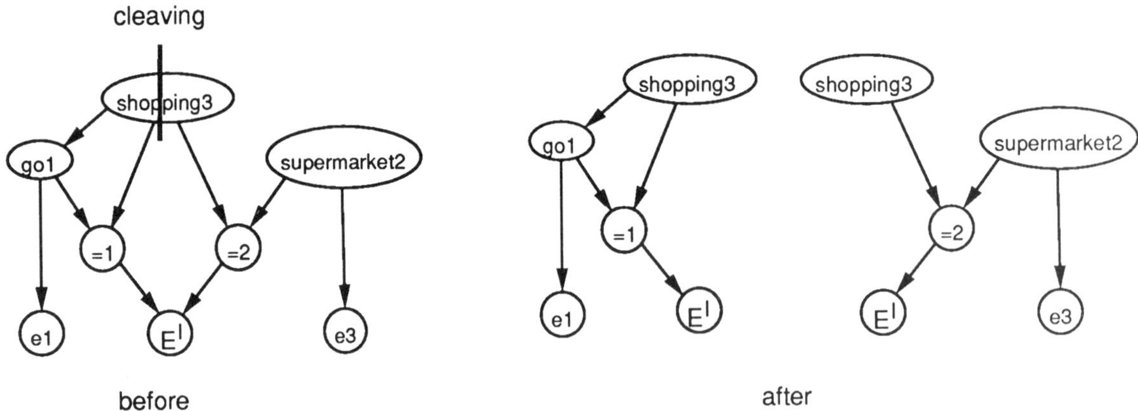

FIG. 4.2. Cleaving a vertebrate Bayesian network.

Acknowledgements

This work has been supported by the National Science Foundation under grant IRI-8911122 and by the Office of Naval Research, under contract N00014-88-K-0589.

References

Alterman, Richard. [1985], "A dictionary based on concept coherence," *Artificial Intelligence* 25, 153–186.

Carroll, Glenn & Charniak, Eugene [1989], "Finding plans with a marker-passer," *Proceedings of the Plan-recognition Workshop, 1989*.

Charniak, Eugene [1983], "Passing markers: A theory of contextual influence in language comprehension," *Cognitive Science* 7.

Charniak, Eugene [1986], "A Single-Semantic-Process Theory of Parsing," Department of Computer Science, Brown University, Technical Report.

Charniak, Eugene & Carroll, Glenn [1991], "A Probabilistic Analysis of Marker-Passing Techniques for Plan-Recognition," Department of Computer Science, Brown University, Technical Report.

Collins, Alan & Quillian, M. Ross [1969], "Retrieval time from semantic memory," *Journal of Verbal Learning and Verbal Behavior* 8, 240–248.

Cooper, Gregory F. [1987], "Probabilistic Inference Using Belief Networks is NP-hard," Stanford University, Technical Report KSL-87-27 Medical Computer Science Group.

Goldman, Robert [1991], "A Probabilistic Approach to Language Understanding," Department of Computer Science, Brown University, Technical Report.

Hendler, James A. [1988], *Integrated Marker-Passing and Problem-Solving*, Lawrence Erlbaum Associates, Hillsdale New Jersey.

Norvig, Peter [1987a], "Inference in text understanding," *Proceedings of the Seventh National Conference on Artificial Intelligence*.

Norvig, Peter [1987b], "Unified Theory of Inference for Text Understanding," Computer Science Division, University of California Berkeley, Report No. 87/339.

Pearl, Judea [1988], *Probabilistic Reasoning in Intelligent Systems: Networks of Plausible Inference*, Morgan Kaufmann, Los Altos, Calf..

Symbolic Probabilistic Inference with Continuous Variables

Kuo-Chu Chang and Robert Fung
Advanced Decision Systems
1500 Plymouth Street
Mountain View, California 94043-1230

Abstract

Research on Symbolic Probabilistic Inference (SPI) [2, 3] has provided an algorithm for resolving general queries in Bayesian networks. SPI applies the concept of dependency-directed backward search to probabilistic inference, and is incremental with respect to both queries and observations. Unlike traditional Bayesian network inferencing algorithms, SPI algorithm is goal directed, performing only those calculations that are required to respond to queries. Research to date on SPI applies to Bayesian networks with discrete-valued variables and does not address variables with continuous values.

In this paper[1], we extend the SPI algorithm to handle Bayesian networks made up of continuous variables where the relationships between the variables are restricted to be "linear gaussian". We call this variation of the SPI algorithm, SPI Continuous (SPIC). SPIC modifies the three basic SPI operations: multiplication, summation, and substitution. However, SPIC retains the framework of the SPI algorithm, namely building the search tree and recursive query mechanism and therefore retains the goal-directed and incrementality features of SPI.

1 Introduction

The Bayesian networks technology provides a language for representing uncertain beliefs and inference algorithms for drawing sound conclusions from such representations. A Bayesian network is a directed, acyclic graph in which the nodes represent random variables, and the arcs between the nodes represent possible probabilistic dependence between the variables. The success of the technology is in part due to the development of efficient probabilistic inference algorithms [5, 6, 7]. These algorithms have for the most part been designed to efficiently compute the posterior probability of each node or the result of simple arbitrary queries. They have not efficiently addressed the more general problem of answering multiple queries with respect to differing sets of evidence.

Recent research in Symbolic Probabilistic Inference (SPI) [2, 3] has made a significant step in this direction. Unlike traditional Bayesian network inference algorithms, SPI algorithm is goal directed, performing only those calculations that are required to respond to queries. In addition, SPI is incremental with respect to both queries and observations. However, the research to date on SPI applies only to Bayesian networks with discrete-valued variables.

There have been several inference algorithms designed to handle networks that are made up of continuous variables where the relationships between the variables are restricted to be "linear gaussian". The algorithms include the distributed algorithm [7] and the influence diagram approach [4, 8].

In this paper, we extend the SPI algorithm to perform this function—handle Bayesian networks with continuous linear gaussian variables. We call the extension, SPI Continuous (SPIC). The framework of this algorithm is the same as that for SPI. However, the basic SPI operations of multiplication, integration and substitution are quite different. Because SPIC stays within the SPI framework, the goal-directed and incrementality features of the algorithm are preserved.

The paper is organized as follows. Section 2 briefly summarize the SPI algorithm which includes the construction of the SPI node tree and the recursive query processing. Section 3 describes the new algorithm with continuous variables. The representation are described as well as the "basic" operations. Finally, some concluding remarks are given in Section 4.

[1]This work is based on research supported by WRDC under Contract F33615-90-C-1482.

2 Overview of the SPI Algorithm

The SPI algorithm consists of several major processing steps. The first step is to organize the nodes of a Bayesian network into a tree structure for query processing. We call these structures SPI trees. In the second step, queries are directed to the root node of the SPI tree. The query is decomposed into queries for the node's subtrees. This recursive procedure continues until a particular query can be answered at the node at which it is directed. The answer is then computed and returned to the next higher level in the SPI tree. Once a node has responses from all of its subtrees it can compute its own response to its predecessor node. This process terminates when the root node processes all the responses from its subtrees.

An SPI tree is constructed by organizing the nodes of a Bayesian network into a tree structure. The only constraint on the construction process is that if there is an arc between two nodes in the original network, then one of the nodes must be a direct or indirect predecessor of the other in the SPI tree. This constraint allows many possible SPI trees.

The first step in building a SPI tree is to choose the root node. This done by computing the maximum node to node distance for each node. The node that has the smallest maximum distance is chosen as the root node. This heuristic is designed to produce a "bushy" SPI tree which can take advantage of distributed processing. The second step is to use maximum cardinality search [9] to build the tree from the root node. This step constructs the tree based on the connectivity principle and guarantees satisfaction of the tree construction constraint.

The general format for a query received by SPI is as a conditional probability, namely, $P\{X|Y\}$, where X and Y are sub sets of nodes in the Bayesian networks. To be processed by SPI, queries of this form are first transformed into another format. The format consists of two set of nodes L and M which satisfy:

$$M = (X \cup Y) \cap D(L) \qquad (1)$$

where $X = M \cap L$, $Y = M \setminus L$, and $D(L)$ is the dimension of the distribution associated with the node set L. Intuitively, L represents the minimum set of node distributions needed to respond to the query and M is dimension of the desired response. L and M can be computed in linear time and are simple to implement [3]. Figure 1 and 2 show a simple Bayesian network and the corresponding SPI tree. For example, if the query is to find the joint probability of a_1 and c_2, the query being sent to the root node will be consisting of $L = \{a_1, a_2, c_1, c_2\}$ and $M = \{a_1, c_2\}$.

The heart of the SPI algorithm is as follows; at any node i, a request arrives for a probability distribution represented by L and M, the algorithm responds to the request by computing the "generalized" distribu-

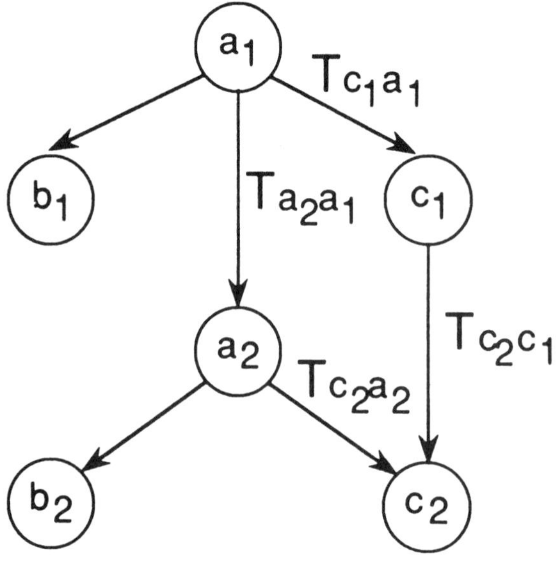

Figure 1: An Example Network

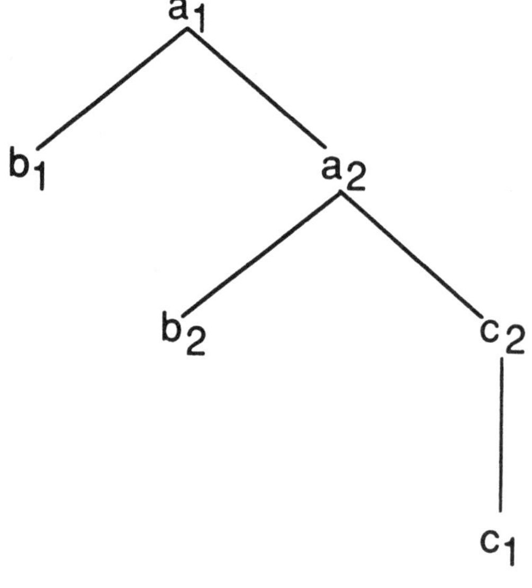

Figure 2: The SPI tree

tion $Q(M)$ [3]. $Q(M)$ is obtained by multiplying the distributions in node L and summing over dimensions $L \setminus M$. If such a distribution had already been computed earlier and cached, it can be returned immediately. However, usually it will be necessary to send requests to node's successors in the SPI tree in order to compute the response. It is obvious that if a particular subtree has nothing to do with the query (i.e., there is no intersection), then no query will be sent to that subtree. For the same example above, the query can be obtained as,

$$Q(a_1, c_2) = \pi_{a_1} \sum_{a_2, c_1} \pi_{a_2} \pi_{c_1} \pi_{c_2} \qquad (2)$$

where π_i represents the probability distribution associated with node i. There are three major operations in SPI algorithm: multiplication, summation and substitution. Multiplication calculates the product of two distributions; summation calculates the sum of a distribution over a set of variables; and substitution calculates the result of substituting an observed value for a node into a distribution. For networks with continuous variables, the SPI algorithm can be applied directly. However the multiplication, summation, and substitution operations must be modified. In the next section, we will describe the corresponding multiplication, integration, and substitution operations for the networks with continuous variables.

3 The SPI with Continuous Variables Algorithm

The continuous SPI (SPIC) algorithm requires redefinition of the SPI operations: multiplication, integration, and substitution. The general mechanism for the continuous SPI algorithm is basically the same as the discrete one except for the caching operation and the handling of evidence. We first describe the representation for conditional probability distributions in linear gaussian continuous variables and then the three operations in detail.

3.1 Node Representation

A SPIC node represents a vector of continuous variables. SPIC restricts the conditional probability distribution of each node to be "linear gaussian". "Linear gaussian" distributions are the sum of a deterministic component and a probabilistic component. The deterministic component is a linear combination of the node's predecessor values. The probabilistic component is restricted to be gaussian (i.e., normal) which can be specified with mean vectors and covariance matrices. For a Bayesian network of this type, the necessary prior information needed before any inference can be drawn are the the prior distributions of the root nodes (i.e., mean and covariance) and the links between nodes in the network.

For example, for a random vector represented by a node x, if it is a root node, only mean $\bar{x}$ and the corresponding covariance matrix Q_x need to be specified. If it is not a root node, and has a set of predecessor nodes $x_1^p, .., x_n^p$, then the relation between x and its predecessors represented by the following linear equation need to be specified,

$$x = B_1 x_1^p + \ldots + B_N x_N^p + w_x \qquad (3)$$

where $B_1, .., B_N$ are constant transition matrices representing the relative contribution made by each of the predecessor variables to the determination of the dependent variable x, and w_x is a noise vector summarizing other factors affecting x. w_x is assumed to be normally distributed with mean $\bar{x}$ and covariance Q_x. For most applications, w_x will have a zero mean. However this is not always true *apriori* and can occur when distributions are multiplied together (e.g., a root node and a non-root node).

For each node x in a network, the sufficient information describing the node itself and the relationship to its predecessors can therefore be represented in the following form:

$$\{\bar{x}, Q_x, (B_1, x_1^p)..(B_N, x_N^p)\} \qquad (4)$$

With this simple representation, we will then describe the multiplication, integration, and substitution operations.

3.2 Multiplication

In this section, we describe the multiplication operation for SPIC. We describe when distributions can be multiplied, what the result will look like, and then describe in detail how each part of the result is computed.

There is a constraint on what distributions can be multiplied. This constraint called "combinability" was developed in [1]. According to the theorem derived in [1], a set of nodes S is "combinable" (i.e., able to be aggregated) if and only if every pair of nodes in the set is combinable. Two nodes are combinable if all nodes in the path(s) between the two nodes are in the set S. It can be shown that if the set of nodes corresponding to the distributions to be multiplied are "combinable", then multiplying the distributions is the same as finding the "joint" distribution of those nodes, or in other words, to find the new probability representation of the "combined" node.

Based on the separation principle in the SPI tree (i.e., any node separate its successors rooted from itself) [3], it can be easily shown that any distributions that will be multiplied from any query request during SPI processing are always combinable. In other words, we can transform the multiplication operation in SPI algorithm into a node combination operation for the continuous nodes.

The dimension of the resulting distribution will be the sum of the dimensions of those nodes to be multiplied. For instance, two representations of nodes (variables) x_1 and x_2 each with dimension $D(x_1)$ and $D(x_2)$ are to be multiplied, the resulting representation will have dimension $D(x_1) + D(x_2)$, which can be interpreted as the description of the combined variable x with x_1 stack over x_2, i.e., $x = \begin{bmatrix} x_1 \\ x_2 \end{bmatrix}$. The question now is how to calculate the new probability representation of x based on the old ones of x_1 and x_2. It is clear that this is nothing but to identify the new predecessors x_i^P of x and calculate the links B_i between x and the new predecessors as well as to calculate the new conditional mean $\bar{x}$ and the associated covariance Q_x.

First of all, the new predecessors of x is just the union of the predecessors of x_1 and x_2 (excluding x_1 or x_2 when one is the direct predecessor of the other). The new linear relation (coefficients) between x and x_i^P are obtained based on the old links. Conceptually, this can be accomplished by first breaking down the combined node into the original element nodes, and then find the relation between the predecessor and the element nodes individually. To do so, all paths between the predecessor and the desired element node are found and then combined together. The contribution of a path is obtained by multiplying the transition matrices of links along the path in the original network.

The mean and associated noise covariance matrix for the combined node is the last part of the representation that needs to be calculated. The first quantity that requires computation is the implicit linear relationship T between the two nodes that are to be multiplied. Based on the SPI tree structure, it can be shown that the T for two nodes is non-zero only when one node is the direct or indirect predecessor of the other. If the nodes do stand in this relation, T can be calculated by first finding all paths between the two nodes and adding the contribution from all paths. As in the process for finding the link coefficients for the new predecessors, the path contributions are obtained by multiplying together the transition matrices of links along the path. Given T, the new mean and covariance matrix of x can be obtained as below, given that x_1 is the direct or indirect predecessor of x_2.

$$\bar{x} = \begin{bmatrix} \bar{x_1} \\ T\bar{x_1} + \bar{x_2} \end{bmatrix} \tag{5}$$

$$Q_x = \begin{bmatrix} Q_{x_1} & Q'_{x_1}T' \\ TQ_{x_1} & TQ_{x_1}T' + Q_{x_2} \end{bmatrix} \tag{6}$$

For example, the results of multiplying π_{c_1} and π_{c_2} of the previous example given in Figure 1 can be represented by

$$c_{12} = \begin{bmatrix} c_1 \\ c_2 \end{bmatrix} = \begin{bmatrix} T_{c_1a_1} \\ T_{c_2c_1}T_{c_1a_1} \end{bmatrix} a_1 + \begin{bmatrix} 0 \\ T_{c_2a_2} \end{bmatrix} a_2 + \begin{bmatrix} W_{c_1} \\ T_{c_2c_1}W_{c_1} + W_{c_2} \end{bmatrix} \tag{7}$$

where c_{12} is the "combined node", T_{xy} are the links (transition matrices) between x and y, and a_1 and a_2 are the new predecessors. In addition to the links obtained as above, the new conditional mean and corresponding covariance are obtained as,

$$\bar{c}_{12} = \begin{bmatrix} \bar{c_1} \\ \bar{c_2} + T_{c_2c_1}\bar{c_1} \end{bmatrix} \tag{8}$$

which is zero since both $\bar{c_1}$ and $\bar{c_2}$ are zeros, and

$$Q_{c_{12}} = \begin{bmatrix} Q_{c_1} & Q'c_1T'_{c_2c_1} \\ T_{c_2c_1}Qc_1 & T_{c_2c_1}Qc_1T'_{c_2c_1} + Q_{c_2} \end{bmatrix} \tag{9}$$

In the discrete case, multiplying distributions can be expensive since the size of the resulting distribution grows exponentially with the number of distribution (nodes) to be multiplied. However, in the linear gaussian case, the resulting representation only increases quadratically. This is because a gaussian distribution can be sufficiently represented by a mean vector and a covariance matrix.

3.3 Integration

The integration operation is relatively simple. All one has to do is to identify and keep the appropriate slots from the representation (i.e., links to predecessors, mean, and covariance) and discard the rest of them. It can be easily shown that the reduced representation precisely describes the resulting distribution after the integration. For example, for the distribution of the combined node c_{12} obtained from the multiplication above. If the goal is to integrate c_1 out of the joint probability representation, all one has to do is to grab the appropriate slots from the links to a_1 and a_2, the mean vector $\bar{c}_{12}$, and the covariance matrix Qc_{12}. These slots are corresponding to the c_2 variable, namely,

$$c_2 = T_{c_2c_1}T_{c_1a_1}a_1 + T_{c_2a_2}a_2 + T_{c_2c_1}W_{c_1} + W_{c_2} \tag{10}$$

$$\hat{c}_2 = \bar{c_2} + T_{c_2c_1}\bar{c_1} \tag{11}$$

and

$$\hat{Q}_{c_2} = T_{c_2c_1}Qc_1T'_{c_2c_1} + Q_{c_2} \tag{12}$$

3.4 Substitution

Evidence is represented in the form of exact observation of the values of variables. The set of variables which have been observed is denoted by E. One easy way of incorporating evidence is to include evidence in the query, for instance, $P\{X|Y,E\}$ and then substitute the observed values E^* for E after the more general query is computed. Suppose the query results before the substitution of the observation is represented as

$$X = \bar{X} + K_Y Y + K_E E \quad (13)$$

with the associated covariance matrix Σ_X. To "substitute" the observation E^*, we first remove the link K_E from the representation, then replace the mean $\bar{X}$ by $\bar{X} + K_E E^*$. The covariance matrix remains the same. It can be easily shown that the new representation correctly describe the results of the query, $P\{X|Y, E = E^*\}$. Other more efficient methods such as to do substitution before query are currently under our investigation.

4 Conclusion

Recent research in Symbolic Probabilistic Inference (SPI) has made a significant step in improving efficiency of general query processing. Unlike traditional inference algorithms, SPI algorithm is goal directed, performing only those calculations that are required to respond to queries. In addition, SPI is incremental with respect to both queries and observations. In this paper, we extent the SPI algorithm to handle Bayesian networks with linear gaussian variables. We call the algorithm SPIC. The framework of this algorithm is the same as that for SPI. However, the basic operations of multiplication, integration and handling observation are quite different. The equivalent operation to the multiplication of discrete case is similar to the "node combination" operation in the continuous case and the equivalent operation to the summation of discrete case is the integration operation. Because SPIC stays within the SPI framework, the goal-directed and incrementality features of the algorithm are preserved.

In this paper, we have only addressed the problem of continuous variables that are restricted to have linear gaussian models. Many real-world problems may require nonlinear or nongaussian models. Classical methods such as approximation with linearization (e.g., extended Kalman filters) or sum of gaussians deserve attention in further investigation. A version of the SPIC algorithm has been implemented, preliminary results show expected performance.

References

[1] K. C. Chang and R. M. Fung. Node aggregation for distributed inference in bayesian networks. In *Proceedings of the 11th IJCAI*, Detroit, Michigan, August 1989.

[2] B. D'Ambrosio. Symbolic probabilistic inference in belief nets. 1990.

[3] R. Shachter A. Del Favero and B. D'Ambrosio. Symbolic probabilistic inference: A probabilistic perspective. *Proceeding of AAAI*, 1990.

[4] C. Robert Kenley. *Influence Diagram Models with Continuous Variables*. PhD thesis, Stanford University, Stanford, California, 1986.

[5] S. L. Lauritzen and D. J. Spiegelhalter. Local computations with probabilities on graphical structures and their application in expert systems. *Journal Royal Statistical Society B*, 50, 1988.

[6] Judea Pearl. Fusion, propagation, and structuring in belief networks. *Artificial Intelligence*, 29, 1986.

[7] Judea Pearl. *Probabilistic Reasoning in Intelligent Systems: Networks of Plausible Inference*. Morgan Kaufmann Publishers, 1988.

[8] Ross D. Shachter and C. Robert Kenley. Gaussian inflience giagrams. *Management Science*, 35, 1989.

[9] R. E. Tarjan and M. Yannakakis. Simple linear time algorithm to test chordality of graphs. *SIAM J. Computing*, 13, 1984.

Symbolic Probabilistic Inference with Evidence Potential

Kuo-Chu Chang and Robert Fung
Advanced Decision Systems
1500 Plymouth Street
Mountain View, California 94043-1230

Abstract

Recent research on the Symbolic Probabilistic Inference (SPI) algorithm[2] has focused attention on the importance of resolving general queries in Bayesian networks. SPI applies the concept of dependency-directed backward search to probabilistic inference, and is incremental with respect to both queries and observations. In response to this research we have extended the evidence potential algorithm [3] with the same features. We call the extension symbolic evidence potential inference (SEPI). SEPI like SPI can handle generic queries and is incremental with respect to queries and observations. While in SPI, operations are done on a search tree constructed from the nodes of the original network, in SEPI, a clique-tree structure obtained from the evidence potential algorithm [3] is the basic framework for recursive query processing.

In this paper, we describe the systematic query and caching procedure of SEPI. SEPI begins with finding a clique tree from a Bayesian network — the standard procedure of the evidence potential algorithm. With the clique tree, various probability distributions are computed and stored in each clique. This is the "pre-processing" step of SEPI. Once this step is done, the query can then be computed. To process a query, a recursive process similar to the SPI algorithm is used. The queries are directed to the root clique and decomposed into queries for the clique's subtrees until a particular query can be answered at the clique at which it is directed. The algorithm and the computation are simple. The SEPI algorithm will be presented in this paper along with several examples.

1 Introduction

The Bayesian networks technology provides a representation language for uncertain beliefs and inference algorithms for drawing sound conclusions from such representations. Bayesian Network is a directed, acyclic graph in which the nodes represent random variables, and the arcs between the nodes represent possible probabilistic dependence between the variables. The success of the representation is mainly due to the development of many probabilistic inference algorithms [3, 4, 5, 6]. While most of the algorithms can efficiently perform simple queries such as the marginal probability of each node given evidence, they have not efficiently addressed the problem of more general queries such as joint or conditional probabilities of any combination of nodes.

The recent work of Symbolic Probabilistic Inference (SPI) [1, 2] has made a significant step in this direction. SPI is a goal-driven method which is incremental with respect to both queries and observations. In response to this research we have extended the evidence potential (EP) algorithm [3] with the same features. We call the extension symbolic evidence potential inference (SEPI). Unlike traditional Bayesian Net inferencing algorithms, both SPI and SEPI are goal directed, performing only those calculations that are required to respond to queries. While in SPI, operations are done on a search tree constructed from the original network, in SEPI, a clique-tree structure obtained from the EP algorithm is the basic framework for recursive query processing.

In SEPI, the EP algorithm [3] is used as the "pre-processing" step in which various probabilities such as "set-chain" conditional [3] and marginal probabilities of each clique are computed based on the clique tree. The second step in SEPI is to process the query with a recursive mechanism similar to the SPI algorithm. A query is directed to the root clique and decomposed into queries for the clique's subtrees. This recursive process continues until a particular query can be answered at the clique at which it is directed. The answer is then computed and returned to the next higher level in the clique tree. Once a clique has responses from all of its subtrees it can compute its own response to its predecessor clique. This process terminates when the root clique processes all the responses from its subtrees.

With similar mechanisms for caching and incorporating evidence as in SPI, the calculation in SEPI is also incremental with respect to both query and evidences. However, since all the necessary probability distributions are stored in the "pre-processing" step, the SEPI algorithm is more efficient.

The paper is organized as follows. Section 2 briefly describes the EP algorithm which includes the construction of the clique tree. Section 3 describes the SEPI algorithm. A systematic recursive query and caching procedure will be presented. Some illustrative examples are given in Section 4, followed by the concluding remarks in Section 5.

2 Evidence Potential Algorithm

In this section, we will briefly review the evidence potential (EP) algorithm [3]. The algorithm first organizes the original network into clique tree, where each clique is a group of nodes not necessary mutually exclusive. It then performs inference by passing messages between cliques in a similar way to the distributed algorithm [4].

The first part of the algorithm is to form a clique tree. This part consists of five steps

1. Marry Parents: link predecessors of a node together
2. Remove Arc Directions: remove directions of all arcs
3. Fill in: generate new arcs between nodes whenever necessary to form a "perfect" graph
4. Find Cliques: form node clusters/cliques
5. Order Cliques, and Find Residuals and Separators: form cluster tree

After the clique tree is formed, the second part of the algorithm is to calculate the marginal probability of each node. Before this can be done, the "evidence potential" and "separator potential" likelihoods [3] are calculated for each cluster.

The second part of the algorithm consists of the following:

1. Calculating Evidence Potentials and Separator potentials: they are calculated from the prior node conditionals in each clique.
2. Calculate Set-Chain Conditionals: namely, the conditional probability of the residuals given the separators of each clique.
3. Calculate Joint Probability for each clique: from joint, we then can calculate individual node posteriors (marginal) probability.

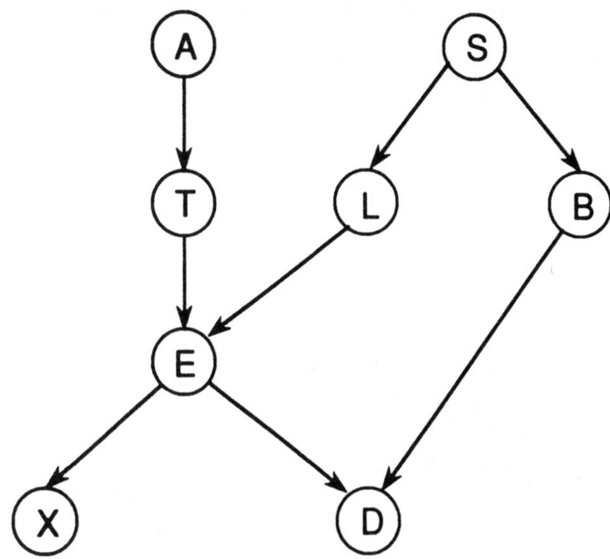

Figure 1: A Example Network

To illustrate this algorithm, the example given in [3] is shown in Figure 1. The corresponding clique tree and the set-chain conditional of each clique is shown in Figure 2. It is clear that the joint probability of the whole network can be obtained by multiplying all the set-chain conditionals together with the marginal probabilities of all the root cliques. Any query can then be obtained from the joint probability. The basic idea of EP algorithm is to decompose and factor the original formulae so that only minimum operations are required to answer the queries.

3 Symbolic Inference with Evidence Potential

The procedure described in the previous section can be considered as the pre-processing step for the generic query algorithm to be described. We call this new algorithm symbolic evidence potential inference (SEPI). In this algorithm, the goal is to calculate the results of arbitrary queries. The idea is to derive an efficient inference algorithm which takes advantage of the clique-tree structure of the EP algorithm.

The SEPI algorithm consists of several major processing steps. The first step is to organize the nodes of a Bayesian network into a clique tree structure and

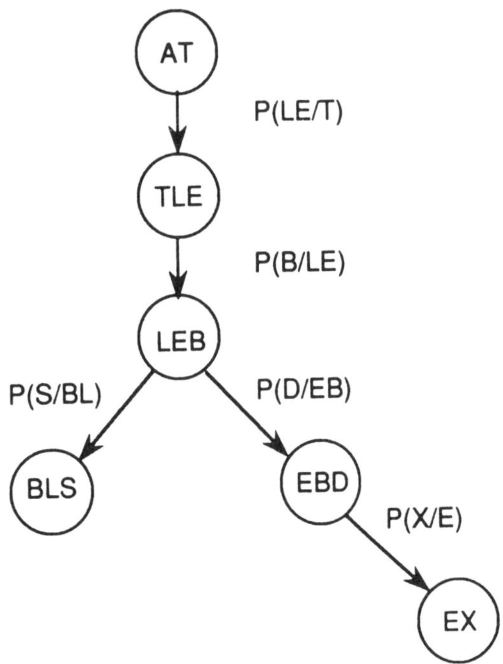

Figure 2: Cluster Tree and Set-Chain Conditional

calculate and store the various probability functions as described in the previous section (e.g., set-chain conditional and joint probability distribution). In the second step, queries from the user are directed to the root clique of the tree. The query is decomposed into queries for the clique's subtrees. This recursive procedure continues until a particular query can be answered.

The general format for a query received by SEPI is as a conditional probability, namely, $P\{X|Y\}$, where X and Y are sets of nodes in the network. This query is first transformed into joint distribution format $P(Z) \doteq P\{X,Y\}$ and directed to the root clique. In order to answer the query, it would be sufficient to calculate $P(Z \setminus C_0|C_0)$, where C_0 is the root clique. This is because we can calculate the query by

$$P(Z) = \sum_{C_0 \setminus Z} P(Z \setminus C_0|C_0)P(C_0) \tag{1}$$

where the prior probability $P(C_0)$ is available at the clique C_0. According to the EP algorithm, the clique tree is organized in a way that the separators are the overlapping nodes between the successor and predecessor cliques. Denote the separators between the root clique and the child clique C_i as S_i, then

$$P(Z \setminus C_0|C_0) = P(Z \setminus C_0|S_i) \tag{2}$$

Define $T(C_i)$ as all the nodes in the subtree rooted from C_i, then the new request to be sent to each child C_i is

$$P((Z \setminus C_0) \cap T(C_i)|S_i) \tag{3}$$

Note that if the successor clique has nothing to do with the query, i.e., $(Z \setminus C_0) \cap T(C_i) = \emptyset$, then no query will be sent to that clique.

At the clique C_i, when the request arrives for a probability distribution represented by $P\{X|S_i\}$, if such a distribution had already been computed earlier and cached, it can be returned immediately. However, usually it will be necessary to send requests to the clique's successors in order to compute the response. Since it can be easily shown that

$$P\{X|S_i\} = \sum_{R_{C_i}} \prod_j P(X \cap T(C_{ij})|S_{ij})P(R_{C_i}|S_i) \tag{4}$$

where R_{C_i} is the residual nodes of C_i, C_{ij} is the $j-th$ child clique of C_i, and S_{ij} is the separators between C_i and C_{ij}, the request to each child C_{ij} will be

$$P(X \cap T(C_{ij})|S_{ij}). \tag{5}$$

The recursive process continues until it reaches the leaf node or the request can be answered from the cached results.

To handle the evidence, just substitute the observed values into all the clique distributions involving the observed node. This operation is very simple in which the particular dimension of the observed value is simply eliminated and the rest of the distribution remain the same. The substitution needs to be done for all the distributions including the cached results stored in each clique which involves the observed node. After the substitution, all the other operations can be applied on distributions with the reduced dimensions.

As in the SPI algorithm, three major operations are needed in the SEPI algorithm: multiplication, summation and substitution. Multiplication calculates the product of two distributions, summation calculates the sum of a distribution over a set of variables, and substitution calculates the result of substituting an observed value for a node into a distribution.

4 Examples

With the network given in Figure 1, we will now illustrate the SEPI algorithm with several query examples. First, assuming the query we are interested is $P(AXS)$, the recursive algorithm works as follows.

- The query $P(AXS)$ is received at the root clique (AT), based on eqn. (2) and (3), a new query $P(XS|T)$ is generated and sent to the successor clique (TLE)
- The query $P(XS|T)$ is received at the clique (TLE); similarly, a new query $P(XS|LE)$ is generated and sent to the successor clique (LEB)
- The query $P(XS|LE)$ is received at the clique (LEB), based on (5), new queries $P(S|BL)$ and $P(X|EB)$ are generated and sent to the successors (BLS) and (EBD) respectively.

- The query $P(S|BL)$ is received at the clique (BLS) which is available in the cache due to the pre-processing.
- The query $P(X|EB)$ is received at clique (EBD), a new query $P(X|E)$ is generated and sent to the successor clique (EX)
- The query $P(X|E)$ is received at clique (EX) which is available.

- At clique (EBD), compute the query $P(X|EB)$ by

$$P(X|EB) = \sum_D P(X|E)P(D|BE) \quad (6)$$

- At clique (LEB), compute the query $P(XS|LE)$ by

$$P(XS|LE) = \sum_B P(S|BL)P(X|EB)P(B|LE) \quad (7)$$

- At clique (TLE), compute the query $P(XS|T)$ by

$$P(XS|T) = \sum_{LE} P(XS|LE)P(LE|T) \quad (8)$$

- At root clique (AT), compute the query $P(AXS)$ by

$$P(AXS) = \sum_T P(XS|T)P(AT) \quad (9)$$

Assume in the second example that the node E is observed and the observed value is E^*. To calculate the posterior probability of the same query, we first substitute the observed value into all the distributions in the cliques related to the observed node. These include $P(D|BE)$, $P(B|LE)$, and $P(LE|T)$ in the cliques (TLE), (LEB), and (EBD) respectively. The substitution operation simply eliminates the particular dimension corresponding to the observed value in the distributions. Then the same procedure as described above to calculate the query can be applied using the distributions with new reduced dimensions. The result is therefore,

$$P(AXS|E = E^*) = \sum_T \sum_L [\sum_B [P(S|BL) \sum_D [p(X|E^*)P(D|BE^*)] P(B|LE^*)] P(LE^*|T)] P(AT) \quad (10)$$

5 Conclusion

SPI algorithm [1, 2] is the latest inference algorithms in which the emphasis is on the efficient generic query. The main goal of these algorithms is to respond to arbitrary queries in an efficient manner. In these algorithms the network is first converted into a search tree and the probabilities are manipulated by symbolically decomposing or factoring the formulae. These methods are incremental with respect to queries and evidence and have good potential for parallel processing.

In this paper, we develop a similar query algorithm based on the combination of evidence potential algorithm and the SPI inference mechanism. Rather than converting the network into a SPI search tree, we construct a "clique tree" based on the evidence potential algorithm. Additionally, the evidence potential algorithm is used as the pre-processing step where all the necessary probability distributions for answering the query are computed and stored in each clique.

Similar to the SPI algorithm, queries are directed to the root clique of the tree. They are decomposed into queries for the clique's subtrees. This recursive procedure continues until a particular query can be answered. The answer is then computed and returned to the next higher level. The algorithm and the computation are simple. With a similar mechanism for caching and incorporating evidence as in the SPI algorithm, the calculation is also incremental with respect to both query and evidence. However, the SEPI algorithm is more efficient since all the necessary probability distributions are stored in the pre-processing step. A version of the SEPI algorithm as well as the SPI algorithm have been implemented, preliminary results from several examples show that with the prep-processing step, the query process of the SEPI algorithm is faster than the SPI algorithm.

References

[1] B. D'Ambrosio. Symbolic probabilistic inference in belief nets. 1990.

[2] R. Shachter A. Del Favero and B. D'Ambrosio. Symbolic probabilistic inference: A probabilistic perspective. *Proceeding of AAAI*, 1990.

[3] S. L. Lauritzen and D. J. Spiegelhalter. Local computations with probabilities on graphical structures and their application in expert systems. *Journal Royal Statistical Society B*, 50, 1988.

[4] Judea Pearl. Fusion, propagation, and structuring in belief networks. *Artificial Intelligence*, 29, 1986.

[5] Judea Pearl. *Probabilistic Reasoning in Intelligent Systems: Networks of Plausible Inference*. Morgan Kaufmann Publishers, 1988.

[6] Ross D. Shachter. Intelligent probabilistic inference. In L.N. Kanal and J.F. Lemmer, editors, *Uncertainty in Artificial Intelligence*. Amsterdam: North-Holland, 1986.

A Bayesian Method for Constructing Bayesian Belief Networks from Databases

Gregory F. Cooper
Section of Medical Informatics
Department of Medicine
University of Pittsburgh
Pittsburgh, PA 15261

Edward Herskovits
Medical Computer Science
Stanford University
Stanford, CA 94305

Abstract

This paper presents a Bayesian method for constructing Bayesian belief networks from a database of cases. Potential applications include computer-assisted hypothesis testing, automated scientific discovery, and automated construction of probabilistic expert systems. Results are presented of a preliminary evaluation of an algorithm for constructing a belief network from a database of cases. We relate the methods in this paper to previous work, and we discuss open problems.

1 INTRODUCTION

Decision making typically is replete with uncertainty. In general, it is important that computer systems that assist in decision making be capable of representing and reasoning with uncertainty. Probabilistic networks provide a precise and concise representation of probabilistic dependencies among variables. In the last few years, significant progress has been made in formalizing the theory of probabilistic networks [Pearl 1988]. Advances also have occurred in improving the efficiency of methods for inference on probabilistic networks [Henrion 1990], although for some complex networks additional improvements are still needed. The feasibility of using probabilistic networks in constructing diagnostic systems has been demonstrated in several domains [Agogino and Rege 1987, Andreassen, Woldbye, et al. 1987, Beinlich, Suermondt, et al. 1989, Heckerman, Horvitz, et al. 1989, Henrion and Cooley 1987, Holtzman 1989, Suermondt and Amylon 1989].

Although substantial advances have been made in developing the theory and application of probabilistic networks, the actual construction of these networks often remains a difficult, time-consuming task. The task is time-consuming because typically it must be performed manually by an expert or with an expert. Some important progress has been made in developing methods to improve the efficiency of knowledge acquisition from experts [Heckerman 1990]. These methods are likely to remain important in domains of small to moderate size in which there are readily available experts. Some domains, however, are large. In others, there are few, if any, available experts. Methods for assisting, or in some cases replacing, the manual expert-based methods of knowledge acquisition are needed.

Databases are becoming increasingly abundant in many areas, including science, engineering, and business. In each of these areas, there are many potential opportunities for using probabilistic networks to provide assistance in decision making. By using databases to assist in constructing probabilistic networks, we may be able to decrease knowledge acquisition time significantly. Automatically generated networks could be used directly to provide decision-making assistance, or used as a starting point for modification by an expert. In the latter case, the editing of a network may require substantially less time than de novo generation of the network by an expert.

The automated construction of probabilistic networks also can provide insight into the probabilistic dependencies that exist among the domain variables. One application is the automated discovery of dependency relationships. The computer program searches for a probabilistic network structure that has a high posterior probability given the database, and outputs the structure and its probability. A related task is computer-assisted hypothesis testing: the user enters a hypothesized structure of the dependency relationships among a set of variables and the program calculates the probability of the structure given a database of cases on the variables. These applications have the potential to affect broad areas of scientific discovery and data evaluation.

As an example, consider the fictitious database of cases shown in Table 1. Suppose that x_1 is an experimental condition and x_2 and x_3 are two experimental outcomes.

Given the database, what are the qualitative dependency relationships among the variables? For example, do x_1 and x_3 influence each other directly, or do they do so only through x_2? What is the probability that x_3 will be present if x_1 is present? Clearly, there are no categorically correct answers to each of these questions. The answers depend on a number of factors, including the model that we use to represent the data, and our prior knowledge about the data in the database and the relationships among the variables. In this paper, we do not attempt to consider all such factors in their full generality. Rather, we specialize the general task by presenting one particular framework for constructing probabilistic networks from databases, as for example the database in Table 1, such that these networks can be used for probabilistic inference, as for instance in calculating $P(x_3 = \text{present} \mid x_1 = \text{present})$. In particular, we focus on using a Bayesian belief network as a model of probabilistic dependency. Our primary goal is to construct such a network (or networks), given a database and a set of explicit assumptions about our prior probabilistic knowledge of the domain, and then use that network (or networks) for inference.

Table 1: A database example. For notational convenience, in the text we sometimes use 0 to denote *absent* and 1 to denote *present*.

	Variable values for each case		
Case	x_1	x_2	x_3
1	present	absent	absent
2	present	present	present
3	absent	absent	present
4	present	present	present
5	absent	absent	absent
6	absent	present	present
7	present	present	present
8	absent	absent	absent
9	present	present	present
10	absent	absent	absent

2 METHODS

In this section, we first briefly review some key concepts about Bayesian belief networks. Then, we present the primary theoretical developments of our work thus far in developing methods for learning the structure of Bayesian belief networks from databases; a more detailed discussion with proofs appears in [Cooper and Herskovits 1991]. Finally, we discuss the empirical results of an algorithm that applies this theory to search for the most likely belief-network structure, given a database.

2.1 BAYESIAN BELIEF NETWORKS

A Bayesian belief-network *structure* B_S is a directed acyclic graph in which nodes represent domain variables and arcs between nodes represent probabilistic dependencies [Cooper 1989, Horvitz, Breese, et al. 1988, Lauritzen and Spiegelhalter 1988, Neapolitan 1990, Pearl 1986, Pearl 1988, Shachter 1988]. A variable in a Bayesian belief-network structure may be continuous [Shachter and Kenley 1989] or discrete. In this paper, we shall focus our discussion on discrete variables. Figure 1a shows an example of a belief-network structure, which we shall call B_{S1}, containing three variables. The arc from x_1 to x_2 indicates that these two variables are probabilistically dependent. Similarly, the arc from x_2 to x_3 indicates a probabilistic dependency between these two variables. The absence of an arc from x_1 to x_3 implies that there is no direct probabilistic dependency between x_1 and x_3. In particular, the probability of each value of x_3 is conditionally independent of the value of x_1 *given* that the value of x_2 is known. Figure 1b shows an alternative structure that expresses different dependency relationships among the three variables. The representation of conditional dependencies and independencies is the essential function of belief networks. For a detailed discussion of the semantics of Bayesian belief networks, see [Pearl 1988].

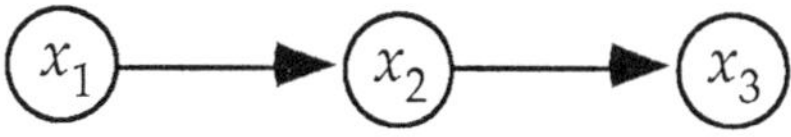

(a) Structure B_{S1}

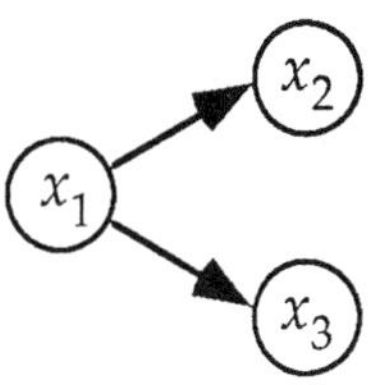

(b) Structure B_{S2}

Figure 1: Two alternative belief-network structures on three variables.

A Bayesian belief-network structure B_S is augmented by conditional probabilities, B_P, to form a Bayesian belief network B. Thus, $B = (B_S, B_P)$. For brevity, we call B a belief network. For each node[1] in the network structure, there is a conditional probability function that relates this node to its immediate predecessors (parents). We shall use π_i to denote the parent nodes of variable x_i. If a node has no parents, then a prior probability function, $P(x_i)$, is specified. A set of probabilities is shown in Table 2 for the belief-network structure in Figure 1a. We shall use the term *conditional probability* to refer to a probability statement, such as $P(x_2 = \text{present} \mid x_1 = \text{present})$. We use the term *conditional probability assignment* to denote a numerical assignment to a conditional probability, as, for example, the assignment $P(x_2 = \text{present} \mid x_1 = \text{present}) = 0.8$. The network structure B_{S1} in Figure 1a and the probabilities B_{P1} in Table 2 together define a belief network, which we denote as B_1.

Table 2: The probability assignments associated with the belief-network structure B_{S1} in Figure 1. We shall denote these probability assignments as B_{P1}.

$P(x_1 = \text{present}) = 0.6$
$P(x_1 = \text{absent}) = 0.4$
$P(x_2 = \text{present} \mid x_1 = \text{present}) = 0.8$
$P(x_2 = \text{absent} \mid x_1 = \text{present}) = 0.2$
$P(x_2 = \text{present} \mid x_1 = \text{absent}) = 0.3$
$P(x_2 = \text{absent} \mid x_1 = \text{absent}) = 0.7$
$P(x_3 = \text{present} \mid x_2 = \text{present}) = 0.9$
$P(x_3 = \text{absent} \mid x_2 = \text{present}) = 0.1$
$P(x_3 = \text{present} \mid x_2 = \text{absent}) = 0.15$
$P(x_3 = \text{absent} \mid x_2 = \text{absent}) = 0.85$

Belief networks can be used to represent the probabilities over any discrete sample space: the probability of any sample point in that space can be computed from the probabilities in the belief network. The key feature of belief networks is their explicit representation of the conditional independence among events. In particular, investigators have shown [Kiiveri, Speed, et al. 1984, Pearl 1988, Shachter 1986] that the joint probability of any particular instantiation[2] of all n variables in a belief network can be calculated as

$$P(X_1, \ldots, X_n) = \prod_{i=1}^{n} P(X_i \mid \pi_i), \tag{1}$$

where each X_i represents an instantiated variable and π_i represents an instantiation of the parents of X_i.

Therefore, the joint probability of any instantiation of all the variables in a belief network can be computed as the product of only n probabilities. In principle, we can recover the complete joint-probability space from the belief-network representation by calculating the joint probabilities that result from every possible instantiation of the n variables in the network. Thus, we can determine any probability of the form $P(Z \mid Y)$, where Z and Y are sets of variables with known values (instantiated variables). For example, for our sample three-node belief network B_1, $P(x_3 = \text{present} \mid x_1 = \text{present}) = 0.75$.

Let us now consider the problem of finding the most probable belief-network structure, given a database. Once such a structure is found, we can derive numerical belief-network probabilities from the database [Cooper and Herskovits 1991]. We can use the resulting belief network for probabilistic inference, such as calculating the value of $P(x_3 = \text{present} \mid x_1 = \text{present})$. In addition, the structure may lend insight into the dependency relationships among the variables in the database, as, for example, possible causal relationships.

To be more specific, let D be a database of cases, Z be the set of variables represented by D, and B_{S_i} and B_{S_j} be two belief-network structures containing exactly those variables that are in Z. In the next section, we develop a method for computing $P(B_{S_i} \mid D)/P(B_{S_j} \mid D)$. By computing such ratios for pairs of belief-network structures, we can rank order a set of structures by their posterior probabilities. To calculate the ratio of posterior probabilities, we shall calculate $P(B_{S_i}, D)$ and $P(B_{S_j}, D)$ and use the following equivalence:

$$\frac{P(B_{S_i} \mid D)}{P(B_{S_j} \mid D)} = \frac{\dfrac{P(B_{S_i}, D)}{P(D)}}{\dfrac{P(B_{S_j}, D)}{P(D)}} = \frac{P(B_{S_i}, D)}{P(B_{S_j}, D)}. \tag{2}$$

2.2 A FORMULA FOR COMPUTING $P(B_S, D)$

Let B_S represent an arbitrary belief-network structure containing just the variables in Z. In this section, we present a method for calculating $P(B_S, D)$. In doing so, we shall introduce five assumptions that render this calculation computationally tractable.

<u>Assumption 1.</u> The process that generated the database is modeled as a belief network containing just the variables in Z, which are discrete.

---

1 Since there is a one-to-one correspondence between a node in B_S and a variable in B_P, we shall use the terms *node* and *variable* interchangeably.

2 An *instantiated variable* is a variable with an assigned value. When we need to designate a particular value v_{ik} of variable x_i, we shall write $x_i = v_{ik}$.

As this assumption states, we shall not consider continuous variables in this paper.

A belief network (structure *plus* conditional probabilities) is sufficient to capture any probability distribution over the variables in Z [Pearl 1988]. A belief-network structure alone, containing just the variables in Z, can capture many—but not all—the qualitative independence relationships that might exist in an arbitrary probability distribution over Z [Pearl 1988]. Assumption 1, therefore, is justified to the extent that the relationships of independence and dependence, among variables in the underlying process that is hidden from us, can be represented by some belief network. In the remainder of this section, we shall write as though database D was generated by Monte Carlo sampling of a belief network with structure B_S that is hidden from us. One of our primary goals will be to use D to try to discover B_S. In this section, we assume that B_S contains just the variables in Z. In [Cooper and Herskovits 1991], we allow B_S to contain variables beyond those in Z.

The application of Assumption 1 yields

$$P(B_S, D) = \int_{B_P} P(D \mid B_S, B_P)\, f(B_P \mid B_S)\, P(B_S)\, dB_P, \qquad (3)$$

where B_P is a vector whose values denote the conditional-probability assignments associated with belief-network structure B_S, and f is the conditional probability density function over B_P given B_S. The integral is over all possible value assignments to B_P. Thus, we are integrating over all possible belief networks that can have structure B_S. The integral in Equation 3 represents a multiple integral and the variables of integration are the conditional probabilities associated with structure B_S.

Assumption 2. Cases occur independently, given a belief network model.

This assumption is equivalent to assuming that the belief network that is generating the data is static, that is, it does not change as cases are being generated. It follows from the conditional independence of cases expressed in Assumption 2 that Equation 3 may be rewritten as

$$P(B_S, D) = P(B_S) \int_{B_P} \left[\prod_{j=1}^{m} P(C_j \mid B_S, B_P)\right] f(B_P \mid B_S)\, dB_P, \qquad (4)$$

where m is the number of cases in D and C_j is the jth case in D.

Assumption 3. Cases are complete, that is, there are no cases that have variables with missing values.

In [Cooper and Herskovits 1991], we relax this assumption. We now introduce additional notation to facilitate the application of Assumption 3. Let D_{ij} denote the value assignment of variable i in case j. Thus, $D_{21} = 0$, since $x_2 = 0$ (i.e., x_2 is absent) in case 1 in Table 1. In B_S, for every variable x_i, there is a set of parents π_i (possibly the empty set). For each case in D, the variables in π_i are each assigned a particular value; call such a case-specific instantiation of all the variables in π_i a π-instantiation. Let ϕ_i denote a list of the unique π-instantiations for the parents of x_i as seen in D. If x_i has no parents, then we define ϕ_i to be the list $(\varnothing)$, where $\varnothing$ represents the empty set of parents. Although the ordering of the elements of ϕ_i is arbitrary, we shall use a list (vector), rather than a set, so that we can refer to members of ϕ_i using an index. For example, consider variable x_2 in B_{S1}, which has parent set $\pi_2 = \{x_1\}$. In this example, $\phi_2 = ((x_1 = 0), (x_1 = 1))$, because there are cases in D where x_1 has the value 0 and cases where it has the value 1. Let $\phi_i[j]$ be the jth element of ϕ_i. Thus, for example, $\phi_2[1]$ is equal to $(x_1 = 0)$. Let $\sigma(i, j)$ be an index function, such that the instantiation of π_i in case j is the $\sigma(i, j)^{\text{th}}$ element of ϕ_i. Thus, for example, $\sigma(2, 1) = 2$, because in case 1 the parent set of variable x_2 — namely $\{x_1\}$ — is instantiated as $x_1 = 1$, which is the second element of ϕ_2. Therefore, $\phi_2[\sigma(2, 1)]$ is equal to $(x_1 = 1)$. Let $q_i = |\phi_i|$. Note that since there are m cases in D, $q_i \le m$. Since, according to Assumption 3, cases are complete, we can apply Equation 1 to represent the probability of a case as follows:

$$P(C_j \mid B_S, B_P) = \prod_{i=1}^{n} P(x_i = D_{ij} \mid \phi_i[\sigma(i,j)], B_P) \qquad (5)$$

Substituting Equation 5 into Equation 4, we obtain

$$P(B_S, D) = P(B_S) \int_{B_P} \left[\prod_{j=1}^{m}\prod_{i=1}^{n} P(x_i = D_{ij} \mid \phi_i[\sigma(i,j)], B_P)\right] \times f(B_P \mid B_S)\, dB_P. \qquad (6)$$

For a given i and j, let $f(P(x_i \mid \phi_i[j], B_P))$ denote our probability distribution over the possible values of

$P(x_i \mid \phi_i[j], B_P)$. That is, the density function $f(P(x_i \mid \phi_i[j], B_P))$ represents our belief about the values to assign the conditional probability function $P(x_i \mid \phi_i[j], B_P)$. For notational convenience, we shall leave the term B_P implicit. We shall assume that our belief about the values to assign to a conditional probability function in a belief network is not influenced by our belief about the values to assign any other conditional probability function. More formally, we can express this assumption as follows:

Assumption 4. For $1 \leq i, i' \leq n$, $1 \leq j \leq q_i$, $1 \leq j' \leq q_{i'}$, if $ij \neq i'j'$ then the distribution $f(P(x_i \mid \phi_i[j]))$ is marginally independent of the distribution $f(P(x_{i'} \mid \phi_{i'}[j']))$.

As an example, Assumption 4 implies that our belief about the assignment of a value to the conditional probability $P(x_3 = 0 \mid x_2 = 0)$ is independent of our assignment of a value to the conditional probability $P(x_2 = 0 \mid x_1 = 0)$, since these two probabilities are components of different conditional probability distributions. However, our belief about $P(x_2 = 0 \mid x_1 = 0)$ must be dependent on our belief about $P(x_2 = 1 \mid x_1 = 0)$, since they are members of the same conditional probability distribution; in particular, since x_2 is a binary variable, $P(x_2 = 0 \mid x_1 = 0) = 1 - P(x_2 = 1 \mid x_1 = 0)$.

Assumption 5. For $1 \leq i \leq n$, $1 \leq j \leq q_i$, the distribution $f(P(x_i \mid \phi_i[j]))$ is uniform.

This assumption states that initially, before we see the data, we are indifferent regarding giving one assignment of values to a conditional probability function versus some other assignment. This probability density function is, however, just a special case of the Dirichlet distribution [deGroot 1970]. In [Cooper and Herskovits 1991] we generalize Assumption 5 by representing $f(P(x_i \mid \phi_i[j]))$ with a Dirichlet distribution.

Assumptions 4 and 5 permit us to define the joint density function $f(B_p \mid B_S)$ using density functions of the form $f(P(x_i \mid \phi_i[j]))$ which are uniform.

We now use Assumptions 1 through 5 in the following theorem, proven in [Cooper and Herskovits 1991], which solves Equation 3 for $P(B_S, D)$:

Theorem Let Z be a set of n discrete variables, where a variable x_i in Z has r_i possible value assignments: $(v_{i1}, \ldots, v_{ir_i})$. Let D be a database of m cases, where each case contains a value assignment for each variable in Z. Let B_S denote a belief-network structure containing just the variables in Z. Each variable x_i in B_S has a set of parents π_i. Let $\phi_i[j]$ denote the jth unique instantiation of π_i relative to D. Suppose there are q_i such unique instantiations of π_i. Define α_{ijk} to be the number of cases in D in which variable x_i is instantiated as v_{ik} and π_i is instantiated as $\phi_i[j]$. Let $N_{ij} = \sum_{k=1}^{r_i} \alpha_{ijk}$. If Assumptions 1 through 5 hold, then

$$P(B_S, D) = P(B_S) \prod_{i=1}^{n} \prod_{j=1}^{q_i} \frac{(r_i - 1)!}{(N_{ij} + r_i - 1)!} \prod_{k=1}^{r_i} \alpha_{ijk}! . \quad (7)$$

❑

Equation 7 allows us to calculate $P(B_S, D)$ using knowledge of $P(B_S)$ combined with simple enumeration over the cases in the database. For example, by applying Equation 7 to the structures in Figure 1 with the data in Table 1, we find that $P(B_{S1}, D) = 8.91 \times 10^{-11}$ and $P(B_{S2}, D) = 8.91 \times 10^{-12}$, if we assume uniform priors on $P(B_S)$. Note that these numbers are small because the probability of seeing *exactly* those data that are in D is small. Given the assumptions in this section, the data imply that B_{S1} is 10 times more likely than B_{S2}. This result is not surprising, because we used B_1 to generate D by the application of Monte Carlo sampling.

Consider the time complexity of computing Equation 7. Let $r = \max_i[r_i]$ for $i = 1$ to n. Define t_{B_S} to be the time required to compute the prior probability of structure B_S, $P(B_S)$. In [Cooper and Herskovits 1991] we show that the time complexity of computing Equation 7 is $O(m\, n^2 r + t_{B_S})$.

Using Equation 7, we can calculate posterior probabilities of belief-network structures as

$$P(B_S \mid D) = \frac{P(B_S, D)}{\sum_{B_S} P(B_S, D)} . \quad (8)$$

Applying Equation 8 to our previous example, we obtain $P(B_{S1} \mid D) = 0.109$, and $P(B_{S2} \mid D) = 0.011$. The remaining probability mass of 0.88 is distributed among the other 23 possible three-node belief-network structures. When there are more than a few variables in the model, the complexity of computing Equation 8 is intractable, due to the large number of belief-network structures. Consider, however, the situation in which $\sum_{B_S \in Y} P(B_S, D) \approx P(D)$, for some set Y of structures, where $|Y|$ is small. If Y can be efficiently located, then

Equation 8 can be efficiently computed to a close approximation.

2.3 FINDING THE MOST PROBABLE BELIEF-NETWORK STRUCTURE

Consider the problem of determining the belief-network structure B_S that maximizes $P(B_S \mid D)$. Knowing such a structure may lend insight into the causal relationships among the model variables, particularly if the structure has a high posterior probability. The structure also may be augmented with numerical probabilities, as we discuss in [Cooper and Herskovits 1991], and used to perform probabilistic inference.

For a given database D, $P(B_S, D) \propto P(B_S \mid D)$, and therefore finding the B_S that maximizes $P(B_S \mid D)$ is equivalent to finding the B_S that maximizes $P(B_S, D)$. We can maximize $P(B_S, D)$ by applying exhaustively Equation 7 for every possible B_S containing just the variables in Z. As a function of the number of variables, the number of possible structures grows super-exponentially. Thus, an exhaustive enumeration of all network structures is not feasible in most domains. In particular, Robinson [Robinson 1976] has derived an efficiently computable recursive function for determining the number of possible belief-network structures that contain n nodes. For $n = 2$, the number of possible structures is 3; for $n = 3$, it is 25; for $n = 5$, it is 29,000; and, for $n = 10$, it is approximately 4.2×10^{18}. Clearly, we need a method that is more efficient than is exhaustive enumeration for locating the B_S that maximizes $P(B_S \mid D)$. In Section 2.3.1, we introduce additional assumptions that reduce the time complexity of enumeration. The complexity, however, remains exponential. Thus, in Section 2.3.2 we introduce and discuss a heuristic method that is polynomial time.

2.3.1 An Exhaustive Search Procedure

Let us assume that we can specify an ordering on all n variables, such that if x_i precedes x_j in the ordering, then we do not allow structures in which there is an arc from x_j to x_i. In some domains, the time precedence of event variables could be used to establish such an ordering. Given an ordering as a constraint, there remain $2^{\binom{n}{2}} = 2^{n(n-1)/2}$ possible belief-network structures. Let $t(n) = 2^{n(n-1)/2}$. For large n, it is not feasible to apply Equation 7 for each of $t(n)$ possible structures. Therefore, in addition to a node ordering, let us assume equal priors on B_S. That is, initially, before we observe the data D, we believe that all structures are equally likely. In that case, we obtain

$$P(B_S, D) = c \prod_{i=1}^{n} \prod_{j=1}^{q_i} \frac{(r_i - 1)!}{(N_{ij} + r_i - 1)!} \prod_{k=1}^{r_i} \alpha_{ijk}! \,, \tag{9}$$

where $c = 1/t(n)$ is our prior probability, $P(B_S)$, for each B_S. To maximize Equation 9, it is sufficient to find the parent set of each variable that maximizes the second inner product. Thus, we have

$$\max_{B_S}[\, P(B_S, D)] =$$

$$c \prod_{i=1}^{n} \max_{\pi_i}\Big[\prod_{j=1}^{q_i} \frac{(r_i - 1)!}{(N_{ij} + r_i - 1)!} \prod_{k=1}^{r_i} \alpha_{ijk}! \,\Big] \,, \tag{10}$$

where the maximization takes place over every possible set of parents π_i of x_i that is consistent with the ordering on the nodes. A generalization of Equation 10, which is discussed in [Cooper and Herskovits 1991], does not assume that $P(B_S)$ is uniform. Although solving Equation 10 is no longer super-exponential in n, it remains exponential in n. Thus, further computational improvements are needed.

2.3.2 A Heuristic Search Procedure

We propose here one polynomial-time heuristic method, among many possibilities, that attempts to find the B_S that maximizes (or nearly maximizes) $P(B_S \mid D)$. We shall use Equation 10 as our starting point, with the attendant assumptions that we have an ordering on the domain variables and that, a priori, all structures are considered equally likely. We shall modify the maximization operation on the right of Equation 10 to use a greedy-search method. In particular, we use an algorithm that begins by assuming that a node has no parents, and that then adds incrementally that parent whose addition most increases the probability of the resulting structure. When the addition of no single parent can increase the probability, we stop adding parents to the node. We shall use the following function:

$$g(i, \pi_i) = \prod_{j=1}^{q_i} \frac{(r_i - 1)!}{(N_{ij} + r_i - 1)!} \prod_{k=1}^{r_i} \alpha_{ijk}! \,, \tag{11}$$

where the α_{ijk} are computed relative to π_i being the parents of x_i and relative to a database D which we leave implicit. Let u be the maximum number of parents allowed for any node. In [Cooper and Herskovits 1991] we show that $g(i, \pi_i)$ can be computed in $O(m\ u\ r)$ time. We also shall use a function $\mathrm{Pred}(x_i)$ that returns the set of nodes that precede x_i in the node ordering. Figure 2 contains the heuristic search algorithm, which we call K2. The algorithm is named K2 because it evolved from a system named Kutató [Herskovits and Cooper 1990] that applies the same search heuristics to construct belief networks; Kutató uses entropy to score network structures .

As shown in [Cooper and Herskovits 1991], the time complexity of K2 is $O(m\ u^2\ n^2\ r)$. This result assumes that the factorials we need in order to apply Equation 11 have been precomputed and stored in an array. We can further improve runtime speed by replacing $g(i, \pi_i)$ and $g(i, \pi_i \cup \{z\})$ in K2 by $log(g(i, \pi_i))$ and $log(g(i, \pi_i \cup \{z\}))$, respectively. The logarithmic version of Equation 11 requires only addition and subtraction rather than multiplication and division. If the logarithmic version of Equation 11 is used in K2 then the logarithms of factorials should be precomputed and stored in an array.

```
procedure K2;
{Input: A set of n nodes, an ordering on the
        nodes, an upper bound u on the
        number of parents a node may have,
        and a database D containing m cases.}
{Output: For each node, a printout of the
         parents of the node.}
for i := 1 to n do
    πi := ∅;
    Pold := g(i, πi); {This function is computed
                       using Equation 11.}
    OKToProceed := true;
    while OKToProceed and |πi| < u do
            let z be the node in Pred(xi) - πi that
                maximizes g(i, πi ∪ {z});
            Pnew := g(i, πi ∪ {z});
            if Pnew > Pold then
                Pold := Pnew;
                πi := πi ∪ {z}
            else OKToProceed := false;
    end {while};
    write('Node: ', xi, ' Parents of this node: ', πi);
end {for};
end {K2};
```

Figure 2: The K2 algorithm heuristically searches for the most probable belief-network structure, given a database of cases and a set of assumptions (see text).

We emphasize that K2 is just one of many possible methods for searching the space of belief networks to maximize the probability metric developed in Section 2.2. Accordingly, the metric developed in Section 2.2 is a more fundamental result than is the K2 algorithm. Nonetheless, K2 has proved valuable as an initial search method for obtaining some preliminary test results, which we shall describe in Section 3.

3 PRELIMINARY RESULTS

In this section we describe an experiment in which we generated a database from a belief network by simulation, and then attempted to reconstruct the belief network from the database. In particular, we applied the K2 algorithm to a database of 10,000 cases generated from the ALARM belief network. Beinlich constructed the ALARM network as a research prototype to model potential anesthesia problems in the operating room [Beinlich, Suermondt, et al. 1989]. ALARM contains 46 arcs and 37 nodes, and each node has from two to five possible values. We generated cases using a Monte Carlo technique [Henrion 1988]. Each case corresponds to a value assignment for each of the 37 variables. The Monte Carlo technique is an unbiased generator of cases, in the sense that the probability that a particular case is generated is equal to the probability of the case according to the belief network. We generated 10,000 such cases to create a database that we used as input to the K2 algorithm. We supplied K2 with an ordering on the 37 nodes that is consistent with the partial order of the nodes as specified by ALARM.

From the 10,000 cases, the K2 algorithm constructed a network identical to ALARM, except that one arc was missing and one arc was added. A subsequent analysis revealed that the missing arc is not strongly supported by the 10,000 cases. The extra arc was added due to the greedy nature of the search algorithm. The total search time for the reconstruction was approximately 16 minutes and 38 seconds on a Macintosh II running LightSpeed Pascal version 2.0. We analyzed the performance of K2 when given the first 100, 200, 500, 1000, 2000 and 3000 cases from the same 10,000-case database. Using only 3,000 cases, K2 produced in about 5 minutes the same belief network as when it used the full 10,000 cases.

Although preliminary, these results are encouraging because they demonstrate that K2 can reconstruct a moderate size belief network rapidly from a set of cases using readily available computer hardware. We currently are investigating the extent to which the performance of K2 is sensitive to the ordering of the nodes. We also are exploring methods that do not require an ordering.

4 SUMMARY OF THE LEARNING METHOD AND RELATED WORK

In the preceding sections, we have described a Bayesian approach to learning the dependency relationships among a set of discrete variables. For notational simplicity, we shall call the approach BLN (Bayesian learning of belief networks). BLN can represent arbitrary belief-network structures and arbitrary probability distributions on discrete variables. BLN calculates the probability of a structure of variable relationships given a database. The probability of multiple structures can be computed and displayed to the user. BLN also can use multiple structures in performing inference, as we discuss in [Cooper and Herskovits 1991]. When the number of domain variables is large, the combinatorics of enumerating all possible belief network structures becomes prohibitively expensive. Developing better methods for efficiently locating highly probable structures remains an open area of research. BLN is able to represent the prior probabilities of belief-network structures. For example, an expert could attach a high probability to the presence of an arc from node x to node y, indicating that—according to current scientific belief—it is very likely that x directly influences y. More generally, a prior probability could be specified for the presence of a *set* of arcs. If prior probability distributions on such structures are not available to the computer, then uniform priors can be assumed.

Previously described methods for learning belief networks from databases are non-Bayesian [Chow and Liu 1968, Fung and Crawford 1990, Geiger, Paz, et al. 1990, Herskovits and Cooper 1990, Pearl and Verma 1991, Rebane and Pearl 1987, Spirtes and Glymour 1990, Spirtes, Glymour, et al. 1990, Srinivas, Russell, et al. 1990, Verma and Pearl 1990, Wermuth and Lauritzen 1983]. With non-Bayesian methods, there is no principled way to attach prior probabilities to individual arcs or sets of arcs. In addition, all of these methods, except [Herskovits and Cooper 1990], rely on having threshold values (e.g., p values) for determining when conditional independence holds among variables. BLN does not require the use of such thresholds. Also, non-Bayesian belief-network methods, as well as classical statistical methods, emphasize finding the single most likely structure, which they then may use for inference. They do not, however, quantify the likelihood of that structure. If a single structure is used for inference, implicitly the probability of that structure is assumed to be 1.

Acknowledgements

We thank Lyn Dupré and Clark Glymour for helpful comments on an earlier draft. This work was supported in part by the National Science Foundation under grant IRI-8703710 and by the U.S. Army Research Office under grant P-25514-EL. Computing resources were provided in part by the SUMEX-AIM resource under grant LM-05208 from the National Library of Medicine.

References

Agogino, A.M. and Rege, A., IDES: Influence diagram based expert system, *Mathematical Modelling* **8** (1987) 227-233.

Andreassen, S., Woldbye, M., Falck, B. and Andersen, S.K., MUNIN — A causal probabilistic network for interpretation of electromyographic findings, In: *Proceedings of the International Joint Conference on Artificial Intelligence,* Milan, Italy (1987) 366-372.

Beinlich, I.A., Suermondt, H.J., Chavez, R.M. and Cooper, G.F., The ALARM monitoring system: A case study with two probabilistic inference techniques for belief networks, In: *Proceedings of the Conference on Artificial Intelligence in Medical Care,* London (1989) 247-256.

Chow, C.K. and Liu, C.N., Approximating discrete probability distributions with dependence trees, *IEEE Transactions on Information Theory* **14** (1968) 462-467.

Cooper, G.F., Current research directions in the development of expert systems based on belief networks, *Applied Stochastic Models and Data Analysis* **5** (1989) 39-52.

Cooper, G.F. and Herskovits, E.H., A Bayesian method for the induction of probabilistic networks from data, Report SMI-91-1, Section of Medical Informatics, University of Pittsburgh, 1991.

deGroot, M.H., *Optimal Statistical Decisions* (McGraw-Hill, New York, 1970).

Fung, R.M. and Crawford, S.L., Constructor: A system for the induction of probabilistic models, In: *Proceedings of AAAI,* Boston, Massachusetts (1990) 762-769.

Geiger, D., Paz, A. and Pearl, J., Learning causal trees from dependence information, In: *Proceedings of AAAI,* Boston, Massachusetts (1990) 770-776.

Heckerman, D.E., *Probabilistic Similarity Networks,* Ph.D. dissertation, Medical Information Sciences, Stanford University (1990).

Heckerman, D.E., Horvitz, E.J. and Nathwani, B.N., Update on the Pathfinder project, In: *Proceedings of the Symposium on Computer Applications in Medical Care* (1989) 203-207.

Henrion, M., Propagating uncertainty in Bayesian networks by logic sampling. In: Lemmer J.F. and

Kanal L.N. (Eds.), *Uncertainty in Artificial Intelligence 2* (North-Holland, Amsterdam, 1988) 149-163.

Henrion, M., An introduction to algorithms for inference in belief nets. In: Henrion M., Shachter R.D., Kanal L.N. and Lemmer J.F. (Eds.), *Uncertainty in Artificial Intelligence 5* (North-Holland, Amsterdam, 1990) 129-138.

Henrion, M. and Cooley, D.R., An experimental comparison of knowledge engineering for expert systems and for decision analysis, In: *Proceedings of AAAI*, Seattle (1987) 471-476.

Herskovits, E.H. and Cooper, G.F., Kutató: An entropy-driven system for the construction of probabilistic expert systems from databases, In: *Proceedings of the Conference on Uncertainty in Artificial Intelligence*, Cambridge, Massachusetts (1990) 54-62.

Holtzman, S., *Intelligent Decision Systems* (Addison-Wesley, Reading, MA, 1989).

Horvitz, E.J., Breese, J.S. and Henrion, M., Decision theory in expert systems and artificial intelligence, *International Journal of Approximate Reasoning* **2** (1988) 247-302.

Kiiveri, H., Speed, T.P. and Carlin, J.B., Recursive causal models, *Journal of the Australian Mathematical Society* **36** (1984) 30–52.

Lauritzen, S.L. and Spiegelhalter, D.J., Local computations with probabilities on graphical structures and their application to expert systems, *Journal of the Royal Statistical Society (Series B)* **50** (1988) 157-224.

Neapolitan, R., *Probabilistic Reasoning in Expert Systems* (John Wiley & Sons, New York, 1990).

Pearl, J., Fusion, propagation and structuring in belief networks, *Artificial Intelligence* **29** (1986) 241-288.

Pearl, J., *Probabilistic Reasoning in Intelligent Systems* (Morgan Kaufmann, San Mateo, California, 1988).

Pearl, J. and Verma, T.S., A theory of inferred causality, In: *Proceedings of the Second International Conference on the Principles of Knowledge Representation and Reasoning*, Boston, MA (1991) 441-452.

Rebane, G. and Pearl, J., The recovery of causal poly-trees from statistical data, In: *Proceedings of the Workshop on Uncertainty in Artificial Intelligence*, Seattle, Washington (1987) 222-228.

Robinson, R.W., Counting unlabeled acyclic digraphs (Note: This paper also discusses counting labeled acyclic graphs.), In: *Proceedings of the Fifth Australian Conference on Combinatorial Mathematics*, Melbourne, Australia (1976) 28-43.

Shachter, R.D., Intelligent probabilistic inference. In: Kanal L.N. and Lemmer J.F. (Eds.), *Uncertainty in Artificial Intelligence* (North-Holland, Amsterdam, 1986) 371-382.

Shachter, R.D., Probabilistic inference and influence diagrams, *Operations Research* **36** (1988) 589-604.

Shachter, R.D. and Kenley, C.R., Gaussian influence diagrams, *Management Science* **35** (1989) 527-550.

Spirtes, P. and Glymour, C., An algorithm for fast recovery of sparse causal graphs, Report CMU-LCL-90-4, Department of Philosophy, Carnegie–Mellon University, 1990.

Spirtes, P., Glymour, C. and Scheines, R., Causal hypotheses, statistical inference, and automated model specification, Unpublished report, Department of Philosophy, Carnegie–Mellon University, 1990.

Srinivas, S., Russell, S. and Agogino, A., Automated construction of sparse Bayesian networks for unstructured probabilistic models and domain information. In: Henrion M., Shachter R.D., Kanal L.N. and Lemmer J.F. (Eds.), *Uncertainty in Artificial Intelligence 5* (North-Holland, Amsterdam, 1990) 295-308.

Suermondt, H.J. and Amylon, M.D., Probabilistic prediction of the outcome of bone-marrow transplantation, In: *Proceedings of the Symposium on Computer Applications in Medical Care* (1989) 208-212.

Verma, T.S. and Pearl, J., Equivalence and synthesis of causal models, In: *Proceedings of the Conference on Uncertainty in Artificial Intelligence*, Cambridge, Massachusetts (1990) 220-227.

Wermuth, N. and Lauritzen, S., Graphical and recursive models for contingency tables, *Biometrika* **72** (1983) 537-552.

Local Expression Languages for Probabilistic Dependence: a preliminary report

Bruce D'Ambrosio
Department of Computer Science
Oregon State University
(503) 737-5563

Abstract

We present a generalization of the local expression language used in the Symbolic Probabilistic Inference (SPI) approach to inference in belief nets [1], [8]. The local expression language in SPI is the language in which the dependence of a node on its antecedents is described. The original language represented the dependence as a single monolithic conditional probability distribution. The extended language provides a set of operators ($*$, $+$, and $-$) which can be used to specify methods for combining partial conditional distributions. As one instance of the utility of this extension, we show how this extended language can be used to capture the semantics, representational advantages, and inferential complexity advantages of the "noisy or" relationship.

1 Introduction

A belief net [5] is a compact, localized representation of a probabilistic model. The key to its locality is that, given a graphical structure representing the dependencies (and, implicitly, conditional independencies) among a set of variables, the joint probability distribution over that set can be completely described by specifying the appropriate set of marginal and conditional distributions over the nodes involved. When the graph is sparse, this will involve a much smaller set of numbers than the full joint. Equally important, the graphical structure can be used to guide processing to find efficient ways to evaluate queries against the model. For more details, see [5], [7], [1]. All is not as rosy at it might seem, though. The graphical level is not capable of representing all interesting structural information which might simplify representation or inference. The only mechanism available for describing antecedent interactions in typical general purpose belief net inference algorithms is the full conditional distribution across all antecedents. However, a number of restricted interaction models have been identified which have lower space and time complexity than the full conditional. The noisy-or [5], [6], [4] for example, can be used to model independent causes of an event, and is linear in both space and time in the number of antecedents. In this paper we show an extension to the local expression language used in Symbolic Probabilistic Inference (SPI) [8] which is capable of directly expressing a noisy-or interaction model, which captures both the space and time advantages of the model, and which permits use of the model within arbitrary belief nets. In the remainder of this paper we first present a very brief overview of SPI. We then present an extension to the representation used to describe the dependence of a node on its antecedents in SPI, and show how it can be used to capture the noisy-or relationship. We then discuss the nature of the changes which must be made to support this extended local expression language. A key issue is the determination of how to distribute conformal product operations over addition and subtraction. We close with some remaining questions.

2 Overview of SPI

In this section we briefly review the essential aspects of the SPI approach to inference in belief nets. For further details, see [1] or [8].

2.1 Overview

Computation of probabilities in a belief net can be done quite straightforwardly, albeit somewhat inefficiently[1]. I illustrate this process with a simple network, shown in figure 1. First, the prior probabilities according to the chain rule:

$p(A) = p(A)$
$p(B) = \sum_A p(B|A) * p(A)$

[1] we ignore evidence for purposes of this introduction. It introduces only minor complications, see [1], [8] for details.

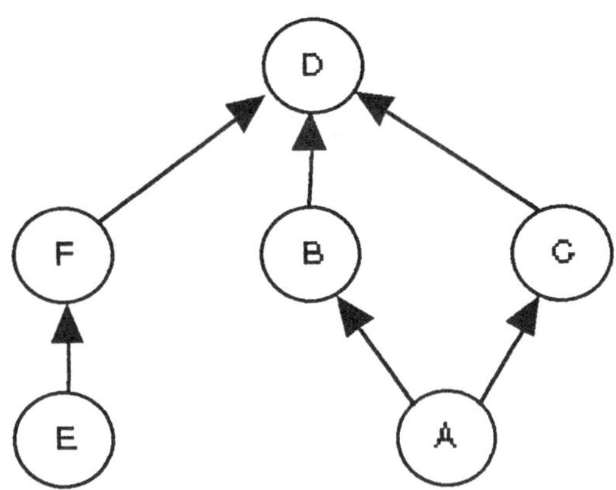

Figure 1: A Simple Belief Net

$p(C) = \sum_A p(C|A) * p(A)$
$p(D) = \sum_{A,B,C,E,F} p(D|B,C,F) * p(F|E)$
$* p(E) * p(C|A) * p(B|A) * p(A)$
$p(E) = p(E)$
$p(F) = \sum_E p(F|E) * p(E)$

Now suppose we wish to compute $p(D)$. The procedure is quite simple. We begin by evaluating the above expression for $p(D)$ from right to left. Once all distributions are combined, we have computed the joint across all six variables, and can derive the marginal over D by summing over all other variables. The actual computation can be optimized somewhat by retaining each dimension only until we have combined with all terms in which the dimension appears (that dimension is a goal of the evaluation, in which case it must be retained throughout the computation). For example, we can sum over A, since it is not needed in the final result, immediately after combining with $p(B|A)$ and $p(C|A)$. Conjunctive queries are easily computed, simply by evaluating the union of the symbolic expressions for the corresponding nodes. SPI essentially follows this process, but can be viewed as a heuristic procedure for developing factorings which minimize the dimension of intermediate results. The factoring is developed incrementally, and factoring is intermixed with expression evaluation. We briefly sketch the process used in the following.

SPI uses a more compact representation, expressing each node marginal only in terms of its conditional distribution and (implicitly) the immediate antecedents needed for computation. For our sample belief net this yields the following expressions:

$$
\begin{aligned}
exp(A) &= p(A) \\
exp(B) &= p(B|A) \\
exp(C) &= p(C|A) \\
exp(D) &= p(D|BCF) \\
exp(E) &= p(E) \\
exp(F) &= p(F|E)
\end{aligned}
$$

It may not be obvious how we can reconstruct the earlier computations from this representation. I will describe the evaluation algorithm shortly.

The next component of the representation is a partitioning of the set of nodes. The partitions are arranged in a tree subject to constraints as described in [8], although note that we permit partitions to contain more than one node in this paper. One valid partition of the example belief-net is shown in fig. 2[2].

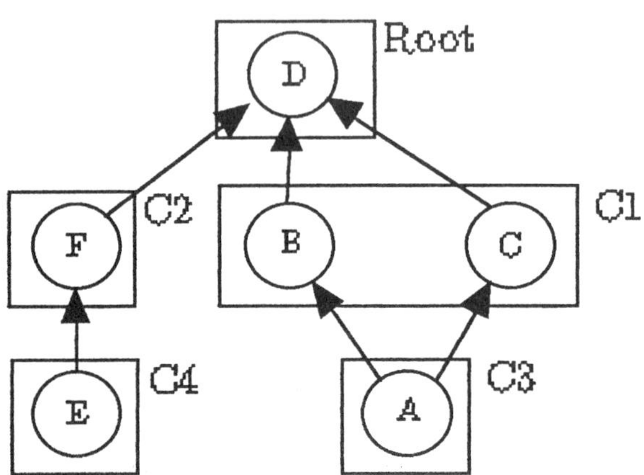

Figure 2: A Partition of the Sample Belief Net

Now consider how we might compute $p(D)$, given this information. The marginal probability of any node can be computed by multiplying the probability expression for the node of interest by distributions across sets of antecedents, subject to the following decomposition constraint: a joint distribution must be computed for antecedents whose corresponding nodes lie in a subtree rooted by the same child partition. Thus, the partitioning describes how to factor any expression at each stage of computation. The expression for D in the root partition, for example, will be decomposed into three groups, $\{p(D|BCF)\}$, $\{p(BC)\}$, and $\{p(F)\}$[3]. $p(D|BCF)$ is known, $p(BC)$ and $p(F)$ will be computed by querying the appropriate child partitions. The identification of the two subqueries that can be processed independently ($p(BC)$ and $p(F)$) is central to the efficiency of SPI. See [8] for proofs of the

[2]The root of the partition tree need not contain only belief net leaf nodes, and subtrees need not contain only antecedent nodes. We present here what we consider the minimal description of SPI needed to understand the extensions described in this paper.

[3]It should be noted that the value returned from a query to a child partition will be a distribution conditioned on all evidence in the subtree rooted by that child, but not conditioned on evidence elsewhere in the partition tree. Attempting to distinguish the various states of conditioning would clutter the representation, so we will not attempt to indicate the set of evidence a distribution has been conditioned with respect to in this paper.

properties which make this possible.

Since the partition graph is a tree, the recursion will terminate (and be evaluable, since all leaf node marginals are defined in the original belief net).

Below I detail this process for evaluating the marginal probability $p(D)$:

1. In the root partition, determine the expansion for $p(D)$:

$$exp(D) = p(D|BCF)$$

2. The following child partition queries are formed according to the antecedent set decomposition criterion:
   - Query to C1: $p(BC)$?
   - Query to C2: $p(F)$?
3. C1 expands $p(BC)$ to:

$$p(B|A)p(C|A)$$

4. This in turn generates a query to C3: $p(A)$?
5. C3 returns $p(A)$.
6. C1 evaluates $\sum_A p(B|A)p(C|A)p(A)$ and returns $p(BC)$.
7. C2 expands $p(F)$ to: $p(F|E)$.
8. This in turn generates the query to C4: $p(E)$?
9. C4 returns $p(E)$.
10. C3 evaluates $\sum_E p(F|E)p(E)$ and returns $p(F)$.
11. Root evaluates $\sum_{BCF} p(D|BCF)p(BC)p(F)$ and returns $p(D)$.

This simple example demonstrates a key feature of the algorithm: each partition deals with a low dimensional subspace of the overall probability space. While six variables are involved, the factoring keeps the dimensionality of intermediate computations down to four. We have made several simplifications in this presentation: we consider only partition trees with all belief net root nodes in partition tree leaves, and we do not consider evidence. See the cited papers for a more complete treatment of the basic algorithm.

3 Local Expression Languages for Probabilistic Knowledge

In this section we extend the local representation in SPI. This extended expression language is useful for compact representation of a number of canonical interaction models among antecedents. In particular, we demonstrate its use in capturing the noisy-or model. The next section describes the extensions needed in the SPI evaluation algorithm.

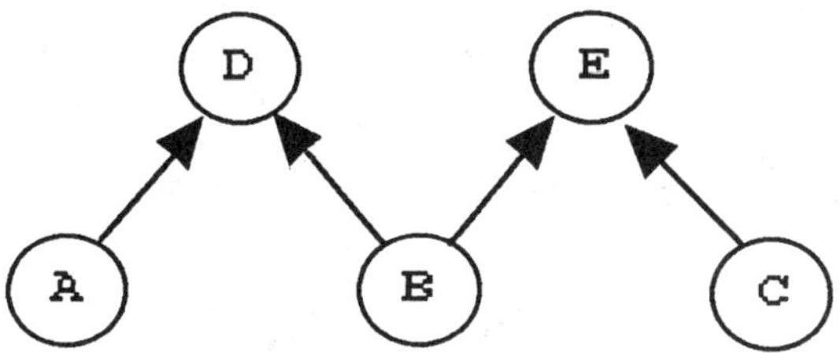

Figure 3: Noisy Or Sample Net

The local expression attached to a node in SPI as described in the previous section is a particularly simple one: it is either a marginal or conditional probability distribution. While this representation is complete (that is, is capable of expressing any coherent probability model), it suffers from both space and time complexity limitations: both the space and time required are exponential in the number of antecedents. However, computation of child probabilities using the noisy-or interaction model is linear in the number of (independent) antecedents in both space and time. When evidence is available on child nodes, computation of the posterior probability of parents is exponential in the number of positive pieces of evidence, but linear in the number of pieces of negative evidence. Heckerman [3] has developed an algorithm, called Quickscore, which provides this efficiency for two level bipartite graphs. However, the author is unaware of any implemented system other than the one reported here which can efficiently incorporate a noisy-or within an arbitrary belief net. If the interaction between the effects of A and B on D in example 3 can be modelled as a noisy-or interaction, then we might write the following expression for the dependence of D on A and B, following Pearl [5]:

$$\begin{aligned} F(D=t) &= 1-(1-c_A(D))(1-c_B(D)) \\ F(D=f) &= (1-c_A(D))(1-c_B(D)) \end{aligned}$$

Where $c_A(D)$ is the probability that D is true given that A is true and B is false. We use c rather than p to emphasize that these are not standard conditional probabilities. Nonetheless, in the following we will show that we can compute with these distributions[4] using an extension to the same mechanisms already in SPI. There are three components of SPI that must be extended:

1. The expression language must be extended to permit direct encoding of those aspects of interaction

[4] As will be noted later, all elements being combined are represented as generalized distributions over some domain. In the case of $c_A(D)$, the domain is the singleton $A = t, D = t$, and A is an antecedent.

models which provide space or time advantages.

2. The symbolic composition operator used to combine local expressions must be extended. This operator previously had one task: to rearrange conformal products of expressions into an efficiently evaluable form, using the commutativity and associativity of the operation. For extended expressions we have distributivity of conformal product over addition and subtraction as an option as well as commutativity and associativity.

3. The numeric evaluation procedure must be extended. First, we must define semantics for the addition and subtraction operators. Second, we must decide how completely to evaluate. The algorithm presented in [8] presumed that it was always appropriate to reduce an expression to the joint distribution over the variables needed in the result. For example, given

$$\sum_{B} F(D|B,C)F(B)F(C)$$

numeric evaluation will yield $F(D,B)$ rather than $F(D|B)F(B)$. While we believe this to be an optimal choice, the situation is less clear for the extended local expression language. Should the goal of expression evaluation always to be return a joint across the target variables, or are there cases in which it is better to return a partially evaluated expression?

In addition, computational complexity of both symbolic and numeric evaluation stages must remain linear, or at least low order polynomial, in the number of independent antecedents (otherwise what is the point!).

In the following we first present a description of the local expression language we have developed. We then proceed to describe the evaluation of queries referencing nodes whose probabilistic dependency on other nodes is defined using expressions from this language. Not all expressions in this language represent coherent probabilistic relationships. We presume that the user starts with a well understood interaction model and simply needs a computational framework that can perform inference with that model.

3.1 BNF for a simple expression language

We present below the BNF for a simple expression language capable of representing noisy-or and a variety of other special-case interaction models:

arithmetic-exp → *term* | (+ *term term-set*)
→ | (− *term term-set*)
→ | (∗ *term term-set*)
term → *arithmetic-exp* | *distribution*.
term-set → *term* | *term term-set*.
distribution → $name_{dimensions}$.
dimensions → *conditioned* "|" *conditioning*.
conditioned → $node\text{-}name_{domain}$
→ $node\text{-}name_{domain}conditioned$.
conditioning → *node-name domain*
→ *node-name domain* | *conditioning*.
domain → | *value* | {*value-set*}.
value-set → *value*. | *value value-set*.

Notice that every term eventually must reduce to one or more *distributions* defined over some domain. As an example, the local expressions for D and E for our sample noisy-or figure are as follows:

$$\begin{aligned} exp(D) &= 1_{D_t} - (1_{D_t} - c_{D_t|A_t}) * (1_{D_t} - c_{D_t|B_t}) \\ &\quad + (1_{D_f} - c_{D_f|A_t}) * (1_{D_f} - c_{D_f|B_t}) \\ exp(E) &= 1_{E_t} - (1_{E_t} - c_{E_t|B_t}) * (1_{E_t} - c_{E_t|C_t}) \\ &\quad + (1_{E_f} - c_{E_f|B_t}) * (1_{E_f} - c_{E_f|C_t}) \end{aligned}$$

The above notation may seem a bit obscure. It is perhaps further obscured by the fact that the actual numbers are not represented. The notation 1_{D_t} denotes a distribution *named* "1," which is defined over the subspace of the joint probability distribution for the network for which node D holds the value t. This distribution contains the single value 1.0 (the actual value is not a necessary consequent of the above notation, but it is convenient to give constants names which correspond to their values.). The expression for D, then, can be read as a straightforward recoding of the noisy-or model. It specifies that the distribution for D can be computed as the sum of two components. The first component computes a value for $F(D=t)$, and the second, on the next line, computes the value for $F(D=f)$. Since these two terms are mutually exclusive (as is obvious in this case, since they are defined over disjoint elements of the domain of D), they can be combined using simple addition. We specify the following semantics for the operators:

- * Conformal product. We assign the same semantics as for standard SPI. When combining distributions defined over differing subspaces of the domain for a node, only those values in the domain for which both distributions are defined need be considered. That is, distributions are implicitly extended with 0.0 in all values for which they are not defined. Thus, 1_{D_T} can be seen to specify the distribution $\{1.0, 0.0\}$ over $\{D=t, D=f\}$.
- +/- sum/difference. Simple sum or difference of the two terms. This assumes that the terms being combined are mutually exclusive. As before, dis-

tributions are extended with zeros for values in the domain over which they are not defined. However, note the following interesting case: how do we compute $1_{D_t} - c_{D_t|A_t}$? The first distribution is defined over D, but the second is defined over D conditioned on A. Unlike the conformal product case, we cannot directly add or subtract distributions over non-identical sets of variables. We first "normalize" the domains by multiplying *both* by $p(A)$. Suppose $p(A) = \{.1, .9\}$, and $c_{D_t|A_t} = .7$. Then the above computation would yield:

D/A	1_{D_t}		$c_{D_t\|A_t}$		Result	
	A=t	A=f	A=t	A=f	A=t	A=f
D=t	.1	.9	.07	0.0	.03	.9

The above is strictly necessary only if A is needed in the result. If it is not, the alternative is to multiply $c_{D_t|A_t}$ by $p(A)$ and then sum over A before subtracting it from 1_{D_t}.

Note that $c_{D_t|A_t}$ and $c_{D_f|A_t}$ represent the same noisy-or parameter. Two copies of this parameter are needed in our current expression language to denote its participation in the computation for $D = t$ and in the computation for $D = f$. We have not had time to investigate ways to eliminate this redundancy. There are doubtless other notations that would serve equally well. The above notation is the one used in our implementation, and serves to unambiguously specify the subspace over which each term is defined.

3.2 Symbolic composition of extended local expressions

In general, query evaluation in each partition consists of three stages, each of which will require modification. The three stages are:

1. Composition of local expressions for all partition nodes involved in the query.
2. Generation of subqueries to each child partition from which information is needed.
3. Numerical evaluation of the results.

In this section we discuss the first of these points, the symbolic composition, and present an algorithm for distributing conformal product over addition and subtraction. This algorithm yields an efficiently evaluable expression under the following restrictions:

1. There are many ways to construct valid partitioning of nodes. The way we currently use, and which we assume here, is to construct a tree with belief net root nodes at the leaves, and with multiple nodes in a partition where permissible under the partitioning constraints. One such partitioning algorithm is described in [1], and the partition tree constructed by that algorithm is shown in figure 4.
2. Queries to child partitions always return a single joint distribution across query nodes.

We will discuss later research in progress on relaxing these restrictions. The algorithm for distribution of conformal product over addition and subtraction begins with the outermost expression, and is as follows:

1. If the operation in the current expression is a conformal product, then
   (a) group terms with overlapping sets of child partitions from which information is needed.
   (b) distribute conformal product one level down in each group, over those terms in the group either separable into subterms which need antecedents from disjoint subtrees, or which require information from only a subset of the child partition set associated with the group.
   (c) repeat this step on the rewritten expression if the operation is still a conformal product. (can occur when terms are themselves conformal products)
2. Recursively apply step 1 to each term if the current expression is a result of performing a distribution operation.

This procedure assumes that the expressions being combined are initially in efficiently evaluable form, as are $exp(D)$ and $exp(E)$ above.

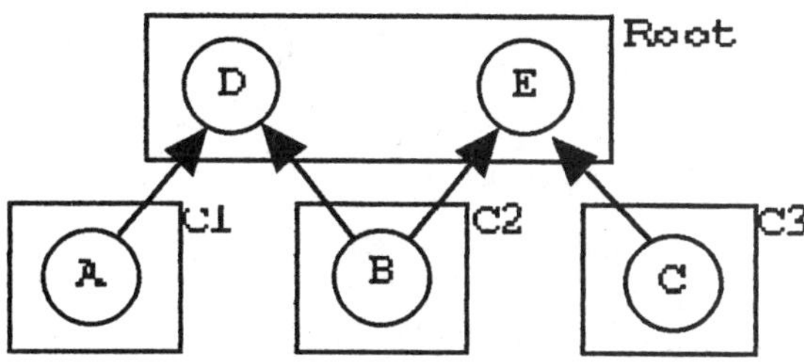

Figure 4: Noisy Or Sample Net Partition

As a simple example, consider the evaluation of the query for $p(D, E)$ in the net shown in Fig.3, where we use the noisy-or model for $\{A, B\}$ and for $\{B, C\}$ (since the queries to child partitions for $p(A)$ through $p(C)$ are trivial, we will ignore them and concentrate on processing in the partitions containing D and E). We concentrate on the processing in the root partition.

Query to root: $p(D, E)$

Composition of local expressions for query nodes:

$$\begin{aligned} p(D,E) \;=\; & ((1_{D_t} - (1_{D_t} - c_{D_t|A_t}) * 1_{D_t} - c_{D_t|B_t})) \\ & +(1_{D_f} - c_{D_f|A_t}) * (1_{D_f} - c_{D_f|B_t})) \\ & *((1_{E_t} - (1_{E_t} - c_{E_t|B_t}) * (1_{E_t} - c_{E_t|C_t})) \\ & +(1_{E_f} - c_{E_f|B_t}) * (1_{E_f} * c_{E_f|C_t})) \end{aligned}$$

Applying the distribution procedure to the above expression for $p(D,E)$ yields, at the first step (for sake of space we list only the terms involving D_t and E_t):

$$\begin{aligned} p(D_t,E_t) \;=\; & (1_{D_t} - (1_{D_t} - c_{D_t|A_t}) * (1_{D_t} - c_{D_t|B_t})) \\ & *(1_{Et} - (1_{Et} - c_{E_t|B_t}) * (1_{E_t} - c_{E_t|C_t})) \end{aligned}$$

Since the top level conformal product in this result contains terms which are separable, it is distributed over those terms. This yields:

$$\begin{aligned} & ((1_{D_t} * 1_{E_t}) + ((1_{D_t} - c_{D_t|A_t}) * (1_{D_t} - c_{D_t|B_t})) \\ & \quad *((1_{E_t} - c_{E_t|B_t}) * (1_{E_t} - c_{E_t|C_t}))) \\ & -((1_{E_t} * ((1_{D_t} - c_{D_t|A_t}) * (1_{D_t} - c_{D_t|B_t}))) \\ & +(1_{D_t} * ((1_{E_t} - c_{E_t|B_t}) * (1_{Et} - c_{E_t|C_t})))) \end{aligned}$$

There are still conformal products which have not been fully distributed. Only one of these, however, contains terms which group together. Distributing that conformal product one level deeper yields:

$$\begin{aligned} & ((1_{D_t} * 1_{E_t}) + ((1_{D_t} - c_{D_t|A_t}) * (1_{D_t} - c_{D_t|B_t}) \\ & \quad *(1_{E_t} - c_{E_t|B_t}) * (1_{E_t} - c_{E_t|C_t}))) \\ & -((1_{E_t} * ((1_{D_t} - c_{D_t|A_t}) * (1_{D_t} - c_{D_t|B_t}))) \\ & +(1_{D_t} * ((1_{E_t} - c_{E_t|B_t}) * (1_{Et} - c_{E_t|C_t})))) \end{aligned}$$

We are done. We can now apply commutativity and associativity to yield the final evaluation form:

$$\begin{aligned} & ((1_{D_t} * 1_{E_t}) + ((1_{D_t} - c_{D_t|A_t}) \\ & \quad *((1_{D_t} - c_{D_t|B_t}) * (1_{E_t} - c_{E_t|B_t})) \\ & \quad *(1_{E_t} - c_{E_t|C_t}))) \\ & -((1_{E_t} * ((1_{D_t} - c_{D_t|A_t}) * (1_{D_t} - c_{D_t|B_t}))) \\ & +(1_{D_t} * ((1_{E_t} - c_{E_t|B_t}) * (1_{Et} - c_{E_t|C_t})))) \end{aligned}$$

None of the conformal products in this final expression meet the criteria for distribution, so we are done, and the expression can be evaluated according to normal SPI methods (the standard SPI local ordering heuristic will group terms appropriately for efficient evaluation, see [1]. The distribution procedure is efficient, and performs well (although not perfectly) at generating an expression which can be efficiently evaluated. We discuss each of these following description of the remaining processing needed.

3.3 Subquery Generation:

It should be clear that during the above process the information needed from each child partition has already been identified. Subquery processing proceeds as in standard SPI. It may seem at first that some savings could be achieved by not computing the full distribution for a node, but only the distribution over the referenced subrange. However, at this time we always generate sub-queries for the full distribution across a node.

3.4 Expression Evaluation:

We have already discussed the semantics of the operators in the local expression language. The only remaining issue is whether evaluation should always reduce an expression to a single joint distribution across the desired set of result variables or stop short of complete evaluation. Our current implementation always reduces expressions to a single joint distribution.

Distribution Procedure Complexity The distribution procedure includes the following steps:

- Grouping of terms - this can be done in $O(nm)$ time, where n is the number of distributions in the expression, and m is the number of child partitions.
- "Separable" test - this can be done in $O(nm)$ time.
- Repetition of these two steps can occur up to $O(l^n)$ times, where l is the length of a node expression, and n is the number of node expressions being composed. For combination of noisy-or expressions as shown above, the overall time will be exponential in the number of expressions being combined which share antecedents.

Evaluation Complexity For noisy-or the above procedure preserves the property that the complexity of numeric evaluation is linear in the number of independent antecedents, since independent antecedents will reside in disjoint subtrees below the partition containing the expression being evaluated. As a result, terms referencing them will not group together, and therefore will not force distribution of the conformal product operator. This property is satisfied for the individual noisy or expressions for D and E. However, is not true for the initial composition of the local expressions for D and E. Correct evaluation of that expression would require that the summation over B be delayed until the subexpressions for D and E had been evaluated and combined. In general, the computation would be exponential in both space and time in the number of shared antecedents. By distributing the conformal product using the algorithm specified above, we reduce the space and time complexity of evaluation of the final expression to linear in the number of shared antecedents. The price we pay, however, is that the expression size, and therefore also evaluation complexity, becomes exponential in the number of nodes being combined. An alternate distribution heuristic might weigh more carefully the costs and benefits of distribution. A few further notes:

1. The "separable" criterion is not perfect. Consider, for example, the expression $((p(D|B,C) +$

$p(E|A,B))*(p(f|A,C)+p(G|B,C)))$ where A, B, and C reside in disjoint partition subtrees. According to our current test, both terms are separable, since no single distribution requires all of the partitions needed to evaluate an entire term. Nonetheless, distributing the conformal product does not yield a more efficiently evaluable expression.

2. It is not always possible to distribute conformal product operators down to a level which permits independent evaluation of each term (for example, terms might be distributions with overlapping sets of antecedents). In this case the same local evaluation heuristic used in [1] is used to group terms and sequence evaluation.

3. Full distribution of $*$ over $+$ and $-$ would not permit efficient evaluation. Were we to fully distribute conformal product, the result would be correct, but we would need to evaluate a number of terms exponential in both the number of antecedents and the number of nodes.

4. Consideration of the example we presented should make it clear that the algorithm reproduces the essential results of Quickscore when applied to two level bipartite (BN2O) graphs: numeric evaluation is linear in the number of antecedents, linear in the number of negative findings, and exponential in the number of positive findings.

4 Discussion

The above procedure is not optimal. It is, however, correct, and therefore provides a method for performing inference using standard interaction models such as noisy-or within SPI. Further, it correctly handles non-independence of antecedents. A review of the example above will reveal that the identification and grouping of the terms involving B did not in any way depend on either the fact that both terms named the same node (B), nor that the terms came from separate local expressions. Similar grouping and distribution of the conformal product operator would have occurred in processing a query for $p(D)$ if A and B were in the same partition subtree below D. We have therefore presented a general method for evaluating arbitrary belief nets which contain noisy or models of antecedent interaction.

Noisy-or is traditionally considered to be of restricted applicability since standard presentations restrict to the case where all nodes take only two values. However, there is a straightforward generalization to the multivalued case which requires $(v-1)^2$ parameters for each antecedent, where v is the number of values a variable can take. The methods presented here support this generalization as well as the simple two-value case.

The work presented here is far from complete. Two major extensions are needed to provide efficient support for the local expression language we describe. First, we must extend the distribution heuristic to cover the case where child partitions contain consequent (child) nodes. We believe this to be a minor extension. More difficult is the question of whether it is always appropriate to reduce an expression to a single joint distribution over the query nodes when performing numeric evaluation. In general we have no reason to believe this is the case. The general problem being solved is to find a factoring of the global expression for the query, as described in [1]. The partition tree indicates how to decompose queries and when nodes can be summed over, but contains little further information to guide evaluation. We are therefore investigating techniques which delay expression reduction as long as possible, only performing in each partition the evaluation necessary to perform summing over nodes not needed higher in the tree.

Also, we do not consider the local expression language to be complete. We have begun to explore further extensions to the local expression language. For example, we are pursuing, in conjunction with R. Fung and R. Shachter, the use of a $CASE$ statement to represent contingencies in belief nets [9].

We began our exploration of probabilistic inference in the context of truth maintenance systems, and at that time used symbolic representation at the level of individual probability mass elements [2]. Later, motivated by efficiency concerns, we changed to a symbolic representation at the distribution level [8]. We now seem to have come full circle: the implementation described here again performs symbolic reasoning on elements as small as individual probabilities. The difference is that we now have a choice of representation grain-size, and can select the grain-size appropriate for the dependence model being described.

5 Conclusion

Belief nets are a compact, intuitive representation for general probabilistic models, but suffer from inability to efficiently represent low level structural details such as asymmetries and noisy-or relationships. We have shown how the SPI framework can be extended to support a wide class of antecedent interaction models. This permits free use of these models within an arbitrary belief net, and provides efficient processing of arbitrary marginal and conditional queries on the resulting belief net. This facility also provides for easy experimentation on new interaction models, since there is no need to write code to perform inference using the new model: one directly describes the interaction using a simple algebraic local expression language. The full expression language has been implemented and is in use at Intel Corp. in a chip fabrication process diagnosis project.

Acknowledgements

Thanks to Bob Fung and Peter Raulefs for many useful discussions. Thanks to NSF (IRI88-21660) for providing the support which made this work possible.

References

[1] B. D'Ambrosio. Symbolic probabilistic inference. Technical report, CS Dept., Oregon State University, 1989.

[2] B. D'Ambrosio. Incremental evaluation and construction of defeasible probabilistic models. *International Journal of Approximate Reasoning*, To Appear 1990.

[3] D. Heckerman. A tractable inference algorithm for diagnosing multiple diseases. In *Proceedings of the Fifth Conference on Uncertainty in AI*, pages 174–181, August 1989.

[4] M. Henrion. Towards efficient probabilistic diagnosis with a very large knowledge-base. In *AAAI Workshop on the Principles of Diagnosis*, 1990.

[5] J. Pearl. *Probabilistic Reasoning in Intelligent Systems*. Morgan Kaufmann, Palo Alto, 1988.

[6] Y. Peng and J. Reggia. A probabilistic causal model for diagnostic problem solving - part 1: Integrating symbolic causal inference with numeric probabilistic inference. *IEEE Trans. on Systems, Man, and Cybernetics: special issue on diagnosis*, SMC-17(2):146–162, 1987.

[7] R. Shachter. Evaluating influence diagrams. *Operations Research*, 34(6):871 – 882, November-December 1986.

[8] R. Shachter, B. D'Ambrosio, and B. DelFavero. Symbolic probabilistic inference in belief networks. In *Proceedings Eighth National Conference on AI*, pages 126–131. AAAI, August 1990.

[9] R. Shachter and R. Fung. Contingent influence diagrams. Tech report, Dept. of Engineering Economic Systems, Stanford University, September 1990. In preparation.

Symbolic Decision Theory and Autonomous Systems

John Fox and Paul Krause
Biomedical Computing Unit
Imperial Cancer Research Fund Laboratories
Lincoln's Inn Fields, London, United Kingdom

Abstract

The ability to reason under uncertainty and with incomplete information is a fundamental requirement of decision support technology. In this paper we argue that the concentration on theoretical techniques for the evaluation and selection of decision options has distracted attention from many of the wider issues in decision making. Although numerical methods of reasoning under uncertainty have strong theoretical foundations, they are representationally weak and only deal with a small part of the decision process. Knowledge-based systems, on the other hand, offer greater flexibility but have not been accompanied by a clear decision theory. We describe here work which is under way towards providing a theoretical framework for *symbolic decision procedures*. A central proposal is an extended form of inference which we call *argumentation*; reasoning for and against decision options from generalised domain theories. The approach has been successfully used in several decision support applications, but it is argued that a comprehensive decision theory must cover autonomous decision making, where the agent can formulate questions as well as take decisions. A major theoretical challenge for this theory is to capture the idea of *reflection* to permit decision agents to reason about their goals, what they believe and why, and what they need to know or do in order to achieve their goals.

1 INTRODUCTION[1]

Medicine has been an important field for developing and testing decision support systems which are capable of reasoning with uncertain and incomplete information. Experiments with numerical techniques for diagnosis and other applications began in the sixties, and produced some early encouraging progress, notably de Dombal's classic work on the diagnosis of abdominal pain [1]. By the end of the seventies, systems such as MYCIN, INTERNIST and CASNET were showing that symbolic techniques for knowledge representation, inference and heuristic reasoning held much promise for decision support systems. While arousing great excitement, these early expert systems were also treated with some skepticism by decision theorists on the grounds that they were somewhat ad hoc in design. This stimulated a great deal of technical activity in developing more rigorous and precise numerical uncertainty handling techniques, but we feel that this has distracted attention from many fundamental issues which still need to be addressed in order to produce flexible and sound decision support systems that will have significant impact in many practical applications.

A major cause of the criticisms levelled at some of the above mentioned systems, was the attempt to incorporate uncertainty handling into a simple rule-based knowledge representation framework. There is, unfortunately, a fundamental conflict between the demands of computational tractability and of semantic expressiveness. The modularity of simple rule-based systems aids efficient data update procedures. However, severe evidence independence assumptions have to be made for uncertainties to be combined and propagated using strictly local calculations. A general and rigorous implementation of a fully intentional system, in which all possible interactions between rules and evidences are taken into account on each data update, could become so computationally intractable that the development of a realistic application would be infeasible

1. This paper is a shortened and revised version of a keynote address given at the IMACS workshop in Qualitative Reasoning and Decision Support Systems, Toulouse, March 13-15, 1991 [8].

[12]. In order to develop computationally tractable, yet rigorous, uncertainty handling mechanisms much recent work has been directed towards the development of graphical structures in which the dependencies and influences between knowledge items are explicitly represented [11], [13]. This has led to a realisation that the correct structuring of the knowledge that is relevant in a given decision making context is as important, *if not more important,* than the numerical values that are propagated through the graph.

In fact, at least for certain classes of applications such as medical diagnostic applications, decision accuracy can be highly insensitive to these values. In [2] for example the performance of a strictly probabilistic approach to diagnosis and a heuristic approach were quantitatively compared. Using a database of medical records of some 400 patients who had been reliably diagnosed as having one of 5 different gastrointestinal conditions, two diagnostic systems were constructed. The first was a simple bayesian procedure for computing posterior probabilities given a set of patient symptoms. The second was a set of categorical production rules for interpreting patterns of symptoms. The rules excluded quantitative information about the associations between symptoms and diseases. A typical rule was:

```
if:   age(elderly) and weight_loss(present)
then: maybe(cancer)
```

It turned out that the diagnostic accuracy of the rule-based system approximately equalled that of the probabilistic system (~70%)[1] while requesting only half the available symptom data. The relative naturalness of the categorical representation did not apparently entail a significant reduction in decision making performance.

There are well documented differences between the performance of different numerical calculi [17], [18]. However, theoreticians have not paid so much attention to studies comparing precise with imprecise methods like the above. There is considerable evidence that the performance of a well structured, largely symbolic system may well be as good as a more rigorous numerical approach [20]. In [28], it was demonstrated that a purely symbolic system only differed in behaviour from a numerical probabilistic system in those cases with an uncommon diagnosis (prior probability ≤ 0.03). Chard's conclusion was that, so long as it could be ensured that a purely symbolic approach could pick up the less common conditions, then it would suffer no performance disadvantage when compared to a bayesian system.

We will go further than simply saying there is no disadvantage; we shall argue that a symbolic approach to decision making has in fact many advantages (other than reducing the purely computational and cost overheads associated with the elicitation and use of large amounts of numerical data). The next section will suggest that a symbolic approach allows us to explicate more of the decision process, including the knowledge required to define, organise and make a decision. It also allows us to explicitly represent decisions, knowledge sources, reasoning strategies and representations, and to reason about the control and inference processes involved in specific tasks. These are all requirements which need to be satisfied if we are to be able to develop systems with an advanced decision making capability. The third section of this paper addresses the requirements of a particularly challenging class of AI system, those capable of making decisions autonomously.

1. This figure is not untypical; in gastroenterology a diagnostic accuracy from the patient history alone is frequently much lower than this because of high intrinsic uncertainty.

2 SYMBOLIC DECISION MAKING UNDER UNCERTAINTY

The *Concise Oxford Dictionary* defines a decision as follows "Decision: settlement of (question etc.), conclusion, formal judgement, making up one's mind". But how should we settle questions, particularly where they involve uncertainty? The view from classical decision theory is quite unequivocal:

"First, the uncertainties present in the situation must be quantified in terms of values called probabilities. Second, the various consequences of the courses of action must be similarly described in terms of utilities. Third that decision must be taken which is expected - on the basis of the calculated probabilities - to give the greatest utility."

Dennis Lindley [3].

Probabilistic inference, or "how degrees of belief are altered by data"[4] is one of the two pillars of classical decision theory. Unfortunately it is widely acknowledged that objective probabilities (e.g. frequency based estimates of the cooccurrence of symptoms and diseases) are impractical for general decision making. Therefore the Bayesian notion of "subjective probability", of a person's willingness to accept a wager, has been formulated in a well-defined way in order to finesse this difficulty.

In reality the (psychological) processes that are involved in the formulation of subjective probabilities, and the formal nature of such numbers, are obscure. Probabilistic inference certainly places clear mathematical requirements on "coherent" belief revision procedures but it pays little attention to the question of what numerical degrees of belief can be said to represent. Unfortunately, heuristic methods may suffer from the reverse problem; while symbolic representational techniques are claimed to capture knowledge of informal domains like medicine quite well, the formal requirements of sound reasoning are not always adequately addressed.

The second pillar of decision theory is utility: roughly a numerical representation of the costs and benefits associated with deciding on a particular option. Unfortunately, as with probability, though for different reasons, it is often difficult to assign objective measures of utility to the consequences of decisions (e.g. the utility of life and death; pain or distress). Even in situations where there seems to be an objective scale (e.g. monetary value) the relationship between subjective and objective scales is not at all clear.

It should also be noted that subjective values are multidimensional not unidimensional, and often qualitative. For example a drug treatment may be desirable because it is painless, because it can be taken at home, and because it is low cost, while it may be less desirable than a surgical procedure because the latter has a higher success rate, though it may compromise long term quality of life. Quantitative representation of values remains, at the very least, controversial.

In this section we will describe techniques for a number of aspects of decision making which are non-quantitative and yet can be clearly formulated. These techniques make use of first-order logic (FOL) to formulate methods for reasoning *for* and *against* decision options; introducing new options; structuring the decision; representing beliefs, values and preferences; taking the decision, and improving communication between decision support systems and their users.

2.1 EXTENDING THE REQUIREMENTS FOR SYMBOLIC REASONING

Inference is the pivot of most kinds of problem solving and decision making is no exception. Classical decision theory emphasises probabilistic inference, and many other techniques (both numerical and logical) are being developed to capture aspects of commonsense inference which are not expressible in standard monotonic logic [22]. However, these formalisations apply to just one (albeit a central one) of the activities associated with decision support. They address the evaluation and selection of decision options. Surrounding this activity are a number of further layers of activities, represented in figure 1 (after Andriole [5]), involving information acquisition, the actual identification of relevant decision options, and so forth. The concentration on the development of formalisms for option evaluation and selection has distracted attention from providing a more formal basis for these other activities [6].

To address the requirements raised by a more eclectic view of decision support we shall have to extend radically our notion of inference to one which can work at the multiplicity of levels represented in figure 1. We need to construct a general inference mechanism which satisfies at least the following requirements:

1. It must be able to construct arguments for decision options using whatever knowledge is productive; we do not wish to restrict reasoning to, nor for it to wholly depend upon, any one kind of inference (such as statistical inference) if this is restrictive.
2. There must be an explicit conceptualisation of *what it means to make a decision* and the roles of different kinds of inference in that process [7].
3. It is desirable to have a simple declarative representation of the decision procedure, decision criteria and application knowledge, permitting greater flexibility and

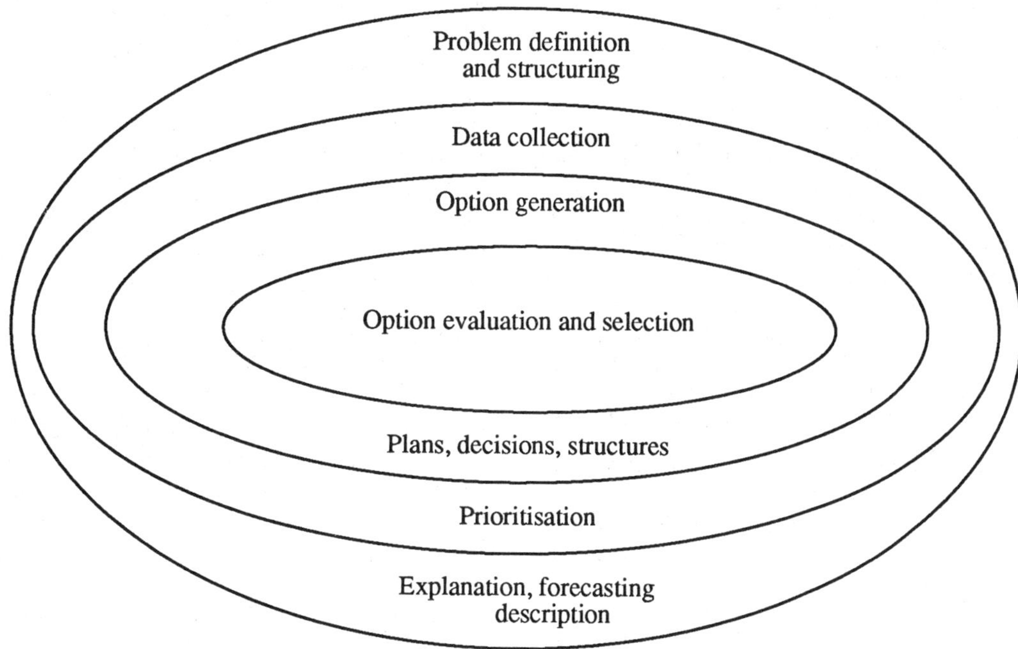

Figure 1: Decision making activities (after Andriole [5]).

more natural understanding by designers and users.

4. Of course we also want our extended inference to be well understood and mathematically sound.

The demand for greater capabilities in decision support systems, and the need to address these requirements is encapsulated in a central goal of our research: achieving a deep understanding of what we have dubbed *symbolic decision procedures (SDPs).* Informally a symbolic decision procedure can be characterised as:

an explicit representation of the knowledge required to define, organise and make a decision, and ... a logical abstraction from the qualitative and quantitative knowledge that is required for any specific application. A SDP may include a specification of when and how the procedure is to be executed [6].

The basic idea of classical decision making is the weighing of quantitative evidence and values for predefined options; the fundamental mechanism of a symbolic decision procedure is a flexible framework for qualitative reasoning that we call argumentation. Argumentation provides a rigorous basis for weighing the pros and cons of decisions but also for structuring the decision and, as we shall see later, for controlling the initiation and execution of a decision process.

2.2 INFERENCE AND "ARGUMENTATION"

Our central thesis is that practical decision making requires diverse sources of domain specific and domain independent knowledge. The relevance and nature of various forms of knowledge may vary with the context and the decision. To accommodate this, we use an extended form of inference, which we call argumentation. Informally we want to capture some of the kinds of argument that are commonly used in decision making, such as "based on the facts that the patient is *elderly* and suffering from *weight loss*, there is *support* for the proposition that *cancer is present*"

Argumentation consists of the identification and appraisal of lines of reasoning about propositions. Argumentation permits the use of whatever theories and sources of knowledge are deemed appropriate. An argument for a proposition P may have an associated *qualifier* or *sign* S_p which represents the certainty of the proposition given that the argument is valid. The *grounds* for the argument, G_p, are also associated with the proposition. These indicate the *facts* used in initiating the argument, and the *theories* used to connect these facts with P.

More formally, if an argument is identified for a proposition P, then we may write

$$KB \vdash (P,S_p,G_p)$$

with S_p and G_p as above. The qualifier S_p and grounds G_p are not merely present to provide useful information to the user. They also satisfy a more formal requirement. Multiple triples will be associated with a proposition P if P can be deduced with different qualifiers S_p, or with the same qualifiers but using different grounds G_p. We say these constitute distinct arguments for P.

The knowledge base, KB, over which the inference engine operates may be partitioned into a number of theories. These may be domain specific theories, consisting primarily of ground facts, or domain independent theories consisting of first order rules for establishing links between knowledge items in a given task. A further knowledge layer may contain information about which theories are relevant to which specific tasks. In our view practical decision making may involve arguing from different points of view (e.g. arguing from a causal theory, an anatomical theory, a theory of physiological function or from statistical knowledge). The kinds of theory that are relevant are determined by the kind of decision that is being taken. We have to keep these theories partitioned because in practice we cannot guarantee that the different views that they embody are globally consistent.

A more detailed discussion on how arguments can be constructed may be found in [9] and [26].

2.3 AGGREGATION OF ARGUMENTS

We have seen that from different grounds it is possible to construct multiple arguments about (for or against) a proposition. If:

$$KB \vdash (P,S_1,G_1)$$
$$KB \vdash (P,S_2,G_2)$$

where $S_1 \neq S_2$, or $G_1 \neq G_2$, then there are two distinct arguments for P. Once two or more distinct arguments have been identified for a proposition P, the associated qualifiers S_i will need to be aggregated to form a global qualification of P.

The process of argumentation allows plenty of scope for the definition of various aggregation operators, both numerical and qualitative. The S_i may be taken from a variety of symbolic or numeric dictionaries. Here we shall focus on a simple 4-valued dictionary:

{confirmed, eliminated, supported, opposed}.

exactly one of which must be associated with each argument.The semantics of these terms is not numerical, but where probabilities (or other numerical certainty data) are available they could be substituted without modification to the basic argumentation framework.

Our interest of course is in the more common situation where those data are not available. A straightforward aggregation operator is simply to add up the arguments for and against each option, and decide on that with the largest ratio of pros to cons. This was the method employed in the gastroenterology example described in the introduction, and such improper linear decision rules are well recognised as effective.

We can also formulate symbolic aggregation operators. Making the grounds explicit in the argument has obvious value in the user interface, but they can also play an important part in aggregation because we can use them in computing states of belief in options (or any proposition). This can be done using logical schemata which demand no numerical coefficients, but which we believe are intuitively appealing and logically coherent.

The following symbolic aggregation rules[1] define logical schemata for assigning propositions to various classes of belief: *conceivable*; *possible*; *plausible*; *confirmed.*

(P, conceivable)
 $\leftarrow$ not $\exists$G • (P, G, eliminated).

(P, possible)
 $\leftarrow$ (P, conceivable) $\wedge$ $\exists$G • (P,G, supported).

(P, plausible)
 $\leftarrow$ (P, possible) $\wedge$ not $\exists$G • (P, G, opposed).

(P, confirmed)
 $\leftarrow$ (P, conceivable) $\wedge$ $\exists$G • (P, G, confirmed).

The aggregation operator defined by this schema allows only a fairly coarse-grained categorisation of decision options. A more complex schema could be defined to allow finer distinctions, but in *The Oxford System of Medicine* (OSM), a decision support system designed to provide flexible assistance for general medical practice (and a specialised derivative for oncology, BOSS) [16], the 4 qualifiers in the dictionary above, together with the belief terms constructible from them, provide an adequate basis for carrying out decision making.

Our contention is that for many problems, where limited statistical data are available, attempts to use numbers to make a fine grained distinction between decision options may be unnecessary, and lead to illusory precision in the final result. A logical approach to arguing for and against and comparing decision options, on the other hand, has a clearly defined semantics which is easily explained to and understood by the user.

2.4 DISCUSSION

Current probabilistic techniques require the prior construction of the graph linking decision options to observables and findings[2]. However, the exact nature of these links may vary with context and the nature of the decision problem at hand, and in general decision systems should be able to construct and revise the graph dynamically as information becomes available and the goals of the problem at hand are identified [15]. Our approach allows for arguing about this graph structure [14],[15]; for example, the discovery that a patient is under medication which can cause an observed abnormality as a side effect may lead to a revision of the graph that had previously been generated.

We have described a purely symbolic approach to identifying and evaluating decision options. Further to this, we aim to develop techniques which address how and when a decision may be taken. As with symbolic terms for representing states of belief, symbolic representations of preference and value may not be arbitrary but must be assigned an explicit semantics. In order to avoid confounding distinct logical ideas like obligations, duties and preferences we are taking an approach in which arguments are constructed from principles of what *must* be done ("deontic" principles) and what *ought* to be done ("praxeological" principles) and pluralistic value theory [10].

It is our intention to strive towards a normative theory of decision making. To achieve this we need "an explicit conceptualisation of what it means to make a decision" (requirement 2 above). A possible approach to this is discussed in the next section.

3 AUTONOMOUS DECISION MAKING UNDER UNCERTAINTY

The central claim of section 2 was that symbolic procedures can significantly extend the capabilities for reasoning about belief and values and structuring the decision as compared with strictly numerical procedures (requirement 1 above). A further advantage we claim is that a symbolic approach allows for an explicit representation of the decision itself. Neither classical decision theory nor work on knowledge based decision aids have placed emphasis on this, apparently because these systems are intended to *assist* in decision making, not to make decisions autonomously. They can rely on knowledgeable users to critically supervise the decision process. In our view this is a serious omission from, and challenge to, theory. For practical reasons and to be confident in our understanding of the limits on decision making capabilities we need to address the problem of building systems that can operate autonomously, without relying on external support.

There is a steadily increasing interest in AI in the development of autonomous agents [23]. In particular SOAR, an "architecture for general intelligence" [21] and HOMER, a simulated submersible capable of receiving task instructions and autonomously planning its solution [24], are projects which are making interesting progress towards autonomous capabilities. Although not developed with either decision theory or uncertainty management in mind they may guide us towards a statement of what the capabilities of an autonomous decision system should be. We first attempt the following definition of an autonomous agent:

An agent is autonomous with respect to its environment if it can set and achieve goals, and respond adaptively to events in its environment, without external advice or assistance.

Practical environments are frequently so complex they can evolve in far more ways than could be allowed for in any *a priori* structuring of a decision. A definite requirement for an autonomous decision maker therefore is that it should be

1. Called "annotation rules" in [6], [14], [15].

2. Although we are grateful to an anonymous referee for drawing our attention to work that is underway to correct this deficiency.

responsive to the arrival of unexpected information. For example, HOMER [24] is given an instruction to collect a package from a pier and constructs a plan to do this. *En route*, however, it finds a large ship on its course; HOMER must perceive this, recognise its implications and replan to achieve its goal.

In general information may at any time become available to a decision maker that has implications for any aspect of a decision *viz*: raising new problems requiring additional decisions; challenging the grounds for current beliefs, or indicating that the current decision can be taken without further information.

Part of the responsiveness of an effective decision maker is the ability to recognise that there is a decision to be taken. The *Concise Oxford Dictionary* relates a decision to the "settlement of a question". Classical decision theory has had much to say about how we should settle a question; the new challenge is to understand how these questions are formulated in the first place. This suggests a revision to our definition:

An agent is an autonomous decision maker if it can pose and resolve questions about the state of its environment or the actions that are desirable to achieve its goals

If a decision maker could ask and answer questions such as the following it would gain great power:

1. The pivotal questions are: *what is the problem? what do I need to know, or do?* As with all AI systems we will necessarily require an explicit representation of the systems goals in order to be able to formulate these questions. Decision theory has taken the question of what a decision is required for entirely for granted. As soon as we address it a cascade of further questions follows.
2. *What do I know that is relevant to this decision?* An agent that has a great deal of knowledge may encounter difficulties in retrieving relevant knowledge during decision making. Explicit representation of theories and their applicability aids search.
3. *What are the possible options? How could I find out?* Symbolic decision procedures can introduce decision options as information is acquired by making use of explicit advice like "in diagnosis, propose possible causes of symptoms as possible diagnoses".
4. *What justifies a belief (value or preference)? Is this argument still valid?* Practical problem solving almost always risks blind-alleys and misunderstandings. The underpinning of beliefs by explicit arguments that record the grounds for those beliefs provides the information necessary for detecting and resolving inconsistencies [25].
5. *Am I thinking about this decision the right way?* All problem solving takes place in a "problem space" which embodies presuppositions about the problem and affects the way problem solving proceeds. If presuppositions or representations are implicit then we are at the mercy of them. If theories and presuppositions are explicit then the agent potentially has the ability to detect when assumptions of validity or relevance are violated.

3.1 REQUIREMENTS AND SKETCH OF AN AUTONOMOUS DECISION MAKER

In this section we summarise some of the principle requirements for a comprehensive decision capability and the main theoretical challenges that they entail. The principle requirements for an autonomous decision maker include the following:

1. It should be able to observe and interpret its environment, and recognise when a decision or sequence of decisions needs to be taken in order to achieve its goals.
2. Goals and decisions should be represented explicitly. One approach (used in the OSM and BOSS) is to represent the "generic" decision as the root class in a generalisation hierarchy. This defines the decision procedure as a set of partially instantiated attribute templates, such as:

   decision_prototype(Decision,Prototype).
   relevant_theories(Decision,Theories).
   relevant_argument_types(Decision,Arguments).
   option_proposal_criteria(Decision,Criteria). ...
3. The decision maker should be able to classify the *types* of decision required. One way to do this is to associate with each class a particular decision_prototype, invoking it when its prototype is satisfied. For example a prototype for a diagnosis decision may specify that if an observation has been made that is abnormal and its cause is not known then a decision of class "diagnosis" is required in the context. Specific classes of decision inherit the generic attributes, but are distinguished from it by the values that instantiate the attribute templates, as in:

   relevant_theories(diagnosis, symptomatology).
   relevant_argument_types(diagnosis,causality).
   option_proposal_criteria(diagnosis,possibility) ...
4. The agent must be able to initiate the decision in the context; this will entail inheriting all the class information to the decision instance, further instantiating it with details of the context (e.g. a patient's name) and presumably executing some control actions.
5. Guiding the decision process. Explicit knowledge of relevant theories and arguments associated with the decision class can be used to guide information acquisition and data interpretation. Decision options (e.g. diagnoses) can be proposed on the basis of criteria associated with the class (in the above example any option is proposed as a candidate if it satisfies the condition for being "possible" (section 2).

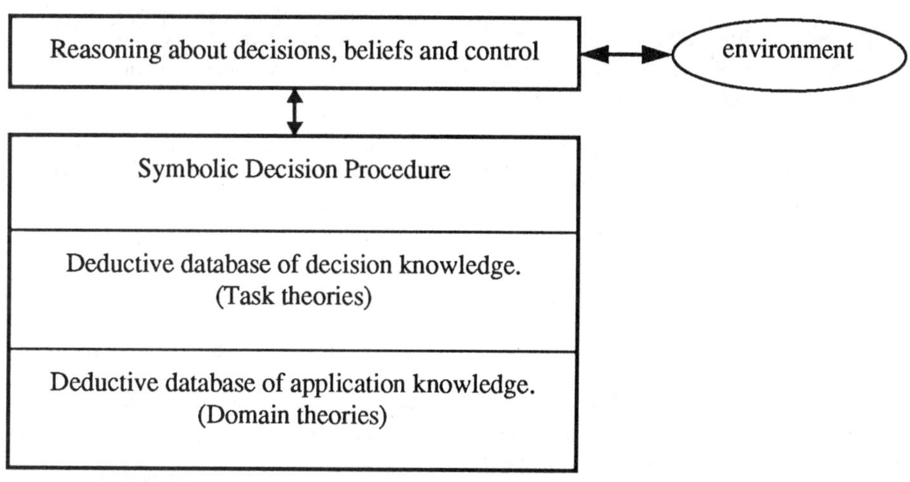

Figure 2: Outline architecture for autonomous decision agents.

6. The decision should be terminated when appropriate. Explicit criteria for formulating decisions also presumably imply criteria for knowing when those decisions can be taken. For example, the criterion given above for requiring a diagnosis decision was that we cannot confirm the cause of an abnormal observation. The opposite is also true; if we can confirm the cause then the diagnosis can be made.

Work is in progress to provide an adequate theoretical basis for these capabilities, and to demonstrate their application. Figure 2 presents a schematic outline of a proposed layered architecture for autonomous decision agents. The ascending layers represent knowledge at increasing levels of abstraction; each layer is capable of manipulating the knowledge in the layers beneath it.

The three lower layers are deductive data bases representing (in ascending order) domain theories (application specific knowledge), task theories (knowledge about decisions), and the symbolic decision procedure itself. The top layer in figure 2 may be described as a control layer; among its functions are to look after interactions with the environment, respond to events, initiate, control and terminate decisions and arguments, and maintain the agent's beliefs and goals. This organisation echoes the traditional distinction between knowledge and action; the symbolic decision procedure and other deductive components can be naturally implemented with a pure logic theorem prover, while the top layer - which operates in time, entails side-effects on the system's knowledge, and has other non-logical features - is procedural in character.

A full explanation of these examples would need a detailed description of an interpreter, which cannot be presented here. Some discussion of techniques to provide this capability can be found in [27].

4 PRINCIPLE RESEARCH DIRECTIONS

It is important to carry out work like this in the context of applications. The OSM and BOSS systems, under development in this laboratory, have been important in forcing us to develop our approaches and in evaluating our ideas. For generality we would like to see applications in domains other than medicine and for decision tasks other than medical decisions. We also hope to build on our approach to look into *compound decisions*, such as planning, design and other tasks. These tasks can be viewed (in part) as complexes of simple selection decisions. Some experimental work on integrating decisions in problem solving is in progress, focusing on planning of cancer treatment and formulation of antibiotic therapy for chest infections [19].

We are in the early stages of formalising argumentation and other aspects of symbolic decision making, focusing on non-autonomous decision support systems. Some work on autonomous systems is in progress, and influences the work, but for the moment is of lower priority.

Perhaps one of the most obvious features of our proposals is the importance we attach to meta-level reasoning, or reflection. To express the questions in section 3 and implement the mechanisms required in section 3.1 it seems clear that considerable capabilities for reflection are needed - reflecting on beliefs, arguments, knowledge, and decisions. Classical decision procedures offer few handholds for developing these ideas. Formalising the concept of reflection will be, we believe, fundamental to significant progress in the field. It is perhaps the most difficult yet most fascinating theoretical challenge before us.

Acknowledgements

We would like to thank all our colleagues in the Biomedical Computing Unit for many useful discussions on this work, but especially Saki Hajnal, Dominic Clark, Andrzej Glowinski, Mike O'Neil and Mirko Dohnal. This work has received an added stimulus with our involvement in and support from the Esprit Basic Research Programme 3085, DRUMS.

P. Krause is supported under the SERC project 1822: a Formal Basis for Decision Support Systems. Our thanks also to Mike Clarke of Queen Mary College who is involved in this project with us.

References

[1] de Dombal, F T "Computer assisted diagnosis of Abdominal pain" in J Rose and J H Mitchell *Advances in Medical Computing*, Edinburgh: Churchill Livingstone,1975.

[2] Fox J, Barber D C, Bardhan K D "Alternatives to Bayes: A quantitative comparison with rule-based diagnosis". *Method of Information in Medicine*, 1980.

[3] Lindley D V *Making decisions* (2nd ed) Wiley 1985.

[4] Lindley D V *Introduction to probability and statistics: part 2. inference.* Cambridge: Cambridge University Press, 1965.

[5] Andriole S J *Handbook of decision support systems*, Blue Ridge: Tab Books, 1989.

[6] Fox J "Symbolic decision procedures for knowledge based systems." Chapter 2 in H Adeli (ed) *Knowledge Engineering*, New York: McGraw Hill, 1989.

[7] Fox J "Formal and knowledge based methods for decision technology" *Acta Psychologica*, 56, 303-331, 1984.

[8] Fox J "Decision Theory and Autonomous Systems" *Proc IMACS workshop*, 1991.

[9] Fox J, Clarke M "Towards a formalisation of arguments in decision making" *Proceedings of Stanford Spring Symposium in AI*, 1991.

[10] Clarke M "A model of practical reasoning for decision support systems" *Proc IMACS workshop*, 1991.

[11] Pearl J *Heuristics: Intelligent Search Strategies for Computer Problem Solving*, Addison-Wesley: Reading MA, 1984.

[12] Pearl J *Probabilistic Reasoning in Intelligent Systems: Networks of Plausible Inference*, Morgan Kaufmann, 1988.

[13] Lauritzen S L and Spiegelhalter D "Local computations with probabilities on graphical stuctures and their application to expert systems" *J Roy. Statist. Soc* B 50 (2), 1988.

[14] Fox J, Glowinski A J, O'Neil M "Decision making from a logical point of view" in B Kelly and A Rector *Research in Expert Systems V*, Cambridge: Cambridge University Press, 1988.

[15] Fox J, Clark D A, Glowinski A J, O'Neil M "Using predicate logic to integrate qualitative reasoning and classical decision theory" *IEEE Trans on Systems Man and Cybernetics*, 20, 347-357, 1990.

[16] Fox J, Gordon C, Glowinski A J and O'Neil M "Logic engineering for knowledge engineering" *Artifical Intelligence in Medicine*, 2, 323-339, 1990.

[17] Heckerman D, "An Empirical Comparison of Three Inference Methods" in Shachter, Levitt, Kanal and Lemmer, eds, *Uncertainty in Artificial Intelligence 4*, Amsterdam: North-Holland, 283-301, 1990.

[18] Henrion M, "Some Practical Issues in Constructing Belief Networks" in Kanal, Levitt and Lemmer, eds, *Uncertainty in Artificial Intelligence 3*, Amsterdam: North-Holland, 161-173, 1989.

[19] O'Neil M "An abstract description of a general approach to problem solving", ICRF technical report, 1991.

[20] O'Neil M, Glowinski A "Evaluating and validating very large knowledge-based systems" *Med. Inform.*, 15, 237-251, 1990.

[21] Laird J, Newell A, Rosenbloom P "SOAR: an architecture for general intelligence" *Artificial Intelligence*, 1987.

[22] Smets P, Mamdani E H, Dubois D, Prade H, *Non-Standard Logics for Automated Reasoning*, Academic Press, 1988.

[23] Seel N R, for example, "From Here to Agent Theory" in *AISB Quarterly, Quarterly Newsletter of the Society for the Study of Artificial Intelligence and the Simulation of Behaviour*, no 72, 1990.

[24] Vere S, Bicknell T "A Basic Agent" *Computational Intelligence*, 6 (1) 41-60, 1990.

[25] Krause P J, Byers P, Hajnal S, Fox J "The use of object-oriented process specification for the validation and verification of decision support systems" in Ayel M and Laurent J-P eds, *Validation, Verification and Test of Knowledge-Based Systems*, Chichester: John Wiley, 1991.

[26] Krause P J and Fox J "Combining symbolic and numerical methods for reasoning under uncertainty" in *AI and Computer Power: The Impact on Statistics*, Unicom Seminars Ltd, 1991.

[27] Fox J, Gordon C, Glowinsk A J, O'Neil M "Expert systems, databases and decision procedures" Proceedings of Medical Informatics Europe, Berlin: Springer 1990.

[28] Chard T "Qualitative probability versus quantitative probability in clinical diagnosis: a study using a computer simulation" *Medical Decision Making*, 1991, 11, 38-41.

A REASON MAINTENANCE SYSTEM DEALING WITH VAGUE DATA

B.Fringuelli, S.Marcugini, A.Milani, S.Rivoira
Dipartimento di Matematica
Università di Perugia
via Vanvitelli, 1
06100 Perugia, ITALY

Abstract

A reason maintenance system which extends an ATMS through Mukaidono's fuzzy logic is described. It supports a problem solver in situations affected by incomplete information and vague data, by allowing nonmonotonic inferences and the revision of previous conclusions when contradictions are detected.

INTRODUCTION

Any reasoning system must deal with belief revision at some extent.

In recent years truth maintenance systems have been proposed as powerful tools able to perform belief revision at a general level.

These systems can be viewed as constraint propagation mechanisms which tell a problem solver what things it is currently obliged to believe, given a single set of premises and a set of deduction constraints, some of which may be nonmonotonic.

Justification-based TMS (Doyle 1979) (McAllester 1980) (McDermott 1983) maintain a single context of belief and support nonmonotonic justifications, while assumption-based TMS (de Kleer 1986) (Martins 1988) avoid the restriction that the overall set of premises is contradiction free, maintaining multiple contexts of belief.

Early truth maintenance systems dealt with certain beliefs only, but several successive works extended them in order to allow handling of some kind of uncertainty.

De Kleer and Williams (de Kleer 1987) have assigned probabilities to assumptions in an ATMS which diagnoses multiple mutually indipendent faults.

Falkenheiner (Falkenheiner 1988) has introduced Dempster-Shafer theory into Doyle's TMS.

D'Ambrosio (D'Ambrosio 1989) has used an ATMS to compute beliefs for a special case of the Dempster-Shafer model.

Provan (Provan 1989) has incorporated belief functions into ATMS and Laskey and Lehner (Laskey 1989) have shown that any Dempster-Shafer inference system can be represented in a ATMS by attaching probabilities to assumptions that represent hypotheses in a background frame.

Dubois et al. (Dubois 1990) extended an ATMS in order to handle uncertainty, pervading justifications or grading assumptions, represented in the framework of possibility and necessity measures.

In this paper we describe a Fuzzy Truth Maintenance System (FTMS) obtained by extending an ATMS through fuzzy logic.

The general idea and motivations of our approach are very close to those of Dubois et al. (Dubois 1990).

The main difference from their work lies in the fact that in our system propositions involve vague predicates which may have intermediary degrees of truth and the underlying logic is truth-functional, while Dubois et al. consider propositions which are true or false, but due to the lack of precision of the available information it can only be estimated to what extent it is possible or necessary that a proposition is true.

In the following the basic definitions and properties of the adopted fuzzy logic are reported and, successively, definitions and functionalities of the FTMS are discussed.

MANY-VALUED LOGICS AND RESOLUTION

The work described in this paper is part of a research aiming to compare existing theories of uncertainty (both logical and probabilistic) from the viewpoint of the efficiency of inference rules and revision mechanisms.

Since the resolution principle (Robinson 1965) encompasses several inference rules in classical logic (modus ponens, modus tollens, disjunctive and hypothetical syllogisms, constructive and desctructive dilemmas) and it is widely used in reasoning systems, we firstly focused our attention on extensions of the resolution principle dealing with some kind of uncertainty.

Dubois and Prade (Dubois 1987) extended the resolution principle in the case of uncertain propositions where the uncertainty involves non-vague predicates and it is modeled in terms of necessity measures.

The first attempt to a theory of fuzzy resolution was proposed by Lee (Lee 1972) for a fuzzy logic defined as follows.

Let [S] denote the truth value of a formula S:

$[S] \in [0,1]$

$[\neg S] = 1-[S]$

$[R \vee S] = \max([R],[S])$

$[R \wedge S] = \min([R],[S])$

$[R \rightarrow S] = [\neg R \vee S] = \max(1-[R],[S])$.

An interpretation I is said to satisfy a formula S if $[S] \geq 0.5$ under I.

The resolution principle corresponds to the following rule of inference:

let $S_1 = x \vee L_1$;

$S_2 = \neg x \vee L_2$;

a logical consequence of $S_1 \wedge S_2$ is the resolvent:

$$R(S_1,S_2) = L_1 \vee L_2$$

and, in fuzzy logic, if $[S_1 \wedge S_2] > 0.5$ then:

$$0.5 < [S_1 \wedge S_2] \leq [R(S_1,S_2)] \leq [S_1 \vee S_2].$$

Basically Lee proved that the resolution principle is complete in fuzzy logic and if every clause in a set has a truth-value greater than 0.5, then all the logical consequences obtained by repeatedly applying the resolution principle will have truth-value at least equal to the most unreliable clause, but never exceeding the truth value of the most reliable one.

These results were extended to a more general case by Mukaidono (Mukaidono 1982) (Mukaidono 1989) which allowed the truth value of all the clauses to be taken in the closed interval [0,1], introducing an inference strategy for fuzzy Prolog based on the following definitions.

The confidence c(S) of a formula S is defined as

$$c(S) =([S] - 0.5) * 2$$

and the fuzzy resolution principle asserts that the *confidence of resolution* c_r of the resolvent $R(S_1,S_2)$ is:

$$c_r(R(S_1,S_2))= (\max([x],[\neg x]) - 0.5) * 2 = |c(x)|$$

where x is the key predicate in the resolution.

If $S_2 = R(S3, S4)$ then

$c_r(R(S1, S2)) = \min(c_r(S2), |c(x)|)$.

The definition $[R \rightarrow S] = [\neg R \vee S] = \max(1-[R],[S])$ adopted for implication in fuzzy logic allows the inference of S from R (or $\neg R$ from $\neg S$) only when

$[R \rightarrow S] \geq [\neg R]$ (or $[R \rightarrow S] \geq [S]$ respectively).

This resolution principle is proved to be complete and significant for any truth value in the closed interval [0,1].

The confidence of resolution of an inferred formula S represents the degree of derivability of S from the formulas used in the inference process.

Mukaidono introduced an additional concept for implication (weight of rule) defined as the product of the confidence values of premise and conclusion:

$$w_{R \rightarrow S} = c(R) * c(S)$$

The weight of rule (usually defined as a closed interval) represents the degree of truth of an implication and it establishes the applicability of the rule, given the confidence of either the premise or the conclusion.

In fact it is easy to prove that a rule R^w->S can be applied if and only if:

$|w| \leq |c(R)|$ and $|w| \leq |c(S)|$.

According to the previous definitions it is possible to derive from a given set of fuzzy Horn clauses all the fuzzy logical consequences, together with their confidences of resolution.

The following example shows the inference mechanism applied to propositional clauses (first order predicate logic can be easily obtained by introducing unification).

From:

r1) $A \rightarrow B$ $\{w1 = 0.3\}$

r2) $B \rightarrow C$ $\{w2 = -0.4\}$

r3) $A \rightarrow D$ $\{w3 = -0.7\}$

r4) $D \rightarrow C$ $\{w4 = 0.1\}$

r5) A $\{[A] = 0.8\}$

it is possible to derive:

$c(A) = ([A]-0.5) * 2 = 0.6$; $c_r(A) = 1$; (from r5)

$c(B) = w1/c(A) = 0.5$ $c_r(B) = \min(c_r(A),|c(A)|) = 0.6$ (from r1, r5)

Since $|w3| > c|(A)|$, r3 cannot be applied.

$c(C) = w2/c(B) = -0.8$; $c_r(C) = \min(c_r(B), |c(B)|) = 0.5$ (from r5,r1,r2)

The fuzzy proposition C is therefore a logical consequence of proposition S r5, r1 and r2. The inferred truth-value of C is:

$$[C] = c(C)/2 + 0.5 = 0.1$$

while its confidence of resolution, that represents the degree of derivability of C from the axioms, is:

$c_r(C) = 0.5$.

The confidence c(P) of a conclusion P and its confidence of resolution $c_r(P)$ can be combined to give the confidence of resolved consequence:

$crc(P) = c(P) * c_r(P)$.

DEFINITION OF A FUZZY TRUTH MAINTENANCE SYSTEM

Extending De Kleer 's definition of ATMS (de Kleer 1986), we define an FTMS in the following way.

Every fuzzy formula introduced or derived by the attached problem solver corresponds to an FTMS **node**.

A special kind of node is represented by the atom $\perp$, corresponding to "falsity", for which $[\perp] = 0$ holds in any interpretation.

A **justification** is a triple:

$<j,c(n),c_r(n)>$

where $j: x_1,x_2,...,x_m \rightarrow n$ is a propositional Horn clause asserting that the consequent node n is derivable from the conjunction of the antecedent nodes $x_1,...,x_m$ and where c(n) and $c_r(n)$ are respectively the confidence and the confidence of resolution established by j for the node n.

A justification $<j,-1,c_r(\perp)>$, where the derived node is falsity, is communicated by the problem solver every time a contradiction is detected.

An **assumption** is a self-justifying node representing the decision of introducing an hypothesis; it is connected to the assumed data through justifications.

An **environment** is a set of logically conjuncted assumptions .

An environment E has **consistency** cs(E) equal to the opposite of the maximal confidence of resolved consequence with which falsity can be derived from E and the current set J of justifications:

$$cs(E) = - \max_j c_r(\perp)_E$$

An FTMS **context** is defined as the set formed by the assumptions of an environment and all the nodes derivable from those assumptions.

The goal of FTMS is to efficiently update the contexts when new assumptions or justifications are provided by the problem solver.

This goal is achieved by associating with every node a description (**label**) of every context in which the node holds.

More formally, a label L_n of the node n is defined as

the set of all the environments from which n can be derived:

$$L_n = \{E_i : E_i \underset{j}{\Rightarrow} n\}$$

In order to save space and time, a problem solver may wish to consider only environments whose consistency is greater than some threshold α and/or from which nodes can be derived with a degree of derivability greater than some threshold β , where α and β depend on the problem domain.

Therefore, given the two lower bounds α and β four important properties can be defined for the labels:

a label L_n is **α-consistent** if the consistency of each of its environments is not less than α;

a label L_n is **β-sound** if n is derivable from each of its environments with a confidence of resolution not less than β;

a label L_n is **α-β-complete** if every α-consistent environment from which n can be derived with a confidence of resolution not less than β is a superset of some environment in L_n;

a label L_n is **minimal** if no environment E_i in L_n is a superset of another environment E_k in L_n with $crc_i(n) \leq crc_k(n)$.

The task of FTMS is to ensure that each label in each node is α-consistent, β-sound, α-β-complete and minimal with respect to the current set of justifications .

This task is performed by invoking the following label-updating algorithm every time the problem solver adds a new justification.

Firstly the justification is recorded and then the new label and new confidence values are evaluated for the justified node.

If the new label or confidence values are different from the old ones, the algorithm considers the datum associated with the node. If it is not the falsity ,then the updating process recursively involves the labels and confidences of all the consequent nodes .

If the newly justified node is falsity , the consistency of each environment in the label is computed and the environment database is updated.

It is worth noticing that the revision of node confidences can make no more significant previously applied rules , forcing the system to retract the corresponding justifications.

Justifications are made retractable by conjoining them with extra assumptions which represent their defeasability.

Only the minimal environment database (MEDB) is maintained in the sense that an environment E_2 is recorded in the database only if no environment E_1 exists such that:

$$(E_1 \subset E_2) \text{ and } (cs(E_1) > cs(E_2)).$$

In contrast with ATMS, where inconsistent environments are removed from every node label, FTMS always keeps the environments in their labels, since consistency can be changed by successive justifications.

FTMS maintains for each fuzzy formula S introduced or derived by an attached problem solver the following information:

-the truth value of S, represented by the confidence established by the justifications of the corresponding node;

-the degree of derivability of S from the current knowledge, represented by the confidence of resolution of the corresponding node;

-the minimal set of environments from which S can be derived, together with their consistency values.

At each step of the reasoning process, the problem solver can therefore rank the partial solutions currently available on the basis of several ordering criteria (truth value, degree of derivability, consistency of the hypotheses), discarding or eliminating solutions which are not enough founded.

The main mechanisms for updating labels and confidences and their possible effects on the reasoning process are illustrated by the following example.

Let us suppose that the problem solver, on the basis of its own domain knowledge and inference procedures, has already derived and communicated to FTMS the justifications reported in figure 1 (where π, ρ, σ, τ are assumptions and $\perp$ indicates falsity) from which FTMS has determined the labels and the minimal environment database reported in figure 2.

The consequent net of dependencies between assumptions and derived propositions is shown in figure 3.

R_5: A,B → E, {w5= 0.2}

R_6: A,C → F, {w6= 0.3}

R_7: E,F → H, {w7= 0.4}

R_8: C,D → F, {w8= 0.4}

R9: B,F → E, {w9= 0.3}

R_{10}: C,B → ⊥, {w10= 0.2}

R_{11}: F,D → G, {w11= 0.2}

R_{12}: A,H → G, {w12= 0.4}

R_{13}: F,G → E, {w13= 0.4}

R_{14}: D,E → ⊥, {w14= 0.5}

figure 1a: set of inference rules

J_1: < π → A, c(A) = 0.6, c_r(A) = 1>

J_2: < ρ → B, c(B) = 0.4, c_r(B) = 1>

J_3: < σ → C, c(C) = 0.4, c_r(C) = 1>

J_4: < τ → D, c(D) = 0.4, c_r(D) = 1>

J_5: <A,B → E, c(E) = 0.5, c_r(E) = 0.5>

J_6: <A,C → F, c(F) = 0.75, c_r(F) = 0.75>

J_7: <E,F → H, c(H) = 0.8, c_r(H) = 0.8>

J_8: <C,D → F, c(F) = 1, c_r(F) = 1>

J_9: <B,F → E, c(E) = 0.75, c_r(E) = 0.75>

J_{10}: <C,B → ⊥, c(⊥) = 0.5, c_r(⊥) = 0.5>

J_{11}: <F,D → G, c(G) = 0.75, c_r(G) = 0.75>

J_{12}: <A,H → G, c(G) = 0.76, c_r(G) = 0.53>

figure 1b: a current set of justifications

L_A = {[(π), cs=1]}

L_B = {[(ρ), cs=1]}

L_C = {[(σ), cs=1]}

L_D = {[(τ), cs=1]}

L_E = {[(π,ρ), cs=1], [(π,σ,τ), cs=-0.5]}

L_F = {[(π,σ), cs=1], [(σ,τ), cs=1]}

L_G = {[(π,ρ,σ), cs=-0.5], [(σ,τ), cs=1]}

L_H = {[(ρ,σ,τ), cs=-0.5]}

figure 2a: the label of each node

MEDB: [(ρ,σ), cs=-0.5]

figure 2b: the minimal environment database

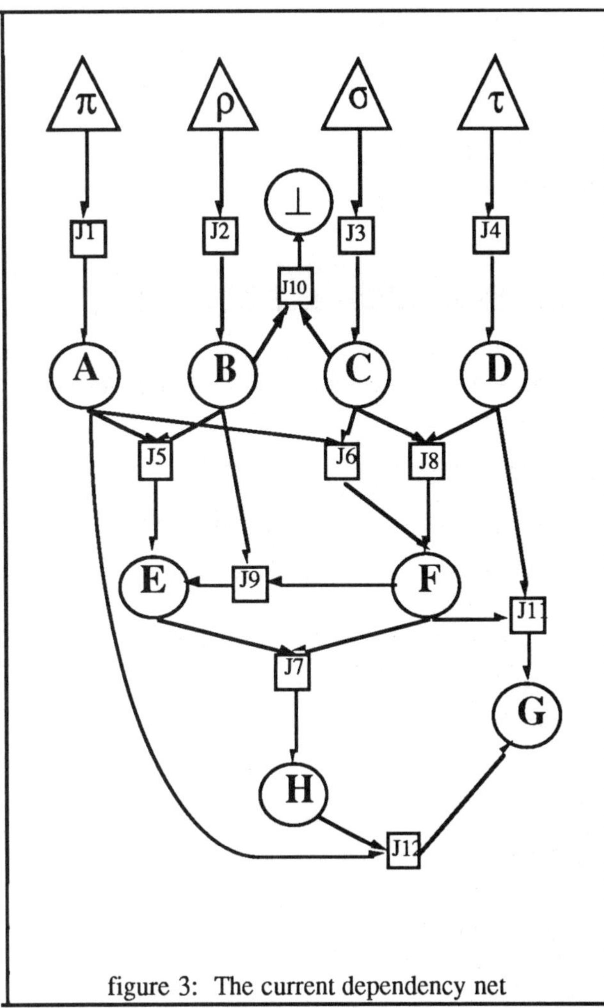

figure 3: The current dependency net

Let now the problem solver adds the justification (see figure 4):

J_{13} <F,G → E, c(E) = 0.8, c_r(E) = 0.75>

Since a new confidence value for E is introduced, it is necessary to update the truth-values of all the consequent nodes. In this case the updating process terminates after the new values for H have been evaluated, because the connfidence in G is not affected.

c(H) = 0.5 c_r(H) = 0.5

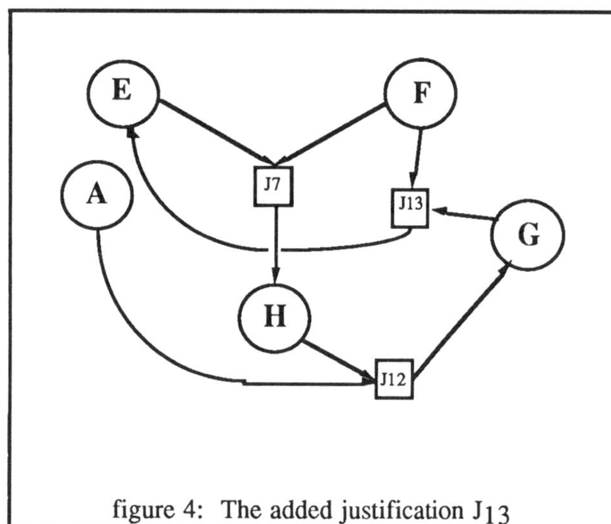

figure 4: The added justification J_{13}

The effect of J_{13} on the labels is the following:

$L_E = \{[(\pi,\rho), cs=1], [(\sigma,\tau), cs=1]\}$

$L_H = \{[(\pi,\rho,\sigma), cs=-0.5], [(\sigma,\tau), cs = 1]\}$

$L_G = \{[(\pi,\rho,\sigma), cs=-0.5], [(\sigma,\tau), cs=1]\}$

Let us finally suppose that a new contradiction, represented by the justification J_{14}, is detected by the problem solver:

J_{14}: $\langle D,E \rightarrow \bot, c(\bot) = 0.4, c_r(\bot) = 0.4\rangle$

This justification modifies the minimal environment database, introducing two new entries:

MEDB:

$[(\sigma,\tau), cs=-0.5]$

$[(\pi,\rho,\tau), cs=-0.4]$

$[(\sigma,\tau), cs=-0.4]$

Therefore the new labels become:

$L_E = \{[(\pi,\rho), cs=1], [(\sigma,\tau), cs=-0.4]\}$

$L_F = \{[(\pi,\sigma), cs=1], [(\sigma,\tau), cs=-0.4]\}$

$L_G = \{[(\pi,\rho,\sigma), cs=-0.5], [(\sigma,\tau), cs=-0.4]\}$

$L_H = \{[(\pi,\rho,\sigma), cs=-0.5], [(\sigma,\tau), cs = -0.4]\}$

CONCLUSION

The system described in this paper supports a problem solver in the task of selecting among several alternatives in situations affected by incomplete information , uncertain knowledge and vague data.

FTMS allows the problem solver to make nonmonotonic inferences, revising previous conclusions if contradictions are detected.

Every derived belief is associated with three parameters: a confidence which shows how much it is true, a confidence of resolution, which tells to what extent it is derivable from the current knowledge, and a consistency, which represents the degree of contradiction of the hypotheses which it relies on.

Dependencies between beliefs are recorded so that when new information is supplied, only the affected beliefs are involved in the updating process.

FTMS has been successfully implemented in Prolog.

Acknowledgements.

The authors wish to thank Settimo Termini fro the valuable discussions about many valued logics.

This work has been supported by P.F. Robotica - Consiglio Nazionale delle Ricerche grant n.90.00556.67 and M.U.R.S.T.- 40% "Tecniche di Ragionamento Automatico e Sistemi Intelligenti".

References

B.D'Ambrosio (1989). A Hybrid Approach to Reasoning Under Uncertainty. In L.N.Kanal, T.S.Levitt, J.F.Lemmer (eds.) *Uncertainty in Artificial Intelligence: 3rd Conference*, North-Holland, pp.267-283.

J.Doyle (1979). A Truth Maintenance System. In *Artificial Intelligence*, **12** (3) ,pp 231- 272.

D.Dubois, J.Lang, H.Prade (1990). Handling Uncertain Knowledge in an ATMS Using Possibilistic Logic. In *Proceeding of ECAI Workshop on Truth Maintenance Systems* ,Stockolm.

D.Dubois, H.Prade (1987). Necessity Measures and the Resolution Principle. In *IEEE Trans. on Systems, Man and Cyberneticss* , vol.SMC-17, n.3, pp.474-478.

B.Falkenheiner (1988). Towards a General Purpose Belief Maintenance System. In J.F.Lemmer, L.N.Kanal (eds.) *Uncertainty in Artificial Intelligence: 2nd Conference,* North-Holland, pp.125-132.

J.de Kleer (1986). An Assumption-based TMS. In *Artificial Intelligence* , 28 (2) , pp.127-162.

J.de Kleer, B.C.Williams (1987). Diagnosing Multiple Faults. In *Artificial Intelligence* , 32, pp. 97-130.

K.B.Laskey, P.E. Lehner(1989). Assumptions, Beliefs and Probabilities. In *Artificial Intelligence* 41, pp. 65-77.

R.C.T.Lee (1972). Fuzzy Logic and the Resolution Principle. In *Journal of ACM*, 19 (1), pp.109-119.

J.P.Martins, S.C.Shapiro (1988). A Model for Belief Revision. In *Artificial Intelligence* , 35, pp. 25-79.

D.McAllester (1980). An Outlook on Truth Maintenance. In *AI Memo* 551, AI Lab., MIT, Cambridge (MA).

D.McDermott (1983). Context and Data Dependencies. In *A Synthesis*, IEEE Trans. Pattern Anal.Mach. Intell., 5 (3), pp. 237-246.

M.Mukaidono (1982). Fuzzy Inference of Resolution Style. In R.R.Yager (Ed.) *Fuzzy Set and Possibility Theory*, Pergamon Press, New York , pp. 224-231.

M.Mukaidono, Z. Shen, L. Ding (1989). Fundamentals of Fuzzy Prolog. In *International Journal of Approximate Reasoning*, 3, pp. 179-193.

G.M. Provan (1989). An Analysis of ATMS-based Techniques for Computing Dempster-Shafer Belief Functions. In *Proceedings of the.9th IJCAI* , Detroit Aug. 1989 , pp. 1115-1120.

J.A.Robinson (1965). A Machine-oriented Logic Based on the Resolution Principle. In *Journal of ACM*, 12 (1), pp. 23-41.

Advances in Probabilistic Reasoning

Dan Geiger
Northrop Research and Technology Center
One Research Park
Palos Verdes, CA 90274

David Heckerman
Departments of Computer Science and Pathology
University of Southern California
HMR 204, 2025 Zonal Ave, LA, CA 94305

Abstract

This paper discuses multiple Bayesian networks representation paradigms for encoding asymmetric independence assertions. We offer three contributions: (1) an inference mechanism that makes explicit use of asymmetric independence to speed up computations, (2) a simplified definition of similarity networks and extensions of their theory, and (3) a generalized representation scheme that encodes more types of asymmetric independence assertions than do similarity networks.

1 Introduction

Traditional probabilistic approaches to diagnosis, classification, and pattern recognition face a critical choice: either specify precise relationships between all interacting variables or make uniform independence assumptions throughout. The first choice is computationally infeasible except in very small domains, while the second, which is rarely justified, often yields inadequate conclusions.

Bayesian networks offer a compromise between the two extremes by encoding independence when possible and dependence when necessary. They allow a wide spectrum of independence assertions to be considered by the model builder so that a practical balance can be established between computational needs and adequacy of conclusions.

Although Bayesian networks considerably extend traditional approaches, they are still not expressive enough to encode every piece of information that might reduce computations. The most obvious omissions are *asymmetric independence* assertions stating that variables are independent for some but not necessarily for all of their values. Such asymmetric assertions cannot be represented naturally in a Bayesian network. Several researchers observed this limitation, however, until recently no effort was made to remove it.

Similarity network paradigm is the first major effort towards the representation of asymmetric independence [Heckerman, 1990]. Contingent influence diagrams is an alternative approach [Fung and Shachter, 1991]. Both schemes employ asymmetric independence to ease the elicitation and improve the quality of probabilistic models.

This article offers three contributions: (1) an inference mechanism that makes explicit use of asymmetric independence to speed up computations, (2) a simplified definition of similarity networks and extensions of their theory, and (3) a generalized representation scheme that encodes more types of asymmetric independence assertions than do similarity networks.

These contributions address problems of knowledge representation, inference, and knowledge acquisition. In particular, Section 2 describes *Bayesian multinets* and how to use them for inference, Section 3 describes knowledge acquisition using *similarity networks* and how to convert them to Bayesian multinets, Section 4 extends these representation schemes to the case where hypotheses are not mutually exclusive and section 5 summarizes the results. We assume the reader is familiar with the definition and usage of Bayesian networks. For details consult [Pearl, 1988].

2 Representation and Inference

2.1 Bayesian Multinets

The following example demonstrates the problem of representing asymmetric independence by Bayesian networks:

> A guard of a secured building expects three types of persons to approach the building's entrance: workers in the building, approved visitors, and spies. As a person approaches the building, the guard notes its gender and whether or not the person wears a badge. Spies are mostly men. Spies always wear badges in order to fool the guard. Visitors

don't wear badges because they don't have one. Female-workers tend to wear badges more often than do male-workers. The task of the guard is to identify the type of person approaching the building.

A Bayesian network that represents this story is shown in Figure 1. Variable h in the figure represents the correct identification. It has three values w, v, and s respectively denoting worker, visitor, and spy. Variables g and b are binary variables representing, respectively, the person's gender and whether or not the person wears a badge. The links from h to g and from h to b reflect the fact that both gender and badge-wearing are clues for correct identification, and the link from g to b encodes the relationship between gender and badge-wearing.

Unfortunately, the topology of this network hides the fact that, independent of gender, spies always wear badges and visitors never do. The network does not show that gender and badge-wearing are conditionally independent given the person is a spy or a visitor. A link between g and b is drawn merely because gender and badge-wearing are related variables when the person is a worker.

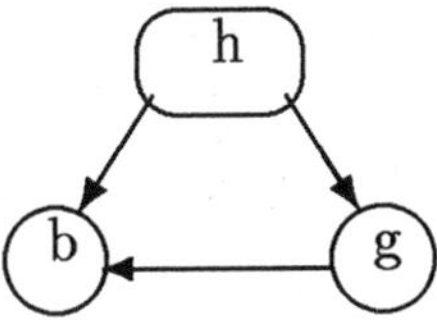

Figure 1: A Bayesian network for the secured-building example.

We can more adequately represent this story using two Bayesian networks shown in Figure 2. The first network represents the cases where the person approaching the entrance is either a spy or a visitor. In these cases, badge-wearing depends merely on the type of person approaching, not on its gender. Consequently, nodes b and g are shown to be conditionally independent (node h blocks the path between them). The links from h to b and from h to g in this network reflect the fact that badges and gender are relevant clues for distinguishing between spies and visitors. The second network represents the hypothesis that the person is a worker, in which case gender and badge-wearing are related as shown.

Figure 2 is a better representation than Figure 1 because it shows the dependence of badge-wearing on gender only in context in which such a relationship exists, namely, for workers. Moreover, the former representation requires 11 parameters while the representation of Figure 2 requires only 9. This gain, due to asymmetric independence, could be substantially larger for real-sized problems because the number of

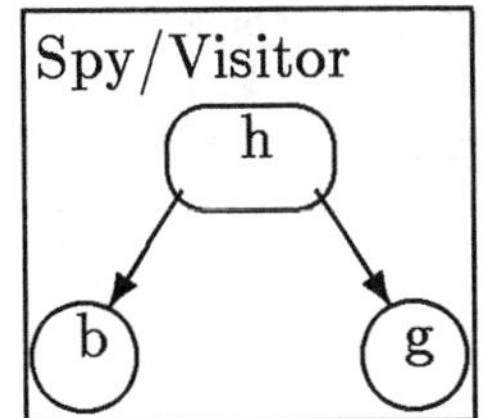

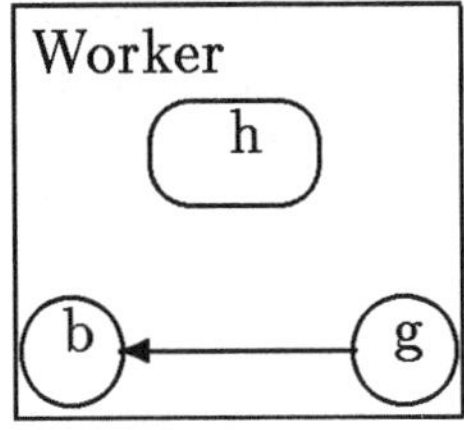

Figure 2: A Bayesian multinet representation of the secured-building story.

parameters needed grows exponentially in the number of variables, whereas the overhead of representing multiple networks grows only linearly.

We call the representation scheme of figure 2, a *Bayesian multinet.*

Definition Let $\{u_1 \ldots u_n\}$ be a finite set of variables each having a finite set of values, P be a probability distribution having the Cartesian product of these sets of values as its sample space, and h be a distinguished variable among the u_i's that represents a mutually-exclusive and exhaustive set of hypotheses. Let $A_1, \ldots, A_k$ be a partition of the values of h. A directed acyclic graph D_i is called a *local network* of P (associated with A_i) if it is a Bayesian network of P given that one of the hypotheses in A_i holds, i.e., D_i is a Bayesian network of $P(u_1 \ldots u_n | A_i)$. The set of k local networks is called a *Bayesian multinet* of P.[1]

In the secured-building example of Figure 2, $\{\{spy, visitor\}, \{worker\}\}$ is a partition of the values of the hypothesis node h, one local network is a Bayesian network of $P(h, b, g| \, worker)$ and the other local network is a Bayesian network of $P(h, b, g| \, \{\text{spy, visitor}\})$. [2]

The fundamental idea of multinets is that of *conditioning*; each local network represents a distinct situation conditioned that hypotheses are restricted to a specified subset. Savings in computations and space occur because, as a result of conditioning, asymmetric independence assertions are encoded in the topology of the local networks. In the example above, conditional independence between gender and badge-wearing is encoded as a result of conditioning on h.

Notably, conditioning may also destroy independence relationships rather then create them [Pearl, 1988]. However, if the distinguished variable is a root node (i.e., a node with no incoming links), conditioning on

[1] A Bayesian multinet roughly corresponds to an *hypothesis-specific similarity network* as defined in Heckerman's dissertation (1990, page 76).

[2] The conditioning set $\{spy, visitor\}$ is a short hand notation for saying that h draws its values from this set, namely, either $h = spy$ or $h = visitor$.

its values never decreases and often increases the number of independence relationships, resulting in a more expressive graphical representation. Other situations are addressed below where the hypothesis variable is not a root node or where more than one node represents hypotheses.

2.2 Representational and Computational Advantages

The vanishing dependence between gender and badge-wearing is an example of an *hypothesis-specific* independence because it is manifest only when conditioning on specific hypotheses, that is, for spies and visitors, but not for workers. The following variation of the secured-building example demonstrates an additional type of asymmetric independence that can be represented by Bayesian multinets as well.

> The guard of the secured building now expects *four* types of persons to approach the building's entrance: executives, regular workers, approved visitors, and spies. The guard notes gender, badge-wearing, and whether or not the person arrives in a limousine (l). We assume that only executives arrive in limousines and that male and female executives wear badges just as do regular workers (to serve as role models).

This story is represented by the two local networks shown in Figure 3. One network represents a situation where either a spy or a visitor approaches the building, and the other network represents a situation where either a worker or an executive approaches the building. The link from h to l in the latter network reflects the fact that arriving in limousines is a relevant clue for distinguishing between workers and executives. The absence of this link in the former network reflects the fact that it is not relevant for distinguishing between spies and visitors.

The vanishing dependence between gender and the hypothesis variable h when h is restricted to a subset of hypotheses {*worker, executive*} is an example of *subset independence*. Similarly, badge-wearing is independent of h when restricted to {*worker, executive*}, and arriving in limousines is independent of h when restricted to {*spy, visitor*}. [3]

Subset independence is a source of considerable computational savings. For example, in lymph-node pathology less than 20% of the potential morphological findings are relevant for distinguishing any given pair of disease hypotheses (among over 60 diseases) [Heckerman, 1990].

[3] Heckerman coined the terms subset independence and hypothesis-specific independence in his dissertation.

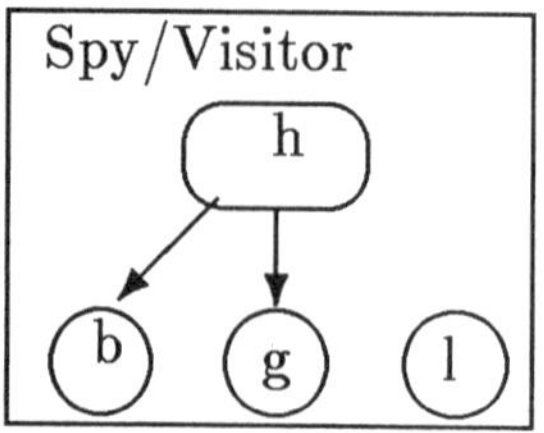

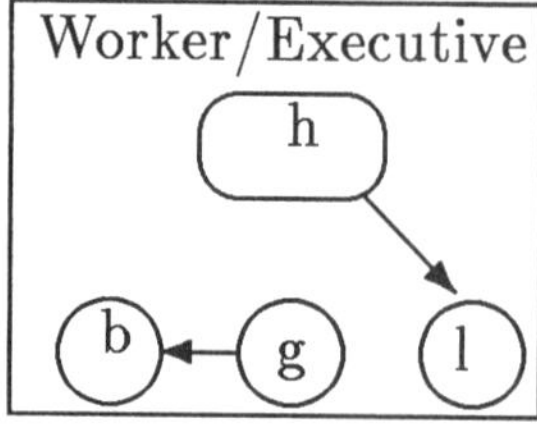

Figure 3: A Bayesian multinet representation of the augmented secured-building story.

Below we demonstrate these computational savings using the simple secured-building example; more savings are obtained in real domains such as lymph-node pathology.

Suppose the guard sees a male (**g**) wearing a badge (**b**) approaches the building and suppose the guard doesn't notice whether or not the person arrives in a limousine. A computation of the posterior probability of each possible identification (*executive, worker, visitor, spy*) based on the Bayesian network of Figure 1 simply yields the chaining rule:

$$P(h|\mathbf{g}, \mathbf{b}) = K \cdot P(h) \cdot P(\mathbf{g}|h) \cdot P(\mathbf{b}|\mathbf{g}, h). \quad (1)$$

where K is the normalizing constant.

Using the representation of Figure 3, however, the following more efficient computations are done instead:

$$P(spy|\mathbf{g}, \mathbf{b}) = K \cdot P(spy) \cdot P(\mathbf{g}|spy) \cdot P(\mathbf{b}|spy) \quad (2)$$

$$P(visitor|\mathbf{g}, \mathbf{b}) = K \cdot P(visitor) \cdot P(\mathbf{g}|visitor) \cdot P(\mathbf{b}|visitor) \quad (3)$$

$$P(worker|\mathbf{g}, \mathbf{b}) = K \cdot P(worker) \cdot P(\mathbf{g}|worker) \cdot P(\mathbf{b}|\mathbf{g}, worker) \quad (4)$$

$$P(\mathbf{g}, \mathbf{b}|executive) = P(\mathbf{g}, \mathbf{b}|worker). \quad (5)$$

Equations 2 and 3 take advantage of an hypothesis-specific independence assertion, namely, that g and b are conditionally independent given, respectively, that $h = spy$ and $h = visitor$. Equation 5 uses a subset independence assertion, namely, that b and g are independent of h restricted to {*worker, executive*}.

More generally, calculating the posterior probability of each hypothesis based on a set of observations $e_1, ..., e_m$ is done in two steps. First, for each hypothesis h_i, the probability $P(e_1, ..., e_m|h_i)$ is computed via standard algorithms such as Spiegelhalter and Lauritzen's (88) or Pearl's (88). Second, these results are combined via Bayes' rule:

$$P(h_i|e_1...e_m) = K \cdot p(h_i)P(e_1...e_k|h_i). \quad (6)$$

Notably, the computation of $P(e_1 \ldots e_k|h_i)$ in the first step uses the local networks as done in Eqs. (2) through

(5) and does not use a single Bayesian network as done in Eq. (1). Consequently, when the values of h are properly partitioned, the extra independence relationships encoded in each local network could considerably reduce computations.

The parameters needed to perform the above computations consist, as we shall see next, of the prior of each hypothesis h_i and the parameters encoded in the local networks:

Theorem 1 *Let $\{u_1 \ldots u_n\}$ be a finite set of variables each having a finite set of values, P be a probability distribution having the Cartesian product of these sets of values as its sample space, h be a distinguished variable among the u_is, and M be a Bayesian multinet of P. Then, the posterior probability of every hypothesis given any value combination for the variables in $\{u_1 \ldots u_n\}$ can be computed from the prior probability of h's values and from the parameters encoded in M.*

According to Eq. 6 above, the only parameters needed for computing the posterior probability of each hypothesis h_i, aside of the priors, are $p(v_2 \ldots v_n|h_i)$ where $v_2 \ldots v_n$ are arbitrary values of $u_2 \ldots u_n$ (assuming without loss of generality that $h = u_1$). Let D_i denote a local network in M, A_i be the hypotheses associated with D_i, and h_i be an hypothesis in A_i. Clearly, $p(v_2 \ldots v_n|h_i)$ is equal to $p(v_2 \ldots v_n|h_i, A_i)$ because h_i logically implies the disjunction over all hypotheses in A_i. The latter probability is computable from the local network D_i by any standard algorithm (e.g., [Pearl, 1988]), thus, the former is also computable as needed. □

For example, $P(\mathrm{g}|$*worker*, {*worker*, *executive*}) is equal to the probability $P(\mathrm{g}|$*worker*) because *worker* logically implies the disjunction *worker* ∨ *executive*. In fact, $P(\mathrm{g}|$*worker*, {*worker*, *executive*}) is also equal to $P(\mathrm{g}|$\{*worker*, *executive*\}) because g and *worker* are independent given {*worker*, *executive*} as shown in Figure 3. In this example, the needed probability $P(\mathrm{g}|$*worker*) is equal to the given one $P(\mathrm{g}|$\{*worker*, *executive*\}), however in general, the needed probabilities are computed via standard inference algorithms.

2.3 Overcoming some Limitations

The multinet approach described thus far is especially beneficial when the hypothesis variable can be modeled as a root node because, then, no dependencies are ever introduced by conditioning on the different hypotheses. However, the hypothesis node cannot always be modeled as a root node. For example, in the secured-building story, suppose there are two independent reports indicating possible spying, say, for military and economical reasons respectively. Such a priori factors for correct identification are modeled as parent nodes of h, called, say, *economics* and *military* having no link between them to show their mutual independence. The resulting network in this case is simply *economics* $\rightarrow h \leftarrow$ *military*.

However when h assumes the value *spy*, an induced link is introduced between its parents *economics* and *military*; one explanation for seeing a spy changes the plausibility of the other explanation, thus making the two variables economics and military be not independent conditioned on h = *spy*. Consequently, an induced link must be drawn between the *economics* and *military* nodes in the local network for spies vs. visitors to account for the above dependency. This link would not appear in the full Bayesian network because economics and military are marginally independent (they become dependent only when conditioning on h = *spy*). Such induced links are often hard to quantify and therefore, constructing a single local network is sometimes harder than constructing the full network, as is the case in the above example.

One approach to handle this situation is to first construct a Bayesian network that represents only a priori factors that influence the hypotheses, ignoring any evidential variables (such as gender, badge-wearing, and limousines). In our example, this network would be *economics* $\rightarrow h \leftarrow$ *military*. Then, use this network to revise the a priori probabilities of the different hypotheses. Finally, construct local networks ignoring a priori factors (as done in Figure 2) and use the resulting multinet with the revised priors of h to compute the posterior probability of h as determined by the evidential clues. This decomposition technique works best if a priori factors are independent of all clues conditioned on the different hypotheses. That is, in situations that can be modeled with Bayesian networks of the form shown in Figure 4 where all paths between a priori factors r_i's and evidential clues f_i's pass through h.

When a network of this form cannot serve as a justifiable model, another approach can be used instead; compose a Bayesian multinet ignoring a priori factors, construct a Bayesian network from the local networks by taking the union of all their links (e.g., the union of all links in Figure 2 yields the Bayesian network of Figure 1). Finally, add a priori factors to the resulting network. This approach was proposed in [Heckerman, 1990].

The disadvantage of this method is that in the process of generating a Bayesian network from a multinet, one encodes asymmetric independence in the parameters rather than in the topology of the Bayesian network. Consequently, these asymmetric assertions are not available to standard inference algorithm to speed up their computations.

Nevertheless, this approach is still the best alternative for decomposing the construction of large Bayesian

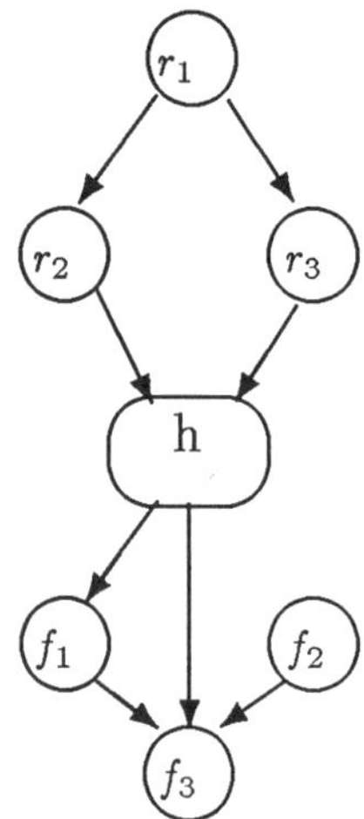

Figure 4: A Bayesian network where all paths between a priori factors r_i's and evidential clues f_i's pass through h.

networks having topologies more complex than that of Figure 4. Such decomposition techniques are crucially needed due to the overwhelming details of real-life problems. Additional issues of knowledge acquisition are discussed below.

3 Knowledge Acquisition/ Representation

3.1 Similarity Networks

Recall the guard that must distinguish between workers, executives, visitors and spies. In this story, some variables do not help distinguish between certain hypotheses. For example, gender and badges do not help distinguish between workers and executives, and limousines do not help distinguish between spies and visitors. In richer domains, large numbers of variables are often not relevant for distinguishing between certain hypotheses.

Unfortunately, the Bayesian multinet approach requires full specification of all variables in each local network even when they are not relevant to distinguish between the hypotheses associated with that local network. For example the relationship between b and g is encoded in the local network for spies vs. visitors although these variables do not help distinguish between this pair of hypotheses (Figure 3). Assessing such relationships, in contexts where they are not relevant, poses insurmountable burden on the expert consulted as is demonstrated by the following quote [Heckerman, 1990]:

> "When the expert pathologist was asked questions of the form
>
> > Given any disease, does observing feature x change your belief that you will observe feature y ?
>
> the expert sometimes would reply
>
> > I've never thought about these two features at the same time before. Feature x is relevant to only one set of diseases, while feature y is only relevant to another set of diseases. These sets of diseases do not overlap, and I never confuse the first set of diseases with the second."

The solution is to simply include in each local network only those variables that are relevant for distinguishing between the hypothesis covered by that local network.

However, by doing so, valuable information for correct identification might be lost. For example, the relationships between badge-wearing and gender in Figure 3 would be lost. To compensate for such losses of information, additional local networks must be constructed.

For example, the secured-building can be represented with three local networks shown in Figure 5 rather than two as in Figure 3. One network is used to distinguish between spies and visitors, another between visitors and workers, and a third between workers and executives. In each local network we include only those variables relevant to distinguishing the hypotheses covered by that local network. In particular, the relationship between badge-wearing and gender is not included in the local network for workers vs. executives as in Figure 3. This relationship, however, is included in the local networks for visitors vs. workers because it helps distinguish between these two hypotheses. The reason for not loosing needed information is that the three local networks are based on a *connected cover* of hypotheses (rather than a partition).

Definition A *cover* of a set A is a collection $\{A_1, ..., A_k\}$ of non-empty subsets of A whose union is A. Each cover is a hypergraph, called the *similarity hypergraph*, where the A_i's are edges and elements of A are nodes. A cover is *connected* if the similarity hypergraph is connected.

In Figure 5, {*spy, visitor*}, {*visitor, worker*}, {*worker, executive*} is a cover of the hypotheses set. This cover is connected because it is simply a four-nodes chain *spy—visitor—worker—executive* which, by definition, is a connected hypergraph. The set {{*spy, visitor*}, {*worker, executive*}} is also a cover but it is not connected. The set {{*worker, executive, visitor*}, {*visitor, spy*}} is an example of a connected cover that is a hypergraph which is not a graph.

Definition Let $U = \{u_1 \ldots u_n\}$ be a finite set of variables each having a finite set of values, P be a

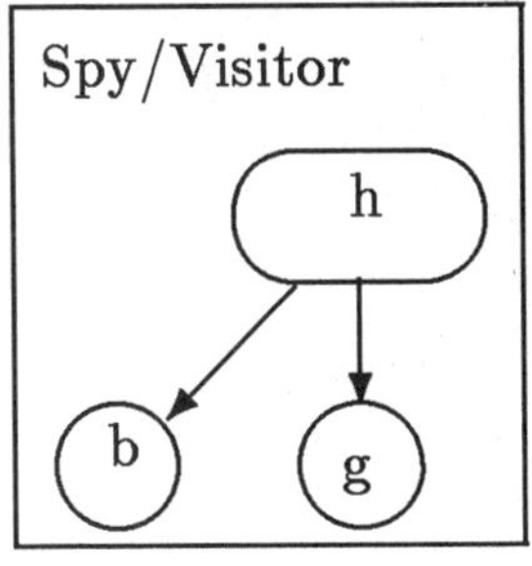

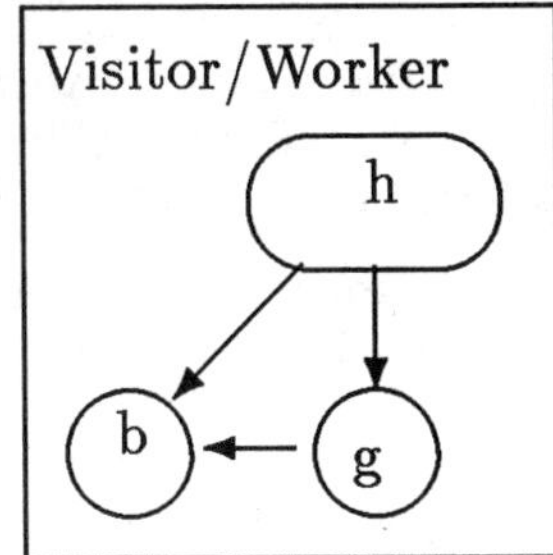

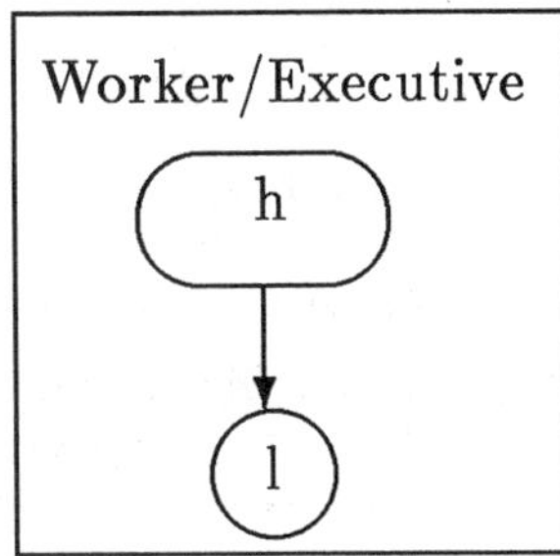

Figure 5: A similarity network representation of the secured-building story.

probability distribution having the cross product of these sets of values as its sample space, and h be a distinguished variable among the u_i's that represents a mutually-exclusive and exhaustive set of hypotheses. Let $A_1, ..., A_k$ be a connected cover of the values of h. A directed acyclic graph D_i is called a *comprehensive local network* of P (associated with A_i) if it is a Bayesian network of P assuming one of the hypotheses in A_i holds, i.e., D_i is a Bayesian network of $P(u_1 \ldots u_n | A_i)$. The network obtained from D_i by removing nodes that are not relevant to distinguishing between hypotheses in A_i is called an *ordinary local network*. The set of k ordinary local networks is called an *(ordinary) similarity network* of P.

For example, the local networks of Figure 5 are ordinary, and together form an ordinary similarity network. Notably, hypotheses covered by each local network are often similar (e.g., spies and visitors), [4] a choice that maximizes the number of asymmetric independence relationships encoded.

Heckerman (1990) shows that under several assumptions, if a cover is connected, one can always remove from each local network variables that do not help distinguish between hypotheses covered by that local network and yet not loose the information necessary for representing the full joint distribution. These assumptions consist of 1) the hypothesis variable is a root node, 2) the cover is a graph and not a hypergraph, 3) the local networks are constrained by the same partial order, and 4) the distribution is strictly positive.

[4]Hence the name: similarity network.

Theses assumptions are relaxed below.

Theorem 2 *Let $\{u_1 \ldots u_n\}$ be a finite set of variables each having a finite set of values, P be a probability distribution having the Cartesian product of these sets of values as its sample space, h be a distinguished variable among the u_is, and S be a similarity network of P. Then, the posterior probability of every hypothesis given any value combination for the variables in $\{u_1 \ldots u_n\}$ can be computed from the parameters encoded in S provided $p(h_i) \neq 0$ for every value h_i of h.*

To prove the above theorem, it suffices to consider the case where h is a root node in all the local networks of S because, otherwise, *arc-reversal* transformations [Shachter 1986] can be applied until h becomes one.

Also note that since the similarity hypergraph is connected, it imposes $n-1$ independent equations among the following n: $p(h_i) = p(h_i|A_i) \cdot \sum_{h_j \in A_i} p(h_j)$, $i = 1 \ldots n$. In addition, $\sum_1^n p(h_i) = 1$. The values for $p(h_i)$ are the unique solution of these linear equations provided $p(h_i) \neq 0$ for $i = 1 \ldots n$.

Aside of the priors, the only remaining parameters needed for computing the posterior probability of each hypothesis h_i, are $p(v_2 \ldots v_n | h_i)$ where $v_2 \ldots v_n$ are arbitrary values of $u_2 \ldots u_n$ (assuming without loss of generality that $h = u_1$). Due to the chaining rule, $p(v_2 \ldots v_n | h_i)$ can be factored as follows:

$$p(v_2 \ldots v_n | h_i) = P(v_2 | h_i) \cdot P(v_3 | v_2\, h_i) \ldots p(v_n | v_1 \ldots v_{n-1}\, h_i).$$

Thus, it suffices to show that for each variable u_j, $p(v_j | v_2 \ldots v_{j-1}\, h_i)$ can be computed from the parameters encoded in S.

Let D_i denote a local network in S, A_i be the hypotheses associated with D_i, and h_i be an hypothesis in A_i. There are two cases; either u_j is depicted in D_i or it is not. Let $A_i, A_{i+1} \ldots A_m$ be a path in the similarity hypergraph where A_m is the only edge on this path associated with a local network that depicts u_j as a node. If u_j is depicted in D_i, then the path consists of one edge A_i which is equal to A_m. If u_j is not depicted in any local network, then u_j does not alter the posterior probability of any hypothesis and is therefore omitted from the computations.

Let D_k be the local netowrk associated with A_k for $k = i+1 \ldots m$ and let $h_{i+1}, h_{i+2} \ldots h_m$ be a sequence of hypotheses such that $h_k \in A_{k-1} \cap A_k$. Due to the definition of similarity networks, since u_j is not depicted in D_k where $k < m$, the following equality must hold:

$$p(v_j | v_2 \ldots v_{j-1}\, h_{k-1}) = p(v_j | v_2 \ldots v_{j-1}\, h_k).$$

Since this equation holds for every k between $i+1$ and m, we obtain,

$$p(v_j | v_2 \ldots v_{j-1}\, h_i) = p(v_j | v_2 \ldots v_{j-1}\, h_m).$$

Moreover,

$$p(v_j | v_2 \ldots v_{j-1}\, h_m) = p(v_j | v'_1 \ldots v'_l\, h_m)$$

where $u'_1 \ldots u'_l$ are the variables depicted in D_m (a subset of $\{u_2 \ldots u_{j-1}\}$) because, due to the definition of similarity network, the variables deleted are conditionally independent of v_j, given the other variables; they are disconnected from all the other variables in D_m. [5]

Finally,

$$p(v_j | v'_1 \ldots v'_l\, h_m) = p(v_j | v'_1 \ldots v'_l\, h_m, A_m),$$

because h_m logically implies the disjunction over all hypotheses in A_m.

The latter probability is computable from the local network D_m by any standard algorithm (e.g., [Pearl, 1988]), thus, due the three equalities above, $p(v_j | v_2 \ldots v_{j-1}\, h_i)$ is also computable as needed. □

For example, to compute $P(g, b, l | spy)$ we use the following two equalities implied by Figure 5: From the first local network, $P(g, b, l | spy) = P(g | spy) \cdot P(b | spy) \cdot P(l | spy)$ and from the absence of l in the first and second local networks, $P(l | spy) = P(l | worker)$. Thus, $P(g, b, l | spy) = P(g | spy) \cdot P(b | spy) \cdot P(l | worker)$, where all the needed probabilities are encoded in the similarity network. In fact, the proof of Theorem 2 provides a general way of factoring any desired probability, thus, the full joint distribution $P(g, b, l, h)$ is encoded in the ordinary similarity network of Figure 5.

Similarity networks have another important advantage not mentioned so far: protecting the model builder from omitting relevant clues. For example, suppose workers and executives often arrive with a smile to work (because the secured building is such a great place to be in) while spies and visitors arrive seriously. Such a clue, smile, is likely to be forgotten when constructing the local networks for spies vs. visitors and for visitors vs. executives because it does not help distinguish between these pairs of hypotheses. However, when constructing the similarity network of Figure 5, which includes a local network for distinguishing visitors from workers, smile is more likely to be recalled because the distinctions between visitors and workers are explicitly in focus.

3.2 Redundancy

Basing the construction of local networks on covers of hypotheses raises the problem of *redundancy*, namely, that some parameters are specified in more than one local network. For example, in Figure 5, the parameter $P(\mathrm{g} | visitor)$ should, in principle, be specified both in the first and in the second local network. This problem is particularly crucial because local networks are actually constructed from expert's judgments rather than from a coherent probability distribution as implied by the definition of similarity networks.

One way to remove redundancy is to automatically-translate a similarity network as it is being constructed to a Bayesian multinet which is never redundant. For example, instead of storing Figure 5, we can actually store Figure 3 which contains no redundant information.

The translation is done by the following algorithm.

Conversion Algorithm

Input: A similarity network S of a probability distribution P.

Output: A Bayesian multinet of P.

1. For each ordinary local network L in S:
   - Add a node for each variable not represented in L.
   - For each added node x, set the parents of x in L to be the union of all parents of x in all other local networks where x originally appeared, excluding variables that were originally in L.
2. Remove enough local networks from S and enough hypotheses from the remaining local networks until a Bayesian multinet is obtained.

(A finer version of this algorithm is forthcoming).

Notably, the user of a similarity network need not know about the conversion to a Bayesian multinet which can be thought of as an internal representation. The user benefits from both the advantages of similarity network for knowledge acquisition, and from an inference algorithm (Section 2) that uses the Bayesian multinet produced by the conversion algorithm.

4 Generalized Similarity Networks

Previous sections assume all hypotheses are mutually exclusive and are, therefore, represented as values of a single hypothesis variable denoted h. Here this assumption is relaxed. We allow several variables to represent hypotheses, as needed by the following example:

> Consider the guard of Section 2 who has to distinguish between workers, visitors, and spies. A *pair* of people approach the building and the guard tries to classify them as they approach. Assume that only workers converse (c) and that workers often arrive with other workers (because they must car-pool to conserve energy).

[5] Geiger and Heckerman (1990) discuss weaker definitions of being irrelevant other than being disconnected.

A Bayesian network representing this situation is shown in Figure 6 where nodes h_1 and h_2 stand for the respective identity of the two persons. (The direction of the link between h_1 and h_2 is arbitrary.)

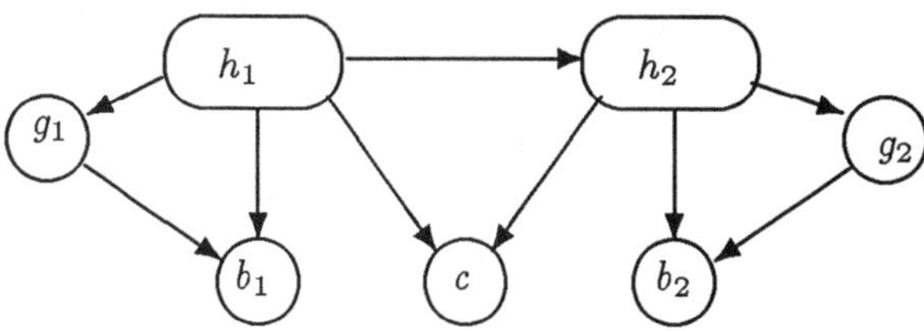

Figure 6: A Bayesian network with two hypothesis nodes h_1 and h_2.

Alternatively, we can represent this example using a *generalized similarity network*, or a *generalized Bayesian multinet.*

Definition Let $\{u_1 \dots u_n\}$ be a finite set of variables each having a finite set of values, P be a probability distribution having the cross product of these sets of values as its sample space, and H be a subset of distinguished variables among the u_i's each representing a set of hypotheses. Denote the Cartesian product of the sets of values of the distinguished variables by *domain(H)*. Let $A_1, \dots, A_k$ be a connected cover of *domain(H)*. A directed acyclic graph D_i is called a *comprehensive local network* of P if it is a Bayesian network of $P(u_1 \dots u_n | A_i)$. The network obtained from D_i by removing nodes that are not relevant to distinguishing between hypotheses in A_i is called an *ordinary local network.* The set of k local networks is called a *generalized similarity network* of P. When $A_1, \dots, A_k$ is a partition of *domain(H)*, then the set of k comprehensive local networks is called a *generalized Bayesian multinet.*

For example, the secured-building story is represented in the generalized similarity network of Figure 7. Note, $H = \{h_1, h_2\}$ and *domain(H)* consists of nine elements (x, y) where both x and y are drawn from the set $\{w, v, s\}$. A connected cover of *domain(H)* upon which Figure 7 is based consists of: $\{(s,s)\,(v,s)\,(s,v)\,(v,v)\}$, $\{(v,v)\,(w,v)\,(v,w)\,(w,w)\}$, and $\{(s,s)\,(s,w)\,(w,s)\}$. This cover is connected.

Most asymmetric independence assertions encoded in Figure 7 were either explained in previous sections or are obvious from the verbal description of the story.

The absence of a link between h_1 and h_2 in the top network encodes the fact that if the guard knew that one person is a spy, this knowledge would not help him/her decide whether the other person is a spy or a visitor. The existence of a link between h_1 and h_2 in the middle network encodes the fact that workers come in pairs more often than do visitors. Hence the knowledge that one person is a worker is a clue for classifying the other person.

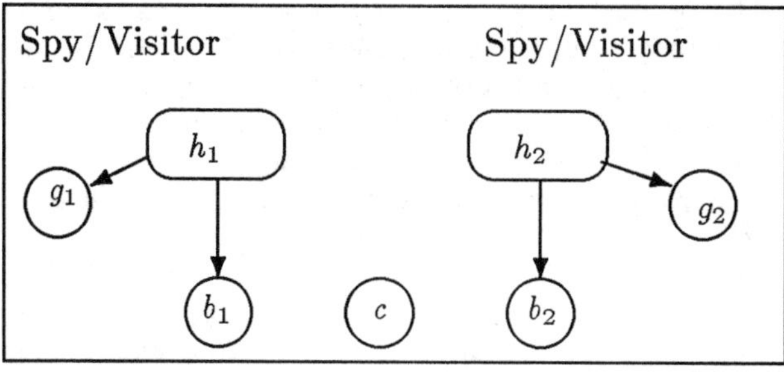

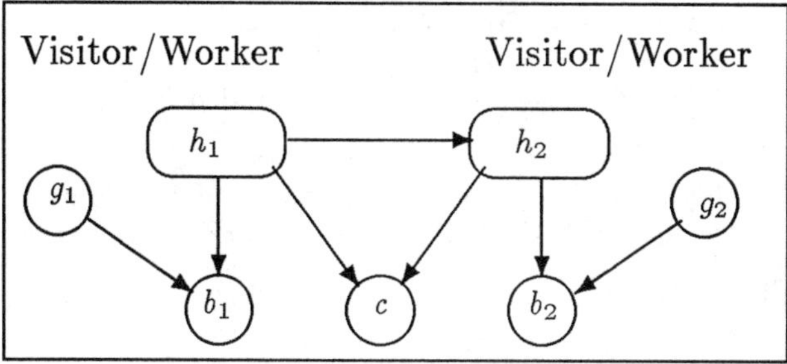

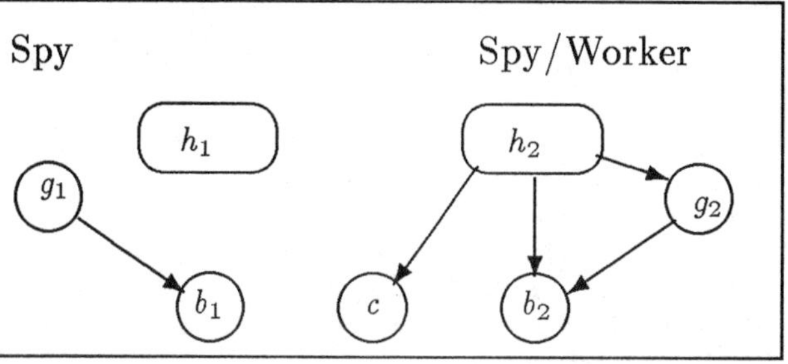

Figure 7: A generalized similarity network with two hypothesis nodes.

The vanishing dependence between hypothesis variables h_1 and h_2 in case of spies vs. visitors is an example of *inter-hypothesis independence.* Such asymmetric assertions cannot be encoded in ordinary similarity networks.

5 Summary

This paper proposes an efficient format for encoding and using asymmetric independence assertions for inference. The model builder is asked to express knowledge about independence by constructing multiple local networks using informal guidelines of causation and time ordering. Like any Bayesian network, local networks possess precise semantics in terms of independence assertions and these can be used to verify 1) whether the network faithfully represents the domain and 2) whether the input is consistent.

Multiple local networks have several advantages compared to a single Bayesian network. The elicitation of several small networks is easier than eliciting a single full-scale Bayesian network because the expert can focus his/her attention to particular subdomains, and hence, provide more reliable judgments. Multiple networks represent a domain better because more knowledge about independence is qualitatively encoded. Algorithms for finding the most likely hypothesis run faster when using multiple networks. And finally, the overall storage requirement of multiple networks is often smaller than that of a single Bayesian network because as independence assertions become more detailed, less numeric parameters are needed for describing a domain.

Notably, when independence assertions in the domain are symmetric, a single Bayesian network is preferable.

The challenges remain to 1) devise additional graphical representation schemes of salient patterns of independence assertions, (2) provide computer-aided elicitation procedures for constructing these representations, and (3) devise efficient inference procedures that make use of the encoded assertions.

References

[Geiger and Heckerman, 1990] Geiger D., and Heckeman, D. (1990). Separable and transitive graphoids. Sixth Conference on Uncertainty in Artificial Intelligence.

[Heckerman, 1990] Heckerman, D. (1990). *Probabilistic Similarity Networks.* PhD thesis, Program in Medical Information Sciences, Stanford University, Stanford, CA.

[Fung and Shachter, 1991] Contingent Influence Diagrams. Submitted for publication.

[Lauritzen and Spiegelhalter, 1988] Lauritzen, S.L.; and Spiegelhalter, D.J. 1988. Local Computations with Probabilities on Graphical Structures and Their Application to Expert Systems (with discussion). *Journal Royal Statistical Society*, B, 50(2):157-224.

[Pearl, 1988] Pearl, J. (1988). *Probabilistic Reasoning in Intelligent Systems: Networks of Plausible Inference.* Morgan Kaufmann, San Mateo, CA.

[Shachter, 1986] Shachter, R. (1986). Evaluating Influence Diagrams. Operations Research 34:871-882.

[Verma and Pearl, 1988] Verma, T. and Pearl, J. (1988). Causal networks: Semantics and expressiveness. In *Proceedings of Fourth Workshop on Uncertainty in Artificial Intelligence,* Minneapolis, MN, pages 352–359. Association for Uncertainty in Artificial Intelligence, Mountain View, CA.

Probability Estimation in face of Irrelevant Information

Adam J. Grove
Department of Computer Science
Stanford University
Stanford, CA 94305
grove@cs.stanford.edu

Daphne Koller
Department of Computer Science
Stanford University
Stanford, CA 94305
daphne@theory.stanford.edu

Abstract

In this paper, we consider one aspect of the problem of applying *decision theory* to the design of agents that learn how to make decisions under uncertainty. This aspect concerns how an agent can estimate probabilities for the possible states of the world, given that it only makes limited observations before committing to a decision. We show that the naive application of statistical tools can be improved upon if the agent can determine which of his observations are truly relevant to the estimation problem at hand. We give a framework in which such determinations can be made, and define an estimation procedure to use them. Our framework also suggests several extensions, which show how additional knowledge can be used to improve the estimation procedure still further.

1 INTRODUCTION

The problem we consider in this paper is how to estimate probabilities for states of the world, so that agents can use the techniques of *decision theory* to make decisions under uncertainty. We illustrate this problem with an example. Suppose we wish to design an agent M whose function is to deliver packages around town as swiftly as possible. We could program M with a set of different methods for doing this; for instance, it can drive between destinations using either the freeway system or city roads, it can walk, it can give the package to the postal service to deliver instead, and so on. Let us ignore the enormous task of implementing each method, which is, in essence, a planning problem and beyond the scope of this work. Here we ask how the agent is to decide between them.

For this example, we might take the following simplistic view of the world. First, we suppose that the time taken to drive depends, in a known way, only on whether traffic is congested. The time taken to walk depends (again, in a known way) on the weather conditions. Posting the package takes constant time. Now we ask M to deliver a particular package. M must commit to a method before finding out about the traffic or whether it will rain. If M can associate a probability with each relevant possibility, then it can calculate expected time for each method and decide accordingly.

We will assume that M has been in situations like this before (presumably this is the case once it has been operational for a while), and so it can estimate probabilities from stored observations. However, M might actually know a lot about the current situation: it could know the time, the day of week, the season, today's weather forecast, the package's weight, the recipient, whether the car has been serviced recently, the price of a postage stamp, and so on. What we really want is the probability of each of the events of interest (such as, it is sunny but traffic is light) conditioned on what is known. This presents a problem because, once we take all of this knowledge into account, most of M's previous data no longer pertains directly. The main issue studied in this paper is how we can decide what information can be safely ignored as being irrelevant, so improving the quality of the estimated probabilities. The agent M might have very little data directly applicable to estimating the chance of "fine weather and light traffic" given all he knows, because it is likely M hasn't been in an identical situation often before. But we know that a lot of M's knowledge—for instance, the nature of the package and the condition of the car—has nothing at all to do with the weather or road conditions. If we estimate probabilities conditional on just relevant data, such as the forecast and the time of day, there will be many more observations that can be used.

The model which stands at the heart of classical decision theory, and on which our work is based, is the decision matrix (see [Savage, 1954] for definitions, and Section 5 for some discussion of related work in AI). As explained in Section 2, applying this technique requires the estimation of the probabilities of the various states of the world that the agent considers possible. Using these probabilities, the agent can estimate the expected utility for each alternative action, and choose the one that maximizes that quantity. Unlike many previous works (e.g. [Simon and Kadane, 1975]), we do not assume that these probabilities are made available by an external source. More realistically, we assume that the agent uses its own experience as the major source of information. The agent will thus learn from experience, by gradually refining its estimates.

Our method for estimating probabilities, which is based on a procedure that attempts to discover irrelevant attributes, is described in Section 3. Some extensions are outlined in Section 4. Our technique combines concepts reminiscent of probabilistic reference hierarchies (see, for example, [Bacchus, 1988]) with statistical tools. It thus enables using statistical data, as well as less precise notions about relevance that the designer might have.

2 THE UNDERLYING MODEL

The decision-making module takes a decision problem, creates a decision-matrix, and uses that matrix to decide on a course of action. Each row of the decision matrix is a possible action under consideration by the agent. For example, agent M's actions might consist of: drive on a freeway, drive on the city roads, walk, and send by mail. Of course, these high-level actions usually represent complex plans consisting of many atomic steps; the model we are using ignores the planning problem of how to determine these steps. The columns of the matrix are possible states of the world, where each state has an associated probability (the probability that it holds in this particular decision situation). These two components of the matrix will be described later in this section. The elements of the matrix are the agent's outcomes for each action/state pair. It is a well-known result of decision theory (see [Savage, 1954]) that in many cases, the agent's preference ordering on outcomes can be expressed by numerical *utilities*. In the particular context of intelligent agents, the utility will often be expressed in terms of certain parameters, such as time, fuel consumption, or money. For example, we might use time as our measure of utility for M. In our paper, we assume that the matrix entries are utilities, and are given in advance. Once the entire decision matrix is available, the agent simply chooses the action with maximum expected utility.

2.1 STATES AND EVENTS

We adopt a framework in which the agent observes and reasons about the world using a fixed set of *attributes*, $\mathcal{A} = \{A_1, \ldots, A_n\}$, which take on values in a finite space. For example, the attribute "day of the week" has a natural set of values; an attribute such as "weather" would be partitioned into values (e.g. raining, cloudy, fine), where the granularity of the partition will depend on the agent's needs. This vocabulary must be chosen carefully, as it greatly affects the performance of the decision-making module The attributes should be chosen to be, in some sense, independent of each other. See Section 4 for further discussion.

The most specific assertion we can make about the world is to announce the value of each $A \in \mathcal{A}$. This exactly determines the world as far as the agent's vocabulary allows it to differentiate. We therefore define a *state* to be an assignment of a value to every attribute in $\mathcal{A}$. In the decision-theoretic paradigm, the agent's uncertainty is modeled via the existence of several states that the agent believes the world could be in.[1] In general, some of the attributes in $\mathcal{A}$ will have no connection to the decision at hand (i.e. will not affect the outcomes of the contemplated actions). For example, although M might have an attribute describing the last time the car was serviced, the value of this attribute would not be relevant to the time it takes M to deliver a certain package. We define an *event* E to be a list of values for a subset $\mathcal{A}'$ of the attributes in $\mathcal{A}$. We say that an event E *obtains* when the true state agrees with E on all attributes in $\mathcal{A}'$.

We assume that the columns of the decision matrix are all events which contain values for some specific subset $\mathcal{A}'$ of $\mathcal{A}$. Ideally, these attributes should be those that have some connection with the actions or the decision under consideration. The smaller $\mathcal{A}'$ is, the easier it is to make the decision.[2] In our example, $\mathcal{A}'$ might consist of the attributes "weather" and "traffic density", and the column events would be all the possible assignments of values to these two attributes.

The initial information I denotes the set of attribute-value pairs that the agent observes in a particular decision making situation, i.e., before an action is chosen and executed. It should be clear that I is also an event.

2.2 PROBABILITY DISTRIBUTION

The decision-theoretic model we are using here assumes the existence of some objective probability distribution on the possible states. That is, let $\mathcal{W}$ be the set of all possible states of the world. We are assuming that $\mathcal{W}$ has the additional structure of a (presumably unknown) probability space $(\mathcal{W}, \pi)$. It is unlikely to be true, in any meaningful sense, that the actual state of the world is a random draw from

[1] This is similar to the familiar concept of "possible worlds".

[2] For choosing $\mathcal{A}'$, all we need is some, possibly incomplete, knowledge about which attributes are "relevant" to an action. It is not necessary to know how or why a certain attribute affects the consequence of the action, or even be certain that it really does.

some probability distribution, but the probabilistic model is often a good approximation to the intricately causal way the world actually works. For further discussion, see, for example, [Cox, 1961; Jaynes, 1968; Savage, 1954].

In our model, a decision-making situation evolves as follows. At the time the agent learns that he is to make a decision, the actual state of the world is regarded as being randomly chosen according to $(\mathcal{W}, \pi)$. The agent has the capability of observing the values of some of the attributes, and so gains some initial information I about the chosen state. It then chooses an action (i.e., makes a decision), and afterwards, perhaps because of the action's execution, it learns more about what the world was like at decision time. That is, it learns the values of more attributes.

2.3 DATA COLLECTION

We assume that the agent has a database $\mathcal{D}$ of observations relating to past experiences (the integration of other types of data into our model will be discussed briefly in Section 4). To be more specific, we assume that every data point $D \in \mathcal{D}$ actually arose from some earlier decision-making episode. Thus D contains, among possibly other things, the values for the attributes that were observed before and during the decision process, i.e., the agent's information about the state of the world holding at the time.

In order to simplify the model, we might make a *complete observability* assumption: the agent always observes the value of every attribute in $\mathcal{A}$. Consider the following example, which illustrates what can go wrong without some such requirement. Suppose that M is sometimes told about baseball games taking place in the city, and that when there is a baseball game M usually decides to walk (perhaps because baseball games generally take place when the weather is fine). Suppose, in violation of complete observability, that if the agent chooses to walk it does not find out about the traffic conditions. Then if the traffic density is in fact heavier on days in which a game takes place, M's estimate for the probability of heavy traffic will be lower than the true value, because most of its observations will be taken on days when there is no game. In general, complete observability avoids this and similar errors because it implies that every observation in $\mathcal{D}$ truly is a random sample from $(\mathcal{W}, \pi)$, free of unwanted bias.

In practice, complete observability can be weakened to *independent observability*, which says that the set of attributes the agent gets to learn about is determined independently of both the actual state of the world, and of any decision the agent takes. In the above example this was violated, because whether or not the traffic was observed depended on whether the agent decided to walk, and it was this that induced bias. Of course, the independent observability requirement by itself offers no guarantee that we ever see enough data to estimate all the required probabilities. So it is also necessary to assume that, whenever $\mathcal{A}'$ defines the set of events for some decision the agent might be asked to make, then the chance of observing this set should be nonzero. Even this requirement can be weakened. For instance, if two attributes are rarely observed together, appropriate assumptions about conditional independence can be used so as to still permit accumulation of sufficient historical data.

In subsequent sections, we shall simplify the presentation by stating our results and techniques in terms of the complete observability assumption only. However, the extensions to the weaker, but more realistic, conditions are straightforward.

In practice, the most restrictive consequences of our model are as follows. First, the requirement that the information observed is an event amounts to assuming that the agent either identifies, without uncertainty, the value of an attribute or else learns nothing at all about it. But we note that if the set $\mathcal{A}$ is chosen well, this assumption should cause relatively little difficulty. The other problem with our model relates to the amount of data stored: there is little obvious scope for data summarization or compression. Currently, our estimation procedure requires every observation to be remembered (or, only slightly better, remember counts for observations that occur frequently). Significant improvements are likely to depend on domain-specific structure.

3 THE ESTIMATION PROBLEM

Let us review the probability estimation problem. We have some initial information I. We have determined a list of events which are the columns of the decision matrix, and wish to estimate $p = Pr(E|I)$ for each event E. Of course, how best to form these estimates is a problem in statistics.

One simple and theoretically sound estimate of p is simply the proportion of data points agreeing with E, among all points that agree with I. This estimate is "good" in several ways: for instance, it is unbiased (i.e., the expected value is exactly p) and its variance decreases to zero as the number of relevant data points grows. The problem is that the number of relevant data points may not grow very quickly because this estimate uses only those observations which agree *exactly* with I. But perhaps situations matching I have not been encountered very often. For instance, if time and date are part of I, there will be no relevant historical data at all. We conclude that this simple estimation procedure is often impractical.

To salvage the approach to decision making we are looking at, we need to be much more clever about how we estimate probabilities. The main result of this section is a technique for probability estimation which can yield substantially better results than the above. It does this by providing a framework which can capture and make use of additional information we have about the structure of the world (see Section 4). The underlying idea is the observation that the less specific the information in I, the more useful data points we will have. Therefore, the estimate would improve if we could (justifiably!) ignore some of the attributes mentioned in I.

It seems to be often true that, in any given context, only a few attributes will be *relevant* to whether some event E occurs. Consider the example in the introduction, where I records, among other things, which day of the week it is. If the attributes in E all refer to natural phenomena, such as the the weather conditions, we would expect the day of the week to be irrelevant to—and, in a sense which is easy to make precise, *independent* of—whether E occurs. In this case, the best estimate of p would pool data for all days, even though this ignores some of the knowledge contained in I. In general, it is not reasonable to require all such information about relevance to be supplied ahead of time. In the example, we would want the estimation procedure to find out for itself whether the day of the week is unimportant.

We begin by looking at the base case of our technique. Suppose I includes the value of some attribute A. Let $I_1, I_2, \ldots, I_k$ be all events which are just like I, except possibly with respect to the value of A; we may assume that $I_1 = I$. Intuitively, we can pool data only if our knowledge about A is irrelevant to p. More formally, we ask whether the conditional probabilities p_i (i.e., $Pr(E|I_i)$) are the same for all i. Our procedure is to test whether this independence is plausible, and then use either the pooled or non-pooled estimate as appropriate. Both the test and the estimate itself can make use of all the observed data in $\mathcal{D}$.

In the following, let N_i be the number of observations in $\mathcal{D}$ agreeing with I_i. Let $\hat{p}_i$ be the proportion of these observations that do in fact agree with the values specified in E. We estimate p either as $\hat{p}_1$ or else as the pooled estimate $\hat{p} = (\sum_{i=1}^{k} \hat{p}_i N_i)/N$, where $N = \sum_{i=1}^{k} N_i$. Note that $\hat{p}_1$ is simply the direct estimate which was mentioned earlier. We decide which of these two possibilities to use on the basis of a hypothesis test (the hypothesis being that $p_i = p_j$, for all i, j.)

One relatively simple hypothesis test we can use for this is the χ^2 test, which is discussed in most statistics texts (such as, [Larsen and Marx, 1981; Sachs, 1982]). The test is based on the value $X^2 = \sum_{i=1}^{k} (\hat{p}_i - \hat{p})^2 N_i / (\hat{p}(1 - \hat{p}))$. If the hypothesis (equal p_i) is true, and the N_i are not too small,[3] then the distribution of X^2 is very well approximated by the χ^2 distribution with $k - 1$ degrees of freedom. In order to perform the test, we must choose some small $\alpha > 0$, which becomes the chance of not pooling data when it really would have been permissible. We accept the hypothesis and use the pooled estimate just if $X^2 < c_\alpha$, where c_α is such that the chance of a random sample from χ^2 exceeding c_α is α. The value c_α can be found from tables. It is generally desirable to have α very small, but note that as α decreases the chance of incorrectly deciding to pool data when this is not justified grows. Later we state two asymptotic properties of our estimation procedure, whose proof assumes that α is $1/N^d$, for some $d > 1$. That is, as the sample size increases we should tolerate less chance of deciding incorrectly not to pool data. It turns out that, so long as α grows smaller no faster than this, the chance of pooling inappropriately also diminishes rapidly.

To recap, the general idea of our procedure is to test for independence and then use the estimate suggested by the result of the test. The hypothesis test can be done in many ways, and we have suggested one possibility, the χ^2 test. We chose this test because its simplicity facilitates the analysis.

This analysis is important because the procedure uses the same data for both the independence test and for the actual estimate. In this way, we can hope to make the best use of scarce data. But reusing sampled data destroys the independence between the outcome of the hypothesis test and the estimate used, and so we must check that the process as a whole gives us a useful result. For example, it is easy to see that both the pooled estimate $\hat{p}$ and the simple estimate $\hat{p}_1$ are unbiased if the hypothesis of equal p_i is in fact true. But it does not follow just from this that the composite estimate is unbiased.[4] Another related issue concerns the estimate's variance: intuitively, we only pool data if all the $\hat{p}_i$ are approximately the same, and so it might seem that the pooled estimate is only used when it provides little additional information over $\hat{p}_1$ anyway.

It turns out that neither of these problems arise: the estimate we give is asymptotically unbiased, and has asymptotic variance that can be much smaller than $\hat{p}_1$. In other words, at least for large N, our estimate is indeed very likely to be close to the true value. Furthermore, if the hypothesis of equal p_i is true, then our estimate has smaller variance than the simple unpooled estimate $\hat{p}_1$ and so is likely to be much closer to p. The formal statement of these results is contained

[3] A frequently stated rule of thumb is that $N_i p_i$ should be larger than 5, for all i.

[4] To illustrate the possible problems, suppose that the test is such that the hypothesis of equal p_i is slightly more likely to be accepted when the observations satisfy $\hat{p} < \hat{p}_1$ than it is otherwise. Then this would bias our estimate. Because we reuse data, the test does get to see the actual values of the estimates $\hat{p}$ and $\hat{p}_1$, and so such behavior cannot be ruled out without deeper analysis.

in the following two theorems (whose proofs are too long for inclusion here).[5]

Theorem 3.1: *If in fact $p_i = p$ for all i, then the estimate we give has mean μ and variance σ^2 such that $\mu \longrightarrow p$ and $\sigma^2 \longrightarrow p(1-p)/N$ as $N \longrightarrow \infty$.*[6] *We note that this asymptotic variance is the best that can be achieved by any unbiased estimate, even if we know for certain that the hypothesis of equal probabilities is true.*

Theorem 3.2: *If in fact $p_i \neq p_j$ for some i, j then the estimate we give has mean μ, and variance σ^2 such that $\mu \longrightarrow p_1$ and $\sigma^2 \longrightarrow p_1(1-p_1)/N_1$ as $N \longrightarrow \infty$. We note that this asymptotic variance is the smallest possible amongst unbiased estimates of p_i (given that observations relating to I_i, for $i \neq 1$, are regarded as being not informative about p_1).*

Although these theorems give asymptotic results only, it seems very likely that the procedure will work well for far smaller sample sizes than were required in our proof. Proving a precise claim about this would be difficult. Instead, we have programmed the technique to run on simulated data, and the results there did confirm this expectation. When the data was generated for each class using the same underlying probability, the decision was made to pool data most of the time. In one typical experiment, 200 data points were successively generated for each of five events, and on average the procedure declined to pool data less than 5% of the time. If the probabilities differ between classes, even by relatively small amounts—and note that the closer the probabilities are to being equal, the less damage is done by incorrect pooling—our procedure rapidly discovered this. In one experiment, where the difference between all probabilities was less than or equal to 0.1, the procedure apparently stabilized on a decision not to pool after each class had accumulated about 150 data points. A similar experiment where the probabilities differed by up to 0.3 stabilized after about 15 data points per event on average.

The procedure so far will, in effect, decide whether to ignore one particular attribute of I. In general, several attributes of I may turn out to be irrelevant. Our technique extends easily to such cases. Suppose that we have decided to ignore some attribute A of I (using a test like that just suggested). That is, we have accepted the hypothesis that $Pr(E|I) = Pr(E|I')$ for all I' that are like I except for the value of A. But from this it also follows that $Pr(E|I) = Pr(E|(I-A))$, where by $I - A$ we mean the event formed from I by omitting A and its value. We have thus reduced our problem to finding a good estimate of the latter probability. The earlier procedure—looking for irrelevant attributes—is immediately applicable again. In this way, we can achieve a substantial increase in the quality of the estimate. Note that we do not require that the attributes be considered in any particular order.

[5]Note that if we did not reuse data, the proof of these theorems would be nearly trivial (because then the hypothesis test would be certain to be independent of both $\hat{p}$ and $\hat{p}_1$). Furthermore, the results would be somewhat tighter; e.g., the composite estimate would be unbiased even for finite sample sizes.

[6]This is not quite correct as stated, because N can grow without bound even as some N_i stays small. The convergence we have in mind here is that, as N tends to infinity, each N_i must be bounded below by N^c for some $c > 0$.

4 JUSTIFICATION AND EXTENSIONS

The success of our technique depends on whether the vocabulary of attributes used to define events really reflects the way the world works. For example, the attributes A_1 = *day of the week* and A_2 = *the weather* seem to be fairly independent of each other; there are many contexts where just one of these is relevant. On the other hand, consider A'_1, which tells us the day of the week if it is Monday or Wednesday and the weather otherwise, and A'_2 which tells us the weather on Monday or Wednesday, and the day otherwise. It is not easy to imagine a context where just one of $\{A'_1, A'_2\}$ is relevant. Both these sets of attributes are equally informative for describing what the world is actually like. Our judgment that $\{A_1, A_2\}$ is better seems to be based on knowledge we have about the causal structure of the world.[7] Our technique is a framework that allows such knowledge to be usefully incorporated into the decision making process. Equally important is that we do not rely on a precise or accurate statement of this knowledge.

Sometimes we have additional knowledge, beyond just a feeling about what a suitable attribute vocabulary should be. A feature of our technique is that it allows easy extensions to cope with many types of extra information. For instance:

- If we are able to provide actual probabilities directly, there is nothing preventing them being used; the estimation procedure can be bypassed when not needed. Similarly, the method can be modified to incorporate statistical data from diverse external sources.
- If we know that some particular attributes can be ignored in certain contexts, then the hypothesis test is redundant and can be omitted. In particular, if some restrictions on the possible relationships between attributes are given to the agent (for example, as a reference hierarchy), this can be used in our process. By avoiding the hypothesis

[7]This is reminiscent of the well-known "grue/bleen" paradox ([Goodman, 1955]), which concerns the attribute vocabulary appropriate for inductive inference.

test, we gain computational efficiency and eliminate the chance of error.

- Suppose we know that if some attribute is relevant, then it must affect probabilities in a particular way. As an example, I am not sure whether the probability of traffic congestion on a particular highway depends on which day of the week it is. I know that, if the day of the week is in fact relevant, then this probability is lower on weekends. This knowledge suggests using a different test for independence. We test the hypothesis that the probability is independent of the day, against the alternatives (which have different probabilities for each day, but definitely lower on Saturday and Sunday). We omit details of such a test here. In general, whenever our knowledge can restrict the possible alternatives, a hypothesis test can achieve the same confidence using less data.
- So far, we have regarded the classes considered for pooling as being implicitly defined by the attribute vocabulary. However, our knowledge about the domain may suggest other classes as well. In our earlier example, to estimate the chance of heavy traffic congestion on a Tuesday it might be useful to consider pooling data over just weekdays (Monday to Friday), as well as over the class of all days. It is even possible to use statistical procedures to suggest useful classes, on the basis of previously collected data (but then we must be careful to use a different set of data for the hypothesis test and estimation procedure, because the results would be statistically invalid otherwise).

Finally, we note that the correctness of our technique depends on the stability over time of the underlying probability distribution. If this cannot be assumed, it would be sensible to ignore or discount older observations. There are several standard ways this might be done. Nevertheless, it is clear that robustness against changes in the underlying distribution can only be obtained at the price of slower or less accurate learning.

5 COMPARISON TO OTHER WORK

Although many techniques of decision theory have been utilized in artificial intelligence, the decision matrix paradigm of separating the probabilities of states from the utilities has been relatively ignored. Many researchers who adopt the concept of maximizing expected utility (see [Etzioni, 1989b; Horvitz, 1988; Wellman, 1990; Russel and Wefald, 1988]) compute the expected utility for each action directly. A separate computation of utilities has the major advantage of allowing additional information about utilities and probabilities, arising from different sources, to be used. The description of a state may be detailed enough so that the utility of an action at that state can be computed using knowledge about causality that the agent might have. For example, the agent might know that when the state of the world is such that there is light traffic and the weather is good, then the action of driving ten miles on a freeway must take about ten minutes, because the average velocity in those conditions is 55 miles per hour. Also, by dividing the estimation process into two stages, more historical data will be usable. For example, the agent might conclude that the exact day of the week (say Friday) is relevant to the probability of having heavy traffic, and will therefore use only the historical data about Friday to compute it. But heavy traffic also occurs on other days (although with different probabilities), so that the agent will be able to use all that additional data to compute the expected driving time given heavy traffic. This leads to more accurate estimates.

While some research in AI has adopted this separation of probabilities and utilities (notably [Haddawy and Hanks, 1990; Simon and Kadane, 1975]), the problem of estimating the probabilities in the face of too much initial information has not, to our knowledge, been attacked directly. Some works [Simon and Kadane, 1975] simply assume that the probabilities are known in advance. Others (e.g. [Bundy, 1984; Lee and Mahajan, 1988]) suggest the concept of sampling, but do not discuss which class to sample. Rendell [Rendell, 1983] deals with the concept of sampling on different classes, but in the very limited context of search trees. Etzioni's work [Etzioni, 1989a] on estimating utilities is based on machine learning techniques, which attempt to discover classes over which the utility is homogeneous. Such homogeneity usually arises due to a deterministic relationship between the properties of the class and the utility (such as the driving time given light traffic described above). These techniques do not carry over to estimating probabilities, because the only way to achieve homogeneity in classes of binary values is to have the entire class be all zeros or all ones. I.e., the class will be such that it deterministically forces the truth value of the event. Typically, it is impossible to find an attribute language precise enough to define such classes.

A different approach to finding the right class for estimating probabilities is to treat the problem of inferring the independence structure as a separate task. For example, [Fung and Crawford, 1990] use techniques similar to ours—classical statistics, and in particular, the χ^2 test—in a system which infers qualitative structure from data, modeling this structure as a *probabilistic network*. Once constructed, the network can be used for several purposes, such as estimation. The major drawback of this technique is that a separate data set is required for the construction of the network. It is not clear how this technique can be safely extended to reuse data. Therefore, larger amounts of data will be needed. Our approach is also better in situations where new data is being constantly accumulated, because the new information could cause us to change our decision as to the relevance of certain attributes.

[Fung and Crawford, 1990] also show how to find the smallest possible set of relevant attributes. This procedure is computationally expensive and relies on strong assumptions about the relationships among the attributes. These assumptions also prevent the procedure in [Fung and Crawford, 1990] from being efficiently used in our framework, because each decision situation will need to be investigated separately. This eliminates the computational advantage of computing the entire independence structure simultaneously. Our approach eliminates the attributes one by one, in an arbitrary order. While not guaranteed to find the minimal set of relevant attributes, this technique is much faster and requires no assumptions.

We conclude this section by comparing our methods to the Bayesian approach. It should be noted that, if prior probabilities are available, Bayesian updating (see [Jaynes, 1968]) can, in a sense, replace the χ^2 test described in Section 3. We have chosen not to assume the existence of prior probabilities, and therefore use a technique from classical statistics. A work similar in outlook to ours, which deals with a different problem using Bayesian techniques is Pearl's work about hierarchies of hypotheses [Pearl, 1986].

6 CONCLUSION

We have investigated the problem of estimating the conditional probability of a state given some initial information I, based on a database of observations. This problem is straightforward when there is plenty of data. However, in many situations, there is little data that exactly matches I. Our main result discusses how to utilize the available data in order to decide which attributes in I are irrelevant, and how to use the information about irrelevance to improve the estimate's quality. A feature of our approach is that it uses all the available data for both this decision and for the actual estimation.

We have discussed in detail the assumptions that are required to make our approach sound. For example, the model is simplified by the (commonly made) assumption we call *complete observability,* that is, that all data points contain observations about every attribute. However, we discuss a relaxation of this, *independent observability,* which is far more realistic yet still permits efficient estimation.

The idea behind our approach to estimation is not limited to finding conditional probabilities. For instance, in the context of decision theory which motivates the work in this paper, another important application would be the estimation of utilities; we believe that this is likely to be a straightforward extension of the present work.

The most important factor in the success of our approach will be the quality of the attribute vocabulary that the agent uses to describe the world. Whether made explicit or not, this theme recurs throughout AI. In our approach, this issue is prominent, and we may hope that our more technical results and discussion will serve to shed some light on this fundamental issue.

Finally, we note that one of the advantages of our framework is that it can be extended in several directions, to make use of other knowledge aside from raw observational data. A few suggestions towards this were described in Section 4, but clearly this does not exhaust all the possibilities.

Acknowledgments

The authors would like to thank Joseph Halpern for comments and discussions relating to this paper.

Some of this work was executed while both authors were employed at IBM Almaden Research Center, 650 Harry Road, San Jose, California 95120-6099. The first author is also supported by an IBM graduate fellowship.

References

[Bacchus, 1988] F. Bacchus. *Representing and reasoning with probabilistic knowledge.* PhD thesis, University of Alberta, 1988. Also issued as Waterloo University Technical Report CS-88-31.

[Bundy, 1984] A. Bundy. Incidence calculus: a mechanism for probabilistic reasoning. Technical Report 216, University of Edinburgh Dept. of Artificial Intelligence, 1984.

[Cox, 1961] R. T. Cox. *The algebra of probable inference.* Baltimore: The Johns Hopkins Press, 1961.

[Etzioni, 1989a] O. Etzioni. Hypothesis filtering: a practical approach to reliable learning. In *Proceedings of the Fifth International Conference on Machine Learning,* 1989.

[Etzioni, 1989b] O. Etzioni. Tractable decision analytic control: an expanded version. Technical Report CMU-CS-89-119, Carnegie Mellon University, 1989.

[Fung and Crawford, 1990] R. M. Fung and S. L. Crawford. Constructor: a system for the induction of probabilistic models. In *Proceedings of the National Conference on Artificial Intelligence (AAAI-90),* pages 762–769, 1990.

[Goodman, 1955] N. Goodman. *Fact, fiction, and forecast,* chapter iii. Harvard University Press, 1955.

[Haddawy and Hanks, 1990] P. Haddawy and S. Hanks. Issues in decision-theoretic planning: symbolic goals and numeric utilities. In *Proceedings of the 1990 DARPA Workshop on Innovative Approaches to Planning, Scheduling, and Control*, 1990.

[Horvitz *et al.*, 1988] E. J. Horvitz, J. S. Breese, and M. Henrion. Decision theory in expert systems and artificial intelligence. *International Journal of Approximate Reasoning*, 2:247–302, 1988.

[Horvitz, 1988] E. J. Horvitz. Reasoning under varying and uncertain resource constraints. In *Proceedings of the National Conference on Artificial Intelligence (AAAI-88)*, pages 111–116, 1988.

[Jaynes, 1968] E. T. Jaynes. Prior probabilities. *IEEE Transactions on Systems Science and Cybernetics*, 4:227–241, 1968.

[Larsen and Marx, 1981] R. J. Larsen and M. L. Marx. *An introduction to mathematical statistics and its applications.* Prentice-Hall, 1981.

[Lee and Mahajan, 1988] K. F. Lee and S. Mahajan. A pattern classification approach to evaluation function learning. *Artificial Intelligence*, 36, 1988.

[Pearl, 1986] J. Pearl. On evidential reasoning in a hierarchy of hypotheses. *Artificial Intelligence*, 28, 1986.

[Rendell, 1983] L. Rendell. A new basis for state-space learning systems and a successful implementation. *Artificial Intelligence*, 20, 1983.

[Russel and Wefald, 1988] S. Russel and E. Wefald. Decision-theoretic control of reasoning: general theory and an application to game playing. Technical Report UCB/CSD 88/435, University of California at Berkeley, 1988.

[Sachs, 1982] L. Sachs. *Applied statistics.* Springer-Verlag, 1982.

[Savage, 1954] L. J. Savage. *Foundations of statistics.* John Wiley & Sons, 1954.

[Simon and Kadane, 1975] H. A. Simon and J. B. Kadane. Optimal problem solving search: all-or-none solutions. *Artificial Intelligence*, 6, 1975.

[Spiegelhalter, 1986] D. J. Spiegelhalter. Probabilistic reasoning in predictive expert systems. In L. N. Kanal and J. F. Lemmer, editors, *Proceedings of the Second Workshop on Uncertainty in Artificial Intelligence*, pages 47–68. Amsterdam, North Holland, 1986.

[Wellman, 1990] M. P. Wellman. *Formulation of tradeoffs in planning under uncertainty.* Pitman, London, 1990.

An Approximate Nonmyopic Computation for Value of Information

David Heckerman
Computer Science and Pathology
University of Southern California
HMR 204, 2025 Zonal Ave
Los Angeles, CA 90033

Eric Horvitz
Palo Alto Laboratory
Rockwell Int Science Center
444 High Street
Palo Alto, California 94301

Blackford Middleton
Section on Medical Informatics
Division of General Internal Medicine
Stanford University Medical Center
Stanford, California 94305

Abstract

Value-of-information analyses provide a straightforward means for selecting the best next observation to make, and for determining whether it is better to gather additional information or to act immediately. Determining the next best test to perform, given a state of uncertainty about the world, requires a consideration of the value of making all possible sequences of observations. In practice, decision analysts and expert-system designers have avoided the intractability of exact computation of the value of information by relying on a *myopic* approximation. Myopic analyses are based on the assumption that only one additional test will be performed, even when there is an opportunity to make a large number of observations. We present a nonmyopic approximation for value of information that bypasses the traditional myopic analyses by exploiting the statistical properties of large samples.

1 INTRODUCTION

A person faced with a decision usually has the opportunity to gather additional information about the state of the world before taking action. Decision-theoretic methods for determining the value of gathering additional information date back to the earliest literature on the principle of maximum expected utility (MEU). These methods form an integral part of many probabilistic expert systems, such as Gorry's congestive-heart-failure program (Gorry and Barnett, 1968) and Pathfinder (Heckerman et al., 1989; Heckerman et al., 1990), an expert system that assists pathologists with the diagnosis of lymph-node diseases. To decide whether or not to perform a test, an expert system computes the value of information of that test. The system recommends that the test be performed if and only if the value of information exceeds the cost of the test.[1]

In most decision contexts, a decision maker has the option to perform several tests, and can decide which test to perform after seeing the results of all previous tests. Thus, an expert system should consider the value of all possible *sequences* of tests. Such an analysis is intractable, because the number of sequences grows exponentially with the number of tests. Builders of expert systems have avoided the intractability of complete value-of-information analyses by implementing *myopic* or *greedy* value-of-information analyses. In such analyses, a system determines the next best test by computing value of information based on the assumption that the decision maker will act immediately after seeing the results of the single test (Gorry et al., 1973; Heckerman et al., 1990). In this paper, we present an approximate nonmyopic analysis. The analysis avoids the traditional myopic assumption by making use of the statistical properties of large samples.

2 VALUE-OF-INFORMATION COMPUTATIONS FOR DIAGNOSIS

We discuss myopic and nonmyopic value-of-information computations in terms of the simple model for diagnosis under uncertainty represented by the influence diagram in Figure 1. In this model, the chance node H represents a mutually exclusive and exhaustive set of possible hypotheses, and the decision node D represents a mutually exclusive and exhaustive set of possible alternatives. The value node U represents the utility of the decision maker, which depends on the outcome of H and the decision D. The chance nodes E_1, E_2, ..., E_n are observable pieces of evidence or tests about the true state of H. This model is identical to that for Pathfinder (Heckerman, 1990).

[1]This prescription for action assumes that the delta property holds. See Section 3.

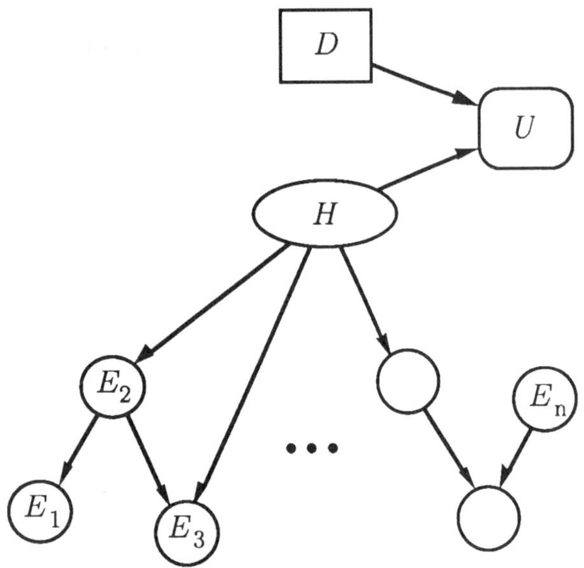

Figure 1: An influence-diagram representation of the problem of diagnosis under uncertainty. The decision-maker's utility (rounded rectangular node, U) depends on a hypothesis (oval node, H) and a decision (square node, D). The variables E_i are pieces of evidence or tests about the true state of H.

We make several simplifying assumptions. First, we assume that H is a binary chance variable and D is a binary decision variable. We use H and $\neg H$ to denote the two outcomes of H, and D and $\neg D$ to denote the two outcomes of D. For definiteness, we assume that the decision maker chooses D (as opposed to $\neg D$), when H occurs. Second, we assume that each piece of evidence, E_1, E_2, ..., E_n, is binary. Finally, we assume that each piece of evidence is conditionally independent of all other evidence, given H and $\neg H$. In Section 6, we relax these assumptions.

Using the assumption of conditional independence of evidence, we can calculate the posterior probability of the hypothesis by multiplying together all of the likelihood ratios, $\frac{p(E_i|H)}{p(E_i|\neg H)}$, with the prior odds, $\frac{p(H)}{p(\neg H)}$.

$$\frac{p(H|E_i,\ldots,E_m)}{P(\neg H|E_i,\ldots,E_m)} = \frac{p(E_1|H)}{p(E_1|\neg H)} \cdots \frac{p(E_m|H)}{p(E_m|\neg H)} \frac{p(H)}{p(\neg H)}$$

We can write this equation more compactly in odds form as

$$O(H|E_i,\ldots,E_m) = O(H)\prod_{i=1}^{m}\lambda_i \quad (1)$$

where λ_i is the likelihood ratio $\frac{p(E_i|H)}{p(E_i|\neg H)}$.

Because D and H are binary, it follows from the MEU principle that there exists a threshold probability p^*, such that we should take action D if and only if the probability of H exceeds p^*. This threshold is the probability of H at which the decision maker is indifferent between acting and not acting. That is, p^* is the point where acting and not acting have equal utility, or

$$\begin{aligned} p^*U(H,D) + (1-p^*)U(\neg H,D) &= \\ p^*U(H,\neg D) + (1-p^*)U(\neg H,\neg D) \end{aligned} \quad (2)$$

In Equation 2, $U(H, D)$ is the decision maker's utility for the situation where H occurs and action D is taken, $U(H,\neg D)$ is the utility when H occurs and action D is not taken, and so on. Solving Equation 2 for p^*, we obtain

$$p^* = \frac{C}{C+B} \quad (3)$$

where C is the *cost* of the decision

$$C = U(\neg H,\neg D) - U(\neg H, D) \quad (4)$$

and B is the *benefit* of the decision

$$B = U(H,D) - U(H,\neg D) \quad (5)$$

If the decision maker has observed pieces of evidence $E_1, E_2, \ldots, E_m$, then the decision maker should choose action D if and only if $p(H|E_1 \ldots, E_m) > p^*$. In terms of the odds formulation, he should act if and only if

$$O(H|E_1,\ldots,E_m) \geq \frac{p^*}{1-p^*} \quad (6)$$

The weight of evidence, w_i, is defined as the log of the likelihood ratio, $\ln \lambda_i$. Mapping likelihood ratios into weights of evidence allows us to update the probability of H through the addition of the weights of evidence. Referring to Equations 1 and 6, we can rewrite the threshold-probability condition in terms of the log-likelihood ratio where $w_i = \ln \lambda_i$. The decision maker should choose action D if and only if

$$W = \sum_{i=1}^{m} w_i \geq \ln\frac{p^*}{1-p^*} - \ln O(H) = W^* \quad (7)$$

In this expression, W^* is the decision threshold in terms of weights of evidence.

3 MYOPIC ANALYSIS

Let us assume that the user of a diagnostic system has instantiated zero or more pieces of evidence in the influence diagram shown in Figure 1. We can propagate the effects of these instantiations to the uninstantiated nodes, and remove the instantiated nodes from the influence diagram. This removal leaves an influence diagram of the same form as that shown in Figure 1. To simplify our notation, we continue to refer to the remaining pieces of evidence as E_1, E_2, ..., E_n; also, we use $p(H)$ to refer to the probability of the hypothesis H, given the instantiated evidence.

The decision maker now considers whether he should observe another piece of evidence before acting. A myopic procedure for identifying such evidence computes, for each piece of evidence, the expected utility of the decision maker under the assumption that *the decision maker will act after observing only that piece of evidence.* In addition, the procedure computes his expected utility if he does not observe any evidence before making his decision. If, for each piece of evidence, the expected utility given that evidence is less than the expected utility given no evidence, then the decision maker acts immediately in accordance with Equation 6. Otherwise, the decision maker observes the piece of evidence with the highest expected utility; then, the myopic procedure *repeats this computation to identify additional evidence for observation.* Because the myopic procedure allows for the gathering of additional evidence, the procedure is inconsistent with its own assumptions. We return to this observation in the next section.

In the remainder of this section, we examine the computation of expected utilities and introduce notation. Let $EU(E, C_E)$ denote the expected utility of the decision maker who will observe E at cost C_E, and then act. Let $CE(E, C_E)$ be the certain equivalent of this situation. That is,

$$U(CE(E, C_E)) = EU(E, C_E) \tag{8}$$

or

$$CE(E, C_E) = U^{-1}(EU(E, C_E)) \tag{9}$$

where $U(\cdot)$ is the decision maker's *utility function*: a monotonic increasing function that maps the value of an outcome (e.g., in dollars) to the decision maker's utility for that outcome. Similarly, let $EU(\phi, 0)$ denote the expected utility of the decision maker if he acts immediately, and let $CE(\phi, 0)$ denote the certain equivalent of this situation. Thus, in the myopic procedure, a decision maker should observe the piece of evidence E for which the quantity

$$CE(E, C_E) - CE(\phi, 0) \tag{10}$$

is maximum, provided it is greater than 0.

In this paper, to simplify the discussion, we assume that the delta property holds.[2] The *delta property* states that an increase in value of all outcomes in a lottery by an amount Δ increases the certain equivalent of that lottery by Δ (Howard, 1967). Under this assumption, we obtain

$$CE(E, C_E) = CE(E, 0) - C_E \tag{11}$$

where $CE(E, 0)$ is the certain equivalent of observing E *at no cost.* Therefore, we have

$$CE(E, C_E) - CE(\phi, 0) = VI(E) - C_E \tag{12}$$

where

$$VI(E) = CE(E, 0) - CE(\phi, 0) \tag{13}$$

[2]The primary result of this research—that we can use the central-limit theorem to make tractable an approximate nonmyopic analysis—is unaffected by this assumption.

is the *value of information* of observing E.[3] The quantity $VI(E)$ represents the largest amount that the decision maker would be willing to pay to observe E. When we compare Expression 10 with Equation 12, we see that, in the myopic procedure, a decision maker should observe the piece of evidence E (if any) for which the quantity

$$VI(E) - C_E \equiv NVI(E) \tag{14}$$

is maximum and positive. We call $NVI(E)$ the *net value of information* of observing E.

The decision maker usually specifies directly the cost of observing evidence. In contrast, we can compute $VI(E)$ from the decision maker's utilities and probabilities. Specifically, from Equations 9 and 13, we have

$$VI(E) = U^{-1}(EU(E, 0)) - U^{-1}(EU(\phi, 0))$$

To simplify notation, we use the abbreviations

$$EU(E, 0) \equiv EU(E) \quad \text{and} \quad EU(\phi, 0) \equiv EU(\phi)$$

Thus, we obtain

$$VI(E) = U^{-1}(EU(E)) - U^{-1}(EU(\phi)) \tag{15}$$

The computation of $EU(\phi)$ is straightforward. We have

$$EU(\phi) = \begin{cases} p(H)U(H, \neg D) + p(\neg H)U(\neg H, \neg D), & p(H) \le p^* \\ p(H)U(H, D) + p(\neg H)U(\neg H, D), & p(H) > p^* \end{cases} \tag{16}$$

by definition of p^*.

To compute $EU(E)$, let us assume that E is defined such that the observation of E increases the probability of H. If $p(H|E) > p^*$ and $p(H|\neg E) > p^*$, then $VI(E) = 0$, because the decision maker will not change his decision if he observes E. Similarly, if $p(H|E) < p^*$ and $p(H|\neg E) < p^*$, then $VI(E) = 0$. Thus, we need only to consider the case where $p(H|E) > p^*$ and $p(H|\neg E) < p^*$. Let us consider separately the cases H and $\neg H$. We have

$$EU(E|H) = p(E|H)U(H, D) + p(\neg E|H)U(H, \neg D) \tag{17}$$

and

$$EU(E|\neg H) = p(E|\neg H)U(\neg H, D) + p(\neg E|\neg H)U(\neg H, \neg D) \tag{18}$$

where $EU(E|H)$ and $EU(E|\neg H)$ are the expected utilities of observing E, given H and $\neg H$, respectively. To obtain the expected utility of observing E, we average these two quantities

$$EU(E) = p(H)EU(E|H) + p(\neg H)EU(E|\neg H) \tag{19}$$

To compute $VI(E)$, we combine Equations 15, 16, and 19.

[3]Other names for $VI(E)$ include the value of perfect information of E and the value of clairvoyance on E.

4 NONMYOPIC ANALYSIS

As we mentioned in the previous section, the myopic procedure for identifying cost-effective observations includes the incorrect assumption that the decision maker will act after observing only one piece of evidence. This myopic assumption can affect the diagnostic accuracy of an expert system because information gathering might be halted even though there exists some set of features whose value of information is greater that the cost of its observation. For example, a myopic analysis may indicate that no feature is cost effective for observation, yet the value of information for one or more feature pairs (were they computed) could exceed the cost of their observation.

There has been little investigation of the accuracy of myopic analyses. In one analysis, Kalagnanam and Henrion, 1990, showed that a myopic policy is optimal, when the decision maker's utility function $U(\cdot)$ is linear, and the relationship between hypotheses and evidence is deterministic. In an empirical study, Gorry, 1968, demonstrated that the use of a myopic analysis does not diminish significantly the diagnostic accuracy of an expert system for congenital heart disease.

In a correct identification of cost-effective evidence, we should take into account the fact that the decision maker may observe more than one piece of evidence before acting. This computation must consider all possible ordered sequences of evidence observation, and is, therefore, intractable.

Let us consider, however, the following nonmyopic approximation for identifying features that are cost effective to observe. Again, we assume that the delta property holds. First, under the myopic assumption, we compute the net value of information for each piece of evidence. If there is at least one piece of evidence that has a positive net value of information, then we identify for observation the piece of evidence with the highest net value of information. Otherwise, we arrange the pieces of evidence in descending order of their net values of information. Let us label the pieces of evidence $E_1, E_2, \ldots, E_n$, such that $NVI(E_i) > NVI(E_j)$, if and only if $i > j$.

Next, we compute the net value of information of each subsequence of $E_1, E_2, \ldots, E_n$. That is, for $m = 1, 2, \ldots n$, we compute the difference between the value of information for observing $E_1, E_2, \ldots, E_m$, and the cost of observing this sequence of evidence. If any such net value of information is greater than 0, then we identify E_1 as a piece of evidence that is cost effective to observe. Once the decision maker has observed E_1, we repeat the entire computation described in this section.

This approach does not consider all possible test sequences, but it does overcome one limitation of the myopic analysis. In particular, the method can identify sets of features that are cost effective for observation, even when the observation of each feature alone is not cost effective.

5 VALUE OF INFORMATION FOR A SUBSET OF EVIDENCE

As in the myopic analysis, we assume that the decision maker can specify the cost of observing a set of evidence. In this section, we show how we can compute the value of information for a set of evidence from the decision maker's utilities and probabilities.

As in the previous section, let us suppose that the decision maker has the option to observe a particular subset of evidence $\{E_1, E_2, \ldots, E_m\}$ before acting. There are 2^m possible instantiations of the evidence in this set, corresponding to the observation of E_i or $\neg E_i$ for every i. Let $\mathcal{E}$ denote an arbitrary instantiation; and let $\mathcal{E}_D$ and $\mathcal{E}_{\neg D}$ denote the set of instantiations $\mathcal{E}$ such that $p(H|\mathcal{E}) > p^*$ and $p(H|\mathcal{E}) \leq p^*$, respectively.

The computation of the value of information for the observation of the set $\{E_1, E_2, \ldots, E_m\}$ parallels the myopic computation. In particular, we have

$$\begin{aligned} &EU(E_1 \ldots E_m) = \\ &\quad p(H)EU(E_1 \ldots E_m|H)+ \\ &\quad p(\neg H)EU(E_1 \ldots E_m|\neg H) \end{aligned} \tag{20}$$

where

$$\begin{aligned} &EU(E_1 \ldots E_m|H) = \\ &\quad \left[\textstyle\sum_{\mathcal{E}\in\mathcal{E}_D} p(\mathcal{E}|H)\right] U(H, D)+ \\ &\quad \left[\textstyle\sum_{\mathcal{E}\in\mathcal{E}_{\neg D}} p(\mathcal{E}|H)\right] U(H, \neg D) \end{aligned} \tag{21}$$

and

$$\begin{aligned} &EU(E_1 \ldots E_m|\neg H) = \\ &\quad \left[\textstyle\sum_{\mathcal{E}\in\mathcal{E}_D} p(\mathcal{E}|\neg H)\right] U(\neg H, D)+ \\ &\quad \left[\textstyle\sum_{\mathcal{E}\in\mathcal{E}_{\neg D}} p(\mathcal{E}|\neg H)\right] U(\neg H, \neg D) \end{aligned} \tag{22}$$

To obtain $VI(E)$, we combine Equations 15, 16, and 20.

When m is small, we can compute directly the sums in Equations 21 and 22. When m is large, we can compute these sums using an approximation that involves the central limit theorem as follows. First we express the sums in terms of weights of evidence. We have

$$\sum_{\mathcal{E}\in\mathcal{E}_D} p(\mathcal{E}|H) = p(W > W^*|H) \tag{23}$$

$$\sum_{\mathcal{E}\in\mathcal{E}_D} p(\mathcal{E}|\neg H) = p(W > W^*|\neg H) \tag{24}$$

$$\sum_{\mathcal{E}\in\mathcal{E}_{\neg D}} p(\mathcal{E}|H)) = 1 - p(W > W^*|H) \tag{25}$$

$$\sum_{\mathcal{E}\in\mathcal{E}_{\neg D}} p(\mathcal{E}|\neg H)) = 1 - p(W > W^*|\neg H) \tag{26}$$

where W and W^* are defined in Equation 7. The term $p(W > W^*|H)$, for example, is the probability that the sum of the weight of evidence from the observation of $E_1, E_2, \ldots, E_m$ exceeds W^*. That is, $p(W > W^*|H)$ is the probability that the decision maker will take action D after observing the evidence, given that H is true.

Next, let us consider the weight of evidence for one piece of evidence. We have

w_i	$p(w_i\|H)$	$p(w_i\|\neg H)$
$\ln \frac{p(E_i\|H)}{p(E_i\|\neg H)}$	$p(E_i\|H)$	$p(E_i\|\neg H)$
$\ln \frac{p(\neg E_i\|H)}{p(\neg E_i\|\neg H)}$	$p(\neg E_i\|H)$	$p(\neg E_i\|\neg H)$

To simplify notation, we let $p(E_i|H) = \alpha$ and $p(E_i|\neg H) = \beta$. The expectation and variance of w, given H and $\neg H$, are then

$$EV(w|H) = \alpha \ln \frac{\alpha}{\beta} + (1-\alpha) \ln \frac{(1-\alpha)}{(1-\beta)} \tag{27}$$

$$Var(w|H) = \alpha(1-\alpha) \ln^2 \frac{\alpha(1-\beta)}{\beta(1-\alpha)} \tag{28}$$

$$EV(w|\neg H) = \beta \ln \frac{\alpha}{\beta} + (1-\beta) \ln \frac{(1-\alpha)}{(1-\beta)} \tag{29}$$

$$Var(w|\neg H) = \beta(1-\beta) \ln^2 \frac{\alpha(1-\beta)}{\beta(1-\alpha)} \tag{30}$$

Now, we take advantage of the additive property of weights of evidence. The central-limit theorem states that the sum of independent random variables approaches a normal distribution when the number of variables becomes large. Furthermore, the expectation and variance of the sum is just the sum of the expectations and variances of the individual random variables, respectively. Because we have assumed that evidence variables are independent, given H or $\neg H$, the expected value of the sum of the weights of evidence for $E_1, E_2, \ldots, E_m$ is

$$EV(W|H) = \sum_{i=1}^{m} EV(w_i|H) \tag{31}$$

The variance of the sum of the weights is

$$Var(W|H) = \sum_{i=1}^{m} Var(w_i|H) \tag{32}$$

Thus, $p(W|H)$, the probability distribution over W, is

$$p(W|H) \sim N(\sum_{i=1}^{m} EV(w_i|H), \sum_{i=1}^{m} Var(w_i|H)) \tag{33}$$

The expression for $\neg H$ is similar.

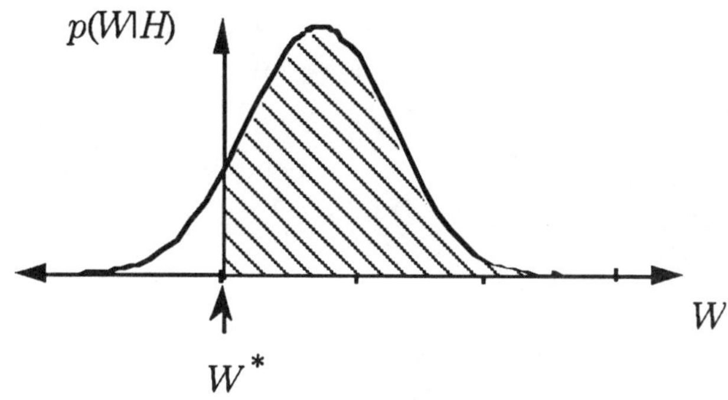

Figure 2: The probability that the total weight of evidence will exceed the threshold weight is the area under the normal curve above the threshold weight W^* (shaded region).

Finally, given the distributions for H and $\neg H$, we evaluate Equations 23 through 26 using an estimate or table of the cumulative normal distribution. We have

$$p(W > W^*|H) = \frac{1}{\sigma\sqrt{2\pi}} \int_{W^*}^{\infty} e^{\frac{-(t-\mu)^2}{2\sigma}} dt \tag{34}$$

where $\mu = EV(W|H)$ and $\sigma = Var(W|H)$. The probability that the weight will exceed W^* corresponds to the shaded area in Figure 2. Again, the expression for $\neg H$ is similar. In this analysis, we assume that no probability ($p(E_i|H)$ or $p(E_i|\neg H)$) is equal to 0 or 1. Thus, all expected values and variances are finite. We relax this assumption in the next section.

6 RELAXATION OF THE ASSUMPTIONS

We can relax the assumption that evidence is two-valued with little effort. In particular, we can extend easily the odds-likelihood inference rule, Equation 1, and its logarithmic transform, to include multiple-valued evidential variables. In addition, the computation of means and variances for multiple-valued evidential variables (see Equations 27 through 30) is straightforward.

In addition, we can relax the assumption that no probability is equal to 0 or 1. For example, let us suppose that

$$0 < p(E_j|H) = \alpha < 1$$
$$p(E_j|\neg H) = \beta = 1$$
$$0 < p(E_i|H) < 1, \qquad i = 1, 2, \ldots, n \ (i \neq j)$$
$$0 < p(E_i|\neg H) < 1, \qquad i = 1, 2, \ldots, n \ (i \neq j)$$

Using Equations 27 through 30, we obtain

$$EV(w_j|H) = +\infty$$

$$\begin{aligned} Var(w_j|H) &= +\infty \\ EV(w_j|\neg H) &< 0 \\ Var(w_j|\neg H) &= 0 \end{aligned}$$

Therefore, although the computation of $p(W > W^*|\neg H)$ is straightforward, we cannot compute $p(W > W^*|H)$ as described in the previous section. Instead, we compute $p(W > W^*|H)$, by considering separately the cases E_j and $\neg E_j$. We have

$$\begin{aligned} p(W > W^*|H) &= p(E_j|H)\, p(W > W^*|HE_j) + \\ &\quad p(\neg E_j|H)\, p(W > W^*|H\neg E_j) \end{aligned} \tag{35}$$

If $\neg E_j$ is observed, $W = +\infty$, and $p(W > W^*|H\neg E_j) = 1$. Consequently, Equation 35 becomes

$$\begin{aligned} p(W > W^*|H) &= p(E_j|H)\, p(W > W^*|HE_j) + \\ &\quad p(\neg E_j|H) \end{aligned}$$

We compute $p(W > W^*|HE_j)$ as described in Equations 31 through 34, replacing $EV(w_j|H)$ with w_j in the summation of Equation 31, and $Var(w_j|H)$ with 0 in the summation of Equation 32. The other terms in the summations remain the same, because we have assumed that evidence variables are independent, given H or $\neg H$. This approach generalizes easily to multiple-valued evidence variables and to cases where more than one probability is equal to 0 or 1.

We can extend our analysis to special cases of conditional dependence among evidence variables. For example, Figure 3 shows a schematic of the belief network for Pathfinder. In this model, there are groups of dependent evidence, where each group is conditionally independent of all other groups. We can apply our analysis to this model by using a clustering technique described by Pearl (Pearl, 1988) (pp. 197-204). As in the previous section, suppose we want to compute the value of information for the set of evidence $S = \{E_1, E_2, \ldots, E_m\}$. For each group of dependent features G^k, we cluster those variables in the intersection of S and G^k into a single variable. Then, we average out all variables in the belief network that are not in S. What remains is a set of clustered variables that are conditionally independent, given H and $\neg H$. We can now apply our analysis—generalized to multiple-valued variables—to this model.

There are special classes of dependent distributions for which the central-limit theorem is valid. We can use this fact to extend our analysis to other cases of dependent evidence. For example, the central-limit theorem applies to distributions that form a Markov chain, provided the transition probabilities in the chain are not correlated (Billingsley, 1968). Thus, we can extend our analysis to belief networks of the form shown in Figure 4. We can generalize the value-of-information analysis even further, if we use the Markov extension in combination with the clustering approach described in the previous paragraph.

(a)

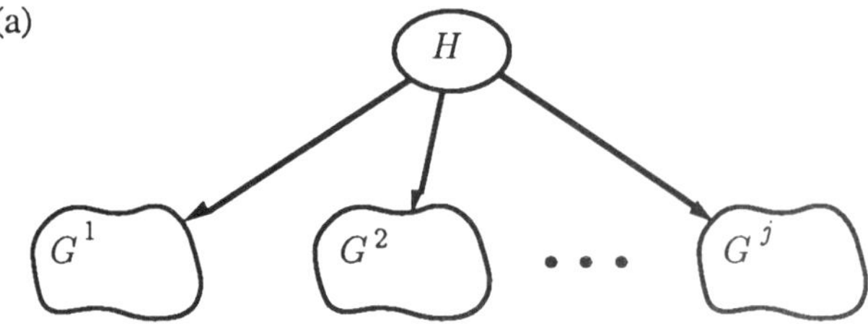

(b)

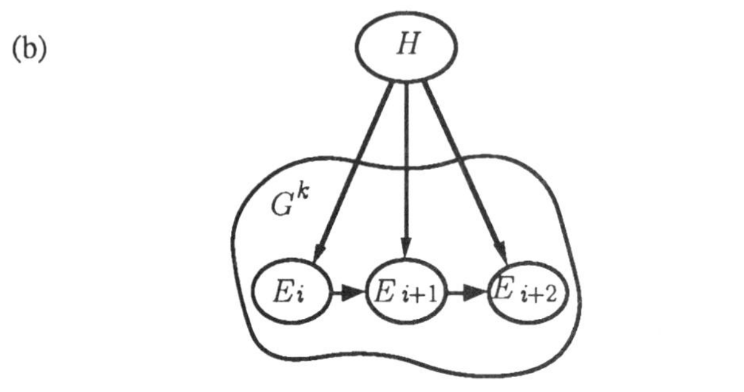

Figure 3: A schematic belief network for Pathfinder. (a) The features in Pathfinder can be arranged into groups of evidence variables $G^1, G^2, \ldots G^j$. The variables within each group are dependent, but the groups are conditionally independent, given the disease variable H. (b) A detailed view of the evidence variables E_i, E_{i+1}, and E_{i+2} within group G^k.

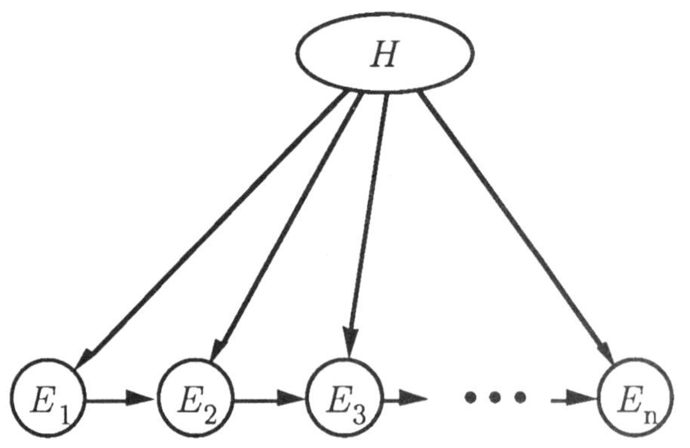

Figure 4: A conditional Markov chain. The evidence variables form a Markov chain conditioned on the variable H. We can extend our analysis involving the central-limit theorem to this case.

It is difficult for us to extend the analysis to include multiple-valued hypotheses and decisions. The algebra becomes more complex, because the simple p^* model for action no longer applies. There is, however, the opportunity for applying our technique to more complex problems. In particular, we can abstract a given decision problem into one involving a binary hypothesis and decision variable. For example, we can abstract the problem of determining which of n diseases is present in a patient into one of determining whether the disease is benign or malignant. In doing so, we ignore details of the decision maker's preferences, and we introduce dependencies among evidence variables. Nonetheless, the benefits of a nonmyopic analysis may outweigh these drawbacks in some domains.

7 SUMMARY AND CONCLUSIONS

We presented work on the use of the central-limit theorem to compute the value of information for sets of tests. Our technique provides a nonmyopic, yet tractable alternative to traditional myopic analyses for determining the next best piece of evidence to observe. Our approach is limited to information-acquisition decisions for problems involving (1) specific classes of dependencies among evidence variables, and (2) binary hypothesis and action variables. Additional research, however, may help to relax these restrictions. For now, we pose the nonmyopic methodology as a new special-case tool for identifying cost-effective observations. We hope to see empirical comparisons of the relative accuracy of the nonmyopic analysis with that of traditional myopic analyses. We expect that the results of such evaluations will be sensitive to the details of the application areas.

Acknowledgments

This work was supported by the National Cancer Institute under Grant RO1CA51729-01A1, and by the Agency for Health Care Policy and Research under Grant T2HS00028.

References

Billingsley, P. (1968). Dependent variables. In *Convergence of Probability Measures*, chapter 4. Wiley and Sons, New York.

Gorry, G. and Barnett, G. (1968). Experience with a model of sequential diagnosis. *Computers and Biomedical Research*, 1:490–507.

Gorry, G., Kassirer, J., Essig, A., and Schwartz, W. (1973). Decision analysis as the basis for computer-aided management of acute renal failure. *American Journal of Medicine*, 55:473–484.

Heckerman, D. (1990). *Probabilistic Similarity Networks*. PhD thesis, Program in Medical Information Sciences, Stanford University, Stanford, CA. Report STAN-CS-90-1316.

Heckerman, D., Horvitz, E., and Nathwani, B. (1989). Update on the Pathfinder project. In *Proceedings of the Thirteenth Symposium on Computer Applications in Medical Care,* Washington, DC, pages 203–207. IEEE Computer Society Press, Silver Spring, MD.

Heckerman, D., Horvitz, E., and Nathwani, B. (1990). Toward normative expert systems: The Pathfinder project. Technical Report KSL-90-08, Medical Computer Science Group, Section on Medical Informatics, Stanford University, Stanford, CA.

Howard, R. (1967). Value of information lotteries. *IEEE Transactions of Systems Science and Cybernetics*, SSC-3(1):54–60.

Kalagnanam, J. and Henrion, M. (1990). A comparison of decision analysis and expert rules for sequential diagnosis. In Shachter, R., Kanal, L., Levitt, T., and Lemmer, J., editors, *Uncertainty in Artificial Intelligence 4*, pages 271–281. North-Holland, New York.

Pearl, J. (1988). *Probabilistic Reasoning in Intelligent Systems: Networks of Plausible Inference.* Morgan Kaufmann, San Mateo, CA.

Search-based Methods to Bound Diagnostic Probabilities in Very Large Belief Nets

Max Henrion

Rockwell International Science Center
Palo Alto Laboratory
444 High Street, #400
Palo Alto, Ca 94301
Henrion@Sumex-AIM.Stanford.EDU

Abstract

Since exact probabilistic inference is intractable in general for large multiply connected belief nets, approximate methods are required. A promising approach is to use heuristic search among hypotheses (instantiations of the network) to find the most probable ones, as in the TopN algorithm. Search is based on the relative probabilities of hypotheses which are efficient to compute. Given upper and lower bounds on the relative probability of partial hypotheses, it is possible to obtain bounds on the absolute probabilities of hypotheses. Best-first search aimed at reducing the maximum error progressively narrows the bounds as more hypotheses are examined. Here, qualitative probabilistic analysis is employed to obtain bounds on the relative probability of partial hypotheses for the BN20 class of networks networks and a generalization replacing the noisy OR assumption by negative synergy. The approach is illustrated by application to a very large belief network, QMR-BN, which is a reformulation of the Internist-1 system for diagnosis in internal medicine.

1 INTRODUCTION

Bayesian belief networks provide a tractable basis for expressing uncertain knowledge at both qualitative and quantitative levels, in a way that is formally sound and intuitively appealing. They are already being used in a wide variety of applications, including knowledge bases of up to about one thousand nodes. A major obstacle to their application for still larger applications is the limitations of available algorithms for diagnostic inference. Exact diagnostic inference in general belief networks has been shown to be NP-hard (Cooper, 1991). Hence, there is considerable interest in the development of methods that provide greater efficiency at the cost of imprecision in the results (Henrion, 1990b).

There have been two main directions in which researchers have sought efficient approximate algorithms. One approach involves random sampling of network instantiations, also known as stochastic simulation (Henrion, 1988). The other involves search among the space of instantiations (hypotheses) to find those that are most probable. Cooper (1984) employed this approach in Nestor, to obtain the most probable hypotheses. Peng and Reggia (1987a, 1987b) and Henrion (1990a) developed more powerful admissability heuristics to prune the search tree, allowing more efficient search of BN2O networks, that is bipartite networks consisting of independent diseases, conditionally independent findings, and noisy ORs, as described in Section 3. These methods are guaranteed to find the most probable composite hypotheses, and their relative probabilities (ratio of posterior probabilities of hypotheses). Peng and Reggia (1989) and Henrion (1990a) also describe methods to bound the absolute probabilities of the composite hypotheses.

Peng and Reggia's approach to abductive reasoning is based on the notion of minimal covering sets of diseases which explain observed findings. They use logical techniques initially to identify covering sets for the given findings, and then use probabilistic methods to find the most probable hypotheses. This scheme assumes zero *leaks*, that is that no findings can occur "spontaneously" in the absence of any explicitly modelled cause. For the QMR-BN application to be described here, and indeed most medical problems, most findings have non-zero leak rates due to false positives, and so an adequate diagnosis does not necessarily all have to explain all observed findings. This makes the covering set approach inapplicable.

Shimony and Charniak (1990) describe a search-based method that finds the MAP (Maximum A-posteriori Probability) assignments to general belief networks. They show how any belief network can be converted to an equivalent weighted boolean function DAG, and that solving the best selection problem (minimum cost assignment) for this network is equivalent to finding the MAP assignment for the belief network. While the best selection problem is also NP-hard, standard best-first search can be relatively efficient in practice.

If the results of diagnostic inference or abductive reasoning are to be used as the basis for making decisions, for example how to treat a patient, or what additional tests to order, knowing the relative probabilities of the most likely complete hypothesis is not enough. We want to know the absolute probabilities, or at least have bounds on them, and we want often want to know the marginal posterior probabilities of individual diseases, or of one or two diseases, rather than of complete assignments which include instantiations of all the other nodes.

To obtain bounds on the absolute probabilities, we need bounds on the relative probabilities of all the hypothesis that we have not explicitly examined in the search. That is we want to find bounds on the sum of the relative probabilities of the possible extensions of a given hypothesis. Given bounds on the relative probabilities of all hypotheses, we can compute bounds on the absolute probabilities. However, to find such bounds requires additional knowledge of properties of the network. Qualitative knowledge about influences (Wellman, 1990; Wellman & Henrion, 1991) is a useful source of information to obtain bounds, as we shall see.

This paper presents improvements and generalizations to the TopN algorithm. First, I will describe the QMR-BN belief network which is the application providing a context and motivation for this work on algorithm design. I then describe a generalization of the noisy-OR assumption of the BN2O networks, to negative product synergy. This forms a basis for generalized bounding theorems, including a new lower bound, that provides a significant improvement on TopN as presented in Henrion (1990b). Qualitative probabilistic analysis, using signs of influence and synergies, provides a clearer and more general basis for obtaining these. I then describe a method to obtain bounds on the posterior probability of hypotheses and for individual diseases. Finally, I present results from application to the QMR-BN network, showing progressive improvement as search is extended.

2 QMR AND INTERNIST-1

QMR (Quick Medical Reference) is a knowledge-based system for supporting diagnosis by physicians in internal medicine (Miller *et al*, 1986). It is a successor to the Internist-1 system (Miller *et al*, 1982). The version of the knowledge-base used here contains information for 576 diseases (of the estimated 750 diseases comprising internal medicine) and over 4000 manifestations, such as patient characteristics, medical history, symptoms, signs, and laboratory results. In this paper, these are referred to generically as *findings*. QMR contains over 40,000 disease-finding associations. It represents about 25 person-years of effort in knowledge engineering and is one of the most comprehensive structured medical knowledge-bases currently existing.

The knowledge-base consists of a *profile* for each disease, that is, a list of the findings associated with it. Each such association between disease d and finding f is quantified by two numbers: The *evoking strength* is a number between 0 and 5 which answers the question "Given a patient with finding f, how strongly should I consider disease d to be its explanation?". The *frequency* is a number between 1 and 5 answering the question "How often does a patient with disease d have finding f?". Associated with each finding f is an *import*, being a number between 1 and 5 answering "To what degree is one compelled to explain the presence of finding f in any patient?".

3 QMR-BN: A PROBABILISTIC INTERPRETATION OF QMR

The aim of this project[1] is to develop a coherent probabilistic interpretation of QMR, which we call QMR-BN (for Belief Network), and eventually a version with treatment decisions and cost or value models, which we call QMR-DT (for Decision Theory). The first goal is to improve the consistency of the knowledge base and to explicate the independence assumptions it incorporates. A second goal is to provide a challenging example to develop and test new algorithms for probabilistic reasoning. The current version is a reformulation of the Internist-1 knowledge-base. See Henrion (1990a), Shwe *et al*, (1991) and Middleton *et al*, (1991) for more details.

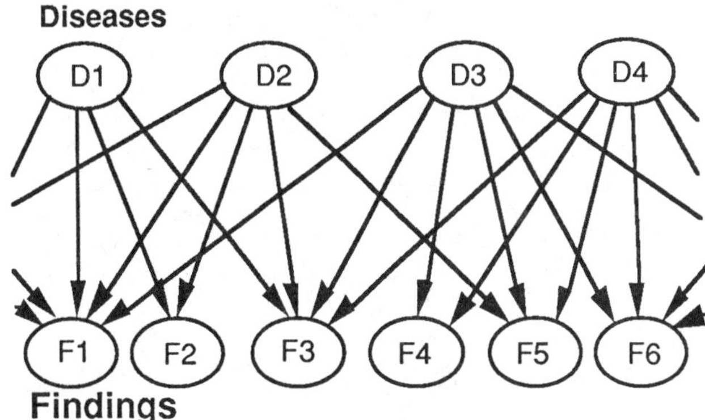

Figure 2: BN2O Belief net

A probabilistic representation can be divided into two aspects: The framework of qualitative assumptions about dependence and independences, and the quantification of the probabilities within that framework. QMR-BN currently follows INTERNIST-1 and QMR in assuming that all diseases and findings are binary variables, being either present or absent, without intermediate values. The initial qualitative formulation incorporates the following assumptions, expressed by the belief net in Figure 2:

Assumption 1 (MID): Diseases are marginally independent.

Assumption 2 (CIF): All findings are conditionally independent of each other given any hypothesis.

---

[1] This project is a collaboration with Gregory Cooper, David Heckerman, Eric Horvitz, Blackford Middleton, and Michael Shwe.

Assumption 3 (LNOG): The effects of multiple diseases on a common finding are combined as a *Leaky Noisy OR Gate*. Suppose S_{df} is the link event that disease d is sufficient to cause finding f.[2] The noisy OR assumption is that finding f will occur if any link event occurs linking a present disease to f, and that these link events are independent. (This is sometimes known as *causal independence*.) With a *leaky* noisy OR an additional leak event L_f is possible, which can cause f to occur even with no explicit disease present.

Definition 1 (BN2O): The class of bipartite belief nets conforming to Assumptions 1, 2 and 3, are termed BN20.

Some of the findings in INTERNIST-1, such as the demographics or family history of a patient, are not actually caused by diseases, but rather circumstances or risk factors that may affect disease probabilities. These variables should rearranged for ease of assessment so that they influence the diseases rather than *vice versa*. Currently, we have done this with age and sex as represented in figure 3.

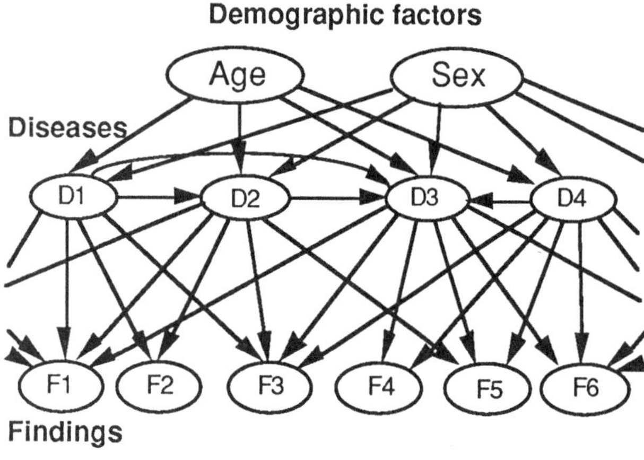

Figure 3: Belief net with causative factors and disease dependencies.

The second stage is to assign probabilities to this framework, either derived from the QMR numbers, or elsewhere. Heckerman & Miller (1986) have demonstrated a fairly reliable monotonic correspondence between the frequency numbers and $P(f/d)$, the link probabilities of a finding f given only disease d. Since there are over 40,000 frequencies in QMR, the ability to use a direct mapping does a great deal to ease the reformulation process by avoiding the need to reassess all the disease-finding relationships. We have also developed a mapping from imports to leak probabilities. Finally, our probabilistic representation requires prior probabilities or prevalence rates for each disease, a quantity with no correspondence in the INTERNIST-1/QMR knowledge base. These were estimated from data compiled by the National Center for Health Statistics on the basis of hospital discharges, conditional on the specified demographic (age and sex) categories. In summary, the qualitative independence assumptions of BN2O, together with the link probabilities, leak probabilities, and disease probabilities conditional on age and sex, specify a reformulation of QMR in coherent probabilistic form.

4 INFERENCE ALGORITHMS

Given this BN2O representation, is there a tractable method for diagnostic inference? To compute the exact posterior probability of any hypothesis, we need to compute the sum of relative probabilities of all hypotheses. Since the set of complete hypotheses (disease combinations) is the powerset of the set of diseases and has cardinality of 2^{576}, this may seem a rather daunting prospect. We have explored at least three different approaches for diagnostic inference for this class of networks. These include an exact method (Quickscore), and two approximate methods, one using a forward sampling or simulation scheme, (likelihood weighting), and one using search of the hypothesis tree with probability bounding (TopN).

The QuickScore algorithm (Heckerman, 1989) uses an ingenious rearrangement of the summation. Its complexity is polynomial in the number of diseases but is exponential in the number of findings observed. In practice it can score cases with 12 findings in about 10 minutes (Lightspeed Pascal on a Mac IIci), but it becomes too slow if there are many more findings. Since BN20 has large numbers of intersecting loops, exact methods seem unlikely to be tractable for larger problems.

Likelihood weighting (Shachter & Peot, 1989; Fung & Chang, 1989) is a development of logic sampling (Henrion, 1988) in which each randomly generated hypothesis is weighted by the likelihood of the observed findings conditional on the hypothesis. Further efficiency is achieved by using importance sampling, in which the sampling probabilities of diseases are iteratively adjusted to reflect the evolving estimate of their actual probabilities. The S algorithm (Shwe & Cooper, 1990) initializes the probabilities with a version of tabular Bayes (assuming mutual exclusivity of diseases) as a starting point for sampling. This version converges to reasonable estimates of the posterior probabilities in about 40,000 samples taking an average of 94 minutes for the SAM cases (on a Macintosh IIci).

The TopN algorithm takes a quite different approach, searching among hypotheses, that is complete instantiations of the diseases. It relies for its efficiency on the assumption that of the vast (2^{576} for QMR-BN) set of possible hypotheses, only a tiny fraction of them account for most of the probability mass. Hypotheses with more than a few diseases (five or six at most) have negligible probabilities, since the improbability of that many

---

[2] Reggia and Peng (1987a) term this the causation event and notate it as f:d.

diseases rapidly outweighs any possible improvement in explaining the observed findings. The second key idea is that, even though computing the *absolute* posterior probability of a hypothesis is intractable in general (requiring summing over all hypotheses), it is easy to compute the *relative* probabilities of two hypotheses (see also Cooper 1984; de Kleer & Williams, 1986; and Peng & Reggia 1987a). The third key element is an admissability heuristic to prune paths that cannot led to the most probable hypothesis (or most probable N hypotheses, hence the name TopN), so that only a small part of the space need be searched. A fourth element are some theorems that allow bounding of the sum of relative probabilities of all extensions of each hypothesis, and hence allow obtaining bounds on the absolute probabilities of hypotheses without examining them all. In the following I will give more detail on these, with some extensions and generalizations of previous results.

5 NOTATION:

I will use the common convention that lower case letters, such as *d*, refer to variables, with uppercase, D and $\overline{D}$, referring to the events *d*=true and *d*=false, respectively. Analogously, if *h* is a set of diseases, then H denotes the event that all diseases in *h* are true (present), and $\mathbb{H}$ denotes the event that all diseases in *h* are false (absent): [2]

$$H = \bigcup_{\forall d \in h} D, \quad \mathbb{G} = \bigcup_{\forall d \in g} \overline{D}$$

Given a set of diseases, $\Delta = \{d_1, d_2, \ldots d_n\}$, a *complete* hypothesis is an event that assigns a value, true or false, to every disease in Δ. A *partial* hypothesis assigns a value to a proper subset of the diseases in Δ, leaving the rest unspecified. If $h \subset \Delta$, then H is a partial hypothesis, since diseases not in *h* remain unspecified.

Adjacency of events denotes conjunction. So the event H$\mathbb{G}$ specifies that all diseases in *h* are present, all those in *g* are absent, and the rest unspecified. (We assume $h \cap g = \varnothing$.)

Underlining makes a complete hypothesis from a partial one, assigning absent to all diseases not specified. Thus $\underline{H}$ denotes the event that all diseases in *h* are present and all others in Δ absent:

$$\underline{H} = \bigcup_{\forall d \in h} D \cup \bigcup_{\forall d \notin h} \overline{D}.$$

[2]Note that $\mathbb{H}$ is not equivalent to $\overline{H}$, the event that at least one of the diseases in *h* is absent.

6 RELATIVE PROBABILITY AND MARGINAL EXPLANATORY POWER

We define $h_0 = \varnothing$ as the empty set of diseases, and $\underline{H}_0$ is the corresponding event that no disease from Δ is present. The *relative probability* of a hypothesis $\underline{H}$ is the ratio of the posterior probability of $\underline{H}$ given findings F to the posterior probability of hypothesis $\underline{H}_0$:

$$R(\underline{H}) = \frac{P(\underline{H} \mid F)}{P(\underline{H}_0 \mid F)} = \frac{P(\underline{H}\ F)}{P(\underline{H}_0\ F)} = \frac{R(\underline{H})}{R(\underline{H}_0)} \qquad [1]$$

TopN starts its search from h_0, extending it by adding one disease at a time. To generate the next candidate hypothesis, it adds to the current hypothesis the disease which leads to the largest relative probability. To identify the *n* most probable hypotheses (hence "TopN"), it applies an admissibility heuristic, which abandons a search path when it provably cannot lead to any hypothesis more probable than the *n*th best so far. TopN's admissibility criterion is based on the concept of Marginal Explanatory Power (MEP).

Definition (MEP): The *Marginal Explanatory Power* (MEP) of a disease *d* with respect to a hypothesis set of diseases, *h*, is the ratio of the posterior probability of the extended hypothesis $h \cup d$ to the posterior of *h* alone:

$$MEP(D, H) = \frac{P(\underline{HD} \mid F)}{P(\underline{H} \mid F)} = \frac{R(\underline{HD})}{R(\underline{H})} \qquad [2]$$

The MEP is a measure of the increase or decrease (according to whether it is greater or less than 1) in the degree to which the hypothesis explains the findings F due to the addition of *d*. The use of the MEP as the basis of an admissable search heuristic depends on the following result (Henrion 1990a):

Theorem 1a (declining MEP): Given a BN2O network, for any disease *d*, and disease sets *h* and *g*, the marginal explanatory power (MEP) of *d* with respect to *h* cannot be less than the MEP of *d* for any extension $h \cup g$, i.e.

$$MEP(D, H) \geq MEP(D, HG) \qquad [3]$$

When searching for the most probable hypothesis from current hypothesis *h*, if MEP(D, H) ≤ 1 then *d* can be eliminated as a path for exploring as an extension to H, since it cannot lead to a more probable hypothesis. It can also be eliminated as a candidate for extending other extensions of H. Thus the only diseases which need to be considered as extensions of H are those for which MEP(D, H) > 1.

7 NEGATIVE PRODUCT SYNERGY AND THE MEP THEOREM

It turns out that Theorem 1a does not require the leaky noisy OR assumption 3 of BN2O, assumed in Henrion

(1990a); a weaker assumption, negative product synergy will suffice. First, we define this property, and then show the more general version of the theorem.

Definition 2a (two cause NPS): Suppose there are two propositions, d and e, and other variable(s) x, that influence finding F according to the conditional probability distribution P(F| d e x), there is *negative product synergy* in the influence of d and e on f, iff

$$\frac{P(F|DE\,x)}{P(F|D\bar{E}\,x)} \leq \frac{P(F|\bar{D}E\,x)}{P(F|\bar{D}\bar{E}\,x)} \quad \forall x. \qquad [4]$$

This is the condition required for disease d to "explain away" the evidence F, that is, given F, there is a negative influence between d and e (Henrion & Druzdzel, 1990):

$$P(E|D\,F\,x) \leq P(E|\bar{D}\,F\,x) \quad \forall x. \qquad [5]$$

It is simple to show that the noisy OR (with or without leaks) exhibits negative product synergy, and so gives rise to this explaining away phenomenon.

Wellman and Henrion (1991) generalize the definition of product synergy for n-ary variables, and discuss its relation to additive synergy. Here we generalize the definition in a different way to apply where there are more than two variables which together influence another variable:

Definition 2b (n cause NPS): Consider a set Δ of propositions which influence finding F, as specified by conditional probability distribution P(F|Δ). The influence exhibits *negative product synergy*, iff for any sets of propositions $x,y,z \subseteq \Delta$, there is negative product synergy between x and y given z, i.e.

$$\frac{P(F|\underline{XYZ})}{P(F|\underline{YZ})} \leq \frac{P(F|\underline{XZ})}{P(F|\underline{Z})}\,. \qquad [6]$$

Assumption 4 (POS): The influence of every disease d on every finding f is positive, that is, for any set of diseases h not containing d,

$$P(F|DH) \geq P(F|\bar{D}H),\ \forall h \subset \Delta, \text{ where } d \notin h$$

Since the inequality is weak, this also allows diseases and findings to be unlinked (independent). Positive influence from disease to finding is an automatic consequence of Assumption 3, the leaky noisy ORs, but not of negative product synergy.

We can now define a class of bipartite belief nets that generalizes the leaky noisy OR of BN20 to positive links with negative product synergy:

Definition 3 (BN2NPS): A bipartite network is said to be BN2NPS if it satisfies Assumption 1 (marginally independent diseases), Assumption 2 (conditionally independent findings), Assumption 4 (positive links), and negative product synergy (NPS) in the influence of the diseases on each finding.

We can now obtain a generalization of Theorem 1a, which applies to BN2NPS:

Theorem 1b (declining MEP): Given a **BN2NPS** network, then, for any disease subsets x, y, z of Δ, the complete set of diseases, the marginal explanatory power (MEP) of x with respect to z cannot be less than the MEP of x for any extension $y \cup z$, i.e.

$$MEP(X, Z) \geq MEP(X, YZ) \qquad [7]$$

Proof: Taking the ratio of the two sides, and substituting the definition of MEP [2],

$$\frac{MEP(X, \underline{Z})}{MEP(X, \underline{YZ})} = \frac{P(F\,\underline{XZ})\,P(F\,\underline{YZ})}{P(F\,\underline{Z})\,P(F\,\underline{XYZ})}$$

$$= \frac{P(F|\underline{XZ})\,P(F|\underline{YZ})}{P(F|\underline{Z})\,P(F|\underline{XYZ})} \times \frac{P(\underline{XZ})\,P(\underline{YZ})}{P(\underline{Z})\,P(\underline{XYZ})} \qquad [8]$$

From the definition of n cause negative product synergy [6] above, we know the first term of the produce above is ≥ 1. From the marginal independence of diseases, we know that

$$P(\underline{XZ}) = P(\underline{Z}) \prod_{d \in z} O(D), \text{ where } O(D) = \frac{P(D)}{1-P(D)}$$

Expanding P($\underline{YZ}$) and P($\underline{XYZ}$) similarly in the second term, the top and bottom cancel out. Hence we are left with the entire ratio as ≥ 1. QED.

8 BOUNDS ON THE PROBABILITY OF EXTENSIONS

We want not just to identify the most probable hypotheses using their relative probabilities, but to obtain bounds on their absolute probabilities. To do this we need to obtain bounds on the relative probabilities of all the extensions of hypotheses in the search tree, so that we can put bound on the contributions of all the hypotheses we do not examine explicitly.

So far we have considered only complete hypotheses, such as $\underline{H}$. The relative probability of a partial hypothesis H is the sum of the relative probabilities of all complete extensions of H, that is all complete hypotheses in which all diseases in h are present, that is,

$$R(H) = \sum_{\forall s \supseteq h} R(\underline{S}) \qquad [9]$$

We also need the relative probabilities of partial hypotheses that contain excluded diseases, such as:

$$R(H\mathbb{G}) = \sum_{\forall s \text{ where } g^c \supseteq s \supseteq h} R(\underline{S}), \qquad [10]$$

where g^c is the complement of g, i.e. the set of diseases in Δ but not in g.

The following result gives an upper bound for the relative probability of a partial hypothesis *h* excluding diseases in *g*. It gives it in terms of the relative probability of the corresponding complete hypothesis and the MEP for candidate extension diseases *d* with respect to *h*, which are relatively easy to compute:

Theorem 2 (UB1):

$$R(H\mathbb{G}) \leq R(\underline{H}) \prod_{\forall d \notin h \cup g} [1+MEP(D, H)]. \quad [11]$$

This follows from the observation that that at most there is no overlap between the findings explained by each disease, and so the MEP(D, H) for each disease d is the same, no matter how many other diseases are in the hypothesis *h* it is extending. It is a generalization of Theorem 2 given in Henrion (1990c) for the BN2O assumptions. The complete proof relies on the Declining MEP Theorem 1b, and so it also follows from the more relaxed BN2NPS assumptions.

$R(\underline{H})$ provides a simple lower bound (LB1) for $R(H\mathbb{G})$. This bound would be attained if all proper extensions $s \supset h$ had probability $R(\underline{S})=0$ (Henrion, 1990c).

An higher lower bound is given by the following:

Theorem 3 (LB2):

$$R(H\mathbb{G}) \geq R(\underline{H}) \prod_{\forall d \notin h \cup g} \frac{1}{1-P(D)}. \quad [12]$$

This follows from Assumption 4 of positive influences, that extending a hypothesis *h* by disease *d* cannot reduce the likelihood of evidence F, that is $P(F|\underline{HD}) \geq P(F|\underline{H})$.

There are often diseases *d* which explain nothing more than hypothesis *h*, that is for which $P(F|\underline{HD})=P(F|\underline{H})$. Since these diseases are independent of the rest conditional on H, it is possible to factor out their contributions to a partial hypothesis $H\mathbb{G}$ thus:

Theorem 4 (Factoring independents):

$$R(H\mathbb{G}) = R(H\mathbb{G}\mathbb{W}) \prod_{\forall d \in w} \frac{1}{1-P(D)},$$

where $w=\{d : P(F|\underline{HD})=P(F|\underline{H})\}$.

This allows us to remove all such independent (non-explanatory) diseases, *w*, from the candidate list as extensions of *h*, while accounting for their contribution. Note that some diseases have relatively high priors (e.g. peptic ulcer with prior 1.6%) and so are not infrequently among the top ten hypotheses even if there is no specific evidence for them. Application of this result prevents them from cluttering up the search process.

Unfortunately the upper bound UB1 is not always a good guide when there are many diseases each of which can explain a lot relative to H_0, i.e. $MEP(D, H_0)>>1$. In the beginning of the search in a case with twenty or more positive findings, UB1 can be very large, for example overflowing an 8 byte floating point number ($>10^{300}$), unless computed as logs. An upper bound avoids this tendency is given by:

Theorem 5 (UB2):

$$R(H\mathbb{G}) \leq R(\underline{H}) + \frac{P(H\mathbb{G}) - P(\underline{H})}{P(F|H_0)P(H_0)} \quad [13]$$

where $P(H\mathbb{G}) - P(\underline{H})$

$$= \prod_{d \in h} P(D) \prod_{d \in g} [1-P(D)] - \prod_{d \in h} P(D) \prod_{d \in h^c} [1-P(D)]$$

$$= \prod_{d \in h} P(D) \left[\prod_{d \in g} [1-P(D)] - \frac{P(H_0)}{\prod_{d \in h} [1-P(D)]} \right].$$

This is based on the observation that at most any extension D to H will completely explain all findings, that is $P(F|\underline{DH}) \leq 1$. This bound is complementary to UB1, with use early in the search in cases with many positive findings.

9 SEARCH METHOD

The search uses a best-first approach, where "best" means the candidate partial hypothesis with the greatest possible contribution to uncertainty about the relative posterior probability. This uncertainty is measured as the *maximum error*, the difference between the lower bound 2 and the least of the upper bounds:

$$MaxErr(h) = Min(UB1(h), UB2(h)) - LB2(h) \quad [14]$$

We order the candidate hypotheses by MaxErr and select the top one as the next one to expand. This is the one for which expansion has the largest scope for reducing its contribution to the overall uncertainty about the relative probability of all unsearched hypotheses. Each time a hypothesis is expanded, this reduces the bounds on its parents. Search terminates, either when the MaxErr is less than a criterion, **Pmin**, expressed as a fraction of the upper bound on the total relative probability, or when the search runs out of space for the hypothesis tree. As in most best-first or A* searches, the algorithm is liable to be memory bound, running out of space before running out of time.

10 OBTAINING ABSOLUTE PROBABILITIES

So far we have obtained bounds on the relative probability of a variety of partial hypotheses, including LBR(H), UBR(H) for each hypothesis H in the search tree, each disease D, LBR(D), UBR(D), and H_0. Note that the partial hypothesis H_0 is all extensions of the no disease hypothesis, i.e. all possible hypotheses, so $P(H_0) = 1$.

$$R(H_0) = \sum_{\forall s \supseteq h_0} R(\underline{S})$$

$$= \sum_{\forall s \supseteq h_0} \frac{P(\underline{S}\ F)}{P(\underline{H}_0\ F)} = \frac{P(F)}{P(\underline{H}_0\ F)} \quad [15]$$

Hence, $P(F) = R(H_0)\ P(\underline{H}_0\ F)$ [16]

The posterior probability of any partial hypothesis H is

$$P(H|F) = \frac{P(H\ F)}{P(F)}$$

Substituting in from the definition of relative probability $P(H\ F) = R(H)\ P(\underline{H}_0\ F)$ and [16] we get

$$P(H|F) = \frac{R(H)}{R(H_0)}. \quad [17]$$

The upper bound for this is when R(H) is at its upper bound UBR(H) and $R(H_0)$ is lower bound $LBR(H_0)$, but note that since the partial hypothesis H_0 includes H, we need replace LBR(H) as a component of $LBR(H_0)$ by the the upper bound of H in the denominator too. Thus, we get the upper bound on the posterior probability of H is:

$$UBP(H|F) = \frac{UBR(H)}{LBR(H_0) - LBR(H) + UBR(H)}, \quad [18]$$

and similarly the lower bound is

$$LBP(H|F) = \frac{LBR(H)}{UBR(H_0) - UBR(H) + LBR(H)}. \quad [19]$$

The maximum total error due to probability of hypotheses not examined in the search is given by

$$\frac{UBR(H_0) - LBR(H_0)}{UBR(H_0)}. \quad [20]$$

TopN also produces a "best" probability estimate for each hypothesis, *h*, defined as the ratio of the sum of the relative probabilities of all complete hypotheses actually examined that contain *h*, to the relative probability of all hypotheses examined, *e*:

$$Best(H) = \frac{\sum_{\forall g \in e \text{ where } g \supseteq h} R(\underline{G})}{\sum_{\forall g \in e} R(\underline{G})} \quad [21]$$

This probability estimate is guaranteed to be between the lower and upper bounds on the absolute probability.

11 PERFORMANCE OF TOPN:

The QMR-BN research team has assembled cases for testing the performance of alternative inference algorithms. These include 16 cases abstracted from the Scientific American Medicine (SAM) Continuing Medical Education Service. More details of the coding process are given in Shwe *et al* (1991).

For analysis of timing and accuracy we examined 12 of the 16 SAM cases in which Quickscore can be run for comparison, that is cases with less than 14 positive findings. These cases have an average 9 positive and 11 negative findings. Table 4 gives results for on the performance of TopN for series of runs using a search precision (**Pmin**) of 10^{-5}. The number of hypotheses examined varies from 277 to 30000. (In two cases search was cut off after 30000 hypotheses due to exhausting memory space.) Since the distributions of hypotheses, time, and precision are highly skewed, Table 1 includes minimum, maximum and median, as well as mean values.

Table 1: Performance on 12 SAM cases using TopN algorithm with a search precision **Pmin** of 10^{-5}

	Min	Max	Mean	Median
Num of findings	9	28	20	22
positive	6	14	9	8
negative	0	20	11	11
Num of hyps	277	30000	11215	3794
Run time (secs)	1.2	65.3	17.8	7.7
Max prob bound	0.008	1.000	0.31	0.21
St. err. of "best"	<0.00001	0.064	0.009	0.005

TopN took an average of 18 seconds (maximum of just over a minute) for the 12 SAM cases. The S sampling algorithm was run for 40,000 samples to achieve adequate convergence for the SAM cases, taking an average of 94 minutes on a Macintosh IIci (about three times faster than the machine used for the Quickscore and TopN runs).

In some cases the maximum probability bound is at or near 1, and quite useless. But it turns out that the actual accuracy of the "best estimate" probabilities is very good when compared with the exact results from QuickScore, with a mean standard error between of 1.2%. Thus it appears that the bounds are highly conservative (much larger than necessary) in most cases. This finding suggests the sampled hypotheses are quite representative in terms of disease probabilities of the unsampled ones. Of course this may not always be true, but it suggests some interesting conjectures about properties of the hypothesis population.

To examine the effect of computational effort on the error, the precision for terminating search **Pmin** was varied by factors of 10 from 10^{-3} to 10^{-7}. Decreasing **Pmin** increases the number of hypotheses explored, and decreases the maximum bound on the probability error. The computation time is approximately linear in the number of hypotheses examined, with 30,000 hypotheses taking about 65 seconds on a plain Macintosh II. Figure 3 shows the effect of increasing the number of hypotheses searched on the error bound for the 16 SAM cases. Most converge satisfactorily according to the error bound by 30,000 hypotheses, but four do not.

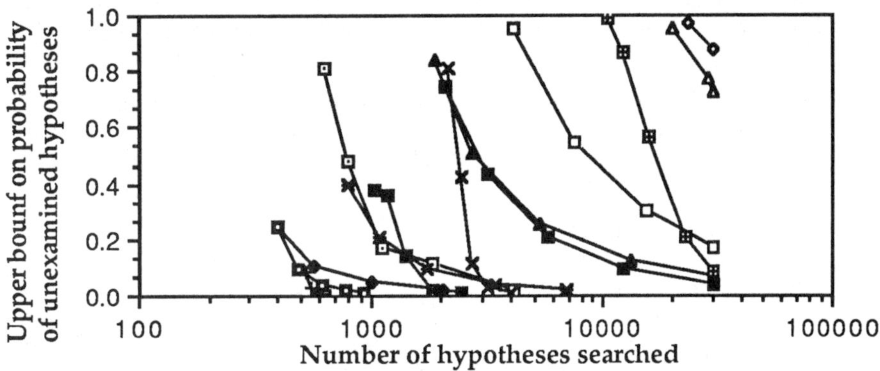

Figure 3: Error bound as maximum probability unaccounted for as a function of the extent of the search for 16 SAM cases.

Figure 3 illustrates how the uncertainty about the computed probabilities decreases as the search of the hypothesis tree is extended, that is as the cumulative probability of all the hypotheses examined approaches one. Thus TopN is an "any time" algorithm: If it is stopped at any point after initialization, it will give bounds on the posterior probabilities; and the longer it runs, the narrower these bounds will be. Given an estimate of the convergence rate, a meta-reasoner could select the run-time to be allocated according to the urgency of the diagnosis, the importance of precision, and the cost of computing.

CONCLUSIONS

The QMR-BN belief network confronts us with the general intractability of exact algorithms for diagnostic inference. Search-based algorithms such as TopN appear a promising approximate approach for such networks. They may be seen as smarter than forward sampling techniques in that they search specifically to find the most probable instantiations. They rely on exact methods for bounding the error in the resulting probabilities instead of the statistical error estimation methods available for some sampling techniques.

We have presented a variety of results that bound the relative probabilities of partial hypotheses in BN2O and BN2NPS networks. These results illustrate the value of applying methods of qualitative probabilistic analysis, based on knowledge of the signs of influences and synergies. For the QMR-BN project, and no doubt others, there remains a need to develop more general results, for example for networks with prior dependences among diseases. The generality of search-based methods for bounding probabilities remains an open question. It seems unlikely that the kind of bounding results used here will be obtainable for completely general networks, but some further generality may be obtainable from knowledge of qualitative probabilistic properties of other classes of network.

Acknowledgements

This work was supported in part by the National Science Foundation under grant IRI-8807061 to Carnegie Mellon, and in part by the Rockwell International Science Center.

References

Cooper, G.F. (1984) "NESTOR: A computer-based medical diagnostic aid that integrates causal and probabilistic knowledge", STAN-CS-84-1031 (PhD Dissertation), Dept of Computer Science, Stanford University.

Cooper, G. F. (1990). “The computational complexity of probabilistic inference using Bayesian belief networks.” *Artificial Intelligence*. **42**(2–3): 393–405.

de Kleer, J & WIlliams, B (1986) Reasoning about multiple faults, *Proc 5th National Conference on AI*, AAAI, Philadelphia, pp132-139.

Fung, R, & Chang, K.-C (1989) "Weighting and integrating evidence for stochastic simulation in Bayesian networks", in M. Henrion (ed.), *Proc of Fifth Workshop on Uncertainty in AI*, Windsor, Ontario, 112-117.

Heckerman, D. & Miller, R.A. (1976) "Towards a better understanding of Internist-1 knowledge bases", in MEDINFO 86, R. Salamon, B. Blum, M. Jorgenson (eds.), IFIP-IMIA, Elsevier Science, North-Holland. pp22-26.

Heckerman, D.E. (1989) "A tractable inference algorithm for diagnosing multiple diseases", in M. Henrion (ed.), *Proc of Fifth Workshop on Uncertainty in AI*, Windsor, Ontario, 174-181.

Henrion, M. (1987) "Uncertainty in Artificial Intelligence: Is probability epistemologically and heuristically adequate?", in *Expert Judgment and Expert Systems*, J.L. Mumpower (ed.) Springer-Verlag, Berlin, pp105-130.

Henrion, M. (1988) "Propagation of uncertainty by probabilistic logic sampling in Bayes' networks", in

Uncertainty in Artificial Intelligence, Vol 2, J. Lemmer & L.N. Kanal (Eds.), North-Holland, Amsterdam. pp149-164.

Henrion, M. (1990a) "Towards efficient probabilistic diagnosis in multiply connected belief networks", in *Influence Diagrams, Belief Nets, and Decision Analysis*, R.M. Oliver & J.Q. Smith (eds.), Wiley, London.

Henrion, M. (1990b). An introduction to algorithms for inference in belief nets. In M.H.&.R. Shachter (Eds.), *Uncertainty in Artificial Intelligence 5* (pp. 129-138). Amsterdam: Elsevier, North Holland.

Henrion, M. (1990c) Towards efficient probabilistic diagnosis with a very large knowledge base. In *Proceedings of International Workshop on Principles of Diagnosis*, Menlo Park, Ca.

Horvitz, E.J., Breese, J.S., & Henrion, M. (1988), "Decision theory in expert systems and artificial intelligence", *Int. J. of Approximate Reasoning*. 2, pp247-302.

Middleton, B.F., M. Shwe, D.E. Heckerman, M. Henrion, E.J. Horvitz, H. Lehmann & G.F. Cooper (1991). "Probabilistic diagnosis using a reformulation of the Internist-1/QMR Knowledge Base: II. Evaluation of Diagnostic Performance." Tech Report. Knowledge Systems Laboratory, Stanford University, Ca.

Miller, R.A., Pople, E.P., & Myers, J.D. (1982) "Internist-1, an experimental computer-based diagnostic consultant for general internal medicine", *New England J. of Medicine*, No 307, Aug 19, pp486-476.

Miller, R.A., McNeil, M.A., Challinor, S.M., Masarie, F.E., & Myers, J.D. (1986) "The Internist1/Quick Medical Reference Project -- Status Report", *The Western J. of Medicine*, No 145, 6, December, pp816-822.

Pearl, J. (1986) "Fusion, propagation, and structuring in belief networks", *Artificial Intelligence*, 29, pp241-88.

Peng, Y. & Reggia, J.A. (1987a) "A probabilistic Causal Model for diagnostic problem solving - Part I: Integrating symbolic causal inference with numeric probabilistic inference", *IEEE Trans. on Systems, Man, and Cybernetics*, Vol SMC-17, No 2, Mar/Apr, pp146-62.

Peng, Y. & Reggia, J.A. (1987b) "A probabilistic Causal Model for diagnostic problem solving - Part 2: Diagnostic strategy", *IEEE Trans. on Systems, Man, and Cybernetics: Special issue for diagnosis*, Vol SMC-17, No 3, May, pp395-406.

Peng, Y. & Reggia, J.A. (1989) "A comfort measure for diagnostic problem-solving", *Information Sciences*, V 47, pp149-184.

Shimony, S.E. and Charniak, E. (1990) "A new algorithm for finding MAP assignments to belief networks", in *Proc of Sixth Conference on Uncertainty in AI*, Cambridge, Ma., p98-103.

Shwe, M. & G. Cooper (1990). An empirical analysis of likelihood weighting simulation on a large, multiply-connected belief network. In *Proceedings of Sixth Conference on Uncertainty in AI*, (pp. 498–508). Cambridge MA: Association for Uncertainty in AI.

Shwe, M., B.F. Middleton, D.E. Heckerman, M. Henrion, E.J. Horvitz, H. Lehmann & G.F. Cooper (1990). "Probabilistic diagnosis using a reformulation of the Internist-1/QMR Knowledge Base: I. The probabilistic model and inference algorithms" Tech Report. Knowledge Systems Laboratory, Stanford University, Ca.

Wellman, M.P. and M. Henrion (1991) "Qualitative Intercausal relations, or Explaining 'Explaining Away'", *KR-91: Principles of Knowledge Representation and Reasoning: Proceedings of the Second International Conference*, Morgan Kaufman, Menlo Park, Calif.

Time-Dependent Utility and Action Under Uncertainty

Eric Horvitz
Palo Alto Laboratory
Rockwell International Science Center
444 High Street
Palo Alto, California 94301

Geoffrey Rutledge
Medical Computer Science Group
Knowledge Systems Laboratory
Stanford University
Stanford, California 94305

Abstract

We discuss representing and reasoning with knowledge about the time-dependent utility of an agent's actions. Time-dependent utility plays a crucial role in the interaction between computation and action under bounded resources. We present a semantics for time-dependent utility and describe the use of time-dependent information in decision contexts. We illustrate our discussion with examples of time-pressured reasoning in Protos, a system constructed to explore the ideal control of inference by reasoners with limited abilities.

1 INTRODUCTION

Decision-theoretic methods have been considered inapplicable for general problem solving because they require agents to possess a utility function that provides a preference ordering over outcomes of action, and to have access to a probability distribution over outcomes associated with each decision (Simon et al., 1987). We have investigated methods for maximizing utility in reasoning systems, given limitations in computational abilities and information. In particular, we have explored the problem of computing probability distributions under resource constraints. To a lesser extent, we have studied the assessment and custom-tailoring of utility models for time-dependent action.

Performing inference to determine a probability distribution can delay an agent's action. Inference-related delays can lead to losses stemming from competition for limited resources, decay of physiological states, and problems with coordination among independent decision makers. Endowing an agent with the ability to trade off the accuracy or precision of an analysis for more timely responses can increase the expected value of that agent's behavior. Growing interest and recent work by several investigators have addressed such tradeoffs in reasoning systems (Doyle, 1988; Horvitz, 1988; Boddy and Dean, 1989; Russell and Wefald, 1989; Breese and Horvitz, 1990).

We constructed the Protos system to experiment with the use of metareasoning procedures to control inference approximation methods (Horvitz et al., 1989a). Protos determines the length of time it should dwell on an inference problem before taking action in the world. Protos iteratively computes a myopic estimate of the expected value of computation (EVC) by balancing the cost of delay with the benefits expected from additional refinement of the probabilities used in a decision problem. The system makes use of information about the convergence of approximate results to exact answers, and about the time-dependent change of the utility of outcomes.

We discuss several aspects of our work on the consideration of time-dependent utility of outcomes. We review background on the Protos system, describe the semantics and assessment procedures for time-dependent utility, and discuss the custom-tailoring of default time-dependent utility models given observations. Finally, we describe the operation of Protos by presenting examples of the system's behavior.

2 A LIMITED REASONER

Determining the expected value of alternate actions under uncertainty requires the assignment of belief, $p(H|E,\xi)$, to one or more relevant hypotheses, H, given observations, E, and background information, ξ. Inference approximation algorithms produce partial results in the form of bounds or second-order probability distributions on relevant probabilities. Let us refer to relevant probabilities as ϕ. If we are forced to act immediately, we should take an action D that maximizes our expected utility, given the mean of $p(\phi)$, $<p(\phi)>$ (Howard, 1970). The utility of this action is equal to the utility of the decision we would make had belief in ϕ been a point probability at the mean of $p(\phi)$. That is,

$$\arg\max_D u(D, p(\phi)) = \arg\max_D u(D, <p(\phi)>)$$

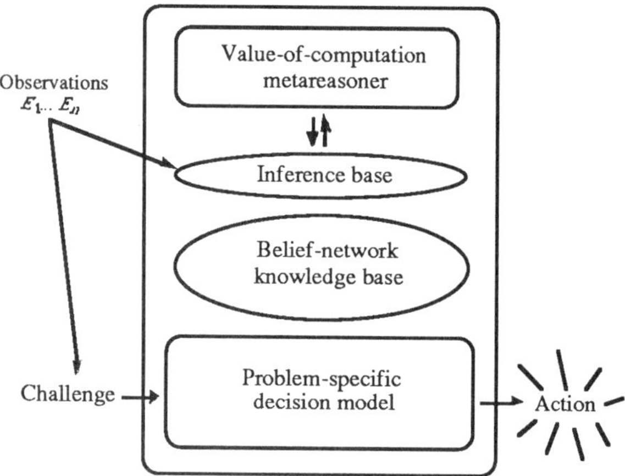

Figure 1: Protos' four components include (1) a metareasoner that considers the benefits of continuing to compute, (2) an inference base containing probabilistic inference procedures, (3) belief networks representing domain domain; and (4) a problem-specific decision model. Inference and time-dependent utility depend on observations.

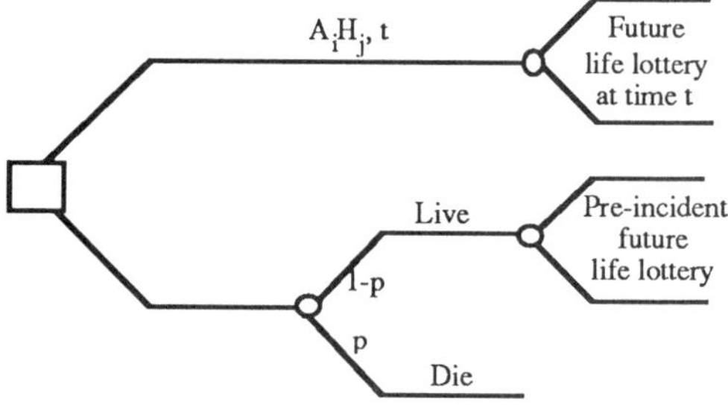

Figure 2: Lottery for assessing time-dependent utilities. We query a decision maker for the probability p of instant, painless death that would make him indifferent between his future life lottery when treated at time t, and having a $1-p$ chance at continuing his life as if the challenge facing him had not occurred.

Additional computation can tighten a second-order distribution. However, the utility of outcomes can diminish with time. Thus, there is a tradeoff between the benefits of making a decision based on a more precise result and the costs associated with delay. An EVC analysis compares the expected utility of instantaneous action with the expected utility of action that might be taken following future computation, including the costs of that computation.

An exact EVC analysis can consume a significant portion of the total computational cost of solving an inference problem. Our investigation on the control of belief-network inference has focused on the use of tractable EVC approximations. Approximate EVC analyses include single-step or *myopic* analyses. In myopic analyses, the EVC is computed under the assumption that an agent will take an action in the world after reasoning for a predetermined increment of time; we undertake a myopic analysis to determine if additional analysis is more valuable than immediate action. One approach to computing the expected utility delaying action is to consider the set of second-order distributions expected with additional computation. For each feasible future distribution, we consider the value of the best action, given that distribution, and weight that utility by the probability of the future distribution.

Protos makes use of myopic EVC analyses. Protos has four major components, pictured schematically in Figure 1: (1) a metareasoner; (2) an inference base containing inference procedures; (3) a domain-specific knowledge base in the form of belief networks; and (4) a problem-specific decision model. At run time, a decision problem containing alternate actions, outcomes, and utilities is passed to Protos. Given a decision problem, Protos initiates an iterative cycle of reasoning and metareasoning. Object-level inference is interleaved with metareasoning about the value of continuing to perform additional inference.

At the start of each cycle, Protos computes the EVC associated with continuing object-level computation for an additional increment of time. If the metareasoner indicates that the EVC associated with the next increment of reasoning is zero or negative computation ceases and the system takes an action indicated by the mean of the second-order probability distribution. Depending on the computational hardware, the structure of the time-dependent utility model, and the expected refinement of the second-order probability distribution by an inference algorithm, Protos may (1) take an immediate reflex action, (2) dictate a best action after some partial inference, or (3) take an action it proves to be dominant. Decision dominance can be proved before inference is completed with the use of a probability bounding algorithm. A decision dominates others when a single action is indicated for the range of probabilities in the interval bordered by an upper and lower bound on the probability.

We have experimented with a tractable myopic approximation named EVC/BC (for *EVC–bounds categorical*) to control probabilistic bounding. With this form of EVC, we compute the value of tightening categorical upper and lower bounds on a probability. EVC/BC hinges on interpreting upper and lower bounds as a second-order probability distribution. The measure is based on a least-commitment interpretation of bounds as a uniform distribution between the upper and lower bounds, with a mean at the midpoint of the bounds interval. The small amount of time required for the EVC/BC analysis is included in the EVC analysis itself. Details about the nature, limitations, and use of EVC/BC are described in (Horvitz, 1990).

3 TIME-DEPENDENT UTILITY

Let us consider the use of Protos to solve time-pressured medical problems. We have worked to represent in Protos the cost of delaying treatment as a function of the time a patient has remained in an untreated acute pathophysiological state. Physicians delivering emergency medical care often rely on knowledge about the cost of delay in treating a patient.

3.1 Semantics and Representation of Time-Dependency

In answer to a query for assistance Protos propagates observations about a patient's symptomatology through a belief network. The system deliberates about whether to make a treatment recommendation immediately, based on a partial analysis, or to defer its action and to continue inference, given its knowledge about the costs of delay.

We represent time-dependent action by considering a continuum of decisions, each defined by initiating an action at a progressively later time, and by assessing the change in utility of the outcome as a function of this time. We use A_iH_j, t to refer to an action, A_i, taken at time t when state H_j is true. We define t in terms of an initial time, t_o, the time a physiological challenge begins. We define the utility of $u(A_iH_j, t)$ at different times t, with an *acute-challenge lottery.* To assess the cost of delaying a treatment, we ask a decision maker to consider a time-pressured problem that he might face in a decision context. Next, we imagine that there is a treatment that can rid him instantly of the acute affliction with probability $1 - p$. Unfortunately, with probability p, the treatment will kill him, immediately and painlessly. We assume that, if a patient wins this lottery, he will continue his life as if the acute incident had not occurred; that is, he faces his preincident future life lottery. To assess the utility, $u(A_iH_j, t)$, at progressively later times t for action, we ask a decision maker for the probability p of instant, painless death that would make him *indifferent* to accepting the uncertain outcome of being treated for an acute illness at time t or having a $1-p$ chance of continuing his life as if the acute incident facing him had never occurred. We take the difference in the probabilities of death for action at time t and at a later time t' as the loss in utility. We can measure the cost of delay in terms of micromorts. A *micromort* is a 10^{-6} chance of immediate, painless death. Alternatively we can assign dollar values to the risks incurred with delay. We can use the *worth-numeraire model* introduced by Howard (Howard, 1980) to convert small probabilities of death to dollars in terms of dollars per micromort.

Beyond assessing utilities for each moment of action, we can model the utility of action at progressively later times with functions that encode a micromort flux for each outcome. The micromort flux is the number of micromorts we incur with each second of delay. We experimented with parametric utility equations and found several to be useful for summarizing the time dependency of alternate outcomes. Two functions we used to model losses with time, are the linear and exponential forms,

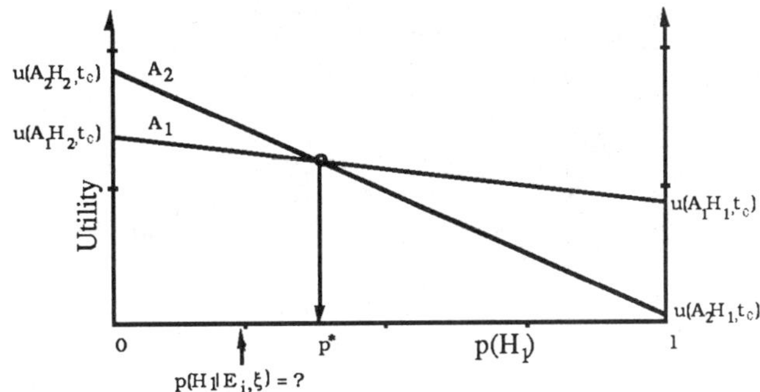

Figure 3: A graphical representation of the utility of two actions under uncertainty. The lines indicate the utilities of action A_1 and action A_2 as a function of the probability of hypothesis H_1. The lines cross at a threshold probability of hypothesis H_1 called p^*.

$$u(A_iH_j, t) = u(A_iH_j, t_o)e^{-k_a t}$$

$$u(A_iH_j, t) = u(A_iH_j, t_o) - c_b t \quad \text{where } u(A_iH_j, t) \geq 0$$

where k_a and c_b are parameter constants derived through fitting a series of micromort assessments to a functional form or are assessed directly. Our language for assessing and representing mathematical models of time-dependence allows decision makers to encode lower bounds on utility over time, and to make statements about the chaining of sequences of functional forms.

3.2 Utility of Action in Time-Pressured Contexts

Given time-dependent utilities, we can compute the expected value of different actions, A_i, in terms of the likelihood of alternative outcomes, H_j. The expected utility (eu) of taking action A_i at time t is

$$eu(A_i, t) = \sum_{j=1}^{n} p(H_j|E, \xi)u(A_iH_j, t)$$

Consider the simple case of a binary time-dependent decision problem. We have two states of the world (e.g., diseases) H_1 and H_2 and two best actions (treatments) A_1 and A_2 to address each state. As an example, the states can be the presence and absence of a disease, and the ideal actions can be treating and not treating for the disease. Under uncertainty, we must consider the utilities of four outcomes: $u(A_2H_2, t)$, $u(A_1H_2, t)$, $u(A_1H_1, t)$, and $u(A_2H_1, t)$. If H_1 and H_2

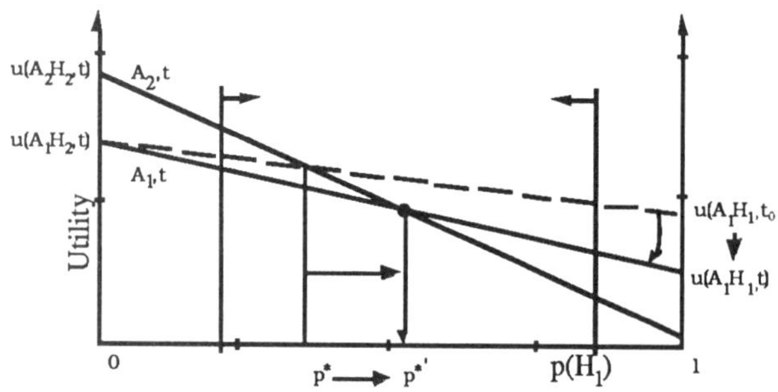

Figure 4: This graph displays how the utility of an outcome can decay as a function of time. In this case, the utility of taking action A_1, in the context of H_1, diminishes with delay. The utility associated with immediate action (broken line) and delaying action (adjacent solid line) is displayed. Note that the decision threshold, p^*, is also a function of time; in this case, p^* increases as the utility of A_1H_1, t decreases.

are mutually exclusive states, the expected utilities of the actions $eu(A_1, t)$ and $eu(A_2, t)$ are:

$$\begin{aligned} eu(A_1,t) &= p(H_1|E,\xi)\,(u(A_1H_1,t) - u(A_1H_2,t)) \\ &\quad +u(A_1H_2,t) \\ eu(A_2,t) &= p(H_1|E,\xi)\,((u(A_2H_1,t) - u(A_2H_2,t)) \\ &\quad +u(A_2H_2,t) \end{aligned}$$

The expected utilities of actions A_1 and A_2, as a function of the probability of H_1, are graphed in Figure 3. Note that the equations specify the expected utility of two action as lines intersecting at a threshold probability of H_1, denoted p^*. As we increase the probability of $p(H_1)$ from zero to 1, the decision with the greatest expected utility shifts, at p^*, from A_1 to A_2. If we must act immediately, we take an action dictated by the mean of the second-order distribution: We take action A_1 if the mean of the second-order distribution over $p(H_1|E,\xi)$ is greater than p^*. Otherwise it is best to take action A_2.

A computational agent rarely is forced to act immediately. An agent can pause to continue inference, or to reflect about the costs and benefits of delaying an action to compute a better decision. The dynamics of reasoning about belief and action under bounded resources is highlighted in Figure 4. The figure shows how the utility of outcome A_1H_1, t might diminish with delay. The dashed line shows the expected utility of taking A_1 in the context of H_1 at an initial time, t_o. The adjacent solid line indicates the diminished expected utility of taking the action at a later time t, given the truth of H_1. Note that, as the utility of taking action A_1 falls, the decision threshold, p^*, increases.

In a time-pressured computational setting the utility of one or more outcomes decay with delay. At the same time, inferential processes may be underway to refine bounds or a second-order distribution over probabilities of interest. Figure 4 shows the concurrent tightening of upper and lower bounds by a bounding algorithm. As the utility lines pivot or sweep down at rates dictated by the decay functions for each outcome approximate inference continues to tighten the bounds, yielding a time-dependent dynamics of belief and action.

3.3 Run-Time Modification of Criticality

Most of the work on Protos has relied on the use of files of utilities assessed for prototypical situations. The utility information is represented in tuples which contain the utility of immediate action, and time dependent decay, indexed by A_iH_J pairs. However, we also have explored the construction of *models* of time-dependent utility. With the modeling approach, we assess utilities that represent preferences for canonical situations and apply a mathematical model to customize "average case" utilities and time-dependencies to a specific decision maker and situation. To handle time-pressured medical decisions, we elicit from an expert decision maker—in our case, an emergency-room physician[1]—functions that modify the micromort flux of relevant outcomes, in response to arguments of discrete and real-valued patient vital signs. We experimented with functions that provide time-dependency parameters as a function of the patient's age, heart rate, blood pressure, and partial pressure of oxygen in the blood (PaO2). In practice, Protos makes use of default time-dependent utility models if no vital signs are observed. Given the observation of vital signs, and the availability of information about the specific class of decision problem, the initial utility and time-dependence are customized.

Our work on customizing time-dependent utility through constructing models of criticality parallels work in the medical decision analysis community on tools for assisting physicians to induce the utility functions of patients by identifying key features of their personalities (McNeil et al., 1982; Jimison, 1990). Our experimentation with deterministic functions for modifying utility models is a modest initial approach to customizing default time-dependent models. In the general case, modeling the utility of decision makers, such as patients receiving time-critical therapy, is a problem of diagnosis under uncertainty.

[1]One of the authors (G.R.) has served as the source of emergency-medicine expertise.

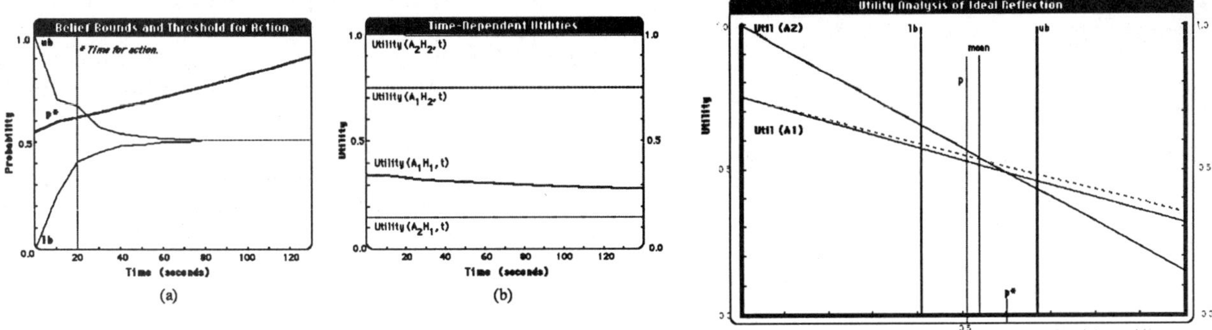

Figure 5: Time-dependent inference and ideal action. (a) Protos displays the convergence of the upper and lower bounds (ub, lb) on a probability of interest and the time-dependent decision threshold (p^*). The vertical line indicates the time for action. (b) The time-dependent utilities for four possible outcomes.

Figure 6: Graphical analysis of action. The utility (crossing solid lines) of treating for hypothesis H_1 (Util(A_1)) and for H_2 (Util(A_2)) as a function of the probability of H_1. Broken lines indicates the utilities of acting at t_o. The vertical line (p) displays the value of the exact probability, computed after the decision to take action A_2 was made.

4 PROTOS IN ACTION

We now examine the behavior of Protos in solving several simplified time-dependent decision problems in medicine. In the examples we determine the ideal time to perform inference with the bounded-conditioning approximation strategy (Horvitz et al., 1989b), given time-dependent changes in the utility of outcomes.

Bounded conditioning is based on the method of conditioning (Pearl, 1988). The method works by decomposing a belief-network inference problem into a set of simpler, singly connected belief-networks and solving these subproblems in order of their contribution to upper and lower bounds on a probability of interest. The more subproblems that are solved, the tighter the bounds. We shall examine decisions based on inference with *Dxnet* and *Alarm*, multiply connected belief networks that were assessed for reasoning about acute medical problems (Beinlich et al., 1989; Rutledge et al., 1989).[2] We note that several approximation algorithms and exact algorithms (such as the clique-tree method of Lauritzen and Spiegelhalter (Lauritzen and Spiegelhalter, 1988)) can solve inference problems with these networks faster than bounded conditioning can perform a complete analysis. However, the incremental and well-characterized convergence of bounds by bounded conditioning gives us the opportunity to explore fundamental interactions between time-dependent belief and utility, and more generally, to develop principles for optimizing the value of actions taken by an agent with limited inferential abilities. Principles of utility-directed control promise to be most valuable for controlling probabilistic inference in larger belief networks, such as the evolving QMR-DT network for internal medicine (Shwe et al., 1990).

[2]Alarm is a 37 node belief network; DxNet has 81 nodes.

4.1 Case Analyses

Figure 5(a) displays the time-dependent decision threshold, p^* and the convergence of the upper and lower bounds (ub,lb) on a probability computed by bounded-conditioning with the Alarm network. Assume we are employing inference to determine the probability of a life-threatening respiratory pathophysiology (H_1), requiring dangerous ventilation therapy, versus a minor acute respiratory reaction that resolves in most cases with minor treatment. We assume that we shall not gather additional information; we shall base our action only on information already collected. A vertical line through the bounds in Figure 5(a) indicates Protos' decision to halt inference after 20 seconds. At this time, the EVC becomes nonpositive. Figure 5(b) displays the time-dependent utilities of four outcomes, constructed as the product of actions and states of the world: We treat (A_1) or do not treat (A_2) the patient with an invasive treatment, and the patient either has (H_1) or does not have the severe respiratory problem (H_2). The time-dependent p^* is a function of the utilities, which were assessed from an expert. In this case, the utility of outcome A_1H_1,t—the utility of acting to treat the patient for the severe respiratory problem—decays significantly with delay.

Figure 6 displays a graph of the utility of actions A_1 and A_2 at the time action was recommended, as a function of the probability of H_1. The broken line, adjacent to the solid utility lines, indicates the utility of A_1 at t_o, allowing us to inspect the effect that delay has had on the value of the time-dependent outcome. The graph displays the upper and lower bounds (ub, lb) at halting time, the mean value between these bounds, and the decision threshold p^* at the time Protos recommended action A_2. The graph also displays the final point probability of H_1, computed after the

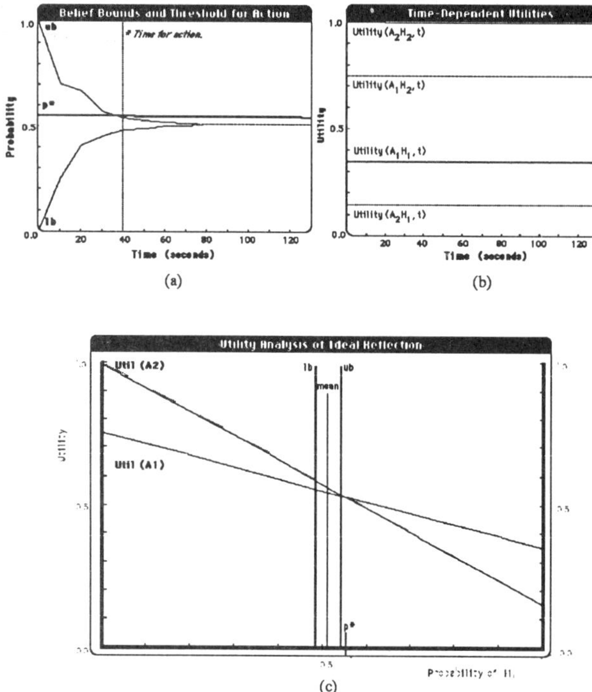

Figure 7: A less critical situation. (a) Here, decision dominance is proved as the upper bound moves below the decision threshold. (b) The time-dependent utilities for the four outcomes. (c) Graphical analysis of the bounds and utility at halting time.

the entire inference problem is solved. The value of the point probability indicates that an instantaneous complete analysis would have recommended the same action. This is not always the case.

To demonstrate the sensitivity of Protos' analysis to changes in time-dependent utilities, we consider the same decision problem with a smaller micromort flux for the utility of outcome, A_1H_1,t. Figure 7(a) displays the convergence of bounds on belief and the trajectory of the decision threshold for the revised problem. The reduced time-dependence of utilities of the outcome are displayed in Figure 7(b). With the revised utility model, which represents a less critical situation, Protos now reasons for 40 seconds before making a recommendation not to treat for H_1. The EVC/BC remains positive until the upper bound passes beneath p^*, proving the dominance of A_2. Figure 7(c) displays graphs of the utilities and bounds at the time action was taken.

Let us now examine Protos' performance on a cardiac decision problem with a focus on the use of default and customized utility models. Consider the case where Protos is challenged with recommending action for a patient who suddenly demonstrates extremely low blood pressure and tachycardia (an extremely fast heart rate). Assume the problem has been narrowed to two mutually exclusive syndromes: *congestive heart failure* (H_1) and *hypovolemia* (H_2). Hypovolemia is a dangerous state of decreased blood volume caused, for example, by dehydration or bleeding. Congestive heart failure (CHF) is a serious condition in which the pumping ability of the heart is weakened; like hypovolemia, it causes low blood pressure and poor oxygenation of tissues. Although hypovolemia and CHF share salient symptomatology, the treatments for these pathophysiological states conflict with each other. The treatment for hypovolemia (A_2) is to give the patient fluids to restore them to a normal level. In contrast, the primary treatment for CHF (A_1) is to reduce the quantity of liquids in the body with a diuretic. Erroneously treating a patient who has CHF with fluid-replacement therapy, or treating a patient who has hypovolemia with diuretic therapy, is life-threatening.

In Protos' default time-dependent utility model for the average case situation, the cost of delaying the treatment of CHF is described by an exponential decay constant that is ten times larger than the constant used to characterize the cost of delay in treating hypovolemia. Protos computes the probability of CHF by propagating observations in the Dxnet belief network. Figure 8(a) shows a trace of the update of the probability of CHF. Here, Protos is considering a new finding that a patient's pulmonary capillary wedge pressure is normal. (Protos was previously informed that the patient displayed low stroke volume and had low central venous pressure.) The vertical line indicates Protos' decision to halt in 115 seconds. At this point, the system recommends that the patient should be treated for CHF. The dominance of this decision is proved when the lower bound crosses the decision threshold p^*.

For this decision problem the micromort flux associated with delaying treatment for CHF is represented as a function of the patient's blood pressure. Let us lower the blood pressure and reevaluate the case. In response to a significant drop in blood pressure, Protos increases the exponential decay of the value for the outcome of treating for CHF, when CHF is indeed present. In this case, the decay of $u(A_1H_1,t)$ is increased from $e^{-.001t}$ to $e^{-.008t}$. Figure 8(b) shows the same probabilistic analysis with the use of the revised time-dependent utility model. Protos now recommends that the patient should be treated for CHF after only 30 seconds of computation. In the more critical case, action is indicated before a decision threshold is reached because the EVC becomes nonpositive before a probability bound crosses the decision threshold.

4.2 Discussion

We have made several observations about Protos' behavior. We have found that, in many cases, a utility-directed analysis of probabilistic inference dictates that actions should be taken after a small fraction of

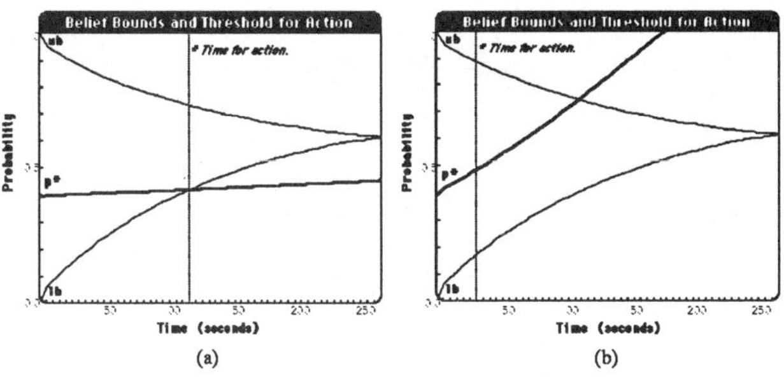

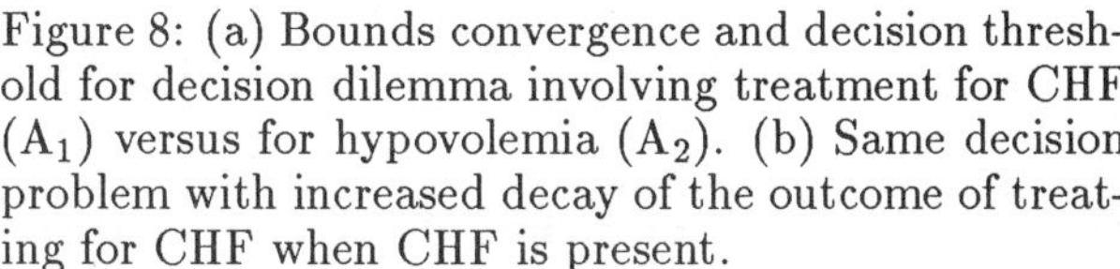
Figure 8: (a) Bounds convergence and decision threshold for decision dilemma involving treatment for CHF (A_1) versus for hypovolemia (A_2). (b) Same decision problem with increased decay of the outcome of treating for CHF when CHF is present.

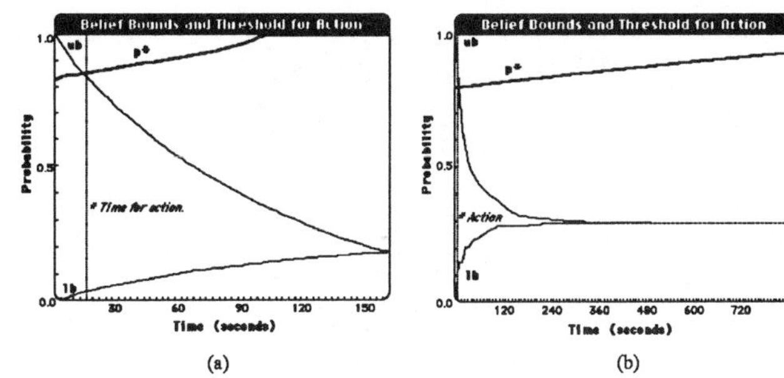

Figure 9: (a) Bounds convergence and decision threshold in the Alarm network for treating possible left-ventricular failure. (b) Bounds convergence and decision threshold in reasoning within the Dxnet belief network to support a decision about treating for a pulmonary embolism.

an analysis has been performed. Thus, even approximation methods with relatively slow convergence can be more valuable than faster exact algorithms. Two salient examples of this phenomena are displayed in Figure 9. In such cases the ideal decision is determined in the first few seconds of an analysis. More generally, we have found that decisions about the ideal length of time to deliberate and the ideal action to take are sensitive to the details of the time-dependent utilities of outcomes, the information about the convergence of an approximation strategy, and the trajectory of partial results generated by approximate inference.

We have observed behaviors that highlight the complexity of the interplay between time-dependent utility and time-consuming inferential processes. Some of the behaviors are explained by the limitations associated with the use of a myopic measure of EVC. We found that dependencies between time-dependent utility and inferential processes can make computation time and recommended actions sensitive to small changes in a time-dependent utility model. In some cases small changes in the time-dependencies in a utility model change the ideal recommended action.[3] We found that increasing the time-dependent decay of the utility of an outcome can *increase* the duration of reflection. In these cases the trajectory of converging bounds surrounds and "keeps step" with an increasing or decreasing p^*. We observed situations where an agent applying a myopic EVC estimate may be in the unlucky situation of continuing, for several steps, to observe a positive EVC, yet see its expected utility continue to diminish with delay. We identified cases where the EVC/BC returns to a positive value after it has been zero or negative. Such nonmonotonicity in the EVC motivated us to implement lookahead analyses that consider two or more future steps of computation. We are experimenting with more advanced lookahead techniques. More generally, we are pursuing the development of methods to monitor and modify behavioral patterns that have roots in the myopic EVC evaluation, and for identifying cases where the results of an analysis are sensitive to small fluctuations in the trajectory of time-dependent utilities or probabilities.

Before concluding, we stress that we have addressed the assignment of belief and utilities by limited agents; we have not discussed the automated construction of decision models. In the current version of Protos, preconstructed decision problems are passed to the system, in reaction to salient observations. We foresee that ongoing work on procedures for constructing decision models (Wellman, 1988; Breese, 1990; Heckerman and Horvitz, 1990) will foster the development of more comprehensive agents that can build as well as solve decision problems under bounded resources.

5 SUMMARY

We described the assessment and use of time-dependent utility in limited computational agents that are charged with taking ideal action in time-critical contexts. Analyses with Protos have demonstrated that the duration of computational analysis and the ideal decisions to make in the world can be sensitive to the time-dependent utilities of relevant outcomes. We discussed the generalization of lottery-based assessment techniques to mathematical models which represent the decay of utility of outcomes with delay. After describing the problem of customizing the time-dependency of default utility models in response to observations, we presented examples of Protos' behavior on time-pressured medical decision problems. Finally, we discussed some of Protos' behaviors and described

[3]Related problems with an optimal decision changing with delay for analysis have been identified previously in the context of decision analysis (McNutt and Pauker, 1987).

ongoing work on the development of nonmyopic inference monitoring and control procedures.

Acknowledgments

This work was supported by NASA under Grant NCC-220-51, by the NSF under Grant IRI-8703710, and by the Palo Alto Laboratory of the Rockwell International Science Center.

References

Beinlich, I., Suermondt, H., Chavez, R., and Cooper, G. (1989). The ALARM monitoring system: A case study with two probabilistic inference techniques for belief networks. In *Proceedings of the Second European Conference on Artificial Intelligence in Medicine, London.* Springer Verlag, Berlin.

Boddy, M. and Dean, T. (1989). Solving time-dependent planning problems. In *Proceedings of the Eleventh IJCAI.* AAAI/International Joint Conferences on Artificial Intelligence.

Breese, J. (1990). Construction of belief and decision networks. Technical Report Technical Memorandum 30, Rockwell International Science Center, Palo Alto, California.

Breese, J. and Horvitz, E. (1990). Ideal reformulation of belief networks. In *Proceedings of Sixth Conference on Uncertainty in Artificial Intelligence, Cambridge, MA*, pages 64–72.

Doyle, J. (1988). Artificial intelligence and rational self-government. Technical Report CS-88-124, Carnegie-Mellon University.

Heckerman, D. and Horvitz, E. (1990). Problem formulation as the reduction of a decision problem. In *Proceedings of Sixth Conference on Uncertainty in Artificial Intelligence, Cambridge, MA.*

Horvitz, E. (1988). Reasoning under varying and uncertain resource constraints. In *Proceedings AAAI-88 Seventh National Conference on Artificial Intelligence, Minneapolis, MN*, pages 111–116. Morgan Kaufmann, San Mateo, CA.

Horvitz, E. (1990). *Computation and Action Under Bounded Resources.* PhD thesis, Stanford University.

Horvitz, E., Cooper, G., and Heckerman, D. (1989a). Reflection and action under scarce resources: Theoretical principles and empirical study. In *Proceedings of the Eleventh IJCAI*, pages 1121–1127. International Joint Conference on Artificial Intelligence.

Horvitz, E., Suermondt, H., and Cooper, G. (1989b). Bounded conditioning: Flexible inference for decisions under scarce resources. In *Proceedings of Fifth Workshop on Uncertainty in Artificial Intelligence, Windsor, ON*, pages 182–193.

Howard, R. (1970). Decision analysis: Perspectives on inference, decision, and experimentation. *Proceedings of the IEEE*, 58:632–643.

Howard, R. (1980). On making life and death decisions. In Howard, R. and Matheson, J., editors, *Readings on the Principles and Applications of Decision Analysis*, volume II, pages 483–506. Strategic Decisions Group, Menlo Park, CA.

Jimison, H. (1990). *A Representation for Gaining Insight Into Clinical Decision Models.* PhD thesis, Stanford University.

Lauritzen, S. and Spiegelhalter, D. (1988). Local computations with probabilities on graphical structures and their application to expert systems. *J. Royal Statistical Society B*, 50:157–224.

McNeil, B. J., Pauker, S. G., Sox, H. C., and Tversky, A. (1982). On the elicitation of preferences for alternative therapies. *New England Journal of Medicine*, 306:1259–62.

McNutt, R. and Pauker, S. (1987). Competing rates of risk in a patient with subarachnoid hemorrhage and myocardial infarction: Its now or never. *Medical Decision Making*, 7(4):250–259.

Pearl, J. (1988). *Probabilistic Reasoning in Intelligent Systems: Networks of Plausible Inference.* Morgan Kaufmann, San Mateo, CA.

Russell, S. and Wefald, E. H. (1989). Principles of metareasoning. In Brachman, R. J., Levesque, H. J., and Reiter, R., editors, *Proceedings of the First International Conference on Principles of Knowledge Representation and Reasoning*, Toronto. Morgan Kaufman.

Rutledge, G., Thomsen, G., Beinlich, I., Farr, B., Kahn, M., Sheiner, L., and Fagan, L. (1989). Ventplan: An architecture for combining qualitative and quantitative computation. In *Proceedings of the Thirteenth SCAMC, Washington, DC.* IEEE Computer Society Press, Los Angeles, CA.

Shwe, M., Middleton, B., Heckerman, D., Henrion, M., Horvitz, E., Lehmann, H., and Cooper, G. (1990). A foundation for normative decision making in internal medicine: A probabilistic reformulation of QMR. Technical Report KSL-90-09, Knowledge Systems Laboratory, Stanford University.

Simon, H., Dantzig, G., Hogarth, R., Plott, C., Raiffa, H., Shelling, T., Shepsle, K., Thaler, R., Tversky, A., and Winter, S. (1987). Decision making and problem solving. *Interfaces*, 17:11–31.

Wellman, M. (1988). *Formulation of Tradeoffs in Planning Under Uncertainty.* PhD thesis, Massachusetts Institute of Technology, Cambridge, MA.

Non-monotonic Reasoning and the Reversibility of Belief Change

Daniel Hunter
3131 E. Highway 246
Santa Ynez, CA 93460

Abstract

Traditional approaches to non-monotonic reasoning fail to satisfy a number of plausible axioms for belief revision and suffer from conceptual difficulties as well. Recent work on *ranked preferential models* (RPMs) promises to overcome some of these difficulties. Here we show that RPMs are not adequate to handle *iterated* belief change. Specifically, we show that RPMs do not always allow for the reversibility of belief change. This result indicates the need for numerical strengths of belief.

1 INTRODUCTION

Makinson (1989) and Kraus, Lehmann, and Magidor (1990) give axioms for a relation of non-monotonic inference and show that most well-known systems for non-monotonic reasoning -- default logic, circumscription, McDermott and Doyle's modal systems -- fail to satisfy one or more of these axioms. Hanks and McDermott (1987) describe anomalies in the application of default rules and circumscription to an intuitive case of non-monotonic reasoning. In general, there is a growing awareness of the inadequacy of traditional approaches to non-monotonic reasoning.

Recent work on preferential and ranked preferential models (Kraus, Lehmann, and Magidor, 1990; Lehmann, 1989; Makinson, 1989) overcomes some of these difficulties. In a preferential model, the worlds or states are related by a binary preference relation $<$. An inference relation $\mid\!\sim$ is defined by saying that $A \mid\!\sim B$ iff B is true in all the most preferred worlds in which A is true. Depending on the properties of $<$, various non-monotonic logics result from this definition. In a ranked preferential model (RPM), the preference relation may be thought of as stemming from a well-ordering of some partition of the worlds (so that where w and v are worlds, $w < v$ iff w occurs in a partition element preceding the partition element to which v belongs). Thus the worlds are in essence *ranked*, with ties permitted.

The purpose of this paper is to show that despite their advantages over other approaches to non-monotonic reasoning, RPMs are still inadequate. In particular, they cannot adequately handle *iterated* belief change, a point already made by Spohn (1988). Here we give a formal proof of this claim. The proof shows that RPMs cannot handle *reversibility* of belief change: sometimes we learn that a piece of information we thought true is not true and we wish to revise our beliefs by going back to the state of belief we had before the information was given.

We first discuss the relation between non-monotonic reasoning and belief change. Next, we demonstrate the inadequacy of RPMs to handle the reversibility of belief change. Finally, we examine one possible way of remedying the deficiency and conclude that it fails.

2 BELIEF CHANGE AND INFERENCE

A *monotonic* inference relation $\vdash$ is one for which the following condition holds:

(M) If $A \vdash C$, then $A\&B \vdash C$.

A *non-monotonic* inference relation is one for which (M) sometimes fails. Common-sense reasoning is generally thought to be non-monotonic, as exemplified by the following ubiquitous example: on learning that Tweety is a bird, I leap to the conclusion that Tweety flies, but on next learning that Tweety is a penguin, I withdraw that conclusion. So in ordinary, or common-sense, reasoning, gaining additional information may cause previous inferences to be withdrawn.

A fruitful way of viewing common-sense reasoning of the non-monotonic variety is as a case of belief revision: one is willing to non-monotonically infer B

from *A* if adding *A* to one's stock of beliefs results in *B*'s being believed. This way of viewing non-monotonic inference suggests an investigation of the rules for rational belief revision, rather than seeking a weakening or modification of the classical relation of logical implication, which concerns static relations between propositions.

Gärdenfors (1988) presents a widely accepted set of axioms for belief revision. Let **B** stand for a person's set of beliefs at a particular time, which set is assumed to be deductively closed (we call such a deductively closed set a *belief set*). We let $\mathbf{B}^*_A$ stand for the belief set that results when a person with belief set **B** comes to believe proposition A -- i.e. it is the result of revising the beliefs in **B** to accommodate belief in A. $\mathbf{B}^*_A$ should be distinguished from what we shall denote as $\mathbf{B}^+_A$, the deductive closure of $\mathbf{B} \cup \{A\}$. The latter contains every proposition in **B**, the former need not if A contradicts the beliefs in **B**. In particular, if **B** contains $\neg A$, the negation of A, $\mathbf{B}^*_A$ will not contain $\neg A$ unless A is contradictory. Gärdenfors' axioms are the following:

(B1) $\mathbf{B}^*_A$ is a belief set.

(B2) $A \in \mathbf{B}^*_A$.

(B3) $\mathbf{B}^*_A \subseteq \mathbf{B}^+_A$.

(B4) If $\neg A \notin \mathbf{B}$, then $\mathbf{B}^+_A \subseteq \mathbf{B}^*_A$.

(B5) $\mathbf{B}^*_A$ is inconsistent iff $\vdash \neg A$.

(B6) If $\vdash A \leftrightarrow B$, then $\mathbf{B}^*_A = \mathbf{B}^*_B$.

(B7) $\mathbf{B}^*_{A\&B} \subseteq (\mathbf{B}^*_A)^+_B$.

(B8) If $\neg B \notin \mathbf{B}^*_A$, then $(\mathbf{B}^*_A)^+_B \subseteq \mathbf{B}^*_{A\&B}$.

(B1)-(B8) are equivalent to the finitary rules for what Lehmann (1989) calls *rational* inference.

Lehmann makes uses of a finitary inference relation $\vdash$, which is taken to be a relation of non-monotonic implication between formulas. Here we regard it as a relation between nonlinguistic propositions. The rules listed in (Lehmann 1989) for $\vdash$ translate into Gärdenfors' terminology of belief set revision by equating $A \vdash B$ with $B \in \mathbf{B}^*_A$. The next section discusses models of belief change satisfying the above axioms.

3 SEMANTICS FOR BELIEF CHANGE

Ranked preferential models provide a semantics for rational belief change. Here we apply RPMs within the general possible worlds framework, taking possible worlds as non-linguistic entities relative to which propositions are true or false. As usual, we identify a proposition with the set of worlds in which it is true and we assume that every set of worlds corresponds to a proposition.

Let W be the set of all possible worlds. Within this framework, an RPM may be considered a well-ordered partition of W, that is, a sequence $E_0, E_1, \ldots$ of disjoint subsets of W such that $\cup_{i=1}^{\infty} E_i = W$[1]. A well-ordered partition of worlds represents a state of belief in the following sense. Worlds within the same partition element are equally equally believable or disbelievable; Worlds in a given partition element are more believable than worlds occurring in succeeding partition elements. The members of the initial partition element E_0 are all the worlds that are not disbelieved -- i.e. no world in E_0 is believed not to hold. The worlds in the remaining partition elements are disbelieved.

A well-ordered partition yields a belief set in the following manner. Recall that a belief set is just a deductively closed set of propositions, representing the beliefs of some agent. The initial element of the well-ordered partition, E_0, is the *total content* of the agent's belief. It can be thought of as the (possibly infinite) conjunction of all the propositions believed by the agent. A proposition is in the belief set of an agent iff it is entailed by the total content of the agent's belief. Within the set-theoretic representation of propositions with which we are working, proposition A entails

[1] We do not distinguish, as does Lehmann (1989), between states and worlds. Given our assumption that the objects of belief and inference are propositions, not sentences, and that a proposition is any subset of worlds, the smoothness condition and the condition that the ranking of worlds be derived from a total order (Lehmann, 1989, p. 215) together imply that the ranking of worlds constitutes a well-ordered partition.

proposition B iff $A \subseteq B$. Thus the belief set of the agent can be defined to be $\{A \subseteq W : E_0 \subseteq A\}$.

An RPM determines how beliefs are to be revised when new information is received. Suppose proposition A comes to be believed. The task is to say what the new total content of belief is. The rule is this: Let E_i be the first partition element whose intersection with A is non-empty (i.e. the first partition element consistent with A). Then the new total content of belief is $E_i \cap A$. Hence proposition B will be believed in the result of revising the agent's beliefs to accommodate A iff $E_i \cap A \subseteq B$.

4 ITERATED BELIEF CHANGE AND REVERSIBILITY

Wolfgang Spohn (1988) criticized the theory of belief change just presented on the grounds that it cannot account for iterated belief change. To handle iterated belief change, argued Spohn, one must know what the new ranking of worlds is after a belief change. RPM semantics only tells us what is believed after a single belief change; it does not tell us how the ranking of worlds changes. The reason this is a problem is that in general the result of a belief change depends, not just upon what is believed, but also upon epistemic preferences among disbelieved propositions. If all we know after a belief change is what propositions are believed, but not what the new ranking of worlds is, there is no way in general to determine the result of future belief changes.

Spohn's solution was to assign numerical degrees of disbelief to worlds together with a rule for revising those degrees of disbelief when new information is obtained. (For details see Spohn, 1988). Given the strong motivation in the non-monotonic reasoning literature to avoid numerical approaches, this solution may appear unsatisfactory to many. Might it not be possible to supplement the theory of ranked preferential models with a rule for revising the ranking of worlds when a belief change occurs? Spohn considered two ways of doing so and showed that both fail. He concluded that accounting for iterated belief change in terms of well-ordered partitions "... looks hopeless" (1988, p. 114). But is it really hopeless? Perhaps there is an acceptable way of revising rankings that Spohn overlooked. The next task is to show that Spohn was correct in his pessimism.

A theorem proved by Lehmann and Magidor (Kraus, Lehmann, and Magidor, 1990, p. 216) appears at first glance to show Spohn wrong. Formulated in terms of belief sets, the theorem says that a belief revision function satisfies (B1)-(B8) if and only if it is defined by some RPM. This result seems to imply that RPMs capture exactly the logic of belief change.

The resolution of this difficulty is that while (B1)-(B8) may completely capture the logic of a single step of belief change, they do not completely capture the logic of *iterated* belief change. To distinguish between RPMs and Spohnian belief revision, additional axioms for iterated belief change are needed. Two axioms for iterated belief change are proposed below, but there is no claim that these axioms are complete.

The first axiom concerns what happens when more precise information is obtained. Suppose the agent comes to believe proposition A and revises her beliefs accordingly. Suppose next that the agent comes to believe B, where B entails A. That is, the agent gets more precise information. What should the agent's beliefs be after receiving the second piece of information? I want to say that her beliefs should be exactly the beliefs she would have had if only the second piece of information had been received. Formally, this amounts to the axiom:

(B9) If $B \vdash A$, then $(\mathbf{B}^*_A)^*_B = \mathbf{B}^*_B$.

Thus according to (B9), if the agent first comes to believe that some object is, say, a tree and then comes to believe that it is a pine tree, her beliefs should be the same as they would have been had she initially come to believe it was a pine tree.

The second axiom is analogous, this time dealing with conflicting pieces of information. If the agent first comes to believe A and next comes to believe B, where A and B are inconsistent, I want to say that the net effect of these two changes is just as if only the latter had occurred. That is, coming to accept a belief that conflicts with a previous piece of information "wipes out" the effect of the previous information. Thus the axiom:

(B10) If $B \vdash \neg A$, then $(\mathbf{B}^*_A)^*_B = \mathbf{B}^*_B$.

Spohn's system of belief revision satisfies both (B9) and (B10).

To show that RPMs are inadequate to handle iterated belief change, assume that some rule for revising rankings of worlds is given for RPMs. (B9) and (B10) imply the following regarding any such rule: that when a belief change involves just the proposition A, the *relative* rankings of worlds within the sets A, $\neg A$ remain the same. That is, if worlds w_1 and w_2 are both in A and w_1 precedes w_2, then after updating on A, w_1 still precedes w_2. Similarly for worlds within $\neg A$. To show this, let **B** be the current belief set, $<$ the precedence relation between worlds, and note that by the updating rule for RPMs the following conditions are equivalent for worlds w_1, w_2:

$w_1 < w_2$.

and

$\mathbf{B}^*_{\{w_1,w_2\}} = \{w_1\}$.

Let < be the old precedence relation and let <' be the new precedence relation determined by revising the old ranking to accommodate belief in proposition A.

Suppose $w_1, w_2 \in$ A and $w_1 < w_2$. By (B9), $(\mathbf{B}^*_A)^*_{\{w_1,w_2\}} = \mathbf{B}^*_{\{w_1,w_2\}}$ and since $w_1 < w_2$, $\mathbf{B}^*_{\{w_1,w_2\}} = \{w_1\}$. Hence $(\mathbf{B}^*_A)^*_{\{w_1,w_2\}} = \{w_1\}$, so $w_1 <' w_2$. A similar argument can be given for the case in which w_1, w_2 belong to ¬A, by appealing to (B10).

To show that RPMs do not allow for the reversibility of belief change in all cases, we must be more precise about what reversibility amounts to. In abstract form, a theory of belief revision is a function *f* from the cross-product space of belief states and epistemic inputs to the space of belief states. Reversibility means that for any belief state *S* and epistemic input *E*, there is an epistemic input *E'* such that *S = f(f(S,E),E')*. What we learn, we can unlearn.

Should any conditions be placed on the epistemic input that returns us to the previous state? It is reasonable, I think, to require that it only involve the proposition that caused the belief change in the first place. Otherwise, there is too much leeway: we could cheat and use information about the starting belief state to pick the right proposition or sequence of propositions to get back to where we started. More formally, let an epistemic input be an ordered pair $\langle A,\alpha\rangle$, where A is a proposition and α is an *epistemic attitude*. In the Spohn system, for example, an epistemic attitude is a strength of belief, so the epistemic input $\langle A,\alpha\rangle$ represents coming to believe coming to believe A with strength α. Then the reversibility condition says:

(R) If *S* is a belief state, *A* a proposition, and α an epistemic attitude, then there exists an epistemic attitude β such that $S = f(f(S,\langle A,\alpha\rangle),\langle A,\beta\rangle)$.

In the case of RPMs, an epistemic input is formally simply a proposition, but it is implicitly understood to be a proposition together with an attitude of belief towards that proposition. More generally, we will say that an epistemic input for an RPM is a proposition together with an attitude of belief, disbelief, or suspension of judgment (neither believing nor disbelieving). To allow numerical degrees of belief as inputs to RPMs would go against the spirit of much research in non-monotonic reasoning, but we will nonetheless later consider the possibility of deriving numerical degrees of belief from RPMs. For the time being, however, we assume that an epistemic input to a RPM is a non-numerical one of the sort just described.

Within the formalism of RPMs, an attitude of belief can be represented as the addition of a proposition (to the stock of beliefs) and the attitude of disbelief also by the addition of a proposition, namely the negation of the proposition disbelieved. A technical problem arises, though, for the attitude of suspension of belief. There seems to be no way to represent coming to suspend judgment in a proposition within the formalism of RPMs. This problem can be skirted if we define the belief set that results from suspending judgment in A as the intersection of the belief set resulting from belief in A with the belief set resulting from belief in ¬A. (That is, what you believe when you suspend judgment in a proposition is exactly what you would believe whether you believed or disbelieved the proposition in question.)

We are now in a position to argue that no belief revision rule for RPMs that satisfies (B9) and (B10) can also satisfy (R). First consider a simple model in which there are only four worlds, the four boolean atoms formed from the atomic propositions A and B. Thus the set of worlds W is {A&B, A&¬B, ¬A&B, ¬A&¬B}. Let RPM r_1 rank the worlds thus: {¬A&B}, {A&B, A&¬B, ¬A&¬B} (the most believable worlds listed first). Let RPM r_2 rank the worlds so: {¬A&B}, {A&B, A&¬B}, {¬A&¬B}. If the revision rule satisfies both (B9) and (B10), then coming to believe A will take both r_1 and r_2 to the RPM r_3 = {A&B, A&¬B}, {¬A&B}, {¬A&¬B}. Are there epistemic inputs involving only proposition A that take r_3 into r_1 and into r_2? Neither belief in A nor suspension of judgment regarding A will take r_3 into either r_1 or r_2. Only disbelief in A -- i.e. belief in ¬A -- will do so. But belief in ¬A cannot simultaneously take r_3 to both r_1 and r_2. Without loss of generality, suppose belief in ¬A takes r_3 into r_2. Then there is no way that r_1 can be recovered -- belief change is irreversible.

This argument can be generalized. Let W be any set of worlds, finite or infinite, with cardinality greater than three. Partition W into four non-empty subsets W_1, W_2, W_3, and W_4. Define A to be $W_1 \cup W_2$. Then coming to believe A will take both the rankings $\langle W_3$,

$\neg W_3$> and <W_3, A, W_4> into the ranking <A, W_3, W_4> and the argument goes through as before.

4.1 USING NUMERICAL STRENGTHS OF BELIEF

It might be suggested that the comparison between the Spohn system and RPMs is unfair because the former makes use of strengths of belief, but such epistemic resources are denied to the latter. Perhaps if the epistemic inputs to RPMs were expressed in terms of strengths of belief, reversibility of belief change could be achieved. This suggestion will not work, however, for the following reason. Consider the equivalent problem of defining degrees of *disbelief* in terms of RPMs. Let d() be a disbelief function over the set of propositions. To derive d() from a given RPM and to maintain consistency with the belief updating rule for RPMs, we must impose the following conditions on d():

(i) For $w \in W$, d(w) is a function of the rank of w.

(ii) For A, $B \subseteq W$, d(A) < d(B) iff where E_i is the first partition element consistent with $A \cup B$, $E_i \cap B = \emptyset$.

The first condition is imposed to capture the idea that knowing the rank of a world determines its degree of disbelief. The second condition is imposed to maintain consistency with the updating rule for RPMs: if the degree of disbelief in A is less than the degree of disbelief in B, then if $A \vee B$ becomes believed, A should be believed but B should still have some positive degree of disbelief; conversely, if coming to believe $A \vee B$ results in a belief state in which A is believed but B is disbelieved, then the initial degree of disbelief in A must have been less than the initial degree of disbelief in B.

These conditions imply that where A is a proposition, d(A) must equal the minimal rank of the worlds in A. (i) and (ii) imply that d()'s range is isomorphic with the set of possible ranks; hence we may as well identify degrees of disbelief with the natural numbers 0, 1, ..., and identify the degree of disbelief in a world with that world's rank. Let A be a proposition and E_A the first partition element consistent with A. Let $w^* \in E_A \cap A$. By the definition of E_A, w* is a world in A of minimal rank. Letting B be {w*} in condition (ii), we see that $d(A) \geq d(w^*)$. Again by (ii), d(w*) < d(A) iff $E_A \cap A$ is empty, which contradicts the definition of E_A. Hence d(A) = d(w*) and we conclude that d(A) = min{rank(w) : $w \in A$}.

Hence we are forced to define the degree of disbelief in a proposition as the minimal degree of disbelief of the worlds in the proposition. But so defined, degrees of disbelief will not help RPMs achieve reversibility of belief change. For in the example given above in which belief in A brought the two rankings r_1 and r_2 into the same ranking r_3, the two initial rankings determine the same degree of belief for A (namely, 1) and for $\neg A$ (namely, 0). But no specification of either of these degrees of disbelief can move r_3 back to both r_1 and r_2.

5 DISCUSSION

Researchers on Uncertainty should find the results presented in this paper of interest because they support the view that an adequate account of belief revision (and of reasoning in general) must involve the notion of degrees of belief, so that numerical uncertainty has a prominence in our reasoning that many have been unwilling to grant it. This should not come as a surprise, though, to those aware of the emphasis in recent years on qualitative aspects of probabilistic reasoning (e.g., see Pearl (1988), especially chapter 10).

A stronger result than that proved in this paper would be a *representation theorem* for the Spohn system: a theorem that says a belief revision function satisfies a certain set of axioms iff it coincides with some Spohnian belief revision function. Future research will look at the possibility of obtaining such a result.

Acknowledgements

I would like to thank Jeff Barnett and Dan Geiger for helpful comments on an earlier version of this paper.

References

Gärdenfors, P. *Knowledge in Flux: Modeling the Dynamics of Epistemic States*, MIT Press, Cambridge, Mass., 1988.

Hanks, S. and McDermott, D., Nonmonotonic logic and temporal projection, *Artificial Intelligence*, 33(3), 379-412, 1987.

Kraus, S., Lehmann, D., and Magidor, M., Nonmonotonic reasoning, preferential models and cumulative logics, *Artificial Intelligence*, 44(1-2), 167-207, 1990.

Lehmann, D., What does a conditional knowledge based entail? in *Proceedings of the Conference on Principles of Reasoning and Knowledge Representation* (R. Brachman and H. Levesque, Eds.), Morgan Kaufmann, 212-222, 1989.

Makinson, D., General theory of non-monotonic reasoning, in *Lecture Notes in Artificial Intelligence 346: Non-monotonic Reasoning*, (M. Reinfrank, J. de Kleer, M. L. Ginsberg, and E. Sandewall, Eds.), Springer Verlag, Berlin, 1-18, 1989.

Pearl, J., *Probabilistic Reasoning in Intelligent Systems*, Morgan Kaufmann, San Mateo, 1988.

Spohn, W., Ordinal conditional functions: a dynamic theory of epistemic states, in *Causation in Decision, Belief Change, and Statistics, II* (W. L. Harper and B. Skyrms, Eds.), Kluwer, Dordrecht, The Netherlands, 105-134, 1988.

Belief and Surprise - A Belief-Function Formulation

Yen-Teh Hsia
IRIDIA, Université Libre de Bruxelles
50 av. F. Roosevelt, CP 194/6
1050, Brussels, Belgium

Abstract

We motivate and describe a theory of belief in this paper. This theory is developed with the following view of human belief in mind. Consider the belief that an event E will occur (or has occurred or is occurring). An agent either entertains this belief or does not entertain this belief (i.e., there is no "grade" in entertaining the belief). If the agent chooses to exercise "the will to believe" and entertain this belief, he/she/it is entitled to a degree of confidence c ($1 \geq c > 0$) in doing so. Adopting this view of human belief, we conjecture that whenever an agent entertains the belief that E will occur with c degree of confidence, the agent will be surprised (to the extent c) upon realizing that E did not occur.

1 INTRODUCTION

Imagine yourself participating in the following "test". At the beginning of the test, your host announces that an internationally renowned company has built a perfect lottery machine with a very large number of black and white balls inside. This machine is capable of performing the following experiment: emit a ball, and then (perhaps upon user instructions) "retake" the emitted ball. However, the machine has been concealed from you so that you do not see how many balls, black or white, are inside the machine. Twenty one thousand experiments have been run on the machine, and you are given the result.

Output	Count
black:	10424
white:	10576

Given these statistics, you are asked to make a judgment about the ratio of black balls versus white balls. You are not allowed to use pen and pencil (or computers or calculators or ...) to make explicit calculations, and you must make up your mind within a very short time (say, in about thirty seconds). Thus, you are forced to use your own intuition to make the kind of judgment you are asked to make (i.e., just think in ways that you do in your everyday life). Before you know it, your host announces the answer: the actual ratio is 1 (black) versus 1 (white) - i.e., the lottery machine contains N black balls and N white balls, where N may be any natural number (and you will not be informed of its value). Now imagine the extent to which you are surprised by this answer, and let us refer to this "extent of surprise" as 0.

Let us start from scratch and redo the whole test (starting with: at the beginning of the test, your host announces that ...), only this time instead of announcing that the answer is "1 versus 1", your host announces that the actual ratio is "1,000,000,000 versus 1". Again, imagine the extent you are surprised by this answer, and let us refer to this extent of surprise as 10 (actually, 10 should correspond to "x, where x approaches infinity, versus 1"; however, we assume the difference is negligible).

Again, we redo the whole test. Again, the host announces a different answer "x versus y" (e.g., "45 versus 17"), where $x > y$, and x and y have no common divider. But this time, you are asked to record your degree of surprise *on a scale of 0 to 10* (with the intuitive meaning of 0 and 10 being what we have just noted above). In doing so, you are not required to use just non-negative integers. Any real number between 0 and 10 can be used.

This, theoretically speaking, allows us to "calibrate" anyone's intuitive degrees of surprise. Once we have made this calibration, we can then use it as a *canonical measurement device* to measure this very same person's degrees of surprise in *any* domain. For example, given the (only) information that the entity we are interested in is a bird, the extent to which we will be surprised by the new information that the entity does not fly may be (judged by us to be) the same as the extent to which we are surprised by the "canonical answer" that the actual ratio is "51 versus 43". If, on a scale of 0 to 10, we recorded the extent of our surprise associated with "51 versus 43" as 4, then the extent to which we will be surprised by the new information that the entity does not fly (given the only information that the entity is a bird) is *measured* 4 (or .4, if we map [0, 10] to [0, 1]). In terms of a notation that we describe in the appendix, we can denote this particular measurement of our intuitive degree of surprise as S([¬FLY] | [BIRD]) = .4. Similarly, if the extent to which we will be surprised by the new information that the entity flies (while previously we were only given the information that it is a bird) is the same as the extent to which we are surprised by the canonical answer that the actual ratio is "1 versus 1", then we can use S([FLY] | [BIRD]) = 0 to denote this measurement. The measurement scheme is clearly subjective, as the extent of surprise associated with "x versus y" (or "not-fly given is-bird") is, in general, different for different people.

Now the reader may be wondering. Why don't we just allow the subject to use pen and pencil (and perhaps even computers) to make whatever calculations he or she feels necessary? Because if the subject is allowed to use probability theory (for example) to make the computations, he or she could have used some probabilistic measure of surprise (e.g., $(\Sigma_j P_j^2)/P_i$, where P_i is the probability of the i-th outcome [Weaver, 1948]) to come up with his or her degree of surprise associated with, say, "51 versus 43". Our answer to this question is as follows. First of all, our purpose here is just to set up an (arguably) useable scheme for the measurement of some one's intuitive degrees of surprise. As far as this purpose is concerned, there is no need to "invoke" the machinery of probability theory here. But even more importantly, what we are trying to do here is to measure some one's intuitive degree of surprise (associated with the occurrence of some event) as what it *is* and not what it *ought to be* (according to some theory). In other words, we want this measurement to be descriptive in some way in characterizing human reasoning. After all, we are entitled to being surprised (according to how we reason and what we actually observe) *without* having to use some formal theory to calculate how surprise we "ought to be".

Why in the world would we want to be able to measure (in a descriptive way) some one's intuitive degrees of surprise? The answer is that we find the following conjecture acceptable.

> **The belief-surprise conjecture:** the *reason* that we are surprised (say, to the extent c > 0) by the occurrence of an event E is that (1) we previously *believed* that E would not occur, and that (2) c was (determined by us to be) the extent to which we were *confident* in entertaining that belief.

Accepting this conjecture, we are led to the following equation:

$$S(\text{"E occurs"}) = Bel(\text{"E does not occur"}) \qquad (1)$$

This means, for instance, our beliefs with respect to the above bird-fly example are Bel(([FLY] | [BIRD]) = .4 and Bel(([¬FLY] | [BIRD]) = 0. And here is our thesis: *As we may feel quite comfortable in assessing our intuitive degrees of surprise, we can, in effect, use these measured degrees of surprise to capture our intuitive notion of belief.*

Some philosophical discussions are now in order. Consider the belief that "FLY is true (in the usual propositional sense)." Here, we are adopting the following view of human belief: *An agent either entertains this belief or does not entertain this belief. And when the agent does entertain this belief, he/she/it is entitled to a degree of confidence (c) in doing so.* Thus, for example, by specifying Bel(([FLY] | [BIRD]) = .4, what we mean is that "*given (the truth of) BIRD, we entertain the belief that FLY is true, and .4 is how confident we are in entertaining this belief.*" In other words, we consider the *act* of believing something a categorical action in itself (either we do it, or we do not do it; there is nothing in between), and the uncertainty consists in how confident we are in exercising our "will to believe" and performing that act. This is, of course, only *one* way to think of human belief, as Bel(([FLY] | [BIRD]) = .4 can also be thought of as "given (the truth of) BIRD, .4 is *the extent to which we believe* that FLY is true." In effect, what this latter view of human belief amounts to is a *graded* concept of "entertaining a belief".

We really have no way of telling which of these two views of human belief is more "correct" (there may even be views of human belief that are not stated here). One can only adopt whichever view that looks more natural to him/her. Nevertheless, some may find Equation 1 above questionable, arguing that surprise is actually a *function* of belief. This really depends on which view of human belief one chooses to adopt. Because if the view we advocate here is adopted, then Equation 1 seems perfectly acceptable. But if some other view of human belief is adopted instead, then of course Equation 1 can easily be refuted. So the question is again: *Which view of belief do you find more natural to adopt?* And whichever view we choose to adopt, it may be important to bear in mind the following: *It may be a methodological error if we try to pass judgment on other views of belief from the perspectives of our own view of belief.*

This said, we now need to somehow defend our theory of belief (even before it is presented). As yet another example of our notion of belief, consider the event that "the restaurant run by the Chang family in Ottawa, Kansas, will hire a new waiter or waitress next month." As we know nothing about the recent situation of the restaurant run by the Chang family, we will not be surprised if this event occurs, nor will we be surprised if this event does not occur. In other words, we do not entertain the belief that this event occur (or does not occur), and we can denote it as Bel([HIRE]) = 0 and Bel([¬HIRE]) = 0. Now, this notion of belief is clearly in violation of the additivity axiom of Bayesian probability theory (i.e., Belp([HIRE]) + Belp([¬HIRE]) = 1, where Belp stands for "probabilistic belief"). As the Bayesian theory is well-known for its normative claim, one might quite legitimately wonder whether our yet-to-be-presented theory of belief should even be considered a theory of belief at all.

To address this issue, we need to somehow clarify what the word 'normative' means. According to [Collins, 1987] (a reasonable source of reference for the English language in our view), 'Normative' means *creating or stating norms or rules of behavior*. However, the normative claim of Bayesians may be more than just a claim of "creating or stating norms or rules of behavior." In the words of Ramsey [1931], "(anyone whose subjective belief violates the axioms of probability theory) could have a book (the so-called Dutch Book) made against him by a cunning bettor, and would then stand to lose in any event." In other words, if making an everyday or non-everyday decision is (setting utility considerations aside) like participating in a bet in which *we decide about* the odds for all possible outcomes and *someone else decides about* who bet on what, then the use of a non-probabilistic belief in the decision making process will have the potential of encountering some cunning opponent that make us lose, whatever the actual outcome may be (which, of course, is not what we want). However, the question here is: *Is making an everyday or non-everyday decision like betting in the above described sense (and if so, who may this cunning bettor be)?* This is actually a (very) philosophical question, and no one is obliged to say "yes" (and who this cunning bettor may be) or "no". If we decide to take the stance that decision making is indeed betting in the above described sense, then there is little doubt that our belief ought to be probabilistic (at least we would like it to be the case). But then, what is the reason or rational that we should take this stance? Apart from this philosophical consideration, Bayesian decision making also assumes that our estimation of belief and our estimation of utility can be made *independently*. This makes it even more difficult to accept the normative claim of Bayesians if we find it difficult to do so. It follows that if we do not take the stance that decision making is betting in the above described sense, then as far as Ramsey's argument is concerned, probability theory is no more normative than any other theory of belief, so long as this other theory of belief also serves to create or state norms or rules of behavior.[1]

Our theory of belief is developed with the specific intention of adopting the view of human belief we advocated above. It is a normative theory in the following sense. Given the various "fragments" of belief specified by the user (e.g., Bel([¬STRIKE]) = .3; Bel([RAIN] | [WET]) = .4; Bel([¬RAIN] | [WET]) = 0; Bel([PARTY]) = Bel([PARTY] | [RAIN]),[2] our system will try to infer what the user's belief *must be* under various circumstances.

Here is how the remainder of this paper is organized. In Section 2, we motivate and describe the use of belief functions [Hsia, 1991; Shafer, 1976; Smets, 1988] to characterize our intuitive notion of surprise. The result we get, then, is a theory of belief - a theory that embodies a completely different view of human belief as compared with the view that is embodied in the Bayesian theory of belief. Section 3 gives an illustration of how our theory of belief may be used in a very special context to help people make judgments. Section 4 contains some discussions. Finally, Section 5 concludes.

2 BELIEF FUNCTIONS AS A GENERAL FORMALIZATION MECHANISM

Given the canonical measurement device we introduced in the last section, we can now use it to measure our intuitive degrees of surprise associated with any domain (theoretically speaking). But what do we do with the measurements we have made? One answer is that we can "feed" these measurements into a system or a machine and ask it to answer queries like "given these measurements, what can we say (or rather, what can you tell us) about the value of Bel([RAIN] | [PARTY])?" To do that, we need a mathematical formalism that can be used to somehow characterize the measurements we have made - a formalism that serves as a postulate in describing the "inner working mechanism" of our intuitive notion of surprise.

For two reasons, we find the formalism of belief functions [Shafer, 1976; Smets, 1988] - in particular, belief functions in the sense of [Hsia, 1991a][3] - attractive. The first reason is that we think belief functions can be viewed as a very general mechanism that is capable of formalizing various different measurements of surprise. The second

[1]Cox [1946] offered another justification for the normative claim of Bayesians. However, Cox has one axiom (about human belief) that we object to - the axiom that our belief in the complement of a proposition is a function of (and thus determined by) our belief in the proposition itself. This axiom is clearly unacceptable, so long as we choose to adopt the view of entertaining beliefs with various degrees of confidence and we also use Equation 1 to measure our degrees of (confidence in entertaining) beliefs. It is easy to find situations in which we are surprised to a different extent by the occurrence of a different event, while being not surprised at all when neither event occurs.

[2]While we use our canonical measurement device to measure the user's degrees of belief, Bayesians may use exchangeable bets to do so.

[3]Hsia [1991a] advocates a "conditioning paradigm" for reasoning with belief functions. In this paradigm, only Dempster's rule of conditioning is used for reasoning, while Dempster's rule of combination is considered something that has to be explicitly justified.

reason is that we think the intuitions underlying the belief-function formalism are in line with our intuitive notion of surprise. Let us first talk about the problem of formalizing various measurements of surprise. Consider the following exemplary measurements.

1. Bel([HIRE $\vee$ ¬HIRE]) = 1

   /* meaning: I will be totally surprised if it turns out that the Changs do not hire any new one, and that they hire some new one. */

2. Bel([HIRE $\wedge$ ¬HIRE]) = 0

   /* meaning: I will not be surprised at all if it turns out that either the Changs do not hire any new one, or that they hire some new one. */

3. Bel([HIRE]) = 0 and Bel([¬HIRE]) = 0

   /* Either way, I will not be surprised. */

4. Bel([Pacifist]) > 0 and Bel([¬Pacifist]) > 0

   /* meaning: I will be surprised if Nixon is not a pacifist (as he is a quaker). I will also be surprised if Nixon is a pacifist (as he is a republican). */

5. Bel([Pacifist]) + Bel([¬Pacifist]) < 1;

   /* meaning: I will only be slightly surprised if Nixon is not a pacifist (as he is also a republican), and I will only be slightly surprised if Nixon is a pacifist (as he is also a quaker). */

6. Bel([TEMP = med $\vee$ TEMP = low]) > Bel([TEMP = med]) + Bel([TEMP = low]);

   /* meaning: I will not be surprised if the temperature is not medium in the spring (as it can be low), nor will I be surprised if the temperature is not low in the spring (as it can be medium). Nevertheless, I will be surprised if the temperature is high in the spring. */

Viewing these measurements as constraints that are to be satisfied, we can find one or more belief functions (defined below) that satisfy these constraints. However, we cannot use probabilities or even possibilities (in the sense of Zadeh [1978]) to characterize these measurements, as no probability satisfies the third, fifth and sixth constraints and no possibility satisfies the fourth constraint (if Bel is equated with the necessity measure of possibility theory).

One might argue that we should have used Bel([Pacifist] | [R $\wedge$ Q]) instead of Bel([Pacifist]) in the above exemplary measurements. However, the point here is that surprise-measurements such as the ones above *could* happen (in particular, rationality requires that all measurements regarding tautologies and unsatisfiable formulas be in the form of the first and second measurements). With regards to the pacifist example, it does seem more natural to use conditionals. But on the other hand, we would also say that a reasoner should be given total freedom in deciding what ought to be regarded as background information (and stay unspecified in the notation) and what ought to be made explicit (by making it part of the frame (defined below) the reasoner is pondering over).

Our second reason for the choice of belief functions as a formalization mechanism is that the intuitions underlying belief functions are in line with our intuitive notion of surprise. To elaborate, we first need some definitions.

Let $\chi = \{X_1, X_2, \ldots, X_N\}$ be a finite non-empty set of *variables* and let $\Theta_1, \Theta_2, \ldots, \Theta_N$ be the respective *frames* of these variables (each Θ_i is a finite non-empty set of values X_i can take; these values are mutually exclusive and exhaustive). X_i is boolean if Θ_i = {Yes, No}. $\Theta = \Theta_1 \times \Theta_2 \times \ldots \times \Theta_N$. We allow the use of *logical formulas* in referring to subsets of Θ, and we list in the appendix the formal correspondence between f, a formula, and [f], f's corresponding subset of Θ.

A *belief function* on Θ is a function Bel: $2^\Theta \rightarrow [0, 1]$ which is characterized by an *m-value function* m_{Bel} (written as "m" whenever confusions can be avoided; m is also called "the m-values of Bel"), where m: $2^\Theta \rightarrow [0, 1]$ satisfies two conditions:

(1) $m(\emptyset) = 0$, and

(2) $\sum_{A:\, A \subseteq \Theta} m(A) = 1$;

and for every subset B of Θ, Bel(B) is defined as $\sum_{A: A \subseteq B} m(A)$.[4] A subset A of Θ is called a *focal element* of Bel if m(A) > 0. When Bel is such that $m(\Theta) = 1$, we call Bel *the vacuous belief function.*

Dempster's rule of conditioning is defined as follows. Let Bel be a belief function on Θ and m be its associated m-values. Let B be a non-empty subset of Θ such that $Bel(B^c) \neq 1$.

$\forall\, C \subseteq \Theta$, **if** $C \subseteq B$

then $m(C \mid B)$ df= $\sum_{D:\, D \subseteq B^c} m(C \cup D) / K$

else $m(C \mid B)$ df= 0,

where $K = 1 - Bel(B^c)$ is the normalization constant.

(Note that for every subset S of Θ, $Bel(S \cap B \mid B) = Bel(S \mid B)$, but in general, $m(S \cap B \mid B) \neq m(S \mid B)$.)

Very abstractly, what the above definition of belief functions says is this. In trying to establish Bel (i.e., to satisfy the specified constraints), we may decide to commit various degrees of intuitive supports (the m-values) to various propositions (i.e., subsets of Θ), and a

[4]This definition is consistent with [Shafer, 1976]. Smets [1988] has a slightly more general definition (called an "open world" definition) in which $m(\emptyset)$ does not have to be 0 and Bel(A) is defined as the sum of the m-values of those *non-empty* subsets of A.

proposition A is allocated some intuitive support s whenever we find the proposition as a whole deserves this much intuitive support and we do not want to further "split" s among the elements (or rather, subsets) of A. A good example of this is (again) the Chang family example we described in the last section. For simplicity, let us assume we only need to worry about one variable HIRE. Clearly, we want the proposition [HIRE $\vee$ $\neg$HIRE] to receive the intuitive support 1. Nevertheless, we do not want to further split this intuitive support among the subsets of [HIRE $\vee$ $\neg$HIRE], as our intuitions satisfy Bel([HIRE]) = 0 and Bel([$\neg$HIRE]) = 0 (i.e., either way, we will not be surprised). What the corresponding belief-function formalization suggests, then, is that we intuitively commit the intuitive support 1 to [HIRE $\vee$ $\neg$HIRE] and we do not commit any intuitive support to anything else. In practice, this may well be what is happening with our intuitions. Of course, there is no way we can generalize this particular example to all possible situations. Nonetheless, the definition of belief functions serves as a (reasonable) postulate, suggesting that we intuitively *do* commit various intuitive supports to various propositions.

Given this notion of intuitively committing various intuitive supports to various propositions, Dempster's rule works as follows. Case 1 ($C \subseteq B$): originally we committed $m(C \cup D) = s$ to $C \cup D$, as we considered $C \cup D$ as a whole deserved this much (s) intuitive support and we did not want to further "split" s among the subsets of $C \cup D$; now we learn that the actual situation is in B; as a result, we let C "inherit" s, as we *still* consider C as a whole deserves this much intuitive support and we *still* do not want to further "split" s among the subsets of C. Case 2 ($C \subseteq B^c$): originally we considered C the most specific subset of Θ that deserves m(C) = v; now we learn that the actual situation is *not* in B^c; as our intuitions satisfy Bel(B | B) = 1 and Bel(C | B) = 0, rationality requires that we make m(C | B) zero and redistribute v in some way; what we do then is that we redistribute v among the focal elements of Bel(. | B) by proportions - a normalization process that is similar in spirit to what the Bayesian rule of conditioning does.

Is this a reasonable concept of conditioning? We think it is. Consider the following example. Suppose we think that one of Tom, Jerry and Pluto broke the window, but are unable to make a further distinction among the three (i.e., we view all three of them as equally likely suspects). However, we are not totally sure about it, as it is also possible that someone else did it. Thus, letting X be the one who broke the window (X=O means "other people did it"), we might specify our belief as Bel([X=T $\vee$ X=J $\vee$ X=P $\vee$ X=O]) = 1, Bel([X=T $\vee$ X=J $\vee$ X=P]) = .6, Bel([X=T $\vee$ X=J]) = 0, Bel([X=T $\vee$ X=P]) = 0, Bel([X=T]) = 0, etc. The underlying intuition, then, is that (for example) if we later discover that neither Tom nor Jerry broke the window, we will not be surprised (as it then means that Pluto is *the* suspect, and we are happy in being able to isolate the suspect). But if what we subsequently discover is that none of these three broke the window (e.g., we are told by Miss White, their school teacher, that all three of them were cleaning the storage room under her supervision during the time in which the window was broken), then we will surely be surprised (with .6 being the extent of our surprise). With the assumption that the only variable we need to worry about is X, we can characterize the above measurements as the belief function that m([X=T $\vee$ X=J $\vee$ X=B $\vee$ X=O]) = .4 and m([X=T $\vee$ X=J $\vee$ X=B]) = .6. In turn, Dempster's rule will give us the expected results. Again, there is no way we can generalize this particular example to all possible situations. Nevertheless, we hope to have convinced the reader in some way that, so far as we are able to tell, Dempster's rule of conditioning seems "compatible" with our intuitive notion of surprise.

Now is a good time to make clear how our notation of belief should be read. By specifying Bel([α] | [β]) = c, where α and β are logical formulas and $1 \geq c > 0$, we mean either (1) or (2) or (3) below, and we do *not* mean either (4) or (5) below.

(1) Given that β is true, I entertain the belief that α is true, and c is how confident I am in entertaining this belief.

(2) Given that β is true, I think α is true, and c is how confident I am in entertaining this belief.

(3) Given that β is true, c is the extent to which I will be surprised upon realizing that α is false.

(4) Given that β is true, c is my belief that α is true (or equivalently, c is my belief in α's being true).

(5) Given that β is true, c is the extent to which I believe that α is true.

We reject (4) as a way to read 'Bel([α] | [β]) = c', because (4) is ambiguous. As such, we feel reading 'Bel([α] | [β]) = c' as (4) has the dangerous potential of inviting some *unintended* view of human belief to "sneak in". This is definitely not how we want our theory of belief to be understood. In the same vein, we reject (5) as a way to read 'Bel([α] | [β]) = c', because we feel (5) really corresponds to the view of human belief that is embodied in the Bayesian theory of belief. For example, if one accepts to read 'Bel([α] | [β]) = c' as (5), then one may want to accept Cox' axioms, while rejecting Equation 1 in the last section. On the other hand, if one accepts to read 'Bel([α] | [β]) = c' as (1) or (2), then one may find Equation 1 perfectly acceptable, while rejecting the one axiom of Cox that we object to in footnote #1.

Similarly, by specifying Bel([α] | [β]) = 0, we mean either (1) or (2) or (3) below.

(1) Given that β is true, I do not entertain the belief that α is true.

(2) Given that β is true, I do not think α is true.

(3) Given that β is true, I will not be surprised (at all) upon realizing that α is false.

We suggest these ways of reading 'Bel($[\alpha] \mid [\beta]$) = 0' because we feel it may be unnatural to assert something like "given that β is true, I entertain the belief that α is true, and I have no confidence whatsoever in doing so."

Having described what belief functions are (from the perspectives of surprise and also from the perspectives of *our* view of human belief), we now need to describe how we can use this formalism for uncertain reasoning. As we have already suggested at the beginning of this section, the basic idea is just to solicit knowledge from the user and then let the system make inferences according to what the belief-function formalism postulates to be the "inner working mechanism of surprise". This amounts to the following two-step reasoning approach.

Step One - knowledge solicitation: the user specifies what his or her intuition satisfies. The result is a set of constraints (e.g., the constraints that Bel([¬STRIKE]) = .3, Bel([RAIN] | [WET]) = .4, Bel([¬RAIN] | [WET]) = 0, and Bel([PARTY]) = Bel([PARTY] | [RAIN])).

Step Two - reasoning: given the specified constraints, the system then infers properties (e.g., Bel([RAIN] | [PARTY]) $\geq$ 0) that are satisfied by *all* belief functions satisfying the user-specified constraints.

We acknowledge that this two-step reasoning approach is not as powerful as what we would like it to be. In particular, we have not provided a methodology which, when followed, would allow the user to make a systematic specification of what his or her intuition satisfies. Nevertheless, this reasoning approach serves as the *backbone* of any future, more refined reasoning approach we may wish to devise. There is already some progress in this direction. Hsia [1991a], for example, suggested the use of the principle of minimum commitment[5] on the part of the system to come up with answers like Bel([RAIN] | [PARTY]) = 0 (instead of Bel([RAIN] | [PARTY]) $\geq$ 0). This allows the system to infer what the user's belief *is* and not what the user's belief *can be* (which is what we are doing here). The principle of minimum commitment is not a panacea, however, as it is not always applicable (i.e., there may not exist a minimum committed belief function in the set of all belief functions satisfying the given constraints). Nevertheless, under this principle, we may be able to devise various specification methodologies that guarantee the existence of a minimum committed belief function satisfying the user-specified constraints. Hsia [1991c] also described a proof theory with belief functions being used in the corresponding model theory. This proof theory is at least as powerful as the system of Pearl and Geffner [1988].

[5]A set of belief functions $\mathbb{B}$ has a minimum committed element σ if and only if $\sigma \in \mathbb{B}$ and σ is such that $\forall\, \tau \in \mathbb{B}$, $\forall\, A \subseteq \Theta$, $\sigma(A) \leq \tau(A)$.

3 A CASE STUDY

In February of 1991, during the Persian Gulf war, the bombs of the Allied forces hit a bunker in which many civilians were taking shelter. The death toll was high, and one can surely imagine that the Allied forces were greatly surprised by the presence of a large number of civilians inside the bunker. To explain why the bunker was attacked, it was later revealed that there were two pieces of evidence suggesting that the bunker was used for military purposes. One piece of evidence was that satellite photographs showed that military personnels were going into and out of the bunker. The other piece of evidence was that there were military communications between this particular bunker and military installations elsewhere.

Our purpose here is not to pass judgment. We mention this particular incidence only because it happens to be a highly specialized situation in which our theory of belief may be of help to people who may need to decide about their beliefs. Consider the following question. Suppose we are in a situation in which we just obtained the *second* piece of evidence (say, the existence of military communications between the bunker and elsewhere, denoted as "E = Yes"). Should our confidence in entertaining the belief that the bunker is a military bunker be raised significantly? Of course, by asking this question, we are assuming that we have already obtained the first piece of evidence (i.e., satellite photographs showing military personnels going into and out of the bunker, denoted as "P = Yes"), and that based on this first piece of evidence, we have decided that our intuitions satisfy Bel([M] | [P]) = c and Bel(¬M] | [P]) = 0, where M (= Yes) stands for "the bunker is used for military purposes." In other words, given the first piece of evidence, we will not be surprised if it turns out that the bunker is for military purposes, and we will be somewhat surprised (to the extent c) if it turns out that the bunker is a civilian shelter (we assume that a bunker is either a military bunker or a civilian shelter). The same thing can be said about the second piece of evidence. That is, we may decide that our intuitions satisfy Bel([M] | [E]) = d and Bel(¬M] | [E]) = 0. The question, however, is what we should decide about Bel([M] | [P $\wedge$ E]) and Bel([¬M] | [P $\wedge$ E]).

As a first step of the analysis, we let χ = {M, P, E}, and the constraints we have for the moment are the following: Bel([M] | [P]) = c, Bel(¬M] | [P]) = 0, Bel([M] | [E]) = d, and Bel(¬M] | [E]) = 0. Let us now try to add more constraints to this set. First, our intuitions may be such that Bel([M]) = 0, Bel([¬M]) = 0, Bel([P]) = 0, Bel([¬P]) = 0, Bel([E]) = 0, and Bel([¬E]) = 0. That is, we do not entertain *any* belief regarding the bunker (at least we try to be so), whether it is a belief regarding what the bunker is for, a belief regarding whether the satellite photographs will show military personnels going into and out of the bunker, or a belief regarding whether there exists any military communication between the bunker and elsewhere. These "vacuous priors" are, in effect, the kinds of "attitudes" we usually try to enforce upon ourselves when performing evidential reasoning. Adding these six constraints to the original set of constraints, we now have a total of ten constraints that have to be satisfied.

Can we do better (in adding more constraints)? It happens that in this particular case, we can. Because our intuitions are also such that Bel([M ⊃ P]) = 1 and Bel([M ⊃ E]) = 1 are satisfied. So, altogether, we now have twelve constraints to be satisfied: Bel([M] | [P]) = c, Bel(¬M] | [P]) = 0, Bel([M] | [E]) = d, Bel(¬M] | [E]) = 0, Bel([M]) = 0, Bel([¬M]) = 0, Bel([P]) = 0, Bel([¬P]) = 0, Bel([E]) = 0, Bel([¬E]) = 0, Bel([M ⊃ P]) = 1 and Bel([M ⊃ E]) = 1.

Next question is guaranteed to be a thorny one: do our intuitions satisfy Bel([¬P] | [¬M]) = c and Bel([¬E] | [¬M]) = d? In other words, given that the bunker is a civilian shelter, will we be surprised (to the extent c) upon seeing military personnels going into and out of the bunker? Similarly, given that the bunker is a civilian shelter, will we be surprised (to the extent d) upon intercepting military communications between the bunker and elsewhere? To answer these two questions, we need to step back and think: why do our intuitions satisfy Bel([M] | [P]) = c (or Bel([M] | [E]) = d) in the first place? Well, our intuitions satisfy Bel([M] | [P]) = c because, given the only information that there were military personnels going into and out of the bunker, we are confident (to the extent c) in thinking that *other* reasons of why there were military personnels in presence can be *ruled out* (and that the reason of P's being true is because the bunker is for military purposes). Now, *if* upon learning that the bunker is a civilian shelter, we are still this confident (to the extent c) in thinking that other possible causes of the presence of military personnels can be ruled out, *then* we are certainly entitled to the expectation (with c being the corresponding confidence in having the expectation) that there will *not* be military personnels going into and out of the bunker. The same thing can be said about Bel([M] | [E]) and Bel([¬E] | [¬M]). Note that we are not suggesting that contrapositions are *always* satisfied. What we are suggesting is that contrapositions are not all that unreasonable as far as evidential reasoning from the perspectives of surprise is concerned. In fact, for this particular example, we tend to accept contrapositions here. Just think: wouldn't you be surprised (to the extent d) if given the only information that the bunker is a civilian shelter, you later intercept military communications between the bunker and elsewhere? (Remember that you already agreed that, given the only information that you intercepted military communications between the bunker and elsewhere, you will be surprised to the extent d if you later learn that it is a civilian shelter.)

Now back to the example. Adding the two contrapositions (i.e., Bel([¬P] | [¬M]) = c and Bel([¬E] | [¬M]) = d) to our set of constraints, we now have fourteen in the set. If we are able to add two additional independence constraints into this set, then it can be shown [Hsia, 1991b] that, given that both P and E are true, we are entitled to a significantly higher confidence in entertaining the belief that M is true. (In effect, this increase is due to the fact that Dempster's rule of combination *happens to be* what we get when we try to satisfy all sixteen constraints.) But unfortunately, this is where the example fails to satisfy.

The two constraints that are in need here are: Bel([¬P] | [¬M]) = Bel([¬P] | [¬M ∧ E]) and Bel([¬E] | [¬M]) = Bel([¬E] | [¬M ∧ P]). What they mean is as follows. Suppose the bunker is a civilian shelter. Then since we accept contraposition here, we will be surprised (to the extent c) upon seeing military personnels going into and out of the bunker. Nevertheless, suppose the bunker is a civilian shelter and we also intercepted military communications between the bunker and elsewhere, then we (probably) will be less surprised upon seeing military personnels going into and out of the bunker, as something fishy may be going on. The same thing can be said about Bel([¬E] | [¬M]) and Bel([¬E] | [¬M ∧ P]). In other words, our intuitions do not satisfy Bel([¬P] | [¬M]) = Bel([¬P] | [¬M ∧ E]) and Bel([¬E] | [¬M]) = Bel([¬E] | [¬M ∧ P]). Thus, our theory can only stop here, as we lack the necessary ingredients to significantly raise the user's degree of confidence in entertaining the belief that M is true. In some sense, this suggests that we ought not make Bel([M] | [P ∧ E]) significantly higher than Bel([M] | [P]) or Bel([M] | [E]).

4 DISCUSSION

When Shafer introduced the theory of belief functions in his 1976 monograph, he had the intention of viewing his theory as a generalization of the Bayesian theory of subjective probability. That is, Shafer's notion of belief is basically what we call *a "graded" concept of entertaining a belief*, and he was, as Fagin and Halpern [1989] observed, extending the Bayesian view of belief from measurable sets to nonmeasurable sets. Smets [1988] also used belief functions to develop a notion of belief along a similar line. Thus, we should not be surprised to see that most of the interpretations of belief functions (e.g., [Black, 1987; Halpern and Fagin, 1990; Kyburg, 1987; Laskey and Lehner, 1989; Nguyen 1978; Pearl, 1988, chapter 9; Shafer and Tversky, 1985]) relate belief functions to probability theory in some way. In other words, all these interpretations share the common goal of trying to generalize the Bayesian view of belief.

Our approach here is completely different. We start with *an entirely different view* of (human) belief, and we "happen" to settle on the use of belief functions to implement (if you will) our particular view of belief. Thus, our theory of belief is (intuitively) *not* a generalization of the Bayesian theory, though formally we cannot deny the fact that probabilities happen to be a special kind of belief functions. In other words, to use our theory of belief for uncertain reasoning, it has to be the case that the user finds our view of belief attractive (and, as a result, wants to adopt it), and it should *not* be the case that the user considers our theory of belief a generalization of the Bayesian theory of belief (as it would then be an outright mistake). So if the question is "why should I use your theory of belief for uncertain reasoning?", then the answer would be "because you agree with us in thinking that the notion of belief consists in entertaining various beliefs with various degrees of confidence."

Up until now, we have maintained that belief functions may be viewed as a very general mechanism for formalizing the notion of surprise. In effect, this just means that we want to keep the versatility of belief functions at our disposal. However, this does not mean that we will always need all the versatility of belief functions when we try to formalize our intuitive notion of surprise associated with some domain. In fact, it may be quite desirable (and also feasible) to impose special constraints when dealing with special domains. For example, in formalizing highly specialized expertise with regards to well-defined domains, we may only need to consider consonant belief functions.[6] And when this is the case, we may then relate belief functions to possibility theory [Dubois and Prade, 1990], as the necessity measure of a possibility is formally equivalent to Bel when Bel is a consonant belief function [Dubois and Prade, 1988]. Similarly, in formalizing common sense, we may only need to consider conjunctive belief functions [Hsia, 1991c].[7] This, in turn, may permit us to make purely qualitative inferences in a logical framework.

In short, belief functions may be "customized" in various ways to permit more efficient specifications as well as inferences. It all depends on whether our domain-of-interest allows us to impose such restrictions.

5 CONCLUSION

There is not just *one* view of human belief. There are at least two views: one that embodies a graded concept of believing in something, and the other that embodies the view of entertaining a belief with some degree of confidence. We can of course adopt the view that we always believe in something to a certain extent, in which case we (most likely) would arrive at the Bayesian theory of belief - a theory that has enjoyed a long history of research and development. On the other hand, we can also adopt the view that we entertain beliefs with various degrees of confidence, in which case we would arrive at our current theory of belief. The two views of belief are equally valid (or rather, neither is more "true" than the other). So which view of belief should we adopt? It is, very simply put, anyone's choice.

We set out to develop our theory of belief for the following reason. Surprise is something that has to do with how we reason and what we actually observe in our everyday life. It is an intuitive concept that we *may* feel quite comfortable in assessing its value. Therefore, by adopting the view of belief we advocate in this paper, we can, in effect, capture the notion of belief using our measured degrees of surprise. Ultimately, this may contribute to efforts in the area of "approximating human expertise with the use of computers," also known as artificial intelligence.

In introducing our theory, we have described a canonical measurement device that can be used for the measurement of surprise (and thus belief), and we have suggested the use of belief functions as a very general mechanism for modeling our notion of belief. As an illustration of how our theory of belief may be of some help to people who need to decide about their beliefs, we also gave an example in (boolean and abductive) evidential reasoning. Unlike probability theory which enjoys a wide spectrum of results and applications, our enterprise of surprise and belief is still at the beginning of its development, and we still need to do (much) more work in order to make this enterprise truly accessible to practitioners of uncertain reasoning.

Acknowledgements

The author thanks Philippe Smets and Paolo Garbolino for ever-enlightening discussions. Robert Kennes and Alessandro Saffiotti also helped to sharpen our views about belief. Thanks also go to one referee who requested that the difference between our theory of belief and the Bayesian theory of belief be clearly specified. This work was supported in part by the DRUMS project funded by the Commission of the European Communities under the ESPRIT II-Program, Basic Research Project 3085.

Appendix - logical formulas and subsets of Θ

Let $X_1, X_2, \ldots, X_N$ be variables and $\Theta_1, \Theta_2, \ldots, \Theta_N$ be their respective frames. X_i is boolean if $\Theta_i = \{\text{Yes, No}\}$. Let $\Theta = \Theta_1 \times \Theta_2 \times \ldots \times \Theta_N$. By the "$X_i$-value" ($1 \le i \le N$) of an element $<a_1, a_2, \ldots, a_N>$ of Θ, we mean a_i. Let $x \in \Theta$ and $a \in \Theta_i$ ($1 \le i \le N$), we recursively define what a formula f is and whether x *satisfies* the formula f below.

Case 1. f is "$X_i = a$": x *satisfies* f if and only if the X_i-value of x is a. ("X_i" is also used as a shorthand for "X_i = Yes" in the case of boolean variables.)

---

[6] A belief function Bel is consonant if we can arrange the focal elements of Bel in a sequence so that each is contained in the following one.

[7] A belief function Bel is conjunctive if $\forall A \subseteq \Theta$, $\forall B \subseteq \Theta$, $\forall C \subseteq \Theta$, if $Bel(A \mid B) > 0$ and $Bel(\Theta \backslash A \mid B) = 0$ and $Bel(C \mid B) > 0$ and $Bel(\Theta \backslash C \mid B) = 0$, then $Bel(A \cap C \mid B) > 0$ and $Bel(\Theta \backslash (A \cap C) \mid B) = 0$.

Case 2. f is "$\neg$g", where g is a formula: x *satisfies* f if and only if x does not satisfy g.

Case 3. f is "g $\vee$ h", where g and h are formulas: x *satisfies* f if and only if x satisfies at least one of g and h.

Case 4. f is "g $\wedge$ h", where g and h are formulas: x *satisfies* f if and only if x satisfies the formula "$\neg(\neg g \vee \neg h)$".

Case 5. f is "g $\supset$ h", where g and h are formulas: x *satisfies* f if and only if x satisfies the formula "$\neg g \vee h$".

Let f be a formula. By *the subset (of Θ) the formula f refers to* (or, alternatively, *the subset (of Θ) the formula f corresponds to*), we mean the set {x: x $\in$ Θ and x satisfies f}, denoted as [f].

References

Black, P.K. (1987). Is Shafer general Bayes? In *Proceedings of the Third Workshop on Uncertainty in Artificial Intelligence*, Seattle, Washington, 2-9.

Collins (1987). COBUILD (COLLINS Birmingham University International Language Database). Collins Publishers, London.

Cox, R.T. (1946). Probability, frequency and reasonable expectation. *American Journal of Physics* **14**, 1-13.

Dubois, D. and Prade, H. (1988). Possibilistic and Fuzzy Logics. In *Non-Standard Logics for Automated Reasoning* (P. Smets, E. H. Mamdani, D. Dubois and H. Prade eds.). Academic Press, London.

Dubois, D. and Prade, H. (1990). Updating with belief functions, ordinal conditional functions and possibility measures. In *Proceedings of the Sixth Conference on Uncertainty in Artificial Intelligence*, Cambridge, Massachusetts, 307-315.

Fagin, R. and Halpern, J.Y. (1989). Uncertainty, belief, and probability. In *Proceedings of the Eleventh International Joint Conference on Artificial Intelligence*, Detroit, Michigan, 1161-1167.

Halpern, J.Y. and Fagin, R. (1990). Two views of belief: Belief as generalized probability and belief as evidence. In *Proceedings of the Eighth National Conference on Artificial Intelligence*, American Association for Artificial Intelligence, Boston, Massachusetts, 112-119.

Hsia, Y.-T. (1991a). Characterizing belief with minimum commitment. In *Proceedings of the Twelfth International Joint Conference on Artificial Intelligence*, Sydney, Australia, (to appear).

Hsia, Y.-T. (1991b). Explanations and surprise - a belief-function approach. Technical Report TR/IRIDIA/91-2, IRIDIA, Université Libre de Bruxelles.

Hsia, Y.-T. (1991c). A Belief-Function Semantics for Cautious Nonmonotonicity. Technical Report TR/IRIDIA/91-3, IRIDIA, Université Libre de Bruxelles.

Kyburg, Jr., H.E. (1987). Bayesian and non-Bayesian evidential updating. *Artificial Intelligence* **31**, 271-293.

Laskey, K. B. and Lehner, P. E. (1989). Assumptions, beliefs and probabilities. *Artificial Intelligence* **41**, 1, 65-77.

Nguyen, H.T. (1978). On random sets and belief functions. *Journal of Mathematical Analysis and Applications* **65**, 531-542.

Pearl, J. (1988). *Probabilistic Reasoning in Intelligent Systems: Networks of Plausible Inference*. Morgan Kaufmann Publishers, Inc., San Mateo, California.

Pearl, J. and Geffner, H. (1988). Probabilistic semantics for a subset of default reasoning. TR CSD-870058 (R-94), Cognitive Systems Laboratory, University of California.

Ramsey, F.P. (1931). Truth and probability. In *The Foundations of Mathematics* (Braithwaite, R.B. ed.), Routledge & Kegan Paul, London, 156-198.

Shafer, G. (1976). *A Mathematical Theory of Evidence*. Princeton University Press.

Shafer, G. and Tversky, A. (1985). Languages and designs for probability judgment. *Cognitive Science* **9**, 309-339.

Smets, P. (1988). Belief functions. In *Non-Standard Logics for Automated Reasoning* (P. Smets, E. H. Mamdani, D. Dubois and H. Prade eds.). Academic Press, London.

Weaver, W. (1948). Probability, rarity, interest and surprise. *Scientific Monthly* **67**, 390-392.

Zadeh, L.A. (1978). Fuzzy sets as a basis for a theory of possibility. Fuzzy Sets and Systems **1**, 3-28.

Evidential Reasoning in a Categorial Perspective: Conjunction and Disjunction of Belief Functions

Robert Kennes[1]
IRIDIA, Université Libre de Bruxelles
Av. F. D. Roosevelt 50 – CP 194/6
B-1050 Brussels, Belgium

Abstract

The *categorial approach* to evidential reasoning can be seen as a combination of the *probability kinematics* approach of Richard Jeffrey (1965) and the *maximum (cross-) entropy inference* approach of E. T. Jaynes (1957). As a consequence of that viewpoint, it is well known that category theory provides natural definitions for logical connectives. In particular, disjunction and conjunction are modelled by general categorial constructions known as *products* and *coproducts*. In this paper, I focus mainly on Dempster-Shafer theory of belief functions for which I introduce a category I call *Dempster's category*. I prove the existence of and give explicit formulas for conjunction and disjunction in the subcategory of separable belief functions. In Dempster's category, the new defined conjunction can be seen as the *most cautious* conjunction of beliefs, and thus no assumption about *distinctness* (of the sources) of beliefs is needed as opposed to Dempster's rule of combination, which calls for *distinctness* (of the sources) of beliefs.

0 INTRODUCTION

J. Halpern and R. Fagin have pointed out [90 p.102] that belief functions can be understood in '*two useful and quite different ways ... The first as a generalized probability ... The second as a way of representing evidence* ...(i.e.) *as a mapping from probability functions to probability functions*'. This can be interpreted by saying that a belief function can be seen either as a static object (i.e., as a state of mind) or as a dynamic entity (i.e., as an evidence transforming a state of mind into another state of mind). The idea of putting together a static component with a dynamic one is not at all a new idea (cf. [Horvitz, Heckerman 86] for a nice survey of this idea). In 1965, Richard Jeffrey coined the term *probability kinematics* to emphasize the idea, although *probability dynamics* would have been a better term.

Actually, there exists a basic and simple mathematical structure encompassing the two foregoing views of belief functions: the *category* structure [Mac Lane 71]. The link between evidential reasoning and category theory can be best summarized by the so-called *Meseguer-Montanari correspondence* [Marti-Oliet, Meseguer 89]:

States $\longleftrightarrow$ *Objects*
Transitions $\longleftrightarrow$ *Morphisms*

where the set of states is a set of admissible *belief states* (or *opinions*) and the transitions from one belief state to a second belief state are the elements of a set of admissible *updatings* (or *adjustment of opinions*) transforming the first state into the second one.

I see two reasons for adopting a categorial viewpoint about evidential reasoning. The first one is related to the *probability kinematics* viewpoint, and the second one is related the *maximum entropy inference* approach to evidential reasoning. Actually, a category can be seen as an abstract view of a dynamic system of beliefs according to the probability kinematics viewpoint. An abstract point of view about beliefs has been advocated among others by Domotor [85]. Although the viewpoint adopted by Domotor is different from ours, the kind of structure he used – a monoid[2] of evidence operating[3] on a set of belief states, which is essentially the abstract view of a *machine* – always determines, in a natural way, a category. The second and more important reason for adopting a categorial viewpoint is: a very powerful way of defining objects is by using *universal properties* which is a generalization of defining objects by *maximum entropy* methods. *Defining an object by a universal property* is the categorist's way to *defining an object by a maximum (or minimum) principle*. Any mathematical objects defined by such a maximum principle live in a category. I also should mention that

[1] The following text presents some research results of the Belgian National incentive-program for fundamental research in artificial intelligence initiated by the Belgian State, Prime Minister's Office, Science Policy Programming. The scientific responsibility is assumed by the author.

[2] A monoid is a set along with a binary operation that is associative and has a neutral element 1.

[3] A monoid (M,*) operates on a set S iff every element m of M determines a transformation $\underline{m}$ of the set S such that for every elements m,n of M and for every element s of S: $(\underline{m*n})(s) = \underline{m}(\underline{n}(s))$ and $\underline{1}(s) = s$

there already exits a maximum (or minimum) property principle known as *Principle of Minimum of Specificity* [Dubois, Prade 87a, 87b], *Principle of Minimum Commitment* [Hsia 91], or *Principle of Maximum Plausibility* [Smets 91] playing an increasing role in Dempster-Shafer theory. Nevertheless, the principle I will be using is not the former one and could be called *the least (or most) updated principle*.
The present paper is structured as following. Section 1 gives a detailed definition of categories. Section 2 presents the Boolean, the Bayesian and the Dempsterian categories of beliefs. Section 3 shows how conjunction and disjunction can be defined by using a maximum (or minimum) principle. Section 4 gives the definition of coproduct and conjunction in any category. Then, section 5 presents the product and disjunction. Finally, in section 6, I study the conjunction and disjunction of separable beliefs functions.
The product (disjunction) and coproduct (conjunction) of beliefs can be considered as an answer to questions raised by P.W. Williams [78, p.383] in his review of Shafer's book [76].
Some categorial approaches to probability theory and to evidential reasoning have already been proposed. Let us just mention F.W. Lawvere [Giry 82], Negoita [85], Goodman and Nguyen [85], Gärdenfors [88]. Contrary to evidential reasoning, the categorial study of fuzzy sets is now – since the work of J. Goguen [69] – a well established part of fuzzy set theory.
The problem of combining non-distinct experts opinions has already been examined in several papers, among them: [Smets 86], [Dubois, Prade 87b], [Hummel, Manevitz 87], [Ling, Rudd 89a,89b], [Wong, Lingras 90] and [Hau, Kashyap 90].
As the categorial framework is not very common among people concerned with evidential reasoning, this paper will be more expository than technical. Only a few technical results will be given and only very elementary notions of category theory will be presented and applied to evidential reasoning.

1 FROM THE DYNAMICS OF BELIEFS TO CATEGORIES OR ... VICE VERSA

The present section can be considered as an introduction to the idea of *category* for belief-minded people or as an introduction to the idea of *probability kinematics* for category-minded people. As a category is essentially a graph-theoretical structure I first need to give a precise definition of a graph (in fact of a directed multigraph):

Definition: a **graph** is defined by the following data:
1. a pair of classes P and A (whose elements are respectively called *points* and *arrows* or *objects* and *morphisms* or ... *states* and *transitions* ... according to our motivations)
2. together with a pair of maps s,t: $A \to P$ (the maps s and t are called *source* and *target* or *origin* and *extremity* or ... *initial state* and *final state*).
Some comments are worth mentioning:
1. The class P can be seen as the *static* component, whereas the class A can be seen as the *dynamic* component of the graph structure.
2. The static and dynamic components are linked together by the maps s and t, specifying the *initial* and *final* state of each arrow.
3. f: $a \to b$ means that f is an arrow whose source or initial state is a and whose target or final state is b. That is: $f \in A$ and $s(f)=a$ and $t(f)=b$.
4. All arrows are directed: they all have an initial point and a final point. (*directed* graph)
5. Many arrows can share the same initial state and the same final state. (*multi* graph)
Definition:
a **category** is defined by the following **data**:
1. a graph s,t: $A \to P$, together with:
2. a map i: $P \to A : a \to i_a$. The arrow i_a: $a \to a$ is called the *identity arrow* at the point a
3. a partial map, called *composition*,
c: $A \times A \to A$: $(f,g) \to c(f,g)=f.g$, f.g is called the *composite* of the arrows f and g (f.g is written in diagrammatic order), f.g is defined iff the target of f equals the source of g.
The preceding data must satisfy the following two **axioms**: for all points a,b and c and all arrows
f: $a \to b$, g: $b \to c$ and h: $c \to d$
(i) $(f.g).h = f.(g.h)$ (associativity of composition)
(ii) $i_a.f = f = f.i_b$ (identities are neutral for composition)
Intuitively, a category is simply a (directed multi-) graph together with a composition rule for *queueing* arrows satisfying associativity and with a neutral arrow at each point.
Examples: Many examples of categories can be classified according to some correspondences.
1. The major examples and motivations at the origins of category theory (in the 40's) were dominated by the following correspondence which could be called the *Klein correspondence* (after the famous Felix Klein 1872 Erlangen Program) :

Structures ⟷ *Objects*
Representations ⟷ *Morphisms*

It is the Klein correspondence which has popularized the view of category as a meta-structure. But, I hasten to add that it is not the only possible view of categories.
Just two very classical examples:
(1) **SET** is the category whose objects are the sets, whose arrows are the usual functions, and the composition is the usual composition of functions. Instead of taking functions as arrows I could as well take the relations or the partial functions as arrows (in that case we are, of course, getting different categories).
(2) **RVECT** is the category whose objects are the real vector spaces, whose arrows are the linear mappings, and the composition is the usual composition of mappings.

In fact, any kind of structure together with a suitable notion of (homo)morphism give rise straightforward to a category.

2. In the late sixties appeared the *Lambek-Lawvere correspondence*:

Formulas ⟷ *Objects*
Proofs ⟷ *Morphisms*

also leading to categories. See [Marti-Oliet, Meseguer 89]

3. Taking into account with [Garvey, Lowrance, Fischler 81], [Hsia 90] and [Provan 90] that a belief function can be considered as a generalized formula and that an updating can be considered as a generalized proof (cf.[Pearl 88,90]), then we get the next correspondence:

Belief States ⟷ *Objects*
Updating ⟷ *Morphisms*

This can also be seen as a particular case of the *Meseguer-Montanari correspondence* (about concurrent systems) which appeared in the late eighties [Marti-Oliet, Meseguer 89]:

States ⟷ *Objects*
Transitions ⟷ *Morphisms*

In particular that correspondence associates a category to any machine.

4. Many important examples of categories do not fit into the preceding correspondences. A category can also be viewed as a common generalization of an algebraic structure: *the monoids*, and of an ordered structure: *the preordered sets*[4]. Explicitly, any monoid can be viewed as a category with only one object (take any object you want), the arrows are the elements of the monoid. Composition is the binary operation of the monoid. Any preordered set can be viewed as a category. The objects are the elements of the set and the arrows are the ordered pairs (a,b) of the preorder. In particular any ordered set[5] and any lattice[6] are (or can be viewed as) categories. Every monoid operating on a set (such an operation can be viewed as a machine) gives rise to a category in the following way: the objects are the elements of the set, and the arrows are the triples (a,m,b) where a and b are elements of the set and m is an element of the monoid such that m(a)=b. So, Domotor's [80] viewpoint is embedded is the categorial viewpoint.

2 CATEGORIES OF "BELIEFS"

I want to show here that there exist a lot of categories of "beliefs". That is, categories whose objects can be thought of as representing belief states (or opinions) of a cognitive agent concerning a particular situation. The general idea is the following one: If I adopt an abstract viewpoint of what should be a system of beliefs (of a cognitive agent), concerning a particular situation, I find natural to:

(i) first, consider a set of admissible *belief states* – whatever this term actually means –which can be taken by an agent, concerning the specific situation at hand.

(ii) second, consider a set of admissible *updatings* – whatever this term actually means – (determined by some evidence), transforming a belief state into another belief state.

(iii) third, the composition of two updatings should be an updating,

(iv) for each belief state there should exist a *trivial* updating, i.e., the one *doing nothing*.

We will get a category of beliefs each time we make clear each of the above notions which have been left vague. Here are some major examples:

The Boolean category of beliefs (induced from a special case of *Boolean machines* of [Domotor 80, p. 391] by the Meseguer-Montanari correspondence).

Let us consider a (finite or infinite) set Ω which can be interpreted as a set of possible values for a variable, or possible answers to a question. The boolean category of beliefs on Ω is defined by the following data:

(i) the objects are the subsets of Ω, i.e., the elements of $\wp\Omega$,

(ii) the arrows $X: A \rightarrow B$ are the subsets X of Ω such that $X \cap A = B$,

in other words $X: A \rightarrow B$ iff $X \cap A = B$

(iii) the composite of $X: A \rightarrow B$ and $Y: B \rightarrow C$ is $X \cap Y: A \rightarrow C$

(iv) the identity arrow at A is $\Omega: A \rightarrow A$.

Intuitively, the Boolean category of beliefs on Ω can be explained the following way: the only admissible belief states that can be entertained are of the kind: *I believe that the answer to the question is in subset X*. The only admissible updatings are those representing the following kind of reasoning: *If I believe that the answer to the question is in subset A, and if I get an evidence which makes me believe that the answer is in subset X, then I will believe that the answer to the question is in subset $X \cap A$.*

The Bayesian category of beliefs (induced from *Bayesian machines* of [Domotor 80, p. 390] by the Meseguer-Montanari correspondence).

The Bayesian category of beliefs (on a set Ω) is defined according to the following definition [Teller 73, p.218]: '*I take bayesianism to be the doctrine which maintains that (i) a set of reasonable beliefs can be represented by a probability function defined over sentences or propositions, and that (ii) reasonable changes of belief can be represented by a process called conditionalization*'.

Let Ω be a (finite or infinite) set which can be interpreted as a set of possible values for a variable, or possible answers to a question. The Bayesian category of beliefs on Ω is defined by the following data:

(i) the objects are the probability functions $P: \wp\Omega \rightarrow [0,1]$, i.e., the functions satisfying the well known Kolmogorov axioms,

(ii) the arrows $X: P \rightarrow Q$ are the subsets X of Ω such that $Q = P(.\,|X)$

---

[4] A preodered set is a set along with a binary relation which is reflexive and transitive.

[5] An ordered set is a set along with a binary relation which is reflexive, transitive and antisymmetric.

[6] A lattice is an ordered set in which every pair of elements has an infimum and a supremum.

(iii) the composition of $X: P \rightarrow Q$ and $Y: Q \rightarrow R$ is $X \cap Y: P \rightarrow R$
(iv) the identity arrow at P is $\Omega: P \rightarrow P$.
So, the only admissible belief states represented by this category are those represented by a probability function on Ω. The only admissible updatings are those representing the following kind of reasoning: *If my belief state (about a situation) is represented by the probability function P, and if I get an evidence which makes me believe that the answer is in subset X, then my new belief state will be represented by the conditional probability function P(. /X).*

Dempster's category of (unnormalized) beliefs
A new kind of category of beliefs was proposed by A. Dempster in the late sixties, and exposed in the seminal work of G. Shafer [76].
Let us first review the two basic notions of Dempster-Shafer theory of belief functions.
The set Ω is finite, and $\wp\Omega$ denotes its power set.
(1) A *mass distribution* m on the set Ω is any function:

$$m: \wp\Omega \rightarrow [0\ 1] \quad \text{such that} \sum_{X \in \wp\Omega} m(X) = 1$$

(2) The key point of the theory is provided by the so-called *Dempster's rule of combination.* It is a binary operation defined on the set of mass distributions on a set Ω: given two mass distributions m_1 and m_2, the rule provides a new mass distribution denoted by $m_1 \otimes m_2$:

$$\forall A \in \wp\Omega: m_1 \otimes m_2(A) = \sum_{X \cap Y = A} m_1(X) \cdot m_2(Y)$$

This product is in fact nothing else than the convolution product of the semi-group algebra of $(\wp\Omega, \cap)$. Before I describe Dempster's category of beliefs, let us note that each subset X of Ω determines a mass distribution denoted by $1_{\{X\}}: \wp\Omega \rightarrow [0,1]$ and defined by $1_{\{X\}}(X) = 1$. I are now ready to describe what I call Dempster's category of (unnormalized) beliefs. As usual, let Ω be a finite set which can be interpreted as a set of possible values for a variable, or possible answers to a question. Dempster's category of beliefs on Ω is defined by the following data:
(i) the objects are the mass distributions $m: \wp\Omega \rightarrow [0,1]$,
(ii) the arrows $e: m_1 \rightarrow m_2$ are the mass distributions e such that: $e \otimes m_1 = m_2$,
(iii) the composite of $e_1: m_1 \rightarrow m_2$ and $e_2: m_2 \rightarrow m_3$ is $e_1 \otimes e_2: m_1 \rightarrow m_3$
(iv) the identity arrow at m is $1_{\{\Omega\}}: m \rightarrow m$.
Some comments are needed:
1. Any *mass distribution* m is bijectively represented by its *Möbius transform* also called its *belief function* bel_m defined by:

$$\forall A \in \wp\Omega: bel_m(A) = \sum_{X \in \wp A - \{\varnothing\}} m(X) = \sum_{X \subseteq A, X \neq \varnothing} m(X)$$

A belief function is sometimes used instead of its mass distribution and vice versa.
2. In Dempster's unnormalized category, the belief states are represented by mathematical objects that are in fact generalized probability functions (see [Fagin, Halpern 89]). But, what makes the situation more intricate is that the updatings (induced by evidences) are represented by the same kind of mathematical objects as belief states are. So, in this framework the phrase of Halpern and Fagin [90, p.102] receives its full meaning, namely that belief functions can be understood in *'two useful and quite different ways ... The first as a generalized probability ... The second as a way of representing evidence ...(i.e.) as a mapping from probability functions to probability functions'.*
3. Another point is the difference between *updating* and *combination*: An updating (transition) is an arrow from a belief state to a belief state, whereas the combination is the composition rule, operating on the arrows of the category. As stressed by Halpern and Fagin [90, p.115] : *'The key point is that updating and combining are different processes; what makes sense in one context does not necessarily make sense in the other.'* And, p.112 : *'It makes sense to think of updating a belief if we think of it as a generalized probability. On the other hand, it makes sense to combine two beliefs (using, say, Dempster' rule of combination) only if we think of the belief functions as representing evidence'.*
4. It is well known that the rule of combination of beliefs is (said to be) valid in case the *'beliefs functions to be combined are actually based on entirely distinct bodies of evidence'* [Shafer 76, p. 57].
5. It is obvious how Dempster's category of beliefs should be interpreted: the belief states are represented by mass distributions (or equivalently by belief functions) on Ω. The updatings represent the following kind of reasoning: *If my belief state is represented by the mass distribution B, and if I get an evidence – based on a body of evidence entirely distinct from the body of evidence on which is based my belief state – represented by the mass distribution E, then my new belief state will be represented by the mass distribution E⊗B.*

Dempster's category of (normalized) beliefs
The differences between this category and the unnormalized Dempster's category of beliefs are the following ones:
(i) the mass distributions are asked to satisfy $m(\varnothing)=0$.
(ii) Dempster product has to be normalized, cf [Shafer 76].

Remark: there exist numerous other categories whose objects are belief functions (or mass distributions). The reader will easily define the *weak-inclusion category of beliefs* and the *strong-inclusion category* or *Yager's category of beliefs*. The main difference between the former categories and the latter ones is that the arrows of the former categories are not induced by evidence. In other words, their arrows are more *descriptive* than *operative*. The two before mentioned categories have already be somehow studied by Yager [86], Dubois and Prade [86,87b,90] and by Kruse and Schwecke [91]. According to the philosophy of category theory, and as observed by

Dubois and Prade [90, p.423], these different categories '*correspond to different views of belief functions*'.

3 DISJUNCTIONS AND CONJUNCTIONS

A slogan for this section could be: *define the logical connectives in terms of minimum (or maximum) principles, i.e., by using universal properties.*
For example, the union and intersection (i.e., disjunction and conjunction) of two sets A and B can be defined without referring to the elements of the sets, using only the inclusion relation, in the following way:
$A \cup B$ is the set included in all sets including A and B,
$A \cap B$ is the set including all sets included in A and B.
Keeping in mind the above example here is, I believe, the essence of the conjuction and disjunction of two pieces of information:
(1) the conjunction is the piece of information *contained* in all pieces of information *containing* the two given pieces of information. More intuitively: it is the most cautious (minimal) piece of information containing the two given pieces of information.
(2) the disjunction is the piece of information *containing* all pieces of information *contained* in the two given pieces of information. More intuitively: it is the most bold (maximal) piece of information contained in the two given pieces of information.
Since Jaynes (1957), a usual approach (at least for conjunction) is the *maximum (cross-) entropy inference* or the *minimum information (gain) inference* approach, which I shall not recall here. That approach can be described as a *quantitative* approach, although only the order relation is used. Another approach, which can be described as a *qualitative* approach, is the categorial approach. Actually, the minimum information (gain) inference approach can be seen as a particular case of the categorial approach. The categorial approach – or better: the universal property approach – is the following: (i) a *piece of information* is interpreted as an object of a category (whose object can be thought of as representing belief states or information states), (ii) A is *contained* in B is interpreted as an arrow X: $A \to B$ of the category. The conjunction is then represented by a construction called the *coproduct* in the category and the disjunction is represented by another construction called the *product* in the category.

4 COPRODUCTS AND CONJUNCTIONS

Let us first define the simplest example of object defined by a universal property: *initial object* of a category.
Definition: an **initial object** of a category is an object I such that for any object X (of the category) there is a unique arrow (of the category) : $I \to X$.
Properties and examples:
1. It can be shown very easily that all initial objects of a category are *isomorphic* (that is: if I1 and I2 are two initial objects,then there exist an arrow f:I1 $\to$ I2 and an arrow g:I2 $\to$ I1 such that $f.g=i_{I1}$ (the identity arrow at I1) and $g.f=i_{I2}$ (the identity arrow at I2).
2. The reader will verify at once that the *vacuous belief function* $1_{\{\Omega\}}$ is the (only) initial object in Dempster's (unnormalized or normalized) category.
3. An initial object can also be defined as a *colimit of the empty diagram* [Goldblatt 84, p. 60]. So, if one *knows nothing* (represented by the empty diagram, as suggested by Negoita [85, p. 8]), the most cautious belief state is the vacuous belief function $1_{\{\Omega\}}$.
4. It is easy to verify that Bayes category has no initial object.
5. The only initial object of Boole category (on Ω) is Ω.
6. The initial object of an ordered set is its minimum (if it exists).
Let us now consider two objects A and B of a category. A *coproduct* of A and B is an object A+B along with two arrows in_A: $A \to A+B$ and in_B: $B \to A+B$, expressing how A+B is related to A and B, satisfying a particular universal property. Intuitively, A+B represents the *fusion* or *aggregation* or *integration* of A and B in the most cautious way, according to the arrows of the category being considered. Here is the definition:
Definition: Let us give two objects A and B (of a category)

A • • B

A **coproduct** of A and B is an object denoted by A+B, along with two arrows:
in_A: $A \to A+B$ and in_B: $B \to A+B$

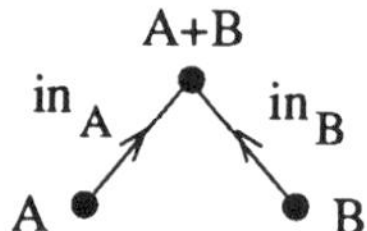

such that for every other object C along with two arrows f: $A \to C$ and g: $B \to C$

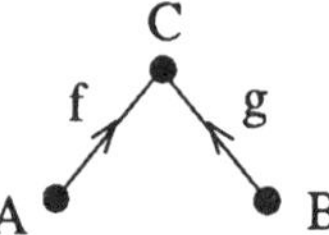

there exists a unique arrow α: $A+B \to C$ such that the following diagram *commutes*: (i.e., $in_A.\alpha=f$ and $in_B.\alpha=g$)

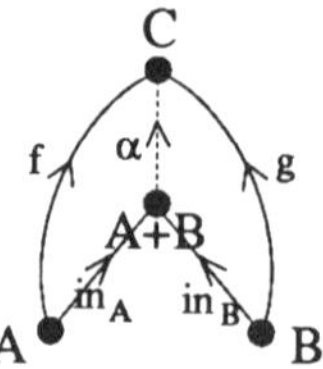

Properties:
1. It can be shown very easily that all coproducts of a given pair of objects are *isomorphic*.
2. [MacLane 71, p. 72-74]: up to isomorphism, the coproduct is an operation satisfying the following properties: (i) Associativity, (ii) Commutativity, (iii) Every initial object is neutral, (iv) Idempotent if the category is a preorder. To say that a category is a preorder

is equivalent to saying that it has at most one arrow between an ordered pair of objects, it is also trivially equivalent to say that every diagram of the category commutes.
3. The initial object of a category can be seen to be the coproduct of ... no object!
4. A priori, there is no guarantee for a pair of objects in a category to have a coproduct. A category is said *to have binary products* if the product of any two objects exists. It is not always a trivial task to show that a category has binary products.
For classical **examples** of coproducts the reader is referred to the literature on category theory. Let us here consider the category $(\wp\Omega,\supseteq)$ which is well known to be a *Boolean lattice*. The objects are the subsets of Ω, and the arrows are the ordered pairs (A,B) such that $A \supseteq B$. The reader can easily verify that the coproduct of A and B is $A \cap B$ (together with the inclusions $A \supseteq A \cap B$ and $B \supseteq A \cap B$). It is trivial to see that in any lattice the coproduct of the elements a and b is the *supremum* or *least upper bound* of a and b.
Let us now examine what happens in our Boolean category of beliefs (on the set Ω). So, let us take two states A and B of the category, at first sight the coproduct of A and B should be $A \cap B$, unfortunately the reader may verify that we get some problems in trying to get commutative diagrams which are asked by the definition of coproduct. The easiest way out of that problem is to consider that all diagrams of the category do commute! Formally, this can be done by identifying all arrows going from one state to another state – that is, by performing a *quotient* of the category. In that way we obtain a *new* category – called the *preorder* of the category – which, in the present case, is (isomorphic to) the Boolean lattice $(\wp\Omega,\supseteq)$. As the Boolean lattice $(\wp\Omega,\supseteq)$ essentially reflects the *logic* of the Boolean category, I will call the preorder of a category its **logic** (warning: this is not a standard definition).
Thus, with the preceding definition we can say that the logic of the Boolean category is a Boolean logic. We can perform the same quotient with Dempster's categories to get the *logics* of Dempster's categories.
Here are the details of the definition of the *logics* of the two Dempster's categories:
(i) the objects are the mass distributions $m: \wp\Omega \rightarrow [0,1]$,
(ii) there is only one arrow $m_1 \rightarrow m_2$ iff there exists at least one "evidence" (mass distribution) e such that: $e \otimes m_1 = m_2$, otherwise there does not exist any arrow $m_1 \rightarrow m_2$.
(iii) the composition rule and (iv) the identity arrows are then uniquely defined.
Dempster's rule of combination is normalized or not according to the category being considered.
Definition: Given two objects A and B of a category, the **conjunction** $A \wedge B$ is the coproduct of A and B in the logic of the category.
More informally, with the vocabulary of "beliefs", the definition of conjunction is the following: the conjunction of two belief states A and B is the *least* (or more precisely: *any* least) common updated belief state of A and of B. '*Least*' means that any other common updated belief state of A and B is an updated state of the conjunction of A and B. The conjunction is thus commutative, associative and idempotent. Moreover, in Dempster's categories the vacuous belief state is neutral for conjunction.
Because of the minimality property of the conjunction there is no need to assume *distinctness* (of the sources) of the combined beliefs.
Remark: Kruse and Schwecke [91] have succeeded in building a category, whose objects are belief functions and whose arrows are *specializations* – a generalization of Yager's inclusion [86] – in which a conjunction of A and B is Dempster's combination of A and B. At first sight this is a remarkable result! Unfortunately, because there are (too) many isomorphisms in Kruse's category, being a conjunction in that category does not characterize Dempster's rule of combination at all.

5 PRODUCTS AND DISJUNCTIONS

The dual notion of initial object is *terminal object*.
Definition: a **terminal object** of a category is an object T such that for any object X there is a unique arrow $X \rightarrow T$.
The only terminal object of the logic of the Boolean category of beliefs is the empty set ∅ which plays the role of the constant FALSE. The reader will verify at once that the belief state defined by $m(\varnothing) = 1$ is the (only) terminal object in the logic of Dempster's unnormalized category. I call that belief function the *total contradiction*, which plays, in this logic, the role of the boolean constant FALSE. Contrary to the unnormalized case, the logic of Dempster's normalized category has no terminal object (i.e., the constant FALSE is not represented in that category).
The product of two objects in a category is simply the coproduct in the *dual* category (i.e., the objects are the same but the arrows are *reversed*). Historically, *products* were first recognized which explains the word *coproduct*.
Let us now consider two objects A and B of a category. A *product* of A and B is an object A×B along with two arrows $p_A: A \times B \rightarrow A$ and $p_B: A \times B \rightarrow B$ (called the *projections*), expressing how A×B is related to A and B, and satisfying a universal property. Intuitively, an interpretation of A×B is the biggest common part of A and B according to the arrows of the category being considered.
The exact definition is the following:
Definition: Let us give two objects A and B (of a category)

A •   • B

A **product** of A and B is an object denoted by A×B, along with two arrows $p_A: A \times B \rightarrow A$ and $p_B: A \times B \rightarrow B$

A •   • B
p_A ↖ ↗ p_B
A×B

such that for every other object C (of the category) along

with two arrows f: C → A and g: C → B

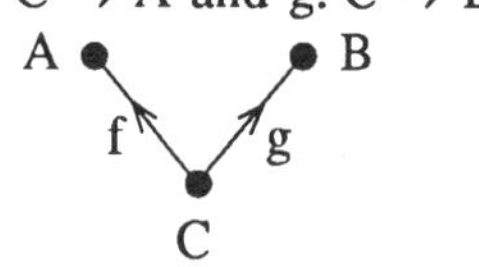

there exists a unique arrow α: C → A×B such that the following diagram *commutes*: (i.e., $\alpha.p_A$=f and $\alpha.p_B$=g)

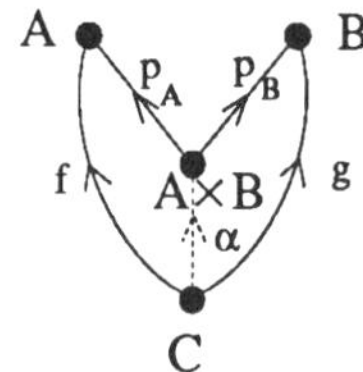

The **properties** of products are dual to those of coproducts. So, I will only remember the most important ones: up to isomorphism, the product is an operation satisfying the following properties: (i) Associativity, (ii) Commutativity, (iii) Every terminal object is neutral, (iv) Idempotent if the category is a preorder.
The reader can verify that, in the category ($\wp\Omega,\supseteq$), the product of A and B is A∪B (together with the inclusions A∪B ⊇ A and A∪B ⊇ B). The preceding example easily extends to any lattice in which the product of the elements a and b is the *infimum* or *greatest lower bound* of a and b.
Definition: Given two objects A and B of a category, the **disjunction** A∨B is the product of A and B in the logic of the category.
More informally, with the vocabulary of "beliefs", the definition of disjunction is the following: the disjunction of two belief states A and B is the *most* (or more precisely: *any* most) updated belief state, such that A and B are updated states of it. '*Most*' means that the disjunction of A and B is an updated state of any state which can be updated into A and B. The disjunction is thus commutative, associative, and idempotent. Moreover, in the logic of Dempster's unnormalized category of beliefs the total contradiction is neutral for the disjunction, which fits well with the idea that the total contradiction contains all informations.

6 SEPARABLE BELIEF FUNCTIONS

In this last section I consider only Dempster's unnormalized category and restrict ourselves to the subcategory whose objects and arrows are separable belief functions. Let us first recall some **definitions** (see [Shafer 76]). The subset A of Ω is a *focal element* of the belief function bel_m: $\wp\Omega \to [0,1]$ iff m(A)>0. The belief function bel_m: $\wp\Omega \to [0,1]$ is a *simple support function* iff bel_m has at most one focal element distinct from Ω. The mass distribution of any simple support function bel_m *focused* on X ≠ Ω will be denoted by m_X. More explicitly, the mass distribution m_X such that $m_X(X) = \alpha$ will be denoted by X^α. The mass allocated to Ω by X^α is thus 1-α. The vacuous belief function $1_{\{\Omega\}}$ will be represented by any expression of the from X^0 where X is not Ω. Note that $\emptyset^\alpha$ denotes a belief function focused on the empty set. A *separable belief function* (called *separable support function* by G. Shafer) is any belief function bel_m such that:

$$m = \bigotimes_{X\in\wp\Omega-\{\Omega\}} m_X$$

Using the just introduced notation we can write:

$$m = \bigotimes_{X\in\wp\Omega-\{\Omega\}} X^{\alpha_X}$$

where $\alpha_X = m_X(X)$
Dempster's rule of combination gets an interesting form for separable belief functions:
Theorem: Given two separable belief functions,

$$\bigotimes_{X\in\wp\Omega-\{\Omega\}} X^{\alpha_X} \text{ and } \bigotimes_{Y\in\wp\Omega-\{\Omega\}} Y^{\beta_Y}$$

then

$$\Big(\bigotimes_{X\in\wp\Omega-\{\Omega\}} X^{\alpha_X}\Big) \otimes \Big(\bigotimes_{Y\in\wp\Omega-\{\Omega\}} Y^{\beta_Y}\Big) = \bigotimes_{X\in\wp\Omega-\{\Omega\}} X^{\alpha_X+\beta_X-\alpha_X.\beta_X}$$

The next theorem states that the conjunction (∧) and disjunction (∨) of two beliefs in the category of separable belief functions always exist and are given by the following formulas:
Theorem[7]: Given two separable belief functions,

$$\bigotimes_{X\in\wp\Omega-\{\Omega\}} X^{\alpha_X} \text{ and } \bigotimes_{Y\in\wp\Omega-\{\Omega\}} Y^{\beta_Y}$$

then

$$\Big(\bigotimes_{X\in\wp\Omega-\{\Omega\}} X^{\alpha_X}\Big) \wedge \Big(\bigotimes_{Y\in\wp\Omega-\{\Omega\}} Y^{\beta_Y}\Big) = \bigotimes_{X\in\wp\Omega-\{\Omega\}} X^{\max(\alpha_X,\beta_X)}$$

$$\Big(\bigotimes_{X\in\wp\Omega-\{\Omega\}} X^{\alpha_X}\Big) \vee \Big(\bigotimes_{Y\in\wp\Omega-\{\Omega\}} Y^{\beta_Y}\Big) = \bigotimes_{X\in\wp\Omega-\{\Omega\}} X^{\min(\alpha_X,\beta_X)}$$

It is interesting to note that the operations induced on the "exponents" by Dempster's rule of combination and the conjunction are T-conorms[8], and the operation induced by the disjunction is a T-norm[9]. The link between T-(co)norms and fuzzy logical connectives has been recognized since a long time ago. This was first recognized by U. Höhle in the late seventies. It can be shown very easily that T-(co)norms is a weakened form of the notion of categorial (co)products in the category [0,1],≤.

7 CONCLUSIONS

The key point expressed in the present paper is that Dempster's rule of combination is less a conjunctive rule

[7] These two formulas - without categorial content - have been brought to my attention by Philippe Smets.

[8] A T-conorm is an operation ∗: [0,1]×[0,1] → [0,1] which is commutative, associative, for which 0 is neutral, monotonic increasing (for the usual order relation ≤ on [0,1] and the product order on [0,1]×[0,1]), and 1∗1=1.

[9] A T-norm is an operation ∗: [0,1]×[0,1] → [0,1] which is commutative, associative, for which 1 is neutral, monotonic increasing, and 0∗0=0.

(of belief states) than the composition rule of a category (composition of evidence). Such a point of view has lead to conjunction and a disjunction for belief functions. Explicit formulas have been given for separable belief functions.

The former key point may also explain a difference between fuzzy logic and Dempster-Shafer theory as follows. In fuzzy logic there exist numerous "combination rules" modelling the logical connectives. People are trying to unify them all by finding a category out of which all these connectives can emerge naturally. Whereas in Dempster-Shafer theory there exists only one combination rule, and people are trying to discover a logic (cf. e.g. [Dubois, Prade 86]) compatible with the combination rule.

Acknowledgments

Philippe Smets once suggested to me to find out an *'idempotent Dempster's rule of combination'* to be used in non-independent situations. The ideas contained in the present paper have grown out of that suggestion for which I am very grateful. I thank Bruno Marchal for his constant encouragement to use a categorial viewpoint and for uncountable many stimulating discussions. I gratefully acknowledge Yen-Teh Hsia and Alessandro Saffiotti for countable many and very fruitful discussions. I am deeply greatful to Yen-Teh for a very careful reading of the paper and for his many comments about it.

References

Domotor Z. (1980), *Probability Kinematics and Representation of Belief Change*. Philosophy of Science 47, 384-403.

Dubois D., Prade H. (1986), *A Set-Theoretic View of Belief Functions - Logical Operations and Approximation by Fuzzy Sets*. Int. J. Gen. Systems 12, 193-226.

Dubois D., Prade H. (1987a), *Properties of Measures of Information in Evidence and Possibility Theories*. Fuzzy Sets and Systems 24, 161-182.

Dubois D., Prade H. (1987b), *The Principle of Minimum Specificity as a Basis for Evidential Reasoning*. In: *Uncertainty in Knowledge-Based Systems* (B. Bouchon, R. R. Yager, editors), LNCS 286, 75-84, Springer-Verlag.

Dubois D., Prade H. (1990), *Consonant Approximations of Belief Functions*. IJAR, 4, 419-449.

Fagin R. , Halpern J.Y., (1989), *Uncertainty, Belief, and Probability*. Proc. of IJCAI-87, 1161-1167.

Gärdenfors P. (1988), *Knowledge in Flux - Modelling the Dynamics of Epistemic States*. MIT Press.

Garvey T.D., Lowrance J.D., Fischler M.A. (1981), *An Inference Technique for Integrating Knowledge from Disparate Sources*. Proc. of IJCAI-81, 319-325.

Giry M. (1982), *A Categorical Approach to Probability Theory*. In: *Categorical Aspects of Topology and Analysis*, Lecture Notes in Mathematics 915, 68-85, Springer-Verlag.

Goguen J.A. (1969), *Categories of V-sets*. Bull. Am. Math. Soc. 75, 622-624.

Goldblatt R. (1984), *Topoi, the Categorial Analysis of Logic* (revised edition). Studies in Logic and the Foundations of Mathematics 98, North Holland.

Goodman I.R., Nguyen H.T. (1985), *Uncertainty Models for Knowledge-Based Systems – A Unified Approach to the Measurement of Uncertainty*. North-Holland.

Halpern J.Y., Fagin R. (1990), *Two Views of Belief: Belief as Generalized Probabilities and Belief as Evidence*. Proc. AAAI-90, 112-119. Full paper is: IBM Research Report RJ 7221.

Hau H.Y., Kashyap R.L. (1990), *Belief Combination and Propagation in a Lattice-Structured Inference Network*. IEEE Trans. on Systems, Man, and Cybernetics 20 (1), 45-58.

Horvitz E., Heckerman D. (1986), *The Inconsistent Use of Measures of Certainty in Artificial Intelligence Research*. In: *Uncertainty in Artificial Intelligence* (Kanal L.N., Lemmer J.F., editors) 137-151, Elsevier Science Publishers.

Hsia Y.-T. (1990), *The Belief Calculus and Uncertain Reasoning*. Proc. of AAAI-90, 120-125.

Hsia Y.-T. (1991), *Characterizing Belief with Minimum Commitment*. To appear in the Proc. of IJCAI-91.

Hummel R.A., Manevitz L.M. (1987), *Combining Bodies of Dependant Information*, Proc. of IJCAI-87, 1015-1017.

Kruse R., Schwecke E. (1991), *Specialization - A new Concept for Uncertainty Handling with Belief Functions*. To appear in International Journal of General Systems.

Ling X., Rudd W.G. (1989a), *Combining Dependent Evidence Using the Shafer Theory of Evidence*. Proc. of the IASTED International Symposium, Expert Systems - Theory and Application, Zürich, June 1989, p. 176.

Ling X., Rudd W.G. (1989b), *Combining Opinions from Several Experts*. Applied Artificial Intelligence 3,439-452.

Mac Lane S. (1971), *Categories for the Working Mathematician*. Springer-Verlag.

Marti-Oliet N., Meseguer J. (1989), *From Petri Nets to Linear Logic*. In: *Category Theory and Computer Science* (D.H. Pitt, D.E. Rydeheard, P. Dybjer, A.M. Pitts and A. Poigné, editors), LNCS 389, 313-337, Springer-Verlag.

Negoita C.V. (1985), *Expert Systems and Fuzzy Systems*. Benjamin/Cummings Publishing Company.

Pearl J. (1988), *Probabilistic Reasoning in Intelligent Systems: Network of Plausible Inference*. Morgan Kaufman.

Pearl J. (1990), *Reasoning with Belief Functions: an Analysis of Compatibility*. IJAR, 4, 363-389.

Provan G.M. (1990), *A Logic-Based Analysis of Dempster-Shafer Theory*. IJAR, 4, 451-495.

Shafer G. (1976), *A Mathematical Theory of Evidence*. Princeton University Press.

Smets P. (1986), *Combining non distinct Evidences*. Proceedings NAFIP86 New Orleans, 544-548.

Smets P. (1988), *Belief Functions*. In: *Non Standard Logics for Automated Reasoning*. (Smets P., Mamdani A., Dubois D. and Prade H., editors), 253-286, Academic Press.

Teller P. (1973), *Conditionalization and Observation*. Synthese 26, 218-258.

Williams P.M. (1978), *On a New Theory of Epistemic Probability*. The British J. for the Philosophy of Science 29, 357-387.

Wong S.K.M., Lingras P. (1990), *Combination of Evidence Using the Principle of Minimum Information Gain*. Proc. of the Sixth Conference on Uncertainty in AI, 450-459, Cambridge, Mass.

Yager R. (1986), *The Entailment Principle for Dempster-Shafer Granules*. Intern. J. of Intell. Syst. 1 (4), 247-262.

Reasoning with Mass Distributions

Rudolf Kruse **Detlef Nauck** **Frank Klawonn**
Dept. of Computer Science
Technical University of Braunschweig
Bueltenweg 74 - 75
W-3300 Braunschweig, Germany

Abstract

The concept of movable evidence masses that flow from supersets to subsets as specified by experts represents a suitable framework for reasoning under uncertainty. The mass flow is controlled by specialization matrices. New evidence is integrated into the frame of discernment by conditioning or revision (Dempster's rule of conditioning), for which special specialization matrices exist. Even some aspects of non-monotonic reasoning can be represented by certain specialization matrices.

1 INTRODUCTION

In this paper we present a suitable theoretical model for handling uncertainty, which is an important problem in the range of knowledge based systems. Uncertainty corresponds to the valuation of some datum, reflecting the faith or doubt in the respective source. So we have to deal with statements being not just simply true or false but with a validity which is a matter of degree. This is caused by the fact that the actual state of the world is not completely determined and we have to rely on a human experts subjective preferences among different possibilities.

Throughout this paper we will restrict ourselves to the treatment of subjective valuations of evidence which requires the use of belief functions measuring the credibility of information although our concept of specialization is very general and can be applied to probabilities as well as possibility measures.

Let Ω, a finite nonempty set be our *frame of discernment.* We assume Ω to be a product space $\Omega^M \triangleq \Omega_1 \times ... \times \Omega_m$ with m characteristics $X^{(1)} \in \Omega_1, ..., X^{(m)} \in \Omega_m$ where Ω_i $(i = 1, ..., m)$ is a finite nonempty set. The partial knowledge is encoded through evidence masses attached to subsets of Ω. Specialization matrices quantify the flow of masses, the concept we prefer to Dempster's rule of conditioning (Shafer 1976).

A mass distribution is considered here as the condensed representation of a (possibly unknown) random set, for other semantics see (Kruse, Schwecke and Heinsohn 1991).

Section 2 provides an overview about mass distributions and belief functions. In section 3 we present our main concept: the flow of evidence masses given by a specialization matrix (Kruse and Schwecke 1990). In section 4 we consider specialization matrices which can be applied to conditioning and revision, and discuss certain aspects of non-monotonic reasoning.

2 REPRESENTING KNOWLEDGE WITH MASS DISTRIBUTIONS

Belief functions aim to model a human decision maker's subjective valuation of evidence. For this purpose we consider an inaccessible, finite probability space Θ of sensors or experts and a sample space Ω containing the possible events. The sensors or experts choose subsets of Ω which they believe to contain the actual state of the world. This means we consider multivalued mappings defined on a probability space, here called random sets (Matheron 1975). With respect to the probability distribution on the sensor space Θ one unit of ''belief'' which we conceive as movable ''evidence mass'' is distributed among the elements of Ω, attributing a greater amount to the more likely elements (the elements chosen by the most or most reliable sensors or experts). That means a *mass distribution m* (basic probability assignment (Shafer 1976)) is specified, which is a mapping from 2^{Ω} to the unit intervall.

Definition 1: *Each function* $m : 2^{\Omega} \rightarrow [0, 1]$ *is called a mass distribution, whenever*

(i) $m(\emptyset) = 0$,

$$(ii) \quad \sum_{A:A \subseteq \Omega} m(A) = 1$$

hold.

The mass $m(A)$ is understood to be the measure of "belief" that is committed exactly to A and corresponds to the support given to A but not to any strict subset of A. Those sets A with $m(A) > 0$ are called *focal elements.* To obtain the *total* measure of belief committed to some set A, we have to sum up the quantities $m(B)$ for all $B \subseteq A$.

Definition 2: *If m is a mass distribution on* 2^Ω, *then the function* $\mathrm{Bel}_m : 2^\Omega \to [0, 1]$,

$$\mathrm{Bel}_m(A) \stackrel{d}{=} \sum_{B:B \subseteq A} m(B),$$

is called the belief function induced by m.

$\mathrm{Bel}_m(A)$ represents the degree to which the actual evidence supports A, i.e. it measures the *credibility* of A. We are also able to calculate the degree to which the evidence fails to refute A, i.e. the degree to which A remains *plausible:*

$$\mathrm{PL}_m(A) \stackrel{d}{=} 1 - \mathrm{Bel}_m(\bar{A})$$

$$= 1 - \sum_{B:B \subseteq \bar{A}} m(B) = \sum_{B:A \cap B \neq \emptyset} m(B).$$

We have

$$\mathrm{Bel}_m(A) \leq \mathrm{Pl}_m(A), \text{ and}$$

$$\mathrm{Bel}_m(A) + \mathrm{Bel}_m(\bar{A}) \leq 1$$

for all $A \subseteq \Omega$.

To measure the evidence mass that can freely move to any element or subset of A we use the concept of *commonality functions.* Let m be a mass distribution defined on 2^Ω. The function

$$Q_m(A) \stackrel{d}{=} \sum_{B:A \subseteq B} m(B)$$

measures the evidence mass which is attached to supersets of A and can move to A or to any of its subsets. Obviously $Q_m(A) = 0$ indicates that there is no mass "above" A, i.e. A cannot receive more evidence mass from its supersets.

To represent *total ignorance* about the domain under consideration, we set $m(\Omega) = 1$ and $m(A) = 0$ for all $A \neq \Omega$ and we obtain $\mathrm{Bel}_m(\Omega) = 1$ and $\mathrm{Bel}_m(A) = 0$ for all $A \neq \Omega$. This belief function is called the *vacuous belief function.* On the other hand setting $m(\{x_i\}) = p_i$, $x_i \in \Omega = \{x_1,..., x_n\}$ and $m(A) = 0$ for all non-elementary sets A leads to a *Bayesian belief function* or, in terms of the probability theory, a discrete probability distribution. We can imagine "belief" as partially movable evidence mass, where $m(A)$ is that amount of mass which can, in the light of new information, move to every subset of A but not to sets with elements outside of A.

The concepts of *conditioning* and *revision* are based on this idea. When we obtain the information that "the truth" is within some set E with certainty, all elements of $\bar{E}$ become impossible. The two concepts differ in their treatments of sets which have a nonempty intersection with E. Conditioning a mass distribution m defined on Ω with respect to a set $E \subseteq \Omega$ means to neglect the evidence mass which is inconsistent with the new information. All masses not attached to subsets of E are omitted and the remaining masses are normalized.

Definition 3: *Let m be a mass distribution on* 2^Ω *and E be a subset of* Ω *with* $\mathrm{Bel}_m(E) > 0$. *The mass distribution*

$$m(.|E): 2^\Omega \to [0, 1]; \quad m(A|E) \stackrel{d}{=} \begin{cases} \dfrac{m(A)}{\mathrm{Bel}_m(E)} & \text{if } A \subseteq E \\ 0 & \text{otherwise} \end{cases}$$

is called conditional[1] *mass distribution.*

The concept of revision is directly based on the idea of partially movable evidence mass. All masses attached to subsets A of Ω float to the sets $A \cap E$ after revision with respect to the set E.

Definition 4: *Let m be a mass distribution on* 2^Ω *and E be a subset of* Ω *with* $\mathrm{Bel}_m(E) > 0$. *The mass distribution*

$$m_E : 2^\Omega \to [0, 1];$$

$$m_E(A) \stackrel{d}{=} \begin{cases} \dfrac{\sum_{D:D \cap E = A} m(D)}{\mathrm{Pl}_m(E)} & \text{if } A \neq \emptyset \\ 0 & \text{otherwise} \end{cases}$$

is called revised[2] *mass distribution.*

Contrary to conditioning revision does not omit the evidence mass attached to sets lying just partially in E. Revising m on E yields the belief function

$$\mathrm{Bel}_{m_E}(A) = \frac{\mathrm{Bel}_m(A \cup \bar{B}) - \mathrm{Bel}_m(\bar{B})}{1 - \mathrm{Bel}_m(\bar{B})}, \quad A \subseteq \Omega$$

and the plausibility function

$$\mathrm{Pl}_{m_E}(A) = \frac{\mathrm{Pl}_m(A \cap B)}{\mathrm{Pl}_m(B)}, \quad A \subseteq \Omega.$$

Remembering our idea of experts or sensors choosing

[1] This concept is also called *strong conditioning* (Dubois and Prade 1986a) or *geometric conditioning.*

[2] This concept is also know as Dempster's rule of conditioning (Shafer 1976).

subsets of Ω the differences between the two concepts conditioning and revision can be made clear quite easily. Conditioning is a very strict treatment of experts whose valuations are inconsistent with the new information E. These experts are now considered as totally unreliable and the evidence mass distributed due to their statements has to be redistributed under the subsets $A \subseteq E$ chosen by the reliable experts.

Revision induces a more optimistic treatment of the experts. The idea is that the valuations which are only partially inconsistent with the new information ($A \not\subseteq E$ but $A \cap E \neq \emptyset$) are now treated as if the expert meant $A \cap E$ and not A. The expert just was not able to express this situation because he had not enough information. So he is still considered to be reliable and the evidence mass attached to A flows completely to the intersection with E. Only those experts whose valuations are totally inconsistent with E are treated as in the case of conditioning.

3 THE CONCEPT OF SPECIALIZATION

In order to compare different frames of discernment we introduce the notion of a refinement (Shafer 1976).

Definition 5: *A set Ω' is a refinement of Ω if there is a mapping $\hat{\Pi} : 2^{\Omega} \to 2^{\Omega'}$ such that*

$$(i) \quad \hat{\Pi}(\{x\}) \neq \emptyset \text{ for all } x \in \Omega,$$

$$(ii) \quad \hat{\Pi}(\{x\}) \cap \hat{\Pi}(\{x'\}) = \emptyset, \text{ if } x \neq x',$$

$$(iii) \quad \bigcup \left\{ \hat{\Pi}(\{x\}) \mid x \in \Omega \right\} = \Omega' \text{ and}$$

$$(iv) \quad \hat{\Pi}(A) = \bigcup \left\{ \hat{\Pi}(\{x\}) \mid x \in A \right\}.$$

$\hat{\Pi}$ is called a refinement mapping. If such a mapping exists, the sets Ω and Ω' are compatible, where the refined space Ω' is able to carry more information than its quotient space Ω. In order to decide for each $\omega \in \Omega$ whether information concerning some set $A' \subseteq \Omega'$ may be of relevance for the valuation of ω or not we define the mapping Π.

Definition 6: *Let Ω' be a refinement of Ω where $\hat{\Pi} : 2^{\Omega} \to 2^{\Omega'}$ is the respective refinement mapping. The mapping*

$$\Pi : 2^{\Omega'} \to 2^{\Omega}, \quad \Pi(A') \stackrel{d}{=} \left\{ \omega \in \Omega \mid \hat{\Pi}(\{\omega\}) \cap A' \neq \emptyset \right\}$$

is called the outer reduction induced by $\hat{\Pi}$.

$\Pi(A')$ contains those $\omega \in \Omega$ which have one or more elements $\omega' \in \hat{\Pi}(\{\omega\})$ within A'. Note that Π essentially is a projection that attaches to each element $\omega' \in \Omega$ that element ω with $\omega' \in \hat{\Pi}(\{\omega\})$. The projection of a mass distribution m' defined on $2^{\Omega'}$ can be obtained by

$$\Pi(m') : 2^{\Omega} \to [0,1]; \quad \Pi(m')(A) \stackrel{d}{=} \sum_{\substack{A' \subseteq \Omega': \\ \Pi(A') = A}} m'(A').$$

If there is a mass distribution m' defined on $2^{\Omega'}$ and a projection $\Pi(m')$ of m' on 2^{Ω}, then m' is a refinement of $\Pi(m')$. The formulation of a mass distribution m on Ω in terms of the refined space Ω' is defined by

$$\hat{\Pi}(m) : 2^{\Omega'} \to [0,1];$$

$$\hat{\Pi}(m)(A') \stackrel{d}{=} \begin{cases} m(A), & \text{if } A' = \hat{\Pi}(A), \\ 0 & \text{otherwise} \end{cases}$$

and is denoted as the *vacuous extension* of m. From the definition it is obvious, that each vacuous extension of a mass distribution is its refinement. In contrast to the projection which generally means a loss of information, the vacuous extension preserves the information borne by the original mass distribution.

The main issue of this chapter is to define the concept of specialization. The intuitive idea of a specialization is the projection of a revision.

Definition 7: *Let s, t be two mass distributions defined on 2^{Ω}. We call s a specialization of t ($s \sqsubset t$), if and only if there are two mass distributions s' and t' on a refinement Ω' of Ω where s' and t' are refinements of s and t, respectively, and if there is an event $E' \subseteq \Omega'$ such that*

$$s'(B') = t'_{E'}(B')$$

holds for each $B' \subseteq \Omega'$.

This definition tells us that we will get all specializations of a given mass distribution on Ω by considering all possible revisions in a refined space Ω'. Relating now the concept of specialization with Dempster's rule of combination we can see, that specialization is bound to the idea of *updating* and not to *aggregation*. Dempster's rule combines two mass distributions (basic probability assignments) which are defined on the same sample space but based on different bodies of evidence. This is a concept of aggregating different expert views.

The change from a mass distribution m to a specialization of m is a different concept, and it is due to an updating of the refinement of m in a refinement of the sample space Ω. We use revision as the updating rule which causes a change of data in the refined space. Those observations A of the experts which are not completely covered by the new evidence E are changed to become $A \cap E$ instead without loosing any evidence mass.

In addition to the definition above the following theorem gives two equivalent characterizations of the specialization relationship. The first one allows to check easily whether $s \sqsubset t$ is valid or not. The second one reflects our intuitive idea of floating evidence masses describing the flow of the mass $t(A)$ onto the subsets of A.

Theorem 1: *Let s, t be two mass distributions on* Ω. *The following three statements are equivalent:*

(i) $s \sqsubset t$,

(ii) $\forall A \subseteq \Omega : \big(Q_t(A) = 0 \Rightarrow Q_s(A) = 0 \big)$,

(iii) *For every* $A \subseteq \Omega$ *there are functions* $h_A : 2^\Omega \rightarrow [0,1]$ *such that*

a) $\sum_{B: B \subseteq \Omega} h_A(B) = t(A)$,

b) $h_A(B) \neq 0 \Rightarrow B \subseteq A$, *for all* $B \subseteq \Omega$, *and*

c) $s(B) = \dfrac{\sum_{A: A \subseteq \Omega} h_A(B)}{1 - \sum_{A: A \subseteq \Omega} h_A(\varnothing)}$ *for all* $\varnothing \neq B \subseteq \Omega$.

$h_A(B)$ specifies that amount of "belief" comitted to A that in the course of refining m to m' floats to the set B. Condition (iii.a) of Theorem 1 assures that no evidence mass is lost, condition (iii.b) requires that the masses flow only to subsets. Those masses floating to the empty set represent partial contradictions, thus have to be neglected and the remaining portions have to be normalized as pointed out in condition (iii.c).

The normalization in condition (iii.c) is due to our treatment of experts whose observations are totally inconsistent with the new evidence (see sect. 2). They are now considered to be unreliable and so the evidence mass bound to their observations has to be redistributed under the consistent observations. Note that we also use a *closed world assumption.* Smets (Smets 1988) considers an *open world assumption* and allows the empty set to bear evidence mass. In this case there is no normalization of the remaining masses because the evidence mass on the empty set is supposed to indicate the belief that the actual state of the world cannot be represented in the chosen frame of discernment. Our perception of the empty set is a different one. The evidence mass that flows to the empty set indicates from our point of view the inconsistency of expert observations at the beginning of the updating process and is not characterizing the current situation. So a normalization has to be made because we don't want to weaken the belief in the consistent observations. Using an open world assumption means that an expert cannot be wrong in spite of inconsistencies due to new information. From our point of view inconsistency arises because of errors made by some of the experts.

A similar concept to the specialization relation is the idea of a containment of "bodies of evidence" introduced in (Yager 1986). A body of evidence is a pair (F,m), where m is a mass distribution defined on Ω and F contains the focal elements of m. A definition of "strong inclusion" can be found in (Dubois and Prade 1986b):

$(F,m) \prec (F',m')$ *if and only if*

(i) $\forall B \in F, \exists A' \in F', B \subseteq A'$

(ii) $\forall A' \in F', \exists B \in F, B \subseteq A'$

(iii) *There exist* $W_{BA'} \in [0,1]$, *for all* B, A' *such that*

$W_{BA'} > 0 \Rightarrow B \subseteq A', \sum_{A',B} W_{BA'} = 1$, *and*

$\forall B \in F, m(B) = \sum_{A': B \subseteq A'} W_{BA'}$,

$\forall A' \in F', m'(A') = \sum_{B: B \subseteq A'} W_{BA'}$.

Specialization is more general than strong inclusion. We have $(F,m) \prec (F', m') \Rightarrow m \sqsubset m'$ but not vice versa. The $W_{BA'}$ are identical to the values $h_{A'}(B)$, but there is no normalization. From considering the definition above and our idea of floating evidence masses, it is obvious that in the case of strong inclusion there is no mass flow to the empty set and that no mass is lost ($\sum W_{BA'} = 1$), so a normalization is not necessary.

4 SPECIALIZATION MATRICES

In order to compute a specialization of a mass distribution m we characterize m as a vector and the respective specialization-relation by a matrix $V : 2^\Omega \times 2^\Omega \rightarrow [0, 1]$ and obtain the more specific mass distribution m' by "multiplying" the vector m with the matrix V. In the following we use square brackets to indicate that we conceive the respective functions as vectors or matrices.

Definition 8: *Let* Ω *be the frame of discernment.*

(i) A matrix $V : 2^\Omega \times 2^\Omega \rightarrow [0, 1]$ *is called a specialization matrix, if and only if*

(a) $\sum_{B: B \subseteq \Omega} V[A,B] = 1$ *for all* $A \subseteq \Omega$

(b) $B \not\subseteq A \Rightarrow V[A,B] = 0$.

(ii) Let V be a specialization matrix and let m be a mass distribution on 2^Ω. *If*

$$c \stackrel{d}{=} \sum_{A: A \subseteq \Omega} \sum_{B: B \neq \varnothing} m[A] \cdot V[A,B] > 0$$

then the mass distribution $m \odot V$ *is defined by*

$$(m \odot V)[B] \stackrel{d}{=} \begin{cases} \frac{1}{c} \cdot \sum_{A:A\subseteq\Omega} m[A] \cdot V[A,B] & \text{if } B \neq \emptyset \\ 0 & \text{otherwise} \end{cases}$$

for all $B \subseteq \Omega$.

In contrast to the mass flow functions h_A, $A \subseteq \Omega$, specialization matrices do not assign absolute portions but relative amounts of mass.

Theorem 2: *Let m and m' be two mass distributions defined on* 2^{Ω}. *We have*

$$m' \sqsubseteq m \Leftrightarrow \exists V : m' = m \odot V,$$

where V is a specialization matrix.

The processes of conditioning and revision, i.e. the change from a mass distribution m to the conditional mass distribution $m(\cdot|E)$ or to the revised mass distribution m_E respectively, are special cases of specialization and can therefore be described by special specialization matrices.

Recall that conditioning with respect to the set $E \subseteq \Omega$ means that those masses bound to sets $A \subseteq E$ remain where they are, while those bound to sets $A \not\subseteq E$ have to be neglected.

Definition 9: *Let* Ω *be the frame of discernment and let* $E \subseteq \Omega$ *be a non-empty set. The conditional matrix* $C(E) : 2^{\Omega} \times 2^{\Omega} \rightarrow [0, 1]$ *is defined by*

$$C(E)[A,B] \stackrel{d}{=} \begin{cases} 1 & \text{if } A \not\subseteq E \text{ and } B = \emptyset \\ 1 & \text{if } A \subseteq E \text{ and } B = A \\ 0 & \text{otherwise} \end{cases}$$

We obtain $m(\cdot|E) = m \odot C(E)$.

Revision with respect to the set E means that the masses attached to sets $A \neq \emptyset$ float to $A \cap E$. Masses attached to sets with $A \cap E = \emptyset$ have to be neglected since they represent (partial) contradictions of the information E and the mass distribution m.

Definition 10: *Let* Ω *be the frame of discernment and let* $E \subseteq \Omega$ *be a non-empty set. The revision matrix* $R(E)$: $2^{\Omega} \times 2^{\Omega} \rightarrow [0, 1]$ *is defined by*

$$R(E)[A,B] \stackrel{d}{=} \begin{cases} 1 & \text{if } B = A \cap E \\ 0 & \text{otherwise} \end{cases}$$

We obtain $m_E = m \odot R(E)$.

The use of specialization matrices leads to a new interesting concept. Some specialization matrix V represents a piece of "structural knowledge". Multiplying a mass distribution m with V means to split the evidence masses in the light of knowledge encoded by V. A rather strict requirement is that the "application" of V to a more specific mass distribution m' should yield a more specific result.

Definition 11: *Let* $V : 2^{\Omega} \times 2^{\Omega} \rightarrow [0, 1]$ *be a specialization matrix. V is called monotonic, if and only if*

$$s \sqsubseteq t \Rightarrow s \odot V \sqsubseteq t \odot V$$

holds for all mass distribution $s, t : 2^{\Omega} \rightarrow [0, 1]$.

The next theorem provides a simple possibility to check whether a given specialization matrix is monotonic or not. It relies on a test, if there is no such set A whose mass flow is completely "outrun" by one of its supersets mass flow.

Theorem 3: *Let* $V : 2^{\Omega} \times 2^{\Omega} \rightarrow [0, 1]$ *be a specialization matrix. V is monotonic, if and only if for all sets A,* $B \subseteq \Omega$ *with* $V[A,B] > 0$, *and for all* $C \supseteq A$ *there is a set* $D \supseteq B$ *with* $V[C,D] > 0$.

Theorem 4: *Let s,t be two mass distributions defined on* 2^{Ω} *and* $s \sqsubseteq t$. *Then there is always a specialization matrix* $V : 2^{\Omega} \times 2^{\Omega} \rightarrow [0, 1]$ *and V is monotonic, such that* $s = t \odot V$.

We want to show in the sequel that also aspects of non-monotonic reasoning can be handled with specialization matrices. From Theorem 3 it is clear that a specialization matrix V is *non-monotonic,* if there exist sets $B \subseteq A \subseteq C$ such that there is a mass flow from A to B and no mass flow from C to supersets of B.

First we want to compare non-monotonic specialization matrices with Yager's non-monotonic compatibility relations (Yager 1988). Yager defines a (type II) compatibility relation on two sets X and Y as a relation R on $2^{X'} \times Y$ such that for each $T \in 2^{X'}$ there exists at least one $y \in Y$ such that $(T,y) \in R$, where $2^{X'}$ is the power set of X minus the empty set. $R(T,y)$ implies that (x,y), for all $x \in T$, are possible states of the world.

Let $W = \{y| R(T,y)\}$ be the subset of Y that contains the $y \in Y$ which are related to any $x \in T$. W is called the "associated set" in Y of T, denoted $T \rightarrow W$. A compatibility relation R is called "irregular" if there exists a triple $T_1 \rightarrow W_1$, $T_2 \rightarrow W_2$ and $T_3 \rightarrow W_3$ with $T_3 = T_1 \cup T_2$ such that W_3 is strictly contained in $W_1 \cup W_2$, $W_3 \subset W_1 \cup W_2$. Yager has proven that every irregular (type II) compatibility relation is *non-montonic.* That means if we have two mass distributions s, t and we have $s \prec t$ (strong inclusion) this does not imply $s \circ R \prec t \circ R$.

Because the concept of specialization matrices is more general than compatibility relations, a non-monotonic compatibility relation R can be easily expressed with a non-monotonic specialization matrix. Let S be a subset of $X \times Y$, let $D_S = \{x \mid \exists\, y, (x,y) \in S, R(x,y)\}$, and let W_{D_S} be the associated set of D_S. A (type II) compatibility relation R can be expressed with a specialization matrix V_R: $2^{X\times Y} \times 2^{X\times Y}$ with

$$V_R[S,S'] = \begin{cases} 1, \text{ if } S' = S \cap \{D_S \times W_{D_S}\} \\ 0, \text{ otherwise} \end{cases}$$

If the relation R is non-monotonic, the same is true for the specialization matrix V_R. If we express any (type II) compatibility relation R with a specialization matrix V_R, and V_R is non-monotonic, the same holds for R.

Now let us take a look at the well known example of the bird Tweety who is not able to fly because he is a penguin. Let $\Omega = \Omega_1 \times \Omega_2$ be our frame of discernemt where Ω_1 = {*birds, fish*} and Ω_2 = {*fly, not fly*}. Now the rule "All birds fly" can be expressed by a specialization matrix V with

$$V[A,B] \overset{d}{=} \begin{cases} 1 & \text{if } B = A - \{(\text{birds, not fly})\} \\ 0 & \text{otherwise} \end{cases}$$

The rule "Penguins don't fly" can only be represented in a refined space, e.g. $\Omega' = \Omega_1' \times \Omega_2$, where Ω_1' = {*eagles, penguins, fish*}. In our refined space the two (partially contradicting) rules "All birds fly" and "Penguins don't fly" are expressed by the following specialization matrix V'.

$$V'[A,B] \overset{d}{=} \begin{cases} 1 & \text{if } A \supseteq \{\text{eagles, penguins}\} \times \{\text{not fly}\} \\ & := H \text{ and } B = A - H, \\ 1 & \text{if } (\text{penguins, fly}) \in A \text{ and } B \\ & = A - \{(\text{penguins,fly})\}, \\ 1 & \text{if } A \not\supseteq H \text{ and } (\text{penguins, fly}) \notin A, \\ 0 & \text{otherwise} \end{cases}$$

The two rules force the mass attached to the set C = {*eagles, penguins*} × {*fly, not fly*} to float to the set D = {*eagles, penguins*} × {*fly*} and the masses attached to A = {*penguins*} × {*fly, not fly*} to B = {*penguin*} × {*not fly*}. We have $C \supseteq A$ but $D \not\supseteq B$. That means the specialization matrix V' is non-monotonic.

5 CONCLUSIONS

With the calculus of mass distributions we presented a suitable theoretical tool for reasoning under uncertainty. We showed that the flow of evidence masses can be conveniently handled by specialization matrices. For the concepts of conditioning and revision (Dempster's rule of conditioning) there exist special specialization matrices. We also demonstrated that certain aspects of non-monotonic reasoning, especially partially contradicting statements can be expressed by non-monotonic specialization matrices. In cooperation with Dornier GmbH the method of reasoning with mass distributions was implemented on a TI-Explorer under KEE.

References

D. Dubois, H. Prade (1986a). 'On the Unicity of Dempster's Rule of Combination'. *Int. J. Intelligent Systems,* 1, 133-142.

D. Dubois, H. Prade (1986b). 'A Set Theoretic View of Belief Functions'. *Int. J. General Systems,* 12, 193-226.

F. Klawonn, R. Kruse, E. Schwecke (1990). 'Belief Functions and Non-monotonic Reasoning'. *Proc. of the 1st DRUMS Workshop on Non-monotonic Reasoning, Marseille, February 1990.*

R. Kruse, E. Schwecke (1990). 'Specialization - A New Concept for Uncertainty Handling with Belief Functions', to appear in: *Int. J. General Systems.*

R. Kruse, E. Schwecke, J. Heinsohn (1991). *Uncertainty Handling in Knowledge Based Systems: Numerical Methods,* Series Artificial Intelligence, Springer, Heidelberg.

G. Matheron (1975). *Random Sets and Integral Geometry,* Wiley, New York.

G. Shafer (1976). *A Mathematical Theory of Evidence,* Princeton University Press, Princeton.

P. Smets (1988). 'Belief Functions'. In P. Smets, E.H. Mamdani, D. Dubois, H. Prade, *Non-Standard Logics for Automated Reasoning,* Academic Press, London, 253-286.

R. R. Yager (1986). 'The entailment principle for Dempster-Shafer granules'. *Int. J. Intelligent Systems,* 1, 247-262.

R. R. Yager (1988). 'Non-monotonic Compatibility Relations in the Theory of Evidence'. *Int. J. Man-Machine Studies,* 29, 517-537.

A Logic of Graded Possibility and Certainty Coping with Partial Inconsistency

Jérôme Lang – Didier Dubois – Henri Prade
Institut de Recherche en Informatique de Toulouse (I.R.I.T.)
Université Paul Sabatier, 118 route de Narbonne
31062 Toulouse Cedex – France

ABSTRACT

A semantics is given to possibilistic logic, a logic that handles weighted classical logic formulae, and where weights are interpreted as lower bounds on degrees of certainty or possibility, in the sense of Zadeh's possibility theory. The proposed semantics is based on fuzzy sets of interpretations. It is tolerant to partial inconsistency. Satisfiability is extended from interpretations to fuzzy sets of interpretations, each fuzzy set representing a possibility distribution describing what is known about the state of the world. A possibilistic knowledge base is then viewed as a set of possibility distributions that satisfy it. The refutation method of automated deduction in possibilistic logic, based on previously introduced generalized resolution principle is proved to be sound and complete with respect to the proposed semantics, including the case of partial inconsistency.

1 INTRODUCTION

Possibilistic logic is a logic of uncertainty tailored for reasoning under incomplete information. At the syntactic level, it handles formulas of propositional or first-order-logic to which lower bounds of degrees of necessity (i.e. certainty) or possibility are attached. The degrees of possibility follows the rules of possibility theory (Zadeh, 1978 ; Dubois and Prade, 1988) and the degrees of necessity are defined from degrees of possibility through a classical duality relationship. A possibilistic knowledge base can thus be viewed as a stratified (or layered) classical knowledge base, where some formulae are more certain, or more possible than others. Resolution rules have been derived in accordance with the axioms of possibility theory (Dubois and Prade, 1987, 1990a) and a refutation technique has been implemented for necessity-valued formulas (Dubois,Prade and Lang, 1987) further on extended to both possibility and necessity-valued formulas (Lang, 1991). The main ideas behind possibilistic logic are : i) the degree attached to a proof path in a possibilistic knowledge-base is the least degree attached to a formula in this proof path, and the degree attached to a consequence of a possibilistic knowledge base is the greatest degree attached to proof-paths yielding this consequence ; ii) when two antagonistic propositions p and ¬p can be derived, the one with the highest degree inhibits the other one. The latter point indicates that possibilistic logic can handle partial inconsistencies. Moreover possibilistic logic proposes a way of handling uncertainty based on the idea of ordering rather than counting, contrary to probabilistic logic.

This paper presents a semantics for possibilistic logic in a fairly general situation, i.e. possibility or necessity-valued clauses, and the presence of partial inconsistency, are allowed. It extends a previous semantics dedicated to necessity-valued propositional clauses only (Dubois et al., 1989). This semantics is based on an extension of the satisfiability notion from sets of interpretations to fuzzy sets of interpretations. The idea of a fuzzy set of interpretations is that some interpretations are preferred to others and enable non-trivial inferences that could not be made if interpretations were equally considered. In this sense, possibilistic logic belongs to the family of non-monotonic logics based on preferential models, whose general setting has been devised by Shoham (1988); see Dubois and Prade (1991) on this point. Possibility distributions are viewed here as a convenient way of encoding a preference relation by attaching a weight to each interpretation of a set of formulas. Possibilistic logic completely contrasts with Ruspini (1991)'s so-called "fuzzy logic" where the semantics relies on the idea of similarity rather than ordering. Ruspini's logic is one of graded indiscernibility between worlds (in the spirit of Pawlak (1982)'s rough sets) while possibilistic logic is a logic of preference between interpretations.

Possibilistic logic is closely related to Shackle (1961)'s degrees of potential surprize, and Spohn (1988)'s ordinal conditional functions. See Dubois and Prade (1990b) on this latter point. Possibility measures can also be viewed as consonant belief functions (Shafer, 1976). However, possibilistic logic is *not* a truth-functional many-valued logic and is not a logic of vagueness (as is fuzzy logic) because it primarily pertains to non-fuzzy propositions the truth of which is uncertain due to incomplete information.

In the next section, a language and a semantics are presented for possibilistic logic, a logic of necessity and possibility-valued (classical) formulas. A version of the semantics, in terms of a possibility distribution on a set of interpretations for the case of consistent knowledge bases is first presented, where consistency refers to the proper assignment of the possibility and necessity degrees (with respect to the axioms of possibility and necessity measures). A generalized semantics, where an extra-element representing the absurd interpretation is added to the referential of the possibility distribution, is then introduced in order to allow for inconsistencies. Section 3 describes an automated deduction procedure based on extended resolution and refutation. Completeness of the deduction procedure holds, with respect to the proposed semantics.

2 POSSIBILISTIC LOGIC : LANGUAGE AND SEMANTICS

2.1 LANGUAGE

A *possibilistic formula* is either a pair $(\varphi\ (N\ \alpha))$ where φ is a classical first-order formula and $\alpha \in (0,1]$, (α should be strictly positive) or a pair $(\varphi\ (\Pi\ \beta))$ where $\beta \in [0,1]$. $(\varphi\ (N\ \alpha))$ expresses that φ is certain at least to the degree α, i.e. $N(\varphi) \geq \alpha$, and $(\varphi\ (\Pi\ \beta))$ expresses that φ is possible at least to the degree β, i.e. $\Pi(\varphi) \geq \beta$, where Π and N are dual measures of possibility and necessity modelling our incomplete state of knowledge (Zadeh, 1978 ; Dubois and Prade, 1988). The right part of a possibilistic formula, i.e. $(N\ \alpha)$ or $(\Pi\ \beta)$, is called the *valuation* of the formula, and is denoted val(φ).

The basic axiom of a possibility measure Π is $\Pi(\varphi \vee \varphi') = \max(\Pi(\varphi),\Pi(\varphi'))$ (on a finite language $\mathcal{L}$ on which formulas are defined). Informally, $\Pi(\varphi) = 0$ means that φ is impossible while $\Pi(\varphi) = 1$ means that φ is consistent with current knowledge. Particularly $\Pi(\varphi) = 0$ when φ is a contradiction. The necessity measure N is defined as $N(\varphi) = 1 - \Pi(\neg\varphi)$, and is such that $N(\varphi \wedge \varphi') = \min(N(\varphi),N(\varphi'))$. $N(\varphi) = 1$ means that φ is sure ; for instance $N(\varphi) = 1$ when φ is a tautology. Since $\forall\ \varphi$, $N(\varphi \vee \neg\varphi) = 1$, we only have $N(\varphi \vee \varphi') \geq \max(N(\varphi),N(\varphi'))$; indeed, for $\varphi' = \neg\varphi$, we may have $N(\varphi) = N(\neg\varphi) = 0$ (i.e. $\Pi(\varphi) = \Pi(\neg\varphi) = 1$). It can be shown that $N(\varphi) \leq \Pi(\varphi)$, generally. More specifically, $\Pi(\varphi) = 1$ as soon as $N(\varphi) > 1$. This is due to the axioms that force $\Pi(\varphi \vee \neg\varphi) = 1 = \max(\Pi(\varphi),\Pi(\neg\varphi))$. When $\Pi(\varphi) = \Pi(\neg\varphi) = 1$, we capture a state of ignorance about φ. Hence since we use lower bounds on possibility or necessity measures, various cases of relative ignorance can be captured ranging from the case where we know that we do not know ($\Pi(\varphi) = \Pi(\neg\varphi) = 1$) to the case where we do not know if we know ($\Pi(\varphi) \geq 0$, $\Pi(\neg\varphi) \geq 0$). Let $\mathcal{V}$ be the set of all possible valuations of possibilistic formulas. Since $N(\varphi) > 0$ entails $\Pi(\varphi) = 1$, and the valuations act as lower bounds, $(\varphi\ (N\ \alpha))$ is stronger than $(\varphi\ (\Pi\ \beta))$ for any $\alpha > 0$, $\beta \geq 0$; this leads us to define the following ordering among valuations :

$$(N\ \alpha) \leq (N\ \beta) \text{ iff } \alpha \leq \beta\ ;\ (\Pi\ \alpha) \leq (\Pi\ \beta) \text{ iff } \alpha \leq \beta\ ;$$
$$(\Pi\ \alpha) \leq (N\ \beta)\ \forall\alpha, \forall\ \beta > 0.$$

Hence the maximal and minimal elements of $\mathcal{V}$ are respectively (N 1) (expressing that a formula is completely certain) and (Π 0) (corresponding to the strongest form of ignorance, since $\Pi(\varphi) \geq 0$ only). A *possibilistic knowledge base* is then defined as a finite set (a conjunction) of possibilistic formulae. $\mathcal{F}^*$ will denote the set of classical formulae obtained from a set of possibilistic formulae $\mathcal{F}$, by ignoring the weights. A possibilistic formula whose valuation is of the form $(N\ \alpha)$ (resp. $(\Pi\ \alpha)$) will be called a *necessity-valued* (resp. *possibility-valued) formula*. Let *LP1* (resp. *LP2*) denote the language consisting of only necessity-valued formulae (resp. where possibility-valued formulae are *also* allowed).

2.2 SEMANTICS UNDER CONSISTENCY

Let $\mathcal{L}$ be a classical language associated with the set $\mathcal{F}^*$ of classical formulae obtained from a set $\mathcal{F}$ of possibilistic formulae, and let Ω be the set of (classical) interpretations for $\mathcal{L}$. Let $\mathcal{L}'$ be the set of closed formulae of $\mathcal{L}$.

Then we define a *possibility distribution* π as a mapping from Ω to [0,1] such that $\exists\ \omega \in \Omega$, $\pi(\omega) = 1$ (*normalization*). This possibility distribution represents the description of an incomplete state of knowledge, such that $\pi(\omega) = 0$ means that ω is forbidden while $\pi(\omega') > \pi(\omega)$ means that ω' is an interpretation preferred to ω. The normalization constraint expresses the natural requirement that there should exist at least one fully possible interpretation in Ω with respect to a consistent (possibly incomplete) state of knowledge. The *possibility measure* Π, induced (in the sense of Zadeh (1978)) by the possibility distribution π is the function from $\mathcal{L}'$ to [0,1] defined by $\forall\ \varphi \in \mathcal{L}'$, $\Pi(\varphi) = \text{Sup}\{\pi(\omega), \omega \models \varphi\}$[1] where $\omega \models \varphi$ means "ω is a model of φ". The dual *necessity measure* N induced by π is defined by $\forall\ \varphi \in \mathcal{L}'$, $N(\varphi) = 1 - \Pi(\neg\varphi) = \text{Inf}\ \{1 - \pi(\omega), \omega \models \neg\varphi\}$[1]. Then, it can be seen that expressing constraints of the form $N(\varphi) \geq \alpha$ or $\Pi(\varphi) \geq \beta$ is equivalent to specify a set of possibility distributions over Ω which are compatible with the corresponding possibilistic formulae. A possibility distribution π on Ω is said to *satisfy* the possibilistic formula $(\varphi\ (N\ \alpha))$, iff $N(\varphi) \geq \alpha$, where N is the necessity measure induced by π. We shall then use the notation $\pi \models (\varphi\ (N\ \alpha))$. In the same manner, we write $\pi \models (\varphi\ (\Pi\ \beta))$ iff $\Pi(\varphi) \geq \beta$, where Π is the possibility measure induced by π. Then, let $\mathcal{F} = \{\Phi_i, i = 1...n\}$ be a set of possibilistic formulae $\Phi_i = (\varphi_i\ v_i)$ where $\varphi_i \in \mathcal{L}'$ and $v_i \in \mathcal{V}$; a possibility distribution π is said to satisfy $\mathcal{F}$, i.e. $\pi \models \mathcal{F}$, iff $\forall\ i = 1,...,n$, π satisfies Φ_i. Then, a possibilistic formula Φ is said to be a *logical consequence* of the set of possibilistic formulae $\mathcal{F}$ iff any possibility distribution satisfying $\mathcal{F}$ also satisfies Φ, i.e. $\forall\pi$, $(\pi \models \mathcal{F}) \Rightarrow (\pi \models \Phi)$.

<u>Example</u> : let $\mathcal{F} = \{(p\ (N\ 0.7)), (\neg p \vee q\ (\Pi\ 0.8))\}$.

---

[1] Sup { } and Inf { } denote the least upper bound and greatest lower bound respectively of the subset of real numbers defined between { }

$\pi \models \mathcal{F}$ iff $N(p) \geq 0.7$ and $\Pi(\neg p \vee q) \geq 0.8$
iff $Inf\{1 - \pi(\omega), \omega \models \neg p\} \geq 0.7$ and
$Sup\{\pi(\omega), \omega \models \neg p \vee q\} \geq 0.8$.

Let [p, q], [¬p, q], [p, ¬q] and [¬p, ¬q] be the 4 different interpretations for the propositional language generated by {p, q} (where [p, q] gives the value True to p and q, etc.). Then, it comes down to

$\pi \models \mathcal{F}$ iff $\pi([\neg p, q]) \leq 0.3$, $\pi([\neg p, \neg q]) \leq 0.3$,
$\pi([p, q]) \geq 0.8$, $\max(\pi([p, q]), \pi([p, \neg q])) = 1$.

Indeed $\Pi(\neg p) \leq 0.3$ and $\Pi(\neg p \vee q) \geq 0.8$
$\Leftrightarrow \max(\pi(\neg p \wedge q), \pi(\neg p \wedge \neg q)) \leq 0.3$,
$\max(\pi(p \wedge q), \pi(\neg p \wedge q), \pi(\neg p \wedge \neg q)) \geq 0.8$,
$\max(\pi(p \wedge q), \pi(\neg p \wedge q), \pi(p \wedge \neg q), \pi(\neg p \wedge \neg q)) = 1$
$\Leftrightarrow \pi(\neg p \wedge q) \leq 0.3$, $\pi(\neg p \wedge \neg q) \leq 0.3$,
$\pi(p \wedge q) \geq 0.8$, $\max(\pi(p \wedge q), \pi(p \wedge \neg q)) = 1$.

It is then obvious that $\mathcal{F} \models (q\ (\Pi\ 0.8))$. Indeed, any possibility distribution π satisfying $\mathcal{F}$ is such that $\pi([p, q]) \geq 0.8$, and thus verifies $\Pi(q) = \max(\pi([p, q]), \pi([\neg p, q])) \geq 0.8$; hence π satisfies $(q\ (\Pi\ 0.8))$. ■

It is worth noticing that *in LP1* there is an equivalence between the consistency of the classical set of formulae $\mathcal{F}^*$ and the existence of a greatest normalized possibility distribution π satisfying $\mathcal{F}$, as shown in (Dubois et al., 1989). Indeed if π is normalized it can be easily checked that $\forall \varphi$, $\min(N(\varphi), N(\neg\varphi)) = 0$ where N is defined from π ; in other words it is impossible that there exists φ such that both φ and $\neg\varphi$ have a strictly positive lower bound for their necessity degrees (i.e. that both φ and $\neg\varphi$ appear in the deductive closure of $\mathcal{F}^*$).

Our semantics is similar to Nilsson's (1986) probabilistic logic semantics. Indeed this author considers a set of probability distributions on the set of interpretations Ω, defining probability measures on the set of closed formulas $\mathcal{L}'$, which are compatible with bounds constraining the probability of formulae in the knowledge base. The notions of logical consequences are similar in both approaches.

2.3 EXTENDING THE SEMANTICS TO PARTIAL INCONSISTENCIES

Let us first take an example : let $\mathcal{G}$ = {(¬p ∨ r (N 0.6)), (¬q ∨ ¬r (N 0.9)), (p (N 0.8)), (q (N 0.3)}. It can be checked that $\pi \models \mathcal{G}$ iff

$\pi([p, q, r]) \leq 0.1$; $\pi([p, q, \neg r]) \leq 0.4$;
$\pi([p, \neg q, r]) \leq 0.7$; $\pi([p, \neg q, \neg r]) \leq 0.4$;
$\pi([\neg p, q, r]) \leq 0.1$; $\pi([\neg p, q, \neg r]) \leq 0.2$;
$\pi([\neg p, \neg q, r]) \leq 0.2$; $\pi([\neg p, \neg q, \neg r]) \leq 0.2$;
$Sup\{\pi(\omega), \omega \in \Omega\} = 1$.

This set of constraints being unsatisfiable (because of the normalization constraint), there is no possibility distribution over Ω satisfying $\mathcal{G}$, which comes down to say that $\mathcal{G}$ is inconsistent. As a consequence, any possibilistic formula is a logical consequence of $\mathcal{G}$.

However, it would not be fully satisfactory to define a logic which handles degrees of uncertainty without allowing for degrees of (partial) inconsistency. Indeed, if we consider the above example where we suppose that p, q and r respectively express "the hostages will be freed" (p) ; "Peter is going to be the victim of an affair" (q) ; "Peter will be elected" (r) respectively. Then the formulas contained in $\mathcal{F}$ express that it is moderately certain that if the hostages are freed then Peter will be elected, that it is almost certain that if Peter is victim of an affair then he will not be elected, that it is rather certain that the hostages are going to be freed and that it is weakly certain that Peter will be the victim of an affair. The inconsistency comes from the beliefs of the experts who gave the information stored in the knowledge base. However, the expert who gave the last formula was only weakly certain of what he said, so that the inconsistency should be relativized. Since the first three formula of $\mathcal{G}$ are strictly more certain than the last one, we would like our logic to behave as if the set of formulas were only partially inconsistent, its inconsistency degree being the valuation of the weakest formula involved in the contradiction ; then, the deduction of a formula with a valuation strictly greater than this inconsistency degree should still be permitted ; since this deduction would involve only a consistent part of the knowledge base made here of the most certain pieces of information in the example, we should still be able to deduce (r (N 0.6)) non-trivially; this is done in Section 3. However a conclusion deduced from a partially inconsistent knowledge base should be regarded as more brittle than what is derived from a consistent one.

We are now going to give a semantics which handles such partial inconsistencies. The problem with the first semantics is that according to the definition of possibility and necessity measures we have (if $\perp$ denotes the contradiction) : $\Pi(\perp) = Sup\{\pi(\omega), \omega \models \perp\} = Sup\ \emptyset = 0$ and $N(\perp) = Inf\{1 - \pi(\omega), \omega \models \neg\perp\} = 1 - Sup\{\pi(\omega), \omega \in \Omega\} = 0$. Hence the solution requires that non-zero values for $\Pi(\perp)$ and $N(\perp)$ be allowed.

The solution we propose consists in adding to the set of interpretations Ω an extra-element, noted $\omega_\perp$ in which any formula is "true", i.e. $\forall \varphi \in \mathcal{L}'$, $\omega_\perp \models \varphi$ which corresponds to the idea of an "absurd interpretation" discussed by Stalnaker (1968)[2] Let $\Omega_\perp = \Omega \cup \{\omega_\perp\}$. A possibility distribution on $\Omega_\perp$ is a mapping $\hat{\pi}$ from $\Omega_\perp$ to [0,1] such that $\exists\, \omega \in \Omega_\perp$, $\hat{\pi}(\omega) = 1$ (normalization over $\Omega_\perp$). Then we define two functions from $\mathcal{L}'$ to [0,1] induced by $\hat{\pi}$: $\hat{\Pi}(\varphi) = Sup\{\hat{\pi}(\omega), \omega \in \Omega_\perp, \omega \models \varphi\}$; $\hat{N}(\varphi) = Inf\{1 - \hat{\pi}(\omega), \omega \in \Omega_\perp, \omega \not\models \varphi\}$. Note that $\hat{N}(\varphi)$ does not take $\hat{\pi}(\omega_\perp)$ into account, while $\hat{\Pi}(\varphi)$ does ;

[2] The idea of adding an extra-element to the referential of a possibility distribution has been already used for dealing with the case of an attribute which does not apply to an item of a data base. However the extensions of the possibility and necessity measures which are used for the evaluations of queries in incomplete information databases differ from the extensions defined here ; see chapter 6 of Dubois and Prade (1988).

particularly $\hat{N}(\varphi) = \inf\{1 - \hat{\pi}(\omega), \omega \in \Omega, \omega \models \neg\varphi\}$, and $\hat{N}(\bot) = 1 - \sup\{\hat{\pi}(\omega), \omega \in \Omega\} \geq 0$; note also that $\omega \not\models \varphi$ is no longer equivalent to $\omega \models \neg\varphi$, since $\omega_\bot \models \varphi$ and $\omega_\bot \models \neg\varphi$.

As it can be easily seen, we have

$$\forall \varphi \in \mathcal{L}', \hat{\Pi}(\varphi) = \max[\hat{\Pi}(\bot), 1 - \hat{N}(\neg\varphi)]$$

Note that $\hat{\Pi}$ and $\hat{N}$ are not possibility and necessity measures with respect to Ω, but only with respect to $\Omega_\bot$.

We now give the inconsistency-tolerant semantics of possibilistic logic. Each possibilistic formula $(\varphi\ (\Pi\ \alpha))$ or $(\varphi\ (N\ \alpha))$, is now considered as meaning $\hat{\Pi}(\varphi) \geq \alpha$ (respectively $\hat{N}(\varphi) \geq \alpha$), i.e. we take into account the absurd interpretation in our understanding of expert statement. For instance, $(\varphi\ (\Pi\ \alpha))$ expresses that "it is possible at least to the degree α that either φ is true or we are in an absurd situation". This leads us to the following definitions :

- *satisfaction* : $\hat{\pi} \hat{\models} (\varphi\ (\Pi\ \alpha))$ iff $\hat{\Pi}(\varphi) \geq \alpha$; $\hat{\pi} \hat{\models} (\varphi\ (N\ \alpha))$ iff $\hat{N}(\varphi) \geq \alpha$, where $\hat{\Pi}$ and $\hat{N}$ are the extended possibility and necessity measures induced by $\hat{\pi}$; $\hat{\pi} \hat{\models} \mathcal{F}$ iff $\hat{\pi}$ satisfies all formulae of $\mathcal{F}$;
- *logical consequence* : $\mathcal{F} \hat{\models} \Phi$ iff $\forall \hat{\pi}$, $\hat{\pi} \hat{\models} \mathcal{F}$ implies $\hat{\pi} \hat{\models} \Phi$.

The inconsistency-tolerant semantics is more general than the first one we introduced. In the case of a consistent possibilistic knowledge base $\mathcal{F}$ (i.e., there exists a possibility distribution π over Ω satisfying $\mathcal{F}$ according to the first semantics), then the two logical consequence relations $\models$ and $\hat{\models}$ are equivalent. This is no longer true if $\mathcal{F}$ is inconsistent (this is the property we wished). For instance, let us consider again $\mathcal{G} = \{(\neg p \vee r\ (N\ 0.6)), (\neg q \vee \neg r\ (N\ 0.9)), (p\ (N\ 0.8)), (q\ (N\ 0.3)\}$ which is inconsistent according to the first semantics ; then, according to the inconsistency-tolerant semantics, $\mathcal{G}$ is consistent since we can find a possibility distribution on $\Omega_\bot$ satisfying $\mathcal{G}$. For example the possibility distribution, $\hat{\pi}_0$ defined by

$\hat{\pi}_0([p, q, r]) = 0.1$; $\hat{\pi}_0([p, q, \neg r]) = 0.4$;
$\hat{\pi}_0([p, \neg q, r]) = 0.7$; $\hat{\pi}_0([p, \neg q, \neg r]) = 0.4$;
$\hat{\pi}_0([\neg p, q, r]) = 0.1$; $\hat{\pi}_0([\neg p, q, \neg r]) = 0.2$;
$\hat{\pi}_0([\neg p, \neg q, r]) = 0.2$; $\hat{\pi}_0([\neg p, \neg q, \neg r]) = 0.2$;
$\hat{\pi}_0(\omega_\bot) = 1$,

satisfies $\mathcal{G}$. Moreover, since $\mathcal{G}$ is not inconsistent according to the inconsistency-tolerant semantics, any formula can no longer be derived from $\mathcal{G}$ contrary to what happened with the first semantics. For example we have $\mathcal{G} \hat{\models} (r\ (N\ 0.6))$ but we do not have $\mathcal{G} \hat{\models} (r\ (N\ 0.7))$; indeed $\hat{\pi}_0 \hat{\models} \mathcal{G}$ but we do not have $\hat{\pi}_0 \hat{\models} (r\ (N\ 0.7))$. Hence the new semantics is definitely more tolerant to inconsistencies than the former one. When a set of possibilistic formulae $\mathcal{F}$ is inconsistent in the sense of the first semantics but not in the sense of the second, then we shall say that $\mathcal{F}$ is *partially inconsistent*. As we are going to show it, we can distinguish between two different types of partial inconsistencies.

Let $\mathcal{F}$ be a set of possibilistic formulae ; considering the possibility distributions on $\Omega_\bot$ satisfying $\mathcal{F}$, three situations may occur :

(i) $\exists\ \hat{\pi} \hat{\models} \mathcal{F}$ such that $\hat{\pi}(\omega_\bot) = 0$: in this case, $\mathcal{F}$ is consistent in both semantics ; $\mathcal{F}$ is then said to be *completely consistent.*

(ii) $\forall\ \hat{\pi} \hat{\models} \mathcal{F}$, $\hat{\pi}(\omega_\bot) > 0$ but $\exists\ \hat{\pi} \hat{\models} \mathcal{F}$ such that $\mathrm{Sup}\{\hat{\pi}(\omega), \omega \neq \omega_\bot\} = 1$: then, for any $\hat{\pi}$ satisfying $\mathcal{F}$, we have $\hat{\Pi}(\bot) = \hat{\pi}(\omega_\bot) > 0$ and $\hat{N}(\bot) = 1 - \mathrm{Sup}\ \{\hat{\pi}(\omega), \omega \neq \omega_\bot\} = 0$. Thus $\mathcal{F}$ induces a "possible inconsistency" (contradiction being possible to a strictly positive degree). The minimal value of $\hat{\Pi}(\bot) = \hat{\pi}(\omega_\bot)$ among the possibility distributions $\hat{\pi}$ on $\Omega_\bot$ satisfying $\mathcal{F}$ gives the *inconsistency degree* of $\mathcal{F}$. Let $\alpha = \mathrm{Inf}\{\hat{\Pi}(\bot), \hat{\pi} \hat{\models} \mathcal{F}\}$; then $\mathrm{Incons}(\mathcal{F}) = (\Pi\ \alpha)$.

(iii) $\forall\ \hat{\pi} \hat{\models} \mathcal{F}$, $\mathrm{Sup}\{\hat{\pi}(\omega), \omega \neq \omega_\bot\} < 1$ (which entails that $\forall\ \hat{\pi} \hat{\models} \mathcal{F}$, $\hat{\Pi}(\omega_\bot) = 1$). In this case, for any $\hat{\pi}$ satisfying $\mathcal{F}$, we have $\hat{\Pi}(\bot) = \hat{\pi}(\omega_\bot) = 1$ and $\hat{N}(\bot) = 1 - \mathrm{Sup}\{\hat{\pi}(\omega), \omega \neq \omega_\bot\} > 0$. Thus $\mathcal{F}$ induces a "(somewhat) necessary inconsistency" ; the minimal value of $\hat{N}(\bot)$ among the possibility distributions $\hat{\pi}$ on $\Omega_\bot$ satisfying $\mathcal{F}$ will give us the *inconsistency degree* of $\mathcal{F}$. Let $\alpha = \mathrm{Inf}\{\hat{N}(\bot), \hat{\pi} \hat{\models} \mathcal{F}\}$; then $\mathrm{Incons}(\mathcal{F}) = (N\ \alpha)$.

$\mathcal{F}$ is thus characterized by its inconsistency degree which is a valuation of the form $(\Pi\ \alpha)$ or $(N\ \alpha)$; if $\mathcal{F}$ is *completely consistent* then $\mathrm{Incons}(\mathcal{F}) = (\Pi\ 0)$. If $\forall\ \hat{\pi} \hat{\models} \mathcal{F}$, $\mathrm{Sup}\{\hat{\pi}(\omega), \omega \neq \omega_\bot\} = 0$ then $\mathrm{Incons}(\mathcal{F}) = (N\ 1)$ and $\mathcal{F}$ is *completely inconsistent*. If $\mathrm{Incons}(\mathcal{F}) = (\Pi\ \alpha)$ with $\alpha > 0$ or $\mathrm{Incons}(\mathcal{F}) = (N\ \beta)$ with $\beta < 1$ then $\mathcal{F}$ is *partially inconsistent.*

The following scale shows the hierarchy of inconsistencies : (see Figure 1)

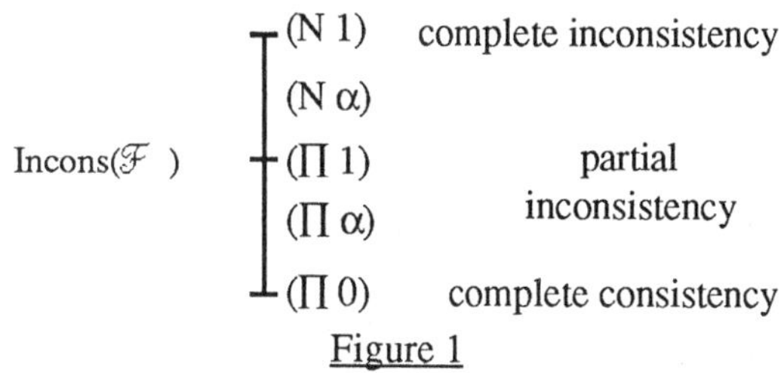

Figure 1

The knowledge base $\mathcal{G}$ gives an example of a degree of inconsistency equal to $(N\ 0.3)$. An example of a knowledge base with a degree of inconsistency of the form $(\Pi\ \alpha)$ is given by $\mathcal{H} = \{(p\ (\Pi\ 0.7)), (\neg p\ (N\ 0.6))\}$. Clearly π satisfies $\mathcal{H} \Leftrightarrow \Pi(p) \geq 0.7$ and $N(\neg p) \geq 0.6 \Leftrightarrow \Pi(p) \geq 0.7$ and $\Pi(p) \leq 0.4$, a contradiction in the first semantics. Using the inconsistency-tolerant semantics, we get for $\omega \neq \omega_\perp$, $\forall\ \omega \models p$, $\hat{\pi}(\omega) \leq 0.4$ and $\exists\ \omega \models \neg p$, $\hat{\pi}(\omega) = 1$; $\hat{\pi}(\omega_\perp) = 0.7$. Hence Incons($\mathscr{H}$) = ($\Pi$ 0.7).

The examples indicate that the inconsistency degree of a possibilistic knowledge base $\mathscr{F}$ is the valuation of the least formula (in the sense of the ordering in $\mathscr{V}$) involved in the strongest contradiction in $\mathscr{F}$. Let w $\in \mathscr{V}$ such that Incons($\mathscr{F}$) = w. It is easy to see that $\forall\ \Phi \in \mathscr{F}$, Incons($\mathscr{F}$ - $\{\Phi\}$) $\leq$ w. Let $\mathscr{F}' \subseteq \mathscr{F}$ such that Incons($\mathscr{F}'$) = Incons($\mathscr{F}$) and $\forall\ \Phi \in \mathscr{F}'$, Incons($\mathscr{F}'$ - $\{\Phi\}$) < Incons($\mathscr{F}'$). $\mathscr{F}'$ is called a smallest maximally inconsistent subset of $\mathscr{F}$. Then the following result holds :

Proposition 1 : The inconsistency of a possibilistic knowledge base $\mathscr{F}$ is the smallest weight of possibilistic formulas in any smallest maximally inconsistent subset $\mathscr{F}'$ of $\mathscr{F}$. More precisely, if Incons($\mathscr{F}$) = (N α) then there exists at least one formula (φ (N α)) $\in \mathscr{F}'$ and $\forall$ (φ' w) $\in \mathscr{F}'$, w $\geq$ (N α). If Incons($\mathscr{F}$) = (Π β) then there is a unique possibility-valued formula in $\mathscr{F}'$ of the form (φ (Π β)).

Proof :

i) *Incons($\mathscr{F}$) = (N α).* Assume $\mathscr{F}' = \{(\varphi_i\ (N\ \alpha_i)), i = 1,m\} \cup \{(\varphi_j\ (\Pi\ \beta_j), j = m + 1,\ldots,n\}$. The inconsistency degree is

$$\alpha = 1 - \sup_{\omega \neq \omega_\perp} \hat{\pi}(\omega)$$

under the constraints

$$\hat{N}(\varphi_i) \geq \alpha_i,\ i = 1,m$$
$$\hat{\Pi}(\varphi_j) \geq \beta_j,\ j = m + 1,\ldots, n$$

Since $\alpha > 0$, $\hat{\pi}(\omega_\perp) = 1$ and the constraints $\hat{\Pi}(\varphi_j) \geq \beta_j$ are ever satisfied. Hence Incons($\mathscr{F}'$) = Incons$\{(\varphi_i\ (N\ \alpha_i)), i = 1,m\}$. The minimality of $\mathscr{F}'$ is thus contradictory with the presence of possibility-valued formulas in $\mathscr{F}'$. Thus $\mathscr{F}'$ is of the form $\{(\varphi_i\ (N\ \alpha_i)), i = 1,n\}$. By assumption any possibility distribution $\hat{\pi}$ satisfying $\mathscr{F}'$ is such that $\hat{\pi}(\omega) \leq 1 - \alpha$ for all $\omega \neq \omega_\perp$. Assume $\alpha_1 = \min_{i=1,m} \alpha_i$. Let us prove that $\alpha_1 = \alpha$. $\hat{\pi}$ satisfies $\mathscr{F}'$ if and only if $\forall$i, $\hat{\pi}(\omega) \leq 1 - \alpha_i$, $\forall\ \omega \models \neg\varphi_i$, $\omega \neq \omega_\perp$; in other words, $\forall \hat{\pi}$, $\hat{\pi} \mathrel{\hat{\models}} \mathscr{F}$ implies $\forall\ \omega \models \neg\varphi_1 \vee \neg\varphi_2 \ldots \vee \neg\varphi_n$, $\hat{\pi}(\omega) \leq \max_i 1 - \alpha_i = 1 - \alpha_1$. Hence, since $\neg\varphi_1 \vee \neg\varphi_2 \ldots \vee \neg\varphi_n = T$, where T denotes the tautology (otherwise $\mathscr{F}'$ would not be inconsistent), $\forall\ \omega \in \Omega$, $\hat{\pi}(\omega) \leq 1 - \alpha_1$ is due to $\hat{\pi} \mathrel{\hat{\models}} \mathscr{F}'$. Hence the inequality $\alpha \geq \alpha_1$. Now let $\hat{\pi}$ be defined by

$\hat{\pi}(\omega) = 1 - \alpha_1$ if $\omega \models \varphi_2 \wedge \varphi_3 \ldots \wedge \varphi_n$, $\omega \neq \omega_\perp$,
$\hat{\pi}(\omega) \leq 1 - \alpha_i$ if $\omega \models \neg\varphi_i$, $\omega \neq \omega_\perp$.

Because $\varphi_2 \wedge \varphi_3 \ldots \wedge \varphi_n \neq \perp$, $\exists\omega$, $\hat{\pi}(\omega) = 1 - \alpha_1$, and $\hat{\pi} \mathrel{\hat{\models}} \mathscr{F}$. Hence $\alpha = \alpha_1$.

ii) *Incons($\mathscr{F}$) = (Π β).* It is obvious that $\mathscr{F}'$ contains at least one possibility valued formula. Let us show that it is unique. The inconsistency degree is now of the form :

$$\beta = \inf \hat{\pi}(\omega_\perp)$$

under the constraints

$$N(\varphi_i) \geq \alpha_i,\ i = 1,m$$
$$\max(\hat{\pi}(\omega_\perp), \Pi(\varphi_j)) \geq \beta_j,\ j = m + 1,\ldots, n$$

Since $\beta > 0$, $\forall\ \hat{\pi} \mathrel{\hat{\models}} \mathscr{F}'$, $\exists$k such that $\Pi(\varphi_k) < \beta_k$, and Incons($\mathscr{F}'$) = β_k for some β_k. In order to minimize this value, let us maximize $\hat{\pi}$ over Ω, so as to make the set $\{j \mid \Pi(\varphi_j) < \beta_j\}$ as small as possible. Let $\hat{\pi}$ be defined by $\hat{\pi}(\omega) = \min\{1 - \alpha_i, \omega \models \neg\varphi_i, \omega \neq \omega_\perp\}$. Clearly, $\hat{\pi} \models \{(\varphi_i\ (N\ \alpha_i)), i = 1,m\}$, $\exists\ \omega \in \Omega$, $\hat{\pi}(\omega) = 1$ (since there is no inconsistency among the N-valued formulas), and $\forall\hat{\pi}'$, $\hat{\pi}' \mathrel{\hat{\models}} \{(\varphi_i\ (N\ \alpha_i)), i = 1,m\} \Rightarrow \forall\ \omega \in \Omega$, $\hat{\pi}'(\omega) \leq \hat{\pi}(\omega)$. The only parameter left is $\hat{\pi}(\omega_\perp)$. Let $\beta_k = \max\{\beta_j \mid \Pi(\varphi_j) < \beta_j\}$ where Π is based on $\hat{\pi}$. Note that the maximality of $\hat{\pi}$ over Ω minimizes the number of (φ_j (Π β_j)) with $\Pi(\varphi_j) < \beta_j$.

For simplicity assume $\beta_k = \beta_{m+1}$. Let us put $\hat{\pi}(\omega_\perp) = \beta_{m+1}$. Then clearly, $\hat{\pi} \mathrel{\hat{\models}} \mathscr{F}'$, since $\forall$j, $\max(\beta_{m+1}, \Pi(\varphi_j)) \geq \beta_j$ by construction. Thus Incons($\mathscr{F}'$) $\leq \beta_{m+1}$. Now, $\forall\varphi_j$ such that $\Pi(\varphi_j) \geq \beta_j$, Incons($\mathscr{F}'$ - $\{(\varphi\ (\Pi\ \beta_j)\}$) = Incons($\mathscr{F}'$) ; the same thing is true for all φ_j such that $\Pi(\varphi_j) < \beta_j < \beta_{m+1}$. If there is another formula (φ_i (Π β_i)) such that $\beta_i = \beta_{m+1}$, dropping one of these formulas still requires $\hat{\pi}(\omega_\perp) = \beta_{m+1}$ for ensuring $\hat{\pi} \mathrel{\hat{\models}} \mathscr{F}'$. Hence, if $\mathscr{F}'$ is really minimal it contains only one possibility-valued formula, i.e. (φ_{m+1} (Π β_{m+1})) and Incons($\mathscr{F}'$) = (Π β_{m+1}). ■

Incons($\mathscr{F}$) acts as a threshold inhibiting all deductions of $\mathscr{F}$ with a valuation $\leq$ Incons($\mathscr{F}$). Indeed, deductions such as $\mathscr{F} \mathrel{\hat{\models}}$ (φ w) where w $\leq$ Incons($\mathscr{F}$) are trivial since $\mathscr{F} \mathrel{\hat{\models}}$ (φ w) comes directly from $\mathscr{F} \mathrel{\hat{\models}}$ ($\perp$ w) and the inequalities $\hat{\Pi}(\varphi) \geq \hat{\Pi}(\perp)$, $\hat{N}(\varphi) \geq \hat{N}(\perp)$ (it easy to check that if for any classical formulae φ and ψ, if $\varphi \models \psi$ then $\hat{\Pi}(\varphi) \geq \hat{\Pi}(\psi)$, $\hat{N}(\varphi) \geq \hat{N}(\psi)$). On the contrary, deductions with a valuation strictly greater than Incons($\mathscr{F}$) are not caused by the partial inconsistency ; these deductions are called non-trivial deductions.

Lastly, the following results are easy to prove (Lang, 1991) : If $\mathscr{F}$ is a set of possibilistic formulae and w a valuation of $\mathscr{V}$, let us note $\mathscr{F}_w = \{(\varphi\ v), v \geq w\}$ and $\mathscr{F}_{\bar{w}} = \{(\varphi\ v), v > w\}$; then

(i) $\mathscr{F} \mathrel{\hat{\models}}$ (φ w) iff $\mathscr{F}_w \mathrel{\hat{\models}}$ (φ w)

(ii) If Incons($\mathscr{F}$) = w, $\mathscr{F}$ is $\hat{\models}$-equivalent to $\mathscr{F}_w$ and to $\mathscr{F}_{\bar{w}} \cup \{(\perp\ w)\}$.

3 AUTOMATED DEDUCTION IN POSSIBILISTIC LOGIC

Two well-known automated deduction methods have been generalized to possibilistic logic : i) resolution (Dubois and Prade, 1990a) and ii) the Davis and Putnam semantic evaluation procedure for propositional logic (Lang, 1990). Here we focus only on resolution for which we give soundness and completeness results.

3.1 CLAUSAL FORM

In order to extend resolution to possibilistic logic, a clausal form is first defined. A possibilistic clause is a possibilistic formula (c w) where c is a first-order or propositional clause and w is a valuation of $\mathcal{V}$. A possibilistic clausal form is a conjunction of possibilistic clauses. If a possibilistic formula $\mathcal{F}$ contains only necessity-valued classical formulae, then there exists a clausal form $\mathcal{C}$ of $\mathcal{F}$ such that Incons($\mathcal{C}$) = Incons($\mathcal{F}$), which generalizes the result holding in classical logic about the equivalence between the inconsistency of a set of formulae and the inconsistency of its clausal form. Indeed possibilistic clausal form $\mathcal{C}$ of $\mathcal{F}$ can be obtained by the following method : if $\mathcal{F} = \{(\varphi_i\ (N\ \alpha_i)),\ i = 1 \ldots n\}$, then put each φ_i into clausal form, i.e. $\varphi_i = (\forall) \wedge_j(c_{ij})$ where c_{ij} is a universally-quantified classical clause ; then $(\forall) \wedge_{i,j}\{(c_{ij}\ (N\ \alpha_i))\}$ is the possibilistic clausal form equivalent to $\mathcal{F}$ [3] . If $\mathcal{F}$ contains also possibility-valued formulae, then generally we cannot compute from $\mathcal{F}$ a clausal form having the same inconsistency degree as $\mathcal{F}$, even in propositional possibilistic logic. For instance, the closest clausal form we can compute from $\mathcal{F} = \{(p \wedge q\ (\Pi\ \alpha)), (\neg p \vee \neg q\ (N\ 1))\}$ $(\alpha > 0)$ is $\mathcal{C} = \{(p\ (\Pi\ \alpha)), (q\ (\Pi\ \alpha)), (\neg p \vee \neg q\ (N\ 1))\}$, but it can be checked that Incons($\mathcal{F}$) = $(\Pi\ \alpha)$ whereas Incons($\mathcal{C}$) = $(\Pi\ 0)$. This negative result comes from the non-compositionnality of possibility measures for conjunction. Indeed $(p \wedge q\ (\Pi\ \alpha))$ is much stronger than $(p\ (\Pi\ \alpha)) \wedge (q\ (\Pi\ \alpha))$, since $(p \wedge q\ (\Pi\ \alpha))$ means $\hat{\Pi}(p \wedge q) \geq \alpha$, i.e. $\exists\ \omega \in \Omega_\perp$ such that $\omega \models p \wedge q$ and $\hat{\pi}(\omega) \geq \alpha$, whereas $(p\ (\Pi\ \alpha)) \wedge (q\ (\Pi\ \alpha))$, means $\exists \omega, \omega' \in \Omega_\perp$ such that $\omega \models p$, $\omega' \models q$ and $\hat{\pi}(\omega) \geq \alpha$, $\hat{\pi}(\omega') \geq \alpha$. This problem, also appears in modal logics (Fariñas and Herzig, 1988) and can be similarly solved in our framework by "coloring" the "Π" valuations. We denote respectively by CLP1 (resp. CLP2) the language consisting in necessity-valued clauses only (resp. necessity- and possibility-valued clauses).

3.2 POSSIBILISTIC RESOLUTION RULES

The following possibilistic resolution rule, between two possibilistic clauses $(c_1\ w_1)$ and $(c_2\ w_2)$, has been established by Dubois and Prade (1987, 1990) :

$$\frac{(c_1\ w_1)\ (c_2\ w_2)}{(R(c_1,c_2)\ w_1 * w_2)} \qquad (R)$$

[3] Indeed, $N(\wedge_i(c_{ij})) \geq \alpha$ is equivalent to $\min_i[N(c_{ij})] \geq \alpha$ and thus to $\wedge_j[N(c_{ij}) \geq \alpha]$; $\mathcal{F}$ is then equivalent to $\wedge_i(\wedge_j\{(c_{ij}\ (N\ \alpha_i))\}\}$, i.e. $\wedge_{ij}\{(c_{ij}\ (N\ \alpha_i))\}$.

where $R(c_1,c_2)$ is a classical resolvent of c_1 and c_2, and $*$ is defined by

$$(N\ \alpha) * (N\ \beta) = (N\ \min(\alpha,\beta))\ ;$$
$$(N\ \alpha) * (\Pi\ \beta) = \begin{cases}(\Pi\ \beta) \text{ if } \alpha + \beta > 1\ ;\\ (\Pi\ 0) \text{ if } \alpha + \beta \leq 1.\end{cases}$$
$$(\Pi\ \alpha) * (\Pi\ \beta) = (\Pi\ 0).$$

The similarity between (R) and resolution patterns existing in modal logics has been pointed out ; see (Dubois and Prade, 1990). The following result can be easily checked

Proposition 2 (soundness of rule (R)) : let $\mathcal{C}$ be a set of possibilistic clauses, and C a possibilistic clause obtained by a finite number of successive applications of (R) to $\mathcal{C}$; then $\mathcal{C} \mathrel{\hat{\models}} C$.

Proof :

(i) If $C = (c_1\ (N\ \alpha))$, $C' = (c_2\ (N\ \beta))$, the application of rule R yields $C'' = (R(c_1,c_2)\ (N\ \min(\alpha,\beta))$. Then $\forall \pi$ satisfying $C \wedge C'$ we have $\hat{N}(c_1) \geq \alpha$ and $\hat{N}(c_2) \geq \beta$, and then $\hat{N}(c_1 \wedge c_2) = \min(\hat{N}(c_1),\hat{N}(c_2)) \geq \min(\alpha,\beta)$ and finally $\hat{N}(R(c_1,c_2)) \geq \hat{N}(c_1 \wedge c_2) \geq \min(\alpha,\beta)$. Thus rule R is sound in this case.

(ii) If $C = (c_1\ (N\ \alpha))$, $C' = (c_2\ (\Pi\ \beta))$, rule R yields $C'' = (R(c_1,c_2)\ (\Pi\ (\alpha * \beta))$; if $\alpha + \beta \leq 1$, $\alpha * \beta = 0$ and then trivially $C, C' \mathrel{\hat{\models}} C''$. If $\alpha + \beta > 1$, $\forall \hat{\pi}$ satisfying $C \wedge C'$ we have $\hat{N}(c_1) \geq \alpha$ and $\hat{\Pi}(c_2) \geq \beta$; but $\hat{\Pi}(c_2) = \max[\hat{\pi}(\omega_\perp), \Pi(c_2)]$, then
- either $\hat{\pi}(\omega_\perp) \geq \beta$ and then $\hat{\Pi}(R(c_1,c_2)) \geq \beta$ and finally $\hat{\pi} \mathrel{\hat{\models}} C''$;
- or $\hat{\pi}(\omega_\perp) < \beta$, then $\hat{\Pi}(c_2) = \Pi(c_2)$; in this case $\Pi(c_2) = \max[\Pi(\neg c_1 \wedge c_2), \Pi(c_1 \wedge c_2)]$; but $\hat{N}(c_1) \geq \alpha$ entails $\Pi(\neg c_1) \leq 1 - \alpha < \beta$, then $\Pi(c_1 \wedge c_2) \geq \beta$ and $\hat{\Pi}(R(c_1,c_2)) \geq \Pi(R(c_1,c_2)) \geq \Pi(c_1 \wedge c_2) \geq \beta$, and finally $\hat{\pi} \mathrel{\hat{\models}} C''$.

Then rule (R) is sound. ■

3.3 REFUTATION BY RESOLUTION

In this section we consider a set $\mathcal{F}$ of possibilistic formulae (the knowledge base) and a formula φ ; we want to know the maximal valuation with which $\mathcal{F}$ entails φ, i.e. $\text{Val}(\mathcal{F},\varphi) = \text{Sup}\ \{w \in \mathcal{V}, \mathcal{F} \mathrel{\hat{\models}} (\varphi\ w)\}$.

This request can be answered by using refutation by resolution, which is extended to possibilistic logic as follows :

Refutation by resolution :

1. Put $\mathcal{F}$ in clausal form $\mathcal{C}$;
2. Put φ in clausal form ; let $c_1, \ldots, c_m$ be the obtained clauses ;
3. $\mathcal{C}' \leftarrow \mathcal{C} \cup \{(c_1\ (N\ 1)), \ldots, (c_n\ (N\ 1))\}$
4. Search for a proof of $(\perp\ \bar{w})$ with $\bar{w}$ maximal , by repeatedly applying the resolution rule (R) from $\mathcal{C}'$;
5. $\text{Val}(\mathcal{F},\varphi) = \bar{w}$

When the knowledge base consists of both necessity-valued and possibility-valued formulae, then since the transformation into clausal form is not complete (it does not preserve the inconsistency degree), *we shall suppose that $\mathcal{F}$ is a set of possibilistic clauses* ; in this case, $\mathcal{C}$ = $\mathcal{F}$ and step 1 is omitted. Soundness and completeness results hold for possibilistic resolution. Let $\mathcal{F}$ be a set of possibilistic clauses, φ a classical formula, $\mathcal{C}$' the set of possibilistic clauses obtained as explained precedently. Then we have the following results :

Proposition 3 *Soundness and completeness of refutation in clausal possibilistic logic* :

$$\mathcal{F} \hat{\models} (\varphi\ w) \Leftrightarrow \mathrm{Incons}(\mathcal{F} \wedge (\neg\varphi\ (N\ 1))) \geq w$$

or equivalently : Incons($\mathcal{F} \wedge (\neg\varphi$ (N 1))) = Val($\mathcal{F}$,φ). See the proof in Annex.

This result allows us to compute Val($\mathcal{F}$,φ) by proving the inconsistency of $\mathcal{F} \wedge (\neg\varphi$ (N 1)).

Note that in Proposition 3 we are not making use of resolution. The two following propositions relate the resolution procedure to the computation of the degree of inconsistency.

Proposition 4 *Soundness and completeness of refutation by resolution in LP1* (Dubois, Lang and Prade, 1989) : let $\mathcal{F}$ be a set of *necessity-valued* first-order formulae and $\mathcal{C}$ the set of necessity-valued clauses obtained from $\mathcal{F}$; then the valuation of the optimal refutation by resolution from $\mathcal{C}$ (i.e. the greatest valuation of the obtained empty clause) is the inconsistency degree of $\mathcal{F}$.

Corollary : let φ be a classical formula and $\mathcal{C}$' the set of possibilistic clauses obtained from $\mathcal{F} \cup \{(\neg\varphi$ (N 1))} ; then the valuation of the optimal refutation by resolution from $\mathcal{C}$' is Val($\mathcal{F}$,φ). This corollary derives immediately from Propositions 3 and 4.

Proposition 5 *Soundness and completeness of refutation by resolution in propositional CLP2* : if $\mathcal{C}$ is a set of *propositional* necessity- or possibility-valued *clauses*, then the valuation of the optimal refutation by resolution from $\mathcal{C}$ is the inconsistency degree of $\mathcal{F}$.

Corollary : let φ be a classical formula and $\mathcal{C}$' the set of possibilistic clauses obtained from $\mathcal{C} \cup \{(\neg\varphi$ (N 1))} ; then the valuation of the optimal refutation by resolution from $\mathcal{C}$' is Val($\mathcal{C}$,φ).

Proposition 5 is a consequence of Propositions 3 and 1 together with the expression of the resolution rule.

N.B. : Proposition 5 does not hold for *first-order* possibilistic clauses; for instance, if $\mathcal{C}$ = {(p(x) (Π α))}, x being a (universally quantified) variable and α > 0, and φ = p(a) ∧ p(b), then there is no (Π α)-refutation by resolution from $\mathcal{C}$ ∧ {(¬p(a) ∨ ¬p(b) (N 1))}, whereas $\mathcal{C} \hat{\models}$ (p(a) ∧ p(b) (Π α)). It does not hold either for possibilistic general formulas, since the tranlation into clausal form does not preserve the inconsistency degree if the knowledge base contains possibility-valued formulas. Completeness can be recovered by indexing the "Π" symbols in the (Π α)-valuations, in the same spirit as in modal logics (Fariñas and Herzig, 1988)).

3.4 ILLUSTRATIVE EXAMPLE

We now give an illustrative example. Let $\mathcal{C}$ be the following knowledge base, concerning an election whose two candidates are Mary and Peter :

C_1 (Elected(Peter) ∨ Elected(Mary) (N 1))
C_2 (¬Elected(Peter) ∨ ¬Elected(Mary) (N 1))
C_3 (¬Former-president(x) ∨ Elected(x) (N 0.5))
C_4 (Former-president(Mary) (N 1))
C_5 (¬Supports(John,x) ∨ Elected(x) (N 0.6))
C_6 (Supports(John, Mary) (Π 0.8))
C_7 (¬Victim-of-an-affair(x) ∨ ¬Elected(x) (N 0.9))

We cannot find any refutation from $\mathcal{C}$; hence, $\mathcal{C}$ is consistent, i.e. Incons($\mathcal{C}$) = (Π 0). Let us now find the best possibility or necessity degree of the formula "Elected(Mary)". Let $\mathcal{C}$'= $\mathcal{C}$ ∪ {(¬Elected(Mary) (N 1))} ; then there exist two distinct refutations by resolution from $\mathcal{C}$', which are :

(¬Elected (Mary) (N 1)) C3
(¬Former-president (Mary) (N 0.5)) C4
(⊥ (N 0.5))
OPTIMAL

(¬Elected (Mary) (N 1)) C5
(¬Supports (John,Mary) (N 0.6)) C6
(⊥ (Π 0.8))
NON-OPTIMAL

Hence we conclude that $\mathcal{C} \hat{\models}$ (Elected(Mary) (N 0.5)), i.e. it is moderately certain that Mary will be elected ; this degree (N 0.5) is maximal, i.e. Val ($\mathcal{C}$, Elected(Mary)) = (N 0.5). Then, we learn that Mary is being the victim of an affair (which is a completely certain information). This leads us to update the knowledge base by adding to $\mathcal{C}$ the possibilistic clause C_8 : (Victim-of-an-affair(Mary) (N 1)). Let $\mathcal{C}_1$ be the new knowledge base, $\mathcal{C}_1 = \mathcal{C} \cup \{C_8\}$. Then, we can find a (N 0.5)-refutation from $\mathcal{C}_1$:

C8 C7 C3 C4
(¬Elected (Mary) (N 0.9)) (Elected (Mary) (N 0.5))
(⊥ (N 0.5))

Hence $\mathcal{F}_1$ is partially inconsistent, with Incons ($\mathcal{C}_1$) = (N 0.5).

The refutation which had given N(Elected(Mary) ≥ 0.5 can always be obtained from $\mathcal{F}_1$ but since its valuation is not greater than Incons($\mathcal{F}_1$), it has become a trivial deduction.

On the contrary, adding to $\mathcal{F}_1$ the possibilistic clause (Elected(Mary) (N 1)), we find this time a (N 0.9)-refutation. And, since (N 0.9) > Incons($\mathcal{F}_1$), we have the non-trivial deduction $\mathcal{F}_1 \hat{\models}$ (¬Elected(Mary) (N 0.9)), and it could be shown that we also have $\mathcal{F}_1 \hat{\models}$ (Elected(Peter) (N 0.9)).

CONCLUSION

Possibilistic logic drastically differs from probabilistic logic since the former is based on the ideas of ordering and preference (only the ordering of numbers is used) while the latter is based on the ideas of measure and counting. Possibilistic logic is a logic of incomplete information that is more robust than classical logic, because it is tolerant to inconsistency. Besides, as advocated elsewhere possibilistic logic is in full accordance with current theories of belief revision based on epistemic entrenchment (Dubois and Prade, 1990b), and with the principles of non-monotonic reasoning (Dubois and Prade, 1991). One of the strength of possibilistic logic is that the proof methods in classical logic still apply, even in the presence of partial inconsistency, and keep all their power, as indicated by the completeness results of this paper. This is would not be the case with a similar probabilistic extension of logic. Moreover efficient strategies for refutation methods have also been implemented (Dubois et al., 1987). Current applications of possibilistic logic include hypothetical reasoning (Dubois, Lang and Prade, 1990), logic programming (Dubois, Lang and Prade, 1991), the automated resolution of combinatorial optimization problems with bottleneck-like objective functions (Lang, 1991) and belief revision.

Among topics for further research is the study of the links between the semantics presented here and the Kripke-like semantics previously proposed for necessity and possibility measures by Dubois, Prade and Testemale (1988). Another issue is to bridge the gap between possibilistic logic (especially the handling of possibility degrees (Π α)) and the semantics proposed by Yager (1987) in default logic for defaults such as "if p is certain and q is possible then r ". It would require to allow for disjunctions of weighted formulas in the language.

Acknowledgements

This work is partially supported by the DRUMS project (Defeasible Reasoning and Uncertainty Management Systems), funded by the Commission of the European Communities under the ESPRIT Basic Research Action Number 3085.

References

D. Dubois, J. Lang, and H. Prade (1987). Theorem-proving under uncertainty – A possibility theory- based approach. *Proc. of the 10th Inter. Joint Conf. on Artificial Intelligence*, Milano, Italy, 984-986.

D. Dubois, J. Lang, and H. Prade (1989). Automated reasoning using possibilistic logic : semantics, belief revision, variable certainty weights. *Preprints of the 5th Workshop on Uncertainty in Artificial Intelligence*, Windsor, Ont., 81-87.

D. Dubois, J. Lang, and H. Prade (1990). Handling uncertain knowledge in an ATMS using possibilistic logic. In Z.W. Ras, M. Zemankova, and M.L. Emrich (eds.), *Methodologies for Intelligent Systems 5*, 252-259. Amsterdam : North-Holland.

D. Dubois, J. Lang, and H. Prade (1991). Towards possibilistic logic programming. *Proc. of the 8th Inter. Conf. on Logic Programming (ICLP'91)*, Paris, June 25-28, MIT Press, to appear.

D. Dubois, and H. Prade (1987). Necessity measures and the resolution principle. *IEEE Trans. on Systems, Man and Cybernetics* 17:474-478.

D. Dubois, and H. Prade (with the collaboration of H. Farreny, R. Martin-Clouaire, and C. Testemale) (1988). *Possibility Theory – An Approach to Computerized Processing of Uncertainty*. New York : Plenum Press.

D. Dubois, and H. Prade (1990a). Resolution principles in possibilistic logic. *Int. J. of Approx. Reason.* 4(1): 1-21.

D. Dubois, and H. Prade (1990b) Epistemic entrenchment and possibilistic logic. In Tech. Report IRIT/90-2/R, IRIT, Toulouse. To appear in *Artificial Intelligence*.

D. Dubois, and H. Prade (1991). Possibilistic logic, preference models, non-monotonicity and related issues. Proc. 12th Int. Joint Conf. on Artif. Intelligence, Sydney.

D. Dubois, H. Prade, and C. Testemale (1988). In search of a modal system for possibility theory. *Proc. Europ. Conf. on Artif. Intelligence (ECAI-88)*, Munich, 501-506.

L. Fariñas del Cerro, and A. Herzig (1988). Quantified modal logic and unification theory. Report LSI n° 293, IRIT, Univ. P. Sabatier, Toulouse, France.

P. Gärdenfors (1988). *Knowledge in Flux – Modeling the Dynamics of Epistemic States*. Cambridge: MIT Press.

J. Lang (1990). Semantic evaluation in possibilistic logic. *Proc. of the 3rd Inter. Conf. Information Processing and Management of Uncertainty in Knowledge-Based Systems (IPMU)*, Paris, France, July 2-6, 51-55.

J. Lang (1991). Logique possibiliste : aspects formels, déduction automatique et applications. PhD Thesis, Université Paul Sabatier, Toulouse.

N.J. Nilsson (1986). Probabilistic logic. *Artificial Intelligence* 28:71-87.

Z. Pawlak (1982). Rough sets. *Int. J. Comput. Inf. Sci.* 11:341-356.

E.H. Ruspini (1991). On the semantics of fuzzy logic. *Int. J. of Approximate Reasoning* 5:45-88.

G.L.S. Shackle (1961). *Decision, Order and Time in Human Affairs*. Cambridge University Press.

G. Shafer (1976). *A Mathematical Theory of Evidence*. Princeton University Press.

Y. Shoham (1988). *Reasoning about Change – Time and Causation from the Standpoint of Artificial Intelligence*. Cambridge, Mass. : The MIT Press.

W. Spohn (1988). Ordinal conditional functions : a dynamic theory of epistemic states. In W. Harper, and B. Skyrms (eds.), *Causation in Decision, Belief Change and Statistics*, 105-134.

R.C. Stalnaker (1981). A theory of conditionals. In W.L. Harper, R. Stalnaker, G. Pearce (eds.), *Ifs*, 41-55. Dordrecht : Reidel

R.R. Yager (1987) Using approximate reasoning to represent default knowledge. *Artificial Intelligence*, 31: 99-112

L.A. Zadeh (1978). Fuzzy sets as a basis for a theory of possibility. *Fuzzy Sets and Systems* 1(1):3-28.

Annex: Proposition 3

$$\mathcal{F} \hat{\models} (\varphi\ w) \Leftrightarrow \text{Incons}(\mathcal{F} \wedge (\neg\varphi\ (N\ 1))) \geq w$$

or equivalently

$$\text{Incons}(\mathcal{F} \wedge (\neg\varphi\ (N\ 1))) = \sup\{w, \mathcal{F} \hat{\models} (\varphi\ w)\}$$

Proof (Lang, 1991):

($\Rightarrow$)

Case (i) : $w = (\Pi\ \alpha)$

Let us suppose that $\mathcal{F} \hat{\models} (\varphi\ (\Pi\ \alpha))$, i.e. $\forall \hat{\pi}$ satisfying $\mathcal{F}$, $\hat{\Pi}(\varphi) = \max[\Pi(\varphi), \hat{\Pi}(\perp)] \geq \alpha$.

Let $\hat{\pi}$ be a possibility distribution satisfying $\mathcal{F} \wedge (\neg\varphi\ (N\ 1))$, i.e. $\forall\ \omega \neq \omega_\perp$ such that $\omega \models \varphi$, $\hat{\pi}(\omega) = 0$; then $\Pi(\varphi) = 0$; but $\hat{\pi}$ also satisfies $\mathcal{F}$ and we have $\max[\Pi(\varphi), \hat{\Pi}(\perp)] \geq \alpha$, thus we get $\hat{\Pi}(\perp) \geq \alpha$; and finally $\text{Incons}(\mathcal{F} \wedge (\neg\varphi\ (N\ 1))) \geq (\Pi\ \alpha)$. ■

Case (ii) : $w = (N\ \alpha)$

Let us suppose that $\mathcal{F} \hat{\models} (\varphi\ (N\ \alpha))$, i.e. $\forall \hat{\pi}$ satisfying $\mathcal{F}$, $\hat{N}(\varphi) \geq \alpha$, or equivalently $\forall\ \omega \neq \omega_\perp$ such that $\omega \models \varphi$, $\hat{\pi}(\omega) \leq 1 - \alpha$. Let $\hat{\pi}$ be a possibility distribution satisfying $\mathcal{F} \wedge (\neg\varphi\ (N\ 1))$, i.e. $\omega \neq \omega_\perp$ such that $\omega \models \varphi$, $\hat{\pi}(\omega) = 0$; but $\hat{\pi}$ also satisfies $\mathcal{F}$ and then $\forall\ \omega \neq \omega_\perp$ such that $\omega \models \neg\varphi$, $\hat{\pi}(\varphi) \leq 1 - \alpha$, which entails $N(\perp) = \inf\{1 - \hat{\pi}(\omega), \omega \neq \omega_\perp\} = \inf\{1 - \hat{\pi}(\omega), (\omega \neq \omega_\perp$ and $\omega \models \varphi)$ or $(\omega \neq \omega_\perp$ and $\omega \models \neg\varphi)\} \geq \alpha$; and finally $\text{Incons}(\mathcal{F} \wedge (\neg\varphi\ (N\ 1))) \geq (N\ \alpha)$. ■

($\Leftarrow$)

Case (i) : $w = (\Pi\ \alpha)$

Let $\mathcal{F} = \{(\Psi_i\ (N\ \alpha_i)), i \in I\} \cup \{(\xi_j\ (\Pi\ \beta_j)), j \in J\}$ and let us suppose $\text{Incons}(\mathcal{F} \wedge (\neg\varphi\ (N\ 1))) \geq (\Pi\ \alpha)$.

Let us suppose that $\hat{\pi}$ satisfies $\mathcal{F}$, i.e.

$\hat{N}(\Psi_i) \geq \alpha_i, \forall\ i \in I$

$\hat{\Pi}(\xi_j) \geq \beta_j, \forall\ j \in J$;

and prove that $\hat{\pi}$ satisfies $(\varphi\ (\Pi\ \alpha))$, i.e. $\hat{\Pi}(\varphi) \geq \alpha$.

Let us define $\hat{\pi}'$ as follows

$\omega \neq \omega_\perp, \omega \models \varphi \Rightarrow \hat{\pi}'(\omega) = 0$

$\omega \neq \omega_\perp, \omega \models \neg\varphi \Rightarrow \hat{\pi}'(\omega) = \hat{\pi}(\omega)$

if $\sup\{\hat{\pi}'(\omega), \omega \neq \omega_\perp\} < 1$ then $\hat{\pi}'(\omega_\perp) = 1$

otherwise $\hat{\pi}'(\omega_\perp) = \max\{\beta_j, j \in J, (\forall\ \omega \neq \omega_\perp, \omega \models \xi_j \Rightarrow \hat{\pi}'(\omega) < \beta_j)\}$

$= \max\{\beta_j, j \in J, \hat{\Pi}'(\xi_j) < \beta_j\}$

Clearly $\sup\{\hat{\pi}'(\omega), \omega \in \Omega_\perp\} = 1$, then $\hat{\pi}'$ is a normalized possibility distribution over $\Omega_\perp$. Let us prove that $\hat{\pi}'$ satisfies $\mathcal{F} \wedge (\neg\varphi\ (N\ 1))$:

– $\forall\ i \in I$, we have $\forall\ \omega \neq \omega_\perp$, $\hat{\pi}'(\omega) \leq \hat{\pi}(\omega)$, then $\hat{N}'(\Psi_i) \geq \hat{N}(\Psi_i) \geq \alpha_i$;

thus $\hat{\pi}'$ satisfies N-valued formulae in $\mathcal{F}$

– $\forall\ j \in J$, $\hat{\Pi}'(\xi_j) = \max[\hat{\pi}'(\omega_\perp), \Pi'(\xi_j)]$ and then

 – either $\Pi'(\xi_j) \geq \beta_j$, and then $\hat{\pi}'$ satisfies $(\xi_j\ (\Pi\ \beta_j))$;

 – or $\Pi'(\xi_j) < \beta_j$; in this case, by definition of $\hat{\pi}'(\omega_\perp)$ we have $\hat{\pi}'(\omega_\perp) \geq \beta_j$, and then $\hat{\Pi}'(\xi_j) \geq \beta_j$;

thus $\hat{\pi}'$ satisfies Π-valued formulae in $\mathcal{F}$

– $\hat{N}(\neg\varphi) = \inf\{1 - \hat{\pi}'(\omega), \omega \neq \omega_\perp, \omega \models \varphi\} = 1$, then $\hat{\pi}'$ satisfies $(\neg\varphi\ (N\ 1))$ Then $\hat{\pi}'$ satisfies $\mathcal{F} \wedge (\neg\varphi\ (N\ 1))$.

But by hypothesis $\text{Incons}(\mathcal{F} \wedge (\neg\varphi\ (N\ 1))) \geq (\Pi\ \alpha)$; hence $\hat{\pi}'(\omega_\perp) \geq \alpha$, or from the definition of $\hat{\pi}'(\omega_\perp)$: $\max\{\beta_j, j \in J, \Pi'(\xi_j) < \beta_j\} \geq \alpha$, which is equivalent to :

$\exists\ j \in J, \Pi'(\xi_j) < \beta_j$ and $\beta_j \geq \alpha$ (a)

But $\Pi'(\xi_j) = \max[\Pi'(\varphi \wedge \xi_j), \Pi'(\neg\varphi \wedge \xi_j)]$

$= \max[0, \Pi'(\neg\varphi \wedge \xi_j)] = \Pi(\neg\varphi \wedge \xi_j)$,

since $\omega \neq \omega_\perp, \omega \models \neg\varphi \Rightarrow \pi'(\omega) = \hat{\pi}(\omega)$ and (a) becomes

$\exists\ j \in J, \Pi(\neg\varphi \wedge \xi_j) < \beta_j$ and $\beta_j \geq \alpha$. (b)

But $\hat{\pi}$ satisfying $\mathcal{F}$, we have $\forall\ j \in J$, $\hat{\Pi}(\xi_j) \geq \beta_j$, i.e.

$\forall j \in J, \max(\hat{\pi}(\omega_\perp), \Pi(\varphi \wedge \xi_j), \Pi(\neg\varphi \wedge \xi_j)) \geq \beta_j \geq \alpha$ (c)

Now (b) and (c) lead to

$\exists\ j \in J, \max(\hat{\pi}(\omega_\perp), \Pi(\varphi \wedge \xi_j)) \geq \beta_j \geq \alpha$ (d)

Then $\hat{\Pi}(\varphi) = \max[\hat{\pi}(\omega_\perp), \Pi(\varphi)] \geq \max[\hat{\pi}(\omega_\perp), \Pi(\varphi \wedge \xi_j)] \geq \alpha$, and then $\hat{\pi}$ satisfies $(\varphi\ (\Pi\ \alpha))$. ■

Case (ii) : $w = (N\ \alpha)$

Let $\mathcal{F} = \{(\Psi_i\ (N\ \alpha_i)), i \in I\} \cup \{(\xi_j\ (\Pi\ \beta_j)), j \in J\}$ let us suppose that $\text{Incons}(\mathcal{F} \wedge (\neg\varphi\ (N\ 1))) \geq (N\ \alpha)$.

Let $\hat{\pi}$ be a possibility distribution satisfying $\mathcal{F}$; we have to show that $\hat{\pi}$ satisfies $(\varphi\ (N\ \alpha))$.

Let us define $\hat{\pi}'$ in the following way :

$\omega \neq \omega_\perp, \omega \models \varphi \Rightarrow \hat{\pi}'(\omega) = 0$

$\omega \neq \omega_\perp, \omega \models \neg\varphi \Rightarrow \hat{\pi}'(\omega) = \hat{\pi}(\omega)$

$\hat{\pi}'(\omega_\perp) = 1$

Clearly $\hat{\pi}'$ satisfies $\mathcal{F} \wedge (\neg\varphi\ (N\ 1))$. Indeed

– $\forall\ i \in I, \forall\ \omega \neq \omega_\perp, \hat{\pi}'(\omega_\perp) \leq \hat{\pi}(\omega_\perp)$,

then $\hat{N}'(\Psi_i) \geq \hat{N}(\Psi_i) \geq \alpha_i$;

– $\forall\ j \in J, \hat{\Pi}(\xi_j) \geq \hat{\pi}'(\omega_\perp) = 1 \geq \beta_j$;

– $\hat{N}(\neg\varphi) = \inf\{1 - \hat{\pi}'(\omega), \omega \neq \omega_\perp, \omega \models \varphi\} = 1$.

By hypothesis, we have $\text{Incons}(\mathcal{F} \wedge (\neg\varphi\ (N\ 1))) \geq (N\ \alpha)$; since $\hat{\pi}'$ satisfies $\mathcal{F} \wedge (\neg\varphi\ (N\ 1))$ we can write

$\forall\ \omega \neq \omega_\perp, \hat{\pi}'(\omega) \leq 1 - \alpha$; then $\hat{N}'(\varphi) = \hat{N}(\varphi) = \inf\{1 - \hat{\pi}'(\omega), \omega \neq \omega_\perp, \omega \models \neg\varphi\} \geq \alpha$,

it enables us to conclude that $\hat{\pi}$ satisfies $(\varphi\ (N\ \alpha))$. ■

Conflict and Surprise: Heuristics for Model Revision

Kathryn Blackmond Laskey
Department of Systems Engineering and C[3]I Center
George Mason University
Fairfax, VA 22030

Abstract

Any probabilistic model of a problem is based on assumptions which, if violated, invalidate the model. Users of probability based decision aids need to be alerted when cases arise that are not covered by the aid's model. Diagnosis of model failure is also necessary to control dynamic model construction and revision. This paper presents a set of decision theoretically motivated heuristics for diagnosing situations in which a model is likely to provide an inadequate representation of the process being modeled.

1 INTRODUCTION

Building a model for an inference problem involves constructing and reasoning within a restricted universe of propositions relevant to the inference problem at hand. Following Savage (1954), I term this restricted universe a *small world* (actually, a small *set* of possible worlds). The small world must obviously include those propositions of direct inferential interest. It also includes certain other propositions which bear on the propositions of interest and about which information may be available, either directly or indirectly. A model for the inference problem specifies relationships (logical or probabilistic) between propositions in the small world, and inference rules for revising beliefs as information is obtained.

The small world includes those propositions represented explicitly in the inference system. But a model of the relationships between these propositions often depends on a background context that is not explicitly represented. The model may make inferences that are seriously in error if these background assumptions are violated. For example, a medical diagnosis system may confidently misdiagnose a patient who is actually suffering from a disease it does not know about. A threat assessment system will be deceived by electronic interference that puts "ghost targets" on the radar screen if the behavior of the interference device is not represented in its knowledge base. A navigation system may go awry if unforseen weather conditions impact the performance of its sensors.

No modeler can hope to cover all possibilities that might arise. If the model is a good one, the situations it cannot handle should be rare. But it is important to be able to recognize such situations when they arise. Even when a system cannot revise its own model of the situation, it can alert the user that its model may be inadequate in the current situation. As research in dynamic model construction matures, model failure indicators will provide an important component of a control strategy for model construction and revision. It may be necessary or desirable not to explore some search paths during network construction, or to prune parts of the network when hypotheses become improbable or nearly independent of the hypotheses of interest. But an improbable hypothesis may become more probable as more evidence is observed. In such situations, a trigger is needed to alert the system that it may be necessary to explore search paths that were initially ignored, or to bring back pruned parts of the network.

2 BACKGROUND

A small world for an inference problem can be represented as a vector $\underline{X}$ of *propositional variables.* Each variable X_i can take on values in the set $X_i \in \{x_{i1}, \ldots, x_{ik_i}\}$. Let $\underline{X}_e$ denote a subvector of $\underline{X}$ whose values have been observed; these are called the *evidence* variables. Let $\underline{X}_t$ denote a subvector of *target* variables, or variables whose values have not been observed, but are of direct interest. Denote the remaining *unobserved* variables as $\underline{X}_u$. Unobserved variables may become evidence variables if their values are observed at a future time, but at present their values are of interest only because of their relationship to the target variables. Assume the variables are ordered so that $\underline{X} = \{\underline{X}_t, \underline{X}_e, \underline{X}_u\}$. The goal of inference is to draw conclusions about the values of the target variables $\underline{X}_t$ given observed values $\underline{x}_e$ for the evidence variables.

A probabilistic model for the small world assigns a probability distribution over the variables in the small world. The *assessed* probability for an assignment of values to the variables is denoted by $P^a(\underline{x})$. Inference within the model consists of conditioning the assessed probability distribution on the observed values for the evidence variables:

$$P^a(\underline{x}_t,\underline{x}_u \mid \underline{x}_e) = \frac{P^a(\underline{x})}{P^a(\underline{x}_e)}, \text{ or}$$

$$P^a(\underline{x}_t \mid \underline{x}_e) = \sum_{\underline{x}_u} P^a(\underline{x}_t,\underline{x}_u \mid \underline{x}_e) \,. \tag{1}$$

A model is at best an approximation of what is being modeled. The distribution $P^a(\cdot)$ is assessed relative to some assumed context; if the assumptions are violated, then the model no longer applies. If $P^a(\cdot)$ is a good approximation, one should feel confident that the assumptions underlying the model are at least approximately correct. Intuitively, the approximation is good if $P^a(\underline{x}_t \mid \underline{x}_e)$ is nearly correct for most $\underline{x}_e$.

This intuitive notion of a good approximation is far from precise, and glosses over some important questions. What does it mean for $P^a(\underline{x}_t \mid \underline{x}_e)$ to be "nearly correct?" What should be the definition of "most $\underline{x}_e$?" I return to these questions later, when I formalize the idea of approximating a model. For now, an intuitive understanding of the quality of an approximation should suffice.

Until recently, research on automated probabilistic inference has focused on computationally efficient methods for computing (1). Much less consideration has been given to the issue of deciding whether (1) is an adequate representation of the data generating process. The statistical community has devoted more attention to this issue, and there is a large literature on the theory of statistical hypothesis testing. However, the statistical hypothesis testing paradigm assumes an explicit, well formulated alternative model against which the current model is tested. In artificial intelligence applications, the purpose of model diagnosis is to initiate search for an alternative model. Requiring explicit representation and computation of the alternative model prior to model diagnosis defeats the purpose of the entire enterprise.

Research on model diagnosis from an AI perspective is beginning to receive more attention. There is general agreement that suspicion should be aroused when a combination of evidence items occurs that was initially assessed to be highly improbable: that is, when $P^a(\underline{x}_e)$ = LOW.[1] The problem with this idea is defining LOW. When there are many uncertain evidence items, the probability of any one combination of values is bound to be quite small. Thus, the definition of a low-probability evidence combination must be relative to the other evidence combinations that might have occurred.

Habbema (1976) suggests identifying a set of "surprising" observations. An observation in the surprising set triggers extra diagnostic attention for the case in question. According to Habbema's definition, each observation identified as surprising must be less probable than all observations not considered surprising; and the total probability of the set of surprising observations must be less than some threshold α. Laskey (1990) suggests comparing $P^a(\underline{x}_e)$ with the expected value $E[P^a(\underline{X}_e)]$ of the probability of the evidence. These suggested approaches do provide measures of relative improbability, but they appear to be computationally intractable for the inference network models common in the literature on uncertainty in AI.

Jensen et al. (1990) suggest a tractable indicator of *conflict* between items of evidence. Their conflict measure can be written:

$$c_J = \log_2\left(\frac{P^a(x_{e1})\cdots P^a(x_{ek})}{P^a(x_{e1},\ldots,x_{ek})}\right). \tag{2}$$

where the x_{ei} are the observed values of the components of the evidence vector $\underline{X}_e = (X_{e1},\ldots,X_{ek})$. This measure is easy to compute using any of the currently popular evidence propagation algorithms. Both the numerator and denominator of (2) can be produced as a natural byproduct of evidence accumulation, if each node stores its original prior probability distribution $P^a(X_i)$ along with its current conditional probability distribution $P^a(X_i \mid \underline{x}_e)$. The numerator of (2) is just the product of the prior probabilities of the observed values of the evidence variables. The denominator is also straightforward to compute as follows. Assume that evidence items $x_{e1}, \ldots, x_{ek-1}$ have been observed, that $P(x_{e1},\ldots,x_{ek-1})$ has been computed, and that the evidence absorption algorithm has resulted in the computation of a revised distribution for X_{ek}, namely $P^a(X_{ek} \mid x_{e1},\ldots,x_{ek-1})$. Now, when x_{ek} is observed, the required joint probability can easily be computed: $P^a(x_{e1},\ldots,x_{ek})=P^a(x_{ek}|x_{e1},\ldots,x_{ek-1})P^a(x_{e1},\ldots,x_{ek-1})$.

Jensen et al. justify c_J heuristically: they simply assert that one would expect the observed evidence to have higher probability than the product of the joint probabilities. Intuitively, if x_{e1} has been observed, it might be reasonable to expect to observe values for X_{e2}

[1] This recommendation appears to violate the likelihood principle, a central tenet of Bayesian theory. According to the likelihood principle, the likelihood of data that might have been observed is irrelevant; all that matters is what was observed. But the likelihood principle applies to the agent's "true" model. The likelihood of unobserved data may indeed be relevant to the issue of whether the current approximation remains tenable.

Figure 1: c_J Positive With Probability .55

P(x,y)

	y1	y2	y3	
x1	.1125	.11	.11	.3325
x2	.1125	.11	.11	.3325
x3	.11	.1125	.1125	.335
	.335	.3325	.3325	

P(x)P(y)

	y1	y2	y3	
x1	.1114	.1106	.1106	.3325
x2	.1114	.1106	.1106	.3325
x3	.1122	.1114	.1114	.335
	.335	.3325	.3325	

c_J given (x,y)

	y1	y2	y3
x1	-.0413	.0073	.0073
x2	-.0413	.0073	.0073
x3	.0289	-.0413	-.0413

that are made more likely by the observation of x_{e1}, that is, values x_{e2} for which

$$P(x_{e2} \mid x_{e1}) > P(x_{e2}) \text{ , or}$$

$$P(x_{e1},x_{e2}) = P(x_{e2} \mid x_{e1})P(x_{e1}) > P(x_{e1})P(x_{e2}) \text{ .} \quad (3)$$

But the example in Table 1 demonstrates that it is not necessarily ture that (3) is satisfied most of the time. In this example, there is a .55 chance that c_J is greater than zero, i.e., there is a better than even chance that the product of the marginal probabilities exceeds the joint probability.

Although it may be probable that c_J is greater than zero, I will show in the next section that very large values of c_J are highly improbable. Furthermore, c_J is never positive in expected value. Its expectation is given by:

$$E[c_J] = -\sum_{\underline{x}_e} P^a(\underline{x}_e)\log_2\left(\frac{P^a(\underline{x}_e)}{P^a(x_{e1})\cdots P^a(x_{ek})}\right) \text{ .} \quad (4)$$

This quantity is the negative of the information theoretic distance from the probability distribution $P^a(\cdot)$ to the distribution $P^i(\cdot)$, in which all the X_{ei} are independent, but their marginal distributions are the same as their marginal distributions under $P^a(\cdot)$. That is, the *expected value* of c_J is a measure of how closely the probability distribution $P^i(\cdot)$ approximates the assessed distribution $P^a(\cdot)$. A well-known result from information theory states that (4) is never positive and is equal to zero only if the distributions $P^a(\cdot)$ and $P^i(\cdot)$ are identical (Kullback, 1959). In other words, the expected value of c_J is more negative the greater the nonindependency among evidence items--that is, the less well $P^i(\cdot)$ approximates $P^a(\cdot)$.

When c_J is positive, the probability $P^i(\underline{x}_e)$ of $\underline{x}_e$ under the independence model is greater than the probability $P^a(\underline{x}_e)$ under the assessed distribution. In other words, a model in which the evidence items are independent fits the observed evidence better than does the assessed distribution. Now, the whole modeling exercise was based on the assumption that the X_{ei} were related to $\underline{X}_t$, and therefore to each other. That is, combinations of evidence items characteristic of a particular $\underline{x}_t$ should tend to occur together. When the independence model fits better than the assessed distribution, it is an indication that the particular combination $\underline{x}_e$ of observed values is characteristic of no $\underline{x}_t$ under the current model.

The next section generalizes c_J to a family of "model suspicion" measures based on comparing how well $P^a(\cdot)$ fits the evidence relative to an alternative model. Unlike formal statistical hypothesis testing, the alternative model is generally not taken seriously as a candidate model for the data generating process. Rather, its purpose is to alert a system or user that the current model may be inadequate given the current situation.

3 THEORETICAL FRAMEWORK

It is now time to develop a formal framework for model approximation and model failure diagnosis. Assume that the small world $\underline{X}$ is embedded within a larger world $\underline{W} = (\underline{X}',\underline{Y})$. The vector $\underline{X}'$ represents the same variables as $\underline{X}$, but each may have additional outcomes in the larger world that are not represented in the small world. That is, $X_i' \in \{x_{i1}, \ldots, x_{ik_i}, x_{i(k_i+1)}, \ldots, x_{ir_i}\}$, where only the first k_i values are also possible values for $\underline{X}$. The vector $\underline{Y}$ corresponds to variables that are not explicitly represented in the small world. Assume that there is some probability distribution $P(\cdot)$ on the larger world which $P^a(\cdot)$ is intended to approximate.

Interpreting the distribution $P(\cdot)$ raises philosophical issues which lie beyond the scope of this paper, but a few words on how I interpret $P(\cdot)$ are appropriate. My main concern is with an automated reasoning system which computes belief values for the target variables $\underline{X}_e$ based on any evidence $\underline{x}_e$ that has been observed to date. Such systems are usually engineered by assessing probabilities from some expert or experts in the domain about which the system reasons. In this context, $P^a(\cdot)$ represents a probability distribution assessed from the expert, who has restricted attention to the small world $\underline{X}$. I assume that $P^a(\cdot)$ approximates some distribution $P(\cdot)$ over $\underline{W}$, in the sense that $P^a(\cdot)$ is obtained from $P(\cdot)$ by conditioning on the small world $\underline{X}$. This does not necessarily mean that $P(\cdot)$ exactly represents the expert's beliefs over $\underline{W}$, or even that the expert has well-defined and coherent "true" probabilities over $\underline{W}$. What I do assume is that if the expert were to make the effort to assess beliefs over the expanded world $\underline{W}$, that this would result in the distribution $P(\cdot)$, and that this distribution is a more accurate representation of the expert's beliefs than the assessed distribution $P^a(\cdot)$. In other words, if computation and assessment burden were not an issue, and if a second system were built using the distribution $P(\cdot)$, the expert would feel more satisfied with the output of the second system than with the output of the system based on the model $P^a(\cdot)$. It is also assumed that the expert thinks it is unlikely that the assumptions underlying the assessments are violated--that is, the expert thinks the small world is probable.

A somewhat different interpretation is appropriate for systems designed for dynamic model revision. Here it is assumed that the full distribution $P(\cdot)$ was assessed from the expert, but is represented only implicitly in the system's knowledge base. The system has explicitly constructed just a small portion of this large implicit joint probability distribution. The assumptions underlying the model the system constructs amount to conditioning on the small world.

Let the proposition q represent the assumptions underlying the assessed distribution. The proposition q includes the restriction of the values of $\underline{X}'$ to $\underline{X}$, as well as some assumptions about the variables $\underline{Y}$:[2]

$$q = (\bigwedge_i X_i' \in \{x_{i1},\ldots,x_{ik}\}) \wedge (\bigvee_{\underline{y}_j} \underline{Y}=\underline{y}_j) . \quad (5)$$

$P^a(\cdot)$ was assessed under the assumption that q was the case. That is, for any $\underline{x}$ in the small world $\underline{X}$:

$$P^a(\underline{x}) = P(\underline{x} \mid q) = \sum_{\underline{y}} P(\underline{x},\underline{y} \mid q) . \quad (6)$$

If q is not the case, the model $P^a(\cdot)$ is not appropriate, and should be replaced by:

$$P^o(\underline{x}) = P(\underline{x} \mid \neg q) = \sum_{\underline{y}} P(\underline{x},\underline{y} \mid \neg q) . \quad (7)$$

Neither the alternative model nor the probability P(q) is assessed explicitly. However, I assume that the context q is assumed because it is thought to be probable, i.e., $P(q) = 1-\varepsilon$, where ε is small. The model $P(\cdot)$, restricted to the variables $\underline{X}'$, can be written:

$$P(\underline{x}) = (1-\varepsilon)P^a(\underline{x}) + \varepsilon P^o(\underline{x}) \quad (8)$$

(where $P^a(\underline{x})$ is understood to be equal to zero if one of the x_i is outside the range of X_i). Because ε is very small, $P^a(\underline{x})$ provides a good approximation to the correct joint probability $P(\underline{x})$.

To summarize, I assume that the small world model $P^a(\cdot)$ over $\underline{X}$ is obtained by a combination of *conditioning* on assumptions thought to be probable (i.e., conditioning on q) and *marginalizing* on variables not of direct interest (i.e., summing over values of $\underline{Y}$).

The goal of inference is to estimate $P(\underline{x}_t \mid \underline{x}_e)$. Because the conditioning operator is nonlinear, there is no guarantee that the approximation error will remain small as evidence is absorbed. The relationship between the actual and estimated posterior probabilities given $\underline{X}_e=\underline{x}_e$ can be seen from the following expression:

$$\begin{aligned} P(\underline{x}_t \mid \underline{x}_e) &= \frac{(1-\varepsilon)P^a(\underline{x}_t,\underline{x}_e) + \varepsilon P^o(\underline{x}_t,\underline{x}_e)}{(1-\varepsilon)P^a(\underline{x}_e) + \varepsilon P^o(\underline{x}_e)} \\ &= (1-\varepsilon^*)P^a(\underline{x}_t \mid \underline{x}_e) + \varepsilon^* P^o(\underline{x}_t \mid \underline{x}_e) , \end{aligned} \quad (9)$$

where

$$\varepsilon^* = \frac{\varepsilon P^o(\underline{x}_e)}{(1-\varepsilon)P^a(\underline{x}_e) + \varepsilon P^o(\underline{x}_e)} .$$

Comparing (8) and (9), it is clear that the "true" prior and posterior probabilities have the same form: both are weighted averages of the assessed model probability $P^a(\cdot)$ and the unknown alternative model probability $P^o(\cdot)$. The prior probability ε of the assessed model is replaced in (9) by ε^*, the posterior probability of the assessed model given that the evidence variables $\underline{X}_e$ take on values $\underline{x}_e$.

Note that

[2]This formulation might seem to preclude assumptions about the relationship between variables in $\underline{X}$ (e.g., that X_i and X_j are independent). However, one could [psot that X_i and X_j are independent conditional on Y_k, where Y_k has high probability.

$$\frac{\varepsilon*}{1-\varepsilon*} = \frac{\varepsilon}{(1-\varepsilon)} \cdot \frac{P^o(\underline{x}_e)}{P^a(\underline{x}_e)} . \qquad (10)$$

Thus, the approximation error becomes large when $P^o(\underline{x}_e)$ is so much larger than $P^a(\underline{x}_e)$ that it swamps the difference in magnitude between ε and 1-ε. The first term in (10) is called the *prior odds ratio*; the second term is called the *likelihood ratio* of the data given the two models being compared.

It would seem straightforward, then, to decide when a model is no longer a good approximation to the observed data. Simply compare the probability of the observations under the approximate model to the probability under the alternative model, and initiate model revision when the ratio of these probabilities becomes too small. But a moment's thought reveals that this will not do: the reason for adopting the approximation in the first place was to avoid the expense of explicitly constructing a detailed model of the many improbable contexts in which $P^a(\cdot)$ does not apply. In other words, you need to have already performed model revision in order to have $P^o(\underline{x}_e)$ available for computing (10).

However, it may be possible to formulate "straw models," which capture some of the expert's intuitions about how the model could go wrong but are computationally much simpler than the fully specified alternate model. The independence model described in Section 2 is just such a model. The following theorem shows that a straw model is unlikely to fit much better than the assessed model in cases for which the assessed model applies.

Theorem 1: Let $P^a(\cdot)$ and $P^s(\cdot)$ be probability distributions over $\underline{X}$. Define the index of surprise at evidence $\underline{x}_e$ under $P^a(\cdot)$ relative to $P^s(\cdot)$ as:

$$c_S = \log_2\left(\frac{P^s(\underline{x}_e)}{P^a(\underline{x}_e)}\right) . \qquad (11)$$

Let π_K be the probability under $P^a(\cdot)$ that c_S is greater than K. Then $\pi_K < 2^{-K}$.

Proof:

$$1 = \sum_{\underline{x}_e} P^s(\underline{x}_e) \geq \sum_{\frac{P^s(\underline{x}_e)}{P^a(\underline{x}_e)} > 2^K} \frac{P^s(\underline{x}_e)}{P^a(\underline{x}_e)} P^a(\underline{x}_e)$$

$$\geq \sum_{\frac{P^s(\underline{x}_e)}{P^a(\underline{x}_e)} > 2^K} 2^K \cdot P^a(\underline{x}_e) = 2^K \pi_K .$$

Therefore, $\pi_K < 2^{-K}$ •

A trivial consequence of Theorem 1 is that high values of conflict are *a priori* unlikely when the assessed model is considered probable. That is, *any* alternative model specified *a priori* is unlikely to fit the data much better than the assessed model.[3]

Corollary 1: If $\underline{X}_e$ is distributed according to $P(\underline{x}_e) = (1-\varepsilon)P^a(\underline{x}_e) + \varepsilon P^o(\underline{x}_e)$, where $P^o(\cdot)$ is a distribution not necessarily the same as $P^s(\cdot)$, then the probability that c_S is less than K exceeds $(1 - \varepsilon)(1 - 2^{-K})$.

The trick is to specify an alternate model that is likely to fit the data better than the assessed model when $P^a(\cdot)$ does *not* apply. That is, we would like for c_S to be large when ε* is large (or at least in the most probable situations in which ε* is large). To construct a model revision indicator, then, the modeler thinks carefully about situations in which the model might not apply, and about how the predictions of the model might fail when this happens. The modeler then formulates a straw model $P^s(\cdot)$ which is computationally simple but captures some important features of situations in which the assessed model is likely to fail.

Consider for example the conflict indicator c_J. The evidence variables $\underline{x}_e$ are predictors of the target variables. They should therefore be expected to be marginally dependent--certain patterns of values of the x_{e_i} are likely to occur together because they indicate a particular target vector $\underline{x}_t$; other combinations of values are unlikely because they are unlikely given *any* target vector. Without formulating an alternate model in detail, the modeler can still use situations in which the independence model fits the data better than the assessed model to diagnose possible problems with the assessed model.

4 REBUTTALS

A general theoretical framework for heuristic model revision indicators has been presented. In summary, the system is assumed to reason under a current model, which is regarded as an approximation to some more accurate model which may or may not be represented implicitly in the system's knowledge base. The approximate model is conditioned on an assumed context which the system regards as highly probable. If the assessed model is an accurate model of the phenomenon in question, it would be expected to fit the data better than other candidate models. A heuristic model revision indicator can be constructed by building

[3]Of course, one can always specify after the fact a model that predicted the observed data exactly. When there are many uncertain evidence items, the observed evidence will have a very low probability, and this "20-20 hindsight" model will fit much better than the assessed model. However, the *a priori* probability that exactly this model would fit the data was extremely low.

an alternate "straw model" which is not necessarily taken seriously as a model of the phenomenon in question, but which is likely to fit better than the assessed model in some class of situations which violate the assumed context.

I have already considered one example of a "straw model" which gives rise to Jensen et al.'s conflict indicator c_J. In this section, I relate another proposed model revision strategy (Laskey, 1990) to the framework proposed in Section 3.

A *Bayesian network* for the probability model $P^a(\cdot)$ is a directed acyclic graph in which each node corresponds to a variable X_i and the directed arcs encode direct conditional dependencies. Suppose that $\mathcal{N}$ is a Bayesian network for $P^a(\cdot)$ and $X_{i_1}, \ldots, X_{i_k}$ is an ordering of the variables such that all predecessors of X_{i_j} in $\mathcal{N}$ are also predecessors in the ordering. Then X_{i_j} is independent of all preceding X_{i_m} given its immediate predecessors in $\mathcal{N}$. The direct parents of the node X_i are denoted by the vector $\underline{X}_{p(i)}$.

A probability model and associated Bayesian network on a set $\underline{X}$ of variables can be completely characterized by its *node models*. A node model for variable X_i is the tuple

$$\mathcal{M}_i = (X_i, \underline{X}_{p(i)}, P^a(X_i \mid \underline{X}_{p(i)})) \tag{12}$$

consisting of the variable, its direct parents in $\mathcal{N}$, and a set of conditional probability distributions for the node, one for each combination of values for its parent variables.

In previous work (Laskey, 1990; see also Laskey, Cohen and Martin, 1989), I have suggested associating *rebuttals* with each node model.[4] A rebuttal is a proposition expressing a condition under which the assessed probability distribution for the node model does not apply. Rebuttals make explicit the contextual assumptions underlying the model: in the terminology of Section 3, the truth of a rebuttal implies $\neg q$. Thus, the system can monitor the rebuttal propositions and trigger model revision when a rebuttal is observed to be true.

However, the system may not have the resources to check rebuttals routinely, or obtaining information about some rebuttals may be costly in time or other resources. Sometimes it might be desirable to associate a general "*ceteris non paribus*" rebuttal with a node model. That is, one allows for the possibility that the node model does not apply, but does not explicitly model the circumstances under which the assumptions are violated (unless the general rebuttal becomes sufficiently probable to warrant such effort).

Let R_i be a variable taking on values $R_i \in \{t_i, f_i\}$, where t_i means that at least one of the rebuttals to $\mathcal{M}_i$ is true, and $f_i = \neg t_i$ means that all rebuttals are false. The assessed node model distribution assumes f_i. That is, $P^a(X_i \mid \underline{X}_{p(i)}) = P(X_i \mid \underline{X}_{p(i)}, f_i)$. To completely specify a model including the rebuttal variable R_i would mean specifying two additional distributions: the distribution of X_i given its parents and t_i, and the distribution of t_i. Additional compications may arise: t_i might imply that X_i depends directly on other nodes in addition to $\underline{X}_{p(i)}$, and R_i might depend on other nodes or other rebuttals (some condition may invalidate more than one node model). The network might become computationally intractable if these complexities were included explicitly (in fact, assuming them away may have been a computationally motivated approximation).

It may be useful to specify a straw model which does not cover all these complexities, but might be expected to fit better than the assessed model when one of the rebuttals is true. Consider the following simplified model. First, a rebuttal is assumed to "break the link" between a node and its parents, so that:

$$P^s(X_i \mid \underline{X}_{p(i)}, t_i) = P^s(X_i \mid t_i) . \tag{13}$$

That is, given t_i, X_i is conditionally independent of all the nodes above it in $\mathcal{N}$, and has the distribution $P^s(X_i \mid t_i)$. Second, the rebuttals for different node models are assumed to be marginally independent of all other nodes in the network (i.e., R_i has no predecessors in $\mathcal{N}$ or among the other R_j).

If the rebuttals are included explicitly in the inference network, the posterior probability $P^s(R_i \mid \underline{x}_e)$ is computed as part of evidence propagation. If the general rebuttal R_i becomes probable, it may flag the system to build a more detailed model of the conditions under which the current node model for X_i is not valid.

However, explicit representation of rebuttals doubles the number of nodes in the network.[5] It is desirable to find a computationally simple method to determine when a rebuttal R_i has become probable. To determine the probability of R_i given evidence, one computes the posterior odds ratio by multiplying the likelihood ratio by the prior odds ratio:

$$\frac{P^s(t_i \mid \underline{x}_e)}{P^s(f_i \mid \underline{x}_e)} = \frac{P^s(\underline{x}_e \mid t_i)}{P^s(\underline{x}_e \mid f_i)} \times \frac{P^s(t_i)}{P^s(f_i)} . \tag{14}$$

When the likelihood ratio is large, the evidence $\underline{x}_e$ increases the posterior probability of t_i relative to its prior probability. This likelihood ratio can be rewritten as:

[4]The term rebuttal is due to Toulmin (e.g., Toulmin et al., 1984); its use in this context is due to Marvin Cohen (cf., Cohen, Laskey and Ulvila, 1987).

[5]No loops are added to the network, so algorithms to find loop cutsets or clique trees need work no harder.

$$\frac{P^s(\underline{x}_e \mid t_i)}{P^s(\underline{x}_e \mid f_i)} =$$

$$\frac{\sum_{(x_i,\underline{x}_{p(i)})} P^s(\underline{x}_e \mid x_i,\underline{x}_{p(i)})\, P^s(x_i \mid t_i)\, P^s(\underline{x}_{p(i)})}{\sum_{(x_i,\underline{x}_{p(i)})} P^s(\underline{x}_e \mid x_i,\underline{x}_{p(i)})\, P^a(x_i \mid \underline{x}_{p(i)})\, P^s(\underline{x}_{p(i)})} \quad . \quad (15)$$

Note that the first and last terms in the summands are the same in numerator and denominator, and that these terms are independent of R_i. If R_i is the only rebuttal in the model, (15) can be reexpressed as:

$$\frac{\sum_{(x_i,\underline{x}_{p(i)})} P^a(\underline{x}_e \mid x_i,\underline{x}_{p(i)})\, P^s(x_i \mid t_i)\, P^a(\underline{x}_{p(i)})}{\sum_{(x_i,\underline{x}_{p(i)})} P^a(\underline{x}_e \mid x_i,\underline{x}_{p(i)})\, P^a(x_i \mid \underline{x}_{p(i)})\, P^a(\underline{x}_{p(i)})}$$

$$= \frac{\sum_{(x_i,\underline{x}_{p(i)})} P^a(\underline{x}_e \mid x_i,\underline{x}_{p(i)})\, P^a(x_i,x_{p(i)}) \dfrac{P^s(x_i \mid t_i)}{P^a(x_i \mid x_{p(i)})}}{P^a(\underline{x}_e)}$$

$$= \sum_{(x_i,\underline{x}_{p(i)})} P^a(x_i,\underline{x}_{p(i)} \mid \underline{x}_e) \frac{P^s(x_i \mid t_i)}{P^a(x_i \mid x_{p(i)})} \quad . \quad (16)$$

When there are rebuttals for other nodes as well, (16) is only approximate. It is a close approximation if the posterior probabilities of all rebuttals other than R_i are small.

The sum (16) will be large when the evidence $\underline{x}_e$ makes probable values of $(x_i,\underline{x}_{p(i)})$ for which the straw model probability $P^s(x_i \mid t_i)$ is much larger than the assessed probability $P^a(x_i \mid \underline{x}_{p(i)})$. This might happen if x_i is a very atypical value of X_i given the values $\underline{x}_{p(i)}$ for the parent variables, but the evidence makes both x_i and $\underline{x}_{p(i)}$ very probable.

Clique tree algorithms automatically keep track of the joint probabilities of the $(x_i, \underline{x}_{p(i)})$; other algorithms can be modified to do so. However, computation of (16) generally amounts to about as much work as explicitly modeling R_i. Computation can be reduced by pre-selecting a subset of $(x_i,\underline{x}_{p(i)})$ for which $P^s(x_i \mid t_i)$ is much larger than $P^a(x_i \mid \underline{x}_{p(i)})$, and monitoring the posterior probability for only the selected subset of values for X_i and its parents.

5 RARE CASES

I have suggested that model revision should be considered when low probability evidence is observed. But even if the model is correct, things which it assigns low probability are occasionally expected to happen. Is there any way to distinguish between rare cases for which the model is correct and cases not covered by the model?

Sometimes the conflict can be explained by some rare hypothesis which is covered by the model. That is, there may be some variable X_k for which the value x_{k_H} would make the observed evidence $\underline{x}_e$ highly probable. The probability of the evidence can be written as:

$$P^a(\underline{x}_e) = P^a(\underline{x}_e \mid x_{k_H})P^a(x_{k_H}) + P^a(\underline{x}_e \mid \bar{x}_{k_H})P^a(\bar{x}_{k_H}) \ .$$

This can be very small even when $P^a(\underline{x}_e \mid x_{k_H})$ is high if x_{k_H} was initially thought to be a very improbable value for X_k. If such a rare hypothesis could explain the conflict, the value of the conflict indicator c_S will typically be decreased by independent evidence for x_{k_H}. That is, one finds an observable variable X_f for which the assessed probability of x_{f_H} is high given $X_k = x_{k_H}$ but low given $X_k \neq x_{k_H}$. Observing X_f may resolve the issue. Precisely speaking, the value $(\underline{x}_e, x_{f_H})$ was assessed to be much more probable relative to other values of $(\underline{X}_e, X_f)$ than was the value $\underline{x}_e$ relative to other values of $\underline{X}_e$. Unless this is also true of the straw model, the conflict will be reduced upon observing $\underline{x}_{f_H}$.

In any case, it is generally wise to single out for special attention cases which occur but were initially assessed to be highly improbable. It may be that, being rare, they were not thought deserving of as close modeling attention. Or it may have been that a heuristic model construction algorithm pruned parts of the network that were independent of the variables of interest given the falsity of the improbable hypotheses. These modeling decisions may need to be reexamined if the hypotheses become more probable than originally thought.

6 DISCUSSION

If probabilistic reasoning methods are to be used on problems where flexible network reconfiguration is necessary, indicators must be constructed that tell the system when its current model appears to be inadequate. Even for static models, it is important to alert users to situations which the system's model was not designed to handle. An exact decision theoretic calculation would require actually revising the model to decide whether model revision is necessary. This is clearly infeasible. This paper presented a class of theoretically justified heuristic model revision indicators. The idea is to construct a computationally simple alternate model which, although not a tenable model for the phenomenon, is likely to fit the evidence better than the current model if the current model is incorrect. Model revision is initiated when the likelihood ratio of the evidence given the alternate model becomes unacceptably large.

Acknowledgements

This work was supported by a grant from the Virginia Center for Innovative Technology to the Center of Excellence in Command, Control, Communications and Intelligence at George Mason University.

References

Cohen, M.S., Laskey, K.B., and Ulvila, J.W., The Management of Uncertainty in Intelligence Data: A Self-Reconciling Evidential Database, Reston, VA: Decision Science Consortium, Inc., 1987.

Jensen, F.V., Chamberlain, B., Nordahl, T. and Jensen F. (1990). Analysis in HUGIN of Data Conflict. In *Proceedings of the Sixth Conference on Uncertainty in Artificial Intelligence*, Boston, MA, 546-554. Association for Uncertainty in Artificial Intelligence, Mountain View, CA.

Habbema, J.D.F. (1976). Models for Diagnosis and Detection of Combinations of Diseases. Decision Making and Medical Care. de Dombal et al. (eds), North Holland.

Kullback, S. (1959). *Information Theory and Statistics*. NY: Wiley.

Laskey, K.B. (1990). A Probabilistic Reasoning Environment. In *Proceedings of the Sixth Conference on Uncertainty in Artificial Intelligence*, Boston, MA, 415-422. Association for Uncertainty in Artificial Intelligence, Mountain View, CA.

Laskey, K.B., Cohen, M.S., and Martin, A.W. (1989). Representing and Eliciting Knowledge about Uncertain Evidence and its Implications. *IEEE Transactions on Systems, Man, and Cybernetics, 19*, 536-545.

Savage, L.J. (1954). *The Foundations of Statistics*. NY: Wiley.

Toulmin, S.E., Rieke, R., and Janik, A. (1984). *An Introduction to Reasoning*. NY: MacMillan.

Reasoning under Uncertainty: Some Monte Carlo Results

Paul E. Lehner
Systems Engineering and C3I Center
George Mason University
Fairfax, VA 22303
plehner@gmuvax2.gmu.edu

Azar D. Sadigh
C3I Center
George Mason University
Fairfax, VA 22303

Abstract

A series of monte carlo studies were performed to compare the behavior of some alternative procedures for reasoning under uncertainty. The behavior of several Bayesian, linear model and default reasoning procedures were examined in the context of increasing levels of calibration error. The most interesting result is that Bayesian procedures tended to output more extreme posterior belief values (posterior beliefs near 0.0 or 1.0) than other techniques, but the linear models were relatively less likely to output strong support for an erroneous conclusion. Also, accounting for the probabilistic dependencies between evidence items was important for both Bayesian and linear updating procedures.

1 INTRODUCTION

Reasoning under uncertainty often involves a great deal of judgmental imprecision. The subjective (or data base retrieved) uncertainty estimates that serve as ingredients of an uncertainty calculus are often perceived as arbitrary, imprecise or uncertain. One consequence of this judgmental imprecision is that many decision makers (and researchers) avoid using an explicit uncertainty calculus for fear of being subject to a garbage in-garbage out problem. In this paper this problem is examined by studying the extent to which several different inference procedures are robustly accurate in the context of increasing levels of judgmental imprecision. This paper updates the preliminary report found in Lehner (1990).

2 METHOD

A series of monte carlo studies were performed in which we iterated through the following steps.

Generate "True" Probabilities - Each run involves an inference problem with one hypothesis (H) node, and either four or seven evidence nodes (A-G). Each node is bi-valued. A "true" probability distribution[1] is defined by randomly assigning (from 0-1 uniform distribution) a value to each instance of P(H=T), P(A=T|H), P(B=T|HA), P(C=T|HAB), etc.[2]

Assigning Belief Values - For each probability distribution, a distribution of belief values was generated by adding random error to the true probabilities. For the runs reported in this paper all the error distributions were uniform. Specifically,

B(x|y) = min + (max-min)*RND,

where

min = maximum[0.0,P(x|y)-(range/2)]
max = minimum[1.0,P(x|y)+(range/2)].

Here P(x|y) is the true conditional probability, B(x|y) is the belief value that is obtained by adding random error to the true probability, RND is a random number and "range" is the range of the error distribution, which we call the error range. When error range = 0.0, the belief values equal the true probabilities. When error range = 2.0, there is no correlation between the true probabilities and the belief values. Our simulation runs used error ranges in the set {0.0, 0.2, 0.4, 0.6, 0.8, 1.0, 1.2, 1.4, 1.6, 1.8, 2.0).

No matter what the error range, the belief values define a fully-specified and coherent distribution. The inputs to

[1] As noted in Lehner (1990) calibration error can be defined without relying the concept of a true probability. Our use of the term "true" is merely a convenience.

[2] A notational note. An expression such P(A=T|H=T&BC) is a template for a set of expressions. In this case, P(A=T|H=T,B=T,C=T), P(A=T|H=T,B=T,C=F), ... are instances of this template.

each of the inference procedures were derived from this underlying distribution of belief values.

Inference Procedures - A variety of inference procedures were examined. Each inference procedure prescribes a mechanism for evaluating evidence to generate a posterior belief value. For example, in Bayesian inference the posterior belief in H=T given A=F, B=T, C=T and D=T (i.e., PB(H=T|A=F B=T C=T D=T)) is determined by Bayes rule, whereas the linear models calculate this by a weighted sum of evidence items that support or contradict H=T. The specific inference procedures are described individually in the results section.

Empirical Evaluation - For each inference procedure we recorded the distribution of posterior belief values for H=T and H=F. Table 1 gives a typical example using the procedure Proper Bayes. Consider the first cell in this table. It indicates that when error range = 0.0, the expected probability that the posterior belief in H=T is less than .11 when in fact H=T is .068. That is

$$P(PB(H=T)<.11|H=T)=.068.$$

In addition, we also calculated normalized difference between the means (d') between the distributions P(PB(H=T)|H=F) and P(PB(H=T)|H=T). This provides an estimate of the extent to which the inference procedure differentiates between the H=T and H=F condition.

Analytical Evaluation - After each monte carlo run we performed an analytical evaluation to explain the results and to identify the extent to which the results are likely to generalize. These analyses were used to design the each new monte carlo run. Rather than execute a series of undirected simulations, each monte carlo run was designed to address a question that the previous analysis left unanswered.

3 RESULTS

Presented below are the principal results of this study.

3.1 BAYESIAN UPDATING

Bayesianism is a school of thought that argues that a rational system of belief values should conform to the probability calculus and that Bayes rule should be the mechanism by which posterior beliefs are calculated (e.g., Pearl, 1988). In Bayesian theory posterior belief values should be conditioned on all available evidence and all probabilistic interactions among those evidence items should be taken into account. In practice it is often necessary to implement simplified Bayesian procedures that ignore some of the interactions between evidence items. In this study we examined the theoretically correct and two simplified Bayesian procedures.

3.1.1 Proper Bayes

Here we used Bayes rule properly. For instance, in the four evidence case for each evidential state

PB(H=T|ABCD) =

$$\sum B(H=T \ \& \ ABCD) / \sum B(HABCD)$$

Table 1 shows the results for three error ranges. Note the shape of the distributions. Proper Bayesian updating consistently resulted in a U-shaped distribution of posterior belief values. This indicates that when H=T, Bayesian updating is more likely to derive an extreme posterior belief value (less than .11) in the wrong direction than an intermediate value (between .44 and .56). The results for H=F are symmetric and are not reported separately.

It is also worth noting that as the error range increased, the proportion of posterior belief values in the middle range (between .33 and .67) did not change substantially. The suggests that proper Bayesian conditioning consistently outputs strong support for some conclusion, and that input error tends to increase the probability that the output values will show strong support for the wrong conclusion.

The U-shaped nature of the posterior belief curve can be accounted for by the fact that Bayesian conditioning is a multiplicative rule applied to likelihood ratios. Whenever the input belief values are very small, there is considerable potential for significant error. We tested this hypothesis by forcing belief values to lie between .05 and .95, and rerunning the simulation. As shown in Table 2, this did have the effect of smoothing out the tail, but as the error range increased the U-shape reappeared.

3.1.2 Naive Bayes

One way to simplify the application of Bayesian inference is to treat the evidence items as though they are conditionally independent of each other. Bayesian models of this type are often called *Naive Bayesian models.* Although recognized as a simplification, this approach does make it easier to apply Bayesian procedures to a large variety of inference problems (e.g., Edwards, et.al., 1968).

Table 1: Average Probability of Posterior Belief Values for Proper Bayes

Posterior Belief	Four Evidence Items 0.00	0.40	1.20	Seven Evidence Items 0.00	0.40	1.20
.00-.11	.068	.075	.151	.047	.058	.159
.11-.22	.050	.055	.082	.031	.037	.065
.22-.33	.048	.053	.071	.029	.035	.052
.33-.44	.049	.052	.063	.030	.034	.049
.44-.56	.053	.057	.066	.033	.039	.051
.56-.67	.063	.066	.072	.039	.046	.056
.67-.78	.080	.087	.083	.054	.060	.068
.78-.89	.122	.127	.114	.088	.097	.100
.89-1.0	.467	.428	.298	.650	.593	.399
d'	1.00	0.88	0.32	1.61	1.34	.046

In our study, we examined two forms of naive Bayesian updating. In both cases we used the marginal probability of each evidence item given H=T and H=F to calculate posterior belief. In the case of Simple Naive Bayes, all evidence items were used to calculate posterior belief values. For Strong Naive Bayes posterior belief was calculated in the same way except that for any evidence item x, if $2/3 < B(x|H=T)/B(x|H=F) < 3/2$ then x was dropped from the calculation (i.e., likelihood ratio set to 1).

Table 3 shows the results for some of the Simple Naive Bayes runs. The Strong Naive Bayes results were nearly identical and are not reported separately. In general, the pattern of results were the same as with Proper Bayes, but the differentiation between the two distributions was considerably less. This is reflected in the lower d' values. Surprisingly, when there are seven evidence items, the distribution of belief values remained almost the same. The d' values for Simple Naive Bayes were .68, .60 and .21 which are close to the d' values in Table 3.

Table 2: Average Probability of Posterior Belief Values for Proper Bayes When Extreme Belief Values Are Suppressed

Posterior Belief	Four Evidence Items 0.00	0.40	1.20
.00-.11	.046	.053	.116
.11-.22	.053	.058	.091
.22-.33	.053	.057	.080
.33-.44	.056	.059	.075
.44-.56	.062	.065	.077
.56-.67	.075	.077	.084
.67-.78	.094	.098	.097
.78-.89	.146	.145	.131
.89-1.0	.414	.387	.249
d'	1.02	0.91	0.34

3.2 LINEAR MODELS

In the judgment and decision making (JDM) research literature there is a tradition of research that focuses on the use of linear models to predict human judgment (see Dawes, 1979 for review; Levi, 1989 for recent example). This work is based on two rather surprising but reliable results. First, in probabilistic domains, linear models are often good predictors of human judgment. Even for tasks that appear to be fundamentally pattern-based (e.g., clinical judgment), a regression model of an expert's judgments is usually a good predictor of that expert's future judgments. Second, linear models of expert judgment usually perform better than the experts from which they were derived. This result even holds for linear models with improper equal-weights.

Here we examined three types of linear models.

Complex Linear. This technique simply adds up pros and cons and normalizes the result to the number of possible evidence items. A pro was defined as any evidence item for which the conditional probability of that evidence item given the hypothesis and *other evidence items* was greater than one. For instance, for the evidential state A=T, B=F, C=T and D=T, evidence item "C=T" was considered a pro if

$$\frac{B(C=T|H=T, A=T, B=F)}{B(C=T|H=F, A=T, B=F).} > 1.0$$

Simple Linear. Same as Complex Liner except that the conditional dependencies between evidence items was ignored. For instance, in the above example "C=T" was counted as a pro if

$$B(C=T|H=T)/B(C=T/H=F) > 1.0.$$

Strong Linear. This is exactly the same as Simple Linear except that we did not count an item as a pro or con if the ratio was near 1 (specifically in the range 2/3 to 3/2).

Table 3: Average Probability of Posterior Belief Values for Simple Naive Bayes

Posterior Belief	Four Evidence Items			Seven Evidence Items		
	0.00	**0.40**	**1.20**	**0.00**	**0.40**	**1.20**
.00-.11	.091	.091	.131	.090	.090	.138
.11-.22	.070	.076	.095	.068	.071	.094
.22-.33	.066	.069	.088	.060	.070	.085
.33-.44	.066	.070	.085	.065	.071	.081
.44-.56	.070	.074	.086	.067	.075	.082
.56-.67	.080	.085	.089	.073	.082	.085
.67-.78	.097	.102	.101	.090	.098	.099
.78-.89	.137	.139	.122	.131	.139	.123
.89-1.0	.321	.294	.203	.356	.304	.212
d'	0.60	0.54	0.19	0.68	0.60	0.21

Weighted Linear. This was the same as Simple Linear except that a weighting scheme was attached that increased the weight on a pro or con as the likelihood ratios deviated from 1.

Tables 4 and 5 show some of the results for the Complex and Simple Linear procedures. The .000 values in some of the cells is an artifact of the limited number of evidence items, so some posterior belief values are logically impossible. The pattern of results for the Strong Linear and Weighted Linear procedures were similar to that of Simple Linear and are not reported separately. Note that the distributions of posterior beliefs are now single peaked and that strong support for either conclusion is rarely observed. This conservatism is even more apparent when the number of evidence items increases. This reflects the inherent conservatism of an additive versus a multiplicative inference procedure.

On the other hand, when the linear procedure does output strong support for some conclusion it is generally more discriminating than the Bayesian procedures. This is shown in Table 6 which shows the likelihood ratio of posterior belief give H=T vs. H=F. Except for the middle range (.44-.56) where the ratio should be 1.0, the ratio for strong linear (indeed all the linear models) was generally more extreme than that of the Bayesian models. When error range = 0.0, the strong linear model was consistently more extreme. This was often true even when we compared the linear models that ignored evidential interactions to Proper Bayes took account of the conditional dependencies between evidence items.

The d' values reflect the same pattern as the Bayesian models. If conditional dependencies between evidence are taken into account, then d' improves substantially as the number of evidence items increases. If conditional dependencies are ignored, then d' remains nearly the same.

TABLE 4 : Average Probability of Posterior Belief Values for Complex Linear

Posterior Belief	Four Evidence Items			Seven Evidence Items		
	0.00	**0.40**	**1.20**	**0.00**	**0.40**	**1.20**
.00-.11	.006	.008	.020	.000	.000	.002
.11-.22	.054	.062	.111	.004	.004	.016
.22-.33	.000	.000	.000	.023	.026	.067
.33-.44	.200	.210	.274	.083	.093	.165
.44-.56	.000	.000	.000	.192	.207	.255
.56-.67	.347	.343	.337	.283	.283	.262
.67-.78	.000	.000	.000	.253	.241	.165
.78-.89	.295	.287	.209	.134	.120	.058
.89-1.0	.101	.091	.050	.028	.025	.010
d'	0.89	0.82	0.32	1.23	1.00	0.45

TABLE 5: Average Probability of Posterior Belief Values for Simple Linear

Posterior	Four Evidence Items			Seven Evidence Items		
Belief	0.00	0.40	1.20	0.00	0.40	1.20
.00-.11	.013	.015	.025	.001	.002	.003
.11-.22	.084	.090	.131	.014	.015	.025
.22-.33	.000	.000	.000	.057	.061	.092
.33-.44	.229	.236	.286	.143	.151	.197
.44-.56	.000	.000	.000	.232	.238	.263
.56-.67	.324	.327	.325	.254	.253	.236
.67-.78	.000	.000	.000	.187	.183	.131
.78-.89	.263	.250	.188	.089	.080	.045
.89-1.0	.088	.082	.045	.023	.017	.008
d'	0.63	0.56	0.19	0.66	0.59	0.19

TABLE 6: P(PB(H=T)|H=T)/P(PB(H=T)|H=F) Four Evidence Nodes

	Error Range = 0.0			Error Range = 1.2		
Posterior Belief	Proper Bayes	Naive Bayes	Strong Linear	Proper Bayes	Naive Bayes	Strong Linear
0.0-.11	0.145	0.285	0.103	0.517	0.654	0.513
.11-.22	0.420	0.521	0.178	0.719	0.796	0.558
.22-.33	0.596	0.675	0.311	0.830	0.844	0.689
.33-.44	0.777	0.796	0.567	0.882	0.933	0.851
.44-.56	0.972	0.980	0.985	0.976	1.005	1.001
.56-.67	1.280	1.204	1.783	1.099	1.064	1.202
.67-.78	1.650	1.452	3.119	1.208	1.194	1.391
.78-.89	2.367	1.920	5.510	1.378	1.280	1.761
.89-1.0	7.129	3.588	9.953	1.949	1.498	1.942

3.3 DEFAULT MODELS

In the AI community there are a number of researchers that advocate the use of qualitative/symbolic approaches to reasoning under uncertainty. The symbolic approach generally involves some form of default reasoning, where a system will jump to default conclusion that can be retracted later if contradictory evidence surfaces (Reiter, 1988).

In our study we examined several default models, all of which involved assigning PB(H=T)=1.0 if any of the LRs exceeded a threshold T and no LRs were less than 1/T; PB(H=T)=0.0 if the reverse occurs; and PB(H=T)=0.5 otherwise. In short, it takes only one piece of confirmatory evidence to jump to a strong conclusion (posterior belief = 1.0 or 0.0), but contradictory evidence leaves the system uncertain (posterior belief = 0.5).

Table 7 shows some of the results for default models where T=3/2 and T=5/2. The principal thing to notice here are the likelihood ratios of posterior belief. When T=3/2, they compare favorably with those generated by the Bayesian procedures, particularly the Naive Bayesian models. In fact the default procedure, using a very mild threshold, was about as discriminating as when the naive Bayes outputs strong (>.89 or <.11) posterior belief values.

Table 7: Average Probability of Posterior Belief Values for Default Models

Posterior Belief	Threshold = 3/2			Threshold = 5/2		
	0.00	0.40	1.20	0.00	0.40	1.20
0.0	.098	.110	.165	.182	.207	.255
0.5	.575	.569	.597	.391	.376	.411
1.0	.327	.322	.237	.426	.417	.334

Perhaps more surprising is the fact that when the threshold for jumping to a conclusion becomes more stringent (increases to T= 5/2) the default reasoning system was more likely to jump to a default conclusion, but was less likely to be correct when doing so. This counter intuitive result is accounted for by the fact that the thresholds are symmetric. A stringent threshold implies that once a default conclusion has been made, it will take a strong piece of evidence to force a retraction of that conclusion. With a less stringent threshold a weaker evidence item is sufficient to get the system to retract a default conclusion. Consequently, with a less stringent threshold, the default reasoning system is less likely to stick to a default conclusion in the context of contradictory evidence.

4 DISCUSSION

4.1 ON SCORING RULES

Before discussing the implications of the above results, we need first to address two possible objections to our study. First, why did we not use a proper scoring rule such as mean squared error (MSE) to evaluate the inference procedures? In fact, in our preliminary studies (Lehner, 1990) we did. However as discussed there the expected MSE score for the Bayesian procedures began increased rapidly as the error range increased. When the error range exceeded 1.0, the expected MSE score for all the Bayesian procedures was greater than .25, which is an MSE score that can be guaranteed by ignoring all evidence and asserting PB(H)=.5 under all conditions. In short, the proper scoring rule indicated that in the context of significant higher order uncertainty, Bayesian updating was worse than useless.

This result can now be explained by the U-shaped PB distribution characteristic of Bayesian inference. Other things being equal, squared error rules will tend to attribute higher error scores to techniques that tend toward extreme PB values. Consequently, despite the fact that MSE is a nondistorting scoring rule, it provided a misleading evaluation.

The second objection has to do with the apparent lack of calibration of our Proper Bayes result. A careful reader might proceed through the following line of thought. Consider the error range = 0.0 column in Table 1. If indeed correct Bayesian procedures are being applied to true probabilities, then the posterior belief values should be the true posterior probabilities. This in turn suggests that if PB(H=T)>.89, then

$$\frac{P(PB(H{=}T)>.89|H{=}T)}{P(PB(H{=}T)>.89|H{=}F)} > \frac{.89}{.11} = 8.1$$

Yet Table 1 shows a ratio of only 7.129. Proper Bayes is not calibrated, and therefore incorrectly implemented.

It turns out that the above analysis is wrong, but for a subtle and interesting reason. Since error range is 0.0, we know that within each run PB(H=T|E) = P(H=T|E). Therefore within each run

$$P(PB(H{=}T){=}x \ \&\ H{=}T)$$

$$= \sum_{E} P(PB(H{=}T){=}x \ |H{=}T \ \&\ E)*P(H{=}T|E)*P(E)$$

$$= \sum_{E|P(H=T|E)=x} x*P(E)$$

here

From this we can derive

$$\frac{P(PB(H{=}T){=}x|H{=}T)}{P(PB(H{=}T){=}x|H{=}F)} = \frac{\mathbf{E}[\Sigma(x*P(E))/P(H{=}T)]}{\mathbf{E}[\Sigma((1-x)*P(E))/P(H{=}F)]},$$

where **E** is the expectation *across runs* and Σ sums over evidential states (E) *within a run* where P(H=T|E)=x.

Now, the values x and P(H=T) are not conditionally independent. Across runs, as P(H=T) is high, the probability of observing an evidential state where P(H=T|E)>.89 decreases. Consequently, one should generally expect that

$$\frac{P(PB(H{=}T){=}x|H{=}T)}{P(PB(H{=}T){=}x|H{=}F)} < \frac{x*E[P(H{=}F)]}{(1-x)*E[P(H{=}T)]}.$$

In our monte carlo runs, E[P(H=T)]=.5, so the observed data is consistent with this inequality.

4.2 IMPLICATIONS

Some of the implications of this study are listed below.

Accounting for evidential interactions is essential - Our simulation results support the common belief that accounting for interactions between the evidence items is essential for effective updating. If interactions are ignored then increasing the amount of evidence available did not substantially improve the ability of either Bayesian or linear updating procedures to discriminate H=T vs. H=F.

If higher order uncertainty exists, update cautiously - Bayesian updating tends toward extreme belief values. If higher order uncertainty exists, then the probability that the posterior values will support an incorrect hypothesis increases rapidly.

Linear updating is accurate, but not very powerful - The results here suggest that simplistic linear update procedures (e.g., add up pros and cons), are a reasonably accurate approach to reasoning under uncertainty. Relative to Bayesian procedures, linear procedures rarely show strong support for the wrong hypothesis. There are however two provisos. First, interactions between the evidence items must be accounted for. Second, the linear procedures often do not show strong support for *any* hypothesis. When this occurs the reasoner should be prepared to execute a more powerful technique.

Default reasoning requires asymmetric thresholds - Implicit in any default reasoning procedure is a conditional probability statement. A knowledge engineer would not add a default rule (if **a** conclude by-default **b**) unless the engineer believed that for the set of applications of the system P(b|a) was high. Our results suggest that as the engineer becomes more conservative in defining defaults (i.e., P(b|a)>T and T increases) the default reasoning system may become *more* likely to make erroneous default conclusions. This is because, once the system has made a default conclusion, the conservatism works in reverse. The system is less likely to retract that conclusion. This suggest that default reasoning systems should have asymetric thresholds. Default reasoning procedures that jump to tentative conclusions should be conservative. Procedures that retract default conclusions should be less conservative.

Perhaps the most interesting question that these results suggest is that of the sufficiency of Bayes rule. Consider the following case. A probability model has been specified that we know reflects true probabilities. Upon observing some evidence, E, we apply Proper Bayes and deduce PB(H=T)=.9. However, using a Strong Linear procedure we deduce PB(H=T)=.1. If we accept PB(H=T)=.9, then we are ignoring the output of the inference procedure which we know is, in general, more discriminating. On the other hand, to accept a posterior value other than .9, is to accept a value which we know to be other than the true probability. Furthermore, it suggests that there is more information in the evidence than coherent updating has extracted. We are currently investigating this issue.

References

Brier, G. "Verification of forecasts expressed in terms of probability," *Monthly Weather Review*, 1950, 75, 1-3.

Dawes, R. "The robust beauty of improperly weighted linear models," *American Psychologist*, 1979, 34(7), 571-582.

Edwards, W., Phillips, L., Hays, W. and Goodman, B. "Probabilistic information processing systems: Design and evaluation, *IEEE Transactions on Systems Science and Cybernetics*, 1968, SCC-4, 248-265.

Lehner, P. "Robust Inference Policies: Preliminary Report," *Proceedings of the sixth Annual Uncertainty in AI Workshop*, Massachusetts Institute of Technology, August 1990.

Levi, K., "Expert systems should be more expert than human experts: Evaluation procedures from human judgment and decision making," *IEEE Transactions on Systems, Man and Cybernetics*, 1989, 19(3), 647-657.

Pearl, J. *Probabilistic Reasoning: Networks of Plausible Inference*, Morgan Kaufmann, 1988.

Reiter, R. "Nonmonotonic Reasoning," *Annual Review of Computer Science*, 1988.

Representation Requirements for Supporting Decision Model Formulation

Tze-Yun Leong
MIT Laboratory for Computer Science
545 Technology Square, room 420
Cambridge, MA 02139
(leong@lcs.mit.edu)

Abstract

This paper outlines a methodology for analyzing the representational support for knowledge-based decision-modeling in a broad domain. A relevant set of inference patterns and knowledge types are identified. By comparing the analysis results to existing representations, some insights are gained into a design approach for integrating categorical and uncertain knowledge in a context-sensitive manner.

1 Introduction

Research in knowledge-based decision systems (KBDS) combines artificial intelligence and decision analysis techniques to solve problems involving choice and uncertainty. The dynamic decision-modeling approach in KBDS advocates that the decision models for different problems should be dynamically constructed from a knowledge base [Breese, 1989, Wellman, 1990a]. This approach facilitates scalability and reusability of the knowledge bases. Moreover, the resulting decision models are context-sensitive and include only the relevant information specific to the problems. To date, however, while much progress has been made in improving the algorithms for manipulating decision models, the automated model construction process remains to be formalized.

This paper characterizes the knowledge for supporting dynamic decision-modeling in medicine. Characterizing such knowledge illuminates the representational and computational requirements for automating decision analysis in a broad domain. Unlike previous efforts, instead of concentrating on the structural components of the decision *model* such as nodes, conditional probabilities, and influences, we focus on the ontological features of the decision *problem* such as contexts, classes of observed events, classes of available actions, classes of possible outcomes, temporal precedence, and probabilistic and contextual dependencies. By gaining insights into the nature of decisions, this exercise serves as a step toward developing a formal methodology for requirement analysis and realizing a uniform representation framework for supporting dynamic decision-modeling in KBDS.

The following discussions are based on the general system architecture depicted in Figure 1. Given a problem description, the *planner* or *decision-maker* constructs a decision model by accessing information contained in the *knowledge base*. The domain and the decision-analytic components of the knowledge base are integrated by the *knowledge-base manager*, which also serves as an interface to the planner.

The decision models considered are *qualitative probabilistic networks* (QPNs) [Wellman, 1990b]. Since QPNs are the qualitative variants of influence diagrams, and since each influence diagram can be transformed into a decision tree, our results are expected to be generalizable to other decision models.

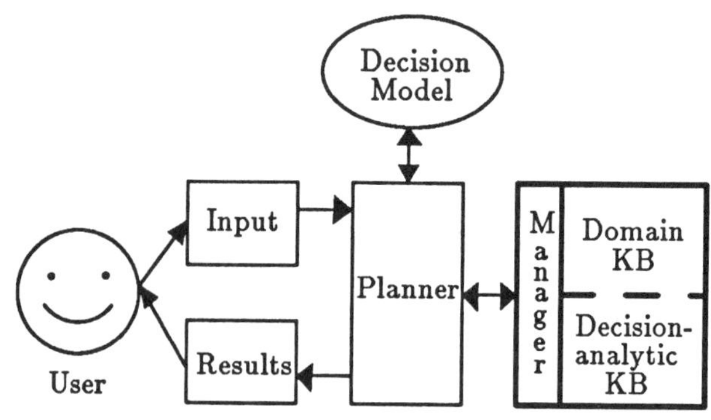

Figure 1: A Knowledge-Based Decision System

In the subsequent sections, we present a medical decision problem and examine the reasoning and representational issues involved in the decision analysis process. Some ideas on integrating context-sensitive categorical and uncertain knowledge will be explored and compared to relevant representation frameworks.

2 An Example

A simplified medical decision problem [Beck and Pauker, 1981, Tsevat *et al.*, 1989] is shown below:

The patient is an 80 year-old woman. She complained of fainting and was found to have irregular heartbeats, or arrythmia. A diagnosis of cardiomyopathy, i.e., disorder of the heart muscles was made. Such a disorder usually leads to embolism, or formation of blood clots in the patient's body. The problem is to determine if anticoagulant therapy should be administered to reduce the chance of embolism, given the high risk of bleeding complications in the elderly.

Each relevant event in the decision problem can be regarded as a *concept*, e.g., 80-year-old, cardiomyopathy, anticoagulant-therapy, etc. A concept is an *event* or a *random variable* in the probabilistic sense; it denotes an abstract description of an object, an attribute, a state of being or a process, depending on the circumstances.

3 The Decision Making Process

Given a set of input concepts, the goal for the proposed KBDS is to construct a decision model such as the one shown in Figure 2, and then evaluate the feasibility of the alternatives with respect to some criteria,e.g., life-expectancy, expected monetary value, etc.

More formally, the decision-analytic approach to decision making can be viewed as a five-step process: 1) Background characterization; 2) context establishment; 3) problem formulation; 4) model construction; and 5) Model evaluation.

3.1 Background Information Characterization

The process begins by classifying the input concepts into the variables concerned, the actions available, and the possible outcomes involved in a decision problem. In the clinical setting, the input concepts can usually be divided into six categories, as shown in Table 1 for our example.

Table 1: Characterized Background Information

Category	Concepts
General history	80 year old, female
Signs and Symptoms	Fainting, arrythmia
Laboratory findings	-
Diseases	Cardiomyopathy
Alternatives	Anticoagulant-therapy
Complications	Embolism, bleeding

The planner can characterize each input concept by asking questions like:

- Is fainting a kind of sign or symptom?
- Is cardiomyopathy a kind of disease?

To answer the above queries, the knowledge-base must support *categorizations* of the relevant domain concepts. A categorization is a grouping of concepts with similar descriptions in a particular dimension. Examples of such groupings include those induced by the specialization (`AKO`) relation, the decomposition (`PARTOF`) relation, etc.

The characterized background information, however, is insufficient for formulating a decision model. For instance, in our example, the relationships among the input concepts are not explicitly stated, the two relevant kinds of embolism being considered, systemic and pulmonary embolisms, are not specified, and the evaluation criteria are not mentioned. The missing information, which may be related to the domain or the decision-analytic methodology, must be derived when necessary.

3.2 Domain Context Establishment

Establishing the context[1] means defining the task environment in which the problem is to be solved. This enables different problem situations to be considered and sets limits on the possible operations that can be applied to a given problem [Kassirer and Kopelman, 1987]. The context is selected with only a few clues [Kassirer and Gorry, 1978]. In the clinical setting, a context is usually indicated by a suspected disease, a syndrome, i.e., a set of signs and symptoms that convey special meanings, or a general diagnostic category, e.g., an acute respiratory disorder [Kassirer and Kopelman, 1987].

In our example, the clinical context is "cardiomyopathy in old-age." This context is established by identifying the suspected diseases and any conditions that might significantly affect their nature.

Given the characterized background information, identifying the suspected diseases simply involves looking them up in the set of input concepts. For now, we assume that other significant conditions, e.g., old-age in our example, are specified by an oracle. Recognizing these conditions automatically requires a very sophisticated planner, and the issues involved are outside the scope of this paper.

The main purpose of establishing a context is to al-

[1] This is different from the *decision context* [Breese, 1989, Holtzman, 1989] which refers to all the assumptions, constraints, variables, and alternatives considered in the decision problem.

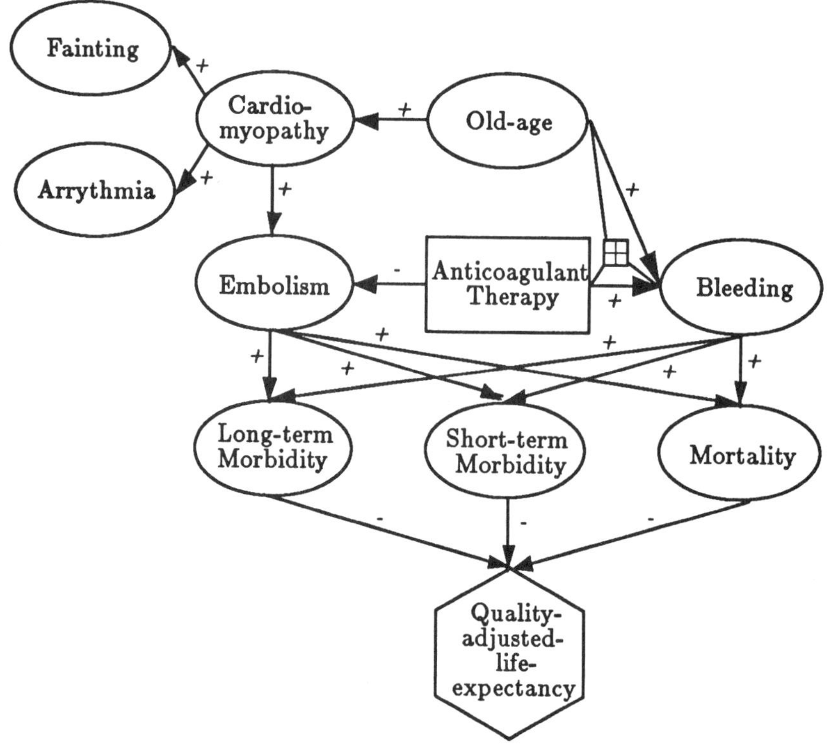

Figure 2: A QPN For The Example

low access to the context-sensitive information. For instance, in older patients, cardiomyopathy may have different manifestations and more severe complications than in younger patients, or in the presence of other diseases. Therefore, such context-sensitive knowledge must be expressible in the knowledge base.

3.3 Decision Problem Formulation

Guided by the characterized background information, a decision problem is formulated within the domain context by identifying:

- all or the most important diseases/hypotheses that may be involved;
- the relative significance of all these concepts;
- all or the most important possible outcomes/complications of these concepts;
- all or the most important actions available;
- the effects of the actions on the concepts and their outcomes and possible complications; and
- the evaluation criteria.

Table 2 shows all the relevant concepts in our example. "Pulmonary embolism" and "systemic embolism" are among the values of the corresponding "embolism" node in Figure 2.

Table 2: Concepts Involved in Decision Problem

Old-age	Anticoagulant-therapy
Cardiomyopathy	Bleeding
Fainting	Long-term-morbidity
Arrythmia	Short-term-morbidity
Embolism	Mortality
Pulmonary-embolism	Quality-adjusted-life-expectancy
Systemic-embolism	

These concepts are derived by asking questions like:

- What are the most common embolisms caused by cardiomyopathy?
- What are the other (if any) complications of anticoagulant-therapy?

To answer the above queries, the knowledge base must, in addition to supporting categorizations of the domain concepts, allow expression of the *interactions*, i.e., the correlational/influential/causal relations, among these concepts. The varying degrees of significance for all these relations in different contexts must also be expressible in the knowledge base. This, together with the varying degrees of temporal and probabilistic dependencies among the interactions, would facilitate derivation of the most relevant information for the problem at hand.

3.4 Decision Model Construction

As mentioned, a decision model for our example is shown in Figure 2.

To construct such a decision model, its structure, e.g., nodes and links in a QPN, and its preference model, e.g., evaluation criteria such as morbidity, mortality, and monetary costs associated with utilities, must be inferrable from the knowledge base. The temporal constraints on the decision model structure, i.e., the order in which the concepts and their consequences are to be considered, should also be inferrable from the interactions of the underlying concepts. Hence, the construction involves asking questions like:

- How are the observable effects of the alternatives relate to the chance events?
- What are the outcomes that affect the evaluation criteria?

To support these queries, the relevant interactions among the concepts must be expressible in the knowledge base. These interactions involve both domain concepts and decision-analytic concepts, e.g., "presence of disease positively-influences morbidity."

3.5 Decision Model Evaluation

Upon completion, the decision model is evaluated by some procedure with respect to the evaluation criteria. Here, evaluation of a decision model refers to solving the model with procedures such as folding back of a decision tree, or graph reduction of a QPN. The evaluation criterion assumed in our example is quality-adjusted life expectancy, i.e., a measure of time remaining in a patient's life, taking into account the inconveniences caused by the illness (morbidity). Given a well-formed decision model, only procedural knowledge is needed in this step.

4 Summary of Inference Patterns and Representation Requirements

The above analysis shows that four types of general inference patterns are involved in the automated decision analysis process:

- (Q1) Does concept A related to concept B in $\mathcal{O}$
- (Q2) What are the concepts related to concept A in $\mathcal{O}$?
- (Q3) Does concept A relate to concept B by i?
- (Q4) What are the concepts related to concept A by i?

where $\mathcal{O}$ is a categorization and i is an interaction.

Three types of knowledge are required to support these inferences: categorical knowledge, uncertain knowledge, and a notion of "context."

4.1 Categorical Knowledge

The categorical knowledge captures the definitional or structural relations of the concepts, allowing expression of facts such as: "cardiomyopathy is a kind of disease" and "pulmonary embolism is a kind of embolism." This type of knowledge should provide the system with the power of abstraction and inheritance. In other words, knowing a class of concepts would allow the planner to derive its subclasses, and vice versa. Furthermore, the generic description for a class of concepts can be specified at an appropriate level of abstraction; portions of this description can be inheritable by its subclasses or superclasses.

4.2 Uncertain Knowledge

The uncertain knowledge captures the interactions, i.e., the correlational, influential, or causal relations among the concepts, allowing expression of facts such as: "presence of anticoagulant-therapy negatively-influences presence of embolism" and "cardiomyopathy causes arrythmia." This type of knowledge should provide the system with the power of differentiation by accommodating a spectrum of temporal and probabilistic dependencies among the concepts. By comparing the relational strengths, the planner would be able to deduce the certainty and usefulness of the information derived from the knowledge base.

4.3 A Contextual Notion

In addition to the categorical and uncertain knowledge, a notion of "context" should be included in the knowledge base. This contextual notion has the following properties:

1. It sets a boundary on the relevant categorical and uncertain knowledge, and can be regarded as a focusing mechanism. This enables the planner to look for different information in different situations. For instance, the old-age of a patient would lead to the focus on a particular set of complications for cardiomyopathy and anticoagulant-therapy.
2. It allows differentiation of the relational significance, both categorical and interactional, among a set of concepts; the relative relevance and importance of the information can thus be distinguished in different situations. For example,

bleeding is the most important complication of anticoagulant-therapy in the context of cardiomyopathy in old-age.

3. It is compositional and can be defined hierarchically. In other words, multiple, interacting contexts may coexist and a context can be defined within another context. For example, "cardiomyopathy" and "old-age" combine to form the context of "cardiomyopathy in old-age"; the latter, in turn, is a subcontext of "disease in old-age."

5 A Representation Design

We now propose a representation design that would meet the requirements for supporting the inferences Q1-Q4 in a context-sensitive manner.

5.1 Representation of Concepts

In our framework, a *concept* is an intensional description of the relational interpretation of an object, a state, a process, or an attribute of these phenomena. In other words, a concept reflects the salient features of the underlying phenomenon through a set of interactions with other concepts. These relevant concepts are called the *properties* of the concept being described. For example, the description of the concept `disease`[2] includes properties such as `severity`, `manifestation`, and `treatment`, as well as interactions such as "`presence-of-disease` causes `presence-of-manifestation-of-disease`" and "`presence-of-treatment-of-disease` negatively-influences `severity-of-disease`."

5.1.1 Properties of Concepts

The properties of a concept include its inherent qualities, characteristics, and other relevant concepts that constitute its description e.g., `size` (of a `tumor`) and `treatment` (of a `disease`). Each property is a concept[3] itself. Each property of a concept has a list of *values*, which are also concepts themselves.

To incorporate context-dependent information, a new concept can be derived from each property of a concept. For example, the concept `treatment-of-cardiomyopathy` is derived from the property `treatment` of `cardiomyopathy`. This new *derived-concept* has a description constrained by the concept it is derived from; the two concepts are related by the *context* (`CXT`) relation to be described below. Compositions of the `CXT` relation enable "chaining" of the derived-concepts, e.g., `duration-of-treatment-of-cardiomyopathy`, `presence-of-complications-of--treatment-of-cardiomyopathy`, etc. , are concepts formable in this way.

The properties of a concept in this framework are analogous to the *roles* in term subsumption languages and the *slots* in frame-based languages. The difference is that the properties alone do not completely describe a concept; they serve only as indices to the interactions that constitute the meaning of a concept. These interactions are expressed in terms of the corresponding derived-concepts, e.g., "`duration-of-treatment-of-cardiomyopathy` negatively-influences `severity-of-cardiomyopathy` is an interaction in the description of `cardiomyopathy`.

5.1.2 Interactions of Concepts

Each interaction between two concepts has two components: *temporal precedence*, with "known" or "unknown" as values, and *qualitative probabilistic influence* [Wellman, 1990b], with "positive," "negative," and "unknown" as values. The interactions can thus be expressed as four types of links in a network interpretation of our framework: *associational* links, which denote probabilistic correlation with an unknown type of influence and unknown temporal precedence; *precedence* links, which denote temporal precedence with unknown type of probabilistic influence; *influential* links, which denote conditional probabilistic dependencies; and *causal/inhibitive* links, which denote known temporal precedence in addition to known type of probabilistic influences.

5.2 Categorization of Concepts

The description of a concept can be constrained by a set of *categorizers*. A categorizer is a categorical or *class* relationship; it is a binary relation that specifies the properties and the interactions of a concept in terms of those of another concept. By imposing a partial order on the related concepts, a categorizer establishes a unique *perspective* for describing each concept. For example, a concept can be described as "a kind of" another concept or "a part of" another concept. Some common categorizers include the specialization (`AKO`) relation, the decomposition (`PARTOF`) relation, and the equivalence (`EQV`) relation.

All the concepts related by a categorizer are said to be in a *categorization*; some categorizations have hierarchical interpretations, while others are more naturally seen as networks. By knowing the position of a particular concept with respect to another concept in a categorization, the description of the former can be inferred from the latter. This descriptive inference in a categorization is called *inheritance*.

For instance, the specialization relation can be defined as follows:

[2] All concepts defined in our framework will be referenced in `typewriter type style`.

[3] Referred to as *property-concept* from now on.

Definition .1 (Specialization) *Let C be the set of all concepts. Let Ω be the set of categorizers. Let $\mathcal{O}_\omega \subseteq C$ be the set of concepts in a categorization related by categorizer $\omega \in \Omega$. For all $a, b \in C$, and for $AKO \in \Omega$ where $AKO \subseteq C \times C$:*

1. $AKO \stackrel{def}{=} \{(a,b)|a \subset b$, i.e., $\forall \alpha, \alpha \in a \Longrightarrow \alpha \in b\}$.
2. *Let $ako : C \longrightarrow 2^C$ be a function defined on AKO:* $ako(a) = \{b|(a,b) \in AKO\}$.

Two major properties are observed for the **AKO** categorizer:

1. $a \in \mathcal{O}_{AKO} \iff \exists b, (a,b) \in AKO$ or $(b,a) \in AKO$.
2. The AKO relation is irreflexive, asymmetric, and transitive.
3. The properties and interactions of the concepts are downward inheritable in the specialization hierarchy.

5.3 Context-Dependent Representation

The categorizers establish some general perspectives for describing a concept. For example, a **pulmonary-embolism** is a kind of **embolism** in general. The description of a concept in these general perspectives is further constrained by a set of *contexts*.

A context (**CXT**) relation can be thought of as a "meta-categorizer;" it is a binary relation that specifies the properties and the interactions of, and hence also the categorizers on a concept in accordance with those of another concept. For example, **treatment-of-cardiomyopathy** is specified as a kind of **treatment-of-disease** because **treatment-of-cardiomyopathy** is defined in the context of **cardiomyopathy**, and **cardiomyopathy** is a kind of **disease**. All concepts are described in some contexts; the descriptions that are valid in general are in the *universal* context. Therefore, the (**CXT**) relation facilitates representation of context-sensitive information, as mentioned earlier, by allowing chaining of derived-concepts and constraining their descriptions. The partial-ordering imposed by this relation forms a *context-hierarchy* of all the concepts in the knowledge base.

6 Supporting General Inferences

Based on the above representation framework, we shall now discuss how the knowledge base of the proposed KBDS would provide answers for the inferences Q1-Q4. In the following discussions:

1. Let C be the set of all concepts.
2. Let $\Omega = \{AKO, ...\}$ = the set of all categorizers.
3. Let $\mathcal{F}_\Omega = \{f_\omega | f_\omega$ is a function defined on $\omega, \forall \omega \in \Omega\} = \{ako, ...\}$ as defined in Section 5.2.
4. Let $\mathcal{I} = \{$*association, precedence, positive-influence, negative-influence, cause, inhibitor*$\}$=the set of all interaction types.
5. $\forall i \in \mathcal{I}$, let $\mathcal{F}_\mathcal{I} = \{f_i | f_i$ is a function defined on $i\}$
6. $\forall f_i \in F_\mathcal{I}, i \in \mathcal{I}, a, b \in C, f_i(a) = \{b|(a,b) \vee (b,a) \in i\}$.

- Q1: Does concept A relate to concept B by <categorizer>?

To find out if two concepts **A** and **B** are related in an categorization, let $\omega_0 \in \Omega$ be the categorizer in question.

$$\text{Answer}_{Q1} = \begin{cases} \text{yes} & \text{if } (A,B) \in \omega_0 \\ \text{no} & \text{otherwise.} \end{cases}$$

An example of the Q1 query is: Does **cardiomyopathy** related to **disease** by specialization? The answer is: yes.

- Q2: What are the concepts related to concept A by <categorizer>?

To find out the concepts related to a concept **A** in an categorization, again let $\omega_0 \in \Omega$ be the categorizer in question.

$$\text{Answer}_{Q2} = f_{\omega_0}(A).$$

An example of the Q1 query is: What are the concepts that are related to **embolism** by specialization? The answers are: **pumonary-embolism** and **systemic-embolism**.

- Q3: What are the concepts that relate to concept A by <interaction>?

To find out the concepts that directly interact with a concept **A** in an interaction, let $i_0 \in \mathcal{I}$ be the interaction in question.

$$\text{Answer}_{Q3} = f_{i_0}(A).$$

An example of the Q3 query is: What are the concepts that relate to **complication-of-anticoagulant--therapy** by positive-influence? The answer is: **presence-of-old-age**.

- Q4: Does concept A relate to concept B by <interaction>?

To find out whether two concepts **A** and tt B are involved in an interaction, again let $i_0 \in \mathcal{I}$ be the interaction in question.

$$\text{Answer}_{Q4} = \begin{cases} \text{yes} & \text{if } (A, B) \in i_0 \\ \text{no} & \text{otherwise.} \end{cases}$$

An example Q4 query is: Does **cardiomyopathy** relate to **fainting** by cause? (Read: Does **cardiomyopathy** cause **fainting**?) The answer is: yes.

For simplicity, all the answers to the above inferences assume a *closed world assumption*, i.e., a negative answer will be returned if a relation is not explicitly derivable from the knowledge base. The context-sensitivity of the answers, though not very obvious, is actually inherent from the underlying representation.

7 Related Work

The major shortcomings of the static decision-modeling approach, i.e., treating pre-enumerated decision models or templates as knowledge bases, result from the rigidity of the knowledge bases. Constrained by the structure of the decision models, e.g., nodes and links of a decision tree, such knowledge bases do not reflect the nature of the domain knowledge.

The different representations used in existing KBDS with the dynamic decision-modeling approach are not very satisfactory, either. The first order logic-like representations, such as those employed by Breese [1987, 1989], and Goldman and Charniak [1990], have no explicit hierarchical dimensions. In these frameworks, multi-level decision models are created by activation of a set of rules; limited contextual information is captured as conditional probabilities matrices in these rules.

In Wellman's [1990a] SUDO-PLANNER system, domain descriptions can be expressed in multiple levels of precision in this framework, thus facilitating decision-modeling in multiple levels of abstraction. The terminological component of this framework, however, is subjected to the limited expressiveness of most *term subsumption languages*. Moreover, the purely probabilistic nature of the effects or influences does not reflect the varying degrees of significance among the concepts with respect to the problem at hand. Although some contextual effects on the influences can be expressed in the *qualitative synergies* defined in QPN, there is no general mechanism for capturing contextual information in the whole framework.

Other relevant representation formalisms include those that incorporate an uncertainty model to a hierarchical representation framework. Most hierarchical representations are designed to support derivation of absolute or categorical answers. To support approximate reasoning, i.e., finding out facts that are not absolutely true or false, but *believed* to a certain degree, some efforts attempt to accommodate an uncertainty model by re-interpreting the semantics of a categorical representation, while others try to couple the two to form a coherent framework.

For instance, in the network representation developed by Lin and Goebel [1990], both subsumption and causal relationships are expressible. Probabilistic interpretations are given to parts of the causal network, called the *scenarios*. These scenarios can be considered as contexts with different probability distributions. Although the scenarios are not hierarchically arranged, their probabilistic rankings are preserved across the subsumption relationships. Nevertheless, this network formalism does not allow the properties, and hence the nature of each node or concept to be explicitly represented.

Yen and Bonissone's [1990] work attempts to generalize the semantics of term subsumption languages with an approximate reasoning model, such as fuzzy logic or possibility theory, to support plausible inferences. Non-definitional relations among the concepts, however, are not expressible in these frameworks. There is also no general notion of context-dependent definitions.

Saffiotti's [1990] hybrid framework, on the other hand, integrates a component that deals with absolute or categorical knowledge and another with the uncertainty of this knowledge. Any formal representation formalism and uncertainty model may constitute the two components in the framework, e.g., first-order logic with Dempster-Shafer theory, term subsumption language with probability theory, etc. We believe this work is an important step toward the theoretical foundations of integrating categorical and uncertain knowledge. The expressiveness and hence the usefulness of the framework, however, depend solely on the component formalisms.

8 Discussion and Conclusion

To support dynamic decision-modeling, the structure of the knowledge base must reflect the nature of both the decision problem and the domain knowledge. In particular, the underlying representation must neither be restricted by the structural components of the decision models, e.g., nodes and links of an influence diagram, nor their evaluation mechanisms, e.g., folding back of a decision tree. By focusing on the ontology of a decision problem, we have identified a set of inference patterns and knowledge types for supporting automated construction of decision models in medicine.

The brief survey on existing representations has shed some light on a design approach for integrating categorical and uncertain knowledge in a context-sensitive manner. We believe such an integration calls for a framework with a terminological component, an assertional component, and a network interpretation. By capturing the context notion via partitioning the network, this framework would allow us to establish taxonomies of structured concepts, state the facts, i.e., the interactions among the concepts, and answer questions about these relations.

We have sketched a design outline of such a representation in this paper; a more detailed exposition is described elsewhere [Leong, 1991]. Many important issues, however, are yet to be explored. In particular, the notion of "context" needs to be more formally defined, many interesting problems arise in the context-sensitive inheritance patterns of the categorical relations, and the context-sensitive probabilistic semantics of the interactions needs to be generalized. Careful examination of these issues, we believe, will lead to the formalization of both the automated decision model formulation process and the domain and decision-analytic knowledge involved.

Acknowledgments

The author would like to thank Peter Szolovits for advice on the project, Mike Wellman for many helpful discussions, Jon Doyle for comments on the mathematical definitions and LaTeXformatting, and the anonymous referees for suggestions on the presentation of this paper.

This research was supported by the National Institutes of Health grant no. 5 R01 LM04493 from the National Library of Medicine.

References

[Beck and Pauker, 1981] J. Robert Beck and Stephen G. Pauker. Anticoagulation and atrial fibrillation in the bradycardia-tachycardia syndrome. *Medical Decision Making*, 1:285–301, 1981.

[Breese and Tse, 1987] Jack Breese and Edison Tse. Integrating logical and probabilistic reasoning for decision making. In *Proceedings of the Workshop on Uncertainty in Artificial Intelligence*, pages 355–362, July 1987.

[Breese, 1989] John S. Breese. Construction of belief and decision networks. Draft manuscript, Rockwell International Science Center, 1989.

[Goldman and Charniak, 1990] Robert P. Goldman and Eugene Charniak. Dynamic construction of belief networks. In *Proceedings of the Sixth Conference on Uncertainty in Artificial Intelligence*, pages 90–97, 1990.

[Holtzman, 1989] Samuel Holtzman. *Intelligent Decision Systems.* Addison-Wesley, 1989.

[Kassirer and Gorry, 1978] J. P. Kassirer and G. A. Gorry. Clinical problem solving: A behavioral analysis. *Annals of Internal Medicine*, 89:245–255, 1978.

[Kassirer and Kopelman, 1987] Jerome P. Kassirer and Richard L. Kopelman. The critical role of context in the diagnostic process. *Hospital Practice*, pages 67–76, August 15 1987.

[Leong, 1991] Tze-Yun Leong. Knowledge representation for supporting decision model formulation in medicine. TR 504, Massachusetts Institute of Technology, Laboratory for Computer Science, 545 Technology Square, Cambridge, MA, 02139, May 1991. Forthcoming.

[Lin and Goebel, 1990] Dekang Lin and Randy Goebel. Integrating probabilistic, taxonomic and causal knowledge in abductive diagnosis. In *Proceedings of the Sixth Conference on Uncertainty in Artificial Intelligence*, pages 40–45, 1990.

[Saffiotti, 1990] Alessandro Saffiotti. A hybrid framework for representing uncertain knowledge. In *Proceedings of the Eighth National Conference on Artificial Intelligence*, pages 653–658, Cambridge, Massachusetts, 1990. American Association for Artificial Intelligence, AAAI Press and The MIT Press.

[Tsevat *et al.*, 1989] J. Tsevat, M. H. Eckman, R. A. McNutt, and S. G. Pauker. Warfarin for dilated cardiomyopathy: A bloody tough pill to swallow. *Medical Decision Making*, 9:162–169, 1989.

[Wellman, 1990a] Michael P. Wellman. *Formulation of Tradeoffs in Planning Under Uncertainty.* Pitman and Morgan Kaufmann, 1990.

[Wellman, 1990b] Michael P. Wellman. Fundamental concepts of qualitative probabilistic networks. *Artificial Intelligence*, 44(3):257–304, 1990.

[Yen and Bonissone, 1990] John Yen and Piero P. Bonissone. Extending term subsumption systems for uncertainty management. In *Proceedings of the Sixth Conference on Uncertainty in Artificial Intelligence*, pages 468–473, 1990.

A Language for Planning with Statistics

Nathaniel G. Martin and James F. Allen
Department of Computer Science
University of Rochester
Rochester, NY

Abstract

When a planner must decide whether it has enough evidence to make a decision based on probability, it faces the *sample size problem*. Current planners using probabilities need not deal with this problem because they do not generate their probabilities from observations. This paper presents an event-based language in which the planner's probabilities are calculated from the binomial random variable generated by the observed ratio of one type of event to another. Such probabilities are subject to error, so the planner must introspect about their validity. Inferences about the probability of these events can be made using statistics. Inferences about the validity of the approximations can be made using interval estimation. Interval estimation allows the planner to avoid making choices that are only weakly supported by the planner's evidence.

1 INTRODUCTION

Planning relies on choosing the future actions most likely to be effective. Because actions are taken after they are planned, a planner's information is uncertain at planning time. Probabilities have been explored as a means of representing and reasoning about this uncertainty. In some domains, the necessary probabilities can be gathered by querying experts in the field. If such experts do not exist, an agent must be able to infer probabilities from observations. This paper develops a language that combines Allen's temporal interval reasoning [Allen, 1984] with statistical inference [Bickel and Doksum, 1977] to facilitate planning using inferences about probabilities.

If a planner must calculate its probabilities, it must decide when it has enough information to be confident of its calculations. Deciding when one is sufficiently confident of probabilities generated from observations is called the *sample size problem*. The sample size problem will be ubiquitous for planners that calculate probabilities from their experience. The most immediate incarnation of this problem is that of deciding whether choices are warranted by the evidence. A planner should make its decisions based on the probabilities about which it has good evidence, and discount the probabilities about which it is uncertain. One application of making decisions based on strength of evidence as well as probability is dealing with facts one is told. A planner may be told that a particular course of actions is better than another, but if its evidence is sufficiently strong, it may choose to ignore this information. The sample size problem also arises when reasoning about specifying actions to an intelligent reactive execution module [Martin and Allen, 1990b]. Here, the planner specifies details of its plans only if it is confident of the probabilities it has calculated. Yet another place the problem arises is in probabilistic solutions to the qualification problem [Martin and Allen, 1990a, Weber, 1989]. The planner adds as many qualifications as it can without making the event about which it is reasoning so specific that there are insufficient statistics to make necessary choices.

Feldman and Sproull [1977] deal with uncertainty by applying decision theory [Raiffa, 1970] to the problem of choosing appropriate actions guiding an A* algorithm. Horvitz [1988] uses decision theory to reason about partial results in planning. Johnson and Schubert [1982] use decision theory to control the cost of planning. More recently, Hartman [1990] has studied the same problem from a more formal perspective. All of these assume that probabilities are known beforehand. Moreover, none of these proposals includes an explicit representation of time.

Kanazawa and Dean [1989] propose a system that uses Bayes nets to make the computation of expected utilities sufficiently efficient to be used in a reactive execution architecture. They suggest using maximum entropy prior distributions as uninformative priors [Dean and Kanazawa, 1988]. Following Jaynes [1979], they choose the distribution that assumes one will receive the minimum amount of information from guessing. Kanazawa [1991] has recently coupled this Bayes net representation with a system for reasoning about probabilities and time.

Hanks [1988, 1990b, 1990a] has developed techniques for combining reasoning about time and probabilities. He is concerned with predicting future events given uncertain observations and actions. The planner then chooses the most effective actions given its beliefs about the state of the world in the future. Hanks also mentions maximum entropy as a guide to appropriate prior distributions.

Haddawy [1990, 1991] develops a formal logic of time and probability in which probability is represented by a modal operator over a temporal language. His system uses objective probabilities, a theory in which history determines chance in a fixed way. The theory of objective probabilities is a theory of causality that makes Bayesian inference valid.

Kanazawa and Hanks both choose a particular distribution from those warranted by their system's experience. The system maintains no information about the amount of evidence on which this distribution is based, so it cannot determine that, even though the probability of one prediction is higher than another, such a prediction rests on shaky foundations. Haddawy assumes an ontology in which probabilities are defined to be determined by the past. If it is used by a planning system, this ontology will rule out the possibility that its knowledge of the probabilities could be erroneous.

This paper explores interval estimation, a standard technique from statistical analysis, to deal with the sample size problem. It develops an event-based first-order language using temporal intervals and confidence intervals for reasoning about plans. Observations of instances of events are used to calculate confidence intervals with which the system represents and reasons about uncertainty. The language developed is similar to the event logic developed by Allen [1991] which is, in turn, based on the temporal logic described in Allen and Koomen [1983] and Allen [1984]. The confidence intervals are used in a manner similar to Kyburg's interval probabilities [Kyburg, 1983]. We provide an example of a planner making decisions based on the amount of evidence it has.

The proposal does not address the problem of generating beliefs from sensor input. It assumes that the beliefs have already been formed from the input, and the planner must decide what probability it should place on projections of its beliefs. We assume that the planner is buffered from the necessity of analyzing raw sensory information and generating control signals by an intelligent reactive system. The planner's task is to monitor the progress of the reactive system and give suggestions based on its observations.

Kaelbling [1990] investigates the possibility of applying interval estimation techniques to learning in embedded systems. She concludes that though learning algorithms that use interval estimation are slightly better than those that use point estimation, they are ill suited to learning in embedded systems because of their computational complexity and the difficulty of applying statistics to situations different from those in which they were gathered. Our use of interval estimation differs from Kaelbling's in that we apply the technique to a strategic planner that is buffered from its situation by its reactive execution module. Moreover, by reasoning about the best description of its current situation, the planner can apply statistics to situations different from those in which they were gathered.

Example As a running example, consider a robot engineer trying to couple two cars. This engineer has a program, **Old**, which it executes whenever it wants to couple cars. It has executed the program 1000 times, but has coupled successfully only 500 times. Recently, a new program, **New** was written and added to the engineer's repertoire. The old program remains an action the engineer can choose. Should the robot try the new program? A conservative guess of the probability of successfully coupling the cars using the new program might be 0.5, so the engineer might try it. If the engineer tries once and fails, it will believe the probability of coupling the cars using the new program is lower than the probability of success using the old program. The engineer could be less conservative and choose a higher prior for the new program, but what should that prior be? In general, how many times should the robot try the new program before concluding that the old program is better? □

2 KNOWLEDGE REPRESENTATION

This paper develops a first-order language that allows one to use statistics to reason about plans and actions. The language is concerned with five kinds of things: actions (**a**), event instances (e_i), temporal intervals (t_i), probability intervals (i_i), and α-levels (α_i). This language is similar to the language developed by Allen [1991]. It differs in the inclusion of probability intervals and α-levels.

An event type is a set of event instances characterized by a sentence that constrains the temporal interval during which the instances of the event type occur. For simplicity, events in this paper are characterized only by their temporal properties. Therefore, a particular event instance can be specified by fixing the time at which the event occurs, *Time*(e). We use the term *event* to represent an event type; event instances will be referred to as such. The characterization of an event is a sentence. We say that one event, e_1, subsumes another, e_2, if the characterization of e_2 is a logical consequence of the characterization of e_1.

Events express context and provide the basis for the calculation of the confidence intervals. Events encode the context of an action in its characterization. For example, being in the same city might characterize an event caused by any execution of the **Old** program. A particular event may also have other properties such as clear weather, but as long as the characterizing sentence is true, the event is said to hold. Probability is defined as the frequency of one event relative to another both in the past and in the future. For example, the probability that the engineer successfully couples two cars is the ratio of the number of successful attempts to the total number of attempts. Statistics about events change as the planner discovers more of the elements that make up the probability, but the probability itself does not change.

The temporal intervals associated with events allow the system to choose actions relative to an event, then order the events, allowing non-linear planning. Plans are generated as described by Allen [1991]. Temporal relations are specified using Allen's interval temporal logic [Allen, 1984]. These temporal intervals allow agents to reason about sequential and concurrent actions. For example, the robot engineer may need to reason that it must keep the coupler open while backing up if it wants to couple two cars.

Actions are the names of programs. When a program is executed, it causes an instance of an event. For example, a planner's program for coupling cars may simply back the engine until it hits a car. Clearly, if the train is on the wrong track, executing this program will not have the desired effect. The predicate Causes $(execute(\mathbf{a}, t), e)$ indicates that the program **a** was executed during time interval t and caused event e. Some of the circumstances that affect the results of executing a program may be specified in the characterization of the event caused by the execution of that program; others may not. The circumstances that are specified in the characterization of such an event express preconditions of the event; those that are not make the events amenable to analysis by probabilities. That is, each event describes a set of event instances, each of which is different (at the very least in its time of occurrence). Ratios of the cardinalities of these sets are the probability of one event relative to another.

Statistics are maintained on the number of occurrences of an event, *occurrences*(*event-type*). The reactive executor updates the planner's knowledge periodically. Each time a new temporal interval is added to the planner's knowledge base, it forward chains on this new information. If, in the process of forward chaining, it proves that an instance of event e has occurred, it increments the value of *occurrences*(*event-type*). As described here, the function *occurrences* is not part of the language; instead, it is used to define the confidence intervals that are part of the language.

Example A single constraint characterizes an event such that an instance of it occurs whenever the agent attempts the **Old** action,

$$\forall(e)[\text{Causes }(execute(\mathbf{Old}, Time(e)), e) \Rightarrow \text{Old-Try }(e)].$$

This event represents all time intervals that match its characterization. A *Couple* event is characterized by,

$$\begin{aligned}\forall \quad (c1, c2, t_1, t_2, e) \quad & [\neg\text{Coupled }(c1, c2, t_1) \wedge \\ & \text{Coupled }(c1, c2, t_2) \wedge \\ & \text{Starts }(t_1, Time(e)) \wedge \\ & \text{Ends }(t_2, Time(e)) \\ \Rightarrow \quad & \text{Couple }(c1, c2, e)].\end{aligned}$$

That is, a couple event is one where before the event the cars were not coupled, and after the event the cars were coupled. We name the events characterized in this way by the characteristic predicate. That is

$$\forall(e)[\text{Couple }(c1, c2, e) \iff e \in Couple(c1, c2)]$$

is always true.

If we assume the planner has seen 1000 *Old-Try* event instances, of which 500 are also *Couple(c1,c2)* event instances, i.e.

$$occurrences(Old\text{-}Try) = 1000$$
$$occurrences(Couple(c1, c2) \cap Old\text{-}Try) = 500$$

then we have characterize the situation of the robot engineer at the beginning of the example mentioned above. The event described by $Couple(c1, c2) \cap Old\text{-}Try$ is the least constrained one that subsumes both *Couple*(*c1*, *c2*) and *Old-Try*.

When the robot is given the new program for coupling cars, it will need to be able to distinguish the event in which it tries this program. This event will be called *New-Try*,

$$\begin{aligned}\forall \quad (e) \quad & [\text{Causes }(execute(\mathbf{New}, Time(e)), e) \\ \Rightarrow \quad & \text{New-Try }(e)].\end{aligned}$$

□

The α-levels are the probability that the parameter being estimated falls outside the confidence interval computed. Confidence intervals are calculated to be of the sizes of the system's α-levels. An α-level confidence interval for a parameter p is a random interval for which the probability that the interval contains p is α. Confidence intervals represent the strongest possible constraints on the location of the parameter given the data observed.

3 INFERENCE

Using statistics on events, the planner can compute constraints on the probability distributions consistent with its knowledge. We define $PCA_{1-\alpha}(e_g, e_a)$ to be the $1-\alpha\%$ confidence interval for the mean of the binomial random variable calculated from the occurrences of two events, e_g and e_a. We call the event in which the action is tried the reference event, the event after which the goal holds the success event.

Such a confidence interval can be approximated using the DeMoivre-Laplace theorem on the approximation of binomial distributions by normal distributions. Given that $z_{\alpha/2}$ is the portion of the standard normal distribution such that

$$P[Z > -z_{\alpha/2}] = P[Z < z_{\alpha/2}] = \alpha/2$$

the confidence interval for n Bernoulli trials with y successes is approximated by:

$$\left[\frac{y+\frac{z^2_{\alpha/2}}{2} - z_{\alpha/2}\sqrt{\frac{y(n-y)}{n}+\frac{z^2_{\alpha/2}}{4}}}{n+z^2_{\alpha/2}}, \frac{y+\frac{z^2_{\alpha/2}}{2} + z_{\alpha/2}\sqrt{\frac{y(n-y)}{n}+\frac{z^2_{\alpha/2}}{4}}}{n+z^2_{\alpha/2}} \right]$$

To use these confidence intervals one must assume that the normal distribution is a good approximation to the binomial. This will be the case when the smaller of np, $n(1-p)$ is less than five, where p is the parameter for the binomial distribution being approximated.

Where there are only a few instances of an event, exact bounds can be computed. The cost of computing these bounds is high, but they can be precomputed and stored in a relatively small table for those cases in which the normal approximation is invalid. The exact α-level confidence interval for the parameter of a binomial random variable generated by n Bernoulli trials with y successes ($y > 0$) will be $[p_l, p_u]$, where p_l is the unique solution to the equation,

$$\sum_{i=y}^{n} \binom{n}{i} {p_l}^i (1-p_l)^{n-i} = \alpha,$$

and p_u is the unique solution to the equation,

$$\sum_{i=0}^{y} \binom{n}{i} {p_u}^i (1-p_u)^{n-i} = \alpha.$$

Tables of confidence intervals for binomial random variables can be found in [Clopper and Pearson, 1934] and [Fisher and Yates, 1963]. There is a discussion of the trade-off between the exact confidence interval and the approximation in [Kendall and Stuart, 1961].

To calculate confidence intervals, the planner needs to know the number of occurrences, n, of instances of the reference event and the number of occurrences, y, of instances of the event subsumed by the reference event that are also subsumed by the success event. That is, the planner will need to know $n = occurrences(e_a)$ and $y = occurrences(e_a \cap e_g)$.

Confidence intervals are represented in the language by constants allowing sentences about the systems constraints on probabilities. One interval is "$\prec$" another if the upper bound of the first is less than the lower bound of the second. The intervals are equal if both bounds correspond. Intervals that overlap are said to be incomparable. That is, $[0.5, 0.6] \prec [0.7, 0.9]$ but $\neg([0.5, 0.6] \prec [0.5, 0.9])$ and $\neg([0.5, 0.9] \prec [0.5, 0.6])$. The planner chooses the action whose confidence interval at a given α-level was the highest among all applicable actions using $\prec$.

A predicate describing the planner's preferred action, Best $(\mathbf{a}, e_g, \alpha)$, can be defined using this language. The planner prefers an action **a** if and only if the statistics it has about the event in which the action occurred give clear indication that **a** is most likely to cause an event that leads to the goal (i.e., Goal(e)). The predicate can be defined by the following conditional:

$$\begin{aligned}(1)\ \forall(e_g, e_a, \alpha, \mathbf{a})\ & [\text{Goal}\ (e_g) \wedge \\ & \quad \text{Causes}\ (execute(\mathbf{a}, Time(e_a)), e_a) \wedge \\ \forall(e_b, \mathbf{b})\ & [\mathbf{a} \neq \mathbf{b} \wedge \\ & \quad \text{Causes}\ (execute(\mathbf{b}, Time(e_b)), e_b) \wedge \\ & \quad PCA_{1-\alpha}(e_g, e_b) \prec PCA_{1-\alpha}(e_g, e_a)] \\ & \Rightarrow \text{Best}\ (\mathbf{a}, e_g, \alpha)]\end{aligned}$$

This predicate says that action **a** is best if and only if the planner's knowledge constrains the probability of its success to be higher than any other action.

Example Suppose the number of occurrences of *New-Try* and *Couple(c1,c2)* are as follows:

$$occurrences(New\text{-}Try) = 2$$
$$occurrences(New\text{-}Try \cap Couple(c1, c2)) = 1.$$

In this example the engineer uses only a .05 α-level to generate its probability constraints. From the number of occurrences of the preceding events, the following constraints on the probability of the successful execution of the actions can be generated:

$$PCA_{.95}(Couple(c1, c2), Old\text{-}Try) = [0.4691, 0.5309]$$
$$PCA_{.95}(Couple(c1, c2), New\text{-}Try) = [0.0254, 0.9747].$$

The planner knows that if these intervals[1] do not overlap it can choose the higher interval, and with probability at least $1-\alpha$, this decision is correct. This information is encoded in (1). Here, the planner can prove neither

Best (*Couple(c1, c2)*, *Try-Old*, .05, **Old**)

nor

Best (*Couple(c1, c2)*, *New-Try*, .05, **New**)

using (1). It must give up. □

[1]The confidence interval for **New** is exact.

When intervals overlap, the statistics do not indicate a clear choice at the $\alpha = .05$ confidence level. When the statistics do not provide clear guidance, the robot might fall back on heuristics. One source of these heuristics might be suggestions by the programmer writing the programs about which the planner reasons.

Example The programmer might tell the robot that the new couple program is better than the old one, since, presumably, this was the reason for writing it. The planner should take this advice only if it does not conflict with its experience. It might therefore translate this advice into a rule saying it should choose the new program only as long as there is no clear evidence that this program is inferior to the old one. Such a rule can be defined by the following conditional:

$$(2)\ \forall(e)\ [\ \neg(PCA_{.95}(Couple(c1, c2), Old\text{-}Try) \prec PCA_{.95}(Couple(c1, c2), New\text{-}Try)) \wedge \neg(PCA_{.95}(Couple(c1, c2), New\text{-}Try) \prec PCA_{.95}(Couple(c1, c2), Old\text{-}Try)) \Rightarrow \text{Best}\ (Coupled, \text{e}, .05\ \mathbf{New})\ ].$$

This sentence states that whenever there is insufficient information to choose between the alternatives it should choose the **New** program. Using it, planner can prove Best $(Couple(c1, c2), e, .05, \mathbf{New})$. □

When the planner has clear evidence that one action is better than another, it need not rely on heuristics. This will be the case when evidence about the effectiveness of the **New** action overwhelms evidence about the effectiveness of the **Old** action. More importantly, the planner will cease to use the **New** action if it gets clear information that this action does not result in improved performance.

Example Suppose, after applying the default rule 100 times, the robot finds that **New** has resulted in cars being coupled 70 times. The number of times instances of the *New-Try* event and the *Couple(c1,c2)* event have occurred are

$$occurrences(New\text{-}Try) = 100$$
$$occurrences(Couple(c1, c2)) = 70,$$

generating new constraints on probability,

$$PCA_{.95}(Couple(c1, c2), New\text{-}Try) = [0.6041, 0.7811].$$

Because $[0.4691, 0.5309] \prec [0.6041, 0.7811]$, the robot chooses the **New** program and will continue to do so unless it discovers that the probability constraints for the **New** program fall below the probability constraints for the **Old** program.

If after the initial two executions of the **New** program, the next seven cause *Couple(c1,c2)* events, the robot stops relying on the heuristic and begins relying on its own experience. The exact confidence intervals for eight successes in nine trials is [0.5709, 0.9944] whereas the exact confidence interval for seven successes in eight trials is [0.5294, 0.9937]. Therefore, seven immediate successes (i.e. the robot has seen eight successes in all) are sufficient to make the robot choose the **New** program without using the heuristic.

Suppose, alternatively, that the robot discovers that it has successfully coupled cars only 30 times after applying the default rule 100 times. Now the number of occurrences of the event in which it tried the **New** program and the event in which the cars were coupled are

$$occurrences(New\text{-}Try) = 100$$
$$occurrences(Couple(c1, c2)) = 30$$

generating new constraints on probability,

$$PCA_{.95}(Couple(c1, c2), \text{New-Try}) = [0.2189, 0.3959].$$

The planner chooses to return the **Old** program because $[0.2189, 0.3959] \prec [0.4691, 0.5309]$.

If after the initial two observations of the *Try-New* event, the next eight event instances are not also instances of the *Couple(c1,c2)* event the robot rejects the heuristic preference for the **New** program. Because [0.0057, 0.4292] is the exact confidence intervals for one success in nine trials and [0.0064, 0.4707] is the interval for one success in eight trials, the robot will need at least eight immediate failures to choose the **Old** action against the advice of the programmer. □

The robot makes a choice when it has enough information to do so; it may reason further or rely on heuristics when it cannot. As the robot gathers more information, it can make more choices based on its information about the probability of success of actions and rely less on guesses.

4 PLANNING

Besides choosing actions, a planner must deal with preconditions and composite actions. Preconditions are important because some details may dramatically affect the probability of success of the action chosen. The planner must be able to take these details into account. The planner cannot take into account everything it knows about the current situation because, in part, there will be only one occurrence of such an event. This is the sample size problem. To solve the problem, the planner chooses the most constrained event that subsumes the current situation for which it has sufficient statistics to make a choice. We call this event the initial event.

To facilitate these solutions, a new event, e_p, which represents the context of the action, is added to the computation of the probability of the goal given the action. The planner computes $PCA_{1-\alpha}(e_g, e_a, e_p)$ from $n = occurrences(e_a \cap e_p)$ and $y = occurrences(e_a \cap e_g \cap e_p)$. The planner chooses the preconditions that produce the highest comparable confidence interval.

Example The engineer is more likely to successfully couple cars if the cars and the engine are in the same city. These constraints can be added to the event against which the success of the action is to be measured. For example, suppose we have a new event called a *Pre-Try* in which the cars and the engine are in the same city. This event will be characterized by:

$$\forall \quad (e, c1, c2, city) \quad [\text{In } (c1, city, Time(e)) \wedge \text{In } (c2, city, Time(e)) \wedge \text{In } (Me, city, Time(e)) \Rightarrow \text{Pre-Try}(e)\ ].$$

Another event, *Any*, describes a situation with no constraints in its characterization.

$$\forall(e)[Any(e)]$$

Since every event that subsumes *Old-Try* ∩ *Any* also subsumes *Old-Try* ∩ *Pre-Try*, the planner will have more evidence for *Old-Try* ∩ *Any*. Since, however, success is unlikely for *Old-Tries* that were not also subsumed by *Pre-Try*, the probability of success will be higher for *Old-Try* ∩ *Pre-Try*.

To choose the appropriate preconditions, the planner will also need to know that both **Old** and **New** are programs whose intention is to couple cars. This can be indicated by generating a new event that is subsumed by either *Try-Old* or *Try-New*, i.e.,

$$\forall(e)[\text{Old-Try } (e) \vee \text{New-Try } (e) \Rightarrow \text{Try } (e)].$$

Suppose that the statistics mentioned above have no particular context and that there are 800 instances of an event that subsumes *Try* ∩ *Pre-Try*. Suppose also that the number of occurrences of the success event described above is the same as the number of occurrences of success for *Try* ∩ *Pre-Try*. That is,

$$occurrences(Try \cap Pre\text{-}Try) = 800$$
$$occurrences(Couple(c1, c2) \cap Try \cap Pre\text{-}Try) = 501$$
$$occurrences(Try \cap Any) = 1002$$
$$occurrences(Couple(c1, c2) \cap Try \cap Any) = 501.$$

These statistics lead to the following probability constraints:

$$PCA_{.95}(Couple(c1, c2), Try, Pre\text{-}Try) = [0.5909, 0.6579]$$
$$PCA_{.95}(Couple(c1, c2), Try, Any) = [0.4691, 0.5309].$$

Since $[0.4691, 0.5309] \prec [0.5922, 0.6591]$, the planner chooses *Pre-Try* as the preconditions to the action. □

The planner ignores preconditions about which it has insufficient information. Even though they may affect the probability of the goal, they can be ignored with relative safety because they occur infrequently. Choosing preconditions in this manner is similar to assuming preconditions as suggested by Allen [1991].

Example Suppose the engineer can recognize when the cars loaded or empty.

$$\forall \quad (e, c1, c2, city) \quad [\text{Loaded } (c1, Time(e)) \wedge \text{Empty } (c2, Time(e)) \wedge \text{In } (c1, city, Time(e)) \wedge \text{In } (c2, city, Time(e)) \wedge \text{In } (Me, city, Time(e)) \Rightarrow \text{Pre-Try2 } (e)]$$

The ability to recognize the state of the cars may be important if the engineer's task is to move cargo. Due to the large number of such events, however, the engineer may have weak statistics on them.

Suppose that there are 100 instances of an event that subsumes *Try* ∩ *Pre-Try2*. Suppose also that 75 of the instances of the success events described above are are instances of *Try* ∩ *Pre-Try2*. That is,

$$occurrences(Try \cap Pre\text{-}Try2) = 100$$
$$occurrences(Couple(c1, c2) \cap Try \cap Pre\text{-}Try) = 75$$

These statistics lead to the following probability constraints:

$$PCA_{.95}(Couple(c1, c2), Try, Pre\text{-}Try2) = [0.6570, 0.8245].$$

Since neither $[0.6570, 0.8245] \prec [0.5922, 0.6591]$ nor $[0.5922, 0.6591] \prec [0.6570, 0.8245]$, the planner chooses *Pre-Try* as the preconditions to the action again. In this case it chooses to ignore a precondition because it does not have enough information about success relative to the precondition. As far as the planner can tell from the statistics, success assuming one event is the same as success assuming the other. □

Once the planner has chosen the appropriate preconditions for its actions, it chooses actions relative to these preconditions as outlined above.

The planner must also deal with sequences of actions. Due to space restrictions, there is only room for a cursory overview of the details of generating such sequences.

When choosing an action in a sequence, the planner chooses relative to a hypothetical event caused by executing the actions chosen earlier. For example, in choosing the second action of a two-action plan (A_1, A_2), it should select the second action in the context of the event caused by the execution of A_1 in the initial event. Since action A_1 may have many possible effects, this new event may be no simpler than was the complete description of the current situation. The planner simplifies this event by reasoning relative to an event for which it has sufficient statistics to choose an appropriate action for the second step of the plan and which subsumes the event caused by executing A_1.

When selecting an event from which to choose subsequent actions, the planner must first recognize that no single action is adequate. Because the effects of actions are uncertain, one possible result of any action is that the goal will hold. As a heuristic the planner might assume that no single action effectively achieves the goal when assuming it performs any single action makes the goal no more likely than assuming it does nothing. Here the planner can be confident that by using time to continue planning, it will miss deadlines. If the goal is part of the current situation, doing nothing is most likely to cause an event in which the goal holds than doing nothing, as it causes an event that subsumes the maximum number of events and is therefore most likely to subsume the current situation.

Once it has realized that it must generate a series of sub-goals to achieve its main goal, it can then deal with each sub-goal as a separate problem. The problems are not really separate, however, because choosing actions that achieve remaining sub-goals may reduce the probability that actions already chosen achieve their sub-goals. The planner avoids such interaction by choosing remaining actions relative to a hypothetical event that subsumes the event caused by executing actions chosen earlier. The order in which the planner chooses actions is unimportant because the temporal logic allows both constraints that precede and constraints that follow the execution of actions.

If the planner has sufficient statistics to reason about sequences of events, it will use them. That is, if it can actually make subsequent choices given the desired results of previous choices, the planner will make the choices. In situations requiring planning, it is unlikely that the planner will have good statistics for long sequences of actions, however. Except for those sequences that are chosen frequently, the statistics are likely to be very weak for the choices the planner must make in long plans. Note that it is the small sample size, not low probability, that makes such decisions untenable. The planner may have actually succeeded every time it chose an action in a very constrained event; it just has not made those choices often enough to be confident in them.

If the planner has insufficient statistics to make subsequent choices, it may rely on heuristics like the one described by formula (2). For example, a good heuristic would be to wait until further information arrives. If a planner has a partial plan it cannot complete, it might simply specify that partial plan to the reactive execution system and hope for the best. Even if the partial plan is insufficient to actually achieve the goal, the planner may have more information when it needs to replan.

If the planner has no applicable heuristics or world knowledge, it will assume the actions are independent. Such an assumption may be incorrect, but a planner that uses statistics will at least have evidence that the plans it is generating are ineffective when the statistics begin to reflect its current strategy's low probability of success. For example, if the planner cannot recognize the event in which the cars and the engine are in the same city, it will continue to try to couple the cars, but will succeed only when the unrecognizable precondition holds. If the engine and cars are rarely in the same city, the probability of success for the engineer's couple programs will fall, and the engineer's confidence in this low probability will increase. Eventually, the planner will become confident enough that the action rarely succeeds that it will stop attempting it.

5 CONCLUSION

A language for reasoning with statistics gives planners the ability to reason about the strength of their evidence. By reasoning about the strength of its evidence, a planner can discount weak evidence as a reason for preferring one action over another. As far as we are aware, no other formalism combines temporal reasoning and reasoning about evidence. Systems that gather information and generate plans based on that information will need this ability.

A shortcoming of the proposal as presented here is the weakness of the statistical tests used. Generating confidence intervals and comparing them is wasteful of the planner's valuable data. We are studying other statistical tests that make better use of the data. Another problem is choosing preconditions based on estimations of the probability of the goal given the preconditions. A better criterion is the information the preconditions provides for the the choice of actions. Measures of information may perform better than do constraints on probability.

An unnecessary restriction of the presentation is its adherence to the frequentist view of probabilities. All of the techniques presented in this paper are equally valid if one uses Bayesian interval estimation rather than confidence intervals. Indeed, even many of the more powerful statistical tests under study have Bayesian correlates.

A shortcoming this proposal shares with others is the large number of events needed for general purpose planning. In this system, events play the part of operators in STRIPS. Still, probabilities may suggest a solution to this problem. One could control the number of events the planner needs to consider by ensuring that the event occurs frequently. If such an assurance can be made, the planner can assume that if it has no statistics about a particular event, that event is rare. Such assurances may be possible if events are generated through cluster analysis. If the events are generated in this way, the planner may safely assume that only rare events will have no statistics.

Acknowledgments

We would like to thank George Ferguson for his many insightful commments on this work. We would also like to thank Steve Hanks and Bulent Murtezaoglu for comments on earlier drafts of the paper. This material is based on work supported by ONR/DARPA under grant number N0014-82-K-0193 and under AF-Rome Air Development Center contract number F30602-92-C-0010.

References

[Allen and Koomen, 1983] James Allen and Johannes Koomen. Planning using a temporal world model. In *IJCAI-83*, pages 741–747, 1983.

[Allen, 1984] James F. Allen. Towards a general theory of action and time. *Artificial Intelligence*, 23(2):123–145, 1984.

[Allen, 1991] James F. Allen. Planning as temporal reasoning. In *KR-91*, pages 3–14, 1991.

[Bickel and Doksum, 1977] Peter J. Bickel and Kjell A. Doksum. *Mathematical Statistics: Basic Ideas and Selected Topics.* Holden-Day, Inc., Oakland, CA, 1977.

[Clopper and Pearson, 1934] C. J. Clopper and E. S. Pearson. The use of confidence or fiducial limits illustrated in the case of the binomial. *Biometrika*, 26:404–413, 1934.

[Dean and Kanazawa, 1988] Thomas Dean and Keiji Kanazawa. Probablistic temporal reasoning. In *AAAI-88*, pages 125–132, 1988.

[Feldman and Sproull, 1977] Jerome Feldman and Robert Sproull. Decision theory and artificial intelligence II: The hungry monkey. *Cognitive Science*, 1:158–192, 1977.

[Fisher and Yates, 1963] R. A. Fisher and F. Yates. *Statistical Tables for Biological Agricultural and Medical Research (6th ed.).* oliver and Boyde, Edinburg, 1963.

[Haddawy, 1990] Peter Haddawy. Time, chance, and action. In *Uncertainty in AI 90*, pages 147–153, 1990.

[Haddawy, 1991] Peter Haddawy. A temporal probability logic for representing actions. In *KR-91*, pages 313–324, 1991.

[Hanks, 1988] Steve Hanks. Representing and computing temporally scoped beliefs. In *AAAI-88*, pages 501–505, 1988.

[Hanks, 1990a] Steve Hanks. Practical temoral projection. In *AAAI-90*, pages 158–163, 1990.

[Hanks, 1990b] Steven John Hanks. *Projecting Plans for Uncertain Worlds.* PhD thesis, Yale University, New Haven, CT, 1990.

[Hartman, 1990] Leo B. Hartman. *Decision Theory and the Cost of Planning.* PhD thesis, University of Rochester, Rochester, NY 14627, 1990.

[Horvitz, 1988] Eric J. Horvitz. Reasoning under varying and uncertain resource constraints. In *AAAI-88*, volume 1, pages 111–116, 1988.

[Jaynes., 1979] E. T. Jaynes. Where do we stand on maximum entropy? In R. D. Levine and M. Tribus, editors, *The Maximum Entropy Formalism*, pages 279–293. MIT Press, 1979.

[Johnson and Schubert, 1982] D. T. Johnson and Lenhart K. Schubert. A planning control strategy that allows for the cost of planning. In *Proc. 6th Eur. Meet. on Cybernetics and Sys. Research*, pages 1–7, 1982.

[Kaelbling, 1990] Leslie Pack Kaelbling. *Learning in Embedded Systems.* PhD thesis, Stanford University, Stanford, CA, 1990.

[Kanazawa and Dean, 1989] Keiji Kanazawa and Thomas Dean. A model for projection and action. In *IJCAI-89*, pages 985–990, 1989.

[Kanazawa, 1991] Kaiji Kanazawa. A logic and time nets for probabilistic inference. In *AAAI-91*, 1991.

[Kendall and Stuart, 1961] M. G. Kendall and A. Stuart. *The Advanced Theory of Statistics Vol II (2nd ed).* Hafner Publishing Co., New York, 1961.

[Kyburg, 1983] Henry E. Kyburg, Jr. The reference class. *Philosophy of Science*, 50:374–397, 1983.

[Martin and Allen, 1990a] Nathaniel G. Martin and James F. Allen. Abstraction in planning: A probabilistic approach. Presented at the Workshop on Automatic Generation of Approximations and Abstractions, 1990.

[Martin and Allen, 1990b] Nathaniel G. Martin and James F. Allen. Combining reactive and strategic planning through decomposition abstraction. In *Workshop on Innovative Approaches to Planning, Scheduling and Control*, pages 137–143, 1990.

[Raiffa, 1970] Howard Raiffa. *Decision Analysis: Introductory Lectures on Choices under Uncertainty.* Addison-Wesley, Reading, MA, 1970.

[Weber, 1989] Jay C. Weber. A parallel algorithm for statistical belief refinement and its use in causal reasoning. In *IJCAI-89*, August 1989.

A Modification to Evidential Probability

Bülent Murtezaoğlu
mucit@cs.rochester.edu
Computer Science Department
University of Rochester
Rochester, NY 14627

Henry E. Kyburg
kyburg@cs.rochester.edu
Computer Science Department
University of Rochester
Rochester, NY 14627

Abstract

Selecting the right reference class and the right interval when faced with conflicting candidates and no possibility of establishing subset style dominance has been a problem for Kyburg's Evidential Probability system. Various methods have been proposed by Loui and Kyburg to solve this problem in a way that is both intuitively appealing and justifiable within Kyburg's framework. The scheme proposed in this paper leads to stronger statistical assertions without sacrificing too much of the intuitive appeal of Kyburg's latest proposal.

1 Overview of the Problem

1.1 An Example

Let us consider a variant of the classic berries example.[1] Suppose a hungry agent has access to the following information:

- Between 70 and 90 percent of the red berries, sampled at some time in the past, were found to be good to eat.
- Between 30 and 50 percent of the berries picked on rainy days were found to be good to eat.
- Between 70 and 75 percent of berries from this region, sampled at some time in the past, were found to be good to eat.
- Between 35 and 45 percent of soft berries, sampled at some time in the past, were found to be good to eat.
- The berries at hand now are both red and soft and picked from this region and furthermore today is a rainy day.

[1] Due to Jerry Feldman.

The agent's problem is deciding whether or not it should eat the berries it has. This decision involves two distinct levels of analysis; the first one is deciding what indeed it can infer from its knowledge about berries in general about the particular berries it has, and the second one is, given its inferred knowledge about the berries it has, whether or not it should eat them.

It may be argued that de-coupling the inference and the decision procedures generally leads agents into lengthy computations even when the relevant utility values and practical concerns would dictate a certain decision, rendering the sophisticated inference procedure futile. In the example the agent may be making a choice between starvation and food poisoning and therefore the utilities involved with the choices would, for a sane agent, dictate that it should eat the berries regardless of what it can infer about their edibility. We will not, however, concern ourselves with such issues in this paper because the proposed method for this restricted case is computationally cheap.

In the example above, the agent has no knowledge of the subset relationships between the candidate reference classes. For instance, if it knew that the red berries that it has statistics about were in fact both red and soft, it could safely disregard the conflicting[2] statistics about soft berries [Kyburg, 1983]. Or if it had access to the joint information about red and soft berries found in this region on rainy days, it would not need to consider the conflicting statistics about the broader classes according to both Reichenbach and Kyburg. Our agent, however, does not have all the necessary bits of information conveniently available.

1.2 The General Case

Suppose we want to compute the probability of some object o having a target property T, and we have knowledge about the classes o belongs to and the in-

[2] *Conflict*, or *disagreement*, between two intervals $[p_1, q_1]$ and $[p_2, q_2]$ is defined as the case where neither $[p_1, q_1] \subseteq [p_2, q_2]$ nor $[p_2, q_2] \subseteq [p_1, q_1]$.

terval valued measure of T in those classes. More formally, our knowledge base contains the following statements:

- Sentences denoting set memberships
  "$x \in Y$"
  where x is an object and Y is a set.
- Sentences denoting subset relationships between classes
  "$Y \subset Z$"
  where Y and Z are sets.
- Sentences concerning proportions of sets of the form
  "$\%(T, S) = [p, q]$"
  where T and S are sets and p and q are some approximate representation of real numbers. These can be read as " the measure or the proportion of elements of set S that have the property T is in the interval $[p, q]$."

Using the above syntax and assumptions, we can state the general problem as follows

- The knowledge base contains the sentences
  "$\%(\mathrm{T}, \mathrm{S}_1) = [\mathrm{p}_1, \mathrm{q}_1]$", "$\%(\mathrm{T}, \mathrm{S}_2) = [\mathrm{p}_2, \mathrm{q}_2]$",
  "$\%(\mathrm{T}, \mathrm{S}_3) = [\mathrm{p}_3, \mathrm{q}_3]$", ...,
  "$\%(\mathrm{T}, \mathrm{S}_{n-1}) = [\mathrm{p}_{n-1}, \mathrm{q}_{n-1}]$", "$\%(\mathrm{T}, \mathrm{S}_n) = [\mathrm{p}_n, \mathrm{q}_n]$"
- and either contains or entails through subset chaining the sentences
  "$\mathrm{o} \in \mathrm{S}_1$", "$\mathrm{o} \in \mathrm{S}_2$", "$\mathrm{o} \in \mathrm{S}_3$", ..., "$\mathrm{o} \in \mathrm{S}_{n-1}$", "$\mathrm{o} \in \mathrm{S}_n$"
- We are interested in finding the probability of
  "$\mathrm{o} \in \mathrm{T}$"

So $S_1, S_2, S_3, \ldots, S_{n-1}, S_n$ are all candidate reference classes for the query. We are assuming that no other knowledge is available; in particular, knowledge about subset relationships between S_i's is not available. If all the intervals $[p_i, q_i]$ nest within each other, the solution is trivial: the candidate with the narrowest interval would be the answer to the query. If, on the other hand, there are conflicts between the intervals, we cannot establish dominance using Kyburg's original rules [Kyburg, 1983] since we do not have the necessary information about the subset relationships. One could give up and return the interval $[0, 1]$ or resort to constructing various subsets of the cross products of the candidate reference classes. The first method is useless, [3] and variations of the second method admit clear-cut counter-examples [Kyburg, 1991].

[3]Though it should be noted that we cannot establish better bounds on the interval by purely set theoretic procedures. It is entirely possible for the probability to be high for two candidate reference classes but very low in their intersection and vice versa. In other words, since we do not know anything about the structures of or the relationships between the candidate reference classes, set theory does not help us come up with non-trivial bounds for their intersection which the object belongs to.

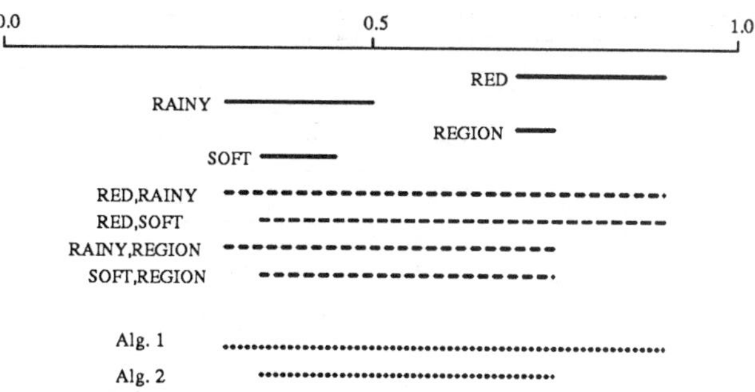

Figure 1: The intervals for the berries example, the dashed lines represent the interval covers of pairs of intervals. The dotted lines are what each algorithm would return. Algorithm 2 is the modified algorithm.

Kyburg used to endorse Loui's approach using subsets of the cross products [Loui, 1986, Kyburg, 1987], but he has changed his mind in recent years [Kyburg, 1991]. He argues that the strongest interval we can justifiably return is the narrowest interval cover that does not conflict with any member of the set of relevant intervals. More formally, given a set of intervals where each member of the set conflicts with at least one other member, we construct an interval using the minimum of the lower endpoints and the maximum of higher endpoints. If there are wide intervals that don't conflict with any other interval in the original set, they can safely be disregarded since they are guaranteed to be as weak or weaker than the narrowest interval cover of the conflicting ones. Thus, in the berries example Kyburg would return the interval $[0.30, 0.90]$ (fig. 1).

2 The Proposed Solution

One can think of the procedure proposed in [Kyburg, 1991] as looking at pairs of candidate reference classes and constructing new candidates by taking the interval covers of the conflicting pairs as a means of settling the conflicts.[4] This procedure can be repeated until there is an interval that does not conflict with any of the others. An inefficient but nevertheless illustrative way of computing the interval cover Kyburg would select is given by the following pseudo-code: [5]

[4]Note that we do not have enough data to choose one candidate over another.

[5]Since no information about the subset relationships between the classes is available, we will deal only with the intervals associated with the classes. Even when enough information is available for using Kyburg's rules, it is conceivable that one could end up with a set of candidates rather than a single reference class. So the proposed procedure can be used as the last step of Kyburg's method in the general case.

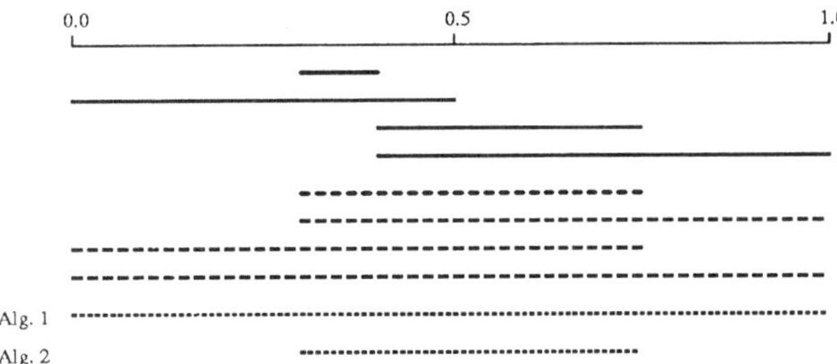

Figure 2: The dashed lines represent the pairwise covers generated in the first iteration of algorithm 1 (elements of $\mathcal{L}'$ after the first iteration). The dotted lines show what each algorithm returns.

Algorithm 1

input: a set $\mathcal{L}$ *of intervals* I_i
repeat
  $\mathcal{L}' := \{\}$
  for every interval pair $I_i = [p_i, q_i], I_j = [p_j, q_j]$ *in* $\mathcal{L}$
    if I_i *conflicts with* I_j *then*
      $I' := [min(p_i, p_j), max(q_i, q_j)]$
      $\mathcal{L}' := \mathcal{L}' \cup \{I'\}$
      mark both I_i *and* I_j
  $\mathcal{L} := \mathcal{L} \cup \mathcal{L}'$
until $\mathcal{L}' = \{\}$
return the narrowest un-marked interval in $\mathcal{L}$

As can be noticed from the pseudo-code, intervals that are no longer candidates (i.e., they are "marked") can still interfere with the selection of other intervals. One upshot of this is that individual "marked" intervals prevent the selection of a narrower cover even when their own cover would not have interfered. This interference from wide intervals is not desirable because it leads us to weaker conclusions. For example, if our set of intervals were $\{[0.3, 0.4], [0.0, 0.5], [0.4, 0.7], [0.4, 1.0]\}$ (Fig. 2), we would have to return [0.0,1.0], but if we look at the set $\mathcal{L}'$ after the first iteration of the algorithm ({[0.3, 0.7], [0.3,1.0], [0.0,0.7], [0.0,1.0]}), it is apparent that [0.3,0.7] is not challenged by any other interval constructed in this iteration. Now, favoring [0.3,0.7] over the conservative but useless [0.0,1.0] is appealing because it leads to a stronger result, but can we justify doing so? We can if we are willing to say that interval covers reflect the information represented by their constituents. In the case of two conflicting intervals [0.0,0.5] and [0.4,0.7], we might argue that the cover [0.0,0.7] encodes all we know, given those two bits of information. If we do not go back and look at its constituents, the cover [0.0,0.7] does not interfere with the stronger cover [0.3,0.7] even though its constituents ([0.0,0.5] and [0.4,0.7]) would.

Considering the presence of conflicting evidence, the widening caused by taking covers of intervals is desirable in terms of the semantics one would like to attribute to intervals. Intuitively, one does expect conflicting piceces of evidence to weaken the conclusions, and the interval cover idea nicely captures that intuition. One may not, however, want the weak pieces of evidence to undermine the stronger conclusions indicated by the stronger pieces of evidence with which they are consistent. One way of preventing the weaker evidence from interfering is to disregard or delete the original intervals once we construct all the covers they cause to be constructed. On the other hand, one wants to use all the information available, and actually deleting the constituents once the cover is constructed is not compatible with that ideal. It is not, however, altogether unreasonable to buy into the former argument while keeping the latter in mind. While professing ignorance is a virtue, one should also be able to make the best of available information.

As is the case with Kyburg's method in [Kyburg, 1991], the reference class associated with the interval we return can be any one of the candidate classes associated with the constituents of the cover.

The modified algorithm, which leads to less conservative conclusions, is as follows:

Algorithm 2

input: a set $\mathcal{L}$ *of intervals* I_i
repeat
  $\mathcal{L}' := \{\}$
  for every interval pair $I_i = [p_i, q_i], I_j = [p_j, q_j]$ *in* $\mathcal{L}$
    if I_i *conflicts with* I_j *then*
      $I' := [min(p_i, p_j), max(q_i, q_j)]$
      $\mathcal{L}' := \mathcal{L}' \cup \{I'\}$
      mark both I_i *and* I_j
  delete all the marked elements of $\mathcal{L}$
  $\mathcal{L} := \mathcal{L} \cup \mathcal{L}'$
until $\mathcal{L}' = \{\}$
return the narrowest un-marked interval in $\mathcal{L}$

This algorithm returns the narrowest interval cover whose set of constituents $\mathcal{S} \subseteq \mathcal{L}$ has the property that for any interval $I \in \mathcal{L} - \mathcal{S}$, there is an interval $I^* \in \mathcal{S}$ that nests in and is at least as narrow as I. Having made that observation, we can write a more efficient version of the algorithm which illustrates this point.

Algorithm 2′

input: a list $\mathcal{L}$ *of intervals* I_i *sorted in ascending order of width*
$\mathcal{L}' := \{\}$
repeat
  extract the first unmarked interval I^* *from* $\mathcal{L}$
  $\mathcal{L}' := \mathcal{L}' \cup \{I^*\}$
  for every remaining un-marked interval I *in* $\mathcal{L}$
    if I *agrees with* I^* *then*
      mark I
until there are no more un-marked intervals in $\mathcal{L}$
return interval cover of the intervals in $\mathcal{L}'$

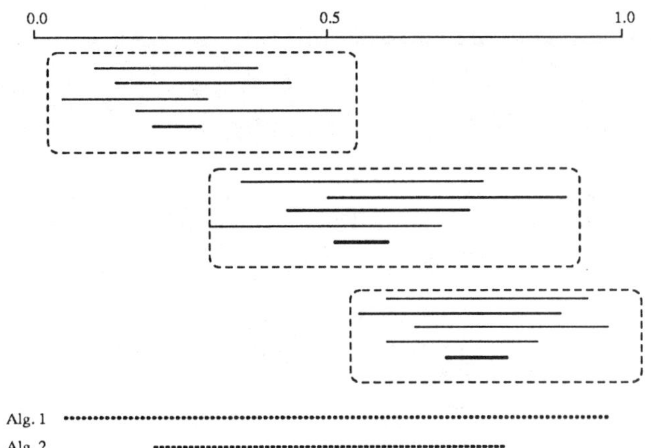

Figure 3: A picture of a more general case with many intervals. The dashed boxes represent sets of intervals with a common narrow sub-interval, which is denoted by a thick line.

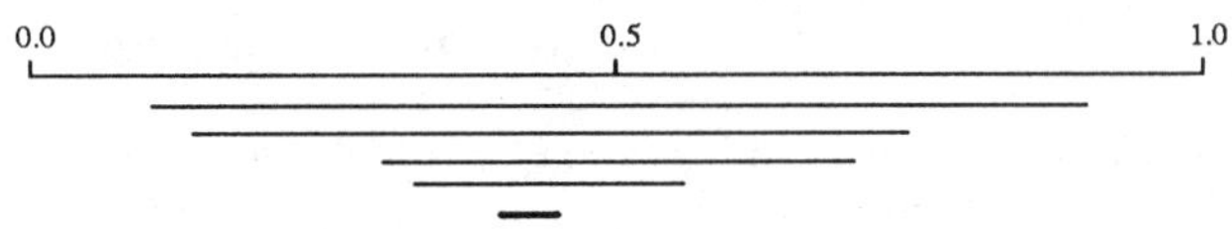

Figure 4: The case where there are no conflicts between the candidates.

One can think of each I^* selected in the algorithm as representing the opinion of an independent agent who has access only to the set of intervals $\mathcal{S}^* \subseteq \mathcal{L}$ such that for every interval $I \in \mathcal{S}^*$, $I^* \subseteq I$ (Fig. 3). The cover of all such I^* would give us the interval on which all such agents would agree.[6] Once again, the point can be made that those agents would not hold those opinions if they had access to what the other agents knew.

2.1 Observations

The interval returned by the modified algorithm is never in conflict with the one returned by the original and is at least as narrow. The modified algorithm does return the same result as the original in such cases as the following:

- When there is no conflict between members of the original set of candidate intervals (Fig. 4). This is the most desirable case in that neither algorithm uses evidence combination to obtain a result.
- When there are no two nesting intervals in the original set of candidates (Fig. 5). Having no agreement at all among the pieces of evidence indicates that a very conservative conclusion is called for.

[6]Note that we are not requiring all members of $\mathcal{S}^*$'s to agree with each other.

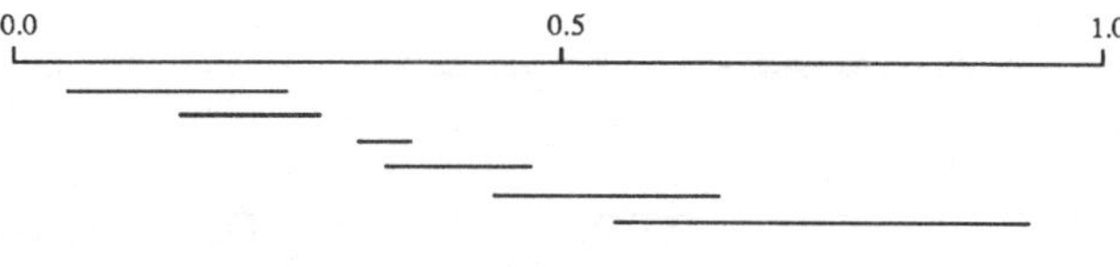

Figure 5: The case where none of the candidates agree.

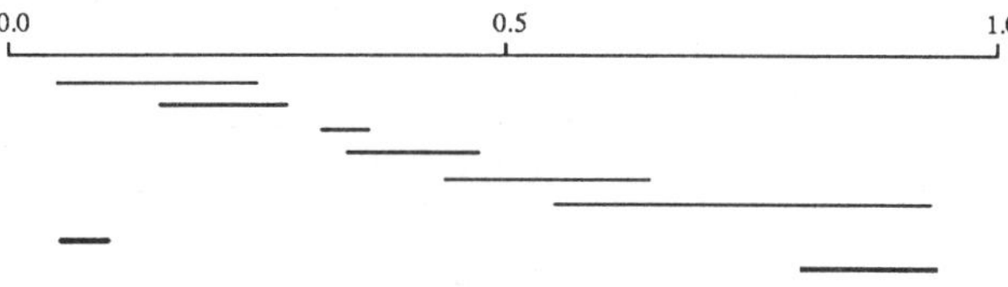

Figure 6: The case where the narrowest intervals (thick lines) are at the extreme ends of the cover of all candidates.

- When the set of narrowest intervals have members that are at the extreme ends of the wider intervals in which they nest (Fig. 6). As can be seen in the figure, having strong but extremely conflicting evidence leads to weak results.

3 Conclusions

Avoiding interference from conflicting unreliable data is a problem for autonomous agents except when the designer can hand pick the relevant information. We think playing it safe with large amounts of conflicting data causes pieces of weak evidence to unnecessarily weaken the results of the inference process. The proposed algorithm leads to stronger results by favoring stronger conclusions when there is enough data to justify them.

Acknowledgments

Research underlying this work has been supported in part by U.S. Army Communication-Electronics Command grant no. DAAB10-87-K-022, and NSF research grant no. IRI-9002659.

References

[Kyburg, 1983] Henry E. Kyburg, Jr. The reference class. *Philosophy of Science*, 50:374–397, 1983.

[Kyburg, 1987] Henry E. Kyburg, Jr. Bayesian and non-bayesian evidential updating. *AI Journal*, (31):271–294, 1987.

[Kyburg, 1991] Henry E. Kyburg, Jr. Evidential probability. In *Proceedings of the Twelfth International Joint Conference on Artificial Intelligence (IJCAI-91)*, 1991.

[Loui, 1986] Ronald P. Loui. Computing reference classes. In *AAAI Uncertainty Workshop*, 1986.

Investigation of Variances in Belief Networks

Richard E. Neapolitan
Computer Science Dept.
Northeastern Illinois University
Chicago, IL 60625

James R. Kenevan
Computer Science Dept.
Illinois Institute of Technology
Chicago, IL 60616

Abstract

The belief network is a well-known graphical structure for representing independences in a joint probability distribution. The methods, which perform probabilistic inference in belief networks, often treat the conditional probabilities which are stored in the network as certain values. However, if one takes either a subjectivistic or a limiting frequency approach to probability, one can never be certain of probability values. An algorithm should not only be capable of reporting the probabilities of the alternatives of remaining nodes when other nodes are instantiated; it should also be capable of reporting the uncertainty in these probabilities relative to the uncertainty in the probabilities which are stored in the network. In this paper a method for determining the variances in inferred probabilities is obtained under the assumption that a posterior distribution on the uncertainty variables can be approximated by the prior distribution. It is shown that this assumption is plausible if their is a reasonable amount of confidence in the probabilities which are stored in the network. Furthermore in this paper, a surprising upper bound for the prior variances in the probabilities of the alternatives of all nodes is obtained in the case where the probability distributions of the probabilities of the alternatives are beta distributions. It is shown that the prior variance in the probability at an alternative of a node is bounded above by the largest variance in an element of the conditional probability distribution for that node.

1 INTRODUCTION

Much recent research in decision analysis and in expert systems which reason under uncertainty has focused on belief networks. A belief network consists of a DAG $= (V, E)$ in which each $v \in V$ represents a set of mutually exclusive and exhaustive events, along with a joint probability distribution, P, on the alternatives of the nodes in V. The fundamental assumption in a belief network is that the value assumed by a node is probabilistically independent of the values assumed by all other nodes in the network, except the descendents of the given node, given values of all parents of the node. It can be shown that, given this restriction on P, P can be retrieved from the product of the conditional distributions of each node given values of its parents; it can further be shown that, if these conditional distributions are freely specified, the product of those distributions, along with the DAG, constitute a belief network. See Heckerman and Horvitz [1987], Neapolitan [1990], Pearl [1988], and Clemen [1991] for discussions of the importance of belief networks in representing problems in expert systems and decision analysis.

Two important problems in belief networks are probability propagation and abductive inference. Probability propagation is the determination of the values of all other nodes in the network given that certain nodes are instantiated for particular values or that evidence is obtained for the values of certain nodes, while abductive inference is the determination of the most probable, second most probable, third most probable, and so on values of a specified set of nodes called the explanation set given that certain nodes are instantiated or that evidence is obtained. Pearl [1986] and Lauritzen and Spiegelhalter [1988] have obtained efficient algorithms for probability propagation for certain classes of networks, while Cooper [1984], Pearl [1987], and Peng and Reggia [1987] have obtained algorithms which perform abductive inference for certain classes of networks. This paper is concerned only with probabilities obtained using probability propagation. Such probabilities will be called inferred probabilities. The development of efficient general purpose algorithms for probability propagation and abductive inference appears unlikely since Cooper [1988] has shown that both these problems are NP-hard. Recent research has therefore centered on development of approximation, special case, and heuristic methods.

The above methods treat the conditional probabilities which are stored in the network as certain values. For example, Chavez and Cooper's [1990] approximation method computes an error relative to an exact value which would be obtained if exact probability propagation were possible (e.g. using the method of Pearl [1986] or Lauritzen and Spiegelhalter [1988].) However, if one takes either a subjectivistic or a limiting frequency approach to probability, one can never be certain of probability values. Only a pure logical approach claims to know probabilities for certain. For example, if a coin were tossed 1000 times and 527 tosses came up heads, the frequentist would obtain a confidence interval for the probability value, while the subjectivist would obtain a posterior probability interval or a beta posterior distribution.

An exact algorithm for probability propagation should not only be capable of reporting inferred probabilities; it should also be capable of reporting the uncertainty in these probabilities relative to the uncertainty in the conditional probabilities which are specified in the network. An approximation algorithm should incorporate this uncertainty into the possible error which is reported for the approximating values. The uncertainty in the conditional probabilities which are specified in the network can be expressed by probability distributions on the probabilities, and the uncertainty in the inferred probabilities can be determined by computing the variances in these probabilities relative to the joint distribution of these distributions. If a belief network includes decision nodes and a value node, (such a belief network is called an influence diagram, see Clemen [1991]), and the system maximizes expected utility, there are two important reasons for reporting the variances. First, the variances can be used to measure the quality of the system. If a decision is based on a probability of .8 when the 'correct' probability is .4, it may not be a good decision. Second, in an individual case, a large variance may indicate that the best decision would be to gather additional information which would decrease the variance. Howard [1970] discusses variances and the value of information. If the system does not maximize expected utility, the variances in the inferred probabilities inform the decision maker as to the system's uncertainty in its probabilities. This uncertainty should be taken into account before a decision is made.

Results of Zabell [1982] show that in many of the situations involving repeatable experiments the uncertainty in probability values must be represented by Dirichlet distributions. Using a method developed by Spiegelhalter [1988], Neapolitan [1990] showed how to 'discretize' the Dirichlet distributions and represent the uncertainty in the conditional probabilities which are specified in the network in the natural framework of the belief network. For example, in Figure 1 the node C represents the uncertainty in the prior probability of A while D and E represent the uncertainty in the conditional probability of B given A. Neapolitan [1990] further showed how to use one of the algorithms for exact probability propagation to compute the variance in an inferred probability relative to the uncertainty in the probabilities which are stored in the network. Neapolitan noted, however, that the number of calculations needed in this computation can grow exponentially with the distance in the graph of a given node from the instantiated node. This is true even in sparsely connected networks for which exact probability propagation is computationally feasible.

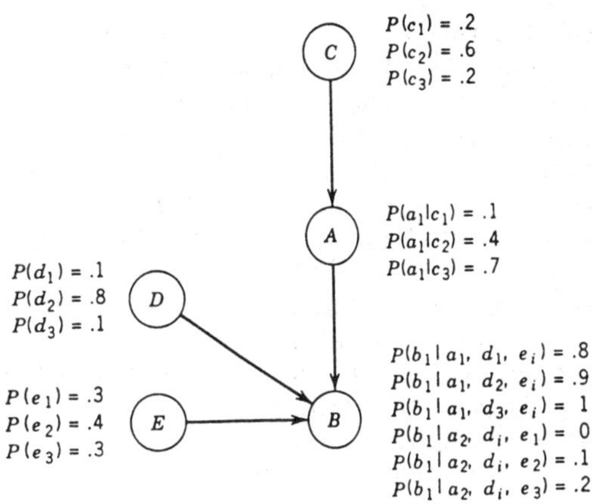

Figure 1: The nodes C, D, and E represent the uncertainty in probabilities.

Thus there still existed a need for a method for determining the variances in inferred probabilities relative to the uncertainty in the stored probabilities. In Neapolitan and Kenevan [1990] a method is given for determining the prior variances (that is, the variances in the marginal probabilities before any evidence is obtained) of the probabilities of all nodes for the case where certain information is available concerning the probability distributions of the conditional probabilities which are specified in the network. It is also shown how to obtain this information when the distributions are Dirichlet. A method for determining the variances of inferred probabilities appears very difficult even in the case of sparsely connected networks. In Section 3, an exact method is obtained for the case where a posterior distribution on the uncertainty variables can be approximated by the prior distribution. It is shown that this approximation is plausible if there is a reasonable amount of confidence in the probabilities which are stored in the network. Note that, even if there is a reasonable amount of confidence in the stored probabilities, there may still be little confidence in the probabilities of the values of a particular node since the uncertainty in these probabilities is relative to the uncertainty in many of the probabilities which are stored in the network. Thus it is still necessary to compute the variances.

One fear concerning belief networks is that, when a probability value is computed for many of the probabilities which are stored in the network, the variance in that probability value might be hopelessly large since it is relative to the uncertainty in many probabilities. Neapolitan and Kenevan [1990] show that if any probability is very large or very small, then the variance in that probability must be small. This is encouraging since, in medical applications for example, information is often obtained until the probability of some explanation is close to 1. However, what of the case where the probability is not large or small? Applications of algorithm in Neapolitan and Kenevan [1990] indicated that the prior variances did not, as one might expect, become hopelessly large as one went down the network. This indication led to the surprising result which is the main theorem at the end of Section 4 of this paper. Namely that, under certain assumptions, the prior variance in the probability of an alternative of a node is bounded above by the largest variance in an element of the conditional distribution which is specified for that node. Therefore, if we have confidence in the conditional probabilities which are specified in the network, we can have confidence in the prior probabilities of all nodes.

2 PRELIMINARY ASSUMPTIONS

It is assumed in what follows that probabilistic assessments in the belief network are made independently. Thus the uncertainties in the assessed probabilities can be represented by a set of mutually independent auxiliary parent nodes. The auxiliary parent of a node, E, will be denoted U_E. For example, in Figure 2, U_E represents the uncertainty in the $P(E)$, the prior probability of E, U_F represents the uncertainty in the $P(F|E)$, the conditional probability of F given E, and U_D represents the uncertainty in the $P(D|F, C)$. Each auxiliary node is actually a set of mutually independent nodes, one for each combination of values of the true parents. For example, U_E consists of one node, if E has three alternatives, U_F consists of three nodes, and if F and C each have two alternatives, U_D consists of four nodes. U will be used to denote the set of all the uncertainty nodes. The underlying distribution is then the joint probability distribution on the members of U and will be denoted by $P(U)$. The probabilistic assessments are random variables on this joint probability distribution. Small p will be used to denote these random variables. For example, $p(e_i)$ is the random variable for the prior probability of e_i. This random variable will also be denoted by $P(e_i|U)$ when it is convenient to do so. Similarly, $p(f_i|e_j)$ is the random variable for the conditional probability of f_i given that E is equal to e_j. This random variable will also be denoted by $P(f_i|e_j, U)$. It is assumed, for example, that $p(e_1)$ is a function only of U_E, and that $p(f_1|e_1)$ is a function only of the first member of U_F, and $p(f_1|e_2)$ is a function only of the second member of U_F. Therefore these random variables are mutually independent. Note however that $p(e_i)$ and $p(e_k)$ are not independent. For example, if E has two alternatives and $p(e_1) = .4$, then $p(e_2)$ must equal .6.

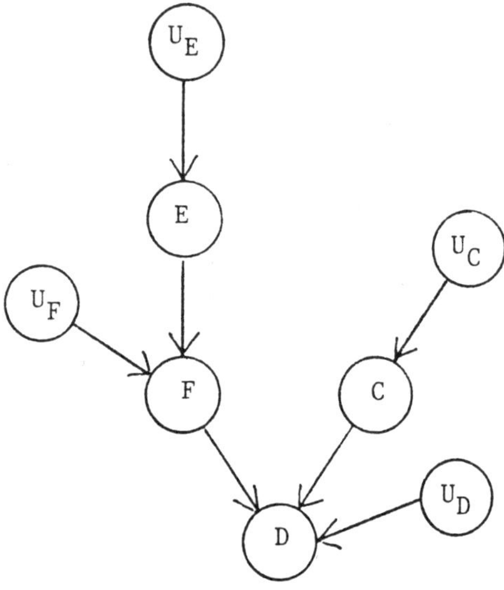

Figure 2: The auxiliary parent nodes represent the uncertainty in probabilities.

The random variable for the probability of a node which is not a root is computed from the assessed random variables. For example,

$$p(f_1) = \sum_i p(f_1|e_i)p(e_i)$$

$$\begin{aligned} p(d_1) &= \textstyle\sum_{i,k} p(d_1|f_i, c_k)p(f_i, c_k) \\ &= \textstyle\sum_{i,k} p(d_1|f_i, c_k)p(f_i)p(c_k) \end{aligned}$$

since $p(f_i)$ and $p(c_k)$ are independent random variables due to the network being singly connected.

If p_i is a random variable for a probability value which is stored in the network (e.g., p_i may be $p(e_i)$ or $p(f_i, e_j)$), it is assumed in this paper that the following information is available for p_i, where E stands for the expected value:

$$E(p_i) \qquad E(p_i^2) \qquad E(p_i p_j) \tag{1}$$

Note that p_i and p_j are random variables for the ith and j^{th} alternatives of the same node. Neapolitan and Kenevan [1990] obtained this information in the case where the distributions are Dirichlet.

3 DETERMINING THE VARIANCES IN INFERRED PROBABILITIES

In this section a method is obtained for computing the posterior variances (i.e., the variances in the inferred probabilities given that certain nodes, W, are instantiated) under the assumption that a posterior distribution on the uncertainty variables, $P(U|V)$, can be approximated by the prior distribution, $P(U)$. Neapolitan [1991] shows that, when nodes are instantiated, the posterior distribution on the uncertainty variables can differ from the prior distribution by no more than a distribution based on the information in one additional trial. Therefore if there is a reasonable amount of confidence in the prior distribution, a posterior distribution can be approximated by the prior distribution. Essentially, we are assuming that we learn nothing about the probabilities which are specified in the network from the current case.

In this section, it is assumed that a variable has exactly two sons for the sake of clarity. The case of an arbitrary number of sons is a straightforward generalization. Furthermore, if W is the set of instantiated variables, E_W will be used to represent an expected value relative to the posterior distribution on the uncertainty variables, while E will continue to represent an expected value relative to the prior distribution.

3.1 THE CASE OF TREES

If W is a set of instantiated nodes, we are interested in the variance of the probability of an uninstantiated node, F, relative to the posterior distribution on the uncertainty variables. This variance is given by

$$V_W(p(f_i|W)) = E_W(p(f_i|W)^2) - (E_W(p(f_i|W))^2.$$

Thus our goal is to compute these latter two quantities. Since

$$E_W(p(f_i|W)) = \int_U P(f_i|W,U)dP(U|W) = P(f_i|W),$$

we could compute $E_W(p(f_i|W))$ using one of the standard methods for computing probabilities. However, the method described here is a generalization of Pearl's [1986] method for computing probabilities, and the determination of $P(f_i|W)$ is a by-product of the determination of $E(p(f_i|W)^2)$. The propagation scheme is based on the following theorem.

Theorem 1 *Let F be an uninstantiated variable, W be the set of instantiated variables, X_F be the set of instantiated variables in the tree rooted at F's left son, V_F be the set of instantiated variables in the tree rooted at F's right son, and let $Y_F = W - X_F - V_F$. Then, with the assumption that a posterior distribution on the uncertainty variables can be approximated by the prior distribution, it is the case that*

$$E_W(p(f_i|W)^2) = \frac{E(p(X_F|f_i)^2)E(p(V_F|f_i)^2)E(p(f_i|Y_F)^2)}{\left(\sum_j P(X_F|f_j)P(V_F|f_j)P(f_j|Y_F)\right)^2}$$

and

$$E_W(p(f_i|W)) = P(f_i|W) = \frac{P(X_F|f_i)P(V_F|f_i)P(f_i|Y_F)}{\sum_j P(X_F|f_j)P(V_F|f_j)P(f_j|Y_F)}.$$

Proof Let U be the set of uncertainty variables, U_X be the subset of those variables which are connected to F through F's left son, U_V be the subset which is connected to F through F's right son, and U_Y be the remainder of the uncertainty variables. Then

$$\begin{aligned} E_W(p(f_i|W)^2) &= \int_U P(f_i|W,U)^2 dP(U|W) \\ &= \int_U \frac{P(W|f_i,U)^2P(f_i|U)^2}{P(W|U)^2}dP(U|W) \\ &= \int_U \frac{P(W|f_i,U)^2P(f_i|U)^2dP(U)^2}{dP(U|W)^2P(W)^2}dP(U|W) \\ &= \int_U \frac{P(W|f_i,U)^2P(f_i|U)^2dP(U)}{dP(U|W)P(W)^2}dP(U) \\ &= \int_U \frac{P(W|f_i,U)^2P(f_i|U)^2dP(U)}{dP(U)P(W)^2}dP(U) \end{aligned}$$

The second to the last equality is due to the assumption that a posterior distribution on uncertainty variables can be approximated by the prior distribution. Thus we have that

$$E_W(p(f_i|W)^2 = \frac{P(Y_F)^2}{P(W)^2}E(p(X_F|f_i)^2E(p(V_F|f_i)^2)E(p(f_i|Y_F)^2).$$

Finally,

$$\frac{P(Y_F}{P(W)} = \frac{P(Y_F)}{P(X_F,V_F,Y_F)} = \frac{P(Y_F)}{P(X_F,V_F|Y_F)P(Y_F)}.$$

Again due to d-separation

$$\begin{aligned} P(X_F,V_F|Y_F) &= \sum_j P(X_F,V_F|Y_F,f_j)P(f_j|Y_F) \\ &= \sum_j P(X_F|f_j)P(V_F|f_j)P(f_j|Y_F), \end{aligned}$$

which proves the first part of the theorem. The second part is proved in the same fashion and does not require the assumption that a posterior distribution on the uncertainty variables can be approximated by the prior distribution. □

Due to Theorem 1, the information which F needs from its parent is

$$P(f_i|Y_F) \quad \text{and} \quad E(p(f_i|Y_F)^2),$$

while the information which F needs from its sons is

$$P(X_F|f_i), \quad E(p(X_F|f_i)^2),$$
$$P(V_F|f_i), \quad E(p(V_F|f_i)^2).$$

First we will show how to obtain the information which F needs from its sons. Suppose that the following information is available for each son, G, of F:

$$P(X_G|g_i), \qquad E(p(X_G|g_i)^2),$$
$$E(p(X_G|g_i)(p(X_G|g_j)),$$
$$P(V_G|g_i), \qquad E(p(V_G|g_i)^2),$$
$$E(p(V_G|g_i)p(V_G|g_j)) \tag{2}$$

Notice that $p(X_G|g_i)$ and $p(X_G|g_j)$ are not in general independent since they both depend on uncertainty variables in the tree rooted at G. Suppose that G is the left son of F. Then the tree rooted at G contains X_F. We shall first consider the case where G is not instantiated. In that case we have, due to d–separation, that

$$E(p(X_F|g_i)^2) = E(p(X_G, V_G|g_i)^2)$$
$$= E(p(X_G|g_i)^2)E(p(V_G|g_i)^2)$$

and similarly that

$$P(X_F|g_i) = P(X_G|g_i)P(V_G|g_i)$$
$$E(p(X_F|g_i)p(X_F|g_j)) =$$
$$E(p(X_G|g_i)p(X_G|g_j))E(p(V_G|g_i)p(V_G|g_j)).$$

Thus if the information listed in (2) is available for G we can compute $E(p(X_F|g_i)^2)$, $P(X_F|g_i)$, and $E(p(X_F|g_i)p(X_F|g_j))$. We will now show that the first half of the information listed in (2) for F can be computed from this latter information. First we have that

$$P(X_F|f_i) = \sum_j P(X_F|g_j)P(g_j|f_i).$$

Since $P(g_j|f_i) = E(p(g_j|f_i))$, and this value is part of the information listed in (1) for $p(g_j|f_i)$, we see that we can compute $P(X_F|f_i)$ from the information listed in (2) for G and the information listed in (1) for distributions which are specified in the network. Next we have that

$$E(p(X_F|f_i)p(X_F|f_j)) =$$
$$E\left(\left(\sum_k p(X_F|g_k)p(g_k|f_i)\right)\left(\sum_k p(X_F|g_k)p(g_k|f_j)\right)\right)$$

This latter expression is the sum of the following kind of terms:

$$E(p(X_F|g_k)^2)E(p(g_k|f_i))E(p(g_k|f_j))$$
and
$$E(p(X_F|g_k)p(X_F|g_r))E(p(g_k|f_i))E(p(g_r|f_j)).$$

The values in these terms are either part of the information listed in (1) for distributions which are specified in the network or, as previously shown, can be computed from the information listed in (2) for G. Finally

$$E\left(p(X_F|f_i)^2\right) =$$
$$E\left(\left(\sum_k p(X_F|g_k)p(g_k|f_i)\right)\left(\sum_k p(X_F|g_k)p(g_k|f_i)\right)\right)$$

This latter expression contains the following kinds of terms:

$$E\left(p(X_F|g_k)^2\right) E\left(p(g_k|f_i)^2\right)$$
$$E(p(X_F|g_k)p(X_F|g_j))E(p(g_k|f_i)p(g_j|f_i)).$$

Therefore $E(p(X_F|f_i)^2)$ can also be computed from the information listed in (2) for G and the information listed in (1) for distributions which are specified in the network.

Next suppose that G is instantiated for g_1. In this case, due to d–separation, we have that

$$\begin{aligned} P(X_F|f_i) &= P(X_G, V_G, g_1|f_i) \\ &= P(X_G|V_G, g_1, f_i)P(V_G|g_1, f_i)P(g_1, f_i) \\ &= P(X_G|g_1)P(V_G|g_1)P(g_1|f_i). \end{aligned}$$

Similarly

$$E\left(p(X_F|f_i)^2\right) =$$
$$E\left(p(X_G|g_1)^2\right) E\left(p(V_G|g_1)^2\right) E\left(p(g_1|f_i)^2\right)$$
$$E\left(p(X_F|f_i)p(X_F|f_j)\right) =$$
$$E\left(p(X_G|g_1)^2\right) E\left(p(V_G|g_1)^2\right)$$
$$E\left(p(g_1|f_i)\right) E\left(p(g_1|f_j)\right).$$

Thus again the information listed in (2) for F can be computed from the information listed in (2) for the sons of F along with the information listed in (1) for distributions which are specified in the network.

Since G d–separates F from the uncertainty variables connected to F through G, it does not seem correct, for example, that $E(p(f_i|W)^2)$ depends on $E(p(X_G|g_1)^2)$ and $E(p(V_G|g_1)^2)$ when G is instantiated for g_1. This apparent dependence was caused by the assumption that a posterior distribution on the uncertainty variables can be approximated by the prior distribution. As shown in Neapolitan [1991] this dependence does not really exist, and when F's son, G, is instantiated for g_1, X_F can be set equal to $\{g_1\}$ in Theorem 3.1 and

$$\begin{aligned} P(X_F|f_i) &= P(g_1|f_i) \\ E\left(p(X_F|f_i)^2\right) &= E\left(p(g_1|f_i)^2\right) \\ E(p(X_F|f_i)p(X_F|f_j)) &= E(p(g_1|f_i))E(p(g_1|f_j)). \end{aligned}$$

These latter values are simply the information listed in (1) for distributions which are specified in the network.

Next we show how to obtain the information which a node, F, needs from its parent, E. We will show that the following information can be obtained from information listed in (1) for distributions which are stored in the network if E is instantiated or, if E is not instantiated, from the corresponding information for E along with the information listed in (2) for E which comes from E's son (since we are assuming that a posterior distribution on the uncertainty variables can be approximated by the prior distribution, notice that this information is the information listed in (1) conditional on Y_F):

$$P(f_i|Y_F), \quad E\left(p(f_i|Y_F)^2\right), \quad E(p(f_i|Y_F)p(f_j|Y_F)). \qquad (3)$$

Since E d-separates F from all of F's ancestors and E's descendents through E's other children, if E is instantiated for e_1 this information is simply equal to

$$P(f_i|e_i) \qquad E\left(p(f_i|e_1)^2\right) \qquad E(p(f_i|e_1)p(f_j|e_1)),$$

which is the information listed in (1) for distributions which are specified in the network. Next assume that E is not instantiated and the information listed in (2) which comes from E's other son and the information listed in (3) is available for E. Due to d-separation

$$P(f_i|Y_F) = \sum_j P(f_i|e_j)P(e_j|Y_F).$$

Assuming that F is the right son of E and that therefore the tree rooted at F contains V_E, in the same way that Theorem 1 is proved it is possible to show that

$$P(e_j|Y_F) = \frac{P(X_E|e_j)P(e_j|Y_E)}{\sum_m P(X_E|e_m)P(e_m|Y_E)},$$

and therefore $P(f_i|Y_F)$ can be computed from the information listed in (2) which comes from E's other son and the information listed in (3) for E along with the information listed in (1) for distributions which are stored in the network. Next we have that

$$E\left(p(f_i|Y_F)^2\right) = E\left(\left(\sum_j p(f_i|e_j)p(e_j|Y_F)\right)^2\right).$$

This latter expression is the sum of the following kinds of terms:

$$E\left(p(f_i|e_j)^2\right) E\left(p(e_j|Y_F)^2\right)$$

and

$$E(p(f_i|e_j))E(p(f_i|e_k))E(p(e_j|Y_F)p(e_k|Y_F)).$$

In the same way that Theorem 1 is proved it is possible to show that

$$E\left(p(e_j|Y_F)^2\right) = \frac{E\left(p(X_E|e_j)^2\right) E\left(p(e_j|Y_E)^2\right)}{\left(\sum_m P(X_E|e_m)P(e_m|Y_E)\right)^2}$$

$$E(p(e_j|Y_F)p(e_k|Y_F)) = \frac{E(p(X_E|e_j)p(X_E|e_k))E(p(e_j|Y_E)p(e_k|Y_E))}{\left(\sum_m P(X_E|e_m)P(e_m|Y_E)\right)^2}.$$

Thus $E(p(f_i|Y_F)^2)$ can be computed from the information listed in (2) for E which comes from E's other son and the information list in (3) for E along with the information listed in (1) for distributions which are specified in the network. Finally

$$E(p(f_i|Y_F)(p(f_i|Y_F)) = E\left(\left(\sum_m p(f_i|e_m)p(e_m|Y_F)\right)\left(\sum_m p(f_j|e_m)p(e_m|Y_F)\right)\right).$$

This latter expression includes the following types of terms:

$$E(p(f_i|e_m)p(f_j|e_m))E(p(e_m|Y_F)^2)$$

and

$$E(p(f_i|e_m))E(p(f_j|e_r))E(p(e_m|Y_F)p(e_r|Y_F)).$$

We have just shown that the information in these terms can be computed from the information listed in (2) which comes from E's other son and the information listed in (3) for E along with the information listed in (1) for distributions which are specified in the network.

Using the theory developed above we can determine variances as follows. First initialize for every node, F, the values of

$$P(X_F|f_i), \quad E(p(X_F|f_i)^2), \quad E(p(X_F|f_i)p(X_F|f_j)),$$
$$P(V_F|f_i), \quad E(p(V_F|f_i)^2), \quad E(p(V_F|f_i)p(V_F|f_j))$$

all to 1. Then since for the root, A,

$$P(a_i|\Phi_A) = P(a_i),$$
$$E(p(a_i|\Phi_A)^2) = E(p(a_i)^2),$$
$$E(p(a_i|\Phi_A)p(a_j|\Phi_A)) = E(p(a_i)p(a_j)),$$

and these values are the information listed in (1) for distributions which are specified in the network, the prior variances can be computed by initiating a propagation flow from the root. At each node the variances are computed using the formulas in Theorem 1. This result agrees with the variances obtained using the exact method described in Neapolitan and Kenevan [1990]. When a node, G, is instantiated, it initiates new propagation down by using the method described above for obtaining the information listed in (3) for each son of G from the son's parent in the case were the parent is instantiated. G's uninstantiated children then continue the propagation flow using the method for the case where the parent is uninstantiated. (Note that instantiated nodes are dead ends for downward propagation.) G also initiates new propagation up by using the method described above to send its parent, F, the portion of the information listed in (2) for F which comes from G. As shown above, this information is stored in the network. If F is uninstantiated, the information listed in (2) for F's parent, which comes from F, is then computed using the method described above for uninstantiated nodes. Instantiated nodes are also dead ends for upward propagation. When an uninstantiated node receives new information from below it not only must send new information up but also must send new information down to each of its other sons using the method described above for obtaining the information in (3) in the case where the parent is not instantiated.

3.2 THE CASE OF SINGLY CONNECTED AND ARBITRARY BELIEF NETWORKS

The method described above can be extended to the case of singly connected networks. This extension appears in Neapolitan [1991]. The case of an arbitrary network can then be handled by using Pearl's [1988] method of clustering as discussed in Neapolitan and Kenevan [1990].

4 OBTAINING AN UPPER BOUND FOR THE PRIOR VARIANCES

As noted in the introduction, Zabell [1982] has shown that in many of the cases which are relevant to expert systems, the probability distribution of a probability must be Dirichlet. In this section it is assumed that there are two alternatives for each node and the distributions stored in the network are all Dirichlet. In the case of two alternatives, the Dirichlet distribution is called the beta distribution. It is given by

$$\mu(p) = \tfrac{(a+b+1)!}{a!b!}p^a(1-p)^b,$$

where a and b are nonnegative parameters.

It is straightforward to show that, in the case of the beta distribution,

$$\begin{aligned} E(p) &= \tfrac{a+1}{a+b+2} \\ E(p^2) &= \tfrac{a+2}{a+b+3}E(p) \\ E(p(1-p)) &= \tfrac{b+1}{a+b+3}E(p) \end{aligned} \qquad (4)$$

where E stands for expected value. Some of these results are needed to obtain the proofs in this section.

The main theorem at the end of this section obtains the upper bounds for the prior variances of the probabilities of all nodes in the network in the case where the network is a tree and the distributions stored in the network are beta. First we must obtain a number of preliminary results.

Lemma 1 *If there are exactly two alternatives, then $V(p_1) = V(p_2)$, however if there are three or more alternatives, the variances are not in general equal.*

Proof Since

$$V(p_1) = \int_U p_1^2 dP(U) - \left(\int_U p_1 dP(U)\right)^2$$

and

$$V(p_2) = \int_U (1-p_1)^2 dP(U) - \left(\int_U (1-p_1) dP(U)\right)^2,$$

the first part of the lemma is proved with simple algebraic manipulations. A counter example using a Dirichlet distribution proves the second part. □

Lemma 2 *Suppose there are exactly two alternatives. Let $E = E(p_1)$, $S = E(p_1^2)$, and $T = E(p_2^2)$. Then $T = 1 - 2E + S$.*

Proof Due to Lemma 1, $V(p_1) = V(P_2)$. Set V be that variance. Since $S = E^2 + V$ and $T = (1-E)^2 + V$, the lemma is proved with straightforward algebraic manipulations. *Box*

Lemma 3 *Suppose there are exactly two alternatives. Let $P = E(p_1 p_2)$, and E and S be as in Lemma 2. Then $P = E - S$.*

Proof

$$\begin{aligned} P &= \textstyle\int_U p_1(1-p_1)dP(U) \\ &= \textstyle\int_U p_1 dP(U) - \int_U p_1^2 dP(U) \\ &= E - S. \quad \square \end{aligned}$$

Lemma 4 *Suppose there are exactly two alternatives for both node A and node B and that A is the only parent of B. Let*

$$\begin{aligned} E &= E(a_1), & E_1 &= E(p(b_1|a_1)), \\ & & E_2 &= E(p(b_1|a_2)), \\ V &= V(a_1), & V_1 &= V(p(b_1|a_1)), \\ & & V_2 &= V(p(b_1|a_2)) \end{aligned}$$

Then

$$V(p(b_1)) = V\left(V_1 + V_2 + (E_1 - E_2)^2\right) + V_2(1-E)^2 + V_1 E^2.$$

Proof Let $S = E(p(a_1)^2)$, $T = E(p(a_2)^2)$, $P = E(p(a_1)p(a_2))$, $S_1 = E(p(b_1|a_1)^2)$, and $S_2 = E(p(b_1|a_2)^2)$. We then have

$$E\left(p(b_1)^2\right) = E\left([p(b_1|a_1)p(a_1) + p(b_1|a_2)p(a_2)]^2\right)$$

which is easily seen to equal

$$\begin{aligned} &E\left(p(b_1|a_1)^2\right) E\left(p(a_1)^2\right) \\ &\quad + 2E(p(b_1|a_1))E(p(b_1|a_2))E(p(a_1)p(a_2)) \\ &\quad + E\left(p(b_1|a_2)^2\right) E\left(p(a_2)^2\right), \end{aligned}$$

and thus

$$E\left(p(b_1)^2\right) = S_1S + 2E_1E_2P + S_2T. \tag{5}$$

Similarly it can be shown that

$$\begin{aligned} (E(p(b_1))^2 = E_1^2E^2 + 2E_1EE_2 - 2E_1E_2E^2 \\ + E_2^2 - 2E_2^2E + E_2^2E^2. \end{aligned} \tag{6}$$

Since

$$V(p(b_1)) = E\left(p(b_1)^2\right) - \left(E(p(b_1))\right)^2,$$

equations (5) and (6), applications of Lemmas 2 and 3, and some algebraic manipulations yield

$$\begin{aligned} V(p(b_1)) = V_2 - 2E_1E_2V - 2EV_2 + S_1S \\ - E_1^2E^2 + S_2S - E_2^2E^2. \end{aligned} \tag{7}$$

Now

$$\begin{aligned} S_1S - E_1^2E^2 &= S_1S - S_1E^2 + S_1E^2 - E_1^2E^2 \\ &= S_1V + E^2V_1, \end{aligned}$$

and an identical result holds for $S_2S - E_2^2E^2$. After inserting these results in equation (7) and performing some more algebraic manipulations we have that

$$\begin{aligned} V(p(b_1)) = V(S_1 + S_2 - 2E_1E_2) \\ + V_2(1-E)^2 + V_1E^2. \end{aligned} \tag{8}$$

Replacing S_1 and S_2 in (8) by $V_1 + E_1^2$ and $V_2 + E_2^2$ respectively proves the lemma. □

Lemma 5 *Let E, S, and V be as in Lemma 2. Then $S \leq (E + E^2)/2$ implies that $V \leq E - S$.*

Proof $V \leq E - S$ means $S - E^2 \leq E - S$, which is true if $2S \leq E + E^2$, which is the condition in the statement of the lemma. □

Lemma 6 *Let E and S be as in Lemma 2. If the distribution is beta, then*

$$S \leq \left(E + 2E^2\right)/3.$$

Proof Let P be as in Lemma 3, and a and b be the parameters for the beta distribution. Then, due to equalities (4),

$$\begin{aligned} P &= \left(\tfrac{b+1}{a+b+3}\right) E \\ &= \left(\tfrac{a+b+2}{a+b+3}\right)\left(\tfrac{b+1}{a+b+2}\right) E \\ &= \left(\tfrac{a+b+2}{a+b+3}\right)(1-E)E \\ &\geq 2\left(E - E^2\right)/3. \end{aligned}$$

Thus due to Lemma 3 we have that $E - S \geq 2(E - E^2)/3$, and the lemma follows from some algebraic manipulations. □

Lemma 7 *If the distribution is beta, then $E \leq (1 + \sqrt{1-12V})/2$.*

Proof In the same way that Lemma 5 was proved, Lemma 6 implies that

$$V \leq \left(E - E^2\right)/3,$$

which implies

$$E^2 - E + 3V \leq 0.$$

The expression $E^2 - E + 3V$ equals 0 at the point $E = (1+\sqrt{1-12V})/2$ and has positive derivative with respect to E at his point and to the right of it. Therefore if $E^2-E+3V \leq 0$, E must be $\leq (1+\sqrt{1-12V})/2$. □

Theorem 2 *Assume the conditions and notations in Lemma 4. Further assume that $S \leq (E+E^2)/2$. Then*

$$V(p(b_1)) \leq Maximum(V_1, V_2).$$

Proof Suppose $V_1 \leq V_2$. Without loss of generality we can assume $E_1 \leq E_2$. For, if this were not the case, we would have

$$E(p(b_2|a_1)) = 1 - E_1 < 1 - E_2 = E(p(b_2|a_2)).$$

However, due to Lemma 1 and the assumption that $V_1 \leq V_2$,

$$\begin{aligned} V(p(b_2|a_1)) &= V(p(b_1|a_1)) = V_1 \\ &\leq V_2 = V(p(b_1|a_2)) = V(p(b_2|a_2)), \end{aligned}$$

and we could proceed in the proof using b_2 instead of b_1. Assuming now that $E_1 \leq E_2$, due to Lemma 4 we have that

$$\begin{aligned} &V(p(b_1)) = \\ &\quad V\left(V_1 + V_2 + (E_2 - E_1)^2\right) + V_2(1-E)^2 + V_1E^2 \\ &\quad \leq V\left(2V_2 + E_2^2\right) + V_2(1-E)^2 + V_2E^2 \\ &\quad \leq V\left(2V_2 + \left(1 + \sqrt{1-12V_2}\right)/2\right) \\ &\qquad + V_2(1-E)^2 + V_2E^2. \end{aligned}$$

The last inequality is due to Lemma 7 and the fact that $E_2^2 \leq E_2$. After some algebraic manipulations we have

$$\begin{aligned} &V(p(b_1)) \\ &\quad \leq V(1 + \sqrt{1-12V_2})/2 \\ &\qquad + V_2(1 + 2V - 2E + 2E^2) \\ &\quad \leq V(1 + \sqrt{1-12V_2})/2 \\ &\qquad + V(1 + 2S - 2E^2 - 2E + 2E^2) \\ &\quad \leq V(1 + \sqrt{1-12V_2})/2 + V_2(1 - 2(E - S)). \end{aligned}$$

Due to Lemma 5 and the assumptions of this theorem we then have

$$V(p(b_1)) \leq V(1+\sqrt{1-12V_2})/2 + V_2(1-2V).$$

Thus $V(p(b_1)) \leq V_2$ if

$$V(1+\sqrt{1-12V_2})/2 + V_2(1-2V) \leq V_2.$$

If $V = 0$, the proof is trivial. Thus this latter inequality is true if $1 + \sqrt{1-12V_2} \leq 4V_2$, which is true if $1-12V_2 \leq 16V_2^2 - 8V_2 + 1$. Since $16V_2^2 + 4V_2 \geq 0$ the theorem is proved. □

Theorem 3 *Assume the conditions and notation in Lemma 4. Furthermore let $S' = E(p(b_1)^2)$ and $E' = E(p(b_1))$. Then $S \leq (E+E^2)/2$ implies that $S' \leq (E'+E'^2)/2$.*

Proof Equation (5) from the proof of Lemma 4 states that

$$S' = S_1 S + 2E_1E_2P + S_2T.$$

It is straightforward that

$$(E' + E'^2) = [E_1E + E_2(1-E) + (E_1E + E_2(1-E))^2]/2.$$

Thus we need show that

$$S_1S + 2E_1E_2P + S_2T \leq [E_1E + E_2(1-E) + (E_1E + E_2(1-E))^2]/2.$$

Algebraic manipulations yield that this is equivalent to showing that

$$(S_1S + E_1E_2P) + (S_2T + E_1E_2P) \leq [E_1E + E_1^2E^2 + E_1EE_2(1-E)]/2 + [E_2(1-E) + E_2^2(1-E)^2 + E_1EE_2(1-E)]/2.$$

We will accomplish this by showing that

$$S_1S + E_1E_2P \leq [E_1E + E_1^2E^2 + E_1EE_2(1-E)]/2. \quad (9)$$

By symmetry we will then also have shown that

$$S_2T + E_1E_2P \leq [E_2(1-E) + E_2^2(1-E)^2 + E_1EE_2(1-E)]/2,$$

and the theorem will be proved. To that end, due to Lemmas 3 and 6,

$$S_1S + E_1E_2P = S_1S + E_1E_2(E-S) \leq (E_1 + 2E_1^2)S/3 + E_1E_2E - E_1E_2S.$$

Thus inequality (9) will hold if

$$S(E_1 + 2E_1^2 - 3E_1E_2)/3 + E_1E_2E \leq [E_1E + E_1^2E^2 + E_1EE_2(1-E)]/2.$$

Eliminating the trivial case when $E_1 = 0$, algebraic manipulations yield that this last inequality is equivalent to

$$2S(1+2E_1-3E_2) \leq 3E(1+E_1E-EE_2-E_2). \quad (10)$$

There are two cases:

Case 1: $1+2E_1-3E_2 \geq 0$. In this casse due to the assumption that $S \leq (E+E^2)/2$, inequality (10) is true if

$$(E+E^2)(1+2E_1-3E_2) \leq 3E(1+E_1E-EE_2-E_2),$$

which, after performing algebraic manipulations and eliminating the trivial case when $E = 0$, is equivalent to $E(1-E_1) \leq 2(1-E_1)$ which proves Case 1.

Case 2: $1+2E_1-3E_2 < 0$. Inequality (10) is equivalent to

$$3E(EE_2 + E_2 - 1 - E_1E) \leq 2S(3E_2 - 2E_1 - 1),$$

where the right side of this inequality is now positive due to the assumption in this case. Since $V \geq 0$, we have $S \geq E^2$ and therefore the last inequality is true if

$$3E(EE_2 + E_2 - 1 - E_1E) \leq 2E^2(3E_2 - 2E_1 - 1).$$

After the trivial case when $E = 0$ is eliminated, algebraic manipulations yield that this inequality is equivalent to

$$2E(1-E_2) + E(E_1 - E_2) \leq 3(1-E_2).$$

Clearly $2E(1-E_2) \leq 2(1-E_2)$. Therefore we need only show that $E(E_1 - E_2) \leq 1 - E_2$. Due to the assumption in this case, $E_1 < (3E_2-1)/2$. Thus we need only show that

$$E((3E_2-1)/2 - E_2) \leq 1 - E_2.$$

Algebraic manipulations yields that this is equivalent to $0 \leq (1-E_2)(2+E)$, which proves this case. □

Theorem 4 (Main Theorem) *If the belief network is a tree, and all distributions stored in the network are beta, then for any node, B,*

$$V(p(b_1)) \leq Maximum(V_1, V_2), \quad (11)$$

where $V_1 = V(p(b_1|a_1))$, $V_2 = V(p(b_1|a_2))$, and A is B's parent.

Proof Due to Lemma 6 and the fact that the distribution for the probability of the root is assumed to be beta, it is easy to show that for the root

$$S \leq (E+E^2)/2. \quad (12)$$

where S and E stand again for the expected value of a probability and the expected value of a probability squared respectively. Thus, due to Theorem 3 and an inductive argument, inequality (12) holds for all nodes in the network. Therefore, due to Theorem 2, inequality (11) holds for all nodes in the network. □

5 FUTURE RESEARCH

There exists a need for a great deal of additional research in this area. First, it should be determined if the results in Section 4 hold when there are more than two alternatives and when the network is not tree. Second, of greater interest than the variance in prior probabilities are the variances in inferred probabilities. If a node is instantiated in a tree, it is easy to see that the results above hold for the descendents of that node. However, in many cases we are more interested in the ancestors of the node. In medicine, for example, instantiated nodes, which represent findings, are often near leaves while the nodes of interest, which represent diseases, are often near roots. It remains to be determined whether the variances become large as we propagate up the network from an instantiated node.

References

R. M. Chavez and G. F. Cooper [1990], "A Randomized Approximation Algorithm for Probabilistic Inference on Bayesian Belief Networks," to appear in *Journal of Networks.*

G. F. Cooper [1984], "'NESTOR': A Computer-Based Medical Diagnostic that Integrates Causal and Probabilistic Knowledge," Technical Report HPP-84-48, Stanford University, Stanford, CA.

G. F. Cooper [1988], "Probabilistic Inference Using Belief Networks is NP-Hard," Technical Report KSL-87-27, Stanford University, Stanford, CA.

D. Heckerman and E. J. Horvitz [1987], "On the Expressiveness of Rule-Based Systems for Reasoning with Uncertainty," *Proceedings of AAAI,* Seattle, Washington.

R. A. Howard [1970], "Decision Analysis: Perspectives on Inference, Decision, and Experimentation," *Proceedings of IEEE,* Vol. 58, No. 5.

S. L. Lauritzen and D. J. Spiegelhalter [1988], "Local Computation with Probabilities on Graphical Structures and Their Applications to Expert Systems," *Journal of the Royal Statistical Society B.,* Vol. 50, No. 2.

R. E. Neapolitan [1990], *Probabilistic Reasoning in Expert Systems: Theory and Algorithms,* Wiley, New York.

R. E. Neapolitan [1991], "Using the Variance as a Measure of the Uncertainty in Inferred Probabilities in Belief Networks," paper in progress.

R. E. Neapolitan and J. R. Kenevan [1990], "Computation of Variances in Causal Networks," Proceedings of 6th International Workshop on Uncertainty in Artificial Intelligence, MIT, Cambridge, MA.

J. Pearl [1986], "Fusion, Propagation, and Structuring in Belief Networks," *Artificial Intelligence,* Vol. 29.

J. Pearl [1987], "Distributed Revision of Composite Beliefs," *Artificial Intelligence,* Vol. 33.

J. Pearl [1988], *Probabilistic Reasoning in Intelligent Systems,* Morgan Kaufmann, San Mateo, California.

Y. Peng and J. A. Reggia [1987], "A Probabilistic Causal Model for Diagnostic Problem Solving — Parts I and II," *IEEE Transactions on Systems, Man, and Cybernetics,* Vol. SMC-17.

R. D. Shachter [1988], "Probabilistic Inference and Influence Diagrams," *Operations Research,* Vol. 36, No. 4.

D. J. Spiegelhalter [1988], "Analysis of Softness," in L. N. Kanal and T. S. Levitt, Eds., *Uncertainty in Artificial Intelligence III,* North-Holland, Amsterdam.

S. L. Zabell [1982], " W. E. Johnson's 'Sufficientness' Postulate," *The Annals of Statistics,* Vol. 10, No. 4.

A Sensitivity Analysis of Pathfinder: A Follow-up Study

Keung-Chi Ng
Department of Pathology
University of Southern California
HMR 204, 2025 Zonal Ave
Los Angeles, CA 90033

Bruce Abramson
Department of Computer Science
University of Southern California
Los Angeles, CA 90089-0782

Abstract

At last year's Uncertainty in AI Conference, we reported the results of a sensitivity analysis study of Pathfinder. Our findings were quite unexpected—slight variations to Pathfinder's parameters appeared to lead to substantial degradations in system performance. A careful look at our first analysis, together with the valuable feedback provided by the participants of last year's conference, led us to conduct a follow-up study. Our follow-up differs from our initial study in two ways: (i) the probabilities 0.0 and 1.0 remained unchanged, and (ii) the variations to the probabilities that are close to both ends (0.0 or 1.0) were less than the ones close to the middle (0.5). The results of the follow-up study look more reasonable—slight variations to Pathfinder's parameters now have little effect on its performance. Taken together, these two sets of results suggest a viable extension of a common decision analytic sensitivity analysis to the larger, more complex settings generally encountered in artificial intelligence.

1 INTRODUCTION

A great deal of recent attention has been focused on the relationship of artificial intelligence (AI) to decision analysis (DA). Most of the work on probability theory as a mechanism for uncertainty management (Cheeseman 1988; Ng and Abramson 1990b), belief networks as representations of uncertainty (Abramson 1990; Howard and Matheson 1984), the propagation of information through a belief network (Pearl 1988; Shachter 1986; Shachter 1987), and the design of systems based on belief networks (Abramson and Finizza 1991; Andereassen, Woldbye, Falck, and Anderson 1987; Heckerman, Horvitz, and Nathwani 1990), falls into this category. These topics are all familiar to decision analysts; they deal with the representation of uncertainty and the derivation of inference. There is, however, a third concern frequently studied in DA: analysis.

In order to be useful, a model and/or system must pass through several stages of development: it must capture the information that it claims to be modeling, it must allow questions to be answered, and it must be (in some sense) validated. Sensitivity analyses fall into this last area of concern. In a classic DA sense, a sensitivity analysis measures the degree to which a decision is sensitive to changes in its inputs. These analyses are generally done one variable at a time. Most well-designed models exhibit a phenomenon known as a *flat maximum;* small (and even medium-sized) changes in input variables rarely lead to changed decisions (von Winterfeldt and Edwards 1986).

Sensitivity analyses are as important to AI systems as they are to DA models. Two characteristics of AI systems, however, force the standard techniques of sensitivity analyses to be rethought: they generate outputs other than decisions, and they include huge numbers of variables. Pathfinder, for example, is an AI system that diagnoses the 63 diseases of the human lymph system; its underlying belief network also contains over 100 distinct symptoms (Heckerman, Horvitz, and Nathwani 1990). In 1990, at the *Sixth Conference on Uncertainty in Artificial Intelligence,* we presented a sensitivity analysis of Pathfinder that led to a surprising conclusion: the system did not exhibit a flat maximum. Instead, it seemed to be highly sensitive to the parameters specified by its contributing expert; even minor changes to these parameters led to drastic declines in the system's performance (Ng and Abramson 1990a). These results were presented with a fairly detailed description of the modified sensitivity analysis techniques upon which our studies were based, and a challenge to the conference participants to suggest possible causes underlying our results. Several useful suggestions were made. This paper revises our modifications to the analysis and provides results that are more in line with previous (empirical) experience.

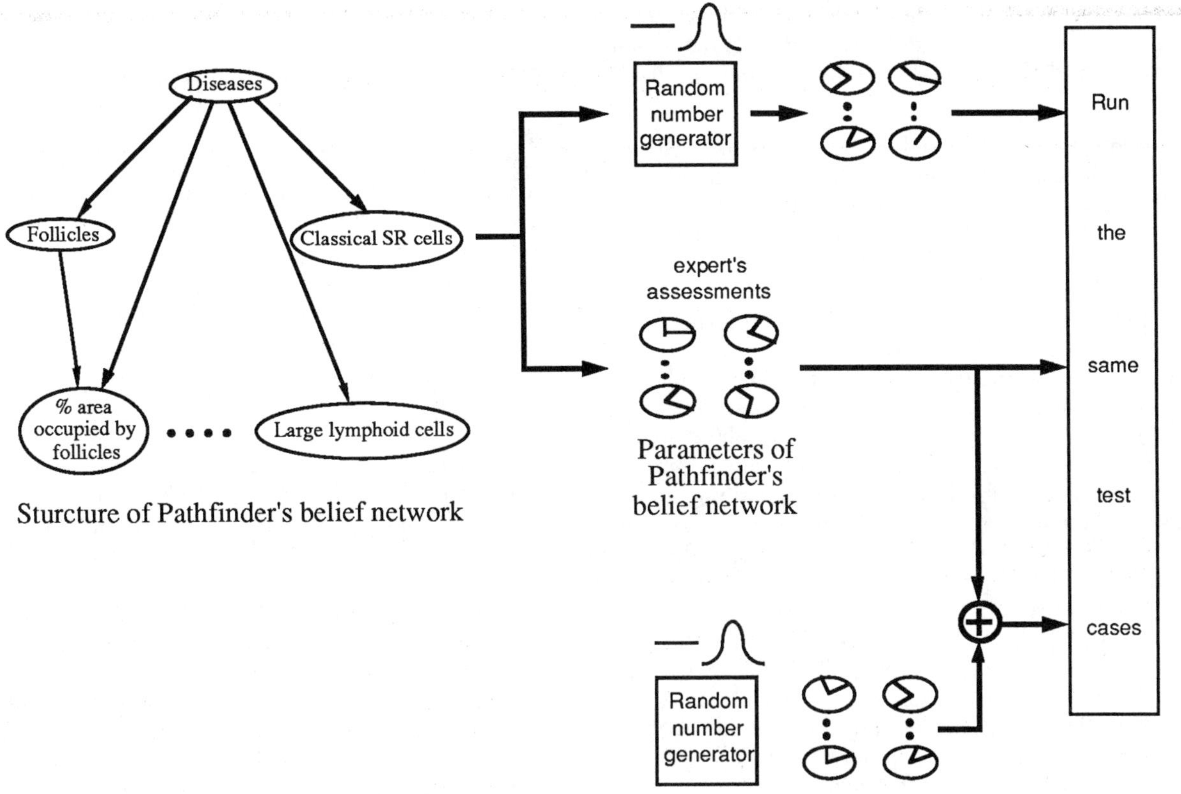

Figure 1: Block diagram of the sensitivity analysis of Pathfinder.

2 DETAILS OF THE ANALYSIS

The goals of a sensitivity analysis are (i) to gain insight into the nature of a problem, (ii) to find a simple and elegant structure that does justice to the problem, and (iii) to check the correctness of the numbers and the need for precision in refining them (von Winterfeldt and Edwards 1986). In most decision problems, once the numbers have reached a certain degree of precision, further refinement of these numbers has little effect on the decisions. Our studies are directed towards determining whether or not similar observations are true for diagnostic systems, (i.e., once the prior and conditional probabilities have reached certain quality, further improvement on these probabilities has little effect on its diagnoses).

A block diagram of the study is shown in Figure 1. In our study, experiments were run on a body of 60 "classic" cases in which the diagnosis was known. Since a network's parameters include prior and conditional probabilities, both sets of probabilities had to be varied. The experiments used two sets of prior probabilities (those specified by the experts and a uniform distribution across all the diseases) and three types of conditionals:

1. The original values, exactly as assessed by experts.
2. Randomly generated probabilities. This class of parameters includes probabilities distributed both uniformly and normally.
3. The values assessed by experts plus randomly generated noise, using both uniformly and normally distributed noise functions.

All the conditional probabilities, either generated or augmented with noise, were renormalized.

Each body of tests served a different purpose; the original knowledge base defined a standard against which others would be judged, the random parameters addressed the relative importance of parameters, and the random noise addressed the issue of sensitivity. The use of two different sets of priors addressed the effect of priors on system performance.

3 THE INITIAL STUDY

The results discussed in this section were first reported at the 1990 Uncertainty in AI Conference (Ng and Abramson 1990a). This study implied that Pathfinder's performance degraded so significantly with randomly generated probabilities that the resultant system had negligible discriminating power. The same results were observed regardless of the choice of distribution function or the selection of priors. These findings led us to conclude that parameters are crucial to a belief network (or at least to Pathfinder's belief network) and that experts are needed to provide the parameters.

Our experiments also studied variations in both prior and conditional probabilities. Priors were fixed either at the expert-assessed set or at a uniform set. Conditionals were varied by augmenting the expert's assessment with randomly generated noise. The resultant conditional probabilities were then renormalized. The random noise functions followed uniform or normal distributions with mean of 0 ($\mu = 0$) and several values of standard deviation (σ). For each noise function, five parameter sets were created. Sixty cases were run on each network, for a total of 300 test cases per noise function. A total of seven noise generating schemes were used, including uniformly generated noise (uniform noise), normally generated noise (normal noise) with σ of 0.005, 0.01, 0.025, 0.05, 0.1, 0.25, all with $\mu = 0$ (to ensure that any probability has equal chance of being increased or decreased). A summary of the test results with expert priors is shown in Table 1. In the table, the percentage of correct diagnoses, (i.e., the number of cases in which the known diagnosis was assigned the highest posterior probability divided by the total number of cases), is intended to provide a measure of the diagnostic power. The average confidence, (average difference in posterior probabilities between the two diseases with the highest posterior probabilities on the differential diagnosis for all the cases run), with respect to the correct diagnosis and incorrect diagnosis,[1] provides a measure of the discriminating power of the leading disease (disease with the highest posterior probability on the differential diagnosis) from the other diseases on the differential diagnosis. It should be pointed out that although the percentage of correct diagnoses is more important than average confidence in system performance, average confidence is also useful in gaging system performance. Systems scoring perfectly (100%) in the correct diagnosis column with 0 average confidence (e.g., all diseases have the same posterior probability with respect to all the test cases) could be as useless a system as one with no correct diagnoses and absolute average confidence (1.0). Also shown in Table 1, in the column headed "Percentage Better," is the percentage of cases in which the noisy network assigned the correct diagnosis with posterior probability that is notably higher than did the original network.

Table 1 indicates that the original knowledge base had the highest score in both percentage of correct diagnoses and average confidence; augmentation with uniform noise produced the lowest scores on both items. Adding normal noise to the original knowledge base produced a system with scores that lie between these extremes, with better results for systems with smaller standard deviations (or less noise). Furthermore, the chance of producing a better diagnosis than the original knowledge base is higher for knowledge bases with less noise than those with more noise. Table 2 summarizes the results of networks with equal priors. The results are similar to those of Table 1.

[1] Correct diagnosis is defined as the situation in which the disease with the highest posterior probability on the differential diagnosis provided by the system is the same as the known diagnosis for a test case; incorrect diagnosis is the situation in which the disease with the highest posterior probability on the differential diagnosis is different from the known diagnosis.

4 THE FOLLOW-UP STUDY

The results summarized in Tables 1 and 2 implied that Pathfinder's belief network did not exhibit a flat maximum. This observation was quite unexpected; flat maxima have been observed in almost all tested models (von Winterfeldt and Edwards 1986). A closer look at our study revealed that one possible reason for this surprise: all probabilities were varied, including those that were equal to 0.0 and 1.0. The variation of these probabilities was undoubtedly a mistake; whereas probabilities in $(0, 1)$ represent degrees of belief that may be varied and refined, probabilities at the endpoints represent ***absolute certainty.*** Although studying perturbations of beliefs is reasonable, studying perturbations of certainty is not. Furthermore, beliefs close to 0.0 and 1.0 are less prone to adjustment than those located elsewhere.

In an attempt to account for this observation, we reran our study using a scheme that generated noise in a slightly different way; the augmented noise function depended on both the random noise function and the actual value of the conditional probability. If the original conditional probability was 0.0 or 1.0 (i.e., the relationship is crisp or definitional), the conditional probability remained unchanged. For other values of conditional probability with normally distributed noise functions, the noise would be more for probabilities close to 0.5 than for those close to either 0.0 or 1.0. The approach that we used is (i) convert the original probability p, with range (0.0, 1.0), to a value v of range $(-\infty, \infty)$, by a function $f(p) = \ln(\frac{p}{1-p})$, (ii) add the generated noise to v to obtain v', and then (iii) convert v' back to a probability by using f^{-1} (the inverse of the function f). With this scheme, the changes in likelihood ratios due to the added noise are comparable for the probabilities that are close to the endpoints (0.0 and 1.0) and those that are close to 0.5, while the actual variations in probabilities are smaller for probabilities that are close to either ends than those near 0.5. The new results are shown in Tables 3 and 4. In these tables, the average improvement in posterior probability for the cases in which the noisy network outperforms the original network is also shown (under the column labelled "average amount better").

	Percentage Correct	Average Confidence Correct (# cases)	Average Confidence Incorrect (# cases)	Percentage Better
Original knowledge base	98.3%	0.7910 (59)	0.8247 (1)	—
Normal noise, SD=0.005	90.0%	0.7329 (270)	0.2511 (30)	22.0%
Normal noise, SD=0.01	87.6%	0.6963 (263)	0.3685 (37)	21.6%
Normal noise, SD=0.025	78.0%	0.6803 (234)	0.2692 (66)	16.3%
Normal noise, SD=0.05	70.7%	0.6997 (212)	0.2541 (88)	15.7%
Normal noise, SD=0.1	61.0%	0.6212 (183)	0.3262 (117)	9.3%
Normal noise, SD=0.25	36.7%	0.5614 (110)	0.2988 (190)	6.0%
Uniform noise	32.7%	0.5417 (98)	0.3142 (202)	5.0%

Table 1: Summary of results of the initial (1990) sensitivity analysis of Pathfinder. In this set, expert-assessed priors were used for all networks. A variety of noise functions were added to the expert's conditional probabilities.

	Percentage Correct	Average Confidence Correct (# cases)	Average Confidence Incorrect (# cases)	Percentage Better
Original knowledge base	88.3%	0.8262 (53)	0.1569 (7)	—
Normal noise, SD=0.005	84.7%	0.7900 (254)	0.1279 (46)	24.3%
Normal noise, SD=0.01	83.0%	0.7688 (249)	0.1444 (51)	17.7%
Normal noise, SD=0.025	80.0%	0.7019 (240)	0.2052 (60)	18.3%
Normal noise, SD=0.05	73.7%	0.6784 (221)	0.1831 (79)	13.7%
Normal noise, SD=0.1	62.3%	0.6458 (187)	0.3019 (113)	10.0%
Normal noise, SD=0.25	42.3%	0.4914 (127)	0.2516 (173)	7.3%
Uniform noise	36.7%	0.4347 (110)	0.2927 (190)	6.0%

Table 2: Summary of results of the initial (1990) sensitivity analysis of Pathfinder. In this set, uniform priors were used for all networks. A variety of noise functions were added to the expert's conditional probabilities.

	Percentage Correct	Average Confidence		Percentage Better (average amount better)
		Correct (# cases)	Incorrect (# cases)	
Original knowledge base	98.3%	0.7910 (59)	0.8247 (1)	—
Normal noise, σ=0.005	96.6%	0.8060 (290)	0.4161 (10)	1.7% (0.0678)
Normal noise, σ=0.01	96.0%	0.8119 (288)	0.3615 (12)	6.3% (0.0293)
Normal noise, σ=0.025	96.0%	0.8101 (288)	0.3624 (12)	10.3% (0.0306)
Normal noise, σ=0.05	95.3%	0.8130 (286)	0.3931 (14)	13.3% (0.0485)
Normal noise, σ=0.1	96.3%	0.8090 (289)	0.4573 (11)	17.0% (0.0680)
Normal noise, σ=0.25	90.3%	0.8270 (271)	0.4204 (29)	18.3% (0.1237)
Uniform noise	65.3%	0.8495 (196)	0.4798 (104)	11.0% (0.1989)

Table 3: Summary of results of the sensitivity analysis of Pathfinder. In this set, expert-assessed priors were used for all networks. A variety of noise functions were added to the expert's conditional probabilities. In this study, more noise was added to probabilities that were close to 0.5 than those that were close to either 0.0 or 1.0, and no change would be made to probabilities that were 0.0 or 1.0.

Table 3 indicates that the percentage of correct diagnoses and average confidence for the original knowledge base and knowledge bases with small noise are comparable. With more noise added to the original knowledge base, the percentage of correct diagnoses drops, but the average confidence remains comparable to that of the original knowledge base. Knowledge bases with more noise, however, have a higher chance of providing better diagnoses and the improvements are more significant (see the column under percentage better)—an average improvement of more than 0.1 in posterior probability for the correct diagnosis over that of the original knowledge base, both for normal noise with $\sigma = 0.25$ and uniform noise. All these observations suggest that although small refinements to the probabilities will not produce significant differences in performance, larger proper refinements may produce stronger results (at least with respect to the test cases). Table 4 summarizes the results of networks with equal priors. The results are similar to those of Table 3.

The results in Table 1 to 4 contain a lot of fine details on our study, which can be nicely summarized through the use of a scoring rule. Table 5 shows the results of our earlier study and this follow-up study evaluated by a quadratic scoring rule (see von Winterfeldt and Edwards 1986 for examples of popular scoring schemes). The scoring rule that we used is

$$score = 2 * p_k - \sum_i (p_i)^2,$$

where p_i denotes the probability assigned to hypothesis i, and p_k is the probability assigned to the correct hypothesis k, which is the correct disease in a test case in our study. It can be observed that *score* can take on values between 1.0 and -1.0, with 1.0 denoting a perfect score—in Pathfinder, this denotes that the system's diagnosis is the same as the diagnosis in the test cases. The values shown in the table are the average scores of each study for the 300 test cases. The results shown in Table 5 revealed the same key message as in Tables 1 to 4, however, the fine details of our results can only be found in Tables 1 to 4.

5 CONCLUSIONS

The results presented in this paper are hardly revolutionary; they indicate that Pathfinder exhibits a flat maximum. They are, however, interesting in several respects. First, they help extend the flat maximum phenomenon beyond decision settings to diagnostic settings. Second, they show how to extend an analysis that is usually conducted one variable at a time to one that can be conducted on all of a domain's variables simultaneously. Third, they reveal the importance of parameters to a belief network, especially those that are close to (or at) 0.0 and 1.0. Fourth, (and of perhaps greatest significance to the authors), they correct results that we have already published. This paper, combined with our earlier one (Ng and Abramson 1990a), then, suggest a viable extension of a common DA analysis to the larger, more complex settings generally encountered in AI.

	Percentage Correct	Average Confidence		Percentage Better (average amount better)
		Correct (# cases)	Incorrect (# cases)	
Original knowledge base	88.3%	0.8262 (53)	0.1569 (7)	—
Normal noise, σ=0.005	86.0%	0.8499 (258)	0.1335 (42)	3.3% (0.0280)
Normal noise, σ=0.01	86.3%	0.8464 (259)	0.1304 (41)	6.3% (0.0238)
Normal noise, σ=0.025	85.7%	0.8562 (257)	0.1388 (43)	12.0% (0.0312)
Normal noise, σ=0.05	86.7%	0.8444 (260)	0.1933 (40)	14.7% (0.0398)
Normal noise, σ=0.1	85.7%	0.8583 (257)	0.2187 (43)	19.7% (0.0616)
Normal noise, σ=0.25	84.0%	0.8331 (252)	0.3793 (48)	16.7% (0.1274)
Uniform noise	66.7%	0.8707 (200)	0.4628 (100)	12.0% (0.2145)

Table 4: Summary of results of the sensitivity analysis of Pathfinder. In this set, uniform priors were used for all networks. A variety of noise functions were added to the expert's conditional probabilities. In this study, more noise was added to probabilities that were close to 0.5 than those that were close to either 0.0 or 1.0, and no change would be made to probabilities that were 0.0 or 1.0.

	First Study		Follow-up Study	
	Expert Priors	Equal Priors	Expert Priors	Equal Priors
Original knowledge base	0.8829	0.8393	0.8829	0.8393
Normal noise, σ=0.005	0.8151	0.8114	0.8837	0.8392
Normal noise, σ=0.01	0.7542	0.7891	0.8835	0.8399
Normal noise, σ=0.025	0.6695	0.7052	0.8824	0.8390
Normal noise, σ=0.05	0.6045	0.6619	0.8774	0.8333
Normal noise, σ=0.1	0.4408	0.4727	0.8809	0.8276
Normal noise, σ=0.25	0.1480	0.2226	0.8255	0.7660
Uniform noise	0.0748	0.1055	0.4923	0.5186

Table 5: A table summarizing our first study and this follow-up study of the sensitivity analysis of Pathfinder. The number in each entry denotes the average score computed by a quadratic scoring rule.

Acknowledgments

This work was supported in part by the National Library of Medicine under grant R01LM04529 and by the NSF under grant IRI-8910173.

References

Bruce Abramson. On Knowledge Representation in Belief Networks. In *Proceedings of the 3rd International Conference on Information Processing and Management of Uncertainty in Knowledge-Based Systems*, July 2-6, 1990.

Bruce Abramson and Anthony J. Finizza. Using Belief Networks to Forecast Oil Prices. *International Journal of Forecasting*, 1991. In press.

S. Andreassen, M. Woldbye, B. Falck, and S. K. Anderson. MUNIN – A Causal Probabilistic Network for the Interpretation of Electromyographic Findings. In *Proceedings of the 10th International Joint Conference on Artificial Intelligence*, pages 366–372, 1987.

Peter Cheeseman. An Inquiry into Computer Understanding. *Computational Intelligence*, 4(1):58–66, 129–142, 1988.

D. E. Heckerman, E. J. Horvitz, and B. N. Nathwani. Toward Normative Expert Systems: The Pathfinder Project. Technical Report KSL-90-08, Stanford University, 1990.

Ronald A. Howard and James E. Matheson. Influence Diagrams. In Ronald A. Howard and James E. Matheson, editors, *Readings on the Principles and Applications of Decision Analysis, vol. II*, pages 721–762. Strategic Decisions Group, 1984.

Keung-Chi Ng and Bruce Abramson. A Sensitivity Analysis of Pathfinder. In *Proceedings of the Sixth Conference on Uncertainty in Artificial Intelligence*, 1990a.

Keung-Chi Ng and Bruce Abramson. Uncertainty Management in Expert Systems. *IEEE Expert*, 5(2):29–48, 1990b.

Judea Pearl. *Probabilistic Reasoning in Intelligent Systems.* Morgan Kaufmann, 1988.

Ross D. Shachter. Probabilistic Inference and Influence Diagram. *Operation Research*, 36:589–604, 1988.

Ross D. Shachter. Evaluating Influence Diagrams. *Operations Research*, 34(6):871–882, 1986.

Detlof von Winterfeldt and Ward Edwards. *Decision Analysis and Behavioral Research.* Cambridge University Press, 1986.

Non-monotonic Negation in Probabilistic Deductive Databases

Raymond T. Ng and **V.S. Subrahmanian**
Department of Computer Science
A. V. Williams Building
University of Maryland
College Park, Maryland 20742, U.S.A.

Abstract

In this paper we study the uses and the semantics of non-monotonic negation in probabilistic deductive databases. Based on the stable semantics for classical logic programming, we introduce the notion of stable formula functions. We show that stable formula functions are minimal fixpoints of operators associated with probabilistic deductive databases with negation. Furthermore, since a probabilistic deductive database may not necessarily have a stable formula function, we provide a stable class semantics for such databases. Finally, we demonstrate that the proposed semantics can handle default reasoning naturally in the context of probabilistic deduction.

1 Introduction

Many frameworks on multivalued logic programming have been proposed to handle uncertain information, such as the ones described in [3, 9, 13, 14, 24]. However, all these approaches are non-probabilistic in nature, as the way they interpret conjunctions and disjunctions is too restrictive for probabilistic data. Since probability theory is well understood, we believe that a probabilistic approach to quantitative deduction in logic programming is important. In [16, 17] we have proposed a framework for probabilistic deductive databases, i.e. logic programs without function symbols. We show that this framework is expressive, as among others, it supports conditional probabilities, classical negation, propagation of probabilities, and Bayesian updates (cf. Example 1).

However, one fundamental issue that remains unaddressed in the framework proposed in [16, 17] is the representation and manipulation of non-monotonic modes of negation. In particular, the framework is incapable of default reasoning and drawing negative conclusions based on the *absence* of positive information. Thus, our focus in this paper is to study the uses and the semantics of non-monotonic negation in probabilistic logic programming.

The semantical approach we adopt is based on the stable semantics of (classical) logic programming with negation [12]. In a nutshell, the stable semantics for classical logic programming makes a "guess" as to the set of formulas provable from the program. Based on this guess, it transforms the program into a new program containing no occurrences of negation, and verifies if this guess satisfies some reasonable criterion. The "guess" is said to be *stable* if it satisfies the criterion.

In this paper we propose a stable semantics that is natural for probabilistic logic programs with non-monotonic negation. We introduce the notion of *stable formula functions*, and examine various connections between this notion of stability and fixpoints of operators associated with this kind of probabilistic logic programs. In effect, stable formula functions provides a fixpoint semantics for probabilistic logic programs with negation. However, similar to the situation in classical logic programming, not all probabilistic logic programs have stable formula functions. Based on the semantics proposed in [2] for classical logic programming, we thus provide a more general notion of *stable classes* of formula functions that applies to all probabilistic logic programs.

Section 2 presents the syntax and uses of probabilistic logic programs (without function symbols) with negation. Section 3 reviews the fixpoint theory for positive probabilistic logic programs presented in [16, 17]. Section 4 presents the notion of stable formula functions. It relates stable formula functions to fixpoints of operators associated with programs with negation. As programs may not have stable formula functions, Section 5 extends the notion of stability to provide semantics for such programs. Section 6 discusses how negation supports default reasoning, and compares our framework with related work. The last section concludes this paper with a discussion on future work.

2 Syntax and Uses of General Probabilistic Logic Programs

2.1 Gp-Clauses and Programs

Let L be a language generated by finitely many constant and predicate symbols. While L does *not* contain any ordinary function symbols, it may contain symbols for a fixed family of interpreted and computable[1] functions, known as *annotation functions* defined as follows.

Definition 1 An *annotation function* f of arity n is a total function of type $([0,1])^n \rightarrow [0,1]$. □

We also assume that L contains infinitely many variable symbols which are partitioned into two infinite subsets. The first subset consists of normal variable symbols in first order logic; they can only appear in atoms. We refer to these variables as *object variables.* The other set consists of *annotation variable* symbols. Annotation variables can only range between 0 and 1. Annotation variable symbols can only appear in *annotation terms*, a concept defined as follows.

Definition 2 1) ρ is called an *annotation item* if it is one of the following:
i) a constant in [0,1], or
ii) an annotation variable in L, or
iii) of the form $f(\delta_1, \ldots, \delta_n)$, where f is an annotation function of arity n and $\delta_1, \ldots, \delta_n$ are annotation items.
2) For real numbers c, d such that $0 \leq c, d \leq 1$, let the *closed interval* $[c, d]$ be the set $\{x \mid c \leq x \leq d\}$.
3) $[\rho_1, \rho_2]$ is called an *annotation (term)* if ρ_i $(i = 1, 2)$ is an annotation item.
If an annotation does not contain any annotation variables, the annotation is called a *c-annotation.* □

Let B_L denote the Herbrand base of L. Since L does not contain any function symbols[2], B_L is finite.

Definition 3 1) A *basic formula*, not necessarily ground, is either a conjunction or a disjunction of atoms. Note that both disjunction and conjunction cannot occur simultaneously in one basic formula.
2) Let $bf(B_L)$ denote the set of all ground basic formulas obtained by using distinct atoms in B_L, i.e. $bf(B_L) = \{A_1 \wedge \ldots \wedge A_n | n \geq 1$ is an integer and $A_1, \ldots, A_n \in B_L$ and $\forall 1 \leq i, j \leq n, i \neq j \Rightarrow A_i \neq A_j\}$ $\bigcup$ $\{A_1 \vee \ldots \vee A_n | n \geq 1$ is an integer and $A_1, \ldots, A_n \in B_L$ and $\forall 1 \leq i, j \leq n, i \neq j \Rightarrow A_i \neq A_j\}$, where all A_i's are ground atoms. □

[1] A function f is computable in the sense that there is a fixed procedure P_f such that if f is n-ary, and $\mu_1, \ldots, \mu_n$ are given as inputs to P_f, then $f(\mu_1, \ldots, \mu_n)$ is computed by P_f in a finite amount of time.

[2] Whenever we say function symbols, we mean exclusively the function symbols in normal first order logic, not including the annotation function symbols defined previously.

Definition 4 1) Let $F_0, \ldots, F_n, G_1, \ldots, G_m$ be basic formulas. Also let $\mu_0, \ldots, \mu_{n+m}$ be annotations such that every annotation variable occurring in μ_0, if any, also appears in one of $\mu_1, \ldots, \mu_{n+m}$. Then the clause

$$F_0 : \mu_0 \leftarrow F_1 : \mu_1 \wedge \ldots \wedge F_n : \mu_n \wedge \neg(G_1 : \mu_{n+1}) \wedge \ldots \wedge \neg(G_m : \mu_{n+m})$$

is called a *general probabilistic clause* (*gp-clause* for short).
2) A *pf-clause* is a gp-clause without negated annotated basic formulas, i.e. $m = 0$ [17]. □

Definition 5 1) A *general probabilistic (gp-)program* is a finite set of gp-clauses.
2) A *pf-program* is a finite set of pf-clauses [17]. □

If the annotation μ is a c-annotation $[c_1, c_2]$, the annotated basic formula $F : \mu$ intuitively means: "The probability of F must lie in the interval $[c_1, c_2]$." Similarly, the negation of the annotated formula, $\neg(G : \mu)$, is to be read as: "It is not provable that the probability of G must lie in the interval μ." Hence, the negation $\neg$ considered here is non-monotonic. Finally, note that to specify that the probability of F is a point c, simply use $F : [c, c]$. The reason why we prefer to support probability ranges to probability points is that given the probabilities of two formulas F_1, F_2, it is generally not possible to *precisely* state the probabilities of $(F_1 \wedge F_2)$ and $(F_1 \vee F_2)$ [16]. It is however possible to precisely state the tightest range within which these probabilities must lie. In [8] Fagin and Halpern also propose using an interval to represent the degree of belief for a nonmeasurable event.

2.2 Uses of Gp-programs

In the following we show a few examples to demonstrate the expressive power of gp-clauses. More examples on default reasoning are included in Section 6.

Example 1 In [17, 18], we show how to use gp-clauses to support propagation of probabilities, classical negation and van Emden's quantitative rule processing[24]. Due to space limitations, here we only show how to support conditional probabilities and Bayesian updates in our framework.
i) (**Support for Conditional Probabilities**:) Suppose the conditional probability of A given B is known to be p. This is equivalent to saying: *Prob*$(A \wedge B) = p * $*Prob*$(B)$. Thus, we can use the pf-clause:

$$(A \wedge B) : [p * V_1, p * V_1] \leftarrow B : [V_1, V_1].$$

Similarly, if to calculate the conditional probability of A given B, denoted by $(A|B)$, we can use:

$$(A|B) : [V_2/V_1, V_2/V_1] \leftarrow (A \wedge B) : [V_2, V_2] \wedge B : [V_1, V_1],$$

assuming that the probability of B is not 0. In [17] we show that these clauses maintain the intended conditional probability relationships.

iii) (**Bayesian Updates:**) Bayes rule states that: $Prob(B|A) = Prob(A|B) * Prob(B) / Prob(A)$ assuming $Prob(A) \neq 0$. Hence, the (updated) conditional probability of B given A, can be calculated by the pf-clause:

$$(B|A) : [V_1 * V_2/V_3, V_1 * V_2/V_3] \leftarrow (A|B) : [V_1, V_1] \wedge B : [V_2, V_2] \wedge A : [V_3, V_3].$$

□

Example 2 Suppose we believe that if it is not provable that the probability of a coin C showing heads is within the range [0.49, 0.51], then there is over 95% chance that the coin is unfair. The gp-clause:

$$unfair(C) : [0.95, 1] \leftarrow \neg(head(C) : [0.49, 0.51])$$

represents our belief. □

Example 3 Suppose we know that there is over 95% chance that a dog can bark, unless the dog is abnormal[3]. We also know that Benjy and Fido are dogs. However, Benjy is unable to bark (his vocal cords were injured at some point). This can be represented as:

$$\begin{aligned} bark(X) : [0.95, 1] &\leftarrow dog(X) : [1, 1] \wedge \neg(abn(X) : [1, 1]) \\ dog(fido) : [1, 1] &\leftarrow \\ dog(benjy) : [1, 1] &\leftarrow \\ bark(benjy) : [0, 0] &\leftarrow \\ abn(X) : [1, 1] &\leftarrow bark(X) : [0, 0] \end{aligned}$$

The last clause says that a dog is certainly abnormal if it *definitely* cannot bark. As we shall see later on (cf. Example 6), we can deduce from these clauses the fact that Fido can bark, but Benjy cannot. □

In [18] we also show how our framework can support mutual exclusion. See [18] for more details. In [17] we propose a fixpoint theory for pf-programs – negation-free gp-programs. Our objective here is to investigate how to extend this theory to handle negation. To do so, we adopt the stable semantical approach[12] for classical logic programming. But before we describe the stable semantics for gp-programs, we review the fixpoint theory we developed for pf-programs.

3 Background: Fixpoint Theory for Pf-programs

In this section we summarize the essential notions and results of the fixpoint theory we developed for probabilistic logic programs without negation as described in [16, 17]. Readers familiar with [16, 17] may skip this section.

[3] Note that this statement is *not* the same as saying: "Over 95% of all dogs bark."

Definition 6 1) Let a *world* W be an Herbrand interpretation, i.e. a subset of B_L. For ease of presentation, assume there is an arbitrary, but fixed enumeration of all possible worlds/subsets of B_L. Such enumerations are possible as L contains no function symbols.
2) A *world probability density function* $WP : 2^{B_L} \longrightarrow [0, 1]$ assigns to each world $W_j \in 2^{B_L}$ a probability $WP(W_j)$ such that for all $W_j \in 2^{B_L}$, $WP(W_j) \geq 0$ and $\sum_{W_j \in 2^{B_L}} WP(W_j) = 1$.
3) To simplify our notation, hereafter we use p_j to denote $WP(W_j)$ for $W_j \in 2^{B_L}$. □

In the context of probabilistic deduction, we assume that the "real" world is definite, i.e. there are some propositions that are true, and some that are false. However, we are uncertain which of the various "possible worlds" is the right one. Thus, we use a world probability density function to define probability densities on the set of all possible worlds. In other words, a world probability density function assigns a probability (i.e. a non-negative number) to each world such that the sum of all probabilities adds up to 1. Our notions of worlds and world probability density functions are similar in essence to the "possible worlds" approach suggested by Nilsson [19]. While Nilsson's enumeration of the possible worlds is based on the given *set of sentences*, ours is based on the Herbrand interpretations of L.

In the study of the semantics of pf-programs, our aim is to use the probability ranges described in a pf-program to find the probabilistic truth values (i.e. point probabilities) of basic formulas. In particular, we use the probability ranges to find world probability density functions that obey those ranges. While the process will be formalized shortly, the following notion of a *formula function* is crucial for the process.

Definition 7 1) Let $\mathcal{C}[0, 1]$ denote the set of all closed sub-intervals of the unit interval [0,1], i.e. the set of all (contiguous) closed intervals $[c, d]$ that are subsets of [0, 1].
2) A *formula function* is a mapping $h : bf(B_L) \longrightarrow \mathcal{C}[0, 1]$. □

The empty interval, denoted by $\emptyset$, is a member of $\mathcal{C}[0, 1]$, because it may be represented as $[c_1, c_2]$ where $c_2 < c_1$. Intuitively, a formula function assigns a probability range to each ground basic formula. Then given a formula function, we can find world probability density functions that obey the ranges assigned by the formula function. This is achieved by setting up a set of linear constraints, as described in the following definition.

Definition 8 1) Let h be a formula function. A set of linear constraints, denoted by $\mathcal{LC}(h)$, is defined as follows. For all $F_i \in bf(B_L)$, if $h(F_i) = [c_i, d_i]$, then

the inequality $c_i \leq \left(\sum_{W_j \models F_i \text{ and } W_j \in 2^{B_L}} p_j \right) \leq d_i$ is in $\mathcal{LC}(h)$ (where p_j's are used as specified in Definition 6). In addition, $\mathcal{LC}(h)$ contains the following 2 constraints: $\sum_{W_j \in 2^{B_L}} p_j = 1$ and $(\forall W_j \in 2^{B_L}), p_j \geq 0$.
2) Let $\mathcal{WP}(h)$ denote the solution set of $\mathcal{LC}(h)$. □

It is easy to see that each solution $WP \in \mathcal{WP}(h)$ (i.e. the solution set of $\mathcal{LC}(h)$) is a world probability density function. Also note that 2^{B_L} consists of all possible worlds, and any two distinct worlds are mutually incompatible as they must differ on at least one atom. Thus, given a world probability density function WP, we can compute the probabilistic truth value of any basic formula F with respect to WP by adding up the probabilities of all the possible worlds in which F is true in the classical 2-valued sense. Hence, it is the set $\mathcal{LC}(h)$ of linear constraints that enables us to find probabilistic truth values that satisfy the ranges assigned by the formula function h. Now we are in a position to define a fixpoint operator T_P for pf-programs P. Hereafter we use the notation $\mathcal{FF}$ to denote the set of all formula functions, and $\mathbf{min_Q}(Exp)$ and $\mathbf{max_Q}(Exp)$ to denote the minimization and maximization of the expression Exp subject to the set of constraints $\mathbf{Q}$.

Definition 9 Suppose P is a pf-program and h is a formula function.
1) Define an intermediate operator $S_P : \mathcal{FF} \longrightarrow \mathcal{FF}$ as follows:
For all $F \in bf(B_L)$, $S_P(h)(F) = \bigcap M_F$ where $M_F = \{\alpha \mid F : \alpha \leftarrow F_1 : \alpha_1 \wedge \ldots \wedge F_n : \alpha_n$ is a ground instance of a clause in P, and for all $1 \leq i \leq n, h(F_i) \subseteq \alpha_i\}$. In particular, if M_F is empty, set $S_P(h)(F) = [0,1]$.

2) Define $T_P : \mathcal{FF} \longrightarrow \mathcal{FF}$ as follows:
i) If $\mathcal{WP}(S_P(h))$ is non-empty (i.e. $\mathcal{LC}(S_P(h))$ has solutions), then for all $F \in bf(B_L)$, $T_P(h)(F) = [c_F, d_F]$ where

$$c_F = \mathbf{min}_{\mathcal{LC}(\mathbf{S_P(h)})} \left(\sum_{W_j \models F \text{ and } W_j \in 2^{B_L}} p_j \right) \text{ and}$$

$$d_F = \mathbf{max}_{\mathcal{LC}(\mathbf{S_P(h)})} \left(\sum_{W_j \models F \text{ and } W_j \in 2^{B_L}} p_j \right).$$

ii) Otherwise, if $\mathcal{WP}(S_P(h))$ is empty, then for all $F \in bf(B_L)$, $T_P(h)(F) = \emptyset$. □

Informally, $S_P(h)$ is a one-step immediate consequence operator that determines the probability ranges of basic formulas by one-step deductions of the pf-clauses in P. But since basic formulas can appear as the heads of pf-clauses, as an example the following situation may arise: $S_P(h)(A \vee B) = [0,0]$, but $S_P(h)(A) = S_P(h)(B) = [1,1]$. By regarding $[1,1]$ as true and $[0,0]$ as false, these range assignments are not consistent. In general, "local" assignments of probability ranges to formulas may not be "globally" consistent. Hence, the linear program $\mathcal{LC}(S_P(h))$ is set up to ensure that all assignments are consistent. Then T_P assigns to each formula a probability range that satisfies every constraint in the linear program.

Given two formula functions h_1 and h_2, we say that $h_1 \leq h_2$ iff $\forall F \in bf(B_L), h_1(F) \supseteq h_2(F)$. As shown in [16], the set $\mathcal{FF}$ of formula functions forms a complete lattice with respect to the ordering $\leq$ defined above. Moreover, the $\top$ element is the formula function h such that $\forall F \in bf(B_L), h(F) = \emptyset$, and the $\perp$ element is the one such that $\forall F \in bf(B_L), h(F) = [0,1]$. In [17] we show that T_P is monontonic, and thus there exists a least fixpoint $lfp(T_P)$ of T_P.

4 Stability of Formula Functions

In the presence of negation, the fixpoint operator associated with a pf-program (cf. Definition 9) must be extended to handle negation. We use T'_P to denote the fixpoint operator associated with a gp-program P.

Definition 10 Suppose P is a gp-program and h is a formula function.
1) Define an intermediate operator $S'_P : \mathcal{FF} \longrightarrow \mathcal{FF}$ as follows:
For all $F \in bf(B_L)$, $S'_P(h)(F) = \bigcap M'_F$ where $M'_F = \{\alpha \mid F : \alpha \leftarrow F_1 : \alpha_1 \wedge \ldots \wedge F_n : \alpha_n \wedge \neg(G_1 : \beta_1) \wedge \ldots \wedge \neg(G_m : \beta_m)$ is a ground instance of a clause in P, for all $1 \leq i \leq n, h(F_i) \subseteq \alpha_i$, and for all $1 \leq j \leq m, h(G_j) \not\subseteq \beta_j\}$. In particular, if M'_F is empty, set $S'_P(h)(F) = [0,1]$.
2) T'_P is obtained from S'_P in exactly the same way as T_P is obtained from S_P. □

The example below shows that T'_P is not monotonic.

Example 4 Consider the gp-program P described in Example 2:

$$p : [0.95, 1] \leftarrow \neg(q : [0.49, 0.51]).$$

Suppose h_1 is a formula function that assigns [0,1] to q, and h_2 is one that assigns [0.5,0.5] to q. Suppose that h_1 and h_2 assign [0,1] to all other basic formulas. Thus, it is the case that $h_1 \leq h_2$. But then, $T'_P(h_1)$ assigns [0.95,1] to p, while $T'_P(h_2)$ assigns [0,1] to p. Therefore, $T'_P(h_1)$ is not necessarily less than or equal to $T'_P(h_2)$. □

In the following we define the notion of *stable formula functions*, adapted from the stable model semantics proposed by Gelfond and Lifschitz [12]. We ultimately show that if there exists a stable formula function with respect to a gp-program P, the formula function is a minimal fixpoint of T'_P.

Definition 11 Given a gp-program P and a formula function h, the *formula-function-transform (ff-transform* for short) of P based on h, denoted by $ff(P,h)$, is defined as follows:
1) Given a ground instance $C' \equiv F : \alpha \leftarrow F_1 : \alpha_1 \wedge \ldots \wedge F_n : \alpha_n \wedge \neg(G_1 : \beta_1) \wedge \ldots \wedge \neg(G_m : \beta_m)$ of a clause in P, if $h(G_j) \not\subseteq \beta_j$ for all $1 \leq j \leq m$, then the clause $C \equiv F : \alpha \leftarrow F_1 : \alpha_1 \wedge \ldots \wedge F_n : \alpha_n$ is included in $ff(P,h)$.
2) Nothing else is in $ff(P,h)$. □

Definition 12 Let P be a gp-program. A formula function h is *stable* with respect to P if h is equal to the least fixpoint of $T_{ff(P,h)}$, i.e. $h = lfp(T_{ff(P,h)})$. □

Example 5 Consider again the gp-program P:

$$p : [0.95, 1] \leftarrow \neg(q : [0.49, 0.51]),$$

where p, q are ground. Then given the formula function h_1 such that $h_1(p) = [0.95, 1]$ and $h_1(q) = [0, 1]$, the ff-transform of P based on h_1 is the single clause:

$$p : [0.95, 1] \leftarrow .$$

Then the least fixpoint $lfp(T_{ff(P,h_1)})$ assigns [0.95, 1] to p and [0,1] to q. Hence, h_1 is stable. In fact, it is easy to show that h_1 is the only stable formula function[18]. □

Example 6 Consider the gp-program P for Benjy and Fido shown in Example 3. Let a formula function h_1 assigns [0,0] to *bark(benjy)*, [1,1] to *abn(benjy)*, [0.95,1] to *bark(fido)*, and [0,1] to *abn(fido)*. Then $ff(P, h_1)$ consists of the following clauses:

$$\begin{aligned} bark(fido) : [0.95, 1] &\leftarrow dog(fido) : [1, 1] \\ dog(fido) : [1, 1] &\leftarrow \\ dog(benjy) : [1, 1] &\leftarrow \\ bark(benjy) : [0, 0] &\leftarrow \\ abn(benjy) : [1, 1] &\leftarrow bark(benjy) : [0, 0] \\ abn(fido) : [1, 1] &\leftarrow bark(fido) : [0, 0]. \end{aligned}$$

It is easy to check that $h_1 = lfp(T_{ff(P,h_1)})$. Therefore, h_1 is stable. In fact, it is easy to verify that h_1 is the only stable formula function for this gp-program. □

The examples below show that there are gp-programs that have none or more than one stable formula function.

Example 7 The gp-program that consists of the single clause below:

$$p : [0.95, 1] \leftarrow \neg(p : [0.95, 1])$$

does not have a stable formula function. See [18] for a proof. □

Example 8 The gp-program that consists of the following clauses:

$$\begin{aligned} p : [0.95, 1] &\leftarrow \neg(q : [0.49, 0.51]) \\ q : [0.49, 0.51] &\leftarrow \neg(p : [0.95, 1]) \end{aligned}$$

has two stable formula functions: i) h_1 such that $h_1(p) = [0.95, 1]$ and $h_1(q) = [0, 1]$, and ii) h_2 such that $h_2(p) = [0, 1]$ and $h_2(q) = [0.49, 0.51]$. □

Intuitively, a stable formula function with respect to a gp-program makes "reasonable" guesses on the probability ranges assigned by the program to basic formulas. In particular, the following theorem shows that a stable formula function with respect to gp-program P is a minimal fixpoint of T'_P (cf. Definition 10).

Theorem 1 Let h be a stable formula function with respect to gp-program P. Then: h is a minimal fixpoint of T'_P, i.e. there does not exist any formula function $h' < h$ such that $T'_P(h') = h'$. □

From Theorem 1, we can conclude that every stable formula function is a minimal fixpoint of T'_P. But the following example shows that the converse is not true.

Example 9 Consider the gp-program P that consists of the following clauses:

$$\begin{aligned} p : [0.95, 1] &\leftarrow \neg(p : [0.95, 1]) \\ p : [0.95, 1] &\leftarrow q : [1, 1] \\ q : [1, 1] &\leftarrow q : [1, 1]. \end{aligned}$$

It is easy to check that the formula function h that assigns [0.95,1] to p and [1,1] to q is a minimal fixpoint of T'_P. However, h is not stable [18]. □

Thus far, we have introduced the notion of stable formula functions which has the desirable property that it is a minimal fixpoint of T'_P. In effect, stable formula functions provide a fixpoint semantics for gp-programs. However, as shown in Example 7, a gp-program does not necessarily have a stable formula function. It is therefore the purpose of the next section to extend our theory of stability to cover those programs.

5 Stable Classes of Formula Functions

In [2] Baral and Subrahmanian propose a stable and extension class theory for logic programs and default logics. Here we adopt an analogous approach in proposing a stable class of formula functions defined as follows.

Definition 13 Let P be a gp-program, and SF be a finite set of formula functions. Then: SF is a *stable class* of formula functions with respect to P iff $SF = \{lfp(T_{ff(P,h_i)}) \mid h_i \in SF\}$. □

Intuitively, a formula function h_i in a stable class is the same as the least fixpoint of an operator associated with the ff-transform of P based on some member h_j in the stable class, i.e. $h_i = lfp(T_{ff(P,h_j)})$. In general, every member in the class is related in the same way with some other member in the class. See [2] for more details on stable class theory. In short, a stable class of formula functions with respect to a gp-program represents a set of "reasonable" guesses on the probability ranges assigned by the program to basic formulas.

Example 10 Consider the gp-program in Example 7 again. A stable class of the program consists of the two formula functions: $h_1(p) = [0.95, 1]$ and $h_2(p) = [0, 1]$. It is easy to check that $h_1 = lfp(T_{ff(P,h_2)})$ and $h_2 = lfp(T_{ff(P,h_1)})$. □

Lemma 1 A formula function h is a stable formula function with respect to gp-program P iff the singleton set $\{h\}$ is a stable class with respect to P. □

The aim of the remainder of this section is to prove that every gp-program has a non-empty stable class of formula functions (cf. Theorem 2).

Definition 14 Let P be a gp-program and h be a formula function. Define the operator $\mathcal{SF}_P : \mathcal{FF} \longrightarrow \mathcal{FF}$ as: $\mathcal{SF}_P(h) = lfp(T_{ff(P,h)})$. □

Lemma 2 The operator $\mathcal{SF}_P$ is anti-monotonic, i.e. $h_1 \leq h_2$ implies $\mathcal{SF}_P(h_2) \leq \mathcal{SF}_P(h_1)$. □

The following theorem is now an immediate consequence of the above lemma and a theorem by Yablo[25] and Fitting[10].

Theorem 2 Every gp-program has a non-empty stable class of formula functions. □

The theorem above states that every gp-program has a non-empty stable class of formula functions. Suppose C_1, C_2 are two sets of formula functions. Recall that the ordering $\leq$ applies to formula functions. We extend this ordering now to *sets* of formula functions (and hence to stable classes) in two ways. Both orderings are well known in algebraic structures called *power domains* due to Hoare and Smyth [23].

Definition 15 Let S_1, S_2 be two sets. We say that:
1) $S_1 \leq_{\mathbf{smyth}} S_2$ iff $(\forall s_1 \in S_1)(\exists s_2 \in S_2)\, s_1 \leq s_2$, and
2) $S_1 \leq_{\mathbf{hoare}} S_2$ iff $(\forall s_2 \in S_2)(\exists s_1 \in S_1)\, s_1 \leq s_2$. □

Definition 16 1) A non-empty stable class C is said to be *Hoare-minimal* iff:
i) C is inclusion-minimal, i.e. there is no non-empty stable class C' such that $C' \subset C$ and
ii) for every inclusion-minimal non-empty finite stable class C', $C' \leq_{\mathbf{hoare}} C$ implies $C' = C$.
2) C is said to be *Smyth-minimal* iff condition (i) above holds and condition (ii) holds with $\leq_{\mathbf{hoare}}$ replaced by $\leq_{\mathbf{smyth}}$. □

We may choose either Hoare-minimal stable classes or Smyth-minimal stable classes as the intended meaning of our program. However, depending on the choice we make, we may get different semantics as shown below.

Example 11 Consider the gp-program:

$$\begin{array}{rcl} p:[1,1] & \leftarrow & a:[1,1] \\ p:[1,1] & \leftarrow & b:[1,1] \\ a:[1,1] & \leftarrow & \neg(b:[1,1]) \\ b:[1,1] & \leftarrow & \neg(a:[1,1]). \end{array}$$

This program has two stable formula functions: i) h_1 that assigns $[1,1]$ to both p and a, and ii) h_2 that assigns $[1,1]$ to both p and b. Furthermore, suppose h_3 is the function that assigns $[1,1]$ to all of p, a, b and h_4 is the function that assigns $[0,1]$ to all of p, a, b. Then the set $\{h_3, h_4\}$ is a stable class of formula functions.

Note that here $\{h_1\}$ and $\{h_2\}$ are both Smyth-minimal stable classes of formula functions. Hence, the Smyth-minimal stable class semantics assigns $[1,1]$ to p. However, $\{h_3, h_4\}$ is the unique Hoare-minimal stable class of formula functions. This Hoare-minimal class only allows us to conclude that p gets the value $[0,1]$. □

In short, we have introduced the notion of a stable class of formula functions for gp-programs. Lemma 1 shows that if h is a stable formula function, then the singleton set $\{h\}$ is a stable class. Thus, the stable class semantics is defined for all gp-programs – whether or not they have stable formula functions.

6 Discussion

Like many researchers, we are interested in the use of numerical estimates in default reasoning. Unfortunately the framework we proposed in [17] is not powerful enough to handle default rules and exceptions. But now with the support of the non-monotonic negation $\neg$, we can specify that a default rule is only applicable in the absence of evidence to the contrary. Example 6 shows that the stable semantics proposed here handles the interaction between default rules and exceptions appropriately. Furthermore, the following examples demonstrate that the proposed semantics can also deal with interacting default rules.

Example 12 In [21], Reiter and Criscuolo consider the following situation: i) that John is a high school dropout, ii) that high school dropouts are typically adults, and iii) that adults are typically employed. Due to transitivity of default rules ii) and iii), the conclusion that John is employed can be deduced. They argue that this conclusion is undesirable.

Now consider the following gp-program P_1:

$$\begin{array}{rcl} adult(X):[0.95,1] & \leftarrow & dropout(X):[1,1] \\ employed(X):[0.95,1] & \leftarrow & adult(X):[1,1] \wedge \\ & & \neg(abn(X):[1,1]) \\ abn(X):[1,1] & \leftarrow & dropout(X):[1,1]. \end{array}$$

Suppose initially P_1 contains the fact: *adult(john)* : $[1,1] \leftarrow$. Then it is easy to check that the only stable formula function with respect to P_1 assigns the range [0,95,1] to *employed(john)* correctly.

Suppose *dropout(john)* : $[1,1] \leftarrow$ is added to P_1. Call this new program P_2. Consider the formula function h that assigns [1,1] to *adult(john)*, *dropout(john)* and *abn(john)*, but [0,1] to *employed(john)*. It is easy to check that h is a unique stable formula function with respect to P_2.

Finally, consider the situation where the only known fact about John is that he is a high school dropout, i.e. deleting the fact about John's adulthood from program P_2. Call this new program P_3. The unique stable formula function with respect to P_3 is the one that assigns: [1,1] to *dropout(john)* and *abn(john)*, [0.95,1] to *adult(john)*, and [0,1] to *employed(john)*. Hence, undesirable conclusions due to transitivity of default rules are avoided. □

The framework proposed by Dubois and Prade [6] also handles the situation discussed in the above example. However, their semantics is different from ours, as their framework is based on possibility logic and their model theory is based on fuzzy sets [26] which are well-known to be non-probabilistic. The following example on interacting default rules has been discussed extensively, but see [11, 20] for a probabilistic treatment on the subject.

Example 13 Consider the situation: i) that tweety is a penguin, ii) that a penguin is a bird, iii) that typically penguins cannot fly, and iv) that birds can typically fly. The situation can be represented by the following gp-program:

$$\begin{aligned}
fly(X):[0.95,1] &\leftarrow bird(X):[1,1]\wedge \\
&\quad\ \neg(abnBird(X):[1,1]) \\
fly(X):[0,0.05] &\leftarrow penguin(X):[1,1]\wedge \\
&\quad\ \neg(abnPeng(X):[1,1]) \\
bird(X):[1,1] &\leftarrow penguin(X):[1,1] \\
abnBird(X):[1,1] &\leftarrow penguin(X):[1,1] \\
penguin(tweety):[1,1] &\leftarrow .
\end{aligned}$$

Consider the formula function h that assigns: [1,1] to *penguin(tweety)*, *bird(tweety)* and *abnBird(tweety)*, [0,0.05] to *fly(tweety)*, and [0,1] to *abnPeng(tweety)*. Again it is easy to show that h is the unique stable formula function with respect to the program. □

Thus far, we have shown several examples on how to handle default reasoning in our framework. But our framework is not as expressive as the probabilistic frameworks proposed by Bacchus[1] and Buntine[4]. For instance, given the above example, their frameworks can conclude that "birds typically are not penguins." Such a conclusion is not deducible in our framework, and in ongoing research we are studying how to extend our theory to handle such cases. However, as the framework of Bacchus extends full first-order logic, it is unclear to us how his framework can be used as a basis for logic programming and deductive databases. Similar comments apply to Buntine's proposal.

There have also been many proposals on multivalued logic programming. These include the works by Blair and Subrahmanian [3], Fitting [9], Kifer et al [13, 14], and van Emden [24]. However, they do not support non-monotonic modes of negation. On the other hand, the integration of logic and probability theory has been the subject of numerous studies [1, 5, 7, 8, 15, 22, 19]. While [16, 17] provides more details on these works, it suffices to point out here that these works have concerns quite different from ours, and that it is unclear how to use these formalisms to support probabilistic logic programs and deductive databases.

7 Conclusions

In this paper we study the semantics and the uses of probabilistic logic programs with non-monotonic negation (i.e. gp-programs). Based on the stable semantical approach for classical logic programming, we investigate the notion of stable formula functions. We show that stable formula functions are minimal fixpoints of operators associated with gp-programs. While some gp-programs may not have stable formula functions, we provide a stable class semantics that applies to all gp-programs. Finally, we demonstrate by examples how the proposed semantics can handle default reasoning appropriately in the context of probabilistic deduction.

In ongoing research, we are studying how to support empirical probabilities in our framework. We are also interested in designing a proof procedure for gp-programs. In particular, we are investigating whether it suffices to augment the proof procedure we developed for positive probabilistic logic programs with some kind of negation as failure rule.

Acknowledgements

This research was partially sponsored by the National Science Foundation under Grant IRI-8719458 and by the "Office of Graduate Studies and Research of the University of Maryland."

References

[1] F. Bacchus. (1988) *Representing and Reasoning with Probabilistic Knowledge*, Research Report CS-88-31, University of Waterloo.

[2] C. Baral and V.S. Subrahmanian. (1990) *Stable and Extension Class Theory for Logic Pro-*

grams and Default Logics, to appear in: Journal of Automated Reasoning. Preliminary version in: Proc. 1990 Intl. Workshop on Non-Monotonic Reasoning, ed K. Konolige, June 1990.

[3] H. A. Blair and V.S. Subrahmanian. (1987) *Paraconsistent Logic Programming*, Theoretical Computer Science, 68, pp 35-54. Preliminary version in: Proc. 7th Conference on Foundations of Software Technology and Theoretical Computer Science, Lecture Notes in Computer Science, Vol. 287, pps 340–360, Springer Verlag.

[4] W. Buntine. (1990) *Modelling Default and Likelihood Reasoning as Probabilistic*, Technical Report FIA-90-09-11-01, NASA Ames Research Center.

[5] A. P. Dempster. (1968) *A Generalization of Bayesian Inference*, J. of the Royal Statistical Society, Series B, 30, pp 205–247.

[6] D. Dubois and H. Prade. (1988) *Default Reasoning and Possibility Theory*, Artificial Intelligence, 35, pp 243-257.

[7] R. Fagin and J. Halpern. (1988) *Uncertainty, Belief and Probability*, in Proc. IJCAI-89, Morgan Kauffman.

[8] R. Fagin, J. Y. Halpern and N. Megiddo. (1989) *A Logic for Reasoning About Probabilities*, to appear in: Information and Computation.

[9] M. C. Fitting. (1988) *Bilattices and the Semantics of Logic Programming*, to appear in: Journal of Logic Programming.

[10] M. C. Fitting. (1990) personal correspondence.

[11] H. Geffner. (1989) *Default Reasoning: Causal and Conditional Theories*, Technical Report 137, Cognitive Systems Laboratory, University of California, Los Angeles.

[12] M. Gelfond and V. Lifschitz. (1988) *The Stable Model Semantics for Logic Programming*, in: Proc. 5th International Conference and Symposium on Logic Programming, ed R. A. Kowalski and K. A. Bowen, pp 1070-1080.

[13] M. Kifer and E. Lozinskii. (1989) *RI: A Logic for Reasoning with Inconsistency*, Proc. 4-th Symposium on Logic in Computer Science, Asilomar, CA, pp. 253-262. Full version to appear in: Journal of Automated Reasoning.

[14] M. Kifer and V. S. Subrahmanian. (1991) *Theory of Generalized Annotated Logic Programming and its Applications*, to appear in: Journal of Logic Programming.

[15] H. Kyburg. (1974) *The Logical Foundations of Statistical Inference*, D. Reidel.

[16] R.T. Ng and V.S. Subrahmanian. (1989) *Probabilistic Logic Programming*, to appear in: Information and Computation. Preliminary version in: Proc. 5th International Symposium on Methodologies for Intelligent Systems, pp 9-16.

[17] R.T. Ng and V.S. Subrahmanian. (1990) *A Semantical Framework for Supporting Subjective and Conditional Probabilities in Deductive Databases*, to appear in: Proc. 1991 International Conference of Logic Programming, ed K. Furukawa, MIT Press. Full version in: Technical Report CS-TR-2563, University of Maryland, College Park.

[18] R.T. Ng and V.S. Subrahmanian. (1990) *Stable Semantics for Probabilistic Deductive Databases*, Technical Report CS-TR-2573, University of Maryland, College Park.

[19] N. Nilsson. (1986) *Probabilistic Logic*, Artificial Inelligence, 28, pp 71-87.

[20] J. Pearl. (1988) *Probabilistic Reasoning in Intelligent Systems: Networks of Plausible Inference*, Morgan Kaufmann.

[21] R. Reiter and G. Criscuolo. (1981) *On interacting Defaults*, in Proc. IJCAI 81, pp 270-276.

[22] G. Shafer. (1976) *A Mathematical Theory of Evidence*, Princeton University Press.

[23] M. Smyth. (1978) *Power Domains*, Journal of Computer and Systems Sciences, 16, 1 pps 23–36.

[24] M.H. van Emden. (1986) *Quantitative Deduction and its Fixpoint Theory*, Journal of Logic Programming, 4, 1, pp 37-53.

[25] S. Yablo. (1985) *Truth and Reflection*, Journal of Philosophical Logic, 14, pps 279–349.

[26] L. A. Zadeh. (1965) *Fuzzy Sets*, Information and Control, 8, pp 338–353.

Management of Uncertainty in the Multi-Level Monitoring and Diagnosis of the Time of Flight Scintillation Array

Robert K. Paasch
Department of Mechanical Engineering
Oregon State University
Corvallis, OR 97331
paasch@kepler.me.orst.edu

Alice M. Agogino
Department of Mechanical Engineering
University of California
Berkeley, CA 94720
aagogino@euler.berkeley.edu

Abstract

We present a general architecture for the monitoring and diagnosis of large scale sensor-based systems with real time diagnostic constraints. This architecture is multi-leveled, combining a single monitoring level based on statistical methods with two model-based diagnostic levels. At each level, sources of uncertainty are identified, and integrated methodologies for uncertainty management are developed. The general architecture was applied to the monitoring and diagnosis of a specific nuclear physics detector at Lawrence Berkeley National Laboratory that contained approximately 5000 components and produced over 500 channels of output data. The general architecture is scalable, and work is ongoing to apply it to detector systems one and two orders of magnitude more complex.

1 INTRODUCTION

The Time of Flight Scintillation Array is a sub-atomic particle detector used at Lawrence Berkeley National Laboratory (LBL) for studies in relativistic heavy-ion physics. With operating costs for these experiments exceeding $60,000 per hour, it is important that this detector operate correctly, and that any failures be identified and remediated as quickly as possible. But with approximately 5000 components, and over 500 output channels producing a Mbyte of data every 10 seconds, the monitoring and diagnosis of this detector system is difficult for human operators to accomplish within the real time constraints.

While the automation of the monitoring and diagnostic process was desirable, the scale of the Time of Flight Scintillation Array combined with real time constraints and uncertain system relationships presented a particular challenge to automated monitoring and diagnosis. The scale of the detector requires the average time spent monitoring an individual output channel (or probe) and diagnosing an individual component be small in order to meet the real time constraints. The uncertain nature of the relationship between the output data and the component states indicates an evidential reasoning approach, which may be contrary to the small average time requirement if applied to every component.

We present a general multi-level architecture developed to efficiently and non-deterministically diagnose large scale sensor-based systems in real time, and describe the implementation of this architecture to diagnose the Time of Flight Scintillation Array. The diagnostic system, the TOF Validation System, combines a single monitoring level with two model-based diagnostic reasoning levels to provide both efficiency and robustness in the face of uncertainty. The system consists of: 1) a statistical monitoring level using traditional chi-squared testing on data samples; 2) a model-based reasoning level operating on Boolean channel states (OK and BAD) with a data base of connectivity information to produce an ordered, reduced set of suspect components; and 3) a model-based reasoning level that extracts considerably more information from the data channels, and uses qualitative behavioral system information operating on the reduced set of suspect components to produce an evidential mapping to individual component failure state beliefs. The system systematically extracts more information from a reduced set of channels to provide a more detailed diagnosis. The system was developed to be scalable to diagnose similar detector systems two orders of magnitude more complex, and ongoing work is directed toward extending the system for use on a Time Projection Chamber at LBL and for possible use on the Superconducting Supercollider.

We believe the TOF Validation System is unique among sensor-based diagnostic expert systems developed to date, first due to the scale and complexity of the TOF Scintillation Array, second due to the multi-level nature of it's diagnostic reasoning, and third in the consideration and management of uncertainty at all levels of reasoning. The general methodology should be applicable to a broad range of monitoring and diagnostic problems where at least a qualitative model of the system is known.

In the following sections we will discuss other related research, describe the TOF Scintillation Array, present the general diagnostic system architecture, then discuss the management of uncertainty at the individual levels. We also describe the implementation of the generalized architecture and methodologies to develop the TOF Validation System.

2 BACKGROUND LITERATURE

In the development of an automated real-time sensor-based multi-level monitoring and diagnostic system, a broad variety of research and implementation issues must be addressed and so there exists a wealth of prior research work that is relevant to this research. This work builds on that of Agogino (1988a, b) and Rege (1986) in the area of real time sensor-based diagnostic expert systems. Rege describes IDES (Influence Diagram Expert System) and an application to a simple sensor-based pump diagnostic problem. Agogino describes the application of IDES to the real time sensor-based diagnosis of a milling machine and Ramamurthy (1990) to drilling applications.

Our view of multi-level diagnostic knowledge is similar to that of Milne (1985, 1987), who states that the diagnostic knowledge can exist at one or more of four levels: compiled, functional, behavioral and structural . Although compiled diagnostic knowledge systems often implicitly contain knowledge about structure and/or function, it is the explicit use of structural, behavioral or functional knowledge that delineates those diagnostic knowledge systems. Milne states that "the basic knowledge required for diagnosis is the set of malfunctions and relations between the observations and malfunctions". A compiled knowledge diagnostic system is a system that has this knowledge explicitly given to it. A structural diagnostic system is a system that is explicitly given structural or connectivity information, and likewise functional and behavioral diagnostic systems are explicitly given functional or behavioral information. While Milne uses multiple levels to categorize knowledge representation, we have explicitly used these same levels to describe a diagnostic architecture.

Chandrasekaran (1983), Davis (1983), Fink (1985a, b, 1987), and Scarl (1987) all address compiled verses deep (structural, behavioral and functional) knowledge based diagnosis. The research by Fink is particularly relevant to this research in that she describes a system that combines knowledge from more than one level, although the application described in that research is several orders of magnitude simpler than the TOF Scintillation Array. Scarl makes explicit use of both structure and function in the development of the diagnostic expert system for the space shuttle described in Scarl (1985).

When a diagnostic reasoning system depends on sensor information, the problem of sensor validation must be addressed. Chandrasekaran (1988) addresses sensor validation in compiled systems, and introduces a "meta-level" of compiled information that constitutes a level of redundancy based on expectations derived during diagnosis. Scarl (1987) shows that with the use of knowledge of structure and function one is able to regard sensor validation as a subset of the more general diagnostic process and therefore validate sensors the same as diagnosing any other component, an observation that we were able to confirm in this research.

3 TIME OF FLIGHT SCINTILLATION ARRAY

The TOF Scintillation Array is part of the Heavy Ion Superconducting Spectrometer (HISS) experiments at Lawrence Berkeley Laboratory. The TOF Scintillation Array consists of 136 plastic scintillation slats, 272 photomultiplier tubes, and associated electronics. As atomic particles produced by an experimental "event" pass through a particular slat, light photons are produced. The duration of an event is measured in nanoseconds, and the associated photons migrate to the ends of the slat and the produce electrical signals in the two photomultiplier tubes that are amplified 106 times. The signal is split and sent to both an Analog to Digital Converter (ADC) and a Time to Digital Converter (TDC). Digital outputs from the ADCs and TDCs are sent directly to magnetic tape, although sampling is possible. Because of the tremendous amount of data produced by and the scale of the TOF Scintillation Array, it can be difficult to monitor and diagnose even for an expert in the Wall's operation. Proposed detector systems for the Superconducting Supercollider would be humanly impossible to monitor and diagnose without assistance.

4 SYSTEM ARCHITECTURE

Difficulty in diagnosing large scale systems comes from a combination of both the complexity of the system and from the external constraints on the time allowed for diagnosis. Diagnostic systems using compiled knowledge (such as heuristic, rule-based systems) are difficult to implement for large scale systems due to the difficulties in acquiring and implementing large numbers of rules, rule conflict resolution, and difficulties in updating and appending the rule base. Also, as the number of rules increases, diagnostic time can increase. If the time to diagnose a failure is of little or no concern, then large, complex rule based systems may be a viable option, but this is not the case for this application.

When a system model is available, model based diagnostic systems can provide increased flexibility in handling system changes. But if the reasoning strategies applied to the entire system are too complex, model based diagnostic systems may also require too much time when diagnosing large scale systems.

The generalizable architecture we propose for large scale sensor-based systems closely mimics the methods by which an expert might diagnose a problem: first a quick look at all the probe outputs to get a general idea of what components might have failed, then a more detailed look at specific probes to determine the exact component and the specific failure type. This architecture consist of four main functional modules as shown in Figure 1.

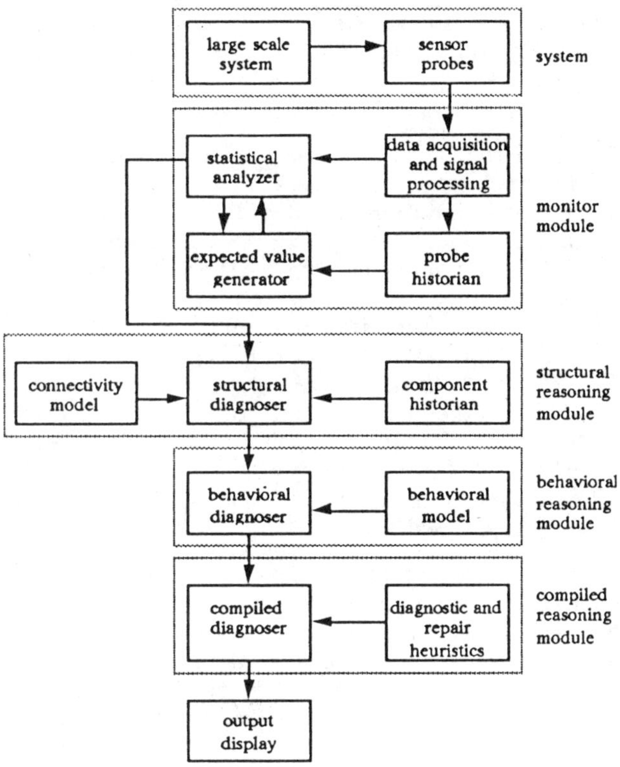

Figure 1: Large Scale System Diagnostic Architecture

A monitoring module would sample the probe (sensor) outputs, comparing these outputs to historical values. When the monitoring module detects an abnormality, the structural reasoning module is alerted. Using a connectivity model of the system and the probe output comparisons from the statistical analyzer, the structural reasoning module performs a "rough cut" diagnosis that produces a short list of suspect components. This short list is sent to the behavioral reasoning module. Using the short list of suspect components, this module retrieves the original probe outputs of all probes related to these components from the statistical analyzer, and using a functional model of the system produces a list of specific failure types for specific suspect components, ordered by degree of belief. A compiled reasoning model provides assistance in interpretation and repair.

Possible applications of this architecture include sensor validation in process control, fault location in complex electomechanical systems and control of food or chemical proccessing. We have applied this architecture to the monitoring and diagnosis of the Time of Flight Scintillation Array. In this implementation of the architecture, a data acquisition and signal processing unit compiles averages for ADC and TDC values for 1000 events, and a statistical analyzer compares these averages to archived values from the expected value generator with a chi-squared test. Probes that fail the test are flagged as "BAD", and the structural reasoning module started. This module assumes structural dependencies among the components based on connectivity (structure).

The term "structural dependency" in this context means that the effective state of a component is dependent on a preceding component. This dependency could occur when a component provides a data output that is the data input to a succeeding component, or if a component cannot operate if the preceding component has failed (such as when the preceding component supplies power to the succeeding component).

From the list of "BAD" probes from the statistical analyzer, and connectivity knowledge stored in the connectivity model, the structural diagnoser produces a short list of suspect components. The behavioral diagnosis module is then started with the list of suspect components. For each suspect component, this module solicits additional information from the statistical analyzer about trending of data from select groups of probes affected by the components under consideration, and compares those trends to expected trending (from the behavioral model) for individual failure types for the specific class of component using evidential algorithms. The final list of suspect components, with the types of failure, is presently sent directly to an output display. The compiled reasoning module has not been implemented.

5 MANAGEMENT OF UNCERTAINTY AT THE MONITORING LEVEL

The monitoring module addresses the question of whether the Time of Flight Scintillation Array is functioning correctly or not. Uncertainty exists at this level due to the highly stochastic nature of particle physics experiments.

In this case the monitoring process is abetted by the tremendous amount of data produced by the experiment. Samples of statistically significant size (typically 1000 events) can be collected rapidly. These samples are compared to expected norms (10 samples of 1000 events collected with the system assumed to be functioning correctly) using standard chi-square testing. These tests establish whether an individual data probe is OK or BAD. Statistical analysis validated the suitability of the chi-square test for determining the state of a probe (Paasch 1990).

6 MANAGEMENT OF UNCERTAINTY AT THE STRUCTURAL REASONING LEVEL

The structural reasoning module has the responsibility for reducing the set of suspect components from a set of all components in the system to a set that can be efficiently diagnosed by the behavioral reasoning module within the real time constraints. The largest reduction in the suspect set occurs in this module. In the TOF Validation System, this module reduces the suspect component set from 5000 components to approximately 10. Detailed information on this module is included in Hall (1989).

The structural reasoning module assumes two possible component states (OK and BAD), and two possible observations per observation probe (OK and BAD). We justify this simplification of component states on the basis of highest common denominator. All components can use OK and BAD, while failure type may be component specific. Also, in the structural reasoning module a rough diagnosis is acceptable, and the lumping of components into either OK or BAD is sufficient. As for the observations per probe, OK or BAD may be all the information available from some extracted features such as the chi-square test used by the monitoring module.

Uncertainty in the probe state is addressed at the monitoring level by statistical methods. Uncertainty in the component state is addressed to some degree at this level, and again at the behavioral reasoning level. At this level we deterministically assume that if a component has all dependent probes in state OK then that component is in state OK and is removed as a suspect. This assumption is justified by the statistical significance of the sample size used in the monitoring module.

If a component has one or more dependent probes in state BAD, then that component can be included as a suspect. Uncertainty about the individual states of the components on the reduced suspect list can be handled by ranking the suspect components by the BAD probe to total probe ratio: a component with four probes dependent upon it and three of those probes assumed BAD would rank ahead of a component with eight dependent probes of which four are BAD.. Multiple component failures would increase the size of the suspect list. The possibility of multiple failures would decrease with the time to collect a sample.

If two or more suspect components have identical signatures (affect the same probes) we cannot discriminate between component failures, an ambiguity would exist, and thus would present a failure class. For the TOF Scintillation Array the worst case is three ambiguous states (i.e. single components failures). Compiled information in the form of prior probabilities can handle this ambiguity, or a secondary diagnosis (detailed in the next section) can be performed.

7 MANAGEMENT OF UNCERTAINTY AT THE BEHAVIORAL REASONING LEVEL

Although the structural reasoning module efficiently produces a limited set of suspect components and can order that list, a more detailed diagnosis may be desired. The structural reasoning module is sensitive to the breakpoint value between BAD and OK channels, in the best of circumstances it may produce a suspect component list with some ambiguity, and it provides no information the specific type of component failure. The behavioral reasoning module was incorporated into the general architecture to address these problems. This module by itself would be adequate for the diagnosis of small scale systems, but is too computationally inefficient to operate on a large set of suspect components in real time.

With the apparent complexity of the system greatly reduced, the behavior module can operate in numerous ways. The behavioral reasoning architecture we present incorporates a behavioral model to produce expected observation values for the different failure types, a methodology to compare expected values to actual values, and a methodology to relate that comparison to the system states. In the TOF Validation System, the later two methodologies are implemented in the behavioral diagnoser.

The behavioral model can exist on many different levels. The compilation of historical data, keeping track of failures by type, would result in a compiled behavioral model relating system state directly to observables. At this level the knowledge would be considered shallow: compiled knowledge of system operation as a whole, with little or no knowledge of deeper system operation. At the other extreme would be the deep analytical model: every component in the system, and every relationship between components is modeled analytically, with a resultant complex mathematical equation for the system rigorously relating system state to observables. Between these two extremes there are a number of possibilities, including qualitative models, data models based on experiential, first principle, compiled knowledge, and hybrid models.

Numerical comparison methodologies such as chi-square or Z distribution can work for numerical observations, and Boolean sensor outputs can be compared directly with expected outputs on a match/no-match basis, with the result mapped directly to increase or decrease a belief.

Relational methodologies would generally involve some sort of mapping from comparison value to evidential value. This mapping could be as simple as a table look up, or could involve qualitative or quantitative relational algorithms.

One possible feature of a behavioral reasoning module, implemented in the TOF Validation System, is the continuous mapping made between data values and hypothesis belief. The structural reasoning module assumes that belief is discrete, as this is a Boolean mapping. For example, if probability were used, $p(t = BAD|y < limit) = 0$ and $p(t = BAD|y > limit) = 1$, where t is a probe state, y is the probe data value, and "limit" is the established breakpoint between OK and BAD. But the argument can be made that the uncertainty mapping in this and other cases is continuous. Intuitively, $p(t = BAD|y)$ might increase as y increases. More importantly, we can relate the individual component failure states, si, to the probe values. For each evidence type for each hypothesis, an algorithm could be found that relates $p(si|y)$ to the value of y. A plot of such an algorithm is shown in Figure 2. In this case the likelihood of the hypothesis, H, increases as the value of the feature, x, increases, but the likelihood might also decrease with an increasing feature value, or it might increase with any feature change, or be related in other ways. The tradeoff to using a continuous evidential approach may be computational complexity and the inability to invert.

Evidential methodologies are used to combine the evidence produced by the relational algorithms, and could be based on Bayesian probabilities, Certainty Factors and Dempster-Shafer, at the preference of the expert or system developers. Each individual observation contributes an individual belief or likelihood for each system state hypothesis, these are then combined to give a final belief or likelihood for each system state hypothesis. The final belief or likelihood for each system state could then be used on either an absolute or relative basis.

The behavioral reasoning module as implemented in the TOF Validation System uses numerical, relational and evidential sub-levels. A qualitative behavioral model is based on the experts first principle and expe-

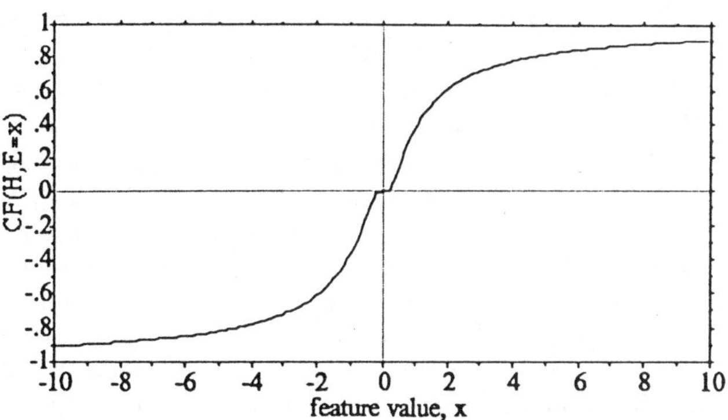

Figure 2: Increase in Belief Associated With Evidence Verses Strength of the Evidence

riential knowledge of the TOF Scintillation Array. To compare current with expected data features a simple Z distribution comparison (z= (x - xavg)/sx) is used. The behavioral diagnoser then uses four continuous quantitative relational algorithms, one for each expected direction of data trending (increasing, decreasing, either direction, and no change) to relate the data to evidential belief. These algorithms are modified for individual component failure state/ data feature relationships by parameters to reflect the desired evidential weighting, slope and cutoff value as determined by the expert. The algorithms can be made to behave in a nearly discrete manner when appropriate. At the preference of the expert, the present implementation uses certainty factors as an evidential methodology. The conversion to Bayesian probabilities is straightforward with the addition of the assessment of prior probabilities (Heckerman 1986).

8 IMPLEMENTATION

The architecture was implemented by the development and testing of individual modules that were then combined to form the TOF validation System. The data acquisition and signal processing unit was coded in a combination of FORTRAN and C. All other modules were coded in C. The system runs on the HISS experiment's VAX computers operating under VMS. A more detailed description of the implementation and use of the validation system may be found in Hall (1989), Olson (1990), and Paasch (1988, 1990).

9 SUMMARY

This paper presents a multi-level diagnostic architecture particularly well suited for the diagnosis of large scale systems with real time constraints. While the idea of multi-level diagnosis is not new, we believe this system is unique in that the inherent complexity and scale of the application required that multiple levels be used in this case to achieve the requisite efficiency while maintaining diagnostic detail and the ability to manage uncertainty.

In implementing a multi-level diagnostic system, we have found that the individual diagnostic levels have strengths and weaknesses that are complementary and generalizable. Structural reasoning systems can be fairly robust, and can be designed in a generic manner so that changes in the structure of the components are reflected as changes in a mapping database. Due to the inherent ambiguity, structural reasoning appears to best lend itself to a rough, first pass, preliminary diagnosis. Uncertainty at this level exists as ambiguity between system states and as uncertainty in the probe feature value to symbolic value mapping.

Behavioral reasoning systems, especially analytic systems derived from first and second engineering principles and incorporating structural knowledge, can be very robust. The construction of a reasoning system from behavioral knowledge can be difficult, however, due to incomplete information on the operation of a complex system and the difficulty in rigorously mapping from evidence to belief. Uncertainty exists in this mapping, and in the accuracy of the system model. Behavioral reasoning systems might need to incorporated various levels of compiled behavioral information, making the design of a general framework more difficult.

We do not feel that compiled systems by themselves are appropriate for the diagnosis of real time large scale systems because of complexity and inflexibility. However, compiled reasoning levels have been considered for this application to interpret the output from the behavioral reasoning module and to guide the repair process.

As the application of diagnostic reasoning systems to more complex systems becomes possible, it becomes apparent that these reasoning systems will incorporate a preprocessing level combined with multiple levels of diagnostic reasoning: structural, behavioral, and compiled. Each level has specific strengths and weaknesses, and in this research a combination has proven to provide the most intelligent, efficient, flexible, and robust system for diagnosing large scale real-time systems like the TOF Scintillation Array and proposed detectors for the Superconducting Supercollider.

Acknowledgements

The authors would like to thank Dennis Hall, Bill Greiman and Doug Olson from Lawrence Berkeley National Laboratory for their guidance and consultation throughout this research. The authors greatly appreciate the support of the Director, Office of Energy Research, Scientific Computing Staff, of the United States Department of Energy, under Contract Number DE-AC03-76SF00098, and by the National Science Foundation, under grant DMC-8451622.

References

Agogino, A. M., S. Srinivas and K. M. Schneider (1988a),"Multiple Sensor Expert System for Diagnostic Reasoning, Monitoring and Control of Mechanical Systems," Mechanical Systems and Signal Processing, Volume 20, Number 2, pages 165 to 185.

Agogino, A. M., R. Guha and S. Russell (1988b), "Sensor Fusion Using Influence Diagrams and Reasoning by Analogy: Application to Milling Machine Monitoring and Control," AIENG88- Third International Conference on Applications of Artificial Intelligence in Engineering, August 8 - 11, 1988, Stanford CA.

Chandrasekaran, B. and W. F. Punch (1988), "Data Validation During Diagnosis, A Step Beyond Traditional Sensor Validation," Proceedings of the Seventh National Conference on Artificial Intelligence, St. Paul, MN, August 1988, pages 778 - 782.

Chandrasekaran, B. and S. Mittal (1983), "Deep Verses Compiled Knowledge Approaches to Diagnostic Problem Solving," International Journal of Man Machine Studies, Volume 19, Number 5, pages 425 - 436.

Davis, R. (1983), "Reasoning from First Principles in Electronic Troubleshooting," International Journal of Man Machine Studies, Volume 19, Number 5, pages 403 - 423.

Davis, R., et al (1982), "Diagnosis Based on Description of Structure and Function," Proceedings of the First National Conference on Artificial Intelligence, Pittsburgh, PA, July 1982, pages 137 - 142.

Fink, P. K. and J. C. Lusth (1987), "Expert Systems and Diagnostic Expertise in the Mechanical and Electrical Domains," IEEE Transactions on Systems, Man, and Cybernetics, Volume 17, Number 3, pages 340 - 349.

Fink, P. K., J. C. Lusth and J. W. Duran (1985a), "A General Expert System Design for Diagnostic Problem Solving," IEEE Transactions on Pattern Analysis and Machine Intelligence, Volume 7, Number 5, pages 553 - 560.

Fink, P. K. (1985b), "Control and Integration of Diverse Knowledge in a Diagnostic Expert System," Proceedings of the Ninth International Joint Conference on Artificial Intelligence, Los Angeles, CA, August 1985, pages 426 - 431.

Hall, D., et al (1989), "A Fault Location System for a Time of Flight Detector Array," Computer Physics Communications, Volume 57, pages 499 - 502.

Heckerman, D. E.(1986),"Probabilistic Interpretations for MYCIN's Certainty Factors," Uncertainty in Artificial Intelligence, Lemmer, J. and Kanal, L., Editors, North Holland, 1986, pages 9 - 20.

Milne, R. (1987), "Strategies for Diagnosis," IEEE Transactions on Systems, Man, and Cybernetics, Volume 17, Number 3, pages 337 - 339.

Milne, R. (1985), "Fault Diagnosis Through Responsibility," Proceedings of the Ninth International Joint Conference on Artificial Intelligence, Los Angeles, CA, August 1985, pages 423 - 425.

Olson, D., et al (1990), "Experience Using an Automated Fault Location System with a Time of Flight Wall Detector Array," Proceeding of the International Conference on Computing in High Energy Physics, Santa Fe, New Mexico, 1990.

Paasch, R. K., and A. Padgaonkar (1988), "Time of Flight Validation System," Preliminary Report, Lawrence Berkeley Laboratory, Berkeley, CA, September 30, 1988.

Paasch, R. K. (1990), "Management of Uncertainty in Sensor Based Diagnostic Expert Systems," Ph.D. Dissertation, Department of Mechanical Engineering, University of California, Berkeley, February 1990.

Ramamurthy, K., D. Shaver and A. M. Agogino (1990), "Real Time Expert System for Predictive Diagnostics and Control of Drilling Operations," Proceedings of the Sixth IEEE Conference on AI Applications, Santa Barbara, CA, March 5-9, 1990, Volume 1 pages 63 - 68 and Volume 2 (visuals) pages 113 - 117.

Rege, A. and A. M. Agogino (1986), "Sensor Integrated Expert System for Manufacturing and Process Diagnostics," Knowledge Based Systems for Manufacturing, S. C.-Y Lu and R. Komanduri, Editors, ASME, PED, Volume 34, pages 67 - 83.

Scarl, E. A., J. R. Jamieson and C. I. Delaune (1987), "Diagnosis and Sensor Validation Through Knowledge of Structure and Function," IEEE Transactions Systems, Man, and Cybernetics, Volume 17, Number 3, pages 360 - 368.

Scarl, E. A., J. R. Jamieson and C. I. Delaune (1985), "A Fault Detection and Isolation Method Applied to Liquid Oxygen Loading for the Space Shuttle," Proceedings of the Ninth International Joint Conference on Artificial Intelligence, Los Angeles, CA, August 1985, pages 414 - 416.

Integrating Probabilistic Rules into Neural Networks: A Stochastic EM Learning Algorithm

Gerhard Paass*
International Computer Science Institute (ICSI)
1947 Center Street, Berkeley, California 94704
E-mail: paass@icsi.berkeley.edu

Abstract

The EM-algorithm is a general procedure to get maximum likelihood estimates if part of the observations on the variables of a network are missing. In this paper a stochastic version of the algorithm is adapted to probabilistic neural networks describing the associative dependency of variables. These networks have a probability distribution, which is a special case of the distribution generated by probabilistic inference networks. Hence both types of networks can be combined allowing to integrate probabilistic rules as well as unspecified associations in a sound way. The resulting network may have a number of interesting features including cycles of probabilistic rules, hidden 'unobservable' variables, and uncertain and contradictory evidence.

1 INTRODUCTION

Probabilistic inference networks (Pearl 1988) have been used to model uncertain causal relations between variables, for instance in a diagnostic system. They consist of a number of rules each of which describes the probabilistic relation of few, typically two to five, variables. Each rule is assumed to model some sort of 'weak' causal dependency. Taken together these rules define the joint probability distribution of a large set of variables. Here we tacitly assume that according to the maximum entropy principle higher order interactions not affected by the rules are set to zero.

The rules should reflect theoretical or empirical knowledge about the corresponding domain. If, however, this knowledge is not available we may capture the probabilistic information in the data by an associative *neural network* (Anderson & Rosenfeld 1988). Pairs of variables of such a network are connected by weighted 'links' modelling their 'correlation'. Its representational power is based upon additional artificial 'hidden' variables used to approximate higher order interactions. The unkown parameters (weights) of a network are automatically adapted to the data by estimation algorithms. Even complex dependencies can be approximated arbitrarily well if the number of hidden variables is sufficiently large (White 1989; Hertz et al. 1991, p.141ff).

The *Boltzmann machine* (Ackley et al. 1985) is a neural network which modifies its variables according to a joint probability distribution. Together with the probabilistic inference network it forms a structure which is able to represent the probabilistic rules as well as the associative data. An example of such a network describing the relation of discrete economic variables is shown in figure 1. All variables are discrete with the '+' meaning an increase of that quantity. The relation between some variables (Taxes+, Deficit+, Interest+, and Stocks+) is described by probabilistic rules based on theoretical considerations. To describe the relation involving the remaining variables (Taxes+, Employ.+, Product.+, and Stocks+) an associative neural network with hidden variables $H_1, \ldots, H_4$ is assumed, as no specific functional relations are known.

The associative data and the probabilistic rules in general will not be compatible. To arrive at a single joint distribution, we have to find some sort of compromise which is formed according to the relative reliability of the input information. The reliability of the information is described with a measurement distribution. The approach developed in this paper is able to combine conflicting information on probabilities and even may process networks with cycles.

The functional form of maximum entropy distributions of discrete variables subject to constraints has been derived twenty years ago by Darroch and Ratcliff (1972). Paass (1989) proposed the integration of neural networks and probabilistic inference

*On leave from German National Research Institute for Computer Science (GMD), D-5205 St. Augustin; E-mail: paass@gmdzi.gmd.de

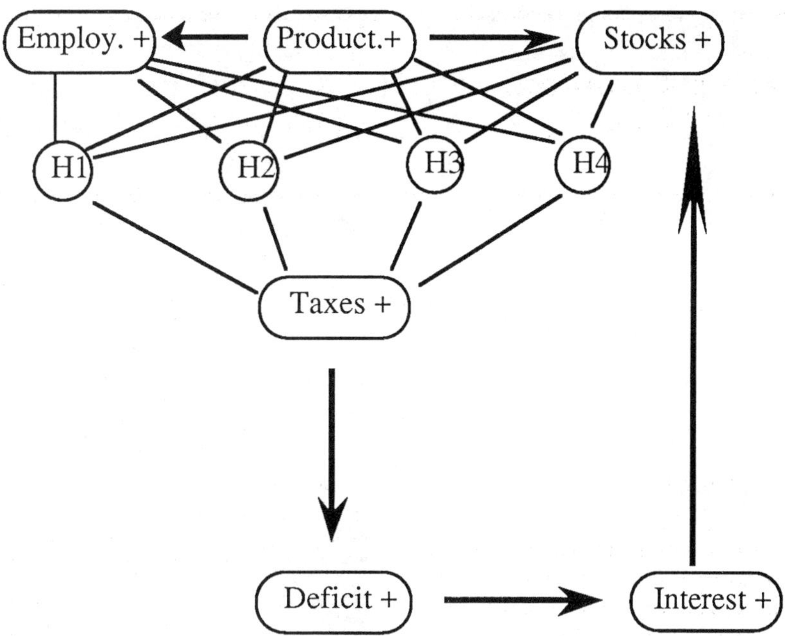

Figure 1: **Combined Network**

networks using a variant of the Boltzmann machine learning algorithm. Recently Hrycej (1990) discussed the relation between Gibbs sampling and probabilistic reasoning. His approach, however, imposes some restrictions, e.g. acyclic network structure, complete knowledge of all conditional probabilities (no truncation), etc, which are not required in this paper.

The next section contains the basic definitions of probabilistic inference networks and the related Boltzmann machine. In section three the maximum likelihood estimation from conflicting evidence is discussed. In section four a stochastic version of the EM-algorithm is used to determine the maximum likelihood estimate. The paper is concluded with a short discussion.

2 PROBABILISTIC NETWORKS

Consider a problem whose relevant features may completely be described in terms of k atomic propositions $A_1, \ldots, A_k$. Corresponding to each A_i, a random variable x_i is defined taking the values 1 if A_i holds and 0 otherwise. The variables are collected in a vector $x := (x_1, \ldots, x_k)$ whose 2^k different values are called 'possible worlds' and form a set $\mathcal{X}$. If $\mathcal{B}$ is the Boolean algebra generated from the A_i, each proposition $B \in \mathcal{B}$ corresponds to the subset of $\mathcal{X}_B \subset \mathcal{X}$ where B holds. To arrive at a simpler notation we write $x \in B$ instead of $x \in \mathcal{X}_B$. The available information on the probability of the propositions is compiled into a joint probability distribution $p : \mathcal{B} \rightarrow [\prime, \infty]$. The probability of some proposition $B \in \mathcal{B}$ is defined as $p(B) := p(\mathcal{X}_B) = \sum_{x \in B} p(x)$.

This setup is used for probabilistic inference networks as well as for associative neural networks. Therefore we can integrate both approaches using the common probability measure $p(x)$. The structure of $p(x)$ is assumed to be known in advance.

Let us first consider a *probabilistic inference network* where the expert's knowledge may be stated in terms of marginal probabilities, e.g. $p(C_r) = q_r$, as well as 'probabilistic rules' which may be interpreted as restrictions on conditional probabilities, e.g. $p(C_r \mid B_r) = q_r$ for propositions $C_r, B_r \in \mathcal{B}$. These restrictions can be reformulated in terms of linear constraints of the form

$$\sum_{x \in \mathcal{X}} b_r(x) p(x) = c_r \qquad r = 1, \ldots, d \tag{1}$$

For marginal probabilities $p(C_r) = q_r$ the term $b_r(x)$ can be defined using the indicator function

$$b_r(x) := [C_r](x) := \begin{cases} 1 & \text{if } x \in C_r \\ 0 & \text{otherwise} \end{cases} \tag{2}$$

and $c_r := p(C_r)$. For conditional probabilities $p(C_r \mid B_r) = q_r$ we set

$$b_r(x) := (1 - q_r)[C_r \wedge B_r](x) - q_r[\neg C_r \wedge B_r](x) \tag{3}$$

and $c_r := 0$. If the constraints are not contradictory[1], there exists a probability distribution $p(x)$, where all of them hold simultaneously.

As in general the number d of constraints is much lower than the number of all 2^k elementary probabilities $p(x)$, there is a large set $\mathcal{P}$ of different probability distributions, which simultaneously satisfy all constraints. Similar to (Cheeseman 1983) we select the distribution from $\mathcal{P}$ which *maximizes the*

[1] Later we are considering inconsistent constraints.

entropy $H(p) = -\sum_{x \in \mathcal{X}} p(x) \log p(x)$ subject to the equality constraints (1), as for this distribution lowest 'interactions' between the variables result. It is unique and has the functional form (Darroch & Ratcliff 1972)

$$p(x) = Z^{-1} \exp\left(\sum_{r=1}^{d} \lambda_r b_r(x)\right) \tag{4}$$

with a multiplicative constant

$$Z := \sum_{x \in \mathcal{X}} \exp\left(\sum_{r=1}^{d} \lambda_r b_r(x)\right)$$

which restricts the sum of probabilities to 1. The parameters λ_r have to be determined in such a way that the constraints (1) hold.

If the parameters λ_r are known, the equation (4) may be used to simulate the distribution $p(x)$ by successively generating new values for the variables exploiting

$$\begin{aligned} & p(x_i{=}1 \mid \bar{x}_i) \qquad (5) \\ &= \frac{1}{1 + p(\bar{x}_{i0})/p(\bar{x}_{i1})} \\ &= \frac{1}{1 + \exp\left(\sum_{r=1}^{d} \lambda_r \left[b_r(\bar{x}_{i0}) - b_r(\bar{x}_{i1})\right]\right)} \end{aligned}$$

where $\bar{x}_i := (x_1, \ldots, x_{i-1}, x_{i+1}, \ldots, x_k)$ and $\bar{x}_{i1} := (x_1, \ldots, x_{i-1}, 1, x_{i+1}, \ldots, x_k)$. The terms $b_r(\bar{x}_{i1})$ and $b_r(\bar{x}_{i0})$ depend only on variables which are involved in restriction r and there difference is zero if x_i is not involved in that restriction. Then (5) shows that $p(x_i{=}1 \mid \bar{x}_i)$ is only dependent on the vector of varibles different from x_i, which simultaneously with x_i are involved in some constraint (1). Such a structure is called a Markov random field (Kindermann & Snell 1980) and corresponds to a a *nearest neighbor Gibbs potential* (Paass 1989; Hrycej 1990). To generate values according to this distribution we may start with an arbitrary vector x, select components x_i at random, and alter their values according to (5). The sequence of vectors evolving from this procedure will have the desired distribution.

The *Boltzmann machine* (Ackley et al. 1985) is a probabilistic *neural network* where some pairs of variables x_{i_r}, x_{j_r}, $r = 1, \ldots, d$, are connected by links with weights $\lambda_r \in \Re$ indicating the mutual dependency or 'correlation' of x_{i_r} and x_{j_r}. Note that $\lambda_r = 0$ if there is no direct dependency. Using

$$b_r(x) := [A_{i_r} \wedge A_{j_r}](x) \tag{6}$$

the probability of a possible world x is defined by (4) (Aarts & Korst 1988, p.207). Hence the Boltzmann machine generates a distribution that has the same form as the maximum entropy distribution subject to the restriction of $p(A_{i_r} \wedge A_{j_r})$, $r = 1, \ldots, d$, to some value. Therefore uncertain reasoning in probabilistic inference networks as well as 'associative reasoning' in neural networks may be combined within one framework. In a neural network some of the variables are *hidden units*, for whom there are no observations available. These hidden units have no simple symbolic interpretation. They are, however, capable to represent arbitrary probabilistic relations, whereas networks without hidden units may only represent linear dependencies. The representational capabilities of neural networks are discussed by Hertz et al. (1991, p.141ff).

3 MAXIMUM LIKELIHOOD ESTIMATION

The structure of the network has to be fixed in advance. Accordingly we have to determine which variables directly interact – as indicated in the example in figure 1. In addition we know the functional form (4) of the probabilities except for the numerical parameters. For each probabilistic inference rule there is a $b_r(x)$-term according to (1), while each bivariate link in an associative 'neural network' substructure corresponds to an appropriate $b_r(x)$-term according to (6).

The probability values assigned to rules and especially the associative data may be subject to some error and in general are contradictory. Therefore these data items, denoted by $\tilde{q}_r$, are *assumed* to originate from independent random samples S_r with n_r elements generated according to the true distribution. If $\tilde{q}_r$ corresponds to the probability of some proposition $p(C_r)$ then we do not know the values for all variables x_i, but we only know whether C_r holds or not. The fraction of records where C_r holds is just our observed probability $\tilde{q}_r$. Hence we have a *missing data* situation. We get the binomial distribution $P(\tilde{q}_r \mid q_{r,\lambda})$ as the 'sampling distribution' describing the deviation of the observed probability $\tilde{q}_r$ from the theoretical value $p(C_r)$. This deviation gets smaller with increasing sample size n_r. As our samples are imaginary[2] we can select n_r in such a way that, for instance, the true probability $p(C_r)$ is contained in a given interval $[a, b]$ with a probability of, say, 0.9.

If $\tilde{q}_r$ corresponds to a probabilistic rule $p(C_r \mid B_r)$, the sample S_r is generated in a twostep procedure. First a sample $\breve{S}_r$ of size N_r is selected from the complete distribution. Then all sample elements where B_r does *not* hold are removed. For each element of the remaining sample S_r of size n_r it is only reported whether C_r holds or not. As part of the population is ignored, S_r is called a *truncated sample*. The deviation between $\tilde{q}_r$ and $p(C_r \mid B_r)$ again is described by a binomial distribution where

[2] In the case that real samples are available, eg. from a statistical survey or a measurement device, we may use them instead.

n_r can be selected to reflect the reliability of the value.

Data on the associative relation between variables also can be understood as an independent sample S_r of size n_r covering a subvector y of visible variables. This time the sample is assumed to stem from real observations of the system in question. There is no special constraint related to S_r as the stochastic relation between the y-variables are communicated by hidden variables not contained in y. To illustrate the situation consider the following example. Assume we have $k = 5$ variables $x_1, \ldots, x_5$ and three pieces of information:

S_1: a sample with $n_1 = 20$ elements on the marginal probability $p(C_1)$ with $C_1 = \{x \mid x_1{=}1\}$ and an observed relative frequency $\tilde{q}_1 = 0.8$.

S_2: a sample with $n_2 = 10$ elements on the conditional probability $p(C_2 \mid B_2)$ with $C_2 = \{x \mid x_4{=}1\}$ and $B_2 = \{x \mid x_1{=}1 \wedge x_2{=}1\}$ and an observed relative frequency $\tilde{q}_2 = 0.3$.

S_3: a sample with $n_3 = 10$ elements on the stochastic relation between the variables $y = (x_2, x_3, x_4)$. To communicate this relation we have symmetric bivariate links between the hidden variable x_5 and the visible variables x_2, x_3, x_4.

We must relate these samples to the joint distribution. While S_1 and S_3 are assumed to cover the joint distribution, the sample S_2 is truncated to the subset where B_2 is valid. Therefore we use the 'extended' sample $\breve{S}^2$ which contains also elements where $\neg B_2$ holds. However, the number $\bar{n}_2$ of these records is unknown. Indicating missing data items by '?' table 1 shows the resulting records in the samples. In the sample $\breve{S}^2$ we even do not know the sample size $N_2 := n_2 + \bar{n}_2$, as part of the records are missing. We may pool together all these samples to a comprehensive sample S which in turn may be as a random sample from our distribution. In our example it is defined as $S := (S_1, \breve{S}^2, S_3)$. Note that there may exist several samples corresponding to different associative sub-networks. Similar to the conditional probabilities of rules these samples may be truncated, i.e. cover specific situations only.

Assuming that all information about the parameters of the distribution is contained in S and that all samples have been obtained independently, we may use the maximum likelihood approach (cf. Paass 1988) to determine the optimal parameter $\hat{\lambda}$ as the solution of

$$\prod_r P(\tilde{q}_r \mid q_{r,\hat{\lambda}}) = \max_{\lambda} \prod_r P(\tilde{q}_r \mid q_{r,\lambda}) \qquad (7)$$

In (Paass 1989) the derivatives of this likelihood function with respect to the parameters λ_r are calculated. Starting with some parameter values we subsequently may use gradient techniques to determine the maximum. The resulting 'generalized Boltzmann machine learning algorithm' has the characteristic that for the current λ-values specific probabilities have to be estimated by stochastic simulation using (5). In addition a non-linear equation system has to be solved for each iteration if cycles are present in the network which involve probabilistic rules.

The Boltzmann machine is very computation intensive. Nevertheless in the area of associative networks they are found to capture the underlying statistical relations in a very effective way. In a detailed comparison on a statistical decision task, Kohonen et al. (1988) found that the Boltzmann machine achieved considerably better accuracy than a backpropagation network. The choice of various process parameters is an active research field (Hertz et al. 1991, p.168ff).

4 THE STOCHASTIC EM-ALGORITHM

As an alternative we consider a sample-based procedure to determine the parameters of $p(x)$. In essence we reconstructs the missing items of the pooled sample $S =: (x_{(1)}, \ldots, x_{(n)})$ described above, whose elements are denoted by $x_{(j)}$. This is just the approach of the stochastic EM-algorithm (Celeux & Diebolt 1988), which is a random version of a general procedure for handling missing data in maximum likelihood problems (Dempster et al. 1977). This algorithm starts with some arbitrary[3] parameter vector $\hat{\lambda}$ and iterates the following steps:

E-step:
Assume $x_{(j)} = (y_{(j)}, z_{(j)})$ is an arbitrary record of the comprehensive sample S and let $y_{(j)}$ be the vector of actually observed values. Then for each $y_{(j)}$ the value of $z_{(j)}$ is randomly generated according to the conditional distribution $p_{\hat{\lambda}}(z_{(j)} \mid y_{(j)})$ given the values $y_{(j)}$ and the current parameter $\hat{\lambda}$. In the case of truncated samples $\breve{S}_i$ the expected value of the sample size $\bar{n}_i$ of the truncated portion is estimated. Hence all missing data items are replaced by imputed values.

M-step:
In this step a maximum likelihood estimation of the parameters λ is performed using the imputed values as if they were actually observed. With the new $\hat{\lambda}$ the E-step is performed again.

The procedure stops if the parameter vector $\hat{\lambda}$ reaches a stationary point. In some sense the sam-

[3]The starting parameters should be different from saddlepoints, as the procedure stops there. For associative data this means that the hidden variables should be dependent on the visible variables, i.e $\lambda_r \neq 0$.

Table 1: **Evidence in the Form of Samples with Missing Values**

Sample	Sample Size	No. of Records	x_1	x_2	x_3	x_4	x_5
S_1	$n_1 = 20$						
		4	0	?	?	?	?
		16	1	?	?	?	?
$\check{S}^2$	$N_2 = 10 + \bar{n}_2$						
		?	0	0	?	?	?
		?	0	1	?	?	?
		?	1	0	?	?	?
		7	1	1	?	0	?
		3	1	1	?	1	?
S_3	$n_3 = 10$						
		1	?	0	0	0	?
		2	?	1	0	0	?
		2	?	1	0	1	?
		4	?	1	1	0	?
		1	?	1	1	1	?

ple S can be understood as a parametrization of the complete distribution. By the law of large numbers the approximation of the distribution gets better if the sample size n is increased, for instance by duplicating each record in S sufficiently often. For $n \to \infty$ the distribution can be represented arbitrarily well.

It has been shown (Celeux & Diebolt 1988) that for $n \to \infty$ under rather general conditions the parameter $\hat{\lambda}$ estimated by the stochastic EM algorithm corresponds to a local minimum of the likelihood function. Empirical evidence shows that the stochastic imputation step allows the algorithm to escape from local minima. The convergence properties of the usual EM-algorithm are discussed by Wu (1983).

To perform the stochastic *E-step* we first have to estimate the weights of trunctated records in truncated samples. These weights simply are selected as the empirical fractions of records with the corresponding values in the current complete sample S. This gives the new sample sizes N_i of the truncated samples. Then we may use (5) together with (4) to generate new values stochastically according to the current value of $\hat{\lambda}$. For each $x_{\langle j \rangle}$ we start with the present values and randomly select a component of $z_{\langle j \rangle}$. Its value is randomly determined using (5). After a number of such modifications $z_{\langle j \rangle}$ fluctuates according to the distribution $p(z_{\langle j \rangle} \mid y_{\langle j \rangle})$. The adaption to the new distribution will be particularly fast as the existing values are used as starting states and the difference between the conditional distributions usually will be small.

For the *M-step* we know that for each variable x_i the conditional probabilities $p(x_i \mid \bar{x}_i)$ should follow the relations (5) and (4). From the binomial distribution we get the log-likelihood function

$$L_i = \sum_{j=1}^{n} L_{ij} \tag{8}$$

$$= \sum_{j=1}^{n} \sum_{m=0}^{1} \tilde{p}(x_{i\langle j \rangle}=m \mid \bar{x}_{i\langle j \rangle}) * \log p(x_{i\langle j \rangle}=m \mid \bar{x}_{i\langle j \rangle})$$

where $\tilde{p}(x_{i\langle j \rangle}=1 \mid \bar{x}_{i\langle j \rangle})$ is the observed probability in record $x_{\langle j \rangle}$, i.e. has the value 0 or 1. The derivative of L_i with respect to λ_r is, using (5), given by

$$\frac{\partial L_{ij}}{\partial \lambda_r} = \left[\frac{\tilde{p}(x_i=1 \mid \bar{x}_i)}{p(x_i=1 \mid \bar{x}_i)} - \frac{1-\tilde{p}(x_i=1 \mid \bar{x}_i)}{1-p(x_i=1 \mid \bar{x}_i)}\right] * \frac{\partial p(x_i=1 \mid \bar{x}_i)}{\partial \lambda_r}$$

We have omitted the index $\langle j \rangle$ for simplicity. Defining $\bar{x}_{i1} := (x_i=1, \bar{x}_i)$ and $R_i := p(x_i=0, \bar{x}_i)/p(x_i=1, \bar{x}_i)$ we find from (5)

$$\frac{\partial p(x_i=1 \mid \bar{x}_i)}{\partial \lambda_r} = \frac{-\frac{\partial R_i}{\partial \lambda_r}}{(1+R_i)^2} \tag{9}$$

As $R_i = \exp\left(\sum_{s=1}^{d} \lambda_s [b_r(\bar{x}_{i0}) - b_r(\bar{x}_{i0})]\right)$ we get

$$\frac{\partial R_i}{\partial \lambda_r} = R_i[b_r(\bar{x}_{i0}) - b_r(\bar{x}_{i0})]$$

Note that R_i can be determined from (5) and (4) using the current parameters λ_s. According to the Hammersley-Clifford theorem (Besag 1974) the distribution $p(x)$ is completely determined if we know the conditional distributions $p(x_i \mid \bar{x}_i)$, $i = 1, \ldots, k$. Hence the estimation of the conditional distributions from our sample completely determines the unkown parameters λ. We evaluate $\frac{\partial L_i}{\partial \lambda_r}$ for each x_i and modify the current values of λ_r according to $\sum_{i=1}^{k} \frac{\partial L_i}{\partial \lambda_r}$. The maximumum likelihood estimates are developed under the assumption that we have for each x_i an independent version of the synthetic sample S. This can be generated by stochastic simulation. However, preliminary experience shows that we may use a single sample for all variables.

An alternative approach uses (4) to express the log-likelihood of the pooled sample S

$$\begin{aligned} \log p(S) &= \sum_{j=1}^{n} \log p(x_{(j)}) \qquad (10) \\ &= \sum_{j=1}^{n} \left(\sum_{s=1}^{d} \lambda_s b_s(x_{(j)}) \right) - \log(Z) \end{aligned}$$

We get the derivatives

$$\frac{\partial \log p(x_{(j)})}{\partial \lambda_r} = b_r(x_{(j)}) - \frac{\partial \log(Z)}{\partial \lambda_r} \qquad (11)$$

$$\begin{aligned} \frac{\partial \log Z}{\partial \lambda_r} &= \frac{1}{Z} \sum_{x \in \mathcal{X}} \exp\left(\sum_{s=1}^{d} \lambda_s b_s(x) \right) b_r(x) \\ &= \sum_{x \in \mathcal{X}} \frac{\exp\left(\sum_{s=1}^{d} \lambda_s b_s(x) \right)}{Z} b_r(x) \\ &= \sum_{x \in \mathcal{X}} p_\lambda(x) b_r(x) \\ &= E_\lambda(b_r) \end{aligned}$$

which is just the expected value of $b_r(x)$ for the current λ. Hence the derivative with respect to λ_r

$$\frac{\partial \log p(S)}{\partial \lambda_r} = \sum_{j=1}^{n} \left[b_r(x_{(j)}) - E_\lambda(b_r) \right] \qquad (12)$$

is just the sum of differences between the mean value of b_r for the distribution with parameter λ and the actual values of $b_r(x_{(j)})$ for the elements of the sample. This is a simplified version of the Boltzmann machine learning algorithm.

5 DISCUSSION

Similar to the Boltzmann machine the stochastic EM-algorithm involves a stochastic simulation of the variables. As only missing data items have to be imputed we have a 'clamped' simulation where the values of variables are used if they are known. In contrast to (Paass 1989) it is not necessary to solve a nonlinear equation system for each iteration. Currently empirical investigations are carried out to determine the relative computational efficiency of the stochastic EM-approach.

The algorithm developed in this paper may be used to incorporate probabilistic rules in a 'soft' way. We may start with a neural network containing only bivariate links (6) and introduce probabilistic rules into a joint sample simply as data as shown in table 1. After the learning algorithm has adapted to the data it should be able reproduce the rules in an approximate way. But the network is only an approximation to the maximum entropy distribution (4) which results if the probabilistic rules are 'hardwired' into the network. The conditional independence assumptions implied by the structure of the rule network may be invalid to some degree. There is more research needed to judge the effect of such errors. The EM-algorithm allows to compare the 'soft' with the 'hardwired' approach in a unified way.

Acknowledgements

This work was supported in part by the German Federal Department of Research and Technology, grant ITW8900A7.

References

Aarts, E., Korst, J. (1988). *Simulated Annealing and Boltzmann Machines.* Wiley, Chichester

Ackley, D., Hinton, G.E., Sejnowski, T.J. (1985). A Learning Algorithm for the Boltzmann machine. *Cognitive Science,* Vol.9 pp.147-169

Anderson, J.A., Rosenfeld, E. (1988). *Neurocomputing: Foundations of Research.* MIT Press, Cambridge, Ma.

Besag, J. (1974). Spatial Interaction and Statistical Analysis of Lattice Systems. *Journal of The Royal Statistical Society,* Series B., p.192-236

Celeux, G., Diebolt, J. (1988). *A Random Imputation Principle: The Stochastic EM Algorithm.* Tech. Rep. No.901, INRIA, 78153 Le Chesnay, France

Cheeseman, P. (1983). A Method of Computing Generalized Bayesian Probability Values for Expert Systems. Proc. *IJCAI'83.* Kaufmann, Los Altos, California.

Darroch, J.N., Ratcliff, D. (1972). Generalized Iterative Scaling for Log-Linear Models. *The Annals of Mathematical Statistics,* Vol.43, p.1470-1480

Dempster, A.P., Laird, N.M., Rubin, D.B. (1977). Maximum Likelihood from Incomplete Data via the EM algorithm (with discussion). *Journal of the Royal Statistical Society,* Vol.B-39, p.1-38

Hrycej, T. (1990). Gibbs Sampling in Bayesian Networks. *Artificial Intelligence.* Vol. 46, p.351-363

Hertz, J., Krogh, A., Palmer, R.G. (1991). *Introduction to the Theory of Neural Computation.* Addison Wesley, Redwood City.

Kindermann, R., Snell, J.L. (1980). *Markov Random Fields and their Applications.* American Math. Society, Providence, R.I.

Kohonen, Barna, G., Chrisley, R. (1988). Statistical Pattern Recognition with Neural Networks: Benchmarking Studies. In proc. *IEEE International Conference on Neural Networks* (San Diego 1988), vol. I, p. 61-68. New York: IEEE.

Paass, G. (1988). Probabilistic Logic. In: Smets, P., A. Mamdani, D.Dubois, H.Prade (eds.) *Non-Standard Logics for Automated Reasoning*, Academic Press, London, p.213-252

Paass, G. (1989). Structured Probabilistic Neural Networks. Proc. *Neuro-Nimes '89* p.345-359

Pearl, J. (1988). *Probabilistic Reasoning in Intelligent Systems,* Morgan Kaufmann, San Mateo, Cal.

White, H. (1989). Some Asymptotic Results for Learning in Single Layer Feedforward Network Models. *J. American Statistical Association.* Vol.84, p.1003-1013.

Wu, C.F. (1983). On the Convergence Properties of the EM algorithm. *Annals of Statistics.* Vol.11, p.95-103.

Representing Bayesian Networks within Probabilistic Horn Abduction

David Poole
Department of Computer Science,
University of British Columbia,
Vancouver, B.C., Canada V6T 1W5
poole@cs.ubc.ca

Abstract

This paper presents a simple framework for Horn-clause abduction, with probabilities associated with hypotheses. It is shown how this representation can represent any probabilistic knowledge representable in a Bayesian belief network. The main contributions are in finding a relationship between logical and probabilistic notions of evidential reasoning. This can be used as a basis for a new way to implement Bayesian Networks that allows for approximations to the value of the posterior probabilities, and also points to a way that Bayesian networks can be extended beyond a propositional language.

1 Introduction

In this paper we pursue the idea of having a logical language that allows for a pool of possible hypotheses [Poole *et al.*, 1987; Poole, 1988], with probabilities associated with the hypotheses [Neufeld and Poole, 1987]. We choose a very simple logical language with a number of assumptions on the structure of the knowledge base and independence amongst hypotheses. This is intended to reflect a compromise between simplicity to implement and representational adequacy. To show that these assumptions are not unreasonable, and to demonstrate representational adequacy, we show how arbitrary Bayesian networks can be represented by the formalism. The main contributions of this embedding are:

- It shows a relationship between logical and probabilistic notions of evidential reasoning. In particular it provides some evidence for the use of abduction and assumption-based reasoning as the logical analogue of the independence of Bayesian Networks. In earlier work [Poole, 1989; Poole, 1990] a form of assumption-based reasoning where we abduce to causes and then makes assumptions in order to predict what should follow is developed; it is a similar mechanism that is used here to characterise Bayesian networks.
- It gives a different way to implement Bayesian networks[1]. The main advantage of this implementation is that it gives a way to approximate the probability with a known error bound.
- Because the underlying language is not propositional, it gives us a way to extend Bayesian networks to a richer language. This corresponds to a form of dynamic construction of Bayesian networks [Horsch and Poole, 1990].

In [Poole, 1991], it is argued that the probabilistic Horn abduction framework provides a good compromise between representational and heuristic adequacy for diagnostic tasks. It showed how the use of variables can be used to extend the purely propositional diagnostic frameworks, and how the use of probabilities can be naturally used to advantage in logical approaches to diagnosis.

2 Probabilistic Horn Abduction

2.1 Horn clause abduction

The formulation of abduction used is a simplified form of Theorist [Poole *et al.*, 1987; Poole, 1988]. It is simplified in being restricted to Horn clauses.

Although the idea [Neufeld and Poole, 1987] is not restricted to Horn clauses (we could extend it to disjunction and classical negation [Poole *et al.*, 1987] or to negation as failure [Eshghi and Kowalski, 1989]), in order to empirically test the framework, it is important to find where the simplest representations fail. It may be the case that we need the extra representational power of more general logics; we can only demonstrate this by doing without the extra representational power.

We use the normal Prolog definition of an atomic sym-

[1] For composite beliefs this is closely related to the algorithm of Shimony and Charniak [1990], but also is developed for finding posterior probabilities of hypotheses (section 3.2)

bol [Lloyd, 1987]. A Horn clause is of the form:

$$\begin{array}{rl} a. & \\ a & \leftarrow a_1 \wedge ... \wedge a_n. \\ \mathit{false} & \leftarrow a_1 \wedge ... \wedge a_n. \end{array}$$

where a and each a_i are atomic symbols. *false* is a special atomic symbol that is not true in any interpretation[2].

An abductive scheme is a pair $\langle F, H\rangle$ where

F is a set of Horn clauses. Variables in F are implicitly universally quantified.

H is a set of atoms, called the "assumables" or the "possible hypotheses". Associated with each assumable is a prior probability.

Here (and in our implementation) we write

$$assumable(h,p).$$

where h is a (possibly open) atom, and p is a number $0 \leq p \leq 1$ to mean that for every ground instance $h\theta$ of h, $h\theta \in H$ and $P(h\theta) = p$.

Definition 2.1 [Poole *et al.*, 1987; Poole, 1988] If g is a ground formula, an **explanation** of g from $\langle F, H\rangle$ is a subset D of H such that

- $F \cup D \models g$ and
- $F \cup D \not\models \mathit{false}$.

The first condition says that, D is a sufficient cause for *obs*, and the second says that D is possible (i.e., $F \cup D$ is consistent).

A **minimal explanation** of g is an explanation of g such that no strict subset is an explanation of g.

2.2 Probabilities

Associated with each possible hypothesis is a prior probability. The aim is to compute the posterior probability of the minimal explanations given the observations. Abduction gives us what we want to compute the probability of and probability theory gives a measure over the explanations [Neufeld and Poole, 1987].

To compute the posterior probability of an explanation $D = \{h_1, ..., h_n\}$ of observation *obs* given observation *obs*, we use Bayes rule and the fact that $P(obs|D) = 1$ as the explanation logically implies the observation:

$$\begin{aligned} P(D|obs) &= \frac{P(obs|D) \times P(D)}{P(obs)} \\ &= \frac{P(D)}{P(obs)} \end{aligned}$$

The value, $P(obs)$ is the prior probability of the observation, and is a constant factor for all explanations. We compute the prior probability of the conjunction of the hypotheses using:

$$\begin{aligned} P(h_1 \wedge ... \wedge h_{n-1} \wedge h_n) &= P(h_n|h_1 \wedge ... \wedge h_{n-1}) \\ &\quad \times P(h_1 \wedge ... \wedge h_{n-1}) \end{aligned}$$

The value of $P(h_1 \wedge ... \wedge h_{n-1})$ forms a recursive call, with $P(true) = 1$. The only other thing that we need to compute is

$$P(h_n|h_1 \wedge ... \wedge h_{n-1})$$

If h_n is inconsistent with the other hypotheses, then the above conditional probability is zero. These are the cases that are removed by the inconsistency requirement. If h_n is implied by the other hypotheses, the probability should be one. This case never arises for minimal explanations.

While any method can be used to compute this conditional probability, we assume that the logical dependencies impose the only statistical dependencies on the hypotheses.

Assumption 2.2 *Logically independent instances of hypotheses are probabilistically independent.*

Definition 2.3 A set D of hypotheses are **logically independent** (given F) if there is no $S \subset D$ and $h \in D \backslash S$ such that

$$F \cup S \models h \quad \text{or} \quad F \cup S \models \neg h$$

The assumptions in a minimal explanation are always logically independent.

Under assumption 2.2, if $\{h_1, ..., h_n\}$ are part of a minimal explanation, then

$$P(h_n|h_1 \wedge ... \wedge h_{n-1}) = P(h_n)$$

thus

$$P(h_1 \wedge ... \wedge h_n) = \prod_{1=1}^{n} P(h_i)$$

To compute the prior of the minimal explanation we multiply the priors of the hypotheses. The posterior probability of the explanation is proportional to this.

The justification for the reasonableness (and universality) of this assumption is based on Reichenbach's *principle of the common cause*:

[2] Notice that we are using Horn clauses differently from how Prolog uses Horn clauses. In Prolog, the database consists of definite clauses, and the queries provide the negative clauses [Lloyd, 1987]. Here the database consists of definite and negative clauses, and we build a constructive proof of an observation.

> "If coincidences of two events A and B occur more frequently than their independent occurrence, ... then there exists a common cause for these events ..." [Reichenbach, 1956, p. 163].

When there is a dependency amongst hypotheses, we invent a new hypothesis to explain that dependence. Thus the assumption of independence, while it gives a restriction on the knowledge bases that are legal, really gives no restriction on the domains that can be represented.

2.3 Relations between explanations

The remaining problem in the probabilistic analysis is in determining the value of $P(obs)$.

When using abduction we often assume that the diagnoses are covering. This can be a valid assumption if we have anticipated all eventualities, and the observations are within the domain of the expected observations (usually if this assumption is violated there are no explanations). This is also supported by recent attempts at a completion semantics for abduction [Poole, 1988; Console *et al.*, 1989; Konolige, 1991]. The results show how abduction can be considered as deduction on the "closure" of the knowledge base that includes statements that the given causes are the only causes. The closure implies the observation are logically equivalent to the disjunct of its explanations. We make this assumption explicit here:

Assumption 2.4 *The diagnoses are covering.*

For the probabilistic calculation we make an additional assumption:

Assumption 2.5 *The diagnoses are disjoint (mutually exclusive).*

It turns out to be straight forward to ensure that these properties hold, for observations that we can anticipate[3]. We make sure that the rules for each possible subgoal are disjoint and covering. This can be done locally for each atom that may be part of an observation or used to explain an observation.

When building the knowledge base, we use the local property that the rules for a subgoal are exclusive and covering to ensure that the explanations generated are exclusive and covering.

Under these assumptions, if $\{e_1, ..., e_n\}$ is the set of all explanations of g:

$$\begin{aligned} P(g) &= P(e_1 \vee e_2 \vee ... \vee e_n) \\ &= P(e_1) + P(e_2) + ... + P(e_n) \end{aligned}$$

[3]Like other systems (e.g., [Pearl, 1988b]), we have to assume that unanticipated observations are irrelevant.

3 Representing Bayesian networks

In this section we give the relationship between Bayesian networks and our probabilistic Horn abduction. We show how any probabilistic knowledge that can be represented in a Bayesian network, can be represented in our formalism.

Suppose we have a Bayesian network with random variables $a_1, ..., a_n$, such that random variable a_i can have values $v_{i,1}, ..., v_{i,n_i}$. We represent random variable a_i having value $v_{i,j}$ as the proposition $a_i(v_{i,j})$.

The first thing we need to do is to state that the values of variables are mutually exclusive. For each i and for each j, k such that $j \neq k$, we have the rule

$$\mathit{false} \leftarrow a_i(v_{i,j}) \wedge a_i(v_{i,k})$$

A *Bayesian network* [Pearl, 1988b] is a directed acyclic network where the nodes represent random variables, and the arcs represent a directly influencing relation. An arc from variable b to variable a represents the fact that variable b *directly influences* variable a; the relation *influences* is the transitive closure of the directly influences relation. *Terminal nodes* of a Bayesian network are those variables that do not influence any other variables. The *depth* of a node is the length of the longest (directed) path leading into the node. A *composite belief* [Pearl, 1987] is an assignment of a value to every random variable.

Suppose variable a is directly influenced by variables $\Pi_a = b_1, ..., b_m$ (the "parents" of a) in a Bayesian network. The independence assumption embedded in a Bayesian Network [Pearl, 1988b] is given by

$$P(a|\Pi_a \wedge v) = P(a|\Pi_a)$$

where v is a variable (or conjunction of variables) such that a does not influence v (or any conjunct in v).

The network is represented by a rule that relates a variable with its parents:

$$a(V) \leftarrow b_1(V_1) \wedge ... \wedge b_m(V_m) \wedge c\_a(V, V_1, ..., V_m)$$

The intended interpretation of $c\_a(V, V_1, ..., V_m)$ is that a has value V because b_1 has value V_1,..., and b_m has value V_m.

Associated with the Bayesian network is a contingency table which gives the marginal probabilities of the values of a depending on the values of $b_1, ..., b_m$. This will consist of probabilities of the form

$$P(a = v|b_1 = v_1, ..., b_m = v_m) = p$$

This is translated into the assertion

$$\mathit{assumable}(c\_a(v, v_1, v_2, ..., v_m), p).$$

Nodes with no parents can be just made assumable, with the appropriate probabilities (rather than inventing a new hypothesis and the above procedure would prescribe).

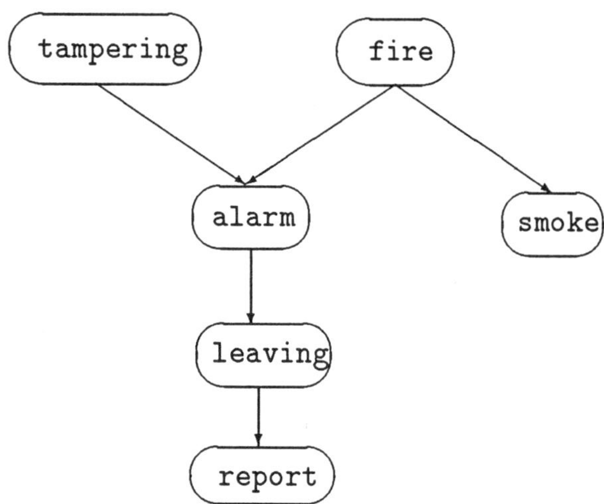

Figure 1: An influence diagram for a smoking alarm.

Example 3.1 Consider a representation of the influence diagram of figure 3.1, with the following conditional probability distributions:

$$\begin{aligned} p(fire) &= 0.01 \\ p(smoke|fire) &= 0.9 \\ p(smoke|\neg fire) &= 0.01 \\ p(tampering) &= 0.02 \\ p(alarm|fire \land tampering) &= 0.5 \\ p(alarm|fire \land \neg tampering) &= 0.99 \\ p(alarm|\neg fire \land tampering) &= 0.85 \\ p(alarm|\neg fire \land \neg tampering) &= 0.0001 \\ p(leaving|alarm) &= 0.88 \\ p(leaving|\neg alarm) &= 0.001 \\ p(\text{report}|leaving) &= 0.75 \\ p(\text{report}|\neg leaving) &= 0.01 \end{aligned}$$

The following is a representation of this Bayesian network in out formalism.

```
assumable( fire(yes), 0.01 ).
assumable( fire(no), 0.99 ).

false <- fire(yes), fire(no).

smoke(Sm) <- fire(Fi),
             c_smoke(Sm,Fi).
false <- smoke(yes),
         smoke(no).

assumable( c_smoke(yes,yes), 0.9 ).
assumable( c_smoke(no,yes), 0.1 ).
assumable( c_smoke(yes,no), 0.01 ).
assumable( c_smoke(no,no), 0.99 ).

assumable( tampering(yes), 0.02 ).
assumable( tampering(no), 0.98 ).

alarm(Al) <- fire(Fi), tampering(Ta),
             c_alarm(Al,Fi,Ta).
false <- alarm(yes),
         alarm(no).

assumable( c_alarm(yes,yes,yes), 0.50 ).
assumable( c_alarm(no,yes,yes),  0.50 ).
assumable( c_alarm(yes,yes,no), 0.99 ).
assumable( c_alarm(no,yes,no),  0.01 ).
assumable( c_alarm(yes,no,yes), 0.85 ).
assumable( c_alarm(no,no,yes),  0.15 ).
assumable( c_alarm(yes,no,no), 0.0001 ).
assumable( c_alarm(no,no,no),  0.9999 ).

leaving(Le) <- alarm(Al),
               c_leaving(Le,Al).
false <- leaving(yes),
         leaving(no).

assumable( c_leaving(yes,yes), 0.88 ).
assumable( c_leaving(no,yes), 0.12 ).
assumable( c_leaving(yes,no), 0.001 ).
assumable( c_leaving(no,no), 0.999 ).

report(Le) <- leaving(Al),
              c_report(Le,Al).
false <- report(yes),
         report(no).

assumable( c_report(yes,yes), 0.75 ).
assumable( c_report(no,yes), 0.25 ).
assumable( c_report(yes,no), 0.01 ).
assumable( c_report(no,no), 0.99 ).
```

3.1 Composite Beliefs

A composite belief [Pearl, 1987] is an assignment of a value to every random variable. The composite belief with the highest probability has also been called a MAP assignment [Charniak and Shimony, 1990]. These composite beliefs have been most used for diagnosis [de Kleer and Williams, 1987; de Kleer and Williams, 1989; Peng and Reggia, 1990] (see [Poole and Provan, 1990] for a discussion on the appropriateness of this).

Lemma 3.2 *The minimal explanations of the terminal variables having particular values correspond to the composite beliefs in the Bayesian network with the terminals having those values. The priors for the explanations and the composite beliefs are identical.*

The proof of this lemma and for lemma 3.4 appears in appendix A.

As the same procedure can be used to get from the priors of composite hypotheses and explanations to the posteriors given some observations, the following theorem is a direct corollary of lemma 3.2.

Theorem 3.3 *If the observed variables include all terminal variables, the composite beliefs with the observed variables having particular values correspond exactly to the explanations of the observations, and with the same posterior probability.*

If the observed variables do not include all terminal values, we need to decide what it is that we want the probability of [Poole and Provan, 1990]. If we want to commit to the value of all variables, we consider the set of possible observations that include assigning values to terminal nodes. That is, if o was our observation that did not not include observing a value for variables $\overline{a}$, then we need to consider the observations $o \wedge \overline{a}(\overline{v})$, for each tuple $\overline{v}$ of values of variables $\overline{a}$. To find the accurate probabilities we need to normalise over the sum of all of the explanations. Whether or not we want to do this is debatable.

3.2 Posterior Probabilities of Propositions

In the previous section, the observations to be explained corresponded exactly to the conditioning variables. This corresponds to the use of "abduction" in [Poole, 1989]. In this section we show a relationship to the combination of abducing to causes and default reasoning to predictions from these causes [Poole, 1989; Poole, 1990].

Let $expl(\alpha)$ be the set of minimal explanations of proposition (or conjunction) α. Define

$$\mathcal{M}(\alpha) = \sum_{E \in expl(\alpha)} P(E)$$

Lemma 3.4 *If H is a set of assignments to variables in a Bayesian Network, and H' is the analogous propositions to H in the corresponding probabilistic Horn abduction system, then*

$$P(H) = \mathcal{M}(H')$$

A simple corollary of the above lemma can be used to determine the posterior probability of a hypothesis based on some observations:

Theorem 3.5

$$P(x_i = v_i | obs) = \frac{\mathcal{M}(obs' \wedge x_i(v_i))}{\mathcal{M}(obs')}$$

The denominator can be obtained by finding the explanations of the observations. The numerators can be obtained by explaining $x_i(v_i)$ from these explanations.

4 Best-first abduction

We are currently experimenting with a number of implementations based on Logic programming technology or on ATMS technology. These are implemented by a branch and bound search where we consider the partial explanation with the least cost (highest probability) at any time.

The implementations keep a priority queue of sets of hypotheses that could be extended into explanations ("partial explanations"). At any time the set of all the explanations is the set of already generated explanations, plus those explanations that can be generated from the partial explanations in the priority queue.

Formally[4], a partial explanation is a pair

$$\langle g \leftarrow C, D \rangle$$

where g is an atom, C is a conjunction of atoms and D is a set of hypotheses.

Initially the priority queue to explain a contains

$$\{\langle a \leftarrow a, \{\}\rangle, \langle false \leftarrow false, \{\}\rangle\}$$

We thus try simultaneously try to find explanations of a and "explanations" of $false$ (forming *nogoods* in ATMS terminology) that can be used to prune other partial explanations.

At each step we choose the element

$$\langle g \leftarrow C, D \rangle$$

of the priority queue with maximum prior probability of D, but when partial explanations are equal we have a preference for explanations of $false$.

We have an explanation when C is the empty conjunction. Otherwise, suppose C is conjunction $a \wedge R$.

There are two operations that can be carried out. The first is a form of SLD resolution [Lloyd, 1987], where for each rule

$$a \leftarrow b_1 \wedge ... \wedge b_n$$

in F, we generate the partial explanation

$$\langle g \leftarrow b_1 \wedge ... \wedge b_n \wedge R, D \rangle .$$

The second operation is used when $a \in H$. In this case we produce the partial explanation

$$\langle g \leftarrow R, \{a\} \cup D \rangle$$

This procedure, under reasonable assumptions, will find the explanations in order of liklihood.

[4]Here we give only the bare-bones of the goal-directed procedure; there is an analogous bottom-up procedure that we are also experimenting with. The analysis is similar for that procedure. We also only give the propositional version here. The lifting to the general case by the use of substitutions is straightforward [Lloyd, 1987].

It turns out to be straight forward to give an upper bound on the probability mass in the priority queue.

If $\langle g \leftarrow C, D\rangle$ is in the priority queue, then it can possibly be used to generate explanations $D_1, ..., D_n$. Each D_i will be of the form $D \cup D'_i$. We can place a bound on the probability mass of all of the D_i, by

$$\begin{aligned} p(D_1 \vee ... \vee D_n) &= p(D \wedge (D'_1 \vee ... \vee D'_n)) \\ &\leq p(D) \end{aligned}$$

This means that we can put an bound on the range of probabilities of an goal based on finding just some of the explanations of the goal. Suppose we have goal g, and we have generated explanations $\mathcal{D}$. Let

$$P_{\mathcal{D}} = \sum_{D \in \mathcal{D}} P(D)$$

$$P_Q = \sum_{D:\langle g \leftarrow C, D\rangle \in Q} P(D)$$

where Q is the priority queue.

We then have

$$P_{\mathcal{D}} \leq P(g) \leq P_{\mathcal{D}} + P_Q$$

As the computation progresses, the probability mass in the queue P_Q approaches zero and we get a better refinements on the value of $P(g)$. This thus forms the basis of an "anytime" algorithm for Bayesian networks.

5 Causation

There have been problems associated with logical formulations of causation [Pearl, 1988a]. There has been claims that Bayes networks provide the right independencies for causation [Pearl, 1988b]. This paper provides evidence that abducing to causes and making assumptions as to what to predict from those assumptions [Poole, 1989; Poole, 1990] is the right logical analogue of the independence in Bayesian networks (based on theorem 3.5).

One of the problems in causal reasoning that Bayesian networks overcome [Pearl, 1988b] is in preventing reasoning such as "if c_1 is a cause for a and c_2 is a cause for $\neg a$, then from c_1 we can infer c_2". This is the problem that occurs in the Yale shooting problem [Hanks and McDermott, 1987]. Our embedding says that this does not occur in Bayesian networks as c_1 and c_2 must already be stated to be disjoint. We must have already disambiguated what occurs when they are both true. If we represent the Yale shooting scenario so that the rules for "alive" are disjoint the problem does not arise.

6 Comparison with Other Systems

The closest work to that reported here is by Charniak and Shimony [Charniak and Shimony, 1990; Shimony and Charniak, 1990]. Theorem 3.3 is analogous to Theorem 1 of [Shimony and Charniak, 1990]. Instead of considering abduction, they consider models that consist of an assignment of values to each random variable. The *label* of [Shimony and Charniak, 1990] plays an analogous role to our hypotheses. They however, do not use their system for computing posterior probabilities. It is also not so obvious how to extend their formalism to more powerful logics.

This work is also closely related to recent embeddings of Dempster-Shafer in ATMS [Laskey and Lehner, 1989; Provan, 1989]. One difference between our embedding of Bayes networks and Dempster Shafer is in the independence assumptions used. Dempster-Shafer assume that different rules are independent. We assume they are exclusive. Another difference is that these embeddings do not do evidential reasoning (by doing abduction), determining probability of hypotheses given evidence, but rather determine the "belief" of propositions from forward chaining.

The ATMS-based implementation is very similar to that of de Kleer and Williams [1987; 1989]. They are computing something different to us (the most likely composite hypotheses), and are thus able to do an $A*$ search. It is not clear that including the "irrelevant" hypotheses gives the advantages that would seem to arise from using an A* search.

7 Conclusion

This paper presented a simple but powerful mechanism for combining logical and probabilistic reasoning and showed how it can be used to represent Bayesian Networks.

Given the simple specification of what we want to compute, we are currently investigating different implementation techniques to determine which works best in practice. This includes using logic programming technology and also ATMS technology. We are also trying to the representational adequacy by building applications (particularly in diagnosis, but also in recognition), and based on this technology.

It may seem as though there is something terribly ad hoc about probabilistic Horn abduction (c.f. the extensional systems of [Pearl, 1988b]). It seems, however, that all of the sensible (where $\sum_j \mathcal{M}(a_i(v_{i,j})) = 1$ for each random variable a_i) representations (propositionally at least) correspond to Bayesian networks. The natural representation tends to emphasise propositional dependencies (e.g., where b is an important distinction when a is true, but not otherwise). These are normal Bayesian networks, but imply more structure on the contingency tables than are normally considered special.

A Proof Outlines of Lemmata

Lemma 3.2 *The minimal explanations of the terminal variables having particular values correspond to the composite beliefs in the Bayesian network with the terminals having those values. The priors for the explanations and the composite beliefs are identical.*

Proof: First, there is a one to one correspondence between the composite beliefs and the minimal explanations of the terminals. Suppose $x_1, ..., x_n$ are the random variables such that variable x_i is directly influenced by $x_{i_1}, ..., x_{i_{n_i}}$. The minimal explanations of the terminal nodes consist of hypotheses of the form

$$c\_x_i(v_i, v_{i_1}, ..., v_{i_{n_i}})$$

with exactly one hypothesis for each x_i, such that $x_{i_j}(v_{i_j})$ is a logical consequence of the facts and the explanation. This corresponds to the composite belief $x_1(v_1) \wedge ... \wedge x_n(v_n)$.

By construction, the proofs for the terminal nodes must include all variables.

Suppose E is a minimal explanation of the terminal variables. To show there is only one hypothesis for each random variable. Suppose that x_i is a variable such that there are two hypotheses

$$c\_x_i(v_i, v_{i_1}, ..., v_{i_{n_i}}), c\_x_i(v'_i, v'_{i_1}, ..., v'_{i_{n_i}})$$

in E. If some $x_{i_j}(v_{i_j})$ or $x_{i_j}(v'_{i_j})$ is not a consequence of $F \cup E$, then the corresponding c_x_i hypothesis can be removed without affecting the explanation, which is a contradiction to the minimality of E. So each $x_{i_j}(v_{i_j})$ and $x_{i_j}(v'_{i_j})$ is a consequence of $F \cup E$. By consistency of E each $v_{i_j} = v'_{i_j}$. The only way these assumptions can be different is if $v_i \neq v'_i$, and so we can derive $x_i(v_i)$ and $x_i(v'_i)$ which leads to *false*, a contradiction to the consistency of E.

Second, the explanations and the composite beliefs have the same prior. Given an assignment of value v_i to each variable x_i, define Π_i by

$$\Pi_i = x_{i_1}(v_{i_1}) \wedge ... \wedge x_{i_{n_i}}(v_{i_{n_i}})$$

where $x_{i_1}, ..., x_{i_{n_i}}$ are the variables directly influencing x_i.

By the definition of a Bayesian net, and the definition of c_x_i, we have

$$\begin{aligned} & P(x_1(v_1) \wedge ... \wedge x_n(v_n)) \\ &= \prod_{i=1}^{n} P(x_i(v_i) | \Pi_i) \\ &= \prod_{i=1}^{n} c\_x_i(v_i, v_{i_1}, ..., v_{i_{n_i}}) \\ &= P(exp) \end{aligned}$$

Where *exp* is the explanation. □

Lemma 3.4 *If H is a set of assignments to variables in a Bayesian Network, and H' is the analogous propositions to H in the corresponding Probabilistic Horn Abduction system, then*

$$P(H) = \mathcal{M}(H')$$

Proof: This is proven by induction on a well founded ordering over sets of hypotheses. This ordering is based on the lexicographic ordering of pairs $\langle h, n \rangle$ where h is the depth of the element of the set with maximal depth, and n is the number of elements of this depth. Each time through the recursion either h is reduced or h is kept the same and n is reduced. This is well founded as both h and n are non-negative integers and n is bounded by the number of random variables.

For the base case, where $h = 1$, we have all of the hypotheses are independent and there is only one trivial explanation. In this case we have

$$P(H) = \mathcal{M}(H') = \prod_{h \in H} P(h)$$

For the inductive case, suppose $a(v)$ is a proposition in H with greatest depth. Let $R = H \backslash a(v)$. Under the ordering above $\Pi_a \cup R < H$, and so we can assume the lemma for $\Pi_a \cup R$. Note also that a does not influence anything in R (else something in R would have greater depth than a).

$$\begin{aligned} P(H) &= P(a = v \wedge R) \\ &= P(a = v | R) \times P(R) \\ &= \left(\sum_{\Pi_a} P(a | \Pi_a \wedge R) \times P(\Pi_a | R) \right) \times P(R) \\ &= \sum_{\Pi_a} P(a | \Pi_a) \times P(\Pi_a | R) \times P(R) \\ &= \sum_{\Pi_a} P(a | \Pi_a) \times P(\Pi_a \wedge R) \\ &= \sum_{\Pi_a} P(c\_a(v, \Pi_a)) \times \mathcal{M}(\Pi'_a \cup R') \\ &= \sum_{\Pi_a} P(c\_a(v, \Pi_a)) \times \sum_{E \in expl(\Pi'_a \wedge R')} P(E) \\ &= \sum_{\Pi_a} \sum_{E \in expl(\Pi_a \wedge R)} P(c\_a(v, \Pi_a)) \times P(E) \\ &= \sum_{E' \in expl(a(v) \wedge R)} P(E') \\ &= \mathcal{M}(a(v) \wedge R') \\ &= \mathcal{M}(H') \end{aligned}$$

□

Acknowledgements

This research was supported under NSERC grant OG-POO44121, and under Project B5 of the Institute for Robotics and Intelligent Systems. Thanks to Michael Horsch for working on the implementations, and to Judea Pearl for pointing out the relationship to Reichenbach's principle.

References

[Charniak and Shimony, 1990] E. Charniak and S. E. Shimony. Probabilistic semantics for cost based abduction. In *Proc. 8th National Conference on Artificial Intelligence*, pages 106–111, Boston, July 1990.

[Console *et al.*, 1989] L. Console, D. Theseider Dupre, and P. Torasso. Abductive reasoning through direct deduction from completed domain models. In W. R. Zbigniew, editor, *Methodologies for Intelligent Systems 4*, pages 175–182. Elsiever Science Publishing Co., 1989.

[de Kleer and Williams, 1987] J. de Kleer and B. C. Williams. Diagnosing multiple faults. *Artificial Intelligence*, 32(1):97–130, April 1987.

[de Kleer and Williams, 1989] J. de Kleer and B. C. Williams. Diagnosis with behavioral modes. In *Proc. 11th International Joint Conf. on Artificial Intelligence*, pages 1324–1330, Detroit, August 1989.

[Eshghi and Kowalski, 1989] K. Eshghi and R. A. Kowalski. Abduction compared to negation by failure. In G. Levi and M. Martelli, editors, *Logic Programming: Proceedings of the Sixth International Conference*, pages 234–254, Lisbon, Portugal, 1989.

[Hanks and McDermott, 1987] S. Hanks and D. V. McDermott. Nonmonotonic logic and temporal projection. *Artificial Intelligence*, 33:379–412, 1987.

[Horsch and Poole, 1990] M. Horsch and D. Poole. A dynamic approach to probabilistic inference using Bayesian networks. In *Proc. Sixth Conference on Uncertainty in AI*, pages 155–161, Boston, July 1990.

[Konolige, 1991] K. Konolige. Closure + minimization implies abduction. technical report, SRI International, Menlo Park, CA, 1991.

[Laskey and Lehner, 1989] K. B. Laskey and P. E. Lehner. Assumptions, beliefs and probabilities. *Artificial Intelligence*, 41(1):65–77, 1989.

[Lloyd, 1987] J. W. Lloyd. *Foundations of Logic Programming*. Symbolic Computation Series. Springer-Verlag, Berlin, second edition, 1987.

[Neufeld and Poole, 1987] E. M. Neufeld and D. Poole. Towards solving the multiple extension problem: combining defaults and probabilities. In *Proc. Third Workshop on Reasoning with Uncertainty*, pages 305–312, Seattle, July 1987.

[Pearl, 1987] J. Pearl. Distributed revision of composite beliefs. *Artificial Intelligence*, 33(2):173–215, October 1987.

[Pearl, 1988a] J. Pearl. Embracing causation in default reasoning. *Artificial Intelligence*, 35(2):259–271, 1988.

[Pearl, 1988b] J. Pearl. *Probabilistic Reasoning in Intelligent Systems: Networks of Plausible Inference*. Morgan Kaufmann, San Mateo, CA, 1988.

[Peng and Reggia, 1990] Y. Peng and J. A. Reggia. *Abductive Inference Models for Diagnostic Problem-Solving*. Symbolic Computation – AI Series. Springer-Verlag, New York, 1990.

[Poole and Provan, 1990] D. Poole and G. Provan. What is an optimal diagnosis? In *Proc. Sixth Conference on Uncertainty in AI*, pages 46–53, Boston, July 1990.

[Poole *et al.*, 1987] D. Poole, R. Goebel, and R. Aleliunas. Theorist: A logical reasoning system for defaults and diagnosis. In N. Cercone and G. McCalla, editors, *The Knowledge Frontier: Essays in the Representation of Knowledge*, pages 331–352. Springer-Verlag, New York, NY, 1987.

[Poole, 1988] D. Poole. Representing knowledge for logic-based diagnosis. In *International Conference on Fifth Generation Computing Systems*, pages 1282–1290, Tokyo, Japan, November 1988.

[Poole, 1989] D. Poole. Explanation and prediction: an architecture for default and abductive reasoning. *Computational Intelligence*, 5(2):97–110, 1989.

[Poole, 1990] D. Poole. A methodology for using a default and abductive reasoning system. *International Journal of Intelligent Systems*, 5(5):521–548, December 1990.

[Poole, 1991] D. Poole. Representing diagnostic knowledge for probabilistic horn abduction. to appear *Proc. 12th International Joint Conf. on Artificial Intelligence*, Sydney, August 1991.

[Provan, 1989] G. Provan. An analysis of ATMS-based techniques for computing Dempster-Shafer belief functions. In *Proc. 11th International Joint Conf. on Artificial Intelligence*, pages 1115–1120, Detroit, August 1989.

[Reichenbach, 1956] H. Reichenbach. *The Direction of Time*. University of California Press, Berkeley and Los Angeles, 1956.

[Shimony and Charniak, 1990] S. E. Shimony and E. Charniak. A new algorithm for finding map assignments to belief networks. In *Proc. Sixth Conf. on Uncertainty in Artificial Intelligence*, pages 98–103, Cambridge, Mass., July 1990.

DYNAMIC NETWORK UPDATING TECHNIQUES FOR DIAGNOSTIC REASONING

G.M.A. Provan
Computer and Information Science Department
University of Pennsylvania
Philadelphia PA 19104-6389
phone:(215) 898-9830; email: provan@cis.upenn.edu

Abstract

A new probabilistic network construction system, DYNASTY, is proposed for diagnostic reasoning given variables whose probabilities change over time. Diagnostic reasoning is formulated as a sequential stochastic process, and is modeled using influence diagrams. Given a set O of observations, DYNASTY creates an influence diagram in order to devise the best action given O. Sensitivity analyses are conducted to determine if the best network has been created, given the uncertainty in network parameters and topology. DYNASTY uses an equivalence class approach to provide decision thresholds for the sensitivity analysis. This equivalence-class approach to diagnostic reasoning differentiates diagnoses only if the required actions are different. A set of network-topology updating algorithms are proposed for dynamically updating the network when necessary.

1 INTRODUCTION

The development of graphical representations for probabilistic models (e.g. belief networks [Pearl, 1988], influence diagrams [Howard and Matheson, 1981; Shachter, 1986; Shachter, 1988]) has enabled efficient probabilistic models to be developed for many tasks, such as diagnostic reasoning [Pearl, 1988; Heckerman and Horvitz, 1990], natural language analysis[Goldman and Charniak, 1990], etc. These representations, by specifying the causal relationships among variables in a causal graph (and not all possible relationships), facilitate efficient inference. A great deal of the recent research in automated probabilistic reasoning has focused on developing more efficient and more general algorithms for causal probabilistic models, and on methods for incrementally constructing belief networks.

However, the application of these techniques and representations to complex diagnostic tasks, such as medical diagnosis, have oversimplified such tasks. A common simplification made in many current approaches is modeling the diagnostic process as a single-stage, static process. This is inadequate, as diagnostic reasoning is a sequential, dynamic process in which feedback is important. Provan and Poole [1991] point out the necessity of considering this complete process, and in particular, the effects of feedback.

This paper extends existing diagnostic models to incorporate the dynamic and sequential nature of diagnostic reasoning. It proposes techniques for constructing sequential belief networks, and of dynamically updating such networks. Many existing techniques for constructing belief networks (e.g. [Goldman and Charniak, 1990; Heckerman and Horvitz, 1990]) model the process for one instant of time.[1] For certain tasks this is adequate, but for tasks in which the probabilistic relationships among variables changes over time, it can be difficult to know when the best model has been constructed. This sometimes produces incorrect answers due to the selection of incorrect probabilities and/or causal relationships. Hence, both the diagnosis and the decision taken given this diagnosis may hinge on whether the best model has been constructed, given the data at a particular time t. Sensitivity analyses may be used to test how the data at different times affects the best decision. If the sensitivity analyses show that a better decision would be made under an alternative model, then the model needs to be updated. It is these sensitivity analyses and model updating techniques that are of interest here. Criteria are proposed to determine when network topology revisions are necessary given time-varying probabilistic and causal relationships. These criteria are based on examining the equivalence of outcomes (e.g. treatments for diseases). Algorithms for conducting the necessary revisions are outlined, including refinement and coarsening techniques [Chang and Fung, 1990], and other network

[1] This is true even for systems in which the models can be constructed incrementally, e.g. [Goldman and Charniak, 1990].

revision algorithms [Pearl, 1988; Srinivas and Breese, 1990].

This approach makes dynamic network updating possible, and formalizes the sequential nature of diagnostic reasoning (e.g. to allow feedback into the network). The explicit introduction of utilities into diagnostic models[2] allows a more realistic formalization of the diagnostic process. In addition, it is expected that the techniques developed for diagnostic reasoning may be applied to other domains, where appropriate.

2 DYNAMICS OF DIAGNOSTIC REASONING UNDER UNCERTAINTY

Treating a diagnostic task as being time-independent can lead to incorrect results in certain domains. Consider medical diagnosis, and in particular the diagnosis of abdominal pain. Constructing a model for the observation of abdominal pain should not be done for a single time interval, since, as noted in [Schwartz *et al.*, 1986], many symptoms take on different meanings as diseases evolve over time, both in terms of their inter-relationships and the diseases indicated by the particular symptoms. In a possible case of appendicitis, the initial symptoms include non-specific abdominal pain (which could be confused with many other ailments), and are often accompanied soon thereafter by gastrointestinal distress and possibly by anorexia and fever. This pain subsequently becomes localized to the right lower quadrant (RLQ) of the abdomen (which then provides a strong indication of appendicitis, along with a high white blood count). If the appendix ruptures, then there are several more symptoms; however, a perforated appendix leads to serious internal complications.[3] Given the evolution of a disease such as appendicitis, the probabilities assigned to network nodes, and even the topology of the network itself, must change over time. For example, Figure 1 shows how the likelihood ratio for the diagnosis of appendicitis might change over time. Clearly, in the initial stages of appendicitis, many other diagnoses are equally likely given the symptoms.

A second aspect of this dynamic nature of (diagnostic) reasoning is the need for modeling the temporal order of observations. In some cases the temporal sequence of observations (as opposed to just an unordered list of the set of observations) can provide strong cues for a diagnosis. For example, if a woman has abdominal pain, noting whether this pain is immediately followed by gastrointestinal distress could help identify a possible case of appendicitis, whereas the absence of such immediate distress would make the presence of a gonohorreal cyst in the right fallopian tube more likely. A second example is the diagnosis of a car which has trouble starting. The sequence of events leading to the inability to start can help identify the problem. Thus, the inability to start only on mornings after it has rained may indicate that moisture is getting under the distributor cap.

Figure 1: Change over time of likelihood ratio for the occurrence of Right-Lower-Quadrant pain given a diagnosis of appendicitis

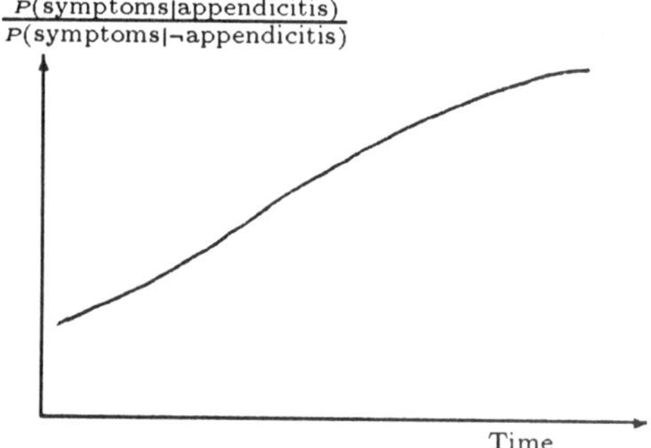

A third aspect is the ability to incorporate the effects of feedback. Feedback can alter not only the probability assignments to a network, but also the topology of the network. For example, consider a network constructed for a case of RLQ abdominal distress. If simple stomach upset is diagnosed, and a treatment of Diovol is administered, the persistence of RLQ abdominal distress will provide feedback to the system that the diagnosis may be incorrect, and the network topology and/or probabilities may need to be updated.

This paper proposes extensions to existing network construction techniques to model diagnostic reasoning as a sequential, dynamic process using the formalism of influence diagrams. This proposal is not intended to be a full temporal calculus based on Bayesian networks, as discussed in [Kanazawa, 1991], for example. Instead, it attempts to build simple networks which will realistically model the dynamics of diagnostic reasoning without necessitating the complicated (and computationally costly) construction and solution of temporal Bayesian networks.

3 SYSTEM ARCHITECTURE

There are many existing systems and theories for model construction. Examples of such network construction frameworks include the proposal of Lehmann [1990], and examples of such systems include QMR-DT [Shwe and Cooper, 1990] and FRAIL3 [Goldman and Charniak, 1990]. In each of these proposals, the

[2] Utility considerations have been ignored in most formal models of diagnostic reasoning, except for approaches such as [Heckerman and Horvitz, 1990].

[3] Most diagnostic procedures attempt to avoid perforation and its resulting complications.

goal is to construct a model which completely characterizes the data. However, this goal conflicts with the need for efficient performance of implemented systems. Solving Bayesian network models is NP-hard [Cooper, 1990], so the networks constructed must be as small as possible to ensure efficiency. The proposal presented in this paper trades off (to some extent) completeness and accuracy for efficiency, as is done in many other systems, such as [Heckerman and Horvitz, 1990].[4]

A new system architecture proposed to model dynamic reasoning tasks is depicted in Figure 2. This system is called DYNASTY, for DYnamic Network Analysis of System TopologY.

Like several existing network construction methods (e.g. QMR-DT, FRAIL3), we start with a Knowledge Base (KB) containing (1) causal rules, and (2) a set of conditional probability tables. From this KB a network is constructed to solve a given task.

The KB for DYNASTY consists of a network of nodes and arcs. Nodes represent state variables, and arcs exist between pairs of nodes related causally and/or temporally.

Associated with the network are probability tables for the conditional probabilities for the network, such as those required for the construction of a Bayesian network. In addition, utility values are stored for decision-making.

Typically, the complete KB for a given domain is quite large,[5] and given a set O of observations, it is necessary to construct a network containing only the data related to O (and not the entire KB).

Within the general model-construction framework (such as that described in Lehmann [1990]), there is always uncertainty in choosing the correct model. That uncertainty may be due to uncertainty in the instruments used to record data, to noise, or to the relationship between data from observations and causes for the observations (e.g. the diseases causing the observed symptoms). This paper examines the uncertainty arising from relating observations and causes, and in particular the temporal uncertainty of this relationship.

The remainder of the paper discusses the algorithms used to create an influence diagram from the KB, and for dynamically altering this influence diagram.

[4]The appropriate balance of resources between meta-analysis of model construction and model solution has been studied by [Horvitz *et al.*, 1989; Breese and Horvitz, 1990].

[5]As an example, the QMR-DT network represents 534 diseases, 4040 manifestations and 40,740 disease-manifestation arcs [Heckerman and Horvitz, 1990].

Figure 2: Network construction methods in DYNASTY

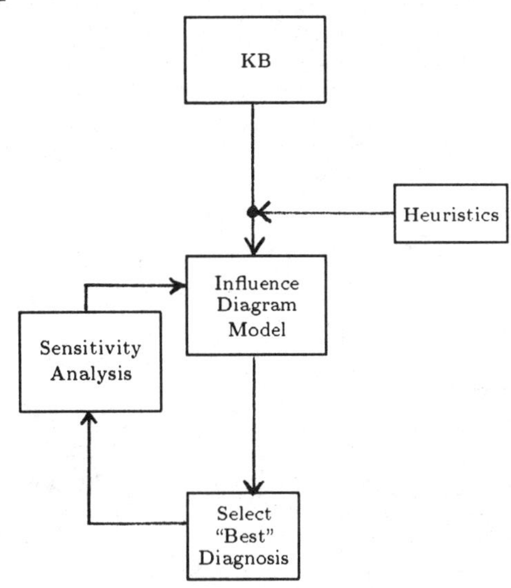

4 MODEL CONSTRUCTION HEURISTICS

4.1 Time Dependence

As noted earlier, diagnostic tasks whose characteristics change over time have not been modeled in earlier approaches. The approach taken in DYNASTY is to discretize the possible times from which the observations could have occurred. Call $\mathcal{D}_{t_i}$ the network (consisting of causes and intermediate causes/observations) which would need to be constructed at time t_i. In full generality, the networks at different times are different, and they can each be quite large for complicated tasks. To fully model a diagnostic task, an influence diagram (ID) containing sub-networks for each time t_i would need to be constructed, given a set O of observations. This is shown in Figure 3.

Figure 3: Most general influence diagram for solving a stochastic diagnostic task

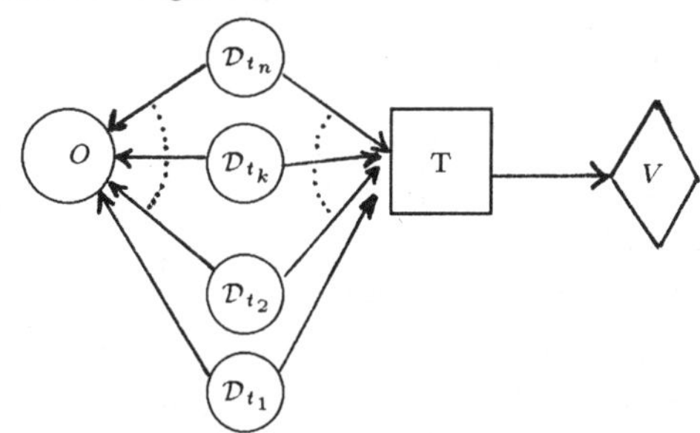

DYNASTY attempts to solve a simplified task: it creates a network for particular time t_j, and then conducts a sensitivity analysis to determine if the action taken is affected by the choice of time t_j. The ID which would be constructed is shown in Figure 4.

Figure 4: Simplified influence diagram for solving a stochastic diagnostic task

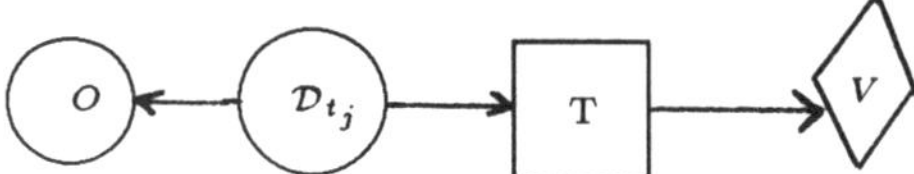

Example 1 Consider the time course of a possible case of appendicitis. Early in the course of appendicitis, the symptoms could appear to be a simple upset stomach. Figure 5 shows the notation necessary to construct IDs for this task. If the observations are nausea and general abdominal pain, then the simple ID shown in Figure 6 may be constructed. This is an easy influence diagram to construct and solve. Given an ID such as this, the possible treatments are the administration of an emetic (for food poisoning) or Diovol (for simple upset stomach).

Figure 5: Notation for constructing Abdominal Pain Influence Diagram

OBSERVATIONS

α	≡	anorexia
N	≡	nausea
F	≡	fever
P	≡	abdominal pain
LLQ	≡	LLQ pain
RLQ	≡	RLQ pain

HYPOTHESES

A	≡	appendicitis
US	≡	upset stomach
FP	≡	food poisoning
GC	≡	gonohorreal cyst

Figure 6: Simple influence diagram for abdominal pain example

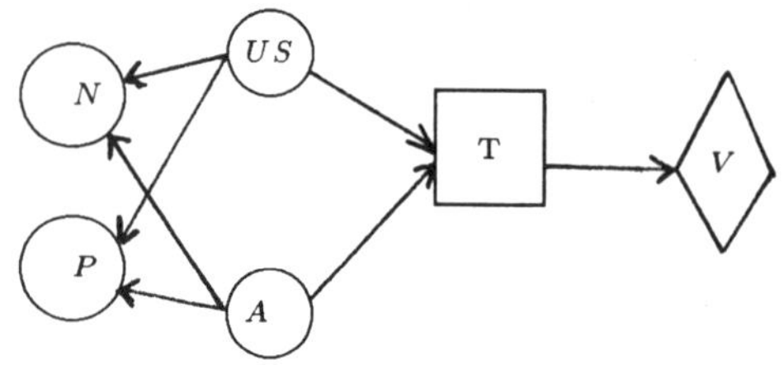

However, these observations may actually be indicative of the early stages of appendicitis. To make sure that a possible case of appendicitis might be diagnosed, the ID shown in Figure 7 must be constructed. This ID bears little relation to the ID shown in Figure 6. The possible treatments include: (1) emetic (for food poisoning), (2) Diovol (for simple upset stomach), (3) removal of appendix (for appendicitis), or (4) treatment or removal of gonohorreal cyst.

Figure 7: More complex influence diagram for abdominal pain example

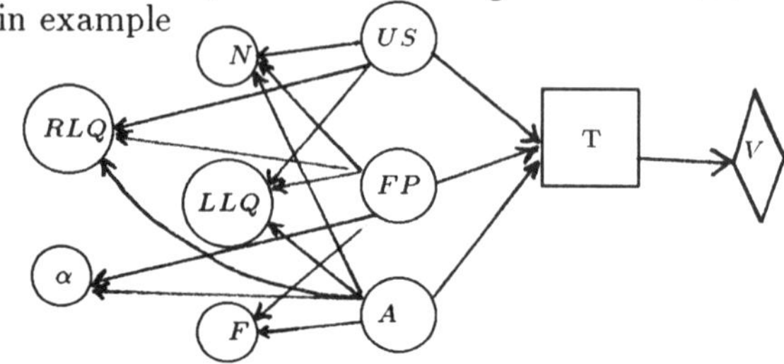

This example shows how, given a set of observations, uncertainty in the time course of possible diseases may require entirely different IDs. ♣

There are a number of heuristics used in DYNASTY for network construction. One heuristic is the use of temporal orderings for probability assignments. This heuristic is best demonstrated by an example. Consider the diagnosis of a car which infrequently has problems starting. The two diagnoses under consideration are a distributor cap problem (DC) or an alternator problem (ALT). The weather (W) may affect the diagnosis, as wet conditions can cause condensation under a distributor cap, thereby causing the failure of the car to start ($\overline{ST}$). Other possible causes of the problems in starting, e.g. the alternator may be faulty and not recharging the battery, are not affected by weather conditions. A simple Bayes network for this problem is shown in Figure 8. Knowledge of the history of the correlation between weather conditions

Figure 8: Bayesian network model for determining the cause of the failure of a car to start

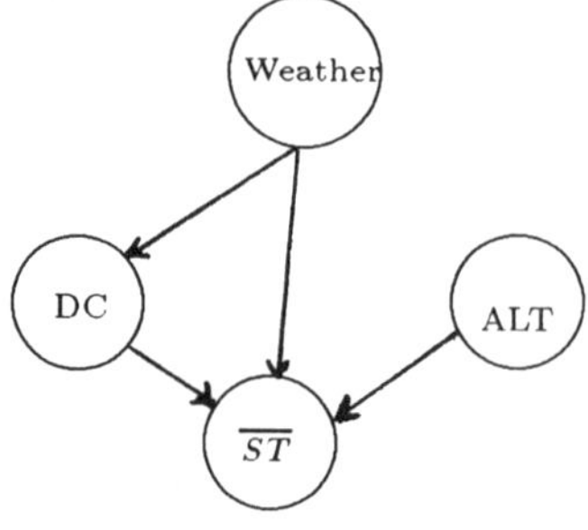

and success in starting the car can significantly affect the probabilities assigned to the network. For example, if the car only gives trouble starting in wet conditions, then the problem is most likely DC; if the car gives trouble with equal probability in both wet and dry conditions, then the problem is most likely ALT. In fact, trouble in a single instance when the weather is dry will lead to the assignment of a low probability to $P(DC|\overline{ST}, W)$. In this case, the *history* of the problem is crucial to the probability assignment.

Hence, the *history heuristic* is the use of temporal history, whenever possible, in selecting the probabilities (from the probability tables) to be assigned to the network in consideration. The temporal history is computed simply by tracing the history for a node in the KB, using revised Truth Maintenance algorithms for computing the justifications for a node in a dependency network [McAllester, 1990]. The history heuristic also uses triggers to guide probability assignments. For example, finding a single instance when the car won't start in dry conditions is a trigger to the assignment of a low probability to $P(DC|\overline{ST}, W)$.

4.2 Sequential Diagnostic Process

The ID framework also allows diagnostic reasoning to be formulated as a sequential diagnostic process. Using a result of Tatman and Shachter [1990], an ID can model a sequential process using dynamic programming, provided that the value function V is separable. In terms of IDs, a value node is separable if it can be represented as the sum or product of multiple subvalue nodes.

Value node separability has been exploited in the design of a sequential process for image understanding [Levitt *et al.*, 1990]. In a similar manner, value node separability is used to model the sequential nature of diagnostic reasoning. In brief, the decision nodes in a DYNASTY ID are called treatments, which may be tests to determine more observations, or actual treatments for hypothesized diseases. In the former case, given an ID shown in Figure 6, the test T can determine a new observation O', creating a new ID with another decision node T' (e.g. another test or a treatment) and another value node V'. In this manner, the sequential nature of tests (or treatments) providing feedback to the diagnostic process can be modeled.[6]

5 MODEL UPDATING

5.1 Overview

In a problem for which probabilities are temporally dependent, the sensitivity of the computed decisions to the temporally-dependent probabilities must be tested. This provides a threshold for determining when a better model is warranted. This may require new probability values (corresponding to a new time t'), or a new network topology corresponding to time t'.

This sensitivity analysis/model updating in DYNASTY occurs in two stages:

Sensitivity Analysis First, a sensitivity analysis is conducted to determine if data from time t' provides a better model than the data from time t.

Model Updating If the network model needs to be updated, then some of the following processes may need to be invoked:

1. New probability values are assigned and propagated to compute a new network equilibrium state.
2. Network topology is altered.
3. A new model is built for a different time t'.

These processes are now discussed in greater detail.

5.2 Equivalence Class Sensitivity Analysis

Given the construction of an ID model at time t, a decision (with accompanying diagnosis) of maximal utility is computed. For example, in the car diagnosis example, the diagnosis might be DC, and the decision *REPLACE-DC*. This decision would maximise the requirement of ensuring that the car no longer has trouble starting.

In the process of computing this best decision, the next-best decision for a different equivalence class is also recorded. In the car example, this is *REPLACE-ALT*. If there is uncertainty concerning which probabilities are correct, then the sensitivity of the decision to this uncertainty must be determined. This is formalised in terms of equivalence classes of decisions as follows.

5.2.1 Analysis of Equivalence Classes

The equivalence class approach to diagnosis, as originally formulated in [Provan and Poole, 1991], is summarised here. The rationale is that there is no point in distinguishing between decision-equivalent diagnoses, i.e. diagnoses for which the decision taken (e.g. administration of drugs to a patient) are the same; as far as the decision-maker is concerned decision-equivalent diagnoses should be considered as the same diagnosis.

The aim of diagnostic reasoning is to provide a treatment for a set of observations. From an equivalence-class point of view, this reduces to refining the set of use-equivalent possibilities; i.e. one does not care about distinct diagnoses, but *distinct treatments* (and their associated distinct equivalence classes). Thus,

[6] Please refer to [Provan, 1991 (forthcoming)] for more details. The presentation here is brief due to space limitations.

use-equivalence induces a partition on the set of diagnoses, where each partition corresponds to a possible distinct decision.

Let $\mathcal{T}$ be the set of all treatments (or decisions).[7] Let $\mathcal{D}$ be the set of all possible diagnoses.

Definition 5.1 The **possible treatment space** $\mathcal{P}$ is a subset of $\mathcal{D} \times \mathcal{T}$. $\langle D, T \rangle \in \mathcal{P}$ means that T is a possible treatment given that the diagnosis is $D \in \mathcal{D}$.

$\mathcal{P}$ induces an equivalence relation on the set of diagnoses. This will be called *strong equivalence* with respect to $\mathcal{P}$. The idea is that equivalent diagnoses have the same set of possible treatments.[8]

Definition 5.2 Two diagnoses D_1 and D_2 are **strongly equivalent** with respect to $\mathcal{P}$, written $D_1 \equiv_{\mathcal{P}} D_2$ if $\forall\ T \in \mathcal{T}$, $\langle D_1, T \rangle \in \mathcal{P}$ if and only if $\langle D_2, T \rangle \in \mathcal{P}$.

5.2.2 Equivalence Class Decision-making

We assume we have a measure $\mu(D,T)$ of the utility of treatment T given diagnosis D. We can define the possible treatment space as the set of diagnoses with the same utility.[9] In this case, "strong use-equivalence" means having the same utility for each treatment.

Let $\mathcal{D}$ be the set of use-diagnoses. For $D \in \mathcal{D}$, every logical model of D has the same utility measure. The following proposition about the expected value, $\mathcal{E}(T)$, of treatment T was proven in [Provan and Poole, 1991]:

$$\mathcal{E}(T) = \sum_{D \in \mathcal{D}} \mu(D,T) \times p(D). \qquad (1)$$

Under this approach to diagnostic reasoning, diagnoses are selected such that the expected utility of the treatment is maximised. That is, the goal is to compute γ_i such that the expected value of the treatment given by equation 1 is maximised.

Consider an ID in which the variables are denoted by $X = \{x_1, ..., x_n\}$, such that any diagnosis D consists of a subset of variables $X' \subseteq X$ which are not functioning normally (cf. [de Kleer *et al.*, 1990; Pearl, 1988; Provan and Poole, 1991] for a further description of such diagnostic models). Then equation 1 can be rewritten in terms of these variables as

$$\mathcal{E}[T] = \sum_{D \in \mathcal{D}} \sum_{D \models x} \mu(x,T) \times p(x), \qquad (2)$$

where $\mu(x,T)$ is the value of $\mu(D,T)$ such that x is true in D.

The notion behind the sensitivity analysis is as follows: consider a model constructed at time t, such that decision T_i is the optimal treatment. Call β the expected utility for decision T_i. If the probabilities of certain variables are time-dependent, then these new probabilities need to be substituted into the model to check if the decision would change. Note that different diagnoses may be computed, but if the decision is unchanged, then, under this use-equivalent approach, no network updating is necessary. For network updating to be necessary, the threshold β must be exceeded by the expected utility of another treatment T_j given probabilities for time t', i.e.

$$\left[\mathcal{E}[T_j] = \sum_{D \in \mathcal{D}} \sum_{D \models x} \mu(x,T) \times p(x)\right] > \beta.$$

This provides a precise bound on when the treatment changes. When the threshold is exceeded, then network alterations may be necessary. These updating methods are now summarised.

5.3 Model Updating Techniques

There are several types of model updating operations, of which two of the most important are: (1) probability value updating, and (2) network topology updating. These are discussed in turn.

5.3.1 Probability Value Updating

This is the simple case of network updating. If no changes to the network topology are required when the model is updated from time t to t', then the required alterations to the probability values are made, and these values are propagated to obtain a new network equilibrium state.

For example, during the early stages of appendicitis diagnosis, probability values may need to be updated given changes in location of abdominal pain. Possible changes in probability assignments are shown in Figure 9(b),(c).

5.3.2 Network Topology Updating

Consider the onset of an entirely new set of symptoms in the observation of a patient with a possible case of the later stages of appendicitis. These are shown in Figure 7. If we started with the model in Figure 6, we see that the topology of the network needs to be altered.

[7] By a treatment we mean a total prescription of what to do (i.e., we do not conjoin different treatments — the conjunction would be one treatment). A treatment may be a test to distinguish abnormalities, the administration of drugs, replacement of circuit components, etc.

[8] Other types of equivalences, e.g. weak equivalence, are also distinguished in [Provan and Poole, 1991]; such cases are not discussed here due to space limitations.

[9] Formally, the treatment in the possible treatment space would be a pair $\langle T, v \rangle$ where $\langle D, \langle T, v \rangle \rangle \in \mathcal{P}$ if $\mu(D,T) = v$.

Figure 9: Early stages of the diagnosis of appendicitis

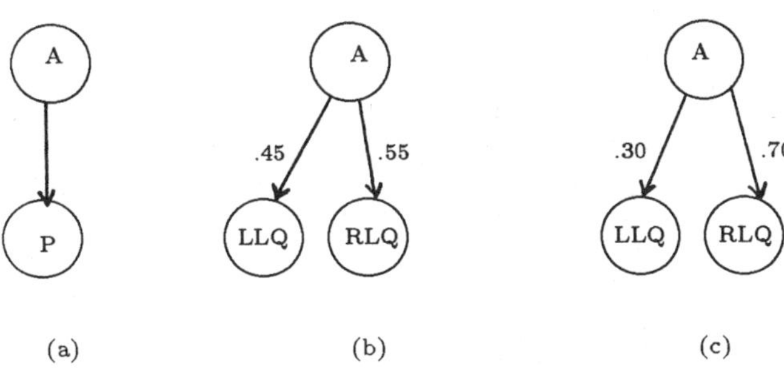

If changes to the network topology are required when the model is updated from time t to t', then one of several algorithms may be used. These algorithms include:

Refinement/coarsening Refinement/coarsening operations [Chang and Fung, 1990] are used to split/merge network nodes respectively. Consider a network refinement necessary to include new alternatives. For example, in abdominal diagnosis, the construction of a network which models only lower abdominal pain may need to be refined to differentiate right-lower quadrant (RLQ) and left-lower quadrant (LLQ) pain. Hence, a node modeling lower abdominal pain needs to be split into nodes for RLQ and LLQ (cf. Figures 9(a),(b)). Or in the car diagnosis example, the single node for weather may need to be split into nodes for wet weather and mixed (wet and dry) weather.

The network changes made for the refinement/coarsening operations are local, and do not involve all nodes in the network. This is formalised as follows. If x is a state node, then we call Π_x the predecessors of x in the network, and Σ_x the successors of x in the network. The Markov boundary of x is the minimal set of nodes which "shield" x from the rest of the network. The Markov boundary $\mathcal{M}(x)$ of node x consists of $\Pi_x \cup \Sigma_x \cup \Pi_{\Sigma_x}$. Hence, ensuring the joint probability distribution of $\mathcal{M}(x)$ is unaffected by the refinement/coarsening or x ensures that the rest of the network will be unaffected as well.

For example, it is shown in [Chang and Fung, 1990] that in a refinement of the values of the state space of variable x, Ω_x, each value $\omega_x \in \Omega_x$ is refined into multiple values $\omega'_x \in R(\omega_x)$. For each value $\omega_x \in \Omega_x$ which is refined into a value $\omega'_x \in R(\omega_x)$,

$$p(\Sigma_x|\omega_x, \Pi_{\Sigma_x})p(\omega_x, \Pi_x) = \sum_{\omega'_x \in R(\omega_x)} p(\Sigma_x|\omega'_x, \Pi_{\Sigma_x})p(\omega'_x, \Pi_x) \quad (3)$$

must be satisfied for all values of Π_x. This provides a set of constraints on how $\mathcal{M}(x)$ must be altered. In an analogous manner, constraints can be defined for the coarsening of the values of the state space of variable x, Ω_x, where multiple values of $\omega_x \in \Omega_x$ are combined into a single value $\omega'_x \in C(\omega_x)$.

The coarsening operation is defined similarly [Chang and Fung, 1990]. The coarsening operation may lose information during the process of node aggregation (i.e. the network probability assignments may be altered). Using the equivalence-class approach, such information loss is acceptable if the equivalence class does not change. Otherwise, approximations may need to be used [Chang and Fung, 1990].

Network additions Instead of splitting and/or merging existing nodes, completely new nodes may need to be added to, or particular nodes deleted from, the network. In such cases a variety of other algorithms are invoked, such as the reduction and clustering algorithms present in the IDEAL system algorithm library [Srinivas and Breese, 1990]. In network addition, the KB is consulted to determine which nodes must be added based on causal relationships.

Network Re-instantiation It may turn out that the network created is inappropriate for the diagnostic task. For example, a simple network may be created which cannot be appropriately augmented to model a more complicated case.[10] In such a situation, a completely new network is constructed from the KB.

5.4 Implementation

The KB is implemented in Common Lisp. Extended Justification-based TMS (e.g. [McAllester, 1990]) data structures and algorithms are used for determining relevant nodes to instantiate given a set of observations. The influence diagrams are implemented using the IDEAL system [Srinivas and Breese, 1990].

It is hoped that the TraumAID system [Webber *et al.*, 1990] will be used as a test-bed for this system. TraumAID is a decision support tool for the management of multiple trauma. Trauma management includes both diagnosis and treatment, and this diagnostic tool achieves these features using two modules: (1) a rule-based reasoner which models the relationships between clinical evidence and diagnostic/therapeutic goals, and (2) a planner which manages the achievement of multiple goals. TraumAID is an excellent system on which to test the theoretical results because, unlike most similar systems, it already contains a no-

[10] If radical changes must be made to an initial network, it can be computationally cheaper to create a new network from scratch than to alter the original network using coarsening/refinement operations.

tion of sequential action and change, key elements of the proposed theory of diagnostic reasoning. Further, efficient incremental management of action and change is necessary for trauma management.

6 CONCLUSIONS

This paper has described a proposed dynamic network construction system which can build models for problems with temporally-dependent probabilities. Heuristics are used to identify the best possible model, and to test the sensitivity of this model to probability values over time. Given the network updating capabilities of DYNASTY, the full diagnostic cycle, which includes feedback from the decisions made, can be incorporated into the network. In addition, the ability to refine/coarsen the network enables different levels of granularity (i.e. the coarseness of the description of the system being modeled) to be examined during the diagnostic process. Most other approaches to diagnostic reasoning (e.g. [de Kleer *et al.*, 1990]) have no way of dynamically altering the granularity of the system description.

Future work includes testing the feasibility of the algorithms in DYNASTY on real-world problems, and extending and optimising these algorithms. The KB for the TraumAID system is the first set of real data for which such tests are proposed.

ACKNOWLEDGEMENTS: The comments of the anonymous reviewers have led to improvements in the paper.

References

[Breese and Horvitz, 1990] J. Breese and E. Horvitz. Ideal Reformulation of Belief Networks. In *Proc. Conf. Uncertainty in Artificial Intelligence*, pages 64–72, 1990.

[Chang and Fung, 1990] K. Chang and R. Fung. Refinement and Coarsening of Bayesian Networks. In *Proc. Conf. Uncertainty in Artificial Intelligence*, pages 475–482, 1990.

[Cooper, 1990] G.F. Cooper. The Computational Complexity of Probabilistic Inference Using Belief Networks. *Artificial Intelligence*, (42):393–405, 1990.

[de Kleer *et al.*, 1990] J. de Kleer, A. Mackworth, and R. Reiter. Characterizing Diagnoses. In *Proc. AAAI*, pages 324–330, 1990.

[Goldman and Charniak, 1990] R. Goldman and E. Charniak. Dynamic Construction of Belief Networks. In *Proc. Conf. Uncertainty in Artificial Intelligence*, pages 90–97, 1990.

[Heckerman and Horvitz, 1990] D. Heckerman and E. Horvitz. Problem Formulation as the Reduction of a Decision Model. In *Proc. Conf. Uncertainty in Artificial Intelligence*, pages 82–89, 1990.

[Horvitz *et al.*, 1989] E. Horvitz, G. Cooper, and Heckerman. Reflection and Action Under Scarce Resources: Theoretical Principles and Empirical Study. In *Proc.IJCAI*, pages 1121–1127, 1989.

[Howard and Matheson, 1981] R.A. Howard and J.E. Matheson. Influence diagrams. In R. Howard and J. Matheson, editors, *The Principles and Applications of Decision Analysis*, pages 720–762, Strategic Decisions Group, CA, 1981.

[Kanazawa, 1991] K. Kanazawa. Logic and Time Nets for Probabilistic Inference. In *Proc. AAAI*, 1991.

[Lehmann, 1990] H.P. Lehmann. A Decision-Analytic Model for Using Scientific Data. In M. Henrion, R. Shachter, L. Kanal, and J. Lemmer, editors, *Uncertainty in Artificial Intelligence 5*, pages 309–318, North Holland, 1990.

[Levitt *et al.*, 1990] T. Levitt, J.M. Agosta, and T. Binford. Model-Based Influence Diagrams for Machine Vision. In M. Henrion, R. Shachter, L. Kanal, and J. Lemmer, editors, *Uncertainty in Artificial Intelligence 5*, North Holland, 1990.

[McAllester, 1990] D. McAllester. Truth Maintenance. In *Proc. AAAI*, pages 1109–1115, 1990.

[Pearl, 1988] J. Pearl. *Probabilistic Reasoning in Intelligent Systems.* Morgan Kaufmann, 1988.

[Provan, 1991 (forthcoming)] G.M. Provan. A Decision-Theoretic Approach to Diagnostic Reasoning. 1991 (forthcoming).

[Provan and Poole, 1991] G. M. Provan and D. Poole. A Utility-Based Analysis of Consistency-Based Diagnosis. In *Proc. Conf. on Knowledge Representation*, pages 461–472, 1991.

[Schwartz *et al.*, 1986] S. Schwartz, J. Baron, and J. Clarke. A Causal Bayesian Model for the Diagnosis of Appendicitis. In L. Kanal and Lemmer J., editors, *Proc. Conf. Uncertainty in Artificial Intelligence*, pages 229–236, 1986.

[Shachter, 1986] R. Shachter. Evaluating Influence Diagrams. *Operations Research*, 34:871–882, 1986.

[Shachter, 1988] R. Shachter. Probabilistic Inference and Influence Diagrams. *Operations Research*, 36:589–604, 1988.

[Shwe and Cooper, 1990] M. Shwe and G.F. Cooper. An Empirical Analysis of Likelihood-Weighting Simulation on a Large, Multiply-Connected Belief Network. In *Proc. Conf. Uncertainty in Artificial Intelligence*, pages 498–508, 1990.

[Srinivas and Breese, 1990] S. Srinivas and J. Breese. IDEAL: A Software Package for Analysis of Influence Diagrams. In *Proc. Conf. Uncertainty in Artificial Intelligence*, pages 212–219, 1990.

[Tatman and Shachter, 1990] J. Tatman and R. Shachter. Dynamic Programming and Influence Diagrams. *IEEE Trans. Systems, Man and Cybernetics*, 20:365–379, 1990.

[Webber *et al.*, 1990] B. Webber, J. Clarke, M. Niv, R. Rymon, and M. Ibanez. *TraumAID: Reasoning and Planning in the Initial Definitive Managment of Multiple Injuries.* Technical Report MS-CIS-90-50, University of Pennsylvania, 1990.

High Level Path Planning with Uncertainty

Runping Qi David Poole
Department of Computer Science
University of British Columbia
Vancouver B. C. Canada V6T 1W5
E-mail: qi@cs.ubc.ca, poole@cs.ubc.ca

Abstract

For high level path planning, environments are usually modeled as distance graphs, and path planning problems are reduced to computing the shortest path in distance graphs. One major drawback of this modeling is the inability to model uncertainties, which are often encountered in practice. In this paper, a new tool, called *U-graph*, is proposed for environment modeling. A U-graph is an extension of distance graphs with the ability to handle a kind of uncertainty. By modeling an uncertain environment as a U-graph, and a navigation problem as a Markovian decision process, we can precisely define a new optimality criterion for navigation plans, and more importantly, we can come up with a general algorithm for computing optimal plans for navigation tasks.

1 INTRODUCTION

For high level path planning, digraphs (distance graphs) are usually used as a tool for environment modeling. In a digraph, vertices denote places (or landmarks), edges — vertex pairs — denote the routes between the place pairs, and the weight of an edge denotes the cost (or distance) between the two vertices of the edge. The path planning problem is formulated as a *shortest path* problem in digraphs.

However, a major drawback of digraphs is the inability to model uncertainties. If there is an edge between two vertices in a digraph, it is assumed that there is a direct route between the places represented by these vertices. But, in reality, we often encounter some situations where we are not sure about something. For example, we may know that there is a door between two rooms, but that door may be locked; we are not sure whether the door is open now, though we know that, according to past experience, the probability of the door being open is about 0.8. Clearly, digraphs are not sufficient to model such situations.

As the first effort to extending the expressive power of digraphs, we propose in this paper a new kind of graphs, called *U-graphs* (uncertain graphs), and investigate path planning problems based on the U-graph model. A U-graph is an ordinary digraph augmented with a new kind of edges: *switches*. Like an edge, each switch connects a vertex pair and has a weight. In addition, each switch has a probability associated with it. The probability associated with a switch represents the probability that the connection between the two vertices of the switch is traversable.

With uncertainty being taken into consideration, the path planning problem is significantly different from the shortest path problem. Instead, a path planner needs to compute a "navigation plan" which can result in an optimal travel with respect to some predefined measures. The main difficulty in computing such an optimal travel strategy largely attributes to the *on-line* nature of the problem, that is, an optimal strategy should be able to tell an agent what is the optimal next step, based on the incomplete knowledge known so far, in any possibly encountered situation.

Traditionally, the quality of an on-line algorithm is measured based on two criteria [Bar-Noy and Schieber, 1991]: *competitive ratio* of the algorithm and worst-case performance. In this paper, we adopt a new optimality criterion in terms of the expected cost for a given task, which we think is very suitable for navigation. We formulate a navigation problem as a *finite state Markovian decision process*. Markovian decision process was studied as a mathematical abstraction of certain types of dynamic systems [Derman, 1970] and as a branch of dynamic programming [Howard, 60] [Denardo, 1982]. With this formulation, the path planning problem amounts to the *optimal first-passage problem* for a Markovian decision process [Derman, 1970]. From this formulation, we derive an algorithm for path planning.

The rest of this paper is organized as follows. In the

next section, U-graphs are formally introduced and world modeling based on U-graphs is briefly discussed. In Section 3, path planning in uncertain environments is addressed and an optimality criterion for navigation plans is informally presented. In Section 4, the path planning problem is formalized and a general path planning algorithm is derived. Section 5 discusses related work, and Section 6 concludes the paper with a brief discussion of our future work.

2 U-GRAPH

Definition 1 *A* U-graph *is* $\langle V, E, S_u, pr, weight\rangle$, *where* V *is a finite set of vertices,* $E \subseteq V \times V$ *is a set of edges,* $S_u \subseteq V \times V$ *is a set of switches,* pr *a probability function from* S_u *to* [0, 1], *and* weight *is a function from* $E \cup S_u$ *to* R^+.

For the purpose of clarity and simplicity, we assume that E and S_u are mutually disjoint.

For a U-graph $\langle V, E, S_u, pr, weight\rangle$, its *pessimistic induced graph* is graph $\langle V, E\rangle$; its *optimistic induced graph* is graph $\langle V, E \cup S_u\rangle$. A U-graph is said to be *disconnected wrt* two vertices if there is no path between the two vertices in the optimistic induced graph.

For high level path planning, the essential knowledge a path planner needs to know about the environment is the topology and connectivity of the environment. The topological structure of an environment can be represented by a set of "interesting places" and the connectivity relationships among these places. These places can be abstracted as vertices and the connectivity relationships abstracted as arcs in a U-graph. If it is uncertain whether the route between the two places is definitely traversable, this uncertainty can be abstracted by a switch. We say a switch is *on* if it is traversable, and a switch is *off* if it is not traversable. The probability that the route being traversable is assigned to the switch. The weight of the switch denotes the cost for an agent to go through the switch provided that it is on.

As an illustration of how to model a practical situation by a U-graph, let us consider a situation as shown in Figure 1-(a), where two places A and B are on the two sides of a river, and usually connected by a bridge. However, it is not sure whether the bridge is broken or not, though it is known that the probability for the bridge being broken is 0.2. If the bridge is not broken, it will take about five minutes to cross the river. The connection between A and B can be represented as a switch, as shown in Figure 1-(b).

In the following discussion we make three assumptions about a U-graph. First, the probabilities of the switches in S_u are mutually independent. Second, the status of the switches in S_u is uncertain to the agent unless the agent is at either end vertex of the switch.

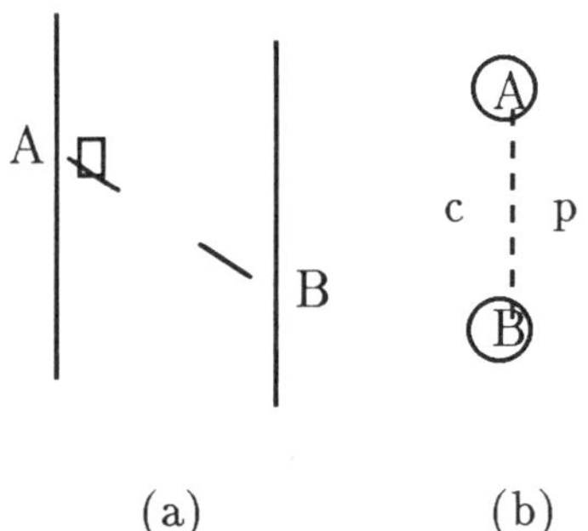

Figure 1: Modeling an uncertain situation by a U-graph

When an agent is at one end of a switch s, the agent can reach the other end through the switch with the cost given by *weight*(s) if the switch is actually on, and cannot otherwise traverse the switch. Third, the status of any switch will not change after the agent discovers it. The first two assumptions are justifiable in most situations. The third assumption is also justifiable because a U-graph is mainly used to represent the overall structure of an environment, and it is reasonable to believe that changes in the overall structure of an environment are comparatively slow.

The third assumption above implies that, when the agent reaches one ending vertex of a switch in S_u, the switch can be replaced by an edge with the same weight if the status of the switch turns out to be on, and can be deleted from the graph otherwise.

3 PATH PLANNING WITH UNCERTAINTY

As a motivating example, let us consider the case shown in Figure 2. Suppose that an agent is at vertex A and is asked to go to vertex B. In order to accomplish this task, the first question to be answered is: "which route should be taken?". Here are some possible answers.

First, if the agent wants to minimize the cost in the worst case, it should take the upper route (edge AB) in the graph.

Second, if the agent would like to minimize the expected cost for accomplishing this task, there are two choices. The first one is to go to B through edge AB. Another one is as follows: go to C first; if CD is actually traversable, go to D then to B; otherwise go back to A, then go to B through edge AB. The expected cost for the first choice is d_1. The expected cost for the second choice is:

$$d_2 + p * (d_4 + d_3) + (1 - p) * (d_2 + d_1)$$

Third, if the agent has a resource limit, it may want to choose a navigation plan which can maximize the

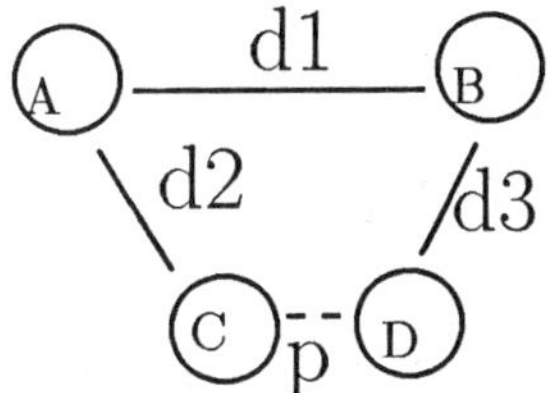

Figure 2: A simple path planning case with uncertainty

probability of reaching the destination within the resource limit.

As we see from the above example, an agent may be subject to various constraints and want to achieve various objectives for a given navigation task. These constraints and objectives determine the optimality criteria of plans. In this paper, we consider path planning problem *wrt* the criterion of minimization of the expected cost for achieving a given task.

More precisely, we state the navigation problem and the optimality criterion as follows. *When given a task of going to vertex q from vertex p in a U–graph representation of an environment, an agent is supposed to systematically explore the environment until either arriving at the goal position or finding out that there is actually no path to the goal position. The path planning problem is to determine a navigation plan which minimizes the expected cost required for exploring the environment.*

4 A FORMAL DEFINITION OF PATH PLANNING

In the present section, we model a navigation problem as a *Markovian decision process* [Derman, 1970], a navigation plan as a *policy* for the Markovian decision process, and give a precise definition of the expected cost for a navigation plan.

4.1 Markovian Decision Model

Informally, a Markovian decision process is an alternating sequence of states of, and actions on, an evolution system. At each point of time, the state of the system can be observed and classified, and an action, based on the observed state, can be taken. A *policy* is a prescription for taking action at each point in time.

Formally, a Markovian decision process is a quadruple $\langle I, K, w, q \rangle$, where I denotes the space of the states that can be observed of a system, $K = \{K_i | i \in I\}$, K_i denotes the set of actions which may be taken in state i, w is a cost function and q is a transition function.

The laws of motion of the system are characterized by the transition function q. Whenever the system is in state i and action a is taken, then, regardless of its history, $q(i,j,a)$ denotes the probability of the system being in state j at the next instant the system is observed. It is assumed that $\sum_j q(i,j,a) = 1$ for any $i \in I$ and $a \in K_i$. A cost structure is superimposed on a Markovian decision process. Whenever the system is in state i and action a is taken, a known cost $w(i,a)$ is incurred.

A deterministic policy for a Markovian decision process can be thought as a function mapping from states to actions. For the purpose of this paper, we will only consider deterministic policies. For a Markovian decision process and a fixed policy R, let $P_R\{Y_t = i\}$ be the probability of M being in state i at time t under the control of policy R. We define a set of random variables $\{W_t, t = 0, 1, ...\}$:

$$W_t = w(i, R(i)) \quad \text{if } Y_t = i.$$

The expected cost at time t *wrt* policy R is:

$$E_R\{W_t\} = \sum_i P_R\{Y_t = i\} w(i, R(i)).$$

Let $Y_0 = i$ be the initial state and let

$$S_{R,T}(i) = E_R \sum_{t=0}^{T} W_t = \sum_{t=0}^{T} \sum_j P_R\{Y_t = j\} w(j, R(j)).$$

$S_{R,T}(i)$ is the expected total cost of operating the system up to and including the time "horizon" $t = T$, given the initial state i and policy R. The *optimal first–passage problem* is to find R that minimizes $\lambda_R(i) = S_{R,\tau}(i)$, where τ denotes the smallest positive value of t such that $Y_t = j$, and j is one of the target states at which the process is stopped. This problem is was first formulated by Eaton and Zadeh [Eaton and Zadeh, 1962].

Let C_D denote a class of all (deterministic) policies. Derman [Derman, 1970] proved that: if $\{w(i,a)\}$ are non–negative, then there exists an $R* \in C_D$ such that

$$\lambda_{R*}(i) = \inf_{R \in C_D} \lambda_R(i), \quad i \in I.$$

For a given policy R, let $X(R,i)$ denote the expected value of the total cost of reaching the target state from state i and $R*$ denote the optimal policy. Thus, we have:

$$X(R*, i) \leq X(R, i) \tag{1}$$

and

$$X(R,i) = E\{w(i,a) + X(R,j)\} \tag{2}$$

or

$$X(R,i) = w(i,a) + \sum_{j \in I} q(i,j,a) * X(R,j) \tag{3}$$

for all $i \in I$, where $a = R(i)$. Furthermore, if there exists another policy R' such that for some state i,

$X(R', i) < X(R, i)$, then R must not be an optimal policy.

The behaviors of a Markovian decision process can be represented as a directed graph. Formally, the *representing graph of the Markovian decision process* $M = (I, K, w, q)$ is a directed graph $RG(M) = \langle V, A_1 \cup A_2 \rangle$ defined as:

$$V = I \cup \{s_{ia} | i \in I; a \in K_i\};$$

$$A_1 = \{\langle i, s_{ia} \rangle | i \in I; a \in K_i\}$$

and

$$A_2 = \{\langle s_{ia}, j \rangle | i, j \in I; a \in K_i; q(i, j, a) > 0\}$$

In such a representing graph, a node $i \in I$, called a *state node*, represents an observable state while node s_{ia}, called a *non-state node*, represents a temporary state resulting from taking action a in state i. The next observable state after the temporary state is determined by a probability distribution $q(i, j, a)$. Therefore we can attach action a as the label for arc $\langle i, s_{ia} \rangle$ and probability $q(i, j, a)$ as the label for arc $\langle s_{ia}, j \rangle$.

The *representing graph for a Markovian decision process* M *starting with state* i_0, denoted by $RG_{i_0}(M)$, is the largest subgraph of $RG(M)$ such that any node in the subgraph is reachable from i_0.

In particular, the behaviors of a Markovian decision process controlled by a particular policy R can be represented by a directed graph $RG(M, R)$ defined as:

$$V = I \cup \{s_{ia} | i \in I; a \in K_i\}$$

and

$$A_1 = \{\langle i, s_{ia} \rangle | i \in I; a \in K_i; R(i) = a\}$$

and A_2 is the same as the above. The representing graph for a Markovian decision process M controlled by policy R starting with state i_0, denoted by $RG_{i_0}(M, R)$, is the largest subgraph of $RG(M, R)$ such that any node in the subgraph is reachable from i_0 in the original graph.

Such a graph representation is quite useful. With this representation, we can study the properties of a Markovian decision process by studying its representing graph. More importantly, it can facilitate the derivation of the algorithm for computing the optimal plan for a given navigation task (see section 4.4).

4.2 Some Related Concepts

A *configuration* is a triple $\langle G, n_c, n_g \rangle$, where G is a U-graph, n_c and n_g are two vertices of the graph, representing the current position and the goal position respectively. An edge is said to be a *current edge* of a configuration if the current vertex of the configuration is one of the vertices of the edge. Similarly, a switch is said to be a *current switch* of a configuration if the current vertex of the configuration is one of the vertices of the switch. Let $CE(C)$ and $CS(C)$ denote the set of current edges and the set of current switches of configuration C respectively.

A *terminal* configuration (or a terminal for short) is a configuration which satisfies either of the following two conditions:

1. the shortest distance between n_c and n_g in the optimistic induced graph $\langle V, E \cup S_u \rangle$ is equal to the shortest distance between n_c and n_g in the pessimistic induced graph $\langle V, E \rangle$;
2. G is disconnected *wrt* to n_c and n_g.

In other words, a terminal is a configuration which is certain enough such that the agent can determine whether there is a path to the goal position, and be able to compute the optimal path if there is any. A terminal satisfying the first condition will be called a "good" terminal. A terminal satisfying the second condition will be called a "bad" terminal. A configuration C is said to be an *uncontrolled configuration* if $CS(C)$ is not empty. A configuration is *controlled* if it is not uncontrolled.

Two kinds of *transitions*, namely *uncontrolled* and *controlled transitions*, can be defined respectively on uncontrolled and controlled configurations. For a controlled configuration $C = \langle G, n_c, n_g \rangle$, suppose $n_1, ..., n_k$ are the k $(k > 0)$ neighbours of n_c; we define k controlled transitions, $t_1, ..., t_k$, corresponding to the k current edges. We denote by $trans(C, t_i)$ the configuration to which the i-th transition t_i can lead from configuration C. We have:

$$trans(C, t_i) = \langle G, n_i, n_g \rangle.$$

For an uncontrolled configuration $C = \langle G, n_c, n_g \rangle$, suppose $G = \langle V, E, S_u, pr, weight \rangle$ and $CS(C) = \{s_1, ..., s_k\}$ is the set of k $(k > 0)$ current switches of C; we define 2^k uncontrolled transitions corresponding to all the possible combinations of the k switches' states. We denote by ONS_{t_i} the set of switches in $CS(C)$ which are on, and by $OFFS_{t_i}$ the set of switches in $CS(C)$ which are off. We denote by p_{t_i} the probability that the transition t_i can happen. Thus,

$$p_{t_i} = \prod_{s \in ONS_{t_i}} pr(s) * \prod_{s \in OFFS_{t_i}} (1 - pr(s))$$

and

$$trans(C, t_i) = \langle G', n_c, n_g \rangle$$

where $G' = \langle V, E', S'_u, pr', weight \rangle$, where $E' = E \cup ONS_{t_i}$ and $S'_u = S_u - CS(C)$.

As an example, Figure 3-(a) shows a controlled configuration where the goal position is vertex q and the current position is indicated by a double-circle. Three

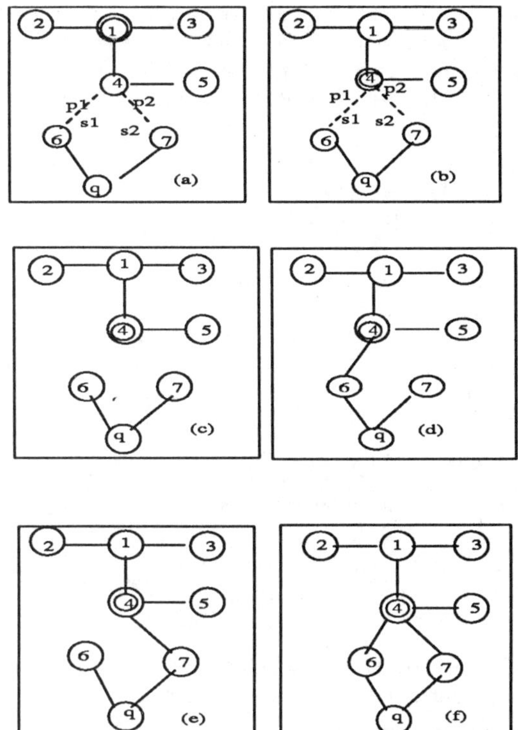

Figure 3: An example for illustrating configuration and transitions

controlled transitions are associated with this configuration, corresponding to going to vertices 2, 3, and 4 respectively. Suppose the transition of going to vertex 4 is chosen, then the next configuration, as shown in Figure 3-(b), is an uncontrolled one. With this uncontrolled configuration, four uncontrolled transitions are associated, corresponding to the possible combinations of the states of switches s_1 and s_2. The possible configurations to which these transitions can lead are shown in Figures 3-(c), 3-(d), 3-(e) and 3-(f) respectively.

A controlled transition sequence $T_{ij} = t^1_{ij}, ..., t^k_{ij}, k \geq 1$ is said to be *a generic transition* from a controlled configuration i to a configuration j, if

$$j = trans(...trans(i, t^1_{ij}), ..., t^k_{ij}).$$

We use $gtrans(i, T)$ to denote the configuration resulting from *taking* generic transition T in i. For the above case, we have $gtrans(i, T_{ij}) = j$. For a controlled transition t, let $c(t)$ denote the cost associated with t. The cost for a generic transition T_{ij}, denoted by $c(T_{ij})$, is the sum of the costs of the constituent transitions of T_{ij}.

Note that, for a given controlled configuration i and a configuration j, there may exist zero, one or many generic transitions from i to j. The *optimal generic transition* from i to j is the one with the least cost. A configuration j is said to be a *generic successor* of a controlled configuration i if there is a generic transition from i to j, and configuration j is either a terminal or is an uncontrolled configuration.

Intuitively, a configuration captures the characteristics of a situation, i.e. where the agent is now, where it wants to go and how much it knows about the environment. When an agent is in a controlled configuration, it can decide which edge to traverse next, and therefore, has control over the selection of the next (controlled) transition. Furthermore, if an agent takes a longer perspective on its navigation in a controlled configuration it can find that it will either enter an uncontrolled configuration first or enter a terminal first. Thus, we can consider the set of the generic transitions from i to the generic successors of i as the set of the possible actions the agent can take in configuration i. Obviously, if an agent wants to reach configuration j, it should take the optimal generic transition from i to j. We use $GT(i)$ to denote the set of the optimal transitions from i to the generic configurations of i.

When an agent is in an uncontrolled configuration, it faces one or more uncertain switches, and it can examine the states of the uncertain switches. When the new information is available to the agent, a new configuration is reached. Thus the agent has no control over which new configuration will be reached.

4.3 Navigation Procedure as a Markovian Decision Process

If we regard all the controlled configurations which may be encountered during a navigation collectively as a state space, all the generic transitions associated with each state as the possible actions which may be taken in that state, and the uncontrolled transitions as the state transitions, then, we can consider a navigation procedure as a Markovian decision process, and a navigation plan as a policy for such a decision process. We now give a formal account of this idea.

For a given U–graph $G = \langle V, E, S_u, pr, weight\rangle$, let $VSG(G)$ denote the following set:
$\{\langle V, E \cup S'_{on}, S'_u, pr, weight\rangle | S'_{on} \cup S'_u \subseteq S_u; S'_{on} \cap S'_u = \phi\}$.
In words, $VSG(G)$ denotes the collection of the variations of U–graph G which are themselves U–graphs obtained by deleting some switches from S_u and moving some of the remaining switches from S_u to E.

For a given task of going from vertex p to vertex q in a U–graph G, let IC be $\langle G, p, q\rangle$, called the *initial* configuration, and I' be the set of all possible controlled configurations defined as:
$I' = \{\langle G', p', q\rangle | G' \in VSG(G), p' \in V, \langle G', p', q\rangle$ is a controlled configuration$\}$. Let f denote a special state called *target state*. Let $I = I' \cup \{f\}$ be the state space.

In our current formulation, we consider $GT(i)$ as the set of the possible actions that can be taken in state i, i.e. $K_i = GT(i)$. We assume further that there exists a special action a_0 which is the only action that could be taken in all the terminals. That is, for any state i corresponding to a terminal configuration, K_i is $\{a_0\}$ and taking action a_0 in state i will result in the target state f.

For any state $i \in I$ and an action $a \in K_i$, the probability $q(i,j,a)$ is defined as:

$$q(i,j,a) = \begin{cases} 1 & \text{if } i \text{ is a terminal, } j = f \\ & \text{and } a = a_0\text{;} \\ 1 & \text{if } j = gtrans(i,a) \\ & \text{and } j \text{ is a terminal;} \\ p_t & \text{if } gtrans(i,a) \text{ is an uncontrolled} \\ & \text{configuration and} \\ & trans(gtrans(i,a),t) = j \\ & \text{for some transition } t \text{ in } gtrans(i,a) \\ 0 & \text{otherwise.} \end{cases}$$

where p_t is the probability of transition t.

For any state $i \in I$, and an action $a \in K_i$, let $w(i,a)$ denote the cost for taking action a in state i, which is defined as:

$$w(i,a) = \begin{cases} c(a) & \text{if } i \text{ is not a terminal;} \\ SD(G', n_i, q) & \text{if } a = a_0 \\ & \text{and } i \text{ is a good terminal;} \\ 0 & \text{otherwise.} \end{cases}$$

where n_i is the current position of configuration i; $c(a)$ is the cost of generic transition a; G' is the pessimistic induced graph of the U-graph of configuration i and $SD(G', n_i, q)$ is the shortest distance from vertex n_i to vertex q in graph G'.

Proposition 2 *For a given navigation task of going from vertex p to vertex q in a U-graph G, let I, w, q, and K_i for each $i \in I$ be constructed as above, and let $K = \{K_i | i \in I\}$ and $M = \langle I, K, w, q\rangle$, then M is a Markovian decision process.*

Definition 3 A navigation plan *for a given navigation task is defined as a policy R for the Markovian decision process corresponding to the task.*

Definition 4 The expected cost *for a plan R is given by $\lambda_R(IC)$, as defined in Section 4.1, where IC is the initial configuration.*

Definition 5 *For a given task,* the path planning problem *is to find a policy which minimizes $\lambda_R(IC)$.*

For a Markovian decision process M derived from a navigation problem, we make the following important observation. That is: *"nature transitions" always lead to new states.* This means that, no matter what history the current state has, if an action (a generic transition) taken in this state will lead to an uncontrolled configuration which in turn will be led to a new controlled configuration (a new state), then this new state is different than any of the states in the history. The intuitive meaning is that whenever an agent reaches an uncontrolled configuration, it will find new information about the states of the uncertain switches, therefore, the resultant configuration must be different than any one encountered before. This implies that $RG_{i_0}(M)$, the representing graph of M, must be a directed acyclic graph (DAG).

4.4 Computing the Optimal Policy for a Navigation Problem

In the literature, the optimal first-passage problem was solved through successive approximations [Derman, 1970] or through computing the fixed point of a set of recursive equations [Denardo, 1982] [Eaton and Zadeh, 1962]. Both approaches involve iterations. The computational complexity of each iteration in these methods is $O(N * K)$, where $N = |I|$ is the size of state space and K is the average number of possible actions that may be taken in a state. There is not a good upper bound for iteration times.

However, we can do much better for our case. As we mentioned earlier, the Markovian decision process M derived from a navigation task with initial state i_0 can be represented by $RG_{i_0}(M)$ which is a DAG. A node in such a DAG represents a configuration which is reachable from the start state (configuration) i_0. The number of nodes in $RG_{i_0}(M)$ is no greater than $|I| + \sum_{i \in I} |K_i|$ even in the worst case. In the average case, the number of nodes is much smaller than the above bound, since, intuitively, many configurations may not be reachable from the initial configuration.

Now, let us consider the structure of an optimal policy $R*$. Obviously, we can assume $X(R*, f) = 0$. Since each state i corresponding to a terminal configuration has only one action a_0, then $R^*(i) = a_0$, thus, $X(R*, i) = w(i, a_0)$, for every state i corresponding to a terminal.

For a state i with possible action set K_i, let J_{ia} denote the set of the possible next states after action a is taken in state i, and $J_i = \cup_{a \in K_i} J_{ia}$ be the possible next states of state i. We have already known that:

$$X(R*, i) \leq X(R, i)$$

and

$$X(R, i) = w(i,a) + \sum_{j \in I} q(i,j,a) * X(R, j)$$

for any policy R and all $i \in I$, where $a = R(i)$. Therefore, for a state i, suppose we already know $X(R*, j)$ for all $j \in J_i$, and suppose $a* = R^*(i)$, then, $w(i, a*) + \sum_j q(i,j,a*) * X(R*, j)$ must equal $\min_{a \in K_i}\{w(i,a) + \sum_j q(i,j,a) * X(R*, j)\}$. Consequently, we have:

$$X(R*, i) = \min_{a \in K_i}\{w(i,a) + \sum_j q(i,j,a) * X(R*, j)\}. \tag{4}$$

This means that the value of $X(R*, i)$ can be computed easily if the values of $X(R*, j)$ are known for those $j \in J_i$.

Based on the above discussion, we obtain the following algorithm for computing $R*$ and $X(R*, i)$ for every i which is reachable from i_0 in $RG_{i_0}(M)$.

Algorithm A1

Input: $RG_{i_0}(M)$;

Output: $RG_{i_0}(M, R*)$ and $X(R*, -)$ defined on the state nodes in $RG_{i_0}(M)$.

1. (Initialization) For each state i corresponding to a terminal configuration, set $R*(i) = a_0$ and $X(R*, i) = w(i, a_0)$.
2. If $X(R*, i_0)$ has been computed, stop, otherwise, go to the next step.
3. For each state–node i, if $X(R*, i)$ has not been computed and for all $j \in J_i$, $X(R*, j)$ has been computed, compute $R*(i)$ and $X(R*, i)$ according to equation (4); cut off all the "non–optimal arcs" incident from i.
4. Go to step 2.

$RG_{i_0}(M, R*)$ can be obtained from the resultant graph by deleting all the nodes which are not reachable from i_0. Obviously, the complexity of the above algorithm is linear in the size of $RG_{i_0}(M)$. However, it should be noted that the size of $RG_{i_0}(M)$ can be exponential in the number of uncertain switches in a given U–graph.

5 RELATED WORK

At the application aspect, our work is related to the large body of research on spatial knowledge representation, path planning and navigation in AI and Robotics community. At the algorithmic aspect, our work is most closely related to some theoretical studies [Papadimitriou and Yannakakis, 1989] [Bar-Noy and Schieber, 1991].

Related work in AI: A number of approaches to path planning and navigation in uncertain environments have been proposed and many navigation systems for mobile robots have been built (e.g. [Arkin, 1989]; [Crowley, 1985]). However, in most of these systems, attention is primarily focused on the problem of how to make a robot capable of moving around in relatively small environments. Some notable exceptions are Kuipers' TOUR model [Kuipers, 1978], Kuipers and Levitt's COGNITIVE MAP [Kuipers and Levitt, 1988] for the representation of spatial knowledge of large scale environments, and Levitt and Lawton's qualitative approach [Levitt and Lawton, 1990] to navigation in large scale environments.

With respect to the express power, our U–graph model can express only the topological aspect of TOUR model in addition to a kind of uncertainty. While TOUR model supports both "highway oriented" navigation and "cross country" navigation, the U–graph supports only the former.

Dean *et al* [Dean *et al.*, 1990] described a navigation system that also makes use of utility theory in navigation planning. However, their stress was on how to coordinate task achieving activities and map building activities so that a group of navigation tasks in an uncertain environment can be efficiently accomplished. In contrast, our planner is primarily concerned with the problem of finding the best way to accomplish a given navigation task.

A major difference between our work and the other related work (e.g. [Levitt and Lawton, 1990]; [Dean *et al.*, 1990]) lies in the fact that the outcome of our path planning algorithm is not just a simple path, but is a comprehensive navigation plan which is highly conditional to the future states of the environment. In fact, the navigation plan generated by our path planner is somewhat similar to Schoppers' Universal Plan [Schoppers, 1989].

Some related theoretical studies: In [Papadimitriou and Yannakakis, 1989] Papadimitriou and Yannakakis first named the problem of travel under uncertainty as the *Canadian Traveller Problem* (CTP). In their formulation, a traveller is given an unreliable graph (map) whose edges may disappear. They also assume that the traveller cannot know whether an edge is actually there unless he/she reaches an adjacent vertex of the edge, and the status of an edge will not change after being revealed. The problem is to devise a travel strategy that results in an optimal travel (according to some predefined measure) from one vertex to another.

There is an obvious difference between our U–graphs and the uncertain graphs of the CTP with respect to environment modeling. In CTP, it is assumed that all the edges in a graph may disappear, and no information is known about the likelihood of the presence of any edge. However, in our U–graphs, we can make an explicit distinction between the "certain edges" and the "uncertain switches". Furthermore, by restricting the uncertain switches to a comparatively small number, we can reasonably assume that the prior probabilities of those uncertain switches can be obtained.

Besides the difference with respect to environment modeling, Papadimitriou and Yannakakis defined their optimality criteria in terms of *competitive ratio*. The competitive ratio is used in the literature to measure the quality of on–line algorithms [Mannasse *et al.*, 1988]. Papadimitriou and Yannakakis showed that devising an on–line travel strategy with a bounded competitive ratio is PSPACE-complete. They also showed that the problem of devising a strategy that minimizes the expected ratio, provided that each edge in a graph has a presence probability, remains hard (#P–hard and solvable in polynomial space).

Bar–Noy and Schieber studied several interesting variations of the CTP [Bar-Noy and Schieber, 1991]. One variation is the *k–Canadian Traveller Problem*, which is a CTP with k as the upper bound on the number of the blocked roads (disappeared edges). They gave a recursive algorithm to compute a travel strategy that guarantees the shortest worst–case travel time. The complexity of the algorithm is polynomial for any given constant k. They also proved that the problem is PSPACE-complete when k is non–constant. Another variation Bar–Noy and Schieber studied is the *Stochastic Recoverable Canadian Traveller Problem.* In this problem, it is assumed that blocked roads can be reopened in certain time. They presented a polynomial algorithm for devising a travel strategy that minimizes the expected travel time, under the assumption that for any edge e in a given graph, the *recover time* of e is less than the weight of any edge adjacent to it in the graph. Unfortunately, it is yet unclear how to relax this unrealistic assumption.

6 CONCLUSION AND FUTURE WORK

In this paper, we present U–graphs as a tool for modeling uncertain environments and formulate a U–graph based navigation problem as a Markovian decision process. This formulation contributes to a better understanding on the problem we try to solve. In addition, we present an optimality criterion for navigation plans and develop an algorithm for computing the optimal navigation plan *wrt* the criterion.

Future work can be carried out in several possible directions. First, we will study some other reasonable optimality criteria for path planning with uncertainty. For example, the optimality criteria could be quite different from the one discussed in this paper if we assume that an agent is subject to a cost limit. Second, we hope that we can make use of the hierarchical property of a given U–graph to cope with the complexity of the path planning with uncertainty. Third, we plan to derive some approximation algorithms having lower complexity, yet being able to compute reasonably good sub–optimal navigation plans for a given problem. Another kind of interesting future work is to incorporate our U–graph model into more general frameworks such as Kuipers' TOUR model [Kuipers, 1978] [Kuipers and Levitt, 1988].

Acknowledgements

We would like to thank Ying Zhang and Andrew Csinger for their valuable comments on this paper. The work presented in this paper was supported in part by NSERC grant under operation number OG-POO44121.

References

[Arkin, 1989] R. C. Arkin. Navigational path planning for a vision based mobile robot. *Robotica*, 7, 1989.

[Bar-Noy and Schieber, 1991] Amotz Bar-Noy and Baruch Schieber. The canadian traveller problem. In *Proc. 2nd Annul ACM–SIAM Symposium on Descrete Algorithms*, 1991.

[Crowley, 1985] J. L. Crowley. Navigation for an intelligent mobile robot. *IEEE Robotics and Automation*, RA-1(1), 1985.

[Dean *et al.*, 1990] T. Dean, K. Basye, R. Chekaluk, S. Hyun, M. Lejter, and M. Randazza. Coping with uncertainty in control system for navigation and exploration. In *Proc. of AAAI–90*, 1990.

[Denardo, 1982] Eric V. Denardo. *Dynamic Programming: models and applications.* Prentice–Hall, Inc., Englewood Cliffs, New Jersey, 1982.

[Derman, 1970] Cyrus Derman. *Finite State Markovian Decision Process.* Academic Press New York and London, 1970.

[Eaton and Zadeh, 1962] J. H. Eaton and L. A. Zadeh. Optimal pursuit strategies in discrete state probabilistic system. *Trans. ASME Ser. D., Journal of Basic Engineering*, 84, 1962.

[Howard, 60] R. A. Howard. *Dynamic Programming and Markov Processes.* Technology Press, Cambridge, Massachusetts, and Wiley New York, 60.

[Kuipers and Levitt, 1988] Benjiamin J. Kuipers and Tod S. Levitt. Navigation and mapping in large–scale space. *AI Magzine*, 9(2), 1988.

[Kuipers, 1978] B. J. Kuipers. Modeling spatial knowledge. *Cognitive Science*, 2, 1978.

[Levitt and Lawton, 1990] T. S. Levitt and D. T. Lawton. Qualitative navigation for mobile robots. *Artificial Intelligence*, 44(3), 1990.

[Mannasse *et al.*, 1988] M. S. Mannasse, L. A. McGeoch, and D. D. Sleator. Competitive algorithms for on–line problems. In *the 20th ACM Symp. on Theory of Computing*, 1988.

[Papadimitriou and Yannakakis, 1989] Christos H. Papadimitriou and Mihalis Yannakakis. Shortest paths without a map. In *Proc. the 16th ICALP, Lecture Note in Comp. Sci. No. 372.* Spring–Verlag, July 1989.

[Schoppers, 1989] Marcel J. Schoppers. Representation and automatic synthesis of reaction plans. Technical Report UIUCDCS–R–89–1546, Department of Computer Science, University of Illinois at Urbana–Champaign, 1989.

Formal Model of Uncertainty for Possibilistic Rules

Arthur Ramer
University of Oklahoma, Norman, OK 73019

Leslie Lander
SUNY-Binghamton, Binghamton, NY 13902-6000

OVERVIEW

Given a universe of discourse X—a domain of possible outcomes—an experiment may consist of selecting one of its elements, subject to the operation of chance, or of observing the elements, subject to imprecision.

A priori uncertainty about the actual result of the experiment may be quantified, representing either the likelihood of the choice of $x \in X$ or the degree to which any such $x \in X$ would be suitable as a description of the outcome. The former case corresponds to a probability distribution, while the latter gives a possibility assignment on X.

The study of such assignments and their properties falls within the purview of possibility theory [DP88, Y80, Z78]. It, like probability theory, assigns values between 0 and 1 to express likelihoods of outcomes. Here, however, the similarity ends. Possibility theory uses the maximum and minimum functions to combine uncertainties, whereas probability theory uses the plus and times operations. This leads to very dissimilar theories in terms of analytical framework, even though they share several semantic concepts. One of the shared concepts consists of expressing quantitatively the uncertainty associated with a given distribution. In probability theory its value corresponds to the gain of information that would result from conducting an experiment and ascertaining an actual result. This gain of information can equally well be viewed as a decrease in uncertainty about the outcome of an experiment. In this case the standard measure of information, and thus uncertainty, is Shannon entropy [AD75, G77]. It enjoys several advantages—it is characterized uniquely by a few, very natural properties, and it can be conveniently used in decision processes. This application is based on the principle of maximum entropy; it has become a popular method of relating decisions to uncertainty.

This paper demonstrates that an equally integrated theory can be built on the foundation of possibility theory. We first show how to define measures of information and uncertainty for possibility assignments. Next we construct an information-based metric on the space of all possibility distributions defined on a given domain. It allows us to capture the notion of proximity in information content among the distributions. Lastly, we show that all the above constructions can be carried out for 'continuous distributions'—possibility assignments on arbitrary measurable domains. We consider this step very significant—finite domains of discourse are but approximations of the real-life infinite domains. If possibility theory is to represent real world situations, it must handle continuous distributions both directly and through finite approximations.

In the last section we discuss a principle of maximum uncertainty for possibility distributions. We show how such a principle could be formalized as an inference rule. We also suggest it could be derived as a consequence of simple assumptions about combining information.

We would like to mention that possibility assignments can be viewed as fuzzy sets and that every fuzzy set gives rise to an assignment of possibilities. This correspondence has far reaching consequences in logic and in control theory. Our treatment here is independent of any special interpretation; in particular we speak of possibility distributions and possibility measures, defining them as measurable mappings into the interval $[0, 1]$.

Our presentation is intended as a self-contained, albeit terse summary. Topics discussed were selected with care, to demonstrate both the completeness and a certain elegance of the theory. Proofs are not included; we only offer illustrative examples.

1 POSSIBILITY DISTRIBUTIONS AND MEASURES

1.1 DISCRETE DOMAINS

We use the model of possibility theory introduced in [Z78]. The domain of discourse can be any finite or finitely measurable set. Here we discuss a finite domain X and define a *possibility distribution* as a function $\pi : X \to [0,1]$ such that $\max_{x\in X} \pi(x) = 1$. It expresses an assignment of possibility values $\pi(x)$ to elementary events $x \in X$. We extend it to arbitrary subsets $Y \subset X$ putting $\pi(Y) = \max_{x\in Y} \pi(x)$. [1]

Given two domains X and Y and two independent possibility assignments $\pi_1 : X \to [0,1]$, $\pi_2 : Y \to [0,1]$ we define a joint distribution

$$\pi_1 \otimes \pi_2 : (x,y) \mapsto \min(\pi_1(x), \pi_2(y)).$$

Given an arbitrary assignment π on a product space $X \times Y$ we define its marginal assignments π' on X and π'' on Y as

$$\pi'(x) = \max_{y\in Y} \pi(x,y), \qquad \pi''(y) = \max_{x\in X} \pi(x,y).$$

It is also convenient to define an *extension* of π from its domain X to a larger set $Y \supset X$. We put $\pi^Y(y) = \pi(y),\ \ y \in X$ and $\pi^Y(y) = 0$ otherwise. Lastly, given $X = \{x_1, \ldots, x_n\}$ and a permutation s of $\{1, \ldots, n\}$, we define a possibility assignment $s(\pi)$

$$s(\pi)(x_i) = \pi(x_{s(i)}).$$

1.2 CONTINUOUS DOMAINS

This structure generalizes to an arbitrary X endowed with a finite (Lebesgue) measure. The assignment becomes a measurable function $f : X \to [0,1]$, defining the possibility of $Y \subset X$ as $\sup_{x\in Y} f(x)$. By analogy with probability theory, we term such structures *continuous* possibility assignments or distributions. Joint, marginal and extended distributions are now defined using *sup* and *inf* instead of *max* and *min*. Lastly, we generalize permutations of X to measure–preserving transformations s, putting $s(f)(x) = f(s(x))$. A transformation corresponding to sorting discrete values is of particular interest. For f defined on X we want $\tilde{f}$ to be a descending equivalent of f, defined on a real interval of the same measure as X. For definiteness, we can make the origin the left end-point of the interval and have $\tilde{f}$ decrease monotonically. Measure-preserving implies that $\tilde{f}$ 'stays' above any given value α, $0 \leq \alpha \leq 1$, over the same space as the original function [2] and leads to a classical construction [HLP34].

We put $P(y) = \mathcal{M}\{x : f(x) \geq y\}$, where $\mathcal{M}$ is a standard measure on $[0,1]$ and define $\tilde{f}(x) = P^{-1}(x)$. As an illustration let us consider two examples.

Example

$$f(x) = \begin{cases} 2x, & 0 \leq x \leq 0.5, \\ 2 - 2x, & \text{otherwise.} \end{cases}$$

Here $P(y) = 1 - y$ and $\tilde{f}(x) = 1 - x$. It is immediate that $\tilde{f}(x) \geq \alpha$ over the set of the same measure as the set where $f(x) \geq \alpha$.

Example $f(x) = 4(x - \frac{1}{2})^2 = 4x^2 - 4x + 1$.
Now $P(y)$ represents the *combined* length of the intervals where $f(x)$ is $\geq y$.

Since $\{x : f(x) \geq y\} = [0, \frac{1-\sqrt{y}}{2}] \cup [\frac{1+\sqrt{y}}{2}, 1]$, we have $P(y) = 1 - \sqrt{y}$. Therefore $y = (1 - P(y))^2$ and $\tilde{f}(x) = (1-x)^2$.

2 INFORMATION FUNCTIONS IN POSSIBILITY THEORY

2.1 UNCERTAINTY

The structure outlined above provides the *possibilistic* context for the quantification of the notions of uncertainty and information. We view the mapping π as assigning a degree of assurance or certainty that an element of X is the outcome of an experiment. That experiment would consist of selecting $x \in X$ as a representative (perhaps unique) object of discourse. A priori we know only the distribution π; to determine $x \in X$ means to remove uncertainty about the result, thus entailing a gain of information. We would be particularly interested in quantifying that gain of information, averaged over the complete distribution π. That would also express the overall value of uncertainty inherent in the complete distribution π. Accordingly, we intend to define an information function I which assigns a nonnegative real value to an arbitrary distribution π. Following established principles of information theory, [AD75, G77] we stipulate that such an information function satisfies certain standard properties. Specifically, we require

additivity	$I(\pi_1 \otimes \pi_2) =$	$I(\pi_1) + I(\pi_2)$
subadditivity	$I(\pi) \leq$	$I(\pi') + I(\pi'')$
symmetry	$I(s(\pi)) =$	$I(\pi)$
expansibility	$I(\pi^Y) =$	$I(\pi)$

It turns out that these properties essentially characterize the admissible information functions [KM87,RL87]. Here we discuss the discrete case of $X = \{x_1, \ldots, x_n\}$. Let $\tilde{p}_1 \geq \tilde{p}_2 \geq \ldots \geq \tilde{p}_n$ be a descending sequence formed from the values $\pi(x_1), \ldots, \pi(x_n)$. Then, up to a multiplicative constant:

Theorem All information functions on X are of the form

$$\begin{aligned} I(\pi) &= \textstyle\sum_{i=1}^{n-1} (\tau(\tilde{p}_i) - \tau(\tilde{p}_{i+1})) \log i \\ &= \textstyle\sum_{i=2}^{h} \tau(\tilde{p}_i) \nabla \log i \end{aligned}$$

where τ is a nondecreasing mapping of $[0,1]$ onto itself. $I(\pi)$ is continuous (as a functional on the space of distributions) iff τ is a continuous deformation of $[0,1]$.

[1] The fuzzy interpretation is obtained by treating the pair (X, π) as a fuzzy subset of X and $\{x : \pi(x) \geq \alpha\}$ as its α-cuts.

[2] All α–cuts [DP88] of f are of the same size (have the same measure) as α–cuts of $\tilde{f}$.

The formula can be derived from functional equations representing the properties of information. In particular, the presence of $\log i$ comes from additivity, while the differences $\tau(\tilde{p}_i) - \tau(\tilde{p}_{i+1})$ reflect the use of the *max* and *min* operations.

By analogy with Shannon theory we may also impose a linear interpolation property on $I(\pi)$ [KM87]. We then obtain a particularly simple expression, named U-uncertainty [HK82]

$$U(\pi) = \sum(\tilde{p}_i - \tilde{p}_{i+1}) \log i = \sum \tilde{p}_i \nabla \log i.$$

It follows by taking τ to be the identity mapping and we shall continue to do that in the remainder of the paper; however, all the results can be extended to an arbitrary τ.

We observe that the distribution which carries the highest uncertainty value consists of assigning possibility 1 to all the events in X. It states that, a priori, every event is fully possible. This distribution, carrying no prior information, can be considered the *most uninformed* one.

2.2 INFORMATION DISTANCE

U-uncertainty serves to define various information distances [HK83, R90] between two distributions π and ρ defined on the same domain X. If $\pi(x) \le \rho(x)$, we put

$$g(\pi, \rho) = U(\rho) - U(\pi).$$

For the general case, given π and ρ, we first define their lattice meet and join

$$\pi \wedge \rho : x \mapsto \min(\pi(x), \rho(x)),$$

$$\pi \vee \rho : x \mapsto \max(\pi(x), \rho(x)).$$

We then put

$$G(\pi, \rho) = g(\pi, \pi \vee \rho) + g(\rho, \pi \vee \rho),$$

$$H(\pi, \rho) = g(\pi \wedge \rho, \pi) + g(\pi \wedge \rho, \rho),$$

$$K(\pi, \rho) = \max(g(\pi, \pi \vee \rho), g(\rho, \pi \vee \rho)).$$

These functions have several attractive properties:

Theorem Both G and K define metric distances on the space of all possibility distributions (on a given domain). H is additive in both arguments

$$H(\pi_1 \otimes \pi_2, \rho_1 \otimes \rho_2) = H(\pi_1, \rho_1) + H(\pi_2, \rho_2).$$

3 DESIGN OF CONTINUOUS POSSIBILITY INFORMATION

We shall now extend the previous definitions to arbitrary measurable domains. To avoid technical complications, we consider only the special, albeit typical case where X is the unit interval. Now a possibility distribution is a function $f : [0,1] \to [0,1]$ such that $\sup_{x \in [0,1]} f(x) = 1$. Although in a variety of practical situations it is sufficient to consider only continuous functions, we do not make that restriction.

As a first step the discrete formula $U(x) = \sum p_i \nabla \log i$ suggests forming an expression like $\int_0^1 \tilde{f}(x) d \ln x$, where $\tilde{f}$ is a suitable 'decreasing sorted' equivalent of f, while $d \ln x$ substitutes $\nabla \log x$. The latter quantity simply represents $x^{-1}dx$, while for $\tilde{f}$ we use a descending rearrangement of f.

Using this definition we can consider $\int_0^1 \frac{\tilde{f}(x)}{x} dx$ as a candidate expression for the value of information. Unfortunately, $\tilde{f}(x)$ is equal to 1 at 0, and the integral above diverges. A solution can be found through a technique that has been used in probability theory [G77], which is to use the information distance between a given density and the uniform one. In possibility theory we consider a constant function $f(x) \equiv 1$ as representing a uniform distribution. It is also the most 'uninformed' one—its discrete form clearly attains maximum U-uncertainty. Our final formula becomes

$$I(f) = \int_0^1 \frac{1 - \tilde{f}(x)}{x} dx.$$

This integral is well defined and avoids the annoying singularity at 0. We demonstrate its use on a class of polynomial functions.

Example Let us consider possibility distributions represented by $f(x) = x^n$, $n = 0, 1, \ldots$. Writing $J_n = I(x^n)$ and remembering that $\tilde{x^n} = (1-x)^n$, let us first compute $J_n - J_{n-1}$

$$\int_0^1 \frac{(1-(1-x)^n) - (1-(1-x)^{n-1})}{x} dx =$$

$$\int_0^1 \frac{(1-x)^{n-1} - (1-x)^n}{x} dx = \int_0^1 (1-x)^{n-1} dx = \frac{1}{n}$$

As $J_0 = 0$ we find that $J_n = 1 + \frac{1}{2} + \cdots + \frac{1}{n} = H_n$, the nth harmonic number.

4 PROPERTIES OF CONTINUOUS INFORMATION MEASURES

We summarize the properties of $I(f)$ in the next two theorems; $f, f_1, \ldots$ stand for continuous distributions, $f_1 \otimes f_2$ for their *min*-product and f' and f'' for the projections of f when it is defined on a product space.

Theorem $I(f)$ is

additive	$I(f_1 \otimes f_2) =$	$I(f_1) + I(f_2)$
superadditive	$I(f) \le$	$I(f') + I(f'')$
symmetric	$I(s(f)) =$	$I(f)$
expansible	$I(f^Y) =$	$I(f)$

Superadditivity of I (replacing subadditivity of U) is due to the minus sign in the formula that defines it.

Using $I(f)$ we can define continuous extensions of the information distances g, G, H and K. As in the discrete case, G and K are metric distances, while H is additive in both arguments. We shall demonstrate additivity of I with an example.

Example We use as an example $f = g = x^\alpha, \quad \alpha \geq 0$. We put $h(x,y) = \min(x^\alpha, y^\alpha)$ and find $\tilde{h}(t) = (1-\sqrt{t})^\alpha$. Then $I(h) = \int_0^1 \frac{1-(1-\sqrt{t})^\alpha}{t} dt$ which, after the substitution $u = \sqrt{t}$ becomes

$$\int_0^1 \frac{1-(1-u)^\alpha}{u^2} \cdot 2u du = 2\int_0^1 \frac{1-(1-u)^\alpha}{u} du = 2I(f).$$

Theorem $I(f)$ can be approximated as a limit of $U(p_n)$, where the p_n are discrete distributions approximating f. [3]

This theorem confirms that we are justified using discrete possibility distributions in uncertainty computations. Their information values approximate consistently an idealized value of a putative continuous distribution. Already a non-trivial example is offered by a linear function.

Example We select $f(x) = 1 - x$ and approximate it using the values at $\frac{1}{n}, \frac{2}{n}, \ldots 1$. The approximating distributions are $\pi^{(n)} = (\frac{n-1}{n}, \frac{n-2}{n}, \ldots 1)$, thus

$$U(\pi^{(n)}) = \sum (p_i - p_{i+1}) \ln i =$$

$$\sum (\frac{n-i+1}{n} - \frac{n-i}{n}) \ln i = \frac{1}{n} \sum \ln i = \frac{1}{n} \ln n!$$

From Stirling's formula $U(\pi^{(n)}) \sim \ln n - 1$ and $I(\pi^{(n)}) = \ln n - U(\pi^{(n)}) = 1$ which agrees with $I(f)$.

5 PRINCIPLE OF MAXIMUM UNCERTAINTY

The decision rule forming the principle of maximum uncertainty can be stated independently of any specific theory used to capture the notions of randomness, vagueness or imprecision [G77, SJ80, J82]. We only need to assume that such randomness, vagueness or imprecision is expressed in the form of a numerical *information* function. The rule can be enhanced if, in addition, an information distance function is available.

The principle offers a method of selecting a distribution subject to certain constraints, usually presented as systems of linear equations on the parameters of an unknown distribution. Such constraints define a set of admissible distributions, and the choice from among those, the reasoning continues, should be made without introducing extraneous information, or should be as 'uninformed' as possible. Thus we should select a distribution of the maximum uncertainty value.

A variation of the rule occurs when we are given a 'prior' distribution and are required to replace it with a 'posterior' distribution, subject to admissibility criteria. Now we select the distribution for which the distance from the current one ('prior') reaches a *minimum.* The earlier case can be viewed as selecting a distribution closest to a hypothetical 'least informed' distribution.

In possibility theory such a principle would state that, given a prior assignment of possibility values and certain constraints on the posterior assignemnt, we should select the latter as the closest admissible assignment. The proximity here is expressed through the possibilistic information distance. If there is no known or assumed prior assignemnt, we should consider the distance from the most 'uninformed' possibility distribution, which is given by assigning a constant value 1 to every element of the domain of discourse. It clearly has the highest value of U-uncertainty; it also agrees with the intuitive perception that, in the absence of constraints, every choice should be accorded maximum possibility.

A similar method of determining distributions holds valid in probability theory [SJ80]. There it can be also shown that any reasonable selection based on maximization must be based on an information measure. Our current research aims to show that also in possibility theory decisions based on information measures stand privileged.

[3] For sufficiently uniform approximations.

REFERENCES

AD75 ACZEL, J. and DAROCZY, Z., 1975, *On measures of information and their characterization*, Academic Press, New York.

DP88 DUBOIS, D. and PRADE, H., 1988, *Possibility theory*, Plenum Press, New York .

DP87 DUBOIS, D. and PRADE, H., 1987, Properties of measures of information in evidence and possibility theories, *Fuzzy Sets Syst.*, 24(2).

G77 GUIASU, S., 1977, *Information Theory and Applications*, McGraw Hill, New York .

HK83 HIGASHI, M. and KLIR, G., 1983, On the notion of distance representing information closeness, *Int. J. Gen. Syst.*, 9(1).

HK82 HIGASHI, M. and KLIR, G., 1982, Measures of uncertainty and information based on possibility distributions *Int. J. Gen. Syst.*, 8(3).

HLP34 HARDY, G., LITTLEWOOD, J. and POLYA, G., 1934, *Inequalities*,

Cambridge University Press, Cambridge .

J82 JAYNES, E., 1982, On the rationale of maximum entropy methods, *Proc. IEEE*, 70.

KM87 KLIR, G. and MARIANO, M., 1987, On the uniqueness of possibilistic measure of uncertainty and information, *Fuzzy Sets Syst.*, 24(2).

R90 RAMER, A., 1990, Structure of possibilistic information metrics and distances, *Int. J. Gen. Syst.*, 17(1), 18(1).

R89 RAMER, A., 1989, Concepts of fuzzy information measures on continuous domains, *Int. J. Gen. Syst.*, 17(2-3).

RL87 RAMER, A. and LANDER, L., 1987, Classification of possibilistic uncertainty and information functions, *Fuzzy Sets Syst.*, 24(2).

SJ80 SHORE, J. and JOHNSON, R., 1980, Axiomatic derivation of the principle of maximum entropy and the principle of minimum cross-entropy, *IEEE Trans.Inf.Theory*, IT-26.

Y80 YAGER, Y., 1980, Aspects of possibilistic uncertainty, *Int. J. Man-Machine Studies*, 12.

Z78 ZADEH, L., 1978, Fuzzy sets as a basis for a theory of possibility, *Fuzzy Sets Syst.*, 3(1).

Deliberation and its Role in the Formation of Intentions*

Anand S. Rao
Australian Artificial Intelligence Institute
Carlton, Victoria 3053
Australia
Email: anand@aaii.oz.au

Michael P. Georgeff
Australian Artificial Intelligence Institute
Carlton, Victoria 3053
Australia
Email: georgeff@aaii.oz.au

Abstract

Deliberation plays an important role in the design of rational agents embedded in the real-world. In particular, deliberation leads to the formation of intentions, i.e., plans of action that the agent is committed to achieving. In this paper, we present a branching-time possible-worlds model for representing and reasoning about, beliefs, goals, intentions, time, actions, probabilities, and payoffs. We compare this possible-worlds approach with the more traditional decision-tree representation and provide a transformation from decision trees to possible worlds. Finally, we illustrate how an agent can perform deliberation using a decision-tree representation and then use a possible-worlds model to form and reason about his intentions.

1 INTRODUCTION

The design of rational agents, situated in a dynamic world and operating effectively under real-time constraints and resource limitations, has been of great interest to researchers in philosophy, artificial intelligence, and computer science [1, 2, 7]. Such rational agents have to balance the time taken thinking against the time needed for acting. In particular, they must balance the frequency of reassessment of options against continuing commitment to previously chosen plans.

Classical planning addresses only one aspect of the above problem; namely, means-end reasoning. Means-end reasoning involves finding a sequence of actions that satisfy a certain end goal (or goals). However, simplifying assumptions are made about the capabilities of the reasoning agents and the worlds they occupy that limit the use of these techniques to essentially static domains.

Classical decision theory, on the other hand, addresses the problem of weighing alternative courses of action and choosing the best plan of action according to some well-defined criteria, such as maximizing expected utility. However, this theory presupposes an ideal agent who can consider and weigh all possible alternative courses of action before making a decision. In real situations, such an assumption is rarely valid—not only does the world undergo continuous change, even as the agent is deliberating, but the agent may not be capable of enumerating all the alternatives.

What is required for the design of rational agents is a combination of symbolic means-end reasoning and numeric decision-theoretic analysis that takes into account the resource-boundedness of rational agents [6]. One such design is provided by the belief-desire-intention (BDI) architecture [2]. This architecture gives primary importance to the attitude of intentions. While most philosophical accounts of rational agency treat intentions as being reducible to beliefs and desires, Bratman [1] argues convincingly that intentions, especially future-directed intentions, play a significant and distinct role in resource-bounded reasoning.

Bratman treats intentions as plans of action that the agent is committed to achieving. Prior intentions constrain the search for possible means for achieving the current intention and thus focus the means-end reasoning process. The notion of commitment, which lends a certain sense of stability to means-end reasoning, is balanced against the notion of reconsideration of intentions, which lends a certain sense of reactivity. This rational balance between commitment and reconsideration is essential for effective means-end reasoning in dynamic domains.[1]

*This research was in part supported by a *Generic Industry Research and Development Grant* from the Department of Industry, Technology and Commerce, Australia and in part by the Australian Civil Aviation Authority.

[1]Some interesting experimental work has recently been done in this area [11].

Intentions play two important roles in resource-bounded decision-theoretic analysis or deliberation [1]. First, prior intentions pose problems for further deliberation, i.e., prior intentions produce the decision problems that the agent needs to consider. Second, prior intentions constrain the deliberation process because they rule out options that conflict with existing intentions. Under this view, the deliberation process is a continuous resource-bounded activity rather than a one-off exhaustive decision-theoretic analysis.

So far, we have discussed the role of intentions in means-ends reasoning and deliberation. However, we have not discussed how the agent arrives at his intentions. Prior intentions, means-ends reasoning, and deliberation are all involved in the formation of intentions. By means-ends reasoning, a prior intention towards an end results in the agent enumerating all the alternative or means of achieving this end; the agent by deliberating on all these alternatives then chooses the best one and commits to it by forming an intention.

We have previously provided [14, 15] a logical framework that describes the role of intentions in means-end reasoning. In this paper, we illustrate how the process of deliberation can lead to the formation of intentions.

2 OVERVIEW

BDI-architectures are formalized by defining notions such as beliefs, goals, intentions, actions, and the inter-relationships between them. We have previously shown how this can be accomplished using a branching-time possible-worlds logic [15].

Briefly, the structure of our logic is as follows: Each world is a temporal structure with a branching time future and a single past called a *time tree* [4]. A particular time point in a particular world is called a *situation*. Event types transform one time point into another. For each situation we associate a set of *belief-accessible*, *goal-accessible*, and *intention-accessible* worlds; intuitively, those worlds that the agent *believes* to be possible, *desires* to bring about, and *commits* to achieving, respectively. Multiple possible worlds result from the agent's lack of knowledge about the state of the world. But within each of these possible worlds, the branching future represents the *choice* of actions available to the agent. Moving from belief to goal to intention worlds amounts to successively pruning the paths of the time tree; intuitively, to making increasingly selective choices about one's future actions. This is captured semantically by requiring that for each belief-accessible world there exists a sub-world which is goal-accessible and, in turn, for each goal-accessible world there exists a sub-world which is intention-accessible (see Figure 1).

In this paper, we extend the expressive power of the above logic to model the process of deliberation by introducing *subjective probabilities* and *subjective payoffs*. For the former, we adopt the formalism of Fagin and Halpern [5] and extend it to a branching-time model. For the latter, we introduce a payoff function that associates numeric values (or payoffs) with certain paths in a time tree. Intuitively, an agent at each situation has a probability distribution on his belief-accessible worlds. He then chooses sub-worlds of these that he considers are worth pursuing and associates a payoff value with each path in these sub-worlds. These sub-worlds are considered to be the agent's goal-accessible worlds. By making use of the probability distribution on his belief-accessible worlds and the payoff distribution on the paths in his goal-accessible worlds, the agent determines the best plan(s) of action for different scenarios. This process will be called *Possible-Worlds(PW) deliberation*. The result of PW-deliberation is a set of sub-worlds of the goal-accessible worlds; namely, the ones that the agent considers best. These sub-worlds are taken to be the intention-accessible worlds that the agent *commits* to achieving.

In contrast to this approach, decision theory represents the problem as a decision tree (or, equivalently, as a payoff matrix or influence diagram). A decision tree consists of three types of nodes: (a) *decision nodes*, which represent the choice of actions; (b) *chance nodes*, which represent the state of uncertainty in the world; and (c) *terminal nodes*, which represent the value of outcomes. Based on the category of decision making – namely, certainty, risk or uncertainty – a particular decision rule is adopted for selecting the best plan(s) of action. We shall refer to this process as *decision-tree (DT) deliberation*.

The main thrust of this paper is to show how decision-tree deliberation can be utilized within a framework that is suited to resource-bounded reasoning in dynamic domains. We first describe the possible-worlds model and the decision tree representation formally. We then provide a transformation from decision trees to the possible-worlds model. From the possible worlds viewpoint, this provides a concrete method for obtaining the probability and payoff distribution on the worlds. From a decision theory viewpoint, the transformation facilitates symbolic manipulation of decision-theoretic entities. Finally, we describe classical decision-tree deliberation and show how it can be used to determine the formation of intentions.

3 POSSIBLE WORLDS MODEL

In our earlier work [15] we extended the propositional branching-time logic CTL* [4] to a possible-worlds framework and introduced modal operators for beliefs, goals, and intentions. In this section, we enhance this logic by introducing operators for probability (similar to that of Fagin and Halpern [5]) and payoffs.

3.1 SYNTAX AND SEMANTICS

Similar to CTL*, we have two types of formulas in our logic: *state formulas* (which are true in a specific world at a particular time point) and *path formulas* (which are true along a specific path). A state formula is defined as follows: (a) any propositional formula is a state formula; (b) if ϕ_1, ..., ϕ_k are state formulas, ψ_1, ..., ψ_k are path formulas, and θ_1, ..., θ_k, α are real numbers, then $\theta_1 \mathsf{PROB}(\phi_1) + \ldots + \theta_k \mathsf{PROB}(\phi_k) \geq \alpha$ and $\theta_1 \mathsf{PAYOFF}(\psi_1) + \ldots + \theta_k \mathsf{PAYOFF}(\psi_k) \geq \alpha$ are also state formulas; (c) if ϕ_1 and ϕ_2 are state formulas, and ψ is a path formula, then $\neg\phi_1$, $\phi_1 \vee \phi_2$, $\mathsf{BEL}(\phi_1)$, $\mathsf{GOAL}(\phi_1)$, $\mathsf{INTEND}(\phi_1)$ and $\mathsf{OPTIONAL}(\psi)$ are state formulas. A path formula can be defined as follows: (a) any state formula is a path formula; (b) if e is an event type then $done(e)$ is a path formula; (c) if ψ_1 and ψ_2 are path formulas, then $\neg\psi_1$, $\psi_1 \vee \psi_2$, and $\Diamond\psi_1$, are path formulas. Event types include primitive event types, $e_1;e_2$, and $?\phi$.

We now define formally the notion of an interpretation in our language.

Definition 1 : An interpretation M = <W, E, T, $\prec$, $\mathcal{B}$, $\mathcal{G}$, $\mathcal{I}$, PA, OA, Φ>. W is a set of worlds, E is a set of primitive event types, T is a set of time points, $\prec$ a binary relation on time points,[2] and Φ is a truth assignment of primitive propositions for any given world and time point. A situation is a world, say w, at a particular time point, say t, and is denoted by w_t. The relations, $\mathcal{B}$, $\mathcal{G}$, and $\mathcal{I}$ map the agent's current situation to her belief, goal, and intention-accessible worlds, respectively. More formally, $\mathcal{B} \subseteq$ W $\times$ T $\times$ W and similarly for $\mathcal{G}$ and $\mathcal{I}$. PA is a probability assignment function that assigns to each time point t and world w a probability function μ_t^w. Each μ_t^w is a discrete probability function on the set of worlds W. OA is a payoff assignment function that assigns to each time point t and world w a payoff function ρ_t^w. Each ρ_t^w is a partial mapping from paths to real-valued numbers.

Definition 2 : Each world w of W is a tuple <T_w, $\mathcal{A}_w$, $\mathcal{O}_w$>, where $T_w \subseteq$ T, $\mathcal{A}_w \subseteq T_w \times T_w$, and $\mathcal{O}_w$: $T_w \times T_w \mapsto$ E. Intuitively, $\mathcal{O}_w$ is an arc function that is a partial mapping from time points to an event and signifies the occurrence of an event. Also, $\mathcal{A}_w$ obeys the ordering of $\prec$. Such worlds are called *time trees*. A *fullpath* in a world w is an infinite sequence of time points (t_0, t_1,...) such that $\forall i$ (t_i, t_{i+1}) $\in \mathcal{A}_w$. We use the notation (w_{t_0}, w_{t_1},...) to make the world of a particular fullpath explicit.

The semantics of the language with interpretation M is as follows:

$M, w_{t_0} \models \mathsf{PROB}(\phi) \geq \alpha$ iff
  $\mu_{t_0}^w(\{w' \in \mathcal{B}_{t_0}^w \mid M, w'_{t_0} \models \phi\}) \geq \alpha$
$M, w_{t_0} \models \mathsf{PAYOFF}(\psi) \geq \alpha$ iff
  $\forall w' \in \mathcal{G}_t^w$ and $\forall x_i$ such that $M, x_i \models \psi$,
  where x_i is a fullpath $(w'_{t_0}, w'_{t_{i1}}, \ldots)$,
  it is the case that $\rho_{t_0}^w(x_i) \geq \alpha$
$M, w_{t_0} \models \mathsf{OPTIONAL}(\psi)$ iff
  there exists a fullpath in w, $(w_{t_0}, w_{t_1}, \ldots)$
  such that $M, (w_{t_0}, w_{t_1}, \ldots) \models \psi$
$M, w_{t_0} \models \mathsf{R}(\phi)$ iff $\forall\ w' \in \mathcal{R}_{t_0}^w$, we have $M, w'_{t_0} \models \phi$.
$M, (w_{t_0}, w_{t_1}, \ldots) \models \phi$ iff $M, w_{t_0} \models \phi$.
$M, (w_{t_0}, w_{t_1}, \ldots) \models \Diamond\phi$ iff
  $\exists k$, $k>0$ such that $M, (w_{t_k}, \ldots) \models \phi$
$M, (w_{t_1}, \ldots) \models done(e)$ iff
  there exists t_0 such that $e \in \mathcal{O}_w(t_0, t_1)$
$M, (w_{t_1}, \ldots) \models done(e_1;e_2)$ iff
  there exists t_0 such that $e_2 \in \mathcal{O}_w(t_0, t_1)$ and
  $M, (w_{t_0}, \ldots) \models done(e_1)$
$M, (w_{t_1}, \ldots) \models done(?\phi)$ iff $M, w_{t_1} \models \phi$.

R and $\mathcal{R}$ indicate the modal operators and relations, respectively, of belief, goal, and intention. We use the abbreviation $\mathcal{R}_t^w$ to denote all the worlds $\mathcal{R}$-accessible from w at t.

The semantics of temporal and modal operators is relatively straightforward. The probability of a formula ϕ is greater than or equal to α if and only if the probability distribution of all the belief-accessible worlds in which ϕ is true is greater than α. The payoff of a formula ψ is greater than or equal to α if and only if the payoff function assigns a value greater than or equal to α to all paths where ψ is true in all goal-accessible worlds.

$\mathsf{INEVITABLE}(\phi)$ is defined as $\neg\mathsf{OPTIONAL}(\neg\phi)$; $\Box\phi$ as $\neg\Diamond\neg\phi$. Additionally, the conditional probability $\mathsf{PROB}(\phi_1 \mid \phi_2) \geq \alpha$ can be represented as $\mathsf{PROB}(\phi_1 \wedge \phi_2) \geq \alpha.\mathsf{PROB}(\phi_2)$ [8].

We shall illustrate the belief- and goal-accessible worlds of an agent using a simple example. Phil, who is currently in the House of Representatives, believes that he can stand for the House of representatives (Rep), switch to the Senate and stand for a Senate seat (Sen), or retire from politics (Ret) [10]. He does not consider the option of retiring seriously and is sure to retain his House seat. He has to make a decision regarding conducting or not conducting an opinion poll, based upon which he has to decide to stand for the House or the Senate. The results of the poll would be either a majority approving his switch to the Senate (yes) or a majority disapproving of his switch (no).

Consider the current situation to be w_t. The four belief-accessible worlds of w_t, shown in Figure 1, correspond to Phil winning or losing the Senate seat based on the majority answering yes or no in the poll. The probabilities of these worlds are shown in the top right hand corner of each world. The propositions *win*, *loss*, *yes*, and *no* are true at the situations shown.

[2] We require that the binary relation be total, transitive and backward-linear to enforce a single past and branching future.

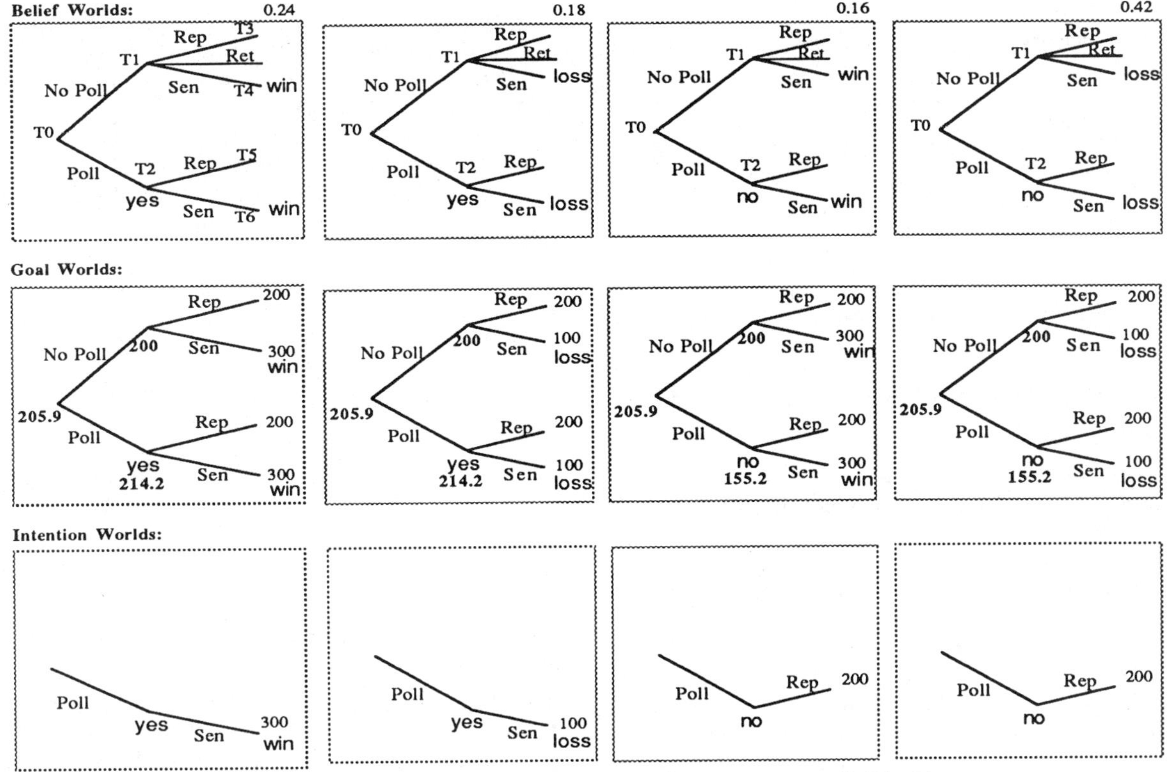

Figure 1: Belief, Goal, and Intention (wrt *maxexpval*) Worlds

Some of the formulas that are satisfiable at w_t are BEL(OPTIONAL($\Diamond done(Sen)$)), i.e., Phil believes that he has the option of eventually standing for the Senate, and PROB(OPTIONAL($\Diamond yes$)) $= 0.42$, i.e., the probability of eventually achieving a yes response is 0.42.

The goal worlds are also shown in Figure 1 (for clarity, we have omitted the time points, which are the same as in the belief worlds). The values at the end of the paths (100, 200, and 300) signify the value of losing a Senate seat, winning a House seat, and winning a Senate seat. This can be expressed as PAYOFF($\Diamond(done(Sen) \wedge loss)$) $= 100$, PAYOFF($\Diamond(done(Sen) \wedge win)$) $= 300$, etc. Other formulas can state other properties of the agent's goals. For example, the goal of the agent to retain his option to eventually stand for a Senate seat is expressed as GOAL(OPTIONAL($\Diamond done(Sen)$)). Note that the option of retiring from politics exists only in belief worlds, not in goal worlds, i.e., Phil believes that retiring is an option, but does not have any goal towards retiring.

3.2 SEMANTIC CONDITIONS

In this section, we give an informal description of some of the semantic conditions that can be imposed on our possible worlds model. Some of these conditions require the definition of a *sub-world*. We define a world to be a *sub-world* of another (denoted by $\sqsubseteq$) if and only if the time points in one are a subset of the other, they share the same history, and everything else is identical. The formal definition of sub-worlds and the axioms corresponding to the following semantic conditions are given elsewhere [13].

If the belief-accessible worlds represent chance, then no level of introspection can change the chance. Thus we require that all belief-accessible worlds have identical probability distributions (Semantic Condition C1). We also require that the probability distribution over belief-accessible worlds add up to one (C2). From C2 we also have that beliefs about inevitable facts have probability one.

We introduce a constraint on our belief, goal, and intention-accessible worlds, called *strong realism* [15]. Strong realism requires that for every belief-accessible world there exists a sub-world which is a goal-accessible world, and for every goal-accessible world there exists a sub-world which is an intention-accessible world (C3). The same restriction can be applied in the reverse direction also (C4). These two conditions essentially ensure that, if the agent intends an option, he has the goal towards that option and also believes in that option. These semantic conditions are very strong and have a significant impact on the inter-relationships between beliefs, goals, and intentions. We show elsewhere [14, 15] how these conditions can be relaxed to solve some of the problems associated with possible-world representations of beliefs, goals, and intentions [3].

More formally, the semantic conditions C1 to C4 can be stated as follows:

(C1) $\forall w' \in \mathcal{B}_t^w$, $\mu_t^w = \mu_t^{w'}$.
(C2) $\mu_t^w(\mathcal{B}_t^w) = 1$.
(C3) $\forall w' \in \mathcal{B}_t^w\ \exists w'' \in \mathcal{G}_t^w$ such that $w'' \sqsubseteq w'$ and $\forall w' \in \mathcal{G}_t^w\ \exists w'' \in \mathcal{B}_t^w$ such that $w'' \sqsubseteq w'$.
(C4) $\forall w' \in \mathcal{G}_t^w\ \exists w'' \in \mathcal{I}_t^w$ such that $w'' \sqsubseteq w'$ and $\forall w' \in \mathcal{I}_t^w\ \exists w'' \in \mathcal{G}_t^w$ such that $w'' \sqsubseteq w'$.

In the remainder of this paper, we shall use this possible-worlds BDI model as a basis for deliberation.

4 DECISION TREES AND GOAL WORLDS

In this section, we give a formal description of a decision tree and show how one can transform a decision tree into a set of goal-accessible worlds. Intuitively, both decision trees and goal-accessible worlds capture the desirable ends or outcomes of the decision problem, the different alternatives or choices available to the agent to achieve those ends, and the chance events controlled by nature. Note that this intuitive mapping is possible only because we have chosen to represent each possible world as a branching-time structure, rather than the more traditional model where each possible world is a linear-time structure [3]. Although one may be able to define a transformation from decision trees to linear-time models, we believe that such a mapping would be less intuitive than the one illustrated here.

The decision tree for our running example is given on the left hand side of Figure 3. Decision nodes are denoted by boxes and chance nodes by circles. The formal definition of a decision tree is as follows:

Definition 3 : A *decision tree* DT = $<\mathcal{N}, \mathcal{E}, \mathcal{S}, \mathcal{PS}, \mathcal{P}, \mathcal{U}, \Phi, \Psi, \Sigma>$. $\mathcal{N}$, is the union of all decision nodes $\mathcal{D}$, all chance nodes $\mathcal{C}$, and all terminal nodes $\mathcal{T}$. Φ is the set of all propositional formulas, Ψ is the set of all probabilistic state formulas (which includes the conditional probability operator in addition to the standard logical operators), and Σ is the set of all primitive event types. $\mathcal{E} \subseteq \mathcal{D} \times \mathcal{N} \times \Sigma$ is an event relation. $\mathcal{S} \subseteq \mathcal{C} \times (\mathcal{D} \cup \mathcal{T}) \times \Phi$ is a chance relation. $\mathcal{PS} \subseteq \mathcal{C} \times (\mathcal{D} \cup \mathcal{T}) \times \Psi$ is a probabilistic state relation. $\mathcal{P}$: $\Psi \rightarrow \Re$ is a probability function that maps probabilistic states to real numbers. $\mathcal{U}$: $\mathcal{T} \rightarrow \Re$ is the payoff function that assigns to a terminal node a real number.

Now we consider the transformation from decision trees to possible worlds. Given a decision tree, we start from the root node and traverse each arc. For each unique state labeled on an arc emanating from a chance node,[3] we create a new decision tree that is identical to the original tree except that (a) the chance node is removed and (b) the arc incident on the chance node is connected to the successor of the chance node. This process is carried out recursively until there are no chance nodes left. Each of the decision trees so obtained consists of only decision nodes and terminal nodes. Each one of these decision trees is then transformed into a possible world structure by appropriately renaming the relations. The payoff function is assigned to paths in a straightforward way, thus yielding a set of goal-accessible worlds.

```
create(t, n, p)
    Case n is a decision node
        For all m such that E(n, m, e)
            create(t, m, p);
    Case n is a chance node
        For all s such that S(n, m, s)
            For all (u q) in remove(t, s, p)
                create(u, m, q);
    Case n is a terminal node
        return(t, p).
remove(t, s, p)
    For all n, m such that S(n, m, s) and PS(n, m, r)
        collect(
        (t - S(n, m, s) - E(k, n, e) + E(k, m, e)), p.r))
```

Figure 2: Functions for Transformation

We obtain the probability distribution over the corresponding belief worlds by associating with each decision tree that is created a value α, which will finally correspond to the probability of a goal world. This probability is essentially the weighted product of all the chance nodes that a particular world represents. This probability distribution is finally passed back onto the corresponding belief-accessible worlds.

The transformation is performed by two functions, **create** and **remove**, which are defined in Figure 2. We have assumed in the function **remove** that the chance node is connected by an arc from a decision node. This is true in all cases except when the chance node is the root node of the decision tree. We have also assumed that the chance states are named uniquely.

The **create** function, when called with a given decision tree, its root node, and a probability value of one, will result in a set of decision trees with appropriate probabilities. The final transformation from these multiple decision trees with no chance nodes to possible worlds is trivial and is given elsewhere [13]. Figure 3 gives the transformation for the running example.

The possible worlds so formed are goal-accessible worlds. The probabilities associated with these worlds are the same as the probabilities of the decision trees

[3] Note that the decision tree is split with respect to the chance states and not with respect to the chance nodes. This is important to avoid invalid goal worlds.

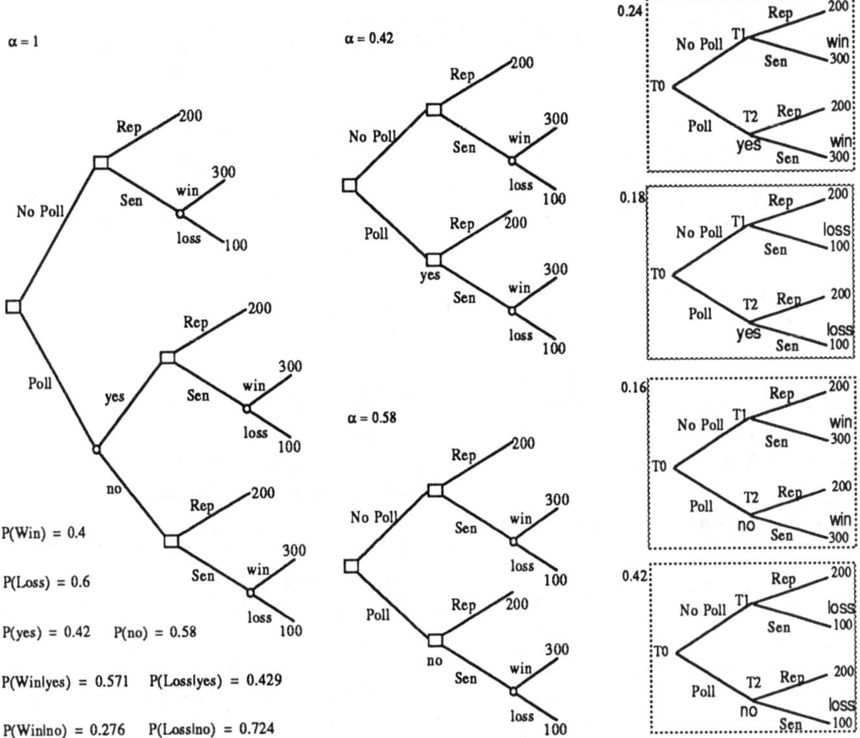

Figure 3: Transformation from Decision Trees to Goal Worlds

from which they are derived. Given our semantic condition earlier that all goal-accessible worlds have corresponding belief-accessible worlds, the probability distribution flows backwards to belief-accessible worlds. This transformation yields the following proposition:

Proposition 1 : *Given a decision tree DT we can create a possible worlds interpretation M such that the information given by the decision tree DT is satisfiable for a particular world y and time t in M. We shall denote this by* transform(*DT*,<*M*,*y*,*t*>).

5 DELIBERATION AND INTENTIONS

Given a decision tree and the above transformation, an agent can make use of standard decision-theoretic techniques such as *maximin* or *maximizing expected value* to deliberate and decide the best plan of action. This best plan of action is what the agent *commits* to and adopts as an intention.

To capture the process of decision theory deliberation, we introduce two generic functions, the *value function*, denoted by $\mathcal{V}$, and the *deliberation function*, denoted by δ. The value function assigns a real-valued number to every node in the decision tree and the deliberation function chooses one or more best sequences of actions to perform at a given node. Both these functions will be parameterised on the particular deliberation procedure used; i.e., maximin deliberation, maximizing the expected utility, or any other deliberation procedure. We shall use the operator ';' to denote sequencing of actions.

First we consider the maximin approach. The value and deliberation functions for this approach is given in Figure 4. For the running example, the maximin deliberation function returns the set {*No Poll;Rep*, *Poll;Rep*}.

Next we examine the principle of maximizing expected value. For decision nodes and terminal nodes, the value function and the deliberation function using the maxexpval principle are identical to the ones under the maximin principle. For chance nodes, the value and deliberation functions are defined as:

$$\mathcal{V}(maxexpval,\, n_i) = \sum_{\{n_j | \mathcal{PS}(n_i, n_j, p_j)\}} P(p_j).\mathcal{V}(n_j)$$

$$\delta(maxexpval,\, n_i) = \{s_j?; \delta(maxexpval, n_j) | \mathcal{S}(n_i, n_j, s_j)\}$$

For the running example the above deliberation function returns {*Poll;yes?;Sen*, *Poll;no?;Rep*}. Actions *yes?* and *no?* are used as conditional tests.

Modifying the modal operator INTEND with a subscript that indicates the decision procedure used, we can state the following theorem which allows an agent to form intentions based on his deliberation.

Theorem 1 : *If an agent with a decision tree DT with*

$$\mathcal{V}(maximin, n_i) = \begin{cases} \min_{\{n_j | \mathcal{S}(n_i,n_j,s_j)\}} \mathcal{V}(n_j) & \text{if } n_i \in \mathcal{C} \\ \max_{\{n_j | \mathcal{E}(n_i,n_j,e_j)\}} \mathcal{V}(n_j) & \text{if } n_i \in \mathcal{D} \\ \mathcal{U}(n_i) & \text{if } n_i \in \mathcal{T} \end{cases}$$

$$\delta(maximin, n_i) = \begin{cases} \{\delta(maximin, n_j) \mid \mathcal{S}(n_i, n_j, s_j) \text{ and } \mathcal{V}(n_j) = \mathcal{V}(n_i)\} & \text{if } n_i \in \mathcal{C} \\ \{e_j; \delta(maximin, n_j) \mid \mathcal{E}(n_i, n_j, e_j) \text{ and } \mathcal{V}(n_j) = \mathcal{V}(n_i)\} & \text{if } n_i \in \mathcal{D} \\ nil & \text{if } n_i \in \mathcal{T} \end{cases}$$

Figure 4: Value and deliberation functions for *maximin*

root node n and deliberation procedure d chooses as a best plan a sequence of actions a, i.e., a $\in \delta(d, n)$*, and the transformation is* transform(*DT*, <*M*,*y*,*t*>) *then* $M, y, t \models$ INTEND$_d$(OPTIONAL($\Diamond$*done*(*a*))).

To prove the above theorem, we need to define the process of deliberation within a possible-worlds model that generates intention-accessible worlds from a given set of goal-accessible and belief-accessible worlds. This definition is given elsewhere [13]. The set of intention-accessible worlds generated by maxexpval deliberation is shown in Figure 1. The possible-worlds deliberation can be shown to be equivalent to the decision tree deliberation [13]. This equivalence together with Proposition 1 establishes the above theorem.

Note that the maximin deliberation function always commits to a particular branch emanating from a chance node; namely, the branch that leads to a minimum value node. This means that δ for *maximin* can always return a sequence of actions without being conditional on any state information. However, this is not true in the case of *maxexpval* deliberation because each chance node is a weighted sum of all its branches. The actions thus have to be conditional on the state of the world. Thus *maximin* deliberation yields unconditional intentions and *maxexpval* deliberation results in conditional intentions.

For the example under discussion, we have the following unconditional maximin intentions and conditional maxexpval intentions: (a) the agent intends by maximin that, in all future paths he will stand for the House of representatives, i.e., INTEND$_{maximin}$ (INEVITABLE ($\Diamond$*done*(*Rep*))); (b) the agent intends by maxexpval that, in all future paths in which he has carried out a poll and the majority have answered yes, he would stand for the Senate, i.e., INTEND$_{maxexpval}$ (INEVITABLE($\Diamond$ (*done*(*Poll*) $\wedge$ *yes* $\supset$ $\Diamond$*done*(*Sen*)))); and (c) the agent intends by maxexpval that, in all future paths inwhich he has carried out a poll and the majority have answered no, he would stand for the House, i.e., INTEND$_{maxexpval}$ (INEVITABLE($\Diamond$ (*done*(*Poll*) $\wedge$ *no* $\supset$ $\Diamond$*done*(*Rep*)))).

So far, we have discussed how deliberation leads to the formation of conditional and unconditional intentions. As discussed in the introduction, intentions play the two important roles of posing decision problems for deliberation and constraining the options open for deliberation. The decision tree and the decision problem that we until now have taken for granted could have been generated because of a top-level intention of Phil to be rich and famous. In other words, a prior intention of the form INTEND(OPTIONAL$\Diamond$(*rich* $\wedge$ *famous*)) followed by means-end reasoning could have resulted in the decision tree to conduct a poll and run for the House or Senate seat. Also, if Phil had the prior intention to stand for a Senate seat, i.e., if INTEND(INEVITABLE$\Diamond$*done*(*Sen*)) were true, then the decision tree would be one without any alternatives for standing for the House. Thus, future-directed intentions constrain the decision problem that has to be considered.

We believe that the formalism we have presented here is general enough to cover a wide range of decision problems. The transformation and equivalence established in this paper should help one to choose the appropriate representation for the appropriate purpose, making use of the results of one representation within the other. For example, one could operate within a possible-worlds BDI framework for reasoning about the interaction of beliefs, goals, and intentions, and how they change with time [15], shift to a decision tree representation for deliberation, and then come back to the possible-worlds framework for reasoning about the intentions so formed.

6 CONCLUSIONS

This paper examines one of the important philosophical aspects of Bratman's theory of rational agency; namely, that deliberation leads to the formation of intentions. We have presented a powerful branching-time possible-worlds model for reasoning about beliefs, goals, intentions, actions, time, probabilities, and payoffs, and provided a transformation from decision trees to structures in this model. We have also shown how the deliberation procedure used determines the intentions adopted by the agent. This formal model of deliberation within a BDI-architecture is one of the main contributions of this paper. Previous work on formalizations of BDI-architectures [3, 12, 15] does not address this issue.

Recent work in real-time reasoning has vigorously pursued the use of decision-theoretic techniques. Russell and Wefald [16] treat computations themselves as actions, with appropriate utilities. These computations have to be chosen from among a number of different alternatives and decision theory is used to choose the best action or computation. This facilitates meta-level reasoning. Haddawy and Hanks [9] explore the relationships between symbolic goals and numeric utilities. In particular, they address the problem of building utility functions. However, neither approach considers the role of decision theory in the formation of intentions, which is the primary focus of this paper.

Fagin and Halpern [5] combine reasoning about knowledge and probabilities by explicitly introducing probability formulas. Haddawy [8] introduces reasoning about probabilities in a branching time model by considering a world to be a future path. The work presented here deals with both future paths in a branching time model and different possible worlds in the epistemic sense. It also introduces explicit reasoning about payoffs and treats payoffs as values the agent places on his future paths within a goal-accessible world. Thus it builds on the existing tradition by combining a possible-worlds BDI framework with decision-theoretic deliberation and explicit reasoning about probabilities and payoffs.

Our future work in this area will focus on the role of intentions in deliberation and reconsideration. We aim to analyze the need for rational agents to reconsider intentions and when they should carry out such reconsideration.

References

[1] M. E. Bratman. *Intentions, Plans, and Practical Reason.* Harvard University Press, Massachusetts, 1987.

[2] M. E. Bratman, D. Israel, and M. E. Pollack. Plans and resource-bounded practical reasoning. *Computational Intelligence*, 4:349–355, 1988.

[3] P. R. Cohen and H. J. Levesque. Intention is choice with commitment. *Artificial Intelligence*, 42(3), 1990.

[4] E. A. Emerson and J. Srinivasan. Branching time temporal logic. In J. W. de Bakker, W.-P. de Roever, and G. Rozenberg, editors, *Linear Time, Branching Time and Partial Order in Logics and Models for Concurrency*, pages 123–172. Springer-Verlag, Berlin, 1989.

[5] R. Fagin and J. Y. Halpern. Reasoning about knowledge and probability: Preliminary report. In M. Y. Vardi, editor, *Second Conference on Theoretical Aspects of Reasoning About Knowledge.* Morgan Kaufmann Publishers, 1988.

[6] M. P. Georgeff and Pollack. M. E. Rational agency project. *CSLI Monthly*, 2(3), 1986.

[7] M.P. Georgeff and F.F. Ingrand. Decision-making in an embedded reasoning system. In *Proceedings of the International Joint Conference on Artificial Intelligence*, Detroit, MI, 1989.

[8] P. Haddawy. Time, chance, and action. In *Proceedings of the Sixth Conference on Uncertainty in Artificial Intelligence*, Cambridge, Mass., U.S.A, July 1990.

[9] P. Haddawy and S. Hanks. Issues in decision-theoretic planning: Symbolic goals and numeric utilities. In *Proceedings of the DARPA Workshop on Innovative Approaches to Planning, Scheduling, and Control*, 1990.

[10] J. M. Jones. *Introduction to Decision Theory.* Richard D. Irwin, Inc., Homewood, Illinois, 1977.

[11] D. Kinny and M. P. Georgeff. Commitment and effectiveness of situated agents. In *Proceedings of the Twelfth International Joint Conference on Artificial Intelligence (IJCAI-91)*, 1991.

[12] K. Konolige and M. Pollack. A representationalist theory of intention. Technical Report (to be published), SRI International, Menlo Park, California, 1990.

[13] A. S. Rao and M. P. Georgeff. Deliberation and the formation of intentions. Technical Report 10, Australian Artificial Intelligence Institute, Carlton, Australia, 1990.

[14] A. S. Rao and M. P. Georgeff. Asymmetry thesis and side-effect problems in linear time and branching time intention logics. In *Proceedings of the Twelfth International Joint Conference on Artificial Intelligence (IJCAI-91)*, 1991.

[15] A. S. Rao and M. P. Georgeff. Modeling rational agents within a BDI-architecture. In J. Allen, R. Fikes, and E. Sandewall, editors, *Proceedings of the Second International Conference on Principles of Knowledge Representation and Reasoning.* Morgan Kaufmann Publishers, San Mateo, 1991.

[16] S. Russell and E. Wefald. Principles of metareasoning. In *Proceedings of the First International Conference on Principles of Knowledge Representation and Reasoning*, Toronto, 1989.

Handling Uncertainty during Plan Recognition in Task-Oriented Consultation Systems

Bhavani Raskutti
Computer Science Department
Monash University
Clayton, VICTORIA 3168
AUSTRALIA

Ingrid Zukerman
Computer Science Department
Monash University
Clayton, VICTORIA 3168
AUSTRALIA

Abstract

During interactions with human consultants, people are used to providing partial and/or inaccurate information, and still be understood and assisted. We attempt to emulate this capability of human consultants in computer consultation systems. In this paper, we present a mechanism for handling uncertainty in plan recognition during task-oriented consultations. The uncertainty arises while choosing an appropriate interpretation of a user's statements among many possible interpretations. Our mechanism handles this uncertainty by using probability theory to assess the probabilities of the interpretations, and complements this assessment by taking into account the *information content* of the interpretations. The information content of an interpretation is a measure of how well defined an interpretation is in terms of the actions to be performed on the basis of the interpretation. This measure is used to guide the inference process towards interpretations with a higher information content. The information content of an interpretation depends on the specificity and the strength of the inferences in it, where the strength of an inference depends on the reliability of the information on which the inference is based. Our mechanism has been developed for use in task-oriented consultation systems. The domain that we have chosen for exploration is that of a travel agency.

1 INTRODUCTION

During task-oriented consultations, a consultant needs to infer a user's requirements from his/her statements in order to provide assistance. To this effect, the consultant needs to interpret a user's statements correctly. However, this task is hindered by the fact that people often provide partial and/or inaccurate information. This requires the consultant to fill in the missing information by using different information sources, such as knowledge of discourse coherence, domain knowledge and knowledge about the user. However, these information sources are not fully reliable, requiring the consultant to draw inferences which are inherently uncertain. As a result, the statements issued by the user may be interpreted in more than one way. Hence, the consultant needs to evaluate the possible interpretations and select the most probable one. In this paper, we present a mechanism for handling the uncertainty arising from the lack of reliability of the various information sources used by the consultant, and for discriminating between multiple interpretations of a user's statements.

An interpretation of a user's statements consists of a sequence of plans that the user proposes to carry out, and a plan consists of an action with a number of parameters defining the action. For instance, in the travel domain, the proposal to fly from Melbourne to Sydney on December 1st, 1990, is a plan, where *flying* is the action, and the parameters *origin*, *destination* and *departure date* are instantiated.

A number of researchers have used plan recognition as a means to response generation during consultation (Grosz 1977, Allen and Perrault 1980, Sidner and Israel 1981, Carberry 1983, Litman and Allen 1987, Pollack 1990). However, the models of plan recognition developed by these researchers cope only with a single interpretation of a user's actions or utterances. Carberry (1990) addresses the problem of multiple interpretations by using default inferences, and by applying Dempster-Shafer theory of evidence (Section 9.1, Pearl 1988) to compute plausibility factors of alternate hypotheses. However, in domains such as travel, where the default assumptions are weak, this approach alone does not cope with the problem of multiple interpretations. Kautz and Allen (1986) use circumscription to generate all possible interpretations during story understanding. However, since all possibilities are constructed, and the search is limited only by the structure of the plan hierarchy, this approach can be very expensive.

Our mechanism applies Bayesian theory of probability in order to address the problem of multiple interpretations which result from uncertain information sources. Probability theory in the form of Bayes Belief Networks (Pearl 1988) was applied by Goldman and Charniak (1989) to model the difference between the effect of objects on plan recognition in stories and in 'real life'. In an earlier research, Goldman and Charniak (1988) combined probability theory with Assumption-based TMS (de Kleer 1986) for plan inference during story understanding. Our mechanism expands on this earlier research with respect to plan inference during task-oriented consultations. We have observed that in these consultations, the user generally provides sufficient information to enable the consultant to help him/her achieve his/her goals. Hence, the better defined the plans in an interpretation, the more likely it is that this is the interpretation intended by the user. Based on this observation, we augment probabilistic reasoning by means of information content considerations, in order to narrow down the number of interpretations produced by the system from a user's statements. The information content of an interpretation is a measure of how well defined an interpretation is in terms of the actions to be performed on the basis of the interpretation. It depends on the specificity and the strength of the inferences in it, where the strength of an inference depends on the reliability of the information source on which it is based.

The use of information content considerations is valid only in intended plan recognition, such as the one occurring in cooperative interactions. In *keyhole* recognition of plans, where the observer infers an agent's plans and goals by unobtrusively observing the agent (Schmidt, Sridharan and Goodson 1978), we cannot assume the same strong desire for communication and hence cannot use the information content of an interpretation to assess its probability.

The subsequent sections describe the inference mechanism with particular reference to the means used for handling the uncertainties arising during the inference process. The actual procedures which draw the inferences are discussed in [Raskutti and Zukerman 1991]. We make use of the following dialogue excerpt to illustrate our approach:

> Traveler: "I want to go to Sydney the day after tomorrow. I am going to Hawaii on the 11:00 am flight. By the way, I'll be leaving from Adelaide."

2 THE INFERENCE MECHANISM

The inference mechanism operates on input provided by a Natural Language Interface (NLI), which consists of predicates, such as FLY and LEAVE, and meta predicates that indicate the modality of the statements, such as CAN and MUST. Based on this input, it generates the intended plans of the user. The inference mechanism consists of three processes: (1) Direct inference, (2) Indirect Inference, and (3) Evaluation of interpretations. In these processes, the uncertainties arising due to partial and possibly unreliable information are handled by using Bayesian theory of probability combined with information content considerations.

The direct inference process generates a set of possible interpretations from the input provided by the NLI, using definitions of domain actions and coherence considerations. During this stage, there are uncertainties arising due to the many possible interpretations of a statement as well as due to the many possible relations between the interpretation of a new statement and the previous discourse. For instance, in the above dialogue excerpt, there is uncertainty as to which trip the departure location 'Adelaide' refers to. This uncertainty is handled by computing the probability of an interpretation of a piece of discourse in terms of the probability of an interpretation of each new statement (Section 3.1), the probability of an interpretation of the previous discourse, and the probability of a relation between the two (Section 3.2). The calculated probabilities are used to prune the set of interpretations (Section 3.3).

The interpretations generated by the direct inference process are usually incomplete. The unspecified details are filled in by indirect inferences based on other information sources, such as domain knowledge and world knowledge. All these sources are not equally reliable and hence the strength of these inferences are not the same. For instance, the desired mode of transport between Sydney and Hawaii may be inferred by taking into consideration typical assumptions about the domain. This type of inference is stronger than an inference based on general 'world knowledge', but weaker than a direct inference. During the indirect inference process, the strength of an inference is used to prevent a weaker inference from refuting the results of a previous stronger inference (Section 4).

A measure of information content is used both after the direct inference process and during the indirect inference process to determine whether the inference process should be continued. This measure is also used after both the direct and the indirect inference process to increase the probability of the interpretations with a high information content and to decrease the probability of those with a low information content (Section 5). The updated probabilities are used to prune the set of interpretations by dropping the interpretations with a low probability (Section 3.3). Thus, the evaluation process prefers those interpretations that are well-defined, i.e., those that were completely specified by the user or those in which the gaps left by the user could be filled in by using the system's knowledge.

3 THE PROBABILITY OF AN INTERPRETATION OF THE DISCOURSE

The probability of an interpretation of a set of statements is a measure of how likely it is that the speaker intended this interpretation when s/he uttered the statements in question. Assume that our discourse S' is composed of the previous discourse S and a new statement s, where s stands for the input returned by the NLI and consists of a predicate and a possibly *nil* meta predicate. Further, assume that S has a set of possible interpretations $\{I_j\}$, and s has a set of possible interpretations $\{i_k\}$. In addition, assume that $\{R_m\}$ is the set of possible relations between an interpretation I_j of S and an interpretation i_k of s. Each relation R_m is one of the possible discourse relations between a statement and previous discourse, namely, Elaboration, Introduction and Correction. In addition, the relations Elaboration and Correction must also refer to a topic or plan that is being elaborated or corrected. Finally, let D be the set of apriori domain knowledge of the listener including the plan-base and the rule-base that are used to generate the set of interpretations. Thus, the probability that the speaker meant an interpretation I_{jkm}, consisting of I_j and i_k and the relation R_m between I_j and i_k, when s/he said S' is $P(I_{jkm}|S', D)$. However, since we are dealing with a closed system where the domain knowledge remains constant throughout the interaction, we can omit D from our calculations, and focus only on $P(I_{jkm}|S')$. This probability is calculated as follows:

$$P(I_{jkm}|S') = P(I_j, i_k, R_m|S, s)$$

According to Bayes Rule for conditional probability:

$$P(I_{jkm}|S') = \frac{P(I_j, i_k, R_m, S, s)}{P(S, s)}$$

Using Bayes Rule for conditional probability, the numerator can be rewritten as follows:

$$P(I_j, i_k, R_m, S, s) = P(S|s, i_k, I_j, R_m) * P(s|i_k, I_j, R_m) * P(R_m|i_k, I_j) * P(I_j|i_k) * P(i_k)$$

- $P(S|s, i_k, I_j, R_m) = P(S|I_j)$, since S is conditionally independent of s, i_k and R_m, given I_j; $P(S|I_j)$ indicates the probability that a user would utter the statements in discourse S when s/he wanted to mean I_j.
- $P(s|i_k, I_j, R_m) = P(s|i_k)$, since s is conditionally independent of I_j and R_m, given i_k; $P(s|i_k)$ indicates the probability that a user would utter the statement s when s/he wanted to mean i_k.
- $P(I_j|i_k) = P(I_j)$, since I_j is the interpretation of statements before s and is independent of i_k.

Using the above results, the expression for $P(I_{jkm}|S')$ may be rewritten as follows:

$$P(I_{jkm}|S') = \frac{P(S|I_j)\, P(s|i_k)\, P(R_m|i_k, I_j)\, P(I_j)\, P(i_k)}{P(S, s)}$$

The application of Bayes Rule to the first two terms of the numerator yields:

$$P(I_{jkm}|S') = \left(\frac{P(I_j|S)\, P(S)}{P(I_j)}\right) * \left(\frac{P(i_k|s)\, P(s)}{P(i_k)}\right) * \left(\frac{P(R_m|i_k, I_j)\, P(I_j)\, P(i_k)}{P(S, s)}\right)$$

The terms $P(s)$, $P(S)$ and $P(S, s)$ represent how often the statement s, the discourse S and the discourse S' consisting of S and s are ever uttered, regardless of the purpose for which they are uttered. These probabilities, in general, can be very difficult to estimate. However, since they are independent of the probabilities of the interpretations, and since we are interested in comparisons of probabilities and not in absolute values, we can define a normalizing constant α, $\alpha = \frac{P(S) \times P(s)}{P(S,s)}$. Hence,

$$P(I_{jkm}|S') = \alpha\, P(I_j|S)\, P(i_k|s)\, P(R_m|i_k, I_j)$$

$P(I_j|S)$ is the probability of the interpretation I_j after processing the discourse S. It is the result of iteratively applying the process described here with respect to the statements in discourse S. $P(i_k|s)$ is the probability of an interpretation i_k of a user's statement s and it is computed as described in Section 3.1. $P(R_m|i_k, I_j)$ links up the new statement's interpretation to the interpretation of the earlier discourse by means of relation R_m. It is determined as described in Section 3.2. The probabilities of the new interpretations, $P(I_{jkm}|S')$, for all the combinations of $\{I_j\}$, $\{i_k\}$ and $\{R_m\}$, are used to prune the set of interpretations.

3.1 PROBABILITY OF AN INTERPRETATION OF A STATEMENT

The input processed by the inference mechanism is a parsed version of the original statements issued by the user, and consists of a predicate and a possibly *nil* meta predicate for each statement. During the direct inference process, interpretations of an input predicate are determined by using an operator library (Fikes and Nilsson 1971) and plan inference rules (Allen and Perrault 1980). The operator library defines the basic actions in the domain. Each operator definition in the library consists of the preconditions, effects and body of an action, where the body defines the composition of the action. The plan inference rules state that all those operators that have the input predicate in their precondition, effect or body must be chosen as possible interpretations of the predicate.

The probability of an interpretation i_k is determined as follows: all the interpretations generated by the same rule, e.g., a body rule, are assigned the same probability; and as more possibilities are generated, each individual one is considered less probable. However, the total probability mass allocated to all the interpretations resulting from the application of a rule depends on two factors: (1) the meta predicate returned by the NLI, and (2) whether other rules gave rise to the inference of any interpretations.

The presence of a meta predicate, such as WANT, enables us to resolve ambiguity when the input predicate appears in both the precondition and the effect of an operator. For instance, if a user's request about BEing at a place is expressed as "I want to be ... " or "I can be ...," but the NLI returns it as BE(...), this predicate can refer either to the precondition or the effect of an operator with equal probability. By taking into consideration the presence of a meta predicate, we increase the bias towards the appropriate inference rule, e.g., if the user had said "I can be ...," then the probability mass of the precondition rule would have been increased. This scheme is implemented by determining in advance the manner in which each of the meta predicates that may be returned by the NLI affects the probability mass assigned to each rule.

A rule which does not match an input predicate fails to infer any interpretations. If one or more rules fail to infer interpretations, the probability mass allocated to the rules that were successful is modified by allocating the apriori mass of the unsuccessful rule proportionally between the successful ones. For instance, if only the effect and precondition rules yield interpretations, then the probability mass allocated to the body rule is 0. This results in the apriori allocation of the body rule being split up proportionally between the effect and precondition rules.

These considerations for determining the probability of an interpretation are domain independent, since the prior probabilities of all the interpretations of a predicate are considered equal, and they are modified using only meta predicates. At this juncture, if domain knowledge is available, it can be used to modify the apriori probabilities of the interpretations of a predicate.

3.2 PROBABILITY OF A RELATION

The possible discourse relations considered by the inference mechanism are as follows: Elaboration, Correction, Digression and Introduction. Digression is a special case of Elaboration, where the probability of elaborating on the last topic is considerably reduced. Hence, the relation R_m can only be one of the other three. In addition, in the case of Elaboration and Correction, R_m also includes the topic that is being referred to. The possible relations and the number of topics that can be referred to lead to a large number of elements in the set $\{R_m\}$. This set is constrained by assigning probabilities to the inferred relations so that normal patterns of discourse are preferred. The following considerations are used while determining the probability of an inferred relation:

1. When a new statement can be interpreted as elaborating on two or more topics discussed earlier, the elaboration of the last referenced topic is preferred to the elaboration of earlier topics. Further, the probability of an earlier topic being referred to falls exponentially as its distance from the current statement increases.

2. A new statement can always be interpreted as introducing a new topic of discussion. However, if the new statement can also be interpreted as elaborating on an earlier topic, the probability of introduction is considerably reduced. This is achieved by assigning a constant and low probability to the introduction relation. If a highly probable elaboration relation is possible, then the relative magnitude of the probability of introduction is reduced.

3. If there are cue words that indicate a particular relation or that point to a particular previous topic, the probability of this relation or this topic increases. For instance, in the statement "*By the way*, I'll be leaving from Adelaide," from the dialogue excerpt presented in Section 1, the italicized cue phrase indicates a digression. Hence, the preferred interpretation is that 'Adelaide' refers to the trip that was mentioned earlier in the discourse, namely the Sydney trip.

4. Correction and digression are never inferred unless the NLI provides evidence to this effect by means of cue phrases, such as "on second thought" and "by the way," respectively.

The above considerations are domain independent, since the probability of a specific relation R_m is determined by the cue words returned by the NLI and by the contents of the interpretations i_k and I_j. Domain knowledge of distances is not taken into consideration while calculating the probability of the relation R_m. However, the probability of going to Hawaii on the way between Sydney and Melbourne is definitely lower than the probability of going to Sydney on the way between Melbourne and Hawaii. If domain knowledge is available, it should be incorporated into the system to update the probabilities obtained using the domain independent considerations discussed above.

3.3 PRUNING THE SET OF INTERPRETATIONS USING THEIR PROBABILITIES

After determining the probabilities of a set of interpretations, the probabilities are normalized. The normalized probabilities are used to prune the set of interpretations by dropping all those interpretations whose probabilities fall below a relative rejection threshold. In principle, the improbable interpretations could be maintained and revisited, if necessary. But, empirically, this has not been necessary since the intended interpretation has been found among the retained interpretations. All the interpretations I that are retained have a probability that satisfies the following condition:

$$\frac{P_I}{P_{max}} \geq Threshold$$

where P_{max} is the maximum of all the normalized probabilities, P_I is the probability of a retained interpretation, and *Threshold* is a number in [0,1] range. This calculation ensures that interpretations with a low probability relative to the most probable interpretation are dropped. For example, with 0.5 as the value for *Threshold*, an interpretation with probability 0.3 is dropped if there is another interpretation with probability 0.7. At the same time, if there is a situation where there are three interpretations with probability 0.4, 0.3 and 0.3, then all three are retained.

By judicious choice of a value for *Threshold*, the system can be tailored to consider more or less possibilities. For instance, currently we have two thresholds. The first one used during the direct inference process is 0.5 and was chosen in line with the probabilities assigned to the discourse relations, so that plausible interpretations are not discarded. The second threshold, which is used to prune the interpretations after the indirect inference process, is 0.7, and was chosen so that fewer possibilities are considered as additional information is brought to bear.

4 STRENGTH OF INFERENCES

We postulate that the strength of an inference is directly proportional to the reliability of the information source that is used as the basis for this inference. Hence, we categorize different information sources that are used to draw inferences and list them below in decreasing order of reliability.

1. *User's Statements* – Direct inferences from what is explicitly stated. While these inferences can be presumed correct, there is still a degree of uncertainty in relating a new statement to the earlier ones due to the different discourse relations possible.
2. *Domain Knowledge* – Indirect inferences that are derived by using the system's beliefs about the user's domain knowledge. A typical example is the inference of the arrival time at the destination once the departure time is known. Such an inference is useful when there are multiple legs in a proposed journey, requiring that departure times at subsequent locations be inferred.
3. *Domain Assumptions* – Indirect inferences that are derived by assuming what is normal in the domain. For example, when no details about the mode of travel are specified, it is possible to derive this information from the usual mode of transport between two places.
4. *User Model* – Indirect inferences that are made on the basis of the system's model of the user. The user model may be a default model describing a typical user, or it may be more specific. In the context of a travel agency, we have adopted a default model based on the assumption that typically, in a travel agency, the information provider cannot form an extensive user model.
5. *Common-Sense* – Indirect inferences that are derived by assuming normal behavior or common notions outside the domain of interest. Typically, such notions are used when we postulate return journeys based on the assumption that people usually do not move from their residence.

The inference types are assigned a strength in the (0,1] range, and this strength is used to calculate the information content of a parameter and also to determine whether a particular parameter should be revised by a new inference during the indirect inference process. The inferences derived from the user's statements have a strength of 1 and all other inference types have a progressively decreasing strength according to the reliability of their source of information. Undefined parameters are assigned a minimum strength. This assignment enables us to distinguish between parameters that are defined inexactly by the user and parameters that are left undefined, and assign less information content to undefined parameters.

In the process of deriving indirect inferences, we emulate one aspect of human behavior whereby once a conclusion is accepted with a particular degree of confidence, people consider it to be certain when drawing subsequent conclusions (Gettys, Kelly and Peterson 1982). Thus, like Carberry (1990), we do not compound the uncertainty in chains of inferences. This approach is different from that used for the computation of confidence factors (CFs) in MYCIN, where the CF of a parameter P is computed by taking into account the CFs of the parameters $P_1, P_2, ..., P_n$ that are used for calculating P (Shortliffe and Buchanan 1975). Our approach is implemented by tagging each parameter, P, in the plans in each interpretation with the type of inference that gave rise to the value of P, without taking into consideration the inference types of $P_1, P_2, ..., P_n$. Since the type of inference indicates the strength of the inference rule, it represents the conditional probability of P, given $P_1, P_2, ..., P_n$.

During the indirect inference process, the strength of the inference in a parameter's tag is compared with the strength of a new inference, before updating the parameter with the new inference. If the strength of the new inference is the same or higher than the strength of the inference type in the tag, the new inference replaces the old one. Otherwise, the old inference is retained. In this manner, a weaker inference is prevented from refuting the results obtained from a stronger inference.

Thus, during the indirect inference process, the gaps left in the interpretations generated by the direct inference process are filled in using the most reliable indirect inference, and unreliable inferences are not maintained. In principle, it is necessary to generate a new interpretation for each new value of a parameter, and process all the generated interpretations. However, this can lead to an exponential explosion of possibilities, and our decision to consider only the strongest inference during the indirect inference process is a trade-off between the benefits of exploring all possibilities and the resource limitations for doing so (Horvitz 1989).

5 INFORMATION CONTENT AND ITS USE

The information content of an interpretation is a measure of the extent of its definition. After both direct and indirect inferences, this measure is used both to determine if the processing is to be continued as well as to modify the probabilities of the interpretations so that the probabilities of interpretations with a higher information content are increased. The modified probabilities are used to prune the set of interpretations as described in Section 3.3.

5.1 THE INFORMATION CONTENT OF AN INTERPRETATION

We define the information content of an interpretation as the sum of the information content of all the plans in the interpretation, and the information content of a plan as the sum of the information content of all the parameters that are necessary for the definition of the plan. The information content of a parameter, in turn, depends on two factors: (1) its specificity, which is defined as the reciprocal of the number of possible values assigned to this parameter, and (2) its strength, which depends on the source of information from which this parameter was obtained. That is, both a parameter with multiple values assigned to it and a parameter derived from an unreliable source of information are deemed to have a low information content.

We borrow from Information Theory (Shannon 1948), to define the information content of a parameter p, $IC(p)$, as follows:

$$IC(p) = \log_2 \frac{S(p)}{N(p)}$$

where $N(p)$ is the number of possible values assigned to p, and $S(p)$ is the strength associated with p. The strength of the parameter is the strength of the inference type that was used to derive the value of the parameter (Section 4.2).

According to this formula, undefined parameters have the least information content, since they can take on all the possible values in the domain, and parameters inferred exactly from a reliable source, such as a direct inference from a user's statement, have a maximum information content. For instance, if we have directly inferred that the departure date for a trip is between the 9th and the 15th of May, 1991, then the information content of this parameter is $log_2\, 1/7$. This measure is additive over multiple plans and it ranges over the negative values, with a maximum information content of 0 when all the parameters which are necessary for the definition of a plan are exactly defined. Thus, the information content of an interpretation I, $IC(I)$, is:

$$IC(I) = \sum_{\{\text{plans } P_j \text{ in } I\}} \; \sum_{\{\text{parameters } p_i \text{ in } P_j\}} \log_2 \frac{S(p_i)}{N(p_i)}$$

5.2 CHECKING COMPLETION

After the direct inference process and during the indirect inference process, the information content measure is used to determine if the processing should be continued. Processing is stopped if at least one complete interpretation, i.e., an interpretation with zero information content is determined. Processing of an interpretation is also stopped if no new inferences can be drawn on the basis of the existing evidence, i.e., the information content of an interpretation cannot be increased further. Thus, the information content measure is used as an *informative stopping rule* (Berger and Berry 1988) to determine if the processing should be stopped.

5.3 UPDATING PROBABILITIES

The information content measure, which ranges over the negative values, is mapped to the [0,1] range and then used to update the probability of an interpretation, $P(I)$. This is performed by means of the following formula:

$$P(I) \leftarrow P(I)\left(1 - \frac{IC(I)}{ICNORM}\right)$$

$ICNORM$ is currently defined to be the minimum possible information content in the domain. In our restricted domain, where the number of possible destinations and origins is low, this choice of $ICNORM$ has a large impact on the probability. However, in a realistic domain, where there is a greater degree of freedom in terms of the values that can be assigned to the parameters, another definition of $ICNORM$ may be preferred. Currently, we are experimenting with $ICNORM$ as the sum of the information content of all the interpretations, and use this definition to update the probabilities when there are multiple interpretations. The update of probabilities using information content is valid only in cooperative information-seeking interactions, such as those occurring at a travel agency, where the user wants his/her intentions to be understood by the listener and hence, interpretations with higher information content are more probable.

6 EXAMPLES

Our system has been implemented to understand discourses in travel domain. The language used for the implementation is Franz Lisp. Our system has a rule-base containing twelve rules and a plan-base containing seven plan operators. The input to the system is in the form of predicates, and the system produces output in the form of possible interpretations consisting of one or more plans that the user proposes to carry out. To illustrate the inference process, we consider two plausible dialogue excerpts at a Melbourne travel agency.

EXAMPLE 1

Traveler: "I want to go to Sydney the day after tomorrow. I am going to Hawaii on the 11:00 am flight. By the way, I'll be leaving from Adelaide."

This chunk of statements issued by a traveler is returned by the NLI as the following four predicates, where the last two predicates are due to the third sentence:

(1) GO (departure_date = *day after tomorrow*, destination = *Sydney*)
(2) FLY (departure_time = *11:00 am*, destination = *Hawaii*)
(3) DIGRESS
(4) LEAVE (origin = *Adelaide*)

The first two domain predicates give rise to an interpretation composed of two plans: (a) to go to *Sydney* and (b) to fly to *Hawaii* at *11:00 am*. The DIGRESS discourse relation in predicate (3) indicates that a plan which precedes the plan currently in focus is likely to be the topic of discussion for the forthcoming predicate. Thus, with the fourth predicate, we have two possible interpretations: I_1 — it elaborates plan (a), or I_2 — it elaborates plan (b). I_1 has a higher probability due to the presence of the DIGRESS discourse relation.

The information content measure rates both these interpretations equally. Hence, both interpretations are retained after the direct inference process. During the indirect inference process, we consider the case where the temporal order of plans is assumed to be the same as the order of presentation during the discourse. Other possible temporal orders are considered and processed in [Raskutti and Zukerman 1991]. The use of indirect inference rules coupled with the assumption for temporal order of plans gives rise to two scenarios:

I_1 : *Adelaide* → *Sydney* → *Hawaii*
I_2 : *Melbourne* → *Sydney* , *Adelaide* → *Hawaii*

I_2 has less information content, since its parameters cannot be inferred due to the need to postulate an additional intervening plan to take the user from *Sydney* to *Adelaide*. Hence its probability is correspondingly decreased and I_1 is chosen as the best interpretation.

EXAMPLE 2

Traveler: "I want to go to Sydney the day after tomorrow. From Sydney I'll be going to Hawaii on the 11:00 am flight. I'll be leaving from Adelaide."

This chunk of statements issued by a traveler is returned by the NLI as the following three predicates.

(1) GO (departure_date = *day after tomorrow*, destination = *Sydney*)
(2) FLY (departure_time = *11:00 am*, origin = *Sydney* destination = *Hawaii*)
(3) LEAVE (origin = *Adelaide*)

The first two domain predicates give rise to an interpretation composed of two plans: (a) to go to *Sydney* and (b) to fly to *Hawaii* from *Sydney* at *11:00 am*. With the third predicate, we have two possible interpretations: I_1 — it elaborates plan (a), or I_2 — it introduces a new plan (c) to go from Adelaide. The probability of I_1 is higher since elaboration is preferred to introduction. However, since the elaboration is that of a plan discussed before, I_2 is retained as a possibility. Thus after the direct inference process, we have two possibilities:

I_1 : *Adelaide* → *Sydney* ,
Sydney → *Hawaii*
I_2 : $?x$ → *Sydney* ,
Sydney → *Hawaii* ,
Adelaide → $?y$

I_1 has higher information content since the origins and destinations of the two proposed trips are known. This coupled with the previous lower probability of I_2 ensures that I_1 is the only possibility carried over to the indirect inference process. Thus, during the indirect inference process, I_1 is completed to yield the same interpretation as the one in the first example.

7 CONCLUSIONS

In this paper, we have described a means for handling uncertainty during plan recognition in task-oriented consultation systems by using Bayesian probability theory augmented by an information content measure. We have used our system on five simple discourse samples similar to the one discussed in Section 6. In each case, the system chooses the same interpretation that people choose, indicating that our tenet of linking specificity and strength of inference to the probability of an interpretation can be valuable in handling real conversations in cooperative interactions. Finally, by modifying the definition of the information content measure to suit different domains, our method may be used for interpreting user's statements in general, as well as in the area of multi-media document retrieval.

Acknowledgments

This research was supported in part by grant Y90/03/22 from the Australian Telecommunications and Electronics Research Board. We thank Prof. J. Roach and D. Sanford from the Virginia Polytechnic Institute and State University for allowing us to use their transcripts of telephone conversations at travel agencies. We also thank Wilson Wen from Telecom Research Laboratories for his advice on probability theory.

References

Allen, J.F. & Perrault, C.R. (1980), Analyzing Intention in Utterances. In *Artificial Intelligence* 15, pp. 143-178.

Berger, J.O. & Berry, D.A. (1988), The Relevance of Stopping Rules in Statistical Inferences. In Gupta, S.S. and Berger, J.O. (Eds.), *Statistical Decision Theory and Related Topics IV*, Vol. 1, Springer Verlag.

Carberry, S. (1983), Tracking User Goals in an Information-seeking Environment. In *Proceedings of the National Conference on Artificial Intelligence*, Washington DC, pp. 59-63.

Carberry, S. (1990), Incorporating Default Inferences into Plan Recognition. In *Proceedings of the National Conference on Artificial Intelligence*, Boston, pp. 471-478.

de Kleer, J. (1986), An Assumption-based TMS. In *Artificial Intelligence* 28, pp. 163-224.

Fikes, R.E. & Nilsson, N.J. (1971), STRIPS: A New Approach to the Application of Theorem Proving to Problem Solving. In *Artificial Intelligence* 2, pp. 189-208.

Gettys, C.F., Kelly III, C. & Peterson, C.R. (1982), The Best-guess Hypothesis in Multistage Inference. In Kahneman, D., Slovic, P., and Tversky, A. (Eds.), *Judgment under Uncertainty: Heuristics and Biases, Cambridge University Press*, pp. 370-377.

Goldman, R. & Charniak, E. (1989), Plan Recognition in Stories and in Life. In *Proceedings of the IJCAI89 Workshop on Uncertainty in Artificial Intelligence*, Windsor, Canada, pp. 54-59.

Goldman, R. & Charniak, E. (1988), A Probabilistic ATMS for Plan Recognition. In *Proceedings of the AAAI-88 Workshop on Plan Recognition*, St. Paul, Minnesota, August 1988.

Grosz, B.J. (1977), The Representation and Use of Focus in Dialogue Understanding. Tech. Note 151, SRI International, Menlo Park, CA.

Horvitz, E.J. (1989), Beliefs and Actions Under Computational Resource Constraints. In Kanal, L.N., Levitt, T.S. and Lemmer, J.F. (Eds.), *Uncertainty in Artificial Intelligence* 3, North Holland.

Kautz, H. & Allen, J.(1986), Generalized Plan Recognition. *Proceedings of the Fifth National Conference on Artificial Intelligence*, Philadelphia, Pennsylvania.

Litman, D. & Allen, J.F. (1987), A Plan Recognition Model for Subdialogues in Conversation. In *Cognitive Science* 11, pp. 163-200.

Pearl, J. (1988), *Probabilistic Reasoning in Intelligent Systems: Networks of Plausible Inference*, Morgan Kaufmann Publishers, San Mateo, California.

Pollack, M. (1990), Plans as Complex Mental Attitudes. In Cohen, P., Morgan, J. and Pollack, M. (Eds.), *Intentions in Communication*, MIT Press.

Raskutti, B. & Zukerman, I. (1991), Generation and Selection of Likely Interpretations during Plan Recognition in Task-oriented Consultation Systems. In *User Modeling and User Adapted Interaction*, an International Journal.

Schmidt, C.F., Sridharan, N.S. & Goodson, J.L. (1978), The Plan Recognition Problem: An Intersection of Artificial Intelligence and Psychology. In *Artificial Intelligence* 10, pp. 45-83.

Shannon, C.E. (1948), A Mathematical Theory of Communications. In *Bell System Technical Journals*, October 1948.

Shortliffe, E.H. & Buchanan, B.G. (1975), A Model of Inexact Reasoning in Medicine, *Mathematical Biosciences* 23, pp. 351-379.

Sidner, C.L. & Israel, D.J. (1981), Recognizing Intended Meaning and Speakers' Plans. In *Proceedings of the Seventh International Joint Conference on Artificial Intelligence*, Vancouver, Canada, pp. 203-208.

TRUTH AS UTILITY: A CONCEPTUAL SYNTHESIS

Enrique H. Ruspini
Artificial Intelligence Center
SRI International
Menlo Park, CA 94025

Abstract

This paper introduces conceptual relations that synthesize utilitarian and logical concepts, extending the logics of preference of Rescher.

We define first, in the context of a possible-worlds model, constraint-dependent measures that quantify the relative quality of alternative solutions of reasoning problems or the relative desirability of various policies in control, decision, and planning problems.

We show that these measures may be interpreted as truth values in a multivalued logic and propose mechanisms for the representation of complex constraints as combinations of simpler restrictions. These extended logical operations permit also the combination and aggregation of goal-specific quality measures into global measures of utility. We identify also relations that represent differential preferences between alternative solutions and relate them to the previously defined desirability measures.

Extending conventional modal logic formulations, we introduce structures for the representation of ignorance about the utility of alternative solutions. Finally, we examine relations between these concepts and similarity-based semantic models of fuzzy logic.

1 Introduction

The ability of logic-based procedures to represent knowledge elements of rather diverse characteristics while identifying, by constructive proof, solutions of a wide variety of problems is the major reason for their appeal as the bases of a class of artificial intelligence methodologies.

Aristotle, who established logic as the discipline concerned with the relations between the truth-values of propositions, was also, as noted by Rescher [Rescher 67], the first student of the notion of preferability ("the worthier of choice"), also a major element of any problem-solving approach.

A large amount of interest has been recently expressed in the artificial intelligence community about the role of the concept of utility in the solution of various problems. Hobbs et al. [Hobbs 90] have, for example, recently proposed measures of cost to assess the quality of interpretations of linguistic utterances. The work of Russell and Wefald [Russell 89] also exemplifies recent interest on the applicability of decision-theoretic principles to the control of reasoning processes. Measures of preference have also been used in intelligent decision planners to control the relaxation of "elastic" constraints [Fox 90].

The appeal that utilitarian notions and structures have as an important element of the problem-solving process lies on their ability to add to the classical logicist concept of rationality—the sound derivation of conclusions from premises— pragmatic principles of rational behavior that aid in the evaluation of the desirability and utility of both assumptions and conclusions, often assisting to determine the relative importance of various constraints. Furthermore, at a metareasoning level, utilitarian considerations are important elements to guide reasoning processes along lines that are likelier to produce the truth values of target hypotheses.

In this paper, we advance a view of truth as utility that follows naturally from considerations about the relative desirability of alternative solutions and that effectively integrates both notions by means of multivalued logic approaches. Our approach is influenced by the "logics of preference" proposed by Rescher [Rescher 67] where the truth-value (usually measured in a $[0, 1]$ scale) of a constraining proposition p represents the desirability of p coming about, or, in other words, the degree by which p is a "good thing." While being close in spirit to the same multivalued-logic ideas, the approach followed by this paper differs from that of Rescher in a number of substantial regards.

First, we seek to develop a model that associates a utility measure, measuring the relative goodness—from a particular perspective—of the solutions of a problem "all other things being equal," to each constraint that defines the problem. Our measures quantify preference between alternatives (e.g., being on this or the other side of the street) from the limited perspective of a single constraint (e.g., we want to hire a taxi). This formulation represents a substantial departure from Rescher's formalism where utilities are simply functions of propositions that measure their "global" relative desirability, regardless of context. This global measure, in Rescher's approach, is given by an average of context-specific desirability values: an assumption that leads to the narrow conclusion that such measures must have the properties of probability distributions.

Second, by introduction of modalities, we enhance the value of multivalued-logic schemes, generalizing both our previous semantic models of fuzzy logic [Ruspini 91] and providing a practical way to represent ignorance about the potential utility of certain choices.

Finally, we provide bases for the rational combination of multiple, goal-specific, measures of utility into a global preference relation that represents their relative importance.

Beyond our objective of expanding and exploring the notions proposed by Rescher, we seek to establish and study formal bases for utility-oriented approaches to problem-solving that depart from classical "optimization" methods that maximize a prespecified measure of performance subject to "hard" constraints. Our formalism, which is also inspired by recent studies on operations research and the foundations of utility theory [Brachinger 90], regards every constraint on the solution of a problem as a source of differential preference relations between alternatives, which are then traded off by a metareasoner capable of *explaining* its solution rationale; a task beyond the ability of current optimization techniques. Furthermore, each such constraint has a "target value," i.e., a quantitative characterization of the "ideal" state of affairs from the single perspective of that restrictive statement.

Our model is based on the mapping of each potential solution of a problem to a set of numbers, each representing the desirability of that alternative from the viewpoint of a different constraint. This perspective on the reasoning problem leads to a uniform characterization of the role that constraints of diverse type have on the determination of the suitability of solutions.

There is no need, for example, to associate two measures, one representing utility and the other representing cost, to each goal or constraint: a most convenient methodological property that is easier to appreciate by noticing that formalisms requiring such one-on-one associations fail to capture complex relations between constraints (i.e., expenditure of some resource contributes to the attainment of multiple goals while attainment of any goal entails use of several resources). Constraints that require attainment of some goal (e.g., "buy nice presents for Jim and Joe") and constraints that limit resource expenditure (e.g., "do not spend too much") are both sources of the same type of measures, which evaluate the desirability of different state of affairs (i.e., "buying presents" is a source of preference measures, and "not spending too much" is another such source). Furthermore, every constraint, including those describing system behavior (e.g., the laws of physics), is the source of utility measures (e.g., as functions of the costs associated with simplifying assumptions that are usually not met by any real system, such as "the container is filled with a perfect gas").

Our ideas also owe much to previous research, which established the close relationships between generalized rankings, operations research, and fuzzy logic [Bellman 80] and similarity-based semantics for that approximate logic [Ruspini 91]. In addition, we have been particularly motivated by the need to provide practical bases for the generation of similarity-measures— the conceptual foundations of analogical reasoning methods— on the basis of the pragmatic rationale for the differentiation between alternative solutions, i.e., two scenarios resemble each other if they are equally preferrable in every relevant regard.

In closing this introduction, it is very important to remark that our synthesis of utilitarian and logical concepts is not the result of a trivial confusion of what is true and what is convenient. We are simply stating that the truth value, measured in a multivalued scale, of propositions of the form:

"The possible world s is an acceptable solution,"

may be interpreted as the relative degree of preference given to s from a specific viewpoint.

2 Possible Worlds and Desirabilities

Our formalism is based on the notion of *possible world*, which will only be given a brief, informal, characterization in this paper. Basically, a possible world, is any conceivable scenario, situation, or behavior that may be used to describe the state of a real-world system. Each such situation is modeled by a function, called a *valuation*, that assigns a conventional truth-value (i.e., either true or false) to every descriptive statement, or proposition, about the system. While we will require that such truth-assignment functions be consistent with the rules of logic, we will not place at this time any other restrictions on the nature of such assignments. Thus, possible worlds may correspond to impossible physical situations, such as the state of idealized systems (e.g., "perfect gases").

The importance of the concept of of possible world, from a reasoning viewpoint, lies on its usefulness to model solutions of reasoning problems as subsets of possible worlds that satisfy certain constraints (i.e., observations, behavioral knowledge) that are usually called "evidence." From such a purely logical viewpoint, a reasoning problem consists of the determination of the set of possible worlds that comply with prescribed constraints. In a classical reasoning problem, the properties of interest are related to the relations of inclusion that hold between the set of possible worlds that satisfy the evidence and sets of possible worlds where some proposition of interest, or *hypothesis* is true. In a number of important cases where such determination is impossible, or *approximate reasoning* problems, applicable approaches, described as approximate reasoning methods, seek to determine certain properties of the set of possible worlds that are consistent with the evidence [Ruspini 90].

Regardless of the nature of our problem, however, we may describe the object of reasoning as being that of assessing if a possible world is worthy of being called a solution. The use of the qualifier "worthy" in the above sentence is not accidental. From a pragmatic point of view, we may say that our aim is to find useful solutions, where "usefulness" is determined by compliance with problem conditions. Given more representational freedom, we may decide to rank (e.g., using some quantitative measures) such usefulness and to speak of the "quality" of a solution.

This notion of utility as cognate of truth is rather easy to understand in connection with engineering problems, where the quality of the solution reflects the ability of a device or system to perform adequately. In general, however, we may regard any problem-solving process as the identification of models (i.e., sets of possible worlds) that meet stated constraints—including those imposed by measurements and observations—to some acceptable degree.

In summary, we may say that we seek solutions with a number of properties, corresponding to compliance with constraints, and that we are willing to pay to different extents to see that those properties come about. At this point, however, it is important to make a few points that are essential to equate measures of desirability with measures of truth.

First, we may note that, in a conventional Boolean context, every proposition p is equivalent to a measure of the solution quality, as measured solely from such a viewpoint (i.e., "other things being equal). In our formalism, we may say that we have a function $\mathbf{D}_p$, called a *desirability* measure. that assigns a value of 1 to every possible world where p is true (denoted $w \vdash p$) and a value of 0 to every possible world where it is false. In this case, this *characteristic function*, in categorical fashion, what is acceptable and what is not. It is often the case, however, that the desirability of a solution is a matter of degree. In such cases, a most natural generalization of the notion of characteristic function will be of value to model such graded preferences: the concept of *fuzzy set* [Zadeh 65].

Second, we must recognize that it will not be difficult to find problems where situation-dependent wishes and desires may not be easily expressed as a single number that quantifies preference. Furthermore, if we aim to associate the truth of any proposition p, not necessarily specified as a problem constraint, with some utilitarian counterpart, we must have some mechanism to indicate that compliance with such proposition is irrelevant to the solution of the problem. The simplest mechanism to represent such irrelevance is to identify a family of *possible* desirability measures to be associated with p, which is easily done by identification of upper and lower bounds for $\mathbf{D}_p$, thus generalizing the notions of possibility and necessity of modal logic.

Finally, we must remark that our functions, which are constraint-dependent, represent relative adequacy of alternative solutions with respect to a set of ideal solutions that attain or exceed some associated "target value." Such ideal solutions are given a relative measure of adequacy that is equal to 1.

It should be clear, however, that the "absolute" usefulness associated with the satisfaction of a particular goal should be given by some "utility" function (defined along some suitable scale of measurement) that, loosely speaking, represents the overall utility associated with its achievement (e.g. if utility is measured in a monetary scale, we may say that the utility of p coming about is \$100). To limit the scope of this paper, however, we shall confine ourselves to the discussion of issues germane to desirability measures, avoiding questions related to the absolute utility associated with their achievement.

3 Desirability and Preference

As informally introduced above, desirability measures quantify the relative value of different solutions from the viewpoint of a single constraint or goal. Although that discussion was confined to "nonelastic" goals, corresponding to subsets of possible worlds, the most interesting applications of utilitarian concepts involve measures ranging over a continuous scale.

3.1 Desirability Measures

The simplest way to formalize the notion of adequacy of a solution is that of a measure that assigns a value of relative desirability to any conceivable solution, as determined solely from the viewpoint of a single, specific goal. In its simplest form, a solution corresponds to some fully specified description (i.e.,a possible world) and it makes sense to start our formalism with a real function defined over possible worlds ranging from 0, representing total inadequacy, to 1, representing total compliance or satisfaction with the goal.

Definition: A *desirability measure* is a function $\mathbf{D} : \mathcal{U} \mapsto [0, 1]$, i.e., a fuzzy set in the universe $\mathcal{U}$ of possible worlds.

The concept of desirability measure is a natural extension of the notion of "hard" or "crisp"constraint. The values $\mathbf{D}(w)$ may also be thought of as the truth-values of the proposition "The solution w is satisfactory." The conceptual synthesis between desirability measures and propositional truth that this explication implies leads to the extension of classical propositional algebra, along well known lines, into a multivalued methodology for their rational combination and aggregation.

Before discussing such methods, however, it is important to remark, once again, that this conceptual unification should not be interpreted as an attempt to reduce issues of factual truth to matters of subjective convenience. Our view of truth as utility stems from the same epistemological principles that led Peter Medawar to describe science as "the art of the solvable." We aim to qualify solution adequacy by measuring the extent by which potential answers fit factual reality and the constraints of the problem. Furthermore, we must stress that desirability measures quantify relative preferences between solutions, from a limited perspective, rather than the overall desirability of a proposition to come about or its importance among various problem constraints.

3.2 Relations between Desirability Measures

It would be rather odd if we were to say that a particular solution w is desirable from the viewpoint of a constraint p, and that it is also desirable from the limited perspective of another constraint q, but that it is rather undesirable from the viewpoint of the conjunction $p \wedge q$. Rational considerations [Trillas 85] show that desirability measures ranking possible worlds by their ability to satisfy the conjunction of two constraints, themselves expressed by means of the desirability functions $\mathbf{D}$ and $\mathbf{D}'$, are related to such measures by the relation

$$(\mathbf{D} \wedge \mathbf{D}')(w) = \mathbf{D}(w) \circledast \mathbf{D}'(w)\,, \quad w \text{ in } \mathcal{U}\,,$$

where the function $\circledast$ is a *triangular norm*.

Similarly, desirability measures quantifying the degree by which solutions meet the disjunction of two restrictions can be seen to be given by

$$(\mathbf{D} \vee \mathbf{D}')(w) = \mathbf{D}(w) \oplus \mathbf{D}'(w)\,, \quad w \text{ in } \mathcal{U}\,,$$

where $\oplus$ is a *triangular conorm*.

Since it is reasonable to ask that the desirability of the conjunction and of the disjunction of two goals should not have an abrupt change when the desirabilities of the arguments are subject to slight variation, we would also require that $\circledast$ and $\oplus$ be continuous functions of both parameters.

Furthermore, desirability measures that rank possible solutions by the degree by which they do *not* meet some constraint (expressed by a desirability $\mathbf{D}$) are given by expressions of the form $\sim \mathbf{D}$, where $\sim$ is a *strong negation function*.

It can also be seen that desirability measures that rank possible worlds by the extent by which they satisfy a conditional constraint of the form $p \rightarrow q$, are related to the desirabilities $\mathbf{D}$ of p and $\mathbf{D}'$ of q by the relation: $(\mathbf{D} \rightarrow \mathbf{D}')(w) = \mathbf{D}'(w) \oslash \mathbf{D}(w)$, where $\oslash$ is the pseudoinverse of a triangular norm $\circledast$.

The discussion above simply restate results in fuzzy-set theory [Bellman 80,Dubois 84,Trillas 85,Valverde 85] that have been recast here in the context of a possible-worlds model to emphasize the parallelism that exists between desirability measures and generalized truth-values. Actual choice of particular T-norms, conorms, and negations depends on the semantics of the problem being considered, as a conjunction $\mathbf{D} \wedge \mathbf{D}'$ modeled using the minimum T-norm has considerably different properties than one being modeled using the product T-norm; being, in the former case, an assertion that minimum standards for $\mathbf{D}$ and $\mathbf{D}'$ must be met, while in the latter declaring that the degree of satisfaction of one goal is exchangeable with the degree of satisfaction of the other.

3.3 Preference Relations

The assignment of desirability values to diverse propositions is often made using comparative measures that assess the advantage that a particular solution w has over a competing alternative w' from the viewpoint of a specific constraint. The ability to define such comparative functions often simplifies the evaluation of the effect of contextual considerations (e.g., the desirability of being in another place, if we are thirsty, depends on how much water we have and how much water is in the other location).

We will formalize this notion by considering functions of the form $\rho(w|w')$ that map pairs of possible worlds to numbers between 0 and 1 so as to quantify the extent to which a possible world w is preferred to another w', from the viewpoint of a particular constraint. We may think of $\rho(w|w')$ as a measure of the amount of resources that we would be willing to spend to be in w rather than in w'. It is easy to see that any definition for ρ must comply with the following rational principles:

1. No resources should be spent to be in w if we are

already in w.

2. If we are willing to spend resources to be in w when we are in w', then we should not spend any resources to be in w' if we were in w
3. The amount that we would be willing to pay to be in w when we are in w'' should be bound by above by a function of the amount that we would be willing to spend to be in w if we were in w' and of the amount that we would be willing to pay to be in w' if we were in w''.

These principles are captured by the following

Definition: A function ρ mapping pairs of possible worlds into numbers between 0 and 1 is called a $\oplus$-*preference* relation if and only if

1. $\rho(w|w) = 0$ for all w in $\mathcal{U}$.
2. If $\rho(w|w') > 0$, then $\rho(w'|w) = 0$ for all w and w' in $\mathcal{U}$.
3. For any possible worlds w, w' and w'' it is
$$\rho(w|w'') \leq \rho(w|w') \oplus \rho(w'|w'').$$

It is also easy to see that if ρ has the semantics of a relation representing graded preference, then $\oplus$ should be a conorm.

3.4 Relations between Desirabilities and Preferences

The combination and aggregation of preference relatons is considerable more complex than that of desirability measures as, for example, the negation $\sim \rho$ of a preference relation ρ is not itself a preference relation. In order to develop an aggregation methodology, it is necessary first to study the relations that exist between both types of utilitarian measures.

The derivation of a $\oplus$-preference relation ρ_D from a desirability measure $\mathbf{D}$ is easily achieved by means of the pseudoinverse $\ominus$ of $\oplus$:
$$\rho_D\,(w|w') = \mathbf{D}(w) \ominus \mathbf{D}(w').$$
The inverse process of derivation of a unique desirability measure from a preference relation is, in general, not possible. One of several representation theorems of Valverde [Valverde 85], exploiting in this case the identity
$$\rho(w|w') = \sup_{w'' \text{ in } \mathcal{U}} \{\rho(w|w'') \ominus \rho(w'|w'')\},$$
assures, however, that there is always a family $\{\mathbf{D}_\alpha\}$ of desirability measures such that
$$\rho(w|w') = \sup_\alpha \{\mathbf{D}_\alpha(w) \ominus \mathbf{D}_\alpha(w')\}.$$

The above representation has a most natural interpretation as the set of constraints (i.e., desirability measures) that are involved in the generalized order defined by a preference relation, i.e., the criteria that make a solution better than another. As it is often the case with conventional constraints, some of these generalized constraints may never be "active," being, in effect, superseded by more specific restrictions. For this reason, the above decomposition is never unique [Jacas 87]. We may, however, always define a unique "canonical decomposition," which is suggested by the proofs of Valverde's theorems. We will call the family of desirability measures $\{\mathbf{D}_w\}$ defined by
$$\mathbf{D}_w(w') = \rho(w'|w), \qquad \text{for every } w \text{ in } \mathcal{U},$$
the *Valverde representation* of ρ.

Note that, although this definition essentially defines a mapping from every possible world w into a desirability measure $\mathbf{D}_w$, the collection of generating functions that is so defined may have a cardinality that is considerably smaller than that of $\mathcal{U}$. The question of whether there exists a unique desirability $\mathbf{D}$ measure that generates ρ, i.e., $\rho(w|w') = \mathbf{D}(w) \ominus \mathbf{D}(w')$, is, in view of the above comments, a matter of rather important practical significance that was studied and solved by Jacas [Jacas 87].

4 Combination of Preference Functions

The ability to express any preference function (i.e. relative adequacy of solutions) in terms of a collection of desirability measures (i.e., criteria for adequacy) also suggests a natural algebraic structure for preference relations.

Definition: Let ρ and ρ' be two preference relations in the universe of discourse $\mathcal{U}$. Furthermore, let $\{\,\mathbf{D}_w\,\}$ and $\{\,\mathbf{D}'_w\,\}$ be the Valverde representations of ρ and ρ', respectively. Then the conjunction and disjunction of ρ and ρ' are the preference functions, denoted $\rho \circledast \rho'$ and $\rho \oplus \rho'$, associated with the generating families $\{\,\mathbf{D}_w \circledast \mathbf{D}'_w\,\}$, and $\{\,\mathbf{D}_w \oplus \mathbf{D}'_w\,\}$, respectively. Furthermore, the complement of ρ is the preference relation $\sim \rho$ associated with the generating family $\{\,\sim \mathbf{D}_w\,\}$. Finally, the implication preference $\rho \rightarrow \rho'$ is the preference relation generated by the family $\{\,\mathbf{D}_w \rightarrow \mathbf{D}'_w\,\}$ of desirability measures.

5 Possibility and Necessity

It is often difficult to assess the adequacy of certain solutions (or particular aspects of such solutions), even from the limited perspective provided by specific problem-solving goals. While steering a mobile robot around an obstacle, for example, it is hard to determine if a particular move is preferrable to another from the viewpoint of a maneuver to be performed much later at a remote location.

Modal logics [Hughes 68], by introduction of notions of possible and necessary truth, permit to represent states of ignorance about the potential truth of the different statements that are being reasoned about. In the formalism presented in this paper, where restrictive propositions have been generalized as relative measures of solution adequacy, the role of the necessity and possibility operators of modal logic is replaced by lower and upper bounds for measures of desirability and preference so as to generalize the modal implications $\mathbf{N}p \rightarrow p \rightarrow \mathbf{\Pi}p$. For example, if we are fully ignorant about the adequacy of w as a solution meeting a constraint represented by the desirability measure $\mathbf{D}$, then we may represent that fact by the bounds $0 \leq \mathbf{D}(w) \leq 1$.

We will say, therefore, that a function $\mathbf{N}_D$ mapping possible worlds w into values between 0 and 1 is a *necessary desirability distribution* for a desirability measure $\mathbf{D}$ if $\mathbf{N}_D(w) \leq \mathbf{D}(w)$ for all w in $\mathcal{U}$. Similarly, we will say that $\mathbf{\Pi}_D$ is a *possible desirability distribution* for $\mathbf{D}$ if $\mathbf{D}(w) \leq \mathbf{\Pi}_D(w)$ for all w in $\mathcal{U}$.

The following results permit to manipulate necessary and possible desirabilities along lines that generalize similar derivation procedures for conventional modal logic:

(a) If $\mathbf{N}_{\sim D}$ is a necessary desirability for the complement $\sim \mathbf{D}$ of $\mathbf{D}$, then $\sim \mathbf{N}_{\sim D}$ is a possible desirability for $\mathbf{D}$. Similarly, if $\mathbf{\Pi}_{\sim D}$ is a possible desirability for the complement $\sim \mathbf{D}$ of $\mathbf{D}$, then $\sim \mathbf{\Pi}_{\sim D}$ is a necessary desirability for $\mathbf{D}$. These relations are the generalization of the well-known duality relations $\neg\mathbf{N}\neg p \equiv \mathbf{\Pi}p$ and $\neg\mathbf{\Pi}\neg p \equiv \mathbf{N}p$.

(b) If $\mathbf{N}_D$ and $\mathbf{N}_{D'}$ are necessary desirability for $\mathbf{D}$ and $\mathbf{D}'$, respectively, then $\mathbf{N}_D \circledast \mathbf{N}_{D'}$ and $\mathbf{N}_D \oplus \mathbf{N}_{D'}$ are necessary desirabilities for $\mathbf{D} \circledast \mathbf{D}'$ and $\mathbf{D} \oplus \mathbf{D}'$, respectively. A similar statement holds for possible desirabilities.

(c) If $\mathbf{N}_D$ is a necessary desirability for $\mathbf{D}$ and if $\mathbf{\Pi}_{D'}$ is a possible desirability for $\mathbf{D}'$, then $\mathbf{N}_D \ominus \mathbf{\Pi}_{D'}$ is a necessary desirability for $\mathbf{D}' \rightarrow \mathbf{D}$. A dual statement also holds for possible desirabilities.

Bounds, called *necessary* and *possible preference functions*, may also be introduced to represent ignorance about relative preference between solutions. Rules for their manipulation, however, are considerably more complex than those for their desirability counterparts. A rather straightforward consequence, nonetheless, of the definition of preference functions is that if if $\mathbf{N}_D$ and $\mathbf{\Pi}_D$ are necessary and possibility desirability distributions for a desirability measure $\mathbf{D}$, then the functions defined by the expressions

$$\mathbf{N}_\rho(w|w') = \mathbf{N}_D(w) \ominus \mathbf{\Pi}_D(w'),$$

and

$$\mathbf{\Pi}_\rho(w|w') = \mathbf{\Pi}_D(w) \ominus \mathbf{N}_D(w'),$$

are necessary and possible preferences for $\rho_D(w|w') = \mathbf{D}(w) \ominus \mathbf{D}(w')$.

It should be also clear that necessary and possible preference functions can always be chosen to satisfy the first two properties (generalized nonreflexivity and antisymmetry) of the definition of preference function. Less obvious is the fact that a possible preference function may always be selected to satisfy the third (or transitive) property. Since then such possible preference relation will be itself a preference relation, it may be represented by a family $\hat{\mathbf{D}}_w$ of desirability measures that is related to the Valverde representation $\mathbf{D}_w$ of ρ by the inequality $\mathbf{D}_w \leq \hat{\mathbf{D}}_w$.

In closing this section, we may note that, in general, it is more likely that a problem-solver will be interested in issues of desirability of a class of solutions or preference between classes of solutions rather than the the corresponding questions for possible worlds. Unfortunately, it is not possible to characterize such general utilitarian concepts using numeric-valued functions as asessments of the utility of a proposition p as a solution depend on the particular world $w \vdash p$ under consideration. It is possible, however, to define bounds

$$\mathbf{N}_D(p) = \inf_{w \vdash p} \mathbf{D}(w), \quad \text{and} \quad \mathbf{\Pi}_D(p) = \inf_{w \vdash p} \mathbf{D}(w),$$

which bound the adequacy of any p-world.

Note also that such bounds may be generated from those of possible and necessary desirability distributions for specific solutions. Conversely, values for $\mathbf{N}_D(p)$ and $\mathbf{\Pi}_D(p)$ defined for every p in an exhaustive, disjoint, partition $\{p_1, p_2, \ldots p_n\}$ of the universe $\mathcal{U}$ may also be used to define possible and necessary possibility distributions by means of the expressions

$$\mathbf{N}_D(w) = \mathbf{N}_D(p_i), \quad \mathbf{\Pi}_D(w') = \mathbf{\Pi}_D(p_i), \quad \text{if } w \vdash p_i.$$

The preference of p-worlds over q-worlds, as measured from the viewpoint of a preference relation ρ, may be similarly defined using the expressions

$$\mathbf{N}_\rho(p|q) = \inf_{w \vdash p} \inf_{w' \vdash q} \rho(w|w'),$$

and

$$\mathbf{\Pi}_\rho(p|q) = \sup_{w \vdash p} \inf_{w' \vdash q} \rho(w|w').$$

6 Preference, Similarity, and Fuzzy Logic

A recent semantic model of the author [Ruspini 91] presented a rationale for the interpretation of the possibilistic structures of fuzzy logic and for its major rule of derivation on the basis of similarity relations between possible worlds. Similarity relations S assign a value $S(w, w')$ between 0 and 1 to every pair of possible worlds w and w' in such a way that

1. $S(w, w) = 1$ for all possible worlds w,
2. $S(w, w') = S(w', w)$ for all possible worlds w and w', and
3. $S(w, w') \leq S(w, w'') \circledast S(w'', w')$ for all possible worlds w, w' and w'', where $\circledast$ is a T-norm.

Two possible worlds w and w' may be considered similar if, from the perspective of all constraints defining a problem, the solutions that they represent have close desirability values. This statement, reflected by the well known relation

$$S(w, w') = \min\left(\sim \rho(w|w'), \sim \rho(w'|w)\right),$$

permits derivation of a similarity relation from a preference relation.

Extensions of the notion of similarity to allow definition of bounds for the resemblance between p-worlds and q-worlds, called *degree of implication* and *degree of consistence*, which are also the result of applying a similar operation to the corresponding preference bounds $\mathbf{N}_\rho(p|q)$ and $\mathbf{\Pi}_\rho(p|q)$, play an essential role in the interpretation of the possibility distributions of fuzzy logic.

Acknowledgements

This work was supported in part by the United States Army Research Office under Contract No. DAAL03-89-K-0156 and in part by a contract with the Laboratory for International Fuzzy Engineering Research. The views, opinions and/or conclusions contained in this note are those of the author and should not be interpreted as representative of the official positions, decisions, or policies, either express or implied, of his sponsors.

The author benefitted from exchanges and conversations with F. Esteva, D. Israel, J. Jacas, J. Lowrance, R. Perrault, E. Trillas, L. Valverde, and L. Zadeh. To all of them, many thanks.

References

[Bellman 80] R. Bellman and L. Zadeh. Decision-making in a fuzzy environment. *Management Science*, 17:B141–B164, 1980.

[Brachinger 90] H.W. Brachinger. Mean-risk Decision Analysis under Partial Information. In T. Kämpke, J. Kohlas, F.J. Radermacher and U. Rieder, editors, *Proceedings of the Workshop on Uncertainty in Knowledge-Based Systems*, Publication FAW-B-90025, FAW, University ofUlm, Germany, 1990.

[Dubois 84] D. Dubois and H. Prade. Criteria aggregation and ranking of alternatives in the framework of fuzzy set theory. In H.J. Zimmerman, L.A. Zadeh, and B.R. Gaines, editors, *Fuzzy Sets and Decision Analysis*, pp. 209–240, North Holland, Amsterdam, 1984.

[Fox 90] M. Fox and K. Sycara. The CORTES Project: A Unified Framework for Planning, Scheduling, Control. In K.P. Sycara, editor, *Proceedings of a Workshop on Innovative Approaches to Planning, Scheduling, and Control*, pp. 412–421. San Diego, California, 1990.

[Hobbs 90] J. Hobbs, M. Stickel, P. Martin and D. Edwards. Interpretation as Abduction. Unpublished report, 1990.

[Hughes 68] Hughes, G. and M. Creswell, *An Introduction to Modal Logic*, Methuen, London, 1968.

[Jacas 87] J. Jacas Moral. Contribució a l'estudi de les relacions d' indistingibilitat i a les seves aplicacions als processos de clasificació. Ph. D. Thesis. Polytechnic University of Barcelona, 1987.

[Rescher 67] N. Rescher. Semantic Foundations for the Logic of Preference. In N. Rescher, editor, *The Logic of Decision and Action*, Pittsburgh, 1967.

[Ruspini 90] E.H. Ruspini. *Approximate Reasoning: Past, Present, Future*. Technical Note No. 492, Artificial Intelligence Center, SRI International, Menlo Park, California, 1990.

[Ruspini 91] E.H. Ruspini. On the Semantics of Fuzzy Logic. *Int.J. Approximate Reasoning*, **5**: 45–88, 1991.

[Russell 89] S. Russell and E. Wefald. Principles of Metareasoning. In *First International Conference on Principles of Knowledge Representation and Reasoning*, pp. 400–411, 1989.

[Trillas 85] E. Trillas and L. Valverde. On mode and implication in approximate reasoning. In M.M. Gupta, A. Kandel, W. Bandler, J.B. Kiszka, editors, *Approximate Reasoning and Expert Systems*, North Holland, Amsterdam, 157–166, 1985.

[Valverde 85] L. Valverde. On the structure of F-indistinguishability operators. *Fuzzy Sets and Systems*, 17: 313–328, 1985.

[Zadeh 65] L. Zadeh. Fuzzy Sets. *Inf. Control*, 8:338–363, 1965.

PULCINELLA

A General Tool for Propagating Uncertainty in Valuation Networks

Alessandro Saffiotti and Elisabeth Umkehrer

IRIDIA - Université Libre de Bruxelles
Av. F. Roosevelt, 50 - CP 194/6
1050 Bruxelles - Belgium
E-mail: r01507@bbrbfu01.bitnet

Abstract

We present PULCinella and its use in comparing uncertainty theories. PULCinella is a general tool for Propagating Uncertainty based on the Local Computation technique of Shafer and Shenoy. It may be specialized to different uncertainty theories: at the moment, Pulcinella can propagate probabilities, belief functions, Boolean values, and possibilities. Moreover, Pulcinella allows the user to easily define his own specializations. To illustrate Pulcinella, we analyze two examples by using each of the four theories above. In the first one, we mainly focus on intrinsic differences between theories. In the second one, we take a knowledge engineer viewpoint, and check the adequacy of each theory to a given problem.

1. INTRODUCTION

A new interest has grown up recently in the uncertainty management community. Moving from consideration of efficiency, ease of representation, and generality, a number of techniques for representing and propagating uncertainty in networks have been proposed (e.g. Chatalic et al., 1987; Lauritzen and Spiegelhalter, 1988; Pearl, 1988; Shafer et al., 1987). Moreover, implementations of these techniques have been developed (e.g. Andersen et al., 1989; Hsia and Shenoy, 1989; Zarley et al., 1988; Xu, 1991). However, all the existing systems only propagate uncertainty values according to a single uncertainty theory. This is unfortunate: if we accept that uncertainty theories should be seen as alternatives, rather than rivals (Fox, 1986; Saffiotti, 1987) then we must also accept that for each problem there is a "most adequate" theory, and this theory is in general different from problem to problem. It would be advisable to have a general tool capable of propagating uncertainty according to different uncertainty theories. This would allow us to use the same piece of software for solving different problems that call for different uncertainty management techniques. Moreover, such a tool would be useful for analyzing and comparing different theories in an experimental way.

In the Platonic world of formal theories, a system having the above characteristics exists. Building on their work on belief function propagation (Shafer et al., 1987), Shafer and Shenoy developed a general framework for local computation (Shafer and Shenoy, 1988b) in which the process of network propagation in itself has been abstracted from what is actually propagated. Shafer and Shenoy have shown (Shafer and Shenoy, 1989a) that their framework is capable of modelling both probability and belief function propagation, and that it can capture other existing propagation schemas (i.e. Lauritzen and Spiegelhalter's and Pearl's). This framework has been further generalized by Shenoy (1989), who proposes a class of languages ("valuation-based languages") for building knowledge-based systems. Besides probability and belief functions, other existing uncertainty theories have already been formalized as valuation languages (e.g. Dubois and Prade, 1990).

In this paper, we introduce PULCinella, a tool for Propagating Uncertainty based on the Local Computation technique of Shafer and Shenoy. Pulcinella is a general implementation of valuation based languages, abstracted from a belief function propagation system (Xu, 1991), and it is fully described in (Saffiotti and Umkehrer, 1991a). As such, it may be instantiated to any of the theories which have been formalized as valuation based languages. In particular, four specialization of Pulcinella have already been implemented, namely for propagating probabilities, belief functions, Boolean values, and possibilities. Moreover, Pulcinella makes it easy to implement new theories in it (provided that they can be modelled in the valuation language formalism). Besides describing the tool and the underlying theory, we illustrate the use of Pulcinella for comparing uncertainty theory. In this sense, the AI researcher will find in this paper an analysis of the different results obtained applying different theories to the same problem; and the knowledge engineer will find a discussion of the pros and cons of using different uncertainty theories for modelling the same test-bed problem. Both discussions are based on the results of experiments carried out using Pulcinella.

The rest of this paper is organized as follows. Section 2 reminds some formal background on valuation-based languages and local computations. Section 3 presents Pulcinella. Section 4 shows two full examples of application of Pulcinella. Section 5 discusses these examples and analyzes the differences detected in using different uncertainty theories. Finally, Section 6 concludes.

2. THEORETICAL BACKGROUND

2.1. VALUATION-BASED LANGUAGES

Shenoy's *valuation-based languages* (Shenoy, 1989) have been abstracted from the axiomatic framework for probabilities and belief functions propagation of Shafer and Shenoy (Shafer, Shenoy and Mellouli, 1987; Shafer and Shenoy, 1988a; Shenoy and Shafer, 1988b). They have been proposed as an alternative to rule-based languages for constructing knowledge-based systems. The language consists of objects, which are used to represent knowledge, and operators, which operate on these objects to make inferences on the knowledge. Two kinds of objects are considered, *variables* and *valuations*, and two operators, *combination* and *marginalization*[1]. We first remind the formal definitions of these elements, and will discuss their interpretation and use later.

Variables, Frames and Configurations. We consider a finite set of variables. Each variable may range over a finite set of possible values, called the *frame* for that variable. A *configuration* of a finite non-empty set of variables is an element of the Cartesian product of the frames of the variables in this set.

Denotations: X for the set of variables; g, h, k for subsets of X; Wg for the set of configurations of g; x,y for single configurations; a,b,c for sets of configurations.

Sometimes we need to project a configuration of one set to another set. A configuration x of g is *projected* to h, $g \supset h$, by dropping all the elements in x belonging to g-h. It is *extended* to k, $k \supset g$, by building the Cartesian product between the configuration and W_{k-g}.

Denotations: $x^{\downarrow h}$ for the projection of x to h; $x^{\uparrow h}$ for the extension of x to h.

Valuations. Given a set of variables h, we consider a set V_h. The elements of V_h are called *valuations* on the set h[2]. In our case, valuations are the objects that represent the uncertainty about a set of variables.

Denotations: V_g for the set of valuations on g; V for the set of all valuations on subsets of X; G, H for single valuations.

Combination is any mapping $\otimes: V \times V \rightarrow V$, such that, if G and H are valuations on g and h, respectively, then $G \otimes H$ is a valuation on $g \cup h$.

Marginalization. For each $h \subseteq X$, there is a mapping $\downarrow h$: $\cup \{V_g \mid h \subseteq g\} \rightarrow V_h$, called *marginalization* to h, such that, if G is a valuation on g and $h \subseteq g$, then $G^{\downarrow h}$ is a valuation on h.

[1] A third operator, *solution*, is used for "decoding" the result obtained the propagation. This operator is not relevant to the present discussion, and so it will not be considered.

[2] For the sake of simplicity, we do not take here into account "proper valuations", a subset of the valuations used to restrict the applicability of operators. Thus, the definitions given here are not complete, but they preserve the basic ideas of valuation-based languages.

2.2. INTERPRETATIONS

It will be useful to give now some examples of possible interpretations for the syntactical entities of a valuation-based language. This will show in which way a valuation-based language can be used for modelling different existing uncertainty theories. For probability theory, belief-functions, and a Boolean case, the mapping of the theory into the concepts of a valuation-based language have been proposed by Shenoy and Shafer (Shenoy and Shafer, 1988b; Shenoy, 1989). For possibility theory, we use the mapping proposed by Dubois and Prade (1990) building on a previous work by Zadeh (1979).

Probability:

Valuations on h are (unnormalized) probability distributions on the configurations of h

Combination: If G and H are probability distributions on g and h, respectively, then their combination is the probability distribution on $g \cup h$ defined by

$$(G \otimes H)(x) = G(x^{\downarrow g})H(x^{\downarrow h}) \quad \text{for all } x \in W_{g \cup h}.$$

Marginalization: If $h \subseteq g$ and G is a probability distribution on g, then the marginal of G for h is the probability distribution on h defined by[3]:

$$G^{\downarrow h}(x) = \Sigma\{G(x,y) \mid y \in W_{g-h}\} \quad \text{for all } x \in W_h$$

Belief Functions:

Valuations on h are basic probability assignment (bpa) functions on sets of configurations of h.

Combination: If G, H are bpa's on g, h –respectively– then their combination is the bpa on $g \cup h$ defined by[4]

$$(G \otimes H)(c) = \sum\{G(a)H(b) \mid (a^{\uparrow(g \cup h)}) \cap (b^{\uparrow(g \cup h)}) = c\}$$
$$\text{for all } c \subseteq W_{g \cup h},\ a \subseteq W_g,\ b \subseteq W_h$$

Marginalization: If $h \subseteq g$ and G is a bpa on g, then the marginal of G for h is the bpa on h defined by

$$G^{\downarrow h}(a) = \sum\{G(b) \mid b \subseteq W_g \text{ such that } b^{\downarrow h} = a\}$$
$$\text{for all } a \subseteq W_h.$$

Boolean:

Valuations on h are functions $H: W_h \rightarrow \{\text{true, false}\}$.

Combination: If G and H are valuations on g and h, respectively, then their combination is the valuation on $g \cup h$ defined, for all $x \in W_{g \cup h}$, by

$$(G \otimes H)(x) = \begin{cases} \text{true} & \text{if } G(x^{\downarrow g}) = \text{true and } H(x^{\downarrow h}) = \text{true} \\ \text{false} & \text{otherwise} \end{cases}$$

Marginalization: If $h \subseteq g$ and G is a valuation on g, then the marginal of G for h is the valuation on h defined, for all $x \in W_h$, by

$$G^{\downarrow h}(x) = \begin{cases} \text{true} & \text{if there is } y \in W_{g-h} \text{ s.t. } G(x,y) = \text{true} \\ \text{false} & \text{otherwise} \end{cases}$$

[3] In all interpretations, we let $G^{\downarrow h}(x) = G(x)$ if h = g..

[4] This corresponds to usual (but un-normalized) Dempster's rule of combination (Dempster, 1966).

Possibility:

Valuations on h are possibility distributions on sets of configurations of h.

Combination: If G and H are possibility distributions on g and h, respectively, then their combination is the possibility distribution on g∪h defined by

$$(G\otimes H)(x) = \min (G(x^{\downarrow g}), H(x^{\downarrow h})) \text{ for all } x\in W_{g\cup h}.$$

Marginalization: If $h\subseteq g$ and G is a possibility distribution on g, then the marginal of G for h is the possibility distribution on h defined by

$$G^{\downarrow h}(x) = \sup \{G(x,y) \mid y\in W_{g-h}\} \text{ for all } x\in W_h.$$

2.3. REPRESENTING PROBLEMS BY VALUATION SYSTEMS

A set of variables, with their frames, together with a set of valuations, is called a *valuation system*. Intuitively, a valuation system corresponds to a knowledge-base. When we want to use a valuation-based language to solve a problem, we first have to define a valuation system that represents our problem. While doing that, we have to keep in mind the intended intuitive meaning of the syntactical entities of valuation-based languages (which holds independently from the interpretation). To this respect, variables can be seen as representing entities of the domain of discourse, and valuations V_h as representing relational knowledge among the entities represented by the variables in h. The combination operator models aggregation of different fragments of knowledge, and the marginalization operator models a narrowing of the focus of interest by concentrating knowledge on a subset of variables. The following is a pictorial representation of the intended interpretation in terms of real world knowledge of variables and valuations.

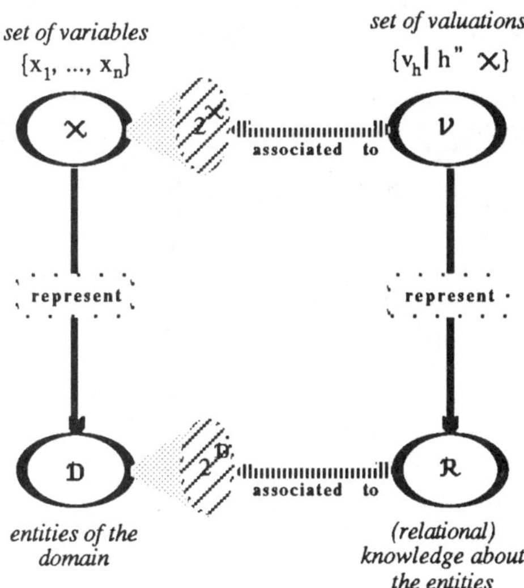

2.4. LOCAL COMPUTATION IN VALUATION SYSTEMS

Having defined a valuation system we want now to evaluate it. This means to compute a global valuation on X obtained by combining together all the valuations in our valuation system, and find the marginals of this global valuation to each variable in X. In terms of knowledge, this corresponds to aggregating all the available knowledge together, and to finding the effect of this knowledge on the individual variables. Computing explicitly the global valuation is often unfeasible from the computational viewpoint. However, Shafer and Shenoy (1988b) proposed a general local computation schema for evaluating valuation systems. The computation is local in the sense that combinations of valuations can be performed without extending each valuation to the whole space of the configurations. Shenoy and Shafer have shown that this schema can be applied if the combination and marginalization operators satisfy the following three axioms:

A1 (Commutativity and associativity of ⊗). Let G, H, K be valuations on g, h and k, respectively. Then:

$$G\otimes H = H\otimes G \text{ and } G\otimes(H\otimes K) = (G\otimes H)\otimes K$$

A2 (Consonance of ↓). Let G be a valuation on g, and suppose $k\subseteq h\subseteq g$. Then:

$$(G^{\downarrow h})^{\downarrow k} = G^{\downarrow k}.$$

A3 (Distributivity of ↓ over ⊗). Let G, H be valuations on g and h, respectively. Then

$$(G\otimes H)^{\downarrow g} = G\otimes(H^{\downarrow g\cap h})$$

All four interpretations described in Section 2.2 satisfy these axioms. Thus, local computations can be used for propagating probabilities, belief functions, Boolean values, and possibilities.

Algorithms based on the above technique have already been proposed and implemented (Zarley et al., 1988; Hsia and Shenoy, 1989; Xu, 1991). These algorithms use a network representation for the valuation system called *Markov Tree*. Mapping a valuation system on a Markov Tree is done in two steps. The first step is to represent the valuation system by a hypergraph: in it, each variable is associated to a node, and each valuation is associated to a hyperedge. The second step is to find a Markov Tree representative of the hypergraph by clustering variables.

3. PULCINELLA

Pulcinella is a system for building and evaluating valuation systems based on Shenoy and Shafer's local computation technique. The system implements the general framework discussed above: it may be specialized to a given uncertainty theory by choosing an interpretation for the objects and the operators. Pulcinella is written in Lisp, and appears as a library of Lisp functions for creating, modifying and evaluating a valuation system. Alternatively, the user can choose to interact with Pulcinella via a graphical interface. The system builds on Hong Xu's implementation of the belief functions propagation technique of Shafer and Shenoy (Xu, 1991). The key move for generalizing Xu's program has been to parametrize it over a set of functions. At the moment, four interpretations of the general framework have been implemented: belief function, probability, Boolean and possibility (in the following, we will use the term "specialization" to refer to an implemented interpretation). By selecting one of these specializations, the user can transform Pulcinella in a probability propagation system, in a belief function propagation system, and so on. Moreover, Pulcinella is meant to be an open system: the set of functions which have to be defined to create a new specialization is very small and with a well defined semantics (reflecting the elements of a valuation-based language). Thus, it is easy for the user to define further specializations. In this Section, we will first show how to use the existing specializations, and then discuss how a new specialization can be created.

3.1 USING A PULCINELLA SPECIALIZATION

As far as modelling quantitative knowledge is not concerned, the way to work with Pulcinella is the same for all specializations. We first describe this common part, and then show how qualitative knowledge is modelled in each of the four provided specializations.

The user can model his problem, either graphically or by calling Lisp functions. In terms of Shafer and Shenoy's framework, modelling the problem means to create a valuation system representing his problem. This modelling process comprises two steps. In the first step, the user specifies the structural knowledge of his problem. This means defining all the variables to be used (along with their frames), and indicating which variables are linked together by a relation. By defining the variables and the relations the user implicitly fixes the subsets of variables for which valuations can be specified in the second step. The second step consists in modelling the quantitative knowledge: i.e. in defining the valuations on (some of) the subsets identified by the structural model created. This step depends from the specialization chosen, and will be discussed below. However, during this step, the user should keep in mind that a default valuation is given by the system to each variable and relation if no valuation is defined by the user. Once the valuation system has been completely defined, the user can evaluate it by asking Pulcinella to start propagation. The user can choose if the results must be shown normalized or unnormalized. If the user wants to apply different uncertainty theories on the same problem, he has to specify the structural knowledge only once. He can use the same variables and relations for different specializations.

Probability Specialization. In the probability specialization, the user models quantitative knowledge by defining probability distributions for single variables and relations. Notice that this means that a dependency between variables is encoded by a joint probability distribution rather than by conditional probabilities. The default valuation is the uniform probability distribution: if nothing is known about a variable or relation, all configurations are considered to have the same probability. A probability distribution is called normalized if the values attached to the configurations adds up to one.

Belief-Function Specialization. In the belief function specialization, the user models the quantitative knowledge by defining basic probability assignment functions on the sets of variables that constitute the structural knowledge. A basic probability assignment function on a set of variables reflects to which extent some subsets of configurations are believed to contain the true configuration, and is expressed by a mapping from subsets of configurations of a set of variables to the interval [0,1]. The value associated to the empty set is always zero. The default valuation is the basic probability assignment function which attach the value 1 to the whole set of configurations. A basic probability assignment function is called normalized if the sum of all its values is 1.

Boolean Specialization. The Boolean specialization can be seen as a way to represent categorical knowledge. The quantitative knowledge is modelled by attaching to the configurations of the defined sets of variables either true or false. These values are better understood in term of satisfaction of constraints: a value true for a configuration means that this configuration is acceptable given the constraints of our problem. Accordingly, a relation among variables will be encoded by selecting all those configurations that are admissible, and by associating true to them. The default valuation attaches true to each configuration: if nothing is known about a set of variables, each configuration could be the case. No normalization is defined for Boolean specialization.

Possibility Specialization. In possibility theory the user models quantitative knowledge by specifying possibility distributions on the defined sets of variables. A possibility distribution on a set of variables reflects to what extent each configuration of the set is regarded as possible, and is expressed by a mapping from configurations to the [0,1] interval. The default possibility distribution attaches to each configuration the value 1: if nothing is known about a set of variables, all configurations are regarded as completely possible. A possibility distribution is called normalized if at least one element of the frame has possibility value 1.

3.2 HOW TO BUILD A NEW SPECIALIZATION

Pulcinella is an open system. The user can build his own specialization with Pulcinella. To build a new specialization the first thing he has to do is to express his theory in terms of the syntactical entities of valuation-based languages, and to prove that the axioms of local computation are satisfied. Having expressed the theory in this way, he may now implement the functions specific to the new specialization. This is made easier by the clear semantics given to these functions: basically, they mirror the concepts and entities of a valuation-based language. These functions may be divided up into three groups:

1. two functions defining the default valuations for variables and relations
2. two functions that implement the combination and marginalization operators.
3. two extra functions for changing the valuations in "some way": one implements the normalization procedure for valuations; the other is called after the

propagation has been completed, and allows the builder of a specialization to do some housekeeping before the results are shown to the user.

4. EXAMPLES

In this section we will give a couple of examples aimed at illustrating the use of Pulcinella for modelling and solving uncertain problems. We will insist on the difference between modelling the structural knowledge of the problem, and modelling its quantitative knowledge. In each example, the same problem will be formalized in all the four specializations discussed above. However, and interestingly, the structural model remains the same for all of them. These examples will highlight how using different uncertainty theories may require different input and produce different results.

4.1. EXAMPLE 1

Our first example is adapted from (Saffiotti, 1987). We want to guess if Francesco will came wearing a black (B), white (W) or polka-dot (P) suite. We do not have any information about Francesco's preference (*state 0*), but we do know that his "Philco" washing machine is out; this makes us believe (say 80%) that he cannot choose W (*state 1*). Later, we remember that Francesco said yesterday that he dislikes mono-chromatic clothes; this is, for the notorious coherence of Francesco, a strong (say 90%) evidence both against B and W (*state 2*).

We first build a structural model for our problem. We define three variables: *Dress*, with frame {B, W, P}; *Philco*, with frame {ok, out}; and *Speech*, with frame {uttered, unuttered}. We then define two relations: *Washing*, between *Philco* and *Dress*; and *Coherence*, between *Speech* and *Dress*. The intended meaning of these elements should be self evident. The following is a graphical representation of our model, as appearing on the screen of Pulcinella:

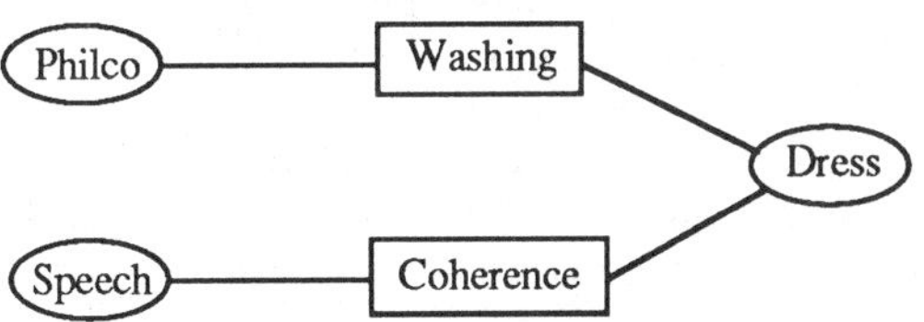

The next step consists in deciding one uncertainty calculus to use, and to specialize Pulcinella to it. Suppose we choose to specialize Pulcinella to probability[5]. We can then enter the (unnormalized) joint probability distributions for our variables and relations. These distributions, which encode the quantitative knowledge in our problem, are shown below[6]:

$\mathcal{P}_{washing}$	B	W	P
ok	1/6	1/6	1/6
out	0.2	0.1	0.2

$\mathcal{P}_{coherence}$	B	W	P
uttered	0.025	0.025	0.45
unuttered	1/6	1/6	1/6

Notice that we are assuming uniform prior distributions whenever no explicit information is available. Finally, we ask Pulcinella to start propagation. The following table gives the marginal probabilities computed for *Dress* at different moments[7]:

Value	*State 0*	*State 1*	*State 2*
B	0.33	0.40	0.051
W	0.33	0.20	0.026
P	0.33	0.40	0.923

Suppose that we now want to try to use belief functions for modelling our problem. All we need to do, is to specialize Pulcinella to belief functions, and to input the quantitative knowledge of our problem in the form of two basic probability assignments for our relations:

Subset (B W P)	$m_{washing}$
ok / out	0.8

Subset (B W P)	$m_{coherence}$
uttered / unuttered	0.9

Intuitively, the subset to which $m_{washing}$ assigns a 0.8 mass represents the fact that the answer to our problem may be any of B, W and P when *Philco* = ok, and any of B and P when *Philco* = out. The remaining 0.2 mass is automatically given to the whole frame. After propagation, we get the following results for the variable *Dress*[8]

Value	*State 0* bel	pl	*State 1* bel	pl	*State 2* bel	pl
B	0	1	0	1	0	0.1
W	0	1	0	0.2	0	0.02
P	0	1	0	1	0.9	1

Next, we consider using possibility theory: we switch Pulcinella accordingly, and enter two possibility distributions for our relations. These distributions, and the one obtained for the variable *Dress* after propagation, are shown below.

$\Pi_{washing}$	B	W	P
ok	1	1	1
out	1	0.2	1

$\Pi_{coherence}$	B	W	P
uttered	0.1	0.1	1
unuttered	1	1	1

Value	*State 0*	*State 1*	*State 2*
B	1	1	0.1
W	1	0.2	0.1
P	1	1	1

Finally, we consider the case in which we collapse uncertainty to true/false values. The following tables show the values for our relations, and the results obtained, with the Boolean specialization[9].

$\mathcal{T}_{washing}$	B	W	P
ok	true	true	true
out	true	false	true

$\mathcal{T}_{coherence}$	B	W	P
uttered	false	false	true
unuttered	true	true	true

[5] In practice, this reduces to selecting a menu item, or to evaluating the form "(specialize-uncertainty 'probability)".

[6] The valuations for variables are obvious, and will not shown.

[7] States in the table refer to the states in the statement of our story.

[8] For greater readability, we show the results using *bel* and *pl* functions (Shafer, 1976). Remind that pl(A) = 1 - bel(~A).

[9] As noticed above, these values are better understood in term of satisfaction of constraints.

Value	*State 0*	*State 1*	*State 2*
B	true	true	false
W	true	false	false
P	true	true	true

4.2. EXAMPLE 2

The next example has been tailored on an experiment made in modelling the uncertainty present in a problem of fault diagnoses in electricity networks (Gallastegui et al., 1989). For the sake of clarity, both the qualitative and the quantitative knowledge have been greatly simplified. The full experiment, and the actual figures used, are reported in (Saffiotti and Umkehrer, 1991b). We consider here the following fragment of an electricity network:

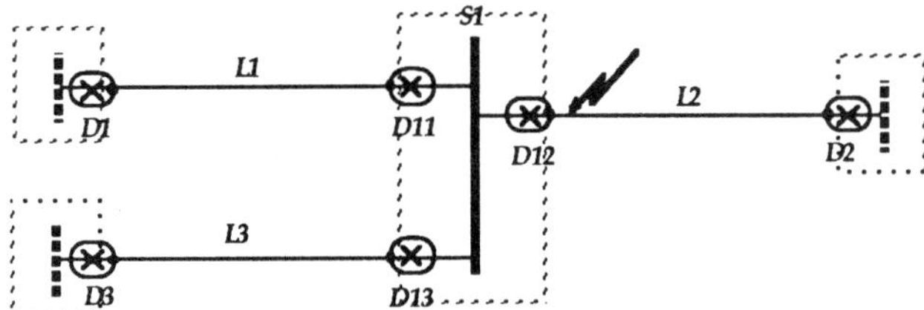

This fragment comprises four "substations", linked by three electricity lines L1, L2 and L3. The substation in the middle includes S1, a big conductive bar used for connecting more lines together. The Di's are "circuit breakers": automatic switches that can isolate two lines when they detect an overload on the part of the network on their "hot" side (marked by a dot in the picture). When an overload is detected, a circuit breaker generate an alarm. There are two kinds of alarm: "instantaneous", for "big" overloads (normally caused by a fault in the line the device is on); or "delayed", for "small" overloads (normally caused by a fault in a neighbour line). All the alarms are sent to the "control room" of some power station. Here, a system engineer is constantly analyzing the incoming alarms to find out what is happening in the network. His goal is to determine if and where there is a fault. We model our electricity network in Pulcinella by the following variables and relations:

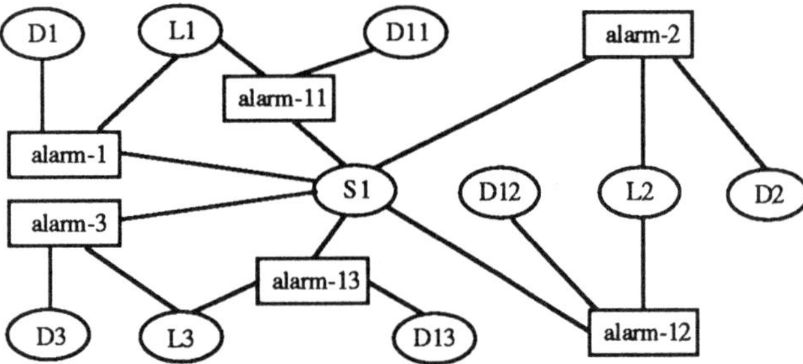

where *Di*'s are variables representing circuit breaker states, with possible values <u>ok</u> (no alarm), <u>del</u> (delayed alarm), and <u>inst</u> (instantaneous alarm); *Li*'s and *S1* represent line states, with frame {<u>ok</u>, <u>fault</u>}; and the *alarm-i*'s relate generation of alarms by breakers with states of neighbour lines.

The quantitative knowledge given by the experts is not very rich. Essentially, it says that:

1. alarms are not very reliable: in roughly 10% of the cases, they do not correspond to the real situation (alarm generated without fault, or fault occurring without alarm);
2. if an instantaneous alarm is generated (correctly), the fault is 70% of the cases in the line the breaker is on, and 30% in the next one; the reverse holds for delayed alarms.

The following tables show how this knowledge has been coded into the relation *alarm-1* by an (unnormalized) joint probability distribution $\mathcal{P}$, a possibility distribution Π, a Boolean constraint $\mathcal{T}$, or a basic probability assignment m, respectively. Distributions for the other *alarm-i*'s are similar; while those for the *alarm-ij*'s are different.

$\mathcal{P}(\bullet)$ — D1

L1, S1	ok	del	inst
ok, ok	0.9	0.1	0.1
ok, fault	0.05	0.6	0.2
fault, ok	0.05	0.2	0.6
fault, fault	0.001	0.1	0.1

$\Pi(\bullet)$

L1, S1	ok	del	inst
ok, ok	1	0.1	0.1
ok, fault	0.1	0.7	0.3
fault, ok	0.1	0.3	0.7
fault, fault	0.1	1	1

$\mathcal{T}(\bullet)$	ok	del	inst
ok, ok	true	false	false
ok, fault	false	true	true
fault, ok	false	true	true
fault, fault	false	true	true

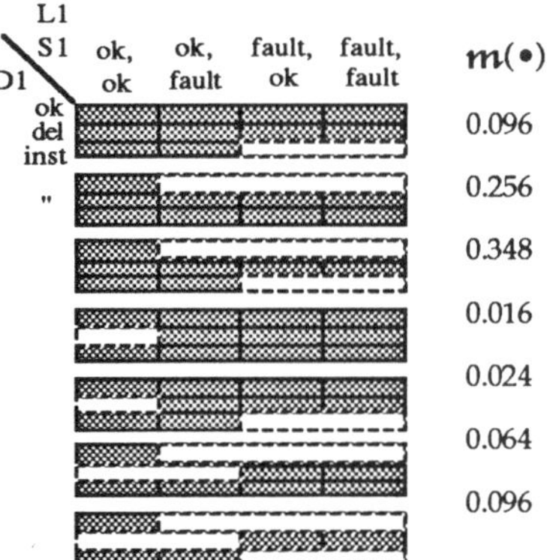

We now imagine a scenario in which a fault occurs on line L2 very near to D12 (see the above picture): as a consequence, a "delayed" alarm is sent by D2, and a "instantaneous" alarm by D12. Moreover, we imagine that D1 has been adjusted incorrectly (it happens), and is too sensitive: thus, also D1 sends a "delayed" alarm.

These three alarms will be received in the control room, and the system engineer will have to find out what has happened. Three main hypotheses are compatible with this set of alarms, shown in order of preference:

1) Fault in L2; alarm from D1 spurious;

2) Fault in S1; missing alarm from D3, and alarm from D12 spurious;

3) Fault in L1; D11 not working (missing alarm & did not open), missing alarm from D3, and alarm from D12 spurious.

The following tables summarize the results obtained for this example with the probability, possibility, Boolean, and belief function specializations of Pulcinella[10]

1. After receiving the alarm from D2

Var	Probab	Possibility		Belief Functions		Boolean	
	$\mathcal{P}$(fault)	N(fault)	Π(fault)	Bel(fault)	Pl(fault)	$\mathcal{T}$(fault)	$\mathcal{T}$(ok)
L1	0.002	0.3	1	0.02	1	true	true
L2	0.226	0.3	1	0.02	1	true	true
L3	0.002	0.3	1	0.02	1	true	true
S1	0.087	0.7	1	0.16	1	true	true

2. After receiving the alarm from D12

Var	Probab	Possibility		Belief Functions		Boolean	
	$\mathcal{P}$(fault)	N(fault)	Π(fault)	Bel(fault)	Pl(fault)	$\mathcal{T}$(fault)	$\mathcal{T}$(ok)
L1	0.002	0.3	1	0.02	1	true	true
L2	0.972	0.9	1	0.60	1	true	false
L3	0.002	0.3	1	0.02	1	true	true
S1	0.013	0.7	1	0.16	1	true	true

3. After receiving the alarm from D1

Var	Probab	Possibility		Belief Functions		Boolean	
	$\mathcal{P}$(fault)	N(fault)	Π(fault)	Bel(fault)	Pl(fault)	$\mathcal{T}$(fault)	$\mathcal{T}$(ok)
L1	0.219	0.3	1	0.03	1	true	true
L2	0.919	0.9	1	0.60	1	true	false
L3	0.002	0.3	1	0.03	1	true	true
S1	0.141	0.7	1	0.29	1	true	true

5. DISCUSSION

Beside illustrating the use of Pulcinella for modelling uncertain problems within a given specialization, the examples above show how Pulcinella may provide useful help in comparing different uncertainty management techniques. The advantage of having this capability is twofold. In theoretical research, Pulcinella allows us to play with uncertainty theories, and to track differences between them. In knowledge engineering, it may be used as a tool for choosing, on an experimental basis, the uncertainty treatment technique that better fits our problem and our needs. The following discussion will illustrate both uses[11]. In our examples, we recognize three basic categories of differences:

1) differences in the data we have to provide (which data, how many, in which form, ...);
2) differences in the results due to differences in the data we provided; and
3) differences in the results due to differences in the mechanisms used in the theories.

We first consider Example 1. Concerning category 1 above, the quantitative knowledge stated in the problem has to be coded differently in the four specializations. In the probabilistic case, the need to specify completely the joint distributions $\mathcal{P}_{washing}$ and $\mathcal{P}_{coherent}$ has obliged us to replace in some way the missing information. In particular, in $\mathcal{P}_{washing}$, the 80% probability of (B∨W) has been converted into exact probability values for B and P individually (assuming equiprobability); a similar operation has been made for $\mathcal{P}_{coherent}$. On the other hand, in both the belief function and the possibilistic specializations knowledge has been expressed at exactly the level of granularity that is available. However, it must be noticed that using basic probability assignments to encode knowledge may sometimes be less intuitive (mainly because we have to work on subsets). Finally, our knowledge has easily been reduced in the obvious way in the Boolean specialization.

Moving now to the analysis of the results (categories 2 and 3 above), we first notice that —as expected— all four specializations agree from the qualitative viewpoint. The major quantitative differences show up between the results of the probabilistic specialization and those of the belief function (or possibilistic) one. These differences must be tracked back to differences in the data used, mainly because of the additional hypotheses (equiprobability) introduced in the probabilistic case. Remarkably, these differences are particularly evident in those cases (States 0 and 1) in which ignorance is predominant: here, in spite of our ignorance, the probabilistic approach needs (and gives) precise figures[12]. Another interesting difference arises between the belief function and the possibilistic cases. Here, differences in results do not originate from differences in the inputs given, but rather from the different combination mechanisms. To wit, consider State 2: the Philco evidence and the Speech evidence are both denying the W hypothesis. These two items of evidence have been combined into one much stronger evidence against W by Dempster's rule in the belief function case, resulting in a very small (0.02) plausibility for W. On the other hand, the stronger of them has simply been selected through the MIN operator in the possibilistic approach, giving a possibility value of 0.1 for W.

The above considerations illustrate how to use Pulcinella for analyzing the different behaviours of uncertainty treating theories. However, we do not have a pragmatic unit for measuring how much do a given theory fits our needs. Still, Pulcinella may be also used as a tool for evaluating uncertainty formalisms in the light of the uses to which they are to be put. To this respect, we now consider Example 2. As before, we first consider the differences in the inputs required by the different techniques (category 1 above), and than the differences in the output produced (categories 2 and 3). However, we try to take here a more "knowledge engineering" viewpoint.

Probability theory requires several values that are not available in our data. It is common practice to produce missing values by resorting to some symmetry consideration, or by using the principle of maximum entropy. Accordingly, we had to introduce a number of

10 For better readability, we show the results of the possibilistic case as necessity/possibility pairs. Remind that N(A) = 1 - Π(~A).

11 This is not meant to be a general comparative analysis of different UR techniques. Our sole aim here is to show how Pulcinella may provide useful information in this perspective.

12 «Wovon man nicht sprechen kann, darüber muß man schweigen» (What we cannot speak about we must consign to silence) (Wittgenstein, 1921).

equiprobability hypotheses for our missing values (e.g. in computing $\mathcal{P}$({ok, ok, fault}). Also, notice that the amount of subjective estimates required by the probabilistic approach greatly increases the risk of inconsistency among them (but see Duda et al., 1986). On the contrary, the process of supplying data is extremely simple in the possibility and the belief function specializations: the expert must supply just the data she knows, and consign the rest to silence. We do not need to force her (or the figures she supplies) to say something they were not meant to. However, in the belief function case, the translation of this data into basic probability assignments may sometimes be hard. The difficulty of the Boolean case is somewhat complementary to that of the probabilistic case: the data given by the expert has to be rounded very roughly, and she may feel uncomfortable with the approximations obtained. A possible reaction to this rude attitude is to try to split general rules into more specific ones. The aim of this would be to reduce uncertainty by explicitly accounting for the possible exceptions to rules. Though this constitutes a stimulus for the expert that may sometimes result in a better explanation of her knowledge, the strongly empirical, tangled and "artistic" nature of electrical fault diagnostic knowledge discouraged us from using the Boolean specialization for our problem.

We now switch to analyzing the results. Our four specializations have produced results that are both quantitatively and qualitatively different. The first phenomenon we notice is that the Boolean specialization does not suggest the possibility of a fault in S1. The causes of this reside both in the input given and in the combination mechanism used. As for the input, the knowledge encoded in our relations allows us to infer that the fault is, e.g., either in S1 or in L1. Yet, no relation encodes knowledge which allows us to infer the S1 hypothesis alone. Discrimination between S1 and L1 is, on the other side, captured by differences in the given weights in the other approaches. As for the mechanism, aggregating knowledge by an AND operation does not allow to perform that "counting" of evidence that seems necessary if we want to accumulate items of weak evidence together. In our example, the evidence given by D2 only partly supports the hypothesis S1; however, we would expect further support for S1 coming from D1 to reinforce the S1 hypothesis. One way to fix this problem in the Boolean specialization is to add new rules (e.g. "IF at least 2 among D1, D2 and D3 send a delayed alarm, THEN S1 is faulty"); but the lesson taken from this story seems to be that considering uncertainty in our problem is necessary, if we want to preserve inferential power without having to drown in a see of specialized rules.

The second qualitative difference we want to notice regards the hypothesis "*L1* = fault", which is suggested by the possibilistic and the probabilistic specializations, but not by the belief function one. The origin of this is again in the way we have coded our data: a delayed alarm does not support, in the belief function case, a fault in the adjacent line ***individually***, but a fault in the adjacent *or* in the next lines[13]. On the contrary, in the possibilistic and the probabilistic cases, the evidence given by the alarm is spread among each hypothesis individually. A related difference concerns the hypothesis "*L3* = fault", suggested by the possibilistic specialization only. This "over-inferencing" is rooted in our rather strong attitude when defining the possibility distributions for the *alarm-i*'s relations (viz. the frequential knowledge about the localization of the fault has been converted to a measure of (im)possibility). A less committed interpretation of our data could lead to the following distribution

$\Pi(\bullet)$	ok	del	inst
ok, ok	1	0.1	0.1
ok, fault	0.1	1	1
fault, ok	0.1	1	1
fault, fault	0.1	1	1

where the information about the relative support given by an alarm to a near fault or a far fault (which is not, strictly speaking, a matter of possibility) has been ignored. Using this encoding, we would get a result suggesting L2 alone (like in the Boolean case). The lesson to be taken here seems to be that possibility theory may provide the additional inference power that we need in our problem, but this power cannot be "fine-tuned" easily.

As for the quantitative differences, the most important one (which might be regarded as qualitative as well) concerns the hypothesis "S1 = fault". This hypothesis is reinforced by the arrival of the alarm from D1 in the probabilistic and belief function specializations, but not in the possibilistic one. The cause here is only the combination mechanism used: like the AND of the Boolean case, the MIN operator does not allow us to perform that "counting", which seems necessary in our problem to accumulate evidence correctly. As a consequence, the answers given by the possibilistic specialization to our problem are meaningful mainly from the qualitative viewpoint (they allow us to focus on those hypotheses which are possible), but they are fairly poor from the quantitative one. To this respect, we notice that the results given by the probabilistic specialization are very rich from the quantitative viewpoint; though, because of our straining the input data, this precision may be somehow unjustified. The belief function specialization seems to provide the trade-off between precision and non-commitment that best fits our knowledge. Yet, the computational complexity inherent in belief functions shows up in running the full experiment: the final choice of the uncertainty treating technique to be used for solving the full scale diagnostic problem will have to take this factor into consideration.

6. CONCLUSIONS

We have presented PULCinella (Propagating Uncertainty using Local Computation), and illustrated its use as a

[13] But notice that, differently from the Boolean case, further evidence may convert this support to one for the adjacent line individually.

comparison tool. The key for Pulcinella's comparison power lies in the separation made between the process of modelling the structural knowledge of a problem, and that of modelling its qualitative knowledge. Once a structural model has been decided, we can superimpose any of the available uncertainty calculi on it. There are at least two places where Pulcinella is expected to be useful. First, on the desk of the theorist involved in the comparative study of uncertain reasoning models. For her, Pulcinella might play the role of a slide-rule when empirically testing the behaviour of uncertainty theories over sample problems of academic interest. The fact that the structural model of the problem is the same for all theories ensures the soundness of the test. Second, on the desk of the knowledge engineer. Here, Pulcinella might prove helpful in checking out different uncertainty management techniques for solving the problem at hands, and then judging—on this experimental basis—which one appears to be the most adequate to our case. In particular, we may test, for each theory, both the input requirements and the results, and evaluate how the available data is accommodated for, or our expectations satisfied.

Acknowledgements

The work reported here has greatly benefit from discussions with (and comments from) Yen-Teh Hsia, Robert Kennes, Bruno Marchal, and Philippe Smets. Hong Xu provided invaluable assistance during the development of Pulcinella. Inaki Laresgoiti and Francesco Ferri have been worthy sources of inspiration for our examples. Work by the first author has been partially supported by the ARCHON project, funded by the Commission of the European Communities under the ESPRIT-II Program, P-2256. Work by the second author has been supported by a grant of IRIDIA, Université Libre de Bruxelles.

References

Andersen, S.K., Olesen, K.G., Jensen, F.V. and Jensen, F. (1989) "HUGIN - a Shell for Building Bayesian Belief Universes for Expert Systems", *Procs. of the 11th Int. Congress on AI* (Detroit).

Chatalic, P., Dubois, D. and Prade, H. (1987) "A System for Handling Relational Dependencies in Approximate Reasoning", *Procs. of the 3rd Int. Expert System Conf.* (London, GB) 495-502.

Dempster, A.P. (1966) "Upper and Lower Probabilities Induced by a Multivalued Mapping", *Annals of Mathematical Statistic* **38**: 325-339.

Dubois, D. and Prade, H. (1990) "Inference in Possibilistic Hypergraphs", Procs. of the 6th IPMU Conference (Paris, Fr).

Duda, R.O., Hart, P.E. and Nilsson, N.J. (1986) "Subjective Bayesian Methods for Rule-Based Inference Systems", *AFIPS Procs.* **45** (New York).

Fox, J. (1986) "Three Arguments for Extending the Framework of Probability", in L. Kanal and J. Lemmer (Eds.) *Uncertainty in AI* (North Holland).

Gallastegui, I., Laresgoiti, I., Perez, J., Amantegui, J., Echavarri, J. (1989) "Operating experience of an expert system for fault analysis in electrical networks", Procs of Int. Working Conf. on Expert Systems in Electr. & Power Systems (Avignon, Fr).

Hsia, Y. and Shenoy, P.P. (1989) "MacEvidence: A Visual Environment for Constructing and Evaluating Evidential Systems", *Working Paper No. 211* (School of Business, Univ. of Kansas, Lw).

Lauritzen, S.L. and Spiegelhalter, D.J. (1988) "Local Computations with Probabilities on Graphical Structures and Their Applications to Expert Systems", *J. of the Royal Stat. Soc. B* **50**(2) 157-224.

Pearl, J. (1988) *Probabilistic Reasoning in Intelligent Systems* (Morgan Kaufman, CA).

Saffiotti, A. (1987) "An AI view of the treatment of uncertainty", *The Knowledge Engineering Review* **2**(2) (Cambridge University Press, UK) 75-97.

Saffiotti, A. and Umkehrer, E. (1991a) "PULCINELLA User's Manual", *Technical Report IRIDIA/91-5*, (Université Libre de Bruxelles, Be).

Saffiotti, A. and Umkehrer, E. (1991b) "What do you want to propagate for breakfast ?", *Technical Report IRIDIA/91-7*, (Université Libre de Bruxelles, Be).

Shafer, G. (1976) *A Mathematical Theory of Evidence* (Princeton University Press, Princeton).

Shafer, G., Shenoy, P.P. and Mellouli, K. (1987) "Propagating Belief Functions in Qualitative Markov Trees", *Int. J. of Approx. Reas.* **1**:349-400.

Shafer, G.R. and Shenoy, P.P. (1988a) "Bayesian and Belief-Function Propagation", *Working Paper No. 192* (School of Business, Univ. of Kansas, LW).

Shenoy, P.P. (1989) "A Valuation-based Language for Expert Systems", *Int. J. of Approx. Reas.* **3**: 383-411.

Shenoy, P.P. and Shafer, G. (1988b) "An Axiomatic Framework for Bayesian and Belief-Function Propagation", Procs. of AAAI Workshop on Uncertainty in AI: 307-314.

Smets, Ph. (1988) "Belief Functions", in: Smets, Ph., Mamdani, E.H., Dubois, D. and Prade, H. (Eds.) *Non-Standard Logics for Automated Reasoning* (Academic Press, London).

Wittgenstein, L. (1921) *Tractatus Logico-Philosophicus* (Annalen der Naturphilosophie).

Xu, H. (1991) "An Efficient Implementation of Belief Function Propagation", *Technical Report IRIDIA/91-4*, (Université Libre de Bruxelles, Be).

Zadeh, L.A. (1979) "A Theory of Approximate Reasoning", in: J.E. Hayes, D. Mitchie, L.I. Mikulich (Eds.) Machine Intelligence 10 (Elsevier) 149-194.

Zarley, D.K., Hsia, Y. and Shafer, G. R. (1988) "Evidential Reasoning using DELIEF", *Working Paper 193* (School of Business, Univ. of Kansas, Lw).

Structuring Bodies of Evidence

Sandra A. Sandri
Université Paul Sabatier-IRIT
118, Route de Narbonne
31062 Toulouse France
sandri@irit.fr

Abstract

In this article we present two ways of structuring bodies of evidence, which allow us to reduce the complexity of the operations usually performed in the framework of evidence theory. The first structure just partitions the focal elements in a body of evidence by their cardinality. With this structure we are able to reduce the complexity on the calculation of the belief functions *Bel*, *Pl*, and *Q*. The other structure proposed here, the Hierarchical Trees, permits us to reduce the complexity of the calculation of *Bel*, *Pl*, and *Q*, as well as of the Dempster's rule of combination in relation to the brute-force algorithm. Both these structures do not require the generation of all the subsets of the reference domain.

1 INTRODUCTION

Evidence Theory (Shafer 1976) is a well-known framework for representing uncertainty in Knowledge-based systems. Its use in practical applications is however compromised by the important complexities involved in its manipulation. In particular, the method used to combine the evidence coming from independent sources, known as the Dempster's rule of evidence, may require a complexity of $2^{2n} - 2^{n+1}$ in the worst case, where n stands for the size of the reference domain. The algorithms proposed in the literature to reduce these complexities impose restrictions either on the pieces of evidence themselves, or on the reference domain of the variables modeling them. In the present paper, we are interested to show that some set-theoretical properties underlying bodies of evidence, the set of pieces of evidence, can be used to produce algorithms that are efficient in the situations where the data cannot be restricted.

The text is divided as follows. Section 2 brings some basic notions on Evidence Theory and discusses some of the algorithms implemented within this framework. In Section 3 we present two ways of structuring bodies of evidence : by partitioning the pieces of evidence on the cardinality relation, and by the use of Hierarchical Trees. In Section 4 we propose an algorithm to implement the Dempster's rule using Hierarchical Trees, and in Section 5 we briefly discuss the use of Hierarchical Trees in the Local Propagation of Information. Section 6 brings the conclusion.

2 BASIC NOTIONS IN EVIDENCE THEORY

In the framework of Evidence Theory, the information supplied by a source about the actual value of a variable x is encoded in a body of evidence on Ω, where Ω stands for the set of all the possible values of x, called the frame of discernment of x. A body of evidence is characterized by a pair $(\mathcal{F}, m)$, where $\mathcal{F}$ is a family ot subsets of Ω, ie $\mathcal{F} \subset \mathcal{P}(\Omega)$, and m (called the mass assignement function) is a mapping of $\mathcal{P}(\Omega)$ to the unit interval, such that $m(A) > 0$ iff $A \in \mathcal{F}$, and $\Sigma\{m(A)/A \subset \Omega\} = 1$. Each element $A \in \mathcal{F}$ is called a focal element, and $m(A)$ represents the amount of evidence focused strictly in A itself, and not in any subset of A. A body of evidence $(\mathcal{F}, m)$ on Ω can also be represented by means of any one of the three following set-functions on $\mathcal{P}(\Omega)$:

$$Bel(A) = \sum\{m(B)/B \subset A, B \neq \emptyset\} \tag{1}$$

$$Pl(A) = \sum\{m(B)/B \cap A \neq \emptyset\} \tag{2}$$

$$Q(A) = \sum\{m(B)/A \subset B\} \tag{3}$$

where $\emptyset$ represents the empty set. The belief function *Bel* (also called a credibility function) gathers the pieces of information which support A. The plausibility function *Pl* gathers the pieces of information which do not contradict A. The commonality function represents to what extent all the elements composing A are plausible (Dubois and Prade 1991). These measures

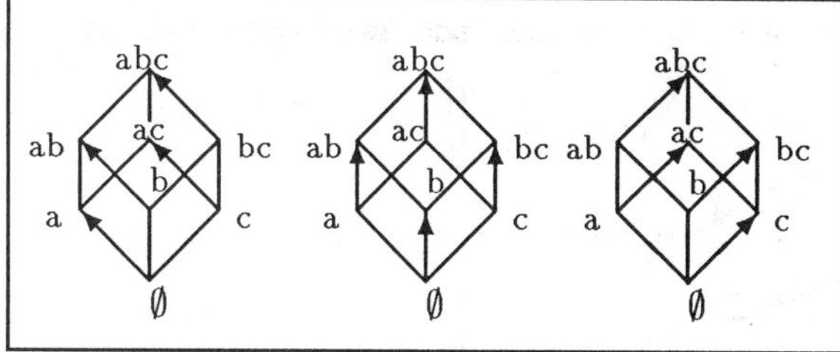

Figure 1: Process of calculation of *Bel* using Moebius Transforms

are strongly inter-related ; for instance, the plausibility function Pl can be calculated from the credibility function Bel using

$$Bel(A) = 1 - Pl(\overline{A}) \tag{4}$$

Fast algorithms for the calculation of Bel, Pl, and Q can be found in (Kennes 1990), (Kennes and Smets 1990a), (Kennes and Smets 1990b), and (Thoma 1991). These algorithms are based on Moebius transforms, and are such that each element of $\mathcal{P}(\Omega)$can be seen as an object that receives and sends information in the form of accumulated evidence. In the calculation of any of the belief functions, each element propagates its accumulated evidence only once. Fig. 1 illustrates the calculation of Bel for all the focal elements in $(\mathcal{F}\ ,\ m)$, on $\Omega = \{a, b, c\}$.

Dempster's rule of combination is the method used for pooling evidence in the framework of Evidence Theory (Shafer 1976). The combination of two given bodies of evidence $(\mathcal{F}_1\ ,\ m_1)$ and $(\mathcal{F}_2\ ,\ m_2)$ on Ω, yields a third body $(\mathcal{F}_3\ ,\ m_3)$ on Ω, where

$$m_3(A) = \sum\{m_1(B) * m_2(C)/B \cap C = A\} \tag{5}$$

This result may be unnormalized, i.e. we might have $m_3(\emptyset) > 0$. Originally, the application of Dempster's rule involves a normalization step, in which the mass assigned to each focal element of $(\mathcal{F}_3\ ,\ m_3)$ is divided by a constant $K = 1 - m_3(\emptyset)$, representing the amount of conflict between the sources. The effective use of this normalization step is however quite controversial (see (Dubois and Prade 1988), (Smets 1988) for discussions over this point).

The use of (5) for the calculation of the Dempster's rule, here called the brute-force strategy, has a complexity of $\mid \mathcal{F}_1 \mid * \mid \mathcal{F}_2 \mid$ in terms of focal elements visited, which gets to $2^{2n} - 2^{n+1}$ in the worst case. Drastic reductions on this complexity are however achieved in some restricted situations. Barnett (1981) treated the case in which the evidence is presented in the form of bodies of evidence having two focal elements : a singleton $f \in \Omega$, and its complement in Ω. Gordon and Shortliffe (1985), and Shafer and Logan (1987) treated the case in which all the possible evidence is hierarchical, in such a way as that all the possible focal elements can be arranged as nodes in a tree, where each father-node represents the union of its son-nodes, and all the nodes having a common father are disjoint. Moreover, in this model, all the bodies of evidence consist of only two focal elements : one representing the reference domain Ω, and another that is either a node of the tree, or the complement of one of its nodes. The continuous case has been treated by Strat (1984), with the restriction that all the focal elements should be closed intervals. A general discussion on the complexity of Dempster's rule can be found in (Orponen 1990).

Another way of implementing Dempster rule, here called the Q-strategy, consists in calculating the commonality functions Q_1 and Q_2 for every set $A \in \Omega$, and then using an important property of the commonality function Q, namely :

$$Q_3(A) = Q_1(A) * Q_2(A) \tag{6}$$

The mass assigment function m_3 can then be recovered by using (Smets 1988) :

$$m(A) = \sum\{(-1)^{|B|}Q(A \cup B), B \subset \overline{A}\} \tag{7}$$

The exact number of operations performed on the Q-strategy with the direct utilization of formulae (6) and (7) is $3^n + 2^{2n+1} - 2^{n+1}$. However, this value comes down to $(n+1)2^n + n2^{n-1} - n$, when Moebius transforms are used (Kennes and Smets 1990a), and (Kennes 1990). The single inconvenience with this strategy is that it requires that he whole set $\mathcal{P}(\Omega)$ be generated, being thus unapplicable when $\mathcal{P}(\Omega)$ is not enumerable.

3 PROPOSAL OF STRUCTURES

We see that efficient algorithms for the calculation of both belief measures and Dempster rule are achieved with restrictions on either the evidence, or on the frame of discernment. Set-theoretical properties underlying the bodies of evidence can however be used to produce efficient algorithms without loss of expressivity.

One of the simplest of such properties is that the focal elements contained in $f \in \mathcal{F}$ are either f itself, or elements having cardinality smaller than f. Based on this property, we propose to structure a body of evidence with $\mathcal{V}(\mathcal{F})$, the partition induced on $\mathcal{F}$, when the focal elements are classified by their cardinality. With this structure we are able to reduce the complexity of the calculation of the belief measures Bel, Pl, and Q.

An important characteristic of $\mathcal{P}(\Omega)$ is that it forms a lattice with the relation $\subset$ (in particular, it is this property that underlies the use of Moebius Transforms in Evidence Theory). Since $\mathcal{F} \subset \mathcal{P}(\Omega)$, $\mathcal{F}$ forms an incomplete lattice with $\subset$. We present here a structure, here, called Hierarchical Trees, that uses this property in order to reduce the complexity of the implementation of Dempster's rule, as well as of Bel, Pl, and Q. This structure establishes an hierarchy in a given body of evidence ; each node f in the tree (representing a focal element A) is connected to a father-node and to a set of sons-nodes, which are respectively greater or smaller than f in the sense of inclusion. Algorithms based on both of the structures proposed here do not require that the whole set $\mathcal{P}(\Omega)$ be generated, and can thus be employed when $\mathcal{P}(\Omega)$ is not enumerable.

3.1 PARTITION $\mathcal{V}(\mathcal{F})$

Let $(\mathcal{F}\ , m)$be a body of evidence on Ω, and A and B be two of its focal elements contained in Ω. We can structure $\mathcal{F}$ with the partition $\mathcal{V}(\mathcal{F}) = \{c_i, 1 \leq i \leq \mid \Omega \mid\}$, where $A\ c_i\ B$, iff $\mid A \mid = \mid B \mid = i$, ie A and B will belong to the same class if they have the same cardinality. The construction of $\mathcal{V}(\mathcal{F})$ is obviously linear with $\mid \mathcal{F} \mid$, and can be done as the input is read.

The credibility function Bel on a set $A \in \mathcal{P}(\Omega), \mid A \mid = j$, in a given body of evidence $(\mathcal{F}\ , m)$, can be calculated from the partition $\mathcal{V}$ corresponding to $\mathcal{F}$ using :

$$Bel(A) = m(A) + \sum_{i=1}^{j-1} \{m(B), B \in c_i, A \supset B\} \quad (8)$$

$Bel(A)$ is calculated by adding its own mass $m(A)$ to the masses of its subsets that can be found lying in the classes below it in $\mathcal{V}$. Each focal element thus visits itself plus the elements with lower cardinality than itself in $\mathcal{V}$. Thus if $\mid c_i \mid$ represents the number of elements of cardinality i present in partition $\mathcal{V}$, the total cost of the algorithm is $\mid \mathcal{F} \mid + \sum_{i=1}^{n} \sum_{j=1}^{i-1} \mid c_i \mid \mid c_j \mid$. The calculation of the plausibility function $Pl(A)$ is similarly done by using formula (4), with the application of (11) in the calculation of $Bel(\overline{A})$. The total cost of calculating Pl for all the elements of $\mathcal{F}$ is $\mid \mathcal{F} \mid + \sum_{i=1}^{n} \sum_{j=1}^{n-i-1} \mid c_i \mid \mid c_j \mid$. The commonality function Q can be calculated using the formula :

$$Q(A) = m(A) + \sum_{i=j+1}^{n} \{m(B), B \in c_i, A \subset B\} \quad (9)$$

leading to a cost of $\mid \mathcal{F} \mid + \sum_{i=1}^{n} \sum_{j=i+1}^{n} \mid c_i \mid \mid c_j \mid$, when applied to all the elements in $\mathcal{F}$.

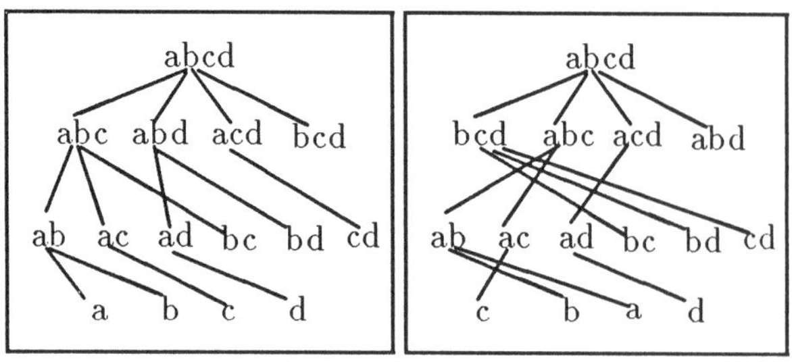

Figure 2: Hierarchical trees on $\mathcal{P}(\Omega)$, $\Omega = \{a, b, c, d\}$

3.2 HIERARCHICAL TREES

Let the set $\mathcal{A}(A) = \{B \mid B \in \mathcal{F}, B \supset A, B \neq A\}$, be the set of ancestors of A in $\mathcal{F}$, ie the set of proper supersets of A in $\mathcal{F}$. Similarly, let $\mathcal{D}(A) = \{B \mid B \in \mathcal{F}, A \supset B, B \neq A, B \neq \emptyset\}$, be the set of descendants of A in $\mathcal{F}$, ie the set of all proper subsets of A (except the empty set) in $\mathcal{F}$. A Hierarchical Tree is a structure that relates the focal elements in $\mathcal{F}$ with their respective ancestors and descendants sets. Let f_i be a node representing a set $A_i \in \mathcal{P}(\Omega)$. A Hierarchical Tree $T = (N, E)$ on the body of evidence $(\mathcal{F}\ , m)$. consists of a set of distinct nodes $N = \{f_i \mid A_i \in \mathcal{F}\}$ and a set of edges $E = \{(f_i, f_j) \mid f_i, f_j \in N, f_i \neq f_j, A_i \supset A_j, \nexists A_i \supset A_k \supset A_j\}$. Set $R = \{f_i \mid \nexists, (f_k, f_i) \in E\}$ denotes the roots of T, and $Sons(f) = \{f_i \mid (f, f_i) \in E\}$ denotes the set of sons of a node f in the Hierarchical Tree T. A Hierarchical Tree may in fact have several roots, thus constituting a forest. Note however that any forest can be transformed into a tree with the addition of a dummy root node u, with $m(u) = 0$, where u represents the union of the focal elements in $\mathcal{F}$. Throughout this paper we suppose that R has a single element. To simplify the notation we make $N = \mathcal{F}$, and $f_i = A_i$.

Hierarchical Trees on $(\mathcal{F}\ , m)$ can be seen as the structures that can be derived from the incomplete lattice induced on $\mathcal{F}$ with the relation $\subset$ when we extract edges in the lattice, in such a way that each node will have at most one father. Thus, from the same set of focal elements $\mathcal{F}$ several Hierarchical trees $T_k = (\mathcal{F}_k\ , m_k)$ may be derived. They are equivalent for our purposes, in the sense that if a focal element A is a node f in T_k, then all the nodes in the path linking f to a root node belong to $\mathcal{A}(A)$, and all the nodes accessible from f belong to $\mathcal{D}(A)$. Moreover, the father of f in T_k refers to a focal element with the smallest cardinality among the nodes in $\mathcal{A}(A)$. Fig. 2 shows some Hierarchical trees derivable from $\mathcal{F} = \mathcal{P}(\Omega), \Omega = \{a, b, c, d\}$. Note that the trees described in both (Gordon and Shortliffe 1985), and (Shafer and Logan 1987) are particular cases of Hierarchical Trees, in which all the nodes in a given level are disjoint focal elements.

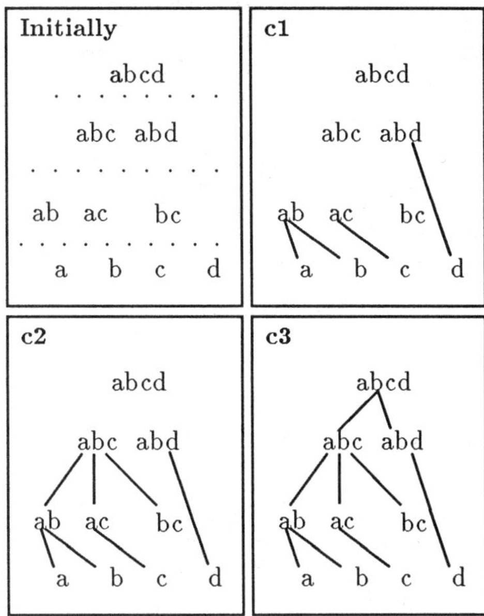

Figure 3: Process of creation of a Hierarchical Tree for $\mathcal{F} = \{abcd, abc, abd, ab, ac, bc, a, b, c, d\}$. Each box refers to the identification of fathers for the nodes in class c_i.

3.2.1 Hierarchical Trees Construction

In order to construct a Hierarchical Tree for a body of evidence $(\mathcal{F}, m)$, we take partition $\mathcal{V}(\mathcal{F})$ and create to each focal element A with cardinality i, a node f_{ij} in T. We start the process of identification of the father of f_{ij} by examining the nodes on class c_{i+1}. If there is no possible father on class c_{i+1}, then f_{ij} is compared with the focal elements on class c_{i+2}, and so successively. If no father can be found, then f_{ij} is set as a root node. Fig. 3 illustrates the application of this algorithm for $\mathcal{F} = \{abcd, abc, abd, ab, ac, bc, a, b, c, d\}$). (Fig 3-a shows partition $\mathcal{V}(\mathcal{F})$).

The tree construction in Fig. 3 requires the examination of 13 nodes, and the complete tree on $\mathcal{P}(\Omega)$, with $\Omega = \{a, b, c, d\}$, would require examining 22 nodes. The exact number of the nodes visited in order to construct the worst possible tree with $|\ \Omega\ |$ elements is (Sandri and Dugat 1991) : $2^n + 2^{n-3} - 2 + \sum_{i=3}^{n-1} \binom{2i}{i-2} 2^{n-i-1}$.

3.2.2 Calculation of Belief Measures

An important characteristic of Hierarchical Trees is that a son-node always "inherits" the ancestors of its father-node. This property can be advantegeously used in the calculation of the Q function, by comparing a Hierarchical Tree on $\mathcal{F}$ with the partition $\mathcal{V}(\mathcal{F})$, as it is seen in the algorithm presented below.

Let f be a node in the tree T, $Q(f)$ be the commonality function of f, and $Sons(f)$ and $Father(f)$ respectively be the immediate sons and the father of f in T. We compute Q recursively for all the nodes in tree T with the application of the following algorithm (initially $f = r$, and $Q(Father(r)) = 0$:

> *If node f (of cardinality i) has at least one son, it is compared to each element f_{ij} of its own class in $\mathcal{V}$. Otherwise, it is only compared to itself. If $f \cap f_{ij} \neq \emptyset$, we update the masses in $\mathcal{V}$ by transfering the mass on f_{ij} to $f \cap f_{ij}$, by making $m(f \cap f_{ij}) \leftarrow m(f \cap f_{ij}) + m(f_{ij})$, and $m(f_{ij}) \leftarrow 0$, if $f \cap f_{ij} \neq f_{ij}$. $Q(f)$ is computed as $Q(Father(f)) + m(f)$, and the algorithm is successively repeated for all the nodes in $Sons(f)$.*

The comparisons that f effectuates in its own level have the sole objective of transfering the masses of elements that might be ancestors of its sons, to subsets of f (note that if $g \in Sons(f)$, and $l \supset g, then (f \cap l) \supset g)$. Each node visits at least itself, and when it has sons, it visits also all of its class neighbours. The maximal number of nodes visited by this algorithm is $2^{n-1} - n + \frac{1}{2}\binom{2n}{n}$, that is closely bounded by $2^{n-1} - n + \frac{2^{2n-1}}{\sqrt{n\pi}}$ (Sandri and Dugat 1991). For instance, the cost of calculating Q for all $\mathcal{F} = \mathcal{P}(\Omega)$ with $|\ \Omega\ |= 5$ is 961 with the usual algorithm, 386 using partition $\mathcal{V}$, and 211 using a Hierarchical Tree : 74 for the tree construction and 137 for the Q algorithm itself (the approximation gives 141 instead of 137 for the Q algorithm).

Bel and *Pl* can be calculated from the commonality function associated with the complement of the body of evidence, as exposed in (Dubois and Prade 1986). The complement of a body of evidence $(\mathcal{F}, m)$ is $(\neg\mathcal{F}, \overline{m})$, defined as $\forall A \subset \Omega, \overline{m}(A) = m(\overline{A})$, so that $\neg\mathcal{F} = \{\overline{A}/A \in \mathcal{F}\}$. Function Q is defined as :

$$\overline{Q}(\overline{A}) = \sum\{\overline{m}(\overline{B})\ /\overline{A} \subset \overline{B}\} \tag{10}$$

The *Bel* function is then calculated using

$$Bel(A) = \overline{Q}(\overline{A}) - m(\emptyset) \tag{11}$$

Finally, function *Pl* is calculated using (10), (11), and (4). In the worst case, the calculation of *Bel* and *Pl* using Hierarchical Trees requires, besides the nodes visited in the calculation of Q, the visit of additional $2^n - 1$ nodes, $|\ \Omega\ | =$ n, due to the derivation of $\neg\mathcal{F}$.

4 DEMPSTER RULE OF COMBINATION

Shafer (1987) comments that an exponential complexity seems to be intrinsic to Dempster's rule.Indeed, the worst case complexity has to be calculated on $|\mathcal{P}(\Omega)|$, since it represents the largest value that $|\mathcal{F}|$ may take. However, using the Q-strategy, the complexity does not decrease when $|\mathcal{F}| << |\mathcal{P}(\Omega)|$, i.e. we are always in a position of the worst case analysis no matter how the evidence is presented. This situation occurs because this strategy requires the generation of the whole set $\mathcal{P}(\Omega)$, and thus deals with more than just the sets $\mathcal{F}_1$, $\mathcal{F}_2$ and $\mathcal{F}_3$ involved in the process. On the other hand, efficient algorithms for the implementation of the brute-force strategy impose restrictions on the evidence. When we recall that bodies of evidence benefit from set-theory properties, it seems natural that there should exist ways of calculating Dempster's rule whose complexity in the mean case depends exclusively on $|\mathcal{F}_1|$ and $|\mathcal{F}_2|$, and that restricts neither the evidence, nor the frame of discernment.

We propose here an algorithm for calculating Dempster's rule using the brute-force strategy that takes advantage of the set-theoretical properties underlying two given bodies of evidence. We divide the process in two phases, the pre-processing phase, and the combination phase in itself.

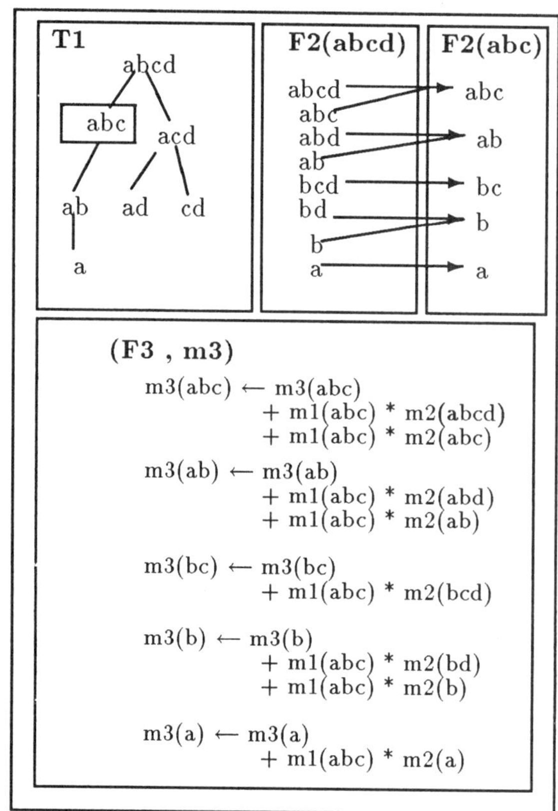

Figure 4: Combination of abc and $\mathcal{F}_2(Father(abc))$

Pre-Processing Phase

Let u_1 and u_2 respectively be the union of the focal elements of $\mathcal{F}_1$ and $\mathcal{F}_2$. It is obvious that the highest possible focal element of the resulting body of evidence $(\mathcal{F}_3, m_3)$ is $u_3 = u_1 \cap u_2$. We can thus reduce any of the bodies $\mathcal{F}_k$ by comparing u_3 to each of its focal elements f_{ij}, and transporting the mass on f_{ij} to $f_{ij} \cap u_3$, ie making $m(f_{ij} \cap u_3) \leftarrow m(f_{ij} \cap u_3) + m(f_{ij})$ and $m(f_{ij}) \leftarrow 0$, if $f_{ij} \cap u_3 \neq f_{ij}$. Note that $\mathcal{F}_k$ remains of the same size in two cases : *a)* $f_{ij} \cap u_3$ is not an element of $\mathcal{F}_k$, and then $f_{ij} \cap u_3$ will be created as f_{ij} will be eliminated (thus modifying $\mathcal{F}_k$ but not its size), or *b)* $f_{ij} = f_{ij} \cap u_3$, and then $\mathcal{F}_k$ is not modified. On the other hand, when $f_{ij} \neq f_{ij} \cap u_3$, and $f_{ij} \cap u_3$ belongs already to $\mathcal{F}_k$, the element f_{ij} is simply eliminated, thus reducing the size of $\mathcal{F}_k$.

In the pre-processing phase we compare u_3 only to the smallest body of evidence between $\mathcal{F}1$ and $\mathcal{F}2$ (the other body of evidence will be implicitly compared to u_3 in the next phase). Thus, if $\mathcal{F}_1$ is the smallest body of evidence, the cost of the pre-processing phase is 1 if $u_1 = u_3$, and $|\mathcal{F}_1|$ otherwise.

Combination Phase

Let us suppose that $\mathcal{F}_1$ is the smallest body of evidence, and T_1 the Hierarchical Tree for $\mathcal{F}_1$ resulting from the construction algorithm as seen in Section 2. Let f be a node in T_1, $Father(f)$ the father-node of f in T_1, and $\mathcal{F}_2(Father(f))$ be the result of the intersection of $Father(f)$ with all the elements of $\mathcal{F}_2$. We will combine each node in T_1 to the focal elements of $\mathcal{F}_2$ by applying the following algorithm, taking the root node as the initial value of f and $\mathcal{F}_2(Father(r))$ as the set $\mathcal{F}_2$ itself :

> *Initially $\mathcal{F}_2(f) = \emptyset$. We compare f to each focal element g in $\mathcal{F}_2(Father(f))$. If $f \cap g \neq \emptyset$, we update $m_2(f \cap g)$ in $\mathcal{F}_2(f)$ with $m_2(g)$, and $m_3(f \cap g)$ with $m_1(f) * m_2(g)$. Then we successively apply the algorithm for the son-nodes of f in T_1 with $\mathcal{F}_2(f)$ as input.*

Fig. 3 illustrates the combination of node $f = abc$ with $\mathcal{F}_2(Father(abc)) = \{abcd, abc, abd, bcd, ab, bd, a, b\}$.

Note that the set of elements $\mathcal{F}_2(Father(f))$ examined by any node f in T_1 is at most the power set $\mathcal{P}(Father(f))$ (the root node examines at most $\mathcal{P}(\Omega)$). The maximal cost of the combination phase is $2^m + 2 * 3^n - 3 * 2^n - 1$, with $n = |u_1|$ and $m = |u_2|$ (Sandri and Dugat 1991). This algorithm turns out to be more efficient the largest is $|\mathcal{F}_1| \times |\mathcal{F}_2|$. For instance, two complete bodies of evidence on Ω, with $| \Omega | = 5$, will require visiting 496 nodes (74 for the tree construction, 1 for the pre-processing phase, and 421 for the combination phase), instead of 961 of the brute-force algorithm. This strategy is specially recommended if, after the pre-processing phase, the maximal cost of constructing a Hierarchical Tree and then of combining it, is found to be greater than $| \mathcal{F}_1 | \times | \mathcal{F}_2 |$. Nevertheless, experimental results show that this strategy is worse than the brute-force algorithm only when T_1 is composed exclusively of a root node r and its immediate sons $Sons(r)$. In this case, all the nodes in T_1 visit all the focal elements in $\mathcal{F}_2$, and thus the additional cost of the tree construction is not justified.

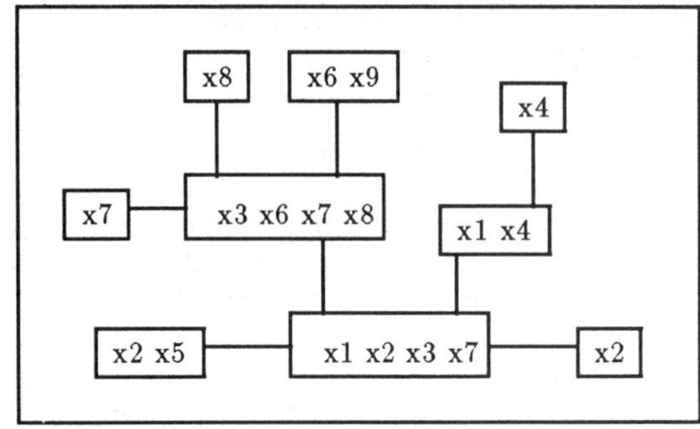

Figure 5: Markov Tree on $\mathcal{X} = \{x_1, x_2, ..., x_9\}$

5 LOCAL PROPAGATION OF INFORMATION

Knowledge Bases are usually composed of individualized pieces of data, each of which regarding a cluster of variables, that together model the system knowledge about the world. When uncertainty is modeled within the framework of Evidence Theory, these pieces of data can be characterized by bodies of evidence on $\Omega_{\mathcal{X}}$, where $\mathcal{X} = \{x_1, x_2, ..., x_n\}$ denotes the set of all the variables in the Knowledge Base. Let $G \subset \mathcal{X}$ be a set of variables in $\mathcal{X}$, $\Omega_G = \Omega_{x_G{}^1 x_G{}^2 ... x_G{}^g} = \Omega_{x_G{}^1} \times \Omega_{x_G{}^2} \times ... \times \Omega_{x_G{}^g}$, $x_G{}^i \in \mathcal{X}$. Each focal element of a body of evidence $(\mathcal{F}_G \ , \ m_G)$ on Ω_G, is then a set of g-uples on $\Omega_{x_G{}^1} \times \Omega_{x_G{}^2} \times ... \times \Omega_{x_G{}^g}$. The extension and projection of a body of evidence $(\mathcal{F} \ , \ m)$are done with the application of the usual set-theoretical extension and projection operations on the set $\mathcal{F}$, and on the additive function m. $(\mathcal{F}_G{}^{\uparrow J} \ , \ m_G{}^{\uparrow J})$ and $(\mathcal{F}_G{}^{\downarrow H} \ , \ m_G{}^{\downarrow H})$ respectively denote the extension and projection of $(\mathcal{F}_G \ , \ m_G)$ to a higher and lower dimensional space, $H \subset G \subset J \subset \mathcal{X}$.

The belief function for a multi-dimensional variable $S \subset \mathcal{X}$, taking into account all the evidence in the Knowledge Base, can be obtained by first calculating the overall belief function on $\mathcal{X}$, and then marginalizing this overall belief function to S. The overall belief function can be obtained by taking all the clusters of variables $G \subset \mathcal{X}$ on Ω_G present in the Knowledge Base, extending each of them to the highest possible frame of discernment $\Omega_{\mathcal{X}} = \Omega_{x1} \times \Omega_{x2} \times ... \times \Omega_{xn}$, and then applying Dempster rule on the resulting set of extended clusters. The cost of the computation of such a procedure is however prohibitive. An alternative is to use the Local Propagation of Information (Shafer and Shenoy 1986), (Shafer and Shenoy 1988a) and (Shafer and Shenoy, 1988b). This strategy requires that the Knowledge Base be partitioned in groups of pieces of knowledge, in such a way as that the variables involved in each group can be arranged as nodes in a Markov Tree (also called a Join Tree in recent literature). In this tree, the nodes are clusters of variables, and the edges are such that, if a variable is contained in two nodes, then it is contained in all the nodes along the path between these two nodes (see Fig. 5).

The process of Local Propagation of Information on a Markov Tree consists on propagating information from the leaf-nodes until the root node, by means of projection/ extension/ combination operations. To obtain the marginal on $S \subset \mathcal{X}$ from the overall belief function, it suffices to propagate information locally on a Markov Tree, setting as root one of the nodes containing S.

When a body of evidence $(\mathcal{F}_G \ , \ m_G)$ on Ω_G is extended to a frame of discernment of higher dimension Ω_J, $J \subset \mathcal{X}$, $G \subset J$, it undergoes only a minor changement ; the focal elements change (a focal element f becomes $f \times \Omega_{J-G}$), but the inter-relationships between the focal elements remain the same. Thus there exists a Hierarchical Tree derivable from $(\mathcal{F}_G{}^{\uparrow J} \ , \ m_G{}^{\uparrow J})$ whose nodes and edges have a one-to-one correspondance with those in the Hierarchical Tree T constructed for $(\mathcal{F}_G \ , \ m_G)$. This tree is in fact the tree that we obtain by changing the label on each node in T with its extension on Ω_J. However, in case of projection of a body of evidence $(\mathcal{F}_G \ , \ m_G)$ on Ω_G to a frame of discernment of lower dimension Ω_H, not only the focal elements will change but also the structure may change to a simpler one, since many focal elements on Ω_J may be projected on the same focal element on Ω_H. As a consequence, only changing the labels of the focal elements of T does not suffice to generate a Hierarchical Tree on $(\mathcal{F}_G{}^{\downarrow H} \ , \ m_G{}^{\downarrow H})$. However, we obtain a Hierarchical Tree T_H on $(\mathcal{F}_G{}^{\downarrow H} \ , \ m_G{}^{\downarrow H})$, directly from T if the projection operation on $(\mathcal{F}_G \ , \ m_G)$ is performed in the following manner. Let f be a node in $\mathcal{F}_G$, $Father(f)$ the father-node of f, and $f^{\downarrow H}$ the projection of f on Ω_H. We start the projection process on the root node, towards the leaf-nodes. Everytime a node $f^{\downarrow H}$ is created in T_H, we take as its father the node $Father(f)^{\downarrow H}$ that represents the projection of the father of f on Ω_H, i.e. we create an edge $(Father(f)^{\downarrow H}, f^{\downarrow H})$ in T_H. At the end of the process we obtain a Hierarchical Tree T_H, that represents the projection of T on Ω_H. More details on the manipulation of Hierarchical Trees in the Local Propagation of Information can be found in (Sandri Dugat 1991).

Thoma (1991) exposes the way Moebius Transforms can be efficiently employed in the application of the Q-strategy in the Local Propagation of Information. As in the case of a single variable, the choice between the brute-force or the Q-strategy for the combination of the information on a node G, depends on whether $\mathcal{P}(\Omega_G)$ is enumerable or not. If there exists a node G in the Markov Tree, such that $\mathcal{P}(\Omega_G)$ is not enumerable then Q-strategy can be used until the process reaches G ; afterwards only the brute-force strategy can be used in the remainder of the propagation process.

6 CONCLUSION

The choice between the brute-force and the Q-strategy should be guided by the relation between $\mid \mathcal{P}(\Omega) \mid$ and $\mid \mathcal{F}_1 \mid * \mid \mathcal{F}_2 \mid$, when $\mathcal{P}(\Omega)$ can be enumerated. In the case where the use of the brute-force strategy is obligatory, and $\mid \mathcal{F}_1 \mid * \mid \mathcal{F}_2 \mid$ is rather large, structuring the bodies of evidence is the only possible way of reducing the computational load, without the imposition of restrictions on the data.

In this article we presented two ways of structuring a body of evidence ; by partitioning its focal elements by their cardinality, and by constructing Hierarchical Trees, that allows us to take into account the set interrelationships existing among the focal elements in a body of evidence. We also presented algorithms for calculating belief measures and the Dempster's rule of combination, that do not require the creation of the whole set of possible focal elements $\mathcal{P}(\Omega)$. These structures do not impose any restrictions on the data, and can be easily manipulated in the Local Propagation of Information.

Acknowledgements

The author is mostly indebted to Vincent Dugat for the help on the calculation of the complexities involved in this work.

References

Barnett J. A. (1981) "Computational Methods For a Mathematical Theory of Evidence", *Proc. 7th IJCAI*, 868-875.

Dubois D. and Prade H. (1986) "A Set-Theoretic View of Belief Functions", *Int. J. General Systems*, **12**, 193-226.

Dubois D. and Prade H. (1988) "Representation and Combination of Uncertainty with Belief Functions and Possibility Measures", *Computational Intelligence*, **4**, 244-264.

Dubois D. and Prade H. (1991) "Fuzzy Rules in Knowledge-Based Systems", *An Introduction of Fuzzy Logic Applications in Intelligent Systems*, (Yager R. R., Zadeh L. A., eds), Kluwer Academic Publishers,to appear.

Gordon J. and Shortliffe E.H. (1985) "A Method for Managing Evidential reasoning", *Artificial Intelligence*,**26**, 323-358.

Kennes R. (1990) "Computational Aspects of the Moebius Transform of a Graph", *Technical Report IRIDIA N° TR/IRIDIA/90-13, Université Libre de Bruxelles*, IRIDIA, Brussels.

Kennes R. and Smets P. (1990a) "Fast Algorithms for Dempster-Shafer Theory", *Proc. 3rd IPMU*, Paris, July 2-6, 99-101.

Kennes R. and Smets P. (1990a) "Computational Aspects of the Moebius Transform", *Proc. 6th Conf. on Uncertainty in Artificial Intelligence*, Cambridge, Mass., 344-351.

Orponen P. (1990) "Dempster's rule of Combination is #P-complete", *Artificial Intelligence*,**44**, 245-253.

Sandri S. and Dugat V. (1991) "Hierarchical Trees", *Tech. Report IRIT*, Université Paul Sabatier, Toulouse, to appear.

Shafer G. (1976) *A Mathematical Theory of Evidence.* Princeton University Press.

Shafer G. and Logan (1987) "Implementing Dempster's rule for Hierarchical Evidence", *Artificial Intelligence*,**33**, 271-298.

Shafer G. and Shenoy P. P. (1986) "Propagating Belief Functions with Local Computation", *IEEE Expert*, **1**(3), 43-51.

Shafer G. and Shenoy P. P. (1988a), *Bayesian and Belief-Function Propagation*, Working Paper N° 192, School of Business, The University of Kansas, Lawrence.

Shafer G. and Shenoy P. P. (1988b) *Local Computation in Hypertrees.* Working Paper N° 201, School of Business, The University of Kansas, Lawrence.

Smets P. (1988) "Belief Functions", In *Non Standard Logics for Automated Reasoning*, (Smets P., Mamdani A., Dubois D. and Prade H., eds), Academic Press, 253-286.

Strat T. M. (1984), "Continuous Belief Functions for Evidential Reasoning", *Proc. AAAI*, 308-313.

Thoma (1991), "Belief Function Computation", In *Conditional Logic in Expert Systems*, (Goodman I. R., Gupta M. M., Nguyen H. T., Rogers G. S. eds), North Holland, 269-308.

On the Generation of Alternative Explanations with Implications for Belief Revision

Eugene Santos Jr.
Department of Computer Science
Brown University
Providence, RI 02912

Abstract

In general, the *best* explanation for a given observation makes no promises on how good it is with respect to other alternative explanations. A major deficiency of message-passing schemes for belief revision in Bayesian networks is their inability to generate alternatives beyond the second best. In this paper, we present a general approach based on linear constraint systems that naturally generates alternative explanations in an orderly and highly efficient manner. This approach is then applied to cost-based abduction problems as well as belief revision in Bayesian networks.

1 INTRODUCTION

We are constantly faced with the problem of explaining the observations we have gathered with our senses. Our explanations are constructed by assuming certain facts or hypotheses which support our observations. For example, suppose I decide to phone my friend Tony at the office. After several rings, no one has answered the phone. From this, I conclude that Tony is not at the office. Our observation in this case is that no one answered the phone. Our explanation for this is that Tony is not at the office. The reasoning process we have just used is called *abductive explanation* (Charniak & Shimony [1990]; Hobbs et al. [1988]; Peng & Reggia [1990]; Selman & Levesque [1990]; Shanahan [1989]). It is often formalized as the process of finding certain hypotheses which can explain or prove the things we observe.

Although we used the word "conclude" in our story, our confidence in our solution may not be absolute. Suppose that I also know for a fact that Tony sometimes disconnects the phone to take a nap in the office. Now, I have an alternative explanation for why the phone was not answered. In general, there are many possible explanations for any given observation, but yet, we often express confidence in one explanation over the others and choose it to be our solution. It is this fact that distinguishes abductive reasoning from deductive reasoning.

In current approaches to modeling abduction, confidence in an explanation is defined by some measure on the set of hypotheses it represents. Such measures include minimal cardinality (Genesereth [1984]; Kautz & Allen [1986]), parsimonious covering theory (Peng & Reggia [1990]), most-probable explanation (Pearl [1988]) and minimal cost proofs (Charniak & Shimony [1990]; Hobbs et al. [1988]; Stickel [1988]). These approaches provide us with a model for choosing a "best" explanation.

In particular, we are interested in *minimal cost proofs* found in the *cost-based abduction model* (Charniak & Shimony [1990]).[1] Under this model, *costs* are associated with individual hypotheses. The use of a hypothesis in an explanation incurs the cost associated with the hypothesis. Thus the cost of an explanation is simply the sum of the costs of the individual hypotheses used. These costs now represent our confidence in each explanation and establishes an ordering on the explanations.

Since cost-based abduction has been shown to be an NP-Hard problem (Charniak & Shimony [1990]), the runtime of standard searching techniques grows exponentially with the size of the problem. In (Santos [1991a]; Santos [1991b]; Santos [1991c]), it was shown that any cost-based abduction problem may be transformed into an equivalent *linear constraint satisfaction problem*, and the latter may be solved by utilizing the highly efficient optimization tools of operations research. Indeed, empirical studies in (Santos [1991a]; Santos [1991c]) showed that the approach is computationally practical and superior to search style techniques. Our linear constraint satisfaction approach actually exhibited a subexponential growth rate.

[1] Cost-based abduction is a minor variant of *weighted abduction* (Hobbs et al. [1988]; Stickel [1988])

Now suppose that we further know that my friend Tony spends nearly all of his time in the office working, sleeping, and eating. This knowledge will significantly increase the likelihood of the phone being disconnected as an alternative explanation. Even though our measures may still choose the initial explanation, they in general make no promises on how good this choice is with respect to our alternative. This issue is especially important in domains such as medical diagnosis where careful consideration of alternative diagnoses/explanations is necessary. Thus, the ability to generate alternative explanations should exist in any complete model of abductive reasoning.

In this regard, a major deficiency of message-passing schemes (Pearl [1988]) for belief revision in Bayesian networks is its inability to generate alternative explanations in an ordered manner beyond the second best. By considering the equivalent problem in terms of constraint systems, we can generate the consecutive next best explanations. In this paper, we present an approach based on our linear constraint systems to generate alternative explanations in order of cost.

In Section 2, we present an overview of constraint systems and cost-based abduction. In Section 3, we present our approach to generating alternative explanations. In Section 4, we consider how our constraint systems may be applied to belief revision in Bayesian networks. Finally, in Section 5, we conclude our discussion and give some final thoughts concerning alternative explanations.

2 CONSTRAINT SYSTEMS

We now present a brief overview of the formulation of cost-based abduction problems as constraint systems. Details and complete proofs can be found in (Santos [1991a]; Santos [1991c]).

NOTATION. $\Re$ denotes the set of real numbers.

DEFINITION 2.1. *A* WAODAG *(or* weighted AND/OR directed acyclic graph*)*[2] *is a 4-tuple* (G, c, r, S), *where:*

1. *G is a directed acyclic graph,* $G = (V, E)$.
2. *c is a function from* $V \times \{\text{true}, \text{false}\}$ *to* $\Re$, *called the* cost function.
3. *r is a function from V to* {AND, OR}, *called the* label. *A node labeled* AND *is called an* AND*-node, etc.*
4. *S is a subset of nodes in V called the* evidence nodes.

NOTATION. V_H is the subset of nodes with zero indegree called the *hypothesis nodes.*

[2]Slight generalization of (Charniak & Shimony [1990]).

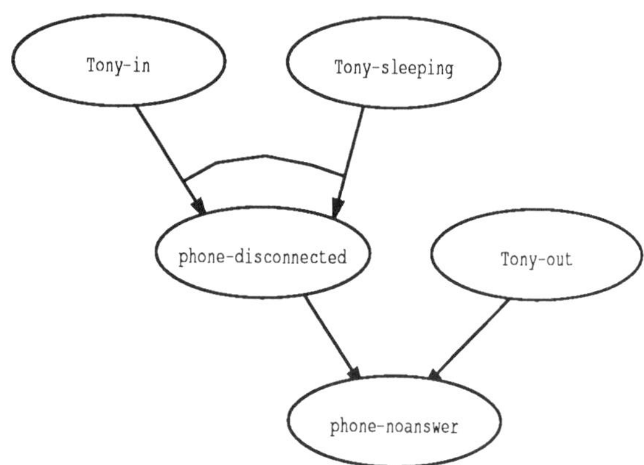

FIG. 2.1. Tony's office habits. phone-disconnected is the only AND-node, phone-noanswer is the only OR-node and the remaining nodes are hypothesis nodes.

DEFINITION 2.2. *A* truth assignment *for a* WAODAG $W = (G, c, r, S)$ *where* $G = (V, E)$ *is a function e from V to* {true, false}. *We say that such a function is* valid *iff the following conditions hold:*

1. *For all* AND*-nodes q,* $e(q) = \text{true}$ *iff for all nodes p such that* (p, q) *is an edge in E,* $e(p) = \text{true}$.
2. *For all* OR*-nodes q,* $e(q) = \text{true}$ *iff there exists a node p such that* (p, q) *is an edge in E and* $e(p) = \text{true}$.

Furthermore, we say that e is an explanation *iff e is valid and for each node q in S,* $e(q) = \text{true}$.

DEFINITION 2.3. *We define the* cost *of an explanation e for* $W = (G, c, r, S)$ *where* $G = (V, E)$ *as*

$$C(e) = \sum_{q \in V} c(q, e(q)).$$

An explanation e which minimizes C is called a best explanation *for W.*

Consider the WAODAG representing the situation with our friend Tony (see Figure 2.1). We first assume that there is no cost for assigning a node to false. Next, assume that assigning Tony-in, Tony-sleeping and Tony-out to true have costs 5, 4 and 8, respectively, and that the costs of assigning true to all non-hypothesis nodes is zero. The minimal cost proof for this WAODAG is the hypotheses set {Tony-out} with a cost of 8.

We now define constraint systems as follows:

NOTATION. For each node q in V, let $D_q = \{p | (p, q) \text{ is an edge in } E\}$, the parents of q. $|D_q|$ is the cardinality of D_q.

DEFINITION 2.4. *A* constraint system *is a 3-tuple* (Γ, I, ψ) *where* Γ *is a finite set of variables, I is a finite set of linear inequalities based on* Γ, *and* ψ *is a function from* $\Gamma \times \{\text{true}, \text{false}\}$ *to* $\Re$. *Given a* WAODAG $W = (G, c, r, S)$ *where* $G = (V, E)$, *we can construct a constraint system* $L(W) = (\Gamma, I, \psi)$ *where:*

1. Γ *is a set of variables indexed by* V, *that is,* $\Gamma = \{x_q | q \in V\}$.
2. $\psi(x_q, X) = c(q, X)$ *for all* $q \in V$ *and* $X \in \{\text{true}, \text{false}\}$.
3. I *is the collection of all inequalities of the forms given below:*

$$x_q \leq x_p \in I \text{ for each } p \in D_q \text{ if } r(q) = \text{AND} \quad (1)$$

$$\sum_{p \in D_q} x_p - |D_q| + 1 \leq x_q \in I \text{ if } r(q) = \text{AND} \quad (2)$$

$$\sum_{p \in D_q} x_p \geq x_q \in I \text{ if } r(q) = \text{OR} \quad (3)$$

$$x_q \geq x_p \in I \text{ for each } p \in D_q \text{ if } r(q) = \text{OR} \quad (4)$$

We say that $L(W)$ *is* induced *by* W. *Furthermore, by including the additional constraints:*

$$x_q = 1 \text{ if } q \in S, \quad (5)$$

we say that the resulting constraint system is induced evidentially *by* W *and is denoted by* $L_E(W)$.

DEFINITION 2.5. *A* variable assignment *for a constraint system* $L = (\Gamma, I, \psi)$ *is a function* s *from* Γ *to* $\Re$. *Furthermore,*

1. *If the range of* s *is* $\{0, 1\}$, *then* s *is a* 0-1 assignment.
2. *If* s *satisfies all the constraints in* I, *then* s *is a* solution *for* L.
3. *If* s *is a solution for* L *and is a 0-1 assignment, then* s *is a* 0-1 solution *for* L.

Given a 0-1 assignment s for $L(W)$, we can construct a truth assignment e for W as follows:

1. For all q in V, $s(x_q) = 1$ iff $e(q) = \text{true}$.
2. For all q in V, $s(x_q) = 0$ iff $e(q) = \text{false}$.

Conversely, given a truth assignment e for W, we can construct a 0-1 assignment s for $L(W)$.

NOTATION. e_s and s_e denote, respectively, a truth assignment e constructed from a 0-1 assignment s, and a 0-1 assignment s constructed from a truth assignment e.

We can show that all explanations for a given WAODAG W have corresponding 0-1 solutions for $L_E(W)$ and vice versa.

THEOREM 2.1. *If* e *is an explanation for* W, *then* s_e *is a solution of* $L(W)$.

THEOREM 2.2. *If* s *is a 0-1 solution of* $L_E(W)$, *then* e_s *is an explanation for* W.

It follows from Theorems 2.1 and 2.2 that 0-1 solutions for constraint systems are the counterparts of explanations for WAODAGs. Thus, by augmenting a WAODAG induced constraint system with a cost function, the notion of the cost of an explanation for a WAODAG can be transformed into the notion of the cost of a 0-1 solution for the constraint system.

DEFINITION 2.6. *Given a constraint system* $L = (\Gamma, I, \psi)$, *we construct a function* Θ_L *from variable assignments to* $\Re$ *as follows:*

$$\Theta_L(s) = \sum_{x_q \in \Gamma} \{s(x_q)\psi(x_q, \text{true}) + (1 - s(x_q))\psi(x_q, \text{false})\}.$$

Θ_L *is called the* objective function *of* L.

DEFINITION 2.7. *An* optimal 0-1 solution *for a constraint system* $L = (\Gamma, I, \psi)$ *is a 0-1 solution which minimizes* Θ_L.

Clearly, Definition 2.6 is identical to Definition 2.3. Thus, it follows from Theorems 2.1 and 2.2 and the relationship between node assignments and variable assignments that an optimal 0-1 solution in $L_E(W)$ is a best explanation for W and vice versa.

As we observed in (Santos [1991a]; Santos [1991c]), I and Θ_L are the elements of a *linear program* in *operations research* (Nemhauser, Kan & Todd [1989]). Extremely efficient and practical optimization techniques such as the *Simplex method* and *Karmarkar's projective scaling algorithm* (Nemhauser, Kan & Todd [1989]) are available for use in minimizing Θ_L with respect to the constraints in I.

Although solving the linear program was sufficient to obtain an optimal 0-1 solution for most of our test problems in (Santos [1991a]; Santos [1991c]), it was sometimes necessary to employ a *branch and bound* technique using the linear program to compute lower bounds. Complete details concerning the branch and bound algorithm can be found in (Santos [1991a]; Santos [1991c]). This technique enables us to avoid searching through all possible solutions by utilizing the lower bounds computed by the linear program as a guide. Experiments performed in (Santos [1991a]; Santos [1991c]) shown the practicality and efficiency of this approach for solving cost-based abduction problems. Also, it can be applied to any constraint system regardless of whether or not they are WAODAG induced.

3 GENERATING ALTERNATIVE EXPLANATIONS

In abductive explanation, having alternative explanations is often useful and sometimes necessary. Having the 2nd best, 3rd best, and so on, can provide a useful gauge on the quality of the best explanation. In this section, we present techniques for extracting alternative explanations in order of their associated costs.

To generate the alternative explanations, we solve a sequence of constraint systems. This sequence consists of constraint systems each of which are derived from the constraint systems earlier in the sequence. The initial constraint system is the original constraint system which determines the first optimal solution. The subsequent constraint systems are generated using the following schema: Consider $L_1 = (\Gamma, I_1, \psi)$, our initial constraint system. Let s_1 be the optimal 0-1 solution of L_1. We define a new problem L_2 as the successor of L_1. L_2 is identical to L_1 except for the additional constraint

$$\sum_{x_q \in \Gamma} F(s_1, x_q) \leq |\Gamma| - 1$$

where for each $x_q \in \Gamma$,

$$F(s_1, x_q) = \begin{cases} x_q & \text{if } s_1(x_q) = 1 \\ (1 - x_q) & \text{if } s_1(x_q) = 0 \end{cases}$$

Note that the new problem does not have s_1 as its optimal 0-1 solution since the variable assignment would violate the new constraint.

Let s_2 be the optimal 0-1 solution, if any, to L_2. This will be the second best 0-1 solution. To continue the search for the next best explanation, we simply define a successor to the last constraint system, in this case, L_2. When the current constraint system does not yield any solution, all possible explanations have been generated and we are finished.

ALGORITHM 3.1. *Given a constraint system $L = (\Gamma, I, \psi)$, generate all the 0-1 solutions for L in order of cost.*

1. *(*Initialization*) Set $I_1 := I$, $L_1 := (\Gamma, I_1, \psi)$ and $k := 1$.*
2. *Compute the optimal 0-1 solution for L_k. If there is no feasible solution, then go to step 7. Otherwise, let s_k be the solution.*
3. *$k := k + 1$.*
4. *Let $I_k := I_{k-1} \cup c_{k-1}$ where c_{k-1} contains the single constraint*

$$\sum_{x_q \in \Gamma} F(s_{k-1}, x_q) \leq |\Gamma| - 1 \qquad (6)$$

where for each $x_q \in \Gamma$,

$$F(s_{k-1}, x_q) = \begin{cases} x_q & \text{if } s_{k-1}(x_q) = 1 \\ (1 - x_q) & \text{if } s_{k-1}(x_q) = 0 \end{cases}$$

5. *Let $L_k := (\Gamma, I_k, \psi)$.*
6. *Go to step 2.*
7. *(*Solutions*) Print $s_1, s_2, \ldots, s_{k-1}$.*

The method we have just described can be classified as a *cutting plane method* in operations research (Nemhauser, Kan & Todd [1989]). Since each derived constraint system differs only in an additional constraint from some previously solved problem, efficient incremental techniques such as the *dual simplex method* can be applied here in a fashion similar to the one which is used in the branch and bound algorithm.

THEOREM 3.1. *Constraint system L_n in Algorithm 3.1 determines the n-th best 0-1 solution for L.*

The algorithm we have just presented can be applied to any constraint system. However, there are certain situations where generating all possible explanations may not be particularly desirable. Returning to our friend Tony above, consider the following additional information: Tony is as likely to be awake as be asleep at any time since he can always get to sleep in any environment. This implies that for the hypothesis that Tony is awake, the difference in the cost of being true and it being false is 0. If we look at our original explanation that Tony is not in the office, we must augment it with our guess as to whether he is asleep or not. With our assumptions, there is no way to choose between asleep and awake. However, since Tony is not in the office, the hypothesis involving his consciousness has no impact towards explaining the observation (see Figure 2.1).

If the algorithm first chooses that Tony is asleep, then the next alternative would be the same set of assignments except for Tony being awake. However, this new alternative explanation is uninteresting. In general, it may be the case that we may run into an overly large number of these types of uninteresting explanations. We now proceed to present an approach to deal with this problem.

DEFINITION 3.1. *Given a* WAODAG *$W = (G, c, r, S)$ where $G = (V, E)$ and $H \subseteq V_H$, an explanation e for W is said to be* consistent *with H iff for all h in H, $e(h) =$* true. *The* base set *$H(e)$ of e is the subset of V_H consisting of all h in V_H where $e(h) =$* true.

In WAODAGs, finding the best explanation is tantamount to finding the best set of hypotheses we need to assume.

DEFINITION 3.2. *The* support-set *$K(e)$ of an explanation e is the set consisting of all nodes m in V such that $e(m) =$* true.

PROPOSITION 3.2. *For every explanation e for W, $H(e) = K(e) \cap V_H$.*

The following propositions follow immediately from the properties of WAODAGs:

PROPOSITION 3.3. *Let e_1 and e_2 be explanations for W. $H(e_1) = H(e_2)$ iff $K(e_1) = K(e_2)$.*

PROPOSITION 3.4. *Let e be an explanation for W. For each $H(e) \subseteq H \subseteq V_H$, there exists an explanation e' for W such that $H(e') = H$.*

THEOREM 3.5. *Let e_1 and e_2 be explanations for W.*

1. $H(e_1) \subseteq H(e_2)$ *iff* $K(e_1) \subseteq K(e_2)$.
2. $H(e_1) \subset H(e_2)$ *iff* $K(e_1) \subset K(e_2)$.

THEOREM 3.6. *There exists a 1-1 and onto mapping between 2^{V_H} and the set of all possible truth assignments for W.*

THEOREM 3.7. *If e is an explanation for W, then there exists at least $2^{|V_H - H(e)|}$ explanations for W which are consistent with H(e).*

In general, we see that there are an exponential number of explanations for a given WAODAG. However, from Theorem 3.7, it seems that the majority of these explanations are formed from a possibly small number of "simpler" and more interesting explanations which utilize smaller numbers of hypotheses. The following question naturally arises: Do these additional explanations provide any new or important information?

DEFINITION 3.3. *A* WAODAG *W is* monotonic *iff for every two explanations e_1 and e_2 for W, $K(e_1) \subseteq K(e_2)$ implies $C(e_1) \leq C(e_2)$. W is* strictly monotonic *iff W is monotonic, and for every two explanations e_1 and e_2 for W, $K(e_1) \subset K(e_2)$ implies $C(e_1) < C(e_2)$.*

PROPOSITION 3.8. *If $c(v, \text{true}) \geq c(v, \text{false})$ for all v in V, then W is monotonic. If $c(v, \text{true}) > c(v, \text{false})$ for all v in V, then W is strictly monotonic.*

THEOREM 3.9. *A* WAODAG *W is monotonic iff for every two explanations e_1 and e_2 for W, $H(e_1) \subseteq H(e_2)$ implies $C(e_1) \leq C(e_2)$. W is strictly monotonic iff W is monotonic, and for every two explanations e_1 and e_2 for W, $H(e_1) \subset H(e_2)$ implies $C(e_1) < C(e_2)$.*

Proposition 3.8 and Theorem 3.9 together show that in a monotonic WAODAG, "simpler" explanations are preferred due to the lower associated costs. The assumption of monotonicity is reasonable in many cases as pointed out by (Charniak & Shimony [1990]) and characterized in (Charniak & Goldman [1988]). Our goal is to generate these explanations in order of cost without having to consider the remaining exponential number of explanations.

DEFINITION 3.4. *e is* cardinal *iff there are no explanations e' such that $H(e') \subset H(e)$.*

Intuitively, a cardinal explanation is among the "simplest" of explanations we wish to consider.

THEOREM 3.10. *If W is strictly monotonic, then any best explanation for W is cardinal.*

All the definitions given above involving WAODAGs can be carried over to WAODAG induced constraint systems.

Similar to Algorithm 3.1, the best cardinal explanation, 2nd best, 3rd best, etc. may be generated by constructing a sequence of constraint systems $L_1, L_2, \ldots$. Instead of introducing the additional constraint (6) to L_k, we introduce

$$\sum_{x_q \in H(s_{k-1})} x_q \leq |H(s_{k-1})| - 1.$$

LEMMA 3.11. *Let W be strictly monotonic. If s_n is the optimal 0-1 solution for the constraint system L_n, then s_n is a cardinal 0-1 solution for L.*

THEOREM 3.12. *Let W be strictly monotonic. The constraint system L_n determines the n-th best cardinal 0-1 solution.*

Our notion of cardinal explanations is very similar to the notion of *irredundancy* found in *parsimonious covering theory* for modeling medical diagnosis (Peng & Reggia [1990]). A *diagnostic problem* (Peng & Reggia [1990]) is a two-layer network consisting of a layer of *manifestations* which are causally affected by a layer of *disorders*. Given a subset of the manifestations as evidence, a subset of disorders must be chosen to best explain the manifestations based on parsimonious covering theory. A collection of disorders which can explain the manifestations is called a *cover*. A cover is said to be irredundant if none of its proper subsets is also a cover.

A limitation of parsimonious covering theory as pointed out by Peng and Reggia (Peng & Reggia [1990]) is the large number of covers which are considered "best". In order to further select from these potential explanations, some additional criteria must be used. Basic parsimonious covering theory is extended to incorporate probability theory. The potential of an explanation is now measured by some probability. With the addition of probabilities, care must be taken in choosing which covers are to be inspected. For example, consider the following analogous problem in cost-based abduction: A set of disorders D can adequately explain manifestations M. Let d be a fairly common disorder which explains manifestation m. Assume d is not in D but m is present in M. Furthermore, assume $c(d, F) > c(d, T)$. Thus, $D \cup \{d\}$ is a better explanation than D, despite the fact that $D \cup \{d\}$ is a superset of D.

Although this modified algorithm works only for W being strictly monotonic, we can modify any non-strictly monotonic problem to make it applicable. In essence, the strict monotonicity simply implies that we should always have a preference for a false assignment over a true assignment. By introducing an arbitrarily small positive difference between the cost for true and the cost for false in the original problem, we can now determine the cardinal solutions of the new problem which turns out to be identical to those of the original.

4 BAYESIAN NETWORKS

Bayesian networks have become an important tool in modeling probabilistic reasoning. The inherent representational power of these networks provides a very promising approach. In particular, *belief revision* in Bayesian networks is the process of finding the best interpretation for some given piece of evidence. This, of course, is a cornerstone of abductive explanation.

Since we are interested in abduction, existing effective algorithms for belief revision should be considered. One such algorithm is given by Pearl in (Pearl [1988]) which is based on a *message passing scheme*. However, except for simple networks such as polytrees, the method is rather complicated to apply. Also, as Pearl points out in Chapter 5 in (Pearl [1988]), this algorithm cannot guarantee the generation of alternative explanations beyond the second best.

Our goal in this section is to apply our linear constraint satisfaction approach to Bayesian networks. This entails constructing a constraint system which is computationally equivalent to the Bayesian network. Although this could be done by first transforming the Bayesian network into a cost-based abduction graph (Charniak & Shimony [1990]) and then transforming the graph into a constraint system (Santos [1991a]; Santos [1991c]), a more natural and straightforward method will be given below. We will show how to directly transform a Bayesian network into an equivalent constraint system.

We first observe that a Bayesian network can be completely described by a finite collection of random variables (or simply, r.v.s) and a finite set of conditional probabilities based on the r.v.s.[3]

Notation. Throughout the remainder of this paper, upper case italicized letters such as $A, B, \ldots$ will represent r.v.s and lower case italicized letters such as $a, b, \ldots$ will represent the possible assignments to the associated upper case letter r.v., in this case, $A, B, \ldots$. Subscripted upper case letters which are not italicized are variables in a constraint system which explicitly represent the instantiation of the associated r.v. with the item in the subscript. For example, $\mathrm{A_a}$ denotes the instantiation of r.v. A with value a.

Notation. Given a r.v. A, the set of possible values for A called the *range* of A will be denoted by $R(A)$.

Given a Bayesian network, we can construct an ordered pair (V, P) where V is the set of r.v.s in the network and P is a set of conditional probabilities associated with the network. $P(A = a | C_1 = c_1, \ldots, C_n = c_n) \in P$ iff $C_1, \ldots, C_n$ are all the immediate parents of A and there is an edge from C_i to A for $i = 1, \ldots, n$ in the network. We can clearly see that (V, P) completely describes the Bayesian network.

Definition 4.1. *Given a Bayesian network $\mathcal{B} = (V, P)$, an* instantiation *is an ordered pair (A, a) where $A \in V$ and $a \in R(A)$. (An instantiation (A, a) is also denoted by $A = a$ and $\mathrm{A_a}$.) A collection of instantiations w is called an* instantiation-set *iff are no two instantiations $(A, a), (A, a')$ in w such that $a \neq a'$.*

An instantiation represents the event when a r.v. takes on a value from its range. Given an instantiation-set, we can define the notion of the *span* of an instantiation-set.

Definition 4.2. *Given an instantiation-set w for a Bayesian network $\mathcal{B} = (V, P)$, we define the* span *of w, $\mathsf{span}(w)$, to be the collection of r.v.s in the first coordinate of the instantiations. Furthermore, an instantiation-set w is said to be* complete *iff $\mathsf{span}(w) = V$.*

Notation. For each r.v. A and each a in $R(A)$, $v_{\mathrm{A_a}}$ is the set of all conditional probabilities in P of the form $P(A = a | C_1 = c_1, \ldots, C_n = c_n)$. For each r.v. A, we define $\mathsf{cond}(A)$ as follows: $B \in \mathsf{cond}(A)$ iff there exists a conditional probability in P of the form $P(A = a | \ldots, B = b, \ldots)$.

Definition 4.3. *Given an instantiation-set $w = \{(A_1, a_1), \ldots, (A_n, a_n)\}$ for a Bayesian network $\mathcal{B} = (V, P)$, we define the probability of w to be*

$$P(w) = P(A_1 = a_1, \ldots, A_n = a_n).$$

The goal of belief revision on Bayesian networks is to determine the complete instantiation-set which maximizes the associated probability under certain conditions. In general, these conditions, called *evidence*, imposes restrictions on what instantiations may be made. The instantiation-set satisfying the evidence with the highest probability is said to be the *most probable explanation* for the evidence. We now formalize this as follows:

Definition 4.4. *Given a Bayesian network $\mathcal{B} = (V, P)$,* evidence *e for $\mathcal{B}$ is an instantiation-set for $\mathcal{B}$.*

Definition 4.5. *Given instantiation-sets w_1, w_2 for a Bayesian network $\mathcal{B}$, w_2 is said to be* consistent *with w_1 iff $w_1 \subseteq w_2$.*

Definition 4.6. *Given evidence e for $\mathcal{B}$, a complete instantiation-set w for $\mathcal{B}$ is an* explanation *for e iff w is consistent with e. Furthermore, w is said to be a* most probable explanation *for e iff for all explanations $w' \neq w$ for e, $P(w') \leq P(w)$.*

Our basic approach in constructing a constraint system from a given Bayesian network is to represent and

[3]We consider prior probabilities to be degenerate cases of conditional probabilities, i.e., $P(A = a) = P(A = a | \phi)$ where ϕ is the empty set.

enforce the constraints that exist between any two or more r.v.s.

Given a Bayesian network $\mathcal{B} = (V, P)$, we construct a constraint system $L(\mathcal{B}) = (\Gamma, I, \psi)$ as follows:

1. For each r.v. A in V, let $R(A) = \{a_1, \ldots, a_n\}$ and construct the variables $\mathsf{A}_{a_1}, \ldots, \mathsf{A}_{a_n}$ in Γ, set $\psi(\mathsf{A}_{a_i}, \mathsf{false}) = \psi(\mathsf{A}_{a_i}, \mathsf{true}) = 0$ and add the following constraint to I:
$$\sum_{i=1}^{n} \mathsf{A}_{a_i} = 1. \quad (7)$$
2. For each r.v. A and some a in $R(A)$, for each conditional probability $P(A = a | C_1 = c_1, \ldots, C_n = c_n)$ in $v_{\mathsf{A_a}}$, construct a variable $q[\mathsf{A_a} \,|\, \mathsf{C}_1 = \mathsf{c}_1, \ldots, \mathsf{C}_n = \mathsf{c}_n]$ in Γ such that (for notational convenience, we will denote $q[\mathsf{A_a} \,|\, \mathsf{C}_1 = \mathsf{c}_1, \ldots, \mathsf{C}_n = \mathsf{c}_n]$ by q in the next two conditions)
   (a) $\psi(q, \mathsf{false}) = 0$, $\psi(q, \mathsf{true}) = -\log(P(A = a | C_1 = c_1, \ldots, C_n = c_n))$, and,
   (b) Add the following constraint to I:
$$q \geq \sum_{k=1}^{n} \mathsf{C}_{k_{\mathsf{c}_k}} + \mathsf{A_a} - n. \quad (8)$$
3. Let $\Upsilon_{\mathsf{A_a}}$ be all the variables q constructed by $v_{\mathsf{A_a}}$ in step (2). For each r.v. A and some a in $R(A)$, add the following constraint to I:
$$\mathsf{A_a} = \sum_{q \in \Upsilon_{\mathsf{A_a}}} q. \quad (9)$$

Definition 4.7. *$L(\mathcal{B})$ constructed above is the constraint system induced by $\mathcal{B}$.*

As we can clearly see, our construction is straightforward and is done in time linear to the size of the Bayesian network. The next theorem show the complexity of our induced constraint system with respect to the Bayesian network.

Theorem 4.1. *Let $\mathcal{B} = (V, P)$ be a Bayesian network and $L(\mathcal{B}) = (\Gamma, I, \psi)$ be the constraint system induced by $\mathcal{B}$. Then*

1. $|\Gamma| = |P| + \sum_{A \in V} |R(A)|$ *and*
2. $|I| = |V| + |P| + \sum_{A \in V} |R(A)|$.

In our construction, (7) guarantees that any r.v. takes on exactly one value. (8) and (9) guarantee that the probability of any complete instantiation-set will be computed with the appropriate set of conditional probabilities. Variables of the form $q[\mathsf{A_a} \,|\, \mathsf{C}_{1_{\mathsf{c}_1}}, \ldots, \mathsf{C}_{n_{\mathsf{c}_n}}]$ are called *conditional variables* in that they explicitly represent the dependencies between r.v.s and will be the mechanism for computing the probability for any instantiation-set.

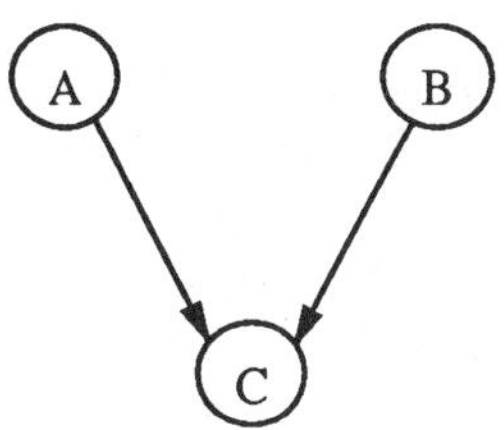

Fig. 4.1. Simple Bayesian network. The distribution is as follows:
$P(C = \mathsf{true} \,|\, A = \mathsf{true}, B = \mathsf{true}) = p_1$
$P(C = \mathsf{true} \,|\, A = \mathsf{true}, B = \mathsf{false}) = p_2$
$P(C = \mathsf{true} \,|\, A = \mathsf{false}, B = \mathsf{true}) = p_3$
$P(C = \mathsf{true} \,|\, A = \mathsf{false}, B = \mathsf{false}) = p_4$
$P(A = \mathsf{true}) = p_9)$
$P(B = \mathsf{true}) = p_{10})$

For example, consider the simple Bayesian network in Figure 4.1. When we have the instantiations $\{A = \mathsf{true}, B = \mathsf{false}, C = \mathsf{true}\}$, its associated probability is $p_2 * p_9 * (1 - p_{10})$. In the induced constraint system, we expect our variables assignments to be $\mathsf{A_{true}} = 1$, $\mathsf{B_{false}} = 1$, $\mathsf{C_{true}} = 1$, $q[\mathsf{C_{true}} \,|\, \mathsf{A_{true}}, \mathsf{B_{false}}] = 1$, and all remaining variables to be 0. Since the only costs are associated with the variables $\mathsf{A_{true}}$, $\mathsf{B_{false}}$ and $q[\mathsf{C_{true}} \,|\, \mathsf{A_{true}}, \mathsf{B_{false}}]$, the cost of this assignment is $-\log(p_9) - \log(1 - p_{10}) - \log(p_2)$ which is equivalent to $-\log(p_2 * p_9 * (1 - p_{10}))$.

Notation. For each r.v. A, let $\Delta(A)$ be the set of variables in the induced constraint system constructed for A.

Theorem 4.2. *Given a 0-1 solution s for $L(\mathcal{B})$, for each set of variables $\Delta(A)$, there exists some $\mathsf{A_a}$ in $\Delta(A)$ such that $\mathsf{A_a} = 1$ and $\mathsf{A_{a'}} = 0$ for all $\mathsf{A_{a'}} \neq \mathsf{A_a}$ in $\Delta(A)$.*

Theorem 4.3. *Given a 0-1 solution s for $L(\mathcal{B})$, for all variables $q[\mathsf{A_a} \,|\, \mathsf{C}_1 = \mathsf{c}_1, \ldots, \mathsf{C}_n = \mathsf{c}_n]$, if $\mathsf{A_a} = \mathsf{C}_{1_{\mathsf{c}_1}} = \ldots = \mathsf{C}_{n_{\mathsf{c}_n}} = 1$, then $q[\mathsf{A_a} \,|\, \mathsf{C}_1 = \mathsf{c}_1, \ldots, \mathsf{C}_n = \mathsf{c}_n] = 1$.*

Theorems 4.2 and 4.3 above verifies our expectations on the legitimate variable assignments. However, $\mathsf{A_a} = \mathsf{C}_{1_{\mathsf{c}_1}} = \ldots = \mathsf{C}_{n_{\mathsf{c}_n}} = 0$ does not necessarily imply that $q[\mathsf{A_a} \,|\, \mathsf{C}_1 = \mathsf{c}_1, \ldots, \mathsf{C}_n = \mathsf{c}_n] = 0$. We could remedy the situation by introducing the following additional constraints:

$$q[\mathsf{A_a} \,|\, \mathsf{C}_1 = \mathsf{c}_1, \ldots, \mathsf{C}_n = \mathsf{c}_n] \leq \mathsf{A_a},$$
$$q[\mathsf{A_a} \,|\, \mathsf{C}_1 = \mathsf{c}_1, \ldots, \mathsf{C}_n = \mathsf{c}_n] \leq \mathsf{C}_{i_{\mathsf{c}_i}} \text{ for } i = 1, \ldots, n.$$

Instead of increasing the number of constraints, we will show that this can be solved through simple restrictions and modifications to the algorithms applied to general constraint systems.

Definition 4.8. *A 0-1 solution s for $L(\mathcal{B})$ is said to be* permissible *if for all variables $q[\mathsf{A_a} \,|\, \mathsf{C}_1 = \mathsf{c}_1, \ldots, \mathsf{C}_n =$*

$c_n]$,

$$q[A_a \mid C_1 = c_1, \ldots, C_n = c_n] = 1 \textit{ only if } A_a = C_{1c_1} = \ldots = C_{nc_n} = 1.$$

Thus our goal is to consider only those 0-1 solutions for $L(\mathcal{B})$ which are permissible. We must now show that calculations on the constructed constraint system are equivalent to those on the Bayesian network for belief revision.

Given a 0-1 solution s for $L(\mathcal{B})$, we can construct a complete instantiation-set w_s for $\mathcal{B}$ as follows: $s(A_a) = 1$ iff $(A, a) \in w_s$. To convert from a complete instantiation-set to a 0-1 solution is slightly trickier. Given a complete instantiation-set w for $\mathcal{B}$, construct a 0-1 solution s_w for $L(\mathcal{B})$ as follows: $(A, a) \in w$ iff $s_w(A_a) = 1$. For each conditional variable q in Υ_{A_a}, set the appropriate value according to w.

THEOREM 4.4. *If s is a 0-1 solution for $L(\mathcal{B})$, then w_s is an instantiation-set for $\mathcal{B}$.*

THEOREM 4.5. *If w is a complete instantiation-set for $\mathcal{B}$, then s_w is a permissible 0-1 solution for $L(\mathcal{B})$.*

From our construction of instantiation-sets from 0-1 solutions, we notice that more than one 0-1 solution can construct the same instantiation-set. This arises from our previous observation that our expectations are not completely met (Theorem 4.3).

COROLLARY 4.6. *There is a 1-1 and onto mapping between permissible 0-1 solutions for $L(\mathcal{B})$ and complete instantiation-sets for $\mathcal{B}$.*

This corollary states that we only need to consider the permissible 0-1 solutions in our calculations of complete instantiation-sets for the Bayesian network.

DEFINITION 4.9. *Let e be some evidence for $\mathcal{B} = (V, P)$. We construct $L_e(\mathcal{B}) = (\Gamma, I_e, \psi)$ from $L(\mathcal{B}) = (\Gamma, I, \psi)$ as follows: Let $I_e = I \cup I'$ where the constraint $A_a = 1$ is in I' iff $(A, a) \in e$. We say that $L_e(\mathcal{B})$ is* induced *by $\mathcal{B}$* with evidence *e*.

PROPOSITION 4.7. $|I_e| = |I| + |e|$.

THEOREM 4.8. *If s is a 0-1 solution for $L_e(\mathcal{B})$, then w_s is an explanation for e.*

THEOREM 4.9. *If w is an explanation for e, then s_w is a permissible 0-1 solution for $L_e(\mathcal{B})$.*

When there is some set of evidence given to be explained, we only want to consider those instantiation-sets which are consistent with the evidence. Theorems 4.8 and 4.9 above guarantee that the evidence also properly restricts the set of possible permissible 0-1 solutions we wish to consider. Now, we must show that the costs associated to each permissible 0-1 solution are directly related to the probability of the corresponding instantiation-set.

For the following theorems, assume that L is induced by a Bayesian network $\mathcal{B}$, w is a complete instantiation-set for $\mathcal{B}$, and s is a permissible 0-1 solution for $L(\mathcal{B})$.

THEOREM 4.10. $\Theta_L(s_w) = -\log(P(w))$.

THEOREM 4.11. *There exists a constant α_e such that for all explanations w for e, $\Theta_{L_e}(s_w) = \alpha_e - \log(P(w|e))$.*

THEOREM 4.12. *w is a most probable explanation for e iff s_w is an optimal 0-1 solution for $L_e(B)$.*

Theorem 4.11 guarantees that the probabilistic ordering of instantiation-sets is exactly reversed from the cost ordering imposed on permissible 0-1 solutions. Furthermore, computing the cost for a permissible 0-1 solution immediately determines the probability of its associated instantiation-set.

THEOREM 4.13. *If $\psi(q, \text{true}) > 0$ for all conditional variables q in $L_e(\mathcal{B})$, then any optimal 0-1 solution for $L_e(\mathcal{B})$ is permissible.*

The condition required in the above theorem can be easily met by increasing the cost of conditional variables with $\psi(q, \text{true}) = 0$ to $\psi(q, \text{true}) = \delta$ where δ is an arbitrarily small but positive value. This still guarantees proper ordering of the permissible 0-1 solutions as compared to the instantiation-sets.

Similarly, we must guarantee that any alternative 0-1 solutions generated must also be permissible. We can accomplish this by modifying the Algorithm 3.1. Again, instead of introducing the new constraint (6) into L_k we introduce

$$\sum_{A_a \in \Delta} F(s_{k_1}, A_a) \leq |\Delta| - 1$$

where $\Delta = \{x | x \in V \text{ and } x \in \Delta(A) \text{ for some r.v. } A\}$.

THEOREM 4.14. *L_n generates the n-th best permissible optimal 0-1 solution for $L_e(\mathcal{B})$.*

With the transformation of belief revision problems into constraint systems, we now have an alternative approach to solving for the best explanation as well as the consecutive next best. With our linear constraint satisfaction approach, we can utilize the highly efficient computational tools of operations research on the NP-Hard problem of belief revision and explanation generation. Furthermore, unlike message-passing schemes requiring preprocessing such as clustering on non-polytree topologies, our approach can be directly applied to any Bayesian network.

5 DISCUSSION

Linear constraint satisfaction has been shown to be an effective and computationally practical approach to solving cost-based abduction (Santos [1991a]; Santos [1991c]). Experimental results comparing our constraint system against existing search style techniques have shown it to be the superior approach.

In this paper, we have presented an approach to generating alternative explanations within our framework of constraint systems. This approach naturally incorporates the computational tools of operations research in an efficient manner. We have also shown how to apply the generation of alternative explanations to cost-based abduction and belief revision in Bayesian networks.

The necessity of having alternative explanations can also be readily seen in natural language processing. Proper handling of problems such as ambiguity requires access to the possible explanations in order of best to worst. For example, the WIMP system (Goldman [1990]; Goldman & Charniak [1991]) uses alternative explanations in order to resolve lexical ambiguities. Our approach is especially well suited to this problem since it is characterized by low prior probabilities making it monotonic within our framework.

Acknowledgments

This work has been supported by the National Science Foundation under grant IRI-8911122 and by the Office of Naval Research, under contract N00014-88-K-0589. Special thanks to Eugene Charniak for critical comments and suggestions. Also, thanks to Solomon Shimony, Glenn Carroll and Moises Lejter for careful review of this paper.

References

Charniak, Eugene & Goldman, Robert [1988], "A Logic for Semantic Interpretation," Proceedings of the AAAI Conference.

Charniak, Eugene & Shimony, Solomon E. [1990], "Probabilistic Semantics for Cost Based Abduction," Proceedings of the 1990 National Conference on Artificial Intelligence.

Genesereth, Michael R. [1984], "The Use of Design Descriptions in Automated Diagnosis," Artificial Intelligence.

Goldman, Robert P. [1990], "A Probabilistic Approach to Language Understanding," Department of Computer Science, Brown University, Ph.D. Thesis.

Goldman, Robert P. & Charniak, Eugene [1991], "Probabilistic Text Understanding," Proceedings of the Third International Workshop on AI and Statistics, Fort Lauderdale, FL.

Hobbs, Jerry R., Stickel, Mark, Martin, Paul & Edwards, Douglas [1988], "Interpretation as Abduction," Proceedings of the 26th Annual Meeting of the Association for Computational Linguistics.

Kautz, Henry A. & Allen, James F. [1986], "Generalized Plan Recognition," Proceedings of the Fifth Conference of AAAI.

Nemhauser, G. L., Kan, A. H. G. Rinnooy & Todd, M. J. [1989], in *Optimization: Handbooks in Operations Research and Management Science Volume 1*, North Holland.

Pearl, Judea [1988], in *Probabilistic Reasoning in Intelligent Systems: Networks of Plausible Inference*, Morgan Kaufmann, San Mateo, CA.

Peng, Y. & Reggia, J. A. [1990], in *Abductive Inference Models for Diagnostic Problem-Solving*, Springer-Verlag.

Santos, Eugene Jr. [1991a], "A Linear Constraint Satisfaction Approach to Cost-Based Abduction," Department of Computer Science, Brown University, in preparation.

Santos, Eugene Jr. [1991b], "Cost-Based Abduction, Linear Constraint Satisfaction, and Alternative Explanations," to appear in Proceedings of the AAAI Workshop on Abduction.

Santos, Eugene Jr. [1991c], "Cost-Based Abduction and Linear Constraint Satisfaction," Department of Computer Science, Brown University, Technical Report CS-91-13.

Selman, Bart & Levesque, Hector J. [1990], "Abductive and Default Reasoning: A Computational Core," Proceedings of the Eighth National Conference on Artificial Intelligence.

Shanahan, Murray [1989], "Prediction is Deduction but Explanation is Abduction," IJCAI-89.

Stickel, Mark E. [1988], "A Prolog-like Inference System for Computing Minimum-Cost Abductive Explanations in Natural-Language Interpretation," SRI International, Technical Note 451.

Completing Knowledge by Competing Hierarchies

Kerstin Schill
Institut f. Med. Psychologie
Ludwig-Maximilians-Universität
Goethestr. 31, 8000 München 2
Germany

Ernst Pöppel
Institut f. Med. Psychologie
Ludwig-Maximilians-Universität
Goethestr. 31, 8000 München 2
Germany

Christoph Zetzsche
Lehrstuhl für Nachrichtentechnik
Technische Universität
Arcisstr. 21, 8000 München 2
Germany

Abstract

A control strategy for expert systems is presented which is based on Shafer's Belief theory and the combination rule of Dempster. In contrast to well known strategies it is not sequentially and hypotheses-driven, but parallel and self-organizing, determined by the concept of information gain. The information gain, calculated as the maximal difference between the actual evidence distribution in the knowledge base and the potential evidence determines each consultation step. Hierarchically structured knowledge is an important representation form and experts even use several hierarchies in parallel for constituting their knowledge. Hence the control strategy is applied to a layered set of distinct hierarchies. Depending on the actual data one of these hierarchies is choosen by the control stratgey for the next step in the reasoning process. Provided the actual data are well matched to the structure of one hierarchy, this hierarchy remains selected for a longer consultation time. If no good match can be achieved, a switch from the actual hierarchy to a competing one will result, very similar to the phenomenon of "restructuring" in problem solving tasks. Up to now the control strategy is restricted to multi-hierarchical knowledge bases with disjunct hierarchies. It is implemented in the expert system IBIG (inference by information gain), being presently applied to acquired speech disorders (aphasia).

1 Introduction

The performance of an expert system is essentially determined by two important factors: the completeness of the knowledge base with respect to the expert knowledge and the ability of the control strategy to make adaquate decisions even in those cases where the actual data are irregularily distributed across the knowledge base. To overcome these problems we shall introduce a knowledge base enabling the incorporation of diverse knowledge structures and a formally derived control strategy. The control strategy is based on the concept of information. Information gain is calculated as the difference between the actual evidence distribution and the potential one, where evidence is handled by Shafer's belief theory and Dempster's rule of combination. In the first section of this paper, we shall introduce the multi-level knowledge base. The control strategy will be described in the second section. The strategy is first derived for a single hierarchy and is then extended to a restricted version of the multi-level model, a model with an arbitrary number of disjunctive hierarchies.

2 The knowledge base

2.1 Common knowledge bases

Common knowledge bases in expert systems with a symbolic knowledge representation can be classified into two categories: single-structure knowledge bases, like the one representing knowledge within one strict hierarchy (e.g., the medical expert system MEDIKS (Chang 1984)), and integrated structures where two or more relationships are linked in one net structure (e.g., the systems EXPERT (Weiss 1979) or CADUCEUS (Miller 1984)). The first category has to deal with the problem that, in most cases, the knowledge of a certain domain is not completely covered by one structure, e.g. one single hierarchy. This implies that necessary inferences cannot be drawn in the reasoning process. Thus, the idea of one best structuring principle for all problems is not suitable (Schill 1986, 1990). The second category has to deal with the problem that no formally derived and transparant method exists to calculate evidence. Since this calculation is not theoretically justified, the same is true for the reasoning process based on it.

Common control strategies for such knowledge bases can be characterized by the principle of partitioning. In rule-based systems a single hypothesis or an agenda with a small number of probable hypotheses are partitioned from all others and control the data collection process (see e.g. MYCIN (Shortliffe 1976)). In hierachically structured knowledge bases a continuous partitioning process starting at the root guides the selection process of the data. The main problem of these partitioning principles arise in unclear consultation cases where the decision has to be taken which of the hypotheses has to be selected from a large list of weak hypotheses. The wrong selection may lead to a "dead end", with no solution or an expensive backtracking.

2.2. A multi-hierarchical knowledge base

Expert knowledge can be characterized by two components, i.e. knowledge entities and the relationships between them. Knowledge entities can be hypotheses or sets of hypotheses, for example diseasecategories or diseases themselves. Typical examples for relationships are hierarchical, causal, or temporal ones. Only both components, entities and relationships together, allow the constitution of expert knowledge. Thus, a knowledge-base structure is required which allows the representation of many diverse relationships for linking the knowledge entities to be made.

In the expert system IBIG (inference by information gain) (Schill 1986), a knowledge-base structure is developed that meets the above-mentioned requirements or supports their further development. The knowledge base is modeled by the parallel representation of an arbitrary number of separate layers. The idea is to represent on each level or layer one specific relationship linking the appropriate knowledge entities. Thus, such a base may have one causal layer, perhaps two different hierarchical ones (knowledge of a certain domain can often be represented by two or more different hierarchies), and a layer characterized by temporally linked knowledge, etc..

A formally derived control strategy applicable to a restricted form, namely a layered set of disjunctive hierarchies, has been developed. Modelling expert knowledge, we have observed that such hierachical structuring is characteristic of many problem-solving situations. As a step towards a complete knowledge representation, not one hierarchy but many distinct ones have to be taken into account for the reasoning process. Thus our actual knowledge base consists of an arbitrary number of strict hierarchies T_i,
where for all hierarchies T_i and T_j, $i \neq j$, i, j=1....n,
if $X_i \subset T_i$ and $X_j \subset T_j$ then $X_i \cap X_j = \emptyset$, for all subsets X_i and X_j. The actual restriction to disjunctive hierarchies is necessary in order to guarantee the consistent distribution of belief induced by pieces of evidence.

To derive our control strategy, first we briefly show the basic formulars of Shafer´s belief theory and Dempster´s combination rule. An approximation of this theory for combining evidence in hierarchies is introduced next. This approach is used to calculate the evidence in IBIG and is a base for the information increment strategy.

3. The control strategy

3.1 Shafer´s Belief theory

Shafer´s Belief Theory (Shafer 1976) is based on subjective belief measures induced in experts given some pieces of evidence. The axiom $Bel(A)+Bel(A^c)\leq 1$ enables one to distinguish betweeen lack of knowledge and nonsupporting knowledge. A set of propositions about the mutually exclusive and exhaustive possibilities in a domain is called the frame of discernment and is denoted by θ. It´s set of subsets is denoted by 2^θ where elements of 2^θ are the general propositions in the domain. It is postulated that some finite amount of belief can be spread among various propositions A of θ according to the available evidence, with one and only one true proposition. This quantity of belief m(A) is allocated to the proposition $A \subset \theta$ and is called basic probability number or basic belief mass (Smets 1988) and represents our exact belief in the proposition represented by A.
A function called basic probability assignment or basic belief assignment assigns to each subset of θ a measure of our belief in the proposition represented by the subset. It is defined whenever

$$m: 2^\theta \text{ --> } [0,1], \quad m(\emptyset) = 0 \text{ and } \sum_{A \subset \theta} m(A) = 1 \text{ is satisfied.}$$

In terms of this basic belief assignment, the belief in a proposition $A \subset \theta$ can be expressed as: $Bel(A) = \sum_{B \subset A} m(B)$

Pieces of evidence are combined by the application of Dempster´s rule of combination on the basic belief assignments. If two distinct pieces of evidence induce two basic belief masses m_1 and m_2, the product of these masses is allocated to the conjunction of the two focal propositions A_i and B_j. Thus, the combination of two basic belief masses is defined by:

$$m_{12}(A) = K * \sum_{\substack{i,j \\ A_i \cap B_j = A}} m_1(A_i) * m_2(B_j)$$

with the normalization constant K

$$K = (1 - \sum_{\substack{i,j \\ A_i \cap B_j = \emptyset}} m_1(A_i) * m_2(B_j))^{-1}.$$

The effects of this normalization with respect to an open or closed world assumption is critically discussed in (Smets 1989).
Since the above shown formulas are the basic one´s for the following derivations for further details see (Shafer 1976).

3.2 The Belief theory applied to hierarchies

Based on Barnett´s approach (Barnett 1981), Gordon and Shortliffe have developed an approximation of the belief theory applicable to strict hierarchical knowledge structures. Later, a correct approach requiring no essential change of the proposed strategy was derived by Shafer and Logan (Shafer 1987). Since the belief approach is applied to 2^θ, the important step of Gordon and Shortliffe for the application to hierarchies was the approximation that pieces of evidence for sets not represented in the tree must be associated with the smallest supersets represented in the tree. The approach is based on simple support functions, a

subclass of belief functions for which the concept of confirming and non-confirming belief has to be introduced. In the approach of Gordon and Shortliffe non-confirming belief for a set in the tree is confirmingly allocated to the set-theoretical complement.
In the following, we briefly show the resulting combination rules with which the calculation of the basic belief mass is provided in a three-step technique. For further details see (Gordon 1985).

Given some pieces of evidence which induce belief masses m_{ij} for a set X_i in our hierarchy, we start by combining these masses to reach a combined belief mass pointed exactely at X_i and no other set in the tree. The same has to be provided for non-confirming belief $m_{ij}{}^c$ and the concerned set $X_i{}^c$ in T' (T' is the set of all set-theoretical complements of T). This first step must be applied to all sets in the tree.

Thus, calculate m_{x_i} for all X_i in T and $m_{x_i}{}^c$ for all $X_i{}^c$ in T' with:

$$m_{x_i}=1-\prod_{j=1}^{n}(1-m_{ij}) \text{ and } m_{x_i}{}^c=1-\prod_{j=1}^{n}(1-m_{ij}{}^c)$$

In the second step, the combination of confirming belief for each set in the hierarchy with respect to all other sets is provided by calculating the aggregated basic belief mass defined by :

$$m_T(X_i) = K * m_{x_i}(X_i) * \prod_{\substack{X_j \not\supset X_i \\ X_j \in T}} m_{x_j}(\theta) \quad \text{if } X_i \in T \text{ or}$$

$$m_T(X_i) = K * \prod_{X_j \in T} m_{x_j}(\theta) \quad \text{if } X_i = \theta$$

In the last step, the combination of nonconfirming belief for all sets in the tree which has attained evidence in any earlier step is provided with the calculation:

$m_T \ominus m_{x_1}{}^c$, then $(m_T \ominus m_{x_1}{}^c) \ominus m_{x_2}{}^c$, etc. for all $X_i{}^c$ in T'.

Case 1: $X_j \subseteq X_i$:

$$m_T \ominus m_{x_i}c(X_j) = K * m_T(X_j) * m_{x_i}c(\theta).$$

Case 2: $X_j \cap X_i = \emptyset$

if $X_j \cup X_i$ is a set in $T \cup \theta$:

$$m_T \ominus m_{x_i}c(X_j) = K * [m_T(X_j) + m_T(X_j \cup X_i) * m_{x_i}c(X_i{}^c)]$$

if $X_j \cup X_i$ is not a set in $T \cup \theta$:

$$m_T \ominus m_{x_i}c(X_j) = K * m_T(X_j).$$

Case 3: $X_j \supset X_i$

if $X_j \cap X_i{}^c$ is not a set in T :

$$m_T \ominus m_{x_i}c(X) = K * m_T(X_j)$$

if $X_j \cap X_i{}^c$ is a set in T :

$$m_T \ominus m_{x_i}c(X_j) = K * m_T(X_j) * m_{x_i}c (\theta).$$

With these three cases, the calculation of belief masses induced by pieces of evidence is provided in IBIG.

3.3 The information increment strategy

The development of our control strategy was guided by two main ideas. First, to make a strategy available which adapts itself to the actually existing data situation and which is not predetermined like most of the known strategies. As mentioned above, these predetermined strategies, characterized by hypotheses-driven behaviour, may culminate in an unsuccessful search whenever data are ambiguous or irregularily distributed over the hierarchy and therefore not represented in one single path. In all these cases, the rigid, top-down partitioning processes are not optimal. The second requirement for our strategy was to make a theory-based strategy available which provides an axiomatic base for further development.

The principles of our strategy first described in (Schill 1986) is to calculate the data one has to collect next to attain the largest information gain with respect to the actual data situation. The information gain is calculated by the difference between the belief distribution in the hierarchy, induced by the available pieces of evidence, and the "potential belief distribution".

Each data item in knowledge base indicating evidence for a set of hypotheses is associated with an a priori belief mass.The potential belief mass is identical with this a priori measure as long as nothing is known about this data item. The following derivations show the influence of all these potential belief masses in the hierarchy on the actual given belief situation. This has to be derived for two extreme cases, namely, the potential confirming belief and the non-confirming belief for these data. In the following, the potential belief of a node or hypotheses set X_i in the tree is designated by $\hat{m}_i$.

In the first case, we assume that all presently unknown or uncollected data, representing evidence which induce confirming belief for a set of hypotheses X_i will be collected and confirmed. Thus, corresponding to Gordon and Shortliffe´s first step, the potential belief is calculated as follows:

$\hat{m}_{x_i}(X_i) = 1 - \prod_{j=1}^{n}(1-\hat{m}_{ij})$, where $\hat{m}_{ij}$ are a priori given maximal potential belief masses.

In the second case, we analogously combine the belief for the potential non-confirming case:

$\hat{m}_{x_i}{}^c(X_i) = 1 - \prod_{j=1}^{n}(1-\hat{m}_{ij}{}^c)$, where $\hat{m}_{ij}{}^c$ are a priori given maximal non-confirming belief masses

Up to now, we have calculated the potential belief masses $(\hat{m}_{x_j}(X_j), \hat{m}_{x_j}{}^c(X_j))$ a node or hypothesis set X_j may reach with respect to all presently unknown data.

The next step is to analyze the influences of this potential belief on the actual belief distribution. For this analysis, we examine elementary evidence situations in the hierarchy consisting of only one node or hypothesis set X_i with actual belief. It is assumed that each more complex belief situation can be approximated by the superposition of elementary evidence situations. Using the approximation of Gordon and Shortliffe, we now calculate the influence of nodes X_j in the tree on the hypothesis set X_i. This is expressed by the potential belief $\hat{m}_T(X_i)$, which X_i attains from X_j proportional to its potential belief mass $\hat{m}_{x_j}$. The information increment for X_i arising from X_j is calculated next by the difference between the belief mass $m_T(X_i)$ and the potential value $\hat{m}_T(X_i)$.

Depending on the intersection possibilities in the hierarchy, the calculation of the information increment is derived in five equations. These five equations include all possible intersections and influences between any node X_j and X_i in the tree. Thus, the information-increment calculation is computed in the following way: On every node or hypothesis set X_i in the hierarchy which has attained evidence, the equations are applied. The information-increment arising from a node X_j is allocated to this node. If more than one equation is applied to X_j, the information increment is added. This superposition has been used to obtain an information increment measure related to the complete evidence distribution. The node or hypothesis set with the largest information gain is the one which determines the data-collection process in the next step. For an extensive derivation of the following five equations see (Schill 1986).

The first equation describes the information increment for the node X_i from X_j with $X_j \not\supseteq X_i$. It is the difference between the belief mass $m_T(X_i)$ and the potential belief mass $\hat{m}_T(X_i) = (K * m_{x_i}(X_i) * \prod_{X_j \not\supseteq X_i,\ X_j \in T} \hat{m}_{x_j}(\theta))$ induced by

he potential confirming belief of X_j. Thus it is calculated by:

Equation 1: $X_j \not\supseteq X_i$

(all nodes without father nodes and the node itself have potential confirming belief)

$$I_{WFC} = |\, m_T(X_i) - (K * m_{x_i}(X_i) * \prod_{\substack{X_j \not\supseteq X_i \\ X_j \in T}} \hat{m}_{x_j}(\theta)) \,|$$

The four other equations are analogously derived.

Equation 2: $X_j \cap X_i = \emptyset$, $X_j \cup X_i$ is in T (binary siblings which have potential nonconfirming belief)

$$I_{SIN} = |\, m_T(X_i) - (K * [m_T(X_i) + m_T(X_i \cup X_j) * \hat{m}_{x_j}{}^c(X_j{}^c)]) \,|$$

Equation 3: $X_j \supseteq X_i$ (the node itself or the father nodes have potential nonconfirming belief)

$$I_{IFN} = |\, m_T(X_i) - (K * m_T(X_i) * \hat{m}_{x_j}{}^c(\theta)) \,|$$

Equation 4: $X_j \subset X_i$, $X_j \cap X_i{}^c \in T$ (X_i is in a binary sibling situation and also the son nodes X_j, which have potential non- confirming belief)

$$I_{SN} = |\, m_T(X_i) - (K * m_T(X_i) * \hat{m}_{x_j}{}^c(\theta)) \,|$$

Equation 5: $X_j = X_i$ (the node itself has still potential confirming belief)

$$I_{NC} = |\, m_T(X_i) - (K * \hat{m}_{x_i}(X_i) * \prod_{\substack{X_k \not\supseteq X_i \\ X_k \in T}} m_{x_k}(\theta)) \,|$$

The suggested information increment, measures the potential change of the knowledge state which can be caused by new, incoming data.

This use of the concept of information is basically comparable to similar recent approaches (Klir 1987, Smets 1983).

4. The application to a multi-hierarchical knowledge base

For a single hierarchy the information increment strategy described above, results in many different adaptive behaviours.Thus e.g. depending on the actual data situation, the control strategy is organizing itself as a parallel search where around the centers of evidence the node that promises the largest information gain is choosen. Another extreme behaviour arises if all data are strictly lying on one single path, in which case the well known top-down partitioning behaviour can be observed.

Given a knowledge base including a number of distinct hierarchies and some preliminary evidence, the information increment strategy calculates in parallel the belief distribution for every hierarchy separately. In the next step, the strategy computes the information gains for each level separately. The hypothesis set with the maximal information gain with respect to all levels determines the next consultation step. The unknown or uncollected data of this node will be collected and, depending on their coincidence, the belief situation is recalculated at all levels in the knowledge base. The control strategy thus applied to the multi-hierarchy structure is an extension of the previous one with one hierarchy. Depending on the actual consultation, the control strategy might operate at one level for the whole reasoning process. This appears whenever the structure of the problem-solving task, e.g. the structure of the disease and the available symptoms, fits optimally into the format of this hierarchical structure. In the extreme opposite case, the information-increment strategy shifts from one hierarchy in the knowledge base to another. New data collected by the largest information increment at one hierarchy allow the strategy to switch to another hierarchy. Cognitively speaking, these switches can be considered as the restructuring of the problem-solving task.

5. Discussion

A knowledge representation scheme enabling the parallel representation of various knowledge relationships has been developed. This type of representation can be regarded as a first step towards the development of knowledge base structures which can exhaustively cover the variety of structural relationships found in knowledge of human experts. In contrast to other approaches the clear separation of the knowledge structures ensures easy consistency checks and knowledge acquisition.

For the restriction to distinct hierarchies, a formally based control strategy was developed which is adaptive with respect to the actual data available. For this control strategy, based on the concept of information, no predetermined direction in the form of a "leading hypothesis" is given. Thus dead-end behaviour arising from the successive hypotheses-driven strategies can be avoided. Depending on the structure of the problem-solving task, the strategy operates by choosing one hierarchy for a longer consultation time or by switching between competing hierarchies, thereby implicitly restructuring the problem-solving task. The calculation of evidence, which is an important basis for the strategy, is provided by an approximation of Shafer´s belief theory and Dempster´s combination rule. This theory allows the use of subjective belief measures of experts and enables one to operate with uncertain knowledge in an adaquate way.

The application has thus far been restricted to knowledge structures in the form of distinct hierarchies in order to guarantee the consistent distribution of belief in the knowledge base. We have implemented this multi-level representation scheme, applying the information-increment strategy in the expert system IBIG which is running on a SUN-3 workstation. With a hypothetical knowledge base consisting of 8 different hierarchies, where each hierarchy represents ca. 300 nodes, the running time for evaluating the largest information gain is 29 seconds. For a "real" medical application the system has already been successfully tested in a small number of cases. Application to a medical area with a larger knowledge base then the one of acquired speech disorders is currently in progress.

Acknowledgements

I thank Christian Freksa and Till Roenneberg for theirs support.

References

L.C. Chang, T.J. Tou (1984). Mediks - a medical knowledge system, *IEEE Transactions on systems, man and cybernetics*, **SMC-14**.

J.A. Barnett (1981). Computational methods for a mathematical theory of evidence, *Proceedings Seventh Intern. Joint Conference on AI*, Vancover Bc, 868-875.

J. Gordon, H. Shortliffe (1985). A method for managing evidential reasoning in a hierarchical hypothesis space, *Artificial Intelligence* **26**.

G.Klir (1987). Where do we stand on measures of uncertainty, ambiguity, fuzziness, and the like, *Fuzzy Sets and Systems* **24**, North-Holland.

R.A. Miller (1984). Internist-1/Caduceus: problems facing expert consultation programs, *Math. Inform. Med.* **.23**.

K. Schill (1986). *Entwurf eines Expertensystems mit dynamischer Strategiewahl im Inferenzmechanismus*, Diplomarbeit, Technische Universität, München.

K. Schill (1990). *Medizinische Expertensysteme, Methoden und Techniken*, R.Oldenbourg Verlag, München.

G. Shafer (1976). *A mathematical theory of evidence*, Princeton University Press, Princton, NJ.

G. Shafer, R. Logan (1987). Implementing Dempsters rule for hierarchical evidence, *Artificial Intelligence* **33**.

E.H. Shortliffe (1976). *Computer based medical consultations: MYCIN* , Elsevier, New York.

Ph. Smets (1983). Information content of an evidence, *Int. J. Man Machine Stuudies* **19**,1983.

Ph. Smets (1988). Belief functions, in Smets, Mamdani, Dubois, Prade (ed.), *Non standard logics for automated reasoning*, Academic Press, 253-286.

Ph. Smets (1989). The combination of evidence in the transferable belief model, *Technical Report No. TR/IRIDIA/89-3*, Universite Libre de Bruxelles.

S. Weiss and C.A. Kulikowski (1979). Expert: a system for developing consultation models, *Proceedings Sixth International Conference on AI*, Tokyo.

A Graph-Based Inference Method for Conditional Independence

Ross D. Shachter
Department of Engineering-Economic Systems
Stanford University
Stanford, CA 94305-4025
shachter@sumex-aim.stanford.edu

Abstract

The graphoid axioms for conditional independence, originally described by Dawid [1979], are fundamental to probabilistic reasoning [Pearl, 1988]. Such axioms provide a mechanism for manipulating conditional independence assertions without resorting to their numerical definition. This paper explores a representation for independence statements using multiple undirected graphs and some simple graphical transformations. The independence statements derivable in this system are equivalent to those obtainable by the graphoid axioms. Therefore, this is a purely graphical proof technique for conditional independence.

1. INTRODUCTION

The graphoid Axioms for conditional independence were originally proposed as the fundamental theme behind statistical inference[Dawid, 1979]. Since then, they have come to be accepted as a complete characterization and definition of conditional independence, applicable to many situations far beyond probabilistic models [Fagin, 1977; Geiger and Pearl, 1990b; Pearl, 1988; Pearl et al., 1990; Smith, 1989; Smith, 1990; Verma and Pearl, 1988].

This article explores a graphical way of representing independence statements using multiple undirected graphs first suggested in [Shachter, 1990]. Its main contribution is showing that repeatedly applying two graphical transformations, node deletion and graph combination, is equivalent to repeatedly applying the graphoid axioms. Consequently a purely graphical method of deriving new independence statements from a given set of such statements is obtained. The graphical operations have the advantage of an intuitive representation in undirected graphs, which makes the structure of independence assumed in a model explicit. They have the potential for making the abstract notion of conditional independence more accessible for teaching and knowledge acquisition. Nonetheless, although the technique is simple to use manually, its complexity is exponential, as are the derivation steps using the graphoid axioms.

The key to these graphical operations is the multiple undirected graph framework developed by Paz[1987; 1988] and Geiger[1987]. Many people have looked at undirected graph representations for the graphoid axioms, but they have always kept the intersection axiom, restricting the applicability to purely positive probability distributions and limiting the possible generalizations beyond probability [Pearl, 1988]. The key result underlying this paper is the development of a system which incorporates the contraction axiom but does not incorporate the intersection axiom.

Section 2 presents the notation and basic principles of the graphoid axioms while Section 3 defines the framework of Multiple Undirected Graphs and the graphical transformations on them. Section 4 proves the equivalence between the two axiom systems. Section 5 extends the graphical operations to some important special cases while Section 6 presents examples of theoretical properties, practical applications, and efficient computational structures which follow from the axioms.

2. NOTATION AND BASIC CONCEPTS

The notation and framework used throughout the paper is described in this section.

The primitive entities in a model are a finite set of **elements** U. In a probabilistic model, these correspond to random variables. A single element or set of elements will be denoted by a capital letter, such as X, Y, or Z. These elements are associated with nodes in an undirected graph. For Sections 3 and 4, it will be assumed that each node corresponds to a single element, but in Section 5 this will be generalized to allow multiple elements to be associated with a single node. For readability, a node will be referred to by the element(s) associated with it. For example, if element X is associated with a particular node, then that node will also be called X.

A **dependency model** over a finite set of elements U is a three place predicate I(X, Z, Y) where X, Z, and Y are disjoint subsets of U. The intended interpretation of I(X, Z, Y) is that X is conditionally independent of Y given Z. Alternatively, having observed Z, no additional information about X could be obtained by also observing Y. For example, in a probabilistic model, I(X, Z, Y) holds if and only if

$$P\{ X \mid Z, Y \} = P\{ X \mid Z \} \text{ whenever } P\{ Z \} > 0$$

for every value of the variables X, Y, and Z.

The realization of I need not necessarily be probabilistic [Fagin, 1977; Geiger and Pearl, 1990a; Geiger and Pearl, 1990b; Geiger et al., 1990; Pearl, 1988; Pearl et al., 1990; Smith, 1989; Smith, 1990; Verma and Pearl, 1988]. All of the those formulations satisfy the following **graphoid** axioms, first proposed by Dawid[1979]:

Symmetry: $I(X, Z, Y) \Leftrightarrow I(Y, Z, X)$;

Decomposition: $I(X, Z, Y \cup W) \Rightarrow I(X, Z, Y)$;

Weak Union: $I(X, Z, Y \cup W) \Rightarrow I(X, Z \cup Y, W)$;

Contraction: $I(X, Z \cup Y, W)$ and $I(X, Z, Y) \Rightarrow I(X, Z, Y \cup W)$.

The essence of these axioms is that learning an irrelevant proposition does not change the status of other facts; every proposition that was irrelevant remains irrelevant and every proposition that was relevant remains relevant. These axioms are not complete for probabilistic independence [Geiger and Pearl, 1990a], but are nevertheless powerful enough to derive useful consequences that generalize from probabilistic independence. We shall next used sets of undirected graphs for deriving such consequences.

3. MULTIPLE UNDIRECTED GRAPHS

The representation of independence by Multiple Undirected Graphs was studied by Paz[1987; 1988] and Geiger[1987]. We will see below how it can be used as a visual technique for deriving new independence statements from a given list of such statements.

Conditional independence is represented in an undirected graph by graph separation: given three disjoint sets of elements from U, X, Y, and Z, Z **separates** X from Y if every path between X and Y contains an element from Z. For example, Z separates X from Y in the graph shown in Figure 1a representing I(X, Z, Y), but there is no independence represented in the graph shown in Figure 1b.

In this section and the following section, it is assumed that each node corresponds to exactly one element. In section 5 this will be generalized to allow multiple elements in a node, and the graph separation rule will apply even when the sets X, Y, and Z are not disjoint.

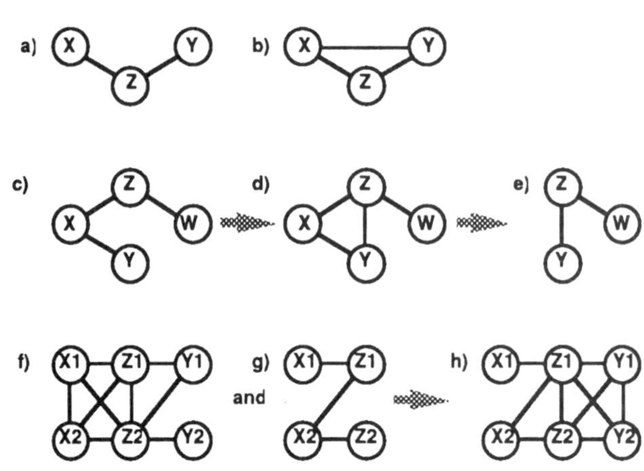

Figure 1: MUGs and Their Basic Operations

A **multiple undirected graph (MUG)** M over U is a dependency model consisting of a set of undirected graphs containing elements from U. An independence statement I(X, Z, Y) holds in M if and only if there exists a graph in M containing $X \cup Y \cup Z$ in which Z separates X from Y. Alternatively, I(X, Z, Y) is said to be **satisfied** by M, or M **satisfies** it. Suppose for example that the graphs shown in Figures 1a and 1b constitute a MUG. Then I(X, Z, Y) even though there is no independence represented in the second graph.

Two dependency models are **equivalent** if they represent the same list of independence statements. The following transformations add undirected graphs to a given MUG, producing a new MUG that is equivalent to the original one. Given any graph G in a MUG, then the MUG obtained by duplicating G and adding any arcs is said to be derived by **arc addition**. Given any graph G in a MUG M, then the MUG obtained from M by duplicating G and deleting any node after adding arcs between all of the nodes which had been adjacent to it is said to be derived by **node deletion**.

Both arc addition and node deletion follow directly from graph separation, since any separation present in the new graph must also have been present in the original graph. In the example graph drawn in Figure 1c an arc is added between Z and Y to obtain the graph shown in Figure 1d. Node X can be deleted from the graph shown in Figure 1c to create the graph shown in 1e, but only after an arc is added between Z and Y, the nodes adjacent to X, to obtain the graph shown in Figure 1d. Although X separates Y from Z ∪ W, that separation can no longer be represented once X is deleted. Instead the fact that there is a path from Z to Y through X requires that X and Y be connected in the new graph. This leads to the following result.

Theorem 1. Let M be a MUG. Then a MUG derived from M by node deletion or arc addition is equivalent to M.

Next we define a new transformation which does not produce an equivalent MUG because it adds independence statements not represented in the original MUG. Let M be a MUG over U, and X, Y, and Z be disjoint subsets of U. If M satisfies I(X, Z, Y) and there is a graph G in M for which X ∪ Z is the set of all of the nodes, then the MUG obtained from M by duplicating G, adding to the new graph nodes for each element in Y, and connecting every pair of nodes in Y ∪ Z with an arc is said to be derived by **graph combination.**

Graph combination synthesizes a new graph from two others. Consider the graph drawn in Figure 1f in which (Z1 ∪ Z2) separates (X1 ∪ X2) from (Y1 ∪ Y2), while the graph drawn in Figure 1g contains only the elements (X1 ∪ X2) ∪ (Z1 ∪ Z2). Using graph combination, a new graph is formed as shown in Figure 1h. In the process, arcs are added between all of the nodes in (Y1 ∪ Y2) ∪ (Z1 ∪ Z2). Note that Z1 separates X1 from (Y1 ∪ Y2) which could not be determined from either of the original graphs.

4. GRAPHICAL REPRESENTATION OF THE GRAPHOID AXIOMS

The thrust of this paper is to show that graph combination and node deletion add all and only those independence statements derivable by the graphoid axioms. Consequently, these transformations provide a graph-based technique for proving all independence statements implied by the graphoid axioms (and none other) from a given input set of independence statements. The input for our proof technique can be specified either by a list of undirected graphs, or a list of independence statements, or a combination thereof. This proof technique is quite useful because the graphoid axioms are strong enough to prove powerful results [Verma and Pearl, 1988].

Theorem 2. Let M be a MUG and let *I* be the set of independence statements satisfied by M. An independence statement I is derivable by the graphoid axioms from *I* if and only if there exists a sequence of node deletions and graph combinations on M that produces a MUG in which I is satisfied.

Proof:

Let I be a statement derived from *I* using the graphoid axioms. Let $\sigma_1 \ldots \sigma_k$ be a derivation chain of I. That is, σ_k equals I and each σ_i is either an independence statement in *I* or it has been derived by the graphoid axioms from $\sigma_1 \ldots \sigma_{i-1}$. Next, we construct a sequence of graphical transformations that would end with a MUG that satisfies I. The proof is done by induction on k.

When k is one, then since σ_1 is in *I*, there exists a graph in M where σ_1 is satisfied. Otherwise, σ_i is derived from previous statements by one of the graphoid axioms. Suppose σ_i is derived from some σ_j (i > jby symmetry. Consider the graph in which σ_j is satisfied. The same graph satisfies σ_i as well since if Z separates X from V it must also separate V from X.

Otherwise, σ_i must have been derived from previous statements using decomposition, weak union, or contraction. To verify that the same statement could be obtained graphically, consider the graphs drawn in Figure 2, representing the graphoid axioms. If the previous statement is I(X, Z, Y ∪ W), as shown in the graph drawn in Figure 2c, then weak union and decomposition , shown in the graphs drawn in Figure 2a and 2b, respectively, are recognized graphically since Z separates X from Y, and Z ∪ Y separates X from W. If the previous statements are I(X, Z ∪ Y, W) and I(X, Z, Y) then a result equivalent to the contraction axiom can be obtained using graph combination. Because I(X, Z ∪ Y, W) and there is a graph containing only X ∪ (Z ∪ Y), that graph can be duplicated, adding to it nodes for W and connecting every pair of nodes in W ∪ (Z ∪ Y) to obtain the graph shown in Figure 2c in which Z separates X from Y ∪ W.

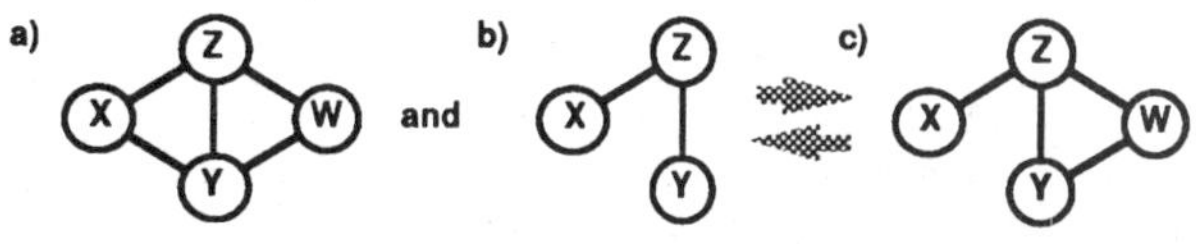

Figure 2: The Graphoid Axioms

Now suppose $M_1 \ldots M_k$ is a sequence of MUGs, M_k satisfies I, and every M_i is obtained from the previous ones by either node deletion or graph combination. It must be shown that I can be derived by the graphoid axioms from the independence statements encoded in M_1, i.e., from *I*. The proof is done by induction on k. The basis k=1 holds since I is satisfied by the given MUG.

Suppose M_i is derived from M_j by node deletion performed on graph G. Let G' be the added graph with a deleted node. Since any statement I represented by G' must also hold in G, it need not be derived.

Similarly, in the case of graph combination, it can be shown that every statement added is derivable using the graphoid axioms. Q. E. D.

5. EXTENSIONS TO THE GRAPHICAL OPERATIONS

In this section, the Graphical Axioms are generalized by relaxing the assumptions, made in Section 3, that each node is associated with a single element, and that independence relations are defined only on disjoint sets. These extensions require no changes to the graphical operations, but they greatly increase their power.

First, it is necessary to generalize the graphoid axioms to define independence relations even when the three sets of elements are not disjoint. This is accomplished through an additional axiom [Pearl, 1988]:

Overlap: $I(X, Z, Y) \Leftrightarrow I(XZ, Z, YZ)$.

Thus I(X, Z, Y) is possible when X, Y, and Z are not disjoint if $X \cap Y \subseteq Z$. No modifications to the graphical operations are required, since Z separates X from Y if every path between X and Y contains an element of Z. This condition can be satisfied when some of the elements of X and Y are also elements of Z. For example, consider the graph shown in Figure 3a). Since Z separates X from Y it follows that I(X, Z, Y), but also $I(X \cup Z, Z, Y \cup Z)$, $I(X \cup Z, Z, Y)$ and $I(X, Z, Y \cup Z)$. It is not usually possible, however, to separate two overlapping sets of elements unless their intersection is included in the separating set.

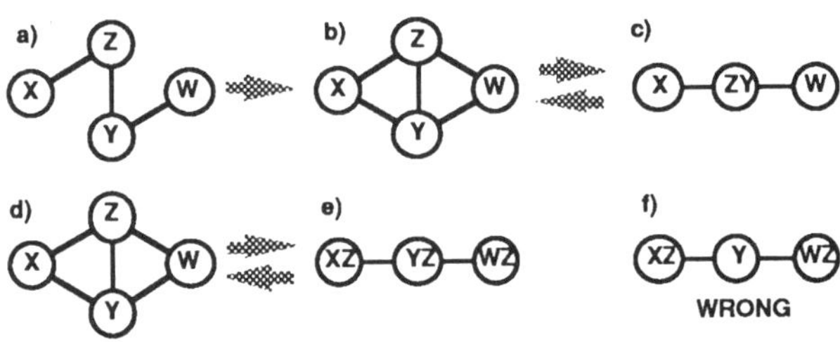

Figure 3: Properties with Multiple Elements in a Node

Now that the definition of independence has been extended, it is possible to have multiple elements be assigned to the same node and also to have the same element assigned to multiple nodes. This leads to two additional graphical transformations. Given any graph G in a MUG M, then the MUG obtained from M by duplicating G and replacing two nodes Z1 and Z2 with one node Z containing the union of the elements associated with Z1 and Z2 is said to be derived by **node merging**. In the new graph, arcs must be drawn between node Z and any node which had been adjacent to node Z1 or node Z2. Given any graph G in a MUG M, then the MUG obtained from M by duplicating G and replacing one node Z with two nodes Z1 and Z2 which together contain all of the elements associated with Z is said to be derived by **node splitting**. In the new graph, arcs must be drawn between nodes Z1 and Z2, and between them and any node which had been adjacent to node Z.

The node merging and node splitting properties follow directly from the extended notion of graph separation, in that any separation present after the change must have been present beforehand. In the case of node merging, separation by the new node is equivalent to separation by both old nodes, while after node splitting, separation by both new nodes is equivalent to separation by the old one. In either case, any path present beforehand will be maintained. Consider the example graphs shown in Figure 3. Arcs are added to the graph drawn in part a) to obtain the graph drawn in part b). The Z and Y nodes are then merged to obtain the graph drawn in part c). The transition from part a) to part c could, of course, be done as a single step. If the ZY node in the graph drawn in part c) is now split, it results in the graph drawn in part b). It would not be possible to infer the graph drawn in part a) from the graph drawn in part c), so conditional independence information is lost in the process of Node Merging. This leads to the following result.

Theorem 3. Let M be a MUG. Then a MUG derived from M by node splitting or node merging is equivalent to M.

An example of a graph with repeated elements is shown in the Figure 3e. Note that if the same element appears in two different nodes, then it should appear in every node on a path between them, since it can only be separated from itself by itself, and thus the graph shown in Figure 3f would usually be in error. A graph G with multiple elements in a node can always be transformed into another graph G' with single elements in a node. An arc should be drawn between two nodes in G' if and only if their elements were in the same or adjacent nodes in G.

6. EXAMPLES

The graphical operations are useful because they allow us to conceptualize abstract conditional independence and to derive easily results which arise from the graphoid Axioms. These sections describe some different types of results which can be derived using the graphical operations.

6.1 ADDITIONAL PROPERTIES

Pearl [Pearl, 1988] describes some additional properties related to conditional independence. The graphical operations allow us to derive easily those which apply and to recognize those which do not. These properties, in independence notation are:

$$\textbf{Mixing:}\ I(X \cup Y, Z, W) \text{ and } I(X, Z, Y) \Leftrightarrow I(X, Z, Y \cup W);$$

$$\textbf{Chaining:}\ I(X \cup Z, Y, W) \text{ and } I(X, Z, Y) \Leftrightarrow I(X, Z, W); \text{ and}$$

$$\textbf{Intersection:}\ I(X, Z \cup Y, W) \text{ and } I(X, Z \cup W, Y) \Leftarrow I(X, Z, Y \cup W).$$

We consider each in turn using the graphs drawn in Figure 4.

The Mixing Property assumptions are represented in the graphs drawn in parts a) and b). Using graph combination, the graph drawn in part c) can be constructed from the one in part b) by adding node W and an arc between Z and W. The resulting graph not only shows that Z separates X from Y ∪ W, but also the symmetry by which Z separates all of the elements from each other. It is simple to verify that the graphs shown in parts a) and b) can be obtained from the graph shown in part c) by either arc addition or node deletion. Mixing is a useful property since it together with symmetry and decomposition have been shown to completely characterize marginal independence [Geiger et al., 1991].

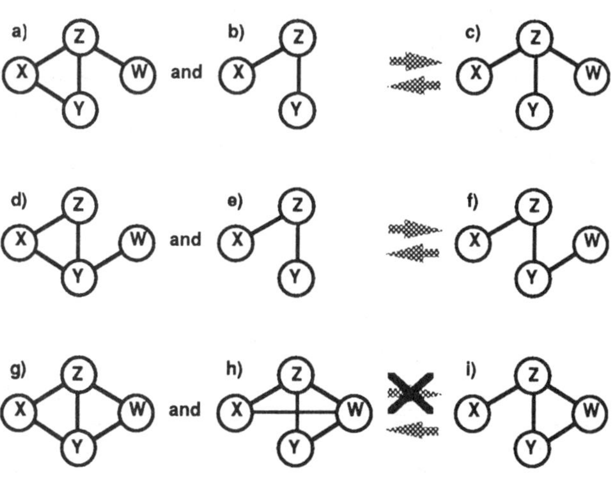

Figure 4: Additional Properties on MUGs

The Chaining Property conditions are represented in the graphs drawn in parts d) and e). Again graph combination allows the graph drawn in part f) to be constructed from the one in part e) by adding node W and an arc between Y and Z. Clearly Z separates X from W in the new valid graph, but it is also more apparent why this is called "chaining." It is again simple to obtain the graphs shown in parts d) and e) from the graph shown in part f) by arc addition and node deletion.

Finally, the conditions for the Intersection Property are satisfied by the graphs drawn in parts g) and h). However, graph combination can not be applied directly, since both graphs are on the same elements, X ∪ Y ∪ Z ∪ W. If any nodes are deleted from either of the graphs, there is no conditional independence remaining, and it is not possible to obtain the graph shown in part i). This is as it should be, because the Intersection Property is not true in general, but rather requires further assumptions. (In the case of probabilistic models, for example, all of the joint probabilities must be strictly positive.) The graph shown in part i) could be obtained if the conditions corresponded to the graphs shown in parts g) and e), rather than g) and h). On the other hand, the graphs shown in parts g) and h) can be obtained from the graph shown in part i) through arc addition.

6.2 DIRECTED GRAPHS, MORAL GRAPHS, AND JOIN TREES

In practice, probabilistic models are most easily assessed in the form of a directed graph, called an influence diagram or belief network [Howard and Matheson, 1984; Pearl, 1986b]. For most efficient computation these models can then be converted into undirected graphs, called **moral graphs** [Lauritzen and Spiegelhalter, 1988], and then into trees of overlapping sets of nodes, called **join** trees [Beeri et al., 1983; Jensen et al., 1990a; Jensen et al., 1990b]. In this section, it is assumed that the reader is familiar with these concepts, so that the focus will be on insights to be gained from the Graphical Axioms.

The directed graph can be thought of as a sequence of conditional independence statements: each element is conditionally independent of the elements listed before it, given its parents in the graph. In fact, the conditional independence does not apply to any particular sequence, but rather to any ordering consistent with the graph. This property is well known [Pearl, 1988; Smith, 1989], but it can also be proven directly through the Graphical Axioms [Shachter, 1990].

This sequence of conditional independence statements can be used to construct the moral graph through repeated application of the Combination Property. Each new element can be added in turn to the undirected graph under construction by adding its node and arcs between it and its parents and among its parents. (This is the marrying of the parents which gives "moral" graphs their name.) Thus the directed graph shown in Figure 5a) has the moral graph shown in part b) (ignoring the dashed (L, B) arc to be discussed below). Moralizing arcs (T, L) and (E, B) are added between the parents of E and D, respectively. Note that we really have a sequence of moral graphs, including the one shown in part c), revealing independence not shown in the full moral graph. This is why the MUG representation is needed in general.

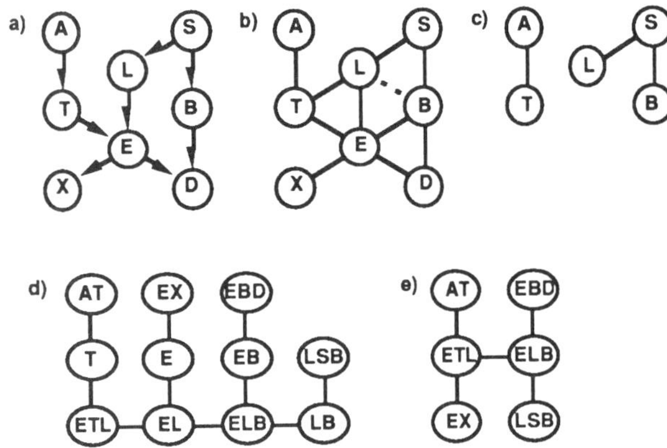

Figure 5: Directed Graph, Moral Graphs, and Join Trees

For efficient inference, it is ideal to have an undirected graph in the form of a tree [Jensen et al., 1990a; Jensen et al., 1990b; Lauritzen and Spiegelhalter, 1988; Pearl, 1988]. In general this cannot be accomplished with nodes corresponding to single elements, but instead requires nodes with sets of elements and some elements assigned to multiple nodes. Such trees are shown in parts d) and e). They are join trees, because whenever an element appears in two different nodes, it appears in every node on the path between them. Recall that this is just the necessary property for assignment of elements to multiple nodes described in Section 5. Note that, given the independence represented in the directed graph, the join tree is a valid graph. To capture all of that independence, however, we need the graph in part d) rather than the one in part e). Notice that through the insertion of *separation sets*, containing the intersection of neighboring node sets, we create a graph in which the only arcs needed for a single element graph such as the one in part b) are between elements in the same node in part d). When we create the graph in part b) in this manner, it has become a *chordal graph* with the addition of the dashed arc (L, B) [Beeri et al., 1983].

6.3 DETERMINISTIC ELEMENTS AND SEPARATION

The independence properties in the directed graph have been extensively studied [Geiger et al., 1989; Geiger et al., 1990; Pearl, 1986a; Pearl, 1988; Shachter, 1988; Shachter, 1990; Verma and Pearl, 1988], but recent work has shown how they can be recognized in the undirected graph [Lauritzen et al., 1990]. Unfortunately, one type of independence appears difficult to represent in the undirected graph: elements which are deterministically related to other elements. Nonetheless the results of Lauritzen et al[1990] can be extended in the undirected graph to recognize independence in models with deterministic elements.

An element in a directed graph is said to be deterministic and drawn with a double oval if it is conditionally independent of all elements, including itself, given its parents. In a probabilistic model, such an element can be described as a deterministic function of its parents. For example, in the diagram shown in Figure 6a), the element B is a deterministic function of A. When an element is deterministic, an operation called deterministic propagation [Shachter, 1988; Shachter, 1990] can be applied to the graph: the children of the deterministic node have their arc from the deterministic node replaced by arcs from its parents. For example, after deterministic propagation, the graph drawn in part a) is transformed into the graph drawn in part b). Such an operation can be interpreted in probabilistic models as substitution of the deterministic function into the children's distributions, but it can also be derived in general using the graphical operations [Shachter, 1990]. In the case of the example, we can justify deterministic propagation by considering the moral graphs for the graphs in parts a) and b) shown in parts c) and d), respectively. To obtain the moral graph shown in part d) from the one shown in part c), first delete the node B, and then use the Combination Property, recognizing that because node B is deterministic, I(B, A, C $\cup$ D).

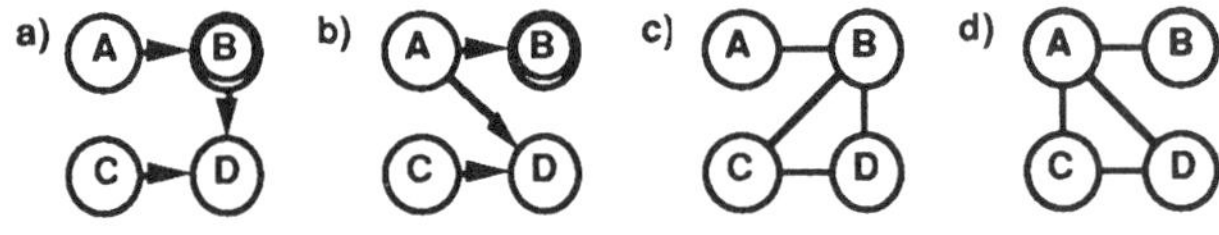

Figure 6: Managing Deterministic Elements

Using the property of deterministic propagation, the independence test of Lauritzen et al[1990] can be generalized to problems with deterministic nodes, to test for what is called D-separation [Geiger et al., 1990; Shachter, 1988; Shachter, 1990]. The procedure to test whether I(X, Z, Y) is satisfied in a directed graph, possibly containing deterministic nodes, is as follows:

1. Discard elements in the directed graph which are not in X $\cup$ Y $\cup$ Z or one of their ancestors in the directed graph.

2. Visiting each element in graph order, perform deterministic propagation on any deterministic element which is not in Z.

3. Form the moral graph of the resulting directed graph.

4. Determine whether Z separates X from Y in the moral graph.

This procedure is applied to some examples as shown in Figure 7. First consider the directed graph shown in part a). There are no deterministic elements and the corresponding moral graph is shown in part b). Clearly I(W, Z, X ∪ Y ∪ V). The entire moral graph is needed to test the independence of element V from other elements, and Z does not separate X from Y ∪ V. However, to just check whether I(X, Z, Y), the element V is discarded from the graph shown in part a) and the moral graph is now the one shown in part c). In fact, in this case, I(X, Z, Y). Another example is the directed graph shown in part d). Its moral graph is shown in part e) and clearly it does not satisfy I(X, Z, Y). If Z were not observed the we would obtain the moral graph shown in part f), so I(X, Ø, Y) is true.

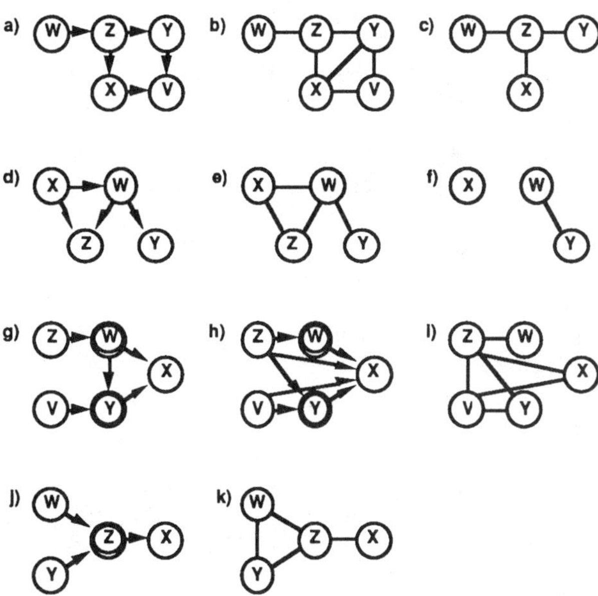

Figure 7: Examples of D-Separation

The next two examples involve deterministic elements. In the directed graph shown in part g), there are two deterministic elements, neither of which is an element in Z. Deterministic propagation results in the directed graph shown in part h), in which arc (W, Y) has been replaced by (Z, Y), (W, X) has been replaced by (Z, X), and (Y, X) has been replaced by (V, X) and (Z, X). The moral graph corresponding to this directed graph is shown in part i). Note that while Z separates W from X ∪ Y ∪ V, Z does not separate X from Y. This is due to the uncertainty introduced into element Y from element V. Finally, although there is a deterministic element in the directed graph shown in part j), deterministic propagation should not be performed because the element is contained in Z. In the corresponding moral graph shown in part k), Z separates X from Y ∪ W. If deterministic propagation had been performed, this independence would not have been recognized.

7. CONCLUSIONS

In this paper, system of graphical transformations on Multiple Undirected Graphs are defined and shown to be equivalent to the graphoid axioms. These axioms have become accepted as the fundamental properties of conditional independence generalized from probabilistic models. These graphical operations are illustrated with examples related to theoretical properties, practical applications, and efficient computations. This representation facilitates the communication and development of intuition for the abstract definition of conditional independence. Although stress has been placed in this paper on the relative benefits of the new approach, its equivalence to the graphoid axioms is especially powerful in that it allows one to use whichever system is convenient for the problem at hand. Unfortunately, the complexity of both methods is exponential.

The essence of this paper is that graph based techniques can help us to reason about independence relations. Pearl and others have shown a dual aspect by which independence helps us to characterize graphical representations. Both views are useful for exploring the connections between separation in graphs and independence in probability.

Acknowledgements

This paper benefitted greatly from the comments of Azaria Paz, Judea Pearl, and an anonymous referee, but it is dedicated to Danny Geiger, without whom it would not exist. He not only encouraged me to pursue this research question in the first place, but he was also most generous with his suggestions and patient tutoring.

References

Beeri, C., Fagin, R., Maier, D., and Yannakakis, M. (1983). On the Desirability of Acyclic Database Schemes. Journal of the Association for Computing Machinery, 30(3), 479-513.

Dawid, A. P. (1979). Conditional Independence in Statistical Theory. Journal Royal Statistical Society, Series B, 41(1), 1-33.

Fagin, R. (1977). Multivalued Dependencies and a New Form for Relational Databases. ACM Transactions on Database Systems, 2(3), 262-278.

Geiger, D. (1987). Towards the Formalization of Informational Dependencies (R-102). Computer Science Department, UCLA.

Geiger, D., Paz, A., and Pearl, J. (1991). Axioms and Algorithms for Inferences Involving Probabilistic Inference. Information and Computation, 91(1), 128-141.

Geiger, D. and Pearl, J. (1990a). Logical and Algorithmic Properties of Independence and Their Application to Bayesian Networks. Annals of Mathematics and Artificial Intelligence, 2, 165-178.

Geiger, D. and Pearl, J. (1990b). On the logic of causal models. In R. D. Shachter, T. S. Levitt, J. F. Lemmer, and L. N. Kanal (Ed.), Uncertainty in Artificial Intelligence 4 (pp. 136-147). Amsterdam: North-Holland.

Geiger, D., Verma, T., and Pearl, J. (1989). d-separation: from theorems to algorithms. Fifth Workshop on Uncertainty in Artificial Intelligence, University of Windsor, Ontario, 118-125.

Geiger, D., Verma, T., and Pearl., J. (1990). Identifying independence in Bayesian networks. Networks, 20, 507-534.

Howard, R. A. and Matheson, J. E. (1984). Influence Diagrams. In R. A. Howard and J. E. Matheson (Ed.), The Principles and Applications of Decision Analysis Menlo Park, CA: Strategic Decisions Group.

Jensen, F. V., Lauritzen, S. L., and Olesen, K. G. (1990a). Bayesian Updating in Causal Probabilistic Networks by Local Computations. Computational Statistics Quarterly, 269-282.

Jensen, F. V., Olesen, K. G., and Andersen, S. K. (1990b). An algebra of Bayesian belief universes for knowledge based systems. Networks, 20, 637-659.

Lauritzen, S. L., Dawid, A. P., Larsen, B. N., and Leimer, H.-G. (1990). Independence properties of directed markov fields. Networks, 20, 491-505.

Lauritzen, S. L. and Spiegelhalter, D. J. (1988). Local computations with probabilities on graphical structures and their application to expert systems. J. Royal Statist. Soc. B, 50(2), 157-224.

Paz, A. (1987). A Full Characterization of Pseudographoids in Terms of Families of Undirected Graphs (R-95). Computer Science Department, UCLA.

Paz, A. and Schulhoff, R. (1988). Closure Algorithms and Decision Problems for Graphoids Generated by Two Undirected Graphs – Abridged Version (R-118). Computer Science Department, UCLA.

Pearl, J. (1986a). A constraint-propagation approach to probabilistic reasoning. In L. N. Kanal and J. F. Lemmer (Ed.), Uncertainty in Artificial Intelligence (pp. 371-382). Amsterdam: North-Holland.

Pearl, J. (1986b). Fusion, propagation and structuring in belief networks. Artificial Intelligence, 29(3), 241-288.

Pearl, J. (1988). Probabilistic Reasoning in Intelligent Systems . San Mateo, CA: Morgan Kaufman.

Pearl, J., Geiger, D., and Verma, T. (1990). The Logic of Influence Diagrams. In R. M. Oliver and J. Q. Smith (Ed.), Influence Diagrams, Belief Nets, and Decision Analysis (pp. 67-87). Chichester: Wiley.

Shachter, R. D. (1988). Probabilistic Inference and Influence Diagrams. Operations Research, 36(July-August), 589-605.

Shachter, R. D. (1990). An Ordered Examination of Influence Diagrams. Networks, 20, 535-563.

Smith, J. Q. (1989). Influence Diagrams for Statistical Modeling. Annals of Statistics, 17(2), 654-672.

Smith, J. Q. (1990). Statistical Principles on Graphs. In R. M. Oliver and J. Q. Smith (Ed.), Influence Diagrams, Belief Nets, and Decision Analysis (pp. 89-120). Chichester: Wiley.

Verma, T. and Pearl, J. (1988). Causal networks: semantics and expressiveness. Fourth Workshop on Uncertainty in Artificial Intelligence, University of Minnesota, Minneapolis, 352-359.

A Fusion Algorithm for Solving Bayesian Decision Problems

Prakash P. Shenoy
School of Business
University of Kansas
Lawrence, KS 66045-2003

Abstract

This paper proposes a new method for solving Bayesian decision problems. The method consists of representing a Bayesian decision problem as a valuation-based system and applying a fusion algorithm for solving it. The fusion algorithm is a hybrid of local computational methods for computation of marginals of joint probability distributions and the local computational methods for discrete optimization problems.

1 INTRODUCTION

The main goal of this paper is to describe a new method for solving Bayesian decision problems. The method consists of representing a Bayesian decision problem as a valuation-based system and applying a fusion algorithm for solving it.

Valuation-based systems are described in Shenoy [1989, 1991c]. In valuation-based system representations of decision problems, we encode utility functions and probability distributions by functions called valuations. We solve valuation-based systems using two operations called combination and marginalization. Solving can be described simply as marginalizing all variables out of the joint valuation. The joint valuation is the result of combining all valuations. The framework of valuation-based systems is powerful enough to include also probability theory [Shenoy, 1991c], Dempster-Shafer theory of belief functions [Shenoy, 1991c], Spohn's theory of epistemic beliefs [Shenoy, 1991a,c], possibility theory [Dubois and Prade, 1990], discrete optimization [Shenoy, 1991b], propositional logic [Shenoy, 1990a], and constraint satisfaction problems [Shenoy and Shafer, 1988].

The fusion algorithm for solving valuation-based representations of decision problems is a hybrid of local computational methods for computation of marginals of joint probability distributions and local computational methods for discrete optimization. Local computational methods for computation of marginals of joint probability distributions have been proposed by, e.g., Pearl [1988], Lauritzen and Spiegelhalter [1988], Shafer and Shenoy [1988], and Jensen et al. [1990]. Local computational methods for discrete optimization are also called non-serial dynamic programming [Bertele and Brioschi, 1972]. Viewed abstractly using the framework of valuation-based systems, these two local computational methods are actually similar. Shenoy and Shafer [1990] and Shenoy [1991b] show that the same three axioms justify the use of local computation in both these cases.

Our method for representing and solving decision problems has many similarities to influence diagram methodology [Howard and Matheson, 1984; Olmsted, 1983; Shachter, 1986; Ezawa, 1986; Tatman, 1986]. But there are also many differences both in representation and solution. A comparison of these two methods is given in [Shenoy, 1990b].

We describe our new method using a diabetes diagnosis problem. Section 2 gives a statement of this problem. Section 3 describes a valuation-based representation of a decision problem. Section 4 describes the method for solving valuation-based systems. Section 5 describes a fusion algorithm for solving valuation-based systems using local computation. Finally, section 6 summarizes the paper.

2 A DIABETES DIAGNOSIS PROBLEM

A medical intern is trying to decide on a policy for treating patients suspected of suffering from diabetes. The intern first observes whether a patient exhibits two symptoms of diabetes—blue toe and glucose in urine. After she observes the presence or absence of these symptoms, she then either prescribes a treatment for diabetes or doesn't.

Table 1 shows the intern's utility function. Also, for the population of patients served by the intern, the prior probability of diabetes is 10%. Furthermore, for patients known to suffer from diabetes, 1.4% exhibit blue toe, and 90% exhibit glucose in urine. On the other hand, for patients known not to suffer from diabetes, 0.6% exhibit

Table 1. The Intern's Utility Function

	Intern's utilities (π)	Act: treat for diabetes (t)	Act: not treat (~t)
State	has diabetes (d)	10	0
	no diabetes (~d)	5	10

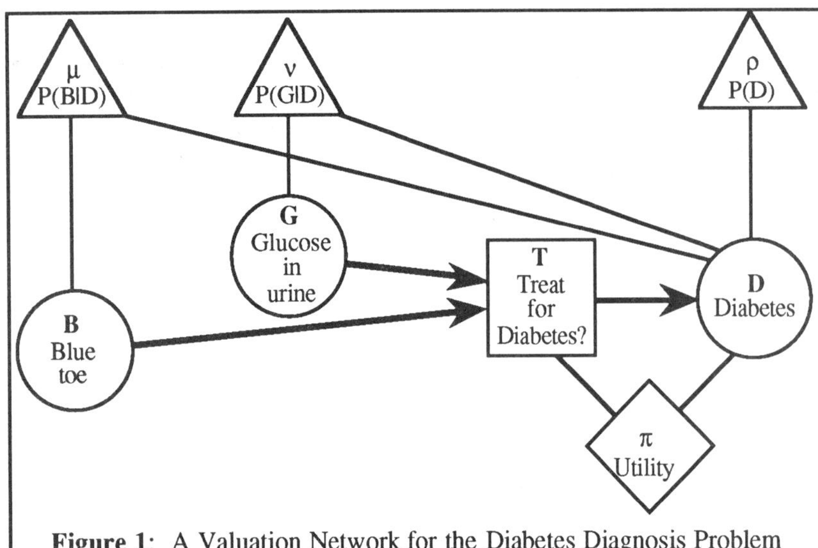

Figure 1: A Valuation Network for the Diabetes Diagnosis Problem

blue toe, and 1% exhibit glucose in urine. We assume that blue toe and glucose in urine are conditionally independent given diabetes.

3 VALUATION-BASED SYSTEM REPRESENTATION

In this section, we describe a valuation-based system (VBS) representation of a decision problem. A VBS representation consists of decision variables, random variables, frames, a utility valuation, potentials, and precedence constraints. A graphical depiction of a VBS is called a *valuation network*. Figure 1 shows a valuation network for the diabetes diagnosis problem.

Variables, Frames and Configurations. A decision node is represented as a variable. The possible values of a decision variable represent the acts available at that point. We use the symbol $\mathcal{W}_D$ for the set of possible values of decision variable D. We assume that the decision-maker has to pick one and only one of the elements of $\mathcal{W}_D$ as their decision. We call $\mathcal{W}_D$ the *frame for D*. Decision variables are represented in valuation networks by rectangular nodes.

In the diabetes diagnosis problem, there is one decision node T. The frame for T has two elements: Treat the patient for diabetes (t), and not treat (~t).

If R is a random variable, we use the symbol $\mathcal{W}_R$ to denote its possible values. We assume that one and only one of the elements of $\mathcal{W}_R$ can be the true value of R. We call $\mathcal{W}_R$ the *frame for R*. Random variables are represented in valuation networks by circular nodes.

In the diabetes diagnosis problem, there are three random variables: Blue toe (B), Glucose in urine (G), and Diabetes (D). Each variable has a frame consisting of two elements.

Let $\mathcal{X}_D$ denote the set of all decision variables, let $\mathcal{X}_R$ denote the set of all random variables, and let $\mathcal{X} = \mathcal{X}_D \cup \mathcal{X}_R$ denote the set of all variables. We will often deal with non-empty subsets of variables in $\mathcal{X}$. Given a non-empty subset h of $\mathcal{X}$, let $\mathcal{W}_h$ denote the Cartesian product of $\mathcal{W}_X$ for X in h, i.e., $\mathcal{W}_h = \times\{\mathcal{W}_X | X \in h\}$. We can think of the set $\mathcal{W}_h$ as the set of possible values of the joint variable h. Accordingly, we call $\mathcal{W}_h$ the *frame for h*. Also, we refer to elements of $\mathcal{W}_h$ as *configurations of h*. We use lower-case, bold-faced letters such as **x**, **y**, etc. to denote configurations. Also, if **x** is a configuration of g and **y** is a configuration of h and $g \cap h = \emptyset$, then (**x**,**y**) denotes a configuration of $g \cup h$.

It is convenient to extend this terminology to the case where the set of variables h is empty. We adopt the convention that the frame for the empty set $\emptyset$ consists of a single configuration, and we use the symbol ♦ to name that configuration; $\mathcal{W}_\emptyset = \{♦\}$. To be consistent with our notation above, we adopt the convention that if **x** is a configuration for g, then (**x**,♦) = **x**.

Valuations. Suppose $h \subseteq \mathcal{X}$. A *utility valuation π for h* is a function from $\mathcal{W}_h$ to $\mathbb{R}$, where $\mathbb{R}$ denotes the set of real numbers. The values of utility valuations are utilities. If $h = d \cup r$ where $d \subseteq \mathcal{X}_D$ and $r \subseteq \mathcal{X}_R$, $\mathbf{x} \in \mathcal{W}_d$, and $\mathbf{y} \in \mathcal{W}_r$, then π(**x**,**y**) denotes the utility to the decision maker if the decision maker chooses configuration **x** and the true configuration of r is **y**. If π is a utility valuation for h, and $X \in h$, then we say that *π bears on X*.

In a valuation network, a utility valuation is represented by a diamond-shaped node. To permit the identification of all valuations that bear on a variable, we draw undirected edges between the utility valuation node and all the variable nodes it bears on. In the diabetes diagnosis problem, there is one utility valuation π as shown in Figure 1. Table 1 shows the values of this utility valuation.

Suppose $h \subseteq \mathcal{X}$. A *potential ρ for h* is a function from $\mathcal{W}_h$ to the unit interval [0, 1]. The values of potentials are probabilities.

In a valuation network, a potential is represented by a triangular node. Again, to identify the variables related by a potential, we draw undirected edges between the potential node and all the variable nodes it bears on.

In the diabetes diagnosis problem, there are three poten-

Table 2: Potentials ρ, μ, and ν

D	ρ
d	.1
~d	.9

μ		B: b	B: ~b
D	d	.014	.986
D	~d	.006	.994

ν		G: b	G: ~b
D	d	.90	.10
D	~d	.01	.99

tials μ, ν, and ρ as shown in Figure 1. Table 2 shows the details of these potentials. Note that μ is a potential for {B, D}, ν is a potential for {G, D}, and ρ is a potential for {D}.

Table 3: Computation of $\mu \otimes \nu \otimes \rho$ and the Joint Valuation $\pi \otimes \mu \otimes \nu \otimes \rho$

$\mathcal{W}_{\{B,G,T,D\}}$	π	μ	ν	ρ	μ⊗ν⊗ρ	π⊗μ⊗ν⊗ρ
b g t d	10	.014	.90	.10	.00126	0.0126
b g t ~d	5	.006	.01	.90	.000054	0.00027
b g ~t d	0	.014	.90	.10	.00126	0
b g ~t ~d	10	.006	.01	.90	.000054	0.00054
b ~g t d	10	.014	.10	.10	.00014	0.0014
b ~g t ~d	5	.006	.99	.90	.005346	0.02673
b ~g ~t d	0	.014	.10	.10	.00014	0
b ~g ~t ~d	10	.006	.99	.90	.005346	0.05346
~b g t d	10	.986	.90	.10	.08874	0.8874
~b g t ~d	5	.994	.01	.90	.008946	0.04473
~b g ~t d	0	.986	.90	.10	.08874	0
~b g ~t ~d	10	.994	.01	.90	.008946	0.08646
~b ~g t d	10	.986	.10	.10	.00986	0.0986
~b ~g t ~d	5	.994	.99	.90	.885654	4.42827
~b ~g ~t d	0	.986	.10	.10	.00986	0
~b ~g ~t ~d	10	.994	.99	.90	.885654	8.86554

Precedence Constraints. Besides acts, states, probabilities and utilities, an important ingredient of problems in decision analysis is information constraints. Some decisions have to be made before the observation of some uncertain states, and some decisions can be postponed until after some states are observed. In the diabetes diagnosis problem, for example, the medical intern doesn't know whether the patient has diabetes or not. And the decision whether to treat the patient for diabetes or not may be postponed until after the observation of blue toe and glucose in urine.

If a decision-maker expects to be informed of the true value of random variable R before they make a decision D, then we represent this situation by the binary relation R→D (read as *R precedes D*). On the other hand, if a random variable R is only revealed after a decision D is made or perhaps never revealed, then we represent this situation by the binary relation D→R.

In the diabetes diagnosis problem, we have the precedence constraints B→T, G→T, T→D. The decision whether to treat the patient for diabetes or not (T) is only made after observing blue toe (B) and glucose in urine (G). And, diabetes (D) is not known at the time the decision whether to treat the patient for diabetes (T) has to be made.

Suppose > is a binary relation on $\mathcal{X}$ such that it is the transitive closure of →, i.e., X > Y if either X → Y, or there exists a Z∈ $\mathcal{X}$ such that X > Z and Z > Y. First, we assume that > is a partial order on $\mathcal{X}$ (otherwise the decision problem is ill-defined and not solvable). Second, we require that this partial order > is such that for any D∈ $\mathcal{X}_D$ and any R∈ $\mathcal{X}_R$, either D>R or R>D. We refer to this second condition as the *perfect recall condition*. The reason for the perfect recall condition is as follows. Given the meaning of the precedence relation →, for any decision variable D and any random variable R, either R is known when decision D has to be made, or not. This translates to either R>D or D>R. (This condition is called "no-forgetting assumption" in influence diagram literature.)

Next, we will define two operations called combination and marginalization. We use these operations to solve the valuation-based system representation. First we start with some notation.

Projection of Configurations. *Projection* of configurations simply means dropping extra coordinates; if (w,x,y,z) is a configuration of {W,X,Y,Z}, for example, then the projection of (w,x,y,z) to {W,X} is simply (w,x), which is a configuration of {W,X}.

If g and h are sets of variables, h⊆g, and **x** is a configuration of g, then we let $\mathbf{x}^{\downarrow h}$ denote the projection of **x** to h. The projection $\mathbf{x}^{\downarrow h}$ is always a configuration of h. If h=g and **x** is a configuration of g, then $\mathbf{x}^{\downarrow h} = \mathbf{x}$. If h=∅, then $\mathbf{x}^{\downarrow h} = \blacklozenge$.

Combination. The definition of combination depends on the type of valuations being combined.

Suppose h and g are subsets of $\mathcal{X}$, suppose ρ_i is a potential for h, and suppose ρ_j is a potential for g. Then the *combination of ρ_i and ρ_j*, denoted by $\rho_i \otimes \rho_j$, is a potential for h∪g obtained by pointwise multiplication of ρ_i and ρ_j, i.e., $(\rho_i \otimes \rho_j)(\mathbf{x}) = \rho_i(\mathbf{x}^{\downarrow h})\rho_j(\mathbf{x}^{\downarrow g})$ for all $\mathbf{x} \in \mathcal{W}_{h \cup g}$. See Table 3 for an example.

Suppose h and g are subsets of $\mathcal{X}$, suppose π_i is a utility valuation for h, and suppose ρ_j is a potential for g. Then the *combination of π_i and ρ_j*, denoted by $\pi_i \otimes \rho_j$, is a utility valuation for h∪g obtained by pointwise multiplication of π_i and ρ_j, i.e., $(\pi_i \otimes \rho_j)(\mathbf{x}) = \pi_i(\mathbf{x}^{\downarrow h})\rho_j(\mathbf{x}^{\downarrow g})$ for all $\mathbf{x} \in \mathcal{W}_{h \cup g}$. See Table 3 for an example.

Note that combination is commutative and associative. Thus, if $\{\alpha_1, ..., \alpha_k\}$ is a set of valuations, we write $\otimes\{\alpha_1, ..., \alpha_k\}$ to mean the combination of valuations in $\{\alpha_1, ..., \alpha_k\}$ in some sequence.

Marginalization. Suppose h is a subset of variables and suppose α is a valuation for h. Marginalization is an operation where we reduce valuation α to a valuation $\alpha^{\downarrow(h-\{X\})}$ for h–{X}. $\alpha^{\downarrow(h-\{X\})}$ is called the *marginal of* α *for h–{X}*. Unlike combination, the definition of marginalization does not depend on the nature of α. But the definition of marginalization does depend on whether X is a decision or a random variable.

Table 4: The Computation of $\tau^{\downarrow\{B,G,T\}}$, $\tau^{\downarrow\{B,G\}}$, Ψ_T, $\tau^{\downarrow\{B\}}$, and $\tau^{\downarrow\varnothing}(\blacklozenge)$

$\mathcal{W}_{\{B,G,T,D\}}$	τ	$\tau^{\downarrow\{B,G,T\}}$	$\tau^{\downarrow\{B,G\}}$	Ψ_T	$\tau^{\downarrow\{B\}}$	$\tau^{\downarrow\varnothing}(\blacklozenge)$
b g t d	0.0126	0.01287	0.01287	t	0.06633	9.864
b g t ~d	0.00027					
b g ~t d	0	0.00054				
b g ~t ~d	0.00054					
b ~g t d	0.0014	0.02813	0.05346	~t		
b ~g t ~d	0.02673					
b ~g ~t d	0	0.05346				
b ~g ~t ~d	0.05346					
~b g t d	0.8874	0.93213	0.93213	t	9.79767	
~b g t ~d	0.04473					
~b g ~t d	0	0.08646				
~b g ~t ~d	0.08646					
~b ~g t d	0.0986	4.52687	8.86554	~t		
~b ~g t ~d	4.42827					
~b ~g ~t d	0	8.86554				
~b ~g ~t ~d	8.86554					

(τ denotes the joint valuation $\pi\otimes\mu\otimes\nu\otimes\rho$)

If R is a random variable, $\alpha^{\downarrow(h-\{R\})}$ is obtained by summing α over the frame for R, i.e., $\alpha^{\downarrow(h-\{R\})}(\mathbf{c}) = \Sigma\{\alpha(\mathbf{c},\mathbf{r}) \mid \mathbf{r} \in \mathcal{W}_R\}$ for all $\mathbf{c} \in \mathcal{W}_{h-\{R\}}$. Here, α could be either a utility valuation or a potential. See Table 4 for an example.

If D is a decision variable, $\alpha^{\downarrow(h-\{D\})}$ is obtained by maximizing α over the frame for D, i.e., $\alpha^{\downarrow(h-\{D\})}(\mathbf{c}) = \text{MAX}\{\alpha(\mathbf{c},\mathbf{d}) \mid \mathbf{d} \in \mathcal{W}_D\}$ for all $\mathbf{c} \in \mathcal{W}_{h-\{D\}}$. Here, α must be a utility valuation. See Table 4 for an example.

We now state three lemmas regarding the marginalization operation. Lemma 3.1 states that in marginalizing two decision variables out of a valuation, the order in which the variables are eliminated does not affect the result. Lemma 3.2 states a similar result for marginalizing two random variables out of a valuation. Lemma 3.3 states that in marginalizing a decision variable and a random variable out of a valuation, the order in which the two variables are eliminated may make a difference.

Lemma 3.1. Suppose h is a subset of $\mathcal{X}$ containing decision variables D_1 and D_2, and suppose α is a utility valuation for h. Then $(\alpha^{\downarrow(h-\{D_1\})})^{\downarrow(h-\{D_1,D_2\})}(\mathbf{c}) = (\alpha^{\downarrow(h-\{D_2\})})^{\downarrow(h-\{D_1,D_2\})}(\mathbf{c})$ for all $\mathbf{c} \in \mathcal{W}_{h-\{D_1,D_2\}}$.

Lemma 3.2. Suppose h is a subset of $\mathcal{X}$ containing random variables R_1 and R_2, and suppose α is a valuation for h. Then $(\alpha^{\downarrow(h-\{R_1\})})^{\downarrow(h-\{R_1,R_2\})}(\mathbf{c}) = (\alpha^{\downarrow(h-\{R_2\})})^{\downarrow(h-\{R_1,R_2\})}(\mathbf{c})$ for all $\mathbf{c} \in \mathcal{W}_{h-\{R_1,R_2\}}$.

Lemma 3.3. Suppose h is a subset of $\mathcal{X}$ containing decision variable D and random variable R, and suppose α is a utility valuation for h. Then $(\alpha^{\downarrow(h-\{D\})})^{\downarrow(h-\{R,D\})}(\mathbf{c}) \geq (\alpha^{\downarrow(h-\{R\})})^{\downarrow(h-\{R,D\})}(\mathbf{c})$ for all $\mathbf{c} \in \mathcal{W}_{h-\{R,D\}}$.

It is clear from Lemma 3.3, that in marginalizing more than one variable, the order of elimination of the variables may make a difference. As we will see shortly, we need to marginalize all variables out of the joint valuation. What sequence should we use? This is where the precedence constraints come into play. We define marginalization such that variable Y is marginalized before X whenever X>Y. Here is a formal definition.

Suppose h and g are non-empty subsets of $\mathcal{X}$ such that g is a proper subset of h, suppose α is a valuation for h, and suppose > is a partial order on $\mathcal{X}$ satisfying the perfect recall condition. The *marginal of* α *for g with respect to the partial order* >, denoted by $\alpha^{\downarrow g}$, is a valuation for g defined as follows: $\alpha^{\downarrow g} =$

$$(((\alpha^{\downarrow(h-\{X_1\})})^{\downarrow(h-\{X_1,X_2\})})\ldots)^{\downarrow(h-\{X_1,X_2,\ldots,X_k\})} \quad (3.1)$$

where $h-g = \{X_1, \ldots, X_k\}$ and $X_1X_2\ldots X_k$ is a sequence of variables in h–g such that with respect to the partial order >, X_1 is a minimal element of h–g, X_2 is a minimal element of h–g–$\{X_1\}$, etc.

The marginalization sequence $X_1X_2\ldots X_k$ may not be

unique since > is only a partial order. But, since > satisfies the perfect recall condition, it is clear from Lemmas 3.1 and 3.2, that the definition of $\alpha^{\downarrow g}$ in (3.1) is well defined.

Strategy. The main objective in solving a decision problem is to compute an optimal strategy. What constitutes a strategy? Intuitively, a strategy is a choice of an act for each decision variable D as a function of configurations of random variables R such that R>D. Let Pr(D) = $\{R \in \mathcal{X}_R \mid R>D\}$. We refer to Pr(D) as the *predecessors of D*. Thus *a strategy* σ is a collection of functions $\{\xi_D\}_{D \in \mathcal{X}_D}$ where ξ_D: $\mathcal{W}_{Pr(D)} \rightarrow \mathcal{W}_D$.

Solution for a Variable. Computing an optimal strategy is a matter of bookkeeping. Each time we marginalize a decision variable out of a utility valuation using maximization, we store a table of optimal values of the decision variable where the maximums are achieved. We can think of this table as a function. We call this function "a solution" for the decision variable. Suppose h is a subset of variables such that decision variable $D \in h$, and suppose π is a utility valuation for h. A function Ψ_D: $\mathcal{W}_{h-\{D\}} \rightarrow \mathcal{W}_D$ is called a *solution for D* (with respect to π) if $\pi^{\downarrow(h-\{D\})}(\mathbf{c}) = \pi(\mathbf{c},\Psi(\mathbf{c}))$ for all $\mathbf{c} \in \mathcal{W}_{h-\{D\}}$. See Table 4 for an example.

4 SOLVING A VBS

Suppose $\Delta = \{\mathcal{X}_D, \mathcal{X}_R, \{\mathcal{W}_X\}_{X \in \mathcal{X}}, \{\pi_1\}, \{\rho_1, ..., \rho_n\}, \rightarrow\}$ is a VBS representation of a decision problem consisting of one utility valuation and n potentials. What do the potentials represent? And how do we solve Δ? We will answer these two related questions in terms of a canonical decision problem.

Canonical Decision Problem. A *canonical decision problem* Δ_C consists of a single decision variable D with a finite frame $\mathcal{W}_D$, a single random variable R with a finite frame $\mathcal{W}_R$, a single utility valuation π for {D,R}, a single potential ρ for {R, D} such that

$$\Sigma\{\rho(\mathbf{d},\mathbf{r}) \mid \mathbf{r} \in \mathcal{W}_R\} = 1 \text{ for all } \mathbf{d} \in \mathcal{W}_D, \quad (4.1)$$

and a precedence relation $\rightarrow$ defined by D$\rightarrow$R.

The meaning of the canonical decision problem is as follows. The elements of $\mathcal{W}_D$ are acts, and the elements of $\mathcal{W}_R$ are states of nature. The potential ρ is a family of probability distributions for R, one for each act $\mathbf{d} \in \mathcal{W}_D$, i.e., $\Sigma\{\rho(\mathbf{d},\mathbf{r}) \mid \mathbf{r} \in \mathcal{W}_R\} = 1$ for all $\mathbf{d} \in \mathcal{W}_D$.

The utility valuation π is a utility function—if the decision maker chooses act **d**, and the state of nature **r** prevails, then the utility to the decision maker is $\pi(\mathbf{d},\mathbf{r})$. The precedence relation $\rightarrow$ states that the true state of nature is revealed to the decision maker only after the decision maker has chosen an act.

Solving a canonical decision problem using the criterion of maximizing expected utility is easy. The expected utility associated with act **d** is $\Sigma\{(\pi\otimes\rho)(\mathbf{d},\mathbf{r}) \mid \mathbf{r} \in \mathcal{W}_R\} = (\pi\otimes\rho)^{\downarrow\{D\}}(\mathbf{d})$. The maximum expected utility (associated with an optimal act, say $\mathbf{d}^*$) is $\text{MAX}\{(\pi\otimes\rho)^{\downarrow\{D\}}(\mathbf{d}) \mid \mathbf{d} \in \mathcal{W}_D\} = ((\pi\otimes\rho)^{\downarrow\{D\}})^{\downarrow\varnothing}(\blacklozenge) = (\pi\otimes\rho)^{\downarrow\varnothing}(\blacklozenge)$. Finally, act $\mathbf{d}^*$ is optimal if and only if $(\pi\otimes\rho)^{\downarrow\{D\}}(\mathbf{d}^*) = (\pi\otimes\rho)^{\downarrow\varnothing}(\blacklozenge)$.

Consider the decision problem $\Delta = \{\mathcal{X}_D, \mathcal{X}_R, \{\mathcal{W}_X\}_{X \in \mathcal{X}}, \{\pi_1\}, \{\rho_1, ..., \rho_n\}, \rightarrow\}$. We will explain the meaning of Δ by reducing it to an equivalent canonical decision problem $\Delta_C = \{\{D\}, \{R\}, \{\mathcal{W}_D, \mathcal{W}_R\}, \{\pi\}, \{\rho\}, \rightarrow\}$. To define Δ_C, we need to define $\mathcal{W}_D$, $\mathcal{W}_R$, π, and ρ. Define $\mathcal{W}_D$ such that for each distinct strategy σ of Δ, there is a corresponding act $\mathbf{d}_\sigma$ in $\mathcal{W}_D$. Define $\mathcal{W}_R$ such that for each distinct configuration **y** of $\mathcal{X}_R$ in Δ, there is a corresponding configuration $\mathbf{r}_\mathbf{y}$ in $\mathcal{W}_R$.

Before we define utility valuation π for {D,R}, we need some notation. Suppose $\sigma = \{\xi_D\}_{D \in \mathcal{X}_D}$ is a strategy, and suppose **y** is a configuration of $\mathcal{X}_R$. Then together σ and **y** determine a unique configuration of $\mathcal{X}_D$. Let $\mathbf{a}_{\sigma,\mathbf{y}}$ denote this unique configuration of $\mathcal{X}_D$. By definition, $\mathbf{a}_{\sigma,\mathbf{y}}^{\downarrow\{D\}} = \xi_D(\mathbf{y}^{\downarrow Pr(D)})$ for all $D \in \mathcal{X}_D$. Consider the utility valuation π_1 in Δ. Assume that the domain of this valuation includes all of $\mathcal{X}_D$. Typically the domain of this valuation will include also some (or all) random variables. Let p denote the subset of random variables included in the domain of the joint utility valuation, i.e., $p \subseteq \mathcal{X}_R$ such that π_1 is a utility valuation for $\mathcal{X}_D \cup p$. Define utility valuation π for {D,R} such that $\pi(\mathbf{d}_\sigma,\mathbf{r}_\mathbf{y}) = \pi_1(\mathbf{a}_{\sigma,\mathbf{y}},\mathbf{y}^{\downarrow p})$, for all strategy σ of Δ, and all configuration $\mathbf{y} \in \mathcal{W}_{\mathcal{X}_R}$. Remember that $\mathbf{a}_{\sigma,\mathbf{y}}$ is the unique configuration of $\mathcal{X}_D$ determined by σ and **y**.

Consider the joint potential $\rho_1\otimes...\otimes\rho_n$. Assume that this potential includes all random variables in its domain. Let q denote the subset of decision variables included in the domain of the joint potential, i.e., $q \subseteq \mathcal{X}_D$ such that $\rho_1\otimes...\otimes\rho_n$ is a potential for $q \cup \mathcal{X}_R$. Note that q could be empty. Define potential ρ for {D,R} such that $\rho(\mathbf{d}_\sigma,\mathbf{r}_\mathbf{y}) = (\rho_1\otimes...\otimes\rho_n)(\mathbf{a}_{\sigma,\mathbf{y}}^{\downarrow q},\mathbf{y})$, for all strategy σ, and all configuration $\mathbf{y} \in \mathcal{W}_{\mathcal{X}_R}$. Δ_C, as defined above, is a canonical decision problem only if ρ satisfies condition (4.1). This motivates the following definition. Δ is a *well-defined VBS representation of a decision problem* if and only if $\Sigma\{(\rho_1\otimes...\otimes\rho_n)(\mathbf{x},\mathbf{y}) \mid \mathbf{y} \in \mathcal{W}_{\mathcal{X}_R}\} = 1$ for every $\mathbf{x} \in \mathcal{W}_q$.

In summary, the potentials $\{\rho_1, ..., \rho_n\}$ represent the factors of a family of probability distributions. It is easy to verify that the VBS representation of the diabetes diagnosis problem is well-defined since $\rho\otimes\mu\otimes\nu$ is a joint probability distribution for {D, B, G}.

The Decision Problem. Suppose $\Delta = \{\mathcal{X}_D, \mathcal{X}_R, \{\mathcal{W}_X\}_{X \in \mathcal{X}}, \{\pi_1\}, \{\rho_1, ..., \rho_n\}, \rightarrow\}$ is a well-defined decision problem. Let $\Delta_C = \{\{D\}, \{R\}, \{\mathcal{W}_D, \mathcal{W}_R\}, \{\pi\}, \{\rho\}, \rightarrow\}$, represent an equivalent canonical decision problem. In the canonical decision problem Δ_C, the two computations that are of interest are (1) the computation of the maximum expected value $(\pi \otimes \rho)^{\downarrow \varnothing}(\blacklozenge)$, and (2) the computation of an optimal act $\mathbf{d}_{\sigma *}$ such that $(\pi \otimes \rho)^{\downarrow \{D\}}(\mathbf{d}_{\sigma *}) = (\pi \otimes \rho)^{\downarrow \varnothing}(\blacklozenge)$. Since we know the mapping between Δ and Δ_C, we can now formally define the questions posed in a decision problem Δ. There are two computations of interest.

First, we would like to compute the maximum expected utility. The maximum expected utility is given by $(\otimes\{\pi_1, \rho_1, ..., \rho_n\})^{\downarrow \varnothing}(\blacklozenge)$. Second, we would like to compute an optimal strategy σ^* that gives us the maximum expected value $(\otimes\{\pi_1, \rho_1, ..., \rho_n\})^{\downarrow \varnothing}(\blacklozenge)$. A strategy σ^* of Δ is *optimal* if $(\pi \otimes \rho)^{\downarrow \{D\}}(\mathbf{d}_{\sigma *}) = (\otimes\{\pi_1, \rho_1, ..., \rho_n\})^{\downarrow \varnothing}(\blacklozenge)$, where π, ρ, and D refer to the equivalent canonical decision problem Δ_C.

In the diabetes diagnosis problem, we have four valuations π, μ, ν, and ρ. Also, from the precedence constraints, we have B>T, G>T, T>D. Thus we need to compute either $((((\pi \otimes \mu \otimes \nu \otimes \rho)^{\downarrow \{B,G,T\}})^{\downarrow \{B,G\}})^{\downarrow \{B\}})^{\downarrow \varnothing}$ or $((((\pi \otimes \mu \otimes \nu \otimes \rho)^{\downarrow \{B,G,T\}})^{\downarrow \{B,G\}})^{\downarrow \{G\}})^{\downarrow \varnothing}$. In either case, we get the same answer.

Tables 3 and 4 display the former computations. As seen in Table 4, the maximum expected utility is 9.864. Also, from Ψ_T, the solution for T (shown in Table 4), the optimal act is to treat the patient for diabetes if and only if the patient exhibits glucose in urine.

Note that no divisions were done in the solution process, only additions and multiplications. But, both decision tree and influence diagram methodologies involve unnecessary divisions, and unnecessary multiplications to compensate for the unnecessary divisions. It is this feature of valuation-based systems that makes it more efficient than decision trees and influence diagrams.

In solving the diabetes diagnosis problem using our method, we do only 11 additions, 28 multiplications and 4 comparisons, for a total of 43 operations. On the other hand, both decision tree and influence diagram methodologies require 17 additions, 38 multiplications, 12 divisions, and 4 comparisons for a total of 71 operations. Thus, for this problem, our method results in a savings of 40 percent over the decision tree and influence diagram methodologies.

5 A FUSION ALGORITHM

In this section, we describe a method for solving a VBS using local computation. The solution for the diabetes diagnosis problem shown in Tables 3 and 4 involves combination on the space $\mathcal{W}_{\mathcal{X}}$. While this is possible for small problems, it is computationally not feasible for problems with many variables. Given the structure of the diabetes diagnosis problem, it is not possible to avoid the combination operation on the space of all four variables, B, G, T, and D. But, in some problems, it may be possible to avoid such global computations.

The basic idea of the method is to successively delete all variables from the VBS. The sequence in which variables are deleted must respect the precedence constraints in the sense that if X>Y, then Y must be deleted before X. Since > is only a partial order, a problem may allow several deletion sequences. Any allowable deletion sequence may be used. All allowable deletion sequences lead to the same answers. But, different deletion sequences may involve different computational costs. We will comment on good deletion sequences at the end of this section.

When we delete a variable, we have to do a "fusion" operation on the valuations. Consider a set of k valuations α_1, ..., α_k. Suppose α_i is a valuation for h_i. Let $Fus_X\{\alpha_1, ..., \alpha_k\}$ denote the collection of valuations after fusing the valuations in the set $\{\alpha_1, ..., \alpha_k\}$ with respect to variable X. Then

$$Fus_X\{\alpha_1, ..., \alpha_k\} = \{\alpha^{\downarrow(h-\{X\})}\} \cup \{\alpha_i \mid X \notin h_i\}, \quad (5.1)$$

where $\alpha = \otimes\{\alpha_i \mid X \in h_i\}$, and $h = \cup\{h_i \mid X \in h_i\}$. After fusion, the set of valuations is changed as follows. All valuations that bear on X are combined, and the resulting valuation is marginalized such that X is eliminated from its domain. The valuations that do not bear on X remain unchanged.

We are ready to state the main theorem.

Theorem 1. Suppose $\Delta = \{\mathcal{X}_D, \mathcal{X}_R, \{\mathcal{W}_X\}_{X \in \mathcal{X}}, \{\pi_1\}, \{\rho_1, ..., \rho_n\}, \rightarrow\}$ is a well-defined decision problem. Suppose $X_1X_2...X_k$ is a sequence of variables in $\mathcal{X} = \mathcal{X}_D \cup \mathcal{X}_R$ such that with respect to the partial order >, X_1 is a minimal element of $\mathcal{X}$, X_2 is a minimal element of $\mathcal{X} - \{X_1\}$, etc. Then $\{(\otimes\{\pi_1, \rho_1, ..., \rho_n\})^{\downarrow \varnothing}\} =$

$$Fus_{X_k}\{... Fus_{X_2}\{Fus_{X_1}\{\pi_1, \rho_1, ..., \rho_n\}\}\}.$$

See [Shenoy, 1990c] for a proof. To illustrate Theorem 1, consider a VBS for a medical diagnosis problem as shown in Figure 2. In this VBS, there are three random variables, D, P, and S, and one decision variable, T. D represents a disease, P represents a pathological state caused by the disease, and S represents a symptom caused by the pathological state. We assume that S and D are conditionally independent given P. The potential ρ is the prior probability of D, the potential ν is the conditional probability of P given D, and the potential μ is the conditional probability of S given P. A medical intern first observes the symptom S and then either treats the patient for the disease and pathological state or not. The utility valuation π bears on the intern's action T, the pathological state P, and the disease D.

Figure 3 shows the results of the fusion algorithm for this

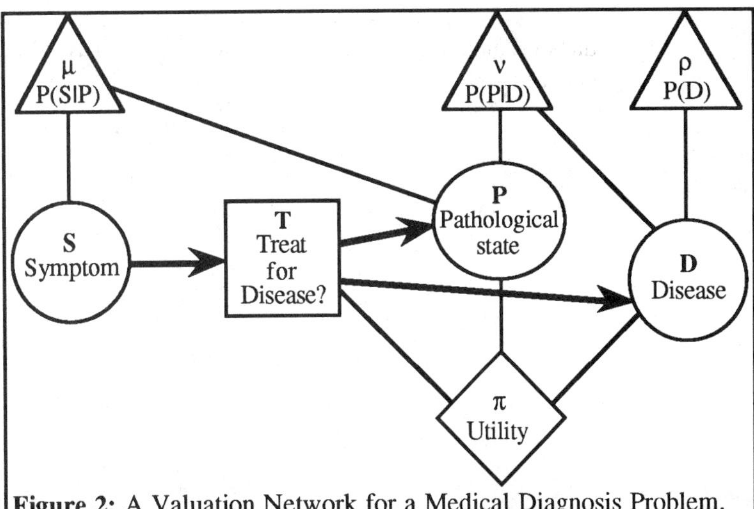

Figure 2: A Valuation Network for a Medical Diagnosis Problem.

problem. The deletion sequence used is DPTS. The first network in Figure 3 is the same as the one in Figure 2. The second network is the result after deletion of D and the resulting fusion. The combination in the fusion operation involves only variables D, P, and T. The third network is the result after deletion of P. The combination operation in the corresponding fusion operation involves only three variables, P, T, and S. The fourth network is the result after deletion of T. There is no combination involved here, only marginalization on the frame of {S, T}. The fifth network is the result after deletion of S. Again, there is no combination involved here, only marginalization on the frame of {S}. The maximum expected utility value is given by $((\pi\otimes\nu\otimes\rho)^{\downarrow\{T,P\}}\otimes\mu)^{\downarrow\varnothing}(\blacklozenge)$. An optimal strategy is given by the solution for T with respect to $((\pi\otimes\nu\otimes\rho)^{\downarrow\{T,P\}}\otimes\mu)^{\downarrow\{S,T\}}$, computed during fusion with respect to T. Note that in this problem, the fusion algorithm avoids computation on the frame of all four variables.

In solving the medical diagnosis problem using our method, we do only 9 additions, 20 multiplications and 2 comparisons, for a total of 31 operations. On the other hand, for this problem, decision tree methodology requires 23 additions, 42 multiplications, 12 divisions, and 2 comparisons for a total of 79 operations. Thus, for this problem, our method results in a savings of 61 percent over the decision tree methodology. If we use the influence diagram methodology for this problem, we do 13 additions, 26 multiplications, 8 divisions, and 2 comparisons, for a total of 49 operations. Thus, for this problem, our method results in a savings of 37 percent over the influence diagram methodology.

The fusion method described in this section applies when there is one utility valuation in the VBS. This method applies unchanged in problems where the utility valuation factors multiplicatively into several utility valuations. In this case, we define combination of utility valuations as pointwise multiplication, i.e., if π_i is a utility valuation for h_i, and π_j is a utility valuation for h_j, then $\pi_i\otimes\pi_j$ is a utility valuation for $h_i\cup h_j$ defined by $(\pi_i\otimes\pi_j)(\mathbf{x}) = \pi_i(\mathbf{x}^{\downarrow h_i})\pi_j(\mathbf{x}^{\downarrow h_j})$ for all $\mathbf{x}\in \mathcal{W}_{h_i\cup h_j}$. This method does not apply directly in problems where the utility valuation decomposes additively. In such problems, we first have to combine all utility valuations before we apply the method described in this section. Thus the fusion method described in this section is unable to take computational advantage of an additive decomposition of the utility valuation. In Shenoy [1990b], we describe a modification of the fusion method that is able to take advantage of an additive decomposition of the utility function. The modification involves some divisions.

Deletion Sequences. Since > is only a partial order, in general, we may have many deletion sequences (sequences that satisfy the condition stated in Theorem 1). If so, which deletion sequence should one use? First, we note that all deletion sequences lead to the same final result. This is implied in the statement of the theorem. Second, different deletion sequences may involve different computational efforts. For example, consider the VBS shown in Figure 3. In this example, deletion sequence DPTS involves less computational effort than PDTS as the former involves combinations on the frame of three variables only whereas the latter involves combination on the frame of all four variables. Finding an optimal deletion sequence is a secondary optimization problem that has shown to be NP-complete [Arnborg et al., 1987]. But, there are several heuristics for finding good deletion sequences [Kong, 1986; Mellouli, 1987; Zhang, 1988].

One such heuristic is called one-step-look-ahead [Kong, 1986]. This heuristic tells us which variable to delete next from amongst those that qualify. As per this heuristic, the variable that should be deleted next is one that leads to combination over the smallest frame. For example, for the VBS in Figure 5, two variables qualify for first deletion, P and D. This heuristic picks D over P since deletion of P involves combination over the frame of {S, D, P, T} whereas deletion of D involves combination over the frame of {T, P, D}. Thus, this heuristic would choose deletion sequence DPTS.

6 CONCLUSIONS

The main objective of this paper is to propose a new method for solving Bayesian decision problems. The VBS representation and solution described here is a hybrid of valuations-based systems for probability propagation [Shenoy, 1991c] and valuation-based systems for optimization [Shenoy, 1991b].

There are several advantages of the VBS representation and solution methodology. First, like influence diagrams, a

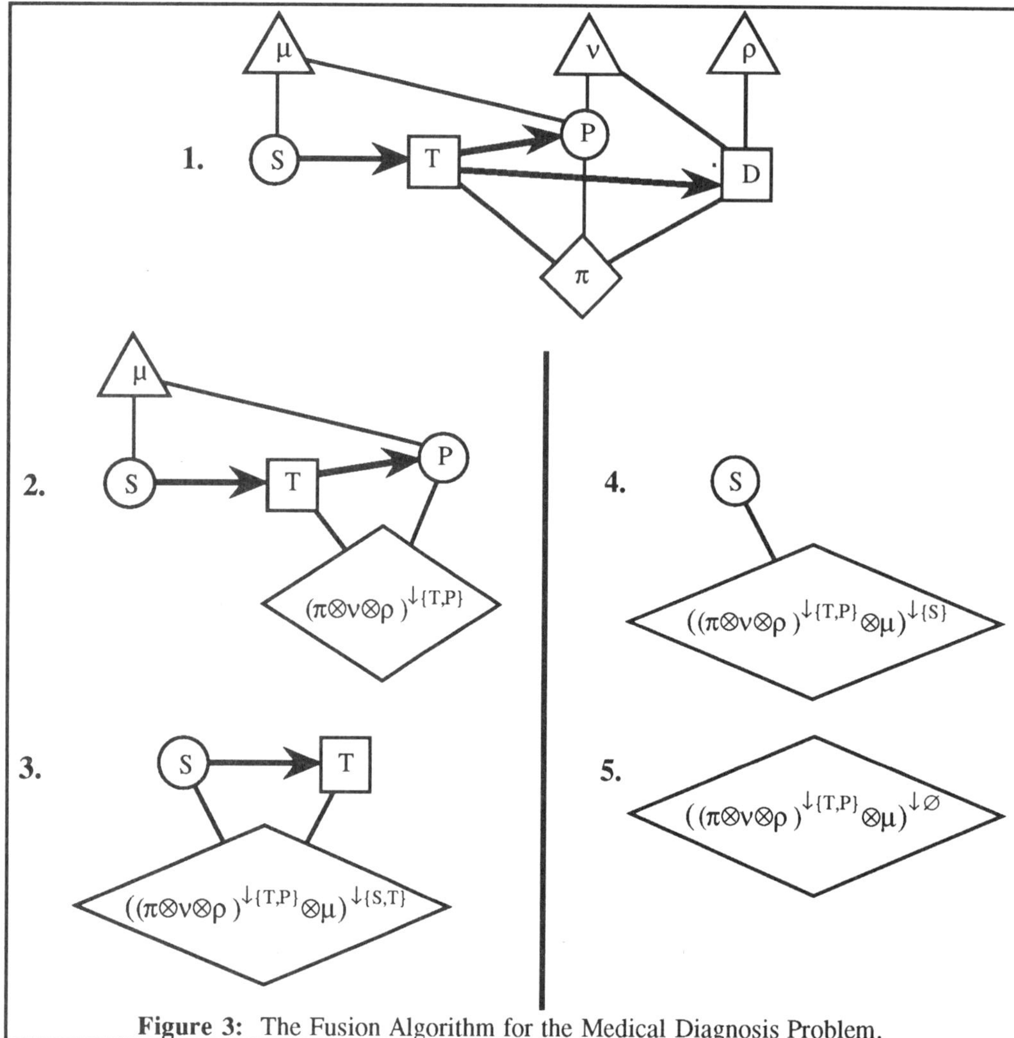

Figure 3: The Fusion Algorithm for the Medical Diagnosis Problem.

valuation network representation is compact when compared to decision trees. A valuation network graphically depicts the qualitative structure of the decision problem and de-emphasizes the quantitative details of the problem. However, both VBSs and influence diagrams are appropriate only for symmetric decision problems. For non-symmetric decision problems, decision tree representation is more flexible.

Second, like influence diagrams, the VBS representation separates the formulation of the problem from its solution.

Third, in symmetric decision problems, the solution procedure of VBSs is more efficient than that of decision trees since it involves minimal divisions. This assumes that the computational procedure of decision trees includes the preprocessing of probabilities. The solution procedure of decision trees includes unnecessary divisions and multiplications. The unnecessary divisions take place during preprocessing of probabilities. The unnecessary multiplications make up for the unnecessary divisions and take place during the averaging-out process. In non-symmetric decision problems, however, decision trees may be more efficient than VBSs.

Fourth, the VBS representation is more powerful than influence diagram representation. Whereas influence diagram representation is only capable of directly representing conditional probabilities, VBS representation is capable of directly representing arbitrary probabilities. (By directly, we mean without any preprocessing.)

Fifth, the solution method of VBSs involves minimal divisions. In comparison, the influence diagram solution method involves unnecessary divisions (in every arc reversal operation) and additional multiplications to compensate for the unnecessary divisions. These unnecessary divisions and multiplications are the same as those in the decision tree solution process. In influence diagrams, these unnecessary operations are performed for semantical considerations. The influence diagram solution process has the property that the diagram resulting from the deletion of a chance node is again an influence diagram. This means that the resulting probabilities in the reduced influence diagram are conditional probabilities. It is this demand for conditional probabilities at each stage that results in the unnecessary divisions and multiplications.

Sixth, the semantics of VBSs are different from the semantics of influence diagrams. Whereas influence diagrams are based on the semantics of conditional independence, VBSs are based on the semantics of factorization.

Seventh, if a decision problem has no random variables, it reduces to an optimization problem. And the solution technique of VBSs reduces to dynamic programming [Shenoy, 1991b].

Eighth, in cases where a decision problem has no decision variables, we may be interested in finding marginals of the joint distribution for each random variable. In such problems, the solution technique described in this paper reduces to the technique for finding marginals [Shenoy, 1991c]. This technique also can revise marginals in light of new observations. We represent each new observation by a potential and then use the fusion algorithm to compute the desired marginals.

Acknowledgements

This research was partially supported by NSF grant IRI-8902444. I have benefitted from discussions with and comments from Dan Geiger, Steffen Lauritzen, Anthony Neugebauer, Pierre Ndilikilikesha, Geoff Schemmel, Glenn Shafer, Philippe Smets, Leen-Kiat Soh, Po-Lung Yu, and Lianwen Zhang.

References

Arnborg, S., D. G. Corneil, and A. Proskurowski (1987), "Complexity of finding embeddings in a k-tree," *SIAM Journal of Algebraic and Discrete Methods*, **8**, 277–284.

Bertele, U. and F. Brioschi (1972), *Nonserial Dynamic Programming*, Academic Press, New York, NY.

Dubois, D. and H. Prade (1990), "Inference in possibilistic hypergraphs," *Proceedings of the Third International Conference on Information Processing and Management of Uncertainty in Knowledge-based Systems (IPMU-90)*, Paris, France, 228–230.

Ezawa, K. J. (1986), "Efficient evaluation of influence diagrams," Ph.D. dissertation, Department of Engineering-Economic Systems, Stanford University.

Howard, R. A. and J. E. Matheson (1984), "Influence diagrams," in Howard, R. A. and J. E. Matheson (eds.), *The Principles and Applications of Decision Analysis*, **2**, 719–762, Strategic Decisions Group, Menlo Park, CA.

Jensen, F. V., K. G. Olesen, and S. K. Andersen (1990), "An algebra of Bayesian belief universes for knowledge-based systems," *Networks*, **20**, 637–659.

Kong, A. (1986), "Multivariate belief functions and graphical models," Ph.D. dissertation, Department of Statistics, Harvard University, Cambridge, MA.

Lauritzen, S. L. and D. J. Spiegelhalter (1988), "Local computations with probabilities on graphical structures and their application to expert systems (with discussion)," *Journal of the Royal Statistical Society*, series B, **50**(2), 157–224.

Mellouli, K. (1987), "On the propagation of beliefs in networks using the Dempster-Shafer theory of evidence," Ph.D. dissertation, School of Business, University of Kansas, Lawrence, KS.

Olmsted, S. M. (1983), "On representing and solving decision problems," Ph.D. dissertation, Department of Engineering-Economic Systems, Stanford University.

Pearl, J. (1988), *Probabilistic Reasoning in Intelligent Systems*, Morgan Kaufmann, San Mateo, CA.

Shachter, R. D. (1986), "Evaluating influence diagrams," *Operations Research*, **34**(6), 871–882.

Shafer, G. and P. P. Shenoy (1988), "Local computation in hypertrees," Working Paper No. 202, School of Business, University of Kansas, Lawrence, KS. To appear as a monograph in *Lecture Notes in Artificial Intelligence* series, Springer-Verlag, 1991.

Shenoy, P. P. (1989), "A valuation-based language for expert systems," *International Journal of Approximate Reasoning*, **3**(5), 383–411.

Shenoy, P. P. (1990a), "Valuation-based systems for propositional logic," in Ras, Z. W., M. Zemankova, and M. L. Emrich (eds.), *Methodologies for Intelligent Systems*, **5**, 305–312, North-Holland, Amsterdam.

Shenoy, P. P. (1990b), "Valuation-based systems for Bayesian decision analysis," Working Paper No. 220, School of Business, University of Kansas, Lawrence, KS.

Shenoy, P. P. (1990c), "A new method for representing and solving Bayesian decision problems," Working Paper No. 223, School of Business, University of Kansas, Lawrence, KS.

Shenoy, P. P. (1991a), "On Spohn's rule for revision of beliefs," *International Journal of Approximate Reasoning*, **5**(2), 149–181.

Shenoy, P. P. (1991b), "Valuation-based systems for discrete optimization," in Bonissone, P. P., M. Henrion, L. N. Kanal, and J. F. Lemmer (eds.), *Uncertainty in Artificial Intelligence*, **6**, North-Holland, Amsterdam, to appear.

Shenoy, P. P. (1991c), "Valuation-based systems: A framework for managing uncertainty in expert systems," Working Paper No. 226, School of Business, University of Kansas, Lawrence, KS.

Shenoy, P. P. and G. Shafer (1988), "Constraint propagation," Working Paper No. 208, School of Business, University of Kansas, Lawrence, KS.

Shenoy, P. P. and G. Shafer (1990), "Axioms for probability and belief-function propagation," in R. D. Shachter, T. S. Levitt, J. F. Lemmer and L. N. Kanal (eds.), *Uncertainty in Artificial Intelligence*, **4**, 169–198, North-Holland, Amsterdam.

Tatman, J. A. (1986), "Decision processes in influence diagrams: Formulation and analysis," Ph.D. dissertation, Department of Engineering-Economic Systems, Stanford University.

Zhang, L. (1988), "Studies on finding hypertree covers of hypergraphs," Working Paper No. 198, School of Business, University of Kansas, Lawrence, KS.

Algorithms for Irrelevance-Based Partial MAPs

Solomon E. Shimony
Computer Science Department
Box 1910, Brown University
Providence, RI 02912
ses@cs.brown.edu

Abstract

Irrelevance-based partial MAPs are useful constructs for domain-independent explanation using belief networks. We look at two definitions for such partial MAPs, and prove important properties that are useful in designing algorithms for computing them effectively. We make use of these properties in modifying our standard MAP best-first algorithm, so as to handle irrelevance-based partial MAPs.

1 INTRODUCTION

Probabilistic explanation, finding causes for observed facts (or evidence), is an extremely important aspect of Artificial Intelligence in general, and probabilistic reasoning in particular. For example, [Charniak and Goldman, 1988], views the understanding of stories as finding high probability facts given the evidence as an explanation of the natural language input text. In automated medical diagnosis (for example the work of [Cooper, 1984], and [Peng and Reggia, 1987]), one wants to find the disease or set of diseases of highest probability given the observed symptoms. In vision processing, recent research formulates the problem in terms of finding some set of objects that have the highest probability given the evidence (the image).

There is, however, no agreement on what should be maximized in finding a good explanation. In fact, Poole discussed six different schemes of probabilistic explanation in [Poole and Provan, 1990], and even these are not exhaustive. One of the schemes discussed was Maximum A-Posteriori models (MAP), which was presented in [Pearl, 1988] by the name of Maximum Probability Explanation (MPE). A MAP is a maximum probability (given the evidence) assignment to *all* the variables. We call such assignments *complete* MAPs, as opposed to *partial* MAPs which are maximum probability assignments to *some* of the variables. MAPs are useful for finding best globally consistent explanations, as argued by Pearl. In [Charniak and Shimony, 1990], we showed that MAPs are useful for explanation by demonstrating that MAP explanations are equivalent to complete assignment cost-based abduction. Cost based abduction is a variant of Hobbs' and Stickel's weighted abduction (see [Hobbs and Stickel, 1988]), which they used for natural language story understanding.

In the rest of this section, we will present the essence of earlier papers: [Shimony and Charniak, 1990] (an algorithm for complete MAPs), and [Shimony, 1991] (definitions of irrelevance-based assignments). The following sections will deal with how we modify the algorithm for complete MAPs to handle partial MAPs. We assume here, as well as in related papers, that the world knowledge is represented as a belief network (Bayesian network).

In [Shimony, 1991], we proposed a new, domain-independent method of highest likelihood explanations called *irrelevance-based (partial) MAPs*. The idea is that the standard MAP solution, that of finding the most-probable complete model given the evidence, suffers from the *overspecification problem* (an instance of which appears in [Pearl, 1988], and [Shimony, 1991]). Our solution is a generalization of Pearl's idea of "circumscribing explanations". Pearl claimed that there is no need to consider the assignment to nodes which have no evidence coming in from below (evidential support).

In many cases the evidential support is insufficient as a criterion for deciding which nodes are irrelevant, as shown in [Shimony, 1991]. In that paper, we defined irrelevance-based assignments as assignments where every unassigned node is irrelevant. We then defined our notion of explanation, irrelevance-based MAP, as the irrelevance-based partial assignment of highest probability (given the evidence).

1.1 IRRELEVANCE-BASED ASSIGNMENTS

We proceeded to give irrelevance a more formal footing, using statistical independence as a criterion for irrelevance. There were two such definitions of irrelevance-based assignments: independence-based partial assignments, and δ-independence based partial assignments; the second being a more general concept that was introduced because independence-based assignments were too restrictive and captured the intuitive meaning of irrelevance only in special cases.

We introduced the notion of independence given a (partial) assignment[1] $\mathcal{A}^S$. We use the notation $In(a, b|\mathcal{A}^S)$ to mean that a and b are independent given an *assignment* $\mathcal{A}^S$, where a and b are either assignments (assignments are used interchangeably with sample-space events), or sets of nodes. Equivalently, we can say that $P(a|\mathcal{A}^S) = P(a|b, \mathcal{A}^S)$. The latter constraint actually is a set of simple constraints, one for each possible assignments to the nodes of a and b. This is similar to Pearl's notation of $I(a, S, b)$ stating that a and b are independent given S, where a, S, b are sets of variables. The difference is that the latter implies the former, but not vice versa. That is because our notion only states that independence occurs given a *particular* assignment to S, whereas Pearl's notion states that independence occurs given *any* assignment to S. That is, $I(a, S, b)$ stands for a set-wise larger set of constraints than $In(a, b|\mathcal{A}^S)$.

An assignment can be seen as a set of pairs, where a pair (v, V) means that node v is assigned the value V. The function *nodes*$(\mathcal{A}^S)$ evaluates to the set of nodes assigned (in this case S). We say that assignment $\mathcal{A}$ *subsumes* assignment $\mathcal{B}$ iff $\mathcal{A} \subseteq \mathcal{B}$. The evidence $\mathcal{E}$ is assumed to be an assignment. We say that an assignment $\mathcal{A}^S$ is *evidentially supported* by $\mathcal{E}$ iff every node $v \in S$ is either an evidence node or there exists a path form v to some evidence node. Likewise, $\mathcal{A}^S$ is properly evidentially supported by $\mathcal{E}$ iff every node $v \in S$ is either an evidence node or there exists a path form v to an evidence node that traverses only nodes in S.

Our definition of irrelevance-based assignments relies on the directionality of belief networks, the "cause and effect" directionality. The potential causes of a node v are its parents, $\uparrow(v)$, and we do not assign (i.e. are not interested in) variables that are irrelevant to the evidence given the causes. We defined our first notion of an irrelevance-based partial assignment formally (and called it *independence-based partial assignment*):

Definition 1 *An assignment $\mathcal{A}^S$ is an* independence-based *assignment (IB assignment for short) iff for every node $v \in S$, $\mathcal{A}^{\{v\}}$ is independent of all its ancestors that are* not *in S, given $\mathcal{A}^{S\uparrow(v)}$.* [2]

If v is independent of its unassigned parents, as in definition 1, we say that the IB constraint holds at v. The idea behind this definition is that the unassigned nodes above each assigned node v should remain unassigned if they cannot affect v (and cannot be used to explain v). Nodes that are not above v are never used as an explanation of v anyway, as we stated implicitly earlier.

Definition 2 *An IB assignment $\mathcal{A}^S$ is an independence based MAP (IB-MAP) w.r.t. to evidence $\mathcal{E}$ iff $\mathcal{A}^S$ is evidentially supported and subsumed by $\mathcal{E}$, and there is no other IB assignment assignment evidentially supported and subsumed by $\mathcal{E}$ of greater probability given the evidence.*

Clearly, since $\mathcal{A}^S$ is subsumed by $\mathcal{E}$, then $P(\mathcal{E}|\mathcal{A}^S) = 1$, whenever $P(\mathcal{A}^S) \neq 0$. In fact, we are only interested in MAPs that are maximal w.r.t. subsumption, because they assign fewer variables and thus lead to "simpler" explanations. This distinction is immaterial if the distribution of the belief network is strictly positive, because then if assignment $\mathcal{A}$ subsumes $\mathcal{B}$ (with $\mathcal{A} \neq \mathcal{B}$) then it also has a strictly greater probability.

We need to maximize $P(\mathcal{A}^S|\mathcal{E})$, the posterior probability. Using Bayes rule, we can write:

$$P(\mathcal{A}^S|\mathcal{E}) = \frac{P(\mathcal{A}^S)P(\mathcal{E}|\mathcal{A}^S)}{P(\mathcal{E})} \tag{1}$$

Since the denominator $P(\mathcal{E}|\mathcal{A}^S)$ is 1 and $P(\mathcal{E})$ is a constant for all the assignments we are comparing, it is sufficient to maximize the prior probability $\mathcal{A}^S$, which is much easier to compute (see section 2).

Definition 2 handles the case where the assigned variables are *exactly* statistically independent of the unassigned variables. There remained the problem that modifying the conditional probabilities very slightly would have a major effect on the solution. In fact, if the correlation factor between effects and potential causes is nearly 0, we would also want to conclude that these potential causes are irrelevant. In order to achieve that, we relax the exact independence constraint by requiring that the equality hold only within a factor of δ. That is (evaluating over all possible assignments for a set of variables), if the maximum conditional probability is within a factor of δ of the minimum conditional probability, then we have δ-independence. Formally:

[1] The superscript over the assignment symbol denotes the set of variables assigned by $\mathcal{A}$. If the assignment assigns values to *all* the nodes of S, we say that $\mathcal{A}$ is complete w.r.t. S.

[2] We use $\uparrow(v)$ to denote the set of immediate predecessors of v. We omit the set-intersection operator between sets whenever unambiguous, thus $S\uparrow(v)$ is the intersection of S with the immediate predecessors of v.

Definition 3 *We say that a is δ-independent of b given $\mathcal{A}^S$, where a, b and S are sets of variables (written $In_\delta(a, b|\mathcal{A}^S)$ for short), iff*

$$\min_{\mathcal{A}^b} P(\mathcal{A}^a|\mathcal{A}^S, \mathcal{A}^b) \geq (1-\delta) \max_{\mathcal{A}^b} P(\mathcal{A}^a|\mathcal{A}^S, \mathcal{A}^b) \quad (2)$$

We expand the definition to include the case of a being a (possibly partial) *assignment* rather than a set of variables, by substituting a for $\mathcal{A}^a$ in the above definition. Likewise for the case of b being an assignment. This definition is parametric, i.e. δ can vary between 0 and 1. We define a δ-independent based assignment as an assignment where each node is δ-independent of its unassigned ancestors given its assigned parents. Formally:

Definition 4 *An assignment $\mathcal{A}^S$ is δ-independence based iff for every $v \in S$, $In_\delta(\mathcal{A}^{\{v\}}, \uparrow^+(v) - S|\mathcal{A}^{S\uparrow(v)})$.*[3]

The case of $\delta = 0$ reduces to the independence-based assignment criterion. A δ-independence based MAP is defined in the same way as independence-based MAPs, using In_δ in place of In.

1.2 BEST-FIRST MAP ALGORITHM

We presented an algorithm for finding complete (rather than partial) MAP assignments to belief networks in [Shimony and Charniak, 1990]. The algorithm finds MAP assignments in linear time for belief networks that are polytrees (when appropriate bookkeeping, not discussed here, is used). The algorithm is potentially exponential time in the general case, as the problem is provably NP-hard.

An agenda of states is kept (or assignments), sorted by current probability, which is a product of all conditional probabilities seen in the current expansion. The operation of the algorithm is shown in the figure 1. An agenda item is *complete* iff all the variables are assigned. Expansion consists of selecting a fringe node (i.e. a node that has unassigned neighbors) and creating a new agenda item for each of the possible assignments to neighboring nodes. The heuristic evaluation function for an agenda item, which is an assignment $\mathcal{A}^S$ to the set of nodes S, is the following product:

$$H(\mathcal{A}^S) = \prod_{v \in G(S)} P(\mathcal{A}^{\{v\}}|\mathcal{A}^{\uparrow(v)}) \quad (3)$$

where $G(S) = \{v | v \in S \wedge \forall w \in \uparrow(v),\ w \in S\}$, i.e. the product is over all assigned nodes which have all their parents assigned as well. Clearly the evaluation function is precise for complete assignments, as the product reduces to exactly the joint distribution of the network in that case. H is also optimistic, because if some nodes are not assigned, it essentially assumes that their probability is 1. Thus, the evaluation function H is heuristically admissible.

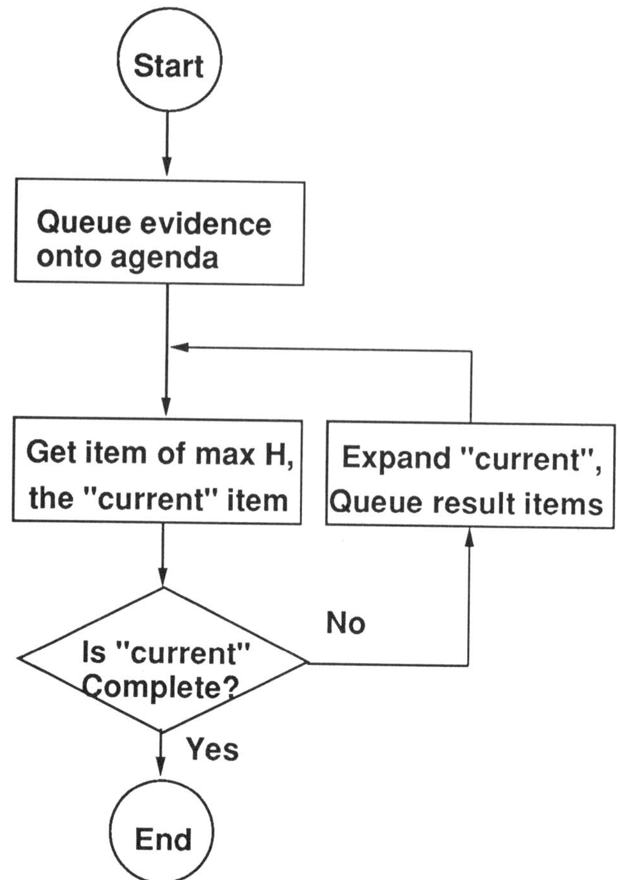

Figure 1: Top Level of Algorithm for Finding MAPs

The advantage of this best-first algorithm is that it can be easily modified to produce the next-best complete assignments in order of decreasing probability. This is done in the following manner (see figure 1): instead of ending with the first complete assignment, output it, and simply continue to loop (getting the next agenda item).

In the following sections, we discuss properties of independence-based and δ-independence-based partial assignments that allow us to use essentially the same algorithm (with only local modifications) to compute them. We then present the modifications required to produce the IB-MAP algorithm. A formal specification of the IB-MAP algorithm and a proof of its correctness follows. We conclude with suggestions of how to modify the algorithm to find δ-independence based MAPs.

[3] We use $\uparrow^+$ to denote the non-reflexive transitive closure of $\uparrow$. Thus $\uparrow^+(v)$ is the set of ancestors of v.

2 IB-MAP ALGORITHM

We begin by informally introducing the changes required to convert the complete MAP algorithm to an IB-MAP algorithm. We then proceed to define the terms and the algorithm formally, and prove its correctness.

2.1 ALGORITHM MODIFICATIONS

The algorithm modifications needed to compute the independence-based partial MAP are in checking whether an agenda item is complete, and in the expansion of an agenda item. Completeness checking in the modified algorithm is different in that an agenda item may be complete even if not all variables are assigned. Specifically, an agenda item is complete iff it is an independence-based (possibly partial) assignment. The other conditions for the agenda item being an IB-MAP are guaranteed because the evidence nodes are assigned initially. Checking whether an assignment is independence-based is easy, due to the following theorem (the locality theorem):

Theorem 1 *If $\mathcal{A}^S$ is a complete assignment to all the nodes of subset S of a belief network B, and for every node $v \in S$, $In(\mathcal{A}^{\{v\}}, \uparrow(v) - S|\mathcal{A}^{S\uparrow(v)})$, then $\mathcal{A}^S$ is an independence-based partial assignment to B.*

The claim is essentially that if conditional independence holds locally (i.e. with respect to just the immediate predecessors, as opposed to *all* ancestors, as in the definition of independence-based partial assignments), then it also holds globally. The theorem allows us to test whether an assignment is independence-based in time linear in the size of the network, and is thus an important theorem to use when we are considering the development of an algorithm to compute independence-based partial MAPs. The following theorem allows us to compute $P(\mathcal{A}^S)$ easily:

Theorem 2 *If $In(v, \uparrow(v) - S|\mathcal{A}^{S\uparrow(v)})$ holds for every node $v \in S$, then the probability of the assignment is:*

$$P(\mathcal{A}^S) = \prod_{v \in S} P(\mathcal{A}^{\{v\}}|\mathcal{A}^{S\uparrow(v)}) \quad (4)$$

Theorem 2 allows us to calculate $P(\mathcal{A}^S)$ in linear time for independence-based partial assignments, as the terms of the product are simply conditional probabilities that can be read off from the conditional distribution array (or any other representation) of nodes given their parents.

Another modification is required because, when extending a node, we may want to leave some of the parents unassigned, as we will show presently. Also, only nodes with unassigned *parents* are considered fringe nodes, since we do not need to assign nodes with no evidence nodes below them.

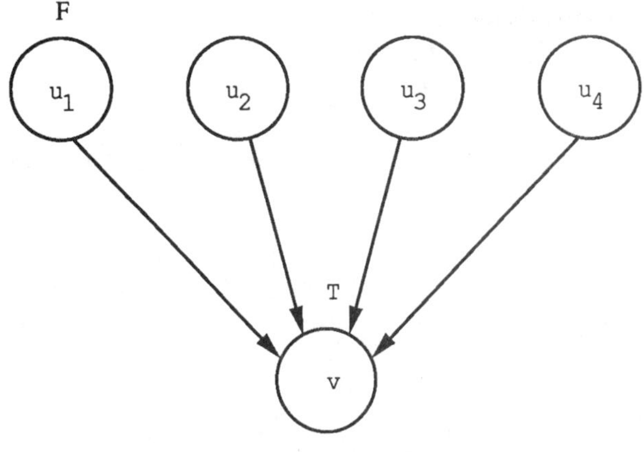

Figure 2: Expanding a Node

To take advantage of theorem 1, we precompute for each node v a set of all the cases where partial independence occurs. We do that in the following manner. The space defined by an assignment to a node v and some of its parents, (where the other parents are not assigned), defines a hypercube $\mathcal{H}$ of possible value assignments. If the probability of v is the same given any assignment in $\mathcal{H}$, then $\mathcal{H}$ is an *independence-based hypercube*. Another way to look at this is: an independence-based hypercube is a sub-space of the conditional distribution array (of v given its parents) with equal conditional probability entries. Consider, for example the "leaky" OR node v of figure 2, where $P(v = T|u_i = T) = 0.9$ for $1 \leq i \leq 4$ is independent of u_j, $j \neq i$. This defines four 3-dimensional hypercubes of "don't-care" values. We also have the 1-dimensional hypercube where all $u_i = F$. When the algorithm expands v, it only assigns values to parents of which v is not independent (given the assignment to its other parents), i.e. it generates one agenda item for each of the above independence-based hypercubes.

Naturally, since a belief net is not always a tree, some nodes may already be assigned. Consider, for example, figure 2. We are at the OR node v, with parents u_1, u_2, u_3, u_4, where v has the value T, and u_1 has already been assigned F. We now have to expand all the states of the nodes u_i, the parents of v. We would, however, like to generate as few new assignments as possible, while guaranteeing that the IB-MAP is still reachable.

In the complete MAP case, we add the following 8 assignments for the nodes (u_2, u_3, u_4):

$$\{(F,F,F),(F,F,T),(F,T,F),(F,T,T),$$
$$(T,F,F),(T,F,T),(T,T,F),(T,T,T)\}$$

That is, all possible complete assignments to these three variables. When we need to find the partial

MAP, however, only the following 4 assignments are added:

$$\{(T, U, U),\ (U, T, U,),\ (U, U, T),\ (F, F, F)\}$$

where U stands for "unassigned". If a hypercube is ruled out by a prior assignment to a parent node (as is the case $u_1 = T$ here), it is ignored. Otherwise, the hypercubes are unified with the prior assignment, as in this case, the 3-dimensional hypercubes are reduced to 2-dimensional hypercubes by the prior assignment of $u_1 = F$. All the other assignments are redundant, because they would assign values to variables that cannot change the probability of v, and are subsumed by the 4 assignments listed above.

Finally, to compute next-best partial assignments in decreasing order, we perform the same simple modification as for the complete MAP algorithm: simply continue to run, producing independence based partial assignments. A useful termination condition is now a probability threshold, i.e. stop producing assignments once the probability of an assignment is below some fraction of that of the first partial MAP produced.

2.2 FORMAL DEFINITION OF THE ALGORITHM

We define the algorithm in terms of an input assignment $\mathcal{E}$, the evidence, and and output IB assignment. We shall define an expansion operator τ, and a termination condition, and show that the algorithm terminates with an IB-MAP.

We assume a total ordering $\mathcal{O}$ on the nodes, such that no node comes before its (possibly indirect) descendents. That is always possible, because belief networks are directed acyclic graphs (DAGs). A fringe node w is minimal in an assignment if it is the first node w.r.t. the ordering $\mathcal{O}$ that has unassigned parents. If w is a fringe node in an assignment, such that the independence-based assignment condition holds at w w.r.t. the assignment, then it is an independence-based inactive (or just inactive, for short) fringe node. If the latter does not hold, then it is an active fringe node. If w is the first active node in the assignment, it is called a minimal active fringe node. Given an assignment and an ordering, the minimal active fringe node is unique. Unless otherwise specified, we shall assume that an implicit ordering $\mathcal{O}$ is present, and define the function *index* $: nodes(B) \to \mathcal{N}$, the index of a node w.r.t. $\mathcal{O}$.

An assignment $\mathcal{A}^{\{w\}\cup X}$ to a node and a subset of its parents ($X \subseteq \uparrow(w)$) is called a *hypercube* based on w. If $\mathcal{A}^{\{w\}\cup X}$ is complete w.r.t. w and X and $P(\mathcal{A}^{\{w\}}|\mathcal{A}^X)$ is independent of the nodes $\uparrow(w) - X$, that is[4]:

$$\exists p\ \forall \mathcal{A}^V \in \mathcal{A}_c^{\uparrow(w)-X} \quad P(\mathcal{A}^{\{w\}}|\mathcal{A}^X, \mathcal{A}^V) = p \qquad (5)$$

[4] $\mathcal{A}_c^{\uparrow(w)-X}$ is the set of all complete assignments to the nodes $\uparrow(w) - X$

then $\mathcal{A}^{\{w\}\cup\uparrow(w)}$ is an independence-based hypercube (acronym IB hypercube), and p is the conditional probability of the hypercube.

Definition 5 *An IB hypercube $\mathcal{A}^{\{w\}\cup X}$ based on w is* maximal *if there does not exist a different independence-based hypercube $\mathcal{B}^{\{w\}\cup Y}$ based on w that subsumes it (i.e. it is maximal with respect to subsumption).*

The maximal IB hypercube based on w is not always unique. Note also that a maximal IB hypercube has the ***smallest*** set of nodes assigned. We currently assume, for computation of hypercubes, that the distribution is strictly positive.

Theorem 3 *If independence-based assignment $\mathcal{A}^S$ is subsumed by the evidence $\mathcal{E}$, but is not evidentially supported w.r.t. $\mathcal{E}$, then there exists an independence-based assignment $\mathcal{A}^{S'}$ that subsumes $\mathcal{A}^S$ and is evidentially supported w.r.t. $\mathcal{E}$.*

Proof: By construction: we show that we can drop all the nodes that have no evidence nodes below them from the assignment $\mathcal{A}^S$. Since the belief network structure is a DAG, then so is any subgraph. Order nodes of S that are not ancestors of some node in E (nodes in E are considered to be ancestors here) in a list such that no node precedes its descendents. Now, proceed to eliminate nodes from the list (and from the assignment), in order of the elements of S. As each node is eliminated, the assignment remains independence-based, as only nodes with no children are eliminated, and the independence-based assignment criterion for each node depends only on ancestor nodes. We can thus eliminate the entire list, and remain with an assignment that is evidentially supported, is still subsumed by $\mathcal{E}$, and is independence-based. Q.E.D.

Theorem 4 *If $\mathcal{A}^S$ is an independence-based assignment that is subsumed by $\mathcal{E}$, then there exists an independence-based assignment $\mathcal{A}^{S'}$ that subsumes $\mathcal{A}^S$ and is properly evidentially supported w.r.t. $\mathcal{E}$.*

Proof: By construction: we show that we can delete from the assignment $\mathcal{A}^S$, all the nodes that have no evidence nodes below them, as well as all nodes for which no path to an evidence node (that traverses only nodes in S) exists. Remove from the assignment $\mathcal{A}^S$ all nodes that are not ancestors of E as in the proof of theorem 3. Then, remove all the nodes T that have no path to a node in E that lies entirely in S, in a similar manner: sort the nodes of T into a list such that no node precedes its descendents. Removing the nodes of T will achieve a properly evidentially supported assignment, if we preserve the independence-based assignment condition. But removing the nodes of T in sequence will always preserve the criterion, because no node v is removed if it has children in the resulting assignment (if it did, then the node v would not have been in T, as there would be a path from v to a node in E). Q.E.D. Theorems 3 and 4 are further support for our intuition for requiring that IB-MAPs be properly evidentially supported.

Let $\mathcal{A}_p$ be the set of all possible (either partial or complete) assignments. We define our expansion operator $\tau : \mathcal{A}_p \cup 2^{\mathcal{A}_p} \rightarrow 2^{\mathcal{A}_p}$, as follows:

Definition 6 *$\tau(\mathcal{S})$ consists of exactly the assignments $\mathcal{A}^S$ that obey the following conditions:*

- *If $\mathcal{S} \in \mathcal{A}_p$, then $\mathcal{S}$ subsumes $\mathcal{A}^S$ and there exists a fringe node $w \in S$ and a maximal IB hypercube $\mathcal{B}^{\{w\} \cup X}$ (based on w, where exactly the nodes $X \subseteq \uparrow(w)$ are assigned), such that both the following conditions hold:*
  1. *$S = nodes(\mathcal{S}) \cup X$*
  2. *$\mathcal{A}^S = \mathcal{S} \cup \mathcal{H}^{\{w\} \cup X}$*
- *If $\mathcal{S} \in 2^{\mathcal{A}_p}$, then exists an assignment $\mathcal{A}^{S'} \in \mathcal{S}$ that subsumes $\mathcal{A}^S$, such that exist a fringe node $w \in S'$ and a maximal IB hypercube $\mathcal{B}^{\{w\} \cup X}$ (based on w, where exactly the nodes $X \subseteq \uparrow(w)$ are assigned), such that both the following conditions hold:*
  1. *$S = S' \cup X$*
  2. *$\mathcal{A}^S = \mathcal{A}^{S'} \cup \mathcal{H}^{\{w\} \cup X}$*

In both cases, the hypercube should not contradict the assignment to variables that are already assigned.

We say that w is the fringe node expanded by τ. Essentially, applying the τ operator is equivalent to taking all the IB-hypercubes at a certain node w, and creating a new assignment for each hypercube. The new assignment is a union of the old assignment and the hypercube.

Theorem 5 *If assignment $\mathcal{A}^S$ is τ-reachable from $\mathcal{E}$, then it is properly evidentially supported by $\mathcal{E}$.*

Proof: By induction on the number of applications of the *tau* operator. The theorem clearly holds for 0 applications, as the only assignment in that case is $\{\mathcal{E}\}$, which is clearly properly evidentially supported. Now, assuming that the theorem holds for n applications of τ, then another application of τ can only assign values to nodes that are in some IB-hypercube based on a node w already assigned. IB-hypercubes assign only direct parents of w, and w is either in E or there exists a path from w to E passing only through assigned nodes, by the induction hypothesis. Hence, there will always by a path from the nodes assigned in the $n+1$ application of τ to E. The theorem follows by induction. Q.E.D.

An assignment $\mathcal{A}^S$ is IB-*terminated* when each assigned node $w \in S$ either has no parents, or the IB condition holds at w. The latter is true iff the assignment for every $w \in S$, $\mathcal{A}^{\{w\} \cup S \uparrow(v)}$ is subsumed by some IB hypercube based on w.

Theorem 6 *Every maximal (w.r.t. subsumption) independence-based assignment $\mathcal{A}^S$ that is properly evidentially supported w.r.t. $\mathcal{E}$ is τ-reachable from $\mathcal{E}$.*

Proof outline: We show that there exists a sequence of assignments $\mathcal{A}^{S'_k}$ of sufficient length, such that each assignment subsumes $\mathcal{A}^S$, $\mathcal{A}^{S'_k} \in \tau(\mathcal{A}^{S'_{k-1}})$, and if v_k is the node expanded by τ, then all the nodes v_i, $i \leq k$, are assigned exactly as in $\mathcal{A}^S$. Thus, for some k, $\mathcal{A}^{S'_k} = \mathcal{A}^S$. The proof of this theorem shows that it is actually sufficient to expand only the minimal fringe node at each state, rather than all fringe nodes.

Using an agenda $\mathcal{S}$ (a set of states, or assignments), evaluation function H, evidence $\mathcal{E}$ (where $E = nodes(\mathcal{E})$) and expansion operator τ, the algorithm is defined formally as follows:

1. Set $\mathcal{S} = \{\mathcal{E}\}$, and $i = min_{v \in E}\ index(v)$.
2. Set $\mathcal{A}^S$ to be a member of $\mathcal{S}$ of maximum $H(\mathcal{A}^S)$, and remove it from $\mathcal{S}$.
3. If $\mathcal{A}^S$, is IB-terminated, halt ($\mathcal{A}^S$ is an IB-MAP).
4. Set $\mathcal{S} = (\mathcal{S} \cup \tau(\mathcal{A}^S)) - \mathcal{A}^S$, and go to step 2.

The evaluation function H is similar the one for the complete MAP algorithm. The only difference is that the (conditional) probability of a node v is included in the product if the IB condition holds at v, as well as when all its parents are assigned:

$$H(\mathcal{A}^S) = \prod_{v \in G(S)} P(\mathcal{A}^{\{v\}} | \mathcal{A}^{\uparrow(v)}) \tag{6}$$

$$\begin{aligned} G(S) &= \{v | v \in S \wedge In(\mathcal{A}^{\{v\}}, \uparrow(v) - S | \mathcal{A}^{S \uparrow(v)})\} \\ &\cup \{v | v \in S \wedge \forall w \in \uparrow(v),\ w \in S\} \end{aligned}$$

H is obviously optimistic, and because of theorem 2, it is exact for IB assignments (the goal states). As the algorithm is implemented, H is actually computed before adding an assignment to the agenda, and the agenda is always kept sorted (e.g. using a heap). We now show that the algorithm is correct.

Theorem 7 *The IB-MAP algorithm terminates, and when it halts it does so with $\mathcal{A}^S$ being the most-probable IB assignment that is properly evidentially supported and subsumed by $\mathcal{E}$.*

Proof: The algorithm terminates, because the number of states added to the agenda in step 3 is finite, and since it always adds nodes to each assignment $\mathcal{A}^S$, it will eventually assign all the nodes above E, in which case the IB condition is vacuously true. Naturally, the runtime may be exponential. The assignment found when the algorithm terminates is IB (that

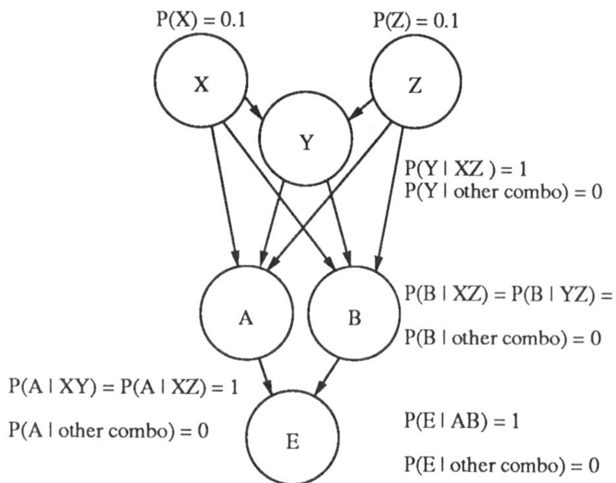

Ordering O = (E, A, B, Y, X, Z)

Minimal assignment: {E, A, B, X, Z}

Expanded node:	Assignment (one possiblity)
E	{E, A, B}
A	{E, A, B, X, Y}
B	{E, A, B, X, Y, Z}

Figure 3: How can a non-maximal assignment occur?

is the termination condition). It is properly evidentially supported (from theorem 5) and the fact that all assignments generated are τ accessible from $\mathcal{E}$. The evaluation function admissible, and all possible maximal properly evidentially supported IB assignments are τ-accessible. The theorem follows from the latter two properties, and from the correctness condition of heuristic search w.r.t. evaluation functions. Q.E.D.

Continuing to run the algorithm after finding a first assignment will find next-best IB-assignments, in decreasing order of probability. Note that theorem 7 does not guarantee a *maximal* (w.r.t. subsumption) IB-MAP. In fact, figure 3 shows a simple counterexample, where all the nodes are binary, E is the evidence node, and is known to be true. Given the set of agenda states shown, the non-maximal assignment, $\{E, A, B, X, Y, Z\}$ is reached. The latter assignment is not maximal w.r.t. subsumption, because the assignment $\{E, A, B, X, Z\}$ subsumes it, and is both IB and properly evidentially supported.

However, for positive distributions, subsumption also implies a higher probability, which guarantees that the IB-MAP found is indeed maximal. For other distributions, to find the maximal IB-MAPs, we need to compare all IB-MAPs with equal probability, which is not hard in most cases. We are assured that the maximal IB-MAP will indeed appear if we continue to run the algorithm, because of theorem 6.

3 δ-IB MAP ALGORITHM

In the case of δ-independence based MAPs, we use essentially the same algorithm again, where we need to pre-compute δ-independence hypercubes, rather than independence hypercubes, as in the previous case. However, once that is done, we can again employ local checking:

Theorem 8 *If $\mathcal{A}^S$ is a complete assignment to all the nodes of subset S of a belief network B, and for every node $v \in S$, $In_\delta(\mathcal{A}^{\{v\}}, \uparrow(v) - S | \mathcal{A}^{S\uparrow(v)})$ (for $0 \leq \delta \leq 1$), then $\mathcal{A}^S$ is a δ-independence-based partial assignment to B.*

Computing the exact probability of a δ-independence based partial assignment seems to be hard (since we cannot use theorem 2, and would need to find posterior probabilities of non-root nodes), but the following easily computable bound inequalities are always true:

$$P(\mathcal{A}^S) \leq \prod_{v \in S} \max_{\mathcal{A}^{U\uparrow(v)}} P(\mathcal{A}^{\{v\}} | \mathcal{A}^S, \mathcal{A}^{U\uparrow(v)}) \qquad (7)$$

$$P(\mathcal{A}^S) \geq \prod_{v \in S} \min_{\mathcal{A}^{U\uparrow(v)}} P(\mathcal{A}^{\{v\}} | \mathcal{A}^S, \mathcal{A}^{U\uparrow(v)})$$

These bounds get better as δ approaches 0, as their ratio is at least $(1-\delta)^{|S|}$.

Since getting the exact probability is hard, but the upper and lower bounds above (denoted $\mathcal{U}(\mathcal{A})^S$ and $\mathcal{L}(\mathcal{A})^S$ respectively) are easily computable, a post-processing step may be needed, to select the most-probable assignment from a number of possible candidates. During the first part of the algorithm, the assignments are sorted in the agenda according to $\mathcal{U}(\mathcal{A})$. We need to collect the *set* of assignments F such that for all assignments $\mathcal{A}$ not in F, $\mathcal{U}(\mathcal{A})$ is smaller than $\mathcal{L}(\mathcal{A})'$, for *some* $\mathcal{A}'$ in F. This assures us that the most-probable assignment is indeed in F. Hopefully, F is a small set (as indeed it will prove to be in almost all cases where one explanation clearly stands out). Then, we evaluate the exact probability of the assignments in F in parallel by adding AND nodes for all of them and evaluating the diagram exactly once. Naturally, if F happens to contain only one assignment, we do not need to post-process the results.

4 FUTURE WORK

The locality property of IB assignments and δ-IB assignments, i.e. the fact that local testing is sufficient to determine whether an assignment is an IB assignment, together with a quick way of computing its probability, makes it possible, in principle, to use other types of algorithm. Future research will determine whether random simulation techniques will prove useful.

Another possibility is to reduce IB-MAP computation to complete MAP computation (on a different belief network). That will allow us to use any complete MAP algorithm, such as belief updating ([Pearl, 1988]), to be used. This may prove to be faster than our algorithms for networks with a small maximal clique size (for using clustering), or a small cutset size (for using conditioning). The algorithm presented in [Santos Jr., 1991a] and [Santos Jr., 1991b] may also prove useful for our purposes, if it can be easily extended to work on multiple-valued nodes.

5 SUMMARY

We introduced irrelevance-based partial MAPs in order to solve the overspecification problem inherent in complete MAP explanation. We defined two methods for defining what nodes are irrelevant, one based on exact independence, the other based on approximate independence. We then discussed properties of the resulting partial MAPs that allowed us to transform an existing best-first search for complete MAPs into one that computes irrelevance-based partial MAPs. The modifications required were minimal.

For independence-based assignments, we showed that we can check whether an assignment is independence based using only local information, (i.e. they are "locally recognizable"). Computation of the probability of such an assignment is also easy, and can be done using only $|S|$ conditional probability array entries. We showed how to adapt our best-first MAP algorithm to compute IB-MAPs, and proved the correctness of the resulting algorithm.

δ-independence-based assignments were shown to be locally recognizable. Computing the exact probability is hard, but good, easily computable bounds are available. It is possible to compute the exact probabilities in parallel, using only one belief-network evaluation (with extra nodes).

We have implemented algorithms for finding IB-MAPs and for finding δIB-MAPs, and their running time seems roughly comparable to the running time of our complete MAP algorithm running on the same networks. That is not surprising, as the additional work required for expansion and for completion testing in small, and the number of states expanded is usually smaller than for complete MAPs.

Acknowledgements

This work has been supported in part by the National Science Foundation under grants IST 8416034 and IST 8515005 and Office of Naval Research under grant N00014-79-C-0529. The author is funded by a Corinna Borden Keen Fellowship. Special thanks to Eugene Charniak for helpful suggestions and for reviewing drafts of the paper.

References

[Charniak and Goldman, 1988] Eugene Charniak and Robert Goldman. A logic for semantic interpretation. In *Proceedings of the ACL Conference*, 1988.

[Charniak and Shimony, 1990] Eugene Charniak and Solomon E. Shimony. Probabilistic semantics for cost-based abduction. In *Proceedings of the 8th National Conference on AI*, August 1990.

[Cooper, 1984] Gregory Floyd Cooper. *NESTOR: A Computer-Based Medical Diagnosis Aid that Integrates Causal and Probabilistic Knowledge.* PhD thesis, Stanford University, 1984.

[Hobbs and Stickel, 1988] Jerry R. Hobbs and Mark Stickel. Interpretation as abduction. In *Proceedings of the 26th Conference of the ACL*, 1988.

[Pearl, 1988] J. Pearl. *Probabilistic Reasoning in Intelligent Systems: Networks of Plausible Inference.* Morgan Kaufmann, San Mateo, CA, 1988.

[Peng and Reggia, 1987] Y. Peng and J. A. Reggia. A probabilistic causal model for diagnostic problem solving (parts 1 and 2). In *IEEE Transactions on Systems, Man and Cybernetics*, pages 146–162 and 395–406, 1987.

[Poole and Provan, 1990] David Poole and Gregory M. Provan. What is an optimal diagnosis? In *Proceedings of the 6th Conference on Uncertainty in AI*, pages 46–53, 1990.

[Santos Jr., 1991a] Eugene Santos Jr. A linear constraint satisfaction approach to cost-based abduction. Technical report, Computer Science Department, Brown University, 1991.

[Santos Jr., 1991b] Eugene Santos Jr. On the generation of alternative explanations with implications. In *Proceedings of the 7th Conference on Uncertainty in AI*, 1991.

[Shimony and Charniak, 1990] Solomon E. Shimony and Eugene Charniak. A new algorithm for finding map assignments to belief networks. In *Proceedings of the 6th Conference on Uncertainty in AI*, 1990.

[Shimony, 1991] Solomon E. Shimony. Explanation, irrelevance and statistical independence. In *AAAI Proceedings*, 1991.

About Updating.

Philippe Smets
IRIDIA, Université Libre de Bruxelles
50 av. F. Roosevelt, CP194/6. B-1050 Brussels, Belgium.

Abstract:

Survey of several forms of updating, with a practical illustrative example.

We study several updating (conditioning) schemes that emerge naturally from a common scenario to provide some insights into their meaning. Updating is a subtle operation and there is no single method, no single 'good' rule. The choice of the appropriate rule must always be given due consideration. Planchet (1989) presents a mathematical survey of many rules.We focus on the practical meaning of these rules. After summarizing the several rules for conditioning, we present an illustrative example in which the various forms of conditioning can be explained.

1. CONDITIONING RULES FOR BELIEF FUNCTIONS.

Let Ω be a finite set with elements $\omega_1, \omega_2, ...\omega_n$. The ω_i are mutually exclusive possible answers to a given question. Let bel: $2^\Omega \rightarrow [0,1]$ be a belief function over Ω, with m its corresponding basic belief mass assignment. For $A \subseteq \Omega$, bel(A) quantifies our degree of belief that the true answer to the question is in A. If the ω_i are an exhaustive list of possible answers, the closed-world assumption prevails (as no solution exists outside Ω), otherwise the open-world assumption prevails (Smets 1988)

Suppose a new piece of evidence that says that the answer is not in $\bar{A}$, where $\bar{A}$ is the set of ω_i that are elements of Ω, but not of A. To say that the answer is not in $\bar{A}$ does not mean that the answer is in A. Under closed-world assumption both statements are equivalent. Under open-world assumption, they are not. Here, the answer might be none of the elements of Ω. When I say "the answer is not in $\bar{A}$", I only eliminate the elements of $\bar{A}$ as possible answer. When I say "the answer is in A", not only I eliminate the elements of $\bar{A}$, but I also claim that the answer is an element of A - a much stronger claim. This distinction is at the origin of the difference between the open-world and the closed-world assumptions.

The updating of bel induced by the information that the answer is not in $\bar{A}$ can be performed variously. It will depend on the interpretation of the problem that bel is supposed to model.

Conditioning C.1. The Unnormalized Dempster's Rule of Conditioning.

For all $X \subseteq \Omega$, the basic belief masses m(X) given to X is transferred to $A \cap X$. The basic belief masses assignment m_A, the belief function bel_A and the plausibility function pl_A obtained after conditioning on A are:

$$m_A(B) = \sum_{X \subseteq \bar{A}} m(B \cup X) \qquad \text{for } B \subseteq A$$

$$m_A(B) = 0 \qquad \text{for } B \not\subseteq A$$

$$bel_A(B) = bel(B \cup \bar{A}) - bel(\bar{A}) \text{ for } B \subseteq \Omega$$

$$pl_A(B) = pl(B \cap A) \qquad \text{for } B \subseteq \Omega$$

This solution is always applicable, even when pl(A) = 0. Notice that $m_A(\emptyset)$ might be non null with this solution. In fact, one has: $m_A(\emptyset) = m(\emptyset) + bel(\bar{A})$.

This rule is the one described in the transferable belief model under open world assumption (Smets 1988).

Conditioning C.2. The Normalized Dempster's Rule of Conditioning.

Masses are transferred as in conditioning C.1, but the result is then proportionally normalized to cope with the masses that would be transferred to the empty set. This avoids ending with a positive mass on $\emptyset$, and guarantees that $bel(\Omega) = 1$. After conditioning, one gets:

$$m_A(B) = c \sum_{X \subseteq \bar{A}} m(B \cup X) \qquad \text{for } B \subseteq A, B \neq \emptyset$$

$$m_A(B) = 0 \qquad \text{for } B \not\subseteq A$$

and for $B \subseteq \Omega$

$$bel_A(B) = c\,(bel(B \cup \bar{A}) - bel(\bar{A}))$$

$$pl_A(B) = c\, pl(B \cap A)$$

where $c^{-1} = bel(\Omega) - bel(\bar{A}) = pl(A)$.

This solution applies only when pl(A)>0. No solution is provided when pl(A)=0.

This rule is the one described in the transferable belief model under closed world assumption. It is the one initially proposed by Shafer (1976a).

Conditioning C.2'. Bayesian solution.

The classical solution with probability function is,

$$P_A(B) = \frac{P(B\cap A)}{P(A)} \qquad \text{for } B\subseteq\Omega.$$

This solution applies only if P(A)>0. If P(A)=0, no solution is provided.

This is a particular case of conditioning C.2. It is obtained when the belief function bel is a probability function.

Conditioning C.3. Yager-Kohlas's Solution.

The basic belief masses are transferred as in C.1, but the masses that could be transferred to the empty set are reallocated to A, so:

$$m_A(B) = \sum_{X\subseteq\overline{A}} m(B\cup X) \qquad \forall B\subseteq A, B\neq A, B\neq\emptyset$$

$$m_A(A) = \sum_{X\subseteq\overline{A}} m(A\cup X) + bel(\overline{A})$$

$$m_A(B) = 0 \qquad \forall B\not\subseteq A$$

$$bel_A(B) = bel(B\cup\overline{A}) - bel(\overline{A}) \qquad \forall B\subseteq A, B\neq A$$

$$bel_A(A) = bel(\Omega)$$

$$pl_A(B) = pl(B\cap A) + bel(\overline{A}) \qquad \forall B\subseteq A$$

This conditioning might seem artificial, but it will be shown that it can be observed sometimes. It was proposed in Yager (1985) and Kohlas (1989). It applies normally only to normalized belief functions (i.e., those with $m(\emptyset)=0$ or equivalently with $bel(\Omega)=1$)

Conditioning C.4. Geometric Rule of Conditioning.

One way to condition belief functions consists in deciding that all basic belief masses not given to subsets of A are nullified, and those given to subsets of A are proportionally normalized so their sum remains one. Then m_A, bel_A and pl_A become:

$$m_A(B) = \frac{m(B)}{bel(A)} \qquad \text{if } B\subseteq A$$

$$= 0 \qquad \text{otherwise}$$

$$bel_A(B) = \frac{bel(B\cap A)}{bel(A)} \qquad \forall B\subseteq\Omega$$

$$pl_A(B) = \frac{pl(B\cup\overline{A}) - pl(\overline{A})}{pl(\Omega) - pl(\overline{A})} \qquad \forall B\subseteq\Omega$$

These relations are described under the closed-world assumption. Their extensions under open-world assumption are obtained by suppressing the denominators in m_A, bel_A and pl_A. The geometrical rule of conditioning has been discussed in Suppes and Zanotti (1977) and Shafer (1976b).

Conditioning C.5. Specialization.

Kruse (1990) has studied a conditioning rule that applies to the transferable belief model and is probably the most general form of conditioning that ties in with the idea of basic belief masses that quantify the part of belief that supports a set A of Ω and cannot support a more specific subset of A through lack of information. The idea is that the basic belief mass given to a set A is distributed among the subsets B of A. This concept was also studied by Yager (1986) and Dubois and Prade (1986) when they introduced the ideas of belief inclusions. These authors work under closed-world assumption. Our presentation is made under the open-world assumption.

For each subset $X\subseteq\Omega$, let c(B, X) $\forall X,B\subseteq\Omega$ be non negative coefficients such that:

$$c(B, X) = 0 \quad \text{if } B\not\subseteq X$$

$$\sum_{B\subseteq X} c(B,X) = 1$$

Then the basic belief masses m* obtained by a specialization based on the c(B, X) coefficients are:

$$m^*(B) = \sum_{B\subseteq X} c(B, X)\, m(X) \qquad \forall B\subseteq\Omega$$

The Dempster and the geometric rule of conditioning are specializations. Suppose we known that the answer to the question about Ω is not in $\overline{A}\subseteq\Omega$.

One obtains the unnormalized Dempster's rule of conditioning when $c(B, B\cup Y) = 1$, $Y\subseteq\overline{A}$. Then:

$$m_A(B) = \sum_{Y\subseteq\Omega} c(B, B\cup Y)\, m(B\cup Y) \qquad \forall B\subseteq A$$

One obtains the unnormalized geometric rule of conditioning if c(B, B) = 1 whenever $B\subseteq A$ and $c(\emptyset, B) = 1$ whenever $B\cap A\neq\emptyset$ otherwise. Normalized rules of conditioning are obtained by further rescaling.

Yager-Kohlas conditioning is not a specialization as the masses given to subsets of $\overline{A}$ are transferred to A.

Remark: the unnormalized Dempster's rule of combination is also a specialization. Suppose there exist two basic belief masses assignment m_1 and m_2 on Ω. Let $m_{12} = m_1\oplus m_2$ and let $c(X, Z) = m_1(X|Z)$. Then (Smets 1991b):

$$m_{12}(X) = \sum_{Y\cap Z=\emptyset\ Y,Z\subseteq\overline{A}} m_1(X\cup Y)\, m_2(X\cup Z) = \sum_{Z\subseteq\Omega} m_1(X|Z)\, m_2(Z)$$

Conditioning C.6. Imaging.

Lewis (1976) considers that probabilities are given to worlds, so each ω_i represents a world. If one learns that a set $\overline{A}$ of world is impossible (does not contain the answer), then the probabilities given to the worlds in $\overline{A}$ are transferred to the 'closest' worlds in A.

Suppose the 'closest' relation $n(\omega, A)$: $\Omega x\Omega\rightarrow\Omega$ with $n(\omega, A)$ being the world in A that is the closest to world ω. So $n(\omega, A)\in A$ and $n(\omega, A)=\omega$ if $\omega\in A$, i.e., the worlds in A are the closest to themselves.

After conditioning on A by the imaging method, the probability $P(\omega)$ given to a world ω is transferred to the world $n(\omega, A)$.

Let $F(\omega_i|\omega_j) = 1$ if $\omega_i= n(\omega_j, A)$
$= 0$ otherwise

Then $P_A(\omega_i) = \sum_{\omega_j\in\Omega} F(\omega_i|\omega_j)\, P(\omega_j) \quad \forall\omega_i\in\Omega.$

Note that $P_A(\omega_i) = 0$ if $\omega_i\in\overline{A}$. We use the conditional probability notation for F to enhance the fact that F behaves as a conditional probability function.

Of course the idea of 'closest' world needs to be defined and most of the criticism against this conditioning rule focusses on criticism of the idea of closeness between worlds (see Gardenfors 1988).

Gärdenfors (1988) generalizes Lewis's imaging. He considers that the probability given to a world that is learned to be impossible is distributed among the remaining worlds according to some probability distribution that somehow reflect closeness between worlds. $F(\omega_i|\omega_j)$ will represent the portion of the probability given to world $\omega_j\in\overline{A}$ that is transferred to world $\omega_i\in A$. So let:

$$F(\omega_i|\omega_j) \begin{cases} = 0 & \text{if } \omega_i\in\overline{A} \\ = 1 & \text{if } \omega_j\in A,\ \omega_i = \omega_j \\ = 0 & \text{if } \omega_j\in A,\ \omega_i \neq \omega_j \\ \geq 0 & \text{if } \omega_j\in\overline{A} \text{ and } \omega_i\in A \end{cases}$$

and $\sum_{\omega_i\in\Omega} F(\omega_i|\omega_j) = 1 \quad \forall\omega_j\in\Omega$

Conditioning on A leads to the relations:

$$P_A(\omega_i) = \sum_{\omega_j\in\Omega} F(\omega_i|\omega_j)\, P(\omega_j) \qquad \forall\omega_i\in\Omega$$

Note that $P_A(\omega_i) = 0$ if $\omega_i\in\overline{A}$.

These relations were described for probability function (under closed-world assumption). They can be generalized in two ways: 1) the requirement $F(\omega_i|\omega_j) = 0$ if $\omega_i\in\overline{A}$ is dropped, and 2) the domain from Ω to 2^Ω is generalized (one assimilates the basic belief masses to probabilities on the power set 2^Ω). Let the relation $F:2^\Omega x2^\Omega\rightarrow[0, 1]$ with: $\sum_{B\subseteq\Omega} F(B|X) = 1 \quad \forall X\subseteq\Omega$

After conditioning on 'not in $\overline{A}$', one gets:

$$m_A(B) = \sum_{X\subseteq\Omega} F(B|X)\, m(X) \qquad \forall B\subseteq\Omega$$

This conditioning relation subsumes all those presented so far.

Specialization is obtained if:
$F(B|X) = 0 \qquad \forall B\cap\overline{A}\neq\emptyset$
Yager-Kohlas conditioning is obtained if:

$$F(B|X) \begin{cases} = 0 & \forall B\cap\overline{A}\neq\emptyset \\ = 1 & B\subseteq A,\ X = B\cup Y\ \forall Y\subseteq\overline{A} \\ = 1 & B=A,\ X\subseteq\overline{A} \end{cases}$$

Conditioning C.7. Upper and Lower Bayesian Conditioning.

Suppose I know only that an unknown probability function P over Ω belongs to a convex subset $\mathcal{P}$ of the set $\mathbb{P}$ of the probability functions defined on Ω. The upper and lower probabilities P^* and P_* define P uniquely, where

$\forall A\subseteq\Omega \quad P^*(A) = \max\{P(A) : P\in\mathcal{P}\}$
$P_*(A) = \min\{P(A) : P\in\mathcal{P}\}.$

Suppose one asks for the value of $P(B|A) = \frac{P(A\cap B)}{P(A)}$. All that can be said is that $P(B|A)$ is between the upper and lower conditional probabilities $P^*(B|A)$ and $P_*(B|A)$, where $\forall A\subseteq\Omega$ (Smets 1987):

$P^*(B|A) = \max\{P(B|A) : P\in\mathcal{P}\}$
$P_*(B|A) = \min\{P(B|A) : P\in\mathcal{P}\}.$

It can be shown that (see Dempster 1967, Fagin and Halpern 1990, Jaffray 1990, Zhang 1989):

$$P^*(B|A) = \frac{P^*(A\cap B)}{P^*(A\cap B)+P_*(A\cap\overline{B})}$$

$$P_*(B|A) = \frac{P_*(A \cap B)}{P_*(A \cap B) + P^*(A \cap \bar{B})}$$

Fagin and Halpern (1990), Jaffray (1990) and Zhang (1989) show that if $P_*(.)$ is a belief function, then $P_*(.|A)$ is also a belief function. Jaffray (1990) also provides the basic belief masses derived from $P_*(.|A)$ by the inverse Moebius transform.

It can be shown that the Upper and Lower Bayesian Conditioning is not a specialization. It is a generalized imaging where the coefficents depend on the basic belief masses of the initial belief function.

2. THE SCENARIO: THE VOTING INTENTIONS STUDY.

To illustrate the meaning of the various rules of conditioning we have described, we present a scenario that deals with objective data, induced objective proportions, and where the various forms of conditioning can be described, depending on the contextual information.

Suppose I organize a study on how people will vote in the next election. Let $\Omega = \{a, b, c, d, e\}$ be the set of candidates. One candidate must be selected by 100 voters. Each voter may vote for only one candidate. Voting will be next Sunday and today, Monday, I shall ask each potential voter to indicate for whom he intends to vote. But voters' opinions, today, are not firmly established and some voters can only point to a subset A of Ω that contains the name of the candidate they will vote for, but they have not yet decided definitively among these candidates in set A. We accept that voters will always vote for one of the candidates belonging to the set they provided to on Monday; opinions can only be made more specific.

Sets Answered	Frequencies	Sets after Conditioning
{a}	5	?
{a, b}	8	?
{a, b, c}	15	{c}
{b, c, d}	21	{c, d}
{a, b, c, d}	29	{c, d}
{d, e}	22	{d, e}

Table 1. Distribution of voters' intentions Monday, and sets of candidates that remain after the conditioning on {c, d, e}. ? indicates ambiguities that are discussed in the various conditioning schemes.

The voting intentions of the 100 voters are summarized in table 1. Note that the data do not result from a survey based on a sample, but from an exhaustive study of the whole population. This prevents problems related to sampling variations.

On Sunday, the 100 voters will vote and their votes will generate a frequency distribution over Ω. Let $\mathbb{P}$ be the set of frequency distributions Prop over Ω, where Prop(a) for $a \in \Omega$ is the proportion of voters who vote a, and Prop(A) $= \sum_{a \in A}$ Prop(a) for $A \subseteq \Omega$[1]. We will neglect the fact that the population is finite, and accept that Prop(A) for $A \subseteq \Omega$ can take any value in [0, 1].

On Sunday, one element of $\mathbb{P}$ will be selected, the one corresponding to the distribution of votes. But today we do not for instance know Prop(a). We know that Prop(a) is at least 5%, at most 78%. Any value in between is acceptable. So all the Monday data says is that Prop belongs to a subset $\mathcal{P}$ of $\mathbb{P}$ where $\mathcal{P}$ contains all those frequency distributions on Ω compatible with the observed frequencies given in table 1. The set $\mathcal{P}$ is uniquely defined by the upper and lower proportions Prop* and $Prop_*$ where $\forall A \subseteq \Omega$

$$\text{Prop}^*(A) = \max\{\text{Prop}(A) : \text{Prop} \in \mathcal{P}\}$$

and $$\text{Prop}_*(A) = \min\{\text{Prop}(A) : \text{Prop} \in \mathcal{P}\}$$

Some upper and lower proportions induced by the data of table 1 are given in table 2. The proportions Prop(A) will be such that $\forall A \subseteq \Omega$:

$$\text{Prop}_*(A) \le \text{Prop}(A) \le \text{Prop}^*(A)$$

Set	$Prop_*$	Prop*
{a}	5 = 5%	5+8+15+29 = 57%
{a, b}	5+8 = 13%	5+8+15+21+29 = 78%
{a, b, c}	5+8+15 = 28%	5+8+15+21+29 = 78%
{c}	0 = 0%	15+21+29 = 65%
{d}	0 = 0%	21+29+22 = 72%
{c, d}	0 = 0%	15+21+29+22 = 87%
{c, d, e}	22 = 22%	15+21+29+22 = 87%

Table 2. Values for some upper and lower proportions induced by the data of table 1.

We are facing a typical case of upper and lower proportions generated by random sets.

3. CONDITIONING.

I collected my data on Monday, but on Tuesday I learn candidates a and b were killed in a car accident during the night. What can I say about Sunday's elections results?

[1]We speak of proportions, not of probablity, in order to avoid any confusion. Probability admits many definitions. Using proportions, and later beliefs, will prevent - hopefully - any confusion.

The 15 voters who answered {a, b, c} will have to vote for c as c is the only remaining candidate and these 15 voters had indicated their willingness to consider a candidate in {a, b, c}. Identically, the 21 and 29 voters who had answered {b, c, d} or {a, b, c, d} will vote for a candidate in {c, d}.
The impact of the conditioning information, a and b are dead, results in a transfer of frequencies similar to the one described in the transferable belief model. The frequency given to a set X is transferred to the set $X \cap \overline{Y}$ once we know that the truth is not in $\overline{Y}$. But what about the 13 voters who answered {a} or {a, b}?

Several scenarios can be considered that lead to the different solutions we wish to illustrate. Some may appear somewhat artificial, but that is not the point. We only wish to give a meaning to each conditioning rule.

The labels of the scenarios are those of the conditioning rules described in section 2.

Scenario C1 : Compulsory Voting.

Suppose we are in Belgium where voting is compulsory (absentees are fined). The 13 voters must cast their votes. If blank voting is allowed, we might consider they will cast blank votes. Table C.1 presents some upper and lower proportions induced after conditioning on {c, d, e}. Note that 13 blank votes will be collected, so Prop∗(Ø)= Prop*(Ø) = 13%.

Set	Prop∗	Prop*
{c}	15 = 15%	15+21+29 = 65%
{d}	0 = 0%	21+29+22 = 72%
{c, d}	15+21+29 = 65%	15+21+29+22 = 87%
{c, d, e}	65+22 = 87%	15+21+29+22 = 87%

Table C.1. Values for some upper and lower proportions induced by the frequencies of table 1 and the conditioning C.1. (65 = 15+21+29)

This conditioning rule is similar to Dempster's rule of conditioning under open world assumption.

Scenario C.2. Free Voting.

Same as Scenario C.1, but we compute proportions among those who do not abstain. This is also the French situation where there is no obligation to vote, in which case the 13 voters would not vote on Sunday. Table C.2 presents some upper and lower proportions induced after conditioning on {c, d, e}

This conditioning rule is similar to Dempster's rule of conditioning under closed-world assumption. It is identical with the C.1 conditioning rule except for the normalization factor (the division by 87).

Set	Prop∗	Prop*
{c}	$\frac{15}{87} = 17.2\%$	$\frac{15+21+29}{87} = 74.7\%$
{d}	$\frac{0}{87} = 0.0\%$	$\frac{21+29+22}{87} = 82.8\%$
{c, d}	$\frac{65}{87} = 74.7\%$	$\frac{65+22}{87} = 100\%$
{c, d, e}	$\frac{65+22}{87} = 100\%$	$\frac{65+22}{87} = 100\%$

Table C.2. Values for some upper and lower proportions induced by the frequencies of table 1 and the conditioning C.2.

Scenario C.3. Compulsory Choice.

Back to Belgium context C.1 (compulsory voting), but blank votes are not allowed. So all I know about the 13 voters that pose a problem is that they will vote for a candidate in {c, d, e}. Table C.3 presents some upper and lower proportions induced after conditioning on {c, d, e}.

Set	Prop∗	Prop*
{c}	15=15%	15+21+29+13=78%
{d}	0=0%	21+29+22+13=85%
{c, d}	15+21+29=65%	65+22+13=100%
{c, d, e}	65+22+13=100%	65+22+13=100%

Table C.3. Values for some upper and lower proportions induced by the frequencies of table 1 and the conditioning C.3.

This conditioning is similar to Yager-Kohlas rule.

Scenario C.4: Geometrical Rule.

Suppose that each voter who had given an answer that contained a or b is so depressed that he commits suicide. Then only 22 voters are left. The proportions among those who had answered a subset of {c, d, e} will be proportionally rescaled. Table C.4 presents some upper and lower proportions induced after conditioning on {c, d, e}.

Set	Prop∗	Prop*
{c, d}	0 = 0%	$\frac{22}{22} = 100\%$
{d, e}	$\frac{22}{22} = 100\%$	$\frac{22}{22} = 100\%$

Table C.4. Values for some upper and lower proportions induced by the frequencies of table 1 and the conditioning C.4.

This conditioning corresponds to the geometrical rule of conditioning, a form also encountered naturally in scenarios based on random sets (Smets 1990a)

Scenario C.5: Specialization

Specialization is obtained when I consider that the information "a and b are dead' allows me to reconsider each voter's answer. For each type of answer, I consider that those who select it will be distributed among its subsets not containing a and b according to a known distribution. The coefficients c of the specialization are these probabilities. As an example, suppose I know (by my knowledge of the political links among the candidates) that: 1) among those who answered {b, c, d}, one third will vote c, one third will vote d, one third is still undecided, 2) among those who answered {a, b, c, d}, half will vote d, the other half is still undecided, and 3) among those who answer {d, e}, half will vote d, the others will vote e. The 13 voters who answer {a} and {a, b} will cast blank votesas in scenario C.1 (normalization can be introduced as in scenario C2). Table C.5 presents some upper and lower proportions induced after conditioning on {c, d, e}.

Set	Prop∗	Prop*
{c}	15+7=22%	15+14+14.5=43.5%
{d}	7+14.5+11=32.5%	14+29+11=54%
{c, d}	65+11=76%	65+11=76%
{c, d, e}	65+22=87%	65+22=87%

Table C.5. Values for some upper and lower proportions induced by the frequencies of table 1 and the conditioning C.5.

This conditioning form corresponds to the specialization.

Scenario C.6.1. Introspective Realloca-tion: level 1.

Maybe I know more about the candidates than their names. I know that a and b had similar political orientations and that among c, d and e, c is politically the closest to a and b. Then I might consider that the 13 voters without a candidate will vote for c. Table C.6.1 presents some upper and lower proportions induced after conditioning on {c, d, e}

Set	Prop∗	Prop*
{c}	15+13=28%	15+21+29+13=78%
{d}	0=0%	21+29+22=72%
{c, d}	65+13=78%	65+22+13=100%
{c, d, e}	65+22+13=100%	65+22+13=100%

Table C.6.1. Values for some upper and lower proportions induced by the frequencies of table 1 and the conditioning C.6.1.

This conditioning generalizes the imaging conditioning introduced by Lewis where:

$\forall Y \subseteq \overline{A}$ $F(B|B \cup Y)$ $= 1$ $B \subseteq A$
$= 0$ otherwise

Scenario C.6.2. Introspective Realloca-ion: level 2.

Generalizing Scenario C.6.1, we might consider c as politically very close to a and b, d as quite similar to a and b, and e totally different. So we might accept that there is a certain proportion of the 13 voters that will vote for c and the remainder will vote for c or d. Let the proportion of people that will vote for c given they had decided to vote for a or b be 0.4, and the others will vote for {c, d}.

Table C.6.2 presents some upper and lower proportions induced after conditioning on {c, d, e}.

Set	Prop∗	Prop*
{c}	15+5.2=20.2%	15+21+29+13=78%
{d}	0=0%	21+29+22+7.8=80%
{c, d}	65+13=78%	65+22+13=100%
{c, d, e}	65+22+13=100%	65+22+13=100%

Table C.6.2. Values for some upper and lower proportions induced by the frequencies of table 1 and the conditioning C.6.2.

This form of conditioning generalizes Gärdenfors's Imaging to power sets, where

$\forall Y \subseteq \overline{A}$ $F(B|Y) \geq 0$ $B \subseteq A$
$= 0$ otherwise

Scenario C.6.3. Introspective Realloca-tion: level 3.

You might be even more subtle in your opinion than in scenario C.6.2. You might consider differently the 5 voters who answered {a} and the 8 who answered {a, b}.

Set	Prop∗	Prop*
{c}	15+6=21%	65+13=78%
{d}	0=0%	21+29+22+5=77%
{c, d}	65+11=76%	65+22+13=100%
{c, d, e}	65+22+13=100%	65+22+13=100%

Table C.6.3. Values for some upper and lower proportions induced by the frequencies of table 1 and the conditioning C.6.3.

They are not identical and you might consider that the distribution of the 5 among {c, d, e} is different from the distribution of the 8. For instance, you might consider that 1) among the 5 voters who answered {a} Monday,

40% (=2) would answer {c} Tuesday, the other (=3) {c, d}, and 2) among the 8 voters who answered {a, b}, half (=4) would answer {c}, one quarter (=2) would answer {c, d} and the last quarter (=2) would answer {c, e}. Table C.6.3 presents some upper and lower proportions induced after conditioning on {c, d, e}.

This corresponds to the generalization of the imaging where

$$
\begin{array}{lll}
F(B|B) & = 1 & \text{if } B \subseteq A \\
F(B|X) & \geq 0 & \text{if } B \subseteq A,\ X \subseteq \bar{A} \\
 & = 0 & \text{otherwise}
\end{array}
$$

Scenario C.7. Upper and Lower Bayesian Conditioning.

Before learning that a and b are dead, i.e., Monday evening, I would like to assess the proportion of those who will vote for c among those who will vote for c or d or e on Sunday. Should I know the frequency distribution of the Sunday votes, I would compute

$$\text{Prop}(\{c\}|\{c, d, e\}) = \frac{\text{Prop}(\{c\})}{\text{Prop}(\{c, d, e\})}$$

But I do not know these values. All I know are upper and lower limits for each Prop. I know that Prop is in a subset $\mathcal{P}$ of $\mathbb{P}$, the set of frequency distributions on Ω. For each Prop in $\mathcal{P}$, I can compute Prop({c}|{c, d, e}).

Set	Prop∗	Prop*
{c}	$\frac{0}{0+21+29+22} = 0\%$	$\frac{65}{65+0} = 100\%$
{d}	$\frac{0}{0+65+22} = 0\%$	$\frac{21+29+22}{21+29+22+0} = 100\%$
{c, d}	$\frac{0}{0+22} = 0\%$	$\frac{65+22}{65+22+0} = 100\%$
{d, e}	$\frac{22}{22+65} = 25.3\%$	$\frac{21+29+22}{21+29+22+0} = 100\%$

Table C.7. Values for some upper and lower conditional proportions induced by the frequencies of table 1 and the conditioning C.7.

Consequently I know that the upper lower limits of Prop({c}|{c, d, e}) are between the upper and lower conditional proportions Prop*(.|{c, d, e}) and Prop∗(.|{c, d, e}) where

$$\text{Prop}^*(A|\{c,d,e\}) = \max\{\frac{\text{Prop}(\{c\})}{\text{Prop}(\{c, d, e\})} : \text{Prop} \in \mathcal{P}\}$$
$$= \frac{\text{Prop}^*(\{c\})}{\text{Prop}^*(\{c\}) + \text{Prop}_*(\{d, e\})}$$
$$\text{Prop}_*(A|\{c,d,e\}) = \min\{\frac{\text{Prop}(\{c\})}{\text{Prop}(\{c, d, e\})} : \text{Prop} \in \mathcal{P}\}$$
$$= \frac{\text{Prop}_*(\{c\})}{\text{Prop}_*(\{c\}) + \text{Prop}^*(\{d, e\})}$$

This conditioning corresponds to the upper and lower bayesian conditioning.

4. BELIEFS INDUCED BY THE PROPORTIONS.

Suppose a voter is going to be selected randomly among the 100 voters (with equiprobability for each voter). The question is to bet on who is the Sunday candidate of this randomly selected voter.

Given the available data, all I can say is that the proportion Prop(A) of voters who will vote for a candidate in set A⊆Ω on Sunday is included between Prop∗(A) and Prop*(A). So the probability P(A) that the selected voters will vote for a candidate in A is included between Prop∗(A) and Prop*(A). Thus I can build upper and lower probabilities P*(A) and P∗(A) for P(A) where P*(A) = Prop*(A) and P∗(A) = Prop∗(A). Given this set of upper and lower probabilities, I can build the pignistic probabilities BetP of the fact that the randomly selected voter will vote for a candidate in A (Smets 1990b), (see also Smets (1991b) for a practical justification of the pignistic transformation).

$$\text{BetP}(A) = \sum_{X \subseteq \Omega} m(X) \frac{|X \cap A|}{|X|}$$

where |X| is the number of candidates in set X⊆Ω. BetP is a probability function, and all bets on Ω are built on it.

But the knowledge of these upper and lower probabilities can also induce a belief in me about the candidate for which the randomly selected voter will vote. As shown in Smets (1991a), the belief function that quantifies my belief about Ω is numerically equal to the lower probabilities function (because mathematically the lower probability happens to be a belief function in the present scenario). This is based on the maximal-minimal isopignistic transformation described in Smets (1991a). The pignistic transformation of this belief function is of course the same as the one derived from the upper and lower probabilities. So analysing the problem directly from the upper and lower probabilities point of view or through the belief function induced by these upper and lower probabilities leads to the same results.

A bet on who will be the Sunday winner is not analysed. It requires a study of our belief concerning the subsets of $\mathbb{P}$. The belief that x is the winner is equal to the belief allocated to those frequency distributions in $\mathcal{P} \subseteq \mathbb{P}$ where x is the most frequent observation. That is a completely different problem altogether and will not be dealt with.

5. CONCLUSIONS.

We have shown that conditioning can be performed by many rules, and through an illustrative example, we have provided scenarios that lead to each form of conditioning. This study is not exhaustive as other forms of updating can - and have been - suggested (Cano and Moral 1990, Moral and De Campos 1990). We hope that these illustrative examples will help the user understand the meaning of the various conditioning rules we have studied.

Acknowledgements.

The following text presents some research results of the Belgian National incentive-programme for fundamental research in artificial intelligence initiated by the Belgian State, Prime Minister's Office, Science Policy Programming. Scientific responsibility is assumed by the author. Research work has been partly supported by the DRUMS project which is funded by a grant from the Commission of the European Communities under the ESPRIT II-Program, Basic Research Project 3085.

Bibliography.

CANO J.E. and MORAL S. (1990) Combination of incomplete probabilistic information. (unpublished manuscript)

DEGROOT M.H. (1970) Optimal statistical decisions. McGraw-Hill, New York.

DEMPSTER A.P. (1967) Upper and lower probabilities induced by a multplevalued mapping. Ann. Math. Statistics 38: 325-339.

DUBOIS D. and PRADE H. (1986) A set theoretical view of belief functions. Int. J. Gen. Systems, 12:193-226.

FAGIN R. and HALPERN J. (1990) A new approach to uptdating beliefs. 6th Conf. on Uncertainty in AI.

GARDENFORS P. (1988) Knowledge in flux. Modelling the dynamics of epistemùic states. MIT Press, Cambridge, Mass.

JAFFREY J.Y. (1990) Bayesian conditioning and belief functions. IPMU-1990.

KOHLAS J. (1989) The reliability of reasoning with unreliable arguments. Inst. Automation and Oper. Research, Univ. Freiburg, Technical report 168.

KRUSE R. and SCHWECKE E. (1990) Specialization: a new concept for uncertainty handling with belief functions. Int. J. Gen. Systems (to appear)

LEWIS D. (1976) Probabilities of conditionals and conditional probabilities. Philosophical Review 85: 297-315.

MORAL S. and DE CAMPOS L.M. (1990) Updating uncertain information. (unpublished manuscript)

PLANCHET B. (1989) Credibility and conditioning. J. Theor. Probabil. 2:289-299.

SHAFER G. (1976a) A mathematical theory of evidence. Princeton Univ. Press. Princeton, NJ.

SHAFER G. (1976b) A theory of statistical evidence. in Foundations of probability theory, statistical inference, and statistical theories of science. Harper and Hooker ed. Reidel, Doordrecht-Holland.

SMETS Ph. (1988) Belief functions. in SMETS Ph, MAMDANI A., DUBOIS D. and PRADE H. ed. Non standard logics for automated reasoning. Academic Press, London p 253-286.

SMETS P. (1987) Upper and lower probability functions versus belief functions. Proc. International Symposium on Fuzzy Systems and Knowledge Engineering, Guangzhou, China, July 10-16, pg 17-21.

SMETS Ph. (1990a) The transferable belief model and random sets. To appear in Int. J. Intell. Systems.

SMETS Ph. (1990b) Construucting the pignistic probability function in a context of uncertainty. Uncertainty in Artificial Intelligence 5, Henrion M., Shachter R.D., Kanal L.N. and Lemmer J.F. eds, North Holland, Amsterdam, , 29-40.

SMETS Ph. (1991a)Belief induced by the knowledge of some probabilities. Submitted for publication.

SMETS Ph. (1991b) Belief functions: the disjunctive rule of combination and the generalized Bayesian theorem. (submitted for publication)

SUPPES P. and ZANOTTI M. (1977) On using random relations to generate upper and lower probabilities. Synthesis 36:427-440.

YAGER R.R. (1985) On the Dempster-Shafer framework and new combination rules. Technical report MII-504, Machine Intelligence Institute, Iona College.

YAGER R.R. (1986) The entailment principle for Dempster-Shafer granules. Int. J. Intell. Systems 1:247-262

ZHANG L (1989) A new proof to theorem 3.2 of Fagin and Halpern's paper. Unpublisshed Memorandum, University of Kansas, Business School.

Compressed Constraints in Probabilistic Logic and Their Revision

Paul Snow
Department of Computer Science
Plymouth State College
P.O. Box 6134
Concord, NH 03303 USA
paulsnow@oz.plymouth.edu

Abstract

In probabilistic logic entailments, even moderate size problems can yield linear constraint systems with so many variables that exact methods are impractical. This difficulty can be remedied in many cases of interest by introducing a three-valued logic (true, false, and "don't care"). The three-valued approach allows the construction of "compressed" constraint systems which have the same solution sets as their two-valued counterparts, but which may involve dramatically fewer variables. Techniques to calculate point estimates for the posterior probabilities of entailed sentences are discussed.

1. PROLIFERATION OF WORLDS

An entailment problem in Nilsson's (1986) probabilistic logic derives an estimate for the prior probability of one sentence (hereafter, the "target") from the priors for a set of other ("source") sentences. The prior beliefs about the source sentences establish constraints of the form

$$\mathbf{P} = \mathbf{V}\mathbf{W}$$

$$\Sigma\, w_i = 1 \qquad \text{sum over all "worlds"}$$

$$w_i \geq 0 \qquad \text{for all "worlds"}$$

Here, **P** is the column vector of the sentences' priors. **V** is a matrix derived from an inventory of all consistent patterns of truth assignments (1 = true, 0 = false) for the source and target sentences. For instance, for source sentences **Q** and **Q=>R**, and target sentence **R**, the consistent patterns (or "possible worlds") are the columns of the matrix:

Q	1	1	0	0
Q=>R	1	0	1	1
R	1	0	1	0

The matrix **V** is the first two rows of the matrix above. The components w_j of the vector **W** are the unknown prior probabilities of the possible worlds, which are constrained by beliefs about the source sentences' priors.

The linear constraint system says that the prior of each sentence is the sum of the priors for the possible worlds in which the sentence is true. The system thus implies a constraint on the target sentence's prior. In the example, the prior for target sentence **R** is $w_1 + w_3$. The linear system, by constraining **W**, also constrains this sum. The estimate for the target may either be a probability interval (computed using two linear programs), or else a point probability (perhaps maximizing entropy over the w_j's).

A practical difficulty with this scheme is the large number of possible worlds that can arise with even a modest number of source sentences: ten sentences can yield a thousand worlds. Exponential complexity is inherent in the approach (Halpern, 1989).

One response to this difficulty is to introduce approximations, as Nilsson himself did. Kane (1989) suggested assessing conditional probabilities (rather than simply zero or one) in the entailment expression for the target sentence. Kane's method doesn't address proliferation of worlds on account of the source sentences, and requires additional assessments beyond priors for the source sentences.

The approach taken in this paper represents prior constraints without approximations or assessments beyond the source priors. Instead, a method is discussed that often derives smaller linear systems to convey constraints on the target sentence probability equivalent to those in Nilsson's original proposal. The effect should be that many moderate-sized entailment problems become practical for solution by exact means.

A method for revision which uses these compressed systems is also discussed. Because of the complicated interaction of conditionals and priors, simplifying assumptions are used.

2. OVERVIEW AND EXAMPLE

The method presented here derives linear constraint systems based on a three-valued logic common in engineering work (true, false, and "don't care," hereafter "d.c."). The opportunity to use the d.c. value arises whenever two worlds' truth assignment vectors differ in only one component, one world having true and the other false. In the example of the last section, worlds 1 and 3 could form one world with assignments [d.c., 1, 1]. In effect, [d.c., 1, 1] is a "shorthand" for the assertion that both [0, 1, 1] and [1, 1, 1] are possible worlds.

For example, consider a modus ponens with a conjunctive antecedent used by Kane (1989). The source sentences are independent **A1**, **A2**, **A3**, and the implication sentence **A1 & A2 & A3 => B**. The target is **B**. In this problem, there are 16 possible worlds:

A1	1 1 0 0 0 0 0 0 0 0 1 1 1 1 1 1
A2	1 1 0 0 0 0 1 1 1 1 0 0 0 0 1 1
A3	1 1 0 0 1 1 0 0 1 1 0 0 1 1 0 0
A1 & A2 & A3 => B	1 0 1 1 1 1 1 1 1 1 1 1 1 1 1 1
B	1 0 1 0 1 0 1 0 1 0 1 0 1 0 1 0

With three-valued logic, these sixteen worlds can be compressed to five. The enumeration of these worlds follows readily from our understanding of the "conjunctive antecedent implies consequent" inference schema. An elementary understanding of what assignments are possible in that schema allows the specification of the possible worlds with **n** conjuncts as follows:

1. one world where all sentences are true;
2. one world where all antecedents are true, and the implication and consequent are false;
3. for each i from 1 through n, a world where:
   - conjunct #i is false
   - conjuncts numbered < i are true
   - conjuncts numbered > i are d.c.
   - the implication is true
   - the consequent is d.c.

Figure 1 shows a semantic tree for three antecedents constructed according to this plan. Figure 2 expresses the same information in a "matrix" format. The resulting five worlds for the example problem can inform a system of ordinary linear constraints. Where the original system contained equation constraints, the new system contains inequalities. Assuming that point priors are available for the **Pr** (A_i)'s, the specific system to bound **Pr (B)** is (in addition to the usual non-negativity and total probability constraints):

Pr (A1)	=	[1, 1, 1, 1, 0] • W′
Pr (A2)	≥	[1, 1, 1, 0, **0**] • W′
Pr (A2)	≤	[1, 1, 1, 0, **1**] • W′
Pr (A3)	≥	[1, 1, 0, **0, 0**] • W′
Pr (A3)	≤	[1, 1, 0, **1, 1**] • W′
Pr (=>)	=	[1, 0, 1, 1, 1] • W′
Pr (B)	≤	[1, 0, **1, 1, 1**] • W′
Pr (B)	≥	[1, 0, **0, 0, 0**] • W′

(Values arising from d.c. assignments are in bold face; the operator "•" indicates the scalar product; **W**′ is the transpose of **W**.) Discussion of the derivation of linear constraints from the semantic tree appears in section 4 below.

The possible solutions for **Pr (B)** in the above system are identical to those that would be found by the corresponding two-valued system. Nevertheless, the "size" of the system (total number of vector or matrix components, a rough but fair estimator of the difficulty of the linear programs) is half that of the original.

3. COMPRESSION USING KNOWLEDGE AND USING SEARCH

Three-valued constraint systems are simplest to construct when they reflect a well-understood inference schema. The "conjunctive antecedent implies consequent" schema is, of course, at the heart of production rule-based systems. From this, the required constraint system can easily be constructed.

Based on the specification described in the last section, we see that **n** antecedents yield only **n**+2 possible worlds. This compares with 2^{n+1} worlds in the two-valued system! (The total size of the linear system will be $O(n^2)$.)

In the case of arbitrary source and target sentences, tree construction will not be guided by an understanding of the possible truth assignments. Standard algorithms, like the Quine-McCluskey procedure, proceed by constructing the ordinary, two-value, semantic tree, and then search that tree for opportunities to combine worlds.

Note that compression may turn out to be impossible. Consider **m** independent sentences S_1 ... S_m as the source and the "parity function" (S_1 **xor** S_2 **xor** ... **xor** S_m) as the target. There are 2^m possible assignments, and each assignment has a Hamming distance of at least 2

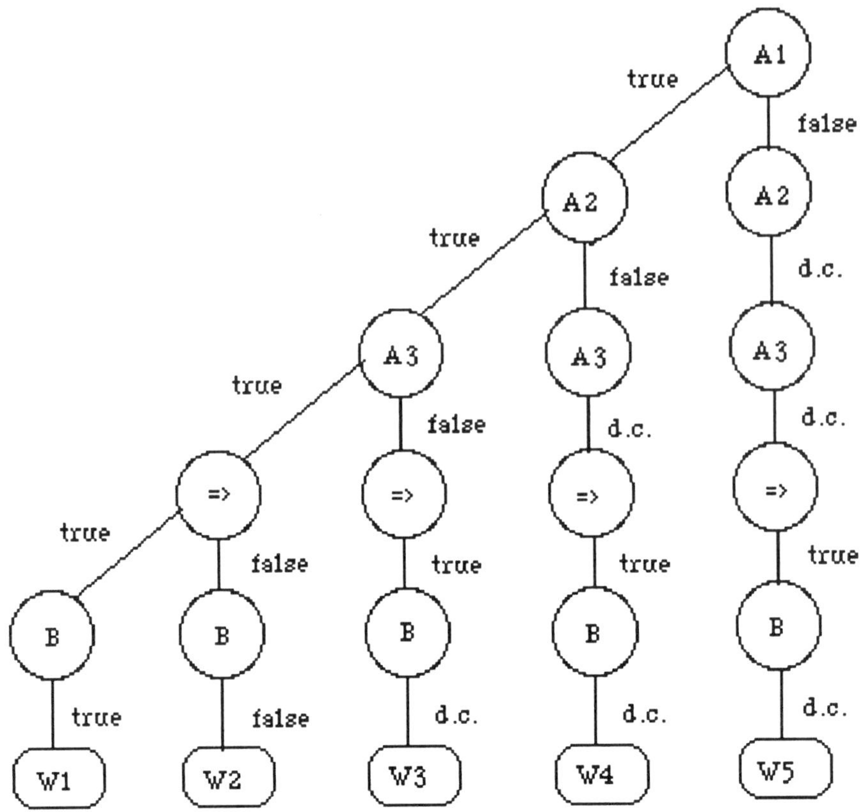

Figure 1. Compressed Semantic Tree for Kane (1989) Example.

	W_1	W_2	W_3	W_4	W_5
A_1	1	1	1	1	0
A_2	1	1	1	0	d.c.
A_3	1	1	0	d.c.	d.c.
$A_1A_2A_3 \Rightarrow B$	1	0	1	1	1
B	1	0	d.c.	d.c.	d.c.

Figure 2. Same Information as Fig. 1, in "Matrix" Format.

from any other assignment. That is, no two assignments differ in only one component, and so no opportunity to use d.c. arises. In other cases, even if some compression were possible, the amount could be disappointing.

The effort involved can be considerable. Just constructing the two-value semantic tree is worst-case exponential, to say nothing of the search. Still, if extensive compression is achieved, the overall effort of the entailment problem may be reduced. That's because the linear programming steps are computationally intensive compared to tree construction, so the potential pay-off for finding a reasonable size constraint system can be handsome.

4. EXPRESSING THE CONSTRAINTS

Once the possible worlds are found, we can derive linear constraints. Returning to the Kane example, sentences like A_1 which have no d.c. values are handled just as they would be in Nilsson's proposal. For a sentence with a d.c. value, A_2, the semantic tree tells us that the possible assignments are [1, 1, 1, 0, d.c.]. This can be read to mean that the prior probabilities w_i of the worlds must be such that there is a number **p** in the closed unit interval where

$$Pr(A_2) = w_1 + w_2 + w_3 + pw_5$$

This reading follows immediately from the way the fifth world was constructed. Of the total weight that was assigned to the original worlds that became world 5, some portion of that weight contributes to the sum that is A_2's prior. For any **p** and **W** which satisfy the equation constraint just given, there is some apportionment of weight to the original worlds that achieves **p** and which satisfies the two-valued system. Conversely, any solution of the two-valued system has a **p** that satisfies the above equation.

The equation, in turn, is equivalent to two simultaneous inequality constraints

$$Pr(A2) \leq w_1 + w_2 + w_3 + w_5$$
$$Pr(A2) \geq w_1 + w_2 + w_3$$

A solution of the equation constraint for any admissible **p** solves both inequalities, and for any solution of the inequalities, there is an admissible **p** that satisfies the equation constraint.

The assignment for sentence A_3, [1, 1, 0, d.c., d.c.], asserts the existence of two numbers (not necessarily distinct) **q** and **r** in the closed unit interval, such that

$$Pr(A_3) = w_1 + w_2 + qw_4 + rw_5$$

Even though **r** above and the earlier **p** pertain to the same compressed world, their values are independent, a fact which follows from the way that the fifth world was constructed. Thus, the two constraints do not interfere with each other when they obtain simultaneously. The last equation can be translated into the inequalities

$$Pr(A_3) \leq w_1 + w_2 + w_4 + w_5$$
$$Pr(A_3) \geq w_1 + w_2$$

These simultaneous inequalities are equivalent to their equation constraint. Further, these inequalities can hold simultaneously with the inequalities derived earlier for the other sentence. (The full translation of this problem into simultaneous linear constraints was given near the end of section 2 above.)

To summarize, each equation constraint involving d.c. assignments can be expanded into two weak inequalities of opposite sense. The upper bounding sum includes the probabilities for the merged worlds; the lower bounding sum omits them. (For source sentences, the quantity being bound is the given prior for the sentence; for the target sentence, the bounds are on the unknown prior being sought).

Prior beliefs can be weak inequalities (for instance, to express bounds on the prior probability for a sentence). A weak inequality expression of belief in the original system yields one weak inequality of the same sense in the new system. If the inequality bounds a prior from above, then any merged worlds contribute to the sum; if from below, they do not.

5. REVISION WITH CONDITIONALS

If evidence **E** is observed that bears on some sentence **S**, then we would wish to revise our probability estimates to reflect our new beliefs. Nilsson assumed that the effect of **E** on any world **j** depended only on whether **S** was true in **j** or not. In particular:

$$Pr(E \mid j) = Pr(E \mid S) \quad \text{if S is true in j} \quad (1a)$$
$$= Pr(E \mid \neg S) \quad \text{if S is false in j} \quad (1b)$$

(Nilsson made the assumption in a different, but equivalent, form: for sentences **S**, **T**, and evidence **E** that bears on **S**, **Pr(T | S, E) = Pr(T | S)** and **Pr(T | ¬S, E) = Pr(T | ¬S)**.) This assumption is frequently encountered in inference work. For a discussion of the motivation of the assumption in an A.I. context, see for example Pearl (1986). The assumption isn't strained, and is surely useful, but its main attraction is its simple relationship between the known conditionals given sentences and the unknown conditionals given worlds.

When **S** is d.c. in **j**, we can extend this assumption by simple probabilistic identities to

$$\Pr(E \mid j) = \Pr(S \mid j) * \Pr(E \mid S) + \Pr(\neg S \mid j) * \Pr(E \mid \neg S) \qquad (2)$$

By the way that the d.c. value was arrived at, knowledge that **j** obtained would provide no constraint on the probability of **S** that depends only on **j** and **S**. This contrasts with the simpler situation when **S** is either definitely true or definitely false in each world.

The sort of revision discussed in Nilsson's original proposal was to find a single feasible **W** vector and then apply Bayes' formula to that prior. This yields a single point posterior for the distribution over worlds, and hence the target posterior. Another useful posterior constraint system describes all posterior distributions consistent with the prior constraints and assumption (1). This kind of estimate can be obtained from the uncompressed system by the straightforward application of a procedure for revising a linear prior system by a point conditional (Snow, 1991). The compressed system, unfortunately, generally doesn't easily support this kind of estimation. The conditional that comports with assumption (1) depends on the prior to which the conditional would be applied.

Revision using a chosen prior solution is not impeded by the interaction of conditionals and priors. The steps are:

- Choose a representative prior which solves the compressed system.
- Use that prior and the tableau (e.g. figure 2) to assess feasible Pr(S | j) values to replace d.c.'s among the sentences about which evidence may be seen.
- When evidence is observed, use equation (2) and the Pr(S | j) values to compute a consistent conditional distribution over worlds.
- Apply Bayes rule using the chosen prior and the consistent conditional to compute the posterior estimate.

6. AN EXAMPLE OF REVISION

A complete inference problem would include estimates for the prior probability of each of the source sentences. Typically, the resulting prior constraint system will have many solutions for **W**, the possible prior distribution over the (compressed) worlds. The method described here doesn't depend on how the analyst selects which solution will serve as the representative prior over the worlds. Possibilities include the maximum entropy solution, or a solution which yields a prior for the target in the middle of its interval of possible values.

Suppose the estimated priors for the source sentences are:

$$\Pr(A_1) = 0.8$$
$$\Pr(A_2) = 0.7$$
$$\Pr(A_3) = 0.6$$
$$\Pr(=>) = 0.8$$

and the analyst chooses from among the solutions for the distributions over the worlds the representative solution

(0.2, 0.2, 0.2, 0.2, 0.2)

This choice is consistent with any estimate for the prior of **B** in the range [0.2, 0.8]. The next step is replace the d.c. markers in figure 2 with estimated values of **Pr(S | j)**. Expecting to view evidence bearing on the source sentences, the analyst replaces their d.c.'s with

$$\Pr(A_2 \mid 5) = 0.5$$
$$\Pr(A_3 \mid 4) = 0.5$$
$$\Pr(A_3 \mid 5) = 0.5$$

These choices aren't unique. They are consistent in the sense that

$$\Pr(A_2) = w_1 + w_2 + w_3 + \Pr(A_2 \mid 5)\, w_5$$
and $0.7 = 0.2 + 0.2 + 0.2 + 0.5 * 0.2$

Now suppose evidence **E** is observed that bears on sentence $\mathbf{A_3}$, and suppose that

$$\Pr(E \mid A_3) = 0.8 \quad \Pr(E \mid \neg A_3) = 0.4$$

Applying (1) and (2) gives as world conditionals

Pr (E | 1) = 0.8
Pr (E | 2) = 0.8
Pr (E | 3) = 0.4
Pr (E | 4) = 0.6
Pr (E | 5) = 0.6

When these conditionals are applied to the representative prior, the corresponding posterior works out to

(0.25, 0.25, 0.12, 0.19, 0.19)

and the posterior estimate for **B** can be anything in the interval [0.25, 0.75].

Note that if evidence were observed that bore directly on **B**, the analyst would also have to assess **Pr(B | j)** for each of the three d.c.'s pertaining to **B**. This, of course, is just what Kane suggested. In that case, there would be a specific point estimate for the entailed posterior of the target, rather than an interval.

7. REVISION USING POSTERIORS

In his original proposal, Nilsson considered revision using posterior probabilities for sentences. The methods developed here for conditional revision can be applied directly to the case where a posterior for sentence **S** given evidence **E** rather than a conditional is known.

Assuming that neither **Pr(S)**, **Pr(¬S)**, nor **Pr(E)** is zero, then we have the probabilistic identities

$$Pr(E \mid S) / Pr(E) = Pr(S \mid E) / Pr(S)$$
$$Pr(E \mid \neg S) / Pr(E) = Pr(\neg S \mid E) / Pr(\neg S)$$

Since we are assumed to know the truth status of **S** in each world, we know (or can assess consistent values for) the priors and any needed **Pr(S | j)**'s. Since division of all conditionals by the same constant (i.e., **Pr(E)**) has no effect on the calculated posterior, we can use the posterior to prior ratios in place of the conditionals in Bayes' formula. If **S** is d.c. in world **j**, and assumption (1) holds, then the appropriate conditional ratio is the average of the posterior to prior ratios weighted by **Pr(S | j)** and its complement, **Pr(¬S | j)**.

8. CONCLUSIONS

The introduction of a third logical value can greatly reduce the number of variables seen in linear constraint systems for entailment in probabilistic logic. The method is most useful when the inference problem involves some easy-to-analyze inference schema, thus avoiding search in the construction of a semantic tree. Modus ponens with a conjunctive antecedent was emphasized here because of its importance in rule-based inference. Similar points could have been made using other common schemata involving modus tollens, modus tollendo ponens and other Latin friends for illustration.

For arbitrary entailments, a resort to search may be needed. The method in that case is something of a gamble: search costs can be heavy, and there is no guarantee that a substantial savings will be realized. Nevertheless, the gamble may be attractive in moderate sized problems which tax the means of linear programming. If successful, the analyst will trade many simple steps to avoid an impractical linear program.

The extra effort of applying the new method is substantially confined to the creation of a suitable three-value semantic tree. The derivation of a linear constraint system from the tree is conceptually simple, and no worse than twice as hard as deriving a two-value system from a conventional semantic tree with the same number of worlds.

Constraints obtained from three-valued systems, like other linear constraint systems, can be revised in the face of evidence using Bayesian approaches. Calculation of a point posterior from a chosen feasible prior is straightforward. Compressed systems do not appear to allow the conceptually easy calculation of an exact posterior constraint system because of the interaction between conditionals and priors. Uncompressed systems do have this capability. This difference between the two kinds of prior constraints is of limited practical import, since the size of uncompressed systems effectively precludes the actual use of the exact posterior system except in small problems.

Literature Cited

Halpern, J. Y., An analysis of first-order logics of probability, *Proceedings IJCAI-89*, 1375-1381, 1989.

Kane, T., Maximum entropy in Nilsson's probabilistic logic, *Proceedings IJCAI-89*, 452-457, 1989.

Levi, I., *The Enterprise of Knowledge*, Cambridge, MA: MIT Press, 1980.

Nilsson, N. J., Probabilistic logic, *Artificial Intelligence* **28**, 71-87, 1986.

Pearl, J., On evidential reasoning in a hierarchy of hypotheses, *Artificial Intelligence* **28**, 9-15, 1986.

Snow, P., Improved posterior probability estimates from prior and conditional linear constraint systems, *IEEE Transactions Systems, Man, & Cybernetics* **21**, April 1991 (to appear).

Detecting Causal Relations in the Presence of Unmeasured Variables

Peter Spirtes
Department of Philosophy
Carnegie Mellon University

Abstract

The presence of latent variables can greatly complicate inferences about causal relations between measured variables from statistical data. In many cases, the presence of latent variables makes it impossible to determine for two measured variables A and B, whether A causes B, B causes A, or there is some common cause. In this paper I present several theorems that state conditions under which it is possible to reliably infer the causal relation between two measured variables, regardless of whether latent variables are acting or not.

1 Introduction

The problem of inferring causal relations from statistical data in the absence of experiments arises repeatedly in many scientific disciplines, including sociology, economics, epidemiology, and psychology. In addition, the building of expert systems could be expedited if background knowledge elicited from experts could be supplemented with automated techniques. Recently, efficient algorithms for determining causal structure (in the form of Bayesian networks) from statistical data when there are no unmeasured or "latent" variables have been proposed. (See Spirtes, Glymour and Scheines 1990, Spirtes and Glymour 1991, Spirtes, Glymour, and Scheines forthcoming, Verma and Pearl 1990, and Pearl and Verma 1991.)

Inferring causal relations when unmeasured variables are also acting is a much more difficult problem. In many cases it is impossible to infer the structure among the latent variables from statistical relations among the measured variables. But the presence of latent variables can also make it difficult to infer the causal relations among the measured variables themselves. One important question for many policy decisions is "Does A cause B?" Statistics about A and B alone do not suffice to answer these questions. When only two variables, A and B, have been measured, and there is a correlation between the two, this does not suffice to establish whether A caused B, B caused A, or there is a third variable causing both A and B. Nevertheless, when more variables are measured, more knowledge about the causal relations between A and B is possible. Drawing upon recent results of Verma and Pearl (Verma and Pearl 1990, and Pearl and Verma 1991), I will prove in Theorem 2 that there are some circumstances in which it is possible to establish that A caused B, rather than that B caused A, or that a third variable caused both A and B; I will prove in Theorem 3 that there are other circumstances in which the possibility that A caused B can be eliminated. The proofs are given in the Appendix. I will also demonstrate that a recent proposal derived from Pearl and Verma (1991) to establish more general conditions for causal pathways in the presence of unmeasured causes is incorrect.

2 Results

Causal processes between a set of random variables **V** are represented by a directed acyclic graph over **V**, where there is an edge from A to B if and only if A is an immediate cause of B relative to **V**. (For a discussion of the meaning of immediate causation, see Spirtes, Glymour and Scheines 1991.) If there is a directed path from A to B in the causal graph, I will say that A is a (possibly indirect) cause of B.

If a distribution is placed over the exogenous variables in a causal process (variables of zero indegree in the causal graph), which in turn affect the values of other random variables, the result is a joint distribution over all of the random variables. In that case, I will say that the causal process generated the joint distribution. Following Pearl (1988) I assume that the distribution generated by a causal process satisfies the Minimality and Markov conditions for the causal graph of that process. In Pearl's terminology (Pearl 1988) the causal graph is a **Bayes network** of any distribution that it generates. (In what follows, I will capitalize random variables, and boldface any sets of variables.)

Markov Condition: Let Descendant(V) be the set of descendants of V in a graph G, and Parents(V) be the set of parents of V in G. A graph G and a probability distribution P on the vertices **V** of G satisfy the Markov condition if and only if for every V in **V**, and every subset

X of **V**, V and **X**\{V} ∪ Descendants(V) are independent conditional on Parents(V).

Minimality Condition: A graph G and a probability distribution P satisfies the minimality condition if and only if G and P satisfy the Markov condition and for every graph H obtained by deleting an edge from G, H and P do not satisfy the Markov condition.

If P satisfies the Markov condition for graph G, and every conditional independence true of the distribution P is entailed by the Markov condition, then we say that P is **faithful** to G.

In a directed graph G, I will write X -> Y if there is an edge from X to Y in G. In an undirected graph U, I will write X - Y if there is an undirected edge between X and Y. X and Y are **adjacent in a directed graph** G if and only if either X -> Y or Y -> X in G. Two edges are **adjacent in an undirected graph** U if and only if X - Y in U. In a directed acyclic graph G, an **undirected path U from X to Y** is a sequence of vertices starting with X and ending with Y such that for every pair of variables A and B that are adjacent to each other in the path, A and B are adjacent in G, and no vertex occurs more than once in U. In a directed acyclic graph G, a **directed path P from X to Y** is a sequence of vertices starting with X and ending with Y such that for every pair of variables A and B that are adjacent to each other in the path in that order, the edge A -> B occurs in G, and no vertex occurs more than once in P. An **edge between X and Y occurs in a path P** (directed or undirected) if and only if X and Y are adjacent in P. If an undirected path U contains an edge between X and Y, and an edge between Y and Z, the two edges **collide** at Z if and only if X -> Y and Z -> Y in G. On an undirected path U, Z is an **unshielded collider** if and only if there exist edges X -> Y and Z -> Y in U, and Z and X are not adjacent in G. X is an **ancestor** of Y and Y is a **descendant** of X if and only if there is a directed path from X to Y.

Pearl and Verma have shown how to calculate the conditional independence relations that are entailed by distributions satisfying the Markov condition for a graph G using the d-separability relation. In graph G, variables X and Y are **d-separated** by a set of vertices **S** not containing X or Y if and only if there exists no undirected path U between X and Y, such that (i) every collider on U has a descendent in S and (ii) no other vertex on U is in S. Disjoint sets of variables **X** and **Y** are d-separated by **S** in G if and only if every member of **X** is d-separated from every member of **Y** by **S** in G. If distribution P satisfies the Markov condition for graph G, then the Markov condition entails that **X** is independent of **Y** conditional on **S** if and only if **X** is d-separated from **Y** by **S** in G (Pearl 1988).

The following algorithm (Spirtes 1990, Spirtes 1991) reconstructs the set of all graphs of causal processes that could have generated a given probability distribution, under the assumptions that no latent variables are present (i.e. every cause of a pair of measured variables is itself measured) and that the distribution is faithful to the graph of the causal process that generated it. The d-separability relations of the graph can be determined either by performing tests of conditional independence on the generated distribution, or in the linear case, tests of zero partial correlations.

Let $\mathbf{A}_C$(A,B) denote the set of vertices adjacent to A or to B in graph C, except for A and B themselves. Let $\mathbf{U}_C$(A,B) denote the set of vertices in graph C on (acyclic) undirected paths between A and B, except for A and B themselves. (Since the algorithm is continually updating C, $\mathbf{A}_C$(A,B) and $\mathbf{U}_C$(A,B) are constantly changing as the algorithm progresses.)

PC Algorithm

A.) Form the complete undirected graph C on the vertex set **V**.

B.)

n = 0.

repeat

For each pair of variables A, B adjacent in C, if $\mathbf{A}_C$(A,B) ∩ $\mathbf{U}_C$(A,B) has cardinality greater than or equal to n and A, B are d-separated by any subset of $\mathbf{A}_C$(A,B) ∩ $\mathbf{U}_C$(A,B) of cardinality n, delete A - B from C.

n = n + 1.

until for each pair of vertices A, B that are adjacent in C, $\mathbf{A}_C$(A,B) ∩ $\mathbf{U}_C$(A,B) is of cardinality less than n.

C.) Let F be the graph resulting from step B. For each triple of vertices A, B, C such that the pair A, B and the pair B, C are each adjacent in F but the pair A, C are not adjacent in F, orient A - B - C as A -> B <- C if and only if A and C are not d-separated by any subset of $\mathbf{A}_F$(A,C) ∩ $\mathbf{U}_F$(A,C) containing B.

D. repeat

If there is a directed edge A -> B, and an undirected edge B - C, and no edge of either kind connecting A and C, then orient B - C as B -> C. If there is a directed path from A to B, and an undirected edge A - B, orient A - B as A -> B.

until no more arrowheads can be added.

We have run this algorithm on as many as 90 variables in randomly generated sparse graphs. In Monte Carlo simulations on linear models, for large sample sizes (on the order of several thousand) on sparse graphs, the percentage of errors of omission or commission for adjacencies is below 2%. Under the same conditions, the percentage of arrowheads that are erroneously omitted is less than 2%, and the percentage of arrowheads that are erroneously added is about 20%. (See Spirtes, Glymour, and Scheines forthcoming for the details of this Monte Carlo study.)

Following Pearl's terminology, the output of the algorithm when there are no unmeasured common causes is a mixture of directed and undirected edges called a

pattern. A pattern Π represents a set of directed acyclic graphs. A graph G is in the set of graphs represented by Π if and only if:

1. G has the same adjacency relations as Π.

2. If the edge between A and B is oriented A -> B in Π, then it is oriented A -> B in G.

3. There are no unshielded colliders in G that are not also unshielded colliders in Π.

A **hybrid graph** may contain contain bidirected edges edges. Such graphs may be used to represented the marginal structure on a set of measured variables when unmeasured common causes have edges that collide (in Verma and Pearl's terminology, are "head to head") with edges between measured variables. When there are unmeasured common causes, the output of the PC algorithm can include such bi-directed edges. X - Y denotes that there is an undirected edge between X and Y in a pattern Π, X o-> Y denotes that X and Y are adjacent and there is at least an arrowhead into Y, X -> Y denotes X o-> Y and not Y o-> X, and X <-> Y denotes X o-> Y and Y o-> X. Two vertices are **adjacent** in a hybrid graph if X - Y, X -> Y, or X <-> Y. Two edges **collide** at Y if and only if each edge has an arrowhead directed into Y. The definitions of directed path, undirected path, and d-separability for hybrid graphs are the same as for directed graphs.

Let D be a directed acyclic graph with vertex set U of which the subset **O** are observable. **The pattern Π of D restricted to O** is the hybrid graph that is the result of applying the PC algorithm to the d-separability relations of D that involve just variables in **O**. From the marginals over **O** of distributions faithful to D, the PC algorithm can be used to construct the pattern of D. (The method that Verma and Pearl use to construct the pattern of D is based upon an earlier algorithm described in Spirtes 1990 for constructing graphs when no latent variables are present given faithful input. It is equivalent in output to the PC algorithm, but is too slow to be used on large numbers of variables, and is less reliable in practice because it requires testing high order conditional independence relations.)

The following theorem is a corollary of a theorem proved by Verma and Pearl:

Theorem 1: Given a graph G over a set of variables **U**, a distribution P that satisfies the Markov condition for G, and some subset **O** of **U**, for **X**, **Y**, and **C** that are disjoint subsets of **O**, the Markov condition entails that **X** is independent of **Y** conditional on **C** if and only if **X** and **Y** are d-separated by **C** in the pattern of G over **O**.

In a pattern Π, a **semi-directed path P from X to Y** is an undirected path from X to Y such that if A occurs before B in P, then in Π the edge from B to A does not have an arrowhead into A. In other words, a semi-directed path can contain both undirected edges and directed edges pointing in the direction from X to Y, but it cannot contain any bidirected edges or edges pointing in the direction from Y to X.

I will show the following;

Theorem 2: Let G be a graph over a set of vertices **U**, and **O** be a subset of **U** containing X and Y, and Π the pattern of G over **O**. If there exists a directed path A from X to Y in G then Π contains a semi-directed path B from X to Y.

Theorem 2 states that if the probability distribution on the set of measured variables is not compatible with a semi-directed path B from X to Y then if that distribution is the marginal of a distribution perfectly represented by a graph on a larger vertex set, the larger graph also contains no directed path from X to Y. In that case, it is possible to know that A is not a cause of B by examining the marginal over the observed variables, even if latent variables are present.

The following theorem states under what conditions it is possible to infer from a pattern the existence of a directed path in a graph G In a directed acyclic graph or a pattern, X , Y, and Z form a **triangle** if and only if X is adjacent to Y and Z, and Z is adjacent to Y.

Theorem 3: Let **O** be a subset of vertices of G containing X and Z, and let the pattern of G for **O** contain a directed edge X -> Z, no triangle containing X and Z, and a variable C such that C o-> X . Then in G there is a directed path from X to Z.

Furthermore:

Corollary 1: Let **O** be a subset of vertices of G containing X and Z, and let the pattern of G for **O** contain a vertex C such that C o-> X , and a directed path A from X to Z such that for no adjacent pair U, W on A is there a triangle in Π containing both U and W. Then in G there is a directed path from X to Z.

Theorem 2 and Corollary 1 state conditions under which it is possible to know that A is a (possibly indirect) cause of B simply by examining the marginal over the observed variables, even if latent variables are present.

3 Can Theorem 3 Be Strengthened?

Verma and Pearl have recently published a claim (Corollary 1 in Pearl 1991) that entails a stronger version of Theorem 3. A consequence of their Corollary 1, translated into the language of this paper is[1]:

Let **O** be a subset of vertices of G containing X and Z, and let the pattern Π of G for **O** contain a directed path P from X to Z, such that for every edge A -> B in P there is a variable C such that C o-> A. Then in G there is a directed path from X to Z.

This claim is false. It is stronger than Theorem 3 because it does not require that each edge in P not be part of a triangle in P order to infer the existence of a directed path

[1] The statement of their Corollary 1 is somewhat ambiguous, so it is not immediately obvious that the correct interpretation entails the consequence stated here. However Pearl (personal communication) has confirmed that the interpretation presented here is the intended one.

from X to Z in G. The graph depicted in Figure 1 (suggested by the proof of Theorem 3) provides a counterexample. In G, there is no directed path from X to Z; however in the pattern of G over the set of variables that does not include T, there is a uni-directed edge from X to Z, and an edge D -> X.

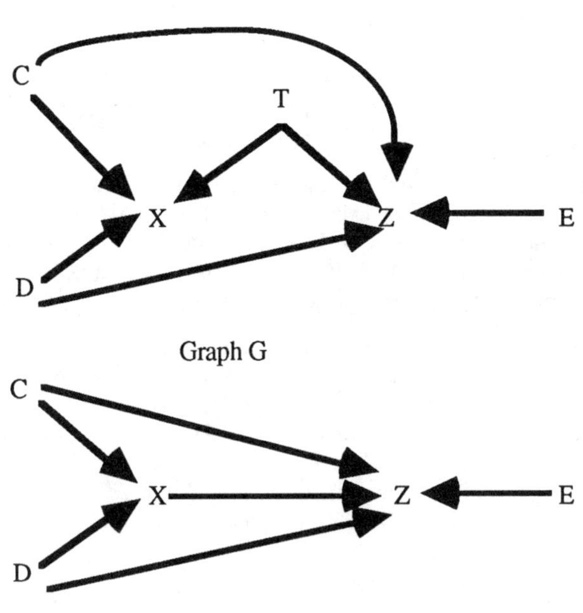

Figure 1

4 Appendix

Lemma 1 (Verma and Pearl): Let **O** be a subset of U, D a directed acyclic graph over U, and Π the pattern of D restricted to O. Two variables A, B in **O** are adjacent in Π if and only if there exists a path P between A and B in D satisfying the following two conditions:

(1) every observable node on P (except the endpoints) is a collider along P; and

(2) every collider along P is a shieldable ancestor of either A or B.

where an ancestor S of A is shieldable if and only if every directed path from S to A contains an observable other than A.

Lemma 2 (Verma and Pearl): For any pattern Π of D over **O**, A o-> B if and only if there is a node C such that either (1) C is adjacent to B and not A (in Π) and both edges A - B and B - C were induced by paths (of D) which ended pointing at B, or (2) C o-> A in Π and B is a descendent of A in D.

Lemma 3: Let G be a directed acyclic graph over a set of vertices **U**, **O** be a subset of **U** containing X and Y, and Π be the pattern of G restricted to **O**. If there is a directed path P_1(X,Y) in G from X to Y that induces an edge between X and Y in Π, then either X -> Y or X - Y in Π.

Proof. The proof is a reductio. Assume that there is a directed path P in G from X to Y that induces and edge between X and Y in Π, but neither X -> Y nor X - Y in Π. It follows that Y o-> X in Π. By lemma 1, there is a vertex Z in **O** such that either Z is adjacent to X and not to Y in Π, and both of the edges between X and Y and X and Z are induced by paths pointing at X, or Z o-> X in Π, and X is a descendant of Y in G. X is not a descendant of Y in G, because Y is a descendant of X in G, and G is acyclic. Suppose then that there is a vertex Z in **O** such that Z is adjacent to X and not to Y in Π, and both of the edges between X and Y and X and Z are induced by paths pointing at X.

Let P(Z,X) be an undirected path between X and Z that points into X and induces an edge between X and Z in Π, and P_2(X,Y) be an undirected path between X and Y that points into X and induces an edge between X and Y in Π. Let R be the first point of intersection of P(X,Z) with P_2(X,Y), P(Z,R) be the subpath of P(Z,X) from Z to R, P(R,Y) be the subpath of P_2(X,Y) from R to Y, and P(Z,Y) be the concatenation of P(Z,R) and P(R,Y). P(Z,Y) is an undirected path because P(Z,R) and P(R,Y) by construction intersect only at R, and hence P(Z,R) and P(R,Y) contain any given vertex at most once.

Every vertex on P(Z,Y) that is in **O** is a collider on P(Z,Y). By lemma 1, every vertex in **O** on P(Z,R) except for Z and R are colliders on P(Z,R), and every vertex in **O** on P_2(R,Y) except for R and Y are colliders on P_2(R,Y) (because they are subpaths of paths that induce edges between Z and X, and X and Y respectively.) This shows that each vertex in **O** with the possible exception of R on P(Z,Y) is a collider on P(Z,Y). I will now show that if R is in **O**, it is also a collider on P(Z,Y). If R is equal to X, then X is a collider on P(Z,Y) because both P(Z,X) and P(X,Y) are into X. If R is not equal to X, and R is in **O**, then R is a collider on both P(Z,X) and P(X,Y); hence R is a collider on P(Z,Y). It follows that every vertex on P(Z,Y) that is in **O** is a collider on P(Z,Y).

Suppose first that every collider on P(Z,Y) is a shieldable ancestor of either Z or Y. By lemma 1, P(Z,Y) induces an edge between Z and Y in Π. It follows from lemma 2 that P(Z,X) and P_2(X,Y) do not induce a Y o-> X orientation. This contradicts the assumption.

Suppose next that there is a collider on P(Z,Y) that is not a shieldable ancestor of either Z or Y, and let W be the first such collider after Z. R is the only vertex on P(Z,Y) that may be a collider on P(Z,Y) but not a collider in either P(Z,X) or P_2(X,Y). Hence W is either equal to R or a collider on P(Z,X) or P_2(X,Y).

In either case Y is a descendant of W. Suppose first that W is a collider on P(Z,X) or P_2(X,Y). Because W is not a shieldable ancestor of either Z or Y, by lemma 1, W is a shieldable ancestor of X. X is an ancestor of Y, and W is an ancestor of X, so W is an ancestor of Y. Suppose next that W is equal to R. In this case R is not equal to X, because X is an ancestor of Y and X is in **O**, and hence X is a shieldable ancestor of Y. Either X is a descendant of R, Y is a descendant of R, or some collider along $P_2(X,Y)$ is a descendant of R. If X is a descendant of R, then Y is a descendant of R, because Y is a descendant of X. If some collider along $P_2(X,Y)$ is a descendant of R, then Y is a descendant of R because each collider on $P_2(X,Y)$ is a shieldable ancestor of either X or Y, and Y is a descendant of X. In any case, then, Y is a descendant of W.

W is an ancestor of Y, but not a shieldable ancestor of Y, so there is a directed path P(W,Y) from W to Y that contains no vertices in **O** other than Y. Let S be the first point of intersection of P(Z,Y) with P(W,Y), P(Z,S) the subpath of P(Z,Y) from Z to S, P(S,Y) the subpath of P(W,Y) from S to Y, and $P_2(Z,Y)$ the concatenation of P(Z,S) and P(S,Y). S is not a collider on $P_2(Z,Y)$ because the first edge P(S,Y) is not directed into S. Hence every collider on P(Z,S) is a collider on $P_2(Z,W)$. W is the first collider on P(Z,Y) that is not a shieldable ancestor of Z or Y, S either equals W or is before W on P(Z,Y), S is not a collider on $P_2(Z,Y)$, and P(S,Y) contains no colliders; hence every collider on $P_2(Z,Y)$ is a shieldable ancestor of either Z or Y.

Every vertex V on $P_2(Z,Y)$ that is in **O** is on P(Z,S). V is not equal to S because S is not in **O**. If V is not equal to S, then V is a collider on P(Z,S), and hence a collider on $P_2(Z,Y)$.

By lemma 1, $P_2(Z,Y)$ induces an edge between Z and Y in P. It follows from lemma 2 that P(Z,X) and $P_2(X,Y)$ do not induce a Y o-> X orientation. This contradicts the assumption.

Theorem 2: Let G be a graph over a set of vertices **U**, and **O** be a subset of **U** containing X and Y, and Π the pattern of G over **O**. If there exists a directed path A from X to Y in G then Π contains a semi-directed path B from X to Y.

Proof. Break the path A in G into a series of subpaths such that only the endpoints of the subpaths are in **O**. Let U be the source and V be the sink of some such arbitrary subpath. There is an edge between U and V in Π by lemma 3. U is prior to V on B. The concatenation of the edges induced by the subpaths are an undirected path B from X to Y in Π. By Lemma 1, it is not the case that V o-> U. By definition of semi-directed path, B is a semi-directed path from X to Y.

Theorem 3: Let **O** be a subset of vertices of G containing X and Z, and let the pattern Π of G for **O** contain a directed edge X -> Z, no triangle containing X and Z, and a variable D such that D o-> X. Then in G there is a directed path from X to Z.

Proof. Since X and Z are adjacent in Π there is a path A in G between X and Z such that every observable node on A is a collider and every collider on A is a shieldable ancestor of X or Z.

If X -> Z in pattern Π arises because of clause (2) of lemma 2, we are done because Z is a descendant of X in G. So suppose X -> Z is oriented by condition (1) of lemma 2. Then there is a path A in G that induces X -> Z and A is into Z in G. If A contains no colliders and is not into X, then A is a directed path from X to Z, and we are done. Otherwise there are two cases: A contains a collider, or A is into X.

First, we consider the case where A is into X. Then there is a path between X and Z that induces an edge in Π, and is into X. By assumption there is a vertex D in Π such that D o-> X. By lemma 2, either there is a vertex C in Π such that C is adjacent to X and not D, and both edges C-X and D-X are induced by paths of G which point at X, or C o-> D in Π and X is a descendant of D in G.

Suppose that the first disjunct is true. In that case, either C is adjacent to Z in Π or it isn't. If it is adjacent to Z, then there is a triangle in Π containing X and Z. If C is not adjacent to Z, then by clause (2) of lemma 2, Z o-> X, contrary to our assumption.

Suppose now that the second disjunct is true. Because X is a descendant of D in G, there is a directed path in G from some variable E in **O** to X that does not contain any variables in **O** other than X and E. This path induces an edge between E and X in Π. If E is adjacent to X in Π, then Π contains a triangle containing X and Z; if E is not adjacent to X in Π, then by clause (2) of lemma 2, Z o-> X, contrary to our assumption.

We now consider the case where A is not into X, but there is a collider on A. Let K be the first collider on A after X. Because A is not into X, then there is a directed path from X to K, and hence no directed path from K to X. This implies that K is not an ancestor, and hence not a shieldable ancestor of X. So by clause (2) of lemma 1, K is a shieldable ancestor of Z. The concatenation of the paths from X to K and from K to Z is a directed path from X to Z.

Corollary 1: Let **O** be a subset of vertices of G containing X and Z, and let the pattern Π of G for **O** contain a vertex C such that C o-> X, and a directed path P from X to Z such that for no adjacent pair U, W on P is there a triangle in Π containing both U and W. Then in G there is a directed path from X to Z.

Proof. Since there is a directed path from X to Z in Π, there is a sequence of edges X -> A -> B ... -> Z in Π. By Theorem 3, there is a directed path from X to A in G. Since X -> A in Π, Theorem 3 can next be applied to A -> B, to show that there is a directed path from A to B in G. Repeating this process in turn for each edge on P implies that there is a directed path from X to Z in G.

Acknowledgements

I wish to thank Clark Glymour for a number of useful discussions and suggestions on the topic of causal inference when latent variables are present. This research was supported in part by a graph with the Office of Naval Research, and the Naval Manpower Research and Development Center under Contract number N00114-89-J-1964. Theorem 3 and a weaker version of Theorem 2 were reported in "Causal Structure among Measured

Variables Preserved with Unmeasured Variables", by Peter Spirtes and Clark Glymour, Laboratory for Computational Linguistics Technical Report No. CMU-LCL-90-5, August, 1990.

References

J. Pearl, *Probabilistic Reasoning in Intelligent Systems*, Morgan Kaufmann, 1988.

J. Pearl and T. Verma, "A Theory of Inferred Causation", in *Principles of Knowledge Representation and Reasoning: Proceedings of the Second International Conference*, ed. by J. Allen, R. Fikes, and E. Sandewall, Morgan Kaufmann, San Mateo CA, 1991.

P. Spirtes, C. Glymour and R. Scheines, "Causality from Probability" Proceedings of the Conference on Advanced Computing for the Social Sciences, Williamsburg, Va. 1990.

P. Spirtes, C. Glymour and R. Scheines, "Causality from Probability" in G. McKee, ed. *Evolving Knowledge in Natural and Artificial Intelligence*, Pitman, 1990.

P. Spirtes and C. Glymour, "An Algorithm for Fast Recovery of Sparse Causal Graphs", *Social Science Computer Review*, 9, 1991.

P. Spirtes, C. Glymour and R. Scheines, *Causality, Statistics and Search*, forthcoming.

T. Verma and J. Pearl, "On Equivalence of Causal Models" Technical Report, R-150, Department of Computer Science, University of California at Los Angeles, April 1990.

A Method for Integrating Utility Analysis into an Expert System for Design Evaluation under Uncertainty

Deborah L. Thurston*
Yun Qi Tian
Decision Systems Laboratory
Department of General Engineering
University of Illinois at Urbana-Champaign

Abstract

In mechanical design, there is often unavoidable uncertainty in estimates of design performance. Evaluation of design alternatives requires consideration of the impact of this uncertainty. Expert heuristics embody assumptions regarding the designer's attitude towards risk and uncertainty that might be reasonable in most cases but inaccurate in others. We present a technique to allow designers to incorporate their own unique attitude towards uncertainty as opposed to those assumed by the domain expert's rules. The general approach is to eliminate aspects of heuristic rules which directly or indirectly include assumptions regarding the user's attitude towards risk, and replace them with explicit, user-specified probabilistic multiattribute utility and probability distribution functions. We illustrate the method in a system for material selection for automobile bumpers.

1. INTRODUCTION

Design evaluation requires simultaneous consideration of several attributes under uncertainty, such as manufacturing cost. At the preliminary design stage, there is frequently a great deal of uncertainty in the estimates of performance levels. In later stages of design, the degree of uncertainty often decreases but might not diminish entirely. This uncertainty has a detrimental impact on the desirability of design alternatives.

* Send all correspondence to: Deborah Thurston Department of General Engineering, 104 S. Mathews Ave., University of Illinois at Urbana-Champaign, Urbana, IL, 61801.
telephone: 216-333-6456,
e-mail: thurston@uxh.cso.uiuc.edu

1.1. EXPERT SYSTEMS FOR MECHANICAL ENGINEERING DESIGN EVALUATION

Mechanical engineering design tasks contain three basic components: (1) determination of a set of needs or conditions to be fulfilled, (2) generation of a set of alternatives, and (3) evaluation of the alternatives. For components manufactured on a large scale, uncertainty as to manufacturing cost can be a significant factor in design evaluation.

Miller and Nevill [1990] use symbolic reasoning for preliminary design. In Dominic, a domain independent iterative redesign system, Dixon and Howe et al. [1986], [Howe, Cohen, et al., 1986] utilize scales to evaluate the current design in the design-evaluate-redesign cycle. Neither of these approaches deal with uncertainty.

1.2 HEURISTICS EMBODY ASSUMED USER ATTITUDE TOWARDS UNCERTAINTY

Embedded in the rules of expert systems for mechanical design are not only heuristics for reducing the search space, but also assumptions regarding the user's attitude towards risk and uncertainty. Since these attitudes can vary significantly depending on the manufacturing scenario, the heuristics might not be accurate and/or impose unnecessary constraints on the user. If differences between users are considered at all, the differences are often categorized into stereotypical situations envisioned by the domain expert. Such a system performs well on cases that match the preconceived user profiles, but fail when an atypical user is presented to the system.

1.3. RELATED WORK

In dealing with uncertainty, decision makers need to measure and represent uncertainty, combine this information into the decision process, construct a decision model, and draw inferences [Bhatnagar & Kanal, 1986], [Holtzman & Breese, 1986]. While there exist several well known methods for representing uncertainty in rule-base expert systems, no universally accepted generic method for "uncertainty handling" exists [Chandrasekaran & Tanner, 1986]. Wise & Henrion [1986] present a method for comparing several well known methods such as MYCIN's certainty factor, Prospector, Bayes' networks, fuzzy set theory, Dempster-Shafer belief functions, and some non-numerical schemes. Several researchers have noted the advantages of combining formal decision theoretic techniques such as utility analysis [von Neumann & Morgenstern, 1947], [Keeney & Raiffa, 1976] with expert system methods [Keeney, 1986], [Henrion & Cooley, 1987], [Kalagnanam & Henrion, 1990]. Other researchers use utility analysis with expert systems [Sykes & White, 1985], [Spillane & Brown, 1986], [Gabbert & Brown, 1987], but do not include consideration of uncertainty.

1.4 COMPARISON BETWEEN UTILITY ANALYSIS AND FUZZY SETS FOR DESIGN EVALUATION

One approach for dealing with this type of uncertainty is fuzzy set analysis [Zadeh, 1975], [Bellman & Zadeh, 1970]. Thurston compares utility and fuzzy set analysis for design evaluation of multiple attributes [Thurston & Carnahan, 1990]. The steps in applying utility analysis and fuzzy set analysis are similar. Each requires the enumeration of relevant attributes, some type of assessment of the relative "value" or "importance" the designer places on each attribute with respect to the other attributes, and the relative attribute performance levels represented by each alternative. Several differences exist:

1. *Quantification of Attributes* - Utility analysis requires that the expected level of performance be quantified, such as dollars, pounds or a numeric scale (such as 1-10). Fuzzy set analysis does not require such quantification, allowing expression in terms of linguistic variables such as "high" and "low."

2. *Monotonicity of Preference* - Fuzzy set analysis permits direct evaluation of attributes whose most desirable level is in the mid-level of the acceptable range, by determining the closeness to a fuzzy goal. Utility analysis requires monotonicity of preference over the attribute range.

3. *Uncertainty* - Both utility and fuzzy set approaches can include consideration of uncertainty as to ultimate performance or attribute levels of a design alternative. Fuzzy sets utilize membership functions, while utility analysis utilizes probability distribution functions to model uncertainty and calculate expected utility.

4. *Relative Importance of Attributes* - Fuzzy set analysis may incorporate "fuzziness" as to the relative "importance" of attributes. Utility analysis does not directly deal with this type of uncertainty, although sensitivity analysis of results on the values of the scaling constants k_j may be performed.

5. *Ordinal Rankings of Alternatives* - Both approaches provide an ordinal ranking of alternatives. However, utility analysis can then be used to quantify beneficial tradeoffs between attributes to guide the iterative design process.

For these reasons, fuzzy sets are more appropriate at the earliest stages of preliminary design configuration when only semantic descriptors of expected design performance are available, and where preliminary design evaluation is being performed by a group, where the use of semantics facilitates reaching consensus. Utility analysis is more appropriate in the later iterative design process that we are concerned with.

2. INTEGRATION OF USER-DEFINED EVALUATION FUNCTION INTO EXPERT SYSTEM

A technique to allow designers to incorporate their own unique attitude towards uncertainty as opposed to those assumed by the expert's rules is presented. We describe a method for integrating quantitative procedures for design evaluation which reflect an individual's unique preferences. The general approach is to identify the aspects of heuristic rules which directly or indirectly include assumptions regarding the user's attitude towards risk and replace them with those of the individual end-user. Multiattribute utility analysis is used to methodically extract, interpret, and manage the user's preferences during the construction of the knowledge base. We present the results of the integration of multiattribute utility analysis with a rule-based system for material selection.

2.1 ANALYSIS OF HEURISTIC RULE BASE

Figure 1 shows the basic steps. The heuristics used to construct a conventional rule base are analyzed in order to separate subjective from objective rules. *Objective rules* contain the expert's technical judgment regarding feasible alternative design configurations, materials and/or manufacturing processes that would satisfy specified performance requirements. They allow or disallow a design option because of mechanical or structural reasons. They describe or embody universal, constant physical laws. Objective rules originate both from expert design engineers and from texts which describe standard practice. These rules do not typically vary between domain experts as they are composed of factual information.

Subjective rules embed assumptions regarding how a particular end-user of the knowledge-based system (KBS) would value a design alternative, including reasonable assumptions as to the user's attitude towards uncertainty. For example, a rule which selects between a traditional versus an innovative new design might reasonably assume that for high volume mass production, long production runs, the financial risk undertaken in committing to a new design whose manufacturing costs are highly uncertain (even if the design offers some advantages) is unacceptable.

These definitions are used as guidelines to separate objective aspects from subjective aspects of rules in the knowledge base. Once the subjective elements of rules are identified and eliminated, expert heuristics are used only to select or eliminate a design configuration based on the technical design requirements.

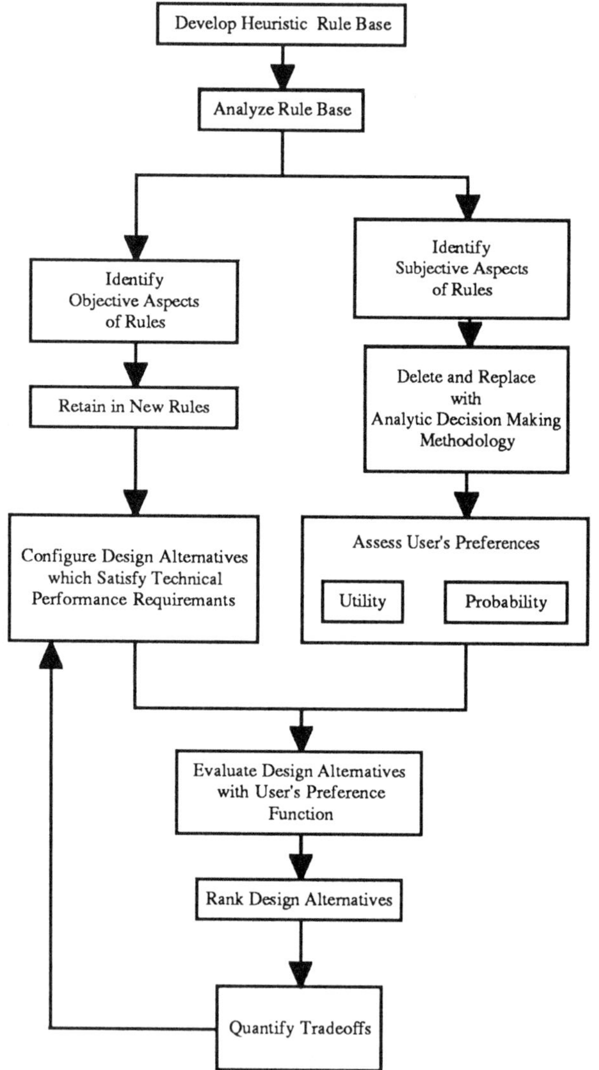

Figure 1. Overview of Steps for Integrating Design Evaluation Procedure into Knowledge Based Systems for Design and Manufacturing

2.2 ASSESSING USER'S UTILITY FUNCTION

We have developed a module that assesses the multiattribute utility function of the user through interactive, mouse-driven software. Responses to a sequence of lottery questions (described by Keeney and Raiffa [1976]) determine the single attribute utility functions and scaling constants. The responses reflect the user's attitude towards uncertainty or degree of risk aversion. An outline appears around the selected option, shown in Figure 2.

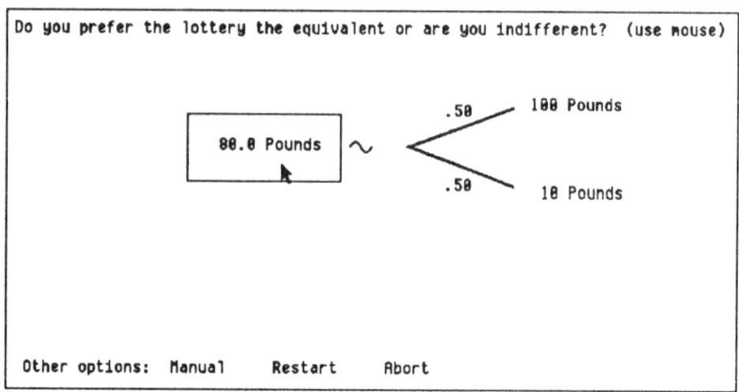

Figure 2. Lottery Question Screen to Determine $u(x_{weight})$

The overall scaling constant K is calculated from equation (2) and the multiplicative multiattribute utility function (after testing for independence conditions) using equation (1).

$$U(X) = \frac{1}{K} [[\prod_{j=1}^{J} \left(Kk_jU_j(x_j)+1\right)]-1] \tag{1}$$

where:

$U(X)$ = overall utility of set of attributes X for each alternative i

$U_j(x_j)$ = single attribute utility function for attribute x_j

x_j = performance level for attribute j

j = 1,2...J attributes

k_j = single attribute scaling constant

K = scaling constant, derived from

$$1 + K = \prod_{j=1}^{J} \left(1 + K\,k_j\right) \tag{2}$$

2.3 UNCERTAINTY IN DESIGN PERFORMANCE

The effect of uncertainty as to attribute levels on the desirability of alternatives is reflected by the degree of risk aversion exhibited in the assessed single attribute utility functions. Probabilistic multiattribute utility analysis can be employed to determine the expected value of the overall utility for the ith alternative, $E[U^i(X)]$. It is calculated from expected values of the single attribute utility functions, $E[Uj(x_j)]$; the latter depend on the probability density functions, $f(x_j)$, for the individual attributes. If the attribute levels are independent random variables, it can be shown that

$$E[U^i(X)] = \frac{1}{K}\{[\prod_{j=1}^{J}\left(Kk_jE[U_j(x_j)]+1\right)] - 1\} \qquad (3)$$

where

$$E[U_j] = \int_{x_{min}}^{x_{max}} U_j(x_j)f(x_j)dx_j \qquad (4)$$

The expected overall utility, $E[U^i(X)]$, is calculated for each of the I alternatives using equation (3), substituting the expected single attribute utility values in place of their deterministic counterparts.

The uncertainty associated with an attribute is characterized by a probability distribution function. The beta distribution is recommended since it may be readily characterized with input from the design decision maker which is fairly straightforward to assess. The beta distribution is part of the theoretical basis for Project Evaluation and Review Technique (PERT) employed to determine the optimal schedule of inter-dependent tasks with user-estimated uncertainty in completion times [Moder & Phillips, 1970], [Sasieni, 1986]. The required inputs are the minimum, maximum, and most probable values.

A beta random variable distributed on the interval (x_L, x_U) has probability density

$$f(x) = \frac{\Gamma(p+q)}{r\,\Gamma(p)\Gamma(q)}\left(\frac{x - x_L}{r}\right)^{p-1}\left(\frac{x_U - x}{r}\right)^{q-1} \quad x_L \le x \le x_U$$
$$= 0 \qquad \text{otherwise} \qquad (5)$$

where the range is $r = x_L - x_U$. If the shape parameters p and q are chosen to be greater than 1, the distribution is unimodal; if they are equal to one the beta distribution degenerates to a uniform distribution. Of course, the gamma function reduces to the ordinary factorial for an integer argument, i. e., $\Gamma(p) = (p-1)!$

For such a beta variate, the mean μ and the mode m can be readily calculated by

$$\mu = x_L + r\,\frac{p}{p+q} \qquad (6)$$

and

$$m = x_L + r\,\frac{p-1}{p+q-2} \qquad (7)$$

where the mode, m, is sometimes referred to as the most probable or "most likely" value. Here x_L, x_U, and m are supplied, so equation 7 defines the relationship between the shape parameters which will produce the requested mode. As p and q vary, however, the probability mass is distributed in a variety of ways about the mode. For instance, when either p or q is large, the density has a pronounced peak near the mode; if both p and q are small, the probability mass is spread over the interval, as shown in Figure 3.

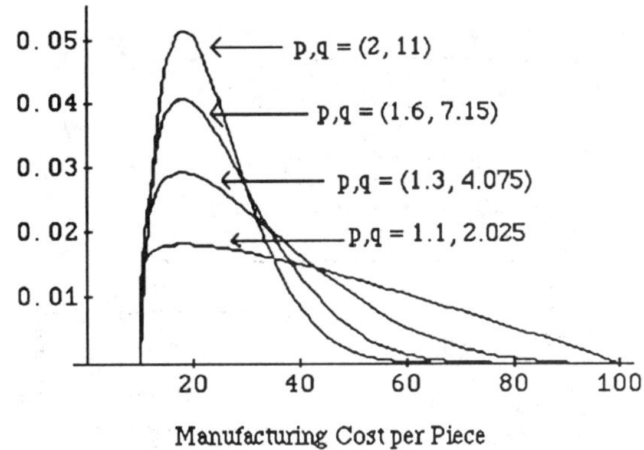

Figure 3. Manufacturing Cost Uncertainty with a Range of Underlying Beta Distribution Parameters p,q

The expected utility for an attribute whose estimated performance level is characterized by a beta probability density function, assuming the interval (x_L, x_U) is contained within (x_{min}, x_{max}), and $U_j(x_j) = a\text{-}be^{cx}$, from equations 4 and 5 is:

$$E[U_j(x_j)] = \frac{\Gamma(p+q)}{r\,\Gamma(p)\Gamma(q)}\int_{x_L}^{x_U}(a - be^{cx})\left(\frac{x - x_L}{r}\right)^{p-1}\left(\frac{x_U - x}{r}\right)^{q-1}dx \qquad (8)$$

which, after the change of variables, $y = (x - x_L)/r$,

$$= \frac{\Gamma(p+q)}{\Gamma(p)\Gamma(q)}\int_0^1 [a - be^{c(ry+x_L)}]\, y^{p-1}(1-y)^{q-1}dy \qquad (9)$$

$$= a - \frac{be^{cx_L}\,\Gamma(p+q)}{\Gamma(p)\Gamma(q)}\left\{\sum_{n=1}^{q}(-1)^{n-1}\binom{q-1}{n-1}\left[(-1)^{n+p-1}\frac{(n+p-2)!}{(cr)^{n+p-1}} + e^{cr}\sum_{i=0}^{n+p-2}(-1)^i\frac{i!\binom{n+p-2}{i}}{(cr)^{i+1}}\right]\right\}. \qquad (10)$$

This expression is valid only when the shape parameters p and q are integers greater or equal to 1. Although the expression is somewhat involved, it requires little computational effort when the shape parameters are small, such as less than 10. The expected value can alternatively be obtained by numerical integration of equation 8.

We have written a subroutine which permits the user to provide parameters used to determine a beta distribution which reflects the uncertainty in estimation of performance levels. The input screen is shown in Figure 4.

Choose Beta Parameters

Lower bound on variable: 10
Upper bound on variable : 100
Explicit value for p : 1.1
Value for q : 2.025
Value of mode : ....
Value of mean : ....

Abort [ ]   Do It [ ]
Find p using mean [ ]   Find p using mode [ ]

Figure 4. User Input Screen to Assess Uncertainty via Beta Distribution

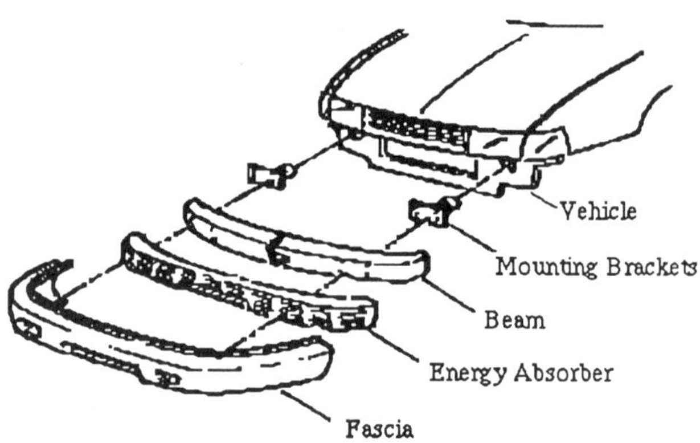

Figure 5. Overview of components of an automobile bumper. [Rusch, 1990]

3. EXAMPLE: AUTOMOTIVE BUMPER MATERIAL SELECTION KBS

Two separate versions of a knowledge-based system (KBS) which performs the task of material selection for an automobile bumper system were developed. The conventional KBS utilizes expert heuristics for all phases of the task. The integrated system substitutes multiattribute utility analysis where rules directly or indirectly deal with uncertainty or evaluate alternative feasible materials.

Bumpers consist of three main components: fascia, bumper beam, and energy absorber (EA), shown in Figure 5. The fascia is an optional outer plastic covering and is made of thermoset or thermoplastic. Vehicles without fascia have either a bright ("chrome") or painted finish.

The energy absorber (EA) allows for energy dissipation without causing permanent damage to the vehicle from low level impacts. The three alternatives are hydraulic strokers, injection molded plastic collapsing column, and expanded bead polypropylene foam. The bumper beam's primary function is to transfer impact energy not dissipated by the energy absorber to the automobile frame. Traditionally beams have been made of steel or aluminum, but reinforced thermosets and unreinforced thermoplastic beams are becoming more common.

3.1. THE CONVENTIONAL KNOWLEDGE-BASED SYSTEM

Knowledge acquisition came from interviews with bumper design engineers, material manufacturers and from trade and technical publications [Berg, et al., 1989], [Collision Estimating Guide Domestic, 1990], [Delco, 1987], [Delmastro, 1989] and product literature. The knowledge base was constructed in OPS5, running on a Texas Instrument microExplorer^{TM}. A mouse-driven menu queries the user for three types of inputs: performance parameters, vehicle characteristics, and manufacturing factors (Figure 6.)

Performance parameters are finish requirements, impact standards, allowable design offset, general bumper shape, and presence or absence of bumper cut-outs. Vehicle characteristics including curb weight, general vehicle model type, and cost range are used to classify the application. Manufacturing data (production volume, length of run, and required lead time) are used both to eliminate materials which could not be manufactured effectively within time requirements, and to estimate manufacturing costs.

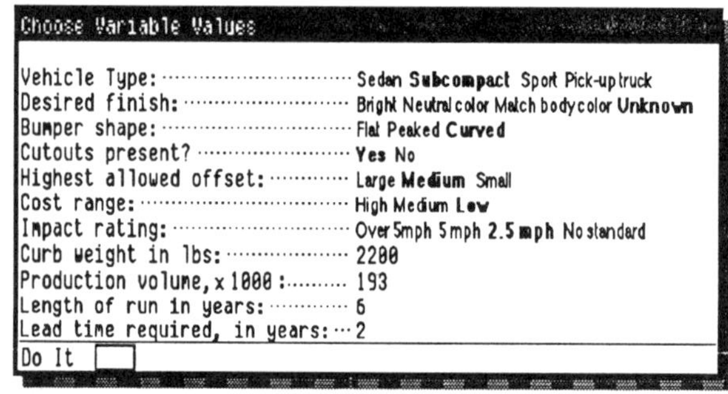
Choose Variable Values

Vehicle Type: .... Sedan **Subcompact** Sport Pick-up truck
Desired finish: .... Bright Neutral color Match body color **Unknown**
Bumper shape: .... Flat Peaked **Curved**
Cutouts present? .... **Yes** No
Highest allowed offset: .... Large **Medium** Small
Cost range: .... High Medium **Low**
Impact rating: .... Over 5mph 5 mph **2.5 mph** No standard
Curb weight in lbs: 2200
Production volume, x 1000 : 193
Length of run in years: 6
Lead time required, in years: ... 2
Do It [ ]

Figure 6. Conventional KBS Bumper Input Menu

Domain knowledge fell into three categories: configuration rules, design restrictions, and applicability considerations.

Design configuration rules restricted certain combinations of materials, since components chosen for one element of the bumper dictate which materials can or cannot be used in another component.

Design restriction rules prevented selection of infeasible material alternatives. For example, if a short start-up time was required, materials that could not be manufactured at the indicated volume in the required time would be eliminated.

Applicability rules selected a material when more than one material could meet the configuration and design parameter requirements.

3.2 THE INTEGRATED SYSTEM

Once the first system was completed and its performance verified, the integrated system was developed. The addition of the probability and utility assessment modules was the only change obvious to the user, while internally the expert system changed significantly. The heuristics used in the original rule base were re-examined to separate subjective from objective rules.

The majority of subjective rules were of the "applicability" type while "design restriction" and "design configuration" rules were primarily objective. The form of the productions in the rule-based system changed from selecting a single material for each component to rejecting materials which did not fall within the stated design parameters and the configuration constraints. Leaving only the objective antecedents in rules resulted in a system that selects a larger number of material alternatives, then ranks these alternatives using the end-user's utility function.

The domain expert's assumptions as to risk aversion characteristics of the user are replaced with the assessed utility function. Domain expert knowledge about possible configurations and minimum performance requirements remains. This allows the revised system to be more responsive to individual user's requirements, especially in instances where the end-user's preference function differs from the stereotypical profile normally assumed by experts.

3.3. COMPARISON BETWEEN CONVENTIONAL KBS AND MAUA/INTEGRATED KBS

A truck designer was characterized in the conventional system as a consistently risk-averse decision maker who was willing to spend very little to achieve higher performance or lower weight. Table 1 compares the results of the conventional KBS with that of the integrated KBS. When the typical truck designer utility and scaling parameters were input into the integrated KBS, the output mirrored the convention KBS: a simple, one piece stamped steel bumper with no fascia and no additional energy absorbing unit.

Method Used to Select Bumper Component Materials

Component	Conventional KBS	Integrated KBS w/typical user	Integrated KBS w/atypical user	System Found on Vehicle
Fascia	None	None	Thermoset	None
Energy Absorber	None	None	Foam	None
Beam	Stamped Steel	Stamped Steel	Stamped Steel	Stamped Steel
Utility of System	Atypical: 0.64	Typical: 0.80	Atypical: 0.80	

Table 1. Comparison of Conventional and Integrated KBS for a Truck Application

Column 3 indicates integrated KBS results using an "atypical" user utility function. "Atypical" users differ from typical users in their toward uncertainty, which is expressed in the degree of risk-aversion exhibited in the utility function. The atypical user in this example showed a much lower degree of risk aversion than the typical user.

When the integrated system used the atypical user profile with the same design parameters as the "typical" designer in the original system, different materials were selected for the fascia and energy absorber. Because design restrictions did not eliminate any of the fascia materials from consideration, the utility module was free to select the material with the highest utility for the user from a list of all possible materials. When the overall utility of the materials was computed, "thermoset," which has the highest appearance ranking, had the highest utility for the "atypical" user. The addition of a fascia allowed foam and collapsing column to be considered as an energy absorbing material, where for the normal user the absence of a fascia eliminated these options from consideration. The energy absorber selected was foam. While no impact standards had to be met, the user still preferred higher impact performance to lower performance. The foam energy absorber provides higher performance than simple fascia support brackets (no EA) at a similar cost.

Both the typical and atypical user had similar utilities for the beam requirements, and the material choice remained the same – stamped steel. The last row in Table 1 indicates that for an atypical user, the overall utility of the system recommended by the integrated KBS, 0.80, is greater than that recommended by the conventional KBS, 0.64, indicating that the integrated system led to a superior alternative.

4. CONCLUSIONS

We have shown that heuristics which embody reasonable assumptions regarding the user's attitude towards risk and uncertainty in evaluating alternatives might be inaccurate for some users.

A tool for assessing the user's attitude and a technique for integrating it into the rule base has been presented. The integration is performed at the individual rule level, and not simply tacked onto the end of the expert system. The heuristic rule base is analyzed, making a clear distinction between aspects of rules which reflect objective technical expertise and aspects which include assumptions as to the user's attitude towards uncertainty.

These attitudes can be successfully dealt with in a more direct manner by eliminating the domain expert's assumptions regarding the user's preferences and replacing them with multiattribute utility analysis. Expert heuristics still play a major role in generating feasible design alternatives from a purely technical viewpoint.

The example showed that this integrated approach can lead to improved selections for the atypical user, without compromising system performance for the more stereotypical designer. Sensitivity to users' preferences is provided without disturbing the original expert's objective knowledge.

An additional benefit is that incorporating new knowledge regarding technological advances is simplified. The only productions that need to be added are configuration restrictions and minimum performance levels, while uncertainty considerations are reflected in the utility and probability assessment modules.

By assessing the utility and probability functions of design engineers and directly incorporating them into the rule base, a computer aid to design has been developed which permits engineers to develop designs which are optimal for their own decision making environment.

Acknowledgment

The author gratefully acknowledges the support of the National Science Foundation under grant DMC-8809829 and PYI award DDM-8957420.

References

Bellman R. E. and Zadeh, L. A., "Decision-Making in a Fuzzy Environment," *Management Science*, Vol. 17B, 1970, pp. 141 - 164.

Berg, J. W., R. E. Morgan, and G. A. Klumb "High Performance RIM Fasica," *Plastics in Automobiles, International Congress and Exposition, Detroit, Michigan, 1989*. p. 33.

Bhatnagar, R. K., Laveen N. Kanal, Handing Uncertain Information: A Review of Numeric and Non-numeric Methods, *Uncertainty in Artificial Intelligence*, Kanal, L.N. et al. (Eds.), Elsevier Science Publishers B. V., 1986, p. 3-26.

Chandrasekaran, B., Michael C. Tanner, Uncertainty Handling in Expert Systems: Uniform vs. Task-Specific formalisms, *Uncertainty in Artificial Intelligence*, Kanal, L.N. et al. (Eds.), Elsevier Science Publishers B. V., 1986, p. 35-46.

Collision Estimating Guide Domestic. Mitchell International, April, 1990.

Delco Products Division of General Motors Corp. *Hard Bar Bumper System Design Manual*, Dec. 14, 1987.

Delmastro, J. "Overview of the North American Car Market for Bumper Applications," *Plastics in Automobiles, International Congress and Exposition, Detroit, Michigan, 1989*. pp. 227-234.

Dixon, J.R., A. Howe, P.R. Cohen, and M.K. Simmons, "Dominic I: Progress Towards Domain Independence in Design by Iterative Redesign," *Proceedings of the ASME 1986 Computers in Engineering Conference, Chicago, Illinois, July, 1986*, Vol I, pp. 199-212.

Gabbert, P., D.E. Brown, A Knowledge-Based Approach to Materials Handling System, *World Probuctivity Forum & 1987 International Industrial Engineering Conference*, May 17-20, 1987, p.445-451.

Henrion, M., D. R. Cooley, "An Experimental Comparison of Knowledge Engineering for Expert Systems and for Decision Analysis," *Proceedings of AAAI-87*, Seattle, WA. 1987, p. 471-476.

Holtzman, S., J. Breese, "Exact Reasoning about Uncertainty: On the Design of Expert Systems for Decision Support," *Uncertainty in Artificial Intelligence*, Kanal, L.N. et al. (Eds.), Elsevier Science Publishers B. V., 1986, p. 339-345.

Howe, A., P. Cohen, J. Dixon, and M. Simmons, "Dominic: A Domain-Independent Program for Mechanical Engineering Design," *Applications of Artificial Intelligence in Engineering Problems Conference, Southampton University, U.K., April, 1986. Vol. 1.* pp. 290-300.

Kalagnanam, Jayant, Max Henrion, A Comparison of Decision Analysis and Expert Rules for Sequential

Diagnosis, *Uncertainty in Artificial Intelligence 4,* R. D. Shachter et al. (Eds.), Elsevier Science Publishers B. V., 1990, p.271-281.

Keeney, R.L. and H. Raiffa, *Decisions with Multiple Objectives: Preferences and Value Tradeoffs.* John Wiley & Sons, Inc., 1976.

Keeney, R. L., Value-Driven Expert Systems for Decision Support, Expert Judgment and Expert Systems, Mnmpower, J.L. et al. (Eds.), 1986, p. 155-171.

Moder, J., and Phillips, C., Project Management with CPM and PERT, Van Nostran Reinhold Co., New York, 1970.

Miller, V.T., Nevill, G.E., "Knowledge Sifting" for Preliminary Design," *Proceedings of the Design Theory and Methodology Conference,* 1990, ASME.

Rusch, K. C. "Overview of Automotive Plastic Bumpers," *Automobile Bumper Systems and Exterior Panels,* 1990, SAE paper 900420.

Sasieni, M., "A Note on PERT Times," *Management Science*, 32, 12, December, 1986.

Spillane, A. R., D. E. Brown, An Intelligent Design Aid for Large Scale Systems with Quantity Discount Pricing, *Proceedings of the 1986 IEEE International Conference in Systems, Man, and Cybernetics,* Oct. 14-17, 1986, p. 1331-1336.

Sykes, E. A., C. C. White, III, Specifications of a Knowledge System for Packet-Switched Data Network Topological Design, *IEEE Expert Systems in Government Symposium,* 1985, p. 102-110.

Thurston, D. L. and Carnahan, J. V., "Fuzzy Ratings and Utility Analysis in Preliminary Design Evaluation of Multiple Attributes," University of Illinois Technical Report, Department of General Engineering, 8/90.

Thurston, D.L., "Multiattribute Utility Analysis in Design Management," *IEEE Transaction on Engineering Management,* Vol. 37, No. 4, November, 1990.

von Neumann, J. and O. Morgenstern, Theory of Games and Economic Behavior, 2nd ed. Princeton University Press, Princeton, N.J., 1947.

Wise, B. P., Max Henrion, A Framework for Comparing Uncertain Inference Systems to Probability, *Uncertainty in Artificial Intelligence,* Kanal, L.N. et al. (Eds.), Elsevier Science Publishers B. V., 1986, p. 69-83.

Zadeh, L. A., "The Concept of a Linguistic Variable and its Application to Approximate Reasoning," *Information Sciences*, Vol. 8, 1975, pp. 199-249.

From Relational Databases to Belief Networks

Wilson X. Wen
AI Systems, Telecom Research Labs.
770 Blackburn Rd, Clayton,
Victoria 3168, Australia

Abstract

The relationship between belief networks and relational databases is examined. Based on this analysis, a method to construct belief networks automatically from statistical relational data is proposed. A comparison between our method and other methods shows that our method has several advantages when generalization or prediction is deeded.

1 INTRODUCTION

It turns out that Relational Database (RD) and Belief Network (BN) are very closely related to each other in many aspects. Spiegelhalter [1986] investigated some of these relationships. He also discussed the issue about "using data to learn about quantitative assessments" so that the conditional probabilities can be revised by data obtained after a BN has been built. Lauritzen, Spiegelhalter [1988], Herskovitz and Copper [1990] used a method based on Maximum Entropy (ME) principle [Shore and Johnson, Jan 1980] to obtain a consistent distribution from empirical data. Spiegelhalter [1986] and Wen [1990b] discussed decomposition of the networks to reduce the computational amount required by probabilistic reasoning.

In this paper, the relationship between RD and BN is investigated and a method to construct BN from statistical RD [Wen, 1990a] is proposed based on the principles of Nearest Neighborhood (NN) [Duda and Hart, 1973] and Occam's Razor (OR) [Blumer *et al.*, 1987]. Most of the contemporary databases are relational, this makes the research in construction of BN from RD interesting and important. A comparison between our method and others is also given.

2 RELATIONAL DATABASES

According to the relational database theory [Ullman, 1982], we have the following basic definitions in RD:

A *relation* r is a subset of the Cartesian product of domains $D_1, ..., D_k$. A *domain* D_i is a set of values taken by an *attribute* A_i. The members of a relation are *tuples*. The value of a tuple t on attribute A is written as $t[A]$. The set of attribute for a relation r is the *relation scheme* R. Let $X \subset R$ and $t \in r$. We write $t[X]$ for the partial tuple of t restricted to X. A collection of relation schemes is a *relational database scheme.* The current values of the relations corresponding to the database scheme are the *relational database.*

Let r and s are relations on relational schemes R and S, respectively, $A \in R$, $a \in D$, and $X \subset R$. We will discuss the following operators on relations.

1. **Select operator:** "Select from r with A equal to a" yields a relation $\sigma_{A=a}(r) = \{t \in r | t[A] = a\}$.

2. **Project operator:** The projection of r onto X is a relation $\pi_X(r) = \{t[X] | t \in r\}$

3. **Join operator:** The **join** of r and s is a relation $r \bowtie s = \{t | t[R] \in r \wedge t[S] \in s\}$

To avoid redundancy and potential inconsistency, RD are often organized in normal forms according to the dependencies existing among the attribute subsets.

Functional dependency (FD): Let X, $Y \subset R$. X functionally determines Y, written $X \rightarrow Y$, if

$$\forall r \; on \; R, \; t, s \in r \wedge t[X] = s[X] \Longrightarrow t[Y] = s[Y].$$

Multivalued dependency (MD): X multidetermines Y, written $X \rightarrow\rightarrow Y$, if $\forall r$ *on* R, $t, s \in r \wedge t[X] = s[X]$ implies that $\exists u, v \in r$ such that (1) $u[X] = v[X] = t[X] = s[X]$, (2) $u[Y] = t[Y]$, and $u[R - X - Y] = s[R - X - Y]$, and (3) $v[Y] = s[Y]$ and $v[R - X - Y] = t[R - X - Y]$.

Join dependency (JD) over $R_1, ..., R_n$, written $\bowtie (R_1, ..., R_n)$, is satisfied by a relation r over $R_1 \cup ... \cup R_n$, if and only if $\pi_{R_1}(r) \bowtie ... \bowtie \pi_{R_n}(r) = r$

Let F be a set of FD's on $R(A_1, ..., A_n)$ and F^+ the closure of F. $K \subset R$ is a *key* of R if $K \rightarrow A_1, ..., A_n \in F^+ \wedge \nexists X \subset K, X \rightarrow A_1, ..., A_n \in F^+$.

To determine keys and calculate F^+, a set of inference rules, which is both complete and sound, called Armstrong's axioms has been developed [Ullman, 1982]. According to these rules $R(A_1, ..., A_n)$ can be decomposed into a collection of subsets $\rho(R_1, ..., R_k)$ such that $R = R_1 \cup, ... \cup R_k$. For a decomposition ρ of R the following properties are always desirable:

Lossless Join (LJ): Suppose D is a set of dependencies in R. ρ has a lossless join w.r.t. D if $\forall r\ on\ R, r = \pi_{R_1}(r) \bowtie ... \bowtie \pi_{R_k}(r)$. With this property any relation can be recovered from its projections.

Dependency Preservation (DP): This requires that D is preserved by the projection $\pi_{R_i}(D)$ of D onto R_i's, where $\pi_{R_i}(D) = \{< X, Y > \mid < X, Y > \in D^+\}$, $XY \subseteq R_i$, $XY = X \cup Y$ and $< X, Y >$ represents either $X \rightarrow Y$ or $X \rightarrow\rightarrow Y$. ρ preserves D if

$$\forall < X, Y > \in D, < X, Y > \in \bar{D}^+, \ \bar{D} = \bigcup_{i=1}^{k} \pi_{R_i}(D).$$

The normal forms we are going to discuss include:

Fourth Normal Form (4NF): R is in 4th normal form if $\forall X \rightarrow\rightarrow Y \in D$,

$$Y \neq \emptyset \wedge Y \not\subseteq X \wedge XY \neq R \Longrightarrow \exists\ a\ key\ K,\ K \subseteq X.$$

Acyclic Databases: The relations of the database form an acyclic hypergraph [Beeri *et al.*, 1983].

The following algorithms [Ullman, 1982] decomposes R into a 4NF decomposition with LJ and DP.

Algorithm 2.1:

Input: Relation scheme R and set of FD and MD $D = \{< X, A >\}$.

Output: A 4NF decomposition ρ of R with LJ and DP.

Method: There are three cases to be discussed:

1. If $\exists A' \in R, \forall < X, A > \in D, A \neq A' \wedge A' \notin X$ then ρ contains a relation scheme with only one element A'.
2. If $\exists < X, A > \in D$, $XA = R$ then the output decomposition is R itself.
3. Otherwise, ρ contains scheme XA for each $< X, A > \in D$.

Finally, ρ should also contain a relation scheme K which is a key of the original relation R. □

Example 1. Sarcophagal Disease

The model [Gallant, 1988] consists of 6 symptoms, 2 diseases, and 3 possible treatments in Table 1. The three columns in Table 1 forms a simple database. All variables are binary variables taking values 1 and -1, except variables u_3 and u_5 which can take values 1, 0, and -1. Here 1 means that the corresponding proposition is true, -1 means false, and 0 means unknown. Suppose that there is a set F of FD on $R(u_1, ..., u_{11})$:

$$\begin{array}{llll} u_1, u_2, u_3 \rightarrow u_7. & u_3, u_4, u_5 \rightarrow u_8. \\ u_6, u_7, u_8 \rightarrow u_9. & u_3, u_7, u_8 \rightarrow u_{10}. \\ u_9, u_{10} \rightarrow u_{11}. & \end{array}$$

Symptom						Disease		Treatment		
u_1	u_2	u_3	u_4	u_5	u_6	u_7	u_8	u_9	u_{10}	u_{11}
1	1	1	-1	0	-1	1	-1	1	-1	1
-1	-1	-1	1	1	-1	-1	1	1	1	-1
-1	-1	1	1	-1	1	1	1	-1	-1	-1
1	1	-1	-1	1	-1	-1	-1	-1	-1	-1
1	-1	0	1	1	1	1	1	-1	1	1
1	-1	-1	1	1	-1	1	1	1	1	-1
1	1	1	-1	-1	1	1	-1	-1	-1	-1
-1	1	1	-1	1	1	-1	1	-1	-1	-1

u_1:Swollen feet u_2:Read ears u_3:Hair loss
u_4:Dizziness u_5:Sensitive aretha
u_6:Placibin allergy u_7:Supercilliosis u_8:Namastosis
u_9 :Placibin u_{10}:Biramibio u_{11}:Posiboost

Table 1: Data Set of Sarcophagal Disease

According to Algorithm 2.1, we have a decomposition of R with a lossless join and preservation of dependencies in F which contains the following relation schemes:

$$\begin{array}{ll} R_1 = \{u_1, u_2, u_3, u_7\}. & R_2 = \{u_3, u_4, u_5, u_8\}. \\ R_3 = \{u_6, u_7, u_8, u_9\}. & R_4 = \{u_3, u_7, u_8, u_{10}\}. \\ R_5 = \{u_9, u_{10}, u_{11}\}. & R_6 = \{u_1, u_2, u_3, u_4, u_5, u_6\}. \end{array}$$

where R_6 is a key of R. Thus, we have a relational sample database in 4th normal form in Table 2. □

u_1	u_2	u_3	u_7	u_3	u_4	u_5	u_8
1	1	1	1	1	-1	0	-1
-1	-1	-1	-1	-1	1	1	1
-1	-1	1	1	1	1	-1	1
1	1	-1	-1	-1	-1	1	-1
1	-1	0	1	0	1	1	1
1	-1	-1	1	-1	1	1	1
1	1	1	1	1	-1	-1	-1
-1	1	1	-1	1	-1	1	1

u_6	u_7	u_8	u_9	u_3	u_7	u_8	u_{10}
-1	1	-1	1	1	1	-1	-1
-1	-1	1	1	-1	-1	1	1
1	1	1	-1	1	1	1	-1
-1	-1	-1	-1	-1	-1	-1	-1
1	1	1	-1	0	1	1	1
-1	1	1	1	-1	1	1	1
1	1	-1	-1	1	1	-1	-1
1	-1	1	-1	1	-1	1	-1

u_9	u_{10}	u_{11}	u_1	u_2	u_3	u_4	u_5	u_6
1	-1	1	1	1	1	-1	0	-1
1	1	-1	-1	-1	-1	1	1	-1
-1	-1	-1	-1	-1	1	1	-1	1
-1	-1	-1	1	1	-1	-1	1	-1
-1	1	1	1	-1	0	1	1	1
1	1	-1	1	-1	-1	1	1	-1
-1	-1	-1	1	1	1	-1	-1	1
-1	-1	-1	-1	1	1	-1	1	1

Table 2: A sample database in 4th normal form

Example 2 [Cooper, 1984]: Metastatic cancer (A) is a possible cause of a brain tumor (C) and is also an explanation for increased total serum calcium (B). In turn, either of these could explain a patient falling into a coma (D). Severe headache (E) is also possibly associated with a brain tumor.

Suppose we have the statistical information in Table 3 from a sample database. Each entry of the table gives the number of occurrences of the records in the database which contain various combinations of the attributes A, B, C, D, and E. This can be obtained by

	$\bar{D}\bar{E}$	$\bar{D}E$	$D\bar{E}$	DE
$\bar{A}\bar{B}\bar{C}$	23104	34656	1216	1824
$\bar{A}\bar{B}C$	128	512	512	2048
$\bar{A}B\bar{C}$	1216	1824	4864	7296
$\bar{A}BC$	32	128	128	512
$A\bar{B}\bar{C}$	1216	1824	64	96
$A\bar{B}C$	32	128	128	512
$AB\bar{C}$	1024	1536	4096	6144
ABC	128	512	512	2048

Table 3: Statistical information in relation ABCDE

a projection of the universal relation of the database on the set $ABCDE$ without eliminating the duplicates. Obviously, the following MD hold on ABCDE:

$$A \rightarrow\rightarrow B,\ A \rightarrow\rightarrow C,\ B,C \rightarrow\rightarrow D,\ C \rightarrow\rightarrow E.$$

Thus, we can use Algorithm 2.1 to decompose ABCDE into 4NF subrelations AB, AC, BCD, CE. Each relation preserves the corresponding dependency and they have a lossless join equal to ABCDE. The statistical information in subrelations is shown in Table 4.

	$\bar{A}$	A
$\bar{B}$	64000	4000
B	16000	16000

(a)

	$\bar{A}$	A
$\bar{C}$	7600	16000
C	4000	4000

(b)

	$\bar{B}\bar{C}$	$\bar{B}C$	$B\bar{C}$	BC
$\bar{D}$	60800	800	5600	800
D	3200	3200	22400	3200

(c)

	$\bar{C}$	C
$\bar{E}$	36800	1600
E	55200	6400

(d)

Table 4: Statistical information in sub-relations

3 BELIEF NETWORKS

In this section, we introduce some concepts of BN based on the theory of discrete Markov random fields

3.1 PROBABILISTIC DEPENDENCY

Data extracted from a RD are called relational data. Although statistical relational data may satisfy MD, it refers to only FD and probabilistic dependency, a special kind of MD.

Definition 3.1: The **frequency** of an attribute subset X of relation scheme R in a relation r on R is $F_X(r) = \{F_{X=x}(r) = \frac{|\sigma_{X=x}(r)|}{|r|}; \forall x \in D_X\}$ where D_X is the domain of X, $|r|$ is the cardinality of r.

Definition 3.2: The **conditional frequency** of X in r given $Y = y$, $Y \subset R$ is $F_{X|Y=y}$:

$$\{F_{X=x|Y=y}(r) = \frac{|\sigma_{X=x\wedge Y=y}(r)|}{|\sigma_{Y=y}(r)|}; \forall x \in D_X\}$$

Definition 3.3: Let $X, Y \subset R$, and $Z = R - XY$. r satisfies the **probabilistic dependency (PD)** $X \mapsto Y$ if $xyz \in r \Longrightarrow$

$$F_{XYZ=xyz}(r) \cdot F_{X=x}(r) = F_{XY=xy}(r) \cdot F_{XZ=xz}(r).$$

According to the law of large numbers, it is reasonable to assume $\lim_{|r|\to\infty} F_X(r) = P(X)$, $\lim_{|r|\to\infty} F_{X|Y=y}(r) = P(X|Y = y)$, and if $X \mapsto Y$ then $P(Y|XZ) = P(Y|X)$, ie. Y and Z are conditionally independent given X. It is easy to prove

Theorem 3.1:

1. $X \rightarrow Y \Longrightarrow X \mapsto Y$ with $P(Y|X) \in \{0,1\}$, and
2. $X \mapsto Y \Longrightarrow X \rightarrow\rightarrow Y$.

In Example 2, we can easily check that the PD $A \mapsto B$, $A \mapsto C$, $B, C \mapsto D$, and $C \mapsto E$ hold.

3.2 BASIC DEFINITIONS OF BELIEF NETWORKS

Consider a probability space $R = \{A_i | i = 1, ...m\}$, which corresponds to a relation scheme R, with $M = a_1 \times ... \times a_m$ possible states $S = \{s_j | j = 1, ..., M\}$ and a probability distribution $p = \{P(s_j) | j = 1, ..., M\}$. Each variable A_i in the space can take a_i values. Suppose according to the dependencies, we have the following constraint set CS on the distribution p of R:

Conditional constraints (CCS):

$$\mu_k = P(A_{k0} | X_{k1,...,kp_k})$$

corresponding to the PD $X_{k1,...,kp_k} \mapsto A_{k0}$, where $k = 1, ..., n$ and $X_{k1,...,kp_k} = \{A_{k1}, ..., A_{kp_k}\} \subset R$.

Marginal constraints (MCS):

$$\nu_{k'} = P(X_{k'1,...,k'p'_{k'}}),\ where\ k' = 1, ...n'.$$

Universal constraint (UCS):

$$\sum_{A_0,...,A_{m-1}} P(A_0, ..., A_{m-1}) = 1.$$

In Example 1, it is easy to extract the CCS in Table 5 from the sample database in Table 2. In Table 5, u stands for $u = 1$, $\bar{u}$ for $u = -1$ and $\hat{u}$ for $u = 0$. Note that all these conditional probabilities are accurate and equal to 1, because all of the dependencies

$$
\begin{array}{llll}
P(\bar{u}_7|\bar{u}_1,\bar{u}_2,\bar{u}_3) & =1, & P(u_7|\bar{u}_1,\bar{u}_2,u_3) & =1 \\
P(\bar{u}_7|\bar{u}_1,u_2,u_3) & =1, & P(u_7|u_1,\bar{u}_2,\bar{u}_3) & =1 \\
P(u_7|u_1,\bar{u}_2,\hat{u}_3) & =1, & P(\bar{u}_7|u_1,u_2,\bar{u}_3) & =1 \\
P(u_7|u_1,u_2,u_3) & =1, & & \\
 & & & \\
P(\bar{u}_8|\bar{u}_3,\bar{u}_4,u_5) & =1, & P(u_8|\bar{u}_3,u_4,u_5) & =1 \\
P(u_8|\hat{u}_3,u_4,u_5) & =1, & P(\bar{u}_8|u_3,\bar{u}_4,\bar{u}_5) & =1 \\
P(\bar{u}_8|u_3,\bar{u}_4,\bar{u}_5) & =1, & P(\bar{u}_8|u_3,\bar{u}_4,\hat{u}_5) & =1 \\
P(u_8|u_3,u_4,\bar{u}_5) & =1, & & \\
 & & & \\
P(\bar{u}_9|\bar{u}_6,\bar{u}_7,\bar{u}_8) & =1, & P(u_9|\bar{u}_6,\bar{u}_7,u_8) & =1 \\
P(u_9|\bar{u}_6,u_7,\bar{u}_8) & =1, & P(u_9|\bar{u}_6,u_7,u_8) & =1 \\
P(\bar{u}_9|u_6,\bar{u}_7,u_8) & =1, & P(\bar{u}_9|u_6,u_7,\bar{u}_8) & =1 \\
P(\bar{u}_9|u_6,u_7,u_8) & =1, & & \\
 & & & \\
P(\bar{u}_{10}|\bar{u}_3,\bar{u}_7,\bar{u}_8) & =1, & P(u_{10}|\bar{u}_3,\bar{u}_7,u_8) & =1 \\
P(u_{10}|\bar{u}_3,u_7,u_8) & =1, & P(u_{10}|\hat{u}_3,u_7,u_8) & =1 \\
P(\bar{u}_{10}|u_3,\bar{u}_7,u_8) & =1, & P(\bar{u}_{10}|u_3,u_7,\bar{u}_8) & =1 \\
P(\bar{u}_{10}|u_3,u_7,u_8) & =1, & & \\
 & & & \\
P(\bar{u}_{11}|\bar{u}_9,\bar{u}_{10}) & =1, & P(u_{11}|\bar{u}_9,u_{10}) & =1 \\
P(u_{11}|u_9,\bar{u}_{10}) & =1, & P(\bar{u}_{11}|u_9,u_{10}) & =1
\end{array}
$$

Table 5: The conditional constraint sets from Table 2

are FD. It may not be the case for PD, ie. the conditional probabilities may not be accurately estimated nor they necessarily equal to 1. Note also that the above set of conditional probabilities is not complete, eg. $P(u_7|\bar{u}_1, u_2, \bar{u}_3)$ is not specified.

According to data dependencies and CCS, we may construct a directed graph, or BN as follows

Definition 3.4: A **Belief Network (BN)** is a directed graph $G =< V, E >$, such that

1. The node set is $V = R$
2. The edge set is $E = \{< A_{kq}, A_{kO} >\}$, such that $\exists CCS\ \mu_k = P(A_{kO}|X_{k1,\ldots,kp}) \in CS, A_{kq} \in X_{k1,\ldots,kp}$.

In Example 1, we have a BN shown in Fig. 1.

Definition 3.5:

A **neighbor system** σ in G is a set of sets $\{\sigma A_i | A_i \in R, \sigma A_i \subseteq R\}$, such that

1. $A_i \notin \sigma A_i$,
2. $A_j \in \sigma A_i \iff \exists\ CCS\ \mu_k = P(A_{kO}|X_{k1,\ldots,kp}) \in CS,\ A_i,\ A_j \in X_{kO,\ldots,kp}$

The **neighbors of a set** $X \subset R$ in G is the set $\sigma X = \{A_i \in R - X | \exists A_j \in X, A_i \in \sigma A_j\}$.

The **neighborhood network** of a BN $G =< V, E >$ is $G_\sigma =< V, E_\sigma >$, where $E_\sigma = \{(A_i, A_j) | A_i \in \sigma A_j\}$.

A set $C \subseteq R$ is called a **clique** if $A_j \in \sigma A_i$ whenever $A_i, A_j \in C$ and $i \neq j$. A clique MC is called **maximal clique** if there is no other clique C, such that $MC \subset C$. Let MCC be the class of all maximal cliques in R.

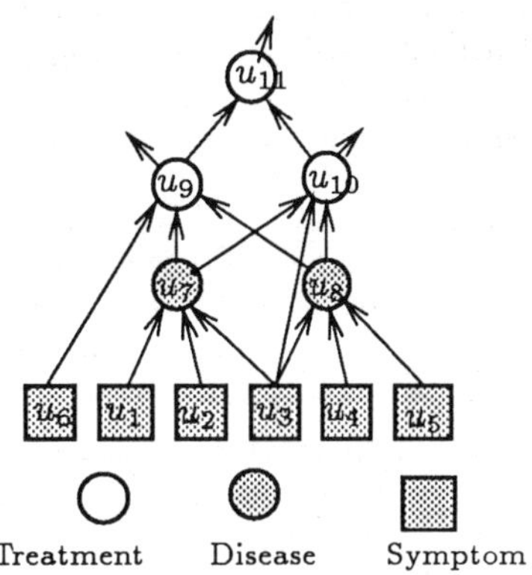

Figure 1: Belief Network of Sarcophagal disease

For Example 1, the neighborhood network is given in Fig. 2.

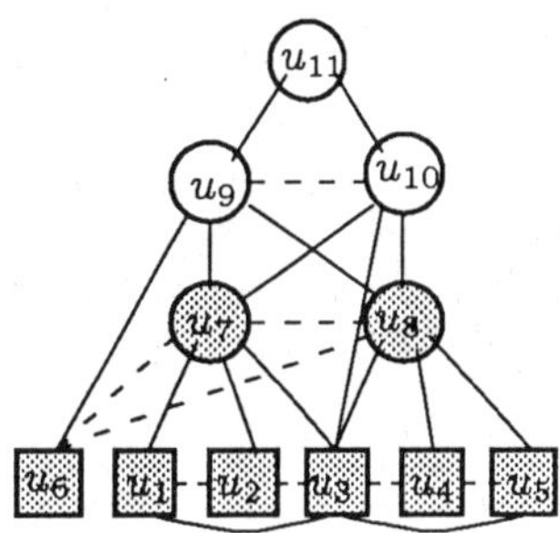

Figure 2: The neighborhood network for Example 2

3.3 DECOMPOSITION OF BELIEF NETWORKS

In order to handle the combinatorial explosion of the number of states in BN, a decomposition may be desired. The concept of neighbor Gibbs field [Wen, 1989] provides a valid factorization of the joint distribution for Markov random fields to localize the computation of the joint ME/MCE distribution of the whole BN within each of the maximal cliques of the neighborhood network. This suggests that the network should be decomposed into a hypergraph with the cliques of the neighborhood network as its hyperedges. To keep consistency among the distributions of the cliques, the results obtained in each clique need to be propagated to other cliques through their intersections. Consequently, it is desired to organize the decomposed result as an acyclic hypergraph [Beeri *et al.*, 1983] to guarantee the termination of the propagation and to avoid other possible anomalies during the propagation.

The decomposition techniques proposed in [Spiegelhalter, 1986; Wen, 1991] are described briefly as follows:

1. Construct a neighborhood network $G_\sigma = < V, E_\sigma >$ for BN $G =< V, E >$.

2. Find a fill-in [Tarjan and Yannakakis, 1984] F of G_σ, such that D_σ, the MCC of $G_f =< V, F \cup E_\sigma >$

- has the minimum $|F|$, for Spiegelhalter's method,
- has the minimum total number of states of all cliques in G_f for our method [Wen, 1991].

D_σ is the decomposition wanted and corresponds to an acyclic hypergraph $< V, D_\sigma >$.

Unfortunately, it has been shown that the problem of optimum belief network decomposition is NP hard under all of the above optimum criteria [Yannakakis, 1981; Wen, 1991]. Therefore, we proposed an algorithm to obtain the optimum belief decomposition based on simulated annealing [Wen, 1991].

In Example 1, it is easy to verify by Graham reduction [Beeri *et al.*, 1983] that the neighborhood network in Fig. 2 has already been an acyclic hypergraph. The decomposition is shown in Fig. 3. There are 6 subnetwroks in the decomposition: $MC_1 = \{u_9, u_{10}, u_{11}\}$, $MC_2 = \{u_7, u_8, u_9, u_{10}\}$ $MC_3 = \{u_6, u_7, u_8, u_9\}$, $MC_4 = \{u_3, u_7, u_8, u_{10}\}$, $MC_5 = \{u_3, u_4, u_5, u_8\}$, and $MC_6 = \{u_1, u_2, u_3, u_7\}$. The total number of states here is 124, comparing $2^9 \times 3^2 = 4608$ states in the original BN.

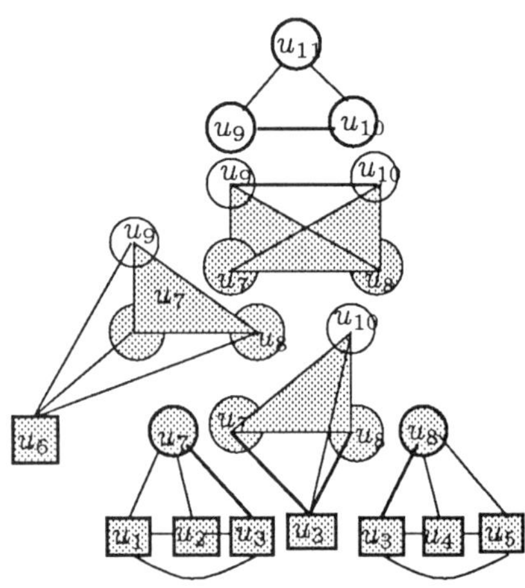

Figure 3: Decomposition of the BN for Example 2

Note that the decomposition corresponding to an acyclic database scheme [Beeri *et al.*, 1983] in Table 6, each relation scheme corresponds to a maximal clique in the decomposition. These relation schemes also satisfy JD and thus have lossless join and running intersection property [Beeri *et al.*, 1983]. In Fig. 3, the intersections between cliques have been shown by bold edges or shaded triangles.

u_1	u_2	u_3	u_7	u_3	u_4	u_5	u_8
1	1	1	1	1	-1	0	-1
-1	-1	-1	-1	-1	1	1	1
-1	-1	1	1	1	1	-1	1
1	1	-1	-1	-1	-1	1	-1
1	-1	0	1	0	1	1	1
1	-1	-1	1	-1	1	1	1
1	1	1	1	1	-1	-1	-1
-1	1	1	-1	1	-1	1	1

u_6	u_7	u_8	u_9	u_3	u_7	u_8	u_{10}
-1	1	-1	1	1	1	-1	-1
-1	-1	1	1	-1	-1	1	1
1	1	1	-1	1	1	1	-1
-1	-1	-1	-1	-1	-1	-1	-1
1	1	1	-1	0	1	1	1
-1	1	1	1	-1	1	1	1
1	1	-1	-1	1	1	-1	-1
1	-1	1	-1	1	-1	1	-1

u_9	u_{10}	u_{11}	u_7	u_8	u_9	u_{10}
1	-1	1	1	-1	1	-1
1	1	-1	-1	1	1	1
-1	-1	-1	1	1	-1	-1
-1	-1	-1	-1	-1	-1	-1
-1	1	1	1	1	-1	1
1	1	-1	1	1	1	1
-1	-1	-1	1	-1	-1	-1
-1	-1	-1	-1	1	-1	-1

Table 6: An acyclic database for Table 2

In [Wen, 1989], we have proven

Theorem 3.2: Belief updating the whole BN with Jeffrey's rule [Wen, 1990b] is equivalent to belief updating the clique in the acyclic decomposition which contains the corresponding constraint set, and Jeffrey belief propagation to all the other cliques through the running intersections.

3.4 THE MAIN OPERATIONS ON BN

There are three main operations on BN:

Belief extracting – Extracting a specified marginal distribution of a distribution. This corresponds to the projection operation in RD.

Updating – Given a new marginal on a subspace and a prior on the whole space, calculate a plausible posterior of the whole space matching with the given marginal. Bayes or Minimum Cross Entropy (MCE) posterior, particularly the posterior obtained by Jeffrey's updating [Wen, 1990b], are considered as plausible. This corresponds to selection operation for RD.

Belief propagation – After updating the marginal of a subspace, propagate the changes to the whole space through the running intersections. This operation corresponds to the join operation in RD.

4 INITIAL DISTRIBUTIONS

For the initial distribution of a decomposed network, two requirements should be satisfied.

1. The distribution should reflect the data in the sample database as faithfully as possible.
2. The distribution should predicate unseen cases as accurately as possible.

4.1 RECALL

There may be many distributions satisfying the fist requirement if the specification is incomplete. The most trivial one can be constructed as follows:

In Table 2, use 0 and 1 to replace of -1 and 1 for binary variables and use 00, 01 and 10 to replace of -1, 0 and 1 for u_3 and u_5, and convert each row in each subrelation into hexadecimal, then we obtain "Index" in Table 7. Suppose all these examples are equally important, or

MC_1		MC_2		MC_3	
Index:	Freq.	Index:	Freq.	Index:	Freq.
5:	0.125	0:	0.125	5:	0.125
6:	0.25	4:	0.125	3:	0.125
0:	0.5	7:	0.125	e:	0.25
3:	0.125	8:	0.125	0:	0.125
		a:	0.125	7:	0.125
		c:	0.125	a:	0.125
		d:	0.125	c:	0.125
		f:	0.125		

MC_4		MC_5		MC_6	
Index:	Freq.	Index:	Freq.	Index:	Freq.
14:	0.25	22:	0.125	1d:	0.25
03:	0.125	0d:	0.25	00:	0.125
16:	0.125	29:	0.125	05:	0.125
00:	0.125	04:	0.125	18:	0.125
0f:	0.125	1d:	0.125	13:	0.125
07:	0.125	20:	0.125	11:	0.125
12:	0.125	25:	0.125	0c:	0.125

Table 7: Prior distributions for cliques

have the same probability, we obtain "Probabilities" in Table 7.

Thus, Table 7 gives all the non-zero probabilities in a distribution satisfying all of the training examples. Using this simple distribution, we can perform all recall-like reasoning. Suppose we are given

$u_1 = 1$: a patient has swollen feet,
$u_3 = 1$: the patient suffers from hair loss,
$u_6 = -1$: the patient is not allergic to placibin.

This corresponds to a constraint set $\{P(u_1) = 1, P(u_3) = 1, P(u_6) = 0\}$. By Jeffrey's updating and belief propagation, we obtain a posterior in Table 8. This implies

(1) $u_2 = u_7 = u_9 = u_{11} = 1$, (2) $u_5 = 0$, (3) $u_4 = u_8 = u_{10} = -1$.

Comparing with the result in [Gallant, Oct 1987]:

$MC_1 : P(u_9 = 1, u_{10} = -1, u_{11} = 1)$	$= 1$
$MC_2 : P(u_7 = 1, u_8 = -1, u_9 = 1, u_{10} = -1)$	$= 1$
$MC_3 : P(u_6 = -1, u_7 = 1, u_8 = -1, u_9 = 1)$	$= 1$
$MC_4 : P(u_3 = 1, u_7 = 1, u_8 = -1, u_{10} = -1)$	$= 1$
$MC_5 : P(u_3 = 1, u_4 = -1, u_5 = 0, u_8 = -1)$	$= 1$
$MC_6 : P(u_1 = 1, u_2 = 1, u_3 = 1, u_7 = 1)$	$= 1$

Table 8: Posterior distributions for cliques

(1) $u_7 = u_9 = u_{11} = 1$, (2) $u_{10} = -1$,

we can see that our method do reasoning in all directions while Gallants can only do reasoning bottom-up.

This method is simple but has some disadvantages:

1. There are still "unseen" cases that cannot be handled by this method.
2. Not all MCS extracted from an RD are always consistent.

To overcome the second difficulty, we should extract a set of conditional probabilities, or *Local Characteristics (LC)*, instead of marginal ones, because any distribution is completely determined by its LC's and a set of non-redundant LC's can be always made consistent.

4.2 PREDICTION OR GENERALIZATION

It is obviously more difficult to predicate unseen cases than to just recall the cases encountered before.

Having constructed a BN, we can use one of the following methods to learn a set of LC's from an incomplete training database:

Frequency Method: A set of LC's can be learned in the same way as that extracting marginal probabilities described in the previous subsection. The disadvantage is that it has no generalization ability at all.

ME/MCE methods assign a uniform conditional distribution to the unseen cases. A special case of ME/MCE methods is so called Dirichlet distribution [Herskovitz and Cooper, 1990] which uses the following formula

$$P(X = x|\Pi_X = \pi_X) = \frac{C(X = x, \Pi_X = \pi_X) + 1}{C(\Pi_X = \pi_X) + V_X}$$

where X is a variable in the underlying BN, x is one of the V_X values can be taken by X, Π_X is the set of parents of X in the BN, π_X is a particular instantiation of Π_X, and $C(\Phi)$ is the number of cases/tuples in the database that match the instantiated set of variables Φ. When the case/tuple does not occur in the database, the above conditional probability becomes $P(X = x|\Pi_X = \pi_X) = \frac{1}{V_X}$ and thus is a uniform one.

The NN/OR Method [Duda and Hart, 1973; Blumer *et al.*, 1987]: For this method, the conditional probability assigned to an unseen case depends on its neighbor conditional distributions. That is, if the unseen case has many neighbors who have high probabilities to occur then it is assigned a relatively high conditional probability, otherwise, a low or even zero conditional probability. When there are neighbors having different probabilities, the NN/OR method prefers the choice making the final result simplest.

4.3 THE NN/OR LEARNING

It has been shown that the decomposed relations preserve all dependencies existing in the original relation. For Example 1, this means that learning can be performed within each relation (see Table 2). For example, in relation $\{u_1, u_2, u_3, u_7\}$, conditional distribution $P(u_7|u_1, u_2, u_3)$ can be learned as follows:

1. Use frequency method to obtain the conditional probabilities for the cases occurring in the training database. For relation (u_1, u_2, u_3, u_7) in Table 2. The result is

$$\begin{array}{llll} P(u_7|\bar{u}_1,\bar{u}_2,\bar{u}_3) & = 0 & P(u_7|\bar{u}_1,\bar{u}_2,u_3) & = 1 \\ P(u_7|\bar{u}_1,u_2,u_3) & = 0 & P(u_7|u_1,\bar{u}_2,\bar{u}_3) & = 1 \\ P(u_7|u_1,u_2,\bar{u}_3) & = 0 & P(u_7|u_1,u_2,u_3) & = 1 \end{array}$$

2. Draw a Karnough-like map for u_1, u_2, u_3 and fill the probability values learned in step 1 into the corresponding entries of the map (see Fig.4 a).

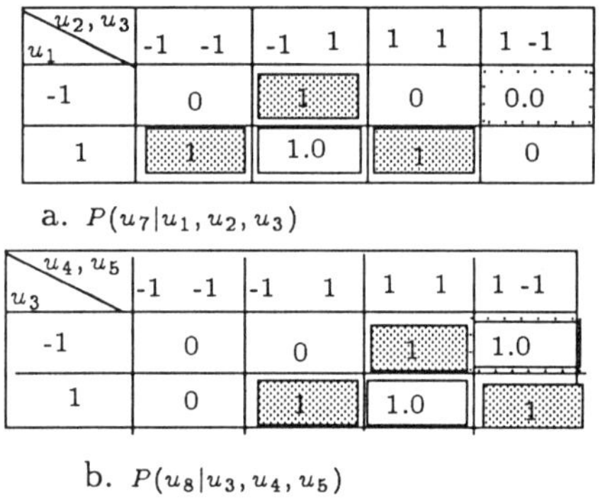

u_2, u_3 \ u_1	-1 -1	-1 1	1 1	1 -1
-1	0	1	0	0.0
1	1	1.0	1	0

a. $P(u_7|u_1, u_2, u_3)$

u_4, u_5 \ u_3	-1 -1	-1 1	1 1	1 -1
-1	0	0	1	1.0
1	0	1	1.0	1

b. $P(u_8|u_3, u_4, u_5)$

Figure 4: The results of learning by NN/OR method

3. For the unseen cases, entry (-1,1,-1) is filled with value 0 because all its nearest neighbors have entry values 0, and entry (1,-1,1) is filled with 1, similarly.

In some cases, the entries in the nearest neighborhood have different values. For example, $P(u_8|\bar{u}_3, u_4, \bar{u}_5)$ (see Fig. 4 b) has two nearest neighbors, (-1,1,1) and (1,1,-1), with values 1 and another one, (-1,-1,-1) with value 0. In this case, the Occam's Razor principle [Blumer *et al.*, 1987] can be used to choose the value for the unseen cases. The principle says

> Among the hypotheses consistent or compatible with the given data set, choose the simplest one.

There are many proposed measures of simplicity, the most common ones are as follows

1. Kolmogorov complexity,
2. Minimum description length, and
3. Logic formula complexity, combinational complexity, and time complexity [Pearl, 1978].

We adopt logic formula complexity which depends on the number of connectives in the logic formula. Trying to assign 0 and 1 to entry $(\bar{u}_3, u_4, \bar{u}_5)$, respectively, we find that logic formula $u_4 + u_3u_5$ corresponding to $P(u_7|\bar{u}_3, u_4, \bar{u}_5) = 1$ is simpler than $u_3u_4 + u_3u_5 + u_4u_5$ corresponding to $P(u_7|\bar{u}_3, u_4, \bar{u}_5) = 0$. Therefore, we choose $P(u_7|\bar{u}_3, u_4, \bar{u}_5) = 1$.

The logical expressions of the 4 possible assignments for unseen cases in Fig. 4 a. are give in Table 9. Obviously, the one obtained by NN/OR method is the simplest and has the shortest code length.

p_2	p_5	Logic expression	Complex.
0	0	$\bar{u}_1\bar{u}_2u_3 + u_1\bar{u}_2\bar{u}_3 + u_1u_2u_3$	8
0	1	$u_1\bar{u}_2 + u_1u_3 + \bar{u}_2u_3$	5
1	0	$\bar{u}_1\bar{u}_2u_3 + u_1\bar{u}_2\bar{u}_3 + u_1u_2u_3 + \bar{u}_1u_2\bar{u}_2$	11
1	1	$u_1\bar{u}_2 + u_1u_3 + \bar{u}_2u_3 + \bar{u}_1u_2\bar{u}_2$	8

$p_2 = P(u_7|\bar{u}_1, u_2, \bar{u}_3)$, $p_5 = P(u_7|u_1, \bar{u}_2, u_3)$

Table 9: Assignments for unseen cases in Fig. 3 a

Fig. 5 gives the results when some statistical information in Table 4 c is missing.

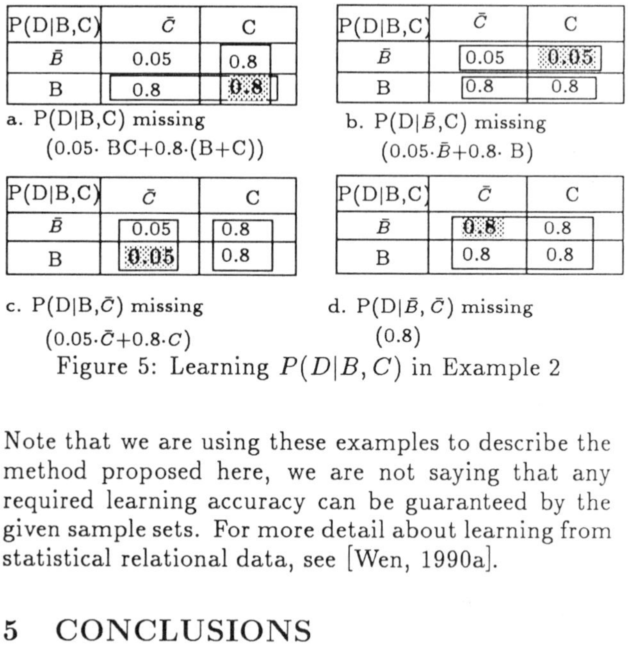

P(D|B,C)	$\bar{C}$	C
$\bar{B}$	0.05	0.8
B	0.8	0.8

a. P(D|B,C) missing (0.05· BC+0.8·(B+C))

P(D|B,C)	$\bar{C}$	C
$\bar{B}$	0.05	0.05
B	0.8	0.8

b. P(D|$\bar{B}$,C) missing (0.05·$\bar{B}$+0.8· B)

P(D|B,C)	$\bar{C}$	C
$\bar{B}$	0.05	0.8
B	0.05	0.8

c. P(D|B,$\bar{C}$) missing (0.05·$\bar{C}$+0.8·C)

P(D|B,C)	$\bar{C}$	C
$\bar{B}$	0.8	0.8
B	0.8	0.8

d. P(D|$\bar{B}$, $\bar{C}$) missing (0.8)

Figure 5: Learning $P(D|B,C)$ in Example 2

Note that we are using these examples to describe the method proposed here, we are not saying that any required learning accuracy can be guaranteed by the given sample sets. For more detail about learning from statistical relational data, see [Wen, 1990a].

5 CONCLUSIONS

The relationship between RD and BN is investigated. Correspondences are discovered between many concepts and operations of RD and BN. A method to construct BN automatically from RD is proposed. It has been shown [Wen, 1990a] that the distributions of discrete Markov fields, eg. BN, are Probably Approximately Correctly (PAC) learnable [Haussler, 1990] when the sizes of the biggest neighborhoods of the variables in the fields are fixed. Hence, our method, is efficient in these circumstances. A comparison between our method and other methods shows that

1. Our method can fulfill the task of recall perfectly just as some other methods.
2. Our method has more plausible result than that of other methods when generalization or prediction is needed. For example, frequency method does not have any prediction capability while ME/MCE methods can not handle the case of functional dependency properly (always assign values $\frac{1}{2}$ to all binary unseen cases).

Acknowledgement

Thanks to A. Jennings and H. Liu for discussions and comments. The permission of the Executive General Manager, TRL, to publish this paper is gratefully acknowledged.

References

[Beeri *et al.*, 1983] Catriel Beeri, Ronald Fagin, David Maier, and Mihalis Yannakakis. On the desirability of acyclic database schemes. *Journal of the ACM*, 30(3):479–513, 1983.

[Blumer *et al.*, 1987] A. Blumer, A. Ehrenfeucht, D. Haussler, and M. K. Warmuth. Occam's razor. *Information Processing Letters*, 24:377–380, Apr. 1987.

[Cooper, 1984] G. F. Cooper. NESTOR: a computer-based medical diagnostic aid that integrates causal and probabilistic knowledge. *Report HPP-84-48, Stanford University*, 1984.

[Duda and Hart, 1973] R. O. Duda and P. E. Hart. *Pattern Classification and Scene Analysis.* John Wiley and Sons, New York, 1973.

[Gallant, 1988] S. I. Gallant. Connectionist expert systems. *Communications of the ACM*, 31(2):152–169, 1988.

[Gallant, Oct 1987] S. I. Gallant. Bayesian assessment of a connectionist model for fault detection. *Technical Report TR MU-CCS-87-25, College of Computer Science, Northeastern University*, Oct. 1987.

[Haussler, 1990] D. Haussler. Probably approximately correct learning. In *Proc. AAAI-90*, volume 2, pages 1101–1108, Boston, MA, July 1990. American Association for Artificial Intelligence, AAAI Press / The MIT Press.

[Herskovitz and Cooper, 1990] E. Herskovitz and G. F. Cooper. Kutato: An entropy-driven system from construction of probabilistic expert systems from databases. In M. Henrion and Bonissone, editors, *Proc. 6th International Conf. on Uncertainty in AI*, Cambridge, MA., July 1990. North Holland.

[Lauritzen and Spiegelhalter, 1988] S. L. Lauritzen and D. J. Spiegelhalter. Local computations with probabilities on graphical structures and their application to expert systems. *J. R. Statist. Soc. B*, 50(2), 1988.

[Pearl, 1978] J. Pearl. On the connection between the complexity and credibility of inferred models. *Int. J. General Systems*, 4:255–264, 1978.

[Shore and Johnson, Jan 1980] J. Shore and R. W. Johnson. Axiomatic derivation of the principle of maximum entropy and the principle of minimum cross entropy. *IEEE Trans. Infor. Theory*, IT-26(1):26–37, Jan 1980.

[Spiegelhalter, 1986] D. J. Spiegelhalter. Probabilistic reasoning in predictive expert systems. *in Uncertainty in artificial intelligence, (ed) L. N. Kanal and J. F. Lemmer, North-Holland, Amsterdam, New York, Oxford, Tokyo*, 1986.

[Tarjan and Yannakakis, 1984] R. E. Tarjan and M. Yannakakis. Simple linear-time algorithms to chordality of graphs, test acyclicity of hypergraphs, and selectively reduce acyclic hypergraphs. *SIAM J. Compt.*, 13(3):566–579, 1984.

[Ullman, 1982] J. D. Ullman. *Principles of Database Systems.* Computer Science Press, Rockville, Maryland, 1982.

[Wen, 1989] W. X. Wen. Markov and Gibbs Fields and MCE Reasoning in General Belief Networks. *Technical Report 89/13, Computer Science, The University of Melbourne*, July 1989.

[Wen, 1990a] W. X. Wen. Learning from statistical relational data. Tech. report, AI Systems, Telecom Research Labs., 770 Blackburn Rd. Clayton, Vic. 3168, Australia., 11 1990.

[Wen, 1990b] W. X. Wen. MCE Reasoning in Recursive Causal Networks. *Uncertainty in Artificial Intelligence 4, (ed) T. Levitt, R. Shachter, J. Lemmer, and L. Kanal, North Holland*, 1990.

[Wen, 1991] W. X. Wen. Optimal decomposition of belief networks. In Max Herion, Piero Bonissone, J. F. Kanal, and J. F. Lemmer, editors, *UNcertainty in Artificial Intelligence 6*. North Holland, 1991.

[Yannakakis, 1981] M. Yannakakis. Computing the minimum fill-in is NP-complete. *SIAM J. Alg. Meth.*, 2:77–79, 1981.

A Monte-Carlo Algorithm for Dempster-Shafer Belief

Nic Wilson
Department of Computer Science
Queen Mary and Westfield College
Mile End Rd., London E1 4NS, UK

Abstract

A very computationally-efficient Monte-Carlo algorithm for the calculation of Dempster-Shafer belief is described. If Bel is the combination using Dempster's Rule of belief functions $\mathrm{Bel}_1, \ldots, \mathrm{Bel}_m$ then, for subset b of the frame Θ, $\mathrm{Bel}(b)$ can be calculated in time linear in $|\Theta|$ and m (given that the weight of conflict is bounded). The algorithm can also be used to improve the complexity of the Shenoy-Shafer algorithms on Markov trees, and be generalised to calculate Dempster-Shafer Belief over other logics.

1 INTRODUCTION

One of the major perceived problems with application of the Dempster-Shafer Theory [Shafer, 76] has been its apparent computational complexity e.g., [Kyburg, 87], [Bonissone, 87]. This is because the Dempster-Shafer theory as usually implemented involves repeated application of Dempster's Rule of Combination, keeping a record at each stage of each subset of Θ with a non-zero mass. For example the combination of m simple support functions can have as many as 2^q non-zero masses where q is the minimum of m and $|\Theta|$, thus making the approach computationally infeasible for large m and $|\Theta|$.

There have been a number of schemes to deal with this; [Barnett, 81] showed how calculation of Dempster-Shafer belief in a very special case, when all the evidence sets are either singletons or complements of singletons, belief could be calculated in linear time. [Gordon and Shortliffe, 85] extended this with an efficient approximation to Dempster-Shafer belief for hierarchically related evidences, and it was shown in both [Shafer and Logan, 87] and [Wilson, 87] that the hierarchical case could be dealt with exactly in a computationally efficient manner. The Shafer-Logan algorithm was generalised to propagation of belief functions in Markov Trees [Shafer and Shenoy, 88] but, although this is a very important contribution, it still requires that the product space associated with the largest clique is small, a condition which will by no means always be satisfied. The hierarchical evidence algorithm in [Wilson, 87] was generalised to arbitrary evidence sets [Wilson, 89] and, because it calculates belief directly without first calculating the masses, it leads to very substantial increases in efficiency (see section 4). However this algorithm appears to have complexity worse than polynomial, which is not surprising since Dempster's Rule is $\#P$-complete [Orponen, 90], [Provan, 90].

This paper describes the Monte-Carlo algorithm given in [Wilson, 89] which also calculates belief directly (or, more accurately, it approximates belief up to arbitrary accuracy). This calculation has very low complexity, showing that the general pessimism about the complexity of Dempster-Shafer Theory is misguided. The use of Monte-Carlo algorithms for calculating Dempster-Shafer belief has also been suggested in [Pearl, 88], [Kämpke, 88] and [Kreinovich and Borrett, 90].

2 THE MONTE-CARLO ALGORITHM

Let $\mathrm{Bel}_1, \ldots, \mathrm{Bel}_m$ be belief functions on a finite frame Θ, and let $\mathrm{Bel} = \mathrm{Bel}_1 \oplus \cdots \oplus \mathrm{Bel}_m$ be their combination using Dempster's Rule. Using the model of [Dempster, 67] Bel_i is represented by a probability function P_i (on a finite set Ω_i) and a compatibility function $\Gamma_i : \Omega_i \mapsto 2^{\Theta}$ where the meaning of Γ_i is 'for $\tau \in \Omega_i$, if τ is true then so is $\Gamma_i(\tau)$'.

The mass function m_i is given by: for $\varepsilon_i \in \Omega_i$, $\mathrm{m}_i(\Gamma_i(\varepsilon_i)) = \mathrm{P}_i(\varepsilon_i)$, and, for $b \subseteq \Theta$,

$$\mathrm{Bel}_i(b) = \mathrm{P}_i(\Gamma_i(\varepsilon_i) \subseteq b), \text{ that is, } \sum_{\varepsilon_i : \Gamma_i(\varepsilon_i) \subseteq b} \mathrm{P}_i(\varepsilon_i).$$

Let $\Omega = \Omega_1 \times \cdots \times \Omega_m$ and for $\varepsilon = (\varepsilon_1, \ldots, \varepsilon_m)$ define $\Gamma(\varepsilon) = \bigcap_{i=1}^{m} \Gamma_i(\varepsilon_i)$. Define the 'independent probability function' P′ on Ω by $P'((\varepsilon_1, \ldots, \varepsilon_m)) = \prod_{i=1}^m P_i(\varepsilon_i)$.

Using [Dempster, 67] it can be seen that

$$\mathrm{Bel}(b) = P'(\Gamma(\varepsilon) \subseteq b | \Gamma(\varepsilon) \neq \emptyset),$$

where e.g. $P'(\Gamma(\varepsilon) \neq \emptyset)$ just means $\sum_{\varepsilon:\Gamma(\varepsilon)\neq\emptyset} P'(\varepsilon)$. $\Gamma(\varepsilon)$ can be viewed as a random set [Nguyen, 78].

The Monte-Carlo algorithm just simulates the last equation.

A large number, N, of trials are performed. For each trial:

1. Randomly pick ε such that $\Gamma(\varepsilon) \neq \emptyset$:
   a. For $i = 1, \ldots, m$
      randomly pick an element of Ω_i, i.e.
      pick ε_i with probability $P_i(\varepsilon_i)$
      Let $\varepsilon = (\varepsilon_1, \ldots, \varepsilon_m)$
   b. **If** $\Gamma(\varepsilon) = \emptyset$ **then** restart trial;
2. **If** $\Gamma(\varepsilon) \subseteq b$ **then** trial succeeds, let $T = 1$
   else trial fails, let $T = 0$

The proportion of trials that succeed converges to Bel(b):

$E[T] = P'(\Gamma(\varepsilon) \subseteq b | \Gamma(\varepsilon) \neq \emptyset) = \mathrm{Bel}(b)$.

$\mathrm{Var}[T] = E[T^2] - (E[T])^2 = E[T] - (E[T])^2 = \mathrm{Bel}(b)(1 - \mathrm{Bel}(b)) \leq \frac{1}{4}$.

Let $\bar{T}$ be the average value of T over the N trials, i.e., the proportion of trials that succeed.

$$E[\bar{T}] = \frac{N\,E[T]}{N} = \mathrm{Bel}(b)$$

$$\text{and} \quad \mathrm{Var}[\bar{T}] = \frac{N\,\mathrm{Var}[T]}{N^2} \leq \frac{1}{4N}$$

Therefore the variance (and so also the standard deviation) for the estimate, $\bar{T}$, of Bel(b) can be made arbitrarily small independently of $|\Theta|$ and m.

Let us say that the estimate $\bar{T}$ of Bel(b) 'has accuracy k' if 3 standard deviations of $\bar{T}$ is less than or equal to k. Then $\bar{T}$ has accuracy k if $N \geq \frac{9}{4k^2}$.

Testing separately if $\Gamma(\varepsilon) = \emptyset$ and if $\Gamma(\varepsilon) \subseteq b$ wastes time; these tests can be combined within the same algorithm (where x_j denotes the jth element of Θ):

For each trial:

```
repeat
  pick ε with probability P′(ε)
  T_∅ := 1; T := 1
  for j = 1 to |Θ|
    if Γ(ε) ∋ x_j then
      T_∅ := 0;        (since Γ(ε) ≠ ∅)
      if x_j ∉ b then T := 0; exit trial;
    end if      (since Γ(ε) ⊈ b)
  end if
  next j
until T_∅ = 0
```

3 COMPUTATION TIME

Picking ε involves m random numbers so takes less than Am where A is constant, approximately the time it takes to generate a random number (with efficient storing of the P_is). Testing if $\Gamma(\varepsilon) \ni x_j$ takes less than Bm for constant B. For a given trial there is a probability $\kappa = P'(\Gamma(\varepsilon) = \emptyset)$ that the **repeat-until** loop will be entered a second time. The expected number of **repeat-until** loops per trial is $\frac{1}{1-\kappa}$; κ is a measure of the conflict of the evidences [Shafer, 76, p65].

Thus the expected time the algorithm takes is less than $\frac{N}{1-\kappa} m(A + B|\Theta|)$, and so the expected time to achieve accuracy k is less than $\frac{9}{4(1-\kappa)k^2} m(A + B|\Theta|)$.

At least for the case where the Bel_is are simple support functions, the condition $\Gamma(\varepsilon) \ni x_j$ can be tested more efficiently; under weak conditions this leads to expected time of less than $\frac{9}{4(1-\kappa)k^2}(Am + C|\Theta|)$ for constant C [Wilson, 89].

4 EXPERIMENTAL RESULTS

The algorithm for the case where the Bel_is are simple support functions has been implemented and tested using the language Modula-2 on a SUN 3/60 workstation. The results showed that the value of A is much bigger than the value of C in this implementation, A being roughly $\frac{1}{4000}$ seconds and C roughly $\frac{1}{50,000}$ seconds. A is essentially the time taken to generate a random number, and $\frac{1}{4000}$ seconds seems rather slow for that. This suggests that very substantial speed-ups (of perhaps an order of magnitude or two) could be achieved by careful choice and use of the random number generator and the use of antithetic runs (so that the random number generator is only used once for several different data items).

The results indicate that, unless the evidences are extremely conflicting, the Monte-Carlo algorithm is practical for problems with large m and Θ. For example, with $\kappa = 0.5$, $m = |\Theta| = 40$, and with 1000 trials, the calculation of the approximate value of Bel(b) would be expected to take 20.6 seconds. The 1000 trials mean that the standard deviation is less than 0.016, and so the confidence interval for the correct value of belief corresponding to 3 standard deviations would be roughly $[b - 0.05, b + 0.05]$. If instead we did 10,000 trials this would take a little over 3 minutes, and give a standard deviation of 0.005. Extrapolating the figures (which seems unlikely to cause problems in this case) gives an approximate time of 1 minute for $m = |\Theta| = 120$, with 1000 trials, and 5 minutes for $m = |\Theta| = 600$.

Also in [Wilson, 89] an exact algorithm for calculating belief is described (related to those described in [Provan, 90]) which involves expressing the event $\Gamma(\varepsilon) \subseteq b$ as a boolean expression and then calculating the probability of this using the laws of boolean algebra. Again this avoids explicit calculation of the masses. The complexity for the simple support function case appears to be approximately of the form $|\Theta|^{\log m}$.

The usual approaches for calculating belief are mass-based: they calculate the combined mass function and use this to calculate the appropriate belief (a good one of these is the fast Möbius transform in [Kennes and Smets, 90]). For large m and Θ this is of necessity very computationally expensive, since if $q = \min(m, |\Theta|)$, there can be as many as 2^q masses. For simplicity it is assumed that the calculation of belief then just does 2^q REAL multiplications. The speed of REAL multiplication was tested on the same workstation and within the same language that the Exact and Monte-Carlo algorithms were tested and implemented on and it was found that it did just over 10^4 REAL multiplications per second. This gives the following results:

m, n	**MC**	**Exact**	**Mass-based $\geq$**
15×15	7 secs	9 secs	3 secs
20×20	11 secs	13 secs	1 min
25×25	13 secs	46 secs	1 hour
30×30	15 secs	3 mins	1 day
35×35	17 secs	8 mins	1 month
50×50	25 secs	2 hours	3000 years

The values for the Monte-Carlo algorithm were based on doing 1000 trials and the contradiction being 0.5. The figure of 2 hours for the Exact in the 50 case is a very rough upper bound derived from insufficient data.

Details of the experiments and the full results and analysis are given in [Wilson, 90b].

5 THE GENERALISED ALGORITHM

The algorithm can be generalised to deal with arbitrary logics [Wilson, 90a]. Let L be the language of some logic. For each i, Bel_i is now a function from L to $[0, 1]$ saying how much the evidence warrants belief in propositions in L and the compatibility function is a function $\Gamma_i : \Omega_i \mapsto L$. The combined compatibility function Γ is now defined by

$$\Gamma((\varepsilon_1, \ldots, \varepsilon_m)) = \bigwedge_{i=1}^{m} \Gamma_i(\varepsilon_i),$$

(or $\Gamma((\varepsilon_1, \ldots, \varepsilon_m))$ = the set $\{\Gamma_i(\varepsilon_i) : i = 1, \ldots, m\}$ if the logic doesn't have conjunction).

For each trial:

1. Randomly pick ε such that
   $\Gamma(\varepsilon)$ is not contradictory:
   a. For $i = 1, \ldots, m$
      randomly pick an element of Ω_i, i.e.
      pick ε_i with probability $P_i(\varepsilon_i)$
   Let $\varepsilon = (\varepsilon_1, \ldots, \varepsilon_m)$
   b. **If** $\Gamma(\varepsilon)$ is contradictory **then** restart trial;
2. **If** b can be deduced from $\Gamma(\varepsilon)$
   then trial succeeds, let $T = 1$
   else trial fails, let $T = 0$

Undecidability and semi-decidability would clearly cause problems, in which case trials which went on for too long would have to be cut short; if T for these trials was given the value 0 then this would lead to a lower bound for $\mathrm{Bel}(b)$. This technique of prematurely halting trials that take too long could be used to increase the efficiency for other cases as well, at the cost of only finding lower and upper bounds for $\mathrm{Bel}(b)$.

The time this algorithm takes is then approximately $\frac{N}{1-\kappa}(Am + R)$ where R is the average time it takes to see if $\Gamma(\varepsilon)$ is contradictory, and if $\Gamma(\varepsilon)$ allows b to be deduced. Given that the weight of conflict of the evidences is bounded this means that the complexity is proportional to that of proof in the logic; it is hard to see how any sensible uncertainty calculus could do better than this (although the complexity for this Monte-Carlo algorithm has a very large constant term if high accuracy is required).

As Shafer points out [Shafer, 90] $|\Theta|$ can be a large product space, making the first algorithm impractical. The generalised algorithm can also be used to greatly improve the complexity of the algorithms for calculating Belief in Markov trees [Shafer and Shenoy, 88]. For each trial, propositions (i.e. belief functions with a single focal element) must be propagated through the Markov tree. The complexity is then proportional to that of propagating propositions, rather than the whole belief functions. Some other propositional cases have been dealt with in [Wilson, 89].

6 DISCUSSION

There are two obvious drawbacks with the Monte-Carlo algorithm:

(i) if very high accuracy is required then the Monte-Carlo algorithm will require a large number of trials (quadratic in the reciprocal of accuracy) so giving a very high constant factor to the complexity;

(ii) when the evidence is highly conflicting the Monte-Carlo algorithm loses some of its efficiency. I don't see this as a great problem since an extremely high weight of conflict would suggest, except in exceptional circumstances, that Dempster's Rule is being applied when it is not valid, e.g. updating a Bayesian prior with a Dempster-Shafer belief function [see Wilson, 91]. I also argue there that, although Dempster's Rule has strong justifications for the combination of a finite number of simple support functions, the more general case has not been convincingly justified: the Monte-Carlo algorithm is guaranteed to give results in accordance with Dempster's Rule, but it remains to be seen if these are always sensible.

It may be important to know which relatively small sets have relatively high beliefs: the Monte-Carlo algorithm can be easily applied to deal with this problem.

Dempster's Rule makes particular independence assumptions, using a single probability function on Ω. By modifying step 1 of the algorithms the beliefs corresponding to other probability functions on Ω can be calculated.

Acknowledgements

I am currently supported by the ESPRIT basic research action DRUMS (3085). Most of the material in this paper was produced in the period Summer '87-Summer '88 when I was employed by the The Hotel and Catering Management, and Computing and Mathematical Sciences Departments of Oxford Polytechnic. Thanks also to Bills Triggs and Boatman for their help during this period, and more recently to Mike Clarke.

References

Barnett, J.A., 1981, Computational methods for a mathematical theory of evidence, in: *Proceedings IJCAI-81*, Vancouver, BC 868-875.

Bonissone, P. P., 1987, 'Reasoning, Plausible' in *Encyclopedia of Artificial Intelligence*. Shapiro, S. C. (Ed.), John Wiley and Sons, 1987.

Dempster, A. P., 67, Upper and Lower Probabilities Induced by a Multi-valued Mapping. *Ann. Math. Statistics* 38: 325-39.

Gordon, J. and Shortliffe, E.H., 1985, A method of managing evidential reasoning in a hierarchical hypothesis space, *Artificial Intelligence* 26, 323-357.

Kämpke, Thomas, 88, About Assessing and Evaluating Uncertain Inferences Within the Theory of Evidence, *Decision Support Systems* 4 433-439.

Kennes, Robert, and Smets, Philippe, 1990, Computational Aspects of the Möbius transform, *Uncertainty in Artificial Intelligence*, July 1990, Cambridge, USA.

Kreinovich, V., and Borrett, W., 90, Monte-Carlo Methods Allow to Avoid Exponential Time in Dempster-Shafer Formalism, Technical Report UTEP-CS-90-5, Computer Science Department, University of Texas at El Paso.

Kyburg, H.E., Jr., 87, Bayesian and Non-Bayesian Evidential Updating, *Artificial Intelligence* 31 271-293.

Nguyen, Hung T., 78, On Random Sets and Belief Functions. *Journal of Mathematical Analysis and Applications* 65: 531-542.

Orponen, Pekka, 90, Dempster's Rule of Combination is $\#P$-complete, *Artificial Intelligence* 44 245-253.

Pearl, Judea, 88, *Probabilistic Reasoning in Intelligent Systems: Networks of Plausible Inference*, Morgan Kaufmann Publishers Inc. 1988, Chapter 9, in particular 455-457.

Provan, G., 90, A Logic-based Analysis of Dempster-Shafer Theory, *International Journal of Approximate Reasoning*, 4, 451-495.

Shafer, G., 76, *A Mathematical Theory of Evidence*, Princeton University Press, Princeton, NJ.

Shafer, G., 90, Perspectives on the Theory and Practice of Belief Functions, International Journal of Approximate Reasoning.

Shafer, G. and Logan, R., 1987, Implementing Dempster's Rule for Hierarchical Evidence, *Artificial Intelligence* 33 271-298.

Shafer, G. and Shenoy, P. P. 1988, Local Computations in Hypertrees, Working Paper No. 201, School of Business, The University of Kansas, Lawrence, KS, 66045, USA.

Wilson, N., 87, On Increasing the Computational Efficiency of the Dempster-Shafer theory, Research Report no. 11, Sept. 1987, Dept. of Computing and Mathematical Sciences, Oxford Polytechnic.

Wilson, Nic, 89, Justification, Computational Efficiency and Generalisation of the Dempster-Shafer Theory, Research Report no. 15, June 1989, Dept. of Computing and Mathematical Sciences, Oxford Polytechnic., to appear in *Artificial Intelligence*.

Wilson, Nic, 90a, Rules, Belief Functions and Default Logic, in Bonissone, P., and Henrion, M., 90, eds *Proc. 6th Conference on Uncertainty in Artificial Intelligence*, MIT, Cambridge, Mass.

Wilson, Nic, 90b, Implementation and Practical Analysis, DRUMS (ESPRIT Basic Research Action 3085) RP3.2, 12 month report, September 1990.

Wilson, Nic, 91, The Combination of Belief: When and How Fast, A Reply to Glenn Shafer's paper Perspectives on the Theory and Practice of Belief Functions, to appear in *International Journal of Approximate Reasoning*.

Compatibility of Quantitative and Qualitative Representations of Belief

S.K.M. Wong, Y.Y. Yao, and P. Lingras
Department of Computer Science, University of Regina
Regina, Saskatchewan, Canada S4S 0A2

Abstract

The compatibility of quantitative and qualitative representations of beliefs was studied extensively in probability theory. It is only recently that this important topic is considered in the context of belief functions. In this paper, the compatibility of various quantitative belief measures and qualitative belief structures is investigated. Four classes of belief measures considered are: the probability function, the monotonic belief function, Shafer's belief function, and Smets' generalized belief function. The analysis of their individual compatibility with different belief structures not only provides a sound basis for these quantitative measures, but also alleviates some of the difficulties in the acquisition and interpretation of numeric belief numbers. It is shown that the structure of *qualitative probability* is compatible with monotonic belief functions. Moreover, a belief structure slightly weaker than that of *qualitative belief* is compatible with Smets' generalized belief functions.

1 INTRODUCTION

Uncertainty is always present in modeling realistic situations. It may stem from a lack of knowledge, the incompleteness or the unreliability of the information at our disposal. In order to draw a meaningful conclusion under uncertain situations, we may have to express our beliefs in a number of propositions. Many approaches have been proposed for representing, measuring, and reasoning with uncertain information. Despite the diversities of these methods, one can divide them into two classes: the quantitative (numeric) and the qualitative (non-numeric) approaches (Bhatnagar and and Kanal, 1986; Spiegelhalter, 1986; Satoh, 1989). In the quantitative approach, a number is associated with each proposition to indicate the degree to which one believes in that proposition. That is, we express our belief in a proposition by a numeric value. To make the quantitative representation of beliefs consistent and meaningful, certain axioms or rules should be observed in expressing one's beliefs. For example, if beliefs are measured by a probability function, the Kolmogorov axioms for probability should be satisfied in order to maintain consistency. In the qualitative approach, beliefs are expressed by a preference relation on a set of propositions. As in quantitative measures of beliefs, such a relation must be consistently defined. For example, if a person believes more in proposition A than in proposition B, and also believes more in B than in C, then it is reasonable to assume that he would believe more in A than in C. In this paper, we are interested in those belief structures which are compatible with some well known belief measures.

Both the quantitative and qualitative approaches are very useful for the management of uncertainty. In fact, probability theory has been extensively studied within the quantitative as well as the qualitative frameworks (Fishburn, 1970; Savage, 1972; Fine, 1973). Given a belief measure and a preference relation, an important question one inevitably would ask is whether they are compatible with each other. This is indeed one of the fundamental issues in measurement theory, which is concerned to a large extent with the mathematical modeling of preferences and beliefs (French, 1986). Depending on the context, a preference relation is also referred to as a comparative probability, possibility, or belief relation. The compatibility of a comparative probability relation and a probability function was investigated by many authors (Fishburn, 1970; Savage, 1972; Fine, 1973). Dubois (1986) studied the compatibility of a comparative possibility relation and a possibility function. Possibility functions were originally proposed by Zadeh (1978) within the framework of fuzzy sets, and they were later shown to be closely related to consonant belief functions introduced in the theory of evidence (Shafer, 1976). Wong et al. (1990) studied the compatibility of a comparative belief relation and a belief function. There is an important class of preference relations referred to as qualitative probability (Savage, 1972). However, until now it is not known which class of belief functions is compatible with qualitative probability relations. Recently, Smets (1988) proposed a generalized version of belief functions. It is interesting to investigate what kind of preference relation is compatible with Smets' generalized belief functions.

In this paper, our discussion will focus on the compatibility of quantitative and qualitative representations of beliefs. In particular, we analyze four classes of quantitative belief measures, namely, the probability function, the monotonic belief function, Shafer's belief function, and Smets' generalized belief function, and their compatibility with different kinds of preference relations. We will show that qualitative probability relations are compatible with monotonic belief functions, and that a preference structure slightly weaker than that of qualitative belief is compatible with generalized belief functions. More importantly, we believe that the study of the compatibility of these qualitative and quantitative representations of beliefs may provide a foundation for developing a generalized utility theory (Jaffray, 1989).

2 QUANTITATIVE BELIEF MEASURES

Based on the notion of belief functions (Shafer, 1976), we will identify four different classes of quantitative measures of belief.

Let $\Theta = \{\theta_1, \ldots, \theta_s\}$ denote a finite set of possible answers to a question, which is referred to as the *frame of discernment* or simply the *frame* defined by the question. Following the convention of representing a proposition by a subset of Θ, the power set 2^Θ denotes the set of all propositions discerned by frame Θ. A quantitative belief measure can be viewed as a mapping from 2^Θ to the real numbers.

Definition 1: A probability function P is a mapping from 2^Θ to the interval $[0,1]$, $P : 2^\Theta \rightarrow [0,1]$, which satisfies the following axioms:

(B1) $P(\emptyset) = 0$,

(B2) $P(\Theta) = 1$,

(B3) For $A, B \in 2^\Theta$ with $A \cap B = \emptyset$,
$$P(A \cup B) = P(A) + P(B).$$

Axiom (B3) is usually referred to as the *additivity* axiom. By replacing this axiom with the *sup-additive* axiom, another class of quantitative belief measures called belief functions (Shafer, 1976) can be defined as follows.

Definition 2: A belief function Bel is a mapping from 2^Θ to the interval $[0,1]$, $Bel : 2^\Theta \rightarrow [0,1]$, which satisfies (B1), (B2), and the sup-additive axiom:

(B3′) For every integer $n > 0$ and every collection $A_1, A_2, \ldots, A_n \in 2^\Theta$,
$$Bel(A_1 \cup A_2 \ldots \cup A_n) \geq \sum_i Bel(A_i) - \sum_{i<j} Bel(A_i \cap A_j) \pm \ldots + (-1)^{n+1} Bel(A_1 \cap A_2 \ldots \cap A_n).$$

A belief function can be equivalently defined by a mapping from 2^Θ to the interval $[0,1]$, $m : 2^\Theta \rightarrow [0,1]$, which is called a basic probability assignment satisfying the axioms:

$$\text{(M1)} \quad m(\emptyset) = 0\,,$$
$$\text{(M2)} \quad \sum_{A \in 2^\Theta} m(A) = 1\,.$$

In terms of the basic probability assignment, the belief in a proposition $A \in 2^\Theta$ can be expressed as:

$$\text{(M3)} \quad Bel(A) = \sum_{B \subseteq A} m(B),$$

where the summation is restricted to the elements B in 2^Θ, which are subsets of A. Conversely, given a belief function one can construct the corresponding basic probability assignment. Therefore, belief functions can be defined either by axioms (B1),(B2), and (B3′) or by axioms (M1)-(M3).

Axioms (B1) and (B2) state that the proposition $\emptyset$ is believed to be false (impossibility) and the proposition Θ is believed to be true (certainty). These two axioms indicate that the *closed* world assumption (Smets, 1988) is in fact used to define the frame of discernment Θ. That is, one has implicitly assumed that the frame Θ consists of *all* possible answers to a given question and only one of these answers is correct. On the other hand, axiom (B3′) indicates that belief functions are sup-additive, and become additive in the degenerated case. Thus, additive probability functions belong to the class of degenerated belief functions.

Note that the additivity axiom implies the monotonicity axiom, namely:

(B4) For $A, B, C \in 2^\Theta$ with $(A \cup B) \cap C = \emptyset$,
$$P(A) > P(B) \Longleftrightarrow P(A \cup C) > P(B \cup C).$$

However, monotonicity does not imply additivity, and axioms (B1), (B2), and (B3′) do not imply monotonicity. This means that belief functions do not necessarily satisfy axiom (B4). In some applications, it is desirable that the monotonicity axiom (B4) is satisfied (Savage, 1972). In that case, we can define another class of belief measures, which falls between the belief functions and the probability functions.

probability function (B1) – (B3)	⊂	monotonic belief function (B1), (B2), (B3′), (B4)	⊂	Shafer's belief function (B1), (B2), (B3′)	⊂	Smets' belief function (B1), (B2′), (B3′)

Figure 1: Relationships Between Quantitative Measures of Belief

Definition 3: A belief function Bel is called a *monotonic* belief function if it satisfies the monotonicity axiom (B4).

We will show that monotonic belief functions are compatible with the qualitative probability relations.

Smets (1988) pointed out that the condition (M1), $m(\emptyset) = 0$, reflects the *closed* world assumption implicitly used in Shafer's definition of belief function; $m(\emptyset) > 0$ reflects the *open* world assumption. With the open world assumption, the probability mass $m(\emptyset)$ can be interpreted as the belief committed exactly to the proposition that the true answer is not in the frame Θ. Smets' belief functions, written bel, satisfy the following axioms:

$$\text{(M2)} \qquad \sum_{A \in 2^\Theta} m(A) = 1,$$

$$\text{(M3}'\text{)} \qquad bel(A) = \sum_{\substack{B \subseteq A \\ B \neq \emptyset}} m(B).$$

The condition $m(\emptyset) > 0$ has also been considered by Dubois and Prade (1986) under a set-theoretic view of belief functions. The generalized belief functions can be equivalently defined as follows.

Definition 4: A generalized belief function bel is a mapping from 2^Θ to the interval $[0, 1]$, $bel : 2^\Theta \longrightarrow [0, 1]$, which satisfies axioms (B1), (B3′), and

$$\text{(B2}'\text{)} \qquad bel(\Theta) = 1 - m(\emptyset),$$

where $0 \leq m(\emptyset) \leq 1$.

In the above discussion, we have considered four classes of quantitative belief measures: the probability function, the monotonic belief function, Shafer's belief function, and Smets' generalized belief function. The relationships between these measures are shown in Figure 1. The set of probability functions is a subset of the set of monotonic belief functions, and so on. In the following section, we will study the preference structures that are compatible with these quantitative belief measures.

3 PREFERENCE RELATIONS VERSUS QUANTITATIVE BELIEF MEASURES

In the qualitative representation of beliefs, it is assumed that one is able to express one's preference on any two propositions $A, B \in 2^\Theta$, without stating numerically how much one prefers proposition A to proposition B. Qualitative judgments can be described in terms of a preference relation $\succ$. By $A \succ B$, we mean that A *is preferred to* B. In the absence of strict preference, i.e., $\neg(A \succ B)$ and $\neg(B \succ A)$, we say that A and B are *indifferent*, written $A \sim B$. We also write $A \succeq B$ if $A \succ B$ or $A \sim B$. The relationship between the quantitative and qualitative representations of beliefs can be formally stated as follows.

Definition 5: Suppose Θ is a frame, f is a function mapping the elements of 2^Θ onto the set of real numbers, and $\succ$ is a preference relation on 2^Θ. We say that f and $\succ$ are *compatible* with each other if for $A, B \in 2^\Theta$,

$$A \succ B \Longleftrightarrow f(A) > f(B).$$

A function f is said to *represent* $\succ$ if it is compatible with $\succ$.

Clearly, whether a preference relation is compatible with a particular quantitative belief measure depends very much on the preference structure representing the qualitative judgments.

Now consider a special class of preference relations characterized by the following two axioms:

(Q1) asymmetric :
$$A \succ B \Longrightarrow \neg(B \succ A)\ ,$$
(Q2) negatively transitive :
$$(\neg(A \succ B), \neg(B \succ C)) \Longrightarrow \neg(A \succ C)\ .$$

Axiom (Q1) suggests that if one commits more belief in A than in B, one should not at the same time commit more belief in B than in A. If this axiom holds for a preference relation $\succ$, then for every $A, B \in 2^\Theta$, $A \succeq B \Longleftrightarrow \neg(B \succ A)$. Axiom (Q2) demands that if one does not commit more belief in A than in B, nor commits more belief in B than in C, one should not commit more belief in A than in C. A preference relation $\succ$ satisfying these two axioms is called a weak order which can be represented by a real-valued function (Fishburn, 1970; Roberts, 1976).

Theorem 1. Suppose Θ is a finite set and $\succ$ a preference relation on 2^Θ. There exists a real-valued function f on 2^Θ such that for every $A, B \in 2^\Theta$,

$$A \succ B \Longleftrightarrow f(A) > f(B)$$

if and only if the relation $\succ$ satisfies axioms (Q1) and (Q2). Moreover, f is uniquely defined up to a strictly monotonic transformation.

This theorem is important because it suggests that any belief characterized by a weak order can be measured in terms of an ordinal scale. Theorem 1 therefore provides a basis for representing various types of preference relations. However, axioms (Q1) and (Q2) alone are not sufficient to guarantee that the preference structure is compatible with any of the belief measures introduced in the last section. Additional conditions are required to differentiate different preference structures.

A special type of preference relation known as *qualitative probability* was studied extensively in probability theory (de Finetti, 1937; Fishburn, 1970; Savage, 1972; Dubois, 1986).

Definition 6: Let Θ be a frame. A preference relation $\succ$ defined on 2^Θ is called a *qualitative probability* relation if it satisfies (Q1), (Q2) and the following additional axioms: for $A, B, C \in 2^\Theta$,

(Q3) nontriviality : $\Theta \succ \emptyset$,

(Q4) improbability of impossibility : $\neg(\emptyset \succ A)$,

(Q5) monotonicity :
$$(A \cup B) \cap C = \emptyset \Longrightarrow (A \succ B \Longleftrightarrow A \cup C \succ B \cup C).$$

Axioms (Q1)-(Q5) are necessary but not sufficient to guarantee the existence of a probability function (Kraft, Pratt, and Seidenberg, 1959). Scott (1964) gave the necessary and sufficient conditions for the existence of a probability function for a finite set. Let μ_A denote the *characteristic function* of a subset A of Θ such that $\mu_A(\theta) = 1$ if $\theta \in A$, and $\mu_A(\theta) = 0$ otherwise. Scott's theorem can be stated as follows.

Theorem 2. Let Θ be a frame and $\succ$ a preference relation on 2^Θ. There exists a probability function, $P : 2^\Theta \to [0,1]$, satisfying: for $A, B \in 2^\Theta$,

$$A \succ B \Longleftrightarrow P(A) > P(B),$$

if and only if $\succ$ satisfies (Q1), (Q3), (Q4) and the following axiom:

(S) For all subsets $A_0, \ldots, A_n, B_0, \ldots, B_n$ of Θ, if $A_i \succeq B_i$ for $0 \leq i < n$, and $\mu_{A_0}(\theta) + \ldots + \mu_{A_n}(\theta) = \mu_{B_0}(\theta) + \ldots + \mu_{B_n}(\theta)$, for all $\theta \in \Theta$, then $B_n \succeq A_n$.

Axiom (S) requires that any element θ of Θ is in exactly as many A_i as B_i. In fact, axiom (S) implies both axioms (Q2) and (Q5) provided that axiom (Q1) holds. For example, let $(A \cup B) \cap C = \emptyset$. Suppose $B \succeq A$. We have: for all $\theta \in \Theta$,

$$\mu_B(\theta) + \mu_{A \cup C}(\theta) = \mu_A(\theta) + \mu_{B \cup C}(\theta).$$

According to axiom (S), $B \cup C \succeq A \cup C$. Similarly, if $B \cup C \succeq A \cup C$, axiom (S) implies $B \succeq A$. Therefore,

$$(A \cup B) \cap C = \emptyset \Longrightarrow (B \succeq A \Longleftrightarrow B \cup C \succeq A \cup C).$$

Recall that axiom (Q1) implies $B \succeq A \Longleftrightarrow \neg(A \succ B)$. Thus,

$$(A \cup B) \cap C = \emptyset \Longrightarrow (A \succ B \Longleftrightarrow A \cup C \succ B \cup C).$$

This means that axiom (S) implies axiom (Q5) if axiom (Q1) holds.

Theorem 2 only suggests the existence of a probability function; there may exist functions other than the probability functions, which are also compatible with a preference relation satisfying (Q1), (Q3), (Q4), and (S).

Since probability functions are a special type of belief functions, it is expected that there exists a weaker preference structure for belief functions.

Definition 7: Let Θ be a frame. A preference relation $\succ$ defined on 2^Θ is called a *qualitative belief* relation if it satisfies (Q1)-(Q3), and the axioms: for $A, B, C \in 2^\Theta$,

(Q4′) dominance : $A \supseteq B \Longrightarrow \neg(B \succ A)$,

(Q5′) partial monotonicity :
$$(A \supset B, A \cap C = \emptyset) \Longrightarrow (A \succ B \Longrightarrow A \cup C \succ B \cup C).$$

Axiom (Q3) eliminates the trivial preference relation, i.e., $A \sim B$ for all $A, B \in 2^\Theta$. The dominance axiom (Q4′) says that one should not commit more belief in a subset than in the set itself. This axiom is stronger than (Q4). Given the axioms (Q1) and (Q2) of a weak order, the dominance axiom can be expressed equivalently as $A \supseteq B \Longrightarrow A \succeq B$. Obviously, axiom (Q5′) is a weaker form of the monotonicity axiom (Q5). It is important to note that (Q1)-(Q3) together with (Q4′)-(Q5′) form a set of independent axioms which completely characterize the qualitative belief relations. The following theorem (Wong et al., 1990) shows that qualitative belief relations are indeed compatible with belief functions.

Theorem 3. Let Θ be a frame and $\succ$ a preference relation on 2^Θ. There exists a belief function, $Bel : 2^\Theta \longrightarrow [0,1]$, satisfying: for $A, B \in 2^\Theta$,

$$A \succ B \Longleftrightarrow Bel(A) > Bel(B)$$

if and only if the preference relation $\succ$ is a qualitative belief relation.

We can prove the *only if* part of the theorem trivially from the properties of belief functions. The *if* part of the theorem can be proved by constructing a belief function compatible with a qualitative belief relation. Axioms (Q1) and (Q2) imply that the induced indifference relation $\sim$ is an equivalence relation (Fishburn, 1970). Since axiom (Q5) holds, based on the relation $\sim$, we can partition 2^Θ into at least two equivalence classes $E_0, \ldots, E_k$ $(k \geq 1)$. An equivalence E_i is also denoted as $[A]$ if $A \in E_i$. For example, E_0 may be written as $[\emptyset]$ and E_k as $[\Theta]$. First we recursively construct a function f on the equivalence classes as follows:

$$\begin{aligned} &\text{(i)} \quad f(E_0) = 0, \\ &\text{(ii)} \quad f(E_{n+1}) = \max\{f'(E_{n+1}), f(E_n) + 1\} \end{aligned}$$

where

$$f'(E_{n+1}) = \max_{A \in E_{n+1}} \{-\sum_{A \supset B} (-1)^{|A-B|} f([B])\}$$

if for every $A \in E_{n+1}$, $A \supset B \Longrightarrow B \notin E_{n+1}$; otherwise $f'(E_{n+1}) = f(E_n) + 1$. The symbol $|\cdot|$ denotes the cardinality of a set. The function thus constructed may be considered as an *unnormalized* belief function which satisfies $A \succ B \Longleftrightarrow f([A]) > f([B])$ for $A, B \in 2^\Theta$. Based on the function f, we can then construct a normalized belief function:

$$Bel(A) = \frac{f([A])}{f([\Theta])}.$$

Theorem 3 shows that if a preference relation is a qualitative belief, i.e., it satisfies axioms (Q1)-(Q3), (Q4′), and (Q5′), then there exists a belief function compatible with the relation. However, these axioms do not guarantee that the class of belief functions is the only kind of functions representing qualitative belief (Smets, 1990). As we mentioned earlier, the same can be said about Scott's theorem. For example, consider a preference relation defined by $\{\theta_1, \theta_2\} \succ \{\theta_2\} \succ \{\theta_1\} \succ \emptyset$. Obviously, this relation satisfies the axioms for qualitative belief as well as those required by Scott's theorem. It can be represented either by a probability function:

$$\begin{aligned} P(\emptyset) &= 0.0, \\ P(\{\theta_1\}) &= 0.4, \\ P(\{\theta_2\}) &= 0.6, \\ P(\{\theta_1, \theta_2\}) &= 1.0, \end{aligned}$$

or by a belief function:

$$\begin{aligned} Bel(\emptyset) &= 0.0, \\ Bel(\{\theta_1\}) &= 0.2, \\ Bel(\{\theta_2\}) &= 0.5, \\ Bel(\{\theta_1, \theta_2\}) &= 1.0. \end{aligned}$$

This relation can also be represented by another function f which is neither a probability function nor a belief function:

$$\begin{aligned} f(\emptyset) &= 0.0, \\ f(\{\theta_1\}) &= 0.6, \\ f(\{\theta_2\}) &= 0.7, \\ f(\{\theta_1, \theta_2\}) &= 1.0. \end{aligned}$$

Certaintly, it will be useful if one can define a set of axioms to characterize a class of preference relations that can be represented only by belief functions. This may, however, be a difficult task in general. For a special type of belief functions known as consonant belief functions, Dubois (1986) gave such a set of axioms.

Based on Definition 7 and Theorem 3, we can now show that the qualitative probability relations are in fact compatible with the monotonic belief functions as defined by Definition 3.

Lemma 1. Suppose Θ is a finite set and $\succ$ a preference relation on 2^Θ. If $\succ$ is a qualitative probability relation, it is also a qualitative belief relation.

Proof: Axioms (Q1), (Q2), and (Q3) are satisfied by both qualitative probability and belief relations. Also, (Q5′) is a weaker version of the monotonicity axiom (Q5). Thus, it will suffice to prove that the dominance axiom (Q4′) follows from those axioms that define qualitative probability. Suppose $A \supseteq B$. Let $A = B \cup C$ and $B \cap C = \emptyset$. From $\neg(\emptyset \succ C)$ and axiom (Q5), it follows that the dominance axiom holds. Therefore, if a preference relation is a qualitative probability relation, it is also a qualitative belief relation. □

Theorem 4. Let Θ be a frame and $\succ$ a preference relation on 2^Θ. There exists a *monotonic* belief function, $Bel : 2^\Theta \longrightarrow [0,1]$, satisfying: for $A, B \in 2^\Theta$,

$$A \succ B \Longleftrightarrow Bel(A) > Bel(B),$$

if and only if the preference relation $\succ$ is a qualitative probability relation.

Proof:

(*only if*) Suppose there exists a monotonic belief function $Bel : 2^\Theta \longrightarrow [0,1]$ such that $A \succ B \Longleftrightarrow Bel(A) > Bel(B)$. Then, the asymmetric and negatively transitive properties of $\succ$ immediately follow from the properties of the relation $>$ on real numbers. In other

probability function (B1)–(B3)	⊂	monotonic belief function (B1), (B2), (B3′), (B4)	⊂	Shafer's belief function (B1), (B2), (B3′)	⊂	Smets' belief function (B1), (B2′), (B3′)
⇕		⇕		⇕		⇕
(Q1), (Q3), (Q4), (S)	⟹	(Q1)–(Q5) qualitative probability	⟹	(Q1)–(Q3), (Q4′), (Q5′) qualitative belief	⟹	(Q1), (Q2), (Q4′), (Q5′)

Figure 2: Relationships between Quantitative and Qualitative Representations of Belief

words, axioms (Q1) and (Q2) hold. The axiom (Q3) of nontriviality, $\Theta \succ \emptyset$, is implied by axioms (B1) and (B2), because $Bel(\Theta) = 1 > 0 = Bel(\emptyset)$. Axiom (Q4) can be trivially proved from the fact that $Bel(\emptyset) = 0$ and $Bel(A) \geq 0$ for all $A \in 2^{\Theta}$. Now suppose $A \cap C = B \cap C = \emptyset$. From the assumption that $A \succ B \Longleftrightarrow Bel(A) > Bel(B)$ and axiom (B4), we obtain:

$$\begin{aligned} A \succ B &\Longleftrightarrow Bel(A) > Bel(B) \\ &\Longleftrightarrow Bel(A \cup C) > Bel(B \cup C) \\ &\Longleftrightarrow A \cup C \succ B \cup C. \end{aligned}$$

That is, the monotonicity axiom (Q5) holds.

(*if*) From Lemma 1, we know that a qualitative probability relation is also a qualitative belief relation. By Theorem 3, there exists a belief function Bel satisfying the condition: $A \succ B \Longleftrightarrow Bel(A) > Bel(B)$ for $A, B \in 2^{\Theta}$. From the monotonicity axiom (Q5), we have: for $A \cap C = B \cap C = \emptyset$,

$$\begin{aligned} Bel(A) > Bel(B) &\Longleftrightarrow A \succ B \\ &\Longleftrightarrow A \cup C \succ B \cup C \\ &\Longleftrightarrow Bel(A \cup C) > Bel(B \cup C). \end{aligned}$$

This means that Bel satisfies axiom (B4). □

Note that axioms (B1) and (B2) imply axiom (Q3), i.e., $\Theta \succ \emptyset$. Thus, (Q3) may be weakened or eliminated under the open world assumption. In fact, the following theorem shows that the preference structure compatible with the generalized belief functions can be defined by a set of axioms without (Q3).

Theorem 5. Let Θ be a frame and $\succ$ a preference relation on 2^{Θ}. There exists a generalized belief function, $bel : 2^{\Theta} \longrightarrow [0, 1]$, satisfying: for $A, B \in 2^{\Theta}$,

$$A \succ B \Longleftrightarrow bel(A) > bel(B),$$

if and only if the preference relation $\succ$ satisfies axioms (Q1)-(Q2) and (Q4′)-(Q5′).

proof:

(*only if*) The proof is similar to that of the *only if* part in Theorem 4.

(*if*) Since the dominance axiom implies $\neg(\emptyset \succ \Theta)$, we only have to consider two separate cases: (i) $\Theta \sim \emptyset$ and (ii) $\Theta \succ \emptyset$. Obviously, the second case with $\Theta \succ \emptyset$ is equivalent to Theorem 3. If $\Theta \sim \emptyset$, from axioms (Q1), (Q2), and (Q4′), one can immediately conclude that for any $A, B \in 2^{\Theta}$, the relationship $A \succ B$ is always false, namely, $A \sim B$ is always true (Wong, Bollmann, and Yao, 1990). In this case, we can construct a generalized belief function by letting $m(\emptyset) = 1$. That is, according to (M3′), $bel(A) = 0$ for all $A \in 2^{\Theta}$. For this belief function bel, the condition $A \succ B \Longleftrightarrow bel(A) > bel(B)$ holds for any $A, B \in 2^{\Theta}$. □

The results of the compatibility of preference relations and belief measures are summarized in Figure 2. It can be seen that the inclusion relation ⊂ between different classes of quantitative belief measures corresponds to the implication relation ⟹ between different sets of axioms defining the various preference relations. The links established here between these belief measures and preference relations provide a better understanding of modeling uncertainty with beliefs.

In this preliminary investigation, we have not considered all the important classes of belief functions. It is worth mentioning here that Dubois (1986) proposed a set of axioms to characterize consonant belief functions. A more detailed analysis of various types of preference relations will be reported in a subsequent paper.

4 CONCLUSION

In this paper, we studied the compatibility of quantitative and qualitative representations of beliefs. In particular, four classes of quantitative belief measures were analyzed, namely, the probability function, the monotonic belief function, Shafer's belief function, and Smets' generalized belief function. We established their individual compatibility with different belief structures. These compatibility relationships not only provide a justification for the use of these quantitative measures, but also alleviate some of the difficulties in the acquisition and interpretation of numeric belief numbers.

We have shown that the qualitative probability structure is compatible with monotonic belief functions, and a belief structure slightly weaker than that of qualitative belief is compatible with Smets' generalized belief functions. More importantly, the qualitative and quantitative representations of beliefs may lead to the development of a generalized utility theory for decision making with belief functions.

Acknowledgements

The authors wish to thank P. Smets and Y.T. Hsia for their critical comments and useful suggestions on the axiomatization of belief structures.

References

Bhatnagar, R.K. and Kanal, L.N. (1986) Handling uncertain information: a review of numeric and non-numeric methods. In Kanal, L.N. and Lemmer, J.F., Eds., *Uncertainty in Artificial Intelligence.* pp. 3-26, North-Holland: New York.

de Finetti, B. (1937) La prévision: ses lois logiques, ses sources subjectives. *Ann. Inst. Poincaré,* **7**, pp. 1-68. English translation in Kyburg, Jr., H.E., Smokler, H.E. (1964), Eds., *Studies in Subjective Probability.* Wiley: New York.

Dubois, D. (1986) Belief structures, possibility theory and decomposable confidence measures on finite sets. *Computers and Artificial Intelligence* (Czechoslovakia), **5**, pp. 403-416.

Dubois, D. and Prade, H. (1986) A set-theoretic view of belief function: logical operations and approximations by fuzzy sets. International Journal of General Systems, **12**, pp. 193-226.

Fine, T.L. (1973) *Theories of Probability: An Examination of Foundations.* Academic Press: New York.

Fishburn, P.C. (1970) *Utility Theory for Decision Making.* Wiley: New York.

French, S. (1986) *Decision Theory – An Introduction to the Mathematics of Rationality.* Ellis Horwood Limited: Chichester.

Jaffray, J.Y. (1989) Linear utility theory for belief functions. *Operations Research Letters,* **8**, pp. 107-112.

Kraft, C.H., Pratt, J.W., and Seidenberg, A. (1959) Intuitive probability on finite sets. *Annals of Mathematical Statistics*, **30**, pp. 408-419.

Roberts, F.S. (1976) *Measurement Theory.* Academic Press: New York.

Satoh, K. (1989) Relative plausibility based on model ordering: preliminary report. In Ras, Z.W., Ed., *Methodologies for Intelligent Systems, 4.* pp. 17-24, North-Holland: New York.

Savage, L.J. (1972) *The Foundations of Statistics.* Dover: New York .

Scott, G. (1964) Measurement structures and linear inequalities. *Journal of Mathematical Psychology,* **1**, pp. 233-247.

Shafer, G. (1976) *A Mathematical Theory of Evidence.* Princeton University Press: Princeton.

Smets, P. (1988) Belief functions. In Smets, P., Mamdani, A., Dubois, D., and Prade, H., Eds., *Non-Standard Logics for Automated Reasoning.* pp. 253-277, Academic Press: New York.

Smets, P. (1990) Private communications.

Spiegelhalter, D.J. (1986) A statistical view of uncertainty in expert systems. In Gale, W.A., Ed., *Artificial Intelligence and Statistics,* pp. 17-55, Reading, MA: Addison-Wesley.

Wong, S.K.M., Bollmann, P., and Yao, Y.Y. (1990) Characterization of qualitative belief structure. Submitted for publication.

Wong, S.K.M., Yao, Y.Y., Bollmann, P., and Bürger, H.C. (1990) Axiomatization of qualitative belief structure. To appear in *IEEE Transaction on Systems, Man, and Cybernetics.*

Zadeh, L.A. (1978) Fuzzy sets as a basis of possibility. *Fuzzy Sets and Systems*, **1**, pp. 3-28.

An Efficient Implementation of Belief Function Propagation

Hong Xu
IRIDIA - Université Libre de Bruxelles
50 av. F. Roosevelt, CP 194/6
B-1050, Brussels, Belgium
Email: r01505@bbrbfu01.bitnet

Abstract

The local computation technique (Shafer et al. 1987, Shafer and Shenoy 1988, Shenoy and Shafer 1986) is used for propagating belief functions in so-called a Markov Tree. In this paper, we describe an efficient implementation of belief function propagation on the basis of the local computation technique. The presented method avoids all the redundant computations in the propagation process, and so makes the computational complexity decrease with respect to other existing implementations (Hsia and Shenoy 1989, Zarley et al. 1988). We also give a combined algorithm for both propagation and re-propagation which makes the re-propagation process more efficient when one or more of the prior belief functions is changed.

1 INTRODUCTION

Dempster-Shafer theory (Shafer 1976, Smets 1988) has been considered as one of the tools for dealing with the problem of uncertain information by the Artificial Intelligence community. The computational complexity of Dempster's rule of combination, the pivot mechanism of the theory, however, is the main obstacle to its effective use. However, several implementations of the Dempster-Shafer theory have recently been developed (Hsia and Shenoy 1989, Zarley 1988, Zarley et al. 1988) based on the observation that an arbitrary belief function network can be represented as a hypergraph (Kong 1986), which can also be embedded in so-called a Markov tree (Zhang 1988). These implementations use the local computation technique (Shafer et al. 1987, Shafer and Shenoy 1988, Shenoy and Shafer 1986) for propagating belief functions in the Markov tree. According to this technique, the belief function propagation can be described as a message-passing scheme: each node in the Markov tree sends its message to one of its neighbours after it has received the messages from all of its other neighbours, and the result of propagation on each node is computed by combining its own belief function (prior belief function) and the messages from all of its neighbours. After the results for all the nodes have been computed, one may want to change one or more of the prior belief functions. Then we have to re-propagate the impact of the changes to all the other nodes. In general, there may be repeated computations during propagation and re-propagation process, which may greatly affect the efficiency of the computation. The goal of this paper is to present an efficient method for the implementation of belief function propagation. The main advantage of this scheme is that it avoids all the redundant computations during propagation, resulting in a reduced computational complexity with respect to that of other existing implementations. It is also shown that making full use of the stored messages passed between the nodes and of stored intermediate information, we can just re-propagate the changed values when some prior belief functions are changed.

The paper is organized as follows. In section 2, some basic concepts about belief function networks are reviewed. In section 3, we describe a straightforward implementation of belief functions propagation using local computation. In section 4, we present our implementation scheme. In section 5, we discuss the problem of updating messages when one or more inputs is changed, and give a combined algorithm for both propagation and re-propagation. Finally, some conclusions are given in section 6.

2 SOME BASIC CONCEPTS ABOUT BELIEF FUNCTION NETWORKS

Dempster-Shafer theory (Shafer 1976, Smets 1988), is concerned with the problem of representing and manipulating incomplete knowledge. In this section, we recall some basic concepts and definitions about belief functions and belief function networks. This presentation follows (Shafer and Shenoy 1988, Shenoy 1989).

Variables and Configurations We use the symbol $\mathcal{W}_X$ for the set of possible values of a variable X, and we call $\mathcal{W}_X$ the *frame for X.* Given a finite non-empty set h of variables, let $\mathcal{W}_h$ denote the Cartesian product of $\mathcal{W}_X$ for X in h: $\mathcal{W}_h = \times\{\mathcal{W}_X \mid X \in h\}$. We call $\mathcal{W}_h$ the *frame for h.* We refer to elements of $\mathcal{W}_h$ as *configurations of h.*

Basic Probability Assignments A *basic probability assignment (bpa)* m on X, is a function which assigns a

value in [0, 1] to every subset $\mathcal{a}$ of $\mathcal{W}_X$ and satisfies the following axioms:
(i) $m(\emptyset) = 0$; and
(ii) $\Sigma\{m(\mathcal{a}) \mid \mathcal{a} \subseteq \mathcal{W}_X\} = 1$

Belief Functions A *belief function* Bel associated with a bpa m, is a function that assigns a value in [0, 1] to every non-empty subset $\mathcal{a}$ of $\mathcal{W}_X$, called "degree of belief in $\mathcal{a}$", defined by

$$Bel(\mathcal{a}) = \Sigma\{m(\mathcal{b}) \mid \mathcal{b} \subseteq \mathcal{a}\}$$

The subsets $\mathcal{a}$ for which $m(\mathcal{a})>0$ are called *focal elements* of Bel. The simplest belief function is the one with $m(\mathcal{W}_X) =1$, called vacuous belief function.

Projection and Extension If g and h are sets of variables, $h \subseteq g$, and **x** is a configuration of g, then we let $\mathbf{x}^{\downarrow h}$ denote the projection of **x** to $\mathcal{W}_h$. $\mathbf{x}^{\downarrow h}$ is always a configuration of h. If $\mathcal{g}$ is a non-empty subset of $\mathcal{W}_g$, then the *projection of* $\mathcal{g}$ *to h*, denoted by $\mathcal{g}^{\downarrow h}$, is obtained by projecting elements of $\mathcal{g}$ to $\mathcal{W}_h$, i.e. $\mathcal{g}^{\downarrow h} = \{\mathbf{x}^{\downarrow h} \mid \mathbf{x} \in \mathcal{g}\}$. By extension of a subset of a frame to a subset of a larger frame, we mean a cylinder set extension. If g and h are sets of variables, $h \subseteq g$, $h \neq g$, and $\mathcal{h}$ is a subset of $\mathcal{W}_h$, then the *extension of* $\mathcal{h}$ *to g* , denoted by $\mathcal{h}^{\uparrow g}$, is $\mathcal{h} \times \mathcal{W}_{g-h}$.

Dempster's Rule of Combination *Dempster's Rule of Combination* is a rule for producing a new bpa from two bpa's. Considering two bpa's m_1 and m_2 on g and h, we let $m = m_1 \oplus m_2$ be the bpa on $g \cup h$ defined by

$$m(\emptyset) = 0 \text{ and}$$
$$m(\mathbf{c}) = K^{-1}\Sigma\{m_1(\mathcal{a})m_2(\mathcal{b}) \mid (\mathcal{a}^{\uparrow(g\cup h)} \cap \mathcal{b}^{\uparrow(g\cup h)}) = \mathbf{c}\}$$

where $K=1-\Sigma\{m_1(\mathcal{a})\, m_2(\mathcal{b}) \mid (\mathcal{a}^{\uparrow(g\cup h)} \cap \mathcal{b}^{\uparrow(g\cup h)}) = \emptyset\}$

K is a normalizing factor, which intuitively measures how much m_1 and m_2 are conflicting. If K = 0, then we say that m_1 and m_2 are not combinable.

Marginalization Suppose m is a bpa on g and suppose $h \subseteq g$, $h \neq \emptyset$. *The marginal of m for h*, denoted by $m_{\downarrow h}$, is a bpa defined by

$$m^{\downarrow h}(\mathcal{a})=\Sigma\{m(\mathcal{b}) \mathcal{b} \subseteq \mathcal{W}_g, \mathcal{b}^{\downarrow h}=\mathcal{a}\} \text{ for all subsets } \mathcal{a} \text{ of } \mathcal{W}_h.$$

A Belief Function Network Using Dempster-Shafer theory, the problem can be represented as a finite set of variables $\mathcal{X}$. A finite frame $\mathcal{W}_X$ is associated with each variable X of $\mathcal{X}$ and the elements of $\mathcal{W}_X$ are mutually exclusive and exhaustive.The relationships of the variables are expressed by subsets of $\mathcal{X}$. The knowledge about the variable X is encoded in the belief function over $\mathcal{W}_X$ or over $\mathcal{W}_h$ where h = {X}. The knowledge about relation among the variables is encoded in the belief function over $\mathcal{W}_h$ of subset h in w hich the variables are included. We call these belief functions as prior belief functions. So, *a belief function network* consists of $\mathcal{X}$, a set of subsets of $\mathcal{X}$: $\mathcal{H}$, and a finite collection of independent belief functions (Bel_1, Bel_2, ..., Bel_k) where each belief function Bel_i is the prior belief function on some subset h, and is stored as a set of focal elements with their values.

Evaluation of a Belief Function Network Suppose we are given a belief function network. To evaluate a belief function network, we have to:
(i) combine all Bel_i in the network, the resulting belief function is called *global belief function* ;
(ii) compute the marginal of the global belief function for each variable in the network.

Because the computational complexity of Dempster's combination is exponential with the size of the frame of belief functions being combined, it will not be feasible to compute the global belief function when there are a large number of variables. In the next section, we will describe an alternative way to evaluate the belief function network by using the local computation technique proposed in (Shafer et al. 1987, Shafer and Shenoy 1988, Shenoy and Shafer 1986).

3 BELIEF FUNCTION PROPAGATION USING LOCAL COMPUTATION

It has been shown that if the belief function network can be represented as certain kind of tree, called Markov tree, the belief functions can be "propagated" in the Markov tree by a local message-passing scheme, producing as a result in the marginals of the global belief function for each of the nodes. We first look at what Markov tree is and how a belief function network can be represented as a Markov tree.

Given a tree $G=(\mathcal{M}, \mathcal{E})$ where each node (also called vertex) $v \in \mathcal{M}$ is a non-empty subset of a finite set V, $\mathcal{E}$ is the set of edges in G. Then G is *Markov* if for any $v \in \mathcal{M}$, such that v separates two other distinct nodes v_i and v_j in G, $(v_i \cap v_j) \subseteq v$. Given three distinct nodes v, v_i and v_j, we say that v *separates* v_i and v_j if v is on the path between v_i and v_j.

Let $\mathcal{H}$ and $\mathcal{X}$ be as defined in the previous section. In the language of graph theory, $\mathcal{H}$ is called a *hypergraph* on $\mathcal{X}$ and each element of $\mathcal{H}$ is called a *hyperedge*. In order to use local computation for propagation, the hypergraph should be arranged in a Markov tree where $V=\mathcal{X}$ and $\mathcal{M} \supseteq \mathcal{H}$. We can always find a method to arrange a hypergraph in a Markov tree. Algorithms for constructing a Markov tree for a hypergraph can be found in (Kong 1986, Mellouli 1987, Zhang 1988). Two examples of Markov tree representatives (on the right hand side of Fig 3.1) for hypergraphs (on the left hand side of Fig 3.1) are shown below. In Example1, $\mathcal{X}_1 = \{a, b, c\}$, $\mathcal{H}_1 = \{\{a\}, \{b\}, \{c\}, \{a, b\}, \{b, c\}\}$, $\mathcal{M}_1 = \mathcal{H}_1$; In Example2, $\mathcal{X}_2 = \{p, q, s, t, r\}$, $\mathcal{H}_2 = \{\{s\}, \{t\}, \{p\}, \{q\}, \{r\}, \{s, p\}, \{p, t\}, \{t, q\}, \{s, q\}, \{p, r\}\}$, where $\mathcal{M}_2 = \mathcal{H}_2 \cup \{\{p, q, t\}, \{s, p, q\}\}$, where {p, q, t} and {s, p, q} are the new nodes added for constructing the Markov tree.

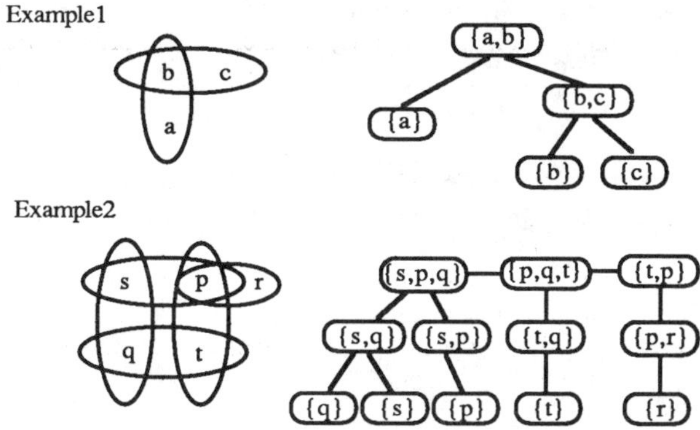

Fig3.1: Markov tree representatives of hypergraphs

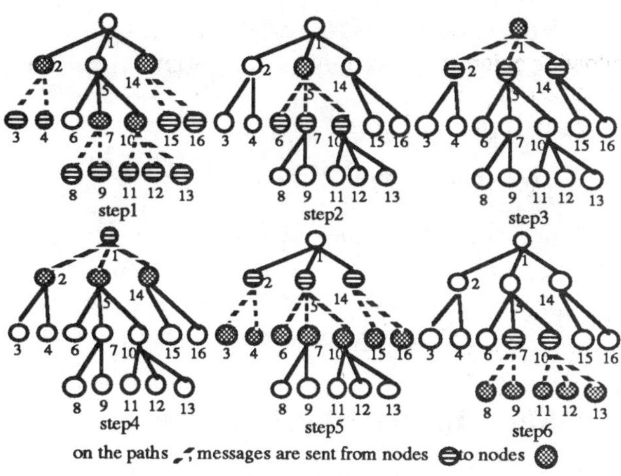

Fig3.2: the message-passing scheme for simultaneous belief function propagation

In the rest of this section, we discuss Shafer, Shenoy and Mellouli's propagation scheme using local computation (Shafer et al. 1987). Suppose we have already arranged the hypergraph in a Markov tree $G=(\mathcal{M}, \mathcal{E})$. For each node v, we let $\mathcal{N}_v=\{v_k|(v_k, v)\in\mathcal{E}\}$ be the set of neighbours of v, Bel_v the prior belief function on v, and $Bel^{\downarrow v}$ the marginal of the global belief function for v. Let L(G) be the leaves of G given some designated node as the root of G. During propagation, each node sends a belief function to each of its neighbours. The belief function sent by v to v_i is referred as a "message" and is denoted by $M^{v\to v_i}$. We define it as:

$$M^{v\to v_i}=((Bel_v\oplus(\oplus\{M^{v_k\to v}|v_k\in(\mathcal{N}_v-\{v_i\})\}))^{\downarrow(v\cap v_i)})^{\uparrow v_i} \quad (3.1)$$

Because a leaf v has only one neighbour, say v_i, then the above expression reduces to:

$$M^{v\to v_i} = ((Bel_v)^{\downarrow(v\cap v_i)})^{\uparrow v_i}$$

Thus, when the propagation starts, the leaves of the Markov tree can send messages to their neighbours right away. The others send a message to one neighbour after they have received messages by all but that one neighbour. And when a node receives a message from that one neighbour, it appropriately (i.e. by using (3.1)) sends messages back to the remaining neighbours. All the messages can be transmitted through the Markov tree in this way.

After node v has received the messages from all the neighbours, the marginal $Bel^{\downarrow v}$ for v is given by

$$Bel^{\downarrow v}=Bel_v\oplus(\oplus\{M^{v_i\to v} \mid v_i\in\mathcal{N}_v\}) \quad (3.2)$$

Because all the variables are included in the Markov tree, as Fig 3.1 illustrated, we can simultaneously compute the marginals of the global belief function for every variables in the belief function network. The whole propagation process is shown in Fig 3.2. For more detail about this propagation scheme, see (Saffiotti 1989, Shafer et al. 1987, Shafer and Shenoy 1988, Shenoy and Shafer 1986).

According to the scheme described above, a typical message-passing situation can be illustrated as in Fig 3.3. A straightforward way for computing the messages between the nodes and the marginals for the nodes is as follows.

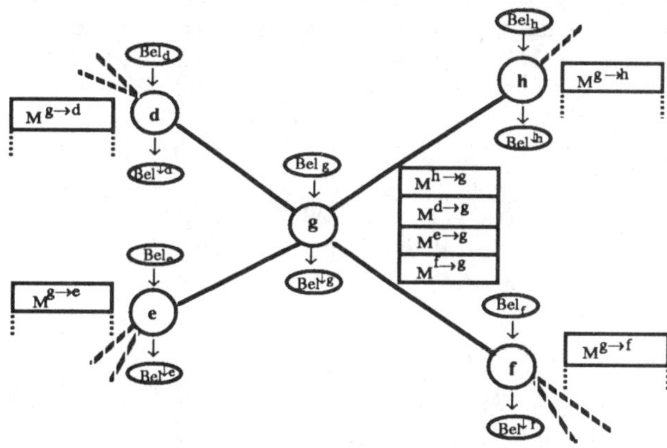

Fig3.3: a typical message-passing situation

<u>Example 3.1:</u> Suppose nodes d, e and f have received messages from all their respective neighbours except node g. Suppose now we want to compute the marginals for d, e and f. According to (3.1), we first compute all $M^{i\to g}$, $i\in\{d, e, f\}$

$$M^{i\to g}=((Bel_i\oplus\{\oplus M^{z\to i}|z\in\mathcal{N}_i-\{g\}\})^{\downarrow(i\cap g)})^{\uparrow g} \quad (3.3)$$

Now g has received the messages by d, e and f, so it can send message to h. Again using (3.1), we have:

$$M^{g\to h}=((Bel_g\oplus M^{d\to g}\oplus M^{e\to g}\oplus M^{f\to g})^{\downarrow(g\cap h)})^{\uparrow h} \quad (3.4)$$

Later, after g has received the message from h, it can send messages back to d, e and f, and the marginals for d, e and f will be computed. Using (3.2), we have

$$Bel^{\downarrow f}=Bel_f\oplus\{\oplus M^{z\to f}|z\in\mathcal{N}_f-\{g\}\}\oplus ((Bel_g\oplus M^{d\to g}\oplus M^{e\to g}\oplus M^{h\to g})^{\downarrow(g\cap f)})^{\uparrow f} \quad (3.5)$$

$$Bel^{\downarrow e}=Bel_e\oplus\{\oplus M^{z\to e}|z\in\mathcal{N}_e-\{g\}\}\oplus ((Bel_g\oplus M^{d\to g}\oplus M^{f\to g}\oplus M^{h\to g})^{\downarrow(g\cap e)})^{\uparrow e} \quad (3.6)$$

$$Bel^{\downarrow d}=Bel_d\oplus\{\oplus M^{z\to d}|z\in\mathcal{N}_d-\{g\}\}\oplus ((Bel_g\oplus M^{e\to g}\oplus M^{f\to g}\oplus M^{h\to g})^{\downarrow(g\cap d)})^{\uparrow d} \quad (3.7)$$

Some repeated computations are found here. e.g. $Bel_f\oplus\{\oplus M^{z\to f}|z\in\mathcal{N}_f-\{g\}\}$ is computed four times in (3.3),(3.5), (3.6) and (3.7). $Bel_g\oplus M^{f\to g}\oplus M^{h\to g}$ is computed twice in (3.6) and (3.7). The solution will be discussed in the next section.

4 A More Efficient Implementation

It is well known that the computation of Dempster's combination involves the most computational expense during the whole propagation process. So the redundant combinations during the propagation should be avoided as much as possible. In this section, we present an algorithm for belief function propagation using local computation which avoids those repeated computations described above.

In our implementation, we assume that once we have chosen a Markov tree representative $G = (\mathcal{M},\mathcal{E})$, G will not change unless the belief function network which it represents is changed. We still make use of the notations defined in the preceding section. We choose one node of G, say v_r, to be the root of the tree, thus the edges in G can be seen as direct edges: we say that an edge (v, v_i) in G is directed from v to v_i whenever node v_i is on the path between node v and v_r. In other words, we can define the parent-children relationship for each node v: let $\mathcal{Ch}_v=\{c_k \mid c_k\in\mathcal{N}_v$, v is on the path between c_k and $v_r\}$ be the children of v and $\mathcal{P}_v$ be the parent of v if $\mathcal{P}_v\in\mathcal{N}_v$ and $\mathcal{P}_v$ is on the path between v and v_r. We also assume that there is an order (arbitrary but fixed) for the elements in $\mathcal{Ch}_v$, and let $\mathcal{Ch}'_v$ denote the same set as $\mathcal{Ch}_v$ but with reverse order. For each $c_k\in\mathcal{Ch}_v$, we let $\mathcal{Lsb}_{c_k}=\{c_j \mid c_j\in\mathcal{Ch}_v, j<k\}$ denote the left hand siblings of c_k, and $\mathcal{Rsb}_{c_k}=\{c_j \mid c_j\in\mathcal{Ch}_v, j>k\}$ denote the right hand siblings of c_k. Furthermore, to remove redundant computations, we associate three intermediate variables $\mathcal{Cur}_v$, $\mathcal{Intm}_v$ and R_v with each node v. Suppose that for a given node v, it is $\mathcal{Ch}_v=\{c_1, c_2, ..., c_m\}$. Then we give below the formulas for computing these intermediate variables:

$$\mathcal{Cur}_v=Bel_v\oplus\{\oplus M^{c_k\to v}|c_k\in\mathcal{Ch}_v\} \quad (4.1)$$

$$\mathcal{Intm}_{c_i}=Bel_v\oplus\{\oplus M^{c_k\to v}|c_k\in\mathcal{Lsb}_{c_i}\} \quad (4.2)$$

$$R_{c_i}=M^{\mathcal{P}_v\to v}\oplus\{\oplus M^{c_k\to v}|c_k\in\mathcal{Rsb}_{c_i}\}$$

Then we compute the marginal for c_i, one of the children of v, as follows:

$$\begin{aligned}Bel^{\downarrow c_i}&=\mathcal{Cur}_{c_i}\oplus((\mathcal{Intm}_{c_i}\oplus R_{c_i})^{\downarrow(v\cap c_i)})^{\uparrow c_i}\\ &=Bel_{c_i}\oplus\{\oplus M^{z\to c_i}|z\in\mathcal{Ch}_{c_i}\}\oplus ((Bel_v\oplus\{\oplus M^{c_k\to v}|c_k\in\mathcal{Lsb}_{c_i}\}\oplus M^{\mathcal{P}_v\to v}\oplus \{\oplus M^{c_k\to v}|c_k\in\mathcal{Rsb}_{c_i}\})^{\downarrow(v\cap c_i)})^{\uparrow c_i}\\ &= Bel_{c_i}\oplus\{\oplus M^{z\to c_i}|z\in\mathcal{Ch}_{c_i}\}\oplus((Bel_v\oplus \{\oplus M^{c_k\to v}|c_k\in\mathcal{N}_v-\{c_i\}\})^{\downarrow(v\cap c_i)})^{\uparrow c_i}\\ &=Bel_{c_i}\oplus\{\oplus M^{z\to c_i}|z\in\mathcal{Ch}_{c_i}\}\oplus\{M^{z\to c_i}|z=\mathcal{P}_{c_i}\}\\ &=Bel_{c_i}\oplus\{\oplus M^{v_j\to c_i}|v_j\in\mathcal{N}_{c_i}\}\end{aligned}$$

which is what (3.2) requires to be the case. For the root v_r, because $\mathcal{Ch}_{v_r}=\mathcal{N}_{v_r}$, so, when node v_r receives the messages from all of its children, the marginal for v_r can be computed immediately, i.e. $Bel^{\downarrow v_r}=\mathcal{Cur}_{v_r}$.

From the analysis in Example 4.1, we will see how the number of applications of Dempster's combination can be reduced to the least. The typical message-passing situation shown in Fig 3.3 above is now as in Fig 4.1. The arrows in the edges are the directions of edges, and two more storages, $\mathcal{Cur}_i$ and $\mathcal{Intm}_i$, are required at each node. Because R_i is used just once, we do not store it at each node, but regard it as a temporary variable.

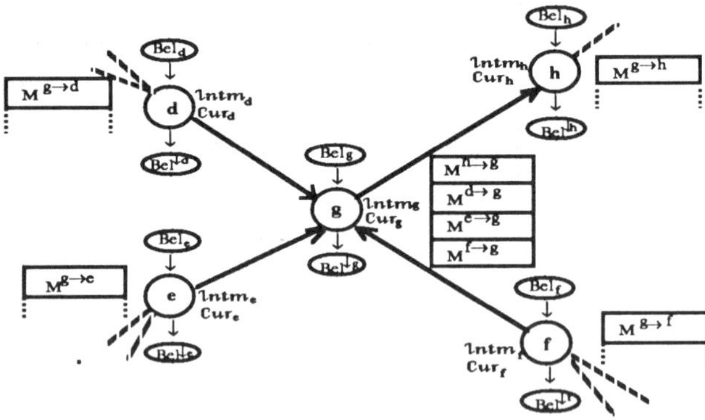

Fig4.1: a typical message-passing situation

<u>Example 4.1:</u> In this example, we consider the same situation as in Example 3.1. Because nodes d, e and f have received all the messages from their children, $\mathcal{Cur}_d$, $\mathcal{Cur}_e$ and $\mathcal{Cur}_f$ can be computed according to (4.1). Then the messages $M^{i\to g}$, i = d, e, f, can be computed as follows:

$$M^{i\to g} = ((\mathcal{Cur}_i)^{\downarrow(i\cap g)})^{\uparrow g}$$

Now g can receive the messages from its children d, e and f in sequence:

$$\mathcal{Intm}_d = Bel_g$$
$$\mathcal{Intm}_e = \mathcal{Intm}_d \oplus M^{d\to g}$$
$$\mathcal{Intm}_f = \mathcal{Intm}_e \oplus M^{e\to g}$$
$$\mathcal{Cur}_g = \mathcal{Intm}_f \oplus M^{f\to g}$$

$$M^{g\to h} = ((\mathbf{Cur}_g)^{\downarrow(g\cap h)})^{\uparrow h}$$

After h has sent the message back to g, g can send the messages back to its children f, e and d, and the marginals for d, e and f can be computed.

$$R_f = M^{h\to g}$$
$$M^{g\to f} = ((\mathbf{Intm}_f \oplus R_f)^{\downarrow(g\cap f)})^{\uparrow f}$$
$$Bel^{\downarrow f} = \mathbf{Cur}_f \oplus M^{g\to f}$$
$$R_e = R_f \oplus M^{f\to g}$$
$$M^{g\to e} = ((\mathbf{Intm}_e \oplus R_e)^{\downarrow(g\cap e)})^{\uparrow e}$$
$$Bel^{\downarrow e} = \mathbf{Cur}_e \oplus M^{g\to e}$$
$$R_d = R_e \oplus M^{e\to g}$$
$$M^{g\to d} = ((\mathbf{Intm}_d \oplus R_d)^{\downarrow(g\cap d)})^{\uparrow d}$$
$$Bel^{\downarrow d} = \mathbf{Cur}_d \oplus M^{g\to d}$$

Thus, all the repeated computation in (3.5), (3.6) and (3.7) of Example 3.1 are avoided by using $\mathbf{Cur}_i$, $\mathbf{Intm}_i$ and R_i. Table 4.1 illustrates the situation (only the number of combinations is compared). In this sense, our approach is an optimal implementation of propagation using local computation.

Table4.1 Comparison of the number of combinations used by our approach and the straightforward one

to compute	Example 3.1	Example 4.1	comparison
$M^{g\to h}$	(1) (2) ⊕ (3) ⊕ (4) ⊕	(1) (2) ⊕ (5) (3) ⊕ (6) (4) ⊕	same
$M^{g\to f}$ and $Bel^{\downarrow f}$	(1) (2) ⊕ (3) ⊕ (7) (8) ⊕ ⊕	(6) (7) (8') ⊕ ⊕	using (6) instead of re-computing (1) ⊕ (2) ⊕ (3)
$M^{g\to e}$ and $Bel^{\downarrow e}$	(1) (2) (7) (4) ⊕ ⊕ (9) ⊕ ⊕	(7) (4) ⊕ (5) (10) (9') ⊕ ⊕	using (5) instead of re-computing (1) ⊕ (2)
$M^{g\to d}$ and $Bel^{\downarrow d}$	(7) (4) ⊕ (3) ⊕ (1) (11) ⊕ ⊕	(10) (3) ⊕ (1) (11') ⊕ ⊕	using (10) instead of re-computing (7) ⊕ (4)

The numbers correspond to: (1): Bel_g, (2): $M^{d\to g}$, (3): $M^{e\to g}$, (4): $M^{f\to g}$, (5): $\mathbf{Intm}_e$, (6): $\mathbf{Intm}_f$, (7): $M^{h\to g}$, (8): $Bel_f \oplus \{\oplus M^{z\to f} \mid z \in \mathcal{N}_f - \{g\}\}$, (8'): $\mathbf{Cur}_f$, (9): $Bel_e \oplus \{\oplus M^{z\to e} \mid z \in \mathcal{N}_e - \{g\}\}$, (9'): $\mathbf{Cur}_e$, (10): R_e, (11): $Bel_d \oplus \{\oplus M^{z\to d} \mid z \in \mathcal{N}_d - \{g\}\}$, (11'): $\mathbf{Cur}_d$,

The following algorithm implements the simultaneous belief functions propagation according to the scheme described above. Note that $\mathcal{Ch}_v$ and $\mathcal{P}_v$ used here always refer to the children and the parent of node v in the same chosen G. In the algorithm, we use "nil" to represent the vacuous belief function. Before propagation, $\mathbf{Cur}_v$ is initiated to Bel_v. The process begins by calling **Propagate** $(\mathcal{M}, \mathcal{E})$.

```
Propagate (𝔐', ℰ')
if 𝔐' ≠ ∅ then
  L := L(𝔐', ℰ')
    /* get the leaves of G' = (𝔐',ℰ') */
  if 𝔐' = {r} then L := 𝔐' end-if
    /* r is the root of G. */
  for i ∈ L     /* for every v in L, do the followings: */
    for k ∈ Ch_i
      /* receive the messages from all its children: */
      Intm_k := Cur_i /* store intermediate result at k*/
      M^{k→i} := ((Cur_k)^{↓(k∩i)})^{↑i}
      /* compute message from k to i */
      Cur_i := Cur_i ⊕ M^{k→i}
      /* combine all the messages from children */
```

```
      end-for
  end-for
  Propagate(𝔐'-L, 𝔈'-{(i, j) | i∈L})
        /* delete the leaves, continue propagation in the
remaining tree */
  for i ∈ L /* for every v in L, do the following: */
    if 𝒫i exists then R := M^(𝒫i→i)
     /* get the message from the parent*/
                 else R := nil
     /* only root has not parent. */
                        Bel↓i := 𝐂𝐮𝐫i
     /* marginal for the root node is computed*/
    end-if
    Q := nil
    for k ∈ 𝐂𝐡'i
      /* send messages back to every child and compute the
marginals for them:*/
      R := R ⊕ Q
      /* combine some messages from i's neighbours */
      M^(i→k) :=((𝐈𝐧𝐭𝐦k⊕R)↓(i∩k))↑k              (4.3)
      /* compute message from i to k by using intermediate
results*/
      Bel↓k := 𝐂𝐮𝐫k ⊕ M^(i→k)
      /* marginal for k is computed*/
      Q := M^(j→i)
    /* get message from k to i for further computation */
    end-for
  end-for
end-if
```

Algorithm1 belief function propagation

We can distinguish two parts in the Algorithm 1, separated by the recursive call. In the first part, each node receives the messages from all of its children, and combines them with its own belief function, because the messages are sent starting from the leaf nodes until the root of G is reached, we call this part "propagation-up". In the second part, after each node has received the message from its parent, it sends messages back to its children and computes the marginals for them; as the messages are sent back from the root until the leaves of G are reached, we call this part "propagation-down". Because the leaves of G have no children to receive messages from, the entire propagation can be invoked by calling. **Propagate($\mathfrak{M}$ -L($\mathfrak{M}$,$\mathfrak{E}$),$\mathfrak{E}$-{(v,v$_j$)| v∈L($\mathfrak{M}$,$\mathfrak{E}$)}).**

From Algorithm 1, we find that the number of applications of Dempster's combination at each node is related to the number of its children. Let |S| denote the size of the set S. Generally, in "propagation-up", there are $|\mathcal{C}h_v|$ combinations at each non-leaf node v; In "propagation-down", there are $2|\mathcal{C}h_{v_r}|-1$ combinations at the root v_r, because v_r has no parent and $3|\mathcal{C}h_v|-1$ combinations at node v which is neither leaf nor root, thus there are altogether $|\mathcal{C}h_v|+(2+|\{\mathcal{P}_v\}|)*|\mathcal{C}h_v|-1$ combinations at non-leaf node v. No combination is needed at leave nodes. In Example 3.1, there are $|\mathcal{C}h_v|*(1+|\mathcal{N}_v|+\Sigma\{|\mathcal{C}h_{c_i}| \mid c_i\in\mathcal{C}h_v, i=1, ..., m, m=|\mathcal{C}h_v|\})$ combinations at each node.

5 UPDATING MESSAGES

Suppose we have already computed the marginals for all the nodes and the Markov tree G is still the same, and we now want to change one or more of the prior belief functions for some reason. Because some of the previous computed intermediate information are stored at each nodes, we can update the marginals for all the nodes without redoing all the work during re-propagation.

For the sake of simplicity, in this section, we use number i to refer to node v_i in the Markov tree, as shown in Fig. 5.1. Node 1 is by convention the root of the tree.

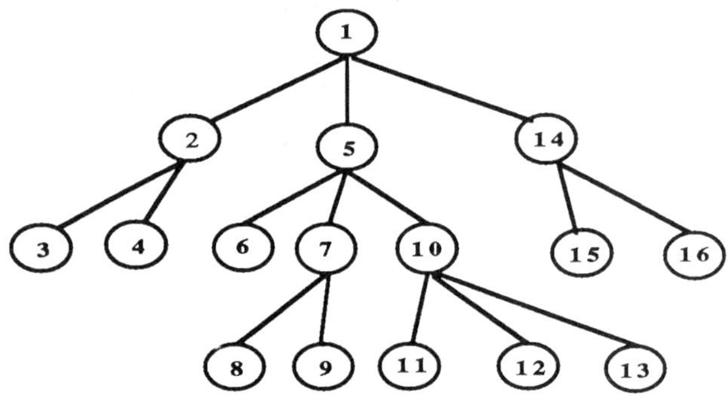

Fig 5.1 a Markov tree representation for a belief function network

Suppose we change one prior belief function, say Bel_{12}. According to (3.1), the generic message $M^{i\to j}$ depends on Bel_i and on $M^{k\to i}$ ($k\in\mathcal{N}_i$, $k\neq j$), thus all the messages $M^{i\to\mathcal{P}_i}$ (if $\mathcal{P}_i$ exists) from any i on the path between node 12 and 1, including node1, will be discarded; Moreover, all the messages $M^{\mathcal{P}_j\to j}$ (if $\mathcal{P}_j$ exists) for all j not lying on the path between 12 and 1, will be discarded as well. The remaining half of the messages can be retained. Now suppose we need to compute the marginals for all nodes again. If we have stored all the previous messages, then only the changed messages should be recomputed, while the unchanged ones can be retained.

As an illustration, let's now focus on the computation of $M^{5\to1}$, a message which has been discarded by the change in Bel_{12}. If there were no $\mathbf{Intm}_{10}$ stored at node 10, we would have to compute $M^{5\to1}$ as follows:

$$\mathbf{Cur}_5 = Bel_5$$
$$\mathbf{Cur}_5 = \mathbf{Cur}_5 \oplus M^{6\to5} \oplus M^{7\to5} \oplus M^{10\to5}$$
$$M^{5\to1} = ((\mathbf{Cur}_5)^{\downarrow(5\cap1)})^{\uparrow1}$$

i.e. three combinations are needed here.

By using the stored $\mathbf{Intm}_{10}$, we compute $M^{5\to1}$ as:

$\mathbf{Cur}_5 = Bel_5$

$\mathbf{Cur}_5 = \mathbf{Intm}_{10} \oplus M^{10\to5}$;as $\mathbf{Intm}_{10}$ is not changed.

$M^{5\to1} = ((\mathbf{Cur}_5)^{\downarrow(5\cap1)})^{\uparrow1}$

i.e. just one combination is needed here.

Formally, suppose that one input Bel_i is changed. According to (3.1), all the messages $M^{k\to\mathcal{P}_k}$ (if $\mathcal{P}_k$ exists) from any k on the path between node i and r (the root), including i, will be discarded; Moreover, all the messages $M^{\mathcal{P}_j\to j}$ (if $\mathcal{P}_j$ exists) for all j not lying on the path between i and r, will be discarded as well. According to (4.1), $\mathbf{Cur}_k$ of node k stores the combination of all the messages sent from the children of k with its own belief function. So only $\mathbf{Cur}_k$ of k lying on the path between i and r, including i and r, will be discarded. According to (4.2), $\mathbf{Intm}_j$ depends on $Bel_{\mathcal{P}_j}$ and $M^{k\to\mathcal{P}_j}$ ($k\in \mathbf{Lsb}_j$), so for any k on the path between i and r, including i, if $j\in\mathbf{Rsb}_k$, then $\mathbf{Intm}_j$ will be discarded. This point is illustrated in Fig. 5.2 by showing some cases when one prior belief function is changed.

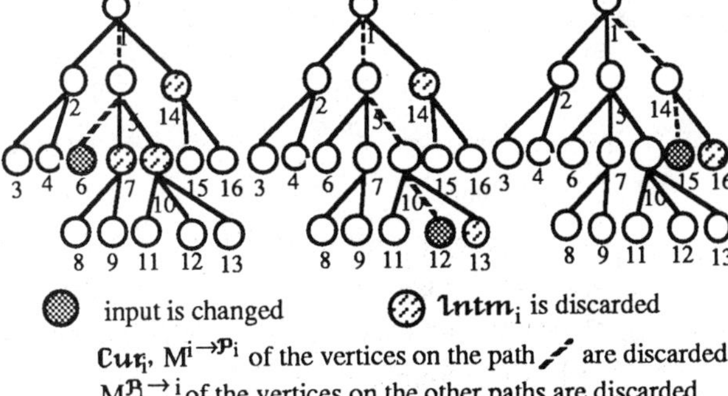

Fig5.2: cases for the changes of the messages

Suppose that for the node i, $\mathbf{Cur}_i$ is not changed, i.e. Bel_i and all the $M^{k\to i}$ ($k\in\mathbf{Ch}_i$) are not changed. As a consequence, all $\mathbf{Intm}_k$ ($k\in\mathbf{Ch}_i$) are not changed. So whenever $\mathbf{Cur}_i$ is unchanged, we can skip the "propagation-up" part for i during re-propagation. e.g. We want to compute $Bel^{\downarrow14}$ now. Because $M^{14\to1}$ does not change, it is desirable not to re-compute $Bel_{14}\oplus M^{15\to14}\oplus M^{16\to14}$ for computing $Bel^{\downarrow14}$. By using $\mathbf{Cur}_{14}$, we just avoid this computation.

Synthesizing all the cases discussed in these two sections, we give a combined algorithm for both simultaneous propagation and re-propagation. This algorithm is based on the assumption that the structure of the Markov tree is not changed when re-propagating and that $M^{i\to j}$, $\mathbf{Intm}_i$, $\mathbf{Cur}_i$ are only discarded when necessary as explained before. In this Algorithm, we will use $Bel^{\downarrow i}$ temporarily to compute $\mathbf{Cur}_i$ in the propagation-up part. Initially, for each node i, $Bel^{\downarrow i}$ is initiated to Bel_i and for the first child c_1 of i, $\mathbf{Intm}_{c_1}$ is initiated to Bel_i. Then the propagation can begin by calling **Propagate**($\mathcal{M}$ -L($\mathcal{M}$, $\mathcal{E}$), $\mathcal{E}$-{(i,j)|i∈ L($\mathcal{M}$, $\mathcal{E}$)}).

```
                    Propagate (M', E')
if M' ≠ ∅ then
  L := L(M', E')    /* get the leaves of G' = (M',E') */
  if M'= {r} then L := M' end-if
    /* r is the root of G. */
  for i ∈ L      /* for every v in L, do the followings: */
    if Cur_i does not exist then
    /* if Cur_i exists, the first part is skipped for i */
      Ch := Ch_i   /* otherwise: */
      for j ∈ Ch_i
      /* find the first child i whose message is discarded */
        if M^{j→i} exists then  Ch := Ch - {j}
                          else  Bel^{↓i} := Intm_j
                                exit loop-for
        end-if
      end-for
      if Ch=∅ then Ch := Ch_i end-if
    /* if all the messages from the children is not changed,
      as Cur_i is discarded, Bel_i is changed. */
      for k ∈ Ch
    /* compute the messages from the rest of children. */
        Intm_k:=Bel^{↓i} /*store intermediate result at k*/
        if M^{k→i} does not exist then
          M^{k→i}:=((Cur_k)^{↓(i∩k)})^{↑i} end-if
    /* compute message from k to i if necessary */
        Bel^{↓i} := Bel^{↓i} ⊕ M^{k→i}
    /* combine all the messages from children */
      end-for
      Cur_i := Bel^{↓i}
    /* store the combination of all the messages from
    children of i with the prior belief function of i at node i*/
    end-if
  end-for
  Propagate(M'-L, E'-{(i, j) | i∈L})
      /* delete the leaves, continue propagation in the
  remaining tree */
  for i ∈ L(M', E')
    /* for every v in L, do the following: */
      if P_i exists then R := M^{P_i→i}
    /* get the message from the parent */
                     else R := nil
      end-if
      Q := nil
      for k ∈ Ch'_i
    /* send messages back to every child and compute the
  marginals for them:*/
        R := R ⊕ Q
    /* combine some messages from i's neighbours */
```

if $M^{i\rightarrow k}$ does not exist then
$M^{i\rightarrow k} := ((\mathbf{Intm}_k \oplus R)^{\downarrow(i\cap k)})^{\uparrow k}$ end-if
/* compute message from i to k by using intermediate results*/
$Bel^{\downarrow k} := \mathbf{Cur}_k \oplus M^{i\rightarrow k}$
/* marginal for k is computed*/
$Q := M^{k\rightarrow i}$
/* get message from k to i for further computation */
end-for
end-for
end-if

Algorithm2 combined algorithm for simultaneous propagation and re-propagation

6 CONCLUSIONS

We have presented an algorithm (Algorithm 1) for belief function propagation based on the local computation technique proposed by Shafer, Shenoy and Mellouli. The advantage of Algorithm 1 is that it decreases the number of applications of Dempster's combination rule during the propagation, thus reducing the overall complexity, which is one of the most serious problems in implementing Dempster-Shafer theory. Moreover, Algorithm 2 makes full use of the already computed messages and intermediate results for re-propagating when one or more of the prior belief functions is changed. A propagation system* has been implemented in Allegro Common Lisp with Common Windows (by Franz Inc) according to Algorithm 2. It runs on a SUN-3/60 Workstation under SUN Operating System 4.0.3. It has shown that the speed of computation can be greatly increased in comparison with an existing implementation such as MacEvidence (Hsia and Shenoy 1989). Because of the generality of the local computation technique (Saffiotti 1989, Shenoy 1989), this approach is not just specific to belief function propagation, but may be used for any case in which the local computation technique may be applied.

Acknowledgements

I am grateful for the support, help and suggestions from Professor Philippe Smets. For the useful discussions and worthy comments on the drafts, I greatly thank Alessandro Saffiotti, Yen-Teh Hsia, Robert Kennes and Elisabeth Umkehrer .This work has been supported by the grant of IRIDIA, Université Libre de Bruxelles.

*The implementation is a property of IRIDIA-Université Libre de Bruxelles, and it is freely available for strictly non-commercial use.

References

Hsia Y. and Shenoy P. P. (1989) *"MacEvidence: A Visual Environment for Constructing & Evaluating Evidential Systems"* Working Paper No. 211, School of Business, University of Kansas, Lawrence, KS.

Kong A. (1986) *"Multivariate Belief Functions & Graphical Models"* Ph.D dissertation, Department of Statistics, Harvard University, Cambridge, MA.

Mellouli K. (1987) *"On the Propagation of Beliefs in Network Using the Dempster-Shafer Theory of Evidence"* Ph.D dissertation, School of Business, University of Kansas, Lawrence, KS.

Saffiotti A. (1989) *"De Propagationibus"* Technical Note IRIDIA/ARCHON/TN-005, IRIDIA, Université Libre de Bruxelles, Brussels.

Shafer G. (1976) *"A Mathematical Theory of Evidence"* Princeton University Press.

Shafer G., Shenoy P. P. and Mellouli K. (1987) *"Propagating Belief Functions in Qualitative Markov Trees"* International Journal of Approximate Reasoning, 1:349-400.

Shafer G.and Shenoy P. P. (1988) *"Local Computation in Hypertrees"* Working Paper No. 201, School of Business, University of Kansas, Lawrence, KS.

Shenoy P. P. and Shafer G. (1986) *"Propagating Belief Functions with Local Computations"* IEEE Expert, 1(3), 43-52.

Shenoy P. P. (1989) *"A Valuation-Based Language for Expert Systems"* International Journal of Approximate Reasoning, 3:383-411.

Smets Ph. (1988) *"Belief Functions"* in "Non Standard Logics for Automated Reasoning" edited by Smets Ph., Mamdani A., Dubois D. and Prade H., Academic Press, London, 253-286.

Zarley D. (1988) *"An Evidential Reasoning System"* Working Paper No. 206, School of Business, University of Kansas, Lawrence, KS.

Zarley D., Hsia Y. and Shafer G. (1988) *"Evidential Reasoning Using DELIEF"* in "Proceedings of the seventh National Conference on Artificial Intelligence" edited by Paul St., MN, 1, 205-209.

Zhang L. (1988) *"Studies on Finding Hypertree Covers of Hypergraphs"* Working Paper No. 198, School of Business, University of Kansas, Lawrence, KS.

A Non-Numeric Approach to Multi-Criteria/Multi-Expert Aggregation Based on Approximate Reasoning

Ronald R. Yager
Machine Intelligence Institute
Iona College
New Rochelle, NY 10801

Abstract

We describe a technique that can be used for the fusion of multiple sources of information as well as for the evaluation and selection of alternatives under multi-criteria. Three important properties contribute to the uniqueness of the technique introduced. The first is the ability to do all necessary operations and aggregations with information that is of a nonnumeric linguistic nature. This facility greatly reduces the burden on the providers of information, the experts. A second characterizing feature is the ability assign, again linguistically, differing importances to the criteria or in the case of information fusion to the individual sources of information. A third significant feature of the approach is its ability to be used as method to find a consensus of the opinion of multiple experts on the issue of concern. The techniques used in this approach are base on ideas developed from the theory of approximate reasoning. We illustrate the approach with a problem of project selection.

1. Introduction

A problem of considerable interest is the so called *information fusion problem.* In this problem one has a number sources of information bearing on a set of hypothesis. The objective here is to aggregate these different sources of information to get some indication of the validity of the individual hypothesis. Pattern recognition can be seen as a special case of this problem. The difficulty of this problem can be somewhat compounded if we allow multiple experts to participate in the validation of hypothesis based upon source information. This becomes even more complicated if each expert can have a different interpretation of the being of a source of information on the validity of a hypothesis as well as attributing a different importance to each of the sources of information. Medical diagnosis is a classic example of this environment. A problem with the exact same structure as the above is the multi-criteria decision problem. In this environment the set of hypothesis are replaced by a set decision alternatives.. The sources of information are replaced by criteria which must be satisfied by good solutions. Again one can also consider an environment in which a number of experts participate in the actual selection process, a kind of consensus, but where each expert has a different degree of importance associated with each criteria. Generically we shall call this class of problems **multi-criteria/ multi-expert aggregation.** We shall here present a procedure for the solution of this problem. The procedure presented here satisfies the added restriction that the information provided by the experts need only be of a linguistic/non-numeric nature. The ability to aggregate nonnumeric information greatly reduces the burden imposed on the experts in providing their information as well as freeing us from the so called tyranny of numbers.

The procedure to be described combines an approach suggested by Yager (1981), which was recently discussed by Caudell (1990), for aggregating fuzzy sets and Yager's recent work on linguistic quantifiers using ordered weighted averaging (OWA) operators (Yager 1988, To Appear). The spirit of this procedure can be said to a formalization of a kind approximate reasoning.

In order more tangible the ideas discussed we of shall consider the description of the technique in the framework of the problem of selecting from a set of alternative project proposals those which are to be funded. Essentially the funding selection process can be seen as a multi-criteria decision process. Central to any multi-criteria decision process is the necessity to aggregate criteria satisfaction. A requirement for aggregation is that the information provided must be on a scale of sufficient sophistication to allow appropriate aggregation operations to be performed. One such scale having this property is the numeric scale. One problem with such a numeric scale is that we become subject to an effect which I shall call *the tyranny of numbers.* The essential issue here is that the numbers take a life and precision far in excess of the ability of the evaluators in providing these scores. The approach we suggest allows for the aggregation of multi-criteria but avoids the tyranny of numbers by using a scale that essentially only requires a linear ordering.

The procedure described here can be seen as a two stage process. In the first stage, individual experts are asked to provide an evaluation of the alternatives, the different proposals. This evaluation consists of providing a measure of how well each of the criteria required of a good solution are satisfied by each of the alternatives. In addition each expert provides an indication of how important he thinks each criteria is. The values to be used for the evaluation of the ratings of the alternatives and importances will be drawn from a linguistic scale making it easier for the evaluator to provide the information. We use a methodology which we developed in (Yager 1981) to provide, for each expert, an overall rating of each alternative for that experts inputted information. In the second stage, we use a methodology, based upon OWA operators, which we introduced in (Yager 1988) and extended in (Yager To Appear) to aggregate the individual experts evaluations to obtain a combined overall rating for each object. This overall evaluation can then be used by the decision maker as an aid in the selection process.

In the application specifically addressed in this paper, we augment the ratings by some textual evaluation. While the need for textual evaluation is not required for the implementation of the procedure described, we feel that it can provide useful additional information in the selection process.

2. PROBLEM FORMULATION

The problem we are interested in addressing can be seen to consist of four components. The first component is a collection $P = \{P_1, \ldots P_n\}$ of proposals from amongst which we desire to select some to be funded. In the information fusion problem this would be our collection of hypothesis.

The second component is a group of experts whose advise is solicited in helping make the decision, we denote this as $A = \{A_1, \ldots A_q\}$. Generally q is much smaller than n.

The third component of the system are the set of criteria to be used in evaluating the suitability of the alternatives. In the information fusion problem instead of criteria we would have the information provided by the different sources of information.

The fourth component of the system is the decision maker who has executive responsibility for using(aggregating) the advise of the experts and then making the final decision.

In this environment, the function of the advisory panel of experts is to provide information to help the decision maker. The following procedure can be used to accomplish this. Each expert is given information about each project and is asked to fill out a form regarding these projects. The form consists of questions relating to that proposal, these questions constitute the criteria. Each question requires a two part answer. The first part consists of a linguistic score drawn from a scale provided and the second part consists of a textual portion. The purpose of the textual portion is to help amplify and clarify the score. The scores play central role in this process. At the very least (and very best) they help make the broad distinction between those proposals that are very bad and those that are very good. They also help provide some ordering amongst the proposals.

It should be noted that in the information fusion problem each of the experts would be provided with the observations from the different sources, instead of the questions or criteria. In addition each would be asked to indicate the degree to which the source supports each of the hypothesis under consideration.

3. A Non-Numeric Technique Multi-Criteria Aggregation

In this section, we shall assume each questionaire, consists of n items. As noted in the previous section each item consists of a criteria of concern in evaluating a proposal. Each expert will select a value from the following scale S:

Perfect (P)	S_7
Very High (VH)	S_6
High (H)	S_5
Medium (M)	S_4
Low	S_3
Very Low	S_2
None	S_1

to indicate the degree to which a proposed project satisfies a criteria.

The use of such a scale provides of course a natural ordering, $S_i > S_j$ if $i > j$. Of primary significance is that the use of such a scale doesn't impose undue burden upon the evaluator in that it doesn't impose the meaningless precision of numbers. The scale is essentially a linear ordering and just implies that one score is better then another. However, the use of linguistic terms associated with these scores makes it easier for the evaluator to manipulate. The use of such a seven point scale appears also to be in line with Miller's (1969) observation that human beings can reasonably manage to keep in mind seven or so items.

Implicit in this scale are two operators, the maximum and minimum of any two scores:

$$\text{Max}(S_i, S_j) = S_i \quad \text{if } S_i \geq S_j$$
$$\text{Min}(S_i, S_j) = S_j \quad \text{if } S_j \leq S_i$$

We shall denote the max by $\vee$ and the min by $\wedge$.

Thus for any arbitrary proposal P_i each expert will provide a collection of n values.

$$(P_{ik}(q_1), P_{ik}(q_2), \ldots P_{ik}(q_n))$$

where $P_{ik}(q_j)$ is the rating of the ith proposal on the jth criteria by the kth expert. Each $P_{ik}(q_j)$ is an element in the set S of allowable scores.

Assuming n = 6, a typical scoring for proposal from one expert would be:

P_{ik}: (high, medium, low, perfect, very high, perfect)

Independent of this evaluation procedure each criteria must be given a measure of importance. Two methods are allowable for the determination of importances. In the first approach the importances are assigned by the experts themselves. In the second approach the executive decision maker assigns a measure of importance to each of the criteria. This information may or may not be available to the evaluators, it is not required by the evaluator.

In either approach the above scale is used to provide the importance associated with the criteria. It should be noted that the only requirement on the assignment of importances is that the most important criteria is given the rating P. We shall use $I(q_j)$ to indicate the importance associated with the criteria. A possible realization for importances could be

$I(q_1) = P$
$I(q_2) = VH$
$I(q_3) = VH$
$I(q_4) = M$
$I(q_5) = L$
$I(q_6) = L$

The next step in the process is to find the overall valuation for a proposal by a given expert.

In order to accomplish this overall evaluation, we use a methodology suggested by Yager (1981). This approach was recently discussed by Caudell (1990).

A crucial aspect of this approach is the taking of the negation of the importances. Yager (1981) introduced a technique for taking the negation on a linear scale of the type we have used. In particular, he suggested that if we have a scale of q items of the kind we are using then

$$Neg(S_i) = S_{q-i+1}$$

We not that this operation satisfies the desirable properties of such a negation as discussed by Dubois & Prade (1985).

(1) Closure
For any $s \in S$, $Neg(s) \in S$
(2) Order Reversal
For $S_i > S_j$, $Neg(S_i) \leq Neg(S_j)$
(3) Involution
$Neg(Neg(S_i)) = S_i$ for all i

For the scale that we are using, we see that the negation operation provides the following

$Neg(P) = N$	$(Neg(S_7) = S_1)$
$Neg(VH) = VL$	$(Neg(S_6) = S_2)$
$Neg(H) = L$	$(Neg(S_5) = S_3)$
$Neg(M) = M$	$(Neg(S_4) = S_4)$
$Neg(L) = H$	$(Neg(S_3) = S_5)$
$Neg(VL) = VH$	$(Neg(S_2) = S_6)$
$Neg(N) = P$	$(Neg(S_1) = S_7)$

The methodology suggested by Yager (1981) which can be used to find the unit score of each proposal by each expert, which we shall denote as P_{ik}, is as follows

$$P_{ik} = Min_j [Neg(I(q_j) \vee P_{ik}(q_j)]$$

In the above $\vee$ indicates the max operation. We first note that this formulation can be implemented on elements drawn from a linear scale as it only involves max, min and negation.

This formulation can be seen as a generalization of a weighted averaging. Linguistically, this formulation is saying that

if the criteria is important then a proposal should score well on it.

Essentially this methodology starts off by assuming each project has a score of perfect and then reduces its evaluation by its scoring on each question. However, the amount of this reduction is limited by the importance of the criteria as manifested by the negation. A more detailed discussion of this methodology can be found in Yager (1981).

Example: We shall use the previous manifestation to provide an example

Criteria:	Q_1	Q_2	Q_3	Q_4	Q_5	Q_6
Importance:	P	VH	VH	M	L	L
Score:	H	M	L	P	VH	P

In this case

$P_{ik} = Min\ [Neg(P) \vee H, Neg(VH) \vee M, Neg(VH) \vee L, Neg(M) \vee P, Neg(L) \vee VH, Neg(L) \vee P]$

$P_{ik} = Min\ [N \vee H, VL \vee M, VL \vee L, M \vee P, H \vee VH, H \vee P]$

$P_{ik} = Min\ [H, M, L, P, VH, P]$

$P_{ik} = L$

The essential reason for the low performance of this object is that it performed low on the third criteria which has a very high importance. We note that if we change the importance of the third criteria to low, then the proposal would evaluate to medium.

The essential feature of this approach is that we have obtained a reasonable unit evaluation of each proposal by each expert using an easily manageable linguistic scale. We had no need to use numeric values and force undue precision on the experts.

4. Combining Expert's Opinions

As a result of the previous section, we have for each proposal, assuming there are r experts, a collection of evaluations $P_{i1}, P_{i2}, \ldots P_{ir}$ where P_{ik} is the unit evaluation of the ith proposal by the kth expert. In this section, we shall provide a technique for combining the expert's evaluation to obtain an overall evaluation for each proposal, which we shall denote as P_i. The technique we shall use is based upon the ordered weighted averaging (OWA) operators introduced by Yager (1988) and extended to the linear environment in Yager (To Appear).

The first step in this process is for the decision maker to provide an aggregation function which we shall denote as Q. This function can be seen as a generalization of the idea of how many experts he feels need to agree on a project for it to be acceptable. In particular for each number i where i runs from 1 to r the decision maker must provide a value Q(i) indicating how satisfied he would be in selecting a proposal that i of the experts where satisfied with. The values for Q(i) should be drawn from the scale $S = \{S_1, S_2, \ldots S_n\}$ described above.

It should be noted that Q(i) should have certain characteristics to make it rational:

(1) As more experts agree the decision maker's satisfaction or confidence should increase;

$$Q(i) \geq Q(j) \quad i > j$$

(2) If all the experts are satisfied then his satisfaction should be the highest possible;

$$Q(r) = \text{Perfect}$$

A number of special forms for Q are worth noting. [4]:

(1) If the decision maker requires all experts to support a proposal

$$Q(i) = \text{none} \quad \text{for } i < r$$
$$Q(r) = \text{perfect}$$

(2) If the support of just one expert is enough to make a proposal worthy of consideration then

$$Q(i) = \text{perfect for all } i$$

(3) If at least m experts' support is needed for consideration then

$$Q(i) = \text{none} \qquad i < m$$
$$Q(i) = \text{perfect} \qquad i \geq m.$$

We note that while these examples only use the two extreme values of the scale S this not at all necessary or preferred.

In the following we shall suggest a manifestation of Q that can be said to emulate the usual arithmetic averaging function. In order to define this function, we introduce the operation Int [a] as returning the integer value that is closest to the number a. In the following, we shall let n be the number of points on the scale (the cardinality of S) and r be the number of experts participating. This function which emulates the average is denoted as Q_A and is defined for all i = 0, 1, . . . r as

$$Q_A(k) = S_{b(k)}$$

where

$$b(k) = \text{Int}\,[1 + (k * \frac{n-1}{r})].$$

We note that whatever the values of n and r it is always the case that

$$Q_A(0) = S_1$$
$$Q_A(r) = S_n.$$

As an example of this function if r = 3 and n = 7 then

$$b(k) = \text{Int}\,[1 + (k * \frac{6}{3})] = \text{Int}\,[1 + 2k]$$

and

$$Q_A(0) = S_1$$
$$Q_A(1) = S_3$$
$$Q_A(2) = S_5$$
$$Q_A(3) = S_7$$

If r = 4 and n = 7 then

$$b(k) = \text{Int}\,[1 + k * 1.5]$$

and

$$Q_A(0) = S_1$$
$$Q_A(1) = S_3$$
$$Q_A(2) = S_4$$
$$Q_A(3) = S_6$$
$$Q_A(4) = S_7$$

In the case where r = 10 and n=7 then

$$b(k) = \text{Int}\,[1 + k * \frac{6}{10}]$$

then

$$Q_A(0) = S_1$$
$$Q_A(1) = S_2$$
$$Q_A(2) = S_2$$
$$Q_A(3) = S_3$$
$$Q_A(4) = S_3$$
$$Q_A(5) = S_4$$
$$Q_A(6) = S_5$$
$$Q_A(7) = S_5$$
$$Q_A(8) = S_6$$
$$Q_A(9) = S_6$$
$$Q_A(10) = S_7$$

Having appropriately selected Q we are now in the position to use the ordered weighted averaging (OWA) method (Yager 1988, To Appear) for aggregating the experts opinions. Assume we have r experts, each of which has a unit evaluation for the ith projected denoted P_{ik}. The first step in the OWA procedure is to order the P_{ik}'s in descending order, thus we shall denote B_j as the jth highest score among the experts unit scores for the project. To find the overall evaluation for the ith project, denoted P_i, we calculate

$$P_i = \text{Max}_{j=1, \ldots r}\,[Q(j) \wedge B_j].$$

In order to appreciate the workings of this formulation we must realize that B_j can be seen as the worst of the jth top scores. Furthermore Q(j) can be seen as an indication of how important the decision maker feels that the support of at least j experts is. The term $Q(j) \wedge B_j$ can be seen as a weighting of an objects j best scores, B_j, and the decision maker requirement that j people support the project, Q(j). The max operation plays a role akin to the summation in the usual numeric averaging procedure. More details on this technique can be found in Yager (1988, To Appear).

Example: Assume we have four experts each providing a unit evaluation for project i obtained by the methodology discussed in the previous section.

$$P_{i1} = M$$
$$P_{i2} = H$$
$$P_{i3} = L$$
$$P_{i4} = VH$$

Reordering these scores we get

$$B_1 = VH$$
$$B_2 = H$$

$B_3 = M$

$B_4 = L.$

Furthermore, we shall assume that our decision maker chooses as his aggregation function the average like function, Q_A. Then with r = 4 and scale cardinality n = 7, we obtain

$Q_A(1) = L \quad (S_3)$

$Q_A(2) = M \quad (S_4)$

$Q_A(3) = VH \quad (S_6)$

$Q_A(4) = P \quad (S_7)$

We calculate the overall evaluation as

$P_i = \text{Max } [L \wedge VH, M \wedge H, VH \wedge M, P \wedge L]$

$P_i = \text{Max } [L, M, M, L]$

$P_i = M$

Thus the overall evaluation of this proposal is medium.

Using the methodology suggested thus far we have obtained for each proposal an overall rating P_i. These ratings allow us to obtain a comparative evaluation of all the projects without resorting to a numeric scale. The decision maker is now in the position to make his selection of projects to be supported. This decision should combine these comparative linguistic overall ratings with the provided textual material. The process used to make this final decision is not subject to a stringent objective procedure but allows for the introduction of the implicit subjective criteria, such as program agenda, held by the decision maker.

The textual material provided should be used to provide a further distinction amongst the projects.

5. CONCLUSION

We have described a methodology to be used in the evaluation of objects which is based upon a non-numeric linguistic scale. The process allows for the multi-criteria evaluation of each object by experts and then a aggregation of this individual experts to obtain an overall object evaluation. This methodology has been suggested as an approach to project funding evaluation where textual material can be used to supplement the selection process. The process can also be used in the information fusion process.

6. REFERENCES

Yager, R. R. (1981). A new methodology for ordinal multiple aspect decisions based on fuzzy sets. Decision Sciences 12, 589-600.

Caudill, M. (1990). Using neural nets: fuzzy decisions. AI Expert, April, 59-64.

Yager, R. R. (1988). On ordered weighted averaging aggregation operators in multi-criteria decision making. IEEE Transactions on Systems, Man and Cybernetics 18, 183-190.

Yager, R. R. (To Appear). Applications and extensions of OWA aggregations. International Journal of Man-Machine Studies.

Miller, G. A. (1969). The organization of lexical memory. In The Pathology of Memory, Talland, G.A. & Waugh, N.C. (Eds.), New York: New York.

Dubois, D. and Prade, H. (1985). A review of fuzzy sets aggregation connectives. Information Sciences 36, 85–121.

Why Do We Need Foundations for Modelling Uncertainties?

Henry E. Kyburg
kyburg@cs.rochester.edu
Department of Computer Science
University of Rochester
Rochester, New York, 14627

1 What Are Foundations?

Surely we want solid foundations. What kind of castle can we build on sand? What is the point of devoting effort to balconies and minarets, if the foundation may be so weak as to allow the structure to collapse of its own weight? We want our foundations set on bedrock, designed to last for generations. Who would want an architect who cannot certify the soundness of the foundations of his buildings?

The architectural analogy is not entirely persuasive, though. It is easy to understand what the foundations of a building are: they are the steel pilings, the stone, the concrete, on which the rest of the edifice physically stands. It stands still. Science is not like that. It is living, dynamic, constantly changing. The foundations of a part of science are themselves open to change.

So what are the foundations of a branch of science? There are the first principles, that everyone can and does (at least for the time being) agree on. The axioms of the discipline. Often these foundations are provided by a different branch of science. Thus engineering takes for granted — uses as a foundation — statics, kinematics, dynamics... In that sense the foundations of uncertainty clearly include logic and mathematics: we don't need to invent the real number system for ourselves.

But there may be something more we want, something more domain specific, on which we can build our science. Some key idea, like the idea of 'force' in physics, or of a 'neighborhood' in topology. We have yet to agree on any such idea or set of ideas: we argue with each other and interrogate our intuitions. And disagree at length. We would liked to find relations, common elements, among the diverse ideas with which we work. But there is no unified theory, no general framework to which we can turn to see the relation between one idea and another.

At the same time, though, we do manage to put together useful systems in which uncertainty figures. In fact people with intense and widely divergent views regarding the nature of uncertainty have been successful in making practical use of their ideas regarding uncertainty, its measurement, procedures for updating uncertainty, its role in decision making, etc. How is this possible? How can you do something right if you start off on the wrong foot? Clearly, since each of n people thinks the other n - 1 are wrong, not more than one can be proceeding correctly. And yet they are getting at least part way to their goals.

2 Do We Need Foundations At All?

In this situation it is easy enough to see why some people are willing to say that we should not bother with foundations at all. A similar situation can be found in logic and mathematics: there are those who *do* mathematics, and then there are those who do a different thing — the *foundations* of mathematics. "It's all very interesting," one might say, "to speculate about foundations, but it's not *serious* work."

In fact this attitude can be raised to the level of a matter of principle. Of course we should be explicit about what our models contain, but it need not be the case that there is any privileged class of models. Different models are useful for different things. To seek a unification of or a foundation for modelling uncertainties is, it might be argued, completely misguided. It can only inhibit free and untrammeled and creative research. "Let a thousand flowers bloom!"

There is a movement in the philosophy of science that leads in the same direction. It can be traced to Paul Feyerabend and Thomas Kuhn [Feyerabend, 1970, Kuhn, 1952], and the gist of the view is that science is driven by practical and also by social goals. The community of scientists accepts a certain 'disciplinary matrix' that embodies rules of evidence, criteria of sound argument, and the like, but these standards change over time. When it comes to science itself, there is no truth of the matter. Scientific argument, for example about the conservation of parity or the measurement of belief, is a formal dance, conforming to temporary rules of argument.

This is a perennial view. A number of years ago, the idea was that there were always 'presuppositions,' so that if you made your presuppositions explicit, you had exercised full foundational responsibility. If my presuppositions differ from yours, why, we have no disagreement after all: one would not expect to reach the same substantive conclusions on the basis of differing presuppositions.

So too, more recently, with the idea of a 'model.' If I argue that the evidence supports the hypothesis that people are expected utility maximizers, and you argue that the evidence doesn't either support that hypothesis, what we must do is to sit down and carefully characterize the models we are respectively employing. Lo and behold: we find that they are not the same model, so of course we are not really disagreeing. What is true on your model is false on mine, and vice versa.

What is nice about all these anti-foundational ploys is that they promote friendship and collegiality; they can be used very effectively to resolve disagreements. After all, if we are using different models of uncertainty, why should we expect to come to the same conclusions?

3 Testability

There are a number of difficulties with the soft friendly world of relativism. For one thing, it conflicts with the persistent nagging feeling that, by gum, there *is* a truth of the matter out there. We know there is, because we have knocked into tables, fallen out of trees, gotten rained on. Reality isn't all bad. We have also basked in the sun, made love, seen magnificent sunsets. The point is that those things, good and bad, are not social constructs: they are the world going about its business.

The view that we must answer to the world as well as to our colleagues is an old and honorable one. Rudolf Carnap, among others, proposed *testability* as a criterion for meaningfulness in the theory of language. [Carnap, 1934] Construed narrowly, the idea of testability is implausible: there are many statements in science that we cannot definitively test. Any universal generalization provides an illustration: we cannot complete an inventory of the universe. Construed broadly, testability might be thought of as the demand that any meaningful statement should be such that you can find evidence supporting it. This begins to get pretty vague.

Karl Popper proposed *falsifiability* as a criterion of meaningfulness. It didn't fare much better. But in both cases, it is assumed that there is a truth of the matter in these controversial issues, and one that is worth pursuing.

4 Proliferation and Communication

The idea that we want to encourage uninhibited creativity in formulating theories and devising structures to represent the world and the activities of intelligent entities in the world is not at all peculiar to the anti-foundational view. Popper and Carnap, for example, both stressed the importance of speculation and invention. The question is partly that of whether or not there are objective standards for evaluating speculations and inventions.

The question is also partly one of communication: it is not only the acceptability or unacceptability of some statement or other, but a question of the very meaning of that statement. If you and I have different paradigms (or models, or assumptions) then when you assert that our robot should be designed to maximize expected utility, and I assert that it should not merely maximize expected utility, we can agree that our disagreement is only apparent, and derives from the difference in our assumptions. When you assert that our robot will avoid risk, how am I to understand that? Without a common framework, how do we even *express* our differences?

In choosing among alternative frameworks, the external world provides a powerful input, according to traditional views. What has been less noticed is that without a shared framework that is tied to the world, we cannot communicate. We can smile and nod, but the empirical value of what you say is lost on me.

Unbounded proliferation, the proliferation of private languages applicable, to all intents and purposes to private worlds, is clearly counterproductive. We can't get very far that way, because we can't communicate and cooperate. That is one reason why we need to consider foundations.

5 Considering Foundations

What is it to 'consider foundations?' One might think it a matter of consulting one's intuitions, and trying to formalize them. Perhaps that is one approach, and if pursued with an awareness of both the history of the subject, and with an alertness to applications in the real world, it can be very interesting.

There are other ways of thinking about foundations that involve looking carefully at ready-made systems. For example, authors often argue that other systems are "special cases" of their own. Shafer [Shafer, 1976] shows that Bayesian propositional probabilities are a special case of his belief functions. It goes the other way, too. Dempster [Dempster, 1965] mentions the possibility that his upper and lower probabilities could be construed as the envelope of a set of classical probability functions, and cites Savage as having suggested that these could be considered convex sets.

The same general view has been endorsed by Isaac Levi [Levi, 1984] under the rubric of "indeterminate probabilities."

David Heckerman [Heckerman, 1985] has shown that MYCIN's certainty factors should (if they are to be fed into decision procedures) be construed in a manner consistent with propositional probabilities.

Updating uncertainties in the light of evidence is a quite different matter. It can be shown that in many cases updating belief functions results in tighter constraints on uncertainty measures than does updating according to Bayes' theorem applied to propositional probabilities [Kyburg, 1989].

One way in which one might want to resolve some of these questions is to adopt the principle of maximizing expected utility as a constraint: that is, it should *not* be the case that the expected utility of an admissible act, under any point-valued probability function that is a *possibility*, is less in every state of nature than the expected utility of some other act.

These results concern the relation of convex sets of probability measures to certainty factors or belief functions. This suggests that one might, more deeply, consider the question of whether convex sets of probability functions are the most useful general representation of uncertainty. Grounds for a negative answer can be found (implicitly) in Pearl's work [Pearl, 1989]. Consider a chance event such as the tossing of a coin. We could be uncertain as to the bias of the coin, but at the same time quite certain as to the independence of the tosses. Since the convex combination of two binomial distributions of heads is not a binomial distribution, we do not want to identify rational belief with

Another foundational issue is whether Bayes' theorem should be applied to the updating of probabilities. This is considered in [Dubois, 1988] as well as [Kyburg, 1990].

6 What Are We Trying to Do?

Different people have different ideas of the goal of modelling uncertainty. Some people are mainly concerned with the representation of human cognition. Others want machines that will handle an uncertain environment with efficiency and grace. These may be two quite different projects (though, presumably, related in some degree). They may call for somewhat different foundational considerations.

For example, if we are interested in how people manage to deal with uncertainty, the idea of a connectionist network may be a very useful one: perhaps that is the basic mechanism we need to embody.

On the other hand, if we are interested in machines that will deal with statistically known uncertain environments, then it may well be that a different foundation is called for: one which depends on a database of statistical knowledge, rather than on being trained by the environment.

The contrast is that between programming a machine to do logic, and constructing a network (which has been done) that will learn logic. I understand that a network has been constructed that learns logic at about the "B" level. It is easy to construct a program that will do logic much better. Which you are interested in depends on your goals. I'm more interested in a pocket calculator that does sums correctly than in one that gets a "B" in third grade arithmetic, but does it the way children do.

7 What Are We Talking About?

One reason for concern with foundations in modelling uncertainty is to enable us to know what we are talking about. If we don't have some foundational framework, some commonality, communication is undermined. If you use 'probability' in one sense and I use it in another, it is clear that we're in for problems. One response has been to proliferate terminology. Thus 'epistemic probability' 'belief function' 'basic probability assignment' 'certainty factor' 'support' ...

But the proliferation of terminology is not necessarily the proliferation of ideas, and does not always enhance communication. It is true that it may help to eliminate or reduce *mis*communication: I won't misinterpret you if you are talking your own language, but avoiding misunderstanding is not the same as successfully communicating.

Is communication so important? Might we proceed along an evolutionary model, in which each of us pursues his own dream, designs his own systems, and eventually, is evaluated by the success of his work? Should we let the thousand flowers bloom, and then let all but one wither? This doesn't seem like science. (Furthermore, if all but one is to die, we'd better make sure that it is self fertile.)

8 Little but the Truth

If, as I think most of us really believe, there is a truth of the matter about the nature (or natures!) of uncertainty, about its representation, and about its modification by evidence or the course of experience (not necessarily the same thing), then foundational issues are clearly important. The closer we can come to an adequate foundation, the more likely we are to be telling the truth when we talk about uncertainty.

This is not at all to say that there is a final foundation, any more than there is a final foundation to physics or to mathematics. It is to say that our work concerning uncertainty will be less likely to contain error. What we pass on will be more likely to be permanent.

9 More of the Truth

We're not merely interested in avoiding falsehoods, however; we are interesting in telling the truth. A better understanding of foundations cannot help but provide insights from which more new results can be obtained. This is particularly the case when the foundational work has shown that two apparently different concepts are simple transformations of one another. Every theorem about the one becomes, with the appropriate transformations, a theorem about the other.

For example, once we have noted that every belief function is equivalent to a convex set of classical probabilities, then theorems concerning convex sets of classical probabilities can be applied to belief functions.

10 Usefulness

We have already noted that, despite the strong divergence of opinion concerning foundations, individuals in a wide variety of camps have managed to produce useful systems, ranging from concrete applications in expert systems to purely abstract shells for representing uncertain inference. This strongly suggests that there is an interesting foundational core underlying those applications.

It does not *entail* that there is a unified foundation; maybe there are *k* foundations for *k* kinds of uncertainty. That's just one of the foundational issues that deserves careful and generous investigation.

If that is the case, however, if these successful applications reflect a unified common core of facts about uncertainty, then having a better understanding of the foundations will provide us with tools for doing things even better.

This observation goes both ways. The more useful applications there are of a certain sort, the stronger the evidence that there is something right in what is being done. This fact should be exploited in the study of foundations. Its exploitation can be neither mechanical nor trivial, however. It is all too easy to take one framework, and to show how a second can be paraphrased in terms of the first.

This is especially the case for the subjectivist Bayesian view. If there is a system that yields decisions on the basis of evidential inputs, and if as I suggested decision procedures should not *conflict* with probabilities, then it is necessarily the case that there are subjective prior probabilities that yield the same decisions.

Does this mean that subjective Bayesianism is the Universal Solvent? Hardly, because there are other desiderata than conformity to the probability calculus that are or may be part of our search for foundations.

11 Practise and Theory

This suggests that practise and theory should go hand in hand. We can engineer applications involving uncertainty that work. We can do so starting from a variety of theoretical and philosophical viewpoints. In view of that variety, we can hardly claim support, on this basis, for any particular foundational view.

On the other hand, the space of possible foundational theories is very large. There is a lot more to be thought about than is involved in any particular engineering development. We must also consult our intuitions — and those of others — in order to have reason to believe that our engineering successes are not accidents.

This doesn't mean that foundational work is a matter of sitting in an armchair thinking deep thoughts. Philosophers are traditionally good at that. But unless the deep thoughts are tested, we can't tell what they have to offer us. Unless the intuitions obtained in the armchair can be put to the test of practise, they can have little persuasiveness.

Practise and theory must go together; to get very far, they must go together systematically, not just accidentally.

12 A Garden

A concern with foundations may be in some small degree conservative — at least in comparison with the radical view of Feyerabend. But there is no one that I know of, in any area, who takes the view that creativity and the proliferation of ideas are to be discouraged. Foundations, even where they exist, are not immutable and unchangeable.

Nor does there have to be uniform agreement on the foundations of uncertainty modelling. The more uniformity we can find, the more agreement we can achieve, the better. A common framework allows us to communicate better, it allows us to transfer results from one part of the theory to another, and we may hope that eventually it will allow us to understand better why the systems that work do work.

Finding a common framework within which many of the current ideas concerning the representation and updating of uncertainty can be related need not inhibit the proliferation of ideas. If we're lucky, it will enhance their effect by enhancing their communication.

Let a thousand flowers bloom; but let them bloom together and cooperatively in a formal garden.

Acknowledgments

Research underlying this work has been supported in part by U. S. Army Communications Command Grant no. DAAB10-87-K-022, and NSF research grant no. IRI-9002659.

References

[Carnap, 1936] Rudolf Carnap. Testability and Meaning I, *Philosophy of Science* **3**: 420-471, 1936.

[Dubois, 1988] Didier Dubois and Henri Prade. *Possibility Theory: An Approach to Computerized Processing of Uncertainty*. Plenum Press, New York, 1988.

[Feyerabend, 1970] Paul Feyerabend. Against Method, in Radner and Winokur (eds), *Minnesota Studies in the Philosophy of Science IV*, 17-130. University of Minnesota Press, Minneapolis, 1970.

[Heckerman, 1985] Heckerman, David E. "Probabilistic Interpretations for MYCIN's Certainty Factors," *Uncertainty in Artificial Intelligence* 167-96, Kanal and Lemmer (eds), North-Holland, Amsterdam, 1986.

[Kuhn, 1960] Thomas S. Kuhn. *The Structure of Scientific Revolutions*, University of Chicago Press, Chicago, 1962.

[Kyburg, 1987] Henry E. Kyburg, Jr. Bayesian and non-Bayesian evidential updating. *AI Journal* 31: 271-294, 1987.

[Kyburg, 1990] Henry E. Kyburg, Jr., Fahiem Bacchus, and Mariam Thalos. Against Conditionalization, *Synthese* **85**: 475–506, 1990.

[Popper, 1959] K.R. Popper. *The Logic of Scientific Discovery*, Hutchinson and Co., London, 1959.

[Shafer, 1976] Glenn Shafer. *A Mathematical Theory of Evidence*, Princeton University Press, Princeton, 1976.

Author Index